INTERNATIONAL HUMAN RIGHTS AND HUMANITARIAN LAW

Treaties, Cases and Analysis

INTERNATIONAL HUMAN RIGHTS AND HUMANITARIAN LAW: TREATIES, CASES AND ANALYSIS introduces law students to the international legal instruments and case law governing the substantive and procedural dimensions of international human rights and humanitarian law, including economic, social, and cultural rights. The textbook also discusses the history and organizational structure of human rights and humanitarian law enforcement mechanisms. Relevant to U.S. audiences, a chapter is devoted to the issues surrounding the incorporation of international law into U.S. law, including principles of constitutional and statutory interpretation, conflict rules, and the self-execution doctrine. Questions and Comments sections provide critical analyses of issues raised in the materials. The last chapter addresses theoretical issues facing contemporary international human rights and humanitarian law and its enforcement.

Francisco Forrest Martin is the president and founder of Rights International, The Center for International Human Rights Law, Inc.

Stephen J. Schnably is the vice-chair and legal director of Rights International, The Center for International Human Rights, Inc. He is also the associate dean and professor of law at the University of Miami School of Law.

Richard J. Wilson is professor of law and director of the International Human Rights Law Clinic at American University Washington College of Law. He is also a legal director of Rights International, The Center for International Human Rights Law, Inc.

Jonathan S. Simon is associate dean and professor of law at the University of California at Berkeley School of Law.

Mark V. Tushnet is the Carmack Waterhouse Professor of Constitutional Law at Georgetown University Law Center.

International Human Rights and Humanitarian Law

TREATIES, CASES AND ANALYSIS

Francisco Forrest Martin
Rights International

Stephen J. Schnably
University of Miami School of Law

Richard J. Wilson
American University Washington College of Law

Jonathan S. Simon
University of California at Berkeley School of Law

Mark V. Tushnet
Georgetown University Law Center

Published under the auspices of  Rights International
The Center for International Human Rights Law, Inc.

CAMBRIDGE UNIVERSITY PRESS
Cambridge, New York, Melbourne, Madrid, Cape Town, Singapore, São Paulo

Cambridge University Press
40 West 20th Street, New York, NY 10011-4211, USA

www.cambridge.org
Information on this title: www.cambridge.org/9780521858861

First published 2006

Printed in the United States of America

A catalog record for this publication is available from the British Library.

Library of Congress Cataloging in Publication Data

International human rights & humanitarian law : treaties, cases, & analysis/
Francisco Forrest Martin ... [et al.].
    p.   cm.
Includes bibliographical references and index.
ISBN-13: 978-0-521-85886-1 (hardback)
ISBN-10: 0-521-85886-0 (hardback)
1. Human rights.   2. Humanitarian law.   I. Title: International human
rights and humanitarian law.   II. Martin, Francisco Forrest.   III. Title.
K3240.I5788   2006
341.4'8 – dc22   2005015710

ISBN-13   978-0-521-85886-1 hardback
ISBN-10   0-521-85886-0 hardback

. . . about

Rights International

This book is published under the auspices of Rights International, The Center for International Human Rights Law, Inc. Rights International is a not-for-profit organization devoted to protecting and furthering the rights recognized in the Universal Bill of Human Rights and other human rights and humanitarian instruments. It seeks to accomplish this mission in two ways.

First, Rights International provides legal assistance to victims of human rights and humanitarian law violations before international tribunals, including those established by the United Nations, the Council of Europe, the Organisation of African Unity, and the Organization of American States.

Second, Rights International trains lawyers and law students in international human rights law and practice. This book represents one component of Rights International's training program.

If you are interested in learning more about Rights International or working on one of our international cases, please visit our website for information about the following programs:

Cooperating Attorney/Firm Program

Frank C. Newman Internship Program

Eric Neisser Project on International Human Rights Law in the United States

Law School Consortium Program

www.rightsinternational.org

WE DEDICATE THIS BOOK TO

Frank and Jonathan Askin
David Fathi
Andrea L. Teitler

– *from Francisco Forrest Martin*

To my wife, Ann

– *from Richard Wilson*

Christina

– *from Jonathan Simon*

ACLU National Prison Project

– *from Mark Tushnet*

Contents

Table of Selected Authorities

Selected International Instrument Citations

UN Instruments

Convention Against Torture and Other Cruel, Inhuman or Degrading Treatment or Punishment, Dec. 10, 1984, G.A. Res. 39/46, 39 UN GAOR, Supp. (No. 51), UN Doc. A/39/51, at 197 (entered into force June 26, 1987).

Convention on the Elimination of All Forms of Discrimination Against Women, Dec. 18, 1979, G.A. Res. 34/180, 34 UN GAOR, Supp. (No. 46), UN Doc. A/34/46, at 193 (entered into force Sept. 3, 1981).

Convention on the Elimination of All Forms of Racial Discrimination, Dec. 21, 1965, 660 U.N.T.S. 195 (entered into force Jan. 4, 1969).

Convention on the Prevention and Punishment of the Crime of Genocide, Dec. 9, 1948, 78 U.N.T.S. no. 1021 (1951).

International Covenant on Civil and Political Rights, Dec. 16, 1966, 999 U.N.T.S. 171 (entered into force Mar. 23, 1976).

International Covenant on Economic, Social and Cultural Rights, G.A. res. 2200A (XXI), 21 UN GAOR Supp. (No. 16) at 49, U.N. Doc. A/6316 (1966), 993 U.N.T.S. 3 (entered into force Jan. 3, 1976).

Statute of the International Court of Justice, 59 Stat. 1005, T.S. 993 (June 26, 1945).

Statute of the International Criminal Court, July 17, 1998, UN Doc. 2187 UNTS 90 (entered into force July 1, 2002).

Statute of the International Criminal Tribunal, S/Res/808 (1993), U.N. Doc. S/25704 (May 3, 1993).

Statute of the International Tribunal for Rwanda, U.N. Doc. S/Res/955, Annex (1994), *reprinted in* 33 I.L.M. 1598, 1602 (1994).

United Nations Charter, June 26, 1945, 59 Stat. 1031, T.S. 993, 3 Bevans 1153 (entered into force Oct. 24, 1945).

Universal Declaration of Human Rights, Dec. 10, 1948, G.A. Res. 217A (III), UN Doc. A/810 (1948).

Vienna Convention on the Law of Treaties, May 23, 1969, 1155 U.N.T.S. 331 (entered into force Jan. 27, 1980).

African Union Instruments

African Charter on Human and Peoples' Rights, June 27, 1981, O.A.U. Doc. CAB/LEG/67/3 Rev. 5 (entered into force Oct. 21, 1986).

Commonwealth of Independent States Instruments

Convention on Human Rights and Fundamental Freedoms of the Commonwealth of Independent States, Council of Europe doc. H(95) 7 rev. and Human Rights Information Sheet No. 36 (Jan.–Jun. 1995) H/Inf (95) 3, pp. 195–206.

European Instruments

Charter of Fundamental Rights of the European Union *in* Treaty Establishing a Constitution for Europe, Dec. 16, 2004, II, 47 Official Journal of the European Union (C 310).

European Convention for the Protection of Human Rights and Fundamental Freedoms, Nov. 4, 1950, 213 U.N.T.S. 221 (entered into force Feb. 3, 1953).

Protocol No. 1, Mar. 20, 1952, E.T.S. 9 (entered into force May 18, 1954).

Protocol No. 11, May 11, 1984, E.T.S. 155 (entered into force 1998).

OAS Instruments

American Convention on Human Rights, Nov. 22, 1969, 1144 U.N.T.S. 123 (entered into force July 17, 1978).

Additional Protocol to the American Convention on Human Rights in the Area of Economic, Social and Cultural Rights (Protocol of San Salvador), Nov. 14, 1988, OAS Treaty Series No. 69.

Protocol to the American Convention on Human Rights to Abolish the Death Penalty, Dec. 15, 1989, OAS Treaty Series, No. 73.

Inter-American Convention to Prevent and Punish Torture, OAS Treaty Series No. 67 (entered into force 28 February 1987), *reprinted in* BASIC DOCUMENTS PERTAINING TO HUMAN RIGHTS IN THE INTER-AMERICAN SYSTEM, OEA/Ser.L.V/II.82 doc.6 rev.1 at 83 (1992).

Inter-American Convention on the Prevention, Punishment and Eradication of Violence Against Women ("Convention of Belem Do Para"), June 9, 1994, *available at* <http://www. oas.org/en/prog/juridico/english/treaties/a-61.htm> (visited 24 July 2000).

Inter-American Convention on the Forced Disappearance of Persons, June 9, 1994, *available at* <http://www.oas.org/en/prog/juridico/english/treaties/a-60.htm> (visited 24 July 2000) (entered into force 28 March 1996).

American Declaration on the Rights and Duties of Man, May 2, 1948, O.A.S. Res. XXX, *reprinted in* BASIC DOCUMENTS PERTAINING TO HUMAN RIGHTS IN THE INTER-AMERICAN SYSTEM, OEA/Ser.L.V/II.82 doc. 6 rev.1 at 17 (1992).

U.S. Instruments

United States Constitution, Sept. 17, 1787 (entered into force June 21, 1788).

Humanitarian Instruments

Geneva Convention (I) for the Amelioration of the Condition of the Wounded and Sick in Armed Forces in the Field, August 12, 1949, 75 U.N.T.S. 31 (entered into force October 21, 1950).

Geneva Convention (IV) relative to the Treatment of Prisoners of War, August 12, 1949, 75 U.N.T.S. 135, 6 U.S.T. 3316. T.I.A.S. No. 3364 (entered into force October 21, 1950).

Geneva Convention Relative to the Protection of Civilian Persons in Time of War, August 12, 1949, 75 U.N.T.S. 287, 6 U.S.T. 3516, T.I.A.S. No. 3365 (entered into force October 21, 1950).

Protocol Additional to the Geneva Conventions of 12 August 1949, and Relating to the Protection of Victims of International Armed Conflicts (Protocol I), December 7, 1978, 16 I.L.M. 1391, (entered into force December 7, 1978).

Protocol Additional to the Geneva Conventions of 12 August 1949, and Relating to the Protection of Victims of Non-International Armed Conflicts (Protocol II), June 8, 1977, 16 I.L.M. 1442, (entered into force December 7, 1978).

Hague Convention (IV) Respecting the Laws and Customs of War on Land, with Annex of Regulations, October 18, 1907, T.S. No. 539, 1 Bevans 631, 36 Stat. 2277 (entered into force January 26, 1910).

Selected Cases, General Comments, & Advisory Opinions

Preface

The fields of international human rights law and international humanitarian law have exploded over the past fifty years. The first few decades after World War II were devoted primarily to the recognition of human rights norms; recent years have witnessed a steady growth in the recognition of humanitarian norms and the creation of mechanisms for enforcing and implementing both human rights and humanitarian norms. Thus, victims of human rights and humanitarian law violations around the world increasingly can find legal protection and redress for their grievances.

This book seeks to integrate the fields of international human rights law and international humanitarian law. Historically, these fields of law have developed in a somewhat disjointed fashion, leading its expositors to view the fields as wholly distinct. However, as we hope will become apparent to the reader, these fields increasingly have become integrated, relying on each other for their own respective coherence. Indeed, a fundamental general principle of international law interpretation demands that states interpret their international legal obligations consistently with their other international legal obligations. Hence, a state's international human rights legal obligations must be construed in conformity with its international humanitarian legal obligations and vice versa.

This integrationist approach is also supported by the texts of international human rights and international humanitarian treaties. For example, human rights treaties explicitly address rights protections during armed conflicts – the customary subject that international humanitarian law governs. And, humanitarian treaties often explicitly prohibit acts (e.g., genocide, crimes against humanity) that occur outside of armed conflicts – the customary period of international human rights law application.

Accordingly, this book will integrate international human rights legal materials with those of international humanitarian law. Specifically, the book will expose the student to substantive, procedural, and theoretical issues through international legal instruments, case law, and literature. We begin with a historical and conceptual overview to provide the student with a social, political, institutional, and ideological context for understanding this law. We then address the formal categories and principles of international law with especial attention to how these relate to international human rights and humanitarian law.

Because this book is primarily designed for a U.S. audience, we have included a section on the incorporation of international law in U.S. law as well as integrated U.S. constitutional legal comparisons with the substantive international human rights law in the following sections because there is much to be gained from such a comparison. Civil liberties and civil rights law in the United States is highly developed, more so than is international human rights law in many areas. At the same time, it is far from perfect. Accordingly, contrasts between U.S. law and international law in specific areas can help highlight any needed areas of improvement in either tradition. Also, the emergence of the United States as the sole superpower in the post–Cold War era makes it ever more vital for the United States to promote international human rights and humanitarian law. Yet the U.S. commitment to human rights and humanitarian law has been tepid at best; a number of important treaties remain unratified, and others have been ratified only with large numbers of reservations, declarations, and understandings designed to limit their impact. The tentativeness of this commitment may well stem in part from the unfamiliarity of human rights and humanitarian law to many in the United States, including a large segment of its legal profession. The comparative analysis with U.S. law may offer a small contribution to demystifying and clarifying to a U.S. audience the ramifications of a full commitment to human rights and humanitarian law.

We then address procedural and substantive law, which constitutes the major proportion of the book. In the sections dealing with substantive law, we have focused on issues the we believe a U.S. law student audience would find especially interesting and timely. Such issues include abortion, the death penalty, torture, gay rights, war crimes, genocide and discrimination, freedom of speech, and economic rights.

Finally, we have placed theoretical materials at the end of the book to suggest that a more abstract and critical treatment of international human rights law and international humanitarian law may be best approached after one has become familiar with the substantive and procedural law. We have attempted to give the reader a taste of different theoretical and critical approaches from a variety of viewpoints.

Beyond the pedagogical purposes of this book, we hope that in exposing the law student to the full range of current human rights and humanitarian legal issues, this book will illuminate the future promise of human rights and humanitarian law as a means of protecting individuals and groups facing persecution. The inspiration of that promise – and the responsibilities it imposes – sustain the efforts of countless advocates for international human rights and humanitarian law.

We invite our readers – faculty, students, practitioners, and others – to send suggestions and comments as well as any corrections. Rights International can be reached through its home page at http://www.rightsinternational.org or by e-mail at <ricenter@ rightsinternational.org>.

Researching International Human Rights Law

It is our hope that the casebook will serve as a research aid for practitioners handling cases, and students and faculty writing about international human rights law topics. Thus, one purpose of this book is to bring together in a convenient arrangement a large portion of the impressive body of international human rights and humanitarian case law.

At the same time, it is clear that no single work can possibly be comprehensive. While the present work provides a useful starting point for research, lawyers and academics will of course need to supplement its efforts. The human rights litigator and academic should be aware that library searches, often through hard copies of poorly indexed and dated materials, will be essential to comprehensive legal analysis. The materials of the United Nations, for example, are among the most daunting and obscure to research.

A number of excellent bibliographies provide systematic guidance to human rights sources. They should be consulted at the outset of any research task. Two noteworthy examples are David Weissbrodt and Marci Hoffman's *Bibliography for Research on International Human Rights Law*, 6 MINN. J. GLOBAL TRADE 200 (1997), and Jack Tobin and Jennifer Green's GUIDE TO HUMAN RIGHTS RESEARCH (1994).

Online databases such as LexisNexis and Westlaw or, increasingly, the Internet, also provide valuable tools for research. Indeed, educated in the era of computers, many law students today tend to conclude that the time for doing research in books, digests, and other hard copies has passed. The conclusion is premature. Students and practitioners alike must still take great care to examine multiple sources, often by digging through the library stacks. Nevertheless, online resources can be essential, particularly for finding the most up-to-date cases.

There are many places to find guidance to online research. The Rights International home page maintains links to many helpful research sources on the Internet.

Note Regarding Editing

To facilitate reading, most footnotes from the case excerpts have been placed in parentheses within the text of the excerpt; however, some footnotes and citations in excerpts from cases and other materials have been omitted. The editors have changed citation styles within case excerpts from the European Court of Human Rights for purposes of consistency, clarity, and brevity. Footnote numbering in excerpts contained in this book may not reflect the original numbering in the excerpt.

The editors' comments generally are enclosed by brackets.

Acknowledgments

We wish to thank the following persons who contributed to the INTERNATIONAL HUMAN RIGHTS LAW AND PRACTICE: CASES, TREATIES AND MATERIALS (Kluwer Law International 1997), from which this present casebook has taken substantial material:

Richard Falk

Edward Koren

Ronald Slye

We also would like to thank Professors Connie De La Vega and George Edwards and an anonymous reviewer for their comments on a draft of this book, John Berger, and Cambridge University Press. Finally, we would like to acknowledge and thank the following authors and publishers who granted permission to reprint excerpts from the following copyrighted material: Philip Alston, *The Commission on Human Rights*, THE UNITED NATIONS AND HUMAN RIGHTS: A CRITICAL APPRAISAL 126 (Philip Alston ed., Oxford Univ. Press, 1992); Abdullah Ahmen An-Na'im, *Human Rights in the Muslim World: Socio-Political Conditions and Scriptural Imperatives*, 3 HARVARD HUMAN RIGHTS JOURNAL 13 (1990); Ian Brownlie, PRINCIPLES OF PUBLIC INTERNATIONAL LAW (Oxford Univ. Press, 4th ed., 1990); Hilary Charlesworth, Christine Chinkin & Shelley Wright, *Feminist Approaches to International Law*, 85 AMERICAN JOURNAL INTERNATIONAL LAW 613 (1991); Andrew Clapham, HUMAN RIGHTS IN THE PRIVATE SPHERE (Oxford Univ.

Press, 1993); Richard Falk, THE END OF WORLD ORDER: ESSAYS ON NORMATIVE INTERNA-
TIONAL RELATIONS 26–30, 277, 288, 289–89 (New York: Holmes & Meier, 1983), copyright
1983 by Holmes & Meier Publishers, Inc. Reproduced by permission of the publisher;
Thomas M. Franck, *Legitimacy in the International System*, 82 AMERICAN JOURNAL OF
INTERNATIONAL LAW 705 (Wash., D.C.: American Society of International Law, 1988);
Laurence R. Helfer, *Consensus, Coherence and the European Convention on Human Rights*,
26 CORNELL INTERNATIONAL LAW JOURNAL 133 (1993), copyright 1993 by Cornell University, All Rights Reserved; Laurence R. Helfer and Alice M. Miller, *Sexual Orientation
and Human Rights: Toward a United States and Transnational Jurisprudence*, 9 HARVARD
HUMAN RIGHTS JOURNAL 61 (1996); Louis Henkin, THE AGE OF RIGHTS (1990), copy-
right 1990 by Columbia University Press; Paul Mahoney, *Judicial Activism and Judicial
Self-Restraint in the European Court of Human Rights*, 11 HUMAN RIGHTS LAW JOURNAL
57 (1990), copyright 1990 by N. P. Engel Publisher, Kehl/Arlington, Va.; Dinah L. Shelton,
Private Violence, Public Wrongs, and the Responsibility of States, 13 FORDHAM INTERNA-
TIONAL LAW JOURNAL 1 (1990); Francisco Forrest Martin, *Delineating a Hierarchical
Outline of International Law Sources and Norms*, 65 SASK. L. REV. 333 (2002); Francisco
Forrest Martin, *Using International Human Rights Law for Establishing a Unified Use of
Force Rule in the Law of Armed Conflict*, 64(2) Sask. L. Rev. 347 (2002); Francisco Forrest
Martin, "U.S. Opposition to the International Criminal Court: What Now?" 1 *Account-
ability* 2–8 (2002); Francisco Forrest Martin, *Our Constitution as Federal Treaty: A New
Theory of United States Constitutional Construction Based on an Originalist Understanding
for Addressing a New World*, 31 HASTINGS CONST. L. QUART. 258 (2004); Francisco Forrest
Martin, CHALLENGING HUMAN RIGHTS VIOLATIONS: USING INTERNATIONAL LAW IN U.S.
COURTS (2001); Francisco Forrest Martin, *The International Human Rights Aspects of the
Forum Non Conveniens Doctrine*, 35 U. MIAMI INTER-AM. L. REV. 101, 106–109 (2003);
Curtis A. Bradley, *The Charming Betsy Canon and Separation of Powers: Rethinking the
Interpretive Role of International Law*, 86 GEO. L. J. 479, 495–533 (1998); Steven R. Ratner,
Corporations and Human Rights: A Theory of Legal Responsibility, 111 YALE L. J. 443 (2001);
John C. Yoo, *Globalism and the Constitution: Treaties, Non-Self-Execution, and the Origi-
nal Understanding*, 99 COLUM. L. REV. 1955 (1999); John C. Yoo, *Rejoinder, Treaties and
Public Lawmaking: A Textual and Structural Defense of Non-Self-Execution*, 99 COLUM. L.
REV. 2218, 2233 *et passim* (1999); Yash Ghai, *Universalism and Relativism: Human Rights
as a Framework for Negotiating Interethnic Claims*, 21 CARDOZO L. REV. 1095–1102 (2000);
David Kennedy, *The International Human Rights Movement: Part of the Problem?* 15 HARV.
HUM. RTS. J. 101 (2002), copyright 2002 by the President and Fellows of Harvard College;
Yash Ghai, *Universalism and Relativism: Human Rights as a Framework for Negotiating
Interethnic Claims*, 21 CARDOZO L. REV. 1095–1102 (2000).

1. An Overview of International Human Rights and Humanitarian Law Development and Their Protection Mechanisms

In this section, we provide a brief overview of the historical and conceptual development of international human rights and humanitarian law. For the student of international human rights and humanitarian law, it is important to note the political, social, and economic conditions giving rise to the conception of international law and the definitional limits imposed by that conception. To this end, we sketch an outline of this development with certain extralegal themes in mind: the nation-state, war, and international transactions. In the next section, we provide an overview of the history, organization, and operation of *present* international human rights and humanitarian law mechanisms of protection.

1.1. The Historical and Conceptual Development of International Human Rights and Humanitarian Law

The "law of nations" (*jus gentium*) is now called "international law." However, the phrase "international law" (*jus inter gentes*) is misleading because it falsely suggests a body of law that only governs relations between nations, and international human rights law most often governs *intra*national matters. *Jus inter gentes* is only a subset of the law of nations. Indeed, the phrase "international law" was not coined until 1780 by Jeremy Bentham. Further contributing to the unfortunate use of the word "international law" is that the word "nation" has become conflated with the meaning of "state," suggesting falsely that international law does not protect and impose duties on a state's own nationals. "Nation" means "people," and a "state" is a particular kind of political body that is defined as such according to its relation with other states. A state sometimes – but not always – is a political organization of a people. Sometimes a state encompasses several peoples. The conflation of "nation" and "state" probably can be attributed to the emergence of independent "nation-states" that resulted from the dismantling of the Holy Roman Empire with the Peace of Westphalia ending the Thirty Years War in 1648. These events initiated an important conceptual approach to the law of nations: international law is a law of nations – not of individuals. On a theoretical level, this conception was strengthened by the use of Roman law by clerks running the chancelleries of these newly emerging nation-states. These clerks earlier had studied law at universities in Padua, Bologna, and Paris where there had been a revival of the study of Roman law that placed primacy on the state's interests – not the individual's.

However, the quasi-private dimension of international law remained and contributed greatly to the growth of the law of nations. One important area of this law was the *lex mercatoria*, and this body of international trade law developed through state-private

1

commercial leagues, such as the Hanseatic League. To reduce transaction costs associated with violations of commercial customs, it was necessary to normalize these practices through treaties.

Rationalization efforts. With the growing number of treaties and customs, legal scholars undertook efforts to rationalize this growing corpus of international law. The first prominent school of thought used natural law (*jus naturale*). The leading natural law scholars were Hugo Grotius (1583–1645), Francisco de Vitoria (1486?–1546), Francisco Suarez (1548–1617), and Samuel Pufendorf (1632–1694). Whereas Vitoria and Suarez based their natural law theories on the laws of God, Grotius had a secular theory based on universal reason rather than divine authority. In his book, DE JURE BELLI AC PACIS (CONCERNING THE LAW OF WAR AND PEACE), Grotius argued that two of the most important principles of the law of nature were (i) restitution must be made for harm done by one party to another and (ii) promises (e.g., treaties) given must be kept (*pacta sunt servanda*). These principles are still present in today's international law.

The next school of thought was Positivism. Its leading exponents were Richard Zouche (1590–1660) and Emerich de Vattel (1714–1767). "The rise of positivism in Western political and legal theory, especially from the latter part of the 18th century to the early part of the 20th century, correspond[ed] to the steady rise of the national state and its increasingly absolute claims to legal and political supremacy."[1] This school focused on positive law as opposed to natural law. With this shift in focus came the primacy of custom and treaties as evidence of the will of nations. Natural law principles were used only where a lacuna existed as to the positive law.

The beginnings of human rights and humanitarian law. The beginnings of human rights and humanitarian law are somewhat disjointed. Human rights law clearly had a beginning in humanitarian law that is strongly associated with international law governing the justification of wars (*jus ad bellum*) and the conduct of war (*jus in bello*). Although the concept of war crimes goes as far back as the fifth century with St. Augustine's discussion of a just war in his treatise, CITY OF GOD, it was not until 1268 that someone was tried and executed for beginning an unjust war.[2] Two hundred years later in 1474, twenty-seven judges of the Holy Roman Empire tried and condemned Peter von Haganbach for crimes his troops committed against civilians.

The conceptual beginnings of international human rights law can be found also in natural law theory. As Professor Louis Henkin has observed:

> Individual rights as a political idea draw on natural laws and its offspring, natural rights. In its modern manifestation that idea is traced to John Locke, to famous articulations in the American Declaration of Independence and in the French Declaration of the Rights of Man and of the Citizen, and to realizations of the idea in the United States Constitution and its Bill of Rights and in the constitutions and laws of modern states.[3]

The conceptual beginning of international human rights law may also owe its existence to the *jus gentium* governing commercial transactions insofar as this law freed up the conceptual limits on international law as confined to a law between nation-states only

---

[1] LOUIS HENKIN, ET AL., INTERNATIONAL LAW: CASES AND MATERIALS xxv (3d ed. 1993).

[2] Christopher L. Blakesley, *Report on the Obstacles to the Creation of a Permanent War Crimes Tribunal*, 18 FLETCHER FORUM OF WORLD AFFAIRS 77 (No. 2, 1994).

[3] LOUIS HENKIN, THE AGE OF RIGHTS 1 (1990).

to allow for the protection of the economic interests of individuals and commercial organizations.

It is in the nineteenth century that an integration of international human rights law and international humanitarian law that reflects and integrates the ideas, events, and conditions outlined emerges. For example, in the nineteenth century, states began to adopt the practice of outlawing the trafficking of slaves – a human rights concern. In 1868, the St. Petersburg Declaration condemned the use of "dum dum" bullets in war, thereby introducing the modern international humanitarian law on which modern international human rights law would be built. In 1898, the Convention on the Laws and Customs of Land War (the "First Hague Convention") was established as the first international codification of laws of land war.

Accordingly, one later begins to see humanitarian law cases and additional treaties. For example, in *The Paquete Habana*,[4] the U.S. Supreme Court held that the seizure of two civilian fishing boats as prizes of war was unlawful under customary international law. In 1920, the Treaty of Sevres provided for Turkey's surrender of persons responsible for the murder of an estimated six hundred thousand Armenians in 1915.

Contributing to the conceptual development of international human rights law was the international law governing the treatment of aliens and national minorities. In 1927, the United States brought an international claim on behalf of a U.S. citizen against Mexico. In *The Chattin Case*,[5] a U.S. citizen had been arrested in Mexico for embezzlement. Under a treaty between Mexico and the United States establishing a claims commission, the United States on behalf of Mr. Chattin claimed that the Mexican authorities had violated several of Chattin's due process rights as recognized under international law. The commission found for the United States (and Chattin). In another Mexican case, the commission found Mexican authorities liable for their failure to take prompt and efficient action in pursuing the murderer of a U.S. citizen working in Mexico.[6] In 1935, the Permanent Court of International Justice issued an advisory opinion finding that a Muslim-dominated Albania unlawfully had discriminated against its Greek Christian minority by closing all private schools – including Christian ones, in violation of its duty as a member of the League of Nations.

Between World Wars I and II, other humanitarian treaties were adopted. The Geneva Conventions of 1929 governed the conduct of war, and the Kellogg-Briand Pact outlawed war of aggression. In 1937, the League of Nations adopted a Convention Against Terrorism, and an optional protocol provided for the establishment of a special international criminal court to prosecute crimes of terrorism, although the convention never came into force.[7]

The World War II tribunals: A watershed in the integration of international human rights law and international humanitarian law. Ten years later, the Nuremberg and Tokyo War Crimes Tribunals would bring together these diverse strands of international law, thereby creating a somewhat more coherent international human rights and humanitarian law. During World War II, many and various gross human rights and

---

[4] 175 U.S. 677 (1900).

[5] *United States of America (B. E.Chattin) v. United Mexican States*, United States-Mexican Claims Commission, 4 U.N.R.I.A.A. 282 (1927).

[6] *United States v. Mexico (Laura M. B. Janes)*, United States and Mexico General Claims Commission, 1926, [1927] Opinions of the Commissioners 108, 4 U.N. Rep. Int'l Arb. Awards 82.

[7] C. OLIVER, THE INTERNATIONAL LEGAL SYSTEM 910 (4th ed. 1995).

humanitarian law violations were perpetrated by both the Allies and Axis powers. However, many atrocities were not covered by the laws of war. These atrocities included Nazi Germany's discrimination against and mass murder of Jews, the Romani, homosexuals, and communists. The U.S. government interned Japanese Americans in concentration camps, an action upheld by the Supreme Court in *Korematsu v. United States*, 323 U.S. 214 (1944). These human rights violations were not covered by the laws of war insofar as they constituted a state's mistreatment of its own citizens, persons believed by many at the time not to be covered by international legal protection.

In the summer of 1945, Allied leaders met in London to discuss the establishment of a war crimes tribunal. Consequently, the Allies signed the London Agreement and Charter[1] that provided for establishing an ad hoc tribunal for prosecution of German war criminals. This tribunal was called the International Military Tribunal (IMT) or Nuremberg War Crimes Tribunal.

Before this agreement, alternative fora were entrusted with the responsibility of trying war criminals. These tribunals were not displaced by the IMT. These trials took place before, during, and after the time of the Nuremberg trials. The most significant of these were the "Subsequent Proceedings" authorized by Control Council Law No. 10 that took place in the U.S. Zone of Occupied Germany. During these proceedings, about two hundred Nazi doctors, lawyers, SS leaders, generals, and diplomats were tried. There were other courts that tried Nazi war criminals as well: local courts throughout Germany, or elsewhere in Europe, and both British and American military courts-martial.

The Allies thought, however, that the IMT was necessary for the prosecution of other Nazi war criminals because the Allies feared that these criminals would escape punishment under domestic law. For example, some of the crimes were committed in a number of European jurisdictions, and it was unclear which country had a better claim to jurisdiction. The IMT's international jurisdiction mooted such jurisdictional issues. Also, many of the courts of the occupied nations used domestic law that allowed an affirmative defense of obedience to superior orders. However, under the London Charter, the IMT disallowed the defense of obeying orders.

In addition to charging defendants with violations of the laws of war, the IMT punished new categories of offenses. The London Charter established other crimes than those earlier identified in The Hague Conventions. These were crimes against peace, conspiracy to commit crimes against peace, and crimes against humanity. The assertion that a person could be held criminally liable under international law for conspiracy was controversial because there was no analogous criminal liability in the civil law traditions of two members of the Allied Powers – France and the Soviet Union. The last of these crimes, crimes against humanity, had some grounding in The Hague Conventions. In the London Charter, they were defined as:

> murder, extermination, enslavement, deportation, and other inhumane acts committed against any civilian population, before or during the war, or persecutions on political, racial or religious grounds in execution of or in connection with any crime within the jurisdiction of the Tribunal, whether or not in violation of the domestic law of the country where perpetrated.[2]

---

[1] (United States, Soviet Union, Great Britain, France) Agreement signed at London August 8, 1945, 59 Stat. 1544, E.A.S. No. 472 (hereafter London Charter).

[2] *Id.* at art. 6(c).

This marked a watershed in the conceptual and institutional development of international human rights and humanitarian law. The treaty law creating and governing the IMT wove together all the different and separate strands of the nascent international human rights and humanitarian law: *jus in bello*, individual standing (and liability), the international arbitrational law governing the treatment of aliens, the international law prohibiting discrimination against national minorities, customary international law outlawing slavery, and even the use of natural law for recognizing international crimes where customary international law arguably had been less than clear.

The Nuremberg trial lasted eleven months. The IMT tried twenty-two individuals and six organizations. Of those tried, the IMT sentenced twelve individuals (including Fritz Sauckel, Arthur Seyss-Inquart, Martin Bormann, Julius Streicher, and Herman Goering) to death by hanging and imprisoned seven others at the Allies' Spandau prison outside Berlin. Three of the six Nazi and German governmental organizations were found guilty as well.

A year after the IMT was established, Gen. Douglas MacArthur, Supreme Allied Commander for the Pacific Theater, established an equivalent tribunal in Tokyo by military order. This tribunal was called the International Military Tribunal for the Far East (IMT-FE). The IMT-FE was very similar to its counterpart in Nuremberg regarding subject-matter jurisdiction. As with the IMT, the IMT-FE had jurisdiction over crimes against humanity, crimes against peace, conspiracy, and other war crimes.[3]

The aftermath of World War II. It has been argued that the Tokyo and Nuremberg trials did not reflect justice but only "victors' vengeance." However, as Professor Ian Brownlie has observed, "whatever the state of law in 1945, Article 6 of the Nuremberg Charter has since come to represent general international law."[4] And, the United Nations (UN) General Assembly subsequently unanimously adopted a resolution affirming "the principles of international law recognized by the Charter of the Nuremberg Tribunal and the judgment of the Tribunal."[5]

After the end of World War II, three intergovernmental organizations were established: the United Nations (1945), the Council of Europe (1949), and the Organization of American States (1948). All three organizations promulgated human rights and humanitarian legal standards and adopted treaties that established protection mechanisms. One of the UN's first contributions was to provide auspices for formulating the basic normative structure of international human rights law. This undertaking took the form of drafting a series of authoritative texts that set forth an agreed corpus of substantive rights: the

---

[3] Besides these tribunals, there were other military commissions responsible for prosecuting violations of the law of war. *See, e.g., In re Yamashita*, 327 U.S. 1, 347 (1946) (recognizing "command responsibility" for failure of a Japanese general to stop war atrocities committed by his troops). Following World War II, there have been some important domestic cases addressing humanitarian law. The foremost case was *Attorney-General of Israel v. Eichmann*, 36 INT'L L. REP. 5 (1968) (District Ct. Jerusalem 1961), in which the former Nazi leader in charge of the "Final Solution" was prosecuted under Israeli law. Another notable case was *United States v. Calley*, 48 C.M.R. 19 (U.S. Ct. Military App. 1973), 48 C.M.R. 19 (U.S. Ct. Military App. 1973), in which a U.S. soldier was convicted of murdering civilians in the My Lai village during the Vietnam War. And, in *Matter of Demjanjuk*, 603 F. Supp. 1468 (N.D. Ohio 1985), an alleged Treblinka concentration camp guard was extradited to Israel to stand trial; however, he subsequently was found not guilty by an Israeli court and ordered to be allowed to return to the United States.

[4] IAN BROWNLIE, PRINCIPLES OF PUBLIC INTERNATIONAL LAW 562 (4th ed. 1990).

[5] *Id.*

foundational documents were the Universal Declaration of Human Rights (1948); the International Covenant on Economic, Social, and Cultural Rights (1966); and the International Covenant on Civil and Political Rights (1966). Together these are often referred to as the Universal Bill of Human Rights. Subsequently, a series of legal instruments were adopted addressing more focused human wrongs and offering the protection of law to vulnerable targets of abuse. These included instruments relating to genocide, racial discrimination, women, children, refugees, victims of torture, and indigenous peoples. Most recently, the UN has established the International Criminal Tribunals for the Former Yugoslavia and Rwanda and the International Criminal Court.

However, regional organizations had been more successful in protecting human rights than the UN because both the United States and the Soviet Union used charges of human rights violations as a political tool to discredit the other. Accordingly, the Council of Europe adopted the European Convention on Human Rights in 1950, which established the European Commission and Court of Human Rights. The Organization of American States adopted the American Declaration on the Rights and Duties of Man in 1948 and the American Convention on Human Rights in 1969 and established the Inter-American Commission and Court of Human Rights. In Africa, the Organisation of African Unity has established the African Commission and Court of Human and Peoples' Rights, charged with enforcing the African Charter on Human and Peoples' Rights.

In the following section, we discuss in greater detail these and other subsequent developments in international human rights and humanitarian law and their enforcement mechanisms.

1.2. Overview of International Protection Mechanisms: History, Organization, and Operations

We now will examine the major international human rights and humanitarian adjudicative and other enforcement mechanisms.

1.2.1. United Nations Mechanisms

The UN's human rights and humanitarian enforcement mechanisms are either UN treaty- or UN Charter-based. The difference between treaty- and Charter-based organizations is important on a very pragmatic level. Charter-based organizations are supported by UN members dues; treaty-based organizations are funded only on a voluntary basis by the states parties to the treaty.

Within the UN enforcement system, there are diverse organs, such as courts/tribunals, committees, special procedural mechanisms, working groups, rapporteurs, experts, and representatives. The only true courts/tribunals at present are the following:

- International Court of Justice ("The Hague" or ICJ)
- International Criminal Court (ICC)
- International Criminal Tribunal for the Former Yugoslavia (ICTY)
- International Criminal Tribunal for Rwanda (ICTR)

Tribunals and courts that have been established or proposed under agreements between the UN and national authorities (so-called hybrid tribunals) include the following:

- Special Court for Sierra Leone
- Crime Panels of the District Court of Dili and Court of Appeals ("East Timor Tribunal")
- UN Interim Administration Mission in Kosovo (UNMIK) "Regulation 64" Panels in the Courts of Kosovo
- Extraordinary Chambers in the Court of Cambodia

These tribunals will be addressed in Section 1.2.3.

The ICJ only considers cases between countries and/or intergovernmental organizations (e.g., World Health Organization, UNICEF). Individuals or nongovernmental organizations (NGOs) cannot bring cases to the ICJ. The International Criminal Court, the International Criminal Tribunals for Yugoslavia and Rwanda, and the other hybrid criminal courts only consider cases prosecuted by their respective prosecutors. Individuals cannot bring private prosecutions. However, these criminal tribunals do consider *amicus curiae* briefs from NGOs and other nongovernmental entities.

There are other adjudicative bodies with quasi-judicial powers that have been established by treaty. These are

- Human Rights Committee
- Committee on the Elimination of Racial Discrimination
- Committee Against Torture
- Committee on the Elimination of Discrimination Against Women

Before these bodies, individuals can bring cases against state's parties to the respective treaties creating these bodies. However, these quasi-judicial bodies can only "recommend" certain measures. They cannot "order" state's parties to comply with their findings. Other UN bodies or procedures have little or no adjudicative power. However, recently the UN Working Group on Detention has begun issuing legally reasoned decisions to develop the international law governing detention.

The opinions issued by these quasi-judicial bodies do provide declaratory relief that is essential for developing the corpus of international human rights and humanitarian law for the UN Security Council and other tribunals with stronger remedial powers. Such "soft law" has "hard law consequences" through other international enforcement mechanisms.

In the following, we briefly describe those bodies and procedures that have been frequently used by human rights and humanitarian law advocates.

1.2.1.1. UN Treaty-Based Tribunals

Although there are numerous human rights and humanitarian declarations, standards, and treaties, presently only five treaties have established either a court or a quasi-judicial body for considering cases: (1) the Treaty of Rome (or ICC Statute) that established the International Criminal Court; (2) the International Covenant on Civil and Political Rights (ICCPR) with its Optional Protocol that established the Human Rights Committee; (3) the Convention Against Torture, Cruel, Inhuman or Degrading Treatment or Punishment that established the Committee Against Torture; (4) the Convention on the Elimination of All Forms of Racial Discrimination that established the Committee on the Elimination of Racial Discrimination; (5) Optional Protocol to the Convention on the Elimination of All Forms of Discrimination Against Women established the Committee on the Elimination of Discrimination Against Women. We will examine only those mechanisms that have individual complaint procedures. Despite the interstate complaint procedure available under these three systems, no state had lodged a complaint against another under these systems as of 1995.[1]

International Criminal Court. In July 1998, the Treaty of Rome ("Statute of the International Criminal Court") was adopted. The ICC was established when the Treaty of Rome came into force on July 1, 2002. The ICC has jurisdiction over the crimes of genocide, crimes against humanity, war crimes, and the crime of aggression.[2] The UN conference that established the ICC declined to give the ICC jurisdiction over crimes of terrorism or illegal drug trafficking.

The UN Security Council or a state party to the Treaty of Rome can refer a case to the ICC prosecutor for investigation. The prosecutor also can initiate an investigation *propio motu.* On the basis of the information gathered by the prosecutor, the ICC's pretrial chamber makes a decision about admissibility. There is also an appeals chamber. In 2004, the ICC prosecutor began investigating international crimes committed in the Democratic Republic of Congo, Central African Republic, and Uganda.

Human Rights Committee. The UN Human Rights Committee was established by the ICCPR in 1976. Its major function is to interpret the ICCPR, which lists many different fundamental rights. Besides examining reports on human rights conditions in particular countries and issuing advisory opinions called "General Comments," the Committee also considers "communications" from individuals in closed meetings under the Optional Protocol to the ICCPR. The eighteen-member committee meets three times a year in Geneva (twice) and New York (once).

Only complaints (called "communications") from person(s) (called "authors") subject to the jurisdiction of a state that is a party to the Optional Protocol can be considered. Of the approximately 130 states parties to the ICCPR, over eighty are parties to the Optional Protocol. If the author's communication is sent to the state party for comment, the author will have an opportunity to reply to the state's comments. The Committee places authors and states parties on equal footing throughout its proceedings.

There is an initial admissibility stage in which the Committee examines the communication to determine whether it has jurisdiction. During this admissibility stage, the Committee examines several issues. As in many international adjudicative systems, the complainant must both exhaust domestic remedies, and the complaint cannot be considered if the same situation involving the same parties is being investigated under another international procedure. Furthermore, the state must have been a state party at the time of the alleged ICCPR violation. The Committee usually takes twelve to eighteen months to declare a communication admissible or inadmissible.

If a communication is found admissible, the Committee then examines the merits of the case. The examination of the merits of the case may take a year or two, depending on the degree of cooperation by states parties and the authors of complaints in submitting all the information needed by the Committee. However, as a matter of practice, oftentimes

---

[1] HENRY J. STEINER & PHILIP ALSTON, INTERNATIONAL HUMAN RIGHTS IN CONTEXT: LAW, POLITICS, MORALS 560 (1996).

[2] Art. 5(1), Statute of the International Criminal Court, U.N Doc. A/CONF.183/9 (17 July 1998).

the Committee examines both the admissibility and merits of the case contemporaneously because the state party addresses both admissibility issues and the merits of the case in its initial comments to the author's complaint.

Subsequently, the Committee makes legal and factual findings on the communication. These findings are called "views." Decisions are usually made by consensus even though members can demand the taking of a vote. If the state party is found to have violated its legal obligations under the ICCPR, the Committee makes a "recommendation" to the state party to correct the matter. Although during the proceedings of the case, parties may not disclose publicly the identity of the parties, after the session at which the findings are adopted parties can publicly be disclosed. The views and recommendations are reproduced in the Committee's annual report to the General Assembly.

Interim protection before the Committee adopts its view is provided by the Committee under Rule 86 of its Regulations. For example, the Committee has advised against a threatened expulsion, for the suspension of a death sentence, or the need for an urgent medical examination.

Because the Committee has no independent fact-finding functions, it can consider only written information made available by the parties. There are no oral hearings. Allegations and counterallegations must be specific and not couched in general terms. In a number of cases dealing with the right to life, torture, and ill-treatment, as well as arbitrary arrests and disappearances, the Committee has established that the burden of proof cannot rest alone on the person who is complaining of the violation of rights and freedoms.

At first, the Human Rights Committee did not receive many communications in part due to the fact that there had been a tacit understanding with human rights NGOs that they would not deluge the Committee with communications. However, in the latter part of the 1980s, growing public awareness of the Human Rights Committee's work under the Optional Protocol multiplied the number of communications it received. In all, 728 communications from individuals involving fifty-two countries have been examined by the Committee as of November 1996. Of these 728 communications, the Committee ruled on the merits in 239 cases and found 181 cases in which there were violations of the ICCPR.

The early decisions of the Human Rights Committee had little if any legal analysis. In the Committee's views, there usually was only a discussion of the facts and an assertion of what ICCPR articles (if any) have been violated. This early lack of legal analysis has been criticized from within and from outside the Committee. Although the Committee has developed some minimal tests for determining the level of deference given to a state party that interferes with a particular ICCPR right, for the most part, the Committee's views were barren of much legal argument. However, in recent years, the Committee's decisions have included more legal analysis.

The effectiveness of the Committee has been mixed. Several countries have changed their laws as a result of Committee recommendations. In a number of cases, prisoner sentences have been commuted and compensation paid to victims of human rights violations. Countries that have complied with their ICCPR obligations include Canada and several Scandinavian countries. However, many countries have simply ignored the Committee's recommendations. Some countries have even refused to answer initial Committee requests for comments on the author's communication. In 1990, the Committee instituted a mechanism whereby it seeks to monitor more closely whether states parties have given effect to its final decisions on the merits.

Committee on the Elimination of Racial Discrimination. Largely in response to Third World pressure against the South African policy of apartheid, the UN General Assembly adopted the Declaration on Racial Discrimination in 1963 and the Convention on the Elimination of All Forms of Racial Discrimination in 1965. The convention entered into force in 1969.

The implementation provisions of the convention were the first such provisions included in the text of a UN human rights convention. Unlike, for example, the ICCPR, the Convention on the Elimination of All Forms of Racial Discrimination incorporates a right of petition for individuals. The Committee on the Elimination of Racial Discrimination (CERD) considers communications from individuals and groups within a state's jurisdiction. If the author has exhausted all domestic remedies, the convention provides notice of the alleged violation to the state party concerned, maintaining the confidentiality of the petitioner. The state is then given a three-month period in which to cure or submit written comments on the allegations. After reviewing all relevant information made available, CERD makes a finding about any violations of the convention. If a violation is found, CERD makes a recommendation to the state party. However, CERD has considered very few communications in all its years even though over 140 countries are states parties. The preferred UN protection mechanism for pressing complaints of racial discrimination has been the UN Human Rights Committee.

CERD also has the task of supervising states parties' implementation of the convention. After a state has notified the committee that another state is not adhering to the provisions of the convention, the Committee is required to transmit the communication to the state concerned and proceed to resolve the issue. In the event that the states parties fail to reach a settlement, an ad hoc conciliation commission of five is appointed by the CERD's chairman to facilitate an amicable solution.

Committee Against Torture. The Committee Against Torture (CAT) was established under Article 17 of the Convention Against Torture and Other Cruel, Inhuman, or Degrading Treatment or Punishment. The convention was adopted by the UN General Assembly in 1984 and entered into force in 1987.

Each party to the convention accepts the affirmative responsibility to take effective legislative, administrative, judicial, and other measures to prevent acts of torture in any territory under its jurisdiction and to submit reports to the CAT on the measures it has taken to fulfill its responsibilities.

The Committee examines and issue reports of CAT violations. Furthermore, Article 22 of the convention creates an individual complaint procedure. On screening out communications that are anonymous or incompatible with provisions of the convention, the Committee brings admissible communications to the attention of the state party concerned and considers the communications in light of all the information made available by the individual and the state party. CAT may then forward its views to both parties and report its views in its annual report to the UN General Assembly.

The convention is distinctive among several treaties in providing for the more intrusive Article 20 remedy, whereby one or more of its members may be called on to undertake a confidential inquiry and to report urgently to CAT in those cases in which it "receives reliable information which appears to it to contain well-founded indications that torture is being systematically practiced in the territory of the State Party." While CERD has an interstate complaint procedure, the CAT interstate complaint procedure is dependent on the specific and separable acceptance by the state of Article 41.

Since its establishment, CAT has considered very few cases. The preferred UN protection mechanism for pressing claims of torture and other cruel, inhuman, or degrading treatment or punishment has been the UN Human Rights Committee.

Committee to Eliminate Discrimination Against Women. The Convention on the Elimination of All Forms of Discrimination Against Women was adopted in 1979 and entered into force in 1981. The Optional Protocol to the Convention to Eliminate Discrimination Against Women was adopted in 1999 and entered into force in 2000. The Optional Protocol allows individuals to submit complaints either on behalf of themselves or others to the Committee to Eliminate Discrimination Against Women (CEDAW) for alleged violations of the Convention. Unlike the convention, the Optional Protocol does not allow reservations.

As in other international adjudicative mechanisms, the complainant must exhaust domestic remedies, and the complaint cannot be pending before or have been examined by another international proceeding. Examination of communications takes place in closed meetings. The CEDAW makes admissibility and merits decisions on the communication. If a violation is found, the state party must respond within six months with what measures it has taken to remedy the situation. As of 2004, only one communication had been examined by the Committee.

Committee on Economic, Social, and Cultural Rights. The Committee on Economic, Social, and Cultural Rights (CESCR), established in 1985, is a body of independent experts responsible for monitoring state party compliance with the International Covenant on Economic, Social, and Cultural Rights. States parties are required under the covenant to submit reports to the Committee on their compliance with the covenant, and the CESCR then examines these reports and issues "concluding observations" addressing its concerns and recommendations.

The CESCR does not consider individual complaints – although a draft protocol is under consideration. The CESCR meets twice yearly and also issues "General Comments" elaborating on the protections guaranteed by the Covenant.

1.2.1.2. UN Charter-Based Tribunals and Other Mechanisms

The following tribunals and other mechanisms receive their authority from the UN Charter.

International Court of Justice. The ICJ succeeded the former Permanent International Court of Justice (PCIJ) established by the League of Nations in 1921. The ICJ probably is the best-known international court because of its age. However, the PCIJ/ICJ, or World Court, has not entertained as many cases/advisory opinions as the European Court of Human Rights, which is considerably younger. It has dealt with a few cases/advisory opinions addressing human rights–related issues, such as genocide, self-determination, and nuclear weapons. The ICJ has jurisdiction over contentious cases between states and intergovernmental organizations. It also issues advisory opinions.

International Criminal Tribunals for the Former Yugoslavia and Rwanda. In response to genocidal practices in the former Yugoslavia and Rwanda in the early 1990s, the UN Security Council established the International Criminal Tribunal for the Former

Yugoslavia (ICT-Y) in 1993 and the International Criminal Tribunal for Rwanda (ICT-R) in 1994. Both are ad hoc tribunals whose life spans are linked to the restoration and maintenance of peace and security in the territories of the former Yugoslavia and Rwanda. Both cover crimes committed in a specific time span.

For each tribunal, there are separate trial chambers. However, both tribunals share the appeals chamber. Both tribunals used to share the same chief prosecutor; however, recently, each tribunal was given a different chief prosecutor. There are no juries. The seat of the ICT-Y is in The Hague, the ICT-R in Arusha, Tanzania. The appeals chamber for both tribunals sits in The Hague.

The ICT-Y's jurisdiction is limited to the former Yugoslavia. The ICT-Y has jurisdiction over grave breaches of the Geneva Conventions, violations of the laws and customs of war, genocide, and crimes against humanity. The ICT-Y does not have jurisdiction over crimes against peace.

The ICT-R's jurisdiction extends to Rwanda and neighboring countries. The ICT-R has jurisdiction over grave breaches of the Geneva Conventions, violations of the laws and customs of war, genocide, and crimes against humanity. Furthermore, the ICT-R can apply certain protocols and articles of the Geneva Conventions, including those relating to noninternational conflicts.[3] Also, unlike the ICT-Y Statute, the ICT-R Statute does not require that crimes against humanity be committed in the context of armed conflict.

Both the ICT-Y and ICT-R have indicted, arrested, and convicted numerous individuals.

UN High Commissioner for Human Rights. In 1994, the first UN High Commissioner for Human Rights was appointed. The High Commissioner has the rank of undersecretary-general and is the principal UN official responsible for promoting human rights worldwide. In this role, the Commissioner supervises the UN Centre for Human Rights in Geneva and seeks to strengthen UN machinery for human rights protection.[4] The first High Commissioner was largely ineffective. In 1997, the former president of the Republic of Ireland replaced the first High Commissioner, and she proved to be very effective. Most recently, the former chief prosecutor for the International Criminal Tribunal, Louise Arbour, became the third High Commissioner.

The UN Human Rights Commission is the principal charter-based human rights organ. It establishes policy and organizes activities surrounding the promulgation of human rights standards. Beginning with the Universal Declaration of Human Rights in the 1940s, the Commission has directed the drafting of declarations and conventions. It also supervises the operations of a number of procedures and agencies.

Procedure under ECOSOC Resolution 1503. The 1503 procedure was established by the Economic and Social Council's Resolution 1503 in 1970. The 1503 procedure was adopted and built on the 1235 procedure and developed as a mechanism for the investigation of specific instances involving civil and political rights violations. Communications under 1503 can be submitted by individuals. Although communications were generally used by the UN primarily as a means of identifying general trends, the adoption of the

---

[3] Statute of the International Tribunal for Rwanda, art. 4, U.N. Doc. S/Res/955, Annex (1994) (hereinafter ICT-R statute).

[4] *The High Commissioner for Human Rights: An Introduction,* U.N. Doc. HR/PUB/HCHR/96/1 (1996).

1503 procedure developed into an individual complaint procedure. The use of the 1503 procedure has been enormously popular: in the first quarter of 1993, over one hundred twenty-five thousand complaints were filed. The following extract explains the procedural aspects:

Philip Alston
The Commission on Human Rights
in Alston (ed.) THE UNITED NATIONS AND HUMAN RIGHTS:
A CRITICAL APPRAISAL
126 (1992)

. . . .

[T]he [1503] procedure currently consists of the following four steps. Firstly, the Communications Working Group of the Sub-Commission begins the procedure by sorting through the various complaints that have been received in the preceding year. The group consists of five Sub-Commission members and each takes primary responsibility for complaints dealing with a specific cluster of rights. . . . The Group requires an affirmative majority vote before any 'situation' can be forwarded on to the Sub-Commission in plenary.

In recent years the Sub-Commission's Working Group has sent its parent a list of about eight to ten countries a year on average. It might also identify a few situations for specific consideration the following year, thus implicitly serving notice on the governments concerned. At the second stage, when the full Sub-Commission considers each of its Working Group's 'nominees', it opts by a simple majority vote to send the country on to the Commission, to drop it, or to reconsider it the following year. While the complainant is not informed at this stage, the government concerned is invited to submit written observations and to defend itself before the Commission, thus creating a clear inequality of opportunities to participate in the proceedings. As the third stage of the procedure, the Commission also establishes a Communications Working Group. Its task is to draft recommendations as to the action which the Commission might wish to take on each country situation that is put before it. At the fourth stage the Commission itself devotes several days at each of its annual sessions to a consideration of all the relevant material. At the end of its deliberations its Chairman announces the names of the countries that have been considered and the names of those that have been let off the hook. He or she does not, however, provide any details as to the nature of the allegations or the specific action taken by the Commission. As to the latter, several options are available – in addition to dropping the case altogether. The first is to keep it 'under review' which means that more evidence will be admitted next year and the government concerned will be called to account again. It also provides an incentive for at least cosmetic measures to be adopted and for strong lobbying to be undertaken in the meantime. The second option is to send an envoy to seek further information on the spot and report back to the Commission. The third is to appoint an ad hoc committee which, with the approval of the state concerned, can conduct a confidential investigation aimed at finding a 'friendly solution'. The Committee then reports to the Commission 'with such observations and suggestions as it may deem appropriate'. This procedure has, as of the end of the 1992 session, never been invoked. The fourth and final option is for the Commission to transfer the case to the 1235 procedure, thereby going public and permitting 'a thorough study by the Commission and a report and recommendations thereon to the Council'. The rule of the Council in this respect has so far proved to be absolutely minimal.

Thus, in the absence of a decision to go public, the entire procedure is shrouded in secrecy, with each of its stages being accomplished in confidential sessions by the bodies concerned. Nevertheless, the details have invariably been leaked to the media for one reason or another and the complete documentation on several country situations has been made available as a result of Commission decisions to release all the relevant documentation in cases concerning Equatorial Guinea, Uruguay, Argentina, and the Philippines.

In statistical terms, the 1503 procedure has 'touched' an impressive number of countries. On the basis of unofficial sources, it seems that at least forty-five countries have been reported to the Commission under the procedure since 1972. More authoritatively, however, it can be said that since the Commission began to officially identify the situations before it, in 1978, thirty-nine States have been subject to scrutiny as of the end of the 1991 sessions. Of these, twelve were in Africa, twelve in Asia, twelve in Latin America, two in Eastern Europe, and one in Western Europe.

∾

The 1503 procedure was more important twenty years ago when it was adopted because the procedure represented a historic first step in the UN's protection of human rights. However, with the development of a wide variety of alternative mechanisms for dealing with complaints, there are more effective protection mechanisms available. There are notable differences between the 1503 procedure and other mechanisms that reflect on 1503's effectiveness. Specifically, 1503 is not intended for dispute resolution. And, like so much of the UN's operations, the 1503 procedure is not "transparent": individual petitioners often cannot learn of the status or outcome of the communication. This last disadvantage has compelled many commentators to seriously criticize its use.

Procedure under ECOSOC Resolution 1235. The Economic and Social Council Resolution 1235 procedure was established in 1967. The 1235 procedure provides the basis on which the UN Commission on Human Rights holds an annual public debate focusing on gross human rights and fundamental freedoms violations in a number of States, including policies of racial discrimination and segregation and of apartheid, in any country, including colonial and other dependent countries, territories, and peoples.

The 1235 procedure authorizes the Commission to examine information relevant to gross systematic violations of human rights and fundamental freedoms. Second, the Commission may make a thorough study of situations that reveal a consistent pattern of human rights violations. Through whatever techniques the Commission deems appropriate, 1235 is also used to permit the studying and investigating of particular situations (or individual cases) raised at the annual debate.

There often needs to be bloodshed or great unrest for the 1235 procedure to be implemented in specific cases. Therefore, 1235 may be seen not only as reactive instead of proactive but also as reactive at a later stage when the stakes are particularly high. In contrast to 1503, there are no admissibility criteria.

Thematic and Country Mechanisms. Besides the 1503 and 1235 procedural mechanisms, there are numerous other UN Charter-based mechanisms for protecting human rights. These mechanisms fall into two categories: thematic or country. A country-specific mechanism (sometimes called a working group, rapporteur, expert, or representative) consists of independent experts assessing a country's overall human rights situation. Thematic mechanisms (called either rapporteurs or working groups) examine specific types of human rights violations *worldwide*. For a thematic mechanism, its "global scope of inquiry increases the likelihood that the government will cooperate with it, as is often not the case when the government feels itself 'pinpointed' for scrutiny" under a country-specific mechanism.[5] Generally, these country and thematic mechanisms operate by visiting individual countries, collecting information about observances or violations of human rights, receiving and forwarding complaints from individuals or organizations to a particular government, reporting on these violations, and formulating policy and/or recommendations.

One very successful mechanism has been the Working Group on Disappearances (WGD). The WGD was created in 1980. Basically, WGD's purpose is to assist families in determining the whereabouts and fate of their missing relatives. Specifically, the WGD undertakes the following measures. It seeks and receives information relating to disappeared persons from governments, intergovernmental organs, and other reliable sources. On receipt of sufficient information, the WGD forwards the information to the government concerned and requests that the government investigate the disappearance and inform WGD on its findings. The names of the "disappeared" remain confidential to protect those individuals from further harm. The WGD encourages governments to invite it to carry out on-site investigations.

The popularity of this mechanism is reflected in the numbers of complaints received: in 1993, the WGD received twenty thousand cases from some fifty countries.[6] Its success may be attributed to the fact that the WGD is not concerned with blaming governments for disappearances.

Another successful mechanism is the Working Group on Arbitrary Detention (WGAD). This group has developed a radically different approach from other thematic mechanisms. The WGAD has adopted a quasi-judicial role in which the investigation of cases takes on an adversarial nature to obtain the cooperation of the country concerned. The WGAD issues "decisions" on communications and adopts formal "deliberations" to develop the doctrinal bases of its work.

International Labour Organisation. The International Labour Organisation (ILO) succeeded the International Labour Office created in 1919, which was autonomously associated with the League of Nations. The ILO seeks to improve labor conditions and the development of independent labor movements. The ILO has two main organs: the General Conference (composed of representatives from each UN member state) and the Governing Body (composed of government, employer, and employee representatives). The Governing Body serves as the executive council and is elected by the General Conference.

---

[5] SHAREEN HERTEL, PROMISES TO KEEP: SECURING HUMAN RIGHTS IN A CHANGING WORLD 11 (New York: United Nations Assn., 1993).

[6] *Id.* at 13.

The ILO has promulgated the International Labour Code that consists of over 250 conventions and recommendations.[7] Upon ratification of an ILO convention, the state party must submit compliance reports to the ILO, and the ILO supervises the state's compliance. Complaints by states and employers' or workers' organizations are reviewed by the ILO's Commission of Inquiry. The Governing Body then makes a recommendation, which is customarily accepted by the General Conference.

UN High Commissioner for Refugees. The post of UN High Commissioner for Refugees (UNHCR) was created by the General Assembly in 1950. The office of UNCHR promotes the protection of refugee rights and supervises state party compliance with the UN Convention Relating to the Status of Refugees (1951) and its Protocol (1967). The UNHRC also provides humanitarian relief, including food, medical care, and the supervision of refugee camps. It also seeks to resettle refugees. For human rights advocates/lawyers, it is important to note that in some cases the UNHRC also issues "individual refugee mandates," which are letters directed to national governments declaring a particular person a "refugee" as defined by the UN Convention Relating to the Status of Refugees and urging the government to provide protection to that person.

1.2.2. Regional Tribunals

There are four major regional international human rights adjudicative systems: the European Court of Human Rights, the Inter-American Commission and Court of Human Rights, the African Commission and Court of Human and Peoples' Rights, and the Caribbean Court of Justice.

European Court of Human Rights. In response to the genocidal horrors of World War II, the European community recognized the need for a regional system for protecting human rights. "The post-mortem by elites and scholars concluded, in part, that disrespect for the rule of law and fundamental individual rights was a transnational destabilizing force with a potentially strong regional reach."[1] Subsequently, Winston Churchill in 1948 called for a European charter of human rights. And in the establishment of the Council of Europe the following year, membership in the Council required that states parties undertake the maintenance and further realization of human rights.[2]

In 1950, the Council of Europe established the Convention for the Protection of Human Rights and Fundamental Freedoms – also called the European Convention on Human Rights (ECHR), which came into force in 1953. The ECHR created the European Commission and Court of Human Rights. States parties to the ECHR may ratify a number of optional protocols that allow an incremental addition of new rights and procedural rules. Of particular interest is the First Protocol that guarantees the enjoyment of property, right to education, and free elections. The Fourth Protocol guarantees freedom of movement, prohibits imprisonment for civil debt, prohibits collective expulsion of

---

[7] Interestingly, states parties to ILO conventions may not make reservations.

[1] Michael Reisman, *Establishment of a Regional Human Rights Arrangement in the Asian and Pacific Region: Experiences of Other Regions*, FOURTH WORKSHOP ON REGIONAL HUMAN RIGHTS ARRANGEMENTS IN THE ASIAN AND PACIFIC REGION: REPORT (KATHMANDU, 26–28 FEBRUARY 1996), UN Doc. HR/PUB/96/3 (1996) at 30–31.

[2] Art. 3, Statute of the Council of Europe.

aliens, and guarantees the right to enter and remain in one's country. The Sixth Protocol abolishes the death penalty in time of peace.

With the Eleventh Protocol coming into force in 1998, the Commission was dismantled and individuals were allowed to take their cases directly to the Court in Strasbourg, France. The Court can receive complaints (known as "applications") from individuals claiming ECHR and protocol violations perpetrated by its states parties. The Court also can receive applications from states parties complaining of ECHR violations by another state party. Presently, over thirty countries recognize the jurisdiction of the Commission, and it now receives five thousand to ten thousand applications annually.

The ECHR requires that applicants exhaust domestic legal remedies and file within six months of exhausting these domestic remedies and that their petition not be pending in another international proceeding. If the Court finds that the application is admissible, it will then examine the merits of the case. If the case is of especial importance, the Grand Chamber will examine the case.

If the Court finds an ECHR violation, it can order compensation; however, it cannot order a state party to undertake specific injunctive measures. It is left to the state party to determine the best way for correcting the conditions giving rise to the violation. The Court also can award costs. The European Court of Human Rights has decided thousands of cases.

Inter-American Commission and Court of Human Rights. The Inter-American Commission and Court of Human Right are the human rights protection mechanisms for the Organization of American States (OAS). The American Declaration of the Rights and Duties of Man ("American Declaration") was adopted by the OAS in 1948. The Inter-American Commission on Human Rights, located in Washington, D.C., was created in 1959. Six years later it was given authority to accept communications from individuals and others, request information from governments, and make recommendations.

In 1969, the OAS adopted the American Convention on Human Rights (ACHR). The ACHR has additional optional protocols dealing with the death penalty; and economic, social, and cultural rights. There are also additional conventions dealing with violence against women and torture. The ACHR created the Inter-American Court of Human Rights, located in San Jose, Costa Rica. The Court came into being in 1978 and rendered its first opinion in 1982.

Under the authority of American Declaration, the Inter-American Commission on Human Rights has competence to examine cases from all states in the Americas. If the Inter-American Commission finds a state in violation of the Declaration, it can make recommendations to "bring about a more effective observance of fundamental human rights."[3] However, it cannot order a state to comply with its recommendations.

The Commission also has jurisdiction to examine cases from countries that have ratified the ACHR. Over two dozen countries have done so. Under Article 44 of the ACHR,

> any person or group of persons, or any non-governmental entity legally recognized in one or more member States of the [OAS], may lodge petitions with the Commission containing denunciations or complaints of violations of [the ACHR] by a State Party.

---

[3] Art. 20(b), Statute of the Inter-American Commission on Human Rights.

Unlike the European Convention on Human Rights, the ACHR allows another person or group to submit a complaint on behalf of a victim to the Commission even though they are not the victim's legal representative. Like the European Convention, the ACHR requires that petitioners exhaust domestic legal remedies and file within six months of exhausting these domestic remedies and that their petition is not pending in another international proceeding.

If the case is found admissible, the Commission transmits the case to the state party for comments. The Commission can hold hearings, take evidence, and make on-site investigations. Most importantly, it can request the president of the Inter-American Court of Human Rights to issue temporary protective orders to a state party to ensure the safety of the petitioner or witnesses. The Commission frequently employs these temporary protective orders.

During this process, the Commission also seeks a friendly settlement between the parties. If a settlement is reached, the Commission sends a short report to the secretary-general of the OAS. If there is no settlement, the Commission draws up a report of its findings and recommendations and submits it to the state party only. If the matter still has not been settled after three months, the Commission can either publish the report in its annual report or refer the case to the Court if the state party has accepted the jurisdiction of the Court. Over a dozen countries have accepted the jurisdiction of the Inter-American Court.

Petitioners before the Court do not have standing – only the Commission. If the case is referred to Court, the Commission sends a "delegate" to argue the case. However, the Court can allow an "adviser" to represent the petitioner at hearings. The Inter-American Court is not bound by the Commission's factual findings. It can make its own factual findings, but this practice has been criticized as unnecessarily time consuming and expensive.[4]

Like the European Court, the Inter-American Court's decisions are binding on states, and the OAS General Assembly is responsible for enforcement of the Court's orders. The Court can order compensation. However, unlike the European Court, the Inter-American Court can order specific injunctive relief. Indeed, the Inter-American Court has ordered a variety of injunctive measures, including the establishment of trust funds and schools. The Court has made some very important and analytically strong decisions and advisory opinions – especially in the area of a state's affirmative obligations to prevent, to investigate, and to punish gross human rights violations. As of 2004, the Court had considered over one hundred cases and advisory opinions.

The Inter-American system has a broader mandate for protecting human rights than other regional systems. Besides its adjudicative mission, the Inter-American Commission also issues reports on countries, conducts visits on-site visits, prepares human rights instruments, and provides technical assistance to states regarding ACHR-related issues. The Commission even has negotiated a hostage crisis. Aside from adjudicating cases, the Inter-American Court has contributed to the promotion of human rights by issuing many advisory opinions. The Inter-American system has been surprisingly effective given the fact that it has had to cover two continents, deal with numerous undemocratic governments, and work within substantial financial and staff restraints.

---

[4] *See, e.g.*, David J. Padilla, *Reparations in Aloeboetoe v. Suriname*, 17 Hum. Rts. Q. 541 (1995).

African Commission and Court of Human and Peoples' Rights. The Organisation of African Unity (OAU) adopted the African Charter on Human and Peoples' Rights ("African Charter," or "Banjul Charter") in 1981 in Banjul, The Gambia. Unlike the European and Inter-American human rights instruments, the African Charter reflects a concern for protecting collective rights. It also imposes duties on individuals.

The African Charter established the African Commission on Human and Peoples' Rights. The Commission has three responsibilities. First, it promotes human rights by conducting studies, organizing symposia, preparing studies regionwide violations, and assisting states parties in the drafting of national legislation. Second, the Commission can issue advisory opinions. Third, it investigates cases submitted by both individuals and states parties.

Under its case procedure, petitioners must exhaust domestic remedies and file their petition "within a reasonable time" from the date of exhaustion or from the date the Commission is made aware of the violation. Petitioners cannot base their complaints solely on news accounts. Complaints cannot be written in disparaging or insulting language directed at the state party and its institutions or the OAU. The Commission is not required to take any action on individual cases; the Commission will consider only those cases in which a simple majority of the commissioners so decide.[5] If one of these cases "reveal[s] the existence of serious or massive violations," the Commission is required to notify the OAU's Assembly of Heads of State and Government.[6]

Under the African Charter, there is no provision for interim protection measures. The complaint procedure remains confidential. The Commission also suffers from a serious lack of funding. For these and other reasons, the Commission has not been effective. When the Commission has issued its views, they have lacked legal analysis important to establishing the Commission's authority and credibility. In 1995, the Commission failed to condemn the Nigerian government's execution of nine leaders of the Ogoni minority, including Ken Saro Wiwa, a Nobel Peace Prize laureate.

Beginning in 1994, the Commission began discussions about establishing an African Court of Human and Peoples' Rights, eventually resulting in the OAU's adoption of the Protocol to the African Charter on Human and Peoples' Rights on the Establishment of an African Court of Human and Peoples' Rights. The Protocol entered into force in 2004.

The African Commission, states parties to the Protocol, and African intergovernmental organizations can bring a claim based on violations of any international human rights instrument that has been ratified by the state party concerned. Furthermore, the Court can exercise its discretion in granting leave to individuals and NGOs to submit petitions directly to the Court if the state party agrees. The Court can award damages and order provisional protective measures and injunctive relief. The African Union (formerly the OAU) Council of Ministers is responsible for monitoring state compliance with the Court's orders. Furthermore, states, African Union (AU) organizations, and any African NGO recognized by the AU can request an advisory opinion.

Caribbean Court of Justice. The Caribbean Community (CARICOM) adopted the Agreement Establishing the Caribbean Court of Justice in 2001, which entered into force in 2002. The Court will be a municipal court of last resort for British Commonwealth

---

[5] Art. 55, African Charter on Human and Peoples' Rights.
[6] *Id.* at art. 58.

states, and, thereby, the Court will effectively replace the United Kingdom's Judicial Committee of the Privy Council for these states. This appellate jurisdiction extends both to criminal and civil matters. Accordingly, individuals will have standing before the Court, and many cases decided under the Court's appellate jurisdiction will involve human rights.

Furthermore, the court is also an international court with original jurisdiction over international legal disputes. States parties to the Agreement Establishing the Caribbean Court of Justice, CARICOM, and nationals of states parties can bring cases to the Court alleging violations of the Treaty Establishing the Caribbean Community.

The Court also has jurisdiction to issue interim measures and advisory opinions. The Court is planned to begin operating in 2005 and to be located in Trinidad and Tobago.

1.2.3. Other Tribunals

Human Rights Commission for Bosnia and Herzegovina. The Dayton Agreement ending the conflict in Bosnia and Herzegovina provided for the establishment of the Human Rights Commission for Bosnia and Herzegovina, whose headquarters are in Sarajevo. The Commission consists of two parts: an Office of Human Rights Ombudsman and the Human Rights Chamber. The Commission is competent to examine and adjudicate cases (called "applications") submitted by individuals, states parties, groups, or NGOs alleging human rights violations as defined by the European Convention on Human Rights committed by any of the states parties. It also is competent to examine and adjudicate cases alleging human rights violations arising from discrimination in the enjoyment of rights guaranteed by several other global and regional human rights treaties addressing genocide, torture, inhuman treatment, refugees, and war crimes.[7] (The Commission is not a criminal tribunal.)

The typical procedure is for the ombudsman to investigate a case submitted by an applicant and to make findings, conclusions, and recommendations. The state party is allowed to submit an explanation of the ombudsman's finding of a violation. If the state party does not comply with the ombudsman's recommendations, the ombudsman publishes a public report disclosing the failure of the state party to comply. The ombudsman also can refer the case to the chamber for adjudication.

If the ombudsman refers the case to the chamber, the chamber first determines whether the application is admissible, examining issues such as whether domestic remedies have been exhausted, whether the application was filed within six months of exhaustion, and whether the case is pending before another international tribunal. During any stage of the proceedings, the chamber may seek a settlement between the parties. If no settlement is reached, the chamber will make a decision on admissibility and the merits. The chamber's decision is binding. Its decision can include injunctive relief, compensation, and costs awards.

As of 2004 and 2005, the mandates of the Chamber and Commission respectively expired, and subsequent human rights cases are submitted to and decided by the Constitutional Court of Bosnia and Herzegovina.

---

[7] Dayton Agreement, *The General Framework Agreement for Peace in Bosnia and Herzegovina*, initialed 21 November 1995 (entered into force 14 December 1995), Annex Six.

Hybrid National-International, Criminal Tribunals. There are a number of hybrid national-international, criminal tribunals. These include the UN Interim Administration Mission in Kosovo (UNMIK) "Regulation 64" Panels in the Courts of Kosovo, the Crime Panels of the District Court of Dili and Court of Appeal ("East Timor Tribunal"), the Special Court for Sierra Leone, and the proposed Extraordinary Chambers in the Court of Cambodia.

The first hybrid tribunal system was established by UNMIK in 2000 following the Kosovo conflict. Regulation 64 Panels were established in the Kosovo courts to ensure equal treatment for Serbian criminal defendants. The panels have jurisdiction over all war crimes cases, as well as all significant cases of organized crime, terrorism, interethnic violence, political assassinations, and corruption. These panels are composed mostly of international judges.

The next hybrid tribunal system to be established was the Crime Panels of the District Court of Dili and Court of Appeal ("East Timor Tribunal"). Following a twenty-four-year occupation of East Timor by Indonesia, East Timor's independence, and the subsequent escalation of atrocities committed by the Indonesian Army and pro-Jakarta militias in 1999, the UN Security Council established the Crime Panels to prosecute persons who committed genocide, crimes against humanity, war crimes, and torture. The Crime Panels also have jurisdiction to try persons who committed murder and sexual offenses under Indonesian law between January 1, 1999, and October 25, 1999. The Crime Panels consist of one East Timorese judge and two international judges.

The Special Court for Sierra Leone was created by an agreement between the government of Sierra Leone and the UN in August 2000 to prosecute persons who bore the greatest responsibility for serious violations of international humanitarian law and Sierra Leonean law committed in the territory of Sierra Leone since November 30, 1996. The Court has jurisdiction over crimes against humanity, violations of common Article 3 of the Geneva Conventions, and other serious violations of international, humanitarian, and Sierra Leonean law addressing the abuse of girls and wanton destruction of property. The Special Court has concurrent jurisdiction with Sierra Leonean courts, but the Special Court has primacy. The Special Court sits in Freetown, Sierra Leone, and has both trial and appeals chambers. At present it is prosecuting a number of persons.

Another hybrid tribunal is the Extraordinary Chambers in the Court of Cambodia. After a delay of years, the Cambodian Parliament entered into an agreement with the UN to create an international criminal tribunal to try the surviving leaders of the Khmer Rouge communist regime for their alleged commission of atrocities that took 1.7 million lives during the late 1970s. As of late 2004, the agreement had not entered into force. The Extraordinary Chambers will have jurisdiction over war crimes, genocide, and crimes against humanity. It will consist of both international and Cambodian judges. Decisions will require a majority plus one vote.

2. Formal Sources and Principles of International Human Rights and Humanitarian Law

The body of law devoted to international human rights and humanitarian issues has exploded in the past two decades, primarily because of renewed interest in international dispute resolution, the decline in traditional doctrines of sovereignty and state-to-state relationships, and the related growth of norms recognizing the enforceability of the rights of individuals against states for the violation of human rights and humanitarian legal norms. The number of institutions that pronounce upon this body of law has increased, and the number of cases addressed each year has increased exponentially. This section includes some of the most important decisions that make up the corpus of international human rights and humanitarian case law.

2.1. Formal Sources

The Statute of the International Court of Justice (ICJ) sets forth the body of international law the Court is to apply to disputes brought before it. The sources of law recognized in the ICJ's statute are universally recognized as constituting a basic description of the general sources of international law.

Article 38
Statute of the International Court of Justice
June 26, 1945, 59 Stat. 1005, T.S. 993

1. The Court . . . shall apply:

(a) international conventions, whether general or particular, establishing rules expressly recognized by the contesting states;

(b) international custom, as evidence of a general practice accepted as law;

(c) the general principles of law recognized by civilized nations;

(d) subject to the provisions of Article 59,[1] judicial decisions and the teachings of the most highly qualified publicists of the various nations, as subsidiary means for the determination of rules of law.

---

[1] Article 59 states: "The decision of the Court has no binding force except between the parties and in respect of that particular case."

Professor Ian Brownlie, in his classic work on international law, discusses Article 38 as follows:

Ian Brownlie
PRINCIPLES OF PUBLIC INTERNATIONAL LAW 3, 4 (4th ed. 1990)

. . . .

These provisions are expressed in terms of the function of the Court, but they represent the previous practice of arbitral tribunals, and Article 38 is generally regarded as a complete statement of the sources of international law. Yet the article itself does not refer to 'sources' and, if looked at closely, cannot be regarded as a straightforward enumeration of the sources. The first question which arises is whether paragraph 1 creates a hierarchy of sources. They are not stated to represent a hierarchy, but the draftsman intended to give an order and in one draft the word 'successively' appeared. In practice the Court may be expected to observe the order in which they appear: (a) and (b) are obviously the important sources, and the priority of (a) is explicable by the fact that this refers to a source of mutual obligations of the parties . . .

. . . Moreover, it is probably unwise to think in terms of hierarchy dictated by order (a) to (d) in all cases. Source (a) relates to *obligations* in any case, and presumably a treaty contrary to a custom or to a general principle part of the *jus cogens* would be void or voidable. Again, the interpretation of a treaty may involve resort to general principles of law or of international law. A treaty may be displaced by a subsequent custom, where such effects are recognized by the subsequent conduct of the parties. . . .

∾

2.1.1. Treaties

International human rights and humanitarian law is, first and foremost, a law of treaties. The law of international agreements – treaties, pacts, protocols (generally supplemental to another agreement), covenants, conventions, charters, and exchanges of notes and concordats (agreements between a nation and the Holy See) – is a law not of cases but predominantly of statutory construction. This is a concept of great familiarity to those who come from a civil law tradition, in which codes and their interpretation play the most prominent role as a source of law and judicial precedent has less value, but this concept is sometimes misunderstood by a litigator trained in a common law system.

What rules govern the statutory construction of treaties? The Vienna Convention on the Law of Treaties[2] provides rules regarding the construction and interpretation of treaties. The most basic rule is that a treaty be interpreted "in good faith in accordance with the ordinary meaning to be given to the terms of the treaty in their context and in the light of its object and purpose."[3] Besides the Vienna Convention, there are other rules of statutory construction,[4] and the legislative history of the treaty (known in international

---

[2] Convention on the Law of Treaties, 23 May 1969, U.N. Doc. A/CONF. 39/27 (1969), 63 A.J.I.L. 875 (1969), 8 I.L.M. 679 (1969) (entered into force on 27 January 1980) (hereafter Vienna Convention).

[3] *Id.* at art. 31.1.

[4] WILLIAM P. STATSKY, LEGISLATIVE ANALYSIS AND DRAFTING (2d ed. 1984).

law as the *travaux préparatoires*[5]) is of great importance. However, this stress on statutory construction and history must be tempered. For example, the European Court of Human Rights (ECHR) interprets the European Convention on Human Rights "as a living instrument which ... must be interpreted in the light of present day conditions."[6] This "evolutive interpretation" has resulted in the Court playing down the importance of the *travaux préparatoires* of the ECHR.[7]

In addition to issues of treaty construction, the student should be alert to other treaty-related issues that are not immediately apparent to students of domestic law. The following is a summary list of concerns for the student:

- *Treaty or Not* – Is the instrument a treaty, making it binding in international law, or is it something less than that? The usual terms used for binding instruments are treaty, convention, pact, covenant, protocol, or other similar language, so long as the document is an "international agreement concluded between States in written form and governed by international law."[8] Nonbinding instruments are often called declarations, but may also be referred to as guidelines, standards, principles, reports, comments, communications, statements, or other such references.
- *Entry Into Force* – Does the treaty itself have enough ratifying parties to enter into effect as formal international law?[9]
- *Ratification/Signature* – What date did the country in question actually agree to be bound by the treaty? The date of signature can also be important, because a country that has signed but not ratified a treaty is obliged to refrain from acts that would "defeat the object or purpose of the treaty."[10]
- *Reservations* – Did the country "exclude or modify the legal effect of certain provisions of the treaty in their application to that State?"[11] Such modifications are effected by "reservations," "declarations," "understandings," or "provisos." It is the nature of the language itself rather than the label placed on it by the state that determines its legal effect.
- *Retroactivity* – Treaties are not generally retroactive, *i.e.*, they do not apply before the date when the treaty enters into force.[12] A country may, however, be subject to an obligation set forth in a treaty prior to the treaty's effective date if it can be shown that that obligation had attained the status of customary international law prior to the effective date.[13]
- *Domestic Legal Effect and Self-Execution* – The fact that a treaty has force in international law does not necessarily define its effect in domestic law. Domestic legal effect is

---

[5] Article 32 of the Vienna Convention on the Law of Treaties recognizes the preparatory work of a treaty as a supplemental means of interpretation.

[6] *Tyrer v. United Kingdom*, 26 Eur. Ct. H.R. (ser. A) (1988) at §31.

[7] *See, e.g., Young, James, and Webster v. United Kingdom*, 44 Eur. Ct. H.R. (ser. A) (1981) (van der Meersch, J. concurring).

[8] Art. 2.1(a), Vienna Convention.

[9] Aspects regarding the entry into force of treaties are dealt with in the Vienna Convention. *Id.* at art. 24.

[10] *Id.* at art. 18(a).

[11] *Id.* at art. 2(d). The formulation of reservations and the effect of objections by another party to the treaty to reservations are dealt with in Section 2 of the Vienna Convention.

[12] *Id.* at art. 28.

[13] *Id.* at art. 43. Also, a peremptory norm of international law (*jus cogens*) that comes into existence after a treaty is adopted renders that treaty void if the treaty's provisions are in conflict with the peremptory norm. *Id.* at art. 64.

usually defined by domestic constitutional provisions and their judicial interpretation. When a state ratifies a treaty, it may promulgate an "understanding" or "declaration" that it is non-self-executing (or its domestic law may so provide generally), which means that domestic courts cannot enforce it in the absence of implementing legislation. Even then, litigants may still ask the court to make use of the treaty as a guide to interpreting domestic law. Although recent U.S. ratifications of human rights treaties contain declarations of non–self-execution, and most U.S. courts have held that treaties dealing with human rights are not self-executing, there is some contrary authority.[14]

- *Derogation* – Many international human rights treaties permit certain of their provisions to be temporarily suspended, or derogated, during periods of national emergency. The process of derogation is a formal one, usually set out in the treaty, and failure to follow it may make the derogation ineffective in international law.

- *Exhaustion of Domestic Remedies* – Most treaties that contain enforcement mechanisms require that the petitioner pursue available remedies in the country where the violation occurred before seeking international relief. This requirement is grounded in the assumption that sovereignty should be honored, and that the local legal system normally is better equipped to resolve the dispute. This is not always true, however, and a significant jurisprudence of exceptions to the exhaustion requirement have developed over time.

Reservations. Another means of limiting international review is the use of reservations. Under Article 2(1)(d) of Vienna Convention on the Law of Treaties, a reservation is "a unilateral statement, however phrased or named, made by a State, when signing, ratifying, acceding to, accepting or approving a treaty, whereby it purports to exclude or to vary the legal effect of certain provisions of the treaty in their application to that State." As a matter of practice, substantive reservations are not common;[15] the exceptions are human rights treaties. Only the UN Convention to Eliminate Racial Discrimination has been free of reservations. At the other end, the UN Convention on the Elimination of All Forms of Discrimination Against Women has been subjected to numerous reservations by states parties.

The ICJ has held that a reservation must be compatible with the object and purpose of the treaty; otherwise, the reserving state may not be considered a party.[16] The ICJ's flexible rule enables the principles in a human rights treaty to acquire authority by allowing more states to accept the treaty in general. Furthermore, if a treaty's principles are broadly accepted, they can become customary international law and, hence, legally binding upon states that are not parties to the convention.

One means of preventing the dilution of a treaty's meaning and enforcement by reservation is allowing other states parties to reject a reservation by another state party. The UN Convention to Eliminate Racial Discrimination allows for two-thirds of the states parties to vote for the rejection of reservations. One commentator has argued in the context of the UN Convention on the Elimination of All Forms of Discrimination Against Women that only those reservations that contemplate the provision of means to move

---

[14] *See, e.g.*, the discussion in Richard B. Lillich, *International Human Rights Law in U.S. Courts*, 2 J. TRANSNAT'L L. & POL'Y 1, 4–12, 19–20 (1993).

[15] John King Gamble Jr., *Reservations to Multilateral Treaties: A Macroscopic View of State Practice*, 74 AM. J. INT'L L. 372 (1980).

[16] 1951 I.C.J. 15.

progressively toward equality of men and women are compatible with the object and purpose of the treaty.[17]

U.S. Reservations, Declarations, and Understandings to the International Covenant on Civil and Political Rights
138 Cong. Rec. S4783–4 (daily ed., April 2, 1992)

I. The Senate's advice and consent is subject to the following reservations:

(1) That Article 20 does not authorize or require legislation or other action by the United States that would restrict the right of free speech and association protected by the Constitution and laws of the United States.

(2) That the United States reserves the right, subject to its Constitutional constraints, to impose capital punishment on any person (other than a pregnant woman) duly convicted under existing or future laws permitting the imposition of capital punishment, including such punishment for crimes committed by persons below eighteen years of age.

(3) That the United States considers itself bound by Article 7 to the extent that "cruel, inhuman or degrading treatment or punishment" means the cruel and unusual treatment or punishment prohibited by the Fifth, Eighth, and/or Fourteenth Amendments to the Constitution of the United States.

(4) That because U.S. law generally applies to an offender the penalty in force at the time the offense was committed, the United States does not adhere to the third clause of paragraph 1 of Article 15.

(5) That the policy and practice of the United States are generally in compliance with and supportive of the Covenant's provisions regarding treatment of juveniles in the criminal justice system. Nevertheless, the United States reserves the right, in exceptional circumstances, to treat juveniles as adults, notwithstanding paragraphs 2(b) and 3 of Article 10 and paragraph 4 of Article 14. The United States further reserves to these provisions with respect to individuals who volunteer for military service prior to age 18.

II. The Senate's advice and consent is subject to the following understandings, which shall apply to the obligations of the United States under this Covenant:

(1) That the Constitution and laws of the United States guarantee all persons equal protection of the law and provide extensive protections against discrimination. The United States understands distinctions based upon race, color, sex, language, religion, political or other opinion, national or social origin, property, birth or any other status – as those terms are used in Article 2, paragraph 1 and Article 26 – to be permitted when such distinctions are, at minimum, rationally related to a legitimate governmental objective. The United States further understands the prohibition in paragraph 1 of Article 4 upon discrimination, in time of public emergency, based "solely" on the status of race, color, sex, language, religion or social origin not to bar distinctions that may have a disproportionate effect upon persons of a particular status.

(2) That the United States understands the right to compensation referred to in Articles 9(5) and 14(6) to require the provision of effective and enforceable mechanisms by which a victim of an unlawful arrest or detention or a miscarriage of justice may

---

[17] Rebecca J. Cook, *Reservations to the Convention on the Elimination of All Forms of Discrimination Against Women*, 30 Va. J. Int'l L. 643 (1990).

seek and, where justified, obtain compensation from either the responsible individual or the appropriate governmental entity. Entitlement to compensation may be subject of the reasonable requirements of domestic law.

(3) That the United States understands the reference to "exceptional circumstance" in paragraph 2(a) of Article 10 to permit the imprisonment of an accused person with convicted persons where appropriate in light of an individual's overall dangerousness, and to permit accused persons to waive their right to segregation from convicted persons. The United States further understands that paragraph 3 of Article 10 does not diminish the goals of punishment, deterrence, and incapacitation as additional legitimate purposes for a penitentiary system.

(4) That the United States understands that subparagraphs 3(b) and (d) of Article 14 do not require the provision of a criminal defendant's counsel of choice when the defendant is provided with court-appointed counsel on grounds of indigence, when the defendant is financially able to retain alternative counsel, or when imprisonment is not imposed. The United States further understands that paragraph 3(e) does not prohibit a requirement that the defendant make a showing that any witness whose attendance he seeks to compel is necessary for his defense. The United States understands the prohibition upon double jeopardy in paragraph 7 to apply only when the judgment of acquittal has been rendered by a court of the same governmental unit, whether the Federal Government or a constituent unit, is seeking a new trial for the same cause.

(5) That the United States understands that this Covenant shall be implemented by the Federal Government to the extent that it exercises legislative and judicial jurisdiction over the matters covered therein, and otherwise by the state and local governments; to the extent that state and local governments exercise jurisdiction over such matters, the Federal Government shall take measures appropriate to the Federal system to the end that the competent authorities of the state or local governments may take appropriate measures for the fulfillment of the Covenant.

III. The Senate's advice and consent is subject to the following declarations:

(1) That the United States declares that the provisions of Articles 1 through 27 of the Covenant are not self-executing.

(2) That it is the view of the United States that States Party to the Covenant should wherever possible refrain from imposing any restrictions or limitations on the exercise of the rights recognized and protected by the Covenant, even when such restrictions and limitations are permissible under the terms of the Covenant. For the United States, Article 5, paragraph 2, which provides that fundamental human rights existing in any State Party may not be diminished on the pretext that the Covenant recognizes them to a lesser extent, has particular relevance to Article 19, paragraph 3, which would permit certain restrictions on the freedom of expression. The United States declares that it will continue to adhere to the requirements and constraints of its Constitution in respect to all such restrictions and limitations.

(3) That the United States declares that it accepts the competence of the Human Rights Committee to receive and consider communications under Article 41 in which a State Party claims that another State Party is not fulfilling its obligations under the Covenant.

(4) That the United States declares that the right referred to in Article 47 may be exercised only in accordance with international law.

IV. The Senate's advice and consent is subject to the following proviso, which shall not be included in the instrument of ratification to be deposited by the President:

Nothing in this Covenant requires or authorizes legislation, or other action, by the United Sates of America prohibited by the Constitution of the United States as interpreted by the United States.

∾

QUESTIONS & COMMENTS

(1) Note that the International Covenant on Civil and Political Rights (ICCPR) makes no allowance for reservations even though numerous states have made them. Are the U.S. government's reservations, declarations, and understandings incompatible with the "object and purpose" of the ICCPR? *See* U.N. Hum. Rts. Ctte., General Comment No. 24, U.N. Doc. CCPR/C/21/Rev. 1 (2 November 1994) (to be reprinted in *Report of the Human Rights Committee*, U.N. GAOR, Hum. Rts. Ctte, 37th Sess., at 124, U.N. Doc. A/50/40. The UN Human Rights Committee commented that

> provisions in the Covenant that represent customary international law (and *a fortiori* when they have the character of peremptory norms) may not be the subject of reservations. Accordingly, a State may not reserve the right to engage in slavery, to torture, to subject persons to cruel, inhuman or degrading treatment or punishment, to arbitrarily deprive persons of their lives, to arbitrarily arrest and detain persons, to deny freedom of thought, conscience and religion, to presume a person guilty unless he proves his innocence, to execute pregnant women or children, to permit the advocacy of national, racial or religious hatred, to deny persons of marriageable age the right to marry, or to deny minorities the right to enjoy their own culture, profess their own religion, or use their own language. And while reservations to particular clauses of Article 14 [due process guarantees] may be acceptable, a general reservation to the right to a fair trial would not be.

Id. at §8. Three U.S. reservations pose potential problems. The U.S. Constitution has been interpreted to permit the advocacy of racial hatred. *Collin v. Smith*, 578 F.2d 1197 (7th Cir. 1978). Also, the U.S. Supreme Court in *Stanford v. Kentucky*, 492 U.S. 361 (1989) allowed the execution of persons who were under the age of 18 when they committed a capital crime. Most importantly, the United States has declared that Articles 1–27 of the ICCPR are not self-executing and that the United States will not expand the recognition of rights beyond those provided by the U.S. Constitution.

2.1.2. Customary International Law

The second source of international law is customary international law, or as defined in the ICJ Statute, "international custom, as evidence of a general practice accepted as law." Customary international law consists of two elements:

(i) a general practice and
(ii) *opinio juris* (*i.e.*, a sense of legal obligation).

Ian Brownlie
Principles of Public International Law 5–7, 10 (4th ed. 1990)[1]

[The following observations are taken from a section entitled "International Custom."]

Evidence. The material sources of custom are very numerous and include the following: diplomatic correspondence, policy statements, press releases, the opinions of official legal advisers, official manuals on legal questions, *e.g.*, manuals of military law, executive decisions and practices, orders to navel forces, *etc.*, comments by governments on drafts produced by the International Law Commission, state legislation, international and national judicial decisions, recitals in treaties and other international instruments, a pattern of treaties in the same form, the practice of international organs, and resolutions relating to legal questions in the United Nations General Assembly. Obviously the value of these sources varies and much depends on the circumstances.

The elements of custom

(a) *Duration.* Provided the consistency and generality of a practice are proved, no particular duration is required: the passage of time will, of course, be a part of the evidence of generality and consistency. A long (and, much less, an immemorial) practice is not necessary, and rules relating to airspace and the continental shelf have emerged from fairly quick maturing of practice. The International Court does not emphasize the time element as such in its practice.

(b) *Uniformity, consistency of the practice.* This is very much a matter of appreciation and a tribunal will have considerable freedom of determination in many cases. Complete uniformity is not required, but substantial uniformity is . . .

. . . .

(c) *Generality of the practice.* This is an aspect which complements that of consistency. Certainly universality is not required, but the real problem is to determine the value of abstention from protest by a substantial number of states in face of a practice followed by some others. Silence may denote either tacit agreement or a simple lack of interest in the issue. . . .

(d) *Opinio juris et necessitatis.* The Statute of the International Court refers to 'a general practice *accepted as law*'. Brierly[2] speaks of recognition by states of a certain practice 'as obligatory', and Hudson[3] requires a 'conception that the practice is required by, or consistent with, prevailing international law'. Some writers do not consider this psychological element to be a requirement for the formation of custom, but it is in fact a necessary ingredient. The sense of legal obligation, as opposed to motives of courtesy, fairness, or morality, is real enough, and the practice of states recognizes a distinction between obligation and usage. The essential problem is surely one of proof, and especially the incidence of the burden of proof.

In terms of the practice of the International Court of Justice – which provides a general guide to the nature of the problem – there are two methods of approach. In many cases the Court is willing to assume the existence of an *opinio juris* on the basis of evidence of a general practice, or a consensus in the literature, or the previous determinations of the Court or other international tribunals. However, in a significant minority of cases the Court has adopted a more rigorous approach and has called for more positive evidence

---

[1] Footnotes omitted. Ed.'s Note.

[2] [Brierly, The Law of Nations 61 (Sir Humphrey Waldock ed., 6th ed., 1963).]

[3] [As quoted in Briggs, The Law of Nations: Cases, Documents, and Notes (2d ed., 1952).]

of the recognition of the validity of the rules in question in the practice of states. The choice of approach appears to depend upon the nature of the issues (that is, the state of the law may be a primary point in contention), and the discretion of the Court.

. . . .

The persistent objector. The way in which, as a matter of practice, custom resolves itself into a question of special relations is illustrated further by the rule that a state may contract out of a custom in the process of formation. Evidence of objection must be clear and there is probably a presumption of acceptance which is to be rebutted. Whatever the theoretical underpinnings of the principle, it is well recognized by international tribunals, and in the practice of states. Given the majoritarian tendency of international relations the principle is likely to have increased prominence.

∾

QUESTIONS & COMMENTS

(1) The emergence of numerous multilateral treaties and intergovernmental organizations in the twentieth century has precipitated a debate in international law over the comparative weight to be given to the two dimensions of customary international law, namely, general state practice and *opinio juris*. The traditional approach is to place greater weight on state practice and use *opinio juris* as a secondary consideration to distinguish between legal and nonlegal obligations. Traditional custom is evolutionary and is identified through an inductive process in which a general custom is derived from specific examples of state practice. This was the Permanent Court of International Justice's approach in *S.S. Lotus*, 1927 PCIJ (ser. A) No. 10, at 18, 29.

The modern approach is to focus on *opinio juris* rather than particular instances of state practice. This approach identifies custom through a deductive process that begins with general statements of rules, as found in, *e.g.*, multilateral treaties and declarations made by intergovernmental organizations that often declare extant customary international legal norms, crystallize emerging customary international legal norms, and/or generate new customary international legal norms. Examples of state practice that are contrary to these rules are merely considered violations of customary international law rather than evidence of state practice generating a new rule. This was the International Court of Justice's approach in *Military and Paramilitary Activities In and Against Nicaragua (Nicar. v. U.S.)*, Merits, 1986 ICJ Rep. 14 (June 27).

Some jurists have argued that this debate has led to an "identity crisis" for customary international law that may be best solved by recognizing these norms as general principles of international law – the third category of law mentioned by Article 38 of the ICJ Statute. *See, e.g.*, Bruno Simma & Philip Alston, *The Sources of Human Rights Law: Custom, Jus Cogens, and General Principles*, 1988–89 AUST. Y.B. INT'L L. 82.

Some jurists have argue that there should be a "sliding scale" between general state practice and *opinio juris*. At one end, evidence of highly consistent state practice would offset any need for providing evidence of *opinio juris*. As the evidence of state practice diminishes, evidence of *opinio juris* becomes more important for demonstrating a customary international legal norm. Determining exactly how much evidence of each is required depends on the importance of the activity in question and the reasonableness of the rule. *See, e.g.*, Frederic L. Kirgis Jr., *Custom on a Sliding Scale*, 81 AM. J. INT'L L. 146 (1987).

This issue is important because many human rights and humanitarian law advocates argue that widely adopted multilateral human rights and humanitarian treaties reflect customary international legal obligations for states that have not explicitly accepted the norms in those treaties. For U.S. human rights and humanitarian advocates, this issue also is important for ensuring successful suits under the Alien Tort Statute, which provides a judicially enforceable means of remedying violations of treaties and the law of nations (which is often equated with customary international law) – especially when the United States has declared that many human rights treaties are non–self-executing.

(2) What are examples of a persistent objection to a customary international legal norm? Can a reservation to a norm in a multilateral treaty that is articulating emerging customary international legal norms be evidence of a persistent objection? Can a state's refusal to sign such a multilateral treaty be evidence of a persistent objection?

(3) Under the United States' constitutional scheme, which branches of the federal government have sole, joint, and/or severable authority to make a persistent objection? Do the individual states of the United States have authority to make a persistent objection?

2.1.3. *Jus Cogens*

Although *jus cogens* ("compelling law") is not mentioned in the ICJ Statute's list of formal international law sources, it increasingly has become recognized as an international law source essential for organizing the comparative authority of international legal norms. Most importantly, *jus cogens* norms are strongly associated with human rights and humanitarian protections. In the following article, Professor Martin discusses the concept of *jus cogens* and its relationship to other sources and norms of international law.

Francisco Forrest Martin

Delineating a Hierarchical Outline of International Law Sources and Norms
65(2) Sask. L. Rev. 333, 341–352 (2002)[1]

A. *JUS COGENS*

The source of international law with the greatest authority is *jus cogens* ("compelling law"). *Jus cogens* is non-derogable, peremptory law. Writing in 1976, Judge Rozakis described the concept of *jus cogens* as "a theoretical inference whose function is actually discernible through the legal norms bearing its peculiar traits."[2] The concept of *jus cogens* (although it was not often referred to by that name) has probably been around since Roman law.[3] Sir Hirsch Lauterpacht introduced the concept of *jus cogens* into International Law Commission discussions by proposing in 1953 that "treaties imposed by force"[4] violated "international public policy."

---

[1] Some cites have been edited and omitted from the original article. Ed.'s Note.

[2] C.L. Rozakis, The Concept of Jus Cogens in the Law of Treaties 11 (Amsterdam: North-Holland, 1976).

[3] L. Haopei, "Jus cogens *and International Law*" in S. Yee & W. Tieya, eds., *International Law in the Post-Cold War: Essays in Memory of Li Haopei* (S. Yee & W. Tieya eds., London: Routledge, 2001) 499 at 499.

[4] *Law of Treaties: Report of the Special Rapporteur*, UN Doc. A/CN.4/63, [1953] 2 Y.B.I.L.C. 90 at 147; Christopher Ford has described the developments that led to the ILC's discussions:

> According to the ILC debates surrounding the drafting of the *jus cogens* clause of the Vienna Convention, three interrelated "developments" were felt to compel the articulation of a theory of peremptory law. First, the international community was rapidly diversifying with the emergence

However, some commentators have argued against the recognition of *jus cogens* because the *Vienna Convention on the Law of Treaties* failed to provide a list of specific *jus cogens* norms and only recognized the category of such norms. Article 53 of the *Vienna Convention* simply states that *jus cogens* "is a norm accepted and recognized by the international community of States as a whole as a norm from which no derogation is permitted and which can be modified only by a subsequent norm of general international law having the same character." Professor Brownlie has written that "more authority exists for the category of *jus cogens* than exists for its particular content," and Egon Schwelb compared Article 53 to a penal code which would provide that crimes shall be punished without saying which acts constitute crimes.

However, Brownlie's and Schwelb's comments are clearly wrong in light of the substantial international human rights and humanitarian case law that has developed over the last forty years, law that addresses most *jus cogens* norms and that is reflected in widely adopted multilateral treaties. There is now no doubt, as a matter of positive law, that *jus cogens* norms exist and contain specific content. The European Court of Human Rights,[5] Inter-American Commission[6] and Court of Human Rights,[7] and the International Criminal Tribunal for the former Yugoslavia (ICTY)[8] have recognized the authority and existence of *jus cogens*. Domestic courts have also recognized *jus cogens* norms.[9]

---

of new states carved out of former European colonial empires or previously excluded from the European-dominated world of "international law." The "international community" was becoming increasingly heterogeneous. International law had once been the "product of the special civilization of modern Europe ... a highly artificial system of which the principles cannot be supposed to be understood or recognized by countries differently civilized." As long as a homogeneous cluster of European powers dominated international relations, the ILC members seemed to assume, explicit articulation of fundamental moral or legal boundary principles was less necessary. Peremptory norms were to a large degree unspoken, but intuitively understood by reference to a common social reservoir of understanding which delineated the crucial line between civilization and barbarity.

With a rapidly expanding international community that included increasing numbers of non-European states, however, the boundary norms of international law – indeed, even the fact that boundary norms *existed in* international law – had to be made more explicit.

. . .

For members of the ILC, "the international public order was merely the superstructure of the international community which resulted from the evolution of international society. It was the minimum of rules of conduct necessary to make orderly international relations possible."

. . .

A second, related factor was the obvious importance of preventing further catastrophic bloodletting in a culturally and ideologically heterogeneous, as well as a technologically advanced world. . . . Third, the atrocities of the Second World War apparently left little doubt that *jus cogens* boundary norms had to exist.

C.A. Ford, "Adjudicating *Jus Cogens*" (1994) 13 Wis. Int'l L.J. 145, 159–61 [footnotes omitted].

[5] *Al-Adsani v. United Kingdom*; see also *Belilos v. Switzerland* (1988), Appl. No. 10328/83, 132 Eur. Ct. H.R. (Ser. A), 10 E.H.R.R. 466 (concurring opinion by de Meyer J.); *Ringeisen v. Austria* (1971), Appl. No. 2614/65, 13 Eur. Ct. H.R. (Ser. A) (separate opinion by Verdross J.).

[6] *Victims of the Tugboat "13 de Marzo" v. Cuba*; *Coard v. United States*; *Pinkerton and Roach v. United States*.

[7] *Aloeboetoe v. Suriname*, at para. 57.

[8] *Prosecutor v. Furundzija*, at para. 155; *Prosecutor v. Delacic*, at para. 454; *Prosecutor v. Kunarac, Kovac, and Vukovic*, at para. 466.

[9] See, e.g., *Committee of United States Citizens Living in Nicaragua v. Reagan*, 859 F.2d 929 (D.C. Cir. 1988) (*jus cogens*); *Siderman de Blake v. Argentina*, 965 F.2d 699 at 714, 92 Cal. Daily Op. Service 4340 (9th Cir. 1992) (*jus cogens*); see *Hawkins v. Comparet-Cassani*, 33 F. Supp.2d 1244 at 1255 (C.D. Cal. 1999) (*jus cogens*); *R. v. Bow Street Metropolitan Stipendiary Magistrate and Others, ex parte Pinochet Ugarte*, [2000] 1 A.C. 147, 2

How does *jus cogens* have greater legal authority than other international law? Unlike customary international law, states do not need to consent to a *jus cogens* norm to be legally bound by that norm. In its discussion of torture, the [International Criminal Tribunal for the former Yugoslavia] described the normative relativity of and obligations emanating from *jus cogens*:

> Because of the importance of the values it protects, [the prohibition of torture] has evolved into a peremptory norm or *jus cogens*, that is, a norm that enjoys a higher rank in the international hierarchy than treaty law and even "ordinary" customary rules. The most conspicuous consequence of this higher rank is that the principle at issue cannot be derogated from by States through international treaties or local or special customs or even general customary rules not endowed with the same normative force.
>
> Clearly, the *jus cogens* nature of the prohibition against torture articulates the notion that the prohibition has now become one of the most fundamental standards of the international community. Furthermore, this prohibition is designed to produce a deterrent effect, in that it signals to all members of the international community and the individuals over whom they wield authority that the prohibition of torture is an absolute value from which nobody must deviate.[10]

1. Substantive Content of Jus Cogens Norms

The next issue is how we determine the content of *jus cogens* norms. Provisions in widely adopted multilateral treaties guaranteeing non-derogable rights can be a source for *jus cogens* norms because these provisions fulfill the definition of *jus cogens* norms by being both peremptory and non-derogable. This is not to say that all rights and duties that are binding during states of emergency are *jus cogens* norms. For example, Article 89 of Geneva Convention IV[11] requires that parties to a conflict allow internees to use tobacco. However, during other times, states could prohibit prisoners from smoking for public health reasons. It would be a stretch to say that the right to smoke is a *jus cogens* norm. What is central to the concept of *jus cogens* is that it is law that is binding in all contexts, whether a state of emergency or not.

Multilateral treaties are especially appropriate sources for *jus cogens* because they are often adopted by a wide majority of states and contain specific language governing the substantive content of the norm. In determining whether a particular provision in a treaty also reflects a *jus cogens* norm, treaties have historically posed evidentiary difficulties because treaties were regarded "more as contracts of private law than as genuine normative instruments." A treaty did not create obligations for non-parties without their consent, and parties to a multilateral convention reserved the general right to denounce it. However, this conception of treaties has changed with the advent of multilateral humanitarian and human rights treaties, many of which do not allow suspension or denunciation. In our contemporary international legal order, the multilateral treaty-making process is legislative in objective but only contractual in method.

All E.R. 97, 2 W.L.R. 827 (H.L.) [hereafter *Pinochet*] (*jus cogens* and norms *erga omnes*); *Nulyarimma et al. v. Thompson; Buzzacott v. Hill et al.*, [1999] F.C.A. 1192, 8 B.H.R.C. 135.

[10] *Furundzija*, at paras. 153–54 [footnotes omitted].

[11] *Geneva Convention [IV] relative to the Protection of Civilian Persons in Time of War*, 12 August 1949, 75 U.N.T.S. 287, 6 U.S.T. 3516, T.I.A.S. No. 3365 (entered into force 21 October 1950).

This brings forth another issue. How many states have to adopt a multilateral treaty in order that its non-derogable provisions reflect *jus cogens*? Although certain non-derogable provisions in multilateral treaties may not initially reflect *jus cogens* because an insufficient number of states (either globally or regionally) have adopted the treaty, generally speaking, in the case of multilateral human rights treaties, these non-derogable provisions do reflect *jus cogens* because these treaties have been widely adopted by a majority of states within either a global or regional treaty regime.

Nevertheless, a numerical threshold of states ratifying a treaty for establishing a *jus cogens* norm is probably higher than that for the rest of conventional customary international law. A "wide majority"[12] or "very large majority"[13] of ratifying states would be required. What exact numerical figure constitutes such a "wide majority" appears not to have been determined by a global court or other global authority. A common-sense figure would probably be about 66–75 per cent. Indeed, in 1987, the Inter-American Commission on Human Rights effectively held that there is a regional *jus cogens* norm against the execution of children on the basis that approximately 70 per cent of OAS members[14] were states-parties to the ACHR, which prohibited the execution of individuals committing capital crimes under the age of eighteen.[15]

Other reasons supporting the pedigree of *jus cogens* norms located in multilateral human rights treaties is that many of these multilateral treaties establish interpretive organs (*e.g.*, courts, tribunals, commissions, committees) that provide greater definition to the norm and that often order compliance with the norm. Perhaps most importantly, some of these treaties do not allow states-parties to withdraw from the treaty itself, which further undermines the state consent aspect of these treaties.

However, unlike *jus cogens* norms reflected in modern multilateral treaties, some *jus cogens* norms are reflected in custom or older treaties. Piracy is such an example. As a consequence of their basis in custom or older treaties, these *jus cogens* norms often lack precise or consistent definition. Accordingly, their pedigree is lesser than those *jus cogens* norms reflected in modern multilateral human rights treaties.

So exactly which rights and duties reflect *jus cogens*? The following represent extant or emerging[16] global *jus cogens* obligations: prohibition of aggression;[17] right to life;[18]

---

12 Rozakis, *supra* note 2 at 79–80 ("wide majority" required).

13 *Restatement of the Law, Third: The Foreign Relations Law of the United States* (St. Paul, Minn.: American Law Institute, 1987) at §102, Reporter's note 6 ("very large majority" required).

14 By 1987, 19 out of 27 OAS members had ratified or acceded to the *American Convention on Human Rights*, 22 November 1969, 1144 U.N.T.S. 123, O.A.S.T.S. No. 36 (entered into force 17 July 1978) [hereinafter ACHR].

15 *See Pinkerton and Roach v. United States.*

16 Unlike the rights and duties found in non-derogable provisions in multilateral human rights treaties, the *jus cogens* character of, for example, the prohibition of aggression, is less clear because it has probably not been sufficiently defined. However, it is, at the least, emerging. The prohibition of aggression is now being defined pursuant to the Treaty of Rome (or *ICC Statute*) establishing the International Criminal Court. The Treaty of Rome also binds states that are not states-parties to the treaty. If a wide majority of states ratify or accede to the Treaty of Rome, the prohibition of aggression will clearly reflect the *jus cogens*.

17 Compare *Case concerning the Barcelona Traction, Light and Power Company, Limited* (*Belgium v. Spain*), [1970] I.C.J. Rep. 3 at 34 (obligation *erga omnes*). Another possible articulation of this *jus cogens* norm is the prohibition of "the use or threat of force in contravention of the principles of the [UN] Charter": Summary Records of the 15th Sess., 682d Mtg., UN Doc. A/CN.4/Ser.A/1963 [1963] 1 Y.B.I.L.C. 55 at para. 2 (Sir Humphrey Waldock, ILC Special Rapporteur).

18 *International Covenant on Civil and Political Rights*, 19 December 1966, art. 6, 999 U.N.T.S. 171, Can. T.S. 1976 No. 47, 6 I.L.M. 368 (entered into force 23 March 1976) [hereinafter ICCPR]; *Commonwealth of*

right to humane treatment;[19] prohibition of criminal *ex post facto* laws;[20] prohibition of genocide;[21] prohibition of war crimes;[22] prohibition of slavery;[23] prohibition of discrimination on the basis of race, color, sex, language, religion, or social origin;[24] prohibition of imprisonment for civil debt;[25] prohibition of crimes against humanity;[26] right to legal personhood;[27] freedom of conscience;[28] and the right to self-determination.[29] Regional *jus cogens* norms include the following: freedom from arbitrary detention;[30] rights of the family;[31] right to a name;[32] rights of the child;[33] right to nationality;[34] and right to participate in government.[35]

What is striking about this list of *jus cogens* norms is that most of them directly address human rights.[36] Some of the others are arguably based on human

---

Independent States Convention on Human Rights and Fundamental Freedoms, 26 May 1995, English trans. Council of Europe doc. H (95) 7 rev., (1996) 17 H.R.L.J. 159, art. 2 (entered into force 11 August 1998) [hereinafter CIS Convention]; ACHR, art. 4(1). The right to life is non-derogable under the ICCPR, art. 4; CIS Convention, art. 35; ACHR, art. 27.

[19] ICCPR, art. 7; *European Convention for the Protection of Human Rights and Fundamental Freedoms*, 4 November 1950, 213 U.N.T.S. 221, Eur. T.S. 5, art. 3, (entered into force 3 September 1953) [hereinafter ECHR]; *CIS Convention*, art. 3; ACHR, art. 5. The right to humane treatment is non-derogable under the ICCPR, art. 4; ECHR, art. 15; CIS Convention, art. 35; ACHR, art. 27.

[20] ICCPR, art. 15; ECHR, art. 7; ACHR, art. 9. The prohibition of criminal *ex post facto* laws is non-derogable under the ICCPR, art. 4; ECHR, art. 15; ACHR, art. 27.

[21] *Convention on the Prevention and Punishment of the Crime of Genocide*, 9 December 1948, 78 U.N.T.S. 277, art. 1 (entered into force 12 January 1951); see *Reservations to the Convention on the Prevention and Punishment of the Crime of Genocide*, Advisory Opinion, [1951] I.C.J. Rep. 15 at 23 ("principles underlying the [Genocide] Convention are principles which are recognized by civilized nations as binding on States, even without any conventional obligation"); compare *Barcelona Traction*, at para. 34 (obligation *erga omnes*). The prohibition of killings constituting genocide is non-derogable: ICCPR, art. 6(3).

[22] *Geneva Convention IV*, arts. 146, 149; see also M.C. Bassiouni, *International Crimes:* Jus Cogens *and Obligation* Erga Omnes 59 L. & Contemp. Probs. 63–74 (1996).

[23] ICCPR, art. 8; ECHR, 64, art. 4; ACHR, art. 6. The prohibition of slavery is non-derogable under the ICCPR, art. 4; ECHR, art. 15; ACHR, art. 27.

[24] ICCPR, art. 4. The prohibition of discrimination is non-derogable under the ICCPR, *id.*

[25] *Id.*, art. 11. The prohibition of imprisonment for civil debt is non-derogable: ICCPR, *id.*, art. 4.

[26] *ICC Statute*, art. 7; see M.C. Bassiouni, Crimes Against Humanity in International Criminal Law, 2d ed. (The Hague: Kluwer Law International, 1999) at 610.

[27] ICCPR, art. 16; ACHR, art. 3. The right to legal personhood is non-derogable: ICCPR, art. 4; ACHR, art. 27.

[28] ICCPR, art. 18; ACHR, art. 12. Freedom of conscience is non-derogable: ICCPR, art. 4; ACHR, art. 27.

[29] See *Western Sahara*, Advisory Opinion, [1975] I.C.J. Rep. 12 (based on a series of General Assembly resolutions and state practice of decolonization).

[30] *Restatement*, §702 (prohibition of prolonged arbitrary detention).

[31] ACHR, art. 17. The right to family is non-derogable: *ibid.*, art. 27.

[32] *Ibid.*, art. 18. The right to a name is non-derogable: *ibid.*, art. 27.

[33] *Ibid.*, art. 19. The rights of the child are non-derogable: *ibid.*, art. 27.

[34] *Ibid.*, art. 20. The right to nationality is non-derogable: *ibid.*, art. 27.

[35] *Ibid.*, art. 23. The right to participate in government is non-derogable: *ibid.*, art. 27.

[36] Other rules have been proposed as *jus cogens* norms. However, there appears to be little – if any – positive law in support of these principles being *jus cogens* norms. These principles include the principles of permanent sovereignty over natural resources, freedom of the seas, the prohibition of piracy, the principles of *pacta sunt servanda* and *rebus sic stantibus*, and the illegality of unequal (or "leonine") treaties. See Summary Records of the 15th Sess., 684th Mtg., UN Doc. A/CN.4/Ser.A/1963, [1963] 1 Y.B.I.L.C. 67; 695th Mtg., *ibid.* at 143; 703d Mtg., *ibid.* at 197; 705th Mtg., *ibid.* at 213; Brownlie, at 513 (suggesting that the principle of sovereignty over natural resources is probably a *jus cogens* norm); M. Janis, "The Nature of Jus Cogens" (1988) 3 Conn. J. Int'l L. 361 (principle of *pacta sunt servanda*); Bassiouni, "International Crimes", at 68 (piracy).

rights.[37] Furthermore, many of these *jus cogens* norms overlap. For example, forced disappearances, a violation of the right to life, are considered crimes against humanity.[38] This strongly suggests that most *jus cogens* norms are inter-related.

2. Derivative Jus Cogens Obligations

Other norms (*e.g.*, rights to due process, food, shelter, and other basic needs) that do not appear in non-derogable provisions of multilateral treaties or other sources have been proposed as having the status of *jus cogens* because of their necessity in ensuring the protection of other *jus cogens* norms. We can call these "derivative *jus cogens* norms." The Inter-American Court of Human Rights opined that judicial guarantees essential for the protection of the enumerated non-derogable rights in the ACHR were also non-derogable in states of emergency,[39] thereby effectively reflecting *jus cogens* status.

However, these other norms have been considered problematic because they entail affirmative duties requiring the availability of resources to give these rights effect. Second and third generation rights are also associated with this problem, and both international[40] and municipal law[41] have historically given greater state deference to how such second and third generation rights are protected. However, most already recognized *jus cogens* norms entail affirmative state duties that may require not only substantial resources but also the reorganization of the domestic political legal regime.[42] Even non–*jus cogens* norms (*e.g.*, right to a fair trial, right to privacy, and respect for family life) may require state affirmative duties. For example, the right to a fair trial demands that the state provide free legal assistance.[43] Therefore, if a right lawfully requires affirmative state action, this does not necessarily bar the right from having *jus cogens* status. It simply means that such *jus*

---

[37] For example, the arguable *jus cogens* prohibition of piracy is designed to protect persons from murder on the high seas, a right to life violation.

[38] *Velásquez Rodríguez Case (Honduras)* (1988), Inter-Am. Ct. H.R. (Ser. C) No. 4, at para. 153.

[39] *Judicial Guarantees in States of Emergency (Arts. 27(2), 25, and 8 of the American Convention on Human Rights)* plain (1987), Advisory Opinion OC-9/97, Inter-Am. Ct. H.R. (Ser. A) No. 9.

[40] *See, e.g.*, ACHR, art. 26:

> The States Parties undertake to adopt measures, both internally and through international cooperation, especially those of an economic and technical nature, with a view to *achieving progressively*, by legislation or other appropriate means, the full realization of the rights implicit in the economic, social, educational, scientific, and cultural standards set forth in the Charter of the Organization of American States as amended by the Protocol of Buenos Aires. [emphasis added]

[41] *See, e.g.*, *Nebbia* v. *New York*, 291 U.S. 502 (1934).

[42] *See, e.g.. Velásquez Rodríguez*, at para. 166:

> The second obligation of the States Parties is to "ensure" the free and full exercise of the rights recognized by the [American Convention on Human Rights] to every person subject to its jurisdiction. This obligation implies the duty of the States Parties to organize the governmental apparatus and, in general, all the structures through which public power is exercised, so that they are capable of juridically ensuring the free and full enjoyment of human rights. As a consequence of this obligation, the States must prevent, investigate and punish any violation of the rights recognized by the Convention and, moreover, if possible attempt to restore the right violated and provide compensation as warranted for damages resulting from the violation.

[43] *See, e.g.*, *Airey v. Ireland* (1979), Appl. No. 6289/73, 32 Eur. Ct. H.R. (Ser. A), 2 E.H.R.R. 305 (recognizing a state's affirmative duty to establish and maintain a program of legal assistance to indigent persons for civil matters regardless of cost).

> On the other hand, other non–*jus cogens* rights may allow consideration of the availability of resources. *See, e.g., Abdulaziz, Cabales and Balkandali v. United Kingdom* (1985), Appl. Nos. 9214/80, 9473/81, 9474/81, 94 Eur. Ct. H.R. (Ser. A), 7 E.H.R.R. 471 at para. 67 (states-parties enjoy a wide margin of appreciation

cogens norms require implementing international instruments and domestic legislation or action, which may in some cases be subject to a certain margin of appreciation or degree of deference. It does not mean that such norms do not have *jus cogens* status.[44]

The term "derivative *jus cogens* norms" does not suggest that these norms by themselves are not *jus cogens* norms and have some status less than *jus cogens*. The use of the word "derivative" merely refers to *how* one can discern them through the lens of international law when international instruments have omitted their description as non-derogable or peremptory. Of course, one must determine from which contexts these norms derive their *jus cogens* status. The issue of derivative *jus cogens* norms is important in the context of not only certain first generation rights (*e.g.*, due process rights) but also second and third generation rights, which impact upon other areas of international law, such as the law of armed conflict, trade and environmental law.

For example, the right to adequate food[45] can impact the international law of trade, and this right has been suggested as a *jus cogens* norm because in order to protect the right to life, adequate food is essential. However, the *jus cogens* status of this right has been challenged on a number of grounds. For example, some have claimed that the right to adequate food is only a negative right (*i.e.*, the state cannot interfere with an individual's

---

in determining steps to be taken to ensure compliance with the ECHR, "with due regard to the needs and resources of the community and of individuals").

[44] The state must provide *some* form of remedy, and failure to do so means that the state has violated its *jus cogens* obligation.

However, decisions from both the ICJ and the European Court of Human Rights, respectively, arguably suggest that the principles of state sovereignty and consular and diplomatic immunity trump either *jus cogens* norms or eliminate the *jus cogens* status of such norms. In the *Case concerning the Arrest Warrant of 11 April 2000 (Democratic Republic of the Congo v. Belgium)*, General List No. 121 (2002), online: <http://www.icj-cij.org/icjwwo/idocket/iCOBE/icobejudgment/icobe_ijudgment_20020214.pdf> (date accessed: 5 July 2002) [hereinafter *DRC v. Belgium*], the ICJ held that Belgium's issue of an international arrest warrant *in absentia* for the DRC's Foreign Minister for war crimes and crimes against humanity. The European Court of Human Rights in *Al-Adsani*, held that it is within a state's margin of appreciation to determine what kind of domestic remedies the state wishes to provide for *jus cogens* violations.

However, these two decisions do not hold that the principles of state sovereignty, and consular and diplomatic immunity trump *jus cogens* norms or eliminate the *jus cogens* status of such norms. As the ICJ itself noted, an international tribunal or the DRC could still prosecute its foreign minister: *DRC v. Belgium* at paras. 60–61. The issue in these cases is what kind of law enforcement action or remedy is appropriate under international law. Although the principle of *restitutio in integrum* requires implementation of the full panoply of necessary remedies, this principle is limited by other principles of international law. One cannot read the substantive law governing rights and duties only through the lens of the law of remedies.

However, in the case of international crimes, it should be noted that there is an essential linkage between the substantive law and the remedy, i.e., between the substantive crime, and prosecution and punishment. The ILC notes,

The absence of any procedural immunity with respect to prosecution or punishment in appropriate judicial proceedings is an essential corollary of the absence of any substantive immunity or defence. It would be paradoxical to prevent an individual from invoking his official position to avoid responsibility for a crime only to permit him to invoke this same consideration to avoid the consequences of this responsibility.

International Law Commission, *Report of the International Law Commission on the Work of its Forty-eighth Session: Draft Code of Crimes Against Peace and Security of Mankind*, UN GAOR, 51st Sess., Supp. No. 10, UN Doc. A/51/10, [1996] 2(2) Y.B.I.L.C. 15 at 27. Therefore, in cases concerning international crimes, the state's margin of appreciation in fashioning remedies should be strictly limited.

[45] *See, e.g.*, *International Covenant on Economic, Social and Cultural Rights*, 19 December 1966, 993 U.N.T.S. 3, Can. T.S. 1976 No. 46, 6 I.L.M. 360, art. 11(1) [hereinafter ICESCR].

efforts to obtain adequate food). However, the affirmative/negative distinction is often a false dichotomy in rights analysis. Even a supposed negative right can require affirmative state action in the form of judicial intervention in order to protect the right. Instead, the issue needs to be framed in terms of whether the state intervention violates the purported negative right.

Some have argued that the state may not have the resources to ensure compliance with its obligation to provide adequate food. However, there are very few states that do not have resources to feed their populations if they appropriately prioritize their legal obligations and resources.

Others have argued that the state has a margin of appreciation in how it goes about providing adequate food. However, although the state may have a margin of appreciation in determining how to best go about providing adequate food, this does not undermine the *jus cogens* status of the right to adequate food if it is indispensable to the protection of another *jus cogens* norm. If an individual has not been provided access to adequate food because of a state's failure to exercise due diligence, his or her right to adequate food has been violated – end of analysis. The failure of the state to establish a competent system of ensuring adequate food does not eliminate the injury. Upon finding the injury, international or domestic tribunals need not order the restructuring or invention of a new system, although arguably the tribunal could lawfully do so under the principle of *restitutio in integrum*. All the tribunal need do is provide monetary damages, an extremely common form of relief under both domestic and international law.

Finally, some have argued that the right to adequate food is ambiguous. However, the right to adequate food is not ambiguous as a matter of law because of the substantial provisions governing the right located in numerous international instruments.[46] Even if the right to adequate food consisted only of the words, "everyone has a right to adequate food", this would still be sufficient in law. Its meaning would be fleshed out by case adjudication. The right to adequate food, like the right against torture, is only shorthand for the articulation of a *jus cogens* norm.

Even the right against torture requires further definition. For example, the right against torture does not include a right against the infliction of batteries with less than aggravated physical or mental suffering. However, the right against torture is always applicable, whether during a state of emergency or not.

The same goes for the right to adequate food. For example, the right to adequate food does not include a right to choose adequate food (*e.g.*, a choice between potatoes and rice). However, the right to adequate food is always applicable, whether during a state of emergency[47] or not.[48] How exactly the state goes about ensuring the provision of adequate food is within the state's margin of appreciation. This does not negate the *jus cogens* status of the right to adequate food.

The point of this example is that, as a matter of international law, we first need to determine how certain rights or duties can trump other rights or duties through, for

---

[46] *See, e.g., Additional Protocol to the American Convention on Human Rights in the Area of Economic, Social and Cultural Rights*, 17 November 1988, O.A.S.T.S. No. 69, 28 I.L.M. 156 (entered into force 16 November 1999).

[47] For example, *Geneva Convention IV*, art. 55, states:

> To the fullest extent of the means available to it, the Occupying Power has the duty of ensuring the food and medical supplies of the population; it should, in particular, bring in the necessary foodstuffs, medical stores and other articles if the resources of the occupied territory are inadequate.

[48] *See, e.g.,* ICESCR, art. 11.

example, a *jus cogens* derivation. How we go about ensuring compliance (*i.e.*, fashioning remedies) is a separate issue, one that may or may not be encumbered by other legal considerations, domestic[49] or international.[50]

∿

Aloeboetoe et al. v. Suriname
Inter-American Court of Human Rights
Judgment of September 10, 1993
Inter-Amer. Ct. H.R. (Ser. C) No. 15 (1994)

[Opinion of the Court]

. . . .

55. In the instant case, there is some difference of opinion between the parties as to who the successors of the victims are. The Commission urges that this decision be made with reference to the customs of the Saramaka tribe, whereas Suriname requests that its civil law be applied.

The Court earlier stated that the obligation to make reparation provided in Article 63(1) of the American Convention is governed by international law, which also applies to the determination of the manner of compensation and the beneficiaries thereof. Nevertheless, it is useful to refer to the national family law in force, for certain aspects of it may be relevant.

56. The Saramakas are a tribe that lives in Surinamese territory and was formed by African slaves fleeing from their Dutch owners. The Commission's brief affirms that the Saramakas enjoy internal autonomy by virtue of a treaty dated September 19, 1762, which granted them permission to be governed by their own laws. It also states that these people "acquired their rights on the basis of a treaty entered into with the Netherlands, which recognizes, among other things, the local authority of the Saramaka (*sic*) over their own territory." The text of the treaty is attached to the brief in question, which adds that "the obligations of the treaty are applicable, by succession, to the state (*sic*) of Suriname."

57. The Court does not deem it necessary to investigate whether or not that agreement is an international treaty. Suffice it to say that even if that were the case, the treaty would today be null and void because it contradicts the norms of *jus cogens superveniens*. In point of fact, under that treaty the Saramakas undertake to, among other things, capture any slaves that have deserted, take them prisoner and return them to the Governor of Suriname, who will pay from 10 to 50 florins per slave, depending on the distance of the place where they were apprehended. Another article empowers the Saramakas to sell to the Dutch any other prisoners they might take, as slaves. No treaty of that nature may be invoked before an international human rights tribunal.

58. The Commission has pointed out that it does not seek to portray the Saramakas as a community that currently enjoys international juridical status; rather, the autonomy it claims for the tribe is one governed by domestic public law.

. . . .

∿

---

[49] For example, the U.S. Constitution's principle of separation of powers and the judicial reluctance to adjudicate economic issues are often domestic legal considerations.

[50] For example, the international legal principles of diplomatic and consular immunity can be international legal considerations. *See, e.g., DRC v. Belgium.*

QUESTIONS & COMMENTS

(1) Article 64 of the Vienna Convention on the Law of Treaties provides that "[i]f a new peremptory norm of general international law emerges, any existing treaty which is in conflict with that norm becomes void and terminates." Article 53 (which defines a peremptory norm as one "accepted and recognized by the international community of States as a whole as a norm from which no derogation is permitted and which can be modified only by a subsequent norm of general international law having the same character") invalidates a treaty that conflicts with a peremptory norm at the time the treaty is concluded. Which provision fits *Aloeboetoe* best? If the 1762 treaty both gave the Saramakas autonomy and obligated them to return slaves, should the court consider the entire treaty invalid, or just the latter obligation? Would the benefits of autonomy be tainted by having been "purchased" by an agreement to return captured slaves?

(2) What other international treaties could be considered a violation of international human rights law?

What are the implications if two regional courts consistently hold contrary interpretations of a right that is expressly recognized in identical language in their respective conventions? As a matter of practice, international courts appear to avoid such conflicts. For example, in *Coeriel v. The Netherlands*, Communication No. 453/1991, views adopted 31 October 1994, petitioners to the Human Rights Committee claimed that the Dutch government's refusal to allow them to adopt Hindi names violated their right to practice their religion and their right to privacy. The Human Rights Committee found that the Dutch government had violated the petitioners' right to privacy but not their right to practice their religion. The petitioners had earlier submitted a claim to the European Commission arguing only a violation of their right to religion. The Commission found no such violation – even though it appears that the right to religion claim was stronger than the privacy claim that eventually the Committee recognized as successful. Was the UN Human Rights Committee attempting to avoid a conflict with the European Commission by finding the religious exercise claim inadmissible yet finding the privacy claim admissible? If you were representing different petitioners before the Human Rights Committee with a similar grievance, how would you address the earlier decision of the European Commission?

Judicial Guarantees in States of Emergency
(Arts. 27(2), 25 and 8 of the American Convention on Human Rights)
Inter-American Court of Human Rights
Advisory Opinion OC-9/87 of October 6, 1987
Inter-Am. Ct. H.R. (Ser. A) No. 9 (1987)

. . . .

THE COURT . . . gives the following Advisory Opinion:

1. By note of September 17, 1986, the Government of Uruguay (hereinafter "the Government") submitted to the Inter-American Court of Human Rights (hereinafter "the Court") an advisory opinion request on the scope of the prohibition of the suspension of the judicial guarantees essential for the protection of the rights mentioned in Article 27(2) of the American Convention on Human Rights (hereinafter "the Convention or "the American Convention").

2. The Government asked the Court "to interpret the scope of the Convention's prohibition of the suspension of 'the judicial guarantees essential for the protection of such rights.' Because even 'in time of war, public danger, or other emergency that threatens the independence or security of a State Party' (Art. 27(1)) it is not possible to suspend 'the judicial guarantees essential for the protection of such rights,' the Government of Uruguay requests the Court's opinion, in particular, regarding: (a) which of these judicial guarantees are 'essential' and (b) the relationship between Article 27(2), in that regard, and Articles 25 and 8 of the American Convention."

. . . .

4. By telex of April 1, 1987, the President [of the Court] asked the Government, pursuant to Article 49(2)(a) of the Rules, to present any additional considerations or reasons that it took into account in deciding to request the advisory opinion. The Government responded by telex of April 24, 1987, in which it expressed the following:

> Under normal circumstances in democratic systems of law in which human rights are respected and regulated, the judicial protection afforded by internal norms is generally recognized in practice.
>
> This is not the case in those systems or situations in which the violation of fundamental rights is not only of a substantive nature but also affects the judicial guarantees which have developed alongside them.
>
> As recognized by the Inter-American Commission and by the Inter-American Court of Human Rights in its Advisory Opinion OC-8, of January 30, 1987, the political history of Latin America shows that it is during states of exception or of emergency that the failure of these judicial guarantees is most serious insofar as the protection of the rights that cannot be suspended even in such situations.

. . . .

III. THE MERITS

18. The Government's request refers to Article 27 of the Convention which reads as follows:

Article 27. Suspension of Guarantees

1. In time of war, public danger, or other emergency that threatens the independence or security of a State Party, it may take measures derogating from its obligations under the present Convention to the extent and for the period of time strictly required by the exigencies of the situation, provided that such measures are not inconsistent with its other obligations under international law and do not involve discrimination on the ground of race, color, sex, language, religion, or social origin.

2. The foregoing provision does not authorize any suspension of the following articles: Article 3 (Right to Juridical Personality), Article 4 (Right to Life), Article 5 (Right to Humane Treatment), Article 6 (Freedom from Slavery), Article 9 (Freedom from Ex Post Facto laws), Article 12 (Freedom of Conscience and Religion), Article 17 (Rights of the Family), Article 18 (Right to a Name), Article 19 (Rights of the Child), Article 20 (Right to Nationality), and Article 23 (Right to Participate in Government), or of the judicial guarantees essential for the protection of such rights.

3. Any State Party availing itself of the right of suspension shall immediately inform the other States Parties, through the Secretary General of the Organization of American States, of the provisions the application of which it has suspended, the

reasons that gave rise to the suspension, and the date set for the termination of such suspension.

19. The Government makes the following request:

3. The Government of Uruguay asks the Court to interpret the scope of the Convention's prohibition of the suspension of "the judicial guarantees essential for the protection of such rights." Because even "in time of war, public danger, or other emergency that threatens the independence or security of a State Party" (Art. 27(1)) it is not possible to suspend "the judicial guarantees essential for the protection of such rights, "the Government of Uruguay requests the Court's opinion, in particular, regarding: (a) which of these judicial guarantees are "essential," and (b) the relationship between Article 27 (2), in that regard, with Articles 25 and 8 of the American Convention.

20. The Court shall first examine what are, according to the Convention, the "essential" judicial guarantees alluded to in Article 27(2). In this regard, the Court has previously defined in general terms that such guarantees are understood to be "those that ordinarily will effectively guarantee the full exercise of the rights and freedoms protected by that provision and whose denial or restriction would endanger their full enjoyment" (Habeas Corpus in Emergency Situations, *supra* [ ] para. 29). Likewise, it has emphasized that the judicial nature of those guarantees implies "the active involvement of an independent and impartial judicial body having the power to pass on the lawfulness of measures adopted in a state of emergency" (*Ibid.*, para. 30).

21. From Article 27(1), moreover, comes the general requirement that in any state of emergency there be appropriate means to control the measures taken, so that they are proportionate to the needs and do not exceed the strict limits imposed by the Convention or derived from it.

22. The Convention provides other criteria for determining the basic characteristics of judicial guarantees. The starting point of the analysis must be the obligation of every State Party to "respect the rights and freedoms recognized (in the Convention) and to ensure to all persons subject to their jurisdiction the free and full exercise of those rights and freedoms" (Art. 1(1)). From that general obligation is derived the right of every person, set out in Article 25(1), "to simple and prompt recourse, or any other effective recourse, to a competent court or tribunal for protection against acts that violate his fundamental rights recognized by the constitution or laws of the state concerned or by this Convention."

23. As the Court has already pointed out, Article 25(1) of the Convention is a general provision that gives expression to the procedural institution known as amparo, which is a simple and prompt remedy designed for the protection of all the fundamental rights (Habeas Corpus in Emergency Situations, supra [ ] para. 32). This article also establishes in broad terms the obligation of the States to provide to all persons within their jurisdiction an effective judicial remedy to violations of their fundamental rights. It provides, moreover, for the application of the guarantee recognized therein not only to the rights contained in the Convention, but also to those recognized by the Constitution or laws. It follows, *a fortiori*, that the judicial protection provided by Article 25 of the Convention applies to the rights not subject to derogation in a state of emergency.

24. Article 25(1) incorporates the principle recognized in the international law of human rights of the effectiveness of the procedural instruments or means designed

to guarantee such rights. As the Court has already pointed out, according to the Convention:

> ... States Parties have an obligation to provide effective judicial remedies to victims of human rights violations (Art. 25), remedies that must be substantiated in accordance with the rules of due process of law (Art. 8(1)), all in keeping with the general obligation of such States to guarantee the free and full exercise of the rights recognized by the Convention to all persons subject to their jurisdictions (Art. 1) (*Velásquez Rodríguez, Fairén Garbi and Solís Corrales* and *Godínez Cruz* Cases, Preliminary Objections, Judgments of June 26, 1987, paras. 90, 90, and 92, respectively).

According to this principle, the absence of an effective remedy to violations of the rights recognized by the Convention is itself a violation of the Convention by the State Party in which the remedy is lacking. In that sense, it should be emphasized that, for such a remedy to exist, it is not sufficient that it be provided for by the Constitution or by law or that it be formally recognized, but rather it must be truly effective in establishing whether there has been a violation of human rights and in providing redress. A remedy which proves illusory because of the general conditions prevailing in the country, or even in the particular circumstances of a given case, cannot be considered effective. That could be the case, for example, when practice has shown its ineffectiveness: when the Judicial Power lacks the necessary independence to render impartial decisions or the means to carry out its judgments; or in any other situation that constitutes a denial of justice, as when there is an unjustified delay in the decision; or when, for any reason, the alleged victim is denied access to a judicial remedy.

25. In normal circumstances, the above conclusions are generally valid with respect to all the rights recognized by the Convention. But it must also be understood that the declaration of a state of emergency – whatever its breadth or denomination in internal law – cannot entail the suppression or ineffectiveness of the judicial guarantees that the Convention requires the States Parties to establish for the protection of the rights not subject to derogation or suspension by the state of emergency.

26. Therefore, any provision adopted by virtue of a state of emergency which results in the suppression of those guarantees is a violation of the Convention.

27. Article 8(1) of the Convention points out that

> Every person has the right to a hearing, with due guarantees and within a reasonable time, by a competent, independent, and impartial tribunal, previously established by law, in the substantiation of any accusation of a criminal nature made against him or for the determination of his rights and obligations of a civil, labor, fiscal, or any other nature.

In the Spanish text of the Convention, the title of this provision, whose interpretation has been specifically requested, is "Judicial Guarantees." ["Right to a Fair Trial" in the English text] This title may lead to confusion because the provision does not recognize any judicial guarantees, strictly speaking. Article 8 does not contain a specific judicial remedy, but rather the procedural requirements that should be observed in order to be able to speak of effective and appropriate judicial guarantees under the Convention.

28. Article 8 recognizes the concept of "due process of law," which includes the prerequisites necessary to ensure the adequate protection of those persons whose rights or obligations are pending judicial determination. This conclusion is justifiable in that

Article 46(2)(a) uses the same expression in establishing that the duty to pursue and exhaust the remedies under domestic law is not applicable when

> the domestic legislation of the state concerned does not afford due process of law for the protection of the right or rights that have allegedly been violated.

29. The concept of due process of law expressed in Article 8 of the Convention should be understood as applicable, in the main, to all the judicial guarantees referred to in the American Convention, even during a suspension governed by Article 27 of the Convention.

30. Reading Article 8 together with Articles 7(6), 25, and 27(2) of the Convention leads to the conclusion that the principles of due process of law cannot be suspended in states of exception insofar as they are necessary conditions for the procedural institutions regulated by the Convention to be considered judicial guarantees. This result is even more clear with respect to habeas corpus and amparo, which are indispensable for the protection of the human rights that are not subject to derogation and to which the Court will now refer.

31. Paragraph 6 of Article 7 (Right to Personal Liberty) recognizes and governs the remedy of habeas corpus. In another opinion, the Court has carefully studied habeas corpus as a guarantee not subject to derogation. It said in that regard:

> (H)abeas corpus performs a vital role in ensuring that a person's life and physical integrity are respected, in preventing his disappearance or the keeping of his whereabouts secret and in protecting him against torture or other cruel, inhumane, or degrading punishment or treatment (Habeas Corpus in Emergency Situations, *supra* [ ] para. 35).

32. Regarding amparo, contained in Article 25(1) of the Convention, the Court asserted the following in the advisory opinion just mentioned above:

> The above text (Art. 25(1)) is a general provision that gives expression to the procedural institution known as "amparo," which is a simple and prompt remedy designed for the protection of all of the rights recognized by the constitutions and laws of the States Parties and by the Convention. Since "amparo" can be applied to all rights, it is clear that it can also be applied to those that are expressly mentioned in Article 27(2) as rights that are non-derogable in emergency situations (*Ibid.*, para. 32).

33. Referring to these two judicial guarantees essential for the protection of the non-derogable rights, the Court held that

> the writs of habeas corpus and of "amparo" are among those judicial remedies that are essential for the protection of various rights whose derogation is prohibited by Article 27(2) and that serve, moreover, to preserve legality in a democratic society (*Ibid.*, para. 42).

34. The Court adds that, moreover, there are other guarantees based upon Article 29(c) of the Convention, which reads as follows:

Article 29. Restrictions Regarding Interpretation

No provision of this Convention shall be interpreted as:

> . . .
> c) precluding other rights or guarantees that are inherent in the human personality or derived from representative democracy as a form of government.

35. The Court has already referred to the rule of law, to representative democracy, and to personal liberty, and has described in detail how essential they are to the inter-American system and in particular to the system for the protection of human rights contained in the Convention (see Compulsory Membership in an Association Prescribed by Law for the Practice of Journalism (Arts. 13 and 29 American Convention on Human Rights), Advisory Opinion OC-5/85 of November 13, 1985. Series A No. 5, para. 66; The Word "Laws" in Article 30 of the American Convention on Human Rights, Advisory Opinion OC-6/86 of May 9, 1986. Series A No. 6, paras. 30 and 34 and Habeas Corpus in States of Emergency, *supra* [ ] para. 20). The Court considers it relevant to reiterate the following:

> In a democratic society, the rights and freedoms inherent in the human person, the guarantees applicable to them and the rule of law form a triad. Each component thereof defines itself, complements and depends on the others for its meaning (Habeas Corpus in Emergency Situations, *supra* [ ] para. 26).
>
> When guarantees are suspended, some legal restraints applicable to the acts of public authorities may differ from those in effect under normal conditions. These restraints may not be considered to be non-existent, however, nor can the government be deemed thereby to have acquired absolute powers that go beyond the circumstances justifying the grant of such exceptional legal measures. The Court has already noted, in this connection, that there exists an inseparable bond between the principle of legality, democratic institutions and the rule of law (*Ibid.*, para. 24; see also The Word "Laws," *supra*, para. 32).

36. The Court also said that the suspension of guarantees must not exceed that strictly required and that

> any action on the part of the public authorities that goes beyond those limits, which must be specified with precision in the decree promulgating the state of emergency, would also be unlawful . . . (Habeas Corpus in Emergency Situations, *supra* [ ] para. 38).
>
> (I)t follows that the specific measures applicable to the rights or freedoms that have been suspended may also not violate these general principles. Such violation would occur, for example, if the measures taken infringed the legal regime of the state of emergency, if they lasted longer than the time limit specified, if they were manifestly irrational, unnecessary or disproportionate, or if, in adopting them, there was a misuse or abuse of power (*Ibid.*, para. 39).

37. Thus understood, the "guarantees . . . derived from representative democracy as a form of government" referred to in Article 29(c) imply not only a particular political system against which it is unlawful to rebel (*Ibid.*, para. 20), but the need that it be supported by the judicial guarantees essential to ensure the legality of the measures taken in a state of emergency, in order to preserve the rule of law (*Ibid.*, para. 40).

38. The Court holds that the judicial guarantees essential for the protection of the human rights not subject to derogation, according to Article 27(2) of the Convention, are those to which the Convention expressly refers in Articles 7(6) and 25(1), considered within the framework and the principles of Article 8, and also those necessary to the preservation of the rule of law, even during the state of exception that results from the suspension of guarantees.

39. When in a state of emergency the Government has not suspended some rights and freedoms subject to derogation, the judicial guarantees essential for the effectiveness of such rights and liberties must be preserved.

40. It is neither possible nor advisable to try to list all the possible "essential" judicial guarantees that cannot be suspended under Article 27(2). Those will depend in each case upon an analysis of the juridical order and practice of each State Party, which rights are involved, and the facts which give rise to the question. For the same reasons, the Court has not considered the implications of other international instruments (Art. 27(1)) that could be applicable in concrete cases.

41. Therefore, THE COURT IS OF THE OPINION

Unanimously,

1. That the "essential" judicial guarantees which are not subject to derogation, according to Article 27(2) of the Convention, include habeas corpus (Art. 7(6)), amparo, and any other effective remedy before judges or competent tribunals (Art. 25(1)), which is designed to guarantee the respect of the rights and freedoms whose suspension is not authorized by the Convention.

Unanimously,

2. That the "essential" judicial guarantees which are not subject to suspension, include those judicial procedures, inherent to representative democracy as a form of government (Art. 29(c)), provided for in the laws of the States Parties as suitable for guaranteeing the full exercise of the rights referred to in Article 27(2) of the Convention and whose suppression or restriction entails the lack of protection of such rights.

Unanimously,

3. That the above judicial guarantees should be exercised within the framework and the principles of due process of law, expressed in Article 8 of the Convention.

~

2.2. Principles of Interpretation

Vienna Convention on the Law of Treaties

Article 31

General rule of interpretation

1. A treaty shall be interpreted in good faith in accordance with the ordinary meaning to be given to the terms of the treaty in their context and in the light of its object and purpose.

2. The context for the purpose of the interpretation of a treaty shall comprise, in addition to the text, including its preamble and annexes:

   (a) any agreement relating to the treaty which was made between all the parties in connexion with the conclusion of the treaty;
   (b) any instrument which was made by one or more parties in connexion with the conclusion of the treaty and accepted by the other parties as an instrument related to the treaty.

3. There shall be taken into account, together with the context:

   (a) any subsequent agreement between the parties regarding the interpretation of the treaty or the application of its provisions;

(b) any subsequent practice in the application of the treaty which establishes the agreement of the parties regarding its interpretation;

(c) any relevant rules of international law applicable in the relations between the parties.

4. A special meaning shall be given to a term if it is established that the parties so intended.

Article 32

Supplementary means of interpretation

Recourse may be had to supplementary means of interpretation, including the preparatory work of the treaty and the circumstances of its conclusion, in order to confirm the meaning resulting from the application of article 31, or to determine the meaning when the interpretation according to article 31:

(a) leaves the meaning ambiguous or obscure; or

(b) leads to a result which is manifestly absurd or unreasonable.

Hague Convention (IV)
Respecting the Laws and Customs of War on Land

[Preamble]

Until a more complete code of the laws of war has been issued, the High Contracting Parties deem it expedient to declare that, in cases not included in the Regulations adopted by them, the inhabitants and the belligerents remain under the protection and the rule of the principles of the law of nations, as they result from the usages established among civilized peoples, from the laws of humanity, and the dictates of the public conscience.

Statute of the International Criminal Court

Article 21

1. The Court shall apply:

(a) In the first place, this Statute, Elements of Crimes and its Rules of Procedure and Evidence;

(b) In the second place, where appropriate, applicable treaties and the principles and rules of international law, including the established principles of the international law of armed conflict;

(c) Failing that, general principles of law derived by the Court from national laws of legal systems of the world including, as appropriate, the national laws of States that would normally exercise jurisdiction over the crime, provided that those principles are not inconsistent with this Statute and with international law and internationally recognized norms and standards.

2. The Court may apply principles and rules of law as interpreted in its previous decisions.

3. The application and interpretation of law pursuant to this article must be consistent with internationally recognized human rights, and be without any adverse distinction founded on grounds such as gender as defined in article 7, paragraph 3, age, race, colour, language, religion or belief, political or other opinion, national, ethnic or social origin, wealth, birth or other status.

"Other Treaties" Subject to the Consultative Jurisdiction of the Court
(Art. 64 of the American Convention on Human Rights)
Advisory Opinion OC-1/82, September 24, 1982
Inter-Am. Ct. H.R. (Ser. A) No. 1 (1982)

. . . .

8. The Government of Peru submitted the following question to the Court concerning Article 64 of the American Convention on Human Rights (hereinafter cited as "the Convention"):

How should the phrase "or of other treaties concerning the protection of human rights in the American states" be interpreted?

With respect to this matter, the Government of Peru requests that the opinion cover the following specific questions:

Does this aforementioned phrase refer to and include:

(a) Only treaties adopted within the framework or under the auspices of the inter-American system? or

(b) The treaties concluded solely among the American states, that is, is the reference limited to treaties in which only American states are parties? or

(c) All treaties in which one or more American states are parties?

9. Article 64 of the Convention reads as follows:

1. The member states of the Organization may consult the Court regarding the interpretation of this Convention or of other treaties concerning the protection of human rights in the American states. Within their spheres of competence, the organs listed in Chapter X of the Charter of the Organization of American States, as amended by the Protocol of Buenos Aires, may in like manner consult the Court.

2. The Court, at the request of a member state of the Organization, may provide that state with opinions regarding the compatibility of any of its domestic laws with the aforesaid international instruments.

10. A reading of the request indicates that the Government of Peru has in effect formulated one question with three possible answers. The main issue consists of defining which treaties may be interpreted by this Court in application of the powers granted it by Article 64 of the Convention. The request requires the Court to determine the limits of its advisory jurisdiction which are not clearly spelled out in Article 64 of the Convention. In analyzing and answering the question presented, the Court will have to determine which international treaties concerning the protection of human rights it has the power to interpret under Article 64 (1); put more precisely, it will have to establish which of the human rights treaties must, a priori, be deemed to be excluded from the Court's advisory jurisdiction.

11. A direct answer to the issue presented implies an analysis of the differences between bilateral and multilateral treaties, as well as between both those adopted within and outside the inter-American system; between those treaties in which only Member States of the system are Parties and those in which Member States of the system are Parties together with non-Member States; as well between treaties in which American States are not, or cannot be, Parties. In dealing with each of these categories, the Court must also distinguish between treaties whose principal purpose is the protection of human rights and those which, although they have another purpose, include human rights provisions.

Once these distinctions are made, the Court will have to determine which of these treaties it is empowered to interpret.

. . . .

32. . . . , the Court can now turn to the specific question presented by the request of the Government of Peru. It seeks to ascertain which treaties fall within the scope of the Court's advisory jurisdiction, which States must be Parties to these treaties, and, to some extent, on the origin of these treaties. According to the Peruvian request, the narrowest interpretation would lead to the conclusion that only those treaties adopted within the framework or under the auspices of the inter-American system are deemed to be within the scope of Article 64 of the Convention. By contrast, the broadest interpretation would include within the Court's advisory jurisdiction any treaty concerning the protection of human rights in which one or more American States are Parties.

33. In interpreting Article 64, the Court will resort to traditional international law methods, relying both on general and supplementary rules of interpretation, which find expression in Articles 31 and 32 of the Vienna Convention on the Law of Treaties.

34. Neither the request of the Peruvian Government nor the Convention itself distinguishes between multilateral and bilateral treaties, nor between treaties whose main purpose is the protection of human rights and those treaties which, though they may have some other principal object, contain provisions regarding human rights, such as, for example, the Charter of the OAS. The Court considers that the answers to the questions posed in paragraph 32 are applicable to all of these treaties since the basic problem consists of determining what international obligations the American States have assumed are subject to interpretation by means of an advisory opinion. The Court, therefore, does not consider that the determining factor is the bilateral or multilateral nature of the treaty; equally irrelevant is the source of the obligation or the treaty's main purpose.

35. The meaning of the phrase "American states" is not defined in Article 64 of the Convention and the Peruvian request does not attempt to explain it. It is the opinion of the Court that, according to the ordinary meaning to be given to the terms of the treaty in their context, the phrase refers to all those States which may ratify or adhere to the Convention, in accordance with its Article 74, *i.e.*, to Member States of the OAS.

36. The issues raised by the Government of Peru lead to the following question, which must be answered consistent with Article 64 and in light of the object and purpose of the treaty: Is it the purpose of the Convention to bar, *a priori*, an advisory opinion of the Court regarding the international human rights obligations assumed by American States simply because the source of such obligations is a treaty concluded outside the Inter-American system, or because non-American States are also Parties to it?

37. The text of Article 64 of the Convention does not compel the conclusion that it is to be restrictively interpreted. In paragraphs 14 through 17, the Court has explained the broad scope of its advisory jurisdiction. The ordinary meaning of the text of Article 64 therefore does not permit the Court to rule that certain international treaties were meant to be excluded from its scope simply because non-American States are or may become Parties to them. In fact, the only restriction to the Court's jurisdiction to be found in Article 64 is that it speaks of international agreements concerning the protection of human rights in the American States. The provisions of Article 64 do not require that the agreements be treaties between American States, nor that they be regional in character, nor that they have been adopted within the framework of the inter-American system. Since a restrictive purpose was not expressly articulated, it cannot be presumed to exist.

38. The distinction implicit in Article 64 of the Convention alludes rather to a question of a geographical-political character. Put more precisely, it is more important to determine which State is affected by the obligations whose character or scope the Court is to interpret than the source of these obligations. It follows therefrom, that, if the principal purpose of a request for an advisory opinion relates to the implementation or scope of international obligations assumed by a Member State of the inter-American system, the Court has jurisdiction to render the opinion. By the same token, the Court lacks that jurisdiction if the principal purpose of the request relates to the scope or implementation of international obligations assumed by States not members of the inter-American system. This distinction demonstrates once again the need to approach the issue presented on a case-by-case basis.

39. The latter conclusion gains special importance given the language of Article 64 (2) of the Convention, which authorizes the Member States of the OAS to request advisory opinions regarding the compatibility of their domestic laws with treaties concerning the protection of human rights in the American States. This provision enables the Court to perform a service for all of the members of the Inter-American system and is designed to assist them in fulfilling their international human rights obligations. Viewed in this perspective, an American State is no less obligated to abide by an international agreement merely because non-American States are or may become Parties to it. The Court can find no good reasons why an American State should not be able to request an advisory opinion on the compatibility of any of its domestic laws with treaties concerning the protection of human rights which have been adopted outside the framework of the Inter-American system. There are, moreover, practical reasons that suggest that the interpretative function be exercised within the Inter-American system even when dealing with international agreements not adopted within its framework. Regional methods of protection, as has been pointed out, "are more suited for the task and at the same time . . . more readily accepted by the states of this hemisphere. . . . " (C. Sepulveda, "Panorama de los Derechos Humanos," Boletín del Instituto de Investigaciones Jurídicas 1053, at 1054 (Mexico, 1982).).

40. The nature of the subject matter itself, however, militates against a strict distinction between universalism and regionalism. Mankind's universality and the universality of the rights and freedoms which are entitled to protection form the core of all international protective systems. In this context, it would be improper to make distinctions based on the regional or non-regional character of the international obligations assumed by States, and thus deny the existence of the common core of basic human rights standards. The Preamble of the Convention gives clear expression to that fact when it recognizes that the essential rights of man "are based upon the attributes of the human personality and that they therefore justify international protection in the form of a convention."

41. A certain tendency to integrate the regional and universal systems for the protection of human rights can be perceived in the Convention. The Preamble recognizes that the principles on which the treaty is based are also proclaimed in the Universal Declaration of Human Rights and that "they have been reaffirmed and refined in other international instruments, worldwide as well as regional in scope." Several provisions of the Convention likewise refer to other international treaties or to international law, without speaking of any regional restrictions. (*See, e.g.*, Convention, Arts. 22, 26, 27, and 29.) Special mention should be made in this connection of Article 29, which contains rules governing the interpretation of the Convention, and which clearly indicates an intention not to restrict

the protection of human rights to determinations that depend on the source of the obligations. Article 29 reads as follows.

"No provision of the Convention may be interpreted as:

a. permitting any State Party, group, or person to suppress the enjoyment or exercise of the rights and freedoms recognized in this Convention or to restrict them to a greater extent than is provided for herein;

b. restricting the enjoyment or exercise of any right or freedom recognized by virtue of the laws of any State Party or by virtue of another convention to which one of the said states is a party;

c. precluding other rights or guarantees that are inherent in the human personality or derived from representative democracy as a form of government; or

d. excluding or limiting the effect that the American Declaration of the Rights and Duties of Man and other international acts of the same nature have.

42. It is particularly important to emphasize the special relevance that Article 29 (b) has to the instant request. The function that Article 64 of the Convention confers on the Court is an inherent part of the protective system established by the Convention. The Court is of the view, therefore, that to exclude, a priori, from its advisory jurisdiction international human rights treaties that are binding on American States would weaken the full guarantee of the rights proclaimed in those treaties and, in turn, conflict with the rules enunciated in Article 29 (b) of the Convention.

43. The need of the regional system to be complemented by the universal finds expression in the practice of the Inter-American Commission on Human Rights and is entirely consistent with the object and purpose of the Convention, the American Declaration and the Statute of the Commission. The Commission has properly invoked in some of its reports and resolutions other treaties concerning the protection of human rights in the American states, regardless of their bilateral or multilateral character, or whether they have been adopted within the framework or under the auspices of the inter-American system. This has been true most recently in the following reports of the Commission the situation of human rights in El Salvador (OEA/Ser.L/V/II.46, doc.23, rev.l, November 17, 1979) at 37–38; the situation of political prisoners in Cuba (OEA/Ser.L/V/II.48, doc.24, December 14, 1979) at 9; the situation of human rights in Argentina (OEA/Ser.L/V/II.49, doc. 19, April 11, 1980) at 24–25; the situation of human rights in Nicaragua (OEA/Ser.L/V/II.53, doc.25, June 30, 1981) at 31; the situation of human rights in Colombia (OEA/Ser.L/V/II.53, doc.22, June 30, 1981) at 56–57; the situation of human rights in Guatemala (OEA/Ser.L/V/II.53, doc.21, rev.2, October 13, 1981) at 16–17; the situation of human rights in Bolivia (OEA/Ser.L/V/II.53, doc.6, rev.2, October 13, 1981) at 20–21; and Case 7481-Acts which occurred in Caracoles (Bolivia), Resolution No. 30/82 (OEA/Ser.L/V/II.55, doc.54, March 8, 1982).

44. This practice of the Commission which is designed to enable it better to discharge the functions assigned to it compels the conclusion that the States themselves have an interest in being able to request an advisory opinion from the Court involving a human rights treaty to which they are parties but which has been adopted outside the framework of the inter-American system. Situations might in fact arise in which the Commission might interpret one of these treaties in a manner deemed to be erroneous by the States concerned, which would then be able to invoke Article 64 to challenge the Commission's interpretations.

45. The Court's interpretation of Article 64, based on the ordinary meaning of its terms viewed in their context and taking into account the object and purpose of the treaty, is confirmed by the preparatory work of the Convention. It can accordingly be relied upon as a supplementary means of interpretation. (Vienna Convention on the Law of Treaties, Art. 32.)

46. As the Court pointed out in paragraph 17, the evolution of the text which ultimately became Article 64 indicates a marked desire to expand the advisory jurisdiction of the Court. The very fact that it was drafted at a time when the narrowly drawn Article 1 of Protocol No. 2 of the European Convention had already been adopted demonstrates that the drafters of the Convention intended to confer on the Court the most extensive advisory jurisdiction, intentionally departing from the limitations imposed upon the European system.

47. During the initial phase of the drafting of the Convention, the majority of the States were clearly opposed to the notion of making a strict distinction between universalism and regionalism.

As a matter of fact, after the International Covenant on Economic, Social and Cultural Rights, the International Covenant on Civil and Political Rights and the Optional Protocol thereto, which were drafted within the framework of the United Nations, were opened for signature, the OAS Council consulted the Member States of the Organization in June 1967 regarding the advisability of continuing the work on an American convention, considering that the UN instruments had been adopted. Ten of the twelve States that replied to the inquiry favored continuing the work on the Convention, it being understood that an effort would be made to draw on the provisions of the UN Covenants. As a result of this poll, the Specialized Inter-American Conference was eventually held in Costa Rica in November 1969. The preparatory work of the Convention consequently demonstrates a tendency to conform the regional system to the universal one, which is evident in the text of the Convention itself.

48. Based on the foregoing analysis, the Court concludes that the very text of Article 64 of the Convention, the object and purpose of the treaty, the rules of interpretation set out in Article 29 of the Convention, the practice of the Commission and the preparatory work all point toward the same result: no good reason exists to hold, in advance and in the abstract, that the Court lacks the power to receive a request for, or to issue, an advisory opinion about a human rights treaty applicable to an American State merely because non-American States are also parties to the treaty or because the treaty has not been adopted within the framework or under the auspices of the inter-American system.

49. A number of submissions addressed to the Court, both by Member States and certain OAS organs, urge a more restrictive interpretation of Article 64. Some of these arguments, already adverted to in paragraph 37, are based on the meaning to be ascribed to the phrase "in the American states." Two other contentions are more substantive in nature. The first is that a broad interpretation would authorize the Court to render opinions affecting States which have nothing to do with the Convention or the Court, and which cannot even be represented before it. As to that issue, the Court has already emphasized that, if a request for an advisory opinion has as its principal purpose the determination of the scope of, or compliance with, international commitments assumed by States outside the inter-American system, the Court is authorized to render a motivated opinion refraining to pass on the issues submitted to it. The mere possibility that the event hypothesized in the above argument might arise, which can after all be dealt with on a

case-by-case basis, is hardly a sufficient enough reason for concluding that the Court, a priori, lacks the power to render an advisory opinion interpreting the human rights obligations assumed by an American State merely because such obligations originate outside the framework of the Inter-American system.

50. The other argument that has been advanced is that the extension of the limits of the Court's advisory jurisdiction might produce conflicting interpretations emanating from the Court and from those organs outside the inter-American system that might be called upon also to apply and interpret treaties concluded outside of that system. The Court believes that it is here dealing with one of those arguments which proves too much and which, moreover, is less compelling than it appears at first glance. It proves too much because the possibility of conflicting interpretations is a phenomenon common to all those legal systems that have certain courts which are not hierarchically integrated. Such courts have jurisdiction to apply and, consequently, interpret the same body of law. Here it is, therefore, not unusual to find that on certain occasions courts reach conflicting or at the very least different conclusions in interpreting the same rule of law. On the international law plane, for example, because the advisory jurisdiction of the International Court of Justice extends to any legal question, the UN Security Council or the General Assembly might ask the International Court to render an advisory opinion concerning a treaty which, without any doubt, could also be interpreted by this Court under Article 64 of the Convention. Even a restrictive interpretation of Article 64 would not avoid the possibility that this type of conflict might arise.

51. Moreover, the conflicts being anticipated, were they to occur, would not be particularly serious. It must be remembered, in this connection, that the advisory opinions of the Court and those of other international tribunals, because of their advisory character, lack the same binding force that attaches to decisions in contentious cases. (Convention, Art. 68.) This being so, less weight need be given to arguments based on the anticipated effects that the Court's opinions might have in relation to States lacking standing to participate in the advisory proceedings here in question. Viewed in this light, it is obvious that the possibility that the opinions of the Court might conflict with those of other tribunals or organs is of no great practical significance; there are no theoretical obstacles, moreover, that would bar accepting the possibility that such conflicts might arise.

52. For these reasons, responding to the request of the Government of Peru for an interpretation of the meaning of the phrase "or of other treaties concerning the protection of human rights in the American states," contained in Article 64 of the Convention,

THE COURT IS OF THE OPINION

Firstly:

"By unanimous vote, that the advisory jurisdiction of the Court can be exercised, in general, with regard to any provision dealing with the protection of human rights set forth in any international treaty applicable in the American States, regardless of whether it be bilateral or multilateral, whatever be the principal purpose of such a treaty, and whether or not non-Member States of the inter-American system are or have the right to become parties thereto."

Secondly:

"By unanimous vote, that, for specific reasons explained in a duly motivated decision, the Court may decline to comply with a request for an advisory opinion if it concludes that, due to the special circumstances of a particular case, to grant the request would exceed the limits of the Court's advisory jurisdiction for the following reasons, *inter alia*: because the issues raised deal mainly with international obligations assumed by a non-American State or with the structure or operation of international organs or bodies outside the inter-American system; or because granting the request might have the effect of altering or weakening the system established by the Convention in a manner detrimental to the individual human being."

∾

QUESTIONS & COMMENTS

(1) The International Court of Justice in *Legal Consequences for States of the Continued Presence of South Africa in Namibia (South West Africa) notwithstanding Security Council Resolution 276 (1970)*, Advisory Opinion, 1971 I.C.J. 16, 31 (1971), opined that "an international instrument must be interpreted and applied within the overall framework of the [international] juridical system in force." (emphasis provided) The Inter-American Court of Human Rights also has opined the same interpretive rule. *Interpretation of the American Declaration of the Rights and Duties of Man within the Framework of Article 64 of the American Convention on Human Rights*, Advisory Opinion OC-10/89, Inter-Am. Ct. H.R. Ser. A, No. 10, at ¶ 37 (1989) (citing ICJ's language from the Namibia Advisory Opinion).

Paul Mahoney
*Judicial Activism and Judicial Self-Restraint
in the European Court of Human Rights:
Two Sides of the Same Coin*
11 Hum. Rts. L. J. 57 (1990)[1]

. . . .

B. Approach of the European Court of Human Rights

The European Court's mandate under the Convention is to interpret and to apply, not to revise. The power of amendment as such rests with the Contracting States. Insofar as some fundamental rights were left unprotected by the Convention at the time of its adoption,[2] the gap is one to be filled by amendment of the text of the Convention. As a matter of principle, the judges should, in order to remain within the limits of their legitimate role, confine themselves to enforcing obligations that are expressly stated or implicit in the written text before them. The difficult question is whether, and if so subject to what conditions, the Court has jurisdiction to extend the existing Convention rights by interpretation into areas or in directions not foreseen by the drafters.

---

[1] Many footnotes and citations removed. Ed.'s. Note.

[2] [Mahoney] *Golder v. United Kingdom*, 21 Feb. 1975, European Court of Human Rights ("ECtHR") Series A Vol. 18, §34, makes clear that the Convention is a selective instrument intended, as the Preamble puts it, to provide a system of "collective enforcement of *certain* of the rights stated in the Universal Declaration."

The European Court has opted for the approach of seeking the current meaning of indeterminate concepts found in the text, employing what is sometimes termed the technique of evolutive interpretation....

....

In 1981 in *Dudgeon v. United Kingdom*, the Court ... relied on an evolutive interpretation to hold that the criminal laws in Northern Ireland which had the effect of proscribing male homosexual practices between consenting adults in private fell foul of the right to respect for private life....

....

[In *Dudgeon*], the drafters of the European Convention could not foresee the developments that would take place in attitudes towards homosexuality. But, in making the justification for any restriction on the right to privacy under Article 8 dependent upon the changeable concept of "necessity in a democratic society," the drafters were perforce giving a variable content to the right. The core of the right may well be stable but its contours will vary with each generation. In the concept of "necessity in a democratic society," which is found in the second, limitative paragraph of Articles 8 to 11 of the Convention, there is written into the very text of the European Convention a mechanism requiring the national law to respond to development needs of society. Although the term "democratic society" may not be explicitly used in other Articles, it is a notion that permeates the whole Convention. As the Preamble shows, for the authors of the Convention democratic society and proper observance of human rights are inseparable.

Democratic society does not stand still, and neither does the way in which democratic society upholds its cherished fundamental values. The drafters must be deemed to have realized this when they made democratic society one of the governing elements of the Convention. They cannot have been blind to the fact that freedom of expression, for example, meant something different in 1950 from what it meant 50 or 100 years earlier. Freedom of expression is a necessarily organic and evolving concept, tied to the growth of democratic society in which it is designed to flourish. Insofar as a Convention provision covers variable social notions of democracy, then the content of the guarantee provided by the Article must necessarily also be subject to variation with each generation.

3. Object and Purpose of the Convention

The European Convention of 1950 was clearly not intended to last for only a day, but to provide for future generations the kind of continuing protection that a national constitution provides for individual liberty. Constitutional documents are *sui generis* and call for special principles of interpretation suitable for their character. In 1819, Chief Justice Marshall of the United States Supreme Court made his oft-quoted dictum that "we must never forget that it is a constitution we are expounding," a "constitution intended to endure for ages to come." As Dickson J. of the Canadian Supreme Court put it some hundred and seventy years later:

> A constitution ... is drafted with an eye to the future. Its function is to provide a continuing framework for the legitimate exercise of government's power and, when joined by a Bill or a Charter of Rights, for the unremitting protection of individual rights and liberties. Once enacted, its provisions cannot easily be repealed or amended. It must, therefore, be capable of growth and development over time to meet new social, political and historical realities often unimagined by its framers.

International instruments protecting fundamental rights call for a similar ongoing interpretative approach. Professor Rudolf Bernhardt, judge on the European Court of Human Rights, has noted that interpretation of human-rights treaties falls into a special category, since the quite distinct object and purpose of a human-rights treaty take on an especial importance. Whilst for some kinds of treaties the original meaning will be decisive, the position is otherwise for human rights treaties. The function of the European Convention, like that of the American Constitution and the Canadian Charter, is "to provide a continuing framework . . . for the unremitting protection of individual rights and liberties." This special purpose and object, and thus the intention of the drafters, would largely be defeated if the Court could not interpret the Convention in the light of present-day conditions.

. . . .

[I]n the view of the present author, the circumstances would have to be highly exceptional for the European Court to declare a common practice or legislative policy of the Contracting States to be contrary to the Convention. A conceivable example might be where there had been a retrogression in comparison to a higher level of protection previously obtaining throughout the Convention community. . . .

. . . .

The judicial power to update the level of human rights protection should be exercised only in full knowledge of the relevant facts. Relevant facts for the European Court include not only (a) the particular circumstances of the individual complainant but also (b) the actual operation of the contested law or practice within the legal order of the respondent State and (c) the approach taken to the problem in question by other democratic societies, especially the Convention counties other than the respondent State. . . .

. . . .

∾

In the following article, Professor Helfer discusses the role of state consensus in the European Court's developing jurisprudence.

Laurence R. Helfer

Consensus, Coherence and the European Convention on Human Rights
26 CORNELL INT'L L.J. 133 (1993)[1]

The European Convention for the Protection of Human Rights and Fundamental Freedoms is widely regarded as the most effective international instrument for the protection of individual rights. The Convention's reputation as a bulwark against arbitrary government interference stems at least in part from the fact that the decisions of its judicial enforcement organs, the European Court of Human Rights ("Court") and the European Commission of Human Rights ("Commission"), are almost universally respected and implemented by the twenty-four European nations ("Contracting States") that have ratified the Convention.[2]

---

[1]   Many citations and footnotes have been removed from this article. Ed.'s Note.

[2]   [Helfer] The Contracting States comply with their Convention obligations by introducing legislative amendments, reopening judicial proceedings, granting administrative pardons, and paying monetary damages to individuals whose rights have been violated. *See* Fredrik G. E. Sundberg, *The European Experience*

The Contracting States' compliance is especially significant given the teleological approach that the Court and Commission (the "tribunals") use to interpret the Convention. Far from being bound by the intention of the drafters, the tribunals interpret the Convention as a modern document that responds to and progressively incorporates changing European social and legal developments. Toward this end, they search for the existence of rights-enhancing practices and policies among the Contracting States that affect human rights. When these practices achieve a certain measure of uniformity, a "European consensus" so to speak, the Court and Commission raise the standard of rights-protection to which all states must adhere. In this way the tribunals have expanded the Convention's reach to groups of individuals whom the drafters did not view as falling within the Convention's protective ambit.

Nearly all those offering commentary on the Court and Commission have viewed this evolutionary interpretation as beneficial to the development of Convention case law, disagreeing only on how far a particular practice must evolve before it should be applied against less progressive states that have failed to modify their laws. Yet little scholarly attention has been devoted to normative aspects of the European consensus inquiry. In particular, few commentators have explored the implications of the tribunals' inability to define the consensus inquiry with precision when articulating the expanding obligations of European governments to protect individual rights.

This Article focuses in depth on the ambiguity in the tribunals' current consensus methodology and its effect on the development of a coherent European human rights jurisprudence. It argues that the failure to articulate with precision the scope and function of the consensus inquiry poses a potentially grave threat to the tribunals' authority as the arbiters of European human rights. Without a consistent definition of the conditions under which emerging human rights principles should be incorporated into the Convention, the tribunals risk judicial illegitimacy whenever they depart from an interpretation based on the intent of the Convention's drafters. The time has come, therefore, to develop a more comprehensive and rigorous methodology for applying the European consensus inquiry.

. . . .

I. The European Convention and the Consensus Inquiry

A. Consensus and the Margin of Appreciation Doctrine

In determining the scope of the obligations that the Convention imposes on the Contracting States, the Court and Commission weigh deference to national decision-makers against their conviction that the treaty must be interpreted in light of progressive European conditions and attitudes. Striking the balance between these two competing goals is difficult, for although the tribunals have indicated that the Convention must be interpreted as a "living instrument" and "in light of present-day conditions," they have also acknowledged that the Contracting States are entitled to a substantial degree of deference, or, to use their words, a "margin of appreciation" for their actions.

The justifications for respect and deference are considerable. The tribunals are keenly aware that the Convention continues to exist solely by consent of the Contracting States.

In an extreme case, a state faced with an unfavorable judgment can choose not to renew the right of individual petition or can withdraw from the Convention altogether. A state can also express its displeasure through less drastic means, for example, by failing to comply with a judgment or by delaying its execution. By contrast, the only genuine enforcement action that other Contracting States may take is to banish the offending state from the Council of Europe, the multi-national organization to which all of the Convention's signatories are members.[3]

The Court and Commission are also aware that they are not national legislatures or courts with plenary authority to strike the balance between competing interests in complex areas of law and public policy. Thus, they will not require a Contracting State to provide what they consider to be the most comprehensive human rights protection possible. Rather, if the laws of a Contracting State are on the "margin" of compatibility with the Convention, the tribunals will defer to the state's judgment in striking the balance between individual rights and the public interest.

The Court and Commission have not, however, allowed these prudential concerns for deference to frustrate their vision of the Convention as a treaty that responds to changing legal thought and practice across Europe. Instead, the tribunals have progressively narrowed the margin of appreciation doctrine by analyzing the degree to which common human rights practices can be discerned among the Contracting States. Where a majority of states have expanded the scope of a right guaranteed by the Convention or broadened the class of individuals to whom it applies, the Court and Commission have been far more likely to find that a state has violated the Convention by enacting or retaining a law which restricts that particular right.

B. Elements of the Consensus Inquiry

Although the tribunals have asserted in numerous cases that this European consensus approach is a "fact" of Convention jurisprudence, they have been less than clear in defining the elements that are relevant to discerning an emerging legal norm. As one commentator recently lamented:

> Especially vexing in any attempt to uncover the meaning of the consensus factor is the consistently unsubstantiated nature of the Court's pronouncements. Each of these opinions relies upon the precedential value of other opinions in which a European consensus, or lack thereof, figured importantly, but a student of the Court is not informed as to how the Court measures the existence or non-existence of any one particular consensus.[4]

A comprehensive survey of the tribunals' judgments, however, reveals that, broadly speaking, the Court and Commission rely on three distinct factors as evidence of

---

[3]   *See* Statute of the Council of Europe, May 5, 1949, 87 U.N.T.S. 103. The Council is composed of two principal bodies. The Parliamentary Assembly, a legislative body composed of representatives appointed by each member state's national Parliament, debates and makes recommendations concerning any matter that affects the Council. *Id.* arts. 23, 25. The Committee of Ministers, composed of the member states' ministers of foreign affairs or their designees, is the Council's executive arm. It enforces the judgments of the Court and has the power to make recommendations to the member states on areas of common concern.

[4]   Howard Charles Yourow, *The Margin of Appreciation Doctrine in the Dynamics of European Human Rights Jurisprudence*, 3 Conn. J. Int'l L. 111, 158 (1987).

consensus: legal consensus, as demonstrated by European domestic statutes, international treaties, and regional legislation; expert consensus; and European public consensus.

Although these elements appear with some regularity in Convention case law, the tribunals have yet to clarify the relative weight that they should be given in determining the presence or absence of an evolving European viewpoint. For example, the Court and the Commission have not specified what percentage of the Contracting States must alter their laws before a right-enhancing norm will achieve consensus status. Nor have they defined the degree to which international treaties and regional legislation are relevant to their analysis.

Rather, the tribunals speak in vague generalities, noting that a state's margin of appreciation varies according to "the existence or non-existence of common ground between the laws of the Contracting States."[5] The Court and Commission are equally ambiguous when examining the consensus factors themselves, referring to "developments and commonly accepted standards"[6] and "modern trends;"[7] or noting that the relevant reforms amount to an "evolution"[8] or a "marked change"[9] in the Contracting States' conception of human rights; or that a "great majority"[10] or a "great number"[11] of states have altered their laws.

II. Jurisprudential Problems with the Consensus Inquiry

One might view this lack of precision as an unremarkable result of the Court's young age (thirty years) and its limited number of judgments (approximately 250 by the end of 1992). Indeed, it seems plausible that as the Court's case load increases, it will have many opportunities to refine the consensus inquiry. But more is at stake here than underdeveloped doctrine. For the consensus methodology is one of the primary tools available for both the Court and Commission to implement the Convention's object and purpose: the protection of individual rights in light of the common European heritage of political traditions, ideals, freedoms, and the rule of law. By allowing the level of rights-protection to evolve with progressive regional standards, the tribunals ensure that their interpretation of protected rights and freedoms is "consistent with 'the general spirit of the Convention, an instrument designed to maintain and promote the ideals and values of a democratic society.'"

This commitment to protecting individual rights is, however, in constant tension with deference to national decision-makers. Therefore, the tribunals must develop persuasive justifications for intruding into the Contracting States' sovereignty. Indeed, if the Court and Commission expect the states to comply with their increasingly rights-protective judgments, they must provide a more precise explanation of the point at which an evolving European viewpoint acquires consensus status.

---

[5] *Rasmussen v. Denmark*, 87 Eur. Ct. H.R. (ser. A) at 15 (1984).

[6] *Tyrer v. United Kingdom*, 26 Eur. Ct. H.R. (ser. A) at 15–16 (1978).

[7] *Öztürk v. Federal Republic of Germany*, 73 Eur. Ct. H.R. (ser. A) at 36 (1984) (Bernhardt, J., dissenting).

[8] *F. v. Switzerland*, 128 Eur. Ct. H.R. (ser. A) at 16 (1987); *Marckx v. Belgium*, 31 Eur. Ct. H.R. (ser. A) at 19 (1979).

[9] *Norris v. Ireland*, 142 Eur. Ct. H.R. (ser. A) at 20 (1988); *Dudgeon v. United Kingdom*, 45 Eur. Ct. H.R. (ser. A) at 24 (1981).

[10] *Dudgeon v. United Kingdom*, 45 Eur. Ct. H.R. (ser. A) at 23–24 (1981).

[11] *Johnston v. Ireland*, 112 Eur. Ct. H.R. (ser. A) at 30 (1986) (quoting preamble to European Convention on the Legal Status of Children Born Out of Wedlock, Oct. 15, 1975, Europ. T.S. No. 85).

A. The Tension Between Precedent and Change

With greater consistency and a more principled approach, the tribunals' practice of treating their prior judgments as authoritative is given enhanced legitimacy. Although the tribunals are not constrained by *stare decisis*, they "usually follow and apply their own precedents, such a course being in the interests of legal certainty and the orderly development of Convention case-law." Since precedent is applied on an interstate basis, a judgment against one Contracting State will be extremely persuasive in a similar factual context against another state.

When the tribunals articulate a rights-protective interpretation of the Convention based on the consensus inquiry, they put other less progressive states on notice that their laws may no longer be compatible with the Convention if their nationals were to challenge them. Although such states may assert that special circumstances in their countries require a different result, in the face of principled and methodical decision-making they will be hard-pressed to articulate a compelling argument, particularly as a greater degree of unity builds across Europe. Thus, when the Court and Commission overrule their previous case law "in order to ensure that the interpretation of the Convention reflects societal changes and remains in line with present-day conditions," in effect they constrain the sovereignty of all Convention signatories.[12]

This broad sovereignty-limiting aspect of the tribunals' decisions argues strongly in favor of a carefully reasoned approach to consensus definition. For if the Contracting States' reliance on a previously valid interpretation of the Convention is to be outweighed by the need to update the provisions enshrined in the treaty, those states that have not participated in the formation of a particular regional norm must have at least some confidence in the tribunals' reasoning. Indeed, such states will have a forceful argument against implementing a judgment where they perceive uncertainty or arbitrariness in the manner in which the Court and Commission have applied the consensus inquiry.

B. Finding a Proper "European" Interpretation

Underlying the tension between adhering to precedent and recognizing change is the tribunals' apprehension over whether they should strive to create an autonomous European interpretation of the Convention rather than a body of unrelated precedents that simply reflect European state practice in discrete subject areas. The tension between these approaches is at the heart of the consensus methodology, which serves very different functions depending on which jurisprudential view is adopted.

At one extreme, the Court and Commission can be seen as a lens through which the existing practices of the Contracting States are reflected. Under this approach, there is little or no room for the tribunals to modernize the Convention on behalf of the states. Rather, they raise the level of human rights protection in accordance with evolving

---

[12] An example of this sovereignty-limiting effect can be seen in the recent debate over repealing the sodomy laws of the Isle of Man. Since at present the Isle of Man does not recognize the right of individual petition for its residents, the laws cannot be declared in violation of the Convention by the Court or Commission absent a complaint by another Contracting State (a relatively rare event in the Convention's history). Nevertheless, the British government has attempted to persuade a very resistant Manx Parliament to amend its criminal code to bring it in line with the Court's rulings that such laws violate a homosexual's right to privacy. *See Keep Ban on Homosexuality, Say Manx MPs*, Assoc. Press Newsfile, Feb. 27, 1991 (*available in* LEXIS, Nexis Library, Current file). In the Spring of 1992, the Parliament finally relented. *See Manx MPs Vote to Legalise Homosexuality*, The Independent, Apr. 1, 1992, at 2.

European norms only where almost all states have adopted the rights-enhancing measures and where it seems apparent that other states have considered reforms and are likely to follow. In the most extreme scenario, the tribunals simply recognize the *de facto* legal changes that have occurred in all states and then incorporate them into the Convention. Such a position requires little theoretical reasoning and poses only a minimal threat to the Court's legitimacy.[13]

At the other extreme, the Court and Commission play a far more aggressive role, highlighting and refining emerging norms and striving to develop a truly pan-European approach. Such activist tribunals might begin to incorporate a newly emerging principle of rights-protection at any time after a significant number of states had modified their domestic laws, with the justifications for judicial intervention growing as more states joined the reform movement. As the degree of European homogeneity increased, the Court and Commission would not allow any state to rely on special circumstances to prevent the formation of a uniform standard.

The tribunals have avoided both of these poles, choosing instead to weigh the need for common standards against the Contracting States' desire to chart a nonconformist course of human rights compliance. In *Cossey v. United Kingdom*,[14] Judge Martens concisely articulated the importance of balancing these two concerns. Arguing in favor of a uniform European approach, he noted that

> the preamble to the Convention, which recalls the aim of achieving greater unity between member States and stresses that Fundamental Freedoms are "best maintained" by a "common understanding and observance of . . . Human Rights," seems to invite the Court to develop common standards. To the extent that the number of member States increases, this side of the Court's mandate gains in weight, for in such a larger, diversified community the development of common standards may well prove the best, if not the only way of . . . ensuring that the Convention remains a living instrument . . .

Yet the judge also underscored the need for a wider degree of deference in certain contexts:

> Judicial self-restraint may, on the other hand, be called for by the special features of the case or the fact that it cannot be decided without taking into consideration special situations obtaining in the defendant State. If, after careful consideration, the Court is convinced that the latter is really the case, then it may be that the State should be left a certain margin of appreciation.

To determine an appropriate degree of deference and judicial self-restraint in specific cases, the Court and Commission have supplemented the consensus inquiry with an understanding of the shifting and context-based nature of a Contracting State's margin of appreciation. As the tribunals have astutely observed, a state's interest in policies or practices that conflict with developing legal norms is likely to vary with the specific human right at issue and with the objectives that are served by restricting the enjoyment

---

[13] It should be noted, however, that even this conservative approach to the consensus inquiry is a departure from traditional principles of treaty construction, which require an express intention by states to limit their sovereignty. *See* Warbrick, [*"Federal" Aspects of the European Convention on Human Rights*, 10 Mich. J. Int'l L. 698, 715 (1989)], at 709.

[14] 184 Eur. Ct. H.R. (ser. A) (1990).

of that right.[15] Thus, where states demonstrate the existence of diverse approaches to protecting a Convention right or where they have challenged the tribunals' proficiency to adjudicate a particular class of disputes, the Court and Commission have granted states discretion to restrict individual rights within widely set parameters.[16] By contrast, where a common interpretive perspective exists, where a Convention article contains especially stringent rights-protective language, or where a right serves a special function in democratic societies, the tribunals have scrutinized such restrictions with a "more extensive European supervision."[17]

. . . .

IV. A Revised Consensus Inquiry for the 1990s

As a first step toward jurisprudential harmony, I offer the following interpretive approach to apply the European consensus inquiry. The proposal responds to the invitation by other scholars to develop a more rigorous methodology for resolving consensus-based disputes. It attempts to synthesize the principles expressed in numerous cases into a flexible framework that weighs the need for common standards to protect individual rights against deference to national decision-makers.

---

[15] *See Leander v. Sweden*, 116 Eur. Ct. H.R. (ser. A) at 25 (1987) (margin of appreciation varies with the nature of the restriction asserted and the nature of the goal pursued by the Contracting State); *Gillow v. United Kingdom*, 109 Eur. Ct. H.R. (ser. A) at 22 (1986) (margin of appreciation "will depend not only on the nature of the aim of the restriction but also on the nature of the right involved"); *see also* Strossen, [*Recent U.S. and International Judicial Protection of Individual Rights: A Comparative Legal Process Analysis and Proposed Synthesis*, 41 HASTINGS L.J. 805, 857 (1990)] ("The Convention tribunals have stated that national government decision-makers are entitled to more deference . . . regarding certain kinds of decisions that are traditionally consigned to a particular community's power of self-determination.").

[16] In *Muller v. Switzerland*, 133 Eur. Ct. H.R. (ser. A) (1988), the Court, after noting that "conceptions of sexual morality have changed in recent years," stated:

> It is not possible to find in the legal and social orders of the Contracting States a uniform European conception of morals. The view taken of the requirements of morals varies from time to time and from place to place, especially in our era, characterised as it is by a far-reaching evolution of opinions on the subject. By reason of their direct and continuous contact with the vital forces of their countries, State authorities are in principle in a better position than the international judge to give an opinion on the exact content of these requirements as well as on the necessity of a "restriction" or "penalty" intended to meet them.

Id. at 22; *see also Mathieu-Mohin & Clerfayt v. Belgium*, 113 Eur. Ct. H.R. (ser. A) at 23 (1987) (manner in which Contracting States hold free elections given broad discretion); *James v. United Kingdom*, 98 Eur. Ct. H.R. (ser. A) at 32 (1986) (Contracting States have wide margin of appreciation to regulate private property in the public interest).

[17] *Sunday Times v. United Kingdom*, 30 Eur. Ct. H.R. (ser. A) at 36 (1979); *see also Soering v. United Kingdom*, 161 Eur. Ct. H.R. (ser. A) at 34 (1989) ("The absolute prohibition of torture and of inhuman or degrading treatment and punishment under the terms of the Convention shows that Article 3 enshrines one of the fundamental values of the democratic societies making up the Council of Europe."); *Abdulaziz, Cabales & Balkandali v. United Kingdom*, 94 Eur. Ct. H.R. (ser. A) at 38 (1985) (requiring "very weighty reasons" to support differential treatment based on gender since "advancement of the equality of the sexes is today a major goal in the member States of the Council of Europe"); *Dudgeon v. United Kingdom*, 45 Eur. Ct. H.R. (ser. A) at 21 (1981) (requiring Contracting States to advance "particularly serious reasons" for an interference with "a most intimate aspect of private life"); *Handyside v. United Kingdom*, 24 Eur. Ct. H.R. (ser. A) at 23 (1976) (noting that "freedom of expression constitutes one of the essential foundations" of a democratic society and "one of the basic conditions for society's progress and for the development of every man"); *Golder v. United Kingdom*, 18 Eur. Ct. H.R. (ser. A) at 17 (1975) ("The principle whereby a civil claim must be capable of being submitted to a judge ranks as one of the universally 'recognized' fundamental principles of law.").

A. Textual and Structural Approaches

Although the consensus inquiry is a vital aspect of Convention jurisprudence, the controversies created by its application argue in favor of using it as an interpretive tool only after structural or textual approaches have been exhausted. Construing the plain meaning of individual articles, their relationship to one another in the Convention as a whole, and where appropriate, writings and statements from the *travaux préparatoires*, may reveal a rights-inclusive or rights-limiting interpretation that, because it is grounded on widely accepted principles of treaty construction, will command large majorities on the Court and Commission.

Yet even where the jurists disagree over whether the existence of a right can be implied from the Convention's object and purpose, proper application of a structural or textual methodology provides greater stability than application of the consensus inquiry. For once the Court has ruled that an unenumerated right is not protected by the Convention, that interpretation will not be subject to reevaluation with the emergence of rights-enhancing law reforms. Rather, the tribunals will respect the conclusion reached by a majority of the Court and allow the Council of Europe to overrule the decision by promulgating an optional Protocol to incorporate the right into the Convention's adjudicatory framework. In addition, a textual or structural method validates the use of the consensus inquiry by limiting it to those human rights concepts that are explicit or implicit in the language of the Convention. . . .

    . . . .

B. The Consensus Continuum

In many if not most cases, however, textual or structural approaches will not resolve the matter before the tribunals. For once they have determined that a particular right is protected by the Convention, they must then define the contours of that right in light of evolving regional trends in human rights. Rather than approach this analysis on an *ad hoc* basis, the Court and Commission should search for such trends along a structured continuum that recognizes the importance of the Convention's text, the extent of domestic law reforms, and the existence of international treaties and regional legislation in assisting the formation of a common European perspective. At each stage along this continuum, the Court and Commission can claim greater authority for accelerating the process of consensus formation and creating a uniform rule of rights-protection.

1. The Text of the Convention

The Convention's text provides the most important starting point for determining the role of the consensus inquiry in the Court's evolutionary jurisprudence. The language of specific articles and the relationship between them should be understood as modifying the tribunals' power to expand the protection of individual rights in Europe using a consensus-based methodology. The ability of the text either to authorize or to circumscribe an evolutionary interpretation can best be grasped by examining a spectrum of positions that illustrate the tribunals' varying authority to impose a construction of the Convention based on shared European values.

At one end of the spectrum are instances in which the Convention expressly authorizes the Contracting States to limit the exercise of individual rights. For example, the language of Article 2 that permits the use of the death penalty provides a seemingly absolute textual limit on the Court's ability to interpret the more open-ended language of Article 3's prohibition against inhuman or degrading punishment. Yet in *Soering v. United Kingdom*,[18] the Court stated that even such a clear textual restriction on an evolutionary interpretation could be overcome by subsequent developments in the penal policies of the Contracting States. In order for the death penalty to fall within the ambit of Article 3, however, the Court concluded that states had to be uniform both in their rejection of capital punishment as an appropriate sanction for criminal conduct and in their understanding of such actions as creating a binding legal obligation to augment the Convention's text. Moreover, the Contracting States' ability to rewrite the Convention through subsequent practices would cease to exist where the states had adopted what the Court referred to as "the normal method of amendment of the text;" that is, where they had drafted an optional Protocol to incorporate the new right or freedom into the Convention system.

A somewhat more centrist position along the spectrum is occupied by such Convention provisions as Article 12, which states that "men and women of marriageable age have the right to marry and to found a family, according to the national laws governing the exercise of this right." As this language makes plain, the Contracting States have broad authority to control the exercise of the right to marry. The Court has modified the consensus inquiry to accommodate this text-based deference to domestic law. Recent cases have demonstrated that evolutionary trends in European law reform will erode a state's power to regulate marriages only when the trends have been widely adopted. Moreover, an expansion of Article 12 to include same sex partnerships will be recognized only where European legal reforms amount to a "general abandonment of the traditional concept of marriage."

At the far end of the spectrum is found a cluster of fundamental rights and freedoms, including respect for private and family life, home, and correspondence; freedom of thought, conscience, and religion; freedom of expression; and freedom of association. These rights are linked not by the content of the substantive norms they enshrine but rather by the similarity of their texts. These Convention articles share two significant features. First, they contain an exclusive list of rationales upon which states may rely to restrict the exercise of the rights the articles protect.[19] Second, each of these articles further circumscribes restrictions upon the rights therein by requiring that the restrictions be "necessary in a democratic society." The Convention drafters left this phrase undefined.

---

[18]   161 Eur. Ct. H.R. (ser. A) (1989).

[19]   Each of these articles consists of two paragraphs. The first enumerates the content of the right while the second lists permissible limitations on its exercise. For example, Article 10 states:

> (1) Everyone has the right to freedom of expression. This right shall include freedom to hold opinions and to receive and impart information and ideas without interference by public authority regardless of frontiers. This Article shall not prevent States from requiring the licensing of broadcasting, television or cinema enterprises.

> (2) The exercise of these freedoms, since it carries with it duties and responsibilities, may be subject to such formalities, conditions, restrictions or penalties as are prescribed by law and are necessary in a democratic society, in the interests of national security, territorial integrity or public safety, for the prevention of disorder or crime, for the protection of health or morals, for the protection of the reputation or rights of others, for preventing the disclosure of information received in confidence, or for maintaining the authority and impartiality of the judiciary.

[Art. 10, ECHR.]

The Court has construed it as requiring a "pressing social need"[20] for limiting any of these rights. As one commentator of the Court has noted:

> In the concept of "necessary in a democratic society" ... there is written into the very text of the European Convention a mechanism requiring the national law to respond to developing needs of society.... Democratic society does not stand still, and neither does the way in which democratic society upholds its cherished fundamental values. The drafters must be deemed to have realised this when they made democratic society one of the governing elements of the Convention.[21]

The variable nature of this reference to democratic values authorizes the Court and Commission to apply the consensus inquiry in an aggressive manner by searching for emerging regional trends and developing common rules for respecting those human rights that the drafters believed should be vigilantly protected by all European nations.

2. Domestic Law Reforms

Having grounded the consensus inquiry in a textual framework, the tribunals must then explore in detail the degree to which common practices appear in the domestic laws of the Contracting States, as well as the views of relevant expert bodies and the European public. The existence of a common perspective provides the tribunals with a motive to modernize the rights enshrined in the Convention by developing a uniform European approach. While it is impossible to specify for every situation a precise formula for the number of states that must have amended their laws, at a minimum, at least half of the Contracting States should have adopted some form of the rights-enhancing measure in question. This majority rule serves as a minimum baseline against which the tribunals can judge the emergence of genuinely regional norms. Beyond this threshold, the justifications for creating a uniform perspective increase.

a. Factors Favoring Deference to National Decision-Makers

As part of their analysis, the Court and Commission must pay careful attention to the specific steps the Contracting States have taken to give effect to emerging European human rights norms. In some cases, a simple head count of legislative developments may satisfy the consensus inquiry, while in other cases states may have used different approaches to address the same issue. In the latter instance, the tribunals' task is far more complicated, for they must consider the various judicial, administrative, and legislative responses states have made and the extent to which such measures represent merely an accommodation of individual claims or a genuine recognition of the binding legal character of a new human rights principle.

Where states have adopted a variety of responses, the Court and Commission should respect their experimentation and encourage diversity by not imposing a single solution, at least until concordant state practice proves such a measure to be clearly preferable to others. During this transitional phase, the tribunals can rightly conclude that states that have made no effort at all to address the concerns raised by emerging regional norms have breached their Convention obligations. But the tribunals must give those states engaged

---

[20] *Handyside v. United Kingdom*, 24 Eur. Ct. H.R. (ser. A) at 22 (1976).

[21] [Paul Mahoney, *Judicial Activism and Judicial Self-Restraint in the European Court of Human Rights: Two Sides of the Same Coin*, 11 Hum. Rts. L.J. 57, 64 (1990).]

in the process of working through a response an opportunity to strike the appropriate balance between individual freedoms and other important concerns.

For example, the tribunals must be sensitive to the unique circumstances in each state that may have prevented it from reforming its laws, even where a majority of states have recognized the existence of an emerging regional norm. In extreme cases, these conditions will have resulted in ratification of the Convention subject to an express reservation. But even where no reservation has been entered, the tribunals should give somewhat greater deference to the policy rationales put forward by non-conforming states in two situations: first, where the tribunals can demonstrate that they lack the institutional competence to adjudicate a particular category of disputes; and second, where the less progressive nations can be separated from their more progressive counterparts by a distinction that divides the Contracting States along common law/civil law lines or according to geo-political sub-regions. During periods of consensus evolution, this additional measure of deference allows states to consider alternative ways of adapting to an emerging legal trend.

b. Factors Favoring an Assertive Role for the Tribunals

The deference to national authorities need not be absolute. As the tribunals have noted, certain rights and freedoms enjoy enhanced judicial protection, either because of their textual composition in the Convention itself or their functional importance in European democratic societies. The Court and Commission should not lightly dismiss any infringement of these Convention guarantees. Moreover, the tribunals can incorporate legal advancements expanding the scope of these highly protected rights into the Convention at an earlier stage than they can for comparable developments in areas where the Contracting States enjoy greater discretion.

The tribunals should also be more reluctant to grant a state a wide margin of appreciation where national decision-makers such as independent law commissions or parliamentary committees have endorsed a rights-enhancing law reform. Similarly, deference may not be necessary where the tribunals can discern a less rights-restrictive means of achieving a Contracting State's objectives that the state itself has acknowledged or applied. They may also claim greater authority where the challenged law or administrative practice is selectively enforced or has fallen into desuetude.

3. International Treaties and Regional Legislation

Admittedly, many close cases will arise in which reasonable jurists will differ over precisely how far a norm has evolved, even after carefully analyzing the Convention's text and national law reform trends. In such cases, the tribunals can look to developments in international law to confirm the existence of a movement toward a common regional perspective in the Contracting States' domestic legislation and to limit an individual state's discretion to adhere to a non-conformist position. International indicia of consensus provide strong evidence that the achievement of European unity with respect to a particular human right is a "major goal in the member states of the Council of Europe," even if the current domestic practice of states does not yet conform to that lofty aspiration.

In resorting to international law beyond the Convention's ambit, not all developments need be given the same weight. Global multilateral treaties relating to human rights which have been widely adopted by European states should be given the greatest force. A heavy burden should be placed on Contracting States attempting to argue against the enforcement of a provision contained in these instruments which the international community recognizes to have developed into customary law or *jus cogens*.

Treaties that have been opened for signature only to the member states of the Council of Europe should also be viewed as convincing evidence of a developing regional perspective on individual rights, particularly where they have been signed or ratified by a large number of states. However, not all such treaties are equally probative of consensus. Instruments that overlap to some degree with the Convention's substantive norms should have the strongest influence on the tribunals' case law, whereas regional treaties that create additional rights beyond the ambit of the Convention should be viewed with caution. For example, the Court has stated that the European Social Charter contains certain substantive provisions that are beyond the scope of the Convention.

Other important regional developments include the recommendations and resolutions of the Committee of Ministers, which are designed to encourage the member states of the Council of Europe to develop harmonious policies on matters of common interest, including human rights. Where such pronouncements purport to interpret or augment the Convention, they can be seen as substantiating a trend toward an evolving European viewpoint. Slightly reduced weight can be accorded similar recommendations and resolutions of the Parliamentary Assembly. These documents are less authoritative because they must first be screened by the Ministers before being sent on to the member states. The persuasive force of both the Ministers' and the Assembly's recommendations becomes more compelling as the Contracting States incorporate their suggestions into domestic law.

C. The Benefits of a More Rigorous Approach

Applying the above framework will permit the tribunals to inject greater rigor into the European consensus inquiry. A clearer exposition of the tribunals' reasoning and balancing of competing factors is necessary, even where the conclusions reached by individual jurists differ. Indeed, the absence of an objective "bright line" rule for deciding when an emerging norm has crystallized into a new rule of rights-protection makes such divergences unavoidable. But if the Court and Commission are committed to using a consensus-based methodology, they must both acknowledge the ambiguity that is a necessary consequence of such an approach and strive to develop general principles for weighing the competing elements of the consensus inquiry and the margin of appreciation doctrine.

. . . .

D. The Benefits of Ambiguity: A Rejoinder

Although there are clear advantages to a more rigorous consensus methodology, the counter-argument to this Article's thesis must be presented and refuted. The struggle for coherence and precision is arguably an unnecessary and improper task for international tribunals that must master the intricacies of twenty-four distinct legal systems. Because the Court and Commission must consider so many applications from this wide array of nations, the argument goes, they would be more effective institutions by remaining elusive about both the elements of the consensus inquiry and the degree of harmonization needed to modernize the Convention.

In this way, the tribunals could exercise an internal, unarticulated control over the scope of the Contracting States' obligations in two opposing situations. First, they might refuse to declare a violation of the Convention as a matter of prudence where such an action would offend a respondent state, even if the indicia of consensus pointed toward that violation; and second, they might use a less precise analysis to enhance the protection of individual rights where the formation of a progressive regional norm had not yet fully emerged. Although this methodology gives the Court and Commission flexibility to reach a desired result, it risks judicial illegitimacy: in the first case by failing to uphold the Convention's objective of providing effective human rights guarantees and in the second by unduly encroaching on the Contracting States' sovereignty.

If such an approach were possible and even desirable when the Convention was still in its infancy and when consensus questions could be resolved by unanimous or nearly unanimous judgments, recent cases on family law, gender equality, and transsexualism reveal that it is no longer tenable. There are substantial disagreements about the scope and function of the consensus inquiry among the judges and the Commission members. States, applicants, and scholars also have cause to question the tribunals' reasoning and results. Given the contingent nature of the Contracting States' participation in the treaty framework, allowing this ambiguity to continue as the Convention becomes progressively more rights-protective may weaken the stature of the tribunals and result in an increasing number of unheeded judgments. . . .

~

QUESTIONS & COMMENTS

(1) As is well known among students of constitutional law, constitutions act as checks on the tyranny of majorities. International human rights conventions also act as checks against the tyranny of majorities, particularly in those countries that lack a domestic constitutional legal order.

Does the European Court's consensus approach to developing international law undercut the important function of international human rights conventions acting as checks on the tyranny of majorities? Should a consensus approach be used only in cases where national authorities have developed their domestic laws with an acute responsiveness to eliminating the oppression of minority or other disenfranchised groups?

(2) Consider the following argument: It is necessary to examine whether a state party's internal legal order incorporates European Commission and Court law to avoid additional harms accruing to other associated rights. Allowing a non-incorporation state party to enjoy a wide margin of appreciation in one area can endanger other rights. European convention law serves to limit harms to other rights associated with a case. This problem is made clearer where a *narrow* margin of appreciation is enjoyed. For example, in the Article 6(1) area of prisoner legal access where state parties are given a narrow margin of appreciation, the European Court and Commission have found repeated violations by the non-incorporation state party (*viz.*, the United Kingdom) of not only identical rights but also associated rights, such as those guaranteed by Article 8.[1] When a

---

[1]   *See e.g., Golder v. United Kingdom*, 18 Eur. Ct. H.R. (ser. A) (1975) (denial of access to solicitor through mail and meetings violated Art. 6(1)); *Hilton v. United Kingdom*, App. No. 5613/72, Eur. Cm. H.R. 177 (1976), 3 E.H.R.R. 104 (1981) (denial of access to solicitor); *Silver v. United Kingdom*, 61 Eur. Ct. H.R. (ser. A) (1983) (Art. 6(1) and 8 violations for stopping mail between solicitor and prisoner); *Campbell*

non-incorporation state party repeatedly violates the same or associated rights, this suggests that non-incorporation itself encourages harms to associated rights. It also suggests that non-incorporation can lead to an unnecessary taxing of the Court and Commission's resources by causing unnecessary litigation.

Accordingly, giving a wide margin of appreciation to state parties who do not incorporate ECHR law into their domestic legal orders fails to discourage harms to other rights. European supervision should operate in such a manner so that no one state party acquires advantages over other state parties because of its peculiar internal legal order; this is particularly important when the advantage of receiving a wide margin of appreciation results in the detriment of fundamental rights recognized by the ECHR, such as the right to respect for family life and legal access.

Consider the case of the United Kingdom. Three of the five European Court cases challenging a state party's failure to recognize transsexual rights have come from the United Kingdom. Two of the these three cases dealt with the Article 8 right to alter one's own birth certificate. The third case addresses an associated Article 8 right to indicate the de facto parent on a birth certificate. Because there is no reason to believe that there are a disproportionate number of transsexuals in the U.K. generating cases, this phenomenon suggests that the United Kingdom's internal legal order should be examined because (i) wide margins of appreciation have been allowed previously and (ii) the United Kingdom does not incorporate ECHR law into its domestic law.

Under U.K. domestic law, Parliament is presumed to legislate in accordance with international law.[2] When a statute is in opposition to a treaty, the statute must prevail. When U.K. judges have used Strasbourg law, it has been used as an aid to statutory interpretation and only where governing law is "straightforward," as reflected in domestic and international law. An example is *ex post facto* criminal legislation *Id.*; see *e.g.*, *Regina v. Miah*, 1 W.L.R. 683 (1974) (first use of ECHR in regard to retrospective criminal legislation). In another case, *Derbyshire County Council v. Times Newspapers Ltd. and Others*, 1 All E.R. 1011 (1993), the U.K. Court of Appeals addressed the issue of whether a newspaper can be held liable for publishing articles critical of government entities. While the Court of Appeals used Article 10 as the principal reference for its reasoning – rather than mere secondary support – the House of Lords found no need to refer to the ECHR and upheld the decision under the common law of England. *Id.* at 1021. Note also that the case hardly addressed a controversial legal issue from an international law point of view. *See Schwabe v. Austria*, 242-B Eur. Ct. H.R. (ser. A) (1993) (criticism of politician); *Castells v. Spain*, 236 Eur. Ct. H.R. (ser. A) (1992) (criticism of government); *Oberschlick v. Austria*, 204 Eur. Ct. H.R. (ser. A) (1991) (criticism of politician); *Lingens v. Austria*, 103 Eur. Ct. H.R. (ser. A) (1986) (criticism of politician); *Report on the Compatibility of "Desacato" Laws with the American Convention on Human Rights*, Inter-Am. C.H.R. 197 (1994), OEA/ser. L./V./11.88, doc.9 rev. (Feb. 17, 1995).

It is insufficient that highly placed government officials, such as Law Lords or the Home Secretary, provide assurances that English law will not violate the Convention. It is doubtful that such good intentions can filter down to those persons responsible for enforcing or interpreting English law consistent with ECHR law in the absence of

---

and *Fell v. United Kingdom*, Eur. Ct. H.R. (ser. A) (1984) (associated right to privacy of meetings violated Arts. 6(1) and 8).

[2] Andrew Clapham, Human Rights in the Private Sphere 24 (1993).

more effective controls. It is much less comforting when sixty-six Parliament members vote for a bill aimed at giving Parliament the right to overrule European regional Court rulings. *See* Terence Shaw & George Jones, "Transsexual Wins Euro Court Fight," THE DAILY TELEGRAPH, 1 May 1996, at 1. To allow the police, bureaucrat, or trial judge a wide margin of appreciation is an ineffective means of allowing law that is in transition to develop in a fashion consistent with the values of the European community.

It is not that the United Kingdom's internal legal order or any other non-incorporation state (namely, Denmark, Iceland, Ireland, Norway, and Sweden) is inherently incompatible with the regimen of the ECHR[3] nor that non-incorporation is wholly dispositive of determining the appropriate level of deference to be given national authorities. The peculiar characteristics of a country's legal culture should be respected as a reflection of the peculiar social, economic, and political conditions obtaining in that country.[4]

Nevertheless, in order for the European Court's margin of appreciation doctrine to function effectively, the Court should take into consideration whether a state party's domestic legal order minimalizes the possibility of additional harms to associated rights and promotes European consensus and unity. This consideration is especially compelling given the fact that the European Court cannot order state parties to alter their domestic legislation.

(3) What other creative ways are there to break out of the conservative confines of international law's requirement of state practice for establishing customary international law? Article 38–2 of the ICJ Statute specifies that the Court may decide a case *ex aequo et bono* ("according to what is just or good") if the parties so agree. This allows a tribunal to decide without regard to technical legal rights.

Assuming that there is nothing in present-day human rights treaties that prohibits such arrangements, under what circumstances might a country agree to this arrangement? Under many human rights treaties, there is a "federal clause" that obligates those states parties having federal forms of government to ensure that provinces/states comply with the international tribunal's ruling. In cases where the federal government opposes a province's practice and supports a petitioner's complaint,[5] the federal government may be in a position in which it could agree to such an arrangement on technical issues, such as the timely filing of the petition.

(4) One should not conclude that all cases in which the European Court limits its review are less protective of human rights. For example, in *C.R v. United Kingdom*, 335-C Eur.Ct.H.R. (ser. A) (1995), the European Court examined whether spousal immunity for rape existed under common law and, if so, whether the United Kingdom's prosecution

---

[3] The mere formal incorporation of ECHR law also can be insufficient, as evidenced by the Italian government's repeated failures to conform its criminal procedures to the requirement of Articles 5 and 6 and the dilatoriness of its proceedings. Jorg Polaciewicz & Valerie Jacob-Foltzer, *The European Convention on Human Rights in Domestic Law: The Impact of the Strasbourg Case-Law in States Where Direct Effect Is Given to the Convention* (first part), 12 H.R.L.J. 65, 84 (1991).

[4] In the United States under its federal scheme of government, states are seen as important laboratories for testing social policy and developing law that is in transition. Nevertheless, even federal-state comity interests recognize that the U.S. Constitution, federal statutory laws, and treaties are the "supreme law of the land." U.S. Const. art. VI §2. Therefore, this federal constitutional law is given direct effect by the states.

[5] *See, e.g., Toonen v. Australia*, UN Hum. Rts. Ctte., Communication No. 488/1992, views adopted 31 March 1994, U.N. Doc. CCPR/C/50/D/488/1992 (Australian federal government opposed the Tasmanian provincial government's outlawing of homosexual conduct).

of a man for raping his wife constituted a violation of Article 7's prohibition of *ex post facto* laws. The Court observed that "it is in the first place for the national authorities, notably the courts, to interpret and apply national law" in determining whether spousal immunity still existed in the English common law. *Id.* at §40. Given that the United Kingdom's Court of Appeal and the House of Lords had held that spousal immunity no longer existed at common law, the European Court accordingly held that the applicant's prosecution for rape did not violate Article 7.

(5) How is the European Court of Human Rights' consensus inquiry similar to determining whether there is a regional norm *erga omnes*?

2.3. Principles of Liability

Dinah L. Shelton
Private Violence, Public Wrongs, and the Responsibility of States
13 FORDHAM INT'L L. J. 1 (1990)[1]

III. STATE RESPONSIBILITY FOR HUMAN RIGHTS VIOLATIONS

. . . . Prior to the establishment of international systems for the protection of human rights at the end of World War II, international law recognized a state's right to bring a claim against another state because of breaches of international law causing injury to the person or property of its nationals. In the *Mavrommatis Palestine Concessions*, the Permanent Court of International Justice states that "[i]t is an elementary principle of international law that a State is entitled to protect its subjects, when injured by acts contrary to international law committed by another State, from whom they have been unable to obtain satisfaction through the ordinary channels."

Although international law during this period imposed an obligation on states to protect foreign nationals and to treat them according to recognized minimum standards, in general it imposed no similar obligation regarding the treatment of a state's own nationals. The great innovation of international human rights law has been to extend the protections formerly afforded aliens, and to some extent, religious minorities, to all individuals.

Today, . . . one of the international obligations imposed upon states by treaty and custom is to "respect and ensure" internationally recognized human rights. Because of this duty, a state's failure to act to prevent or remedy human rights violations committed by private entities, such as death squads, may give rise to liability in circumstances where, in earlier times, liability was found only under the law of state responsibility for injury to aliens.

A. Acts and Omissions

Acts contrary to international law involve a breach or nonperformance of an international obligation. Breach includes both "acts" and "omissions" according to the type of conduct covered by the rule in question because both are included in the concept of non-performance of an international obligation.

International practice has long made clear that both acts and omissions may give rise to international liability, depending on the duty imposed under international law. In fact,

---

[1] Some footnotes and citations omitted; others renumbered. Ed.'s Note.

one United Nations report noted that "the cases in which the international responsibility of a State has been invoked on the basis of an omission are perhaps more numerous than those based on action taken by a State."...

B. Fault

The issue of standard of care necessarily arose when a state's liability for the safety of foreign nationals was considered. It similarly arises in the context of human rights protections. Neither doctrine nor case law has arrived at a definitive determination of the limits of state responsibility, especially where the acts of private individuals are concerned. It has been questioned whether the state is strictly liable for human rights violations or whether there must be a basis in fault for attributing the violation to the state.

With regard to most international law violations, writers and tribunals, including the Inter-American Court of Human Rights, have generally adopted the principle of fault. Accordingly, Grotius noted that "[t]he liability of one for the acts of his servants without fault of his own does not belong to the law of nations ... but to municipal law; and that [is] not a universal rule."

In practice, it appears that strict liability is generally avoided and responsibility is not imposed for the acts of private persons unless fault on the part of state organs or officials is established. ...

With regard to aliens, a state was and is not held to guarantee the safety of an alien, but is responsible for injury when police protection falls below a minimum standard of reasonableness. What constitutes reasonable police protection depends on all the circumstances. Of course, the state is also responsible for injuries resulting from private violence encouraged by government officials. ...

In order for the state to be liable, however, there must be a harmful act committed by an individual or group. In addition, it must also be possible to attribute to the state some conduct with respect to the act that implies the non-performance of an international duty. As early as 1598, Gentili wrote that

> [o]ne who knows of a wrong is free from guilt only if he is not able to prevent it. Therefore the state, which knows because it has been warned, and which ought to prevent the misdeeds of its citizens, and through its jurisdiction can prevent them, will be at fault and guilty of a crime if it does not do so.[2]

C. Due Diligence

The duty of states has traditionally been formulated in terms of the concept of due diligence with regard to the protection of aliens. The Harvard Law School Draft on State Responsibility (the "Harvard Draft") provides that, where criminal conduct is concerned, "failure to exercise due diligence to afford protection to an alien, by way of preventive or deterrent measures, against any act wrongfully committed by any person" gives rise to state responsibility, as does failure to exercise due diligence to apprehend and to hold any person committing such an act.

The due diligence standard establishes that a state is not responsible for purely private harm. ...

---

[2] 2 A. Gentili, De Jure Belli Libri Tres 100 (J. Rolfe trans. 1933).

Liability for lack of due diligence results from more than mere negligence on the part of state officials and, of course, from wilful conduct. Due diligence consists of the reasonable measures of prevention that a well-administered government could be expected to exercise under similar circumstances. In U.S. tort law terms, "the [danger] reasonably to be perceived defines the duty to be obeyed."

It is not lightly assumed that a state is responsible. "In other words, a State is not responsible unless it displayed, in the conduct of its organs or officials, patent or manifest negligence in taking the measures which are normally taken in the particular circumstances to prevent or punish the injurious acts." Thus, a state's responsibility is not engaged by the private injurious act, but as a consequence of the response of its authorities to the act.

D. Arrest and Prosecution

A state's additional obligation operates after an impermissible act has been committed. The state cannot ignore a wrong even where it has no initial responsibility. It must undertake all reasonable measures to pursue, arrest, and bring the criminal to justice.... Neither immediate arrest nor conviction are required. However, the prosecution, trial, and verdict must follow ordinary standards of justice....

E. Rationale

It may prove difficult to draw the line between direct responsibility for complicity in wrongful acts and failure to exercise due diligence to protect against private violence. It is sometimes stated that the rationale for imposing liability on a state for failure to act to prevent or to remedy wrongful private conduct derives from a sense of the state's complicity in the wrongful acts. In the *Janes* arbitration,[3] the Commissioners cautioned against too great a reliance on this factor in explaining why the Mexican government should be held liable for failing to apprehend and punish the killers of a United States national:

> At times international awards have held that, if a State shows serious lack of diligence in apprehending and/or punishing culprits, its liability is a derivative liability, assuming the character of some kind of complicity with the perpetrator himself and rendering the State responsible for the very consequences of the individual's misdemeanor.... The reasons upon which such a finding of complicity is usually based in cases in which a Government could not possibly have prevented the crime, is that the nonpunishment must be deemed to disclose some kind of approval of what has occurred, especially so if the Government has permitted the guilty parties to escape or has remitted the punishment by granting either pardon or amnesty. A reasoning based on presumed complicity may have some sound foundation in cases of nonprevention where a Government knows of an *intended* injurious crime, might have averted it, but for some reason constituting its liability did not do so. The present case is different; it is one of nonrepression.... [T]he Government is liable for not having measured up to its duty of diligently prosecuting and properly punishing the offender.... Even if the nonpunishment were conceived as some kind

---

[3] Laura M.B. Janes (U.S. v. Mex.) United States and United Mexican States Claims Commission, Op. of Comm'rs 108 (1927).

of approval – which in the Commission's view is doubtful – still approving of a crime has never been deemed identical with being an accomplice to that crime; and even if nonpunishment of a murderer really amounted to complicity in the murder, still it is not permissible to treat this derivative and remote liability not as an attenuate form of responsibility, but as just as serious as if the Government had perpetrated the killing with its own hands.[4]

~

QUESTIONS & COMMENTS

(1) *A* is physically beaten by *X*; *B* is beaten by *Y*. *X* is a police officer making an arrest; *Y*, a private citizen. Both *X* and *Y* acted in violation of state law. Is the state responsible for the injury to *A*? To *B*? Should the two be treated differently? Do states have the same degree of control over the actions of private individuals as they do over their employees? Why should that matter? Is it a question of "fairness" to the state, or concern that making the state too broadly responsible for private conduct would put impossible burdens on it or perhaps force it to regulate that conduct to a degree that would threaten liberty?

(2) How distinguishable are private acts from public acts? Does the state action requirement mean that private acts could never lead to international responsibility? Note that a state is responsible for "official inaction" as well as "official action." Could *state* inaction ever cause harm to a victim where no *private* actor (whom the victim had a right to expect that the state would restrain) had caused him or her harm? Alternatively, is there any claim against a private actor for injury that could not logically be recharacterized as a grievance against the state for failing to prevent the private actor from causing the harm? If so, then is the real question the extent to which the state should be held responsible in particular circumstances for private wrongs?

(3) Suppose a state's law forbids torture. A military officer who engages in torture would seem to be acting *ultra vires*. Would the state be responsible for the torture? Suppose a military officer in uniform tortured someone out of a personal vendetta. Would the state be responsible?

(4) Suppose a human rights group were writing a report on a state that had been wracked by a guerrilla insurgency and government counterinsurgency for a number of years. Suppose, further, that there had been many reports of torture, particularly of people who had been disappeared by paramilitary groups. The military had, however, operated to a large degree free from civilian control, and most judges were either too intimidated by or too sympathetic with the army to take any action that might challenge its authority. Finally, suppose the government were receiving extensive military aid from the United States, which sought to prevent a victory by the insurgents. Would it be sufficient for the human rights group simply to call on the government to cease engaging in torture? What other measures might it want to recommend? How difficult would they be to implement – and what light might those difficulties cast on the conception of the right to be free from torture as a negative right, capable of being implemented immediately?

---

[4] Id. at 114–15, ¶¶ 19–20 (emphasis in original).

(5) Suppose a couple from the United States traveled to the hypothetical state of Paragua hoping to adopt a child there. As they left the government adoption agency offices, they were attacked by a mob of ordinary citizens who had been infuriated by rumors that had been widespread for the past few months that wealthy Americans were kidnapping Paraguan children to use their bodies for organ transplants. There happened to be a police officer nearby, who tried in vain to protect the couple, but he was outnumbered. The two Americans were seriously injured. The day before, the head of the Paraguan Congress had made a fiery speech denouncing Americans "who steal our children" and called on Paraguans "to put an end to this abomination, even if that means taking matters into our own hands." The Paraguan President, asked to comment on the speech immediately after it had been delivered, had simply remarked, "He's entitled to his opinion." Would the Paraguan government incur any international responsibility as a result of this incident? If there is any responsibility, how would the *Janes* arbitrators characterize it? What measures would the Paraguan government be required to take?

(6) Andrew Clapham gives the following example of how privatization raises questions of the application of human rights:

> [I]n 1987 the United Kingdom Government hired the ship MV *Earl William* from the Sealink company, which had been recently privatized. The ship was moored at Harwich and was used to hold Tamils and other asylum seekers. Operations on board the ship were handled by the private security firm Securicor. Should we consider that the alleged abuse and maltreatment by the guards do not come within the sphere of international human rights protection, as the perpetrators are not real policemen but a private security firm? . . .

ANDREW CLAPHAM, HUMAN RIGHTS IN THE PRIVATE SPHERE 126 (1993). How would you answer his question?

2.3.1. State Liability

This section explores the doctrinal basis and scope of the "state action" requirement. That traditionally there has been such a requirement should come as no surprise, given the state-oriented focus of international law. But what does it mean? That a state can be responsible only for action and not inaction? Is there a meaningful difference between them? If there is an affirmative duty to protect human rights, does it mean that every time they are violated by an actor not directly under the state's control, there is a violation? Or must the state somehow be at fault?

International Covenant on Civil and Political Rights

Article 2

1. Each State Party to the present Covenant undertakes to respect and to ensure to all individuals within its territory and subject to its jurisdiction the rights recognized in the present Covenant, without distinction of any kind, such as race, colour, sex, language, religion, political or other opinion, national or social origin, property, birth or other status.

2. Where not already provided for by existing legislative or other measures, each State Party to the present Covenant undertakes to take the necessary steps, in accordance with its constitutional processes and with the provisions of the present Covenant, to adopt such

legislative or other measures as may be necessary to give effect to the rights recognized in the present Covenant.

3. Each State Party to the present Covenant undertakes:

(a) To ensure that any person whose rights or freedoms as herein recognized are violated shall have an effective remedy, notwithstanding that the violation has been committed by persons acting in an official capacity;

(b) To ensure that any person claiming such a remedy shall have his right thereto determined by competent judicial, administrative or legislative authorities, or by any other competent authority provided for by the legal system of the State, and to develop the possibilities of judicial remedy;

(c) To ensure that the competent authorities shall enforce such remedies when granted.

American Convention on Human Rights

Article 1. OBLIGATION TO RESPECT RIGHTS.

1. The States Parties to this Convention undertake to respect the rights and freedoms recognized herein and to ensure to all persons subject to their jurisdiction the free and full exercise of those rights and freedoms, without any discrimination for reasons of race, color, sex, language, religion, political or other opinion, national or social origin, economic status, birth, or any other social condition.

2. For the purposes of this Convention, "person" means every human being.

Article 2. DOMESTIC LEGAL EFFECTS.

Where the exercise of any of the rights or freedoms referred to in Article I is not already ensured by legislative or other provisions, the States Parties undertake to adopt, in accordance with their constitutional processes and the provisions of this Convention, such legislative or other measures as may be necessary to give effect to those rights or freedoms.

Article 25. RIGHT TO JUDICIAL PROTECTION.

1. Everyone has the right to simple and prompt recourse, or any other effective recourse, to a competent court or tribunal for protection against acts that violate his fundamental rights recognized by the constitution or laws of the state concerned or by this Convention, even though such violation may have been committed by persons acting in the course of their official duties.

2. The States Parties undertake:

a. To ensure that any person claiming such remedy shall have his rights determined by the competent authority provided for by the legal system of the state;

b. To develop the possibilities of judicial remedy; and

c. To ensure that the competent authorities shall enforce such remedies when granted.

European Convention on Human Rights

ARTICLE 1

The High Contracting Parties shall secure to everyone within their jurisdiction the rights and freedoms defined in Section I of this Convention.

ARTICLE 13

Everyone whose rights and freedoms as set forth in this Convention are violated shall have an effective remedy before a national authority notwithstanding that the violation has been committed by persons acting in an official capacity.

Charter of Fundamental Rights of the European Union

Article 43

Ombudsman

Any citizen of the Union and any natural or legal person residing or having its registered office in a Member State has the right to refer to the Ombudsman of the Union cases of maladministration in the activities of the Community institutions or bodies, with the exception of the Court of Justice and the Court of First Instance acting in their judicial role.

Article 44

Right to petition

Any citizen of the Union and any natural or legal person residing or having its registered office in a Member State has the right to petition the European Parliament.

Article 47

Right to an effective remedy and to a fair trial

Everyone whose rights and freedoms guaranteed by the law of the Union are violated has the right to an effective remedy before a tribunal in compliance with the conditions laid down in this Article. . . .

African Charter on Human and Peoples' Rights

Article 1

The Member States of the Organization of African Unity parties to the present Charter shall recognize the rights, duties and freedoms enshrined in this Chapter and shall undertake to adopt legislative or other measures to give effect to them.

Convention Against Torture and Other Cruel, Inhuman or Degrading Treatment of Punishment

Article 2

1. Each State Party shall take effective legislative, administrative, judicial or other measures to prevent acts of torture in any territory under its jurisdiction.

2. No exceptional circumstances whatsoever, whether a state of war or a threat or war, internal political instability or any other public emergency, may be invoked as a justification of torture.

3. An order from a superior officer or a public authority may not be invoked as a justification of torture.

Article 4

1. Each State Party shall ensure that all acts of torture are offences under its criminal law. The same shall apply to an attempt to commit torture and to an act by any person which constitutes complicity or participation in torture.

2. Each State Party shall make these offences punishable by appropriate penalties which take into account their grave nature.

Article 5

1. Each State Party shall take such measures as may be necessary to establish its jurisdiction over the offences referred to in article 4 in the following cases:

(a) When the offences are committed in any territory under its jurisdiction or on board a ship or aircraft registered in that State;

(b) When the alleged offender is a national of that State;

(c) When the victim is a national of that State if that State considers it appropriate.

2. Each State Party shall likewise take such measures as may be necessary to establish its jurisdiction over such offences in cases where the alleged offender is present in any territory under its jurisdiction and it does not extradite him pursuant to article 8 to any of the States mentioned in Paragraph 1 of this article.

3. This Convention does not exclude any criminal jurisdiction exercised in accordance with internal law.

Article 6

1. Upon being satisfied, after an examination of information available to it, that the circumstances so warrant, any State Party in whose territory a person alleged to have committed any offence referred to in article 4 is present, shall take him into custody or take other legal measures to ensure his presence. The custody and other legal measures shall be as provided in the law of that State but may be continued only for such time as is necessary to enable any criminal or extradition proceedings to be instituted.

2. Such State shall immediately make a preliminary inquiry into the facts.

3. Any person in custody pursuant to paragraph 1 of this article shall be assisted in communicating immediately with the nearest appropriate representative of the State of which he is a national, or, if he is a stateless person, to the representative of the State where he usually resides.

4. When a State, pursuant to this article, has taken a person into custody, it shall immediately notify the States referred to in article 5, paragraph 1, of the fact that such person is in custody and of the circumstances which warrant his detention. The State which makes the preliminary inquiry contemplated in paragraph 2 of this article shall promptly report its findings to the said State and shall indicate whether it intends to exercise jurisdiction.

Article 12

Each State Party shall ensure that its competent authorities proceed to a prompt and impartial investigation, wherever there is reasonable ground to believe that an act of torture has been committed in any territory under its jurisdiction.

Inter-American Convention to Prevent and Punish Torture

Article 4

The fact of having acted under orders of a superior shall not provide exemption from the corresponding criminal liability.

Article 6

In accordance with the terms of Article 1, the States Parties shall take effective measures to prevent and punish torture within their jurisdiction.

The States Parties shall ensure that all acts of torture and attempts to commit torture are offenses under their criminal law and shall make such acts punishable by severe penalties that take into account their serious nature.

The States Parties likewise shall take effective measures to prevent and punish other cruel, inhuman, or degrading treatment or punishment within their jurisdiction.

Inter-American Convention on the Forced Disappearance of Persons

ARTICLE IV

The acts constituting the forced disappearance of persons shall be considered offenses in every State Party. Consequently, each State Party shall take measures to establish its jurisdiction over such cases in the following instances:

a. When the forced disappearance of persons or any act constituting such offense was committed within its jurisdiction;
b. When the accused is a national of that state;
c. When the victim is a national of that state and that state sees fit to do so.

Every State Party shall, moreover, take the necessary measures to establish its jurisdiction over the crime described in this Convention when the alleged criminal is within its territory and it does not proceed to extradite him.

This Convention does not authorize any State Party to undertake, in the territory of another State Party, the exercise of jurisdiction or the performance of functions that are placed within the exclusive purview of the authorities of that other Party by its domestic law.

ARTICLE VIII

The defense of due obedience to superior orders or instructions that stipulate, authorize, or encourage forced disappearance shall not be admitted. All persons who receive such orders have the right and duty not to obey them.

The States Parties shall ensure that the training of public law-enforcement personnel or officials includes the necessary education on the offense of forced disappearance of persons.

ARTICLE IX

Persons alleged to be responsible for the acts constituting the offense of forced disappearance of persons may be tried only in the competent jurisdictions of ordinary law in each state, to the exclusion of all other special jurisdictions, particularly military jurisdictions.

The acts constituting forced disappearance shall not be deemed to have been committed in the course of military duties.

Privileges, immunities, or special dispensations shall not be admitted in such trials, without prejudice to the provisions set forth in the Vienna Convention on Diplomatic Relations.

Inter-American Convention on the Prevention, Punishment, and Eradication of Violence Against Women
CHAPTER III
DUTIES OF THE STATES

Article 7

The States Parties condemn all forms of violence against women and agree to pursue, by all appropriate means and without delay, policies to prevent, punish and eradicate such violence and undertake to:

a. refrain from engaging in any act or practice of violence against women and to ensure that their authorities, officials, personnel, agents, and institutions act in conformity with this obligation;

b. apply due diligence to prevent, investigate and impose penalties for violence against women;

c. include in their domestic legislation penal, civil, administrative and any other type of provisions that may be needed to prevent, punish and eradicate violence against women and to adopt appropriate administrative measures where necessary;

d. adopt legal measures to require the perpetrator to refrain from harassing, intimidating or threatening the woman or using any method that harms or endangers her life or integrity, or damages her property;

e. take all appropriate measures, including legislative measures, to amend or repeal existing laws and regulations or to modify legal or customary practices which sustain the persistence and tolerance of violence against women;

f. establish fair and effective legal procedures for women who have been subjected to violence which include, among others, protective measures, a timely hearing and effective access to such procedures;

g. establish the necessary legal and administrative mechanisms to ensure that women subjected to violence have effective access to restitution, reparations or other just and effective remedies; and

h. adopt such legislative or other measures as may be necessary to give effect to this Convention.

U.S. Constitution

Amendment I

Congress shall make no law . . . abridging . . . the right of the people . . . to petition the Government for a redress of grievances.

Amendment XIV

Section 1. All persons born or naturalized in the United States, and subject to the jurisdiction thereof, are citizens of the United States and of the State wherein they reside. No State shall make or enforce any law which shall abridge the privileges or immunities of citizens of the United States; nor shall any State deprive any person of life, liberty, or property, without due process of law; . . .

Velásquez Rodríguez v. Honduras
Inter-American Court of Human Rights
Judgment of July 29, 1988, Ser. C No. 4

. . . .

147. The Court now turns to the relevant facts that it finds to have been proven. They are as follows:

a. During the period 1981 to 1984, 100 to 150 persons disappeared in the Republic of Honduras, and many were never heard from again. . . .

b. Those disappearances followed a similar pattern, beginning with the kidnapping of the victims by force, often in broad daylight and in public places, by armed men in civilian clothes and disguises, who acted with apparent impunity and who used vehicles without any official identification, with tinted windows and with false license plates or no plates. . . .

c. It was public and notorious knowledge in Honduras that the kidnappings were carried out by military personnel or the police, or persons acting under their orders. . . .

d. The disappearances were carried out in a systematic manner, regarding which the Court considers the following circumstances particularly relevant:

i. The victims were usually persons whom Honduran officials considered dangerous to State security. . . . In addition, the victims had usually been under surveillance for long periods of time . . . ;

ii. The arms employed were reserved for the official use of the military and police, and the vehicles used had tinted glass, which requires special official authorization. In some cases, Government agents carried out the detentions openly and without any pretense or disguise; in others, government agents had cleared the areas where the kidnappings were to take place and, on at least one occasion, when government agents stopped the kidnappers they were allowed to continue freely on their way after showing their identification . . . ;

iii. The kidnappers blindfolded the victims, took them to secret, unofficial detention centers and moved them from one center to another. They interrogated the victims and subjected them to cruel and humiliating treatment and torture. Some were ultimately murdered and their bodies were buried in clandestine cemeteries . . . ;

iv. When queried by relatives, lawyers and persons or entities interested in the protection of human rights, or by judges charged with executing writs of habeas corpus, the authorities systematically denied any knowledge of the detentions or the whereabouts or fate of the victims. That attitude was seen even in the cases of persons who later reappeared in the hands of the same authorities who had systematically denied holding them or knowing their fate . . . ;

v. Military and police officials as well as those from the Executive and Judicial Branches either denied the disappearances or were incapable of preventing or investigating them, punishing those responsible, or helping those interested discover the whereabouts and fate of the victims or the location of their remains. The investigative committees created by the Government and the Armed Forces did not produce any results. The judicial proceedings brought were processed slowly with a clear lack of interest and some were ultimately dismissed . . . ;

e. On September 12, 1981, between 4:30 and 5:00 p.m., several heavily-armed men in civilian clothes driving a white Ford without license plates kidnapped Manfredo Velásquez from a parking lot in downtown Tegucigalpa. Today, nearly seven years later, he remains disappeared, which creates a reasonable presumption that he is dead. . . .

f. Persons connected with the Armed Forces or under its direction carried out that kidnapping. . . .

g. The kidnapping and disappearance of Manfredo Velásquez falls within the systematic practice of disappearances referred to by the facts deemed proved in paragraphs a–d. To wit:

i. Manfredo Velásquez was a student who was involved in activities the authorities considered "dangerous" to national security. . . .

ii. The kidnapping of Manfredo Velásquez was carried out in broad daylight by men in civilian clothes who used a vehicle without license plates.

iii. In the case of Manfredo Velásquez, there were the same type of denials by his captors and the Armed Forces, the same omissions of the latter and of the Government in investigating and revealing his whereabouts, and the same ineffectiveness of the courts where three writs of habeas corpus and two criminal complaints were brought. . . .

h. There is no evidence in the record that Manfredo Velásquez had disappeared in order to join subversive groups, other than a letter from the Mayor of Langue, which contained rumors to that effect. The letter itself shows that the Government associated him with activities it considered a threat to national security. However, the Government did not corroborate the view expressed in the letter with any other evidence. Nor is there any evidence that he was kidnapped by common criminals or other persons unrelated to the practice of disappearances existing at that time.

148. Based upon the above, the Court finds that the following facts have been proven in this proceeding: (1) a practice of disappearances carried out or tolerated by Honduran officials existed between 1981 and 1984; (2) Manfredo Velásquez disappeared at the hands of or with the acquiescence of those officials within the framework of that practice; and (3) the Government of Honduras failed to guarantee the human rights affected by that practice.

X

. . . .

153. International practice and doctrine have often categorized disappearances as a crime against humanity. . . .

154. Without question, the State has the right and duty to guarantee its security. It is also indisputable that all societies suffer some deficiencies in their legal orders. However, regardless of the seriousness of certain actions and the culpability of the perpetrators of certain crimes, the power of the State is not unlimited, nor may the State resort to any means to attain its ends. The State is subject to law and morality. Disrespect for human dignity cannot serve as the basis for any State action.

155. The forced disappearance of human beings is a multiple and continuous violation of many rights under the Convention that the States Parties are obligated to respect and guarantee. [The Court found that disappearances violate Articles 7 (right to personal liberty), 5 (right to humane treatment), and 4 (right to life).] . . .

158. The practice of disappearances, in addition to directly violating many provisions of the Convention, such as those noted above, constitutes a radical breach of the treaty in that it shows a crass abandonment of the values which emanate from the concept of

human dignity and of the most basic principles of the inter-American system and the Convention. The existence of this practice, moreover, evinces a disregard of the duty to organize the State in such a manner as to guarantee the rights recognized in the Convention, as set out below.

XI

. . . .

161. Article 1(1) of the Convention provides:

Article 1. Obligation to Respect Rights

1. The States Parties to this Convention undertake to respect the rights and freedoms recognized herein and to ensure to all persons subject to their jurisdiction the free and full exercise of those rights and freedoms, without any discrimination for reasons of race, color, sex, language, religion, political or other opinion, national or social origin, economic status, birth, or any other social condition.

162. This article specifies the obligation assumed by the States Parties in relation to each of the rights protected. Each claim alleging that one of those rights has been infringed necessarily implies that Article 1(1) of the Convention has also been violated.
. . . .

164. Article 1(1) is essential in determining whether a violation of the human rights recognized by the Convention can be imputed to a State Party. In effect, that article charges the States Parties with the fundamental duty to respect and guarantee the rights recognized in the Convention. Any impairment of those rights which can be attributed under the rules of international law to the action or omission of any public authority constitutes an act imputable to the State, which assumes responsibility in the terms provided by the Convention.

165. The first obligation assumed by the States Parties under Article 1(1) is "to respect the rights and freedoms" recognized by the Convention. The exercise of public authority has certain limits which derive from the fact that human rights are inherent attributes of human dignity and are, therefore, superior to the power of the State. . . .

166. The second obligation of the States Parties is to "ensure" the free and full exercise of the rights recognized by the Convention to every person subject to its jurisdiction. This obligation implies the duty of the States Parties to organize the governmental apparatus and, in general, all the structures through which public power is exercised, so that they are capable of juridically ensuring the free and full enjoyment of human rights. As a consequence of this obligation, the States must prevent, investigate and punish any violation of the rights recognized by the Convention and, moreover, if possible attempt to restore the right violated and provide compensation as warranted for damages resulting from the violation.

167. The obligation to ensure the free and full exercise of human rights is not fulfilled by the existence of a legal system designed to make it possible to comply with this obligation – it also requires the government to conduct itself so as to effectively ensure the free and full exercise of human rights.

168. The obligation of the States is, thus, much more direct than that contained in Article 2, which reads:

Article 2. Domestic Legal Effects

Where the exercise of any of the rights or freedoms referred to in Article 1 is not already ensured by legislative or other provisions, the States Parties undertake to adopt, in accordance with their constitutional processes and the provisions of this Convention, such legislative or other measures as may be necessary to give effect to those rights or freedoms.

169. According to Article 1(1), any exercise of public power that violates the rights recognized by the Convention is illegal. Whenever a State organ, official or public entity violates one of those rights, this constitutes a failure of the duty to respect the rights and freedoms set forth in the Convention.

170. This conclusion is independent of whether the organ or official has contravened provisions of internal law or overstepped the limits of his authority: under international law a State is responsible for the acts of its agents undertaken in their official capacity and for their omissions, even when those agents act outside the sphere of their authority or violate internal law. . . .

172. Thus, in principle, any violation of rights recognized by the Convention carried out by an act of public authority or by persons who use their position of authority is imputable to the State. However, this does not define all the circumstances in which a State is obligated to prevent, investigate and punish human rights violations, nor all the cases in which the State might be found responsible for an infringement of those rights. An illegal act which violates human rights and which is initially not directly imputable to a State (for example, because it is the act of a private person or because the person responsible has not been identified) can lead to international responsibility of the State, not because of the act itself, but because of the lack of due diligence to prevent the violation or to respond to it as required by the Convention.

173. Violations of the Convention cannot be founded upon rules that take psychological factors into account in establishing individual culpability. For the purposes of analysis, the intent or motivation of the agent who has violated the rights recognized by the Convention is irrelevant – the violation can be established even if the identity of the individual perpetrator is unknown. What is decisive is whether a violation of the rights recognized by the Convention has occurred with the support or the acquiescence of the government, or whether the State has allowed the act to take place without taking measures to prevent it or to punish those responsible. Thus, the Court's task is to determine whether the violation is the result of a State's failure to fulfill its duty to respect and guarantee those rights, as required by Article 1(1) of the Convention.

174. The State has a legal duty to take reasonable steps to prevent human rights violations and to use the means at its disposal to carry out a serious investigation of violations committed within its jurisdiction, to identify those responsible, to impose the appropriate punishment and to ensure the victim adequate compensation.

175. This duty to prevent includes all those means of a legal, political, administrative and cultural nature that promote the protection of human rights and ensure that any violations are considered and treated as illegal acts, which, as such, may lead to the punishment of those responsible and the obligation to indemnify the victims for damages. It is not possible to make a detailed list of all such measures, since they vary with the law and the conditions of each State Party. Of course, while the State is obligated to prevent human rights abuses, the existence of a particular violation does not, in itself, prove the failure to take preventive measures. On the other hand, subjecting a person to official,

repressive bodies that practice torture and assassination with impunity is itself a breach of the duty to prevent violations of the rights to life and physical integrity of the person, even if that particular person is not tortured or assassinated, or if those facts cannot be proven in a concrete case.

176. The State is obligated to investigate every situation involving a violation of the rights protected by the Convention. If the State apparatus acts in such a way that the violation goes unpunished and the victim's full enjoyment of such rights is not restored as soon as possible, the State has failed to comply with its duty to ensure the free and full exercise of those rights to the persons within its jurisdiction. The same is true when the State allows private persons or groups to act freely and with impunity to the detriment of the rights recognized by the Convention.

177. In certain circumstances, it may be difficult to investigate acts that violate an individual's rights. The duty to investigate, like the duty to prevent, is not breached merely because the investigation does not produce a satisfactory result. Nevertheless, it must be undertaken in a serious manner and not as a mere formality preordained to be ineffective. An investigation must have an objective and be assumed by the State as its own legal duty, not as a step taken by private interests that depends upon the initiative of the victim or his family or upon their offer of proof, without an effective search for the truth by the government. This is true regardless of what agent is eventually found responsible for the violation. Where the acts of private parties that violate the Convention are not seriously investigated, those parties are aided in a sense by the government, thereby making the State responsible on the international plane.

178. In the instant case, the evidence shows a complete inability of the procedures of the State of Honduras, which were theoretically adequate, to carry out an investigation into the disappearance of Manfredo Velásquez, and of the fulfillment of its duties to pay compensation and punish those responsible, as set out in Article 1(1) of the Convention.

179. As the Court has verified above, the failure of the judicial system to act upon the writs brought before various tribunals in the instant case has been proven. Not one writ of habeas corpus was processed. No judge had access to the places where Manfredo Velásquez might have been detained. The criminal complaint was dismissed.

180. Nor did the organs of the Executive Branch carry out a serious investigation to establish the fate of Manfredo Velásquez. There was no investigation of public allegations of a practice of disappearances nor a determination of whether Manfredo Velásquez had been a victim of that practice. . . . The offer of an investigation in accord with Resolution 30/83 of the Commission resulted in an investigation by the Armed Forces, the same body accused of direct responsibility for the disappearances. This raises grave questions regarding the seriousness of the investigation. The Government often resorted to asking relatives of the victims to present conclusive proof of their allegations even though those allegations, because they involved crimes against the person, should have been investigated on the Government's own initiative in fulfillment of the State's duty to ensure public order. This is especially true when the allegations refer to a practice carried out within the Armed Forces, which, because of its nature, is not subject to private investigations. No proceeding was initiated to establish responsibility for the disappearance of Manfredo Velásquez and apply punishment under internal law. All of the above leads to the conclusion that the Honduran authorities did not take effective action to ensure respect for human rights within the jurisdiction of that State as required by Article 1(1) of the Convention.

181. The duty to investigate facts of this type continues as long as there is uncertainty about the fate of the person who has disappeared. Even in the hypothetical case that those individually responsible for crimes of this type cannot be legally punished under certain circumstances, the State is obligated to use the means at its disposal to inform the relatives of the fate of the victims and, if they have been killed, the location of their remains.

182. The Court is convinced, and has so found, that the disappearance of Manfredo Velásquez was carried out by agents who acted under cover of public authority. However, even had that fact not been proven, the failure of the State apparatus to act, which is clearly proven, is a failure on the part of Honduras to fulfill the duties it assumed under Article 1(1) of the Convention, which obligated it to ensure Manfredo Velásquez the free and full exercise of his human rights.

183. The Court notes that the legal order of Honduras does not authorize such acts and that internal law defines them as crimes. The Court also recognizes that not all levels of the Government of Honduras were necessarily aware of those acts, nor is there any evidence that such acts were the result of official orders. Nevertheless, those circumstances are irrelevant for the purposes of establishing whether Honduras is responsible under international law for the violations of human rights perpetrated within the practice of disappearances.

. . . .

185. The Court, therefore, concludes that the facts found in this proceeding show that the State of Honduras is responsible for the involuntary disappearance of Angel Manfredo Velásquez Rodríguez. Thus, Honduras has violated Articles 7, 5 and 4 of the Convention.

. . . .

[The Court also held that there had been a violation of the duty under Article 1(1) to protect the rights under each of those articles. Finally, it ordered Honduras "to pay fair compensation to the next-of-kin of the victim."]

⌀

QUESTIONS & COMMENTS

(1) The central holding in *Velásquez Rodríguez* – that a state has a duty to investigate and prosecute disappearances – has been reiterated in subsequent cases. *See, e.g., Godínez Cruz*, Inter-Am. Ct. H.R., Ser. C, No. 4 (Judgment of January 20, 1989); *Neira Alegria v. Peru*, 20 Inter-Am. Ct. H.R, Ser. C (Judgment of January 1, 1995). Prior to the *Velásquez Rodríguez* case, the Inter-American Commission also had previously held that states have a duty to investigate and prosecute disappearances on a number of occasions.

The UN Human Rights Committee similarly has recognized a duty to investigate and prosecute. In *Celis Laureano v. Peru*, U.N. Doc. CCPR/C/56/D/540/1993 (1996) (views adopted 25 March 1996), the Committee addressed a case involving a 16-year-old who had been kidnapped by the Shining Path and escaped, then detained by the military, released by a judge, and finally abducted by paramilitary forces acting together with the military. The Committee stated:

8.3 In respect of the alleged violation of article 6, paragraph 1, the Committee recalls its General Comment 6 [16] on article 6 which states, *inter alia*, that States parties should take measures not only to prevent and punish deprivation of life by criminal acts, but also to prevent arbitrary killing by their own security forces. States parties should also take specific and effective measures to prevent the disappearance of individuals and establish effective facilities and procedures to investigate thoroughly, by an appropriate and impartial body, cases of missing and disappeared persons in circumstances which may involve a violation of the right to life.

. . . .

9. The Human Rights Committee, acting under article 5, paragraph 4 of the Optional Protocol to the International Covenant on Civil and Political Rights, is of the view that the facts before the Committee reveal violations of articles 6, paragraph 1; 7; and 9, paragraph 1, *all juncto* article 2, paragraph 1; and of article 24, paragraph 1, of the Covenant.

10. Under article 2, paragraph 3, of the Covenant, the State party is under an obligation to provide the victim and the author with an effective remedy. The Committee urges the State party to open a proper investigation into the disappearance of Ana Rosario Celis Laureano and her fate, to provide for appropriate compensation to the victim and her family, and to bring to justice those responsible for her disappearance notwithstanding any domestic amnesty legislation to the contrary.

The UN Human Rights Committee also has found a state affirmative duty to investigate a wounding allegedly perpetrated by police. *García Fuenzalida v. Ecuador*, Communication No. 480/1991, views adopted 12 July 1996, U.N. Doc. CCPR/C/57/D/480/1991 (1996).

(2) In *Velásquez Rodríguez*, the Court speaks sweepingly of "the duty to organize the State in such a manner as to guarantee the rights recognized in the Convention." What limitations can reasonably be put on the Court's holding? What role should the dichotomy between private versus governmental duties play in this context?

(3) A state might incur international responsibility where it carries out or is otherwise complicit in the disappearance. Suppose it takes no part in the disappearance. What does *Velásquez Rodríguez* say about the state's responsibility in that situation? On this issue, see *X. & Y. v. The Netherlands*, 91 Eur. Ct. H.R. (ser. A) (1985), reproduced below.

(4) What precise measures must a state take to fulfill its obligation to secure the protection of human rights in the disappearances context? What specific factors made Honduras' investigation inadequate, in the view of the Court?

(5) What measures are adequate to satisfy the state's duty to respond to disappearances? Would it be enough, for example, to dismiss members of the military who took part in disappearing someone? Why or why not? Consider *Bautista de Arellana v. Colombia*, U.N. Doc. CCPR/C/55/D/1993 (1995) (views adopted 27 October 1995). The victim, a member of Colombia's M-19 guerrilla movement, was abducted in 1987 by armed men dressed as civilians, tortured, mutilated, and buried. When her body was later identified in 1990, disciplinary proceedings were begun against some members of the military and then dropped. In 1993, her relatives filed a petition with the UN Human Rights Committee. In 1994, formal proceedings were instituted before the National Delegate for Human Rights, a Colombian official. In July 1995, the delegate issued a decision holding Col. Velandia Hurtado and Sgt. Ortega Araque responsible for the disappearance and requesting their summary dismissal from the armed forces. Following the delegate's findings, the Administrative Tribunal of Cundinamarca awarded the victim's family damages, and the president dismissed Col. Velandia Hurtado from the armed forces (although the order was subject to appeal). The criminal investigation was still pending as of 1995. The Committee noted:

8.2 In its submission of 14 July 1995, the State party indicates that Resolution 13 of 5 July 1995 pronounced disciplinary sanctions against Messrs. Velandia Hurtado and Ortega Araque, and that the judgment of the Administrative Tribunal of Cundinamarca of 22 June 1995 granted the claim for compensation filed by the family of Nydia Bautista. The State party equally reiterates its desire to guarantee fully the exercise of human rights and fundamental freedoms. These observations would appear to indicate that, in the State party's opinion, the above-mentioned decisions constitute an effective remedy for the family of Nydia Bautista. The Committee does not share this view, because purely disciplinary and administrative remedies cannot be deemed to constitute adequate and effective remedies within the meaning of article 2, paragraph 30 of the Covenant, in the event of particularly serious violations of human rights, notably in the event of an alleged violation of the right to life.

(6) Suppose the state undertakes an investigation that is not on its face inadequate, but the victim's whereabouts remain undiscovered and no one is punished. In *Caballero-Delgado v. Colombia*, Series C, No. 17 (Judgment of December 8, 1995), the Inter-American Court found that the Colombian army and its collaborators had disappeared Isidro Caballero-Delgado and María del Carmen Santana six years earlier; they had never been seen again. At the time of the disappearance, a judge denied a writ of habeas corpus, apparently after detention centers denied having detained Caballero-Delgado. Three members of the army were detained for alleged involvement in the crime but released by the court for insufficient evidence. One of those three was later discharged from the military for disappearing other individuals in a nearby region. The criminal investigation was reopened twice, but at the time of the Inter-American Court's decision, no one had been convicted. The Court found that Colombia had violated Articles 7 and 4 in conjunction with Article 1(1), as well as Article 5, and then held:

57 In the instant case, Colombia has undertaken a prolonged judicial investigation, not free of defects, to find and sanction those responsible for the detention and disappearance of Isidro Caballero-Delgado and María del Carmen Santana, and those proceedings have not been closed....

58....Nevertheless, to fully ensure the rights recognized in the Convention, it is not sufficient that the Government undertake an investigation and try to sanction those guilty; rather it is also necessary that all this Government activity culminate in the reparation of the injured party, which in this case has not occurred.

59. Therefore, as Colombia has not remedied the consequences of the violations carried out by its agents, it has failed to comply with the duties that the above-cited Article 1(1) of the Convention imposes on it....

69. In the instant case, reparations should consist of the continuation of the judicial proceedings inquiring into the disappearance of Isidro Caballero-Delgado and María del Carmen Santana and punishment of those responsible in conformance with Colombian domestic law.

Dissenting, Judge Nieto-Navia accused the majority of applying, in effect, a strict liability standard:

It is not enough that there be a violation to say that the State failed to prevent it. To interpret the Convention in this manner obviously goes farther than what the States accepted on subscribing to it, because it would imply that it is sufficient that the act of State which violates a protected right be present for the State to have to answer for it....

The record of this case does not prove that "reasonable" steps to prevent acts of this nature, do not exist, or if they do exist, that they have not been taken....

One cannot attribute to the Republic of Colombia negligence or indolence in the investigation. Moreover, the fact that those implicated have been absolved in the first proceeding does not signify that there is "collusion" between them and the Public Power given that the rules that criminal judges must apply require that doubts be resolved in favor of the accused. Nor has it been demonstrated that the judges were not independent.

Similarly, in *Bautista de Arellana v. Colombia* (discussed above), the Human Rights Committee noted:

8.6 The author has finally claimed a violation of article 14, paragraph 3(c), on account of the unreasonable delays in the criminal proceedings instituted against those responsible for the death of Nydia Bautista. As the Committee has repeatedly held, the Covenant does not provide a right for individuals to require that the State criminally prosecute another person.[1] The Committee nevertheless considers that the State party is under a duty to investigate thoroughly alleged violations of human rights, and in particular forced disappearances of persons and violations of the right to life, and to prosecute criminally, try and punish those held responsible for such violations. This duty applies *a fortiori* in cases in which the perpetrators of such violations have been identified.

Should it be acceptable for the state to close a disappearance case without having found the victim's body? Convicted anyone? Does it depend on whether there is simply an allegation of a disappearance, or a finding by the Court that the state has disappeared someone?

(7) Compare the discretion that the Prosecutor of the International Criminal Court has under its Statute.

Article 13
Exercise of jurisdiction

The Court may exercise its jurisdiction with respect to a crime referred to in article 5 in accordance with the provisions of this Statute if:
(a) A situation in which one or more of such crimes appears to have been committed is referred to the Prosecutor by a State Party in accordance with article 14;
(b) A situation in which one or more of such crimes appears to have been committed is referred to the Prosecutor by the Security Council acting under Chapter VII of the Charter of the United Nations; or
(c) The Prosecutor has initiated an investigation in respect of such a crime in accordance with article 15.

Article 14
Referral of a situation by a State Party

1. A State Party may refer to the Prosecutor a situation in which one or more crimes within the jurisdiction of the Court appear to have been committed requesting the Prosecutor to investigate the situation for the purpose of determining whether one or more specific persons should be charged with the commission of such crimes.

2. As far as possible, a referral shall specify the relevant circumstances and be accompanied by such supporting documentation as is available to the State referring the situation.

---

[1] *See* the decisions on cases No. 213/1986 (*H.C.M.A. v. the Netherlands*), adopted 30 March 1989, para. 11.6; No. 275/1988, (*S.E. v. Argentina*), adopted 26 March 1990, para. 5.5; Nos. 343–345/1988 (*R.A., V.N. et al. v. Argentina*), adopted 26 March 1990, ¶ 5.5.

Article 15
Prosecutor

1. The Prosecutor may initiate investigations *proprio motu* on the basis of information on crimes within the jurisdiction of the Court.

2. The Prosecutor shall analyse the seriousness of the information received. For this purpose, he or she may seek additional information from States, organs of the United Nations, intergovernmental or non–governmental organizations, or other reliable sources that he or she deems appropriate, and may receive written or oral testimony at the seat of the Court.

3. If the Prosecutor concludes that there is a reasonable basis to proceed with an investigation, he or she shall submit to the Pre-Trial Chamber a request for authorization of an investigation, together with any supporting material collected. Victims may make representations to the Pre-Trial Chamber, in accordance with the Rules of Procedure and Evidence.

How does the ICC Statute comport with the international human rights law that establishes state liability for failure to investigate, to prosecute, and to punish gross human rights violations? Should the prosecutor be held liable for failure to investigate gross human rights violations? Should intergovernmental bodies be held liable as states are?

(8) Under the ICC Statute, ICC can exercise jurisdiction over cases in which the domestic courts have been unwilling and/or incompetent to prosecute (Article 17). In such a case and assuming that the state is a party to the ACHR or ECHR, how much weight should be given to the ICC's admissibility decision in a case on the merits before the Inter-American or European Courts of Human Rights? What kind of factors should the Inter-American or European Courts consider in transposing an admissibility decision in a criminal matter to a decision on the merits in a quasi-civil matter?

Francisco Forrest Martin
"U.S. Opposition to the International Criminal Court: What Now?"
1 *Accountability* 2–8 (2002)

So far, the United States apparently has been partly successful in ensuring that its nationals will not be brought before the International Criminal Court. The U.S. withdrew its signature from the Rome Statute of the International Criminal Court.[1] It enacted the American Servicemembers' Protection Act.[2] The Bush Administration successfully lobbied the UN Security Council for exemption of U.S. peacekeeping forces from ICC prosecution,[3] and exerted pressure on other states to enter into so-called "Article 98 agreements"[4] disallowing transfer of U.S. nationals to the ICC.[5] The Bush Administration has publicly justified these measures on the ground that the unfettered discretionary authority of the ICC prosecutor can lead to politically-motivated charges against U.S. servicemembers under

---

[1] 17 July 1998, U.N. Doc. A/CONF.183/9 (entered into force 1 July 2002) [hereinafter ICC Statute].

[2] H.R. 4775, 107th Cong., 2d Sess. (2002).

[3] S.C. Res. 1422, U.N. Doc. SC/1422 (2002).

[4] These agreements are supposedly based on Article 98 of the ICC Statute that allows states to not surrender persons to the ICC if such surrender would violate the sending state's international legal obligations. However, the legal validity of these agreements is subject to debate because they may violate the object and purpose of the ICC Statute. *See* Coalition for the International Criminal Court website: <http://www.iccnow.org/html/pressarticle9820020903.doc> (visited 12 Sept. 2002).

[5] As of this article's publication date, Israel, Romania, and Tajikistan had agreed to these treaties.

the ICC Statute.[6] In light of the Bush Administration's so-far successful efforts to immunize U.S. nationals from prosecution for international crimes before the International Criminal Court, what do we do now to ensure that the U.S. will prosecute U.S. nationals before its own courts?

It is ironic that the very complaint of prosecutorial discretionary authority proffered by the Bush Administration against the ICC is often the same made by victims of international crimes – just inversely. Federal prosecutors exercising their discretionary authority often *refuse* to prosecute powerful persons because they lack the political will, hence the need for the ICC and other special prosecutors. It is also ironic that in its efforts to immunize U.S. nationals from prosecution for international crimes, the Bush Administration may have misdirected its attack by aiming its fire abroad while overlooking potentially more harmful prosecutions here at home over which the Administration may not have any control. What the Bush Administration may have missed is that under U.S. international human rights and humanitarian law obligations, federal prosecutors have no absolute or exclusive discretionary authority for prosecuting many of the same international crimes covered by the ICC Statute.[7] Most importantly, U.S. federal criminal law sets harsher sentences – including the death penalty – for these crimes than those sentences set by the ICC Statute.[8]

Eliminating domestic prosecutorial discretion for international crimes

Under the *Geneva Conventions*, the U.S. has an affirmative duty to prosecute persons alleged to have committed or ordered to be committed grave breaches of the Conventions.[9] Furthermore, under the U.S.' international human rights legal obligations – whether

---

6   However, the Bush Administration may be even more motivated by another, less than admirable reason: its desire to criminally and civilly immunize U.S. businessmen for the commission of international crimes. Recently, the Administration has included *private* U.S. nationals for protection by its Article 98 agreements and asked a federal court to dismiss a suit against ExxonMobil's executives for their alleged gross human rights violations in Indonesia that effectively amounted to international crimes. *See* Letter from Wm. H. Taft IV (State Dept. Legal Advisor) to Hon. Louis F. Oberdorfer (7/29/02) in *Doe et al. v. ExxonMobil Corp. et al.*, No. 01-1357 CIV (D.D.C. filed 20 June 2001) (requesting dismissal of Alien Tort Claims Act suit against ExxonMobil executives for participation in torture, rape, and murder in Indonesia on basis that suit would compromise United States' war against terrorism).

7   For a detailed discussion of this argument, see Francisco Forrest Martin, Challenging Human Rights Violations: Using International Law in U.S. Courts 81–115 (2001).

8   Compare ICC Statute, art. 77 (maximum life-sentence) with 18 U.S.C. §§241 (death penalty for constitutional rights violations), 242 (death penalty for conspiracy to violate constitutional rights), 1091 (death penalty for genocide), and 2441 (death penalty for war crimes). Furthermore, if the sentencing practices of the International Criminal Tribunals for the former Yugoslavia and Rwanda are any indication of the future sentencing practice of the ICC, then ICC defendants will fare better in terms of prison sentences given the lenient sentencing practices of the Tribunals. *See, e.g., Prosecutor v. Akayesu (Sentencing Appeals Decision)*, No. ICTR-96-4-A (1 June 2001) (life imprisonment for war crimes, genocide, and crimes against humanity); *Prosecutor v. Tadic (Sentencing Appeals Decision)*, No. IT-94-1-A (15 July 1999) (20 years sentence for both murder and inhuman treatment constituting crimes against humanity and war crimes); *Prosecutor v. Erdemovic (Sentencing Decision)*, No. IT-96-22 (5 March 1998) (5 years for murdering 70–100 persons constituting war crime).

9   *See, e.g., Geneva Convention Relative to the Protection of Civilian Persons in Time of War*, 12 August 1949, art. 146, 75 U.N.T.S. 287 (entered into force 21 October 1950) [hereinafter GC4]: "The High Contracting Parties undertake to enact any legislation necessary to provide effective penal sanctions for person committing, or ordering to be committed, any of the grave breaches of the present Convention.... Each High Contracting Party shall be under the obligation to search for persons alleged to have committed, or to have ordered to be committed, such grave breaches, and shall bring such persons, regardless of their nationality, before its own courts."

under the *International Covenant on Civil and Political Rights* [ICCPR][10] or customary international law,[11] the U.S. has an affirmative duty to prevent, investigate, and punish violations of the rights to life, humane treatment, and liberty or personal security. The U.S. does not enjoy prosecutorial discretionary authority in such cases when they constitute international crimes. These crimes also happen to overlap with much of the International Criminal Court's jurisdiction[12] by including some of the worse sorts of war crimes, genocidal acts, and crimes against humanity.[13]

For example, if a U.S. national wilfully kills or inhumanely treats a civilian or other person who is taking no active part in the hostilities, this would constitute a war crime under the ICC Statute[14] as well as a violation of U.S. criminal law.[15] If a U.S. national kills or tortures members of a group with the specific intent to destroy, in whole or in substantial part, such a national, ethnic, racial, or religious group as such, this would constitute genocide under the ICC Statute[16] as well as a violation of U.S. criminal law.[17] If a U.S. national murders or tortures another person "as part of a widespread or systemic attack directed against any civilian population, with knowledge of the attack," that is "pursuant to or in furtherance of a State or organizational policy to commit such attack," this constitutes a crime against humanity under the ICC Statute.[18] Although there is no federal criminal statute establishing "crimes against humanity" as such, there are other federal criminal statutes effectively covering many of these crimes.[19] Therefore, many of the most serious crimes under the ICC Statute are also crimes under U.S. federal law, and the U.S. has no discretionary authority in choosing whether to prosecute these crimes or not because the U.S. has an affirmative state duty to prosecute under its international legal obligations.

Prosecutorial discretionary authority under U.S. law

There is an old fallacy that prosecutors have absolute and exclusive discretionary authority in initiating or stopping prosecutions and determining which crimes will be prosecuted.

---

[10]   16 December 1966, arts. 6, 7, and 9, 999 U.N.T.S. 171 (entered into force 23 March 1976) [hereinafter ICCPR] (rights to life, humane treatment, and liberty and personal security); *Celis Laureano v. Peru*, U.N. Doc. CCPR/C/56/D/540/1993 (1996) (views adopted 25 March 1996) (state affirmative duty to prevent and punish violations of rights to life, humane treatment, and liberty and personal security committed by state and non-state actors); *Bautista de Arellana v. Colombia*, U.N. Doc. CCPR/C/55/D/1993 (1995) (views adopted 27 October 1995) (violation of right to life requires criminal punishment).

[11]   *Velásquez Rodríguez v. Honduras*, Inter-Am. Ct. H.R., Ser. C No. 4 at §161–77 (Judgment of 29 July 1988) (affirmative state duty to prevent, investigate, and punish violations of rights to life, humane treatment, liberty, and personal security); *Godínez Cruz v. Honduras*, Inter-Am. Ct. H.R., Ser. C, No. 4 (Judgment of 20 January 1989) (same).

[12]   ICC Statute, art. 5 (jurisdiction over genocide, crimes against humanity, and war crimes).

[13]   There are potentially more crimes, but for the sake of brevity and clarity, this article will focus only on those crimes for which there is clear international law establishing a state affirmative duty to prosecute and U.S. federal law establishing criminal jurisdiction. For example, conspiracy to violate constitutional rights (18 U.S.C. §241), torture (18 U.S.C. §114), genocide (18 U.S.C. §1091), and war crimes (18 U.S.C. §2441 and 10 U.S.C. §§818 and 821) constitute federal criminal law violations.

[14]   ICC Statute, art. 8 (grave breach under GC4, art. 147).

[15]   18 U.S.C. §2441 (c) (1) and (3) (grave breaches and common article 3 violations).

[16]   ICC Statute, art. 6.

[17]   18 U.S.C. §1091(a).

[18]   ICC Statute, art. 7.

[19]   *See* 18 U.S.C. §§114 (crime to commit torture within U.S. territorial jurisdiction), 241 (crime to conspire to injure person in enjoyment of rights guaranteed by federal law within U.S. territorial jurisdiction), 242 (crime for state actor to injure person in the deprivation of rights guaranteed by federal law within U.S. territorial jurisdiction), 1091 (genocide), and 2441 (war crimes).

The U.S. Supreme Court in *Wade v. United States* held that federal district courts have authority to compel a prosecutor to not prosecute.[20] However, there is other substantial case law establishing near absolute and exclusive discretionary authority in choosing to prosecute. This case law is based on interpretations of Article II of the Constitution,[21] the Judiciary Act of 1789[22] (and subsequent re-codifications),[23] and U.S. and English common law.[24] What is striking about these decisions is that they are based on either constitutional and/or statutory language that says *nothing* about prosecutorial discretion. This law is purely judge-made law. Most importantly, none of these decisions ever addressed the international law governing prosecutorial discretionary authority.

Construing constitutional and federal statutory law in conformity
with international law

Under the *Charming Betsy* Rule, federal law must be interpreted consistently with international law when the federal law is ambiguous.[25] Therefore, the arguably ambiguous language in both federal statutory and common law must be construed in conformity with the international human rights and humanitarian law requiring states to prosecute persons for international crimes.[26]

However, the issue of constitutional interpretation is problematic. There is no *Charming Betsy* Rule for construing constitutional provisions. The proper interpretation of the President's prosecutorial authority under Article II probably will depend on the consideration of several factors. On the one hand, there is a "textually demonstrable commitment"[27] to the executive branch in the Constitution for the prosecution of federal crimes. However, as already noted, Article II makes no mention of this commitment being absolute or exclusive. Indeed, private individuals can "execute" federal human rights and humanitarian law respectively through civil rights actions,[28] habeas corpus

---

[20] 504 U.S. 181 (1992) (prosecutor's failure to file substantial assistance motion based on unconstitutional motive subject to review and remedy by district courts).

[21] The Constitution states: "The executive power shall be vested in a President of the United States of America.... [The President] shall take Care that the Laws be faithfully executed.... " U.S. Const. arts. II §§(1)–(3). *See Pugach v. Klein*, 193 F. Supp. 630 (S.D.N.Y. 1961) (writ of mandamus compelling U.S. district attorney to prosecute denied on basis of Art. II).

[22] *Confiscation Cases*, 74 U.S. (7 Wall.) 454 (1868) (interpreting Section 35 of Judiciary Act governing district attorney's duty to prosecute prize cases to be exclusive).

[23] 28 U.S.C. §501 *et seq.* is the re-codification of the Judiciary Act of 1789. Section 547 details the duties of the U.S. district attorneys: "Except as otherwise provided by law, each United States Attorney, within his district, shall – (1) prosecute for all offenses against the United States; (2) prosecute or defend, for the Government, all civil actions, suits or proceedings in which the United States is concerned." *Smith v. United States*, 375 F. 2d 243, 247 (5th Cir. 1967) (interpreting Judiciary Act to require exclusive prosecutorial discretionary authority).

[24] *United States v. Brokaw*, 60 F. Supp. 100 (S.D. Ill. 1945) (using U.S. and English common law for establishing exclusive prosecutorial discretionary authority).

[25] *Murray v. The Schooner Charming Betsy*, 6 U.S. (2 Cranch.) 64 (1804) (congressional acts must be construed in conformity with customary international law); *Weinberger v. Rossi*, 456 U.S. 25 (1982) (federal statutes enacted prior to treaty must be construed in conformity with treaty obligations).

[26] Moreover, even if this federal law was not ambiguous and established exclusive prosecutorial discretionary authority, the last-in-time rule still would require that this international human rights law trump the federal statutory law because both the ratification of the ICCPR and the emergence of customary international law recognizing a state's affirmative duty to prosecute came after the enactment of the Judiciary Act of 1789 or any of its re-codifications. *Whitney v. Robertson*, 124 U.S. 190 (1888) (last-in-time rule).

[27] *Goldwater v. Carter*, 444 U.S. 996, 997 (1979) (Powell, J., *concurring*).

[28] *E.g.*, 42 U.S.C. §1983 (against state actors); *Bivens* suits (against federal actors).

petitions,[29] or the Alien Tort Claims Act.[30] Most importantly, the President is required "to take Care that the laws be faithfully executed"[31] and, therefore, to comply with international law as federal law.[32] This would mean that the President must comply with international human rights and humanitarian law establishing an affirmative state duty to prosecute. Moreover, a U.S. Court of Appeals has stated in dicta that *jus cogens* norms could have domestic effect equal to that of the Constitution,[33] and the international human rights law[34] establishing a state's affirmative duty to prosecute reflects *jus cogens* because this law is non-derogable.[35] Accordingly, constitutional provisions also probably should be construed in conformity with *jus cogens* establishing the state affirmative duty to prosecute.

Several other factors support the elimination of prosecutorial discretionary authority. First, the crimes for which there is no prosecutorial discretionary authority are some of the worse possible crimes: genocide, crimes against humanity, and war crimes. The international human rights law eliminating exclusive prosecutorial discretionary authority reflects an appreciation of the fact that governments themselves often lack the political will to prosecute powerful political or economic elites when the victims are disempowered or marginalized. Second, the elimination of exclusive prosecutorial discretionary authority ensures greater law enforcement – *a fortiori* in cases where federal prosecutors are reluctant to prosecute, such as those involving powerful persons in the political or business realms.[36] Third, interpreting Article II to eliminate prosecutorial discretionary authority would be consistent with the extant delegation of traditionally governmental, criminal justice functions to private individuals and organizations in *qui tam* suits[37] and to the privitization of jails and prisons.[38] Therefore, Article II should be construed in conformity with U.S. international human rights legal obligations eliminating exclusive prosecutorial discretionary authority.

Strategies

In cases where the victim is an alien, the best apparent method for compelling a U.S. attorney to prosecute a U.S. national for the commission of these international crimes

---

[29] *United States v. Noriega*, 808 F. Supp. 791, 797 (S.D. Fla. 1992) (dictum).

[30] As the U.S. government argued in an early Alien Tort Claims Act case, "[l]ike many other areas affecting international relations, the protection of fundamental human rights is not committed exclusively to the political branches of government." Memorandum for the United States as *Amicus Curiae, Filartiga v. Pena-Irala*, 630 F.2d 876 (2d Cir. 1980) (No. 79-6090), *reprinted in* 19 I.L.M. 585, 603 (1980) (citations omitted).

[31] U.S. Const. art. II §1.

[32] U.S. Const. art. VI, cl. 2 (Supremacy Clause establishing international law as federal law).

[33] *Committee of United States Citizens Living in Nicaragua v. Reagan*, 859 F.2d 929, 941 (D.C. Cir. 1988).

[34] *See, e.g.*, ICCPR, art. 4 (rights to life and humane treatment are non-derogable).

[35] C.L. Rozakis, The Concept of Jus Cogens in the Law of Treaties 70 (1976) (non-derogable provisions in treaties reflect *jus cogens*).

[36] However, it is unclear whether there is no prosecutorial discretion under international law concerning the President, Secretary of State, and U.S. diplomatic officers in cases where these persons are prosecuted before their own national courts. *Cf. Case concerning the Arrest Warrant of 11 April 2000 (Democratic Republic of the Congo v. Belgium)*, General List No. 121 (2002), available at <http://www.icj-cij.org/icjwww/idocket/iCOBE/icobejudgment/icobe_ijudgment_20020214.PDF> (visited 24 Sept. 2002) (issuance of arrest warrant by third-party state for foreign minister held violative of consular and diplomatic immunity).

[37] *See* 31 U.S.C. §§3729–3732.

[38] The U.S. historically has delegated international criminal justice functions to private citizens as exemplified by its use of informants in prize cases. *See Confiscation Cases*, 74 U.S. (Wall.) 454.

is to add a *Bivens*[39] claim against the federal prosecutor in an Alien Tort Claims Act[40] suit against the U.S. national committing such crimes – whether this U.S. national is a private or state actor.[41] In cases where the victim is a U.S. national, the best apparent method is to add a *Bivens* claim against the federal prosecutor in a suit against the U.S. national (whether a federal, state, or private actor) responsible for the commission of these international crimes. If the U.S. national is a federal actor, a *Bivens* claim would be appropriate; if a state actor, a 42 U.S.C. §1983 claim;[42] if a private individual, a state tort claim.

Whether there is the presence of "judicially discoverable and manageable standards"[43] for judicial oversight to prosecutions compelled by private plaintiffs and an absence of compelling prudential considerations counseling for judicial abstention in regulating prosecutorial discretionary authority, most likely will turn on the facts in the specific case. However, there are a few points to remember. First, private plaintiffs are not the ones prosecuting the case; judicial intervention is only required to initiate and supervise a prosecution that otherwise would not have taken place because of unconstitutional motive or the lack of political will. Second, the disclosure of sensitive national security evidence to a private plaintiff through civil discovery as s/he proves their case can be regulated by *in camera* judicial review as in any civil suit.[44]

It should be advantageous for victims to join such a claim for injunctive relief on a number of grounds. First, greater civil discovery may be available under the *Hague Convention on the Taking of Evidence Abroad in Civil and Commercial Matters*[45] that would allow the collection of more evidence than would otherwise be available to governmental criminal prosecutors. Second, civil trials are better than criminal trials because of plaintiffs' greater control over the civil trial process.[46] Civil plaintiffs also have greater control over how their story is told. Finally, there may be some political advantage by joining governmental prosecutors and international criminal suspects as co-defendants.

Conclusion

The Bush Administration's efforts to undermine the ICC's ability to prosecute U.S. nationals may end up backfiring by pressuring private victims to not only seek civil damages but also compel federal prosecutors to go after these suspects, thereby exposing defendants to even greater penalties than would be available under the ICC Statute or the present

---

[39] *Bivens v. Six Unknown Named Agents*, 403 U.S. 388 (1971) (federal courts have authority to create private cause of action against federal authorities committing constitutional violations in absence of statute creating such cause of action). Even prior to *Bivens*, the Supreme Court had permitted suits for injunctive relief brought directly under the Constitution for violation of plaintiff's constitutional rights. *See Bolling v. Sharpe*, 347 U. S. 497 (1954); *Philadelphia Co. v. Stimson*, 223 U. S. 605 (1912).

[40] 28 U.S.C. §1350 (hereinafter ATCA) states: "The district courts shall have original jurisdiction of any civil action by an alien for a tort only, committed in violation of the law of nations or a treaty of the United States."

[41] *See Jama v. United States Immigration & Naturalization Serv.*, 22 F. Supp.2d 353 (D.N.J. 1998) (ATCA available against federal and private actors).

[42] *Shoshone-Bannock Tribes v. Fish & Game Comm'n*, Idaho, 42 F.3d 1278 (9th Cir. 1994) (treaty rights violation may be pursued under 42 U.S.C. §1983); *Wyatt v. Ruck Constr., Inc.*, 117 Ariz. 186, 191 (Ariz., Ct. App. 1977) (treaty rights covered by 42 U.S.C. §1983).

[43] *Goldwater v. Carter*, 444 U.S. at 998.

[44] *See* Challenging Human Rights Violations, *supra* note 7, at 110–111.

[45] 23 U.S.T. 2555, 847 U.N.T.S. 231 (entered into force 18 March 1970).

[46] *See* Jose E. Alvarez, *Lessons of the Tadic Judgment*, 96 Mich. L. Rev. 2031, 2102 (1998).

sentencing practices of international criminal tribunals. It would be ironic indeed that the Bush Administration finds itself surrendering U.S. nationals to the ICC in order to ensure that they receive less punishment. Although private suits compelling U.S. district attorneys to prosecute powerful, international criminal suspects undoubtedly will face tremendous political opposition as well as legally conceptual challenges, international and U.S. law – at least in principle – supports the elimination of exclusive prosecutorial discretionary authority.

~

QUESTIONS & COMMENTS

(1) Professor Martin wrote that "the issue of constitutional interpretation is problematic" because "[t]here is no *Charming Betsy* Rule for construing constitutional provisions." If the U.S. Constitution is a treaty that must be construed in conformity with customary international law, would the issue of constitutional interpretation no longer be problematic? If so, why?

(2) In *REINICIAR v. Colombia*, the Inter-American Commission held the following:

> the State has the nonderogable and nondelegable duty to prosecute public action crimes ("*delitos de acción pública*"), crimes for which the State has exclusive power to prosecute, in order to preserve public order and ensure the right to justice.

Report No. 5/97, Case 11.227, ANNUAL REPORT OF THE INTER-AMERICAN COMMISSION ON HUMAN RIGHTS 1996 99, OEA/Ser.L/V/II.95, Doc. 7 rev. (14 March 1997) at 113 n. 30. If a State under its domestic law has the exclusive power to prosecute, does that undercut the argument that private individuals have standing to compel prosecutors in the United States to prosecute individuals for gross human rights violations? If not, why?

X. and Y. v. The Netherlands
European Court of Human Rights
91 Eur. Ct. H.R. (ser. A) (1985)
8 E.H.R.R. 235 (1986)

[In this case, the European Court of Human Rights reviewed a state's response to a claim of sexual violence. A sixteen-year-old Dutch girl with mental disabilities had been allegedly raped by an acquaintance. Being incompetent under the law, the police concluded that the girl could not file a complaint, instead directing that her father file on her behalf. The prosecutor's office declined to file charges against the alleged rapist on the condition that the latter not commit a similar offence within the next two years. The father appealed this decision, and asked the court to direct that the prosecutor institute proceedings against the suspect. The Dutch court refused, and raised questions about whether a charge of rape could be proved in this case. The Dutch court also noted that the father was not legally empowered to file a complaint since his daughter was over the age of sixteen (complaints involving individuals over sixteen could only be filed by the victim under Dutch law), and thus there was no official complaint upon which the prosecutor could act.]

. . . .

21. According to the applicants, the impossibility of having criminal proceedings instituted against Mr B violated Article 8 of the Convention, which reads:

1. Everyone has the right to respect for his private and family life, his home and his correspondence.

2. There shall be no interference by a public authority with the exercise of this right except such as is in accordance with the law and is necessary in a democratic society in the interests of national security, public safety or the economic well-being of the country, for the prevention of disorder or crime, for the protection of health or morals, or for the protection of the rights and freedoms of others.

The Government contested this claim; the Commission, on the other hand, agreed with it in its essentials.

22. There was no dispute as to the applicability of Article 8: the facts underlying the application to the Commission concern a matter of 'private life', a concept which covers the physical and moral integrity of the person, including his or her sexual life.

23. The Court recalls that although the object of Article 8 is essentially that of protecting the individual against arbitrary interference by the public authorities, it does not merely compel the State to abstain from such interference: in addition to this primarily negative undertaking, there may be positive obligations inherent in an effective respect for private or family life. (*Airey v. Ireland*, §32.) These obligations may involve the adoption of measures designed to secure respect for private life even in the sphere of the relations of individuals between themselves.

1. Necessity for criminal-law provisions

24. The applicants argued that, for a young girl like Miss Y, the requisite degree of protection against the wrongdoing in question would have been provided only by means of the criminal law. In the Government's view, the Convention left it to each State to decide upon the means to be utilised and did not prevent it from opting for civil-law provisions.

The Court, which on this point agrees in substance with the opinion of the Commission, observes that the choice of the means calculated to secure compliance with Article 8 in the sphere of the relations of individuals between themselves is in principle a matter that falls within the Contracting States' margin of appreciation. In this connection, there are different ways of ensuring 'respect for private life', and the nature of the State's obligation will depend on the particular aspect of private life that is at issue. Recourse to the criminal law is not necessarily the only answer.

25. ...

The Government stated that under Article 1401 of the Civil Code, taken together with Article 1407, it would have been possible to bring before or file with the Netherlands courts, on behalf of Miss Y:

– an action for damages against Mr B for pecuniary or non-pecuniary damage;
– an application for an injunction against Mr B, to prevent repetition of the offence;
– a similar action or application against the directress of the children's home.

The applicants considered that these civil-law remedies were unsuitable. They submitted that, amongst other things, the absence of any criminal investigation made it harder to furnish evidence on the four matters that had to be established under Article 1401, namely a wrongful act, fault, damage and a causal link between the act and the damage. Furthermore, such proceedings were lengthy and involved difficulties of an emotional nature for the victim, since he or she had to play an active part therein.

. . . .

27. The Court finds that the protection afforded by the civil law in the case of wrong-doing of the kind inflicted on Miss Y is insufficient. This is a case where fundamental values and essential aspects of private life are at stake. Effective deterrence is indispensable in this area and it can be achieved only by criminal-law provisions; indeed, it is by such provisions that the matter is normally regulated.

Moreover, as was pointed out by the Commission, this is in fact an area in which the Netherlands has generally opted for a system of protection based on the criminal law. The only gap, so far as the Commission and the Court have been made aware, is as regards persons in the situation of Miss Y; in such cases, this system meets a procedural obstacle which the Dutch legislature had apparently not foreseen.

. . . .

III. Alleged Violation of Article 3, taken alone or in conjunction with Article 14, as regards Miss Y

33. According to the applicants, Miss Y suffered at the hands of Mr B 'inhuman and degrading treatment' contrary to Article 3 of the Convention. They maintained that, for the purposes of this provision, the State was in certain circumstances responsible for the acts of third parties and that the chronic psychological trauma caused to Miss Y had attained such a level as to fall within the ambit of that Article.

34. According to the Commission, Article 3 had not been violated since there was no close and direct link between the gap in the Dutch law and 'the field of protection covered' by the Article.

At the hearings, the Government adopted this opinion and submitted that they were not answerable for the treatment inflicted on Miss Y.

Having found that Article 8 was violated, the Court does not consider that it has also to examine the case under Article 3, taken alone or in conjunction with Article 14.

. . . .

VI. Article 50

38. Under Article 50 of the Convention,

> If the Court finds that a decision or a measure taken by a legal authority or any other authority of a High Contracting Party is completely or partially in conflict with the obligations arising from the . . . Convention, and if the internal law of the said Party allows only partial reparation to be made for the consequences of this decision or measure, the decision of the Court shall, if necessary, afford just satisfaction to the injured party.

In her letter of 27 August 1984, Ms van Westerlaak explained that 'approximately seven years after the event, the girl in question is still experiencing daily the consequences of the indecent assault of which she was the victim' and that 'this is the source of much tension within the family'. Ms van Westerlaak stated at the hearings that non-pecuniary damage was still being suffered.

The Commission did not comment on these allegations.

The Government also did not challenge the allegations as such, but they argued that the suffering was the result of the act committed by Mr B and not of the violation of the Convention. Accordingly, there was no reason to afford just satisfaction.

39. The Court notes that the claim is confined to non-pecuniary damage and does not relate to the costs of the proceedings.

40. No one contests that Miss Y suffered damage. In addition, it is hardly deniable that the Dutch authorities have a degree of responsibility resulting from the deficiency in the legislation which gave rise to the violation of Article 8.

The applicants left it to the Court's discretion to determine a standard for compensation.

The damage in question does not lend itself even to an approximate process of calculation. Assessing it on an equitable basis, as is required by Article 50, the Court considers that Miss Y should be afforded just satisfaction which it fixes at 3,000 Dutch guilders.

For these reasons, THE COURT unanimously

1. Holds that there has been a violation of Article 8 as regards Miss Y;

2. Holds that it is not necessary to give a separate decision:

   (a) on her other complaints;
   (b) on the complaints of Mr X;

3. Holds that the respondent State is to pay to Miss Y three thousand (3,000) Dutch guilders under Article 50.

∾

QUESTIONS & COMMENTS

(1) Note that the European Court of Human Rights did not order the Dutch Government to investigate, prosecute, and punish the alleged rapist in *X. & Y. v. The Netherlands* unlike the Inter-American Court of Human Rights has done repeatedly in disappearance cases. Instead, the European Court limits its forms of relief to money damages and declaratory relief. However, as part of its declaratory relief, the European Court often does declare that certain measures if undertaken by the state-party would bring the government into conformity with its obligations under the ECHR.

(2) The Court concludes that it need not reach the Article 3 claim in light of its holding on Article 8. If the Court had gone on to reach the merits on Article 3, what should it have held?

(3) The European Court of Human Rights has declared that states parties have affirmative duties in other criminal law contexts. *See, e.g., Assenov v. Bulgaria*, Eur. Ct. H.R. (ser. A) (1998) (state duty to investigate police brutality); *Ergi v. Turkey*, Eur. Ct. H.R. (ser. A) (1998) (duty to investigate circumstances of applicant's death during security force operation); *Güleç v. Turkey*, Eur. Ct. H.R. (ser. A) (1998) (duty to investigate applicant's death during clash with police during demonstration).

(4) Article 2 of the ICCPR, provides that states have a general duty to enact legislation to protect the rights recognized by the Covenant. The European Convention on Human Rights has no similar provision requiring legislation. Instead, it is left to the state party to

determine exactly how to bring itself into compliance with its ECHR obligations. *McGoff v. Sweden*, 83 Eur. Ct. H.R. 22, 28 (ser. A) (1984), 8 E.H.R.R. 246, 250 (1986).

(5) The problem in *X & Y* is that there was a gap in the Dutch law concerning sexual assaults, such that there was no way to prosecute Mr B. Does the European Court hold that every instance of harm to one's private life by another private party must be covered by the law in order to avoid liability under Article 8? In other words, must all gaps be filled?

(6) What is a "gap"? Does it include an inability to seek redress because the statute of limitations has expired? In *Stubbings & Others v. United Kingdom*, 23 E.H.R.R. 213 (1997) (judgment of October 22, 1996), Leslie Stubbings asserted that since 1976 she had experienced severe psychological problems as a result of having been sexually abused a number of times between 1959 and 1971 by her adoptive father and brother, in whose care she had been placed by a local authority in 1959 when she was 2 years old. She filed a damages action against her parents and brother in 1987, three years after she said she first understood in therapy the connection between her childhood abuse and her emotional problems. The House of Lords held that a six-year statute of limitations applied and began to run in 1975 when she had turned 18. Consequently, her action had become time-barred when she turned 24. Criminal charges were, however, brought against her father, who pled guilty in 1991 to a charge of indecent assault. (There was no statute of limitations for the criminal offense.) In response to Stubbings' claim that Britain had violated Article 8, the European Court of Human Rights reiterated that Article 8 "does not merely compel the State to abstain from . . . interference [with private life]: there may, in addition to this primary negative undertaking, be positive obligations inherent in an effective respect for private or family life." *Id.* at §60. It added that "[c]hildren and other vulnerable individuals are entitled to State protection, in the form of effective deterrence, from such grave types of interference with essential aspects of their private lives." *Id.* at §62. At the same time, it noted:

> 61. There are different ways of ensuring respect for private life and the nature of the state's obligation will depend on the particular aspect of private life that is in issue. It follows that the choice of means calculated to secure compliance with this positive obligation in principle falls with the Contracting States' margin of appreciation. . . .
>
> 63. . . . The abuse of which the applicants complained is regarded most seriously by the English criminal law and subject to sever maximum penalties. . . .
>
> 64. . . . It is . . . true that under the domestic law it was impossible for the applicants to commence civil proceedings against their alleged assailants after their twenty-fourth birthdays. However, . . . Article 8 does not necessarily require that State fulfill their positive obligation to secure respect for private life by the provision of unlimited civil remedies in circumstances where criminal law sanctions are in operation.

Suppose that the statute of limitations had expired on the criminal charges as well. How would that have affected the Court's decision?

Andrew Clapham
HUMAN RIGHTS IN THE PRIVATE SPHERE 93, 104 (1993)

. . . [W]hat is clear is that individuals do have *duties* under international law. This was established with the introduction of legal instruments outlawing slavery and piracy, and with the regulation of the high seas and outer space. In the context of human rights, the Charter of the International Military Tribunal (at Nuremberg) clearly fixes duties on individuals for crimes against humanity.

On 1 October 1946 the Nuremberg Tribunal delivered a judgment in which the concept of individual responsibility was clearly recognized. It stated that individuals had duties to obey international law: that international law imposes duties and liabilities upon individuals as well as upon States has long been recognized ... Crimes against international law are committed by men, not by abstract entities, and only by punishing individuals who commit such crimes can the provisions of international law be enforced.

The principles of international law recognized by the Nuremberg Tribunal were affirmed in a Resolution of the General Assembly of the UN on 11 December 1946. On the same day the Assembly passed a Resolution on the crime of genocide which states in part that "Genocide is a crime under international law which the civilized world condemns, and for the commission of which principals and accomplices – *whether private individuals*, public officials or statesmen, and whether the crime is committed on religious, racial, political or any other grounds are punishable" (emphasis added).

The subsequent Convention on the Prevention and Punishment of the Crime of Genocide (signed on 9 December 1948) states in Article IV that private individuals will be punished for the crime of genocide. Genocide is a crime under international law and can be tried in any court; the fact that private individuals can be held responsible must colour interpretations of the Universal Declaration of Human Rights signed the next day, on 10 December 1948. The first few lines after the preamble to the Declaration run as follows:

The General Assembly proclaims this Universal Declaration of Human Rights as a common standard of achievement for all peoples of all nations, to the end that *every individual* and every organ of society, keeping this Declaration constantly in mind, shall strive by teaching and education to promote respect for these rights and freedoms and by progressive measures, national and international, to secure their universal recognition and observance. (emphasis added)

The Declaration then specifically states in Article 29(1) that everyone has duties to the community.

. . . .

Some evidence of the future direction of international law can be found in the work of the International Law Commission (ILC) in its Draft Code of Crimes against the Peace and Security of Mankind. The Commentary to draft Article 21 on human rights states:

It is important to point out that the draft article does not confine possible perpetrations of the crimes to public officials or representatives alone. Admittedly, they would in view of their official position, have far-reaching factual opportunity to commit the crimes covered by the draft article; yet the article does not rule out the possibility that private individuals with de facto power or organized in criminal gangs or groups might also commit the kind of systematic or mass violations of human rights covered by the article; in that case their acts would come under the draft code.

Similarly, the draft provisions before the ILC concerning complaints before the proposed international criminal court state: 'It shall be immaterial whether the person against whom a complaint is directed acted as a private individual or in an official capacity.'

. . . .

∽

QUESTIONS & COMMENTS

(1) How far can nondemocratic states impose legal duties upon individuals who have no effective right to participate in formulating public policy?

(2) Some general conclusions might be drawn concerning state action and affirmative duties. First, it is clear that international human rights law is not confined to negative rights against the state. The state has a duty to secure the protection of human rights, and human rights law may apply directly to individuals in some cases.

The duty to secure human rights law is evolving, but at the very least one can say that while enacting legislation and taking other administrative measures is necessary, a state cannot satisfy its obligation to protect people simply by outlawing certain conduct. Enforcement is necessary – the state must vigorously investigate and prosecute persons who commit violations even when the state is not responsible for the violation in the first place.

Should there be a state action "requirement"? Why isn't a state as much responsible for its choice not to prohibit conduct as it is for a choice to outlaw it? In none of the cases in this section did anything of significance turn on whether or not there was a finding of "state action." That does not mean, of course, that every wrong by a private individual is a human rights violation. The state's choice *not* to intervene may, after all, be entirely consistent with human rights norms.

There are, of course, cases where the state does not have a choice – because international human rights norms would bar it from prohibiting the conduct in question. Determining when the state should properly be treated as not having a choice is the same exercise as determining the parameters of a state action doctrine. Once again, nothing is gained by characterizing the issue as one of state action.

While formulating the issue in terms of state action appears unhelpful, it regularly recurs in human rights cases and theorizing.[1] There appear to be two fundamental reasons for the persistence.

In part, state action doctrine reflects deeply embedded social practices, practices that sorely need reexamination. One such practice is gender discrimination. It is hard to see how anything other than a failure to respect women's interests could account for the way in which human rights law has tended to downplay the systematic violence committed against women in the domestic sphere, violence that is supported in a myriad of ways by the state. Even the notion that there is no state action where the state has failed to

---

[1] To be sure, state action doctrine is less of a barrier to protection under international human rights law than under U.S. constitutional law. No international human rights tribunal would cast human rights law in terms of purely negative rights against the state in the same way that the U.S. Supreme Court read the Fourteenth Amendment in *DeShaney v. Winnebago County Dept. of Social Services*, 489 U.S. 189 (1989). Perhaps the difference is a product of the language of human rights treaties, which are more easily read to recognize affirmative rights and regulate the private sphere than is the Constitution.

intervene does not hold up on close analysis. It is as much "action" for a police officer to walk away from a battered woman's house on the ground that the dispute is just a domestic dispute as it is for the officer to arrest the husband.

At the same time, state action doctrine does reflect some valid concerns; perhaps the most important is the role of judicial bodies. Although the distinction between positive and negative rights is easily overdrawn, it is true that in many instances judicial enforcement is not a particularly appropriate way to implement positive rights. Further, abandoning the idea of state action as a general limit on the scope of rights means facing deep questions about the proper scope of individual freedom. Is a court or other human rights tribunal the best forum in which to decide such questions? In the end, state action doctrine may point as much to the limits of judicial enforcement as it does to any delimitation of state responsibility.

2.3.2. Individual Liability: State and Nonstate Actors

Universal Declaration of Human Rights

Article 29.

(1) Everyone has duties to the community in which alone the free and full development of his personality is possible.

(2) In the exercise of his rights and freedoms, everyone shall be subject only to such limitations as are determined by law solely for the purpose of securing due recognition and respect for the rights and freedoms of others and of meeting the just requirements of morality, public order and the general welfare in a democratic society.

(3) These rights and freedoms may in no case be exercised contrary to the purposes and principles of the United Nations.

American Declaration on the Rights and Duties of Man

Article XXIX. Duties to society.

It is the duty of the individual so to conduct himself in relation to others that each and every one may fully form and develop his personality.

Article XXX. Duties toward children and parents.

It is the duty of every person to aid, support, educate and protect his minor children, and it is the duty of children to honor their parents always and to aid, support and protect them when they need it.

Article XXXI. Duty to receive instruction.

It is the duty of every person to acquire at least an elementary education.

Article XXXII. Duty to vote.

It is the duty of every person to vote in the popular elections of the country of which he is a national, when he is legally capable of doing so.

Article XXXIII. Duty to obey the law.

It is the duty of every person to obey the law and other legitimate commands of the authorities of his country and those of the country in which he may be.

Article XXXIV. Duty to serve the community and the nation.

It is the duty of every able-bodied person to render whatever civil and military service his country may require for its defense and preservation, and, in case of public disaster, to render such services as may be in his power.

It is likewise his duty to hold any public office to which he may be elected by popular vote in the state of which he is a national.

Article XXXV. Duties with respect to social security and welfare.

It is the duty of every person to cooperate with the state and the community with respect to social security and welfare, in accordance with his ability and with existing circumstances.

Article XXXVI. Duty to pay taxes.

It is the duty of every person to pay the taxes established by law for the support of public services.

Article XXXVII. Duty to work.

It is the duty of every person to work, as far as his capacity and possibilities permit, in order to obtain the means of livelihood or to benefit his community.

Article XXXVIII. Duty to refrain from political activities in a foreign country.

It is the duty of every person to refrain from taking part in political activities that, according to law, are reserved exclusively to the citizens of the state in which he is an alien.

American Convention on Human Rights

Article 32. RELATIONSHIP BETWEEN DUTIES AND RIGHTS.

1. Every person has responsibilities to his family, his community, and mankind.

2. The rights of each person are limited by the rights of others, by the security of all, and by the just demands of the general welfare, in a democratic society.

African Charter of Human and Peoples' Rights

Chapter II – Duties

Article 27

1. Every individual shall have duties towards his family and society, the State and other legally recognized communities and the international community.

2. The rights and freedoms of each individual shall be exercised with due regard to the rights of others, collective security, morality and common interest.

Article 28

Every individual shall have the duty to respect and consider his fellow beings without discrimination, and to maintain relations aimed at promoting, safeguarding and reinforcing mutual respect and tolerance.

Article 29

The individual shall also have the duty:

  1. to preserve the harmonious development of the family and to work for the cohesion and respect of the family; to respect his parents at all times, to maintain them in case of need;

2. To serve his national community by placing his physical and intellectual abilities at its service;
3. Not to compromise the security of the State whose national or resident he is;
4. To preserve and strengthen social and national solidarity, particularly when the latter is threatened;
5. To preserve and strengthen the national independence and the territorial integrity of his country and to contribute to its defence in accordance with the law;
6. To work to the best of his abilities and competence, and to pay taxes imposed by law in the interest of the society;
7. to preserve and strengthen positive African cultural values in his relations with other members of the society, in the spirit of tolerance, dialogue and consultation and, in general, to contribute to the promotion of the moral well being of society;
8. To contribute to the best of his abilities, at all times and at all levels, to the promotion and achievement of African unity.

Charter of the International Military Tribunal

Article 6.

The Tribunal established . . . for the trial and punishment of the major war criminals of the European Axis countries shall have the power to try and punish persons who, acting in the interests of the European Axis countries, whether as individuals or as members of organizations, committed any of the following crimes. [Crimes Against Peace, War Crimes, Crimes Against Humanity]

Leaders, organizers, instigators and accomplices participating in the formulation or execution of a common plan or conspiracy to commit any of the foregoing crimes are responsible for all acts performed by any persons in execution of such plan.

Article 7.

The official position of defendants, whether as Heads of State or responsible officials in Government Departments, shall not be considered as freeing them from responsibility or mitigating punishment.

Article 8.

The fact that the Defendant acted pursuant to order of his Government or of a superior shall not free him from responsibility, but may be considered in mitigation of punishment if the Tribunal determines that justice so requires.

Article 9.

At the trial of any individual member of any group or organization the Tribunal may declare (in connection with any act of which the individual may be convicted) that the group or organization of which the individual was a member was a criminal organization.

After the receipt of the Indictment the Tribunal shall give such notice as it thinks fit that the prosecution intends to ask the Tribunal to make such declaration and any member of the organization will be entitled to apply to the Tribunal for leave to be heard by the Tribunal upon the question of the criminal character of the organization. The Tribunal shall have power to allow or reject the application. If the application is allowed, the Tribunal may direct in what manner the applicants shall be represented and heard.

Article 10.

In cases where a group or organization is declared criminal by the Tribunal, the competent national authority of any Signatory shall have the right to bring individual to trial for membership therein before national, military or occupation courts. In any such case the criminal nature of the group or organization is considered proved and shall not be questioned.

Article 11.

Any person convicted by the Tribunal may be charged before a national, military or occupation court, referred to in Article 10 of this Charter, with a crime other than of membership in a criminal group or organization and such court may, after convicting him, impose upon him punishment independent of and additional to the punishment imposed by the Tribunal for participation in the criminal activities of such group or organization.

Convention on the Prevention and Punishment of Genocide

Article I

The Contracting Parties confirm that genocide, whether committed in time of peace or in time of war, is a crime under international law which they undertake to prevent and to punish.

Article IV

Persons committing genocide or any of the other acts enumerated in Article III shall be punished, whether they are constitutionally responsible rulers, public officials or private individuals.

Article V

The Contracting Parties undertake to enact, in accordance with their respective Constitutions, the necessary legislation to give effect to the provisions of the present Convention and, in particular, to provide effective penalties for persons guilty of genocide or any of the other acts enumerated in Article III.

Article VI

Persons charged with genocide or any of the other acts enumerated in Article III shall be tried by a competent tribunal of the State in the territory of which the act was committed, or by such international penal tribunal as may have jurisdiction with respect to those Contracting Parties which shall have accepted its jurisdiction.

Statute of the International Criminal Tribunal [for the Former Yugoslavia]

Article 6

Personal jurisdiction

The International Tribunal shall have jurisdiction over natural persons pursuant to the provisions of the present Statute.

Article 7

Individual criminal responsibility

1. A person who planned, instigated, ordered, committed or otherwise aided and abetted in the planning, preparation or execution of a crime referred to in articles 2 to 5 of the present Statute, shall be individually responsible for the crime.

2. The official position of any accused person, whether as Head of State or Government or as a responsible Government official, shall not relieve such person of criminal responsibility nor mitigate punishment.

3. The fact that any of the acts referred to in articles 2 to 5 of the present Statute was committed by a subordinate does not relieve his superior of criminal responsibility if he knew or had reason to know that the subordinate was about to commit such acts or had done so and the superior failed to take the necessary and reasonable measures to prevent such acts or to punish the perpetrators thereof.

4. The fact that an accused person acted pursuant to an order of a Government or of a superior shall not relieve him of criminal responsibility, but may be considered in mitigation of punishment if the International Tribunal determines that justice so requires.

Article 8

Territorial and temporal jurisdiction

The territorial jurisdiction of the International Tribunal shall extend to the territory of the former Socialist Federal Republic of Yugoslavia, including its land surface, airspace and territorial waters. The temporal jurisdiction of the International Tribunal shall extend to a period beginning on 1 January 1991.

Statute of the International Criminal Tribunal for Rwanda

Article 5

Personal jurisdiction

The International Tribunal for Rwanda shall have jurisdiction over natural persons pursuant to the provisions of the present Statute.

Article 6

Individual criminal responsibility

1. A person who planned, instigated, ordered, committed or otherwise aided and abetted in the planning, preparation or execution of a crime referred to in articles 2 to 4 of the present Statute, shall be individually responsible for the crime.

2. The official position of any accused person, whether as Head of State or Government or as a responsible Government official, shall not relieve such person of criminal responsibility nor mitigate punishment.

3. The fact that any of the acts referred to in articles 2 to 4 of the present Statute was committed by a subordinate does not relieve his or her superior of criminal responsibility if he or she knew or had reason to know that the subordinate was about to commit such acts or had done so and the superior failed to take the necessary and reasonable measures to prevent such acts or to punish the perpetrators thereof.

4. The fact that an accused person acted pursuant to an order of a Government or of a superior shall not relieve him or her of criminal responsibility, but may be considered

in mitigation of punishment if the International Tribunal for Rwanda determines that justice so requires.

Article 7

Territorial and temporal jurisdiction

The territorial jurisdiction of the International Tribunal for Rwanda shall extend to the territory of Rwanda including its land surface and airspace as well as to the territory of neighbouring States in respect of serious violations of international humanitarian law committed by Rwandan citizens. The temporal jurisdiction of the International Tribunal for Rwanda shall extend to a period beginning on 1 January 1994 and ending on 31 December 1994.

Statute of the International Criminal Court

Article 23

Nulla poena sine lege

A person convicted by the Court may be punished only in accordance with this Statute.

Article 25

Individual criminal responsibility

1. The Court shall have jurisdiction over natural persons pursuant to this Statute.
2. A person who commits a crime within the jurisdiction of the Court shall be individually responsible and liable for punishment in accordance with this Statute.
3. In accordance with this Statute, a person shall be criminally responsible and liable for punishment for a crime within the jurisdiction of the Court if that person:

(a) Commits such a crime, whether as an individual, jointly with another or through another person, regardless of whether that other person is criminally responsible;
(b) Orders, solicits or induces the commission of such a crime which in fact occurs or is attempted;
(c) For the purpose of facilitating the commission of such a crime, aids, abets or otherwise assists in its commission or its attempted commission, including providing the means for its commission;
(d) In any other way contributes to the commission or attempted commission of such a crime by a group of persons acting with a common purpose. Such contribution shall be intentional and shall either:

(i) Be made with the aim of furthering the criminal activity or criminal purpose of the group, where such activity or purpose involves the commission of a crime within the jurisdiction of the Court; or
(ii) Be made in the knowledge of the intention of the group to commit the crime;

(e) In respect of the crime of genocide, directly and publicly incites others to commit genocide;
(d) Attempts to commit such a crime by taking action that commences its execution by means of a substantial step, but the crime does not occur because of circumstances independent of the person's intentions. However, a person who abandons the effort to commit the crime or otherwise prevents the completion of

the crime shall not be liable for punishment under this Statute for the attempt to commit that crime if that person completely and voluntarily gave up the criminal purpose.

4. No provision in this Statute relating to individual criminal responsibility shall affect the responsibility of States under international law.

Article 26

Exclusion of jurisdiction over persons under eighteen

The Court shall have no jurisdiction over any person who was under the age of 18 at the time of the alleged commission of a crime.

Article 27

Irrelevance of official capacity

1. This Statute shall apply equally to all persons without any distinction based on official capacity. In particular, official capacity as a Head of State or Government, a member of a Government or parliament, an elected representative or a government official shall in no case exempt a person from criminal responsibility under this Statute, nor shall it, in and of itself, constitute a ground for reduction of sentence.

2. Immunities or special procedural rules which may attach to the official capacity of a person, whether under national or international law, shall not bar the Court from exercising its jurisdiction over such a person.

Article 28

Responsibility of commanders and other superiors

In addition to other grounds of criminal responsibility under this Statute for crimes within the jurisdiction of the Court:

1. A military commander or person effectively acting as a military commander shall be criminally responsible for crimes within the jurisdiction of the Court committed by forces under his or her effective command and control, or effective authority and control as the case may be, as a result of his or her failure to exercise control properly over such forces, where:

(a) That military commander or person either knew or, owing to the circumstances at the time, should have known that the forces were committing or about to commit such crimes; and
(b) That military commander or person failed to take all necessary and reasonable measures within his or her power to prevent or repress their commission or to submit the matter to the competent authorities for investigation and prosecution.

2. With respect to superior and subordinate relationships not described in paragraph 1, a superior shall be criminally responsible for crimes within the jurisdiction of the Court committed by subordinates under his or her effective authority and control, as a result of his or her failure to exercise control properly over such subordinates, where:

(a) The superior either knew, or consciously disregarded information which clearly indicated, that the subordinates were committing or about to commit such crimes;
(b) The crimes concerned activities that were within the effective responsibility and control of the superior; and

(c) The superior failed to take all necessary and reasonable measures within his or her power to prevent or repress their commission or to submit the matter to the competent authorities for investigation and prosecution.

Article 30

Mental element

1. Unless otherwise provided, a person shall be criminally responsible and liable for punishment for a crime within the jurisdiction of the Court only if the material elements are committed with intent and knowledge.

2. For the purposes of this article, a person has intent where:

(a) In relation to conduct, that person means to engage in the conduct;
(b) In relation to a consequence, that person means to cause that consequence or is aware that it will occur in the ordinary course of events.

3. For the purposes of this article, "knowledge" means awareness that a circumstance exists or a consequence will occur in the ordinary course of events. "Know" and "knowingly" shall be construed accordingly.

Superior Responsibility

Benavides Cevallos v. Ecuador
Inter-American Court of Human Rights
Memorial *Amicus Curiae* submitted by Rights International (1998)

. . . .

Aside from its failure to fulfill its affirmative obligations under Article 1(1), ACHR, the State of Ecuador also has violated customary international law that imposes individual criminal liability under a command responsibility model, for its failure to prosecute both the material and intellectual authors of the human rights violations committed against Prof. Benavides.

A. Customary International Law Employs the Principle of Command Responsibility for the Illegal Acts of a Superior's Subordinates Which Were Ordered or Tolerated by the Superior Officer.

It is a well-established principle of international law that individuals who violate international criminal law may be held individually responsible. As the Appeals Chamber of the International Criminal Tribunal for the Former Yugoslavia has noted "[c]rimes against international law are committed by men, not by abstract entities, and only by punishing individuals who commit such crimes can the provisions of international law be enforced." *Prosecutor v. Tadic*, Appeals Chamber Decision on the Defence Motion for Interlocutory Appeal on Jurisdiction ("Int'l Criminal Tribunal for the Former Yugo.") at 68 (2 Oct. 1995) (citing *The Trial of Major War Criminals: Proceedings of the Int'l Military Tribunal Sitting at Nuremberg Germany*, Part 22, at 447 (1950)). Often such crimes are committed by state agents under direct orders from the offender's commanding officer or are committed with the knowledge and/or consent of the offender's superiors. In such a context, customary international law requires that if the superior officer had knowledge of and control over the illegal acts of his subordinates, the superior officer also may be held criminally liable for the subordinate's criminal acts.

Most significantly, the recently enacted Statutes of the International Tribunals for the Former Yugoslavia and Rwanda impose command responsibility[1] for international crimes of the same kind perpetrated in the instant case. Under the Statute of the International Criminal Tribunal for Yugoslavia [hereinafter, ICT-Y Statute], these crimes include "wilful killing," "torture or inhuman treatment," "wilfully causing great suffering or serious injury to body," and "wilfully depriving... a civilian of the rights of fair and regular trial." *Report of Secretary General Pursuant to Paragraph 2 of Security Council Resolution 808 (1993)*, U.N. Doc. S/25704 (3 May 1993), Annex, Art. 2 (Grave Breaches of Geneva Conventions of 1949). Under the Statute of the International Criminal Tribunal for Rwanda [hereinafter, ICT-R Statute], these crimes include murder and extra-judicial executions. S/Res/955 (1994) (8 Nov. 1994), Annex, Articles 3 (murder) and 4 (extra-judicial executions). Article 7 of the ICT-Y Statute stipulates that:

1. A person who planned, instigated, *ordered*, committed *or otherwise aided and abetted* in the planning, preparation or execution of a crime referred to in article 2 ... *shall be individually responsible* for the crime.

2. The official position of any accused person ... shall not relieve such person of criminal responsibility nor mitigate punishment.

3. *The fact that any of the acts referred to in article[ ] 2 ... was committed by a subordinate does not relieve his superior of criminal responsibility if he knew or had reason to know that the subordinate was about to commit such acts or had done so and the superior failed to take the necessary and reasonable measures to prevent such acts or to punish the perpetrators thereof...*

Art. ICT-Y Statute (emphases added). Article 6 of the ICT-R Statute uses nearly identical language.[2]

The general principle of law that commanders are individually criminally responsible for the violations committed by their subordinates had its beginnings as early as 1474

---

[1] The UN Security Council's establishment of the International Tribunal for Yugoslavia authorized only the use of *already existing* international humanitarian law, including the command responsibility doctrine. As the UN Secretary General in his accompanying report to the Statute of the International Tribunal for Yugoslavia noted,

the Security Council would not be creating or purporting to 'legislate' [international humanitarian] law. Rather, the International Tribunal would have the task of applying existing international humanitarian law.

Report of Secretary General Pursuant to Paragraph 2 of Security Council Resolution 808 (1993), U.N. Doc. S/25704 (3 May 1993), ¶ 29.

[2] Article 6 states in relevant part:

1. A person who planned, instigated, ordered, committed or otherwise aided and abetted in the planning, preparation or execution of a crime referred to in articles 2 to 4 of the present Statute, shall be individually responsible for the crime.

2. The official position of any accused person, whether as Head of State or Government or as a responsible Government official, shall not relieve such person of criminal responsibility nor mitigate punishment.

3. The fact that any of the acts referred to in articles 2 to 4 of the present Statute was committed by a subordinate does not relieve his or her superior of criminal responsibility if he or she knew or had reason to know that the subordinate was about to commit such acts or had done so and the superior failed to take the necessary and reasonable measures to prevent such acts or to punish the perpetrators thereof.

Art. 6, ICT-R Statute.

when Peter von Hagenbach was convicted and executed for atrocities committed under his command in Breisach, Austria. Timothy L.H. McCormack, *From Sun Tzu to the Sixth Comm.: The Evolution of an Int'l Criminal Law Regime, in* THE LAW OF WAR CRIMES: NATIONAL AND INTERNATIONAL APPROACHES (Timothy L.H. McCormack & Gerry J. Simpson eds, 1997).... Several centuries later, the American Colonies adopted a similar approach in the Articles of War which required:

> Every Officer Commanding ... shall keep good order, and to the utmost of his power, redress all such abuses or disorders which may be committed by any Officer or Soldier under his command; if upon complaint made to him of Officers or Soldiers beating or otherwise ill-treating any person ... the said commander, who shall refuse or omit to see justice done to this offender ... [shall] be punished ... in such manner as if he himself had committed the crimes or disorders complained of.

American Articles of War, Article XII, June 30, 1775 (cited in William H. Parks, *Command Responsibility*, 62 MIL. L. REV. 1, 5 (1973)). This principle was first employed by the United States in the 1800s. *See, e.g., The Trial of Captain Henry Wirz*, 8 Amer. State Trials 666 (1865) (commandant of prisoner-of-war camp convicted and executed for ordering torture, maltreatment and execution of war prisoners in his custody).

The Treaty of Versailles was the first international instrument to articulate in express terms the legal requirement of prosecuting commanders for the illegal acts of his subordinates. Articles 227 and 228 of the Treaty of Versailles created a tribunal to prosecute high ranking German officials for violations the law and customs of war during World War I.[3] In response to those provisions, the Germans agreed to administer war crime trials under German law.[4]

---

[3] As a signatory to the Treaty of Versailles, Ecuador has adopted the international law principle of command responsibility. Treaty of Peace Between the Allied and Associated Powers and Germany, signed at Versailles, Mar. 28, 1919, *reproduced in* THE TREATY OF VERSAILLES AND AFTER: ANNOTATIONS OF THE TEXT OF THE TREATY (1947). Therefore, Ecuador is not a persistent objector for purposes of opting out of the formation of a customary international norm. *See* Ian Brownlie, PRINCIPLES OF PUBLIC INTERNATIONAL LAW 10 (4th ed. 1990).

[4] The German Supreme Court of Leipzig held that "if the execution of an order in the ordinary course of duty involves such a violation of the law as is punishable, the superior officer issuing such order is alone responsible." *The Dover Castle Case*, cited in 1 THE LAW OF WAR, *supra*[ ], at 868, 881. While the German Court did limit criminal responsibility to the superior officer *alone*, in a subsequent case, the *Llandovery Castle Case*, the same German court did not recognize such a limitation. *Llandovery Castle Case*, S.Ct. Liepzig, Judgement of 16 July 1921, 16 AM. J. INT'L LAW 708, 722 (1922). Indeed, international law does not either. International principles that deal with criminal responsibility mandate as a general principle of law that if an individual commits an act which is recognized as a crime under international law, even if the actor's commander is criminally responsible, the subordinate may also be held criminally accountable. *See* Principles of the Nuremberg Charter and Judgment Formulated by the Int'l Law Comm'n, and adopted by G.A. Res. 177 (II) (a), 5 U.N. GAOR, Supp. No. 12, at 11–14, para. 99, U.N. Doc. A/1316 (principle I states that "Any person who commits an act which constitutes a crime under international law is responsible therefor and liable to punishment ... s." This principle was adopted by the United Nations General Assembly and is recognized as customary international law. JORDAN J. PAUST, INTERNATIONAL CRIMINAL LAW 1043–44 (1996)); *see also* article 7 of the Statute of the International Tribunal for the Former Yugoslavia ("[a] person who ... committed ... a crime referred to in articles 2 to 5 of the present statute, shall be individually responsible for the crime ... [and] the fact that an accused person acted pursuant to an order of a ... superior shall not relieve him of criminal responsibility ... "). Article 7, 32 I.L.M. 1192 (1993); M. CHERIF BASSIOUNI, THE LAW OF THE INTERNATIONAL CRIMINAL TRIBUNAL FOR THE FORMER YUGOSLAVIA 381 n. 103 (1997) (absolute defense of obedience to superior orders no longer "carr[ies] much weight").

Subsequently during World War II in reaction to mistreatment of prisoners of war, a number of national and international laws were enacted establishing command responsibility. Article 3 of the Law of August 2, 1947 of the Grand Duchy of Luxembourg, on the Suppression of War Crimes imposed responsibility on "superiors in rank who have tolerated the criminal activities of their subordinates.... " United Nations War Crimes Comm'n, IV Law Reports of Trials of War Criminals 87 (hereinafter cited as "– L.R.T.W.C. – ") (1948). Article 4 of the French Ordinance of August 28, 1944 required that when a subordinate was prosecuted as the actual perpetrator of a war crime, his superiors also would be considered as accomplices insofar as they had tolerated the criminal acts of their subordinates. III L.R.T.W.C. 94. Article II(2) of Law No. 10 of the Allied Control Council provided that "[a]ny person ... is deemed to have committed a crime ... if he ... ordered or abetted the [crime]s.... " I Trials of War Criminals Before the Nuremberg Military Tribunals Under Control Council No. 10 (hereinafter cited as "– T.W.C. – ") XVI (1948).

After World War II, the Allies conducted trials in Germany and Japan which convicted and sentenced commanding officers from World War II under the principle of command responsibility. In the *High Command Case* of the Trials of War Criminals Before the Nuremberg Military Tribunals under Control Council Law No. 10, the tribunal defined the standard by which command responsibility should be found. "For a defendant to be held criminally responsible, there must be a breach of some moral obligation fixed in international law, a personal act voluntarily done with knowledge of its inherent criminality under international law." XI T.W.C. 510. The tribunal specified that for a order to be "inherently criminal" it must be "one that is criminal on its face, or which [the commander] is shown to have known was criminal." *Id.* at 510–11.

In the International Japanese War Crimes Trial Before the International Military Tribunal for the Far East, twenty-two former Japanese leaders were charged with violating crimes against peace, murder, conspiracy to commit murder, war crimes, and crimes against humanity during World War II and were tried on the basis of command responsibility. In defining command responsibility, the tribunal stated that:

> [T]he principle of command responsibility to be that, if this accused knew, or should by the exercise of ordinary diligence have learned, of the commission by his subordinates ... of the atrocities ... or of the existence of a routine which would countenance such, and, by his failure to take any action to punish the perpetrators, permitted the atrocities to continue, he has failed in his performance of his duty as a commander and must be punished.

William H. Parks, *Command Responsibility*, 62 Mil. L. Rev. 1, 72 (1973) (citing 19 *United States v. Soemu Toyoda* 5005–06 [Official Transcript of Record of Trial]).

In a case adjudicated in the United States, a United States Military Commission found Japanese General Tomoyuki Yamashita individually criminally responsible for atrocities committed under his command during World War II in the Philippines. In reviewing the case, the United States Supreme Court found that under international law there exists a duty of a military commander to "to take such appropriate measures as are within his power to control the troops under his command for the prevention of [criminal] acts." *In re Yamashita*, 327 U.S. 1, 15 (1946).[5] The Court noted that this duty does not just extend to prisoners of war, but to civilian populations as well. *Id.* at 16.

In 1976, the United Nations International Convention on the Suppression and Punishment of the Crime of Apartheid entered into force. This convention places criminal responsibility on individuals and their superiors for the crime of apartheid.[6] This convention, which has been ratified by Ecuador, was the first international document to recognize the principle of command responsibility regardless of whether the crime was committed within the context of war or not. This is a significant development since it illustrates that command responsibility is not limited to international war crimes but to other international crimes as well.

"The doctrine of 'command responsibility' now clearly exists in conventional and customary international law." M. CHERIF BASSIOUNI, CRIMES AGAINST HUMANITY IN INTERNATIONAL LAW 389 (1992). It is a principle that is now at least five centuries old. Recent developments such as the International Tribunals for Yugoslavia and Rwanda and the Apartheid Convention have provided guidance on just how far-reaching command responsibility extends and further reinforce its status as a general principle of international humanitarian law as well as human rights law.[7]

. . . .

~

QUESTIONS & COMMENTS

(1) On 19 June 1998, in a hearing before the Inter-American Court of Human Rights, the parties in *Benavides v. Ecuador* reached a friendly settlement. Among other aspects of the judgment, the Court required that Ecuador "continue the investigations to sanction all of those persons responsible for violations of human rights" discussed in the decision. The family received $1 million in damages – the largest settlement in the Court's history at that time. *Benavides v. Ecuador*, Inter-Am. Ct. H.R., Judgment of 19 June 1998, at 15.

(2) In *The Prosecutor v. Jean-Paul Akayesu*, Case No. ICTR-96–4-T, Int'l Crim Trib.-Rwanda, Judgment (2 September 1998), the trial chamber examined the *mens rea* requirement for command responsibility. It held that in cases where the commander failed to stop

---

[5] It should be noted that the *Yamashita Case* has been criticized that the facts did not support Gen. Yamashita's conviction; however, the principle of command responsibility has not been criticized.

[6] As a prerequisite to command responsibility in the Apartheid Convention, however, the illegal act must be in response to an order. Mere knowledge of the act would not be sufficient. Article 3 of the Convention states in relevant part:

> International criminal responsibility shall apply . . . to individuals, members of organizations . . . and representatives of the state . . . whenever they:

> Commit, participate in, *directly incite or conspire* in the commission of [acts of apartheid] . . .

> Directly abet, *encourage* or co-operate in the commission of the crime of apartheid.

> G.A. Res. 3068, U.N. GAOR, art. 3 (1973) (emphases added).

[7] As the Preamble of the Inter-American Convention on the Forced Disappearances of Persons recognizes, "the systematic practice of the forced disappearance of persons constitutes a crime against humanity", and, thereby, a violation of humanitarian law. Here, the distinction between international humanitarian law and international human rights law disappears.

(as opposed to ordered) his/her troops committing humanitarian law violations, there must be "malicious intent, or, at least, . . . negligence . . . so serious as to be tantamount to acquiescence or even malicious intent."

(3) Consider *The Prosecutor v. Delalic and Delic (The Celebici Case)*, Case No. IT-96–21-T, Int'l Crim. Trib.-Yugo., Judgment (16 November 1998). The trial chamber recognized that the doctrine of command responsibility encompasses "not only military commanders, but also civilians holding positions of authority (. . .)" and "not only persons in de jure positions but also those in such position de facto (. . .)." Consider the following case in which the ICTR addresses this distinction in greater detail.

Prosecutor v. Kayishema & Ruzindana
Case No. ICTR-95-1-A
International Criminal Tribunal for Rwanda – Appeals Chamber
1 June 2001

. . . .

3. Kayishema's responsibility under Article 6(3)

280. Kayishema submits that the Trial Chamber committed errors of fact and of law that invalidate the decision and occasion a miscarriage of justice (Grounds 2 and 3) in its assessment of the *préfet*'s status and powers.

281. It is Kayishema's core contention that the Chamber erred when it found, as ground for the accused's responsibility under Article 6(3), that the various entities present during the massacres were the *préfet*'s subordinates. The Appellant thus sets out to show that, given his status and powers, the *préfet* could not reasonably be held responsible for the reprehensible acts of the assailants, pursuant to Article 6 (3), and therefore could neither prevent nor punish the purported perpetrators of the massacres, considered by the Trial Chamber to have acted under his authority.

282. The Appeals Chamber observes that the Appellant therefore not only seems to call into question the findings of the Trial Chamber regarding the *préfet*'s *de jure* authority, but also attempts to show that, since the *préfet* had no *de jure* authority, he could not in fact, and worse still, in the Rwandan context of 1994, exercise any such authority.

(i) Interpretation of the concept of subordinate

a. Arguments of the Parties

283. In his Appellant's Brief, Kayishema mainly raises the issue of the Trial Chamber's assessment of Kayishema's position as hierarchical superior over the various groups of assailants. In substance, he asserts that whatever the powers of the *préfet* were, the context of the time reduced them *de facto* to nothing.

284. The Defence attempts to show that an analysis of the relevant [Rwandan] statutory instruments [ ] lead to the conclusion that, given the Rwandan context of the time, the accused, as a *préfet*, had no subordinate.[ ] The Defence submits that political changes which occurred as from 1992 caused considerable disruption in the *préfet*'s overall situation in the [ ] sense that the hierarchical link with the decentralized services was already cut down [ ] and, on the other hand, that the relation between the *préfets* and the *bourgmestres* in the context of 1994 implied a form of tutelage (monitoring of lawfulness) and not a hierarchical power structure. [ ]

285. Relying on Professor Guibal's testimony, [ ] the Defence argues that "*préfets* [were] in a position of great theoretical power and in a situation of real practical weakness", [ ] which therefore rendered 'those civil servants legally impotent'". Kayishema thus contends that the Trial Chamber "artificially creat[ed] a powerful *préfet*", [ ] which, according to him, constitutes an error of law.

286. As concerns the powers of the *préfet*, the Defence examined consecutively the powers of the *préfet* in general, and then his powers over the *bourgmestre*, the communal police, and the *gendarmerie*.

287. Kayishema proceeds with an analysis of legal provisions to show the *préfet's* lack of power, making it impossible for him to assert himself within the context of 1994. [ ] He reiterates the argument that the legal provisions organizing the administrative functioning of the *préfecture*, which remained in force in 1994, were totally ill-adapted to multiparty politics established in 1994, [ ] to show that it is impossible to establish any direct link between the *préfet* and the crimes charged. The Defence thus submits that, since Kayishema was not a "camp commander or commander of a warring group", he was not responsible for "the victims for which he is being held to account". [ ]

288. As concerns the *préfet's* power over the *bourgmestre* [ ] and therefore over the communal police, [ ] Kayishema once again invokes legal provisions to show the non-existence of hierarchical powers of the *préfet* over mayors, contrary to the findings of the Chamber which, in his view, erred in law. [ ] According to him, the *préfet* certainly has hierarchical power over the *bourgmestre* but this is absolutely not the power of a superior over his subordinate, for he contends, "hierarchy does not mean subordination". [ ] Kayishema submits, therefore, that the notion of hierarchy does not include that of superiority.

289. As for the communal police, Kayishema contends that "the very basis of the decision rendered is undermined", for according to him, the Trial Chamber "undertook a succinct examination [ ] of the 1991 constitution and of the Arusha Accords". [ ] He argues that the legal instruments do not allow for the conclusion that the *préfet* has indirect authority over the communal police through the *bourgmestre*. [ ] After an analysis of the relevant legal provisions . . . , Kayishema concludes that the *préfet* can only requisition the communal police in case of "public disasters and disturbances". He therefore contends that the communal police could not effectively intervene in the 1994 events. Legally, the *préfet* can certainly ask the communal police to intervene, but Kayishema denies the existence of any hierarchical authority. Moreover, Kayishema avers that "the concept of indirect subordination is a construction which does not exist in law", [ ] that "authority is direct or it is not, and responsibility is never indirect; it either is or is not". [ ]

290. Lastly, Kayishema disagrees with the Trial Chamber for having misconstrued the *préfet's* [ ] power of requisition, that is, the relationship between the *gendarmes* and the *préfet*. In this section, Kayishema also carries out an analysis of the relevant legal provisions to show that the *préfet* is not the hierarchical superior of the *gendarmes* [ ] since "the legislation requires mutual cooperation". [ ] Kayishema further submits that a requisition does not give the *préfet* any coercive power since, on the one hand, the latter must justify his request and, on the other hand, the request may be turned down. [ ]

291. Kayishema asserts that "it must first be demonstrated that Kayishema had *de jure* authority and that, at the time, he had a *de facto* authority to be able to exercise his authority. [ ] Consequently, the Defence concludes, "if no *de jure* authority exists, there is no subordinate and, therefore, no *de facto* authority". [ ]

292. During the hearing on appeal, the Prosecution contended that the grounds of appeal raised by the Appellant were factual grounds, [ ] and that the Defence did not provide evidence to show that the accused had no power over the various groups of attackers. The Prosecution asserts that Kayishema exercised effective authority and control over his subordinates. It concludes that the Trial Chamber has already adjudicated reasonably on the arguments, which arguments it does not consider convincing.[ ] The Prosecution contends, referring to "a well-established principle: [that] the absence of *de jure* authority does not prevent a finding of *de facto* authority". [ ] The Prosecution is of the view that the arguments presented by the Defence were not convincing and further asserts that said arguments had been adjudicated upon by the Trial Chamber. It argues that the fact that the *bourgmestre* was legally responsible in Rwanda does not mean that the *préfet* does not have *de facto* authority.[ ] The Prosecution further argues that, even if the Appeals Chamber decided to come back on the fact that Kayishema had no *de jure* authority over the *bourgmestre*, the communal police and the *gendarmes*, the fact remains that he was indeed in a position of authority, which gave him *de facto* power. Accordingly, the Prosecution submits that "[…] no good cause has been shown on appeal to justify a re-examination of the factual findings of the Trial Chamber".[ ]

(ii) Discussion

293. Kayishema alleges both legal and factual errors in the findings of the Trial Chamber with respect to his *de jure* authority over his subordinates. The Appeals Chamber understands his main argument to be that unless there is *de jure* authority there cannot be criminal responsibility under Article 6(3) of the Statute. [ ] Kayishema appears to be contesting whether a *de facto* status can be determined without first establishing the *de jure* status.

294. Article 6(3) of the Statute on "Individual criminal responsibility", provides that:

> The fact that any of the acts referred to in Articles 2 to 4 of the present Statute was committed by a subordinate does not relieve his or her superior of criminal responsibility if he or she knew or had reason to know that the subordinate was about to commit such acts or had done so and the superior failed to take the necessary and reasonable measures to prevent such acts or to punish the perpetrators thereof.

With respect to the nature of the superior-subordinate relationship, the Appeals Chamber refers to the relevant principles expressed in the _Celebici Appeal Judgement in relation to the identical provision in Article 7(3) of ICTY Statute, as follows:

> (i) [A] superior is "one who possesses the power or authority in *either* a *de jure* or a *de facto* form to prevent a subordinate's crime or to punish the perpetrators of the crime after the crime is committed". [ ] Thus, "[t]he power or authority to prevent or to punish does not solely arise from *de jure* authority conferred through official appointment."[ ]
>
> (ii) "In determining questions of responsibility it is necessary to look to effective exercise of power or control and not to formal titles.[…]. In general the possession of *de jure* power in itself may not suffice for the finding of command responsibility if it does not manifest in effective control, although a court may presume that possession of such power *prima facie* results in effective control unless proof to the contrary is produced. [T]he ability to exercise effective control is necessary for the

establishment of *de facto* command or superior responsibility and [...] the absence of formal appointment is not fatal to a finding of criminal responsibility, provided certain conditions are met." [ ]

(iii) "The showing of effective control is required in cases involving both *de jure* and *de facto* superiors." [ ]

This Appeals Chamber accepts these statements and notes that the Trial Chamber, in its Judgement, applied a similar approach when it found that:

> [E]ven where a clear hierarchy based upon *de jure* authority is not present, this does not prevent the finding of command responsibility. Equally, as we shall examine below, the mere existence of *de jure* power does not always necessitate the imposition of command responsibility. The culpability that this doctrine gives rise to must ultimately be predicated upon the power that the superior exercises over his subordinates in a given situation.[ ]

Thus, "as long as a superior has effective control over subordinates, to the extent that he can prevent them from committing crimes or punish them after they committed the crimes, he would be held responsible for the commission of the crimes if he failed to exercise such abilities of control". [ ] Therefore, Kayishema's argument that without *de jure* authority, there can be no subordinate and hence, no *de facto* authority, is misconceived. This question turns on whether the superior had effective control over the persons committing the alleged crimes. The existence of effective control may be related to the question whether the accused had *de jure* authority. However, it need not be; such control or authority can have a *de facto* or a *de jure* character.[ ]

295. As to the remainder of Kayishema's arguments, the Appeals Chamber is of the view that they concern the allegation of an error on the part of the Trial Chamber in its evaluation of the evidence regarding the existence of *de jure* authority. This poses a question of fact and, in respect of a factual error, the Appeals Chamber recalls that the relevant "test" is that of reasonableness. Thus, "[i]t is only where the evidence relied on by the Trial Chamber could not reasonably have been accepted by any reasonable person that the Appeals Chamber can substitute its own finding for that of the Trial Chamber." [ ] In paragraphs 479–516 of the Trial Judgement, a thorough analysis of the evidence led the Trial Chamber to conclude that Kayishema exercised clear, definitive control, both *de jure* and *de facto*, over the assailants at every massacre site set out in the indictment. Kayishema, who now disputes this conclusion on appeal, must persuade the Appeals Chamber that the conclusion is one which could not have reasonably been made by a reasonable tribunal of fact, so that a miscarriage of justice has occurred.

296. The Appeals Chamber notes that during the closing arguments at trial, Counsel for Kayishema had argued to the effect that Kayishema did not enjoy *de jure* control over the appropriate administrative bodies and law enforcement agencies. [ ] On appeal, he repeats these arguments both in the Kayishema Brief and during the hearing on appeal.

297. Kayishema argues that the Trial Chamber erred in its assessment of the testimony of Professor Guibal with respect to "crisis multi-partyism", the exceptional climate that reigned in 1994 and their effect on the existing legal texts on which the function and powers of the *préfet* were based. Having considered the testimony of Professor Guibal as confirming the *de jure* power of the *préfet*, [ ] the Trial Chamber went on to consider the conclusion of Professor Guibal's testimony to the effect that such power was "emptied of

any real meaning when the ministers, the ultimate hierarchical superiors to the police, *gendarmes* and army, were of a different political persuasion. [ ] This conclusion led the Trial Chamber to find that:

> [S]uch assertions clearly highlight the need to consider the *de facto* powers of the Prefect between April and July 1994. Such an examination will be conducted below. However, the delineation of power on party political grounds, whilst perhaps theoretically sound, should only be considered in light of the Trial Chambers findings that the administrative bodies, law enforcement agencies, and even armed civilians were engaged together in a common genocidal plan. The focus in these months was upon a unified, common intention to destroy the ethnic Tutsi population. Therefore, the question of political rivalries must have been, if it was at all salient, a secondary consideration. [ ]

The Appeals Chamber considers that it has not been shown that the Trial Chamber erred in its assessment of the testimony of Professor Guibal. The Trial Chamber adequately considered such testimony with respect to the events occurring at the material period and, hence, reasonably concluded that possession of *de jure* power would not suffice in the circumstances for the determination of effective control.

298. Kayishema submits that the *de jure* relationship between the *préfet* and *bourgmestre* (*i.e.* the hierarchical powers) under Rwandan law cannot be construed as one of a superior and a subordinate. Kayishema further relies on an analysis of the relevant legal text to claim, (i) that the *préfet* does not exercise an indirect *de jure* authority [ ] over the communal police and (ii) that the *préfet*'s restricted powers of requisition over the *gendarmerie* refute a finding of *de jure* authority over the same. He submits that these arguments show that the Trial Chamber erred in ascribing criminal responsibility to Kayishema under Article 6(3) of the Statute. The Appeals Chamber notes that Kayishema's arguments are entirely premised on his main assertion that a finding of *de jure* authority is required for criminal responsibility under Article 6(3) of the Statute. As the Appeals Chamber has considered above that the argument is misplaced, it will not address Kayishema's arguments but, rather, it will briefly consider whether the Trial Chamber reasonably concluded that he exercised effective control over the assailants.

299. In the case of the *bourgmestre*, the Trial Chamber looked at the following factors (both *de jure* and *de facto*) to establish that Kayishema exercised effective authority: the legislative provisions of two Rwandan Statutes, [ ] the actions of Kayishema himself showing the continued subordination of the *bourgmestres* to his *de jure* authority; [ ] Kayishema's own evidence on his relationship with the *bourgmestre* of Gishyita *commune* indicating the importance of his presence at a scene and evidencing that the *préfet* was a "well-known, respected and esteemed figure within his community". [ ] Similarly, Kayishema was also found to have effective control over the communal police and the *gendarmerie*, as evidenced by legislative provisions, [ ] and the actual control he wielded over all the assailants including the *gendarmes*, soldiers, prison wardens, armed civilians and members of the *Interahamwe*[1] as demonstrated by the identification of Kayishema as leading, directing, ordering, instructing, rewarding and transporting them to carry out the attacks. [ ] The Trial Chamber found that the facts of the case established that Kayishema exercised *de facto*

---

[1] [The Interahamwe was the militia of the Mouvement révolutionnaire national pour le développement [MRND]. Ed.'s note.]

control over all of the assailants.[ ] At paragraph 504 of the Trial Judgement it was stated that:

> All of the factual findings need not be recounted here. These examples are indicative of the pivotal role that Kayishema played in leading the execution of the massacres. It is clear that for all crime sites denoted in the Indictment, Kayishema had *de jure* authority over most of the assailants, and *de facto* control of them all.

The Appeals Chamber is satisfied that it was open to the Trial Chamber to find that Kayishema exercised effective control through its consideration of the *de jure* and *de facto* status of the authority enjoyed by him. Kayishema has sought to challenge the findings of the Trial Chamber with respect to command responsibility under Article 6(3) of the Statute, exclusively through an allegation of error in its findings of his *de jure* authority. Consequently, the Appeals Chamber finds that Kayishema has not shown that the Trial Chamber's findings with regard to his effective control were unreasonable so as to result in a miscarriage of justice.

(b) The issue of the *préfet*'s power to punish and prevent crime

(i) Arguments of the parties

300. Kayishema maintains that, given the prevailing context at the time, it emerges clearly that he could neither prevent the crimes committed in Kibuye *préfecture* nor punish the perpetrators thereof. [ ] To this effect, he recalls the findings of Professor Guibal, who holds the opinion that "the powers of administrative policing and of direct penalization of the *préfet* [...] were reduced and, in some cases, even disappeared". [ ]

301. Kayishema recognizes that Article 10 of the legislative decree of 11 March 1975 provides that the *préfet*, in some cases, "could have a power which could be qualified as judicial since he may prosecute and punish". [ ] But that provision cannot be relied upon as a ground for the responsibility of the accused under Article 6 (3). The Defence holds the view that Kayishema could neither control, contain, prevent nor even punish the assailants since he had neither the authority nor the necessary means to do so.[ ]

(ii) Discussion

302. The Appeals Chamber notes that, in substance, Kayishema alleges a lack of means to prevent or punish, based on a similar argument of lack of *de jure* authority and, hence, an absence of *de facto* means, in the light of the circumstances of the material period. His submissions on this point are set out in general terms.

Article 6 (3) of the Statute establishes a duty to prevent a crime that a subordinate was about to commit or to punish such a crime after it is committed, by taking "necessary and reasonable measures". The Appeals Chamber recalls that the interpretation of "necessary and reasonable measures" has been considered in previous cases before ICTY. The *Celebici* Trial Judgement found that:

> [A] superior should be held responsible for failing to take such *measures that are within his material possibility*... [T]he lack of formal legal competence to take the necessary measures to prevent or repress the crime in question does not necessarily preclude the criminal responsibility of the superior.[ ]

The Appeals Chamber agrees with this interpretation and further notes that the Trial Chamber applied a similar approach when it found that:

In order to establish responsibility of a superior under Article 6 (3), it must also be shown that the accused was in a position to prevent or, alternatively, punish the subordinate perpetrators of those crimes. Clearly, the Trial Chamber cannot demand the impossible. Thus, *any imposition of responsibility must be based upon a material ability of the accused to prevent or punish* the crimes in question. [ ]

Thus, it is the effective capacity of the Accused to take measures which is relevant. Accordingly, in the assessment of whether a superior failed to act, it is necessary to look beyond formal competence to actual capacity to take measures. Kayishema's argument that he lacked the means to prevent or punish crime in the context of the material period through an absence of formal competence or *de jure* authority, is once again misplaced.

303. In particular, the Appeals Chamber also notes that the Trial Chamber found as follows:

No evidence was adduced that he attempted to prevent the atrocities that he knew were about to occur and which were within his power to prevent. [ ]

On the issue of Kayishema's failure to punish the perpetrators, the Defence submitted that the only power held by the *préfet* in this respect was the ability to incarcerate for a period not exceeding 30 days. The Trial Chamber concurs with the Defence's submission that this would not be sufficient punishment for the perpetrators of the alleged crimes (though possibly sufficient as a short-term measure to help prevent further atrocities). However, the Trial Chamber is mindful that there is no evidence to suggest that in the 3 months between the start of these attacks and Kayishema's departure from Rwanda, no action was commenced which might ultimately have brought those barbarous crimes to justice. [ ]

(c) Conclusion

304. In the light of the foregoing, the Appeals Chamber finds that Kayishema's arguments are unfounded. The Appeals Chamber, therefore, holds that it has not been demonstrated that the Trial Chamber erred as alleged. Consequently, Grounds Two and Three in relation to Kayishema's individual criminal responsibility under Article 6 (3) of the Statute are dismissed.

. . . .

～

QUESTIONS & COMMENTS

(1) In *Kadic v. Karadzic*, 70 F.3d 232 (2d Cir. 1995), *cert. denied*, 116 S. Ct. 2524 (1996), Muslim and Croat citizens brought an Alien Tort Claims Act lawsuit in federal district court against President Radovan Karadzic of "Srpska," the self-proclaimed Bosnian Serb republic. They alleged that he had directed a campaign of "brutal acts of rape, forced prostitution, forced impregnation, torture, and summary execution" in the course of ethnic cleansing. Because no state other than Serbia recognized Sprska, the question arose whether the state action requirement had been satisfied – that is, whether Karadzic had acted under color of state law. The Court of Appeals for the Second Circuit held that plaintiffs should have the opportunity to prove that Srpska had the attributes of a

state under international law, and remanded the case (which had been dismissed) to the lower court. It also held that state action was not required as to genocide as well as the war crimes prohibited under customary law as codified in the Geneva Conventions. But "torture and summary execution – when not perpetrated in the course of genocide or war crimes – are proscribed by international law only when committed by state officials or under color of state law." In other words, private individuals who commit torture or summary execution cannot be held directly liable under international law.

The distinction appears to be grounded on the fact that the Genocide Convention and the Geneva Conventions, as well as other international instruments, clearly contemplate that individuals should be held liable for violations. The ICCPR and regional human rights conventions are nowhere near as clear. Note, however, that Article 4 of the Torture Convention requires a state to make acts of torture criminal offences. *See* also Inter-American Convention on Forced Disappearance of Persons, Article III (same for disappearances). Would it be desirable, in your view, for international human rights law to move in the direction of making torture and summary execution acts that engage individual responsibility? Should all such violations be treated that way? If not, what criteria would you use to distinguish between those that require state action and those that do not?

2.3.3. Conspiracy and Corporate Responsibility

Judgment for the Trial of German Major War Criminals
International Military Tribunal
1946

[The Law as to the Common Plan or Conspiracy]

. . . .

In the previous recital of the facts relating to aggressive war, it is clear that planning and preparation had been carried out in the most systematic way at every stage of the history.

Planning and preparation are essential to the making of war. In the opinion of the Tribunal aggressive war is a crime under international law. The [London] Charter defines this offence as planning, preparation, initiation or waging of a war of aggression "or participation in a common plan or conspiracy for the accomplishment . . . of the foregoing." The Indictment follows this distinction. Count One charges the common plan or conspiracy. Count Two charges the planning and waging of war. The same evidence has been introduced to support both counts. We shall therefore discuss both counts together, as they are in substance the same. The defendants have been charged under both counts, and their guilt under each count must be determined.

The "common plan or conspiracy" charged in the Indictment covers twenty-five years, from the formation of the Nazi party in 1919 to the end of the war in 1945. The party is spoken of as "the instrument of cohesion among the defendants" for carrying out the purposes of the conspiracy the overthrowing of the Treaty of Versailles, acquiring territory lost by Germany in the last war and "lebensraum"[1] in Europe, by the use, if necessary, of armed force, of aggressive war. The seizure of power by the Nazis, the use of terror, the destruction of trade unions, the attack on Christian teaching and on churches,

---

[1] "Living space." Ed's. Note.

the persecution of the Jews, the regimentation of youth – all these are said to be steps deliberately taken to carry out the common plan. It found expression, so it is alleged, in secret rearmament, the withdrawal by Germany from the Disarmament Conference and the League of Nations, universal military service, and seizure of the Rhineland. Finally, according to the Indictment, aggressive action was planned and carried out against Austria and Czechoslovakia in 1936–1938, followed by the planning and waging of war against Poland; and, successively, against ten other countries.

The Prosecution says, in effect, that any significant participation in the affairs of the Nazi Party or Government is evidence of a participation in a conspiracy that is in itself criminal. Conspiracy is not defined in the Charter. But in the opinion of the Tribunal the conspiracy must be clearly outlined in its criminal purpose. It must not be too far removed from the time of decision and of action. The planning, to be criminal, must not rest merely on the declarations of a party programme, such as are found in the twenty five points of the Nazi Party, announced in 1920, or the political affirmations expressed in "Mein Kampf" in later years. The Tribunal must examine whether a concrete plan to wage war existed, and determine the participants in that concrete plan.

It is not necessary to decide whether a single master conspiracy between the defendants has been established by the evidence. The seizure of power by the Nazi Party, and the subsequent domination by the Nazi State of all spheres of economic and social life must of course be remembered when the later plans for waging war are examined. That plans were made to wage wars, as early as 5th November, 1937, and probably before that, is apparent. And thereafter, such preparations continued in many directions, and against the peace of many countries. Indeed the threat of war – and war itself if necessary – was an integral part of the Nazi policy. But the evidence establishes with certainty the existence of many separate plans rather than a single conspiracy embracing them all. That Germany was rapidly moving to complete dictatorship from the moment that the Nazis seized power, and progressively in the direction of war, has been overwhelmingly shown in the ordered sequence of aggressive acts and wars already set out in this Judgment.

In the opinion of the Tribunal, the evidence establishes the common planning to prepare and wage war by certain of the defendants. It is immaterial to consider whether a single conspiracy to the extent and over the time set out in the Indictment has been conclusively proved. Continued planning, with aggressive war as the objective, has been established beyond doubt. The truth of the situation was well stated by Paul Schmidt, official interpreter of the German Foreign Office, as follows:

> The general objectives of the Nazi leadership were apparent from the start, namely the domination of the European Continent to be achieved first by the incorporation of all German speaking groups in the Reich, and secondly, by territorial expansion under the slogan 'Lebensraum.' The execution of these basic objectives, however, seemed to be characterised by improvisation. Each succeeding step was apparently carried out as each new situation arose, but all consistent with the ultimate objectives mentioned above.

The argument that such common planning cannot exist where there is complete dictatorship is unsound. A plan in the execution of which a number of persons participate is still a plan, even though conceived by only one of them; and those who execute the plan do not avoid responsibility by showing that they acted under the direction of the man who conceived it. Hitler could not make aggressive war by himself. He had to have the co-operation of statesmen, military leaders, diplomats, and business men. When they, with knowledge of his aims, gave him their co-operation, they made themselves parties to the plan he had initiated. They are not to be deemed innocent because Hitler made use of them, if they knew what they were doing. That they were assigned to their tasks by a dictator does not absolve them from responsibility for their acts. The relation of leader and follower does not preclude responsibility here any more than it does in the comparable tyranny of organised domestic crime.

Count One, however, charges not only the conspiracy to commit aggressive war, but also to commit war crimes and crimes against humanity. But the Charter does not define as a separate crime any conspiracy except the one to commit acts of aggressive war. Article 6 of the Charter provides:

> Leaders, organisers, instigators and accomplices participating in the formulation or execution of a common plan or conspiracy to commit any of the foregoing crimes are responsible for all acts performed by any persons in execution of such plan.

In the opinion of the Tribunal these words do not add a new and separate crime to those already listed. The words are designed to establish the responsibility of persons participating in a common plan. The Tribunal will therefore disregard the charges in Count One that the defendants conspired to commit war crimes and crimes against humanity, and will consider only the common plan to prepare, initiate and wage aggressive war.

. . . .

Article 9 of the Charter provides:

> At the trial of any individual member of any group or organisation the Tribunal may declare (in connection with any act of which the individual may be convicted) that the group or organisation of which the individual was a member was a criminal organisation.

> After receipt of the Indictment the Tribunal shall give such notice as it thinks fit that the prosecution intends to ask the Tribunal to make such declaration and any member of the organisation will be entitled to apply to the Tribunal for leave to be heard by the Tribunal upon the question of the criminal character of the organisation. The Tribunal shall have power to allow or reject the application. If the application is allowed, the Tribunal may direct in what manner the applicants shall be represented and heard.

Article 10 of the Charter makes clear that the declaration of criminality against an accused organisation is final, and cannot be challenged in any subsequent criminal proceeding against a member of that organisation. Article 10 is as follows:

> In cases where a group or organisation is declared criminal by the Tribunal, the competent national authority of any Signatory shall have the right to bring individuals to trial for membership therein before national, military or occupation courts. In any such case the criminal nature of the group or organisation is considered proved and shall not be questioned.

The effect of the declaration of criminality by the Tribunal is well illustrated by Law Number 10 of the Control Council of Germany passed on the 20th day of December, 1945, which provides:

Each of the following acts is recognised as a crime:

(d) Membership in categories of a criminal group or organisation declared criminal by the International Military Tribunal.

. . . .

In effect, therefore, a member of an organisation which the Tribunal has declared to be criminal may be subsequently convicted of the crime of membership. . . . This is not to assume that international or military courts which will try these individuals will not exercise appropriate standards of justice. This is a far-reaching and novel procedure. Its application, unless properly safeguarded, may produce great injustice.

Article 9, it should be noted, uses the words "The Tribunal may declare" so that the Tribunal is vested with discretion as to whether it will declare any organisation criminal. This discretion is a judicial one and does not permit arbitrary action, but should be exercised in accordance with well settled legal principles one of the most important of which is that criminal guilt is personal, and that mass punishments should be avoided. If satisfied of the criminal guilt of any organisation or group this Tribunal should not hesitate to declare it to be criminal because the theory of "group criminality" is new, or because it might be unjustly applied by some subsequent tribunals. On the other hand, the Tribunal should make such declaration of criminality so far as possible in a manner to insure that innocent persons will not be punished.

A criminal organisation is analogous to a criminal conspiracy in that the essence of both is cooperation for criminal purposes. There must be a group bound together and organised for a common purpose. The group must be formed or used in connection with the commission of crimes denounced by the Charter. Since the declaration with respect to the organisations and groups will, as has been pointed out, fix the criminality of its members, that definition should exclude persons who had no knowledge of the criminal purposes or acts of the organisation and those who were drafted by the State for membership, unless they were personally implicated in the commission of acts declared criminal by Article 6 of the Charter as members of the organisation. Membership alone is not enough to come within the scope of these declarations.

Since declarations of criminality which the Tribunal makes will be used by other courts in the trial of persons on account of their membership in the organisations found to be criminal, the Tribunal feels it appropriate to make the following recommendations:

1. That so far as possible throughout the four zones of occupation in Germany the classifications, sanctions and penalties be standardised. Uniformity of treatment so far as practical should be a basic principle. This does not, of course, mean that discretion in sentencing should not be vested in the court; but the discretion should be within fixed limits appropriate to the nature of the crime.

2. Law No. 10, to which reference has already been made, leaves punishment entirely in the discretion of the trial court even to the extent of inflicting the death penalty. The De-Nazification Law of 5th March, 1946, however, passed for Bavaria, Greater-Hesse and Wuerttemberg-Baden, provides definite sentences for punishment in each type of offence. The Tribunal recommends that in no case should punishment imposed under Law No. 10 upon any members of an organisation or group declared by the Tribunal to be criminal exceed the punishment fixed by the De-Nazification Law. No person should be punished under both laws.

3. The Tribunal recommends to the Control Council that Law No. 10 be amended to proscribe limitations on the punishment which may be imposed for membership in a criminal group or organisation so that such punishment shall not exceed the punishment prescribed by the De-Nazifiction Law.

The Indictment asks that the Tribunal declare to be criminal the following organisations: The Leadership Corps of the Nazi Party; ... and The General Staff and High Command of the German Armed Forces.

THE LEADERSHIP CORPS OF THE NAZI PARTY

Structure and Component Parts: The Indictment has named the Leadership Corps of the Nazi Party as a group or organisation which should be declared criminal. The Leadership Corps of the Nazi Party consisted, in effect, of the official organisation of the Nazi Party, with Hitler as Fuehrer at its head. The actual work of running the Leadership Corps was carried out by the Chief of the Party Chancellery (Hess, succeeded by Bormann) assisted by the Party Reich Directorate, or Reichsleitung, which was composed of the Reichleiters, the heads of the functional organisations of the Party, as well as of the heads of the various main departments and offices which were attached to the Party Reich Directorate. Under the Chief of the Party Chancellery were the Gauleiters, with territorial jurisdiction over the main administrative regions of the Party, the Gaus. The Gauleiters were assisted by a Party Gau Directorate or Gauleitung, similar in composition and in function to the Party Reich Directorate. Under the Gauleiters in the Party hierarchy were the Kreisleiters with territorial jurisdiction over a Kreis, usually consisting of a single county, and assisted by a Party of Kreis Directorate, or Kreisleitung. The Kreisleiters were the lowest members of the Party hierarchy who were full time paid employees. Directly under the Kreisleiters were the Ortsgruppenleiters, then the Zellenleiters and then the Blockleiters. Directives and instructions were received from the Party Reich Directorate. The Gauleiters had the function of interpreting such orders and issuing them to lower formations. The Kreisleiters had a certain discretion in interpreting orders, but the Ortsgruppenleiters had not, but acted under definite instructions. Instructions were only issued in writing down as far as the Ortsgruppenleiters. The Block and Zellenleiters usually received instructions orally. Membership in the Leadership Corps at all levels was voluntary.

On 28th February, 1946, the Prosecution excluded from the declaration all members of the staffs of the Ortsgruppenleiters and all assistants of the Zellenleiters and Blockleiters. The declaration sought against the Leadership Corps of the Nazi Party thus includes the Fuehrer, the Reichsleitung, the Gauleiters and their staff officers, the Kreisleiters and their staff officers, the Ortsgruppenleiters, the Zellenleiters and the Blockleiters, a group estimated to contain at least 600,000 people.

Aims and Activities: The primary purposes of the Leadership Corps from its beginning was to assist the Nazis in obtaining and, after 30th January, 1933, in retaining control of the German State. The machinery of the Leadership Corps was used for the widespread dissemination of Nazi propaganda and to keep a detailed check on the political attitudes of the German people. In this activity the lower Political Leaders played a particularly important role. The Blockleiters were instructed by the Party Manual to report to the Ortsgruppenleiters, all persons circulating damaging rumours or criticism of the regime. The Ortsgruppenleiters, on the basis of information supplied them by the Blockleiters and Zellenleiters, kept a card index of the people within their Ortsgruppe which recorded the factors which would be used in forming a judgment as to their political reliability. The Leadership Corps was particularly active during plebiscites. All members of the Leadership Corps were active in getting out the vote and insuring the highest possible proportion of "yes" votes. Ortsgruppenleiters and Political Leaders of higher ranks often collaborated with the Gestapo[2] and SD[3] in taking steps to determine those who refused to vote or who voted "no", and in taking steps against them which went as far as arrest and detention in a concentration camp.

Criminal Activity: These steps, which relate merely to the consolidation of control of the Nazi Party, are not criminal under the view of the conspiracy to wage aggressive war which has previously been set forth, But the Leadership Corps was also used for similar steps in Austria and those parts of Czechoslovakia, Lithuania, Poland, France, Belgium, Luxembourg and Yugoslavia which were incorporated into the Reich and within the Gaus of the Nazi Party. In those territories the machinery of the Leadership Corps was used for their Germanisation through the elimination of local customs and the detection and arrest of persons who opposed German occupation. This was criminal under Article 6 (b) of the Charter in those areas governed by the Hague Rules of Land Warfare and criminal under Article 6 (c) of the Charter as to the remainder.

The Leadership Corps played its part in the persecution of the Jews. It was involved in the economic and political discrimination against the Jews, which was put into effect shortly after the Nazis came into power. The Gestapo and SD were instructed to co-ordinate with the Gauleiters and Kreisleiters the measures taken in the pogroms of the 9th and 10th November in the year 1938. The Leadership Corps was also used to prevent German public opinion from reacting against the measures taken against the Jews in the East. On the 9th October, 1942, a confidential information bulletin was sent to all Gauleiters and Kreisleiters entitled "Preparatory Measures for the Final Solution of the Jewish Question in Europe. Rumours concerning the Conditions of the Jews in the East." This bulletin stated that rumours were being started by returning soldiers concerning the conditions of Jews in the East which some Germans might not understand, and outlined in detail the official explanation to be given. This bulletin contained no explicit statement that the Jews were being exterminated, but it did indicate they were going to labour camps, and spoke of their complete segregation and elimination and the necessity of ruthless severity. Thus, even at its face value, it indicated the utilisation of the machinery of the Leadership Corps to keep German public opinion from rebelling at a programme which was stated to involve condemning the Jews of Europe to a lifetime of slavery. This information continued to be available to the Leadership Corps. The August, 1944, edition of "Die Lage", a publication which was circulated among the Political Leaders, described the deportation of 430,000 Jews from Hungary.

The Leadership Corps played an important part in the administration of the Slave Labour Programme. A Sauckel decree dated 6th April 1942, appointed the Gauleiters as Plenipotentiary for Labour Mobilisation for their Gaus with authority to co-ordinate all agencies dealing with labour questions in their Gaus, with specific authority over the employment of foreign workers, including their conditions of work, feeding and housing. Under this authority the Gauleiters assumed control over the allocation of labour in their Gaus, including the forced labourers from foreign countries. In carrying out this

---

[2] "*Die Geheime Staatspolizei*" or state police. Ed's. Note.

[3] "*Die Sicherheitsdienst des Reichsfuehrer SS*," the intelligence agency for security police. Ed's. Note.

task the Gauleiters used many Party offices within their Gaus, including subordinate Political Leaders. For example, Sauckel's decree of the 8th September, 1942, relating to the allocation for household labour of 400,000 women labourers brought in from the East, established a procedure under which applications filed for such workers should be passed on by the Kreisleiters, whose judgment was final.

Under Sauckel's directive the Leadership Corps was directly concerned with the treatment given foreign workers, and the Gauleiters were specifically instructed to prevent "politically inept factory heads" from giving too much consideration to the care of Eastern workers. The type of question which was considered in their treatment included reports by the Kreisleiters on pregnancies among the female slave labourers, which would result in an abortion if the child's parentage would not meet the racial standards laid down by the SS[4] and usually detention in a concentration camp for the female slave labourer. The evidence has established that under the supervision of the Leadership Corps, the industrial workers were housed in camps under atrocious sanitary conditions, worked long hours and were inadequately fed. Under similar supervision, the agricultural workers, who were somewhat better treated were prohibited transportation, entertainment and religious worship, and were worked without any time limit on their working hours and under regulations which gave the employer the right to inflict corporal punishment. The Political Leaders, at least down to the Ortsgruppenleiters, were responsible for this supervision. On the 5th May, 1943. a memorandum of Bormann instructing that mistreatment of slave labourers cease was distributed down to the Ortsgruppenleiters. Similarly on the 10th November, 1944, a Speer circular transmitted a Himmler directive which provided that all members of the Nazi Party, in accordance with instructions from the Kreisleiter, would be warned by the Ortsgruppenleiters of their duty to keep foreign workers under careful observation.

The Leadership Corps was directly concerned with the treatment of prisoners of war. On 5th November, 1941, Bormann transmitted a directive down to the level of Kreisleiter instructing them to insure compliance by the Army with the recent directives of the Department of the Interior ordering that dead Russian prisoners of war should be buried wrapped in tar paper in a remote place without any ceremony or any decorations of their graves. On 25th November, 1943, Bormann sent a circular instructing the Gauleiters to report any lenient treatment of prisoners of war. On 13th September, 1944, Bormann sent a directive down to the level of Kreisleiter ordering that liaison be established between the Kreisleiters and the guards of the prisoners of war in order "to better assimilate the commitment of the prisoners of war to the political and economic demands". On 17th October, 1944, an OKW[5] directive instructed the officer in charge of the prisoners of war to confer with the Kreisleiters on questions of the productivity of labour. The use of prisoners of war, particularly those from the East, was accompanied by a widespread violation of the rules of land warfare. This evidence establishes that the Leadership Corps down to the level of Kreisleiter was a participant in this illegal treatment.

The machinery of the Leadership Corps was also utilised in attempts made to deprive Allied airmen of the protection to which they were entitled under the Geneva Convention. On 13th March, 1940, a directive of Hess transmitted instructions through the Leadership

---

[4] "*Die Schutzstaffeln Der Nationalsocialistischen Deutschen Arbeiterpartei*," the internal security police of the Nazi Party. Ed's. Note.

[5] German acronym for High Command. Ed's. Note.

Corps down to the BIockleiter for the guidance of the civilian population in case of the landing of enemy planes or parachutists, which stated that enemy parachutists were to be immediately arrested or "made harmless". On 30th May, 1944, Bormann sent a circular letter to all Gau and Kreisleiters "reporting instances of lynchings of Allied low level fliers" in which no police action was taken. It was requested that Ortsgruppenleiters be informed orally of the contents of this letter. This letter accompanied a propaganda drive which had been instituted by Goebbels to induce such lynchings, and clearly amounted to instructions to induce such lynchings or at least to violate the Geneva Convention by withdrawing any police protection. Some lynchings were carried out pursuant to this programme, but it does not appear that they were carried out throughout all of Germany. Nevertheless, the existence of this circular letter shows that the heads of the Leadership Corps were utilising it for a purpose which was patently illegal and which involved the use of the machinery of the Leadership Corps at least through the Ortsgruppenleiter.

Conclusion

The Leadership Corps was used for purposes which were criminal under the Charter and involved the Germanisation of incorporated territory, the persecution of the Jews, the administration of the slave labour programme, and the mistreatment of prisoners of war. The defendants Bormann and Sauckel, who were members of this organisation, were among those who used it for these purposes. The Gauleiters, the Kreisleiters, and the Ortsgruppenleiters participated, to one degree or another, in these criminal programmes. The Reichsleitung as the staff organisation of the Party is also responsible for these criminal programmes as well as the heads of the various staff organisations of the Gauleiters and Kreisleiters. The decision of the Tribunal on these staff organisations includes only the Amtsleiters who were heads of offices on the staffs of the Reichsleitung, Gauleitung and Kreisleitung. With respect to other staff officers and party organisations attached to the Leadership Corps other than the Amtsleiters referred to above, the Tribunal will follow the suggestion of the Prosecution in excluding them from the declaration.

The Tribunal declares to be criminal within the meaning of the Charter the group composed of those members of the Leadership Corps holding the positions enumerated in the preceding paragraph who became or remained members of the organisation with knowledge that it was being used for the commission of acts declared criminal by Article 6 of the Charter, or who were personally implicated as members of the organisation in the commission of such crimes. The basis of this finding is the participation of the organisation in war crimes and crimes against humanity connected with the war, the group declared criminal cannot include therefore, persons who had ceased to hold the positions enumerated in the preceding paragraph prior to 1st September, 1939.

   ....

GENERAL STAFF AND HIGH COMMAND

The prosecution has also asked that the General Staff and High Command of the German Armed Forces be declared a criminal organisation. The Tribunal believes that no declaration of criminality should be made with respect to the General Staff and High Command. The number of persons charged ... is ... so small that individual trials of these officers would accomplish the purpose here sought better than a declaration such as is requested. But a more compelling reason is that in the opinion of the Tribunal the

General Staff and High Command is neither an "organisation" nor a "group" within the meaning of those terms as used in Article 9 of the Charter.

Some comment on the nature of this alleged group is requisite. According to the Indictment and evidence before the Tribunal, it consists of approximately 130 officers, living and dead, who at any time during the period from February, 1938, when Hitler reorganised the Armed Forces, and May, 1945, when Germany surrendered, held certain positions in the military hierarchy. These men were high-ranking officers in the three armed services: OKH-Army, OKM-Navy, and OKL-Air Force. Above them was the over-all armed forces authority, OKW-High Command of the German Armed Forces with Hitler as the Supreme Commander.[6] The Officers in the OKW, including defendant Keitel as Chief of the High Command were in a sense Hitler's personal staff. In the larger sense they co-ordinated and directed the three services, with particular emphasis on the functions of planning and operations.

The individual officers in this alleged group were, at one time or another, in one of four categories: (1) Commanders-in-Chief of one of the three services; (2) Chief of Staff of one of the three services; (3) "Oberbefehlshabers", the field commanders-in-chief of one of the three services, which of course comprised, by far the largest number of these persons; or (4) an OKW officer, of which there were three, defendants Keitel and Jodl, and the latter's Deputy Chief, Warlimont. This is the meaning of the Indictment in its use of the term "General Staff and High Command".

The Prosecution has here drawn the line. The Prosecution does not indict the next level of the military hierarchy consisting of commanders of army corps, and equivalent ranks in the Navy and Air Force, nor the level below, the division commanders or their equivalent in the other branches. And the staff officers of the four staff commands of OKW, OKH, OKM, and OKL are not included, nor are the trained specialists who were customarily called General Staff officers.

In effect, then, those indicted as members are military leaders of the Reich of the highest rank. No serious effort was made to assert that they composed an "organisation" in the sense of Article 9. The assertion is rather that they were a "group", which is a wider and more embracing term than "organisation".

The Tribunal does not so find. According to the evidence, their planning at staff level, the constant conferences between staff officers and field commanders, their operational technique in the field and at headquarters was much the same as that of the armies, navies and air forces of all other countries. The over-all effort of OKW at co-ordination and direction could be matched by a similar, though not identical form of organisation in other military forces, such as the Anglo-American Combined Chiefs of Staff.

To derive from this pattern of their activities the existence of an association or group does not, in the opinion of the Tribunal, logically follow. On such a theory the top commanders of every other nation are just such an association rather than what they actually are, an aggregation of military men, a number of individuals who happen at a given period of time to hold the high-ranking military positions.

Much of the evidence and the argument has centred around the question of whether membership in these organisations was or was not voluntary; in this case, it seems to the Tribunal to be quite beside the point. For this alleged criminal organisation has one characteristic, a controlling one, which sharply distinguishes it from the other five indicted.

---

6   OKW, OKH, OKM, and OKL are German acronyms for their respective military branches. Ed's. Note.

When an individual became a member of the SS for instance, he did so, voluntarily or otherwise, but certainly with the knowledge that he was joining something. In the case of the General Staff and High Command, however, he could not know he was joining a group or organisation, for such organisation did not exist except in the charge of the Indictment. He knew only that he had achieved a certain high rank in one of the three services, and could not be conscious of the fact that he was becoming a member of anything so tangible as a "group," as that word is commonly used. His relations with his brother officers in his own branch of the service and his association with those of the other two branches were, in general, like those of other services all over the world.

The Tribunal therefore does not declare the General Staff and High Command to be a criminal organisation.

Although the Tribunal is of the opinion that the term "group" in Article 9 must mean something more than this collection of military officers, it has heard much evidence as to the participation of these officers in planning and waging aggressive war, and in committing war crimes and crimes against humanity. This evidence is, as to many of them, clear and convincing.

They have been responsible in large measure for the miseries and suffering that have fallen on millions of men, women and children. They have been a disgrace to the honourable profession of arms. Without their military guidance the aggressive ambitions of Hitler and his fellow Nazis would have been academic and sterile. Although they were not a group falling within the words of the Charter they were certainly a ruthless military caste. The contemporary German militarism flourished briefly with its recent ally, National Socialism, as well as or better than it had in the generations of the past.

Many of these men have made a mockery of the soldier's oath of obedience to military orders. When it suits their defence they say they had to obey; when confronted with Hitler's brutal crimes, which are shown to have been within their general knowledge, they say they disobeyed. The truth is they actively participated in all these crimes, or sat silent and acquiescent, witnessing the commission of crimes on a scale larger and more shocking than the world has ever had the misfortune to know. This must be said.

Where the facts warrant it, these men should be brought to trial so that those among them who are guilty of these crimes should not escape punishment.

. . . .

~

QUESTIONS & COMMENTS

(1) In U.S. federal law, the Racketeer Influenced Corrupt Organizations (RICO) Act establishes both criminal and civil sanctions for enterprises involved in a variety of criminal acts. Enterprises can include partnerships, corporations, associations, unions, or group of individuals associated in fact although not a legal entity (28 U.S.C. §1961(4)). Would either the Nazi Party Leadership Corp or the General Staff and High Command in the *Judgment for the Trial of German Major War Criminals* have met the enterprise definition in the RICO Act?

(2) Is there a need under international criminal law to define an organization as criminal? The ICT-Y, ICT-R, and ICC have jurisdiction only over natural persons (Art. 6, ICT-Y

Statute; Art. 5, ICT-R Statute; Art. 25(1), ICC Statute). They do not have authority to declare an organization criminal.

How important is such authority for seizing the assets of a criminal organization? Both Article 24 of the ICT-Y Statute and Article 23 of the ICT-R Statute allow their respective tribunals to order the return of any property and proceeds acquired by criminal conduct. The ICC Statute goes further (Art. 77(2), ICC Statute):

> 2. In addition to imprisonment, the Court may order:
>
>> (a) A fine under the criteria provided for in the Rules of Procedure and Evidence;
>> (b) A forfeiture of proceeds, property and assets derived directly or indirectly from that crime, without prejudice to the rights of bona fide third parties.

Should the ICT-Y, ICT-R, and ICC have the authority to declare an organization criminal? How would you argue that there is a customary international law norm allowing the seizure of assets from criminal organizations?

(3) Given the fact that conspiracy law was a foreign notion to many of the Allied countries, how would you have argued in 1940 that there was a customary international law norm allowing criminal liability for conspiracy?

(4) The U.S. Supreme Court and other federal courts have recognized accomplice liability for international law violations. *See, e.g., Talbot v. Janson*, 3 U.S. 133 (1795) (defendant liable for aiding in unlawful capture of neutral ship); *Henfield's Case*, 11 F. Cas. 1099 (C.C.D. Pa. 1793) (No. 6360) (liability for "committing, aiding or abetting hostilities" in violation of law of nations).

Steven R. Ratner

Corporations and Human Rights: A Theory of Legal Responsibility
111 Yale L. J. 443 (2001)

. . . .

V. Circumscribing Corporate Duties: A Theory in Four Parts

[T]he theory adopted here for developing a model of enterprise liability is based on an inductive approach that reflects the actual operations of business enterprises. It appraises the ways in which corporations might affect the human dignity of individuals and posits a theory that is sensitive to the corporations' diverse structures and modes of operating within a particular country. This theory asserts that corporate duties are a function of four clusters of issues: the corporation's relationship with the government, its nexus to affected populations, the particular human right at issue, and the place of individuals violating human rights within the corporate structure.

A. The Company's Relationship to the Government

[T]he doctrine of state responsibility has recognized that the government may act through a variety of actors in breaching its international obligations. International decisionmakers evaluate the connections between these actors and the government to determine whether the state has violated international law. The reverse applies as well, *i.e.,* the ties between the government and the TNE[7] play a major role in determining the obligations of the corporation. Where an enterprise has close ties to the government, it

---

7   [Transnational Enterprise. Ed's. note]

has prima facie a greater set of obligations in the area of human rights. This proposition follows from the government's possession of the greatest set of resources capable of violating human dignity – police and military forces, with accompanying weapons, as well as judicial processes capable of curtailing human rights. It also reflects the likelihood that such ties reduce the state's desire and ability to regulate the conduct effectively, necessitating the recognition of responsibility under international law. The critical issue then becomes determining the sort of ties to the state that are relevant for deriving corporate duties. I begin my analysis from the standpoint of state responsibility rules that describe the consequences of ties between states and private actors; I then consider the relationships that states and corporations are most likely to have and the legal ramifications of these relationships for the company.

1. State Responsibility – The Mirror Image

As an initial matter, the extant rules of state responsibility that make the state liable for the acts of some private actors can provide for the responsibility of those private actors as well. That is, because the state is responsible for certain acts of private actors, those actors can also be held responsible for that same conduct under international law. This principle already has some basis in domestic law. For instance, certain important U.S. statutes hold private defendants civilly and criminally liable for violations of civil rights on the theory that such entities may be acting "under color of law." U.S. courts have applied a variety of tests to determine whether the acts of private individuals were so closely linked with the state as to make them liable. These cases demonstrate the rather obvious proposition that when a private entity acts, in some sense, on behalf of the state, it is as liable as the state for violations of human rights. In recent years, courts have applied these tests to determine whether acts of private corporations violate international law for purposes of the Alien Tort Claims Act (based on the view among those courts that most violations of international law require state action). For the most part, these tests set a relatively high standard, as a result of which plaintiffs have lost key cases. . . .

As significant as these cases are, any international law theory must transcend American notions of state action. International decisionmakers have also recognized a variety of ways in which private entities can become agents of the state. Some of these decisions do not entail affirmative findings of liability by the private actor because the particular forum – an international court or arbitral body – permits only suits against states; but other venues, such as international criminal courts, do reach such conclusions directly. Yet the multitude of arenas for law interpretation at the international level renders the task more difficult than simply restating clearly accepted principles of domestic law. I consider here three sets of relationships.

Governments, international courts, and others have devoted significant time to appraising the legal implications of a state serving as a principal to private agents. A key issue here is the degree of control that a government must have over private actors in order to be responsible for their actions. In the Nicaragua case, the International Court of Justice held that the United States could be held responsible for the acts of the Contras in their war against the Nicaraguan government in the 1980s only if it had "effective control of the military or paramilitary operations in the course of which the alleged violations were committed." In 1999, in *Prosecutor v. Tadic*, the first appeal brought before the International Criminal Tribunal for the Former Yugoslavia (ICTY), the Appeals Chamber had to determine whether the Bosnian Serb army was part of the armed forces of Serbia; a positive finding would mean that the war in Bosnia was an interstate war and would thereby trigger the protections of civilians in the 1949 Geneva Conventions and make certain breaches of that treaty war crimes. The court criticized the Nicaragua test and adopted a looser formula – that the acts of an armed group are attributable to a state as long as the state "has a role in organising, coordinating or planning the military actions" of the group, not necessarily controlling its particular operations. At the same time, the Chamber said that the acts of nonmilitary private groups were attributable to the state only if "specific instructions concerning the commission of that particular act had been issued" by the state, or the state "publicly endorsed or approved ex post facto" the conduct, a test very close to the ICJ's Nicaragua test.

In another forum, the European Court of Human Rights adopted an even looser test for attribution. It found Turkey responsible for the acts of the authorities of the self-styled "Turkish Republic of Northern Cyprus" on the basis of the Turkish army's "effective" and "overall" control of that part of the island. The members of the International Law Commission, for their part, seem to favor the strictness of the Nicaragua test, with the ILC's latest proposal on state responsibility positing responsibility of the state if a person or group is "in fact acting on the instructions of, or under the direction or control of, that State in carrying out the conduct."

As a least common denominator, then, if we posit that the responsibility of the principal entails the responsibility of the agent, this jurisprudence means that private enterprises would be liable for human rights violations where the government has instructed them to engage in those violations. This may well have been the case with some of the World War II business defendants. But as a practical matter, such a relationship probably characterizes a fairly small category of corporate activity, either because governments do not typically make many such bald requests or because corporations do not comply with them. It would, however, cover an episode where the government has asked a company, through its private security force, to detain someone for interrogation where there is reason to believe that the detention will lead to a violation of human dignity (*e.g.*, torture, disappearance, summary execution, or unfair trial).

Beyond responsibility emanating from governmental control over the particular violator, the secondary rules of state responsibility also provide that the state is responsible if private groups more broadly exercise governmental authority as empowered by the law of the state, or in the absence or default of official authorities. (U.S. law on state action recognizes similar tests.) The first category covers a very important class of parastatal actors; while the second covers those filling in for the government, a situation that the doctrine has considered quite exceptional on the theory that governments do not typically relinquish such power. Yet with respect to corporations, both scenarios prove more than speculative. The practices of South American states and Indonesia with respect to foreign corporations would appear to amount, in essence, to granting these companies de jure or de facto control over the areas of the concessions. Under this view, private corporations have duties to protect the human rights of those under their control when they exercise quasi-state authority. The extent of the duties would depend on the extent of control.

3. Corporations as Complicit with Governments

Beyond situations where the private entity is an agent – *de facto* or *de jure* – of the state, other links might characterize the state-enterprise relationship. International law also accepts notions of complicity, whereby one entity engages in otherwise lawful conduct that serves to aid other entities in violating norms. With respect to state responsibility, numerous decisionmakers have held, either in the course of deriving or interpreting primary or secondary rules of conduct, that a state can be responsible for the acts of another state, based on a variety of tests involving its cooperation. Statements of the liability of states for complicity in illegal acts have emanated from decisions of the ICJ, authoritative resolutions of the General Assembly and Security Council, and ample state practice. The ILC has attempted to codify such a standard too and has recently suggested that responsibility hinges upon a requirement that the state "aids or assists" another state "with knowledge of the circumstances" of the illegal act.

The law on individual responsibility has long recognized notions of complicity as well. Thus, for example, Article III of the 1948 Genocide Convention states that conspiracy to commit genocide and complicity in genocide also constitute crimes. The statutes of the International Criminal Tribunals for the Former Yugoslavia and for Rwanda make culpable those who "planned, instigated, ordered, committed or otherwise aided and abetted in the planning, preparation or execution" of one of the enumerated crimes. The 1998 Statute of the International Criminal Court offers a detailed schema, providing for responsibility for a broad range of associated crimes, but conditioning guilt for certain of these crimes on completion of various acts or possession of various mental states. The ICTY has interpreted its statute to mean that an accomplice is guilty if "his participation directly and substantially affected the commission of that offence through supporting the actual commission before, during, or after the incident," and that guilt extends to "all that naturally results" from the act; as for *mens rea*, the court required that the defendant act with knowledge of the underlying act.

Deriving duties of corporations from the law's recognition that states are responsible for their complicity in illegal acts by others states, and that individuals are responsible for complicity in illegal acts by other individuals, must be done with care. Nevertheless, at a minimum, both the state (civil) and individual (criminal) standards clearly recognize such responsibility as long as the underlying activity is illegal and the state or individual involved in the illegal activity has, in some sense, knowledge of it. With respect to corporate activity, this view would suggest that if a business materially contributes to a violation of human rights by the government with knowledge of that activity, it should be held responsible as a matter of international law – to put it conversely, that a business has a duty not to form such complicit relationships with governments.

Such a standard does not suggest that any ties, or even any significant ties, between the government and the corporation per se create corporate responsibility for the government's acts (although other standards might suggest so). The international legal standards for complicity would, for instance, require a corporation not to lend its equipment to government forces with knowledge that it will be used to suppress human rights. Recognition of such duties would address many, perhaps most, of the ongoing concerns about corporate involvement in human rights abuses, for example, accusations of corporate involvement in harassment of government critics and loans of corporate equipment to military units suspected of human rights abuses. But it would not require a corporation to divest, or not invest in the first place, in a country whose government abuses its citizens. Nor would it require, for instance, a paper company (or a soft drink company for that matter) to stop selling to a governmental bureaucracy that violates human rights insofar as this activity does not "directly and substantially" contribute to the violations. Nor would it even suggest that close personal or business ties between the government and the TNE give rise to the latter's responsibility. More would have to be shown than such loose ties.

Indeed, these sorts of distinctions proved critical to the South African Truth and Reconciliation Commission's appraisal of the role of business in apartheid. The Commission drew lines establishing three levels of involvement: (1) companies that "played a central role in helping design and implement" apartheid, in particular, mining firms; (2) companies "that made their money by engaging directly in activities that promoted state repression," with knowledge thereof, such as the arms industry; and (3) companies that "benefited indirectly by virtue of operating" in apartheid society. The TRC found the first two levels reprehensible per se and thereby rejected many claims by business leaders of innocence based on their nonstate status. Yet its nuanced conclusions regarding other businesses reflected an appreciation of the extent to which apartheid clearly benefited them and of the complexity of business interactions with the government. In the end, while concluding that government and business "co-operated in the building of an economy that benefited whites," it rejected both a condemnation of all business people as collaborators as well as an exculpation of them for taming and helping end the system. Although the TRC was not in a position to impose – or eliminate – legal, let alone criminal, liability upon corporations, its sophisticated analysis represents an important element of state practice in favor of a duty on corporations to avoid complicit relationships.

One could go much further than the existing norms of international law for deriving corporate duties – for instance, by working from a moral starting point that a corporation has a duty not to invest at all in a repressive society, or a duty to ensure that it does not in any way benefit from the government's lax human rights policy. During the years of apartheid, many states and nonstate actors asserted such a duty with respect to South Africa, resulting in the divestment of many corporations from that country. And those opposing investment in Burma today might well be seeking to advance such a legal duty. A note of caution, however, is required. To the extent that international actors have accepted the notion of complicity, they have generally hinged it on the direct involvement of the individual or state in violations of law. To extend complicity to corporations seems a reasonable – although, certainly in the view of many, unorthodox – step in the development of international norms. To ignore completely the extant notions of legal responsibility in favor of a concept of accomplice liability that has little support in state practice risks defeating the entire enterprise. I do not wish to exclude such responsibility as a possibility for the future, nor would I advise corporations to develop ties with repressive regimes that fall short of legal complicity. But this version of corporate responsibility would need to derive from an acceptance by governments and other actors of a broader notion of complicity than they have expressed to date.

4. Corporations as Commanders?

The need for care in transposing notions of individual responsibility into the corporate area is demonstrated by a special, significant form of culpability that international law recognizes for acts of omission – the doctrine of superior or command responsibility. It extends the liability of a military commander or civilian superior for acts of subordinates beyond those covered through the notion of accomplice liability to those where the superior plays a more passive role by failing to prevent certain actions of subordinates. The rationale for such responsibility is that, by virtue of a hierarchical relationship between superior and subordinate, the former should be held criminally liable for failure to exercise his duties when the result is the commission of offenses by subordinates. In general, the doctrine holds that a superior is responsible for the acts of subordinates if (1) he knew or should have known that the subordinate had committed, or was about to commit, the acts, and (2) he did not take necessary and reasonable measures to prevent the acts or punish the subordinate. This general starting point nonetheless leaves unanswered numerous questions regarding the precise scope of the superior's responsibility, including the definition of a superior and the scope of his duty to be aware of activities by subordinates.

NGOs have made claims against corporations based on the corporations' failure to inform themselves of certain conduct by the government. Because all traditional forms of complicity assume knowledge of the illegal activity, the NGO claims stem essentially from a notion of superior responsibility. And inherent in such a claim is the belief that the company is effectively the superior and the state the agent. This starting point flips the traditional doctrine of state responsibility on its head insofar as the law generally works from the presumption that nonstate actors are the agents rather than the principal. But it may accurately reflect some enterprise-state relations. If, for instance, the company utilized governmental forces to maintain security around the perimeter of a mine, and those forces engaged in serious human rights abuses, one can speak of a form of superior responsibility of the company for the acts of the governmental forces. Utilizing, as an example, the standard in the ICC Statute for the responsibility of civilian superiors for acts of subordinates, the corporation would be liable for acts of those under its "effective authority and control" where it "knew, or consciously disregarded information which clearly indicated, that the subordinates were committing or about to commit such crimes" and where "the crimes concerned activities that were within the effective responsibility and control of the superior."

Determining "effective responsibility and control" and what sort of information "clearly indicates" the commission of human rights abuses is, of course, no simple matter. Hard cases would arise if, for instance, the business agreed to invest in exchange for a government promise to "secure" (so to speak) an area from opponents of the investment or the regime, and if the investor knew what that term in fact meant. Human rights NGOs involved in the drafting of the Rome Statute found even its standard of knowledge too high. Indeed, if my theory is to derive a set of duties applying to corporations generally rather than simply those duties that give rise to criminal liability, a lower standard of knowledge seems justifiable, one more akin to the negligence standard imposed on military commanders. But, regardless of how these details are resolved, command responsibility itself seems a justifiable basis for corporate duties in situations where corporations are indeed superiors to governmental actors.

B. The Corporation's Nexus to Affected Population

The second element in a theory of corporate responsibility arises from a fundamental distinction between states and companies. States generally have human rights obligations toward all persons on their territory, although some duties do not run to nonnationals. This stems from an assumption that governmental control and jurisdiction is determined on a territorial basis. For TNEs, however, a territorial scope for determining the universe of relevant rightholders will not work insofar as businesses do not exercise such a geographically fixed form of jurisdiction. Therefore, the determination of enterprise duties must address the company's links with individuals possessing human rights. My analysis of this factor is grounded in premises from moral philosophy about interpersonal duties and is buttressed by extant international practice.

The extent to which obligations of one actor toward other actors turn on the former's ties with the latter has engaged moral philosophers for centuries. Contemporary scholars have framed the debate in terms of partiality and impartiality. In its purist (and indeed most extreme or absurd) form, impartiality is seen by its supporters to flow inevitably from Kant's Categorical Imperative and to endorse equal treatment of all persons under all circumstances (regardless of family or group connections); partiality, on the other hand, would favor overt identification with close relatives and limited moral duties toward others. Nonetheless, many philosophers have rejected pure impartiality as unrealistic and pure partiality as immoral, and have instead found common ground that explicitly acknowledges the morality of certain preferences toward family, community, association, or country. Arguing in different ways, scholars such as Alan Gewirth and Brian Barry have shown that partialist conceptions of duties are not inconsistent with – and indeed can flow from – an overall moral theory of impartiality and equal respect for all persons. Communitarian political philosophers such as Michael Walzer and Yael Tamir have adopted similar ideas to demonstrate how liberalism and nationalism need not collide. Without delving into the philosophical differences among these and other thinkers, the overall conclusion remains that the idea of equal respect for all humans, central in human rights theory and law, is consistent with the notion that, under certain circumstances, individuals and institutions owe greater duties to those with whom they have special associative ties than to others beyond that sphere.

In the corporate context, this premise argues for viewing the ties as falling within concentric circles emanating from the enterprise, with spheres enlarging from employees to their families, to the citizens of a given locality otherwise affected by their operation (admittedly a broad and amorphous category), and eventually to an entire country. This, of course, represents an oversimplification in the case of TNEs, since by their very nature they operate in different localities and different countries. But in general, as the circles widen, the duties of the corporation will diminish. In Gewirth's terms, these circles represent social groupings, with the bonds (and corresponding intra-group structures and rules) strongest among the corporation and its employees and weaker with respect to other communities. (Certain members of the groupings, such as neighbors of a plant, may not have chosen to be part of the social group, just as family members do not choose to be a part of a social group, but this does not diminish – indeed it arguably increases – the enterprise's duties toward them.)

The nexus factor thus suggests, all other things being equal, that as the proximity of the corporation to individuals – the extent to which the enterprise and the population form a meaningful association – lessens, the duties of the corporation toward those individuals lessen as well. For example, the ICCPR's requirement that the law prohibit any discrimination based on "race, colour, sex, language, religion, political or other opinion, national or social origin, property, birth or other status" would suggest a duty upon corporations not to discriminate on these grounds in their employment practices – their relations with the group enjoying the closest nexus to the corporation.

Moving further out in the spheres of influence, the corporation's duties to its customers might well suggest an obligation to ensure that the product is sold (perhaps through its franchisers or distributors) in a way that does not entail those invidious forms of discrimination. At a certain point, however, the nexus to the affected population fails to generate duties concerning this right – it would be difficult to conclude, for example, that the corporation has a duty to ensure that its product is sold in all parts of the country in order to ensure access for all different religious, national, or social groups.

The nexus factor might also have a purely territorial element to it, such that a corporation's duties depend upon the extent to which the corporation physically controls a certain area. Thus, where the enterprise effectively manages a particular piece of territory, as in the case of mineral or timber concessions, it would have a certain, presumably larger, set of duties to those living within that territory, distinct from those to persons living outside it. The enterprise operates as a quasi-state whose special obligations to those under its control are accepted in both moral philosophy and international law doctrine. On the other hand, insofar as the corporation has important ties with persons within a broader area, it would have some duties to them as well. For instance, if the activities of the corporation poisoned the only supply of drinking water of an adjacent area, then the human right to "the highest attainable standard of physical and mental health" would appear to place some duties on the corporation to prevent or respond to such damage. Similar examples might apply to the duties of the corporation to those persons in the immediate vicinity of a factory as compared to those living further away from it.

States have already accepted this concept through the development of international labor standards. Whatever one's view on whether those treaties place direct or merely indirect duties on companies, their promulgation by institutions such as the ILO suggests that governments, labor unions, and business leaders view the sphere of employer-employee relations as an appropriate target for detailed international regulation (one that, as noted, preceded the international human rights movement by a generation). International law has not, for the most part, extended these duties to cover larger spheres potentially influenced by private enterprises, although ILO Convention No. 169 Concerning Indigenous and Tribal Peoples in Independent Countries, while principally drafted to impose obligations on governments, does at least hint of corporate duties toward those groups.

More recently, the United Nations, the OECD, the EU, and human rights and corporate NGOs have endorsed such an approach. For instance, the UN Secretary-General, in establishing in 1999 the UN's Global Compact program (a joint project of the UN and world business leaders), noted two distinct sets of duties of corporations: to respect human rights "within their sphere of influence" and to avoid being "complicit in human rights abuses" – the latter term referring to corporate involvement in governmental action. The OECD's 2000 Code of Conduct for TNEs urges companies to "[r]espect the human rights of those affected by their activities consistent with the host government's international obligations and commitments." The European Commission's Directorate of Employment and Social Affairs has noted, in the context of the reach of corporate codes of conduct, that "[w]hat seems to matter is the degree of control a company has over the employment conditions of all workers employed by its subcontractors." Both Amnesty International and the Prince of Wales Business Leaders Forum have distinguished corporate responsibility for a company's own operations from duties extending to the broader environment in the state.

But is there a circularity here? Are these institutions and I simply asserting that as long as the corporation engages in activities that trigger duties, it will have duties? Is not the notion of ties so amorphous that the spheres themselves are not fixed but merely move with the given human right? For example, what happens if corporate agents were physically to attack persons who were seemingly unrelated to the company's operations but were in fact representing some sort of threat to the company? Would the theory argue that these persons are beyond some objective sphere of influence and thus the corporation owes no duty to them, or that the corporation would have effectively extended its sphere of influence, and thus the violation of their physical integrity would render the company liable? The theory addresses this question in the important "all other things being equal" qualification to the premise noted above. In general, the corporation's duties can be defined in spheres. However, there may well be circumstances (or certain rights) for which the spheres of influence factor is irrelevant. Gewirth and Raz, for instance, have both written of certain absolute rights, such that, in the former's words, "agents and institutions are absolutely prohibited from degrading persons, treating them as if they had no rights or dignity." For such rights, the corporation may well have equal duties toward all.

C. The Substantive Rights at Issue

Once decisionmakers identify the corporation's connections to the government and to affected populations, they must turn to the nature of the right being impinged. For any particular human right may well place a different set of duties upon a corporation than the sort of duties that the primary rules of state responsibility place on states. I argue below that, for those rights that business enterprises can infringe, corporate duties turn on a balancing of individual rights with business interests and rights. This approach circumscribes corporate duties in a manner that considers the nature of business activity.

1. Can the Corporation Infringe the Right?

A preliminary issue in appraising how particular rights give rise to duties is whether the corporation can even have a duty with respect to all human rights. [F]or some human rights, the government represents the principal dutyholder insofar as only the government can directly infringe upon those rights. Thus, I sought to differentiate between those sorts of rights that the corporation can directly infringe and those that only the government can directly infringe, for example, between the right against cruel, inhuman, or degrading treatment and the right to cross-examination in criminal trials. The duties of the corporation with regard to the latter are only the complicity-based duties discussed in Section V.A [ ]. Thus, for those rights that only the government can directly infringe, the links between the corporation and government (the first factor in the theory) are a necessary factor for the derivation of company duties. Indeed, the links with the government would seem to be a sufficient factor for determining enterprise duties so that the issue of the corporation's nexus to the victims (the factor in Section V.B [ ] becomes irrelevant. In such cases, the state is violating the rights of its citizens, and the enterprise has a duty not to be complicit in this effort, whether the affected population consists of its own employees or individuals far from its normal sphere of influence.

Which other rights belong in this category? In addition to many rights concerning criminal defendants, others would include the right to enter one's country without arbitrary restrictions; the right of a child to nationality, registration, and a name; the right to marry; the right to vote and run for office; and the right to equality before the law. Of course, the scope of this list can itself be the subject of some dispute. Purists opposed to a notion of corporate duties might argue that the vast majority of human rights, especially in the civil and political realm, are capable of being violated only by the state. They might argue that the right to leave one's country can be directly infringed only by the state (through its interior ministry or immigration bureaucracy) and that it therefore gives rise to corporate duties only through the notion of complicity. Yet private actors are capable, through physical force, of preventing their employees from leaving the country, as the problem of forced prostitution makes clear.

But what of the large number of rights that do not belong in this category, that is, those that are capable of direct infringement by private actors and corporate entities, as well as by the state? As a preliminary matter, it bears clarifying that the complicity-based duties that arise when the government can directly abuse rights also arise when both the government and the corporation can abuse the rights. As long as the state can violate the right, the corporation has a duty not to be complicit in such conduct.

More important, because other human rights are capable of direct infringement by business actors, they give rise to obligations on those actors beyond the duty to avoid complicity in the government's violation of them. But in order to derive the duties from all those other rights – whether the right to life, liberty, and security of the person, to free association, free assembly, and free speech, or to participation in public affairs – we need to take into account the differences between corporations and states, as well as the various types of duties that can arise from the same right.

2. The Imperative of Balancing Interests

Human rights law is generally based on a balancing between the interests of the state and the rights of the individual. As Raz notes from a jurisprudential perspective, a right does not simply translate into some corresponding duty. Rather, "[i]t is the ground of a duty, ground which, if not counteracted by conflicting considerations, justifies holding that other person to have the duty." The ICCPR (and its regional counterparts in Europe and Latin America) identifies these interests – national security (including preservation of the nation in the event of a national emergency), public order, public health or morals, and the rights or freedoms of others – although it also recognizes that some rights cannot be suspended under any circumstances. Business enterprises, however, have different goals and interests that fundamentally rest on the need to maintain a profitable income stream. To talk about duties of business entities vis-à-vis individuals necessitates taking into account not only the rights of the individuals, but also these interests. Indeed, as noted earlier, businesses themselves have some human rights, including privacy and association rights that, when exercised, inevitably have an impact upon individuals with whom they interact.

Consequently, the company's responsibility must, as an initial matter, turn on a balancing of the individual right at issue with the enterprise's interests and on the nexus between its actions and the preservation of its interests. Such a view simply parallels the basic notion of human rights law that the state may limit many rights to the extent "necessary in a democratic society," with its concomitant notion of proportionality between means and ends. To give a simple example, the right to free speech requires governments to refrain from penalizing individuals for speech critical of the government (as well as much other speech); but it would not require a company to refrain from penalizing employees for public speech that insults the company to consumers, lures away employees, or gives away trade secrets, since these actions impinge on core interests of the company. In general, however, it would bar a company from taking disciplinary measures against an employee for his speech critical of the government.

Just as domestic constitutional courts, regional human rights courts, and UN human rights bodies grapple with determining the limits of lawful governmental interference with individual liberties, so the balancing of corporate interests and individual rights may prove difficult. For example, with respect to the right against arbitrary or unlawful interference with privacy, family, home, or correspondence, a corporation would not be able to use its resources to break into anyone's home, wiretap conversations there, or intercept mail, since the means are disproportionate to the ends. The corporation would not, however, be violating the human rights of employees by videotaping them surreptitiously while on the job in order to prevent pilfering of products.

Decisionmakers would also apply the balancing test if the corporation's rights were at issue. One difficult example would concern whether a media company's rights to free speech violated the individual's right to privacy if it published embarrassing information about celebrities, politicians, or criminal suspects. One might argue that the individual is too far removed from the corporation – that their associative ties are too weak – to create any duties in the latter. Some decisionmakers might, however, regard their ties (given the nature and purpose of the media company's business) as close enough to justify corporate duties; in that case, they would have to balance the reputational harm to the individual against the right of a business to speak. This individual rights/business rights balancing – what might be called horizontal balancing – seems by its nature more difficult than the individual rights/business interests – *i.e.*, vertical – balancing more akin to the sort done by human rights bodies and domestic constitutional courts. Yet the former sort of balancing takes place all the time when legislatures and courts grapple with issues of libel and other so-called private law. Indeed, the use of the third-party effect doctrine by German and Dutch courts as well as by the European Court of Justice in cases concerning exclusively private parties suggests that balancing that considers the rights (or interests) of private parties faces no larger theoretical bar than do the more paradigmatic cases of balancing governmental interests with individual rights.

In the end, the balancing test offers a uniform approach for those deriving specific corporate duties – whether through domestic statute, treaty, or soft law. Of course, one set of decisionmakers, such as a legislature, might prove unwilling to do the balancing itself, leaving the final determinations to administrative officials or courts. That balancing does not guarantee uniform outcomes is no more an argument against corporate duties than it is against governmental duties in the human rights area, which are derived by the same methodology and may assume different contours from region to region.

Beyond balancing, certain rights with which the state may never interfere – such as the right to life and physical integrity and the rights against torture, slavery, or debt imprisonment – would be just as nonderogable against the corporation. The nature of those rights determines their nonderogability, such that no state or corporate interests can override them.

While some readers may see such balancing as too theoretically complex for its own good, decisionmakers may well find as a practical matter that deriving a set of corporate duties based on balancing is hardly an unmanageable exercise. Corporations have already begun this task. For instance, the Norwegian Confederation of Business and Industry has derived a list of twelve human rights, primarily based on the Universal Declaration, and suggested various obligations they might put on corporations. The list notably prohibits corporations from interfering with individual political freedoms and proscribes corporal punishment.

Beyond not violating rights directly, how far do corporate duties extend? Under the International Covenant on Civil and Political Rights and its regional counterparts, states must not only directly refrain from abuses; they must also "respect and ensure" the rights in the Convention, which include in particular the obligation to provide an "effective remedy" in the event of a violation of the right. The UN Human Rights Committee has, for instance, stated that many rights give rise not only to duties on the government not to impinge them directly, but positive duties as well (*e.g.*, the right against torture implies a state duty to train police and prison guards in order to prevent torture). The question thus arises whether, for example, the right against torture creates a duty on corporations to train their security personnel properly. Or does the human right to form a family create a duty upon a corporation to provide a certain amount of paid or unpaid maternal and paternal leave to the parents? Or a duty not to discriminate on the basis of pregnancy or maternal status in hiring and promotion? Beyond these derivative duties . . . regional human rights courts have required states to prevent certain abuses by private actors on their territory.

The scope of such related duties turns in part on the extent to which fulfillment of the derivative duty is necessary for compliance with the principal duty. In the case of torture, the close link between training security personnel and preventing torture argues strongly for such a duty. As for the right to form a family, this right does not, in the current state of international human rights law, create an obligation on states to provide parental leave, so it would not create such an obligation on businesses. In addition, these duties turn on the enterprise's nexus to affected individuals, as discussed in Section V.B [ ]. The closer the nexus, the greater the extent of corporate duties. If, for example, the corporation enjoys control over territory equivalent to that of a state, it has duties beyond the duty not to infringe directly the right itself, more akin to those of states. It would also have some duties to protect the welfare of those closest to it, such as employees, and to ensure that actors, whether private or governmental, do not violate their human rights. The Prince of Wales Business Leaders Forum and Amnesty International, for example, have asserted that if labor activists are arrested, state security forces abuse rights at a TNE site, or a worker disappears, "for a [company] not to raise these concerns . . . with government officials, while adopting the argument of political neutrality or cultural relativism, is to fail to fulfill its responsibility to uphold international human rights standards." In the many situations short of these sorts of ties, the company's duties will be significantly less.

As a practical matter, the nexus analysis suggests that the company will usually have only negative duties or those positive measures clearly necessary to effect them. That is, the company's duties will typically be to avoid directly infringing upon the right based on the balancing test above, including through some prophylactic measures. Other derivative duties might be appropriate where the nexus between the enterprise and the individual is particularly close. But to go further than this position would effectively ignore the functional differences between states and businesses; it would thereby ask too much of the corporation, especially at this stage of the international legal process, when the broad notion of business duties in the human rights area is just emerging.

This position *a fortiori* calls into question the applicability to business entities of state duties under human rights law to go beyond immediate preventive action (such as the training of security forces) and promote respect for human rights generally. Promotion is a secondary duty compared to directly respecting or protecting rights, as it calls upon the dutyholder to create a general atmosphere or public consciousness of human rights, rather than to refrain from the conduct itself or to undertake necessary measures to ensure that it will not engage in the conduct. In the end, improvement of the overall human rights situation of the population seems attenuated from the corporation's key purposes, whereas it is one of the central purposes of government (or at least of liberal government). The business enterprise might have resources at its disposal that, if improperly used, could violate human rights, thus necessitating the derivation of duties to ensure that it does not do so; and it may well be both good corporate policy as well as good human rights policy to encourage corporations to promote human rights, especially when they operate in countries with poor human rights records. But to extend their duty away from a dictum of "doing no harm" – either on their own or through complicity with the government – toward one of proactive steps to promote human rights outside their sphere of influence seems inconsistent with the reality of the corporate enterprise.

D. Attribution Principles: The Relevance of Corporate Structures

The final element of the theory of responsibility addresses the structure of the enterprise as an actor and the place of the human rights violator (or person(s) complicit with the government) within that structure. This Section derives a set of attribution principles that connect individual violators to the company. These critical secondary rules of corporate responsibility must confront the reality of the modern business organization.

... part of the difficulty of transplanting notions of state responsibility to the corporate area lies in the differences between states and corporations. The former are constituted and organized in overtly legal terms – through constitutions, statutes, regulations, policies, and practices, all defining the relationship of the various parts to the whole. This characteristic of states forms the basis for a core secondary rule of state responsibility – that states are responsible for the acts of all state organs and state officials acting as such, however low or high in the governmental hierarchy and however close or far from the state's governmental center.

The business entity, however, is defined in more diverse ways. The status of many individuals as direct employees justifies attribution of their company-related acts to the corporation based on ideas of state responsibility (although questions of the standard of fault arise in this connection, an issue considered below. Beyond employees, other relationships are more complex. As Blumberg and Strasser note, the subsidiary's relationship with the corporation turns upon a number of distinct factors, namely, stock ownership, economic integration, administrative, financial, and employee interdependence, and a common public persona. The corporate group may extend beyond this paradigm to include a variety of enterprises with which the main corporation maintains close relations, such as franchisees and licensees.

The relations among parts of a business enterprise can make the determination of the very boundaries of that entity difficult. A corporate entity may operate through joint ventures with other businesses, contractors, and subcontractors; and it may rely upon obtaining inputs from certain suppliers and selling outputs to certain buyers, each creating a variety of economic ties. In some cases, these links originate in contracts establishing long-term relationships; in others, the economic interactions result from the economic importance of the corporation to the supplier or purchaser. A theory of corporate duties must take these relationships into account through some guidelines regarding attribution.

The touchstone for determining the relevance of enterprise structures for duties must be the element of control. As Hugh Collins writes, corporate relations are not merely a function of ownership (subsidiaries) or contractual ties (contractors, distributors, or franchisees). Rather, they extend to a variety of what he calls "authority relations" that "arise wherever the economic dependence of one party upon the other effectively requires compliance with the dominant party's wishes." In such situations, attributing to the controller actions of the controlled entity is entirely appropriate. This concept, of course, resonates with principles of state and individual responsibility noted above; in the corporate realm, it is gaining some acceptance as a basis for assessing corporate responsibility under domestic law.

Several issues immediately arise concerning the role of control. First, control is not a monolithic concept. A corporation's control over its wholly-owned subsidiary might be total, requiring the former to assume responsibility for all the latter's acts. But what of a corporation's control over a joint venture partner, subcontractor, supplier, or buyer? As a first take, one might distinguish between the corporation's control over the contractor and subcontractor for human rights abuses related to the particular contract, and its control over the contractor for acts on a project not involving that corporation. With respect to the former, the corporation might be said to control the contractor; with respect to the latter, it would not.

Yet such a dichotomy is too simple insofar as it might not accurately take into account the question of economic interdependence central to Collins's theory. Thus, what if demand for particular contractors so exceeded supply that the corporation effectively had to work with the contractor on the latter's terms and had no real control of its operations? Do the contractual links between them alone serve to make the enterprise responsible for the acts of the contractor? Conversely, what if supply for particular contractors so exceeded demand, or the corporation provided such a large part of the contractor's business, that the contractor effectively had to work with the corporation on the latter's terms? In that case, the corporation would appear in a position to control the contractor, even on the contractor's projects not involving that corporation.

One approach to this problem would lie in a set of rebuttable presumptions: The corporation would be prima facie responsible for acts of contractors and subcontractors concerning the contracted-for projects, and prima facie not responsible for other acts by those entities. The two presumptions could be overcome if it were shown, respectively, that the corporation did not exercise real control over the execution of the contracted-for project, or, conversely, that it had actual dominion over the contractor.

Dependence may also turn upon technical cooperation arrangements among entities. If, for example, one TNE lends numerous expert personnel to a local entity such that the latter becomes dependent upon it for its effective functioning, then the TNE is, for all intents and purposes, exercising control over the latter. But even here, actions by individuals within the local entity who have no real connection to the expert personnel would not give rise to responsibility by the corporation. Deriving such presumptions for suppliers and purchasers based on a linchpin of control proves more difficult. Does one attribute to the corporation the abuses of a buyer of its products simply by virtue of the corporation's having supplied a core input? Are the acts of a seller to the company attributable to the latter simply if the company is the seller's largest customer? These difficulties might be resolved by ascribing a certain knowledge standard to the company. Indeed, at a certain point, the rules of attribution – determining the scope of the corporation's component entities – begin to merge with the principles of agency and complicity discussed above. (The difference between this scenario and that discussed in Section V.A is that we are now considering the liability of a company for acts of another company, rather than complicity by one company in the acts of the government.) The test for determining the responsibility of a company for acts of a buyer or seller (or even of a contractor or subcontractor) may thus turn on the mindset of the company rather than merely on economic ties. I do not seek to resolve these issues here, but merely point out the possible limitations of a test that hinges on control.

Of course, such a proposition could also be attacked from the other side, *i.e.*, that the mere presence of economic contacts between the corporation and other entities suffices to attribute to the corporation the acts of all those with whom it works. But this seems far too slender a reed upon which to hang a theory of responsibility. It would require as a general matter that enterprises cut off all ties from entities that might abuse human dignity, even if the abuses stem from activities completely unrelated to the enterprises' connection with the violator entities. To extract a general notion of attribution (just like complicity) from economic ties alone has no basis in domestic or international law.

Second, economic dependence must take account of the attenuated influence of the corporation as one moves further down the chain of production. If a multinational corporation making shoes in Vietnam hires a contractor to make the cotton laces, who hires a subcontractor to provide the cotton cloth, who hires a subcontractor to grow the cotton, who hires a subcontractor to actually pick the cotton, and this last actor uses forced labor in his practices, can the corporation be said to be responsible for his activities – even if each was somehow dependent upon the entity directly above it for its continuing livelihood? If one were to base a theory of responsibility upon multiplying the degree of dependency, an eighty-five percent dependency for four levels of dependency translates to just over fifty percent. (If the cotton-picker were acting in his spare time, the conduct would clearly be totally private.)

Finally, the control test might not suffice for determining the responsibility of joint venture partners for the activities of their newly created entity. If four companies joined forces to create a local mining company, with each owning twenty-five percent of the company's shares and appointing a quarter of its directors or senior managers, none might control the entity in the sense of being able to force through decisions or block the decisions of others. Yet state responsibility principles increasingly recognize the concept of joint and several liability for such joint acts by states. The extension of this principle to joint ventures seems justified on the same underlying ground, namely that because the companies have created the joint venture specifically for the purpose of gaining the benefits of cooperation from its conduct, they assume the risks should the venture violate human dignity.

E. A Brief Word on Fault

Lastly, any discussion of corporate duties must address the degree of fault (if any) that creates enterprise responsibility. Governments, international institutions, and legal scholars have long wrestled with the standards of fault required for determining whether the state has violated international law. Treaties, courts, arbitral bodies, individual governments, and other decisionmakers have adopted various standards in elaborating primary rules of state and individual responsibility. As a general matter, fault is not required for violations by states. Thus, for instance, human rights courts do not require victims to demonstrate that the government was negligent in restraining its officials; rather, the acts of such officials are simply attributed to the state (a secondary rule) and the state is liable for the violation. For other primary rules binding on states, such as duties to prevent certain injuries to individuals by wholly private actors, courts and other decisionmakers have found violations only after finding the state at fault in its failure to exercise due diligence.

With respect to individual responsibility, international criminal law conventions and cases include the defendant's *mens rea* as part of the definition of a crime. Intent and knowledge are typically required, although the extent of the defendant's knowledge and intent regarding each element of the crime can vary from crime to crime; and under the concept of superior responsibility, the defendant need not have had either intent or knowledge regarding the underlying act.

Can either of the above approaches to standards of care be shifted to the corporate sector? On the one hand, the individual accountability standards require such a significant level of fault as to be inappropriate for a general scheme of corporate responsibility that goes beyond criminal sanctions. Even with respect to criminal liability, different national systems have adopted sharply contrasting concepts of the degree of fault (if any) required of the corporation for criminal liability, suggesting the absence of general principles of law upon which one might rely. On the other hand, we can ask whether the state responsibility standard, which generally does not require fault, should apply to corporations. Perhaps, as the discussion on attribution makes clear, the business enterprise is different enough from the state that the former should be liable only if it fails to exercise due diligence over its agents, including by not engaging in corrective measures after the fact. Moreover, business enterprises will likely resist any standard of strict liability.

In the end, it would seem that the ultimate standard of care will turn upon the particular forum in which the norms are formulated, whether civil, penal, administrative, or otherwise. The state responsibility approach seems most appealing as a general matter insofar as it views the business enterprise, like the state, as a unit engaged in a particular function, with its own internal structures. In that sense, it seems appropriate that it should be *per se* responsible for all its components acting under color of corporate authority without any separate requirement of fault by the business. For those duties for which the corporation might have to prevent actions by persons not connected with the business enterprise, a lesser standard, such as due diligence, would apply, as the human rights courts have recognized. If, however, severe sanctions were envisioned, it would seem justifiable to limit the enterprise's responsibility to situations where it failed to exercise due diligence over its agents.

. . . .

∿

2.3.4. Defenses

Statute of the International Criminal Court

Article 31

Grounds for excluding criminal responsibility

1. In addition to other grounds for excluding criminal responsibility provided for in this Statute, a person shall not be criminally responsible if, at the time of that person's conduct:

> (a) The person suffers from a mental disease or defect that destroys that person's capacity to appreciate the unlawfulness or nature of his or her conduct, or capacity to control his or her conduct to conform to the requirements of law;
>
> (b) The person is in a state of intoxication that destroys that person's capacity to appreciate the unlawfulness or nature of his or her conduct, or capacity to control his or her conduct to conform to the requirements of law, unless the person has become voluntarily intoxicated under such circumstances that the person knew, or disregarded

the risk, that, as a result of the intoxication, he or she was likely to engage in conduct constituting a crime within the jurisdiction of the Court;

(c) The person acts reasonably to defend himself or herself or another person or, in the case of war crimes, property which is essential for the survival of the person or another person or property which is essential for accomplishing a military mission, against an imminent and unlawful use of force in a manner proportionate to the degree of danger to the person or the other person or property protected. The fact that the person was involved in a defensive operation conducted by forces shall not in itself constitute a ground for excluding criminal responsibility under this subparagraph;

(d) The conduct which is alleged to constitute a crime within the jurisdiction of the Court has been caused by duress resulting from a threat of imminent death or of continuing or imminent serious bodily harm against that person or another person, and the person acts necessarily and reasonably to avoid this threat, provided that the person does not intend to cause a greater harm than the one sought to be avoided. Such a threat may either be:

(i) Made by other persons; or

(ii) Constituted by other circumstances beyond that person's control.

2. The Court shall determine the applicability of the grounds for excluding criminal responsibility provided for in this Statute to the case before it.

3. At trial, the Court may consider a ground for excluding criminal responsibility other than those referred to in paragraph 1 where such a ground is derived from applicable law as set forth in article 21. The procedures relating to the consideration of such a ground shall be provided for in the Rules of Procedure and Evidence.

Article 33

Superior orders and prescription of law

1. The fact that a crime within the jurisdiction of the Court has been committed by a person pursuant to an order of a Government or of a superior, whether military or civilian, shall not relieve that person of criminal responsibility unless:

(a) The person was under a legal obligation to obey orders of the Government or the superior in question;

(b) The person did not know that the order was unlawful; and

(c) The order was not manifestly unlawful.

2. For the purposes of this article, orders to commit genocide or crimes against humanity are manifestly unlawful.

State and official immunity

Al-Adsani v. United Kingdom
Application No. 35763/97
European Court of Human Rights
[2001] ECHR 752 (21 November 2001)

. . . .

10. The applicant, who is a trained pilot, went to Kuwait in 1991 to assist in its defence against Iraq. During the Gulf War he served as a member of the Kuwaiti Air Force and,

after the Iraqi invasion, he remained behind as a member of the resistance movement. During that period he came into possession of sex videotapes involving Sheikh Jaber Al-Sabah Al-Saud Al-Sabah ("the Sheikh"), who is related to the Emir of Kuwait and is said to have an influential position in Kuwait. By some means these tapes entered general circulation, for which the applicant was held responsible by the Sheikh.

11. After the Iraqi armed forces were expelled from Kuwait, on or about 2 May 1991, the Sheikh and two others gained entry to the applicant's house, beat him and took him at gunpoint in a government jeep to the Kuwaiti State Security Prison. The applicant was falsely imprisoned there for several days during which he was repeatedly beaten by security guards. He was released on 5 May 1991, having been forced to sign a false confession.

12. On or about 7 May 1991 the Sheikh took the applicant at gunpoint in a government car to the palace of the Emir of Kuwait's brother. At first the applicant's head was repeatedly held underwater in a swimming-pool containing corpses, and he was then dragged into a small room where the Sheikh set fire to mattresses soaked in petrol, as a result of which the applicant was seriously burnt.

13. Initially the applicant was treated in a Kuwaiti hospital, and on 17 May 1991 he returned to England where he spent six weeks in hospital being treated for burns covering 25% of his total body surface area. He also suffered psychological damage and has been diagnosed as suffering from a severe form of post-traumatic stress disorder, aggravated by the fact that, once in England, he received threats warning him not to take action or give publicity to his plight.

B. The civil proceedings

14. On 29 August 1992 the applicant instituted civil proceedings in England for compensation against the Sheikh and the State of Kuwait in respect of injury to his physical and mental health caused by torture in Kuwait in May 1991 and threats against his life and well-being made after his return to the United Kingdom on 17 May 1991. On 15 December 1992 he obtained a default judgment against the Sheikh.

15. . . . He was not, however, granted leave to serve the writ on the State of Kuwait.

16. The applicant submitted a renewed application to the Court of Appeal, which was heard *ex parte* on 21 January 1994. Judgment was delivered the same day.

The court held, on the basis of the applicant's allegations, that there were three elements pointing towards State responsibility for the events in Kuwait: firstly, the applicant had been taken to a State prison; secondly, government transport had been used on 2 and 7 May 1991; and, thirdly, in the prison he had been mistreated by public officials. It found that the applicant had established a good arguable case, based on principles of international law, that Kuwait should not be afforded immunity under section 1(1) of the State Immunity Act 1978 ("the 1978 Act": see paragraph 21 below) in respect of acts of torture. In addition, there was medical evidence indicating that the applicant had suffered damage (post-traumatic stress) while in the United Kingdom. It followed that the conditions [ ] of the Rules of the Supreme Court had been satisfied [ ] and that leave should be granted to serve the writ on the State of Kuwait.

17. The Kuwaiti government, after receiving the writ, sought an order striking out the proceedings. The application was examined *inter partes* by the High Court on 15 March 1995. In a judgment delivered the same day the court held that it was for the applicant to show on the balance of probabilities that the State of Kuwait was not entitled to immunity under the 1978 Act. It was prepared provisionally to accept that the Government was

vicariously responsible for conduct that would qualify as torture under international law. However, international law could be used only to assist in interpreting lacunae or ambiguities in a statute, and when the terms of a statute were clear, the statute had to prevail over international law. The clear language of the 1978 Act bestowed immunity upon sovereign States for acts committed outside the jurisdiction and, by making express provision for exceptions, it excluded as a matter of construction implied exceptions. As a result, there was no room for an implied exception for acts of torture in section 1(1) of the 1978 Act. Moreover, the court was not satisfied on the balance of probabilities that the State of Kuwait was responsible for the threats made to the applicant after 17 May 1991. As a result, the exception provided for by section 5 of the 1978 Act could not apply. It followed that the action against the State should be struck out.

18. The applicant appealed and the Court of Appeal examined the case on 12 March 1996. The court held that the applicant had not established on the balance of probabilities that the State of Kuwait was responsible for the threats made in the United Kingdom. The important question was, therefore, whether State immunity applied in respect of the alleged events in Kuwait. Lord Justice Stuart-Smith finding against the applicant, observed:

> Jurisdiction of the English court in respect of foreign States is governed by the State Immunity Act 1978. Section 1(1) provides:
>
>> "A State is immune from the jurisdiction of the courts of the United Kingdom except as provided in the following provisions of this Part of this Act...."
>
> ... The only relevant exception is section 5, which provides:
>
>> "A State is not immune as respects proceedings in respect of
>>
>> (a) death or personal injury...caused by an act or omission in the United Kingdom."
>
> It is plain that the events in Kuwait do not fall within the exception in section 5, and the express words of section 1 provide immunity to the First Defendant. Despite this, in what [counsel] for the Plaintiff acknowledges is a bold submission, he contends that that section must be read subject to the implication that the State is only granted immunity if it is acting within the Law of Nations. So that the section reads: 'A State *acting within the Law of Nations* is immune from jurisdiction except as provided...'
>
> ... The argument is...that international law against torture is so fundamental that it is a *jus cogens*, or compelling law, which overrides all other principles of international law, including the well-established principles of sovereign immunity. No authority is cited for this proposition.... At common law, a sovereign State could not be sued at all against its will in the courts of this country. The 1978 Act, by the exceptions therein set out, marks substantial inroads into this principle. It is inconceivable, it seems to me, that the draughtsman, who must have been well aware of the various international agreements about torture, intended section 1 to be subject to an overriding qualification.
>
> Moreover, authority in the United States at the highest level is completely contrary to [counsel for the applicant's] submission. [Lord Justice Stuart-Smith referred to the judgments of the United States courts, *Argentine Republic v. Amerada Hess Shipping*

Corporation and *Siderman de Blake v. Republic of Argentina,* cited in paragraph 23 below, in both of which the court rejected the argument that there was an implied exception to the rule of State immunity where the State acted contrary to the Law of Nations.] ... [Counsel] submits that we should not follow the highly persuasive judgments of the American courts. I cannot agree.

... A moment's reflection is enough to show that the practical consequences of the Plaintiff's submission would be dire. The courts in the United Kingdom are open to all who seek their help, whether they are British citizens or not. A vast number of people come to this country each year seeking refuge and asylum, and many of these allege that they have been tortured in the country whence they came. Some of these claims are no doubt justified, others are more doubtful. Those who are presently charged with the responsibility for deciding whether applicants are genuine refugees have a difficult enough task, but at least they know much of the background and surrounding circumstances against which the claim is made. The court would be in no such position. The foreign States would be unlikely to submit to the jurisdiction of the United Kingdom court, and in its absence the court would have no means of testing the claim or making a just determination.... "

The other two members of the Court of Appeal, Lord Justice Ward and Mr Justice Buckley, also rejected the applicant's claim. Lord Justice Ward commented that "there may be no international forum (other than the forum of the *locus delicti* to whom a victim of torture will be understandably reluctant to turn) where this terrible, if established, wrong can receive civil redress".

19. On 27 November 1996 the applicant was refused leave to appeal by the House of Lords. His attempts to obtain compensation from the Kuwaiti authorities via diplomatic channels have proved unsuccessful.

II. RELEVANT LEGALMATERIALS

....

B. The State Immunity Act 1978

21. The relevant parts of the State Immunity Act 1978 provide:

1. (1) A State is immune from the jurisdiction of the courts of the United Kingdom except as provided in the following provisions of this Part of this Act.
....
5. A State is not immune as regards proceedings in respect of-

(a) death or personal injury;

...

caused by an act or omission in the United Kingdom ...

C. The Basle Convention

22. The above provision (section 5 of the 1978 Act) was enacted to implement the 1972 European Convention on State Immunity ("the Basle Convention"), a Council of Europe instrument, which entered into force on 11 June 1976 after its ratification by three States. It has now been ratified by eight States (Austria, Belgium, Cyprus, Germany,

Luxembourg, the Netherlands, Switzerland and the United Kingdom) and signed by one other State (Portugal). Article 11 of the Convention provides:

> A Contracting State cannot claim immunity from the jurisdiction of a court of another Contracting State in proceedings which relate to redress for injury to the person or damage to tangible property, if the facts which occasioned the injury or damage occurred in the territory of the State of forum, and if the author of the injury or damage was present in that territory at the time when those facts occurred.

Article 15 of the Basle Convention provides that a Contracting State shall be entitled to immunity if the proceedings do not fall within the stated exceptions.

D. State immunity in respect of civil proceedings for torture

23. In its Report on Jurisdictional Immunities of States and their Property (1999), the working group of the International Law Commission (ILC) found that over the preceding decade a number of civil claims had been brought in municipal courts, particularly in the United States and United Kingdom, against foreign governments, arising out of acts of torture committed not in the territory of the forum State but in the territory of the defendant and other States. The working group of the ILC found that national courts had in some cases shown sympathy for the argument that States are not entitled to plead immunity where there has been a violation of human rights norms with the character of *jus cogens*, although in most cases the plea of sovereign immunity had succeeded. The working group cited the following cases in this connection: (United Kingdom) *Al-Adsani v. State of Kuwait* 100 International Law Reports 465 at 471; (New Zealand) *Controller and Auditor General v. Sir Ronald Davidson* [1996] 2 New Zealand Law Reports 278, particularly at 290 (per Cooke P.); Dissenting Opinion of Justice Wald in (United States) *Princz v. Federal Republic of Germany* 26 F 3d 1166 (DC Cir. 1994) at 1176–1185; *Siderman de Blake v. Republic of Argentina* 965 F 2d 699 (9th Cir. 1992); *Argentine Republic v. Amerada Hess Shipping Corporation* 488 US 428 (1989); *Saudi Arabia v. Nelson* 100 International Law Reports 544.

24. The working group of the ILC did, however, note two recent developments which it considered gave support to the argument that a State could not plead immunity in respect of gross human rights violations. One of these was the House of Lords' judgment in *ex parte Pinochet (No. 3)* (see paragraph 34 below). The other was the amendment by the United States of its Foreign Sovereign Immunities Act (FSIA) to include a new exception to immunity. This exception, introduced by section 221 of the Anti-Terrorism and Effective Death Penalty Act of 1996, applies in respect of a claim for damages for personal injury or death caused by an act of torture, extra-judicial killing, aircraft sabotage or hostage-taking, against a State designated by the Secretary of State as a sponsor of terrorism, where the claimant or victim was a national of the United States at the time the act occurred.

In its judgment in *Flatow v. the Islamic Republic of Iran and Others* (76 F. Supp. 2d 16, 18 (D.D.C. 1999)), the District Court for the District of Columbia confirmed that the property of a foreign State was immune from attachment or execution, unless the case fell within one of the statutory exceptions, for example that the property was used for commercial activity.

. . . .

B. Compliance with Article 6 §1

1. Submissions of the parties

50. The Government contended that the restriction imposed on the applicant's right of access to a court pursued a legitimate aim and was proportionate. The 1978 Act reflected the provisions of the Basle Convention (see paragraph 22 above), which in turn gave expression to universally applicable principles of public international law and, as the Court of Appeal had found, there was no evidence of a change in customary international law in this respect. Article 6 §1 of the Convention could not be interpreted so as to compel a Contracting State to deny immunity to and assert jurisdiction over a non-Contracting State. Such a conclusion would be contrary to international law and would impose irreconcilable obligations on the States that had ratified both the Convention and the Basle Convention.

There were other, traditional means of redress for wrongs of this kind available to the applicant, namely diplomatic representations or an inter-State claim.

51. The applicant submitted that the restriction on his right of access to a court did not serve a legitimate aim and was disproportionate. The House of Lords in *ex parte Pinochet (No. 3)* (see paragraph 34 above) had accepted that the prohibition of torture had acquired the status of a *jus cogens* norm in international law and that torture had become an international crime. In these circumstances there could be no rational basis for allowing sovereign immunity in a civil action when immunity would not be a defence in criminal proceedings arising from the same facts. Other than civil proceedings against the State of Kuwait, he complained that there was no effective means of redress available to him. He had attempted to make use of diplomatic channels but the Government refused to assist him, and although he had obtained judgment by default against the Sheikh, the judgment could not be executed because the Sheikh had no ascertainable recoverable assets in the United Kingdom.

2. The Court's assessment

52. In *Golder v. the United Kingdom* (judgment of 21 February 1975, Series A no. 18, pp. 13–18, §§28–36) the Court held that the procedural guarantees laid down in Article 6 concerning fairness, publicity and promptness would be meaningless in the absence of any protection for the pre-condition for the enjoyment of those guarantees, namely, access to a court. It established this as an inherent aspect of the safeguards enshrined in Article 6, referring to the principles of the rule of law and the avoidance of arbitrary power which underlie much of the Convention. Thus, Article 6 §1 secures to everyone the right to have any claim relating to his civil rights and obligations brought before a court.

53. The right of access to a court is not, however, absolute, but may be subject to limitations; these are permitted by implication since the right of access by its very nature calls for regulation by the State. In this respect, the Contracting States enjoy a certain margin of appreciation, although the final decision as to the observance of the Convention's requirements rests with the Court. It must be satisfied that the limitations applied do not restrict or reduce the access left to the individual in such a way or to such an extent that the very essence of the right is impaired. Furthermore, a limitation will not be compatible with Article 6 §1 if it does not pursue a legitimate aim and if there is no reasonable relationship of proportionality between the means employed and the aim

sought to be achieved (see *Waite and Kennedy v. Germany* [GC], no. 26083/94, §59, ECHR 1999-I).

54. The Court must first examine whether the limitation pursued a legitimate aim. It notes in this connection that sovereign immunity is a concept of international law, developed out of the principle *par in parem non habet imperium*, by virtue of which one State shall not be subject to the jurisdiction of another State. The Court considers that the grant of sovereign immunity to a State in civil proceedings pursues the legitimate aim of complying with international law to promote comity and good relations between States through the respect of another State's sovereignty.

55. The Court must next assess whether the restriction was proportionate to the aim pursued. It reiterates that the Convention has to be interpreted in the light of the rules set out in the Vienna Convention on the Law of Treaties of 23 May 1969, and that Article 31 §3 (c) of that treaty indicates that account is to be taken of "any relevant rules of international law applicable in the relations between the parties". The Convention, including Article 6, cannot be interpreted in a vacuum. The Court must be mindful of the Convention's special character as a human rights treaty, and it must also take the relevant rules of international law into account (see, *mutatis mutandis, Loizidou v. Turkey* (merits), judgment of 18 December 1996, *Reports* 1996-VI, p. 2231, §43). The Convention should so far as possible be interpreted in harmony with other rules of international law of which it forms part, including those relating to the grant of State immunity.

56. It follows that measures taken by a High Contracting Party which reflect generally recognised rules of public international law on State immunity cannot in principle be regarded as imposing a disproportionate restriction on the right of access to a court as embodied in Article 6 §1. Just as the right of access to a court is an inherent part of the fair trial guarantee in that Article, so some restrictions on access must likewise be regarded as inherent, an example being those limitations generally accepted by the community of nations as part of the doctrine of State immunity.

57. The Court notes that the 1978 Act, applied by the English courts so as to afford immunity to Kuwait, complies with the relevant provisions of the 1972 Basle Convention, which, while placing a number of limitations on the scope of State immunity as it was traditionally understood, preserves it in respect of civil proceedings for damages for personal injury unless the injury was caused in the territory of the forum State (see paragraph 22 above). Except insofar as it affects claims for damages for torture, the applicant does not deny that the above provision reflects a generally accepted rule of international law. He asserts, however, that his claim related to torture, and contends that the prohibition of torture has acquired the status of a *jus cogens* norm in international law, taking precedence over treaty law and other rules of international law.

58. Following the decision to uphold Kuwait's claim to immunity, the domestic courts were never required to examine evidence relating to the applicant's allegations, which have, therefore, never been proved. However, for the purposes of the present judgment, the Court accepts that the ill-treatment alleged by the applicant against Kuwait in his pleadings in the domestic courts, namely, repeated beatings by prison guards over a period of several days with the aim of extracting a confession (see paragraph 11 above), can properly be categorised as torture within the meaning of Article 3 of the Convention (see *Selmouni v. France* [GC], no. 25803/94, ECHR 1999-V, and *Aksoy*, cited above).

59. Within the Convention system it has long been recognised that the right under Article 3 not to be subjected to torture or to inhuman or degrading treatment or

punishment enshrines one of the fundamental values of democratic society. It is an absolute right, permitting of no exception in any circumstances (see, for example, *Aksoy*, cited above, p. 2278, §62, and the cases cited therein). Of all the categories of ill-treatment prohibited by Article 3, "torture" has a special stigma, attaching only to deliberate inhuman treatment causing very serious and cruel suffering (ibid., pp. 2278–79, §63, and see also the cases referred to in paragraphs 38–39 above).

60. Other areas of public international law bear witness to a growing recognition of the overriding importance of the prohibition of torture. Thus, torture is forbidden by Article 5 of the Universal Declaration of Human Rights and Article 7 of the International Covenant on Civil and Political Rights. The United Nations Convention against Torture and Other Cruel, Inhuman and Degrading Treatment or Punishment requires, by Article 2, that each State Party should take effective legislative, administrative, judicial or other measures to prevent torture in any territory under its jurisdiction, and, by Article 4, that all acts of torture should be made offences under the State Party's criminal law (see paragraphs 25–29 above). In addition, there have been a number of judicial statements to the effect that the prohibition of torture has attained the status of a peremptory norm or *jus cogens*. For example, in its judgment of 10 December 1998 in *Furundzija* (see paragraph 30 above), the International Criminal Tribunal for the Former Yugoslavia referred, *inter alia*, to the foregoing body of treaty rules and held that "[b]ecause of the importance of the values it protects, this principle [proscribing torture] has evolved into a peremptory norm or *jus cogens*, that is, a norm that enjoys a higher rank in the international hierarchy than treaty law and even 'ordinary' customary rules". Similar statements have been made in other cases before that tribunal and in national courts, including the House of Lords in the case of *ex parte Pinochet (No. 3)* (see paragraph 24 above).

61. While the Court accepts, on the basis of these authorities, that the prohibition of torture has achieved the status of a peremptory norm in international law, it observes that the present case concerns not, as in *Furundzija* and *Pinochet*, the criminal liability of an individual for alleged acts of torture, but the immunity of a State in a civil suit for damages in respect of acts of torture within the territory of that State. Notwithstanding the special character of the prohibition of torture in international law, the Court is unable to discern in the international instruments, judicial authorities or other materials before it any firm basis for concluding that, as a matter of international law, a State no longer enjoys immunity from civil suit in the courts of another State where acts of torture are alleged. In particular, the Court observes that none of the primary international instruments referred to (Article 5 of the Universal Declaration of Human Rights, Article 7 of the International Covenant on Civil and Political Rights and Articles 2 and 4 of the UN Convention) relates to civil proceedings or to State immunity.

62. It is true that in its Report on Jurisdictional Immunities of States and their Property (see paragraphs 23–24 above) the working group of the International Law Commission noted, as a recent development in State practice and legislation on the subject of immunities of States, the argument increasingly put forward that immunity should be denied in the case of death or personal injury resulting from acts of a State in violation of human rights norms having the character of *jus cogens*, particularly the prohibition on torture. However, as the working group itself acknowledged, while national courts had in some cases shown some sympathy for the argument that States were not entitled to plead immunity where there had been a violation of human rights norms with the character of

jus cogens, in most cases (including those cited by the applicant in the domestic proceedings and before the Court) the plea of sovereign immunity had succeeded.

63. The ILC working group went on to note developments, since those decisions, in support of the argument that a State may not plead immunity in respect of human rights violations: first, the exception to immunity adopted by the United States in the amendment to the Foreign Sovereign Immunities Act (FSIA) which had been applied by the United States courts in two cases; secondly, the *ex parte Pinochet (No. 3)* judgment in which the House of Lords "emphasised the limits of immunity in respect of gross human rights violations by State officials". The Court does not, however, find that either of these developments provides it with a firm basis on which to conclude that the immunity of States *ratione personae* is no longer enjoyed in respect of civil liability for claims of acts of torture, let alone that it was not enjoyed in 1996 at the time of the Court of Appeal's judgment in the present case.

64. As to the amendment to the FSIA, the very fact that the amendment was needed would seem to confirm that the general rule of international law remained that immunity attached even in respect of claims of acts of official torture. Moreover, the amendment is circumscribed in its scope: the offending State must be designated as a State sponsor of acts of terrorism, and the claimant must be a national of the United States. The effect of the FSIA is further limited in that after judgment has been obtained, the property of a foreign State is immune from attachment or execution unless one of the statutory exceptions applies (see paragraph 24 above).

65. As to the *ex parte Pinochet (No. 3)* judgment (see paragraph 24 above), the Court notes that the majority of the House of Lords held that, after the UN Convention and even before, the international prohibition against official torture had the character of *jus cogens* or a peremptory norm and that no immunity was enjoyed by a torturer from one Torture Convention State from the criminal jurisdiction of another. But, as the working group of the ILC itself acknowledged, that case concerned the immunity *ratione materiae* from criminal jurisdiction of a former head of State, who was at the material time physically within the United Kingdom. As the judgments in the case made clear, the conclusion of the House of Lords did not in any way affect the immunity *ratione personae* of foreign sovereign States from the civil jurisdiction in respect of such acts (see in particular, the judgment of Lord Millett, mentioned in paragraph 34 above). In so holding, the House of Lords cited with approval the judgments of the Court of Appeal in *Al-Adsani* itself.

66. The Court, while noting the growing recognition of the overriding importance of the prohibition of torture, does not accordingly find it established that there is yet acceptance in international law of the proposition that States are not entitled to immunity in respect of civil claims for damages for alleged torture committed outside the forum State. The 1978 Act, which grants immunity to States in respect of personal injury claims unless the damage was caused within the United Kingdom, is not inconsistent with those limitations generally accepted by the community of nations as part of the doctrine of State immunity.

67. In these circumstances, the application by the English courts of the provisions of the 1978 Act to uphold Kuwait's claim to immunity cannot be said to have amounted to an unjustified restriction on the applicant's access to a court.

It follows that there has been no violation of Article 6 §1 of the Convention in this case.

. . . .

Joint Dissenting Opinion of Judges Rozakis and Caflisch joined by Judges Wildhaber, Costa, Cabral Barreto and Vajiç

We regret that we are unable to concur with the Court's majority in finding that, in the present case, there has not been a violation of Article 6 of the Convention in so far as the right of access to a court is concerned. Unlike the majority, we consider that the applicant was unduly deprived of his right of access to English courts to entertain the merits of his claim against the State of Kuwait although that claim was linked to serious allegations of torture. To us the main reasoning of the majority – that the standards applicable in civil cases differ from those applying in criminal matters when a conflict arises between the peremptory norm of international law on the prohibition of torture and the rules on State immunity – raises fundamental questions, and we disagree for the following reasons.

1. The Court's majority unequivocally accept that the rule on the prohibition of torture had achieved at the material time, namely at the time when civil proceedings were instituted by the applicant before the English courts, the status of a peremptory rule of international law (*jus cogens*). They refer to a number of authorities which demonstrate that the prohibition of torture has gradually crystallised as a *jus cogens* rule. To this conclusion we readily subscribe and in further support of this we refer to the Statutes of the *ad hoc* Tribunals for the Former Yugoslavia and Rwanda, and to the Statute of the International Criminal Court, which also gives a definition of the crime [*See* Article 7 §2 (e) of the Statute of the International Criminal Court]. State practice corroborates this conclusion [*See, inter alia*, the judgment of the Swiss *Tribunal Fédéral* in the case of *Sener c. Ministère public de la Confédération et Département fédéral de justice et police* where, as early as 1983, the tribunal accepted that the rule of the prohibition of torture of the European Convention on Human Rights is a rule of *jus cogens* [ ] By accepting that the rule on prohibition of torture is a rule of *jus cogens*, the majority recognise that it is hierarchically higher than any other rule of international law, be it general or particular, customary or conventional, with the exception, of course, of other *jus cogens* norms. For the basic characteristic of a *jus cogens* rule is that, as a source of law in the now vertical international legal system, it overrides any other rule which does not have the same status. In the event of a conflict between a *jus cogens* rule and any other rule of international law, the former prevails. The consequence of such prevalence is that the conflicting rule is null and void, or, in any event, does not produce legal effects which are in contradiction with the content of the peremptory rule.

2. The Court's majority do not seem, on the other hand, to deny that the rules on State immunity; customary or conventional, do not belong to the category of *jus cogens*; and rightly so, because it is clear that the rules of State immunity, deriving from both customary and conventional international law, have never been considered by the international community as rules with a hierarchically higher status. It is common knowledge that, in many instances, States have, through their own initiative, waived their rights of immunity; that in many instances they have contracted out of them, or have renounced them. These instances clearly demonstrate that the rules on State immunity do not enjoy a higher status, since *jus cogens* rules, protecting as they do the "*ordre public*", that is the basic values of the international community, cannot be subject to unilateral or contractual forms of derogation from their imperative contents.

3. The acceptance therefore of the *jus cogens* nature of the prohibition of torture entails that a State allegedly violating it cannot invoke hierarchically lower rules (in this case,

those on State immunity) to avoid the consequences of the illegality of its actions. In the circumstances of this case, Kuwait cannot validly hide behind the rules on State immunity to avoid proceedings for a serious claim of torture made before a foreign jurisdiction; and the courts of that jurisdiction (the United Kingdom) cannot accept a plea of immunity, or invoke it *ex officio*, to refuse an applicant adjudication of a torture case. Due to the interplay of the *jus cogens* rule on prohibition of torture and the rules on State immunity, the procedural bar of.State immunity is automatically lifted, because those rules, as they conflict with a hierarchically higher rule, do not produce any legal effect. In the same vein, national law which is designed to give domestic effect to the international rules on State immunity cannot be invoked as creating a jurisdictional bar, but must be interpreted in accordance with and in the light of the imperative precepts of *jus cogens*.

4. The majority, while accepting that the rule on the prohibition of torture is a *jus cogens* norm, refuse to draw the consequences of such acceptance. They contend that a distinction must be made between criminal proceedings, where apparently they accept that a *jus cogens* rule has the overriding force to deprive the rules of sovereign immunity from their legal effects, and civil proceedings, where, in the absence of authority, they consider that the same conclusion cannot be drawn. Their position is well summarised in paragraph 66 of the judgment, where they assert that they do not find it established that "there is yet acceptance in international law of the proposition that States are not entitled to immunity in respect of civil claims for damages for alleged torture committed outside the forum State". Hence, "[t]he 1978 Act, which grants immunity to States in respect of personal injury claims not inconsistent with those limitations generally accepted by the community of nations as part of the doctrine of State immunity".

In our opinion, the distinction made by the majority and their conclusions are defective on two opinion grounds.

Firstly, the English courts, when dealing with the applicant's claim, never resorted to the distinction made by the majority. They never invoked any difference between criminal charges or civil claims, between criminal and civil proceedings, in so far as the legal force of the rules on State immunity or the applicability of the 1978 Act was concerned. The basic position of the Court of Appeal – the last court which dealt with the matter in its essence – is expressed by the observations of Lord Justice Stuart-Smith who simply denied that the prohibition of torture was a *jus cogens* rule. In reading the Lord Justice's observations, one even forms the impression that if the Court of Appeal had been convinced that the rule of prohibition of torture was a norm of *jus cogens*, they could grudgingly have admitted that the procedural bar of State immunity did not apply in the circumstances of the case.

Secondly, the distinction made by the majority between civil and criminal proceedings, concerning the effect of the rule of the prohibition of torture, is not consonant with the very essence of the operation of the *jus cogens* rules. It is not the nature of the proceedings which determines the effects that a *jus cogens* rule has upon another rule of international law, but the character of the rule as a peremptory norm and its interaction with a hierarchically lower rule. The prohibition of torture, being a rule of *jus cogens*, acts in the international sphere and deprives the rule of sovereign immunity of all its legal effects in that sphere. The criminal or civil nature of the domestic proceedings is immaterial. The jurisdictional bar is lifted by the very interaction of the international rules involved, and the national judge cannot admit a plea of immunity raised by the defendant State as an element preventing him from entering into the merits of the case and from dealing with the claim of the applicant for the alleged damages inflicted upon him.

Under these circumstances we believe that the English courts have erred in considering that they had no jurisdiction to entertain the applicant's claim because of the procedural bar of State immunity and the consequent application of the 1978 Act. Accordingly, the applicant was deprived of his right to have access to the English court to entertain his claim of damages for the alleged torture suffered by him in Kuwait, and Article 6 §1, has, in our view, been violated.

~

QUESTIONS & COMMENTS

(1) Do you find the Court's analysis convincing? Consider the following questions. Does the *jus cogens* prohibition of torture include the victim's right to compensation from a state? If so, does this right extend to seeking redress through national courts? If so, does this further right extend to *any* national court? If state immunity from damages is available in courts of a state where the torture did not take place, what reasons does the European Court of Human Rights give?

(2) Do you find the dissenting opinion convincing?

(3) The defense of head of state or official immunity generally is not available before international criminal courts. In cases of gross human rights/humanitarian law violations, this immunity is not available because such violations far exceed ordinary domestic crimes. *See, e.g.,* Art. 31, Vienna Convention on Diplomatic Relations, 500 U.N.T.S. 95, adopted 18 April 1961 (entered into force 24 April 1964). Most importantly, these violations break both customary international law and *jus cogens*. Accordingly, any domestic law or treaty providing such immunity would be invalid. However, in the following case, consider how the ICJ differentiates between immunity from domestic criminal jurisdiction and impunity.

Case Concerning Arrest Warrant of 11 April 2000
(Democratic Republic of Congo v. Belgium)
International Court of Justice
[2002] ICJ 1 (14 February 2002)

[In this case, a Belgian investigating magistrate issued "an international arrest warrant in absentia" against the incumbent Minister for Foreign Affairs of the Congo, alleging grave breaches of the Geneva Conventions of 1949 and of its Additional Protocols, and crimes against humanity. The warrant was circulated through Interpol. The Congolese Minister of Foreign Affairs subsequently left the office.]

. . . .

51. The Court would observe at the outset that in international law it is firmly established that, as also diplomatic and consular agents, certain holders of high-ranking office in a State, such as the Head of State, Head of Government and Minister for Foreign Affairs, enjoy immunities from jurisdiction in other States, both civil and criminal. For the purposes of the present case, it is only the immunity from criminal jurisdiction and

the inviolability of an incumbent Minister for Foreign Affairs that fall for the Court to consider.

52. A certain number of treaty instruments were cited by the Parties in this regard. These included, first, the Vienna Convention on Diplomatic Relations of 18 April 1961, which states in its preamble that the purpose of diplomatic privileges and immunities is "to ensure the efficient performance of the functions of diplomatic missions as representing States". It provides in Article 32 that only the sending State may waive such immunity. On these points, the Vienna Convention on Diplomatic Relations, to which both the Congo and Belgium are parties, reflects customary international law. The same applies to the corresponding provisions of the Vienna Convention on Consular Relations of 24 April 1963, to which the Congo and Belgium are also parties.

. . . .

53. In customary international law, the immunities accorded to Ministers for Foreign Affairs are not granted for their personal benefit, but to ensure the effective performance of their functions on behalf of their respective States. In order to determine the extent of these immunities, the Court must therefore first consider the nature of the functions exercised by a Minister for Foreign Affairs. He or she is in charge of his or her Government's diplomatic activities and generally acts as its representative in international negotiations and intergovernmental meetings. Ambassadors and other diplomatic agents carry out their duties under his or her authority. His or her acts may bind the State represented, and there is a presumption that a Minister for Foreign Affairs, simply by virtue of that office, has full powers to act on behalf of the State (see, *e.g.*, Art. 7, para. 2 *(a)*, of the 1969 Vienna Convention on the Law of Treaties). In the performance of these functions, he or she is frequently required to travel internationally, and thus must be in a position freely to do so whenever the need should arise. He or she must also be in constant communication with the Government, and with its diplomatic missions around the world, and be capable at any time of communicating with representatives of other States. The Court further observes that a Minister for Foreign Affairs, responsible for the conduct of his or her State's relations with all other States, occupies a position such that, like the Head of State or the Head of Government, he or she is recognized under international law as representative of the State solely by virtue of his or her office. He or she does not have to present letters of credence: to the contrary, it is generally the Minister who determines the authority to be conferred upon diplomatic agents and countersigns their letters of credence. Finally, it is to the Minister for Foreign Affairs that *chargés d'affaires* are accredited.

54. The Court accordingly concludes that the functions of a Minister for Foreign Affairs are such that, throughout the duration of his or her office, he or she when abroad enjoys full immunity from criminal jurisdiction and inviolability. That immunity and that inviolability protect the individual concerned against any act of authority of another State which would hinder him or her in the performance of his or her duties.

55. In this respect, no distinction can be drawn between acts performed by a Minister for Foreign Affairs in an "official" capacity, and those claimed to have been performed in a "private capacity", or, for that matter, between acts performed before the person concerned assumed office as Minister for Foreign Affairs and acts committed during the period of office. Thus, if a Minister for Foreign Affairs is arrested in another State on a criminal charge, he or she is clearly thereby prevented from exercising the functions of his or her office. The consequences of such impediment to the exercise of those official

functions are equally serious, regardless of whether the Minister for Foreign Affairs was, at the time of arrest, present in the territory of the arresting State on an

> "official" visit or a "private" visit, regardless of whether the arrest relates to acts allegedly performed before the person became the Minister for Foreign Affairs or to acts performed while in office, and regardless of whether the arrest relates to alleged acts performed in an "official"

capacity or a "private" capacity. Furthermore, even the mere risk that, by travelling to or transiting another State a Minister for Foreign Affairs might be exposing himself or herself to legal proceedings could deter the Minister from travelling internationally when required to do so for the purposes of the performance of his or her official functions.

....

56. The Court will now address Belgium's argument that immunities accorded to incumbent Ministers for Foreign Affairs can in no case protect them where they are suspected of having committed war crimes or crimes against humanity. In support of this position, Belgium refers in its Counter-Memorial to various legal instruments creating international criminal tribunals, to examples from national legislation, and to the jurisprudence of national and international courts.

Belgium begins by pointing out that certain provisions of the instruments creating international criminal tribunals state expressly that the official capacity of a person shall not be a bar to the exercise by such tribunals of their jurisdiction.

Belgium also places emphasis on certain decisions of national courts, and in particular on the judgments rendered on 24 March 1999 by the House of Lords in the United Kingdom and on 13 March 2001 by the Court of Cassation in France in the *Pinochet* and *Qaddafi* cases respectively, in which it contends that an exception to the immunity rule was accepted in the case of serious crimes under international law. Thus, according to Belgium, the *Pinochet* decision recognizes an exception to the immunity rule when Lord Millett stated that "[i]nternational law cannot be supposed to have established a crime having the character of a *jus cogens* and at the same time to have provided an immunity which is co-extensive with the obligation it seeks to impose", or when Lord Phillips of Worth Matravers said that "no established rule of international law requires state immunity *rationae materiae* to be accorded in respect of prosecution for an international crime". As to the French Court of Cassation, Belgium contends that, in holding that, "under international law as it currently stands, the crime alleged [acts of terrorism], irrespective of its gravity, does not come within the exceptions to the principle of immunity from jurisdiction for incumbent foreign Heads of State", the Court explicitly recognized the existence of such exceptions.

57. The Congo, for its part, states that, under international law as it currently stands, there is no basis for asserting that there is any exception to the principle of absolute immunity from criminal process of an incumbent Minister for Foreign Affairs where he or she is accused of having committed crimes under international law.

In support of this contention, the Congo refers to State practice, giving particular consideration in this regard to the *Pinochet* and *Qaddafi* cases, and concluding that such practice does not correspond to that which Belgium claims but, on the contrary, confirms the absolute nature of the immunity from criminal process of Heads of State and Ministers for Foreign Affairs. Thus, in the *Pinochet* case, the Congo cites Lord Browne-Wilkinson's statement that "[t]his immunity enjoyed by a head of state in power and an ambassador in post is a complete immunity attached to the person of the head of state or ambassador and rendering him immune from all actions or prosecutions . . . ". According to the Congo, the French Court of Cassation adopted the same position in its *Qaddafi* judgment, in affirming that "international custom bars the prosecution of incumbent Heads of State, in the absence of any contrary international provision binding on the parties concerned, before the criminal courts of a foreign State".

As regards the instruments creating international criminal tribunals and the latter's jurisprudence, these, in the Congo's view, concern only those tribunals, and no inference can be drawn from them in regard to criminal proceedings before national courts against persons enjoying immunity under international law.

. . . .

58. The Court has carefully examined State practice, including national legislation and those few decisions of national higher courts, such as the House of Lords or the French Court of Cassation. It has been unable to deduce from this practice that there exists under customary international law any form of exception to the rule according immunity from criminal jurisdiction and inviolability to incumbent Ministers for Foreign Affairs, where they are suspected of having committed war crimes or crimes against humanity.

The Court has also examined the rules concerning the immunity or criminal responsibility of persons having an official capacity contained in the legal instruments creating international criminal tribunals, and which are specifically applicable to the latter (see Charter of the International Military Tribunal of Nuremberg, Art. 7; Charter of the International Military Tribunal of Tokyo, Art. 6; Statute of the International Criminal Tribunal for the former Yugoslavia, Art. 7, para. 2; Statute of the International Criminal Tribunal for Rwanda, Art. 6, para. 2; Statute of the International Criminal Court, Art. 27). It finds that these rules likewise do not enable it to conclude that any such an exception exists in customary international law in regard to national courts.

Finally, none of the decisions of the Nuremberg and Tokyo international military tribunals, or of the International Criminal Tribunal for the former Yugoslavia, cited by Belgium deal with the question of the immunities of incumbent Ministers for Foreign Affairs before national courts where they are accused of having committed war crimes or crimes against humanity. The Court accordingly notes that those decisions are in no way at variance with the findings it has reached above.

In view of the foregoing, the Court accordingly cannot accept Belgium's argument in this regard.

59. It should further be noted that the rules governing the jurisdiction of national courts must be carefully distinguished from those governing jurisdictional immunities: jurisdiction does not imply absence of immunity, while absence of immunity does not imply jurisdiction. Thus, although various international conventions on the prevention and punishment of certain serious crimes impose on States obligations of prosecution or extradition, thereby requiring them to extend their criminal jurisdiction, such extension of jurisdiction in no way affects immunities under customary international law, including those of Ministers for Foreign Affairs. These remain opposable before the courts of a foreign State, even where those courts exercise such a jurisdiction under these conventions.

60. The Court emphasizes, however, that the *immunity* from jurisdiction enjoyed by incumbent Ministers for Foreign Affairs does not mean that they enjoy *impunity* in respect of any crimes they might have committed, irrespective of their gravity. Immunity from criminal jurisdiction and individual criminal responsibility are quite separate concepts.

While jurisdictional immunity is procedural in nature, criminal responsibility is a question of substantive law. Jurisdictional immunity may well bar prosecution for a certain period or for certain offences; it cannot exonerate the person to whom it applies from all criminal responsibility.

61. Accordingly, the immunities enjoyed under international law by an incumbent or former Minister for Foreign Affairs do not represent a bar to criminal prosecution in certain circumstances.

First, such persons enjoy no criminal immunity under international law in their own countries, and may thus be tried by those countries' courts in accordance with the relevant rules of domestic law.

Secondly, they will cease to enjoy immunity from foreign jurisdiction if the State which they represent or have represented decides to waive that immunity.

Thirdly, after a person ceases to hold the office of Minister for Foreign Affairs, he or she will no longer enjoy all of the immunities accorded by international law in other States. Provided that it has jurisdiction under international law, a court of one State may try a former Minister for Foreign Affairs of another State in respect of acts committed prior or subsequent to his or her period of office, as well as in respect of acts committed during that period of office in a private capacity.

Fourthly, an incumbent or former Minister for Foreign Affairs may be subject to criminal proceedings before certain international criminal courts, where they have jurisdiction. Examples include the International Criminal Tribunal for the former Yugoslavia, and the International Criminal Tribunal for Rwanda, established pursuant to Security Council resolutions under Chapter VII of the United Nations Charter, and the future International Criminal Court created by the 1998 Rome Convention. The latter's Statute expressly provides, in Article 27, paragraph 2, that

> [i]mmunities or special procedural rules which may attach to the official capacity of a person, whether under national or international law, shall not bar the Court from exercising its jurisdiction over such a person.

. . . .

[The Court concluded that the circulation of the warrant violated the incumbent Congolese Minister of Foreign Affairs' immunity from criminal jurisdiction guaranteed by international law.]

∼

QUESTIONS & COMMENTS

(1) Would not the *jus cogens* prohibition of such international crimes trump the customary international law of head of state (or foreign minister) immunity in the same way as the dissenting opinion in *Al-Adsani v. United Kingdom* argued in regard to the *jus cogens* prohibition of torture trumping the customary international law of state immunity? Or, is the ICJ in *DRC v. Belgium* and the European Court of Human Rights in *Al-Adsani v. United Kingdom* effectively arguing, respectively, that state immunity and head of state (or foreign minister) immunity are *jus cogens* norms? If so, did the *jus cogens* prohibitions of torture and genocide emerge after the *jus cogens* norms of state immunity and head of state immunity? If so, would not the newer *jus cogens*

prohibitions of genocide and torture replace the older *jus cogens* norms of immunity, as Article 53 of the Vienna Convention on the Law of Treaties states (*jus cogens* norm "can be modified only by a subsequent norm of general international law having the same character")?

(2) The Genocide Convention (arts. V–VII) requires its states parties to extradite and punish persons perpetrating acts of genocide. Do these articles have the status of *jus cogens*?

Combat Immunity

Geneva Convention (III) relative to the Protection of Prisoners of War

Article 87

Prisoners of war may not be sentenced by the military authorities and courts of the Detaining Power to any penalties except those provided for in respect of members of the armed forces of the said Power who have committed the same acts.

. . . .

Article 99

No prisoner of war may be tried or sentenced for an act which is not forbidden by the law of the Detaining Power or by international law, in force at the time the said act was committed.

Article 4

A. Prisoners of war, in the sense of the present Convention, are persons belonging to one of the following categories, who have fallen into the power of the enemy:

(1) Members of the armed forces of a Party to the conflict as well as members of militias or volunteer corps forming part of such armed forces.

(2) Members of other militias and members of other volunteer corps, incuding those of organized resistance movements, belonging to a Party to the conflict and operating in or outside their own territory, even if this territory is occupied, provided that such militias or volunteer corps, including such organized resistance movements, fulfil the following conditions:

(a) that of being commanded by a person responsible for his subordinates;

(b) that of having a fixed distinctive sign recognizable at a distance;

(c) that of carrying arms openly;

(d) that of conducting their operations in accordance with the laws and customs of war.

(3) Members of regular armed forces who profess allegiance to a government or an authority not recognized by the Detaining Power.

(4) Persons who accompany the armed forces without actually being members thereof, such as civilian members of military aircraft crews, war correspondents, supply contractors, members of labour units or of services responsible for the welfare of the armed forces, provided that they have received authorization from the armed forces which they accompany, who shall provide them for that purpose with an identity card similar to the annexed model.

(5) Members of crews, including masters, pilots and apprentices, of the merchant marine and the crews of civil aircraft of the Parties to the conflict, who do not benefit by more favourable treatment under any other provisions of international law.

(6) Inhabitants of a non-occupied territory, who on the approach of the enemy spontaneously take up arms to resist the invading forces, without having had time to form themselves into regular armed units, provided they carry arms openly and respect the laws and customs of war.

B. The following shall likewise be treated as prisoners of war under the present Convention:

(1) Persons belonging, or having belonged, to the armed forces of the occupied country, if the occupying Power considers it necessary by reason of such allegiance to intern them, even though it has originally liberated them while hostilities were going on outside the territory it occupies, in particular where such persons have made an unsuccessful attempt to rejoin the armed forces to which they belong and which are engaged in combat, or where they fail to comply with a summons made to them with a view to internment.

(2) The persons belonging to one of the categories enumerated in the present Article, who have been received by neutral or non-belligerent Powers on their territory and whom these Powers are required to intern under international law, without prejudice to any more favourable treatment which these Powers may choose to give and with the exception of Articles 8, 10, 15, 30, fifth paragraph, 58–67, 92, 126 and, where diplomatic relations exist between the Parties to the conflict and the neutral or non-belligerent Power concerned, those Articles concerning the Protecting Power. Where such diplomatic relations exist, the Parties to a conflict on whom these persons depend shall be allowed to perform towards them the functions of a Protecting Power as provided in the present Convention, without prejudice to the functions which these Parties normally exercise in conformity with diplomatic and consular usage and treaties.

. . . .

Protocol Additional to the Geneva Conventions of 12 August 1949, and Relating to the Protection of Victims of International Armed Conflicts (Protocol I)

SECTION II.-COMBATANT AND PRISONER-OF-WAR STATUS

Article 43.-Armed forces

1. The armed forces of a Party to a conflict consist of all organized armed forces, groups and units which are under a command responsible to that Party for the conduct of its subordinates, even if that Party is represented by a government or an authority not recognized by an adverse Party. Such armed forces shall be subject to an internal disciplinary system which, inter alia, shall enforce compliance with the rules of international law applicable in armed conflict.

2. Members of the armed forces of a Party to a conflict (other than medical personnel and chaplains covered by Article 33 of the Third Convention) are combatants, that is to say, they have the right to participate directly in hostilities.

3. Whenever a Party to a conflict incorporates a paramilitary or armed law enforcement agency into its armed forces it shall so notify the other Parties to the conflict.

Article 44.-Combatants and prisoners of war

1. Any combatant, as defined in Article 43, who falls into the power of an adverse Party shall be a prisoner of war.

2. While all combatants are obliged to comply with the rules of international law applicable in armed conflict, violations of these rules shall not deprive a combatant of his right to be a combatant or, if he falls into the power of an adverse Party, of his right to be a prisoner of war, except as provided in paragraphs 3 and 4.

3. In order to promote the protection of the civilian population from the effects of hostilities, combatants are obliged to distinguish themselves from the civilian population while they are engaged in an attack or in a military operation preparatory to an attack. Recognizing, however, that there are situations in armed conflicts where, owing to the nature of the hostilities an armed combatant cannot so distinguish himself, he shall retain his status as a combatant, provided that, in such situations, he carries his arms openly:

    (a) During each military engagement, and

    (b) During such time as he is visible to the adversary while he is engaged in a military deployment preceding the launching of an attack in which he is to participate.

Acts which comply with the requirements of this paragraph shall not be considered as perfidious within the meaning of Article 37, paragraph 1 (c).[1]

4. A combatant who falls into the power of an adverse Party while failing to meet the requirements set forth in the second sentence of paragraph 3 shall forfeit his right to be a prisoner of war, but he shall, nevertheless, be given protections equivalent in all respects to those accorded to prisoners of war by the Third Convention and by this Protocol. This protection includes protections equivalent to those accorded to prisoners of war by the Third Convention in the case where such a person is tried and punished for any offences he has committed.

5. Any combatant who falls into the power of an adverse Party while not engaged in an attack or in a military operation preparatory to an attack shall not forfeit his rights to be a combatant and a prisoner of war by virtue of his prior activities.

6. This Article is without prejudice to the right of any person to be a prisoner of war pursuant to Article 4 of the Third Convention.

7. This Article is not intended to change the generally accepted practice of States with respect to the wearing of the uniform by combatants assigned to the regular, uniformed armed units of a Party to the conflict.

8. In addition to the categories of persons mentioned in Article 13 of the First and Second Conventions, all members of the armed forces of a Party to the conflict, as defined in Article 43 of this Protocol, shall be entitled to protection under those Conventions if they are wounded or sick or, in the case of the Second Convention, shipwrecked at sea or in other waters.

---

[1] [*Viz.*, The feigning of civilian, non-combatant status. Ed.'s Note.]

Article 45.-Protection of persons who have taken part in hostilities

1. A person who takes part in hostilities and falls into the power of an adverse Party shall be presumed to be a prisoner of war, and therefore shall be protected by the Third Convention, if he claims the status of prisoner of war, or if he appears to be entitled to such status, or if the Party on which he depends claims such status on his behalf by notification to the detaining Power or to the Protecting Power. Should any doubt arise as to whether any such person is entitled to the status of prisoner of war, he shall continue to have such status and, therefore, to be protected by the Third Convention and this Protocol until such time as his status has been determined by a competent tribunal.

2. If a person who has fallen into the power of an adverse Party is not held as a prisoner of war and is to be tried by that Party for an offence arising out of the hostilities, he shall have the right to assert his entitlement to prisoner-of-war status before a judicial tribunal and to have that question adjudicated. Whenever possible under the applicable procedure, this adjudication shall occur before the trial for the offence. The representatives of the Protecting Power shall be entitled to attend the proceedings in which that question is adjudicated, unless, exceptionally, the proceedings are held in camera in the interest of State security. In such a case the detaining Power shall advise the Protecting Power accordingly.

3. Any person who has taken part in hostilities, who is not entitled to prisoner-of-war status and who does not benefit from more favourable treatment in accordance with the Fourth Convention shall have the right at all times to the protection of Article 75 of this Protocol. In occupied territory, an such person, unless he is held as a spy, shall also be entitled, notwithstanding Article 5 of the Fourth Convention, to his rights of communication under that Convention.

Article 46.-Spies

1. Notwithstanding any other provision of the Conventions or of this Protocol, any member of the armed forces of a Party to the conflict who falls into the power of an adverse Party while engaging in espionage shall not have the right to the status of prisoner of war and may be treated as a spy.

2. A member of the armed forces of a Party to the conflict who, on behalf of that Party and in territory controlled by an adverse Party, gathers or attempts to gather information shall not be considered as engaging in espionage if, while so acting, he is in the uniform of his armed forces.

3. A member of the armed forces of a Party to the conflict who is a resident of territory occupied by an adverse Party and who, on behalf of the Party on which he depends, gathers or attempts to gather information of military value within that territory shall not be considered as engaging in espionage unless he does so through an act of false pretences or deliberately in a clandestine manner. Moreover, such a resident shall not lose his right to the status of prisoner of war and may not be treated as a spy unless he is captured while engaging in espionage.

4. A member of the armed forces of a Patty to the conflict who is not a resident of territory occupied by an adverse Party and who has engaged in espionage in that territory shall not lose his right to the status of prisoner of war and may not be treated as a spy unless he is captured before he has rejoined the armed forces to which he belongs.

Article 47.-Mercenaries

1. A mercenary shall not have the right to be a combatant or a prisoner of war.

2. A mercenary is any person who:

(a) Is specially recruited locally or abroad in order to fight in an armed conflict;

(b) Does, in fact, take a direct part in the hostilities;

(c) Is motivated to take part in the hostilities essentially by the desire for private gain and, in fact, is promised, by or on behalf of a Party to the conflict, material compensation substantially in excess of that promised or paid to combatants of similar ranks and functions in the armed forces of that Party;

(d) Is neither a national of a Party to the conflict nor a resident of territory controlled by a Party to the conflict;

(e) Is not a member of the armed forces of a Party to the conflict; and

(f) Has not been sent by a State which is not a Party to the conflict on official duty as a member of its armed forces.

QUESTIONS & COMMENTS

(1) Would members of the Taliban receive combat immunity under the Third Geneva Convention? What about Protocol I?

Superior Orders, Coercion, and Duress

In re Ohlendorf and Others (Einsatzgruppen Case)
U.S. Military Tribunal at Nuremberg
15 I.L.R. 656 (1948)

[The defendants, twenty-four members of the SS *Einsatzgruppen* (mobile killing units), were charged with crimes against humanity, war crimes, and membership in a criminal organization for the murder and mistreatment of PoWs and civilians in German-occupied countries during World War II. All twenty-four defendants were found guilty of at least one charge.]

. . . .

Those of the defendants who admit participation in the mass killings which are the subject of this trial, plead that they were under military orders and, therefore, had no will of their own. As intent is a basic prerequisite to responsibility for crime, they argue that they are innocent of criminality since they performed the admitted executions under duress, that is to say, superior orders. The defendants formed part of a military organization and were, therefore, subject to the rules which govern soldiers. It is axiomatic that a military man's first duty is to obey. If the defendants were soldiers and as soldiers responded to the command of their superiors to kill certain people, how can they be held guilty of crime? This is the question posed by the defendants. The answer is not a difficult one.

The obedience of a soldier is not the obedience of an automaton. A soldier is a reasoning agent. He does not respond, and is not expected to respond, like a piece of machinery. It is a fallacy of wide-spread consumption that a soldier is required to do everything his superior officer orders him to do. A very simple illustration will show to what absurd extreme such a theory could be carried. If every military person were required, regardless of the nature of the command, to obey unconditionally, a sergeant could order the corporal to shoot the lieutenant, the lieutenant could order the sergeant to shoot the captain, the captain could order the lieutenant to shoot the colonel, and in each instance the executioner would be absolved of blame. The mere statement of such a proposition is its own commentary. The fact that a soldier may not, without incurring unfavorable consequences, refuse to drill, salute, exercise, reconnoiter, and even go into battle, does not mean that he must fulfill every demand put to him. In the first place, an order to require obedience must relate to military duty. An officer may not demand of a soldier, for instance, that he steal for him. And what the superior officer may not militarily demand of his subordinate, the subordinate is not required to do. Even if the order refers to a military subject it must be one which the superior is authorized, under the circumstances, to give. The subordinate is bound only to obey the lawful orders of his superior and if he accepts a criminal order and executes it with a malice of his own, he may not plead superior orders in mitigation of his offense. If the nature of the ordered act is manifestly beyond the scope of the superior's authority, the subordinate may not plead ignorance to the criminality of the order. If one claims duress in the execution of an illegal order it must be shown that the harm caused by obeying the illegal order is not disproportionally greater than the harm which would result from not obeying the illegal order. It would not be an adequate excuse, for example, if a subordinate, under orders, killed a person known to be innocent, because by not obeying it he himself would risk a few days of confinement. Nor if one acts under duress, may he, without culpability, commit the illegal act once the duress ceases.

The International Military Tribunal, in speaking of the principle to be applied in the interpretation of criminal superior orders, declared that –

"The true test, which is found in varying degrees in the criminal law of most nations, is not the existence of the order, but whether moral choice was in fact possible."

The Prussian Military Code, as far back as 1845, recognized this principle of moral choice when it stated that a subordinate would be punished if, in the execution of an order, he went beyond its scope or if he executed an order knowing that it "related to an act which obviously aimed at a crime".

This provision was copied into the Military Penal Code of the Kingdom of Saxony in 1867, and of Baden in 1870. Continuing and even extending the doctrine of conditional obedience, the Bavarian Military Penal Code of 1869 went so far as to establish the responsibility of the subordinate as the rule, and his irresponsibility as the exception.

The Military Penal Code of the Austro-Hungarian Monarchy of 1855 provided –

Article 158. "A subordinate who does not carry out an order is not guilty of a violation of his duty of subordination if (*a*) the order is obviously contrary to loyalty due to the Prince of the Land; (*b*) if the order pertains to an act or omission in which evidently a crime or an offense is to be recognized."

In 1872 Bismarck attempted to delimit subordinate responsibility by legislation, but the Reichstag rejected his proposal and instead adopted the following as Article 47 of the German Military Penal Code:

Article 47. "If through the execution of an order pertaining to the service, a penal law is violated, then the superior giving the order is alone responsible. However, the obeying sub-[. . . ordinate] shall be punished as accomplice (1) if he went beyond the order given to him, or (2) if he knew that the order of the superior concerned an act which aimed at a civil or military crime or offense."

This law was never changed, except to broaden its scope by changing the word "civil" to "general", and as late as 1940 one of the leading commentators of the Nazi period, Professor Schwinge wrote –

"Hence, *in military life,* just as in other fields, *the principle of absolute, i.e., blind obedience, does not exist.*"

 . . . .

Superior Orders Defense Must Establish Ignorance of Illegality

To plead superior orders one must show an excusable ignorance of their illegality. The sailor who voluntarily ships on a pirate craft may not be heard to answer that he was ignorant of the probability he would be called upon to help in the robbing and sinking of other vessels. He who willingly joins an illegal enterprise is charged with the natural development of that unlawful undertaking. What SS man could say that he was unaware of the attitude of Hitler toward Jewry?

 . . . .

Duress Needed for Plea of Superior Orders

But it is stated that in military law even if the subordinate realizes that the act he is called upon to perform is a crime, he may not refuse its execution without incurring serious consequences, and that this, therefore, constitutes duress. Let it be said at once that there is no law which requires that an innocent man must forfeit his life or suffer serious harm in order to avoid committing a crime which he condemns. The threat, however, must be imminent, real, and inevitable. No court will punish a man who, with a loaded pistol at his head, is compelled to pull a lethal lever. Nor need the peril be that imminent in order to escape punishment. But were any of the defendants coerced into killing Jews under the threat of being killed themselves if they failed in their homicidal mission? The test to be applied is whether the subordinate acted under coercion or whether he himself approved of the principle involved in the order. If the second proposition be true, the plea of superior orders fails. The doer may not plead innocence to a criminal act ordered by his superior if he is in accord with the principle and intent of the superior. When the will of the doer merges with the will of the superior in the execution of the illegal act, the doer may not plead duress under superior orders.

If the mental and moral capacities of the superior and subordinate are pooled in the planning and execution of an illegal act, the subordinate may not subsequently protest that he was forced into the performance of an illegal undertaking.

Superior means superior in capacity and power to force a certain act. It does not mean superiority only in rank. It could easily happen in an illegal enterprise that the captain guides the major, in which case the captain could not be heard to plead superior orders in defense of his crime.

If the cognizance of the doer has been such, prior to the receipt of the illegal order, that the order is obviously but one further logical step in the development of a program which he knew to be illegal in its very inception, he may not excuse himself from responsibility for an illegal act which could have been foreseen by the application of the simple law of cause and effect. From 1920, when the Nazi Party program with its anti-Semitic policy was published, until 1941 when the liquidation order went into effect, the ever-mounting severity of Jewish persecution was evident to all within the Party and especially to those charged with its execution. One who participated in that program which began with Jewish disenfranchisement and depatriation and led, step by step, to deprivation of property and liberty, followed with beatings, whippings, and measures aimed at starvation, may not plead surprise when he learns that what has been done sporadically; namely, murder, now is officially declared policy. On 30 January 1939, Hitler publicly declared in a speech to the Reichstag that if war should come it would mean "the obliteration of the Jewish race in Europe". One who embarks on a criminal enterprise of obvious magnitude is expected to anticipate what the enterprise will logically lead to. In order successfully to plead the defense of superior orders the opposition of the doer must be constant. It is not enough that he mentally rebel at the time the order is received. If at any time after receiving the order he acquiesces in its illegal character, the defense of superior orders is closed to him.

. . . .

~

QUESTIONS & COMMENTS

(1) Three related viable defenses are those of superior orders, coercion, and duress. The defense of superior orders is also known as "the Nuremberg defense" in which the offender claims that she or he was just following orders and, thereby, is excused. After the *Einsatzgruppen Case*, this defense also was rejected by the IMT in *Matter of Von Leeb and Others (German High Command Trial)*, 15 I.L.R. 376 (1949), 11 Trials of War Criminals (1950). However, this defense may be viable in certain circumstances. For example, the defense of duress may provide a partial defense "only by way of mitigation" in cases where the defendant faced a real risk that she or he would face execution had she or he disobeyed an order. *See The Prosecutor v. Erdemovic*, Int'l Crim. Trib.-Yugo., Appeals Chamber (5 March 1998), *reported in* Int'l Crim. Trib.-Yugo. 20 *Bulletin* 2 (20 March 1998).

Other Viable and Nonviable Defenses

There are a number of other viable and nonviable defenses. For example, self-defense and the defense of others can be aspects of the coercion defense, discussed in the *Einsatzgruppen Case*. Again, to plea such defenses successfully, one must show that the criminal act was proportional and the harm to oneself or others was imminent, real, and inevitable. *See* ICC Statute, art. 31.

Nonviable defenses include double jeopardy between two sovereigns and *tu quoque*. The defense of double jeopardy between two sovereigns refers to the prosecution of the same crime by different sovereigns. The *tu quoque* ("you also") defense refers to the prosecution of offenders by persons/states that also have committed the same crimes. The IMT held that this defense was not valid in *Matter of Von Leeb and*

Others (German High Command Trial). 15 I.L.R. 376 (1949), 11 Trials of War Criminals (1950).

Amnesty laws have posed an obstacle to punishment and/or to accountability – although amnesty laws have been justified by some commentators as necessary for preventing *further* human rights violations. Some have argued that such a consideration is a legitimate and lawful concern for determining punishment or accountability. Many countries[1] have used amnesty laws to induce repressive regimes and rebel groups to achieve political stability and stop committing human rights violations, but amnesty laws violate states' international law obligations by preventing individuals from exercising their right to a remedy that includes the investigation and prosecution of persons responsible for human rights violations. All of the major human rights treaties require states to "respect and ensure" against violations of protected rights[2] and require states to provide effective remedies for their violation.[3] The repetition and consistency of these obligations create a strong presumption that states also have a customary law obligation to provide remedies for human rights violations. Accordingly, governments over the past fifty years have compromised by providing amnesty in conjunction with truth or investigatory

---

[1] States that have enacted such amnesty laws include Argentina, Brazil, Chile, Czech and Slovak Republics, El Salvador, France, Hungary, Italy, Nicaragua, Portugal, Russia, South Africa, South Korea, Spain, Uruguay, and Zimbabwe. Fauzia Shariff, *Comparative Chart on the Use of Amnesty Legislation, Truth Commissions and Compensation Mechanisms*, 10 INTERIGHTS BULLETIN 96–98 (1996).

[2] Art. 2(1), ICCPR ("[e]ach State Party to the present Covenant undertakes to respect and ensure to all individuals within its territory and subject to its jurisdiction the rights recognized in the present Covenant . . . "); Art. 1(1), ACHR ("[t]he States Parties to this Convention undertake to respect the rights and freedoms recognized herein and to ensure to all persons subject to their jurisdiction the free and full exercise of those rights and freedoms . . . "); Art. 13, ECHR ("[t]he High Contracting Parties shall secure to everyone within their jurisdiction the rights and freedoms defined in Section I of this Convention").

[3] Article 8, Universal Declaration of Human Rights, G.A. Res. 217 (III), U.N. Doc. A/810, at 71 (1948), states:

> [e]veryone has the right to an effective remedy by the competent national tribunals for acts violating the fundamental rights granted him by the constitution or by law.

Article 2(3), ICCPR, states:

> Each State Party to the present Covenant undertakes:
> To ensure that any person whose rights or freedoms as herein recognized are violated shall have an effective remedy, notwithstanding that the violation has been committed by persons acting in an official capacity;
> To ensure that any person claiming such a remedy shall have his right thereto determined by competent judicial, administrative or legislative authorities, or by any other competent authority provided for by the legal system of the State, and to develop the possibilities of judicial remedy;
> To ensure that the competent authorities shall enforce such remedies when granted;

Article 25(1), ACHR, states:

> [e]veryone has the right to simple and prompt recourse, or any other effective recourse, to a competent court or other tribunal for protection against acts that violate his fundamental rights recognized by the constitution or laws of the state concerned or by this Convention, even though such violation may have been committed by persons acting in the course of their official duties.

Article 13, ECHR, states:

> [e]veryone whose rights and freedoms as set forth in this Convention are violated shall have an effective remedy before a national authority notwithstanding that a violation has been committed by persons acting in an official capacity.

commissions[4] and/or compensation.[5] Besides pecuniary compensation, some governments have provided credit grants, housing, and employment as part of a compensation
package.[6] Other mechanisms include the barring of former perpetrators of human rights
violations from quasi-state or state positions.[7]

These approaches have had mixed results. Most of these schemes have been unsatisfactory as a matter of both international law and political stability. Both the Inter-
American Commission of Human Rights and the UN Human Rights Committee have
found amnesty laws to be in conflict with states' international human rights obligations.
In reference to the prohibition of torture in Article 7 of the ICCPR, the Human Rights
Committee has expressed the view that "[a]mnesties are generally incompatible with
the duty of States to investigate [torture]; to guarantee freedom from such acts within
their jurisdiction; and to ensure that they do not occur in the future."[8] In examining the
amnesty laws of Argentina, El Salvador, and Uruguay, the Inter-American Commission
ruled that all three laws violated rights protected by the American Convention, including the obligation to investigate.[9] And, many of those countries – such as El Salvador,
Nicaragua, and Russia – that have enacted amnesty laws in conjunction with other mechanisms have failed to achieve political stability. Even die-hard advocates of *realpolitik*
recognize that there is "no peace without justice" in the long run: the long-term success
and stability of a successor government to a repressive regime must ensure individualized
justice that entails a right to remedies criminal, declarative, compensatory, and injunctive. With the recent establishment of the ICT-Y and ICT-R; the establishment of the
ICC; the Pinochet extradition and domestic prosecution by Spain, France, and Belgium;
the domestic prosecution of Fidel Castro by France; and the prosecution of the Khmer
Rouge leadership by Cambodia, the rule of international criminal law has acquired a very
real and considerable geopolitical force that can be brought to bear on both state and
nonstate powers.

Finally, it is important to note that U.S. courts have rejected the "political question"
defense to international crimes. *See, e.g., Abebe-Jira v. Negewo,* 72 F.3d 844, 848 (11th Cir.
1996); *Kadic v. Karadzic,* 70 F.3d 232, 249–50 (2d Cir. 1995). U.S. courts also have rejected

---

[4]   Truth or investigatory commissions have been used by Argentina, Brazil, Chad, Chile, El Salvador, Ethiopia,
      Germany, Hungary, Lithuania, Nicaragua, Philippines, South Africa, Uganda, and Zimbabwe. Shariff, *supra*,
      at n. 1.

[5]   Compensatory mechanisms have been used by Albania, Argentina, Bulgaria, Czech and Slovak Republics,
      Germany, Hungary, Lithuania, Russia, and South Africa. *Id.*

[6]   Bulgaria has such a package. *Id.*

[7]   The former Czechoslovakia enacted such a law in 1991.

[8]   General Comment 20, U.N. Doc. HRI/GEN/1/Rev.3 (1997), ¶ 15.

[9]   Report 28/92 (Argentina), ANNUAL REPORT OF THE INTER-AMERICAN COMMISSION ON HUMAN RIGHTS
      1992–1993, OEA, Ser.L/V/II/.83, Doc. 14, corr. 1 (12 March 1993), ¶ 50, (finding a violation of the right to
      a fair trial [Art. 8] and the right to judicial protection [Art. 25] "in relation to the obligation of the States to
      guarantee the full and free exercise of the rights recognized in the Convention [Art. 1.1]"); Report 26/92 (El
      Salvador), ANNUAL REPORT OF THE INTER-AMERICAN COMMISSION ON HUMAN RIGHTS 1992–1993, OEA,
      Ser.L/V/II/.83, Doc. 14, corr. 1 (12 March 1993) (finding a violation of the right to life [Art. 4], the right
      to personal security and integrity [Art. 5], the right to due process [Art. 8], and the right to due judicial
      protection [Art. 25]); Report 29/92 (Uruguay), ANNUAL REPORT OF THE INTER-AMERICAN COMMISSION
      ON HUMAN RIGHTS 1992–1993, OEA, Ser.L/V/II/.83, Doc. 14, corr. 1 (12 March 1993) (finding a violation
      of the right to a fair trial [Art. 8.1], the right to judicial protection [Art. 25], and the obligation to investigate
      [Art. 1.1]).

the "acts of state" defense. *See, e.g., Hilao v. Estate of Marcos*, 25 F.3d 1467, 1470–72 (9th Cir. 1994); *Kadic v. Karadzic*, 70 F.3d at 250.

In conclusion, consider the following quotation:

> Kill one person, they call you a murderer.
>
> Kill a dozen people, they call you serial killer.
>
> Kill a thousand people, and they invite you to a peace conference.
>
> – attributed to Haris Silajdzic

3. Incorporation of International Human Rights and Humanitarian Law in U.S. Law

U.S. Constitution

Article I, §8

The Congress shall have Power . . .

(10) To define and punish Piracies and Felonies committed on the high Seas, and Offences against the Law of Nations;

(11) To declare War, grant Letters of Marque and Reprisal, and make Rules concerning Captures on Land and Water. . . .

Article I, §10, cl. 1.

No State shall enter into any Treaty, Alliance, or Confederation; grant Letters of Marque and Reprisal. . . .

Article II, §2, cl. 2

[The President] shall have Power, by and with the Advice and Consent of the Senate, to make Treaties, provided two thirds of the Senators present concur. . . .

Article VI, cl. 2

This Constitution, and the Laws of the United States which shall be made in Pursuance thereof; and all Treaties made, or which shall be made, under the Authority of the United States, shall be the supreme Law of the Land; and the Judges in every State shall be bound thereby, any Thing in the Constitution or Laws of any State to the Contrary notwithstanding.

3.1. Construction Rules

In this section, we examine different rules for construing the Constitution, federal statutes, and state law in conformity with international law.

3.1.1. Constitutional Construction

In the following subsection, we examine different rules of construing U.S. constitutional provisions in conformity with the United States' international legal obligations as a means of incorporating international law.

3.1.1.1. Mandatory International Legal Construction Rule

Francisco Forrest Martin

Our Constitution as Federal Treaty: A New Theory of United States
Constitutional Construction
Based on an Originalist Understanding for Addressing a New World
31 Hastings Const. L. Quart. 258 (2004)[1]

Introduction

In the face of growing globalization, can our Constitution adequately address the forces of globalization that have been created by a host of recent technological and geopolitical developments? The effective erosion of national frontiers, the increasing interdependence of states, and the multiplication of multilateral approaches to global problems demand a construction of the Constitution that can respond to these new challenges – this New World. Our Constitution should be up to the task. After all, it originally was designed for a New World, albeit an earlier and somewhat different one.

Fortunately, the Constitution often is cast in general language that allows adaptability to new circumstances. However, such general language requires further definition, and properly construing the Constitution is of paramount importance for ensuring the Constitution's vitality when confronted with novel situations. In our present New World, construing the Constitution in conformity with international law would appear to enable the Constitution to meet the test of globalization because international law generally provides a uniformity of norms across frontiers. Also, because it has embedded values common to the global community, international law enables multilateral, integrated approaches to conflicts, catastrophes, and other challenges. However, most constitutional construction by the courts has been textually and nationally insular. Such a hermeneutic approach has hermetically sealed the Constitution from international law and mystified the Constitution's meaning.

To meet the challenges of this New World, I will propose a new paradigm of constitutional construction based on an originalist understanding of the Constitution.[2] This Article will argue that the Constitution is a federal treaty.[3] As a treaty, the Constitution

---

[1] [Many footnotes have been omitted. Ed.'s note.]

[2] By "an originalist understanding," I mean the public understanding of the Constitution's meaning around the time of its ratification as garnered from, e.g., the proceedings of the Continental Congress, Constitutional Convention, and state constitutional conventions; writings by the Founding Fathers (including the Federalist and Anti-Federalist Papers); speeches, resolutions, and laws from the early Congress; statements by the early Executive Branch; and early judicial opinions. See Keith Whittington, Constitutional Interpretation: Textual Meaning, Original Intent, and Judicial Review (2001) (discussing originalist theories). However, it is important to note that this Article departs from originalism when it fails to accept the Constitution's status as a treaty and its consequent legal implications as a treaty.

[3] During the Constitution's framing and ratification period, it was not controversial that the Constitution was a treaty. Only later during the 19th century nullification debate did a controversy emerge over whether the Constitution was a treaty. [ ] There are writings among early nineteenth century states' rights advocates and a modern foreign international jurist explicitly arguing that the Constitution was a "treaty." See, e.g., Congressional Resolution introduced by Pennsylvania (11 Jan. 1811) (drafted by Roane) (declaring Constitution "to all intents and purposes" was "a treaty among sovereign states"), in John Marshall's Defense of McCulloch v. Maryland 150 (Gerald Gunther ed., 1969); Torkel Opsahl, An "International Constitutional Law"? 10 Int'l. & Comp. L.Q. 760, 771 (1961) (Constitution was a treaty). However, there

must be construed in conformity with the United States' law of nations obligations – specifically those constituting customary international law. I will call this new theory "International Legal Constructionism [ILC]."

Although the Supreme Court has held that Congress is assumed to legislate in conformity with its international legal obligations and that ambiguous federal statutes must be construed in conformity with such obligations, few jurists have argued that the Constitution *should* be construed in conformity with the law of nations, and the U.S. Supreme Court also has cited international legal authorities in construing the Constitution. Even fewer have argued that the Constitution *must* be construed in conformity with the law of nations. None have provided a justification based on the Constitution's text for why the Constitution must be construed in conformity with the law of nations.

ILC has the advantage of providing a unique prescriptive methodology of constitutional construction that is derived inherently from the kind of legal instrument that the Constitution is (*viz.*, a federal treaty) and in whose text the Constitution is indicated as such.[4] ILC is truly "textualist" in both senses of the word. First, ILC is textualist in that it relies upon what the Constitution's text expressly *states*. Second, ILC is textualist in that it relies on what the Constitution as a text *is*.

It is this last sense of "textualist" that provides the prescriptive nexus between the Constitution and the use of extra-constitutional authorities for construing it that often is lacking in other theories of constitutional construction. When some theories do address the issue of what the Constitution is, such theories cannot show where in the Constitution's text that the Constitution says it is such. For example, Judge Bork (a textualist) has referred to the Constitution as a "social compact," but the Constitution never refers to itself as such. Of course, theories based on the "living Constitution" principle do rely upon the Constitution's text denoting it as a constitution, but such theories merely beg the question because such theories merely point out that the Constitution *qua* constitution must be construed in a fashion that constitutes the government of the United States. Such theories cannot show how the use of particular extra-constitutional authorities are required by the nature of the Constitution as a constitution and cannot show any text in the Constitution requiring the use of such authorities.

. . . .

1. The Formation of the United States and Eventual Establishment of the Constitution within the Context of an International Legal Process

To properly understand the formation of the United States and the eventual establishment of the Constitution, it is necessary to place them in the context of an international legal process that began with the Declaration of Independence. The Declaration of Independence (1776), Articles of Confederation (1778), and the Constitution (1788) are three

---

appears to be no literature explicitly referring to the Constitution as a "federal treaty." Furthermore, the writings of these early states rights advocates reflect incorrect conceptions of both the Constitution and the international law governing treaties. Most recently, a political scientist has argued that in view of the political circumstances facing the Founders, the Constitution could be viewed as a treaty-like arrangement. See DAVID C. HENDRICKSON, PEACE PACT: THE LOST WORLD OF THE AMERICAN FOUNDING (2003).

[4] *See* U.S. CONST. art. VII ("Constitution between the States").

different kinds of international legal instruments building upon the previous one in order to ensure the political and legal viability of the United States.

1.1 The Declaration of Independence and Articles of Confederation

The Declaration of Independence was an international declaration to other nation-states setting forth the thirteen colonies' complaints against the British Crown justifying their independence under international law, announcing their independence from Great Britain, and declaring their rights under international law "to levy War, conclude Peace, establish Commerce, and to do all other Acts and Things which Independent States of right may do."[5] ... As a practical matter, an international declaration was needed in order that the thirteen colonies could be recognized as states by other foreign states. Under the law of nations, members of a state could dissolve their relations with their prince if the prince failed to protect them, and establish an independent state:

> The state is obliged to defend and preserve all its members ...; and the prince owes the same assistance to his subjects. If, therefore, the state or the prince refuses or neglects to succour a body of people who are exposed to imminent danger, the latter, being thus abandoned, become perfectly free to provide for their own safety and preservation in whatever manner they find most convenient, without paying the least regard to those who, by abandoning them, have been the first to fail in their duty. The country of Zug, being attacked by the Swiss in 1352, sent for succour to the duke of Austria, its sovereign; but that prince, being engaged in discourse concerning his hawks, at the time when the deputies appeared before him, would scarcely condescend to hear them. Thus abandoned, the people of Zug entered into the Helvetic confederacy.[6]

The British Crown repeatedly had failed to protect the colonies in a number of different ways; therefore, under the law of nations, the thirteen colonies could declare their independence and establish a confederacy. Indeed, a primary purpose of the Declaration was to seek alliances through treaties with other states, such as France, in order to fight the British in securing the colonies' independence, and this purpose could only be accomplished if other nation-states recognized the U.S.[7] The Declaration of Independence served to give notice to other foreign states that the thirteen colonies were now independent states and provided the reasons for their independence.

Subsequently, the Articles of Confederation were adopted establishing a government. The Articles of Confederation was a regional, multilateral, federal, constitutional treaty between the thirteen – now sovereign – states. It was a "regional" treaty in that it bound states in the North American region as well as invited Canada to become a member.[8] It was a multilateral, federal, constitutional treaty in that it bound thirteen sovereign

---

[5] THE DECLARATION OF INDEPENDENCE paras. 5–32 (U.S. 1776) (complaints against Crown), 34 (rights of independent states); see David Armitage, The Declaration of Independence and International Law, 59 WM. & MARY Q. 1, 39 (2002) (Declaration of Independence recognized as international instrument in 18th century).

[6] [1 EMMERICH DE VATTEL, THE LAW OF NATIONS §202 (1758) (hereinafter Vattel).]

[7] See, e.g., Treaty of Alliance, Feb. 6, 1778, U.S.-Fr., 2 T.I.A.S 35; Treaty of Amity and Commerce, Oct. 8, 1782, U.S.-Neth., 2 T.I.A.S. 59; Treaty of Amity and Commerce Apr. 3, 1783, U.S.-Swed., T.I.A.S. 123; Treaty of Amity and Commerce, July 9, 1785, U.S.-Fr., 8 Bevans 78.

[8] THE ARTICLES OF CONFEDERATION art. XI (U.S. 1781) (inviting Canada to become member).

states into a confederacy and constituted a federal government. For example, the Articles Congress referred to the Articles as a "national constitution," and the Commissioners at the Annapolis Convention and Madison in THE FEDERALIST No. 40 both referred to the Articles as a "constitution of the federal government." And, like other similar multilateral treaties, it established a league of friendship, trade, and mutual defense. The thirteen states were just the same as other foreign states, but they had placed themselves into a federal arrangement.

However, the Articles were less than perfect in ensuring that the thirteen states acted uniformly in their international relations between themselves and foreign states, no doubt in part because the Confederation was a diplomatic body, according to John Adams and because states (with three exceptions[9]) failed to employ the boards of commissioners or federal courts provided by the Articles of Confederation for resolving inter-state disputes. States enacted trade barriers and entered into treaties with each other, and violated treaties with Great Britain, France and Holland.

1.2 The Constitution as Federal Treaty

As a result of these problems, the people of the United States "in Order to form a more perfect Union" replaced the Articles with another regional, multilateral, federal, constitutional treaty – viz., the Constitution. Whereas the individual states of the United States were to remain intact, the government under the Articles was replaced with a different government under the Constitution. The legal status of the thirteen states under the Articles of Confederation as states did not change under the Constitution. They were still sovereign states with international legal personalities. As under the Articles,[10] states still could enter into agreements with foreign states and each other with Congressional approval under the Constitution.[11] Only the legal relations between the states, and between the states and federal government were altered through the adoption of the Supremacy Clause that ensured the supremacy of federal law (which included treaties) over state law.[12] The compulsory original jurisdiction of the U.S. Supreme Court ensured

---

[9]   Connecticut v. Pennsylvania, 24 JOURNALS OF THE CONTINENTAL CONGRESS 6–32 (1912) (1783 dispute over Wyoming Valley adjudicated by federal court established under the Articles); Massachusetts v. New York, 33 JOURNALS OF THE CONTINENTAL CONGRESS 617–29 (territorial dispute adjudicated by federal court established under the Articles and subsequently settled); Georgia v. South Carolina, 31 JOURNALS OF THE CONTINENTAL CONGRESS 651 (congressional resolution approving establishment of federal court for resolving territorial dispute).

[10] ARTICLES OF CONFEDERATION, art. VI ("No State, without the consent of the United States in Congress assembled, shall ... enter into any conference, agreement, alliance or treaty with any King, Prince or State. ... No two or more States shall enter into any treaty, confederation or alliance whatever between them, without the consent of the United States in Congress assembled, specifying accurately the purposes for which the same is to be entered into, and how long it shall continue.").

[11] U.S. CONST. art. I, §10, cl. 1 ("No State shall enter into any Treaty, Alliance, or Confederation. ...") and 3 ("No State shall, without the Consent of Congress, ... enter into any Agreement or Compact with another State, or with a foreign power. ...").

[12] U.S. Const. art. VI, §2 ("This Constitution, and the Law of the United States which shall be made in Pursuance thereof; and all Treaties made, or which shall be made, under the Authority of the United States, shall be the supreme Law of the Land; and the Judges in every State shall be bound thereby, any Thing in the Constitution or Laws of any State to the Contrary notwithstanding.").

It is interesting to note that the Supremacy Clause ensures that state judges can apply treaties and federal law as the supreme law of the land. This was to ensure that state courts had lawful jurisdiction to apply federal law that, otherwise, they could not apply. Recall that although British courts could apply customary

that inter-state conflicts and treaty violations were to be resolved and not allowed to fester, as they had under the Articles.[13] Only the constitutional law compliance mechanism had been altered for the states – not the states themselves. Again, like under the Articles of Confederation, the states were the same as foreign states, but they had placed themselves in a federal arrangement. If the Framers had wanted to make the thirteen states not "states" in the international legal sense, they would have done so by calling the states something else. They did not.

For the Framers, using a treaty was the proper vehicle for joining the thirteen states into the United States and the peoples therein as one nation because it was the customary legal instrument for uniting states and consolidating peoples.[14] Of course, the U.S. Constitution was not the first treaty establishing a constitution. Earlier examples included the Articles of Confederation and the Union of Utrecht (1579). As one Anti-Federalist put it, "Who is it that does not know, that by treaties in Europe the succession and constitution of many sovereign states, ha[ve] been regulated?" In arguing for the adoption of the Constitution, Jay made a favorable comparison of the consolidation of the American people under the Constitution with the consolidation of the British people by implicit reference to the Treaty of Union (1707) between England and Scotland. Like the Treaty of Union, the Constitution as a treaty operated to unify states and consolidate peoples. As James Madison in 1833 pointed out in his letter to Daniel Webster, the states were "parties" to the Constitution, and the Constitution made the American people "one people, [*i.e.,*] nation."

However, Madison made two statements during his life appearing to suggest that the Constitution was not a treaty. During the Constitutional Convention, he is reported

---

international law, they could not apply treaties without implementing legislation from Parliament. *See* 3 Vattel, n. (172) ("And in Great Britain, no municipal court, whether of common law or equity, can take cognizance of ... any question respecting the infraction of treaties be directly agitated before courts of law. ..." (Ed.'s note)). To avoid this scenario, the Supremacy Clause guaranteed that state courts could directly apply treaties and federal statutory law (a species of international law). [ ]Furthermore, state courts – like the British courts – already could apply customary international law. *See, e.g.*, Respublica v. De Longchamps, 1 U.S. (1 Dall.) 114 (Pa. Oyer and Terminer, 1784); Nathan v. Commonwealth of Virginia, 1 U.S. (1 Dall.) 77, 78 (Common Pleas, Philadelphia County, 1781). VATTEL, *Preliminaries*, n. (1) ("The law of nations is adopted in Great Britain in its full and most liberal extent by the common law, and is held to be part of the law of the land; and all statutes relating to foreign affairs should be framed with reference to that rule. (Ed.'s note, citing 4 BLACKSTONE'S COMMENTARIES ON THE LAWS OF ENGLAND 67.)) Hence, there was no need to include the customary law of nations in the Supremacy Clause.

13   *See* U.S. CONST. art. III, §2, cl. 2 ("In all Cases affecting Ambassadors, other public Ministers and Consuls, and those in which a State shall be a Party, the supreme Court shall have original Jurisdiction.")

14   The Declaration of Independence earlier also stated that the people of the different colonies were one people. DECLARATION OF INDEPENDENCE para. 6 ("We ... the Representatives of the United States of America ... do, in the Name, and by Authority of the good People of these Colonies, solemnly publish and declare, That these United Colonies are, and of Right ought to be Free and Independent States. ...").

It is important to note the difference between "nations" and "states." Nations are peoples. States are bodies politic. When a nation and state are joined, they constitute a "nation-state." The American people were the people in the United States under both the Articles of Confederation and the Constitution. Sometimes nations are not organized into states (as is the case of the Kurdish people in Turkey and Iraq). Also, a state may include multiple nations. For example, Florida includes both the American and Seminole nations.

There also is a difference between states and governments. The government of a state can change without eliminating the state. For example, the recent change of government in Iraq did not eliminate the state of Iraq. The United States were not eliminated when the government under the Articles of Confederation was replaced with the Constitution's government.

to have stated that "[h]e considered the difference between a system founded on the Legislatures only, and one founded on the people, to be the true difference between a *league* or *treaty*, and a *Constitution*." Later in his 1833 letter to Daniel Webster, he also stated the following:

> It is fortunate when disputed theories, can be decided by undisputed facts. And here the undisputed fact is, that the Constitution was made by the people, but as imbodied into the several states, who were parties to it and therefore made by the States in their highest authoritative capacity. They [*i.e.*, the states] might, by the same authority & by the same process have converted the Confederacy into a mere league or treaty; or continued it with enlarged or abridged powers; or have imbodied the people of their respective States into one people, nation or sovereignty; or as they did by a mixed form make them one people, nation, or sovereignty, for certain purposes, and not so for others.

It is important to note in the above two excerpts that Madison is not saying that the Constitution is not a "treaty" in its sense of being a legal instrument. Madison was using the term "treaty" to refer to the political system of a league or alliance or confederacy – another, somewhat arcane, meaning of the word "treaty."

Indeed, there appears to be *no* evidence during the drafting and ratification of the Constitution that the Founders thought that the Constitution was *not* a treaty. The Founders operated under the assumption that the Constitution was a treaty. The issue was non-controversial.

1.2.1. The Dissolution of the Articles of Confederation and Ratification of the Constitution Governed by the Law of Treaties

Furthermore, the only legal instrument that could have dissolved the Articles of Confederation was another treaty because only a treaty could replace the reciprocal obligations under an earlier treaty made between the same states and addressing the same subject-matter.[15] Otherwise, the states would have been violating their obligations under the law of nations, and the states recognized the law of nations.[16]

. . . .

The issue of how many state convention ratifications were legally necessary for replacing the Articles with the Constitution deeply concerned the Framers because the Articles of Confederation was a treaty whose obligations were to be observed. Madison

---

[15] *Cf.* 2 VATTEL, §205 ("as treaties are made by the mutual agreement of the parties, they may also be dissolved by mutual consent, at the free will of the contracting powers"); *Vienna Convention*, art. 59 ("A treaty shall be considered as terminated if all the parties to it conclude a later treaty relating to the same subject matter and . . . it appears from the later treaty or is otherwise established that the parties intended that the matter should be governed by that treaty. . . .").

   The Articles and the Constitution addressed the same subjects. *Compare, e.g.*, ARTICLES OF CONFEDERATION, arts. IV–VI, IX, and XII–XIII (full faith and credit, establishment of Congress, limitations on states, Congressional declaration of war, previous debts, supremacy of constitutional law) *with* U.S. CONST. arts. I, IV, and VI (same).

[16] *See, e.g.*, *Respublica*, 1 U.S. (1 Dall.) at 120 (Pa. Oyer and Terminer, 1784) ("principles of the laws of nations . . . form part of the municipal law of Pennsylvania"); Nathan v. Commonwealth of Virginia, 1 U.S. (1 Dall.) 77, 78 (Common Pleas, Philadelphia County, 1781) (law of nations part of common law and "consequently extended to Pennsylvania"). Indeed, in *Rutgers v. Waddington*, the New York City Mayor's Court in 1784 recognized that customary international law trumped a New York statute.

recognized that treaty law governed both subjects of voiding the Articles and of the Constitution's ratification:

> It is an established doctrine on the subject of treaties, that all the articles are mutually conditions of each other; that a breach of any one article is a breach of the whole treaty; and that a breach committed by either of the parties absolves the others; and authorizes them, if they please, to pronounce the treaty violated and void. Should it unhappily be necessary to appeal to these delicate truths for a justification for dispensing with the consent of particular States to a dissolution of the federal pact, will not the *complaining parties* find it a difficult task to answer the MULTIPLIED and IMPORTANT *infractions with which they* may be confronted?

A thirteen-state rule legally was unnecessary because some states had violated the Articles. Madison's notes from the Constitutional Convention indicate that the Convention's delegates supporting a non-unanimity rule did so on two bases: (i) to ensure that a minority of states could not frustrate a majority of states wishing to establish a new constitution and (ii) to continue the Articles' nine-state rule for deciding important issues, including the ratification of treaties. The Constitutional Convention eventually adopted the nine-state convention rule – a modification of the nine-state treaty rule under the Articles. Of course, the Convention did not state exactly which nine states conventions were needed to ratify the Constitution because this probably would have been a difficult question to resolve given that states probably would not admit or did not believe that they had violated the Articles. To require the Constitution to name which states conventions were required to ratify the Constitution would have embarrassed the other states conventions whose ratifications were not required and would have served to provoke the latter to not ratify.

In summary, a treaty still was required to replace the Articles, but practical and legal considerations allowed a non-unanimity rule to be implemented for the ratification of the new treaty – *viz.,* the Constitution. The nine-state rule appeared to have been sufficiently legal even to those states that initially opposed the Constitution (such as North Carolina and Rhode Island) because such states did not avail themselves of their opportunity to sue the other states for their ratifications of the Constitution in an Articles federal court before the Constitutional government went into operation in March of 1789. What is important to recognize from all of this is that the replacement of the Articles of Confederation was governed by the international law governing treaties and that the Articles as a treaty only could be replaced by another treaty that could ensure the same reciprocal legal relations. A unanimity rule was not legally applicable because the Articles were not being altered. Instead, a new treaty (*viz.,* the Constitution) was being adopted and an earlier government replaced, and the nine-state rule was the applicable rule under the Articles for adopting a new treaty.

In the end, it is not so important to this Article's thesis that the Constitution is a treaty whether the Framers got it right about whether the Constitution's specific ratification process conformed to the international law governing treaties – although they did get it right. *What is dispositive to determining whether the Constitution is a treaty is the fact that the Framers presumed (correctly) that the international law of treaties governed the Articles' dissolution and the Constitution's establishment.*

Consequently, the Constitution was "ratified" as other treaties are "ratified." Also as a treaty, the Constitution came into force when a certain pre-determined number of state conventions had ratified the Constitution, thereby – as the language of the Constitution puts it – "[e]stablishing...this Constitution *between* the States." After all, treaties are agreements made "between" states and "governed by international law."[17]

It is a mistake to claim that the Constitution is not a treaty because its Preamble says that it was "ordain[ed] and establish[ed]" by the people. It is important to note that the Constitution was ratified by individual state conventions – not by the American people as a whole. There was no single constitutional convention attended by all of the American people residing in the thirteen individual states. The ordination and establishment of the Constitution by the people could only take place after the Constitution's ratification by individual state conventions. Indeed, the American people as a whole could not ratify the Constitution according to its terms. The Constitution expressly required ratification by individual state conventions.

To claim that the Constitution is not a treaty because it was ordained and established by the people is to flagrantly ignore its ratification process – a process that established it as a treaty and a process that the Framers explicitly stated was governed by the law of treaties. However, the Preamble's "We the People" *legally* serves to preclude the possibility that the replacement of the Articles was illegal because the law of nations recognized that the original locus of sovereignty resided in the people.[18] An appeal to merely domestic social contract theory would have been legally insufficient because such theory did not apply to inter-state relations. Any remaining question as to the lawfulness of the Constitution's establishment was mooted.

1.2.2. *Being a Treaty, the Constitution Is Governed by Customary International Legal Norms Through Their Incorporation in the Constitution.*

For the Framers, the Constitution could not violate customary international law. For example, Randolph, Madison, and others argued that the Constitution did not allow Congress to violate state navigational rights because this would violate the law of nations – even if there was no explicit prohibition in the Constitution. During the Virginia state constitutional convention, Governor Randolph stated:

> The gentleman wishes us to show him a clause [in the Constitution] which shall preclude Congress from giving away this right [to navigation on the Mississippi River]. It is first incumbent upon him to show where the right is given up. There is a prohibition naturally resulting from...the law of...nations, to yield the most valuable right of a community, for the exclusive benefit of one particular part of it.

The Constitution as a treaty could not violate the law of nations.[19] Although few treaties explicitly require that they be governed by international law, treaties often incorporate international legal norms. After all, if a treaty is a written agreement between states

---

[17] The *Vienna Convention on the Law of Treaties* defines a treaty as "an international agreement concluded between States in written form and governed by international law." *Vienna Convention*, art. 2(1)(a).

[18] J.J. Burlamaqui, 2 The Principles of Natural and Politic Law, pt. II, ch. VI, §VI (1748) (Thomas Nugent trans., 5th ed., Cambridge Univ. Press 1807) (1748) ("sovereignty resides originally in the people") [hereinafter Burlamaqui]; Francisco de Vitoria, On the Law of War (1557).

[19] *Cf.* 2 Vattel, §165:

> A sovereign already bound by a treaty cannot enter into others contrary to the first. The things respecting which he has entered into engagements are no longer at his disposal. If it happens that a posterior treaty be found, in any particular point, to clash with one of more ancient date, the new treaty is null and void with respect to that point, inasmuch as it tends to dispose of a thing that is no longer in the power of him who appears to dispose of it. (We are here to be understood as speaking of treaties made with different powers.)

"*governed by international law*," the best way to ensure that the agreement is governed by international law is to explicitly *write such international law into the agreement*. It is no different with the Constitution. For example, the Supremacy Clause explicitly states that treaties (like the Constitution) are part of "the supreme Law of the Land." Furthermore, the Constitution incorporates many substantive international legal norms. For example, the Constitution has incorporated the international legal principle of state co-equality[20] guaranteeing full faith and credit between the states. Also incorporating the law of nations, the Constitution did not allow the federal government to violate the territorial integrity of the states (without their consent).[21] As under the Articles of Confederation (a treaty), the Constitution guarantees that states retained their international legal personality by being able to enter into agreements with each other and with foreign states, subject to Congressional approval.[22] The Constitution also incorporates the international legal doctrine of state succession regarding continuity of treaty obligations by expressly recognizing that the U.S. is still bound by treaties that the U.S. entered into under the Articles of Confederation.[23] The Eleventh Amendment also effectively ensured the retention of state sovereign immunity (guaranteed by the law of nations) from federal suits prosecuted by citizens of another state, or citizens or subjects of foreign states.[24]

Furthermore, the substantive text of the Constitution addresses a plethora of international legal matters appropriate for a treaty. In terms of legal hierarchy and jurisdiction, the Constitution expressly establishes that treaties are part of the supreme law of the land, that the President can make treaties (with Senate consent), that the Supreme Court has jurisdiction over cases involving treaties, and that Congress can define and punish violations of the law of nations. In terms of substantive content, the Constitution addresses customary international legal matters such as war, piracy, ambassadors, naturalization, and trade.

Perhaps most revealing about the Constitution's incorporation of international law is that the Constitution explicitly states that it was established by "the people," which was the original locus of sovereignty according to international law. The Constitution's Preamble

---

[20] *See, e.g.*, VATTEL, *Preliminaries*, at §18 ("[s]mall republic is no less a sovereign state than the most powerful kingdom."); *UN Charter*, art. 2(1) (sovereign equality of states).

[21] U.S. CONST. art. IV, §3; 2 VATTEL, §93 (prohibition of usurpation of territory); *UN Charter*, art. 2, para. 4 (prohibiting states from threatening or using force against state's territorial integrity or political independence).

[22] U.S. CONST. art. I, §9, cl. 3. However, other federal nation-states, such as Germany and Switzerland, allow their constitutive states to enter into treaties among themselves without approval from their respective central governments.

[23] U.S. CONST. art. VI, §2 ("[A]ll Treaties *made*... shall be the supreme Law of the Land.") (emphasis added); 2 Vattel, §191; SAMUEL PUFENDORF, OF THE LAW OF NATURE AND NATIONS, bk. VIII, ch. ix, §8 (James Brown Scott ed., 1933) (1672) (recognizing successor state responsibility for complying with treaties entered into by earlier state) [hereinafter PUFENDORF].

[24] U.S. CONST. amend. XI. The Eleventh Amendment was ratified in response to the U.S. Supreme Court's decision in *Chisholm v. Georgia*. 2 U.S. (2 Dall.) 419 (1793). After the adoption of the Eleventh Amendment, *Chisholm* was dismissed. Hollingsworth v. Virginia, 3 U.S. (3 Dall.) 378 (1798). Although the Eleventh Amendment did not ensure absolute state sovereign immunity from federal suits, states (U.S. or foreign) often surrender aspects of their sovereignty (including immunity from suits). This surrender does not alter their status as states. As Justice Jay stated in *Chisholm* even before the adoption of the Eleventh Amendment, "suability and state sovereignty are not incompatible." 2 U.S. (2 Dall.) at 473 (Jay, J.). Indeed, the very recognition of statehood is premised on a state's recognition of international legal norms that inherently limit state sovereignty.

placed the Constitution's foundation on the international legal principle of popular sovereignty forward and center. Indeed, the Constitution's ratification process through individual state conventions may have reflected a more legally authentic ratification process than that of most other treaties. The ratification process of most other treaties often involved the participation of fewer representatives of the people. For example, ratification of most treaties only required the consent of the crown.

When the Constitution's preamble states "[w]e the People of the United States, in Order to form a more perfect Union," these clauses denoted that the "people" singular (as sovereign in relations both external and internal to the Union) were confirming[25] the lawful establishment of a new government for the "nation-states" plural – not a "nation-state" singular. In this way the American people could make a social compact that disabled the states from withdrawing from the Constitution if one of them should violate it. Only the people as a whole could dissolve the constitutional compact – not the individual states (nor their respective citizens). The states *per se* retained a residual sovereignty derivative of their respective citizens, but their external sovereignty was limited because that external sovereignty resided more fully in the consolidated people of the United States exercised through the federal government. However, as under the Articles of Confederation (a treaty), the fact that states *qua* states were retained indicates that the Constitution is a treaty, too. After all, if the Constitution was not a treaty between states and binding on the states, why retain the states as states? At least one Framer considered the possibility of not retaining the states as states. James Patterson had considered proposing the elimination of the states at the Constitutional Convention, but he eventually rejected this idea because such action would have diminished the sovereignty of the states, which he – as author of the New Jersey Plan – wanted to avoid. Also during the Constitutional Convention, Rufus King analogized the Constitution's retention of states to the Treaty of Union between the English and Scottish states.

. . . .

4. Why Must the Constitution Be Construed in Conformity with the U.S.'s Customary International Legal Obligations?

Why should we go further and conclude that our federal Constitution must be construed according to the U.S.'s customary international legal obligations? From an originalist viewpoint, the Founders believed that the Constitution must be construed in conformity with the law of nations, of which customary international law constituted a substantial proportion. From an international law perspective, the simple answer is that treaties (such as the Constitution) generally must be construed in conformity with the law of nations. Treaties as international legal instruments must be first construed in conformity with the other laws suitable to its genre, namely, the law of nations. As numerous international

---

[25] The people of the United States only "confirmed" the legitimacy of the new government established by the Constitution. The "People" (*i.e.*, nation) and the "United States" existed prior to the Constitution's ratification. The Declaration of Independence earlier had declared a new nation and new states in 1776. DECLARATION OF INDEPENDENCE, para. 5 ("We, therefore, the Representatives of the *United States* of America, in General Congress, Assembled, . . . do, in the Name, and by Authority of the good *People* of these Colonies. . . ." (emphasis added)); ARTICLES OF CONFEDERATION, art. IV ("The better to secure and perpetuate mutual friendship and intercourse among the *people of the different States in this Union*, the free inhabitants of each of these States, paupers, vagabonds, and fugitives from justice excepted, shall be entitled to all privileges and immunities of free citizens in the several States. . . ." (emphasis added)).

courts and tribunals have held, "an international instrument must be interpreted and applied within the overall framework of the [international] juridical system in force at the time of the interpretation."[26]

Treaties generally cannot violate extant customary international legal norms binding on a treaty's parties for a couple of reasons. First, to violate a customary international legal norm by implementing a conflicting treaty norm is to violate the principle of *pacta sunt servanda* that establishes the basis for most of international law – whether treaty law or customary international law that is reflected by treaties. One cannot say that s/he promises to abide by a certain norm and subsequently promise to abide by a conflicting norm because the later promise is not credible. Second, implementing a treaty norm that conflicts with a customary international legal norm would result in the unraveling of the international legal order through a "domino-effect" of state withdrawals

---

[26] Legal Consequences for States of the Continued Presence of South Africa in Namibia (South West Africa) notwithstanding Security Council Resolution 276 (1970), Advisory Opinion, 1971 I.C.J. 16, 31 (1971); Interpretation of the American Declaration of the Rights and Duties of Man within the Framework of Article 64 of the American Convention on Human Rights, Advisory Opinion OC-10/89, Inter-Am. Ct. H.R. Ser. A, No. 10, at ¶ 37 (1989); Coard v. United States, Inter-Am. Cm. H.R., No. 109/99 at ¶ 40 (1999), available at <http://www.cidh.oas.org/annualrep/99eng/Merits/UnitedStates10.951.htm> (last visited 15 Feb. 2003); *see also Vienna Convention*, art. 31(3) (c) (treaty must be interpreted in light of "any rules of international law applicable in the relations between the parties"); *Vienna Convention-SIO*, art. 31(3)(c) (treaty between intergovernmental organization and state must be interpreted in light of "any relevant rules of international law applicable in the relations between the parties"). Geofroy v. Riggs, 133 U.S. 258, 271 (1890) (meaning of treaty language "to be taken in their ordinary meaning, as understood in the public law of nations").

As the International Court of Justice's Advisory Opinion notes, a treaty must be interpreted according to *present* customary international law – not outdated customary international law in force at the time the treaty came into force. If a treaty were to be construed in conformity with customary international legal norms present at the time of the treaty coming into force but that were no longer valid, the treaty may conflict with the state's present international legal obligations not only with other states but with its treaty partner. *Cf.* Aloeboetoe et al. v. Suriname, Inter-Am. Ct. H.R. (Ser. C) No. 15, at §§56–57 (1994) (recognizing that 1762 Netherlands-Saramaka treaty allowing sale of slaves – which had been protected by contemporary customary international law – "would be today null and void" because treaty violates present *jus cogens*).

Furthermore, a treaty cannot be construed in conformity *only* with those customary international legal norms that existed at the time of a treaty coming into force (and which are still valid) because a treaty must be interpreted and applied within the "*overall* framework" of international law, according to the International Court of Justice's advisory opinion. If a treaty were to be construed only in conformity with the customary international law existing at the time of the treaty entering into force, the implementation of the treaty may violate present customary international legal norms with not only other states but also with the original treaty partner.

Therefore, the Constitution as a treaty cannot be construed in conformity with outdated invalid customary international legal norms or only in conformity with those customary international legal norms that were recognized by the Framers in 1789 and persist today.

In the context of federal statutory law, Judge Robert Bork has argued that violations of international law over which the Alien Tort Statute provides jurisdiction should be limited to only those international legal violations recognized in 1789, the date of the Alien Tort Statute's enactment. *Tel-Oren v. Libya*, 726 F.2d 774, 813 (D.C. Cir. 1984) (Bork, J. concurring). If this were to be the case, an alien today seeking compensation for the loss of his slaves freed in another country would have a colorable claim covered by the Alien Tort Statute because the law of nations protected slavery in 1789. *See* The Antelope, 23 U.S. (10 Wheat.) 66 (1825) (law of nations protects slavery); 3 Vattel, §152 (law of nations allows enslavement of prisoners of war). Indeed, one of the first reported cases that addressed the Alien Tort Statute involved this very issue. *See* Bolchos v. Darrel, 3 F.Cas. 810 (D.S.C.1795) (No. 1607) (suit for restitution for loss of slaves available under Alien Tort Statute).

from their customary international legal obligations with the violating states. The only exception to this general rule of international law is when the norm is of a human rights or humanitarian nature because such norms transcend the inter-state dimensions of international law.[27]

Another, more theoretical answer to why the Constitution must be construed in conformity with the law of nations is that in recognizing the validity of the very social contract that authorizes the federal government to govern the American people – namely, our Constitution – we are logically committed to recognizing that the federal government cannot violate our reciprocal arrangements with other nations that is embedded in the law of nations. To allow the federal government to commit such violations would allow these other nation-states, in turn, to violate our rights recognized by these treaties and customary international law. Construing our Constitution to allow that such international rights lawfully could be violated would make our Constitution a "suicide pact" in so far as our rights are concerned. By violating our treaty and customary international legal obligations, the federal government violates its social compact with its own people by placing their rights at peril. Recall that some of the complaints in the Declaration of Independence that justified the American people "dissolving" the social contract with the British government was the British government's violation of rights possessed not only by the American people but also by foreign peoples that were guaranteed by the law of nations, such as those involving freedom of trade and the seas. To put it another way, the Brits broke *brith* not only with the American people but also with foreign peoples.

Furthermore, international lawmaking can be more advantageous to the American people than the Congressional lawmaking or amendment making mechanisms. International lawmaking allows both the articulation and recognition of rights that otherwise would be unavailable under the Congressional lawmaking or amendment making mechanisms because such rights require acceptance from foreign states for their observance. Such rights include (but are necessarily restricted to) those having an extraterritorial extension in other countries or in international spaces. Although the Congressional lawmaking and amendment lawmaking mechanisms can articulate such rights, the recognition of those rights often necessarily relies upon other foreign states for their enforcement in the territories of these states and in international spaces.

Furthermore, unlike most of the Constitution's rights protections (as presently construed), international law can be more advantageous to the American people because it often creates affirmative state duties for protecting fundamental individual rights.[28] Also, attempts through the State Commerce Clause and the penumbras of the Fourth, Fifth, and Ninth Amendments to recognize other fundamental rights (such as workers'

---

[27] *See* UN Human Rights Committee, General Comment No. 24, U.N. Doc. HRI/GEN/1/Rev.3 at ¶ 8 (1997) ("Although treaties that are mere exchanges of obligations between States allow them to reserve *inter se* applications of rules of general international law, it is otherwise in human rights treaties, which are for the benefit of persons within their jurisdiction. . . ."); *Vienna Convention*, art. 60 (5) (termination or suspension of humanitarian treaty not justified by breach).

[28] *See, e.g.*, Velásquez Rodríguez v. Honduras, Inter-Am. Ct. H.R., Ser. C., No. 4 at ¶ 172 (1988) (state affirmative duty to prevent right to life, humane treatment, and liberty violations committed by private or state actor); Osman v. United Kingdom, 29 E.H.R.R. 245 (2000) (affirmative state duty to prevent right to life violations committed by private actor); A. v. United Kingdom, 27 E.H.R.R. 611 (1999) (affirmative state duty to prevent right to humane treatment violations committed by private actor).

and privacy rights) are controversial because of their loose constructions of the Constitution. Hence, such attempts often fail. However, international law guarantees such fundamental rights. Construing the State Commerce Clause, and the Fourth, Fifth, and Ninth Amendments in conformity with U.S. international legal obligations ensures the protection of such rights. Indeed, for Ninth Amendment construction, the use of the law of nations is especially appropriate given that this law protects the fundamental rights of nations, *i.e.*, peoples, such as those shared by the American people that cannot be denied or disparaged by the enumeration of other rights in the Constitution.

On the other hand, what if the President and Senate make a treaty that undermines these international rights? For example, what if the treaty eroded individual human rights at the expense of securing corporate trade advantages that harmed the natural environment in which the American people lived? The solution to this problem is found on the international law level. As John Jay noted in FEDERALIST No. 64, such a treaty "would be null and void by the law of nations." Furthermore, international law creates a hierarchy of norms on top of which sit *jus cogens* norms that are strongly identified with fundamental human rights norms, such as the rights to life, humane treatment, liberty, and non-discrimination (among others). Such *jus cogens* norms invalidate provisions of treaties that conflict with these norms. Even those human rights norms that do not reflect *jus cogens* still can trump provisions of treaties that violate human rights because many human rights norms have derivative *jus cogens* status by virtue of the fact that their observance is essential for the protection of *jus cogens* norms. Although the Constitution does not guarantee *jus cogens* norms as such, treaties can and do.

Another reason why the Constitution as a treaty must be construed with the law of nations is because the contemporary conventional customary international law is often more specific than the general language of the Constitution. Both international and domestic laws require that specific law prevail over general law. The Constitution contains many vague provisions that require further definition that can be found in modern customary international law.

Finally, construing the Constitution in conformity with customary international law accommodates the Constitution *per se*. Customary international law recognizes that a treaty (such as the Constitution) must be construed according to the ordinary meaning of the treaty's terms in their context, and that the context must be construed in conformity with "any relevant rules of international law applicable in the relations between the parties" (*i.e.*, the states of the Union).[29] Indeed, one correctly can say that general rules of constitutional construction represent general rules of regional (*i.e.*, American) international law because of the Constitution's status as a regional inter-state treaty. However, a global (or more widely accepted regional) rule generally would trump such regional rules for a couple of reasons. First, as discussed above, violating the global (or more widely accepted regional) rule would dismantle the larger international legal order.[30] Second,

---

[29] *Vienna Convention*, art. 31 (1). Consistent with this international law principle, the U.S. Supreme Court repeatedly has held that international law governs the relations between states of the Union. Arkansas v. Tennessee, 310 U.S. 563, 570 (1940); Wisconsin v. Michigan, 295 U.S. 455, 461 (1935); Connecticut v. Massachusetts, 282 U.S. 660, 670 (1931); Kansas v. Colorado, 185 U.S. 125, 143 (1902).

[30] *See, e.g.*, Prosecutor v. Kovacevic, Case No. IT-97-24-AR73, Int'l Crim. Trib., Appeals Chamber (29 May 1998) (customary international legal principle governing arrangements with supernational body trumps customary international law governing relations only between states); *cf. UN Charter*, art. 103 (obligations under global *UN Charter* prevails over any other treaty obligation).

the global (or more widely accepted regional) rule often has a better pedigree because more states have observed the rule, thereby providing stronger evidence of its objective normativity. This is especially true if such a rule reflects a new customary international law norm or *jus cogens* because such a rule respectively would replace or supercede the constitutional regional rule.

Although the present text of Constitution does not necessarily conflict with the United States' customary international legal obligations, some U.S. courts have construed certain constitutional provisions effectively to allow for violations of customary international legal and *jus cogens* norms that emerged after the ratifications of the Constitution and its Amendments. Therefore, these judicial constructions are unconstitutional because the relevant constitutional provisions were not construed in conformity with the U.S.' customary international legal or *jus cogens* obligations.

It is important to note that although certain textual provisions in the Constitution arguably may violate present customary international law in general, those textual provisions can be considered evidence of the United States' persistent objection to those norms when they were emerging; hence the U.S. is not bound by these new customary international legal norms. For example, the constitutional authority to issue letters of marque and reprisal (art. I, §8, cl. 11), to suspend the writ of habeas corpus (art. I, §9, cl. 2), and to effectively deny U.S. citizens residing in the District of Columbia the right to elect representatives to the House and Senate (art. I, §8, cl. 17) represent persistent objections to norms that subsequently may have emerged as customary international law.

However, customary international law often will be silent on a particular issue, providing no *lex specialis* to apply. In such cases, the already existing, substantial body of constitutional jurisprudence will fill the vacuum, and it is only appropriate that it should because this jurisprudence is also international law, albeit only a regional American international law.

≈

QUESTIONS & COMMENTS

(1) Professor Martin generally limits his international legal contructionism approach to the use of customary international law. What about other international legal authorities recognized by the ICJ Statute, namely, treaties, "general principles of law recognized by civilized nations," and "judicial decisions and the teachings of the most highly qualified publicists of the various nations"? Why do you think he limited his approach to customary international law? What are the difficulties in using other such international legal authorities?

3.1.1.2. Persuasive Authority Rule

Lawrence v. Texas
U.S. Supreme Court
539 U.S. 558 (2003)

. . . .

The question before the Court is the validity of a Texas statute making it a crime for two persons of the same sex to engage in certain intimate sexual conduct.

In Houston, Texas, officers of the Harris County Police Department were dispatched to a private residence in response to a reported weapons disturbance. They entered an apartment where one of the petitioners, John Geddes Lawrence, resided. The right of the police to enter does not seem to have been questioned. The officers observed Lawrence and another man, Tyron Garner, engaging in a sexual act. The two petitioners were arrested, held in custody over night, and charged and convicted before a Justice of the Peace.

The complaints described their crime as "deviate sexual intercourse, namely anal sex, with a member of the same sex (man)."[ ] The applicable state law is Tex. Penal Code Ann. §21.06(a) (2003). It provides: "A person commits an offense if he engages in deviate sexual intercourse with another individual of the same sex." The statute defines "[d]eviate sexual intercourse" as follows:

"(A) any contact between any part of the genitals of one person and the mouth or anus of another person; or

"(B) the penetration of the genitals or the anus of another person with an object." §21.01(1).

The petitioners exercised their right to a trial *de novo* in Harris County Criminal Court. They challenged the statute as a violation of the Equal Protection Clause of the Fourteenth Amendment. . . .

. . . .

The sweeping references by Chief Justice Burger [in *Bowers*[31]] to the history of Western civilization and to Judeo-Christian moral and ethical standards did not take account of other authorities pointing in an opposite direction. . . .

Of even more importance, almost five years before *Bowers* was decided the European Court of Human Rights considered a case with parallels to *Bowers* and to today's case. An adult male resident in Northern Ireland alleged he was a practicing homosexual who desired to engage in consensual homosexual conduct. The laws of Northern Ireland forbade him that right. He alleged that he had been questioned, his home had been searched, and he feared criminal prosecution. The court held that the laws proscribing the conduct were invalid under the European Convention on Human Rights. *Dudgeon* v. *United Kingdom*, 45 Eur. Ct. H. R. (1981) ¶ 52. Authoritative in all countries that are members of the Council of Europe (21 nations then, 45 nations now), the decision is at odds with the premise in *Bowers* that the claim put forward was insubstantial in our Western civilization.

. . . .

To the extent *Bowers* relied on values we share with a wider civilization, it should be noted that the reasoning and holding in *Bowers* have been rejected elsewhere. The European Court of Human Rights has followed not *Bowers* but its own decision in *Dudgeon* v. *United Kingdom*. *See P. G. & J. H.* v. *United Kingdom*, App. No. 00044787/98, ¶ 56 (Eur. Ct. H. R., Sept. 25, 2001); *Modinos* v. *Cyprus*, 259 Eur. Ct. H. R. (1993); *Norris* v. *Ireland*, 142 Eur. Ct. H. R. (1988). Other nations, too, have taken action consistent with an affirmation of the protected right of homosexual adults to engage in intimate,

---

[31] The U.S. Supreme Court earlier in *Bowers v. Hardwick* had held that a Georgia criminal statute prohibiting sodomy did not violate the Fourteenth Amendment.

consensual conduct. See Brief for Mary Robinson et al. as *Amici Curiae* 11–12. The right the petitioners seek in this case has been accepted as an integral part of human freedom in many other countries. There has been no showing that in this country the governmental interest in circumscribing personal choice is somehow more legitimate or urgent.

. . . .

The judgment of the Court of Appeals for the Texas Fourteenth District is reversed, and the case is remanded for further proceedings not inconsistent with this opinion.

∾

QUESTIONS & COMMENTS

(1) Does the Supreme Court give a sufficient justification for using international law for construing constitutional rights? Does Professor Martin's ILC approach provide a better justification?

3.1.2. Federal and State Statutory Construction

In the following subsection, we examine the different rules governing the construction of federal and state statutes with the United States' international legal obligations as a means of incorporating international law.

3.1.2.1. Federal Mandatory Rule: The *Charming Betsy* and *Rossi* Rules

Weinberger v. Rossi
U.S. Supreme Court
456 U.S. 25 (1982)

. . . .

It has been a maxim of statutory construction since the decision in *Murray v. The Charming Betsy*, 2 Cranch 64, 118 (1804), that "an act of congress ought never to be construed to violate the law of nations, if any other possible construction remains. . . ." In *McCulloch v. Sociedad Nacional de Marineros de Honduras*, 372 U.S. 10, 20–21 (1963), this principle was applied to avoid construing the National Labor Relations Act in a manner contrary to State Department regulations, for such a construction would have had foreign policy implications. The *McCulloch* Court also relied on the fact that the proposed construction would have been contrary to a "well-established rule of international law." Id., at 21. While these considerations apply with less force to a statute which by its terms is designed to affect conditions on United States enclaves outside of the territorial limits of this country than they do to the construction of statutes couched in general language which are sought to be applied in an extraterritorial way, they are nonetheless not without force in either case.

. . . .

∾

QUESTIONS & COMMENTS

(1) Note that the *Charming Betsy* Rule requires federal statutes to be construed in conformity with the law of nations, whereas the *Rossi* Rule requires federal statutes to be construed in conformity with the United States' treaty law obligations.

(2) The Supreme Court in *Charming Betsy* provided no authority for such a statutory construction rule. On what constitutional text do you think the Supreme Court bases the *Charming Betsy* and *Rossi* Rules? If the Constitution is a treaty that must be construed in conformity with the United States' customary international legal obligations, then doesn't it follow that federal statutes implementing constitutional provisions must also be construed in conformity with such customary international law?

Curtis A. Bradley

The Charming Betsy Canon and Separation of Powers:
Rethinking the Interpretive Role of International Law

86 GEO. L. J. 479, 495–533 (1998)[1]

. . . .

II. TWO COMMON CONCEPTIONS OF THE CANON

In this Part, I describe two common conceptions of the role of the Charming Betsy canon....

A. LEGISLATIVE INTENT CONCEPTION

One common conception of the canon is that it facilitates the implementation of congressional intent. This "legislative intent conception" rests on the assumption that Congress generally does not wish to violate international law because, among other things, such violations might offend other nations and create foreign relations difficulties for the United States. Consequently, when the text of a statute is unclear, the canon purportedly increases the likelihood of a correct construction, and thereby assists courts in acting as faithful agents of congressional will. This conception does not claim that Congress considered international law in enacting the statute, just that Congress would not have wanted to violate international law if it had considered it. The legislative intent conception thus attributes "an internationally law-abiding character to the law-giver whose unclear enactments are at issue." . . . .

B. INTERNATIONALIST CONCEPTION

. . . .

Some judges and commentators, including Professor Steinhardt, have nevertheless argued for what could be called an "internationalist conception" of the canon. In essence, this conception views the canon as a means of supplementing U.S. law and conforming it to the contours of international law. Under this view, courts should use the canon not primarily to implement legislative intent, but rather to make it harder for Congress to violate international law, and to facilitate U.S. implementation of international law. In this sense, courts are to act as "agents of the international order" rather than as agents of Congress. This conception, akin to the "monist" view of international law, might call for "essentially rewrit[ing] a statute to conform it with international law," or for construing

---

[1] [Many footnotes have been omitted. Ed.'s note.]

a statute broadly to mirror international law, even if such a construction is not necessary in order to avoid a violation of international law.

. . . .

III. CHANGES SINCE THE CANON'S ADOPTION

. . . .

In this Part, I focus on certain changes in the context. Specifically, I discuss three developments during this century that are relevant to the continued validity of the Charming Betsy canon: first, the post-realist defense of canons of construction; second, alterations in the structure and content of customary international law; and third, the redefinition of federal court power in *Erie Railroad v. Tompkins*. In light of these changes, neither the legislative intent conception nor the internationalist conception provides an adequate justification for contemporary use of the canon.

A. POST-REALIST DEFENSE OF CANONS OF CONSTRUCTION

Canons of construction have long been a prominent feature of American, as well as English, statutory interpretation. Many of the nineteenth-century American and English treatises on statutory interpretation were organized around well-accepted canons. The leading American treatise on statutory interpretation during this century – the Sutherland treatise – contains a multivolume description of various canons. In addition, canons have been and continue to be routinely invoked by federal and state courts.

During the latter half of this century, however, commentators have heavily criticized the use of canons. Canons were a common target of the legal realist commentators during the 1940s through the 1960s. The most prominent critic was Karl Llewellyn, who purported to demonstrate that "there are two opposing canons on almost every point." More recently, some commentators, including Judge Posner, have cited to law and economics and public choice scholarship, with its focus on the realities of legislative bargaining and the costs of legislation, as further undermining the legitimacy of canons. In 1989, Professor Sunstein observed that "[a]lmost no one has had a favorable thing to say about the canons in many years."

There are three principal criticisms of canons. First, critics claim that canons do not provide any meaningful restraint on judicial decisionmaking. Because of the existence of counter-canons and the selective use of canons by judges, critics argue that canons "are useful only as facades, which for an occasional judge may add lustre to an argument persuasive for other reasons." Second, critics claim that canons do not accurately reflect likely congressional intent. They argue that canons either rely on factors unlikely to be considered by legislators or assume an attention to detail by the drafters that is inconsistent with the realities of the legislative process. A related criticism questions the existence and discoverability of legislative intent. Finally, critics claim that the canons promote judicial activism by allowing judges to ignore the plain meaning of statutes. Although Congress has the ability to overturn statutory decisions with which it disagrees, this can be politically difficult and costly. Canons may also promote activism, some critics argue, by allowing judges to use ostensibly value-free rules to hide their true policy considerations.

Despite these criticisms, there recently has been a resurgence of academic and judicial support for canons. Prominent scholars, including Professors Eskridge, Shapiro, and Sunstein have written in support of canons. Furthermore, the Supreme Court seems to be relying more heavily on certain types of canons – most notably, "clear statement" rules – than ever before. Instead of treating the canons as an "undifferentiated lump," recent academic supporters of canons divide them into numerous categories, which roughly boil down to two sets – "descriptive canons" and "normative canons." Descriptive canons, which include rules of syntax and grammar, "involve predictions as to what the legislature must have meant, or probably meant, by employing particular statutory language." Normative canons, by contrast, "direct courts to construe any ambiguity in a certain way in order to further some policy objective." Commentators typically classify the Charming Betsy canon with the normative canons.

B. THE NEW CUSTOMARY INTERNATIONAL LAW

The second change that is relevant to the continued legitimacy of the Charming Betsy canon concerns the structure and content of customary international law. . . . To understand the recent changes in the nature of customary international law, it is necessary to understand what customary international law was historically. For this purpose, it is useful to distinguish between two periods of U.S. history: the eighteenth century through the early-nineteenth century, which I will call the "early historical period," and the mid-nineteenth century through World War II, which I will call the "late historical period."

In the early historical period, customary international law – referred to as part of the "law of nations" – was closely linked by courts and commentators with natural law. Blackstone, for example, described the law of nations as "a system of rules, deducible by natural reason," and said that it "result[s] from those principles of natural justice, in which all the learned of every nation agree." Similarly, Emerich de Vattel's famous international law treatise, frequently relied upon by the Supreme Court and counsel during this period, asserts that international law can be ascertained by "a just and rational application of the law of nature to the affairs and conduct of nations or sovereigns." Consistent with this view, the Supreme Court in 1814 referred to the law of nations as "founded on the great and immutable principles of equity and natural justice."

Another feature of the law of nations during the early historical period was the lack of a sharp distinction between public and private international law. The law of nations encompassed not only the law governing the relations among nations, but also the "law merchant," maritime law, and the law of conflict of laws. Moreover, even with respect to interstate matters, the law of nations regulated to some extent the behavior of individuals. For example, it governed individual breaches of neutrality and attacks on foreign diplomats.

Finally, customary law, rather than treaty law, was the principal source of international law during this period. Many important areas of international law were unregulated by treaty, and the existing treaties were generally bilateral rather than multilateral. . . .

International law changed during the late historical period. As the nineteenth century progressed, courts and commentators began to embrace positivism. As a result, the natural law conception of international law faded and was replaced by an emphasis on state practice and consent. As early as 1825, the Supreme Court held, in an opinion by Chief Justice Marshall, that a practice contrary to the law of nature does not automatically violate the law of nations, because the law of nations is derived from "the usages, the national acts, and the general assent" of the nations of the world. Commentators during this period similarly began describing the law of nations in terms of state practice and consent. This view was well-settled doctrine by the time of *The Paquete Habana* decision, in which the Court described the law of nations as derived from "the customs and usages of civilized nations." As a result, the determination of customary international law was primarily inductive; "[t]he question of what states ought to do was answered primarily by what they have done."

Also during this period, there came to be a separation between public and private international law. As part of this separation, the private law components of the law of nations – the law merchant, conflict of laws, and maritime law – gradually were absorbed into domestic law. The law of nations came to regulate primarily the relations among states, not the rights and duties of individuals. During this period, "it was thought to be antithetical for there to be international legal rights that individuals could assert against states, especially against their own governments." A final change during this period, particularly during the latter part of the period, was the proliferation of treaties and statutes. The late historical period saw a significant increase in the number and types of treaties, as well as the advent of general international lawmaking by means of multilateral treaties. It also saw the incorporation of many treaty obligations into federal statutory law. As a result, much of the traditional customary international law began to be codified. This eventually happened, for example, with respect to foreign sovereign and diplomatic immunity. Other traditional customary international law, such as prize law, became irrelevant during this period.

This history helps place in context the radical changes in customary international law after World War II.... [T]here have been at least three fundamental changes in the nature of customary international law: it can arise much more quickly; it is less tied to state practice and consent; and it increasingly regulates the ways in which nations treat their own citizens. These changes were the result of, among other things, the Nuremberg trials and the establishment of the United Nations and other international organizations.

In some ways, the new customary international law looks a lot like the law of nations in the early historical period. In particular, the new customary international law appears to be linked at least implicitly with natural law concepts. Thus, whereas the customary international law of the late historical period was derived from state practice and consent, the new customary international law, like the law of nations in the early historical period, is derived to some extent from principles of morality. This linkage with natural law is most evident with regard to international human rights law.

But there are also important differences between the new customary international law and the law of nations in the early historical period. The principal difference is the content. For the first time, customary international law is viewed as providing a host of rights that individuals can assert against their own governments. This change has been called the most "radical development in the whole history of international law." ... It is precisely these rights that proponents of the internationalist conception of the Charming Betsy canon are seeking to advance.

C. ERIE AND THE REDEFINITION OF FEDERAL COURT POWER

The third change that is relevant to the continued viability of the Charming Betsy canon is the redefinition of federal court power resulting from the Supreme Court's decision in *Erie Railroad v. Tompkins*. *Erie* fundamentally altered the role of the federal courts in this country. The federal courts in the nineteenth century felt free to develop their own common law, independent of the common law developed by state courts, except with respect to subjects considered "local" in nature. In overruling the *Swift v. Tyson* decision that had approved this practice, the Court declared that "[t]here is no federal general common law." The Court held, consistent with its reading of the Rules of Decision Act, that "[e]xcept in matters governed by the Federal Constitution or by Acts of Congress, the law to be applied in any case is the law of the State."

Erie reflects two shifts from nineteenth-century legal thinking. The first is the shift from natural law thinking to legal positivism, in particular the variant of legal positivism that views all law as emanating from a sovereign source. As Justice Frankfurter later explained, *Erie* "did not merely overrule a venerable case. It overruled a particular way of looking at law." The Court in *Erie* concluded that the practice of the federal courts in developing their own general common law rested on a fallacy. This fallacy involved the assumption, in the words of Justice Holmes, that "there is 'a transcendental body of law outside of any particular State but obligatory within it unless and until changed by statute.'" . . .

The second shift is the legal realist shift from viewing judges as finding law to viewing them as making it. The *Erie* Court, for example, quoted Justice Field's observation that federal general common law "is often little less than what the judge advancing the doctrine thinks at the time should be the general law on a particular subject." The Court therefore emphasized the need to identify the source of the authority being exercised by the federal courts, noting, for example, that "no clause in the Constitution purports to confer [general common-lawmaking] power upon the federal courts."

It is the combination of these two theoretical shifts that made federal general common law so objectionable. This law was now viewed as being made, and it was viewed as being made by federal judges. The result, given the absence of a proper delegation of such power to the federal courts, was "an unconstitutional assumption of powers by courts of the United States." The constitutional problem in *Erie* concerned not only federalism, but also separation of powers. . . . The Court in *Erie* indicated that even if the federal government had the power to make general common law binding on the states, this did not mean that the federal courts had this power. . . .

Notwithstanding *Erie*, the federal courts have continued to create some common law. This post-*Erie* "federal common law" differs from the earlier general common law in that it is considered part of supreme federal law under Article VI of the Constitution, and thus is binding on the states. Although scholars differ significantly regarding the proper scope of federal common law, many agree that, in light of *Erie*, this lawmaking is proper only if authorized in some fashion by either the Constitution or federal legislation. As Justice Jackson put it, "[f]ederal common law implements the federal Constitution and statutes, and is conditioned by them." This authorization requirement could be construed broadly or narrowly. Recent decisions by the Supreme Court, however, suggest a narrow view of the scope of federal common-lawmaking power. In both *Atherton v. FDIC* and *O'Melveny & Myers v. FDIC*, for example, the Court emphasized that federal common law is appropriate only in rare instances and that the decision whether to exercise preemptive federal power is primarily for Congress, not the courts. The Court also emphasized that the creation of federal common law is normally inappropriate in the absence of a "significant conflict" between state law and "an identifiable federal policy or interest." Finally, the Court expressed an unwillingness to base federal common law merely on generalized policy arguments, such as a purported need for uniformity.

D. EFFECT OF THE CHANGES

For a number of reasons, these and related changes tend to render questionable both the legislative intent and internationalist conceptions of the Charming Betsy canon. As a result, if the canon is to be retained, a different conception may be necessary.

1. Post-Realist Defense of Canons of Construction

The legislative intent conception of the Charming Betsy canon does not sit well with the post-realist defense of canons. The post-realist defense, particularly with respect to "normative" canons like Charming Betsy, rests not primarily on legislative intent but rather on substantive and institutional values. This is in part because, as the critics of canons have pointed out, any attempt to ground such canons in legislative intent encounters substantial conceptual and empirical difficulties. Thus, to establish that the Charming Betsy canon reflects likely congressional intent, one would have to address difficult questions, such as: Does Congress as a whole have an intent regarding international law? If so, how does one ascertain this intent, or even the likely intent? Can one generalize with respect to Congress's intent concerning all ambiguous statutes? Which Congress counts for purposes of this generalization – the one that enacted the statute or the one at the time of the litigation? How does a judge assess congressional intent if a statute clearly violates international law in some respects but is ambiguous in others?

In addition to these questions, an intent-based account of the Charming Betsy canon would have to confront problematic empirical evidence suggesting that compliance with international law is often not the political branches' paramount concern. The recent Helms-Burton Act and Iran-Libya Sanctions Act, for example, have been widely condemned around the world as violating the GATT and NAFTA trade agreements and customary international law rules concerning prescriptive jurisdiction. The failure by Congress during the last several years to authorize timely payment of United States dues to the United Nations similarly has been seen by many observers as a breach of this country's international obligations. Consider also the provision in the Maritime Drug Law Enforcement Act that denies standing to any person charged under the Act from raising a defense under international law. Similar prominent examples with respect to the Executive branch include the abduction at issue in Alvarez-Machain, the activities in support of the contras in the Nicaragua cases litigated before both the International Court of Justice and domestic courts well as the U.S. disregard of the ICJ judgment and the announcement by the Clinton Administration that it would not participate in the World Trade Organization's dispute settlement proceedings concerning the validity of the Helms-Burton Act....

. . . .

2. The New Customary International Law

The post–World War II changes in the structure and content of customary international law undermine both the legislative intent and internationalist conceptions of the Charming Betsy canon. They undermine the legislative intent conception because, even if it is fair to say that Congress has in the past legislated against the backdrop of the canon, or has acquiesced in the canon, the effect of the canon may be quite different when applied to the new customary international law. The nature of international law, particularly customary international law, is now radically different, and there is an increasing possibility of inconsistency and conflict between international law and domestic law.

Moreover, regardless of how one construes the attitude of the political branches with respect to international law in general, we have fairly specific evidence of their attitude concerning the new customary international law, particularly in the human rights area. The purported customary international human rights norms are largely derived from, or codified in, multilateral treaties. It is noteworthy that the United States has so far declined to ratify many of these treaties. In addition, for the treaties that it has ratified, the United States has consistently attached a series of reservations, understandings, and declarations ("RUDs") that purport to limit the treaties' domestic effect. One motivation for these RUDs, which the government included in the face of substantial domestic and foreign opposition, "was a desire not to effectuate changes in domestic law."

Some commentators have criticized these RUDs as being in violation of international law. They argue that, by refusing to allow changes to domestic law, the RUDs are incompatible with the object and purpose of the treaties, and are thereby invalid pursuant to Article 19 of the Vienna Convention on the Law of Treaties. Professor Henkin has also suggested that the frequent use of non–self-executing clauses is unconstitutional, or at least "'anti-Constitutional' and highly problematic as a matter of law," because it subverts Article VI, which states that treaties are the supreme law of the land.

These criticisms, if accepted, may have the effect, unintended by the critics, of negating the U.S. ratifications, both on the international plane and as a matter of domestic politics. They may also have the effect of reducing the likelihood of future U.S. ratification of human rights treaties. As David Stewart has explained, it is likely that the RUDs were needed in order to obtain the political support required for ratification. In any event, these RUDs make clear that the political branches are not receptive to treating the human rights treaties – the genesis of much of the customary international law of human rights – as an independent source of domestic law. As Professor Henkin himself has observed, "By its reservations, the United States apparently seeks to assure that its adherence to a convention will not change, or require change, in U.S. laws, policies, or practices, even where they fall below international standards." Consequently, the empirical claim that the political branches wish to comply with international law may be particularly suspect in this context of the new customary international law.

This evidence also undermines the internationalist conception of the canon. The approach of the political branches to the human rights treaties is, for better or worse, a rejection of internationalism. Far from approving the judicial enhancement of domestic law with international norms, the political branches have insisted – at least in the context of international human rights law, which is the principal focus of the internationalist conception – that domestic law be preserved unless and until the political branches incorporate the international norms. . . . This development may be regrettable, but it is nevertheless a fact that should be considered when determining the proper treatment of international law by the federal judiciary.

3. *Erie* and the Redefinition of Federal Court Power

The reasoning in *Erie* and the resulting restrictions on post-*Erie* federal common law also tend to preclude an internationalist conception of the Charming Betsy canon. Although customary international law was treated in the nineteenth century in something of an internationalist fashion, the framework for this treatment – pre-positivistic general common law – was repudiated in *Erie*. In addition, *Erie* requires that all law applied by the federal courts be either federal or state law, which means that federal courts can no longer apply international law of its own force. Erie thus negates the premise of the internationalist conception "that the [international law] norms operate without the mediation of a political branch." The natural law character of the new customary international law further heightens the separation of powers problem because this law is even more clearly being made rather than found. Finally, although it has become accepted after *Erie* that some federal law can emanate from the federal courts themselves, the authorization requirement underlying the post-*Erie* federal common law further precludes the sort of independent federal court application of such law envisioned by the internationalist conception.

In light of this, it should not be surprising that the recent Supreme Court, which has been sensitive to the separation of powers aspect of *Erie*, has been generally unreceptive to internationalist-type claims concerning the interpretive role of international law. For example, as discussed above, the Court in *Amerada Hess* was unwilling to restrict the statutory immunity of foreign states based on international law. In *Stanford v. Kentucky*, the Court rejected the argument that it should consult international practice in construing the Eighth Amendment, "emphasiz[ing] that it is American conceptions of decency that are dispositive." And in *Sale v. Haitian Centers Council*, the Court refused to interpret a U.S. immigration statute as providing rights to refugees on the high seas, even though the Court acknowledged that providing such rights might be consistent with the "spirit" of international law. These decisions, like the actions of the political branches described above, have been heavily criticized by those who advocate a larger role for international law in the U.S. legal system. They are nevertheless part of the contemporary legal landscape, and they should therefore be considered in evaluating the future scope and viability of the Charming Betsy canon.

IV. THE SEPARATION OF POWERS COMPROMISE

In this Part, I propose an alternate conception of the Charming Betsy canon, which I call the "separation of powers conception." This conception has support in recent case law and, unlike the other conceptions, is strengthened rather than undermined by the changes described above. This conception nevertheless requires a compromise of the very separation of powers values that it seeks to promote. Although the question is a close one, for a variety of reasons I conclude that such a compromise is warranted. I also explain how this conception sheds light on the proper relationship between the Charming Betsy canon and state law.

A. SEPARATION OF POWERS CONCEPTION

It is well settled that "[t]he conduct of the foreign relations of our Government is committed by the Constitution to the Executive and Legislative – 'the political' – Departments of the Government." This principle reflects both formal and functional considerations. The formal considerations include the Constitution's express assignment of policymaking and foreign affairs powers to the political branches and the Executive's head-of-state role in representing the United States in relations with other nations. The functional considerations include the political branches' advantages vis-à-vis the courts in obtaining foreign affairs information and in responding to changing world conditions.

Against this backdrop, the separation of powers conception views the Charming Betsy canon as a means of both respecting the formal constitutional roles of Congress and the President and preserving a proper balance and harmonious working relationship among the three branches of the federal government. The canon arguably does this in several ways. First, it is a means by which the courts can seek guidance from the political branches concerning whether and, if so, how they intend to violate the international legal obligations of the United States. Second, the canon reduces the number of occasions in which the courts, in their interpretation of federal enactments, place the United States in violation of international law contrary to the wishes of the political branches. Third, by requiring Congress to decide expressly whether and how to violate international law, the canon reduces the number of occasions in which Congress unintentionally interferes with the diplomatic prerogatives of the President.

This conception differs from the other two conceptions because it emphasizes institutional relationships rather than legislative intent or respect for international law. The separation of powers conception, like the other two conceptions, acknowledges that the violation of international law can create foreign relations difficulties for the United States. But it takes no view as to whether particular violations of international law are desirable or undesirable from the U.S. perspective. Nor does it agree with the internationalist conception that courts should supplement U.S. positive law with international law. It simply rests on the belief that, for formal and functional reasons, the political branches should determine when and how the United States violates international law.

The separation of powers conception also agrees with the legislative intent conception that, when Congress wishes to violate international law, it has the institutional capacity to make this intent clear. But it does not agree that the principal function of the canon is to implement likely congressional intent, or even that assessing "likely congressional intent" is possible. Rather, it simply holds that, when faced with ambiguous statutes, the division of power among the federal branches is best served by interpreting such statutes so as not to violate international law.

Unlike the other two conceptions of the Charming Betsy canon, the separation of powers conception is strengthened rather than undermined by the changes discussed above. Its emphasis on institutional values is consistent with the modern shift in emphasis from intent-based accounts of canons to values-based accounts. Its traditional, restraint-oriented view of the canon avoids the potential conflict with the political branches that may be entailed by the more affirmative internationalist conception. Its emphasis on structural constitutional considerations rather than on the importance of international law per se is consistent with the redefinition of federal court power resulting from *Erie*. Indeed, *Erie* itself was premised on similar separation of powers considerations....

Moreover, there is decisional support for this conception of the canon. Most directly, the Supreme Court has in recent years cited the Charming Betsy decision for another canon – that statutes are to be construed if possible to avoid serious constitutional questions. The Court has stated that this constitutional canon "has its roots" in the Charming Betsy decision, and is "the essence" of that decision. While these statements are somewhat cryptic, the Court appears to be suggesting that the Charming Betsy canon is designed to avoid difficult separation of powers problems associated with judicial speculation over whether Congress intended to violate international law.

More generally, recent Supreme Court decisions suggest that the Court increasingly favors and uses interpretive rules like the Charming Betsy canon to accomplish judicial restraint in the area of foreign affairs. This practice stems both from concerns regarding the lack of judicial competence, as well as from the expectation that restraint may produce additional guidance from the political branches. For example, in *EEOC v. Arabian American Oil Co.*, the Court was called upon to decide whether Title VII of the Civil Rights Act of 1964 applied to discriminatory conduct occurring in another country. In concluding that the statute did not apply to such conduct, the Court applied a strong presumption against extraterritoriality, whereby federal statutes will be construed to apply only within the territorial borders of the United States unless an "affirmative intention of the Congress clearly expressed" can be found to the contrary. In doing so, the Court noted both that an extraterritorial reading of Title VII would raise "difficult issues of international law," and that "Congress, should it wish to do so, may . . . amend Title VII and in doing so will be able to calibrate its provisions in a way that we cannot."

. . . .

B. OBJECTIONS

Despite the above decisional support, the separation of powers conception is not free from question. Although they have not considered the precise framework described above, both Professor Steinhardt and Professor Turley have argued that separation of powers is an inadequate basis for the canon.

. . . .

Professor Turley advances a . . . criticism of the separation of powers conception. He argues correctly that use of the canon does not in fact eliminate separation of powers concerns: "By interpreting international sources and defining 'conflicts' between municipal and international laws, the court is actively engaged in a transnational dispute regardless of its ultimate decision under the canon."

Thus, as he argues, the separation of powers conception seems to contradict itself. It justifies the use of the Charming Betsy canon on the basis of judicial deference to the political branches in the area of foreign affairs. But at the same time, the canon that it endorses requires that the courts make some assessment of international law. This assessment means that the courts will to some extent be making foreign policy judgments. In addition, their assessment may conflict with the interpretation of international law that would be reached by the political branches. It therefore is not a sufficient defense of the canon simply to note, as one book does, that the canon helps "prevent the judicial branch from placing the United States in violation of its international legal obligations when that result was not intended by the political branches."

In considering this line of criticism, it is important to keep in mind several factors that reduce the separation of powers concerns associated with use of the canon. First, there is a difference between evaluating the content of international law and evaluating the proper U.S. stance toward this law. The canon involves primarily the former, something that is less political and more consistent with the traditional judicial role and competence than the latter. Second, the canon, as traditionally applied, invokes international law primarily to avoid conflicts, not to give international law independent, affirmative effect. It thus does not pose a significant danger of committing the country to international law in a way not intended by the political branches. Third, the canon applies only when legislation is ambiguous; if a statute is clear, the courts will apply it regardless of any violation of international law. The ultimate authority to determine the country's relationship with international law therefore rests with the political branches. Finally, potential conflicts between the branches are further reduced by the traditional judicial practice of giving substantial weight to the views of the political branches, especially the Executive, regarding the content of international law.

Although these factors reduce the separation of powers concerns, they probably do not negate them. The judiciary, under this conception of the canon, is still making judgments relating to this country's interpretation of and relationship with international law. As a result, the decision whether to retain the canon may depend on a weighing of the separation of powers benefits against the separation of powers costs. It is to this balancing issue that I now turn.

C. THE CONSTITUTIONAL BALANCE

The separation of powers balance with respect to the Charming Betsy canon appears to be a close question. Although the canon may result in separation of powers benefits, it also entails separation of powers costs – costs that might be avoided simply by eliminating the canon. Nevertheless, in my view several factors tilt the constitutional balance in favor of retaining the Charming Betsy canon. First, the separation of powers costs associated with judicial error without the canon probably are greater than with the canon. In its traditional form, the Charming Betsy canon has been used primarily as a braking mechanism. If judges do not use the canon, they are more likely to err in favor of over-enforcing statutes because international law will no longer be exercising a brake on their interpretation. If they use the canon, they are more likely to err in favor of under-enforcement, because they will apply it as a brake in some cases in which Congress actually did want to violate international law (or would have wanted to if it had considered the matter). Erroneous under-enforcement of federal enactments may have negative domestic effects. It may, for example, confer less protection to U.S. business interests overseas than Congress desired – for example, by limiting an intellectual property statute to U.S. borders. But erroneous over-enforcement may have both negative domestic effects and foreign relations consequences. It may, for example, give more protection to business interests than Congress desired, and thereby harm consumer interests by reducing competition. In addition, over-enforcement has the potential for generating adverse foreign relations consequences associated with violating international law, such as reduced credibility and influence around the world. These additional consequences may be large or small, and may or may not be material in any particular case. But in the face of uncertainty regarding the appropriate balance, it is sensible, from a separation of powers perspective, for the courts to err in the direction of under-enforcement. This is particularly true given the lack of judicial competence and constitutional authority in the foreign affairs area.

Second, although the legislative intent conception is not strong, particularly with respect to the new customary international law, it probably still carries some force. It seems likely that, at least in a weak sense, the political branches (particularly the Executive) still care about international law, if for no other reason than that violations of international law may have negative effects on the relationship between the United States and other countries. As a result, when confronted with ambiguous statutes, the Charming Betsy canon probably continues to be one useful consideration in judicial efforts to faithfully implement federal enactments.

. . . .

Notwithstanding these factors, the separation of powers costs in question suggest that courts should exercise some caution in applying the canon. There are several specific steps that the courts probably should take in this regard. First, courts should continue to give deference to the political branches concerning the content of international law. Second, when applying the canon, courts should require clear evidence of the international law principles alleged to be violated, particularly with respect to the new customary international law. Finally, courts should reject internationalist versions of the canon, and apply the canon only in its traditional, violation-avoidance form.

. . . .

~

QUESTIONS & COMMENTS

(1) Note that Professor Bradley relies on the constitutionality of Congress' authority to violate the United States' international legal obligations in arguing for a separation of powers conception of the *Charming Betsy* Rule that limits the federal courts' use of international law. Consider the problems with the last-in-time rule in Section 3.2.1. If Congress constitutionally cannot enact legislation that supercedes the United States' treaty and customary international legal obligations, does not this seriously undercut Professor Bradley's arguments?

(2) As Professor Bradley correctly notes, the codification of modern customary international human rights law is characterized by the use of multilateral treaties, and many commentators have argued that the President/Senate has attached reservations to these treaties that violate the United States' extant customary international legal obligations. If Congress constitutionally cannot attach such reservations, it may be the case that the United States would not be considered a party to such treaties. If so, does this not alter the fact that the United States is still bound by the customary international legal norms that such treaties happen to codify? And, does this issue now turn to whether these norms are self-executing?

(3) If the U.S. earlier had signed a human rights treaty effectively signaling the United States' acceptance of a customary international human rights legal norm codified in the treaty, has not a political branch of the government already given its view as to the content of this norm, thereby addressing Professor Bradley's concern for ensuring that federal courts give a political branch substantial deference regarding its view of the content of international law? If so, why could not the federal courts use such a conventional customary international legal norm for construing a federal statute – a construction that is not strict but one that ensures the United States' international legal obligations are observed completely?

3.1.2.2. Persuasive Authority Rule

Laurence R. Helfer and Alice M. Miller

Sexual Orientation and Human Rights: Toward a United States and Transnational Jurisprudence

9 HARV. HUM. RTS. J. 61, 82–84 (1996)[1]

Advocates litigating cases under the ICCPR's privacy clause must remember that it is the text of the Covenant, rather than the decisions of the Human Rights Committee, to which the United States is bound as a State Party. Therefore, even if the treaty is self-executing, a U.S. court considering a Covenant-based challenge to state sodomy statutes is not compelled to follow the Committee's views and can advance a different interpretation of the treaty. Given the practice of other States in respecting the Committee's decisions, however, a court in the United States should view the Committee's opinion in the *Toonen*[2]

---

[1] Footnotes and citations omitted. Ed.'s Note. Laurence R. Helfer and Alice M. Miller *Sexual Orientation and Human Rights: Toward a United States and Transnational Jurisprudence,* 9 HARV. HUM. RTS. J. 61, 82–84 (1996).

[2] [The UN Human Rights Committee in *Toonen v. Australia* held that a Tasmanian anti-sodomy statute violated right to privacy as guaranteed by the ICCPR. Ed.'s Note.]

case as "highly persuasive evidence" that sodomy laws violate our nation's binding treaty obligations.

. . . .

Several recent cases decided by the Court seem to reflect disdain for international law generally and for human rights in particular as a means of resolving close cases of constitutional interpretation or statutory construction. *See Sale v. Haitian Centers Council, Inc.,* 113 S. Ct. 2549, 2565 (1993) (finding that statute and treaty prohibiting repatriation of aliens does not apply to individuals intercepted outside U.S. territorial waters, although such actions may "violate the spirit" of the treaty); *United States v. Alvarez-Machain,* 504 U.S. 655, 666–69 (1992) (refusing to interpret U.S.-Mexico extradition treaty "against the backdrop of customary international law" as informed by U.N. Charter and Charter of the Organization of American States); *Stanford v. Kentucky,* 492 U.S. 361, 369 n.1 (1989) (plurality opinion) (rejecting reliance on foreign or international human rights law in construing "evolving standards of decency" for purposes of Eighth Amendment).

Prospects for using the ICCPR to inform state constitutional provisions appear more promising. As the Supreme Court has limited federal constitutional rights doctrines, state constitutions have become a vanguard of civil liberties protection in many areas, including gay and lesbian rights. In the more than eight years since Hardwick, courts in three states have struck down sodomy statutes on state constitutional law grounds. [*Commonwealth v. Wasson,* 842 S.W.2d 487 (Ky. 1993); *State v. Morales,* 826 S.W.2d 201 (Tex. Ct. App. 1992), *rev'd on other grounds,* 869 S.W.2d 941 (Tex. 1994); *City of Dallas v. England,* 846 S.W.2d 957 (Tex. Ct. App. 1993); *see also* "County Judge Strikes Down Michigan Sodomy Law," UPI, July 10, 1990, available in LEXIS, NEWS Library, UPSTAT File (discussing *Michigan Organization for Human Rights v. Kelley,* No. 88-815820 (Wayne County Cir. Ct. July 9, 1990)).] And in a recent and highly celebrated decision, the Supreme Court of Hawaii ruled that the express prohibitions against sex discrimination in that state's constitution required strict scrutiny and a presumption of unconstitutionality for laws restricting marriage to opposite sex couples. [*Baehr v. Lewin,* 852 P.2d 44, 67–68 (Haw. 1993).]

The ICCPR may be particularly useful where state constitutions contain provisions, such as a privacy clause, that have no federal analog or where a state supreme court has already construed a "mirror image" constitutional text to provide greater protections than its federal counterpart. [For a recent example of a state supreme court justice relying on international human rights law to inform her analysis of constitutional provisions unique to the state constitution, *see Moore v. Ganim,* 660 A.2d 742, 780–82 (Conn. 1995) (Peters, C.J., concurring) (relying on international treaties' guarantees of a right to a minimum standard of subsistence to interpret Connecticut Constitution's preamble and "social compact" clause).] In such cases, the Covenant and the decisions of the Committee and other human rights tribunals can provide guidance to state supreme courts wrestling with the question of whether the right of privacy or to equal protection should extend to consensual homosexual conduct. Of course, as in the self-executing scenario described above, the Committee's views interpreting the ICCPR are merely persuasive rather than binding authority.

A final advantage of urging state courts to give effect to the *Toonen* decision is the consistency of this approach with the United States' understanding on federalism adopted by the Senate when ratifying the Covenant. To preserve the balance of power in federal-state relations, the United States explained that the treaty "shall be implemented by the

Federal Government to the extent that it exercises legislative and judicial jurisdiction over the matters covered therein, and otherwise by state and local governments." Inasmuch as legal issues of concern to lesbians and gay men, such as criminal and family law, are matters traditionally within the competence of the states, looking to state courts as the primary agents to give effect to the treaty is congruent with the Senate's interpretation of the United States' legal obligations. . . .

~

QUESTIONS & COMMENTS

(1) Can the UN Human Rights Committee's opinions reflect customary international legal norms?

3.2. Conflict Rules

In the following subsections, we examine different rules for determining when treaty or customary international law applies when it conflicts with federal statutory law and executive orders.

3.2.1. Treaties and Federal Statutes: The Last-in-Time Rule

In this subsection, we examine the last-in-time rule that places treaty law and federal statutory law on equal authoritative basis. The rule holds that a previously enacted federal statute is superceded by a later ratified treaty, and a earlier ratified treaty is superceded by a later enacted federal statute.

Chae Chan Ping v. United States (The Chinese Exclusion Case)
U.S. Supreme Court
130 U.S. 581 (1889)

[In 1844 and 1858, the United States and China entered into treaties, respectively, pledging peace and friendship between the two nations, promising protection to all citizens of the United States in China peaceably attending to their affairs, and stipulating to security for Christians in the profession of their religion. In 1868, the United States and China added additional articles to the 1858 treaty addressing migration and emigration of their respective citizens and subjects. The additional articles, respectively, guaranteed the "inherent and inalienable right of man to change his home and allegiance, and also the mutual advantage of the free migration and emigration of their citizens and subjects respectively from the one country to the other for purposes of curiosity, of trade, or as permanent residents" (art. 5); and the rights of "[c]itizens of the United States visiting or residing in China [to] enjoy the same privileges, immunities, or exemptions in respect to travel or residence as may there be enjoyed by the citizens or subjects of the most favored nation; and, reciprocally, [the rights of] Chinese subjects visiting or residing in the United [to] enjoy the same privileges, immunities, and exemptions in respect to travel or residence as may there be enjoyed by the citizens or subjects of the most favored nation." (art. 6).

In 1888, Congress enacted a statute prohibiting Chinese laborers from entering the United States who earlier had received permission from the United States to return, in effect expelling them in violation of these earlier treaties as well as their rights vested in them under earlier federal statutes.

In upholding the constitutionality of the federal statute prohibiting Chinese laborers from entering the United States, the Supreme Court held that federal statutes could supercede treaties if enacted after the ratification of a treaty.]

. . . .

But notwithstanding these strong expressions of friendship and good will [articulated in the U.S.-China treaties], and the desire they evince for free intercourse, events were transpiring on the Pacific coast which soon dissipated the anticipations indulged as to the benefits to follow the immigration of Chinese to this country. The previous treaties of 1844 and 1858 were confined principally to mutual declarations of peace and friendship, and to stipulations for commercial intercourse at certain ports in China, and for protection to our citizens while peaceably attending to their affairs. It was not until the additional articles of 1868 were adopted that any public declaration was made by the two nations that there were advantages in the free migration and emigration of their citizens and subjects, respectively, from one country to the other, and stipulations given that each should enjoy in the country of the other, with respect to travel or residence, the "privileges, immunities, and exemptions" enjoyed by citizens or subjects of the most favored nation. Whatever modifications have since been made to these general provisions have been caused by a well-founded apprehension – from the experience of years – that a limitation to the immigration of certain classes from China was essential to the peace of the community on the Pacific coast, and possibly to the preservation of our civilization there. A few words on this point may not be deemed inappropriate here, they being confined to matters of public notoriety, which have frequently been brought to the attention of congress.

The discovery of gold in California in 1848, as is well known, was followed by a large immigration thither from all parts of the world, attracted not only by the hope of gain from the mines, but from the great prices paid for all kinds of labor. The news of the discovery penetrated China, and laborers came from there in great numbers, a few with their own means, but by far the greater number under contract with employers, for whose benefit they worked. These laborers readily secured employment, and, as domestic servants, and in various kinds of outdoor work, proved to be exceedingly useful. For some years little opposition was made to them, except when they sought to work in the mines, but, as their numbers increased, they began to engage in various mechanical pursuits and trades, and thus came in competition with our artisans and mechanics, as well as our laborers in the field. The competition steadily increased as the laborers came in crowds on each steamer that arrived from China, or Hong Kong, an adjacent English port. They were generally industrious and frugal. Not being accompanied by families, except in rare instances, their expenses were small; and they were content with the simplest fare, such as would not suffice for our laborers and artisans. The competition between them and our people was for this reason altogether in their favor, and the consequent irritation, proportionately deep and bitter, was followed, in many cases, by open conflicts, to the great disturbance of the public peace. The differences of race added greatly to the difficulties of the situation. Notwithstanding the favorable provisions of the new articles of the treaty of 1868, by which all the privileges, immunities, and exemptions were extended to subjects of China in the United States which were accorded to citizens or subjects of the most favored nation, they remained strangers in the land, residing apart by themselves, and adhering to the customs and usages of their own country. It seemed impossible for them to assimilate with our people, or to make any change in their habits or modes of living. As they grew in numbers each year the people of the coast saw, or believed they saw, in the facility of immigration, and in the crowded millions of China, where population presses upon the means of subsistence, great danger that at no distant day that portion of our country would be overrun by them, unless prompt action was taken to restrict their immigration. The people there accordingly petitioned earnestly for protective legislation.

In December, 1878, the convention which framed the present constitution of California, being in session, took this subject up, and memorialized congress upon it, setting forth, in substance, that the presence of Chinese laborers had a baneful effect upon the material interests of the state, and upon public morals; that their immigration was in numbers approaching the character of an Oriental invasion, and was a menace to our civilization; that the discontent from this cause was not confined to any political party, or to any class or nationality, but was well nigh universal; that they retained the habits and customs of their own country, and in fact constituted a Chinese settlement within the state, without any interest in our country or its institutions; and praying congress to take measures to prevent their further immigration. This memorial was presented to congress in February, 1879. So urgent and constant were the prayers for relief against existing and anticipated evils, both from the public authorities of the Pacific coast and from private individuals, that congress was impelled to act on the subject. Many persons, however, both in and out of congress, were of opinion that, so long as the treaty remained unmodified, legislation restricting immigration would be a breach of faith with China. A statute was accordingly passed appropriating money to send commissioners to China to act with our minister there in negotiating and concluding by treaty a settlement of such matters of interest between the two governments as might be confided to them. [ ] Such commissioners were appointed, and as the result of their negotiations the supplementary treaty of November 17, 1880, was concluded and ratified in May of the following year. [ ]

. . . .

The government of China thus agreed that, notwithstanding the stipulations of former treaties, the United States might regulate, limit, or suspend the coming of Chinese laborers, or their residence therein, without absolutely forbidding it, whenever in their opinion the interests of the country, or of any part of it, might require such action. Legislation for such regulation, limitation, or suspension was intrusted to the discretion of our government, with the condition that it should only be such as might be necessary for that purpose, and that the immigrants should not be maltreated or abused. On the 6th of May, 1882, an act of congress was approved, to carry this supplementary treaty into effect. 22 St. 58, c. 126. It is entitled 'An act to execute certain treaty stipulations relating to Chinese.' Its first section declares that after 90 days from the passage of the act, and for the period of 10 years from its date, the coming of Chinese laborers to the United States is suspended, and that it shall be unlawful for any such laborer to come, or, having come, to remain within the United States. . . .

The enforcement of this act with respect to laborers who were in the United States on November 17, 1880, was attended with great embarrassment, from the suspicious nature, in many instances, of the testimony offered to establish the residence of the parties, arising from the loose notions entertained by the witnesses of the obligation of an oath. This fact led to a desire for further legislation restricting the evidence receivable. . . . To prevent the possibility of the policy of excluding Chinese laborers being evaded, the act of October 1, 1888, the validity of which is the subject of consideration in this case, was passed. It is entitled 'An act a supplement to an act entitled 'An act to execute certain treaty stipulations relating to Chinese,' approved the 6th day of May, eighteen hundred and eighty-two.' 25 St. p. 504, c. 1064. It is as follows: 'Be it enacted by the senate and house of representatives of the United States of America, in congress assembled, that from and after the passage of this act it shall be unlawful for any Chinese laborer who shall at any time heretofore have been, or who may now or hereafter be, a resident within the United States, and who shall have departed, or shall depart, therefrom, and shall not have returned before the passage of this act, to return to or remain the United States. Sec. 2. . . .

The validity of this act, as already mentioned, is assailed, as being in effect an expulsion from the country of Chinese laborers, in violation of existing treaties between the United States and the government of China, and of rights vested in them under the laws of congress. The objection that the act is in conflict with the treaties was earnestly pressed in the court below, and the answer to it constitutes the principal part of its opinion. [ ] Here the objection made is that the act of 1888 impairs a right vested under the treaty of 1880, as a law of the United States, and the statutes of 1882 and of 1884 passed in execution of it. It must be conceded that the act of 1888 is in contravention of express stipulations of the treaty of 1868, and of the supplemental treaty of 1880, but it is not on that account invalid, or to be restricted in its enforcement. The treaties were of no greater legal obligation than the act of congress. By the constitution, laws made in pursuance thereof, and treaties made under the authority of the United States, are both declared to be the supreme law of the land, and no paramount authority is given to one over the other. A treaty, it is true, is in its nature a contract between nations, and is often merely promissory in its character, requiring legislation to carry its stipulations into effect. Such legislation will be open to future repeal or amendment. If the treaty operates by its own force, and relates to a subject within the power of congress, it can be deemed in that particular only the equivalent of a legislative act, to be repealed or modified at the pleasure of congress. In either case the last expression of the sovereign will must control.

The effect of legislation upon conflicting treaty stipulations was elaborately considered in the Head-Money Cases, and it was there adjudged 'that, so far as a treaty made by the United States with any foreign nation can become the subject of judicial cognizance in the courts of this country, it is subject to such acts as congress may pass for its enforcement, modification, or repeal.' 112 U.S. 580, 599, 5 S. Sup. Ct. Rep. 247. This doctrine was affirmed and followed in Whitney v. Robertson, 124 U.S. 190, 195, 8 S. Sup. Ct. Rep. 456. It will not be presumed that the legislative department of the government will lightly pass laws which are in conflict with the treaties of the country; but that circumstances may arise which would not only justify the government in disregarding their stipulations, but demand in the interests of the country that it should do so, there can be no question. Unexpected events may call for a change in the policy of the country. Neglect or violation of stipulations on the part of the other contracting party may require corresponding action on our part. When a reciprocal engagement is not carried out by one of the contracting parties, the other may also decline to keep the corresponding engagement. In 1798 the conduct towards this country of the government of France was of such a character that congress declared that the United States were freed and exonerated from the stipulations of previous treaties with that country. Its act on the subject was as follows:

'An act to declare the treaties heretofore concluded with France no longer obligatory on the United States. Whereas, the treaties concluded between the United States and France have been repeatedly violated on the part of the French government, and the just claims of the United States for reparation of the injuries so committed have been refused, and their attempts to negotiate an amicable adjustment of all complaints between the two nations have been repelled with indignity; and whereas, under authority of the French government, there is yet pursued against the United States a system of predatory violence, infracting the said treaties, and hostile to the rights of a free and independent nation: be it enacted by the senate and house of representatives of the United States of America, in congress assembled, that the United States are of right freed and exonerated from the stipulations of the treaties, and of the consular convention, heretofore concluded between the United States and France, and that the same shall not henceforth be regarded as legally obligatory on the government or citizens of the United States.' 1 St. 578.

This act, as seen, applied in terms only to the future. Of course, whatever of a permanent character had been executed or vested under the treaties was not affected by it. In that respect the abrogation of the obligations of a treaty operates, like the repeal of a law, only upon the future, leaving transactions executed under it to stand unaffected. The validity of this legislative release from the stipulations of the treaties was, of course, not a matter for judicial cognizance. The question whether our government is justified in disregarding its engagements with another nation is not one for the determination of the courts. This subject was fully considered by Mr. Justice CURTIS, while sitting at the circuit, in Taylor v. Morton, 2 Curt. 454, 459, and he held that, while it would always be a matter of the utmost gravity and delicacy to refuse to execute a treaty, the power to do so was prerogative, of which no nation could be deprived without deeply affecting its independence; but whether a treaty with a foreign sovereign had been violated by him, whether the consideration of a particular stipulation of a treaty had been voluntarily withdrawn by one party so as to no longer be obligatory upon the other, and whether the views and acts of a foreign sovereign, manifested through his representative, had given just occasion to the political departments of our government to withhold tax execution of a promise contained in a treaty or to act in direct contravention of such promise, were not judicial questions; that the power to determine them has not been confided to the judiciary, which has no suitable means to execute it, but to the executive and legislative departments of the government; and that it belongs to diplomacy and legislation, and not to the administration of existing laws. And the learned justice added, as a necessary consequence of these conclusions, that if congress has this power it is wholly immaterial to inquire whether it has, by the statute complained of, departed from the treaty or not; or, if it has, whether such departure was accidental or designed; and, if the latter, whether the reasons therefor were good or bad. These views were reasserted and fully adopted by this court in Whitney v. Robertson, 124 U.S. 190, 195, 8 S. Sup. Ct. Rep. 456. And we may add, to the concluding observation of the learned justice, that, if the power mentioned is vested in congress, any reflection upon its motives, or the motives of any of its members in exercising it, would be entirely uncalled for. This court is not a censor of the morals of other departments of the government; it is not invested with any authority to pass judgment upon the motives of their conduct. When once it is established that congress possesses the power to pass an act, our province ends with its construction and its application to cases as they are presented for determination. . . . We do not mean to intimate that the moral aspects of legislative acts may not be proper subjects of consideration. Undoubtedly they may be, at proper times and places, before the public, in the halls of congress, and in all the modes by which the public mind can be influenced. Public opinion thus enlightened, brought to bear upon legislation, will do more than all other causes to prevent abuses; but the province of the courts is to pass upon the validity of laws, not to make them, and, when their validity is established, to declare their meaning and apply their provisions. All else lies beyond their domain.

There being nothing in the treaties between China and the United States to impair the validity of the act of congress of October 1, 1888, was it on any other ground beyond the competency of congress to pass it? If so, it must be because it was not within the power of congress to prohibit Chinese laborers who had at the time departed from the United States, or should subsequently depart, from returning to the United States. Those laborers are not citizens of the United States; they are aliens. That the government of the United States, through the action of the legislative department, can exclude aliens from its territory is a proposition which we do not think open to controversy. Jurisdiction over its own territory to that extent is an incident of every independent nation. It is a part of its independence. If it could not exclude aliens it would be to that extent subject to the control of another power. As said by this court in the case of The Exchange, 7 Cranch, 116, 136, speaking by Chief Justice MARSHALL: 'The jurisdiction of the nation within its own territory is necessarily exclusive and absolute. It is susceptible of no limitation not imposed by itself. Any restriction upon it, deriving validity from an external source, would imply a diminution of its sovereignty to the extent of the restriction, and an investment of that sovereignty to the same extent in that power which could impose such restriction. All exceptions, therefore, to the full and complete power of a nation within its own territories, must be traced up to the consent of the nation itself. They can flow from no other legitimate source.'

While under our constitution and form of government the great mass of local matters is controlled by local authorities, the United States, in their relation to foreign countries and their subjects or citizens, are one nation, invested with powers which belong to independent nations, the exercise of which can be invoked for the maintenance of its absolute independence and security throughout its entire territory. The powers to declare war, make treaties, suppress insurrection, repel invasion, regulate foreign commerce, secure republican governments to the states, and admit subjects of other nations to citizenship, are all sovereign powers, restricted in their exercise only by the constitution itself and considerations of public policy and justice which control, more or less, the conduct of all civilized nations. As said by this court in the case of Cohens v. Virginia, 6 Wheat. 264, 413, speaking by the same great chief justice: 'That the United States form, for many, and for most important purposes, a single nation, has not yet been denied....'

.... To preserve its independence, and give security against foreign aggression and encroachment, is the highest duty of every nation, and to attain these ends nearly all other considerations are to be subordinated. It matters not in what form such aggression and encroachment come, whether from the foreign nation acting in its national character, or from vast hordes of its people crowding in upon us. The government, possessing the powers which are to be exercised for protection and security, is clothed with authority to determine the occasion on which the powers shall be called forth; and its determinations, so far as the subjects affected are concerned, are necessarily conclusive upon all its departments and officers. If, therefore, the government of the United States, through its legislative department, considers the presence of foreigners of a different race in this country, who will not assimilate with us, to be dangerous to its peace and security, their exclusion is not to be stayed because at the time there are no actual hostilities with the nation of which the foreigners are subjects. The existence of war would render the necessity of the proceeding only more obvious and pressing. The same necessity, in a less pressing degree, may arise when war does not exist, and the same authority which adjudges the necessity in one case must also determine it in the other. In both cases its determination is conclusive upon the judiciary. If the government of the country of which the foreigners excluded are subjects is dissatisfied with this action, it can make complaint to the executive head of our government, or resort to any other measure which, in its judgment, its interests or dignity may demand; and there lies its only remedy.

The power of the government to exclude foreigners from the country whenever, in its judgment, the public interests require such exclusion, has been asserted in repeated instances, and never denied by the executive or legislative departments. . . .

The power of exclusion of foreigners being an incident of sovereignty belonging to the government of the United States as a part of those sovereign powers delegated by the constitution, the right to its exercise at any time when, in the judgment of the government, the interests of the country require it, cannot be granted away or restrained on behalf of any one. The powers of government are delegated in trust to the United States, and are incapable of transfer to any other parties. They cannot be abandoned or surrendered. Nor can their exercise be hampered, when needed for the public good, by any considerations of private interest. The exercise of these public trusts is not the subject of barter or contract. Whatever license, therefore, Chinese laborers may have obtained, previous to the act of October 1, 1888, to return to the United States after their departure, is held at the will of the government, revocable at any time, at its pleasure. Whether a proper consideration by our government of its previous laws, or a proper respect for the nation whose subjects are affected by its action, ought to have qualified its inhibition, and made it applicable only to persons departing from the country after the passage of the act, are not questions for judicial determination. If there be any just ground of complaint on the part of China, it must be made to the political department of our government, which is alone competent to act upon the subject. The rights and interests created by a treaty, which have become so vested that its expiration or abrogation will not destroy or impair them, are such as are connected with and lie in property capable of sale and transfer, or other disposition, not such as are personal and untransferable in their character. Thus, in the Head-Money Cases, the court speaks of certain rights being in some instances conferred upon the citizens or subjects of one nation residing in the territorial limits of the other, which are 'capable of enforcement as private parties in the courts of the country.' 'An illustration of this character,' it adds, 'is found in treaties which regulate the mutual rights of citizens and subjects of the contracting nations in regard to rights of property by descent or inheritance, when the individuals concerned are aliens.' 112 U.S. 580, 598, 5 S. Sup. Ct. Rep. 247. The passage cited by counsel from the language of Mr. Justice WASHINGTON in Society v. New Haven, 8 Wheat. 464, 493, also illustrates this doctrine. There the learned justice observes that, 'if real estate be purchased or secured under a treaty, it would be most mischievous to admit that the extinguishment of the treaty extinguished the right to such estate. In truth, it no more affects such rights than the repeal of a municipal law affects rights acquired under it.' Of this doctrine there can be no question in this court; but far different is this case, where a continued suspension of the exercise of a governmental power is insisted upon as a right, because, by the favor and consent of the government, it has not heretofore been exerted with respect to the appellant or to the class to which he belongs. Between property rights not affected by the termination or abrogation of a treaty, and expectations of benefits from the continuance of existing legislation, there is as wide a difference as between realization and hopes.

    . . . .

~

QUESTIONS & COMMENTS

(1) The last-in-time rule often is stated categorically: any federal statute that is enacted after a treaty supercedes the treaty. What possible exceptions to this rule are suggested by the Supreme Court in the *Chinese Exclusion Case*? What about the lack of a fundamental change of circumstances? What about a treaty that does not require implementing legislation? If so, why? What about the property rights of aliens? Can the exception of alien property rights be extended to human rights?

(2) The Supreme Court in the *Chinese Exclusion Case* indicates that certain areas of sovereign interest (*e.g.*, the powers to declare war, make treaties, suppress insurrection, repel invasion, regulate foreign commerce, secure republican governments to the states, and admit subjects of other nations to citizenship) are "restricted in their exercise only by the constitution itself and considerations of public policy and justice which control, more or less, the conduct of all civilized nations." Is the Supreme Court being inconsistent here given that international law represents such a consideration?

Francisco Forrest Martin
Our Constitution as Federal Treaty: A New Theory of United States Constitutional Construction
Based on an Originalist Understanding for Addressing a New World
31 HASTINGS CONST. L. QUART. 258 (2004)[3]

    . . . .

    . . . . It is textually clear that the President with the two-thirds of the Senate can make treaties. It is less textually clear that the federal government can un-make treaties because treaties can only be made with the consent of other nations. The structure of the treaty process indicates that the federal government can un-make treaties under certain circumstances according to the *lex specialis* governing the treaty process. This *lex specialis*, namely, the conventional and customary international law of treaties, recognizes that the federal government can withdraw its consent or dissolve the treaty on a number of grounds, including treaty violation by its treaty partner, a fundamental change of circumstances, and – most importantly – if the treaty manifestly violates constitutional law.[4] The

---

[3] [Many footnotes have been omitted. Ed.'s note.]

[4] 2 EMMERICH DE VATTEL, THE LAW OF NATIONS (1758) (hereinafter Vattel) at §§202 (breach) and 296 (change of circumstances); *Vienna Convention*, arts. 46 (fundamental law), 60 (breach), and 62 (fundamental change of circumstances); Vienna Convention on the Law of Treaties Between States and International Organizations or Between International Organizations, Mar. 21, 1986, arts. 46, 60, and 62, U.N. Doc. A/CONF.129/15, 25 I.L.M. 543 (fundamental law, breach, change of circumstances).

    The U.S. State Department has recognized the *Vienna Convention*'s substantive provisions "as the authoritative guide to current treaty law and practice." S. Exec. Doc. L. 92d Cong., 1st Sess. (1971) p.1; *see, e.g.*, Weinberger v. Rossi, 456 U.S. 25, 29 (1982) (using *Vienna Convention*); Legal Consequences for States of the Continued Presence of South Africa in Namibia (S.W. Africa) Notwithstanding Security Council Resolution No. 276 (1970), 1971 I.C.J.16 at 47 (*Vienna Convention* reflects customary international law).

federal government also can un-make treaties if the treaty itself allows it. But, the federal government cannot lawfully unilaterally "violate" its treaty obligations. Furthermore, the Constitution's Supremacy Clause made it clear that the individual states of the Union could not violate the United States' treaty law obligations.

Contrast the Supremacy Clause's language dealing with federal laws with that of treaties. In regard to federal law, the Supremacy Clause says that "the Laws of the United States which shall be made in Pursuance [of the Constitution] . . . shall be the supreme Law of the Land." In regard to treaties, the Supremacy Clause says that "all Treaties made, or which shall be made, under the authority of the United States, shall be the supreme Law of the Land." Federal laws are only made in *pursuance* of the Constitution. On the other hand, treaties are made under the *authority of the United States.*

The language of the Supremacy Clause indicates that treaties have greater authority than federal laws by virtue of treaties being made under the authority of the United States, whereas the authority of federal laws is only derivative from the Constitution. The Constitution only says how treaties are to be made under the authority of the United States (*viz.*, by the President with the advice and consent of two-thirds of Senators present). The authority to make treaties (both the Constitution and other kinds of treaties) is inherent in the attribute of sovereignty, which resides in the people. Treaties and the Constitution are ordained by the American people. Federal laws only implement the Constitution and, sometimes, treaties.[5] Therefore, implementing legislation in pursuance of the Constitution has only a derivative authority unlike that authority of the Constitution and other treaties. Also, if the Constitution was to be dissolved, treaties (but not federal statutes) would continue to bind the United States in the same way that treaties made by the Articles Congress continue to bind the United States according to the Supremacy Clause and international law. However, the Constitution has authoritative primacy over other treaties because it was ordained and established by the people of the United States, whereas other treaties are made through the manner prescribed by the Constitution and only derivatively through the people of the United States.[6]

Although federal courts subsequently have held that federal statutes can trump . . . earlier treaties, these precedents are fraught with a litany of insurmountable problems. In cases where federal courts have held that federal statutes can supercede earlier ratified treaties, this last-in-time rule is problematic because of its racist and anti-immigrant etiology,[7] its incompatibility with multilateral treaties,[8] its violation of the separation of

---

[5] *Cf.* Missouri v. Holland, 252 U.S. 416, 433 (1920) ("Acts of Congress are the supreme law of the land only when made in pursuance of the Constitution, while treaties are declared to be so when made under the authority of the United States. It is open to question whether the authority of the United States means more than the formal acts prescribed to make the convention.").

[6] A treaty, strictly speaking, cannot violate the Constitution. Reid v. Covert, 354 U.S. 1, 15–19 (1957).

[7] *See, e.g.,* The Cherokee Tobacco, 78 U.S. (11 Wall.) 616 (1871) (breaking treaty with Cherokee nation by charging tax on tobacco); Head Money Cases, 112 U.S. 580 (1884) (breaking friendship treaties by charging head tax on entering aliens); Chae Chan Ping v. United States (The Chinese Exclusion Case), 130 U.S. 581 (1889) (breaking treaty with China by excluding Chinese immigrants); Thomas v. Gay, 169 U.S. 264 (1898) (breaking treaty with Cherokee nation by denying self-government); Stephens v. Cherokee Nation, 174 U.S. 445 (1899) (breaking treaty with Cherokee nation by taking land); *see also* Howard Tolley, *The Domestic Applicability of International Treaties in the United States,* 17 REV. JUR. U.P.R. 403 (1983).

[8] How does one determine whether a multilateral treaty is the last-in-time or not when the treaty provides for an interstate complaint procedure that creates mutual obligations between parties? As states become new parties to the multilateral treaty creating new obligations for the U.S. *vis-a-vis* these new states-parties,

powers principle,[9] its failure to recognize a number of grounds allowed by the law of nations for states to withdraw from treaties,[10] and its conflict with the original understanding of the Framers and early Supreme Court precedent.[11] Indeed, the last-in-time rule in regard to federal statutes superceding treaties is a continuation of the *Plessy v. Ferguson*[12] legacy of racist constitutional construction. The same Supreme Court that embraced a "separate but equal" construction of the Fourteenth Amendment's Equal Protection Clause in regard to African-Americans also embraced a last-in-time rule construction of the Article II treaty clause in regard to Native-Americans, Chinese and other aliens.[13] Therefore, the last-in-time rule has serious constitutional infirmities.

. . . .

The Founders did not adhere to an American exceptionalism in international law and affairs. For example, in response to certain states of the United States violating the Paris Peace Treaty, the Articles Congress wrote a letter to Great Britain in 1787 clearly stating that neither the U.S. nor its individual states could violate its obligations under either treaties or the law of nations.

> Our national constitution having committed to us the management of the national concerns with foreign States and powers, it is our duty to take care that all the rights which they ought to enjoy within our Jurisdiction by the laws of nations and the faith of treaties remain inviolate. . . . For as the Legislature only which constitutionally passes a law has power to revise and amend it, so the sovereigns only who are parties to the treaty have power, by mutual consent and posterior Articles to correct or explain it. . . . As the treaty of peace so far as it respects the matters and things provided for in it, is a Law to the United States, which cannot by all or any of [the United States] be altered or changed, . . .[14]

The Founders' belief that the United States' international legal obligations could not be violated by either the federal government or the individual states was not limited to the

---

any prior legislation is nullified in respect to these new parties. Therefore, the last-in-time rule's application becomes problematic. *See, e.g., ICCPR*, art. 41 (interstate complaint procedure). Also, many multilateral treaties do not allow party withdrawal. General Comment No. 26, UN Human Rights Committee, 61st Sess., 84 ¶ 2, U.N. Doc. CCPR/C/21/Rev.1/Add.8 (1997) (state-party cannot denounce or withdraw from *ICCPR*).

[9] If the last-in-time rule was valid, Congress alone without the President's approval could invalidate the treaty by subsequent legislation if the bill received 2/3 of votes from each House. If such a federal statute violated the law of nations, this would exceed Congress' limited authority to only "define" offenses against the law of nations and only make laws that are "necessary and proper."

[10] [*See* note 22.]

[11] [*See infra* discussion.]

[12] Plessy v. Ferguson, 163 U.S. 537 (1896).

[13] *Compare, e.g., Chae Chan Ping*, 130 U.S. at 595 ("the presence of Chinese laborers had a baneful effect upon the material interests of the state, and upon public morals; that their immigration was in numbers approaching the character of an Oriental invasion, and was a menace to our civilization"), *with Plessy*, 163 U.S. at 544 ("Laws permitting, and even requiring, [the separation of Whites and Negroes], in places where they are liable to be brought into contact, do not necessarily imply the inferiority of either race to the other. . . .").

[14] 32 JOURNALS OF THE CONTINENTAL CONGRESS 177, 177–81 (1912) (letter to Great Britain dated Apr. 13, 1787).

government under the Articles of Confederation but also extended to the Constitution.[15] In FEDERALIST No. 64, Jay stated:

> They who make laws may, without doubt, amend or repeal them; and it will not be disputed that they who make treaties may alter or cancel them; but still let us not forget that treaties are made, not by only one of the contracting parties, but by both; and consequently, that as the consent of both was essential to their formation at first, so must it ever afterwards be to alter or cancel them. The proposed Constitution, therefore, has not in the least extended the obligation of treaties. They are just as binding, and just as far beyond the lawful reach of legislative acts now, as they will be at any future period, or under any form of government.[16]

---

[15] Madison stated that "[t]he powers relating to ... treaties ... are all vested in the existing Congress by the Articles of Confederation. The proposed change [by the Constitution] does not enlarge these powers; it only substitutes a more effectual mode of administering them." THE FEDERALIST No. 45, at ¶ 11 (James Madison) (1788).

[16] THE FEDERALIST No. 64, at ¶ 12 (John Jay) (1788). During the North Carolina Constitutional Convention, William Davie stated, "although treaties are mere conventional acts between the contracting parties, yet, by the law of nations, they are the supreme law of the land to their respective citizens or subjects. All civilized nations have concurred in considering them as paramount to an ordinary act of legislation." ELLIOT's DEBATES at 119 (July 28, 1788). Hamilton later would write that it was "understood by all" during the Constitutional Convention that the Constitution's treaty power was "competent to ... controul and bind the legislative power of Congress" and that "no objection was made to the idea of its controuling future exercises of the legislative power." Alexander Hamilton, *The Defence No. 38* (1795), *in* 20 THE PAPERS OF ALEXANDER HAMILTON 22, 25 n.* (H. Syrett ed., 1974).

In 1791, James Wilson argued that the reason for why a nation could not violate its treaties with other nations was because such a violation was a disservice to the nation's own members:

> When men have formed themselves into a state or nation, they may reciprocally enter into particular engagements, and, in this manner, contract new obligations in favour of the members of the community; but they cannot, by this union, discharge themselves from any duties which they previously owed to those, who form no part of the union. They continue under all the obligations required by the universal society of the human race – the great society of nations. The law of that great and universal society requires, that each nation should contribute to the perfection and happiness of the others. It is, therefore, a duty which every nation owes to itself, to acquire those qualifications, which will fit and enable it to discharge those duties which it owes to others.[ ]

During the Jay Treaty controversy five years later, U.S. Supreme Court Chief Justice Oliver Ellsworth wrote that "a Treaty cannot be repealed or annulled by Statute because it is a compact with a foreign power, and one party to a compact cannot dissolve it without the consent of the other." William Casto, *Two Advisory Opinions*, 6 GREENBAG 414 (2003) (letter dated Mar. 13, 1796 to John Trumbull); *see* ANNALS OF CONGRESS 479, 4th Cong. 2nd Sess. (Mar. 1796) (Roger Griswold: treaty superior to Congressional act and, consequently, treaty provision cannot be repealed by mere Congressional act). However, also during the Jay Treaty controversy, Treasury Secretary Oliver Wolcott opined that Congress lawfully could enact a law to "repeal" an earlier treaty, but it is important to note that Wolcott used the example of a Congressional declaration of war "repealing" an earlier treaty. 1 OLIVER WOLCOTT, MEMOIRS OF THE ADMINISTRATIONS OF WASHINGTON AND JOHN ADAMS 1796 (1846). Wolcott was effectively correct. As noted above, under the law of nations, a state lawfully could "terminate" (not "repeal") a treaty on the grounds that another state had violated either its treaty or customary international legal obligations with the first state. Violations of treaty or customary international legal obligations could be sufficient grounds under the law of nations for waging war. [ ] Madison during the Jay Treaty controversy staked out a middle ground that created a dilemma. He argued that federal statutes could not violate treaties, but he also argued that treaties could not violate federal statutes. ANNALS OF CONGRESS 479, 4th Cong. 2nd Sess. (Mar. 1796).

However, Thomas Jefferson later wrote that legislative acts constitutionally could violate treaties.[17] In this regard, it is important to note that Jefferson was not a Framer. He was in France during the drafting and ratification of the Constitution, and his understanding of the Constitution was flawed. Furthermore, Jefferson contradicted himself because he had indicated that the Constitution was a treaty and that federal legislation lawfully could not violate it.[18]

The Supreme Court a few years later would state that "[w]hen the United States declared their independence, they were bound to receive the law of nations." "[T]he United States by taking a place among the nations of the earth [became] amenable to the law of nations." Most importantly, the U.S. Supreme Court in 1812 held that civilized nations could not violate treaties. In *The Antelope*, the Court stated the following:

> In almost every instance, the treaties between civilized nations contain a stipulation to this effect in favor of vessels driven in by stress of weather or other urgent necessity. In such cases the sovereign is bound by compact to authorize foreign vessels to enter his ports. The treaty binds him to allow vessels in distress to find refuge and asylum in his ports, and *this is a license which he is not at liberty to retract*.[19]

It was clear that the U.S. government could not violate either the law of nations or its treaties. When the United States in its early years did stop complying with its treaty obligations, it did so because its treaty partner had breached the treaty[20] or the treaty itself allowed termination;[21] treaty breach by one of its parties or unilateral withdrawal per a treaty's provisions is sufficient ground to void a treaty under the law of nations.[22]

. . . .

~

3.2.2. Customary International Law and Other Federal Law: The *García-Mir* Rule

In this subsection, we examine rules governing conflicts between customary international law and other federal law, such as federal statutes and executive orders.

---

[17] THOMAS JEFFERSON, A MANUAL OF PARLIAMENTARY PRACTICE: FOR THE USE OF THE SENATE OF THE UNITED STATES §LII (1812) ("Treaties being declared, equally with the laws of the United States, to be the supreme law of the land, it is understood that an act of the legislature alone can declare them infringed and rescinded.").

[18] Letter from Thomas Jefferson to Edward Everett (Apr. 8, 1826), *in* THE POLITICAL WRITINGS OF THOMAS JEFFERSON 151 (E. Dumbauld ed., 1955) (Constitution is a compact between independent nations); Kentucky Resolution at ¶ 1 (1799) (drafted by Jefferson), *available at* http://www.yale.edu/lawweb/avalon/enres.htm (last visited Oct. 5, 2003) (stating that federal Alien and Sedition Acts were unconstitutional).

[19] 11 U.S. (7 Cranch) 116, 141 (1812) (emphasis provided).

[20] *See, e.g.*, An Act to Declare the Treaties Heretofore Concluded with France, no Longer Obligatory on the United States, 1 Stat. 578 (1798) (repeated treaty violations by France and French failure to compensate for violations justifies U.S. voiding of treaties).

[21] For example, President Polk in 1846 requested that Congress approve his authority to withdraw from the Oregon Territory Treaty (1827) with Great Britain and notify the British government of the U.S.' withdrawal *per* the Treaty's terms. Congress did so in Joint Resolution of April 27, 1846, 9 Stat. 109–110 (1846).

[22] 2 Vattel §202 (breach); *Vienna Convention*, arts. 42 (2) (withdrawal according to treaty provisions) and 60 (breach).

García-Mir v. Meese
U.S. Court of Appeals for the 11th Circuit
788 F.2d 1446 (11th Cir. 1986)

[The appellees–cross appellants were Cuban refugees from the Mariel Boatlift that had been accorded parole. Subsequently, their parole was revoked, and they were being detained indefinitely in the Atlanta federal penitentiary. They challenged their indefinite detention as being violative of customary international law.]

. . . .

The public law of nations was long ago incorporated into the common law of the United States. The Paquete Habana, 175 U.S. 677, 700 (1900); The Nereide, 13 U.S. (9 Cranch) 388, 423 (1815); Restatement of the Law of Foreign Relations Law of the United States (Revised) §131 comment d (Tent. Draft No. 6, 1985) [hereinafter cited as "Restatement 6"]. To the extent possible, courts must construe American Law so as to avoid violating principles of public international law. Murray v. The Schooner Charming Betsy, 6 U.S. (2 Cranch) 64, 102, 118 (1804); Lauritzen v. Larsen, 345 U.S. 571, 578 (1958). But public international law is controlling only "where there is no treaty and no controlling executive or legislative act or judicial decision. . . ." 175 U.S. at 700. Appellees argue that, because general principles of international law forbid prolonged arbitrary detention,[1] we should hold that their current detention is unlawful.

We have previously determined that "the general deportation statute, 8 U.S.C.A. §1227(a) (1985), does not restrict the power of the Attorney General to detain aliens indefinitely." Fernandez-Roque II, 734 F.2d at 580 n.6. But this does not resolve the question whether there has been an affirmative legislative grant of authority to detain. As to [those Appellees-Cross Appellants who are guilty of crimes committed in Cuba before the boatlift or who are mentally incompetent] there is sufficiently express evidence of congressional intent as to interdict the application of international law: 8 U.S.C.A. §1522 note.[2]

The trial court found, correctly, that there has been no affirmative legislative grant to the Justice Department to detain [those other Appellees-Cross Appellants whose paroles were later revoked on other grounds] without hearings because 8 U.S.C.A. §1227(c) does not expressly authorize indefinite detention. Fernandez-Roque v. Smith, 622 F. Supp. 887, 902 (N.D Ga. 1985). Thus we must look for a controlling executive act. The trial

---

[1] *See, e.g.*, Restatement 6 §702(e), comment h; Rodriguez-Fernandez v. Wilkinson, 654 F.2d 1382, 1388 (10th Cir. 1981).

[2] That enactment provides:

The Congress finds that the United States Government has already incarcerated recently arrived Cubans who are admitted criminals, are security threats, or have incited civil disturbances in Federal processing facilities. The Congress urges the Executive branch, consistent with United States law, to seek the deportation of such individuals.

Admittedly, the legislation encourages the Executive Branch to act in accordance with United States law. That would implicitly incorporate international law prohibiting detention without a hearing, assuming for argument's sake that the international norm appellees invoke actually applies to circumstances of this sort. But the language suggests that Congress clearly anticipated that the First Group was being and would continue to be held until they could be deported. Congress made no attempt to undo what the Justice Department has already done. In fact they encouraged it to deport these persons. We hold that the First Group is subject to a controlling legislative enactment and hence unprotected by international law.

court found that there was such a controlling act in the Attorney General's termination of the status review plan and in his decision to incarcerate indefinitely pending efforts to deport. Id. at 903. The appellees and the amicus[ ] challenge this by arguing that a controlling executive act can only come from an act by or expressly sanctioned by the President himself, not one of his subordinates.[ ] They rely for that proposition upon *The Paquete Habana* and upon the Restatement of the Law of Foreign Relations Law of the United States (Revised) §131 comment c (Tent. Draft No.1, 1980) [hereinafter cited as "Restatement 1"].

As to *The Paquete Habana*, that case involved the capture and sale as war prize of several fishing boats during the Spanish-American War. The Supreme Court found this contrary to the dictates of international law. The amicus characterizes the facts of the case such that the Secretary of the Navy authorized the capture and that the Supreme Court held that this did not constitute a controlling executive act because it was not ordered by the President himself. This is a mischaracterization. After the capture of the two vessels at issue, an admiral telegraphed the Secretary for permission to seize fishing ships, to which the Secretary responded that only those vessels "'likely to aid enemy may be detained.'" [ ] Seizing fishing boats aiding the enemy would be in obvious accord with international law. But the facts of *The Paquete Habana* showed the boats in question to be innocent of aiding the Spanish. The Court held that the ships were seized in violation of international law because they were used solely for fishing. It was the admiral who acted in excess of the clearly delimited authority granted by the Secretary, who instructed him to act only consistent with international law. Thus *The Paquete Habana* does not support the proposition that the acts of cabinet officers cannot constitute controlling executive acts. At best it suggests that lower level officials cannot by their acts render international law inapplicable. That is not an issue in this case, where the challenge is to the acts of the Attorney General.

As to the Restatement 1, the provision upon which amicus relies[3] has been removed in subsequent drafts. The most recent version of that provision notes that the President, "acting within his constitutional authority, may have the power under the Constitution to act in ways that constitute violations of international law by the United States." The Constitution provides for the creation of executive departments, U.S. Const. art. 2, §2, and the power of the President to delegate his authority to those department to act on his behalf is unquestioned.[ ] .... Thus we hold that the executive acts here evident constitute a sufficient basis for affirming the trial court's finding that international law does not control.

Even if we were to accept, *arguendo*, the appellees' interpretation of "controlling executive act," *The Paquete Habana* also provides that "the reach of international law will be interdicted by a controlling judicial decision." In *Jean v. Nelson*, we interpreted the Supreme Court's decision in *Mezei* to hold that even an indefinitely incarcerated alien "could not challenge his continued detention without a hearing."[ ] This reflects the obligation of the courts to avoid any ruling that would "inhibit the flexibility of the political branches of government to respond to changing world conditions. . . ." Mathews v. Diaz,

---

[3] Amicus cites to Restatement 1, §131, Comment C to the effect that a controlling executive act within the meaning of *The Paquete Habana* can come only from the President himself.

426 U.S. 67, 81, 48 L. Ed. 2d 478, 96 S. Ct. 1883 (1976). We find this decision sufficient to meet the test of *The Paquete Habana.*

. . . .

∾

QUESTIONS & COMMENTS

(1) In *Sosa v. Alvarez-Machain,* _ U.S. _, 124 S. Ct. 2739, 159 L. Ed. 2d 718 (2004), the U.S. Supreme Court stated in dicta that Congress may "at any time (explicitly, or implicitly by treaties or statutes that occupy the field)" modify or cancel a law of nations' norm in the context of federal court jurisdictional statutes, namely, the Alien Tort Statute that provided jurisdiction over torts committed in violation of the law of nations or treaties. The Court provided no authority or reason in support of this claim. However, given the fact that Congress has the constitutional authority to determine federal court jurisdiction, this claim is arguably valid. *See* U.S. Const. art. I, §8, cl. 9 (Congress shall have power "[t]o constitute Tribunals inferior to the supreme Court. . . ."); and art. III, §2, cl. 2 ("In all the other Cases before mentioned, the supreme Court shall have appellate Jurisdiction, both as to Law and Fact, with such Exceptions, and under such Regulations as the Congress shall make."). On the other hand, if there is a customary international legal norm guaranteeing a private cause of action for international human rights violations, should the Supreme Court's dicta should be narrowly construed?

(2) Note that the Supreme Court has yet to rule whether the President can supercede an extant customary international legal norm through executive orders.

Francisco Forrest Martin
Our Constitution as Federal Treaty: A New Theory of United States Constitutional Construction Based on an Originalist Understanding for Addressing a New World
31 HASTINGS CONST. L. QUART. 258 (2004)[1]

. . . .

. . . . The Constitution states that Congress may only "define" offenses against the law of nations, and the records from the Constitutional Convention make it clear that the word "define" meant "clarify" – not "create."[2] It only makes sense that the U.S. (or any other foreign state) cannot unilaterally make the law of nations because, by definition, such law is made by "nations" plural. All the U.S. can do, is to "contribute" to the formation of the law of nations by making or refusing to sign treaties, or acquiescing or objecting to an emerging customary international law norm.[3]

. . . .

---

[1] [Many footnotes have been omitted. Ed.'s note.]

[2] 2 THE RECORDS OF THE FEDERAL CONVENTION OF 1787 61 (ed. Max Farrand 1937) ("To pretend to define the law of nations which depended on the authority of all the Civilized Nations of the World, would have a look of arrogance. that would make us ridiculous. Mr. Govr: The word define is proper when applied to offences in this case; the law of nations being often too vague and deficient to be a rule."). . . .

[3] A method of explicitly accepting an emerging customary international law norm is to enter into a treaty that recognizes the norm. The customary method of effectively objecting to an emerging customary

[R]ecent federal court practice seems to suggest that federal statutes and executive orders always trump customary international law regardless of when it emerged.[4] However, this recent rule is also fraught with insurmountable problems, such as its basis on a paraphrasing of dicta in the U.S. Supreme Court's *The Paquete Habana*[5] that is overreaching,[6] its failure to recognize earlier conflicting case law and authorities,[7] its absurd results (such as indefinite detention),[8] its mischaracterization of customary international law as merely common law that can be superceded by statute,[9] its displacement of customary international law by treaty law as a superior authority of law,[10] and – again – its conflict with the original understanding of the Founders. Therefore, this rule has serious constitutional infirmities.[11]

. . . .

～

3.3. Self-Execution Doctrine

In this subsection, we examine when a treaty or customary international law requires or does not require federal legislation to implement it.

3.3.1. Treaties

In the following materials, consider what kind of treaties – if any – constitutionally would require implementing legislation. And, if so, what kind of implementing legislation would be constitutionally required or allowed.

---

international law norm is to not enter into a treaty recognizing the norm or make a reservation concerning the treaty norm and attach it to the ratified treaty when deposited.

[4] *See, e.g.*, Galo-Garcia v. Immigration & Naturalization Serv., 86 F.3d 916, 918 (9th Cir. 1996) (federal statute supercedes customary international law); Comm. of U.S. Citizens Living in Nicar. v. Reagan, 859 F.2d 929, 938 (D.C. Cir. 1988) (federal statute supercedes customary international law); U.S. v. Merkt, 794 F.2d 950, 964 (5th Cir. 1986) (federal statute supercedes customary international law); Garcia-Mir v. Meese, 788 F.2d 1446, 1455 (11th Cir. 1986) (federal statutes and executive orders supercede customary international law); U.S. v. Howard-Arias, 679 F.2d 363 (4th Cir. 1982) (federal statute supercedes customary international law); Tag v. Rogers, 267 F.2d 664, 666 (D.C. Cir. 1959) (federal statute supercedes customary international law).

[5] 175 U.S. 677, 700 (1900) (dictum) ("where there is no treaty and no controlling executive or legislative act or judicial decision, resort must be had to the customs and usages of civilized nations").

[6] For example, some federal courts have overreached the dictum's meaning by adding the word "only," as in "[o]nly 'where there is not treaty and no controlling executive or legislative act or judicial decision,' resort will be made to the customary international law." *In re* Extradition of Cheung, 968 F. Supp. 791, 803 n. 17 (D. Conn. 1997); *see also* Dimon-Sainz v. U.S., No. 97-3117-RDR, 1999 U.S. Dist. LEXIS 18582, *5 (D. Kan. 1999) (same); *Tag*, 267 F.2d at 666 (same).

[7] *See, e.g.*, Macintosh v. U.S., 283 U.S. 605, 622 (1931) (dictum) (Congress under war powers authority cannot violate international law); *see also* Jordan Paust, *Rediscovering the Relationship Between Congressional Power and International Law: Exceptions to the Last in Time Rule and the Primacy of Custom*, 28 Va. J. Int'l L. 393 (1988), for additional authorities cited therein.

[8] *See, e.g.*, *Garcia-Mir*, 788 F.2d at 1455 (indefinite detention).

[9] *See, e.g.*, Louis Henkin, *The Constitution and United States Sovereignty: A Century of Chinese Exclusion and Its Progeny*, 100 Harv. L. Rev. 853 (1987) [hereinafter Henkin, *Chinese Exclusion*] (disputing customary international law as being only federal common law).

[10] If federal statutes as well as treaties have equal authority – as the last-in-time rule holds – then treaties trump customary international law. However, this inference violates international law.

[11] [*See* Section 3.2.1 (discussing last-in-time rule governing treaties as being inconsistent with originalist understanding).

Francisco Forrest Martin
CHALLENGING HUMAN RIGHTS VIOLATIONS: USING INTERNATIONAL LAW IN U.S. COURTS 9–14, 17–30 (2001)

. . . .

Treaties are part of the "supreme Law of the Land."[1] The U.S. Constitution grants the President power to enter into treaties with the advice and consent of the Senate.[2]

. . . .

In the following sections, we will examine the issue of self-executing treaties. . . .

i. Self-Executing and Non-Self-Executing Treaties

From the outset, one should note the following:

> The Framers' criticisms of the government established by the Articles of Confederation show that they understood that treaties, as international instruments, operated on states as bodies politic and were enforceable only by military force. They described the Articles as a "mere treaty" for these reasons.
>
> The new government that the Framers established, by contrast, was one of "law": its acts, treaties, and the Constitution were all three declared to be "laws." To the Framers, this meant that all three would be operative on individuals, not just on states, and would be enforceable in the courts. This was the mechanism by which the new government sought to secure compliance with its acts. The Supremacy Clause transformed instruments that had previously been operative on states as political bodies and enforceable only by military force into instruments operative on individuals and enforceable in the courts.[3]

This observation acquires especial relevance in the context of human rights and humanitarian treaties that recognize and/or create rights for individuals. One must keep in mind the Framers' perception of treaties when examining the domestic legal effect of treaties.

In the 1829 case of *Foster v. Neilson*,[4] the U.S. Supreme Court held that treaties can be either self-executing or non-self-executing. . . . In discussing non-self-executing treaties, Chief Justice John Marshall stated that these treaties are addressed "to the political, not the judicial department; and the legislature must execute the contract (*i.e.*, the treaty) before it can become a rule for the Court."[5] . . . .

Professor Vazquez has distinguished four doctrines of non-self-execution. They are the following:

> First, legislative action is necessary if the parties to the treaty (or perhaps the U.S. treaty makers alone) intended that the treaty's object be accomplished through intervening acts of legislation. Second, legislative action is necessary if the norm the treaty establishes is "addressed" as a constitutional matter to the legislature.

---

[1] U.S. CONST. art. VI, cl. 2.

[2] U.S. CONST. art. II, §2, cl. 2.

[3] Carlos Manuel Vazquez, *Treaty-Based Rights and Remedies of Individuals*, 92 COLUM. L. REV. 1082, 1096–97 (1992).

[4] 27 U.S. (2 Pet.) 253 (1829).

[5] *Id.* at 314.

Third, legislative action is necessary if the treaty purports to accomplish what under our Constitution may be accomplished only by statute. Finally, legislation is necessary if no law confers a right of action on a plaintiff seeking to enforce the treaty.[6]

The RESTATEMENT states that a treaty or agreement is non-self-executing if: (i) the agreement itself manifests an intention that it shall not be effective domestically until implemented through further legislation; (ii) the Senate in giving consent, or Congress by resolution, requires implementing legislation; or (iii) if implementing legislation is constitutionally required, such as for a declaration of war or an appropriation.[7]

In the context of human rights and humanitarian treaties, the political branches have attempted to limit or eliminate the domestic effect of the rights invested by these treaties in individuals. The political branches have done so simply by declaring such treaties as non-self-executing in very sweeping and vague fashion. What the political branches have intended exactly is often ambiguous.

Sometimes the political branches ratify a treaty declaring that the treaty is non-self-executing and claiming that the treaty adds nothing to human rights protection under extant U.S. law. (If the treaty does provide additional protection, a reservation is deposited eliminating this additional protection.) Consequently, Congress enacts no implementing legislation. This is the case with the ICCPR, and, as we shall see, this interpretation is invalid.

Sometimes the political branches declare the treaty as non-self-executing to mean that the rights *themselves* guaranteed by the treaty require legislation to be enacted before or after ratification in order for these rights to have *any* domestic legal effect. An example of this approach was the Senate's requirement that implementing legislation be enacted before ratification of the Genocide Convention.

The constitutional authority of the political branches to make a declaration limiting the ability of the federal courts to enforce treaty rights has been challenged by leading scholars. Since the U.S. Constitution gave treaty-making power to the President with the Senate, to the exclusion of the House or Congress, allowing a Congressional resolution or Senatorial act to render a treaty domestically inapplicable appears to violate the Constitution. Commentators question whether this practice "is contrary to both the letter and spirit of the Constitution, and to the distribution of power between the Senate and the House intended by the Framers."[8] Sometimes a non-self-execution declaration can be considered a "counteroffer" to the other parties to a treaty.[9] However, the Constitution does not give the Senate the authority to make counteroffers or negotiate treaties. Accordingly, such declarations would violate the separation of powers principle between

---

[6] Carlos Manuel Vazquez, *The Four Doctrines of Self-Executing Treaties*, 89 AM. J. INT'L L. 695, 696–97 (1995).

[7] RESTATEMENT §111(4).

[8] LOUIS HENKIN ET AL., INTERNATIONAL LAW: CASES AND MATERIALS 219 (3d ed. 1993) (hereinafter HENKIN, CASEBOOK); *see* Lori Fisler Damrosch, *The Role of the United States Senate Concerning "Self-Executing" and "Non-Self-Executing" Treaties*, 67 CHI.-KENT. L. REV. 515, 526 (1991) ("[a] Senate declaration purporting to negate the legal effect of otherwise self-executing treaty provisions is constitutionally questionable as a derogation from the ordinary application of Article VI of the Constitution. . . .").

[9] *See, e.g., Treaties and Executive Agreements: Hearings on S.J. Res. I ad S.J. Res. 43 Before a Subcomm. of the Senate Comm. on the Judiciary*, 83rd Cong., 1st Sess. 7, at 922 (1953) (testimony of U.S. Attorney General Brownell).

the President and the Senate. Most importantly, as Professor Paust has stated,

> It is the judiciary, not Congress, that has been granted the power . . . under Article III
> of the Constitution to apply treaty law in cases or controversies otherwise properly
> before the courts.[10]

Citing the U.S. Supreme Court case of *Owings v. Norwood's Lessee*,[11] Professor Paust
argues that the "reason for inserting that clause [Art. III, §2, cl. 1] . . . was, that all persons
who have real claims under a treaty should have their causes decided."[12] Therefore, such a
non-self-execution declaration would violate the separation of powers principle between
Congress and the federal judiciary.

Generally, a treaty that creates a duty to refrain from acting or confers specific rights
will be considered self-executing.[13] Human rights treaties – like Amendments 1–8 or
federal civil rights statutes – is federal law not requiring further legislation. It is like
saying that a constitutional provision or federal statute that creates or recognizes rights
requires a subsequent federal statute as implementing legislation to give domestic legal
effect to these rights. This is an unnecessary duplication of law-making. Provisions of the
U.S. Constitution, such as the due process guarantee in the Fourteenth Amendment, are
often drafted in general terms. Nevertheless, these provisions are enforced in the courts
without enabling legislation. Congress is allowed to enforce constitutional provisions
through legislation (such as 42 U.S.C. §1983), but such measures are not necessary to
give domestic legal effect to rights recognized/created by the Constitution. Congress has
the authority to enact subsequent legislation *only to guide* enforcement. However, the
availability of judicial decisions for interpreting treaty provisions obviates the need for
implementing legislation to guide interpretation.[14] In the context of international human
and humanitarian rights, legislation is not needed to guide enforcement. There is ample
international case law giving guidance and meaning to international human rights and
humanitarian law.

Sometimes a treaty is ratified that later is considered to be non-self-executing because
only the political branches can competently enforce the rights and fulfill the duties guaranteed by the treaty. Examples of such treaties are the humanitarian treaties, such as the
Hague and Geneva Conventions. Such treaties raise the political question doctrine under
the principle of separation of powers. However, whether the political question doctrine is
relevant and a claim under the treaty is justiciable will depend upon the particular treaty
provisions being addressed.

Finally, the political branches sometimes declare a human rights treaty non-self-
executing in the sense that the treaty does not create a private cause of action.[15] An

---

[10] Jordan J. Paust, *Self-Executing Treaties*, 82 Am. J. Int'l L. 760, 775 (1988).

[11] 9 U.S. (5 Cranch) at 348–349 (1809).

[12] Paust, *supra*, at 766 n. 41.

[13] Restatement §111 reporters' note 5.

[14] *See Warren v. United States*, 340 U.S. 523, 526–28 (1951). In *Warren v. United States*, the U.S. Supreme
Court held that a treaty provision at issue was self-executing, despite the Secretary of State's view to
the contrary. The Supreme Court rejected the Secretary of State's interpretation of a provision of the
Shipowners' Liability Convention as being non-self-executing because general maritime law established
by judicial decisions provided sufficient interpretive guidance.

[15] *See, e.g., In re Estate of Ferdinand E. Marcos Human Rights Litig.*, 978 F.2d 493, 503 (9th Cir. 1992) ("No
private cause of action can ever be implied from a non-self-executing treaty."); *cf. Goldstar (Panama) S.A.
v. United States*, 967 F.2d 965, 968 (4th Cir. 1992) ("Courts will only find a treaty to be self-executing if the

example of this is when the political branches declared the Convention to Eliminate All Forms of Racial Discrimination to be non-self-executing in that it did not create new or independent private causes of action. However, although a treaty may not *create* a private cause of action, a treaty can be self-executing if it *recognizes* that extra-treaty sources establishing a private cause of action for treaty violations already exist. Such sources may be statutory or common law causes of action.[16] Anyway, regardless whether a human rights treaty creates or recognizes a private cause of action, the substantive provisions of human rights treaties could still be used as a defense.[17]

The U.S. Ninth Circuit Court of Appeals in *Islamic Republic of Iran v. Boeing Co.*[18] developed a four-part test for determining whether and to what extent a treaty is self-executing. Although this test probably is too restrictive for the reason discussed below,[19] we shall use the test to demonstrate how human rights and humanitarian treaties still would have domestic legal effect. The four factors under the *Boeing* test to be considered are the following:

1. "the purposes of the treaty and the objectives of its creators;"
2. "the existence of domestic procedures and institutions appropriate for direct implementation;"
3. "the immediate and long-range social consequences of self- or non-self-execution;" and
4. "the availability and feasibility of alternative enforcement methods."[20]

The first factor is the only factor for determining whether a treaty is self-executing.[21] The U.S. Court of Appeals decision in *Islamic Republic of Iran v. Boeing Co.* effectively adopts the "Object and Purpose Rule" in Article 19 of the Vienna Convention on the Law of Treaties (Vienna Convention-T)[22] for determining whether a treaty is self-executing or non-self-executing.[23] The Vienna Convention-T is universally accepted to be a codification of general principles of international treaty law.[24] According to its provisions,

---

document, as a whole, evidences an intent to provide a private right of action."); *see also* David Sloss, *The Domestication of International Human Rights: Non-Self-Executing Declarations and Human Rights Treaties,* 24 YALE J. INT'L L. 129, 152–53 (1999) (describing shifting understandings of concept of self-executing treaties through Carter, Bush, and Clinton presidential administrations).

16 *See* Vazquez, *supra*, at 1141–57.

17 *See* Vazquez, *supra*, at 719–22.

18 771 F.2d 1279 (9th Cir. 1985).

19 *See infra* text accompanying note [64].

20 771 F.2d at 1283 (quoting *People of Saipan v. United States Dep't of Interior*, 502 F.2d 90, 97 (9th Cir. 1974).

21 *Id.*

22 *See* Vienna Convention on the Law of Treaties, signed 23 May 1969, U.N. Doc. A/CONF/.39/27 (entry into force 27 January 1980) (hereinafter Vienna Convention-T).

23 771 F.2d at 1283.

24 Although the U.S. has not ratified the treaty, it is a signatory. The State Department has said that "the Convention is already generally recognized as the authoritative guide to current treaty law and practice" with respect to its substantive provisions. S. Exec. Doc. L. 92d Cong., 1st Sess. (1971) p. 1. The U.S. Solicitor General has stated that the Vienna Convention-T "is generally considered to be consistent with current treaty law and practice as recognized by the United States." *Domingues v. Nevada,* No. 98-8327, On petition for a writ of certiorari to the Supreme Court of Nevada, Brief for the United States as Amicus Curiae at 8 (October 1999). Federal courts have frequently applied its provisions when dealing with questions of treaty interpretation. *See Weinberger v. Rossi,* 456 U.S. 25, 29 (1982); *Sale v. Haitian Ctrs. Council, Inc.,* 509 U.S. 155, 194–95 (1993) (Blackmun, J., dissenting); *Siderman de Blake v. Argentina,* 965 F.2d 699, 714 (9th Cir. 1992); *Day v. Trans World Airlines, Inc.,* 528 F.2d 31, 33 (2d Cir. 1975); *United States v. Cadena,* 585

countries are allowed to enter reservations to a treaty except in a few circumstances, including where the reservation is prohibited by the treaty or incompatible with the object and purpose of the treaty. The Vienna Convention-T states:

> A State may, when signing, ratifying, accepting, approving or acceding to a treaty, formulate a reservation unless:
>
> (a) the reservation is prohibited by the treaty;
> (b) the treaty provides that only specified reservations, which do not include the reservation in question, may be made; or
> (c) in cases not falling under sub-paragraphs (a) and (b), the reservation is incompatible with the object and purpose of the treaty.[25]

The other three factors in the test articulated in *Islamic Republic of Iran v. Boeing Co.* are relevant for determining the extent to which the treaty is self-executing,[26] including the availability of a private cause of action.

. . . .

i. International Covenant on Civil and Political Rights

A major international human rights treaty to which the U.S. is a party is the International Covenant on Civil and Political Rights (ICCPR). The U.S. deposited the instrument of ratification with the UN on 8 June 1992.[27] Attached to the instrument was a series of reservations, understandings, and declarations. Most significantly was a declaration that Articles 1–27 of the ICCPR (which lists the human rights guaranteed by the ICCPR) were non-self-executing. It is interesting to note that the Bush Administration appears to have used two conceptions of "non-self-executing." "The Bush Administration presented different explanations at different times, shifting back and forth between the Foster[[28]] concept and the 'private cause of action' concept."[29] The Senate had made its consent to the ICCPR's ratification conditioned upon these same reservations, understandings, and declarations,[30] which, in turn, had been proposed by President Bush.

F.2d 1252, 1261 (5th Cir. 1978); *Committee of U.S. Citizens Living in Nicaragua v. Reagan*, 859 F.2d 929, 940 (D.C. Cir. 1988); *Doe I v. UNOCAL Corp.*, 963 F. Supp. 880, 890 (C.D. Cal. 1997); *Acrilicos v. Regan*, 617 F. Supp. 1082, 1086 (Ct. Int'l Trade 1985).

    The U.S. appears to have never objected to the legal authority of the Object and Purpose Rule.

[25] Vienna Convention-T, art. 19.

[26] 771 F.2d at 1283.

[27] Multilateral Treaties Deposited with the Secretary General: Status as at 31 Dec. 1992, at 132, U.N. Doc. ST/LEG/SER.E/11 (1993) (hereinafter Multilateral Treaties).

[28] The Foster concept refers to the understanding of self-executing treaties in *Foster v. Neilson*, 27 U.S. (2 Pet.) 253, 314 (1829): "[W]hen the terms of [a treaty] import a contract, when either of the parties engages to perform a particular act, the treaty addresses itself to the political, not the judicial department, and the legislature must execute the contract before it can become a rule for the Court."

[29] David Sloss, *The Domestication of International Human Rights: Non-Self-Executing Declarations and Human Rights Treaties*, 24 Yale J. Int'l L. 129, 153 (1999).

[30] U.S. Reservations, Declarations, and Understandings to the International Covenant on Civil and Political Rights, 138 Cong. Rec. S4783-4 (daily ed., 2 April 1992).

    The Senate has defined the terms "reservation," "understanding," and "declaration" in the following manner: "A reservation is usually defined as a unilateral statement made by a contracting party which purports to exclude or modify the terms of a treaty or the legal effect of certain provisions." S. Exec. Rep. No. 99-2, at 16 (1985). "An understanding is generally defined as a statement which interprets or clarifies the obligation undertaken by a party to a treaty." *Id.* "A declaration is generally defined as a formal statement, explanation or clarification made by a party about its opinion or intentions relating to issues raised

a. Articles 1–27 of the Covenant Self-Executing Under Islamic Republic of Iran v. Boeing Co.

The only condition for establishing whether the ICCPR is self-executing under *Islamic Republic of Iran v. Boeing Co.* is to examine the treaty's object and purpose to determine whether it was designed to recognize/create self-executing rights.[31] Under the Object and Purpose Rule, Articles 1–27 are self-executing. The object and purpose of the ICCPR as reflected in its text is to recognize and protect rights and to give these rights domestic effect. Article 2 states:

> 1. Each State Party to the present Covenant undertakes to respect and to ensure to all individuals within its territory and subject to its jurisdiction the rights recognized in the present Covenant. . . . [32]

Articles 1–27 expressly guarantee these rights. There is no need to enact enabling legislation to provide further meaning to these rights in order to guide enforcement because there already is substantial case law[ ] interpreting these rights.[33]

President Bush's (and Senate's) non-self-execution declaration was designed to not allow the ICCPR to provide any further substantive human rights protection. The declaration is effectively a reservation because it seeks to eliminate or modify the ICCPR's provisions. In areas where ICCPR rights did appear to provide greater protection than U.S. law in 1992, the U.S. deposited a reservation. The President (and Senate) believed that most U.S. law and practices already were in conformity with the ICCPR. Of course,[. . .] the President (and Senate) clearly failed to recognize the numerous areas in which the United States's law and practices were *not* in conformity with the ICCPR – regardless of the United States' reservations.[34] Such a mistaken interpretation cannot be controlling.

---

by the treaty under consideration. Ordinarily, declarations do not touch upon a party's obligations under a treaty." *Id.* at 17.

Regardless of these definitions, many of the ICCPR's "understandings" and "declarations" arguably appear to be designed to "exclude or to modify the legal effect of certain provisions." Hence, these "understandings" and "declarations" are properly classified as "reservations" under international law. *See* Vienna Convention-T, art. 2 (1) (d) ("a unilateral statement, however phrased or named, made by a State, when signing, ratifying, accepting, approving or acceding to a treaty, whereby it purports to exclude or to modify the legal effect of certain provisions of the treaty in their application to that State").

Whether the non-self-execution declaration is a reservation or not depends on the definition of non-self-execution being used. When the President (or Senate) defined the non-self-execution declaration in the sense that the U.S.' obligations under ICCPR would provide no further substantive rights protection, this definition clearly would make the declaration a reservation. On the other hand, when the declaration is defined in the sense that the U.S.' obligations under the ICCPR would not create new private causes of action, the declaration is not a reservation.

[31] 771 F.2d 1279, 1283 (9th Cir. 1985).

[32] ICCPR, art. 2(1).

[33] *Cf. Warren v. United States*, 340 U.S. 523, 526–28 (1951) (treaty provisions are self-executing because no Act of Congress is needed to guide enforcement of treaty provisions in light of judicial decisions).

The *travaux préparatoires* of the ICCPR do not indicate that the U.S. delegations ever objected to the self-executing nature of the ICCPR. Therefore, the object and purpose of the ICCPR as partially reflected by the U.S. delegation's ambiguous position does not provide much insight. Only until two years after the ICCPR came into force did the President propose that Articles 1–27 should not be considered self-executing. Message from the President of the United States Transmitting Four Treaties Pertaining to Human Rights, S. Exec. Docs. C, D, E and F, 95–2, at vi (1978).

[34] One commentator has observed that regardless of the Executive Branch's repeated assurances to the Senate that "the conditions included in the U.S. instruments of ratification had successfully eliminated any

Although interpretations by the political branches are given great weight,[35] the U.S. Supreme Court has rejected invalid interpretations of treaties by the political branches.[36]

Moreover, the non-self-execution declaration as a reservation is invalid under the Object and Purpose Rule, which reflects customary international law, and U.S. law[37] and policy.[38] ... [T]he Constitution recognizes and enforces customary international law as federal law. Accordingly, the constitutional treaty-making authority should be subject to the "Object and Purpose Rule" recognized by both the Vienna Convention-T and customary international law.[39]

Furthermore, the Vienna Convention-T states:

> When a treaty is a constituent instrument of an international organization and unless it otherwise provides, a reservation requires the acceptance of the competent organ of that organization.[40]

---

discrepancy between treaty requirements and preexisting domestic law, thereby ensuring that the United States could comply fully with its treaty obligations without having to domesticate the treaties," the United States' law and practices are in conflict with its international human rights treaty obligations. David Sloss, *The Domestication of International Human Rights: Non-Self-Executing Declarations and Human Rights Treaties*, 24 YALE J. INT'L L. 129, 135 (1999).

[35] *See Kolovrat v. Oregon*, 366 U.S. 187, 194 (1961) ("While courts interpret treaties for themselves, the meaning given them by the departments of government particularly charged with their negotiation and enforcement is given great weight."); *see also Cameron Septic Tank Co. v. City of Knoxville*, 227 U.S. 39, 48–50 (1913) (placing great weight on the views expressed by Congress and the Executive Branch in supporting its conclusion that the treaty provision at issue was not self-executing).

[36] *See, e.g., Kolovrat v. Oregon*, 366 U.S. at 192 ("This Court has many times set its face against treaty interpretations that unduly restrict rights a treaty is adopted to protect.").

[37] *Islamic Republic of Iran v. Boeing Co.*, 771 F.2d 1279 (9th Cir. 1985).

[38] The State Department has said that "the Convention is already generally recognized as the authoritative guide to current treaty law and practice" with respect to its substantive provisions. S. Exec. Doc. L. 92d Cong., 1st Sess. (1971) p. 1. The U.S. Solicitor General has stated that the Vienna Convention-T "is generally considered to be consistent with current treaty law and practice as recognized by the United States." *Domingues v. Nevada*, No. 98-8327, On petition for a writ of certiorari to the Supreme Court of Nevada, Brief for the United States as Amicus Curiae at 8 (October 1999). Federal courts have frequently applied its provisions when dealing with questions of treaty interpretation. *See Weinberger v. Rossi*, 456 U.S. 25, 29 (1982); *Sale v. Haitian Ctrs. Council, Inc.*, 509 U.S. 155, 194–95 (1993) (Blackmun, J., dissenting); *Siderman de Blake v. Argentina*, 965 F.2d 699, 714 (9th Cir. 1992); *Day v. Trans World Airlines, Inc.*, 528 F.2d 31, 33 (2d Cir. 1975); *United States v. Cadena*, 585 F.2d 1252, 1261 (5th Cir. 1978); *Committee of U.S. Citizens Living in Nicaragua v. Reagan*, 859 F.2d 929, 940 (D.C. Cir. 1988); *Doe I v. UNOCAL Corp.*, 963 F. Supp. 880, 890 (C.D. Cal. 1997); *Acrilicos v. Regan*, 617 F. Supp. 1082, 1086 (Ct. Int'l Trade 1985).

[39] The International Law Commission while commenting on the original draft version of the Object and Purpose Rule under Article 19, Vienna Convention-T suggested that the rule is not an independent barrier to reservation acceptance by other nations under Article 20. *See* Documents of the Conference on the Vienna Convention, A/CONF.39/11/Add.2. During later negotiations, many nations proposed amendments to the Vienna Convention-T to clarify that the Object and Purpose Rule was an absolute bar to reservations, but these amendments were all rejected. *See* Catherine Redgwell, *Universality or Integrity? Some Reflections on Reservations to General Multilateral Treaties*, 64 BRIT. Y. B. INT'L L. 245, 255–60 (1993). Regardless of the Object and Purpose Rule's apparent ambiguity as an independent bar to reservations, the UN Human Rights Committee in addressing the validity of reservations to the ICCPR (which expressly authorizes the Committee to issue general comments under Article 40, ICCPR) has commented that the Object and Purpose Rule does act as an independent bar. Therefore, the International Law Commission's ambiguous position is not controlling on the ICCPR because (i) the only organ authorized by the ICCPR to interpret the ICCPR – the UN Human Rights Committee – has held that the Object and Purpose Rule does bar reservations, and (ii) the International Law Commission is interpreting general international law.

[40] Vienna Convention-T, art. 20 (3).

In the case of the ICCPR, it is the "constituent instrument" of an intergovernmental organization – *viz.*, the UN Human Rights Committee. The ICCPR created the UN Human
Rights Committee, and the UN Human Rights Committee is an intergovernmental organization because the ICCPR was adopted by the UN, its staff are provided by the UN, and
Committee members are elected by an intergovernmental meeting convened by the UN
Secretary General for states-parties. The Committee happens also to be the "competent
organ" for accepting or rejecting reservations to the ICCPR. The non-self-execution declaration, which is effectively a reservation, did not receive the Committee's affirmative
approval. Therefore, there is a legal presumption that the non-self-execution declaration
is invalid under the Vienna Convention-T.[41]

Finally, the non-self-execution declaration probably also violates a customary international law prohibition on general reservations. In *Belilos v. Switzerland*,[42] the European
Court of Human Rights held that Switzerland's interpretive declaration was too general
and vague to be valid. The Swiss declaration stated the following.

> The Swiss Federal Council considers that the guarantee of fair trial in Article 6(1) of
> the Convention, in the determination of civil rights and obligations or any criminal
> charge against the person in question is intended solely to ensure ultimate control
> by the judiciary over the acts or decisions of the public authorities relating to such
> rights or obligations or the determination of such a charge.[43]

The European Court held that declaration was invalid because it was impossible to ascertain exactly the scope of obligations that Switzerland was undertaking, in particular as
to which categories of dispute were included and as to whether or not the "ultimate control by the judiciary" takes in the facts of a case.[44] In *Belilos*, the Swiss government's
declaration was even more precise than the U.S. declaration, which sweepingly and
unclearly states that Articles 1–27 are non-self-executing. As argued below, the European
Court of Human Rights' decisions reflect customary international law which is binding
on the U.S.[ ] Therefore, the U.S. declaration is invalid because it is too general and
vague.

The next issue for examination under *Islamic Republic of Iran v. Boeing Co.* is what *extent*
is the ICCPR self-executing? Are there "domestic procedures and institutions appropriate
for direct implementation,"[45] such as extant statutory and judicial authorities providing
or recognizing private causes of action?

Article 2, ICCPR, expressly recognizes that such "domestic procedures and institutions"
may be already available for providing direct implementation of the rights guaranteed by
Articles 1–27. Article 2 requires the U.S. to give domestic effect to these rights.

---

[41] In a analogous case to the ICCPR, the Inter-American Court of Human Rights has opined that the ACHR
is "not the constituent instrument of an international organization" for purposes of Article 20(3) of the
Vienna Convention-T, which means that the Court is not the organ envisaged by Article 20(3). However,
the Court's conclusion was a summary involving no analysis. *See The Effect of Reservations on the Entry
Into Force of the American Convention on Human Rights (Arts. 74 and 75)*, Advisory Opinion OC-2/82 of
September 24, 1982, Inter-Am.Ct.H.R. (Ser. A) No. 2 (1982) at §27.

[42] 132 Eur. Ct. H.R. (ser. A) §60 (1988) (Switzerland still bound by ECHR regardless of invalidity of interpretive
declaration made upon ratification).

[43] *Id.* at §29.

[44] *Id.* at §55.

[45] 771 F.2d at 1283 (quoting *People of Saipan v. United States Dep't of Interior*, 502 F.2d 90, 97 (9th Cir. 1974).

2. *Where not already provided for by existing legislative or other measures*, each State Party to the present Covenant undertakes to take the necessary steps, in accordance with its constitutional processes and with the provisions of the present Covenant, to adopt such legislative or other measures as may be necessary to give effect to the rights recognized in the present Covenant.

3. Each State Party to the present Covenant undertakes:

(a) To ensure that any person whose rights or freedoms as herein recognized are violated shall have an effective remedy, notwithstanding that the violation has been committed by persons acting in an official capacity;

(b) To ensure that any person claiming such a remedy shall have his right thereto determined by competent judicial, administrative or legislative authorities, or by any other competent authority provided for by the legal system of the State, and to develop the possibilities of judicial remedy;

(c) To ensure that the competent authorities shall enforce such remedies when granted.[46]

It is the object and purpose of the ICCPR for states-parties to undertake the necessary steps to give domestic effect to these rights if such measures have not already been taken. As we will see later,[ ] the U.S. already had taken such measures in the form of statutes and judicial decisions that recognize the domestic legal effect of such rights. The domestic effect provided by these statutes and judicial decisions include the recognition of private causes of action for violations of treaty rights.

Nevertheless, several U.S. federal[47] and state[48] courts have held that Articles 1–27 of the ICCPR are non-self-executing, relying upon (i) the ICCPR's text itself and/or (ii) the U.S. declaration that these articles are not self-executing. In regard to the reliance upon the ICCPR's text, a U.S. district court in *White v. Paulsen*[49] concluded from the language of Article 2 that the ICCPR was non-self-executing because the ICCPR

expressly require[s] party-states take steps under their municipal laws to enforce the rights described in [the ICCPR], suggesting strongly that parties to [the ICCPR] did not intend for [it] to be self-executing.[50]

Furthermore, the district court stated that "the existence of the various domestic law remedies...counsels against reading into [the ICCPR and CAT] an intent to create a domestic private right of action."

The district court failed to understand that the ICCPR was not *creating* a private cause of action but *recognizing* the extant availability of such private causes of action. Article 2(2) stated: "Where not already provided for by existing legislative or other measures...." For example, federal *habeas corpus* statutes, 42 U.S.C. §1983, and the Alien Tort Claims Act create private causes of action for treaty claims.[ ] And, for those areas in which

---

[46] ICCPR, art. 2 (2)-(3) (emphasis provided).

[47] *See, e.g., Igartua de la Rosa v. United States*, 32 F.3d 8, 10 n.1 (1st Cir. 1994); *Ralk v. Lincoln Country, Georgia*, 81 F. Supp. 2d 1372 (S.D. Ga. 2000) (relying on declaration); *Heinrich v. Sweet*, 49 F. Supp. 2d 27, 44 (D. Mass. 1999) (relying on declaration and text); *In the Matter of the Extradition of Cheung*, 968 F. Supp. 791, 803 n.17 (D. Conn. 1997).

[48] *See, e.g., Domingues v. State of Nevada*, 114 Nev. 783; 961 P.2d 1279 (1998) (relying on declaration).

[49] 997 F. Supp. 1380 (E.D. Wash. 1998).

[50] *Id.* at 1386.

there are no legislative measures giving effect to the rights guaranteed by Articles 1–27, "other" – including judicial – measures already are available.[ ] Therefore, Articles 1–27 are self-executing because there already are legislative or other measures giving them effect.

This raises another question. Did the Bush Administration (and Senate) want to not create new private causes of action or did it want to eliminate already existing private causes of action? If the Bush Administration (and the Senate) did not want to *create new* private causes of action, the declaration poses no problem for establishing that the ICCPR is self-executing because the ICCPR, nevertheless, recognizes already existing private causes of action based on extra-ICCPR sources. However, if the Bush Administration (and Senate) intended to *eliminate already existing* private causes of action, then the declaration not only would be unconstitutional but also extremely far-reaching with consequences probably unintended by the President (and Senate).

The U.S. cannot by virtue of its non-self-execution declaration withdraw the domestic legal effect of the very rights whose protection is the object and purpose of the ICCPR because this would violate the Object and Purpose Rule, which is recognized as customary international law, and U.S. law and policy. Therefore, the Bush Administration's declaration as interpreted to mean the withdrawal of extant statutory and judicial private causes of action is invalid because it would violate the Object and Purpose Rule.

This raises the third factor to consider under *Islamic Republic of Iran v. Boeing Co.*: "the immediate and long-range social consequences of self- or non-self-execution." It is hard to believe that the President (and Senate) would have intended the declaration to eliminate extant private causes of action because of the enormous reach of such an intended effect. If the declaration were to be considered constitutional, the ICCPR as interpreted by the non-self-execution declaration would have the effect of superceding numerous statutory provisions establishing private causes of action for ICCPR violations.[51] Among the many important federal statutes whose provisions would be superceded are, as noted earlier, the Alien Tort Claims Act (ATCA), 42 U.S.C. §1983, and the *habeas corpus* statutes.[ ] Indeed, under the *Foster* approach to the declaration, the consequences would be even further far-reaching. The protection available through sources other than private causes of action would be eliminated. For example, *any* executive or legislative act would be trumped by the ICCPR as interpreted by the declaration.[52] Such consequences weigh against the declaration being given such an interpretation.

On the other hand, does the invalidity of the U.S.' declaration void the U.S.' agreement to become a party to the ICCPR? First, it is important first to note that regardless of the invalidity of the declaration under this interpretation, the U.S. would still be bound by the ICCPR according to the UN Human Rights Committee[53] and the Vienna

---

[51] Of course, the Senate and President constitutionally cannot eliminate federal and state judicial sources for recognizing private causes of action for ICCPR claims because this respectively would violate the principles of federalism and separation of powers.

[52] This may have been the kind of scenario that the U.S. Court of Appeals for the D.C. Circuit wanted to avoid in *Power Authority of New York v. Federal Power Commission.* 247 F.2d 538 (D.C.Cir.), *vacated & remanded with directions to dismiss as moot*, 355 U.S. 64 (1957). By interpreting a Senate reservation to *not* be a necessary condition for Senate consent to a U.S-Canada treaty, the U.S. Court of Appeals avoided invalidating the Federal Power Commission's pre-existing licensing authority under federal statutory law.

[53] *See* General Comment 26, U.N. GAOR Hum. Rts. Comm., 53d Sess., Supp. No. 40, P 5, U.N. Doc. A/53/40 (1998) (states-parties to ICCPR cannot withdraw).

Convention-T,[54] as well as – probably – other international law reflected by the European Court of Human Rights' decisions in *Loizidou v. Turkey*[55] and *Belilos v. Switzerland*.[56] Although the International Court of Justice in a 1951 Advisory Opinion opined that if a state makes a reservation incompatible with the object and purpose of the Genocide Convention, the state "cannot be regarded as being a party to the Convention," this opinion no longer reflects the general customary international law regarding reservations.[57] Given the date of the ICJ's opinion relative to the dates of the adoption of the Vienna Convention-T (1969), the European Court of Human Rights decisions in *Loizidou v. Turkey* (1995) and *Belilos v. Switzerland* (1988), and the UN Human Rights Committee's General Comment 26 (1998), the ICJ's opinion probably no longer reflects the general customary international law regarding reservations. Most importantly, unlike the ICCPR and ECHR, the Genocide Convention did not create an interpretive body. Under Article 20(3) of the Vienna Convention-T, a reservation to a treaty constituting such a body must be approved by the body.

Second, although consent is important in international law, it is not always controlling.[58] According to the Vienna Convention-T, before a treaty is ratified, a signatory state "must refrain from acts which would defeat the object and purpose" of the treaty.[59] Such acts would include the United States' deposit of reservations, understandings, and declarations that violate the Object and Purpose Rule.

The issue of the United States' consent must be analyzed according to constitutional principles – not the generally irrelevant principles of traditional contract law. The U.S. Supreme Court in *Foster v. Neilson* rejected the contractual law conceptualization of self-executing treaties under the Supremacy Clause.[60] The contract law approach is especially inappropriate in the context of multilateral human rights treaties. Multilateral human rights treaties impose *trans*-national obligations that recognize the rights of individuals and are not merely "exchanges of obligations" between two states.[61] A contract creates mutual obligations between the parties. Multilateral human rights treaties do not primarily create mutual duties between states-parties. Multilateral human rights treaties generally do not create mutual duties between the state-party and the protected individual. Also, the state-party receives no consideration from the protected individual. As Professor Stein has observed about the contemporary international legal

---

[54] Article 56 of the Vienna Convention-T states: "A treaty which contains no provision regarding its termination and which does not provide for denunciation or withdrawal is not subject to denunciation or withdrawal...." The ICCPR contains no such provision.

[55] 310 Eur. Ct. H.R. (ser. A) (1995) (Turkey still bound by ECHR regardless of reservation's invalidity). However, the European Court inferred that Turkey originally intended to be bound to the ECHR regardless of the reservation's invalidity.

[56] 132 Eur. Ct. H.R. (ser. A) §60 (1988) (Switzerland still bound by ECHR regardless of invalidity of interpretive declaration made upon ratification). However, the European Court concluded that Switzerland intended to continue being bound by the ECHR.

[57] *Reservations to the Genocide Convention*, [1951] I.C.J. REP. 15, 18.

[58] For example, state consent is not required to establish the state's legal obligation to observe *jus cogens* norms....

[59] Vienna Convention-T, art. 18 (a).

[60] *See* 27 U.S. (2 Pet.) at 314.

[61] UN Hum. Rts. Ctte. General Comment 24, U.N. Doc. HRI/GEN/1/Rev.3 ¶ 8 (1997) (recognizing difference between those treaties that are "mere exchanges of obligations between States" and human rights treaties, "which are for the benefit of persons within their jurisdiction....").

order, "the multilateral treaty-making process is legislative in objective but contractual in method."[62]

Moreover, reservations to treaties usually require subsequent re-negotiation with other states parties that is difficult – if not impossible – in cases involving multilateral, global treaties – especially sixteen years after the treaty comes into force, as in the case of the U.S. ratification of the ICCPR.[63] For states-parties to begin re-negotiation with the U.S. over its reservations (including the declaration) is impractical. In the case of the U.S. ratification of the ICCPR in 1992, there already were over 100 states-parties to the ICCPR. It is no wonder that there has been no attempt to re-negotiate with the U.S.

The appropriate understanding of the Senate's consent is to place it in the context of law-making. Treaties become federal law in similar ways to Congressional bills becoming federal law. The Senate's consent to a treaty takes place through vote-taking as is the passage of Congressional bills. For both treaties and Congressional bills, the President's signature is required (except for those bills that can override the President's veto). If subsequently a federal court finds that certain provisions (*e.g.*, a declaration or reservation) of the treaty – like a federal statute – are unconstitutional, then those provisions cannot have domestic legal effect. This view makes more commonsense because human rights treaty-making is more similar to law-making then it is to contract-making, which may not involve any fundamental rights or third-party beneficiaries.

In any event, all of this is mooted by the fact that the ambiguity of the declaration's reach regarding the elimination of extant private causes of action requires that the declaration be interpreted to not conflict with international law under the *Charming Betsy* Rule. There is no clear indication that the President (and Senate) intended to eliminate extant legislative private causes of action giving domestic legal effect to the ICCPR Therefore, the declaration should not be interpreted to mean that it eliminates already existing private causes of action.

Finally, the last issue to consider under *Islamic Republic v. Boeing, Co.* is "the availability and feasibility of alternative enforcement methods."[64] This last factor probably is invalid because if treaties are federal law like federal statutes and different federal statutes can duplicate rights protection, then human rights treaties that duplicate constitutional or federal statutory protection should not be a reason for not giving domestic legal effect to such treaty rights....

. . . .

b. Regardless of Constitutional Validity, U.S. Non-Self-Execution Declaration Does Not Extend to Non-Article III Tribunals

Regardless of whether the non-self-executing declaration has lawful effect or not, the declaration cannot apply to tribunals not established under Article III of the Constitution. In discussing non-self-executing treaties in *Foster v. Nielson*, Chief Justice John Marshall stated that these treaties are addressed "to the political, not the judicial department."[65] Accordingly, those tribunals that are not part of the judicial department, *i.e.*,

---

[62] Ted Stein, *The Approach of a Different Drummer: The Principle of the Persistent Objector in International Law*, 26 HARV. INT'L L. J. 457, 465 (1985).

[63] *Cf. Belilos v. Switzerland*, 132 Eur. Ct. H.R. (ser. A) at §53 (1988) (rejecting government's argument that objection to declaration 15 years after deposit and after subsequent case law was wrong.)

[64] 771 F.2d 1279, 1283 (9th Cir. 1985).

[65] 27 U.S. (2 Pet.) 253, 314 (1829).

not established under Article III, are not affected by the non-self-executing declaration. Such non-Article III tribunals include administrative and state courts.

c. Non-Self-Execution Declaration Not Applicable to State Governments Under Principles of Separation of Powers and Federalism

Regardless of whether the Senate's declaration that the ICCPR is or is not self-executing in regard to the federal government, the declaration does not apply to the individual states under the principles of separation of powers and federalism. The doctrine of self-execution emanates from the separation of powers doctrine.[66] Federal courts find treaties to be non-self-executing because it would not be appropriate, as a matter of separation of powers (specifically, the proper role of the courts) to act on their own, without Congressional authorization. Federal separation of powers doctrine simply does not apply to state courts. Congress may have the power to decide the proper role of federal courts, but not of state courts. States retain "a residuary and inviolable sovereignty."[67] Allowing the declaration's application to a state would directly impair a state court's general jurisdiction. Therefore, it would not make sense for the Senate to declare that the ICCPR is non-self-executing for the individual states.

Even assuming, for the sake of argument, that the Senate could preclude the state courts from using the ICCPR, in light of Tenth Amendment[68] concerns, there probably should have to be a clear and express statement by the Senate that it meant the state courts to be encompassed by the declaration under a *Charming Betsy*-type Rule.[69] There is no such express statement in either the text of the declaration or its legislative history.[70]

---

[66] *See* Vásquez, *supra*, at 717 (calling for doctrine of self-execution that takes into account underlying separation of powers doctrine).

[67] *Printz v. United States*, 521 U.S. 898, 919 (1997) (quoting THE FEDERALIST No. 39, at 245 (J. Madison)).

[68] The Tenth Amendment states:

> The powers not delegated to the United States by the Constitution, nor prohibited by it to the States, are reserved to the States respectively, or to the people.

U.S. CONST. amend. X.

[69] *See Murray v. The Schooner Charming Betsy*, 6 U.S. (2 Cranch.) 64, 118 (1804). The author wishes to thank Prof. Stephen Schnably for this insight.

[70] Furthermore, the legislative history of the Senate's declaration discloses an intent to ensure that the ICCPR was implemented within the restraints of U.S. notions of federalism. The Senate reported the following:

> 5. Article 50 (federalism)
> In light of Article 50 ("The provisions of the present Covenant shall extend to all parts of federal States without any limitations or exceptions"), it is appropriate to clarify that, even though the Covenant will apply to state and local authorities, *it will be implemented consistent with U.S. concepts of federalism.*
> The following recommended understanding is a modification of the understanding adopted on the same point in connection with the Torture Convention:

> The United States understands that this Convention shall be implemented by the Federal Government to the extent that it exercises legislative and judicial jurisdiction over the matters covered therein, and otherwise by the State and local governments; to the extent that State and local governments' exercise jurisdiction over such matters, the Federal Government shall take measures appropriate to the Federal system to the end that the competent authorities of the State or local governments may take appropriate measures for the fulfillment of the Convention.

> The proposed understanding serves to emphasize domestically that *there is no intent to alter the constitutional balance of authority between the State and Federal governments or to use the provisions of*

d. Regardless of Whether Covenant Recognizes Private Causes of Action, Rights Guaranteed by Articles 1–27 Can Be Used Defensively

Regardless of whether Articles 1–27 are self-executing or not, an individual can still use the ICCPR as a defense. The U.S. Supreme Court has accepted treaty-based defenses with respect to the application of state laws that were inconsistent with treaty agreements.[71] In another line of cases, the Supreme Court has permitted the use of treaty provisions as defenses to personal jurisdiction.[72] In *United States v. Duarte Acero*,[73] the U.S. Eleventh Circuit Court of Appeals indicated that the ICCPR arguably could be used for defensive purposes. There appears to be no case law contrary to this point. However, the defendant-appellant did not succeed on this claim on the facts in the case. It should be noted that such defenses could be used in either civil or criminal cases.

e. Although President May Deposit Reservations with Instrument of Ratification, Such Reservations Cannot Violate Extant International Law to Have Constitutional Effect

Treaty reservations must be limited according to the President's constitutional duties. Article II, §2, cl. 3[74] of the Constitution probably must be interpreted in conformity with international law because the President must obey federal law, of which international law is one aspect. Accordingly, the effect of Presidential reservations should not conflict with

---

the Covenant to "federalize" matters now within the competence of the States. (During the negotiation of the Covenant, the "federal-state" issue assumed some importance because there were legally justified practices, at the State and local level, which were both manifestly inconsistent with the Covenant and beyond the reach of Federal authority under the law in force at that time; that is no longer the case.)

A reservation is not necessary with respect to Article 50 since the intent is not to modify or limit U.S. undertakings under the Covenant but rather to put our future treaty partners on notice with regard to the implications of our federal system concerning implementation. Moreover, an attempt to reserve to this article would likely prove contentious. For example, in the face of objections from other States Parties, Australia recently withdrew its initial reservation to Article 50 (to the effect that implementation of the Covenant would be a matter for the authorities of its constituent States where the subject-matter was within the States' legislative, executive and judicial jurisdiction), replacing it with a declaration that, since it has a federal system, the Covenant will be implemented by Commonwealth, State and Territorial authorities having regard to their respective constitutional powers and arrangements concerning their exercise. The proposed understanding is similarly intended to signal to our treaty partners that the U.S. will implement its obligations under the Covenant by appropriate legislative, executive and judicial means, federal or state as appropriate, and that the Federal Government will remove any federal inhibition to the States' abilities to meet their obligations.

Senate Comm. on Foreign Relations, Report on the International Covenant on Civil and Political Rights, S. Exec. Rep. No. 23, 102d Cong., 2d Sess. 6–20 (1992), reprinted in 31 I.L.M. 645 (1992) (emphases provided).

As discussed below in connection with customary international law and *jus cogens*, the U.S.' ratification of the ICCPR did not "'federalize' matters within the competence of the States because the U.S.' customary international law and *jus cogens* obligations already had done that before 1992, the date of the U.S.' ratification of the ICCPR.

[71] *See, e.g., Kolovrat v. Oregon,* 366 U.S. 187 (1961) (allowing the use of the treaty as defense to escheatment of property); *Patsone v. Pennsylvania,* 232 U.S. 138 (1914) (recognizing use of treaty as defense, but ultimately concluding treaty did not conflict with state law).

[72] *Cook v. United States,* 288 U.S. 102 (1933) (recognizing right to assert treaty as defense and holding that trial court lacked personal jurisdiction over defendant); *Ford v. United States,* 273 U.S. 593 (1927); *United States v. Rauscher,* 119 U.S. 407 (1886) (recognizing defense by ruling that U.S. had violated treaty by trying defendant on charge different from that which Great Britain had granted extradition).

[73] 208 F.3d 1282 (11th Cir. 2000).

[74] The President has the duty to "take Care that the Laws be faithfully executed." U.S. Const. art. II, §2, cl. 3.

other extant treaty,[75] customary international law[76] (*e.g.*, the "object and purpose" rule[77] or the right to life as guaranteed under Article 6, ICCPR[78]), or *jus cogens*[79] (*e.g.*, the right against torture[80] as guaranteed by Article 7, ICCPR) obligations of the U.S. . . .

In the case of the ICCPR, President Bush did attach certain reservations (which includes the non-self-execution declaration), but these reservations should be given no effect under the Constitution because they were unlawful as a matter of international law at the time of their deposit. . . . [81] Although the Executive Branch's interpretation of a treaty should be given strong consideration, a U.S. Court of Appeals has held that it is less inclined to withhold review of such an interpretation when "individual liberty, rather than economic interest, is implicated."[82]

. . . .

〜

QUESTIONS & COMMENTS

(1) Can the United States constitutionally make a treaty that has absolutely no domestic effect? Or, does the doctrine of nonexecution still allow certain treaty provisions to govern certain branches of the federal and state governments and private individuals?

(2) If a treaty norm provision is considered non-self-executing because it lacks specificity, how can such specificity be provided? Case law interpreting treaty provisions can provide specificity. Furthermore, similar norms in other treaties can provide specificity. For example, the right-to-life provision in the ECHR provides greater specificity than the right-to-life provision in the ICCPR. Also, the ICJ Statute includes the teachings of the most highly qualified publicists of the various nations as a source of interpreting international legal norms, including treaty and customary international legal norms.

(3) In light of Professor Martin's argument that the Constitution is a treaty that must be construed in conformity with the United States' customary international human rights

---

[75] If a reservation violates a provision of an extant treaty law obligation, the reservation has no legal effect because although the President arguably may unilaterally terminate or suspend this earlier treaty, s/he cannot modify its terms. *See* RESTATEMENT §339 comment a.

[76] *United States v. Buck*, 690 F. Supp. 1291 (S.D.N.Y 1988) (customary international law trumps controlling executive acts) (dictum).

[77] *See* Vienna Convention-T, art. 19 (c); *Advisory Opinion on Reservations to the Convention on the Prevention and Punishment of the Crime of Genocide*, 1951 I.C.J. REP. 15 (28 May 1961) (affirming Object and Purpose Rule).

[78] The right to life was recognized as a customary international law norm by the time it was codified in the ICCPR in 1966. *See* Joan F. Hartman, *"Unusual" Punishment: The Domestic Effects of International Norms Restricting the Application of the Death Penalty*, 52 U. CIN. L. REV. 655, 671–72 (1983) (ICCPR's *travaux préparatoires* indicate Art. 6 as codifying already existing customary international law).

[79] *See, e.g.*, JORDAN J. PAUST, INTERNATIONAL LAW AS LAW OF THE UNITED STATES 368 (1996) ("an attempted 'reservation' or 'declaration' which conflicts with a *jus cogens* norm must also be void, and such is the case" with respect to non-self-executing declarations).

[80] *See In re Estate of Ferdinand E. Marcos Human Rights Litigation*, 978 F.2d 493, 500 (9th Cir. 1992) (torture violation of *jus cogens*).

[81] This is not to say that the President should not attach those reservations that violate international law. Reservations can serve as evidence of a state's persistent objection to customary international law reflected in a treaty that eventually can serve to undermine the norm.

[82] *United States v. Decker*, 600 F.2d 733, 738 (9th Cir.), *cert. denied*, 444 U.S. 855 (1979).

legal obligations, is not the issue of non-self-execution mooted in the case where such purportedly non-self-executing human rights treaty obligations that reflect customary international law are used merely to construe similar constitutional provisions that are considered themselves to be self-executing?

John C. Yoo

Globalism and the Constitution: Treaties, Non-Self-Execution, and the
Original Understanding
99 COLUM. L. REV. 1955, 1959 *et passim* (1999)[1]

. . . .

[A] developing academic consensus has emerged that sharply criticizes non-self-execution. These scholars argue that the Supremacy Clause requires courts to automatically enforce treaties, just as with constitutional and statutory provisions. Any exception for non-self-executing treaties is a narrow one, if it exists at all. Professor Carlos Vazquez, the most thorough critic of non-self-executing treaties, argues that the Supremacy Clause makes treaties law, on a par with the Constitution and federal statutes, that must be enforced by courts in properly brought suits by individuals. Professor Louis Henkin has gone so far as to declare that a "tendency in the Executive branch and in the courts to interpret treaties and treaty provisions as non-self-executing runs counter to the language, and spirit, and history of . . . the Constitution." These critics accuse treatymakers who attach non-self-executing reservations to treaties, and judges who respect such provisions, of negating the supremacy of treaty law. According to Henkin, "that recent practice, accepted without significant discussion, is 'anti-Constitutional' in spirit and highly problematic as a matter of law." I refer to these scholars as "internationalists" because their approach to treaties results in the tight integration of international and domestic law, and frees international agreements from many of the constitutional restraints that apply in the ordinary public lawmaking process.

. . . . An argument in favor of non-self-execution takes a more functional approach, based in the text and structure of the Constitution, in judicial doctrine, and in the practice of the political branches and the need for governmental efficiency. Defenders of the new academic consensus of self-execution usually respond to such pragmatic arguments, made by courts and the political branches, by citing the Framers' intent, rather than by addressing these claims on their merits.

This Article seeks to resolve the debate concerning the self-executing nature of treaties by providing a more complete account of the original understanding of the place of treaties within the American legal system. It agrees with the methodology employed by critics of non-self-execution. To understand the interaction of the Treaty Clause, the Supremacy Clause, and Article I, Section 8, one must first look at the Framing of the Constitution. The results of such an inquiry, however, provide a different, more nuanced story than the standard internationalist account. Upon closer examination, the original understanding does not compel a reading of the Supremacy Clause that immediately makes treaties law within the United States, but instead allows the branches of government to delay execution of a treaty until Congress as a whole can determine how treaty obligations are to be implemented. Non-self-execution maintains a clear separation between the power

---

[1] [Many footnotes have been omitted. Ed.'s note.]

to make treaties and the power to make domestic law, and it gives Congress the means to limit the potentially unbounded Treaty Clause. This Article will present a complex theory of the concept of federal supremacy, one that shows that non-self-execution is not at odds with the Supremacy Clause. It will also demonstrate that non-self-execution is consistent with the Framers' notions of democratic self-government and popular sovereignty.

. . . .

. . . . While the original understanding does not definitively show that all treaties must be non-self-executing, neither does it require the opposite conclusion. . . .

. . . .

[A] significant textual difference between a treaty and a law is found in the treaty power's placement in Article II, which vests the executive power in the President, rather than in Article I, which vests all "legislative Powers herein granted" to the Congress. The Treaty Clause's location suggests that treaties are executive, rather than legislative, in nature. The Senate's participation alone does not convert treaties into legislation, just as the Senate's participation in appointments does not transform them into legislative acts. Instead, the Constitution appears to include the Senate both to dilute the unitariness of executive action in the area of treaties, and perhaps to impart more continuity and wisdom to the conduct of foreign affairs. With their six-year terms (two years longer than the President's), Senators would provide "a sense of national character" and stability, much like that supplied by the privy council in England and the governors' councils in the states, and would restrain abuses of power by the executive.

[The Author proceeds to give a rich description and discussion of the law of nations, British law, political theory, the Articles of Confederation, the Constitutional and State Conventions, the Constitution, early Supreme Court practice, and early U.S. treaty practices under the Articles and Constitution. Ed.'s note.]

This article's review of the Framing Period shows that the Framers did not understand the Constitution to compel the self-execution of treaties in American law. Emerging from the political thought and the British constitutional struggles of the seventeenth and eighteenth centuries, non-self-execution embodied a deeper structural principle that separated the executive power, which controlled treatymaking, from the legislative power, which regulated domestic conduct. Americans during the Colonial and early National Periods sought to maintain this distinction, which checked the power of the central government and ensured that local representatives promulgated the laws. Dissatisfaction with the inability to enforce treaties, however, contributed to the calling of the Constitutional Convention. While some leaders believed that treaties were supreme law and should be enforced by state judges, others, particularly James Madison, sought to establish a truly representative national government that would make, and enforce, treaties by its own means. Tradition and history established a constitutional rule that treaties were not to take domestic effect without legislative implementation; Madison sought to work within this rule by establishing sufficient legislative power at the national level to enforce treaties directly.

Events during and after the Constitutional Convention further undermine claims that the Framers chose to make all treaties self-executing. While the Convention adopted the Supremacy Clause rather than the negative on state laws, it also put into place the mechanisms of a national government that could act directly on individuals. During the ratification debates, Anti-Federalists charged that the Treaty Clause, combined with the Supremacy Clause, threatened to give the executive branch a legislative power that would soon prove despotic. Federalists responded in the most politically significant states that treaties could not infringe upon areas within Congress's legislative powers; this would place an additional check upon the exercise of the treaty power. In certain states, both Federalists and Anti-Federalists seemed to reach agreement on this point, even as they continued to disagree on whether this would amount to a sufficient check on federal powers. What had begun as an idea to invigorate the national government's powers had transformed, in the heat of the ratification battle, into an important element of the separation of powers in foreign affairs. Events after ratification, culminating in the Jay Treaty and *Foster v. Neilson*, confirmed this understanding of the relationship between the treatymaking power and Congress's power to legislate.

Internationalists, then, cannot find full support in the Framers' Constitution for their efforts to eliminate the line between international agreements and domestic, statutory law. Rather, the original understanding demonstrates that two themes emerged from the Framing; while some (perhaps a minority) believed that the Constitution made treaties immediately part of domestic law, other Federalists publicly argued in the most crucial moments of ratification that the American rule would follow that of the British. Treaties would remain an executive action of the government that would require the passage of implementing legislation by Congress before they could have any domestic effect. A presumption of non-self-execution enforces the distinction between the power to make treaties and the power to legislate, it includes the most democratic branch of government in the establishment of rules that apply to the conduct of private citizens, and it allows the judiciary to defer to the political branches in the management of American foreign relations. If anything, early constitutional history falls on the side of the arguments in favor of non-self-execution, rather than self-execution.

The presence of both non-self-execution and self-execution themes during the Framing Period suggests the rules that courts and the political branches might apply today. Internationalists would do away with the distinction between international and domestic regulation, but in the process they undermine the difference between domestic lawmaking and treaties. If adopted, this approach would generate severe textual and structural constitutional difficulties, and would fail to account for the practice of the President, Congress, and the courts. At the very least, courts should obey the presumption that when the text of a treaty is silent, courts ought to assume that it is non-self-executing. This would obviate the potential conflicts between the growing demands of the international system and the expanding scope of treaties by maintaining the House's control over domestic legislation, which the Framers thought so important. Such a presumption also has the additional virtue of leaving foreign affairs in the hands of the political branches, keeping the judiciary out of a policymaking role, and providing the national government with the constitutional flexibility to determine how best to live up to our international obligations. Non-self-execution responds to globalization by enhancing the democratic safeguards on the making of international agreements, an important value as treaties come to mimic and even replace statutes in the regulation of domestic affairs.

Such an approach would consider favorably the recent efforts of the President and Senate to render multilateral treaties non-self-executing by reservation. Much like a judicial presumption in favor of non-self-execution, RUDs[2] preserve the House's control

---

[2] ["RUDs" are "Reservations, Understandings, and Declarations" made by the President and/or Senate and often attached to the treaty after its ratification. Ed.'s note.]

over legislation. The original understanding also supports efforts similar to those that occurred during the Jay Treaty. Rather than imposing a fixed rule of self-execution, the Constitution may allow the House and Senate to use their constitutional and political powers over legislation and funding to prevent direct treaty implementation. Congress may use its powers in specific cases to establish the broad principle that any treaty that infringes upon the scope of the domestic legislative power must be implemented by legislation, or it can use its powers on a case-by-case basis to ensure that it plays a central role in treaty implementation. After this process of cooperation or struggle, the branches may even arrive at a rule of complete non-self-execution, depending on historical and international circumstances, the relative power of the branches, and the people's wishes.

The original understanding also could support a stricter approach toward treaties, one that a presumption in favor of non-self-execution is designed to advance. From the historical evidence examined in this article, it appears that the President and Senate cannot use the Treaty and Supremacy Clauses to exercise powers that ordinarily would fall within the scope of Congress's authority over legislation. The House can give effect to this original understanding by refusing to fund or support treaties that attempt to exert domestic legislative effects without its approval. The federal courts similarly could refuse to enforce, pursuant to the modern doctrine of non-self-execution, treaties that infringe on Congress's enumerated powers under Article I. As Congress's powers have expanded under the Commerce Clause, this approach would render non-self-executing many of the multilateral regulatory treaties under consideration in areas such as the environment, the economy, or human rights. But it also would have the effect of ensuring that the most democratically elected branch of government would retain its control over the imposition of rules that regulate the conduct of its citizens.

Even if one believes that the evidence presented here from the original understanding does not compel non-self-execution, it still undermines academic arguments in favor of self-execution. In criticizing the practice of the courts and the political branches, internationalist scholars rely to a great degree on the original understanding. Their work, however, has focused too narrowly on a small set of sources and has paid insufficient attention to the course of the Constitution's ratification. A more comprehensive examination of the ratification, in its historical context, demonstrates that the evidence relied upon by internationalists is neither conclusive nor definitive concerning the original understanding of the Framers. At the very least, the reconstruction of the original understanding presented here should shift the debate on treaty execution toward textual, structural, or doctrinal arguments, rather than the Framers' intent.

. . . .

~

QUESTIONS & COMMENTS

(1) Do you find Professor Yoo's textualist argument that the placement of the treaty-making power in Article II rather than Article I indicates that treaties are not self-executing? Consider the following. According to Article II, the President's constitutional "Power . . . to make treaties" is only "*by* . . . the Senate." (emphasis provided) The President's power to make treaties is only derivative of the Senate's power. The original plan

submitted by the Committee of Detail on August 6, 1787 provided that only "the Senate of the United States shall have power to make treaties. . . ."[3] Not until September 7th (ten days before the Convention's final adjournment) did the Constitutional Convention give the President derivative power to make treaties.[4] Doesn't this suggest that treaty-making is legislative because the President's authority to make treaties is only derivative of the Senate, whose authority to legislate is clear? Furthermore, given the last moment inclusion of the President in treaty-making and the placement of treaty-making authority in Article II, is it probable that the Committee of Detail's placement of the treaty-making power in Article II was a stylistic device to reflect that treaty law-making begins with the President negotiating treaties with other states and to ensure that the President's role in treaty law-making was clear? After all, it was stylistically appropriate to place federal statute-making provisions in Article II because such law-making begins with Congress notwithstanding the President's subsequent role in such law-making. The Framers did not place the President's authority to approve/veto federal legislation in Article II as they did not place the Senate's treaty consent authority in Article I. Doesn't this all suggest that there is a presumption that treaties are self-executing like federal statutes – albeit this presumption is subject to rebuttal depending on the particular treaty provision as is the case even with federal statutory provisions?

John C. Yoo

Rejoinder, Treaties and Public Lawmaking: A Textual and Structural Defense of Non-Self-Execution
99 Colum. L. Rev. 2218, 2233 *et passim* (1999)[1]

. . . .

. . . . [S]elf-execution would have the unfortunate effect of reading out of our Constitution important aspects of the separation of powers and federalism, and would also undermine the principle of popular sovereignty. The doctrine of self-execution vests in the executive branch a legislative power that is broader in scope than that enjoyed by Congress. Self-executing treaties arguably are free of the constraints of federalism and the separation of powers – threatening to disrupt our constitutional structure. Non-self-execution, in contrast, harmonizes the relevant constitutional clauses, and maintains the important distinction between foreign relations and domestic lawmaking.

Vazquez's theory of self-execution would distort an executive power into a legislative one. Article II, Section 1 provides that the "executive Power shall be vested in a President of the United States." As Justice Scalia has written, this "does not mean some of the executive power, but all of the executive power." Others also read Article II to constitute a broad grant of power, analogizing it to Article III's Vesting Clause, which is the only textual source for the federal judiciary's powers. The powers enumerated in Section 2, such as command of the military, pardons and execution of the laws, are executive in nature. Section 2 defines the broad grant of executive power to the President – it does not create new executive-legislative powers. By its placement in Article II, therefore, treatymaking is clearly an executive power.

---

[3] Max Farrand, 2 The Records of the Federal Convention of 1787 183 (1911).
[4] *Ibid.* at 538–39.
[1] [Many footnotes have been omitted. Ed.'s note.]

To be sure, the Constitution does not embody a pure separation of powers in which each branch solely exercises all functions peculiar to it. Nonetheless, the Senate's participation in treatymaking and appointments reflects the Framers' effort to dilute the unitary nature of the executive branch in those areas, rather than to transform these functions into legislative powers. While the Constitution reduces executive power in favor of the legislature, it does not transfer what were considered legislative powers to Article II. When the Constitution grants the executive a power that is legislative in nature, such as the veto power, it does so in Article I, not in Article II, because Article I alone describes the finely balanced method for making federal laws.[2] The Constitution centralizes public lawmaking into a tortuous process to make the exercise of legislative authority more difficult, thereby protecting the states and the people from unwarranted exercises of federal power. In the few cases articulating the distinction between legislative and executive power, the Supreme Court has defined the executive power by its very lack of the power to make laws.

Moreover, self-execution invites a conflict between the textual grants of the executive and legislative powers and resolves the clash by allowing the treatymaking authority to trump Congress's Article I powers. According to internationalists, the President and Senate may resort to the treaty process to address any matter, so long as it is "an agreement between two or more states or international organizations that is intended to be legally binding and is governed by international law." If treaties enjoy this broad scope, and if, as Vazquez argues, they are always self-executing, then the treatymakers can regulate any area that lies within Article I's enumerated powers. For example, a self-executing treaty could make certain actions federal crimes, despite the Constitution's allocation to Congress of authority to "define and punish Piracies and Felonies committed on the high Seas, and Offences against the Law of Nations." Likewise, the treatymakers would be free to establish new commercial or environmental regulations, though the power to regulate interstate commerce is vested in Congress. If the United States forges multilateral agreements addressing problems that were once domestic in scope, treaties could replace legislation as a vehicle for domestic regulation.

Recognizing these problems, the Restatement and leading internationalist scholars admit that certain exceptions must exist from their general principle. For example, the Restatement declares that treaties cannot take direct effect as American law if legislation is "constitutionally required." Yet internationalists argue that the treatymakers can exercise the Commerce Clause power, among others, without resorting to statute. If Vazquez is correct that the treatymakers can exercise a single Article I, Section 8 power granted to Congress, then the treatymakers must be able to exercise all of Congress's legislative powers. The constitutional text, which treats all of these powers in Article I, Section 8, does not make any distinctions among them. Internationalists concede that legislation may be necessary to implement a treaty if it calls for a declaration of war, an appropriation of money, the raising of taxes, or the punishment of criminal conduct. Yet, neither the Restatement nor internationalists provide any principled distinctions between those areas

---

[2] While no one can deny that the executive branch also makes law through administrative regulations, this occurs due to the delegation of authority by Congress, subject to clear and manageable standards, rather than by direct constitutional authorization. *See, e.g.,* Clinton v. New York, 524 U.S. 417 (1998), Mistretta v. United States, 488 U.S. 361, 372 (1989). Of course, whether the "intelligible principle" standard of these cases actually imposes a real check on executive discretion in public administration is another question. *See* Edward L. Rubin, *Law and Legislation in the Administrative State,* 89 Colum. L. Rev. 369, 380–85 (1989).

that can be the subject of treaties, and those areas that cannot be. As Madison argued during the Jay Treaty debates, "if the Treaty-power alone could perform any one act for which the authority of Congress is required by the Constitution, it may perform every act for which the authority of that part of the Government is required."

In making treaties self-executing, Vazquez and other internationalists would create a potentially limitless legislative power. While Article I, Section 8, vests Congress with enumerated plenary powers, the Constitution subjects these grants to the limitations of Article I, Section 9. Even some important elements of the Bill of Rights apply textually only to Congress. If Vazquez is right that the treatymakers can exercise legislative power without resort to Article I's lawmaking process, then self-execution allows the federal government to legislate without opposition from the textual checks on congressional powers. As Madison worried, "if the legislative powers specifically vested in Congress, are to be no limitation or check to the Treaty power, it was evident that the exceptions to those powers, could be no limitation or check to the Treaty power." While the Supreme Court has rejected the argument that treaties can infringe on individual rights,[3] textually the Constitution would seem to permit this result, once we agree with Vazquez that treaties are self-executing.

Self-execution also may permit the treatymakers to act outside the constraints of the separation of powers, which internationalists believe do not apply to treaties. If they are right, the treatymakers could delegate to international organizations powers that ordinarily inhere in the executive branch, such as authority over law enforcement or administrative rulemaking. Or a treaty could transfer authority from Congress to the executive branch or to an international organization, as some argue that the U.N. Charter actually does, when a statute could not. According to internationalist logic, the treatymakers could delegate lawmaking or law-execution authority from the national government to international agencies in ways that would violate either the Appointments Clause, the vesting clauses, or the non-delegation doctrine, if a statute were used. If treaties are interchangeable with statutes as domestic law, as Vazquez would have it, but are free from the usual structural constraints of the separation of powers, then the treatymakers could restructure government to regulate domestic affairs in ways not permitted to Congress.

Self-execution also would free the treatymakers from federalism limitations, which internationalists claim do not apply to treaties. Leading commentators assert that the President and Senate can make policy for the whole nation on any subject, regardless of the limited enumeration of federal powers or the Tenth Amendment.[4] The Tenth Amendment presents no bar, these authorities argue, because its reservation of powers is inapplicable to the treaty power, which was expressly delegated to the federal government. Anything that the treaty power can touch upon is, by definition, excluded from the Tenth Amendment. In *Missouri v. Holland*, the Supreme Court suggested its agreement with this proposition. According to an opinion by Justice Holmes, the treaty power was not to be limited in the same manner as Congress's Article I, Section 8 powers, because treaties concerned "a national interest of very nearly the first magnitude," the power over which had to be vested somewhere in the national government. *Holland*'s expansive reading of

---

[3] *See* Reid v. Covert, 354 U.S. 1 (1957) (plurality opinion).

[4] [The Tenth Amendment states: "The powers not delegated to the United States by the Constitution, nor prohibited by it to the States, are reserved to the States respectively, or to the people." Ed.'s note.]

the treaty power's scope underscores the severe textual and structural difficulties created by Vazquez's theory of self-execution. When combined with Vazquez's claims that all treaties have the same legal force as statutes, that they automatically preempt inconsistent state law, and that they are to be immediately enforced by the federal and state courts, the treaty power becomes an unlimited authority to legislate on any subject.

B. Self-Execution and the Public Lawmaking Process

Self-executing treaties conflict not just with the constitutional text and the structure of our government, but also with the principle of popular sovereignty underlying the Constitution. In almost all domestic spheres of activity over which the federal government has jurisdiction, the Constitution grants the power to legislate to Congress. As a matter of accountability, when the government imposes rules of conduct on individuals, those rules ought to be made by members of the legislature who directly represent the people. Non-self-execution, therefore, better promotes democratic government in the lawmaking process by requiring the consent of the most directly democratic part of the government, the House of Representatives, before the nation can implement treaty obligations at home. To be sure, the President provides a safeguard against an anti-majoritarian treaty, but presidential participation is not a complete protection for majority rule, especially during a second term. Establishing a process in which the House takes part through implementing legislation provides yet another safeguard for popular sovereignty.

Non-self-execution also produces benefits for the system of public lawmaking described by different theories of the legislative process. Some students of legislation believe that Congress primarily acts as a forum for the making of deals between interest groups. Although some public choice scholars are dubious that the legislative process advances the "public interest," pluralists view interest groups as desirable because they facilitate stability, moderation, and broad satisfaction with the political system. Other theories of the legislative process suggest that if international agreements are implemented by the full Congress, more committees and groups will become involved, bringing to bear greater legislative and policy expertise, producing more information on legislative choices, and fostering communication between the different political players. The more steps that exist in implementing treaties, the more open the process and the greater the chances for reasoned discussion about the policies involved. A requirement that treaties receive implementing legislation exposes international agreements to the benefits of a more open political process, which promotes stable policymaking and broader political acceptance.

Invoking the words of the Framers,[5] Vazquez and other internationalists argue that the House is ill-suited for the secrecy needed for diplomacy. These secrecy concerns no longer seem compelling, due to the large size of the Senate, the role of the House in foreign affairs, and the nature of modern regulatory treaties, which resemble domestic legislation in purpose and effect. Furthermore, the Senate never assumed the active role in diplomatic negotiations that some Framers may have hoped for. The Senate's formal role in treatymaking has become one of after-the-fact consent, while the President assumes primary responsibility for setting foreign policy and conducting diplomatic negotiations.

---

[5] *See, e.g.,* The Federalist No. 75, at 483 (Alexander Hamilton) (explaining exclusion of House from formal role in treatymaking).

Giving treaties self-executing effect distorts the public lawmaking process by removing the procedural checks on the exercise of legislative authority. In place of the parallel House and Senate procedures for studying and adopting legislation, in which the President exercises a final veto, the treatymaking process shifts the center of policymaking from Congress to a President unencumbered by bicameralism. The development of treaty provisions and the understanding of treaty negotiation and drafting is dominated by the President, rather than by the legislature, as would be the case with domestic statutes. The termination of treaties also demonstrates how treaties would distort the public lawmaking process. Statutes require the consent of both houses of Congress and the President, or two-thirds of Congress without the President, before they can be repealed. Although the Constitution is silent on the question, and even though it once was thought that breaking treaties required the consent of two-thirds of the Senate, today most commentators, courts and government entities accept that the President unilaterally may terminate treaties. As with treaty formation, the President retains this authority due to his preeminent position in foreign affairs and his structural superiority in managing international relations. If the nation regulates certain domestic conduct by statute, the President cannot terminate the rules without congressional approval. If the nation should regulate the same conduct by treaty, however, the President may terminate the regulation at will.

Furthermore, under the consensus view, the "last-in-time" rule allows treaties to supersede earlier statutes, and subsequent statutes to override earlier treaties. In other words, if the terms of a statute and of a treaty come into conflict, the provision that was enacted most recently will preempt the earlier version. Allowing treaties and statutes to supersede each other in this way seems inconsistent with the formalist approach to lawmaking articulated by the Supreme Court in *I.N.S. v. Chadha*. In *Chadha*, the Court invalidated Congress's creation of the legislative veto, which was used in that case to overturn the Attorney General's determination, pursuant to his statutorily delegated power, not to deport an alien. It reasoned that Congress could enact legislation – which it defined as legislative action affecting the rights of individuals outside of Congress – only by passing laws that survived bicameralism and presentment to the President. A decision to repeal earlier legislation – as was the case with the use of the legislative veto in *Chadha* – requires a new law. Viewed in *Chadha*'s light, the last-in-time rule violates the Constitution's structural principles of lawmaking, because it allows the treatymakers to counteract an earlier action by the President, Senate, and House. During the Jay Treaty debates, Madison rejected this possibility out of hand because "it involved the absurdity of an Imperium in imperio; or of two powers both of them supreme, yet each of them liable to be superseded by the other."

. . . .

～

QUESTIONS & COMMENTS

(1) Do all treaties constitutionally need implementing legislation? What about treaties that address subjects over which Congress has no constitutional authority to legislate? For example, what about treaties addressing space exploration?

(2) Assume for the sake of argument that Professor Yoo's conclusion that treaties should not be implemented as domestic law without the participation of the House

of Representatives to ensure better democratic accountability in public lawmaking. How does this have an opposite effect? Consider the following: Human rights treaties not only impose obligations on the United States, but they also guarantee human rights that make the U.S. government more accountable in areas where Congress has failed to legislate. Requiring federal legislation to implement these treaty rights provides the House an opportunity to undermine the protection of these rights, thereby undercutting such accountability.

(3) In *Foster v. Neilson*, the Supreme Court held that a treaty norm provision is considered non-self-executing in the federal courts when the norm requires action from one of the political branches of the federal government. What does this mean exactly? If a legal instrument (*e.g.*, Constitution, federal statute, treaty) recognizes a human right that has been violated by the executive branch, only the president can take the requisite action for remedying the violation. Does this mean that the legal instrument is non-self-executing and federal courts cannot give the right effect? This conclusion appears to be patently incorrect because the president must comply with federal law.

What if the legal instrument requires remedial action that the Constitution appears to place exclusively with a political branch. For example, the power to declare war under Article 1, Section 8 appears to be given exclusively to Congress. If the President (with the Senate) makes a mutual defense treaty that binds the United States to declaring war when one of its treaty partners is attacked by another state, the treaty would be considered non-self-executing because a declaration of war requires approval by both Houses.

Is there any principled distinction between the two aforementioned examples? Professor Yoo would appear to not think so. However, consider the difference between the two treaties. The mutual defense treaty is a treaty whose execution would have to be conditioned upon congressional approval. The execution of the human rights treaty is not conditional upon approval by any branch of the federal government because there is no explicit human rights provisions in Article I, Section 8 suggesting the requirement of such approval.

Although Congress has the Article I, Section 8 authority to define offenses against the law of nations – which certainly includes human rights violations – the authority is limited to *clarifying* the offense – not creating it[6] – through legislation and only if such legislation is "necessary and proper."[7] Accordingly, a human rights or humanitarian law treaty whose provisions are vague would require implementing legislation to clarify such provisions.

However, Congress also does have the Article I, Section 8 authority to punish offenses against the law of nations, which includes serious human rights or humanitarian law violations prohibited by treaty. Accordingly, a human rights or humanitarian treaty that recognizes certain crimes and/or establishes penalties for the commission of such crimes would require Congress to enact implementing legislation establishing it as a crime and setting penalties for its commission.

---

[6] *See* 2 THE RECORDS OF THE FEDERAL CONVENTION OF 1787 61 (Max Farrand ed., 1937) ("To pretend to define the law of nations which depended on the authority of all the Civilized Nations of the World, would have a look of arrogance that would make us ridiculous. Mr. Govr: The word define is proper when applied to offences in this case; the law of nations being often too vague and deficient to be a rule.").

[7] U.S. CONST. art. 1, §9.

The Thirteenth (prohibiting slavery), Fourteenth (guaranteeing equal protection and due process of law), Fifteenth (right to vote regardless of race), Nineteenth (right to vote regardless of sex), and Twenty-sixth (right to vote) Amendments all provide that Congress has the power to enforce these amendments. This suggests that treaty human rights provisions require implementing legislation in areas covered by these amendments. However, Congress already has provided implementing legislation for these amendments, and the *Charming Betsy* Rule requires that the federal statutes be construed in conformity with the United States' international legal obligations, thereby mooting the issue of whether the human rights treaties require implementing legislation. For example, 42 U.S.C. §1983 establishes a private cause of action for constitutional violations, and 18 U.S.C. §242 establishes criminal penalties for constitutional violations.

(4) Professor Yoo does not like the last-in-time rule when it allows treaties to supercede earlier legislation. Recall the difficulties with the last-in-time rule's application to treaties. Is not the solution to Professor Yoo's difficulty with the last-in-time rule's application to treaties to recognize that treaties are not inferior to federal statutory law (as he suggests) but superior?

Francisco Forrest Martin

Our Constitution as Federal Treaty: A New Theory of United States Constitutional Construction

Based on an Originalist Understanding for Addressing a New World

31 HASTINGS CONST. L. QUART. 258 (2004)[1]

. . . .

A treaty, constitutional provision, or statute sometimes requires an additional law (such as a statute, executive or administrative agency order, or judicial order) in order to give the instrument effect because the instrument needs further definition.[2] Sometimes a statute is needed to provide a private cause of action for the violation of a constitutional provision.[3] The instrument also may require additional action from another branch or sub-branch of the government. For example, Congress often must enact implementing legislation to set penalties for treaty violations.[4] Another example is that the House of Representatives must introduce appropriations legislation to implement federal law requiring funding.[5]

However, not all legal instruments require additional law for their execution. For example, many treaty and constitutional provisions are self-executing.[6] Whether a legal

---

[1] [Many footnotes have been omitted. Ed.'s note.]

[2] Blessing v. Freestone, 520 U.S. 329, 340–41 (1997) (ambiguous federal statute); Vázquez, *Four Doctrines*, *supra* note 232, at 713–15 (ambiguous treaties).

[3] *See, e.g.*, 42 U.S.C. §1983 (providing private cause of action for constitutional violations committed by state authorities).

[4] *See, e.g.*, "War Crimes Act of 1996," 18 U.S.C. §2441(a) (implementing penalty legislation for Hague and Geneva Conventions).

[5] U.S. CONST. art. I, §7, cl. 1.

[6] *See, e.g.*, Bivens v. Six Unknown Named Agents, 402 U.S. 388 (1971) (recognizing availability of damages relief for Fourth Amendment violations committed by federal authorities); Bolling v. Sharpe, 347 U.S. 497 (1954) (recognizing availability of injunctive relief for Fifth Amendment violations committed by federal authorities); United States v. Percheman, 32 U.S. (7 Pet.) 51 (1833) (United States-Spain treaty provision self-executing).

instrument is self-executing turns on constitutional restraints, the language of the particular instrument,[7] and/or the contemporaneous practice of the parties in the instrument's implementation.[8] Use of the instrument's legislative history may only be used as a supplemental means of interpretation.[9]

However, the execution doctrine becomes problematic when one tries to apply it by using a separation of powers doctrine extrapolated only from the text and structure of the Constitution. For example, when one tries to determine whether treaty provisions are self-executing or non-self-executing by appealing only to the text and structure of the Constitution, a dilemma results. The same dilemma results for customary international legal norms because treaties can serve as evidence of extant customary international legal norms or signal the acceptance of emerging customary international legal norms. On the one hand, to allow the President with the Senate to make self-executing federal law through their joint treaty making authority under Article II sometimes can appear to circumvent and usurp the House of Representative's essential role in lawmaking and intrude upon areas of lawmaking that historically have been assigned to both Houses under Article I. These areas include declaring war, raising taxes, and imposing criminal penalties. Such a construction of the treaty making power arguably violates the separation of powers principle. On the other hand, to allow Congress to make self-executing law that intrudes upon the President's and Senate's treaty making power also violates the separation of powers doctrine.[10] Examples of such usurpation could take the form of statutes violating

---

[7] The *Vienna Convention* states:

   1. A treaty shall be interpreted in good faith in accordance with the ordinary meaning to be given to the terms of the treaty in their context and in light of its object and purpose.

   2. The context for the purpose of the interpretation of a treaty shall comprise, in addition to the text, including its preamble and annexes:

   a) any agreement relating to the treaty which was made between all the parties in connexion with the conclusion of the treaty;

   b) any instrument which was made by one or more parties in connexion with the conclusion of the treaty and accepted by the other parties as an instrument related to the treaty.

   3. There shall be taken into account, together with the context:

   c) any subsequent agreement between the parties regarding the interpretation of the treaty or the application of its provisions;

   ...

   Vienna Convention, art. 31 (1)–(3).

[8] *Vienna Convention*, art. 31 (3) (b) ("any subsequent practice in the application of the treaty which establishes the agreement of the parties regarding its interpretation"). As the Supreme Court stated in the context of constitutional construction:

   The construction placed upon the Constitution by the first act of 1790, and the act of 1802, by the men who were contemporary with its formation, many of whom were members of the convention which framed it, is of itself entitled to very great weight, and when it is remembered that the rights thus established have not been disputed during a period of nearly a century, it is almost conclusive.

   Burrow-Giles Lithographic Co. v. Sarony, 111 U.S. 53, 57 (1884).

[9] Central Bank of Denver v. First Interstate Bank of Denver, 511 U.S. 164 (1994); Hart & Wechsler, The Federal Courts and the Federal System 840–41 (4th ed. 1996).

[10] A construction using the Necessary and Proper Clause does not solve this dilemma. Congress may only enact legislation that is necessary and proper for executing treaties, but what is "necessary and proper" depends on how one interprets the separation of powers principle. If all treaties (regardless if their provisions are self-executing) require implementing legislation in order to avoid a separation of powers conflict, then

a previously ratified treaty or the form of statutes addressing any area in which treaties could govern.[11] Therefore, both constructions of the separation of powers principle in relation to the self-execution or non-self-execution of treaties founders on the horns of a dilemma created by relying solely upon the text and structure of the Constitution.[12]

Consider another related separation of powers dilemma. Take the example of the Senate conditioning its consent to a treaty on the acceptance of a reservation that certain treaty provisions are non-self-executing.[13] On the one hand, the Constitution makes no mention of conditional consent. Either two-thirds of the Senate gives its consent to a treaty, or it does not; therefore, such conditional consent arguably could be a violation of the separation of powers principle.[14] Furthermore, if the reservation requires a certain interpretation of the treaty, the reservation arguably would run afoul of the judicial branch's final authority to interpret federal law.[15] If the Senate's reservation requires the President to submit this reservation upon the treaty's ratification, the Senate's reservation arguably would intrude upon the President's ratification authority.

On the other hand, the Constitution is designed to ensure efficient lawmaking. For example, the Constitution allows the Senate to propose amendments to appropriations bills which do not originate in the Senate but are still subject to the Senate's consent for becoming law.[16] This process is designed to avoid inefficiency resulting from rein-troduction of appropriations bills whose earlier versions did not meet conditions for Senate approval. It would appear that the treaty-making process should also reflect such efficiency by allowing the Senate to condition its consent to a treaty by way of submitting a reservation to ensure that the treaty's implementation is consistent with Senate intent. Hence, applying a separation of powers principle based merely on the text and structure of the Constitution creates constitutionally internal contradictions by both allowing and disallowing the Senate to condition its consent through the submission of reservations.

---

this legislation is proper and necessary. On the other hand, if Congress cannot legislate in areas already covered by the treaties made under the authority of the President and Senate, any legislation that attempts to usurp or circumvent these treaties violates the separation of powers principle, and such legislation is neither necessary or proper.

[11] One easily can imagine a vague federal trade statute that would require a trade treaty to give the statute definition. Indeed, the *Charming Betsy* Rule requires that federal statutes be construed in conformity with United States treaty obligations. Weinberger v. Rossi, 456 U.S. 25 (1982).

[12] Even an appeal to democratic accountability and state equality as the underlying justifications for the separation of powers principle does not get one off the horns of this dilemma. Both a Presidential/Senatorial exclusive treaty-making power and an extension of Congressional lawmaking power to international affairs are subject to democratic accountability and state co-equality. Both constructions of the execution doctrine incorporate state co-equality and at least different but roughly equal measures of democratic accountability. The plenary treaty making power is checked by the state equality in the Senate and by the people in a President elected by an electoral college whose members are chosen according to the numbers of citizens in each state. The extension of Congressional lawmaking power to international affairs is also checked by state equality in the Senate as well as by the people in the House of Representatives whose members are elected according to the numbers of citizens in each state. Therefore, both Presidential/Senatorial and Congressional authorities have equal claims to reflecting democratic accountability and state equality that do not resolve whose lawmaking authority trumps the other.

[13] *See, e.g.*, U.S. Reservations, Declarations, and Understandings to the International Covenant on Civil and Political Rights, 138 Cong. Rec. S4783–4 (daily ed., April 2, 1992) (declaring that substantive individual rights provisions in articles 1–27 of *ICCPR* as non-self-executing).

[14] *Cf.* Clinton v. City of New York, 524 U.S. 417 (1998) (Presidential line-item veto held unconstitutional.)

[15] *Cf.* City of Boerne v. Flores, 521 U.S. 507 (1997) (judicial branch has exclusive final authority in interpreting Constitution).

[16] U.S. Const. art. I, §7, cl. 1.

The solution to these constitutional conundrums is *not* to figure out where one branch's power ends and another begins. As earlier discussed, treaties and customary international law have superior legal authority over federal statutory law, and therefore, the treaty-making authority of the President and Senate must not be conceived as being able to intrude upon the House's inferior lawmaking role. Although international law often accommodates the separation of powers principle,[17] the solution is to construe the Constitution in conformity with the United States' modern customary international law and treaty obligations.

In the case where a treaty (or customary international legal norm) is being used to construe a constitutional provision that is itself self-executing in the sense that it does not need a federal statute to provide a private cause of action, the issue of whether a treaty (or customary international legal norm) is self-executing is moot because it is not the treaty (or customary international legal norm) *per se* that is being implemented. The constitutional provision already provides a private cause of action, and the treaty (or customary international legal norm) is being used only for the provision's construction.

In the case of a constitutional provision that is non-self-executing in the sense that it requires definition or does not provide a private cause of action, the provision can become implemented by construing it in conformity with a treaty (or customary international legal norm). After all, the notion of non-self-execution means that the legal instrument requires action from a political branch of the government for the instrument to be implemented, and in the case of a non-self-executing constitutional provision, the President and Senate can take such action through their treaty-making authority.

In the case where a treaty (or customary international law) addresses a substantive area to which the Constitution does not speak (*e.g.*, space exploration), the norm is self-executing unless legislation is necessary for its execution. Such legislation could be that which provides, *e.g.*, needed clarification to the international law's provisions, a private cause of action for ensuring the international law's enforcement by persons whose rights have been violated, or appropriations for the execution of the international law's provisions. If such legislation arguably is necessary, then Congress is under as much a constitutional duty to enact such legislation as it is under a constitutional duty to execute other federal law – be it constitutional or federal statutory law. Indeed, under the Object and Purpose Rule, Congress' power "[t]o make all Laws which shall be necessary and proper for carrying into Execution" the treaty power, must be construed in conformity with the Constitution's Preamble, and the Preamble states that the Constitution's objects and purposes, *inter alia*, are to "establish Justice, provide for the common defence, [and] promote the general Welfare" – objects and purposes that often require Congress to enact laws.[18]

---

[17] For example, the right to an impartial hearing under international human rights law requires the functional independence – but not necessarily formal separation – of the judiciary and political branches. Procola v. Luxembourg, 326 Eur. Ct. H.R. (ser. A) (1995); *see also*, A. v. United Kingdom, Application No. 35373/97, at §77 (2002) (parliamentary immunity enjoyed by Minister of Parliament pursued legitimate aims of protecting free speech in Parliament and maintaining separation of powers between legislature and judiciary). International law provides states a degree of deference (known as the "margin of appreciation doctrine") in fashioning their domestic measures of complying with their international legal obligations that is scaled according to, *inter alia*, the amount of interference with the particular human right. *See* Laurence R. Helfer, *Consensus, Coherence and the European Convention on Human Rights*, 26 CORNELL INT'L L.J. 133 (1993) (discussing margin of appreciation doctrine).

[18] *Vienna Convention*, 31(1) (object and purpose rule); U.S. CONST. pmbl., art. I, §8, cl. 10, and art. I, §9.

If Congress fails to do so, then there is a presumption that no legislation is needed, and the federal courts have the constitutional obligation to apply the international legal norm and – if a violation is found – fashion remedies. The constitutional authority of a federal court to perform a United States international legal obligation is acquired by construing its statutory jurisdictional grant in conformity with customary international law guaranteeing judicial remedies *per* the *Charming Betsy* Rule.[19] At the very least, the performance of such international legal obligations by federal courts would include a declaration that the United States has failed to comply with its international legal obligations. Also, the court must award monetary damages, the quantum of which would depend on the measure of harm incurred by the victim. Further relief, such as punitive damages, criminal prosecution, and other injunctive relief, will depend on the factual circumstances of the case and the limits of the United States' international legal obligations.

Even in cases where a treaty (or customary international law) addresses a subject over which Congress has been given the specific authority, *e.g.*, under Article I, Section 8 to legislate (*e.g.*, declaring war, taxation, defining and punishing offenses against the law of nations) or under the Fourteenth Amendment to enact implementing legislation,[20] there is no constitutional requirement for implementing legislation – unless such legislation is necessary. If such legislation is arguably necessary, then Congress is under a constitutional obligation to enact proper legislation. Again, if Congress fails to do so, then there is a presumption that no legislation is needed, and the federal courts are free to apply the treaty (or customary international legal norm) and fashion remedies. This conclusion even extends to cases in which the House of Representatives has the exclusive authority to introduce appropriations bills. If the House has failed to introduce appropriations necessary for the execution of the United States' international law obligations, then a state or individual victim can sue in federal court and obtain a money judgment against the United States.

In the case of the proper reach of the Senate's treaty making authority in the context of conditional consents, the solution is to conceptualize the Constitution as treaty, and as a treaty, the Constitution becomes "amenable to the law of nations."[21] Customary international law establishes that the conclusion of a treaty can be invalidated by a party on the basis of error or fraud.[22] Evidence of such error or fraud could be established by an interpretive declaration submitted by the President and/or Senate. Otherwise, the

---

[19] *See infra* note [25] (discussing customary international law guaranteeing effective judicial remedies); *see, e.g.*, 28 U.S.C. §1331 ("The district courts shall have original jurisdiction of all civil actions arising under the Constitution, laws, or treaties of the United States."); Murray v. the Schooner Charming Betsy, 6 U.S. (2 Cranch.) 64, 118 (1804) (federal statutory law must be construed in conformity with customary international law).

    However, the U.S. Supreme Court recently in *Sosa v. Alvarez-Machain* noted in dicta that federal question jurisdiction under 28 U.S.C. §1331 might not be available for customary international law claims. – U.S. – n.19, 124 S.Ct. 2739, 159 L. Ed. 2d 718 (2004) (dicta). However, the Court failed to consider the *Charming Betsy* Rule's application to such jurisdictional statutes that would provide a statutory construction requiring the recognition of jurisdiction for individual claims. And, because other customary international legal norms also must be used to construe the substantive constitutional rights, individuals would have a private cause of action under those federal statutes (*e.g.*, 42 U.S.C. §1983) or judicial remedies (*e.g.*, Bivens v. Six Unknown Named Agents, 402 U.S. 388 (1971) (recognizing private cause of action for constitutional violations)) that implement such constitutional rights.

[20] *See* U.S. Const. amend. XIV, §5 ("The Congress shall have power to enforce, by appropriate legislation, the provisions of this article.").

[21] Chisholm v. Georgia, 2 U.S. (2 Dall.) 419 (1793).

[22] *Vienna Convention*, arts. 48 (error) and 49 (fraud).

ordinary meaning of the treaty's terms in their context and in light of the treaty's object and purpose governs. However, if the interpretation given by one of the state-parties to the treaty conflicts with the ordinary meaning of the treaty or clearly violates the treaty's object and purpose, the interpretation is just not valid. Hence, an interpretive reservation made by the Senate (or President) that conflicts with the meaning of the treaty or violates the treaty's object and purpose is not valid.[23] For example, if the reservation states that a provision in a human rights treaty will not be self-executing by providing a private cause of action, the reservation may not be valid[24] because states must provide individuals with an effective and sufficient domestic judicial remedy under international human rights law.[25]

---

[23] *Vienna Convention*, art. 19(c).

[24] *See* Kolovrat v. Oregon, 366 U.S. 187, 194 (1961) ("While courts interpret treaties for themselves, the meaning given them by the departments of government particularly charged with their negotiation and enforcement is given great weight."). However, the Supreme Court has rejected interpretations that clearly conflict with the language of the treaty. *Id.* at 192 ("This Court has many times set its face against treaty interpretations that unduly restrict rights a treaty is adopted to protect.").

[25] International law generally requires that states provide full reparations, including money damages and, if necessary, injunctive relief when they have committed an illegal act. *See* Chorzow Factory Case, 1928 P.C.I.J. (ser. A) No. 17, at 47 (13 Sept.) (recognizing *restitutio in integrum* principle). International human rights law guarantees that individuals have a remedy enforceable in domestic courts. For example, the International Covenant on Civil and Political Rights states:

> 2. Where not already provided for by existing legislative or other measures, each State Party to the present Covenant undertakes to take the necessary steps, in accordance with its constitutional processes and with the provisions of the present Covenant, to adopt such legislative or other measures as may be necessary to give effect to the rights recognized in the present Covenant.
>
> 3. Each State Party to the present Covenant undertakes:
>
> (a) To ensure that any person whose rights or freedoms as herein recognized are violated shall have an effective remedy, notwithstanding that the violation has been committed by persons acting in an official capacity;
>
> (b) To ensure that any person claiming such a remedy shall have his right thereto determined by competent judicial, administrative or legislative authorities, or by any other competent authority provided for by the legal system of the State, and to develop the possibilities of judicial remedy;
>
> (c) To ensure that the competent authorities shall enforce such remedies when granted.

ICCPR, art. 2 (2)-(3); *see* UN Hum. Rts. Ctte., General Comment No. 24 (52), General comment on issues relating to reservations made upon ratification or accession to the Covenant or the Optional Protocols thereto, or in relation to declarations under article 41 of the Covenant, §§3 and 12, U.N. Doc. CCPR/C/21/Rev.1/Add.6 (1994) (state-party cannot make reservation denying remedy – including judicial remedy – for human rights violations).

The American Convention on Human Rights states:

> Article 25. Right to Judicial Protection.
>
> 1. Everyone has the right to simple and prompt recourse, or any other effective recourse, to a competent court or tribunal for protection against acts that violate his fundamental rights recognized by the constitution or laws of the state concerned or by this Convention, even though such violation may have been committed by persons acting in the course of their official duties.
>
> 2. The States Parties undertake:
>
> a. To ensure that any person claiming such remedy shall have his rights determined by the competent authority provided for by the legal system of the state;
>
> b. To develop the possibilities of judicial remedy; and
>
> c. To ensure that the competent authorities shall enforce such remedies when granted.

ACHR, art. 25. *See* Martin, Challenging, *supra* note 9, at 77–78 (discussing individual's right to remedy entails judicial remedy).

Although, generally speaking, international law often allows states to exercise a certain amount of discretion in fashioning how they provide a domestic remedy for international legal violations, international human rights tribunals have strictly limited this deference and have required a judicial remedy because other remedies (such as those provided by the political branches) are most often ineffective and/or inadequate and a judicial remedy is the only remedy that can provide complete restitution.[26] For example, in cases where individuals have committed gross human rights violations, international human rights law creates an affirmative state duty to punish such persons.[27] Only a judicial remedy could provide the required punishment of individuals committing such human rights violations. If the reservation violates extant customary international law or *jus cogens*, then the reservation is invalid because the political branches are violating the Constitution as construed according to customary international law or *jus cogens*.[28]

. . . .

In conclusion, ILC allows us to do an "end-run" around these execution and political question dilemmas. This interpretive move releases us from the internally contradictory constraints of a separation of powers principle that relies solely upon the Constitution's text and structure. First, the claim that treaties (or customary international law) are unenforceable in United States courts absent an express statement to the contrary or implementing legislation[ ] is effectively mooted because the determination of whether such treaties (or customary international law) are enforceable is not exclusively tied to the Constitution's ambiguous text and structure but also is tied to customary international law – the appropriate source of law for construing Constitution as a treaty. In the case of treaties requiring an express statement that the treaty is self-executing, such a statement is effectively not required when customary international law (as reflected in treaties or judicial decisions construing such treaties) already speaks to the matter.[29]

---

[26] *See, e.g.,* Anguelova v. Bulgaria, Application No. 38361/97, Eur. Ct. H.R. at §161 (2002) (states allowed "some discretion" as to how they provide remedy to individuals for international law violations); M.J. Bossuyt, Guide to the "Travaux Préparatoires" of the International Covenant on Civil and Political Rights 67 (1987); Darmburg v. Suriname, Case No. 10.117, Res. No. 19/89, Inter-Am. Cm. H.R. 138, OEA/ser.L/V.II.76, doc. 10 (1988–89); Tumilovich v. Russia, Application No. 47033, Eur. Ct. H.R. (1999) (domestic remedy depending on discretionary powers do not constitute effective domestic remedy).

[27] *See, e.g.,* Velásquez Rodríguez v. Honduras, Inter-Am. Ct. H.R., Ser. C., No. 4 at ¶ 172 (1988) (state affirmative duty to punish rights to life and humane treatment); Celis Laureano v. Peru, U.N. Doc. CCPR/C/56/D/540/1993 (1996) (views adopted March 25, 1996) (state affirmative duty to punish violations of rights to life, humane treatment, and liberty and personal security committed by state and non-state actors).

[28] [ ] However, a reservation's invalidity does not abrogate the United States' customary international legal obligations under the treaty if the United States already effectively has acquiesced to the treaty's norms through, *e.g.,* its signature to the treaty. A way in which a state arguably could lawfully make a reservation to a customary international legal norm in a treaty is if the treaty creates an enforcement organ and if the reservation is interpreted to mean only that the state-party does not recognize the organ's competence to interpret the norm in regard to claims against the state-party. *See* UN Hum. Rts. Ctte., General Comment No. 24 (52), General comment on issues relating to reservations made upon ratification or accession to the Covenant or the Optional Protocols thereto, or in relation to declarations under article 41 of the Covenant, §17, U.N. Doc. CCPR/C/21/Rev.1/Add.6 (1994) ("The principle of inter-State reciprocity has no place, save perhaps in the limited context of reservations to declarations on the Committee's competence" to consider inter-state complaints.); Belilos v. Switzerland, 10 E.H.R.R. 466 (1988) (de Meyer, J., concurring).

[29] *Cf.* Warren v. United States, 340 U.S. 523, 526–28 (1951) (no Act of Congress required to guide enforcement of treaty provisions because judicial decisions provided sufficient definition to treaty provisions).

In cases where constitutional text is being construed with a treaty (or customary international law), implementing legislation is not required. It is not legally relevant if the treaty (or customary international law) requires implementing law (for it to be enforced by United States courts) in order for the treaty (or customary international law) to, in turn, be used to construe the Constitution's text. Such treaty law (or customary international law) is not being implemented *per se*.[30] The relevant issue is whether the particular Constitutional provision itself is self-executing. For some constitutional provisions, no implementing legislation is required, *e.g.*, to provide definition to the provision, a private cause of action for its violation, or some other action constitutionally addressed to another branch of the federal government. For example, the United States Supreme Court has held that the human rights guarantees contained in the first eight Amendments to the Constitution are self-executing in the sense of not constitutionally requiring a private cause of action.[31] Accordingly, these constitutional rights – even if construed according to treaty or customary international legal norms – still are self-executing. Even in cases where constitutional provisions require implementing legislation to provide definition, such provisions do not need such implementing legislation if they have been construed in light of a treaty (or customary international law or any other extra-constitutional authority). The issue of whether the constitutional provision is self-executing or not is made moot by this international legal construction. In cases where Congress has arguably failed to fulfill its constitutional duty, as construed by the Object and Purpose Rule, to provide necessary implementing legislation for a treaty (or customary international legal norm), federal courts are free to apply the treaty (or customary international legal norm) and fashion remedies.

. . . .

∼

---

[30] Indeed, under customary international law governing treaties, courts sometimes can construe a treaty in conformity with other treaties that do not share any states-parties with the treaty being construed and, hence, do not constitute binding law for a party to the treaty being construed. *See, e.g.*, Legal Consequences for States of the Continued Presence of South Africa in Namibia (South West Africa) notwithstanding Security Council Resolution 276 (1970), Advisory Opinion, 1971 I.C.J. 16, 31 (1971) ("an international instrument must be interpreted and applied within the *overall* framework of the [international] juridical system in force" (emphasis provided)); Interpretation of the American Declaration of the Rights and Duties of Man within the Framework of Article 64 of the American Convention on Human Rights, Advisory Opinion OC-10/89, Inter-Am. Ct. H.R. Ser. A, No. 10, at ¶ 37 (1989) (same). The Inter-American Court of Human Rights has recognized that even non-Inter-American treaties properly can be used to complement and construe Inter-American treaties.

   The need of the regional system to be complemented by the universal finds expression in the practice of the Inter-American Commission on Human Rights and is entirely consistent with the object and purpose of the Convention, the American Declaration and the Statute of the Commission. The Commission has properly invoked in some of its reports and resolutions "other treaties concerning the protection of human rights in the American states," regardless of their bilateral or multilateral character, or whether they have been adopted within the framework or under the auspices of the inter-American system.

   "Other Treaties" Subject to the Consultative Jurisdiction of the Court (Art. 64 of the American Convention on Human Rights), Advisory Opinion OC-1/82, Inter-Am. Ct. H.R. (Ser. A) No. 1, at §43(1982).

[31] *See* City of Bourne v. Flores, 521 U.S. 507, 524 (1997) ("first eight Amendments to the Constitution set forth self executing prohibitions on governmental action"); Bivens v. Six Unknown Named Agents, 402 U.S. 388 (1971) (recognizing private cause of action for Fourth Amendment violations); Bolling v. Sharpe, 347 U.S. 497 (1954) (recognizing private right to injunctive relief for Fifth Amendment violations).

3.3.2. Customary International Law

In the following materials, consider what kind of customary international law – if any – constitutionally requires implementing legislation. Also, consider how specific a customary international legal norm must be for U.S. courts to give it effect.

Sosa v. Alvarez-Machain

U.S. Supreme Court

– U.S. –, 124 S. Ct. 2739, 159 L. Ed. 2d 718 (2004)

. . . .

. . . . In 1985, an agent of the Drug Enforcement Administration (DEA), Enrique Camarena-Salazar, was captured on assignment in Mexico and taken to a house in Guadalajara, where he was tortured over the course of a 2-day interrogation, then murdered. Based in part on eyewitness testimony, DEA officials in the United States came to believe that respondent Humberto Alvarez-Machain (Alvarez), a Mexican physician, was present at the house and acted to prolong the agent's life in order to extend the interrogation and torture. *Id.*, at 657.

In 1990, a federal grand jury indicted Alvarez for the torture and murder of Camarena-Salazar, and the United States District Court for the Central District of California issued a warrant for his arrest. 331 F.3d 604, 609 (CA9 2003) (en banc). The DEA asked the Mexican Government for help in getting Alvarez into the United States, but when the requests and negotiations proved fruitless, the DEA approved a plan to hire Mexican nationals to seize Alvarez and bring him to the United States for trial. As so planned, a group of Mexicans, including petitioner Jose Francisco Sosa, abducted Alvarez from his house, held him overnight in a motel, and brought him by private plane to El Paso, Texas, where he was arrested by federal officers. *Ibid.*

Once in American custody, Alvarez moved to dismiss the indictment on the ground that his seizure was "outrageous governmental conduct," *Alvarez-Machain*, 504 U.S. at 658, and violated the extradition treaty between the United States and Mexico. The District Court agreed, the Ninth Circuit affirmed, and we reversed, *id.*, at 670, holding that the fact of Alvarez's forcible seizure did not affect the jurisdiction of a federal court. The case was tried in 1992, and ended at the close of the Government's case, when the District Court granted Alvarez's motion for a judgment of acquittal.

In 1993, after returning to Mexico, Alvarez began the civil action before us here. He sued Sosa, . . . So far as it matters here, Alvarez sought damages . . . from Sosa under the ATS [Alien Tort Statute, 28 U.S.C. §1350], for a violation of the law of nations. The [ATS] provides in its entirety that "[t]he district courts shall have original jurisdiction of any civil action by an alien for a tort only, committed in violation of the law of nations or a treaty of the United States." §1350.

The District Court granted . . . awarded summary judgment and $25,000 in damages to Alvarez on the ATS claim. A three-judge panel of the Ninth Circuit then affirmed the ATS judgment, . . .

. . . [F]or the ATS claim, the court called on its own precedent, "that [the ATS] not only provides federal courts with subject matter jurisdiction, but also creates a cause of action for an alleged violation of the law of nations." *Id.*, at 612. The Circuit then relied upon what it called the "clear and universally recognized norm prohibiting arbitrary arrest and detention," *id.*, at 620, to support the conclusion that Alvarez's arrest amounted to a tort in violation of international law....

. . . .

III

Alvarez has also brought an action under the ATS against petitioner, Sosa, who argues (as does the United States supporting him) that there is no relief under the ATS because the statute does no more than vest federal courts with jurisdiction, neither creating nor authorizing the courts to recognize any particular right of action without further congressional action. Although we agree the statute is in terms only jurisdictional, we think that at the time of enactment the jurisdiction enabled federal courts to hear claims in a very limited category defined by the law of nations and recognized at common law. We do not believe, however, that the limited, implicit sanction to entertain the handful of international law *cum* common law claims understood in 1789 should be taken as authority to recognize the right of action asserted by Alvarez here.

A

Judge Friendly called the ATS a "legal Lohengrin," *IIT v. Vencap, Ltd.*, 519 F.2d 1001, 1015 (CA2 1975); "no one seems to know whence it came," *ibid.*, and for over 170 years after its enactment it provided jurisdiction in only one case. The first Congress passed it as part of the Judiciary Act of 1789, in providing that the new federal district courts "shall also have cognizance, concurrent with the courts of the several States, or the circuit courts, as the case may be, of all causes where an alien sues for a tort only in violation of the law of nations or a treaty of the United States." Act of Sept. 24, 1789, ch. 20, §9(*b*), 1 Stat. 79.[ ]

The parties and *amici* here advance radically different historical interpretations of this terse provision. Alvarez says that the ATS was intended not simply as a jurisdictional grant, but as authority for the creation of a new cause of action for torts in violation of international law. We think that reading is implausible. As enacted in 1789, the ATS gave the district courts "cognizance" of certain causes of action, and the term bespoke a grant of jurisdiction, not power to mold substantive law. See, *e.g.*, The Federalist No. 81, pp. 447, 451 (J. Cooke ed. 1961) (A. Hamilton) (using "jurisdiction" interchangeably with "cognizance"). The fact that the ATS was placed in §9 of the Judiciary Act, a statute otherwise exclusively concerned with federal-court jurisdiction, is itself support for its strictly jurisdictional nature. Nor would the distinction between jurisdiction and cause of action have been elided by the drafters of the Act or those who voted on it. As Fisher Ames put it, "there is a substantial difference between the jurisdiction of courts and rules of decision." 1 Annals of Cong. 807 (Gales ed. 1834). It is unsurprising, then, that an authority on the historical origins of the ATS has written that "section 1350 clearly does not create a statutory cause of action," and that the contrary suggestion is "simply frivolous." Casto, The Federal Courts' Protective Jurisdiction Over Torts Committed in Violation of the Law of Nations, 18 Conn. L. Rev. 467, 479, 480 (1986) (hereinafter Casto, Law of Nations); Cf. Dodge, The Constitutionality of the Alien Tort Statute: Some Observations on Text and Context, 42 Va. J. Int'l L. 687, 689 (2002). In sum, we think the statute was intended as jurisdictional in the sense of addressing the power of the courts to entertain cases concerned with a certain subject.

But holding the ATS jurisdictional raises a new question, this one about the interaction between the ATS at the time of its enactment and the ambient law of the era. Sosa would have it that the ATS was stillborn because there could be no claim for relief without a further statute expressly authorizing adoption of causes of action. *Amici* professors of federal jurisdiction and legal history take a different tack, that federal courts could entertain claims once the jurisdictional grant was on the books, because torts in violation of the law of nations would have been recognized within the common law of the time. Brief for Vikram Amar et al. as *Amici Curiae.* We think history and practice give the edge to this latter position.

1

"When the *United States* declared their independence, they were bound to receive the law of nations, in its modern state of purity and refinement." *Ware v. Hylton*, 3 Dall. 199, 281 (1796) (Wilson, J.). In the years of the early Republic, this law of nations comprised two principal elements, the first covering the general norms governing the behavior of national states with each other: *"the science which teaches the rights subsisting between nations or states, and the obligations correspondent to those rights,"* E. de Vattel, The Law of Nations, Preliminaries §3 (J. Chitty et al. transl. and ed. 1883) (hereinafter Vattel) (footnote omitted), or "that code of public instruction which defines the rights and prescribes the duties of nations, in their intercourse with each other," 1 James Kent Commentaries *1. This aspect of the law of nations thus occupied the executive and legislative domains, not the judicial. See 4 W. Blackstone, Commentaries on the Laws of England 68 (1769) (hereinafter Commentaries) ("[O]ffenses against" the law of nations are "principally incident to whole states or nations").

The law of nations included a second, more pedestrian element, however, that did fall within the judicial sphere, as a body of judge-made law regulating the conduct of individuals situated outside domestic boundaries and consequently carrying an international savor. To Blackstone, the law of nations in this sense was implicated "in mercantile questions, such as bills of exchange and the like; in all marine causes, relating to freight, average, demurrage, insurances, bottomry...; [and] in all disputes relating to prizes, to shipwrecks, to hostages, and ransom bills." *Id.*, at 67. The law merchant emerged from the customary practices of international traders and admiralty required its own transnational regulation. And it was the law of nations in this sense that our precursors spoke about when the Court explained the status of coast fishing vessels in wartime grew from "ancient usage among civilized nations, beginning centuries ago, and gradually ripening into a rule of international law...." *The Paquete Habana*, 175 U.S. 677, 686 (1900).

There was, finally, a sphere in which these rules binding individuals for the benefit of other individuals overlapped with the norms of state relationships. Blackstone referred to it when he mentioned three specific offenses against the law of nations addressed by the criminal law of England: violation of safe conducts, infringement of the rights of ambassadors, and piracy. 4 Commentaries 68. An assault against an ambassador, for example, impinged upon the sovereignty of the foreign nation and if not adequately redressed could rise to an issue of war. *See* Vattel 463–464. It was this narrow set of violations of the law of nations, admitting of a judicial remedy and at the same time threatening serious consequences in international affairs, that was probably on minds of the men who drafted the ATS with its reference to tort.

2

Before there was any ATS, a distinctly American preoccupation with these hybrid international norms had taken shape owing to the distribution of political power from independence through the period of confederation. The Continental Congress was hamstrung by its inability to "cause infractions of treaties, or of the law of nations to be punished," J. Madison, Journal of the Constitutional Convention 60 (E. Scott ed. 1893), and in 1781 the Congress implored the States to vindicate rights under the law of nations. In words that echo Blackstone, the congressional resolution called upon state legislatures to "provide expeditious, exemplary, and adequate punishment" for "the violation of safe conducts or passports,... of hostility against such as are in amity,... with the United States,... infractions of the immunities of ambassadors and other public ministers..." [and] "infractions of treaties and conventions to which the United States are a party." 21 Journals of the Continental Congress 1136–1137 (G. Hunt ed. 1912) (hereinafter Journals of the Continental Congress). The resolution recommended that the States "authorise suits... for damages by the party injured, and for compensation to the United States for damage sustained by them from an injury done to a foreign power by a citizen." *Id.*, at 1137; cf. Vattel 463–464 ("Whoever offends... a public minister... should be punished..., and... the state should, at the expense of the delinquent, give full satisfaction to the sovereign who has been offended in the person of his minister"). Apparently only one State acted upon the recommendation, see First Laws of the State of Connecticut 82, 83 (J. Cushing ed. 1982) (1784 compilation; exact date of Act unknown), but Congress had done what it could to signal a commitment to enforce the law of nations.

Appreciation of the Continental Congress's incapacity to deal with this class of cases was intensified by the so-called Marbois incident of May 1784, in which a French adventurer, Longchamps, verbally and physically assaulted the Secretary of the French Legion in Philadelphia. *See Respublica v. De Longchamps*, 1 Dall. 111 (O. T. Phila. 1784). [ ] Congress called again for state legislation addressing such matters, and concern over the inadequate vindication of the law of nations persisted through the time of the constitutional convention. *See* 1 Records of the Federal Convention of 1787, p. 25 (M. Farrand ed. 1911) (speech of J. Randolph). During the Convention itself, in fact, a New York City constable produced a reprise of the Marbois affair and Secretary Jay reported to Congress on the Dutch Ambassador's protest, with the explanation that "the federal government does not appear... to be vested with any judicial Powers competent to the Cognizance and Judgment of such Cases." Casto, Law of Nations 494, and n. 152.

The Framers responded by vesting the Supreme Court with original jurisdiction over "all Cases affecting Ambassadors, other public ministers and Consuls." U.S. Const., Art. III, §2, and the First Congress followed through. The Judiciary Act reinforced this Court's original jurisdiction over suits brought by diplomats, see 1 Stat. 80, ch. 20, §13, created alienage jurisdiction, §11 and, of course, included the ATS, §9. *See* generally Randall, Federal Jurisdiction over International Law Claims: Inquiries into the Alien Tort Statute, 18 N. Y. U. J. Int'l L. & Pol. 1, 15–21 (1985) (discussing foreign affairs implications of the Judiciary Act); W. Casto, The Supreme Court in the Early Republic 27 – 53 (1995).

3

Although Congress modified the draft of what became the Judiciary Act, see generally Warren, New Light on the History of the Federal Judiciary Act of 1789, 37 Harv. L. Rev. 49 (1923), it made hardly any changes to the provisions on aliens, including what became the ATS, see Casto, Law of Nations 498. There is no record of congressional discussion about private actions that might be subject to the jurisdictional provision, or about any need for further legislation to create private remedies; there is no record even of debate on the section. Given the poverty of drafting history, modern commentators have necessarily concentrated on the text, remarking on the innovative use of the word "tort," see, *e.g.,* Sweeney, A Tort only in Violation of the Law of Nations, 18 Hastings Int'l & Comp. L. Rev. 445 (1995) (arguing that "tort" refers to the law of prize), and the statute's mixture of terms expansive ("all suits"), see, *e.g.,* Casto, Law of Nations 500, and restrictive ("for a tort only"), see, *e.g.,* Randall, *supra,* at 28–31 (limiting suits to torts, as opposed to commercial actions, especially by British plaintiffs). [ ] The historical scholarship has also placed the ATS within the competition between federalist and antifederalist forces over the national role in foreign relations. *Id.,* at 22–23 (nonexclusiveness of federal jurisdiction under the ATS may reflect compromise). But despite considerable scholarly attention, it is fair to say that a consensus understanding of what Congress intended has proven elusive.

Still, the history does tend to support two propositions. First, there is every reason to suppose that the First Congress did not pass the ATS as a jurisdictional convenience to be placed on the shelf for use by a future Congress or state legislature that might, some day, authorize the creation of causes of action or itself decide to make some element of the law of nations actionable for the benefit of foreigners. The anxieties of the preconstitutional period cannot be ignored easily enough to think that the statute was not meant to have a practical effect. Consider that the principal draftsman of the ATS was apparently Oliver Ellsworth, [ ] previously a member of the Continental Congress that had passed the 1781 resolution and a member of the Connecticut Legislature that made good on that congressional request. *See* generally W. Brown, The Life of Oliver Ellsworth (1905). Consider, too, that the First Congress was attentive enough to the law of nations to recognize certain offenses expressly as criminal, including the three mentioned by Blackstone. *See* An Act for the Punishment of Certain Crimes Against the United States, §8, 1 Stat. 113–114 (murder or robbery, or other capital crimes, punishable as piracy if committed on the high seas), and §28, *id.,* at 118 (violation of safe conducts and assaults against ambassadors punished by imprisonment and fines described as "infract[ions of] the law of nations"). It would have been passing strange for Ellsworth and this very Congress to vest federal courts expressly with jurisdiction to entertain civil causes brought by aliens alleging violations of the law of nations, but to no effect whatever until the Congress should take further action. There is too much in the historical record to believe that Congress would have enacted the ATS only to leave it lying fallow indefinitely.

The second inference to be drawn from the history is that Congress intended the ATS to furnish jurisdiction for a relatively modest set of actions alleging violations of the law of nations. Uppermost in the legislative mind appears to have been offenses against ambassadors, see *id.,* at 118; violations of safe conduct were probably understood to be actionable, *ibid.,* and individual actions arising out of prize captures and piracy may well have also been contemplated. *Id.,* at 113–114. But the common law appears to have understood only those three of the hybrid variety as definite and actionable, or at any rate, to have assumed only a very limited set of claims. As Blackstone had put it, "offences against this law [of nations] are principally incident to whole states or nations," and not individuals seeking relief in court. 4 Commentaries 68.

4

The sparse contemporaneous cases and legal materials referring to the ATS tend to confirm both inferences, that some, but few, torts in violation of the law of nations were understood to be within the common law. In *Bolchos v. Darrel,* 3 F. Cas. 810 (No. 1,607)

(S. C. 1795), the District Court's doubt about admiralty jurisdiction over a suit for damages brought by a French privateer against the mortgagee of a British slave ship was assuaged by assuming that the ATS was a jurisdictional basis for the court's action. Nor is *Moxon v. The Fanny*, 17 F. Cas. 942 (No. 9, 895) (Pa. 1793), to the contrary, a case in which the owners of a British ship sought damages for its seizure in United States waters by a French privateer. The District Court said in dictum that the ATS was not the proper vehicle for suit because "[i]t cannot be called a suit for a tort only, when the property, as well as damages for the supposed trespass, are sought for." *Id.*, at 948. But the judge gave no intimation that further legislation would have been needed to give the District Court jurisdiction over a suit limited to damages.

Then there was the 1795 opinion of Attorney General William Bradford, who was asked whether criminal prosecution was available against Americans who had taken part in the French plunder of a British slave colony in Sierra Leone. 1 Op. Atty. Gen. 57. Bradford was uncertain, but he made it clear that a federal court was open for the prosecution of a tort action growing out of the episode:

> "But there can be no doubt that the company or individuals who have been injured by these acts of hostility have a remedy by a *civil* suit in the courts of the United States; jurisdiction being expressly given to these courts in all cases where an alien sues for a tort only, in violation of the laws of nations, or a treaty of the United States...." *Id.*, at 59.

Although it is conceivable that Bradford (who had prosecuted in the Marbois incident, see Casto, Law of Nations 503, n. 201) assumed that there had been a violation of a treaty, 1 Op. Atty. Gen., at 58, that is certainly not obvious, and it appears likely that Bradford understood the ATS to provide jurisdiction over what must have amounted to common law causes of action.

B

Against these indications that the ATS was meant to underwrite litigation of a narrow set of common law actions derived from the law of nations, Sosa raises two main objections. First, he claims that this conclusion makes no sense in view of the Continental Congress's 1781 recommendation to state legislatures to pass laws authorizing such suits. Sosa thinks state legislation would have been "absurd," Reply Brief for Petitioner Sosa 5, if common law remedies had been available. Second, Sosa juxtaposes Blackstone's treatise mentioning violations of the law of nations as occasions for criminal remedies, against the statute's innovative reference to "tort," as evidence that there was no familiar set of legal actions for exercise of jurisdiction under the ATS. Neither argument is convincing.

The notion that it would have been absurd for the Continental Congress to recommend that States pass positive law to duplicate remedies already available at common law rests on a misunderstanding of the relationship between common law and positive law in the late 18th century, when positive law was frequently relied upon to reinforce and give standard expression to the "brooding omnipresence"[ ] of the common law then thought discoverable by reason. As Blackstone clarified the relation between positive law and the law of nations, "those acts of parliament, which have from time to time been made to enforce this universal law, or to facilitate the execution of [its] decisions, are not to be considered as introductive of any new rule, but merely as declaratory of the old fundamental constitutions of the kingdom; without which it must cease to be a part of the civilized world." 4 Commentaries 67. Indeed, Sosa's argument is undermined by the 1781 resolution on which he principally relies. Notwithstanding the undisputed fact (per Blackstone) that the common law afforded criminal law remedies for violations of the law of nations, the Continental Congress encouraged state legislatures to pass criminal statutes to the same effect, and the first Congress did the same, *supra*, at 23.[ ]

Nor are we convinced by Sosa's argument that legislation conferring a right of action is needed because Blackstone treated international law offenses under the rubric of "public wrongs," whereas the ATS uses a word, "tort," that was relatively uncommon in the legal vernacular of the day. It is true that Blackstone did refer to what he deemed the three principal offenses against the law of nations in the course of discussing criminal sanctions, observing that it was in the interest of sovereigns "to animadvert upon them with a becoming severity, that the peace of the world may be maintained," 4 Commentaries 68. [ ] But Vattel explicitly linked the criminal sanction for offenses against ambassadors with the requirement that the state, "at the expense of the delinquent, give full satisfaction to the sovereign who has been offended in the person of his minister." Vattel 463–464. Cf. Stephens, Individuals Enforcing International Law: The Comparative and Historical Context, 52 DePaul L. Rev. 433, 444 (2002) (observing that a "mixed approach to international law violations, encompassing both criminal prosecution . . . and compensation to those injured through a civil suit, would have been familiar to the founding generation"). The 1781 resolution goes a step further in showing that a private remedy was thought necessary for diplomatic offenses under the law of nations. And the Attorney General's Letter of 1795, as well as the two early federal precedents discussing the ATS, point to a prevalent assumption that Congress did not intend the ATS to sit on the shelf until some future time when it might enact further legislation.

In sum, although the ATS is a jurisdictional statute creating no new causes of action, the reasonable inference from the historical materials is that the statute was intended to have practical effect the moment it became law. The jurisdictional grant is best read as having been enacted on the understanding that the common law would provide a cause of action for the modest number of international law violations with a potential for personal liability at the time.

IV

We think it is correct, then, to assume that the First Congress understood that the district courts would recognize private causes of action for certain torts in violation of the law of nations, though we have found no basis to suspect Congress had any examples in mind beyond those torts corresponding to Blackstone's three primary offenses: violation of safe conducts, infringement of the rights of ambassadors, and piracy. We assume, too, that no development in the two centuries from the enactment of §1350 to the birth of the modern line of cases beginning with *Filartiga v. Pena-Irala*, 630 F.2d 876 (CA2 1980), has categorically precluded federal courts from recognizing a claim under the law of nations as an element of common law; Congress has not in any relevant way amended §1350 or limited civil common law power by another statute. Still, there are good reasons for a restrained conception of the discretion a federal court should exercise in considering a new cause of action of this kind. Accordingly, we think courts should require any claim based on the present-day law of nations to rest on a norm of international character accepted by the civilized world and defined with a specificity comparable to the features of the 18th-century paradigms we have recognized. This requirement is fatal to Alvarez's claim.

A

A series of reasons argue for judicial caution when considering the kinds of individual claims that might implement the jurisdiction conferred by the early statute. First, the prevailing conception of the common law has changed since 1789 in a way that counsels restraint in judicially applying internationally generated norms. When §1350 was enacted, the accepted conception was of the common law as "a transcendental body of law outside of any particular State but obligatory within it unless and until changed by statute." *Black and White Taxicab & Transfer Co. v.* Brown and Yellow Taxicab & Transfer Co., 276 U.S. 518, 533 (1928) (Holmes, J., dissenting). Now, however, in most cases where a court is asked to state or formulate a common law principle in a new context, there is a general understanding that the law is not so much found or discovered as it is either made or created. Holmes explained famously in 1881 that

> "in substance the growth of the law is legislative . . . [because t]he very considerations which judges most rarely mention, and always with an apology, are the secret root from which the law draws all the juices of life. I mean, of course, considerations of what is expedient for the community concerned." The Common Law 31–32 (Howe ed. 1963).

One need not accept the Holmesian view as far as its ultimate implications to acknowledge that a judge deciding in reliance on an international norm will find a substantial element of discretionary judgment in the decision.

Second, along with, and in part driven by, that conceptual development in understanding common law has come an equally significant rethinking of the role of the federal courts in making it. *Erie R. Co. v. Tompkins*, 304 U.S. 64 (1938), was the watershed in which we denied the existence of any federal "general" common law, *id.*, at 78, which largely withdrew to havens of specialty, some of them defined by express congressional authorization to devise a body of law directly, *e.g.*, *Textile Workers v. Lincoln Mills of Ala.*, 353 U.S. 448 (1957) (interpretation of collective-bargaining agreements); Fed. Rule Evid. 501 (evidentiary privileges in federal-question cases). Elsewhere, this Court has thought it was in order to create federal common law rules in interstitial areas of particular federal interest. *E.g.*, *United States v. Kimbell Foods, Inc.*, 440 U.S. 715, 726–727 (1979). And although we have even assumed competence to make judicial rules of decision of particular importance to foreign relations, such as the act of state doctrine, see *Banco Nacional de Cuba v. Sabbatino*, 376 U.S. 398, 427 (1964), the general practice has been to look for legislative guidance before exercising innovative authority over substantive law. It would be remarkable to take a more aggressive role in exercising a jurisdiction that remained largely in shadow for much of the prior two centuries.

Third, this Court has recently and repeatedly said that a decision to create a private right of action is one better left to legislative judgment in the great majority of cases. *Correctional Services Corp. v. Malesko*, 534 U.S. 61, 68 (2001); *Alexander v. Sandoval*, 532 U.S. 275, 286–287 (2001). The creation of a private right of action raises issues beyond the mere consideration whether underlying primary conduct should be allowed or not, entailing, for example, a decision to permit enforcement without the check imposed by prosecutorial discretion. Accordingly, even when Congress has made it clear by statute that a rule applies to purely domestic conduct, we are reluctant to infer intent to provide a private cause of action where the statute does not supply one expressly. While the absence of congressional action addressing private rights of action under an international norm is more equivocal than its failure to provide such a right when it creates a statute, the possible collateral consequences of making international rules privately actionable argue for judicial caution.

Fourth, the subject of those collateral consequences is itself a reason for a high bar to new private causes of action for violating international law, for the potential implications for the foreign relations of the United States of recognizing such causes should make courts particularly wary of impinging on the discretion of the Legislative and Executive Branches in managing foreign affairs. It is one thing for American courts to enforce constitutional limits on our own State and Federal Governments' power, but quite another to consider suits under rules that would go so far as to claim a limit on the power of foreign governments over their own citizens, and to hold that a foreign government or its agent has transgressed those limits. Cf. *Sabbatino, supra,* at 431–432. Yet modern international law is very much concerned with just such questions, and apt to stimulate calls for vindicating private interests in §1350 cases. Since many attempts by federal courts to craft remedies for the violation of new norms of international law would raise risks of adverse foreign policy consequences, they should be undertaken, if at all, with great caution. Cf. *Tel-Oren v. Libyan Arab Republic,* 726 F.2d 774, 813 (CADC 1984) (Bork, J., concurring) (expressing doubt that §1350 should be read to require "our courts [to] sit in judgment of the conduct of foreign officials in their own countries with respect to their own citizens").

The fifth reason is particularly important in light of the first four. We have no congressional mandate to seek out and define new and debatable violations of the law of nations, and modern indications of congressional understanding of the judicial role in the field have not affirmatively encouraged greater judicial creativity. It is true that a clear mandate appears in the Torture Victim Protection Act of 1991, 106 Stat. 73, providing authority that "establish[es] an unambiguous and modern basis for" federal claims of torture and extrajudicial killing, H. R. Rep. No. 102-367, pt. 1, p. 3 (1991). But that affirmative authority is confined to specific subject matter, and although the legislative history includes the remark that §1350 should "remain intact to permit suits based on other norms that already exist or may ripen in the future into rules of customary international law," *id.,* at 4, Congress as a body has done nothing to promote such suits. Several times, indeed, the Senate has expressly declined to give the federal courts the task of interpreting and applying international human rights law, as when its ratification of the International Covenant on Civil and Political Rights declared that the substantive provisions of the document were not self-executing. 138 Cong. Rec. 8071 (1992).

B

These reasons argue for great caution in adapting the law of nations to private rights. Justice Scalia, *post,* p. 1 (opinion concurring in part and concurring in judgment) concludes that caution is too hospitable, and a word is in order to summarize where we have come so far and to focus our difference with him on whether some norms of today's law of nations may ever be recognized legitimately by federal courts in the absence of congressional action beyond §1350. All Members of the Court agree that §1350 is only jurisdictional. We also agree, or at least Justice Scalia does not dispute, *post,* at 2, 7, that the jurisdiction was originally understood to be available to enforce a small number of international norms that a federal court could properly recognize as within the common law enforceable without further statutory authority. Justice Scalia concludes, however, that two subsequent developments should be understood to preclude federal courts from recognizing any further international norms as judicially enforceable today, absent further congressional action. As described before, we now tend to understand common law not as a discoverable reflection of universal reason but, in a positivistic way, as a product of human choice. And we now adhere to a conception of limited judicial power first expressed in reorienting federal diversity jurisdiction, see *Erie R. Co. v. Tompkins,* 304 U.S. 64 (1938), that federal courts have no authority to derive "general" common law.

Whereas Justice Scalia sees these developments as sufficient to close the door to further independent judicial recognition of actionable international norms, other considerations persuade us that the judicial power should be exercised on the understanding that the door is still ajar subject to vigilant doorkeeping, and thus open to a narrow class of international norms today. *Erie* did not in terms bar any judicial recognition of new substantive rules, no matter what the circumstances, and post-*Erie* understanding has identified limited enclaves in which federal courts may derive some substantive law in a common law way. For two centuries we have affirmed that the domestic law of the United States recognizes the law of nations. See, *e.g., Sabbatino,* 376 U.S., at 423 ("[I]t is, of course, true that United States courts apply international law as a part of our own in appropriate circumstances"); [ ] *The Paquete Habana,* 175 U.S., at 700 ("International law is part of our law, and must be ascertained and administered by the courts of justice of appropriate jurisdiction, as often as questions of right depending upon it are duly presented for their determination"); *The Nereide,* 9 Cranch 388, 423 (1815) (Marshall, C. J.) ("[T]he Court is bound by the law of nations which is a part of the law of the land"); see also *Texas Industries, Inc. v. Radcliff Materials, Inc.,* 451 U.S. 630, 641 (1981) (recognizing that "international disputes implicating . . . our relations with foreign nations" are one of the "narrow areas" in which "federal common law" continues to exist). It would take some explaining to say now that federal courts must avert their gaze entirely from any international norm intended to protect individuals.

We think an attempt to justify such a position would be particularly unconvincing in light of what we know about congressional understanding bearing on this issue lying at the intersection of the judicial and legislative powers. The First Congress, which reflected the understanding of the framing generation and included some of the Framers, assumed that federal courts could properly identify some international norms as enforceable in the exercise of §1350 jurisdiction. We think it would be unreasonable to assume that the First Congress would have expected federal courts to lose all capacity to recognize enforceable international norms simply because the common law might lose some metaphysical cachet on the road to modern realism. Later Congresses seem to have shared our view. The position we take today has been assumed by some federal courts for 24 years, ever since the Second Circuit decided *Filartiga* v. *Pena-Irala,* 630 F.2d 876 (CA2 1980), and for practical purposes the point of today's disagreement has been focused since the exchange between Judge Edwards and Judge Bork in *Tel-Oren v. Libyan Arab Republic,* 726 F.2d 774 (CADC 1984), Congress, however, has not only expressed no disagreement with our view of the proper exercise of the judicial power, but has responded to its most notable instance by enacting legislation supplementing the judicial determination in some detail. See *supra,* at 34 (discussing the Torture Victim Protection Act).

While we agree with Justice Scalia to the point that we would welcome any congressional guidance in exercising jurisdiction with such obvious potential to affect foreign relations, nothing Congress has done is a reason for us to shut the door to the law of nations entirely. It is enough to say that Congress may do that at any time (explicitly, or implicitly by treaties or statutes that occupy the field) just as it may modify or cancel any judicial decision so far as it rests on recognizing an international norm as such.[32]

C

We must still, however, derive a standard or set of standards for assessing the particular claim Alvarez raises, and for this case it suffices to look to the historical antecedents. Whatever the ultimate criteria for accepting a cause of action subject to jurisdiction under §1350, we are persuaded that federal courts should not recognize private claims under federal common law for violations of any international law norm with less definite content and acceptance among civilized nations than the historical paradigms familiar when §1350 was enacted. See, *e.g.*, *United States v. Smith*, 5 Wheat. 153, 163–180, n. *a* (1820) (illustrating the specificity with which the law of nations defined piracy). This limit upon judicial recognition is generally consistent with the reasoning of many of the courts and judges who faced the issue before it reached this Court. See *Filartiga*, *supra*, at 890 ("[F]or purposes of civil liability, the torturer has become – like the pirate and slave trader before him – *hostis humani generis*, an enemy of all mankind"); *Tel-Oren*, *supra*, at 781 (Edwards, J., concurring) (suggesting that the "limits of section 1350's reach" be defined by "a handful of heinous actions – each of which violates definable, universal and obligatory norms"); see also *In re Estate of Marcos Human Rights Litigation*, 25 F.3d 1467, 1475 (CA9 1994) ("Actionable violations of international law must be of a norm that is specific, universal, and obligatory"). And the determination whether a norm is sufficiently definite to support a cause of action [ ] should (and, indeed, inevitably must) involve an element of judgment about the practical consequences of making that cause available to litigants in the federal courts.[33]

---

[32] Our position does not, as Justice Scalia suggests, imply that every grant of jurisdiction to a federal court carries with it an opportunity to develop common law (so that the grant of federal-question jurisdiction would be equally as good for our purposes as §1350)[ ]. Section 1350 was enacted on the congressional understanding that courts would exercise jurisdiction by entertaining some common law claims derived from the law of nations; and we know of no reason to think that federal-question jurisdiction was extended subject to any comparable congressional assumption. Further, our holding today is consistent with the division of responsibilities between federal and state courts after *Erie*[ ], as a more expansive common law power related to 28 U.S.C. §1331 might not be.

[33] This requirement of clear definition is not meant to be the only principle limiting the availability of relief in the federal courts for violations of customary international law, though it disposes of this case. For example, the European Commission argues as *amicus curiae* that basic principles of international law require that before asserting a claim in a foreign forum, the claimant must have exhausted any remedies available in the domestic legal system, and perhaps in other fora such as international claims tribunals. See Brief for European Commission as *Amicus Curiae* 24, n. 54 (citing I. Brownlie, Principles of Public International Law 472-481 (6th ed. 2003)); cf. Torture Victim Protection Act of 1991, §2(b), 106 Stat. 73 (exhaustion requirement). We would certainly consider this requirement in an appropriate case. Another possible limitation that we need not apply here is a policy of case-specific deference to the political branches. For example, there are now pending in federal district court several class actions seeking damages from various corporations alleged to have participated in, or abetted, the regime of apartheid that formerly controlled South Africa. See *In re South African Apartheid Litigation*, 238 F. Supp. 2d 1379 (JPML 2002) (granting a motion to transfer the cases to the Southern District of New York). The Government of South Africa has

Thus, Alvarez's detention claim must be gauged against the current state of international law, looking to those sources we have long, albeit cautiously, recognized.

[W]here there is no treaty, and no controlling executive or legislative act or judicial decision, resort must be had to the customs and usages of civilized nations; and, as evidence of these, to the works of jurists and commentators, who by years of labor, research and experience, have made themselves peculiarly well acquainted with the subjects of which they treat. Such works are resorted to by judicial tribunals, not for the speculations of their authors concerning what the law ought to be, but for trustworthy evidence of what the law really is. *The Paquete Habana*, 175 U.S., at 700.

To begin with, Alvarez cites two well-known international agreements that, despite their moral authority, have little utility under the standard set out in this opinion. He says that his abduction by Sosa was an "arbitrary arrest" within the meaning of the Universal Declaration of Human Rights (Declaration), G. A. Res. 217A (III), U. N. Doc. A/810 (1948). And he traces the rule against arbitrary arrest not only to the Declaration, but also to article nine of the International Covenant on Civil and Political Rights (Covenant), Dec. 19, 1996, 999 U. N. T. S. 171,[34] to which the United States is a party, and to various other conventions to which it is not. But the Declaration does not of its own force impose obligations as a matter of international law. See Humphrey, The UN Charter and the Universal Declaration of Human Rights, in The International Protection of Human Rights 39, 50 (E. Luard ed. 1967) (quoting Eleanor Roosevelt calling the Declaration "'a statement of principles ... setting up a common standard of achievement for all peoples and all nations'" and "'not a treaty or international agreement ... impos[ing] legal obligations'" [ ] And, although the Covenant does bind the United States as a matter of international law, the United States ratified the Covenant on the express understanding that it was not self-executing and so did not itself create obligations enforceable in the federal courts. [ ] Accordingly, Alvarez cannot say that the Declaration and Covenant themselves establish the relevant and applicable rule of international law. He instead attempts to show that prohibition of arbitrary arrest has attained the status of binding customary international law.

Here, it is useful to examine Alvarez's complaint in greater detail. As he presently argues it, the claim does not rest on the cross-border feature of his abduction.[ ] Although the District Court granted relief in part on finding a violation of international law in taking

---

said that these cases interfere with the policy embodied by its Truth and Reconciliation Commission, which "deliberately avoided a 'victors' justice' approach to the crimes of apartheid and chose instead one based on confession and absolution, informed by the principles of reconciliation, reconstruction, reparation and goodwill." Declaration of Penuell Mpapa Maduna, Minister of Justice and Constitutional Development, Republic of South Africa, reprinted in App. to Brief for Government of Commonwealth of Australia et al. as *Amici Curiae* 7a, ¶ 3.2.1 (emphasis deleted). The United States has agreed. See Letter of William H. Taft IV, Legal Adviser, Dept. of State, to Shannen W. Coffin, Deputy Asst. Atty. Gen., Oct. 27, 2003, reprinted in *id.*, at 2a. In such cases, there is a strong argument that federal courts should give serious weight to the Executive Branch's view of the case's impact on foreign policy. Cf. *Republic of Austria* v. *Altmann,* 541 U.S. ___, ___ (2004) (slip op., at 23–24) (discussing the State Department's use of statements of interest in cases involving the Foreign Sovereign Immunities Act of 1976, 28 U.S.C. §1602 *et seq.*)

[34] Article nine provides that "[n]o one shall be subjected to arbitrary arrest or detention," that "[n]o one shall be deprived of his liberty except on such grounds and in accordance with such procedure as are established by law," and that "[a]nyone who has been the victim of unlawful arrest or detention shall have an enforceable right to compensation."[ ]

Alvarez across the border from Mexico to the United States, the Court of Appeals rejected that ground of liability for failure to identify a norm of requisite force prohibiting a forcible abduction across a border. Instead, it relied on the conclusion that the law of the United States did not authorize Alvarez's arrest, because the DEA lacked extraterritorial authority under 21 U.S.C. §878 and because Federal Rule of Criminal Procedure 4(d)(2) limited the warrant for Alvarez's arrest to "the jurisdiction of the United States."[ ] It is this position that Alvarez takes now: that his arrest was arbitrary and as such forbidden by international law not because it infringed the prerogatives of Mexico, but because no applicable law authorized it.[ ]

Alvarez thus invokes a general prohibition of "arbitrary" detention defined as officially sanctioned action exceeding positive authorization to detain under the domestic law of some government, regardless of the circumstances. Whether or not this is an accurate reading of the Covenant, Alvarez cites little authority that a rule so broad has the status of a binding customary norm today.[35] He certainly cites nothing to justify the federal courts in taking his broad rule as the predicate for a federal lawsuit, for its implications would be breathtaking. His rule would support a cause of action in federal court for any arrest, anywhere in the world, unauthorized by the law of the jurisdiction in which it took place, and would create a cause of action for any seizure of an alien in violation of the Fourth Amendment, supplanting the actions under Rev. Stat. §1979, 42 U.S.C. §1983 and *Bivens* v. *Six Unknown Fed. Narcotics Agents*, 403 U.S. 388 (1971), that now provide damages remedies for such violations. It would create an action in federal court for arrests by state officers who simply exceed their authority; and for the violation of any limit that the law of any country might place on the authority of its own officers to arrest. And all of this assumes that Alvarez could establish that Sosa was acting on behalf of a government when he made the arrest, for otherwise he would need a rule broader still.

Alvarez's failure to marshal support for his proposed rule is underscored by the Restatement (Third) of Foreign Relations Law of the United States (1987), which says in its discussion of customary international human rights law that a "state violates international law if, as a matter of state policy, it practices, encourages, or condones . . . prolonged arbitrary detention." *Id.,* §702. Although the Restatement does not explain its requirements of a "state policy" and of "prolonged" detention, the implication is clear. Any credible invocation of a principle against arbitrary detention that the civilized world accepts as binding customary international law requires a factual basis beyond relatively

---

[35] Specifically, he relies on a survey of national constitutions, Bassiouni, Human Rights in the Context of Criminal Justice: Identifying International Procedural Protections and Equivalent Protections in National Constitutions, 3 Duke J. Comp. & Int'l L. 235, 260–261 (1993); a case from the International Court of Justice, *United States v. Iran,* 1980 I. C. J. 3, 42; and some authority drawn from the federal courts, see Brief for Respondent Alvarez-Machain 49, n. 50. None of these suffice. The Bassiouni survey does show that many nations recognize a norm against arbitrary detention, but that consensus is at a high level of generality. The *Iran* case, in which the United States sought relief for the taking of its diplomatic and consular staff as hostages, involved a different set of international norms and mentioned the problem of arbitrary detention only in passing; the detention in that case was, moreover, far longer and harsher than Alvarez's. See 1980 I. C. J., at 42, ¶ 91 ("detention of [United States] staff by a group of armed militants" lasted "many months"). And the authority from the federal courts, to the extent it supports Alvarez's position, reflects a more assertive view of federal judicial discretion over claims based on customary international law than the position we take today.

brief detention in excess of positive authority. Even the Restatement's limits are only the beginning of the enquiry, because although it is easy to say that some policies of prolonged arbitrary detentions are so bad that those who enforce them become enemies of the human race, it may be harder to say which policies cross that line with the certainty afforded by Blackstone's three common law offenses. In any event, the label would never fit the reckless policeman who botches his warrant, even though that same officer might pay damages under municipal law. *E.g.*, *Groh* v. *Ramirez*, 540 U.S. __ (2004).[ ]

Whatever may be said for the broad principle Alvarez advances, in the present, imperfect world, it expresses an aspiration that exceeds any binding customary rule having the specificity we require.[ ] Creating a private cause of action to further that aspiration would go beyond any residual common law discretion we think it appropriate to exercise.[36] It is enough to hold that a single illegal detention of less than a day, followed by the transfer of custody to lawful authorities and a prompt arraignment, violates no norm of customary international law so well defined as to support the creation of a federal remedy.

. . . .

~

QUESTIONS & COMMENTS

(1) The Supreme Court in dicta states that the ICCPR is not self-executing in the sense that it cannot be enforced by the federal courts. Does the United States' declaration actually say that? Professor Sloss has argued that the Senate and Presidents Carter and Bush had vacillating notions of what they meant by the ICCPR was "non-self-executing." *See* David Sloss, *The Domestication of International Human Rights: Non-Self-Executing Declarations and Human Rights Treaties*, 24 YALE J. INT'L L. 129, 152–53 (1999).

(2) How does the Supreme Court's claim that the Universal Declaration of Human Rights does not reflect customary international law square with a U.S. Court of Appeals' claim to the contrary in *Filártiga v. Peña-Irala*, 630 F.2d 876 (2d Cir. 1980), which the Court cites approvingly on other issues?

(3) How is the Supreme Court using the term "universal" in requiring customary international legal norms to be such? Does the Court mean "general" as opposed to "all inclusive?" Which definition conforms with the ICJ Statute?

Consider that the Supreme Court in *United States v. Smith* did not require uniformity as to all aspects of the definition of piracy for the law of nations to give it constitutionally sufficient definition. It was sufficient that the commentators on the law of nations agreed that the core definition of piracy was "robbery upon the sea."

---

[36] Alvarez also cites, Brief for Respondent Alvarez-Machain 49–50, a finding by a United Nations working group that his detention was arbitrary under the Declaration, the Covenant, and customary international law. See Report of the United Nations Working Group on Arbitrary Detention, U. N. Doc. E/CN.4/1994/27, pp. 139–140 (Dec. 17, 1993). That finding is not addressed, however, to our demanding standard of definition, which must be met to raise even the possibility of a private cause of action. If Alvarez wishes to seek compensation on the basis of the working group's finding, he must address his request to Congress.

(4) How would one demonstrate that a norm was sufficiently specific to be a customary international legal norm? Does case law provide specificity, or is such judicial interpretation begging the question?

(5) The Alien Tort Statute only provides protection to aliens. How would U.S. nationals have a cause of action for customary international legal violations? If the Constitution is a treaty whose provisions must be construed in conformity with the United States' customary international legal obligations, does the Supreme Court's requirement of specificity for establishing a tort in violation of a customary international legal norm become moot because a *Bivens* action would be available? What about those customary international legal norms that provide no assistance in construing constitutional provisions? Is such specificity then required?

(6) However, what about those human rights treaty norms that find no explicit counterparts in the Constitution? Can the Ninth Amendment be construed in conformity with such customary international human rights law to ensure that such rights are self-executing? The Ninth Amendment states that "[t]he enumeration in the Constitution, of certain rights, shall not be construed to deny or disparage others retained by the people." Does such a construction extend protection to non-U.S. nationals?

(7) Justice Antonin Scalia (with Mr. Chief Justice William Rehnquist) states the following in his dissenting opinion in *Alvarez-Machain*:

> The notion that a law of nations, redefined to mean the consensus of states on *any* subject, can be used by a private citizen to control a sovereign's treatment of *its own citizens* within *its own territory* is a 20th-century invention of internationalist law professors and human-rights advocates. [*citing* Curtis A. Bradley & Jack L. Goldsmith, *Customary International Law as Federal Common Law: A Critique of the Modern Position*, 110 Harv. L. Rev. 815 (1997)] The Framers would, I am confident, be appalled by the proposition that, for example, the American peoples' democratic adoption of the death penalty . . . could be judicially nullified because of the disapproving views of foreigners.

Is Scalia (and Bradley & Goldsmith) characterizing the earlier law of nations fairly? Is the law of nations merely the views of foreigners? What about role of the persistent objector rule in exempting the United States from emerging customary international legal norms held by other states?

(8) What do you make of the Supreme Court's apparent rather summary dismissal of the UN Working Group's finding that Alvarez-Machain's detention did violate customary international law?

(9) What do you think of the Restatement's claim that detention must be prolonged to reflect a violation of a customary international legal norm?

(10) The Supreme Court in *Sosa* in dicta leaves open the possibility that ATS plaintiffs may have to exhaust remedies available through foreign domestic fora and even international claims tribunals. Would this exhaustion requirement always apply to U.S. defendants? Consider that the ATS itself is a domestic remedy itself and that international human rights tribunals themselves require the exhaustion of domestic remedies for a case to be admissible.

Also, would the international remedy exhaustion requirement apply to foreign non-state defendants? Consider that international human rights tribunals only consider cases against states. However, given that states also can incur liability for failing to prevent and punish certain gross human rights violations, would the international remedy exhaustion requirement still apply to foreign nonstate defendants for their alleged commission of such gross human rights violations?

Finally, would the domestic remedy exhaustion requirement apply in cases where such remedies are not real, effective, or sufficient – as is often the case in countries having poor human rights records?

4. International Human Rights Tribunal Procedure and Remedies

4.1. Jurisdiction

Generally speaking, for an international human rights tribunal to have jurisdiction (called "competence" in international law) over a case, the following requirements must be met:

(i) the state respondent must have ratified the treaty and any protocols recognizing the competence of the tribunal to decide the case;

(ii) the state respondent must have ratified the treaty before the alleged human rights violations occurred;

(iii) the complainant is alleging violations of rights from which the state party has not derogated during a state of emergency, nor of which the state party has made reservations;

(iv) the complainant has exhausted or constructively exhausted domestic remedies;

(v) the complaint has been filed within the prescribed time from the date of exhausting domestic remedies; and

(vi) the subject-matter of the complaint is not pending before another international proceeding.

Other requirements can include that the complaint not be anonymous,[1] that the complaint include the complainant's profession and domicile,[2] that the complaint not be based exclusively on news media reports,[3] and/or that the complaint not use insulting language.[4]

There are exceptions to these general rules, which will be discussed in greater detail. Concerning exhaustion of domestic remedies, the absence of legal aid and unreasonably prolonged domestic proceedings constructively exhaust. Reservations cannot be inconsistent with the object and purpose of the treaty. The subject matter of a complaint can be pending before another international proceeding if that proceeding does not have the character of a human rights tribunal. The limitations period for filing can be suspended if the violation is ongoing[5] or if the life, personal integrity, or health of a person is in imminent danger.

---

[1] Art. 46, ACHR.

[2] *Id.*

[3] Art. 56, African Charter on Human and Peoples' Rights.

[4] *Id.*

[5] *DeBecker v. Belgium*, 4 Eur. Ct.H.R. (ser. A) (1962).

Another exception to these rules is the case of the American Declaration of the Rights and Duties of Man. In the following advisory opinion, the Inter-American Court explains why OAS members are legally bound by the American Declaration and why the Inter-American Commission has jurisdiction over cases against OAS members even though the Declaration is not a treaty.

Interpretation of the
American Declaration of the Rights and Duties of Man
Within the Framework of Article 64 of the
American Convention on Human Rights
Inter-American Court of Human Rights
Advisory Opinion OC-10/89 of July 14, 1989
Inter-Am. Ct. H.R. (Ser. A) No. 10 (1989)

. . . .

THE COURT [. . .] renders the following Advisory Opinion:

. . . .

2. The Government [of Colombia] requests a reply to the following question:

Does Article 64 authorize the Inter-American Court of Human Rights to render advisory opinions at the request of a member state or one of the organs of the OAS, regarding the interpretation of the American Declaration of the Rights and Duties of Man, adopted by the Ninth International Conference of American States in Bogota in 1948?

The Government adds:

The Government of Colombia understands, of course, that the Declaration is not a treaty. But this conclusion does not automatically answer the question. It is perfectly reasonable to assume that the interpretation of the human rights provisions contained in the Charter of the OAS, as revised by the Protocol of Buenos Aires, involves, in principle, an analysis of the rights and duties of man proclaimed by the Declaration, and thus requires the determination of the normative *status* of the Declaration within the legal framework of the inter-American system for the protection of human rights.

The applicant Government points out that

for the appropriate functioning of the inter-American system for the protection of human rights, it is of great importance to know what the juridical status of the Declaration is, whether the Court has jurisdiction to interpret the Declaration, and if so, what the scope of its jurisdiction is within the framework of Article 64 of the Convention.

. . . .

29. The Court will now address the merits of the question before it.

30. Article 64(1) of the Convention authorizes the Court to render advisory opinions "regarding the interpretation of this Convention or of other treaties concerning the protection of human rights in the American states." That is, the object of the advisory opinions of the Court are treaties (*see generally* ["Other Treaties" Subject to the Advisory

Jurisdiction of the Court (Art. 64 American Convention on Human Rights), Advisory Opinion OC-1/82 of September 24, 1982. Series A No. 1]).

31. According to the Vienna Convention on the Law of Treaties of 1969:

... "treaty" means an international agreement concluded between States in written form and governed by international law, whether embodied in a single instrument or in two or more related instruments and whatever its particular designation (Art. 2(1)(a)).

32. The Vienna Convention of 1986 on the Law of Treaties among States and International Organizations or among International Organizations provides as follows in Article 2(1)(a):

... "treaty" means an international agreement governed by international law and concluded in written form:

  (i) between one or more States and one or more international organizations; or
  (ii) between international organizations,

whether that agreement is embodied in a single instrument or in two or more related instruments and whatever its particular designation.

33. In attempting to define the word "treaty" as the term is employed in Article 64(1), it is sufficient for now to say that a "treaty" is, at the very least, an international instrument of the type that is governed by the two Vienna Conventions. Whether the term includes other international instruments of a conventional nature whose existence is also recognized by those Conventions (Art. 3, Vienna Convention of 1969; Art. 3, Vienna Convention of 1986), need not be decided at this time. What is clear, however, is that the Declaration is not a treaty as defined by the Vienna Conventions because it was not approved as such, and that, consequently, it is also not a treaty within the meaning of Article 64(1).

34. Here it must be recalled that the American Declaration was adopted by the Ninth International Conference of American States (Bogotá, 1948) through a resolution adopted by the Conference itself. It was neither conceived nor drafted as a treaty. Resolution XL of the Inter-American Conference on the Problems of War and Peace (Chapultepec, 1945) expressed the belief that in order to achieve the international protection of human rights, the latter should be listed and defined "in a Declaration adopted as a Convention by the States." In the subsequent phase of preparation of the draft Declaration by the Inter-American Juridical Committee and the Ninth Conference, this initial approach was abandoned and the Declaration was adopted as a declaration, without provision for any procedure by which it might become a treaty (Novena Conferencia Internacional Americana, Actas y Documentos. Bogotá: Ministerio de Relaciones Exteriores de Colombia, 1953, vol. I, pp. 235–236). Despite profound differences, in the Sixth Committee of the Conference the position prevailed that the text to be approved should be a declaration and not a treaty (see the report of the Rapporteur of the Sixth Committee, Novena Conferencia Internacional Americana, 1948, Actas y Documentos. Bogotá: Ministerio de Relaciones Exteriores de Colombia, 1953, vol. V, p. 512).

In order to obtain a consensus, it was agreed that:

... the initial system of protection considered by the American states as being suited to the present social and juridical conditions, not without a recognition on their part that they should increasingly strengthen that system in the international field as conditions become more favorable (American Declaration, Fourth Considerandum).

This same principle was confirmed on 26 September 1949, by the Inter-American Committee of Jurisconsults, when it said:

> It is evident that the Declaration of Bogotá does not create a contractual juridical obligation, but it is also clear that it demonstrates a well-defined orientation toward the international protection of the fundamental rights of the human person (C.J.I., Recomendaciones e informes, 1949–1953 (1955), p. 107. *See also* U. S. Department of State, Report of the Delegation of the United States to the Ninth International Conference of American States, Bogotá, Colombia, March 30–May 2, 1948, at 35–36 (Publ. No. 3263, 1948)).

35. The mere fact that the Declaration is not a treaty does not necessarily compel the conclusion that the Court lacks the power to render an advisory opinion containing an interpretation of the American Declaration.

36. In fact, the American Convention refers to the Declaration in paragraph three of its Preamble which reads as follows:

> *Considering* that these principles have been set forth in the Charter of the Organization of the American States, in the American Declaration of the Rights and Duties of Man, and in the Universal Declaration of Human Rights, and that they have been reaffirmed and refined in other international instruments, worldwide as well as regional in scope.

And in Article 29(d) which indicates:

Restrictions Regarding Interpretation

> No provision of this convention shall be interpreted as:
>
> . . . .
>
> d. excluding or limiting the effect that the American Declaration of the Rights and Duties of Man and other international acts of the same nature may have.

From the foregoing, it follows that, in interpreting the Convention in the exercise of its advisory jurisdiction, the Court may have to interpret the Declaration.

37. The American Declaration has its basis in the idea that "the international protection of the rights of man should be the principal guide of an evolving American law" (Third Considerandum). This American law has evolved from 1948 to the present; international protective measures, subsidiary and complementary to national ones, have been shaped by new instruments. As the International Court of Justice said: "an international instrument must be interpreted and applied within the overall framework of the juridical system in force at the time of the interpretation" (*Legal Consequences for States of the Continued Presence of South Africa in Namibia (South West Africa) notwithstanding Security Council Resolution 276 (1970)*, Advisory Opinion, I.C.J. Reports 1971, p. 16 ad 31). That is why the Court finds it necessary to point out that to determine the legal status of the American Declaration it is appropriate to look to the inter-American system of today in the light of the evolution it has undergone since the adoption of the Declaration, rather than to examine the normative value and significance which that instrument was believed to have had in 1948.

38. The evolution of the here relevant "inter-American law" mirrors on the regional level the developments in contemporary international law and especially in human rights law, which distinguished that law from classical international law to a significant extent. That is the case, for example, with the duty to respect certain essential human rights, which is today considered to be an *erga omnes* obligation (*Barcelona Traction, Light and Power Company, Limited,* Second Phase, Judgment, I.C.J. Reports 1970, p. 3. For an analysis following the same line of thought *see also Legal Consequences for States of the Continued Presence of South Africa in Namibia (South West Africa) notwithstanding Security Council Resolution 276* (1970) *supra* 37, p. 16 ad 57; *cfr. United States Diplomatic and Consular Staff in Tehran,* I.C.J. Reports 1980, p. 3 ad 42).

39. The Charter of the Organization refers to the fundamental rights of man in its Preamble ((paragraph three) and in Arts. 3.j), 16, 43, 47, 51, 112 and 150, Preamble (paragraph four), Arts. 3.k), 16, 44, 48, 52, 111 and 150 of the Charter revised by the Protocol of Cartagena de Indias), but it does not list or define them. The member states of the Organization have, through its diverse organs, given specificity to the human rights mentioned in the Charter and to which the Declaration refers.

40. This is the case of Article 112 of the Charter (Art. 111 of the Charter as amended by the Protocol of Cartagena de Indias) which reads as follows:

> There shall be an Inter-American Commission on Human Rights, whose principal function shall be to promote the observance and protection of human rights and to serve as a consultative organ of the Organization in these matters.
>
> An inter-American convention on human rights shall determine the structure, competence, and procedure of this Commission, as well as those of other organs responsible for these matters.

Article 150 of the Charter provides as follows:

> Until the inter-American convention on human rights, referred to in Chapter XVIII (Chapter XVI of the Charter as amended by the Protocol of Cartagena de Indias), enters into force, the present Inter-American Commission on Human Rights shall keep vigilance over the observance of human rights.

41. These norms authorize the Inter-American Commission to protect human rights. These rights are none other than those enunciated and defined in the American Declaration. That conclusion results from Article 1 of the Commission's Statute, which was approved by Resolution No. 447, adopted by the General Assembly of the OAS at its Ninth Regular Period of Sessions, held in La Paz, Bolivia, in October 1979. That Article reads as follows:

> 1. The Inter-American Commission on Human Rights is an organ of the Organization of the American States, created to promote the observance and defense of human rights and to serve as consultative organ of the Organization in this matter.
> 2. For the purposes of the present Statute, human rights are understood to be:
>
> > a. The rights set forth in the American Convention on Human Rights, in relation to the States Parties thereto;
> > b. The rights set forth in the American Declaration of the Rights and Duties of Man, in relation to the other member states.

Articles 18, 19 and 20 of the Statute enumerate these functions.

42. The General Assembly of the Organization has also repeatedly recognized that the American Declaration is a source of international obligations for the member states of the OAS. For example, in Resolution 314 (VII-O/77) of June 22, 1977, it charged the Inter-American Commission with the preparation of a study to "set forth their obligation to carry out the commitments assumed in the American Declaration of the Rights and Duties of Man." In Resolution 371 (VIII-O/78) of July 1, 1978, the General Assembly reaffirmed "its commitment to promote the observance of the American Declaration of the Rights and Duties of Man," and in Resolution 370 (VIII-O/78) of July 1, 1978, it referred to the "international commitments" of a member state of the Organization to respect the rights of man "recognized in the American Declaration of the Rights and Duties of Man." The Preamble of the American Convention to Prevent and Punish Torture, adopted and signed at the Fifteenth Regular Session of the General Assembly in Cartagena de Indias (December 1985), reads as follows:

> Reaffirming that all acts of torture or any other cruel, inhuman, or degrading treatment or punishment constitute an offense against human dignity and a denial of the principles set forth in the Charter of the Organization of American States and in the Charter of the United Nations and are violations of the fundamental human rights and freedoms proclaimed in the American Declaration of the Rights and Duties of Man and the Universal Declaration of Human Rights.

43. Hence it may be said that by means of an authoritative interpretation, the member states of the Organization have signaled their agreement that the Declaration contains and defines the fundamental human rights referred to in the Charter. Thus the Charter of the Organization cannot be interpreted and applied as far as human rights are concerned without relating its norms, consistent with the practice of the organs of the OAS, to the corresponding provisions of the Declaration.

44. In view of the fact that the Charter of the Organization and the American Convention are treaties with respect to which the Court has advisory jurisdiction by virtue of Article 64(1), it follows that the Court is authorized, within the framework and limits of its competence, to interpret the American Declaration and to render an advisory opinion relating to it whenever it is necessary to do so in interpreting those instruments.

45. For the member states of the Organization, the Declaration is the text that defines the human rights referred to in the Charter. Moreover, Articles 1(2)(b) and 20 of the Commission's Statute define the competence of that body with respect to the human rights enunciated in the Declaration, with the result that to this extent the American Declaration is for these States a source of international obligations related to the Charter of the Organization.

46. For the States Parties to the Convention, the specific source of their obligations with respect to the protection of human rights is, in principle, the Convention itself. It must be remembered, however, that, given the provisions of Article 29(d), these States cannot escape the obligations they have as members of the OAS under the Declaration, notwithstanding the fact that the Convention is the governing instrument for the States Parties thereto.

47. That the Declaration is not a treaty does not, then, lead to the conclusion that it does not have legal effect, nor that the Court lacks the power to interpret it within the framework of the principles set out above.

48. For those reasons,

THE COURT, unanimously DECIDES

That it is competent to render the present advisory opinion.

unanimously

IS OF THE OPINION

That Article 64(1) of the American Convention authorizes the Court, at the request of a member state of the OAS or any duly qualified OAS organ, to render advisory opinions interpreting the American Declaration of the Rights and Duties of Man, provided that in doing so the Court is acting within the scope and framework of its jurisdiction in relation to the Charter and Convention or other treaties concerning the protection of the human rights in the American states.

. . . .

≈

Bankoviç and Others v. Belgium and Others (Admissibility Decision)
European Court of Human Rights (Grand Chamber)
Application no. 52207/99
41 I.L.M. 517, at P 70 (2001)

[The Applicants sought damages for the killing and injury of their family members (who were civilians) that resulted from the NATO aerial missile attack on the Serbian television and radio station in Belgrade during the Kosovo Conflict. In addressing the admissibility of their application, the Grand Chamber of the European Court of Human Rights examined whether the ECHR applied extraterritorially under its jurisdictional provision in Article 1, which reads: "The High Contracting Parties shall secure to everyone within their jurisdiction the rights and freedoms defined in Section I of this Convention."]

. . . .

3. The drafting history of Article 1 of the Convention

19. The text prepared by the Committee of the Consultative Assembly of the Council of Europe on legal and administrative questions provided, in what became Article 1 of the Convention, that the "member States shall undertake to ensure to all persons residing within their territories the rights . . . ". The Expert Intergovernmental Committee, which considered the Consultative Assembly's draft, decided to replace the reference to "all persons residing within their territories" with a reference to persons "within their jurisdiction". The reasons were noted in the following extract from the *Collected Edition of the* Travaux Préparatoires *of the European Convention on Human Rights* (Vol. III, p. 260):

> "The Assembly draft had extended the benefits of the Convention to 'all persons residing within the territories of the signatory States'. It seemed to the Committee that the term 'residing' might be considered too restrictive. It was felt that there were good grounds for extending the benefits of the Convention to all persons in the territories of the signatory States, even those who could not be considered as

residing there in the legal sense of the word. The Committee therefore replaced the term 'residing' by the words 'within their jurisdiction' which are also contained in Article 2 of the Draft Covenant of the United Nations Commission."

20. The next relevant comment prior to the adoption of Article 1 of the Convention, made by the Belgian representative on 25 August 1950 during the plenary sitting of the Consultative Assembly, was to the effect that

"henceforth the right of protection by our States, by virtue of a formal clause of the Convention, may be exercised with full force, and without any differentiation or distinction, in favour of individuals of whatever nationality, who on the territory of any one of our States, may have had reason to complain that [their] rights have been violated".

21. The *travaux préparatoires* go on to note that the wording of Article 1 including "within their jurisdiction", did not give rise to any further discussion and the text as it was (and is now) was adopted by the Consultative Assembly on 25 August 1950 without further amendment (the above-cited Collected Edition (Vol. VI, p. 132).

. . . .

54. The Court notes that the real connection between the applicants and the respondent States is the impugned act which, wherever decided, was performed, or had effects, outside of the territory of those States ("the extra-territorial act"). It considers that the essential question to be examined therefore is whether the applicants and their deceased relatives were, as a result of that extra-territorial act, capable of falling within the jurisdiction of the respondent States.[ ]

(a) The applicable rules of interpretation

55. The Court recalls that the Convention must be interpreted in the light of the rules set out in the Vienna Convention [on the Law of Treaties].

56. It will, therefore, seek to ascertain the ordinary meaning to be given to the phrase "within their jurisdiction" in its context and in the light of the object and purpose of the Convention (Article 31 §1 of the Vienna Convention 1969 and, amongst other authorities, Johnston and Others v. Ireland judgment of 18 December 1986, Series A no. 112, §51). The Court will also consider "any subsequent practice in the application of the treaty which establishes the agreement of the parties regarding its interpretation" (Article 31 §3 (b) of the Vienna Convention 1969 and the above-cited Loizidou judgment (*preliminary objections*), at §73).

57. Moreover, Article 31 §3 (c) indicates that account is to be taken of "any relevant rules of international law applicable in the relations between the parties". More generally, the Court recalls that the principles underlying the Convention cannot be interpreted and applied in a vacuum. The Court must also take into account any relevant rules of international law when examining questions concerning its jurisdiction and, consequently, determine State responsibility in conformity with the governing principles of international law, although it must remain mindful of the Convention's special character as a human rights treaty (the above-cited Loizidou judgment (*merits*), at §§43 and 52). The Convention should be interpreted as far as possible in harmony with other principles of international law of which it forms part (*Al-Adsani v. the United Kingdom*, [GC], no. 35763, §60, to be reported in ECHR 2001).

58. It is further recalled that the *travaux préparatoires* can also be consulted with a view to confirming any meaning resulting from the application of Article 31 of the Vienna Convention 1969 or to determining the meaning when the interpretation under Article 31 of the Vienna Convention 1969 leaves the meaning "ambiguous or obscure" or leads to a result which is "manifestly absurd or unreasonable" (Article 32). . . .

(b)　The meaning of the words "within their jurisdiction"

59. As to the "ordinary meaning" of the relevant term in Article 1 of the Convention, the Court is satisfied that, from the standpoint of public international law, the jurisdictional competence of a State is primarily territorial. While international law does not exclude a State's exercise of jurisdiction extra-territorially, the suggested bases of such jurisdiction (including nationality, flag, diplomatic and consular relations, effect, protection, passive personality and universality) are, as a general rule, defined and limited by the sovereign territorial rights of the other relevant States (Mann, "*The Doctrine of Jurisdiction in International Law,*" RdC, 1964, Vol. 1; Mann, "*The Doctrine of Jurisdiction in International Law, Twenty Years Later,*" RdC, 1984, Vol. 1; Bernhardt, *Encyclopaedia of Public International Law,* Edition 1997, Vol. 3, pp. 55–59 "*Jurisdiction of States*" and Edition 1995, Vol. 2, pp. 337–343 "*Extra-territorial Effects of Administrative, Judicial and Legislative Acts*"; Oppenheim's *International Law,* 9th Edition 1992 (Jennings and Watts), Vol. 1, §137; P. M. Dupuy, *Droit International Public,* 4th Edition 1998, p. 61; and Brownlie, *Principles of International Law,* 5th Edition 1998, pp. 287, 301 and 312–314).

60. Accordingly, for example, a State's competence to exercise jurisdiction over its own nationals abroad is subordinate to that State's and other States' territorial competence (Higgins, *Problems and Process* (1994), at p. 73; and Nguyen Quoc Dinh, *Droit International Public,* 6th Edition 1999 (Daillier and Pellet), p. 500). In addition, a State may not actually exercise jurisdiction on the territory of another without the latter's consent, invitation or acquiescence, unless the former is an occupying State in which case it can be found to exercise jurisdiction in that territory, at least in certain respects (Bernhardt, cited above, Vol. 3 at p. 59 and Vol. 2 at pp. 338–340; Oppenheim, cited above, at §137; P. M. Dupuy, cited above, at pp. 64–65; Brownlie, cited above, at p. 313; Cassese, *International Law,* 2001, p. 89; and, most recently, the "*Report on the Preferential Treatment of National Minorities by their Kin-States*" adopted by the Venice Commission at its 48th Plenary Meeting, Venice, 19–20 October 2001).

61. The Court is of the view, therefore, that Article 1 of the Convention must be considered to reflect this ordinary and essentially territorial notion of jurisdiction, other bases of jurisdiction being exceptional and requiring special justification in the particular circumstances of each case (see, *mutatis mutandis* and in general, Select Committee of Experts on Extraterritorial Criminal Jurisdiction, European Committee on Crime Problems, Council of Europe, "*Extraterritorial Criminal Jurisdiction,*" Report published in 1990, at pp. 8–30).

62. The Court finds State practice in the application of the Convention since its ratification to be indicative of a lack of any apprehension on the part of the Contracting States of their extra-territorial responsibility in contexts similar to the present case. Although there have been a number of military missions involving Contracting States acting extra-territorially since their ratification of the Convention (*inter alia,* in the Gulf, in Bosnia and

Herzegovina and in the FRY[1]), no State has indicated a belief that its extra-territorial actions involved an exercise of jurisdiction within the meaning of Article 1 of the Convention by making a derogation pursuant to Article 15 of the Convention. The existing derogations were lodged by Turkey and the United Kingdom in respect of certain internal conflicts (in south-east Turkey and Northern Ireland, respectively) and the Court does not find any basis upon which to accept the applicants' suggestion that Article 15 covers all "war" and "public emergency" situations generally, whether obtaining inside or outside the territory of the Contracting State. Indeed, Article 15 itself is to be read subject to the "jurisdiction" limitation enumerated in Article 1 of the Convention.

63. Finally, the Court finds clear confirmation of this essentially territorial notion of jurisdiction in the *travaux préparatoires* which demonstrate that the Expert Intergovernmental Committee replaced the words "all persons residing within their territories" with a reference to persons "within their jurisdiction" with a view to expanding the Convention's application to others who may not reside, in a legal sense, but who are, nevertheless, on the territory of the Contracting States (§19 above).

64. It is true that the notion of the Convention being a living instrument to be interpreted in light of present-day conditions is firmly rooted in the Court's case-law. The Court has applied that approach not only to the Convention's substantive provisions[ ] but more relevantly to its interpretation of former Articles 25 and 46 concerning the recognition by a Contracting State of the competence of the Convention organs (the above-cited Loizidou judgment (*preliminary objections*), at §71). The Court concluded in the latter judgment that former Articles 25 and 46 of the Convention could not be interpreted solely in accordance with the intentions of their authors expressed more than forty years previously to the extent that, even if it had been established that the restrictions at issue were considered permissible under Articles 25 and 46 when the Convention was adopted by a minority of the then Contracting Parties, such evidence "could not be decisive".

65. However, the scope of Article 1, at issue in the present case, is determinative of the very scope of the Contracting Parties' positive obligations and, as such, of the scope and reach of the entire Convention system of human rights' protection as opposed to the question, under discussion in the Loizidou case (*preliminary objections*), of the competence of the Convention organs to examine a case. In any event, the extracts from the *travaux préparatoires* detailed above constitute a clear indication of the intended meaning of Article 1 of the Convention which cannot be ignored. The Court would emphasise that it is not interpreting Article 1 "solely" in accordance with the *travaux préparatoires* or finding those *travaux* "decisive"; rather this preparatory material constitutes clear confirmatory evidence of the ordinary meaning of Article 1 of the Convention as already identified by the Court (Article 32 of the Vienna Convention 1969).

66. Accordingly, and as the Court stated in the Soering case:

"Article 1 sets a limit, notably territorial, on the reach of the Convention. In particular, the engagement undertaken by a Contracting State is confined to 'securing' ('*reconnaître*' in the French text) the listed rights and freedoms to persons within its own 'jurisdiction'. Further, the Convention does not govern the actions of States not Parties to it, nor does it purport to be a means of requiring the Contracting States to impose Convention standards on other States."

---

[1] ["FRY" is the acronym for the Federal Republic of Yugoslavia. Ed.'s Note.]

(c) Extra-territorial acts recognised as constituting an exercise of jurisdiction

67. In keeping with the essentially territorial notion of jurisdiction, the Court has accepted only in exceptional cases that acts of the Contracting States performed, or producing effects, outside their territories can constitute an exercise of jurisdiction by them within the meaning of Article 1 of the Convention.

68. Reference has been made in the Court's case-law, as an example of jurisdiction "not restricted to the national territory" of the respondent State (the Loizidou judgment (*preliminary objections*), at §62), to situations where the extradition or expulsion of a person by a Contracting State may give rise to an issue under Articles 2 and/or 3 (or, exceptionally, under Articles 5 and or 6) and hence engage the responsibility of that State under the Convention (the above-cited Soering case, at §91, Cruz Varas and Others v. Sweden judgment of 20 March 1991, Series A no. 201, §§69 and 70, and the Vilvarajah and Others v. the United Kingdom judgment of 30 October 1991, Series A no. 215, §103).

However, the Court notes that liability is incurred in such cases by an action of the respondent State concerning a person while he or she is on its territory, clearly within its jurisdiction, and that such cases do not concern the actual exercise of a State's competence or jurisdiction abroad (see also, the above-cited *Al-Adsani* judgment, *at* §39).

69. In addition, a further example noted at paragraph 62 of the Loizidou judgment (*preliminary objections*) was the Drozd and Janousek case where, citing a number of admissibility decisions by the Commission, the Court accepted that the responsibility of Contracting Parties (France and Spain) could, in principle, be engaged because of acts of their authorities (judges) which produced effects or were performed outside their own territory (the above-cited Drozd and Janousek judgment, at §91). In that case, the impugned acts could not, in the circumstances, be attributed to the respondent States because the judges in question were not acting in their capacity as French or Spanish judges and as the Andorran courts functioned independently of the respondent States.

70. Moreover, in that first Loizidou judgment (*preliminary objections*), the Court found that, bearing in mind the object and purpose of the Convention, the responsibility of a Contracting Party was capable of being engaged when as a consequence of military action (lawful or unlawful) it exercised effective control of an area outside its national territory. The obligation to secure, in such an area, the Convention rights and freedoms was found to derive from the fact of such control whether it was exercised directly, through the respondent State's armed forces, or through a subordinate local administration. The Court concluded that the acts of which the applicant complained were capable of falling within Turkish jurisdiction within the meaning of Article 1 of the Convention.

On the merits, the Court found that it was not necessary to determine whether Turkey actually exercised detailed control over the policies and actions of the authorities of the "Turkish Republic of Northern Cyprus" ("TRNC"). It was obvious from the large number of troops engaged in active duties in northern Cyprus that Turkey's army exercised "effective overall control over that part of the island". Such control, according to the relevant test and in the circumstances of the case, was found to entail the responsibility of Turkey for the policies and actions of the "TRNC." The Court concluded that those affected by such policies or actions therefore came within the "jurisdiction" of Turkey for the purposes of Article 1 of the Convention. Turkey's obligation to secure the rights and freedoms set out in the Convention was found therefore to extend to northern Cyprus.

In its subsequent *Cyprus v. Turkey* judgment (cited above), the Court added that since Turkey had such "effective control", its responsibility could not be confined to the acts of its own agents therein but was engaged by the acts of the local administration which survived by virtue of Turkish support. Turkey's "jurisdiction" under Article 1 was therefore considered to extend to securing the entire range of substantive Convention rights in northern Cyprus.

71. In sum, the case-law of the Court demonstrates that its recognition of the exercise of extra-territorial jurisdiction by a Contracting State is exceptional: it has done so when the respondent State, through the effective control of the relevant territory and its inhabitants abroad as a consequence of military occupation or through the consent, invitation or acquiescence of the Government of that territory, exercises all or some of the public powers normally to be exercised by that Government.

72. In line with this approach, the Court has recently found that the participation of a State in the defence of proceedings against it in another State does not, without more, amount to an exercise of extra-territorial jurisdiction (*McElhinney v. Ireland and the United Kingdom* (dec.), no. 31253/96, p. 7, 9 February 2000, unpublished). The Court said:

> "In so far as the applicant complains under Article 6 . . . about the stance taken by the Government of the United Kingdom in the Irish proceedings, the Court does not consider it necessary to address in the abstract the question of whether the actions of a Government as a litigant before the courts of another Contracting State can engage their responsibility under Article 6 . . . The Court considers that, in the particular circumstances of the case, the fact that the United Kingdom Government raised the defence of sovereign immunity before the Irish courts, where the applicant had decided to sue, does not suffice to bring him within the jurisdiction of the United Kingdom within the meaning of Article 1 of the Convention."

73. Additionally, the Court notes that other recognised instances of the extra-territorial exercise of jurisdiction by a State include cases involving the activities of its diplomatic or consular agents abroad and on board craft and vessels registered in, or flying the flag of, that State. In these specific situations, customary international law and treaty provisions have recognised the extra-territorial exercise of jurisdiction by the relevant State.

(d) Were the present applicants therefore capable of coming within the "jurisdiction" of the respondent States?

74. The applicants maintain that the bombing of RTS[2] by the respondent States constitutes yet a further example of an extra-territorial act which can be accommodated by the notion of "jurisdiction" in Article 1 of the Convention, and are thereby proposing a further specification of the ordinary meaning of the term "jurisdiction" in Article 1 of the Convention. The Court must be satisfied that equally exceptional circumstances exist in the present case which could amount to the extra-territorial exercise of jurisdiction by a Contracting State.

75. In the first place, the applicants suggest a specific application of the "effective control" criteria developed in the northern Cyprus cases. They claim that the positive obligation under Article 1 extends to securing the Convention rights in a manner proportionate to the level of control exercised in any given extra-territorial situation. The Governments contend that this amounts to a "cause-and-effect" notion of jurisdiction

---

2 [RTS was the Serbian television and radio station in Belgrade. Ed.'s Note.]

not contemplated by or appropriate to Article 1 of the Convention. The Court considers that the applicants' submission is tantamount to arguing that anyone adversely affected by an act imputable to a Contracting State, wherever in the world that act may have been committed or its consequences felt, is thereby brought within the jurisdiction of that State for the purpose of Article 1 of the Convention.

The Court is inclined to agree with the Governments' submission that the text of Article 1 does not accommodate such an approach to "jurisdiction". Admittedly, the applicants accept that jurisdiction, and any consequent State Convention responsibility, would be limited in the circumstances to the commission and consequences of that particular act. However, the Court is of the view that the wording of Article 1 does not provide any support for the applicants' suggestion that the positive obligation in Article 1 to secure "the rights and freedoms defined in Section I of this Convention" can be divided and tailored in accordance with the particular circumstances of the extra-territorial act in question and, it considers its view in this respect supported by the text of Article 19 of the Convention. Indeed the applicants' approach does not explain the application of the words "within their jurisdiction" in Article 1 and it even goes so far as to render those words superfluous and devoid of any purpose. Had the drafters of the Convention wished to ensure jurisdiction as extensive as that advocated by the applicants, they could have adopted a text the same as or similar to the contemporaneous Articles 1[3] of the four Geneva Conventions of 1949 [ ].

Furthermore, the applicants' notion of jurisdiction equates the determination of whether an individual falls within the jurisdiction of a Contracting State with the question of whether that person can be considered to be a victim of a violation of rights guaranteed by the Convention. These are separate and distinct admissibility conditions, each of which has to be satisfied in the afore-mentioned order, before an individual can invoke the Convention provisions against a Contracting State.

76. Secondly, the applicants' alternative suggestion is that the limited scope of the airspace control only circumscribed the scope of the respondent States' positive obligation to protect the applicants and did not exclude it. The Court finds this to be essentially the same argument as their principal proposition and rejects it for the same reasons.

77. Thirdly, the applicants make a further alternative argument in favour of the respondent States' jurisdiction based on a comparison with the Soering case (cited above). The Court does not find this convincing given the fundamental differences between that case and the present as already noted at paragraph 68 above.

78. Fourthly, the Court does not find it necessary to pronounce on the specific meaning to be attributed in various contexts to the allegedly similar jurisdiction provisions in the international instruments to which the applicants refer because it is not convinced by the applicants' specific submissions in these respects [ ]. It notes that Article 2 of the American Declaration on the Rights and Duties of Man 1948 [ ] contains no explicit limitation of jurisdiction. In addition, and as to Article 2 §1 the CCPR[4] 1966 [ ], as early as 1950 the drafters had definitively and specifically confined its territorial scope and it is difficult to suggest that exceptional recognition by the Human Rights Committee of certain instances of extra-territorial jurisdiction (and the applicants give one example

---

[3] [Common Article 1 of the Geneva Conventions requires the Contracting Parties to undertake "to respect and to ensure respect for the present Convention in all circumstances". Ed.'s Note.]

[4] [Article 2 (1) reads: "Each State Party to the present Convention undertakes to respect and to ensure to all individuals within its territory and subject to its jurisdiction the rights recognised in the present Covenant . . . " Ed.'s Note.]

only) displaces in any way the territorial jurisdiction expressly conferred by that Article of the CCPR 1966 or explains the precise meaning of "jurisdiction" in Article 1 of its Optional Protocol[5] 1966 [ ]. While the text of Article 1 of the American Convention on Human Rights[6] 1978 [ ] contains a jurisdiction condition similar to Article 1 of the European Convention, no relevant case-law on the former provision was cited before this Court by the applicants.

79. Fifthly and more generally, the applicants maintain that any failure to accept that they fell within the jurisdiction of the respondent States would defeat the *ordre public* mission of the Convention and leave a regrettable vacuum in the Convention system of human rights' protection.

80. The Court's obligation, in this respect, is to have regard to the special character of the Convention as a constitutional instrument of *European* public order for the protection of individual human beings and its role[ ] is to ensure the observance of *the engagements undertaken* by the Contracting Parties (the above-cited Loizidou judgment (*preliminary objections*), at §93). It is therefore difficult to contend that a failure to accept the extra-territorial jurisdiction of the respondent States would fall foul of the Convention's *ordre public* objective, which itself underlines the essentially regional vocation of the Convention system....

It is true that, in its above-cited *Cyprus v. Turkey* judgment (at §78), the Court was conscious of the need to avoid "a regrettable vacuum in the system of human-rights protection" in northern Cyprus. However, and as noted by the Governments, that comment related to an entirely different situation to the present: the inhabitants of northern Cyprus would have found themselves excluded from the benefits of the Convention safeguards and system which they had previously enjoyed, by Turkey's "effective control" of the territory and by the accompanying inability of the Cypriot Government, as a Contracting State, to fulfil the obligations it had undertaken under the Convention.

In short, the Convention is a multi-lateral treaty operating, subject to Article 56[7] of the Convention, in an essentially regional context and notably in the legal space (*espace*

---

5 [Article 1 reads: "A State Party to the Covenant that becomes a Party to the present Protocol recognises the competence of the Committee to receive and consider communications from individuals subject to its jurisdiction who claim to be victims of a violation by that State Party of any of the rights set forth in the Covenant...." Ed.'s Note.]

6 [Article 1 reads: "The States Parties to this Convention undertake to respect the rights and freedoms recognised herein and to ensure to all persons subject to their jurisdiction the free and full exercise of those rights and freedoms, without any discrimination...." Ed.'s Note.]

7 Article 56 reads:

(1) Any State may at the time of its ratification or at any time thereafter declare by notification addressed to the Secretary General of the Council of Europe that the present Convention shall, subject to paragraph 4 of this Article, extend to all or any of the territories for whose international relations it is responsible.

(2) The Convention shall extend to the territory or territories named in the notification as from the thirtieth day after the receipt of this notification by the Secretary General of the Council of Europe.

(3) The provisions of this Convention shall be applied in such territories with due regard, however, to local requirements.

(4) Any State which has made a declaration in accordance with paragraph 1 of this article may at any time thereafter declare on behalf of one or more of the territories to which the declaration relates that it accepts the competence of the Court to receive applications from individuals, non-governmental organisations or groups of individuals as provided by Article 34 of the Convention.

[Ed.'s Note.]

juridique) of the Contracting States. The FRY clearly does not fall within this legal space. The Convention was not designed to be applied throughout the world, even in respect of the conduct of Contracting States. Accordingly, the desirability of avoiding a gap or vacuum in human rights' protection has so far been relied on by the Court in favour of establishing jurisdiction only when the territory in question was one that, but for the specific circumstances, would normally be covered by the Convention.

81. Finally, the applicants relied, in particular, on the admissibility decisions of the Court in the above-cited *Issa* and *Öcalan* cases. It is true that the Court has declared both of these cases admissible and that they include certain complaints about alleged actions by Turkish agents outside Turkish territory. However, in neither of those cases was the issue of jurisdiction raised by the respondent Government or addressed in the admissibility decisions and in any event the merits of those cases remain to be decided. Similarly, no jurisdiction objection is recorded in the decision leading to the inadmissibility of the *Xhavara* case to which the applicants also referred [ ]; at any rate, the applicants do not dispute the Governments' evidence about the sharing by prior written agreement of jurisdiction between Albania and Italy. The *Ilascu* case, also referred to by the applicants and cited above, concerns allegations that Russian forces control part of the territory of Moldova, an issue to be decided definitively on the merits of that case. Accordingly, these cases do not provide any support for the applicants' interpretation of the jurisdiction of Contracting States within the meaning of Article 1 of the Convention.

4. The Court's conclusion

82. The Court is not therefore persuaded that there was any jurisdictional link between the persons who were victims of the act complained of and the respondent States. Accordingly, it is not satisfied that the applicants and their deceased relatives were capable of coming within the jurisdiction of the respondent States on account of the extra-territorial act in question.

 . . . .

For these reasons, the Court unanimously

Declares the application inadmissible.

∿

Francisco Forrest Martin
*The International Human Rights Aspects
of the Forum Non Conveniens Doctrine*
35 U. Miami Inter-Am. L. Rev. 101, 106–109 (2003)

 . . . .

 . . . . Recently, the European Court of Human Rights in *Bankovic* held that the European Convention's rights guarantees did not extend extraterritorially to areas not under the "effective overall control" of a state party.[1] *Bankovic* addressed the NATO bombing of the Serbian radio and television station in Belgrade during the Kosovo Conflict. . . . [T]his article submits that this "effective overall control" test articulated by the European Court in Bankovic is manifestly incorrect for several reasons. . . .

---

[1] Bankovic and Others v. Belgium, App. No. 52207/99, Eur. Ct. H.R., 41 I.L.M. 517, at P 70 (2001), available at www.ehcr.coe.int/eng.

First, the European Court contradicted itself in its decision in *Bankovic*. The Court held that ECHR jurisdiction is primarily territorial, basing its decision on a general principle of international law as articulated by international law experts.[2] Although the Court recognized that there are extraterritorial exceptions, such as flag, nationality, diplomatic and consular relations, it held that these exceptions did not include jurisdiction over armed attacks against extraterritorial targets because the jurisdictional language in the Geneva Conventions governing such attacks is different from the jurisdictional language in the ECHR. Article 1 of the ECHR, governing jurisdiction, states that: "the High Contracting Parties shall secure to everyone within their jurisdiction the rights and freedoms defined in [the ECHR]." [ ] Common Article 1 of the Geneva Conventions states: "The High Contracting Parties undertake to respect and to ensure respect for the present Convention in all circumstances."[3]

The European Court, however, contradicts itself. The language in treaties establishing extraterritorial jurisdiction for those exceptions that the Court already recognized is often different from the jurisdictional language of the ECHR. First, the provisions in the U.N. Convention on the Law of the Sea [UNCLOS],[4] which governs jurisdiction over ships on the high seas, has different jurisdictional language from that of the ECHR, but the Court recognized that the ECHR applied to ships on the high seas flying the flag of a state-party to the ECHR.[5]

Second, the European Court incorrectly rejected the *lex specialis* governing jurisdiction established by the customary international law reflected in Protocol I to the Geneva Conventions [Protocol I], which governs extraterritorial attacks. Instead of relying on the language in Protocol I, the Court relied upon an incomplete *lex generalis* having nothing to do with extraterritorial attacks. Article 49 (2) of Protocol I states: "The provisions of this Protocol with respect to attacks apply to all attacks in whatever territory conducted, including the national territory belonging to a Party to the conflict but under the control of an adverse Party."[6] The jurisdictional language of the ECHR says nothing about extraterritoriality or armed attacks. Because specific law applies over general law, the Court's failure to follow the language of Protocol I made its argument invalid. The jurisdictional language of Protocol I is the *lex specialis* that should have been used to construe the jurisdictional language of the ECHR.

Third, the *Bankovic* decision contradicts the substantial case law of both the Inter-American Commission on Human Rights and the UN Human Rights Committee that recognizes jurisdiction over such extraterritorial attacks. For example, the Inter-American Commission in *Alejandre et al. v. Cuba* and *Salas and Others v. United States*, as well as the

---

[2] *Id.* at para. 59.

[3] Geneva Convention for the Amelioration of the Condition of the Wounded and Sick in Armed Forces in the Field, Aug. 12, 1949, art. 1, 75 U.N.T.S. 31, 32 (entered into force Oct. 21, 1950); Geneva Convention for the Amelioration of the Condition of Wounded, Sick and Shipwrecked Members of Armed Forces at Sea, art. 1, 75 U.N.T.S. 85, at 86 (entered into force Oct. 21, 1950); Geneva Convention Relative to the Treatment of Prisoners of War, art. 1, 6 U.S.T. 3316, at 3318, 75 U.N.T.S. 135, at 136 (entered into force Oct. 21, 1950); Geneva Convention Relative to the Protection of Civilian Persons in Time of War, art. 1, 6 U.S.T. 3516, at 3518, 75 U.N.T.S. 287 at 288 (entered into force Oct. 21, 1950) [hereinafter Fourth Geneva Convention].

[4] U.N. Convention on the Law of the Sea, 1833 U.N.T.S. 397, U.N. Doc. A/CONF.62/122 (entered into force Nov. 16, 1994) (1982) [hereinafter UNCLOS].

[5] Compare UNCLOS, supra[ ], arts. 86, 92(1), 94(1), and ECHR,[ ] art. 1.

[6] Protocol Additional to the Geneva Conventions of August 12, 1949, and Relating to the Protection of Victims of International Armed Conflicts (Protocol I), June 8, 1977, art. 49 (2), 16 I.L.M. 1391, (entered into force Dec. 7, 1978) [hereinafter Geneva Convention-Protocol I].

UN Human Rights Committee in *Saldias de Lopez v. Uruguay* and *Celiberti de Casariego v. Uruguay* recognized the extraterritorial application of international human rights law.[7] It is well-established in international law that "an international instrument must be interpreted and applied within the overall framework of the [international] juridical system in force at the time of the interpretation."[8] The European Court failed to do this and, instead, invented its own law. The result will be the emergence of conflicting international legal norms across both regional and global adjudicative systems, as well as state confusion over what international legal obligations will be imposed.

Fourth, by refusing to recognize extraterritorial jurisdiction over areas in which a state does not exercise "effective overall control," it violates other provisions in the ECHR that explicitly recognize such jurisdiction, such as the right to receive information "regardless of frontiers."[9] A treaty cannot be interpreted to produce a result that conflicts with its other provisions. This would violate the object and purpose of the treaty, which is a violation of international law.[10]

Finally, the Bankovic standard of "effective overall control" is ambiguous. The Court did not explain how much control was necessary, nor did it explain over how much territory the standard applied. Such a standard is indeterminate.

In conclusion, the Bankovic decision is problematic. . . .

. . . .

∽

4.2. Standing

Generally speaking, complainants must be directly harmed or at risk of being harmed by violations of their rights to have "standing" or "victim status."[1] An *actio popularis*

---

[7] *See, e.g.*, Alejandre et al. v. Cuba, Case 11.589, Report No. 86/99, OEA/Ser.L/V/II.106 Doc. 3 rev. at 586 (1999) (recognizing jurisdiction over Cuban extraterritorial use of disproportionate force and violation of right to life); Salas and Others v. United States, Case 10.573, Report No. 31/93, OEA/Ser.L/V/II.85 Doc. 9 rev. at 312 (1994) (recognizing jurisdiction over U.S. extraterritorial attacks in Panama); Case 9.239, United States, 986–87 Annual Report of the IACHR, OEA Ser. L/V/II.71, doc. 9 rev. 1, Sept. 22, 1987, p. 184 (recognizing jurisdiction over U.S. extraterritorial attacks in Grenada); Saldias de Lopez v. Uruguay, Comm. No. 52/1979, U.N. Doc. CCPR/C/OP/1 (1985) (views adopted July 29, 1981) (recognizing extraterritorial jurisdiction over detention and torture in Argentina); Celiberti de Casariego v. Uruguay, Comm. No. 56/1979, U.N. Doc. CCPR/C/OP/1 at 92 (1984).

[8] Legal Consequences for States of the Continued Presence of South Africa in Namibia (South West Africa) notwithstanding Security Council Resolution 276 (1970), Advisory Opinion, 1971 I.C.J. Reports 16, 31 (1971); Interpretation of the American Declaration of the Rights and Duties of Man within the Framework of Article 64 of the American Convention on Human Rights, Advisory Opinion OC-10/89, Inter-Am. Ct. H.R. Ser. A, No. 10, at P 37 (1989); Coard v. United States, Inter-Am. Cm. H.R., No. 109/99 at P 40 (1999), available at http://www.cidh.oas.org/annualrep/99eng/Merits/UnitedStates10.951.htm (last visited Feb. 15, 2003); see also Vienna Convention on the Law of Treaties, May 23, 1969, art. 31 (3) (c), 1155 U.N.T.S. 331 (entered into force Jan. 27, 1980) (hereinafter Vienna Convention) (treaty must be interpreted in light of "any rules of international law applicable in the relations between the parties"); Geofroy v. Riggs, 133 U.S. 258, 271 (1890) (meaning of treaty language "to be taken in their ordinary meaning, as understood in the public law of nations").

[9] ECHR,[ ] art. 10 (1).

[10] Vienna Convention, supra[ ], art. 31 (1) ("A treaty shall be interpreted in good faith in accordance with the ordinary meaning to be given to the terms of the treaty in their context and in the light of its object and purpose").

[1] We use "standing" to refer to "victim status" in this section. Recall that before the Inter-American Court, only state parties and the Inter-American Commission have standing *in strictu sensu*.

is not allowed. Only the Inter-American system allows third-parties (either individuals or NGOs legally recognized in one of the member states of the OAS) to submit complaints on behalf of a victim.[2] However, corporation shareholders cannot submit petitions to the Inter-American Commission. The European Court has recognized in *dicta* that shareholders may have standing in exceptional circumstances. Only individuals – not associations, corporations, and other organizations – can submit communications to the UN Human Rights Committee. Corporations can submit applications to the European system; however, it is not clear what kind of corporations do not have standing to submit complaints to the Inter-American system. The African Commission does accept cases from NGOs.

A group of associations . . . v. Italy
UN Human Rights Committee
Communication No. 163/1984
Views adopted 10 April 1984
2 Selected Decisions of the Human Rights Committee
under the Optional Protocol 47
U.N. Doc. CCPR/C/OP/2 (1990)

. . . .

1. The authors of the communication, dated January 1984, are a group of associations for the defence of the rights of disabled and handicapped persons in Italy (a non-governmental organization hereinafter referred to as the "Coordinamento") and the representatives of those associations, who claim that they are themselves disabled or handicapped or that they are parents of such persons. Although the representatives are primarily acting for the Coordinamento, they also claim to act on their own behalf.

2. The authors challenge article 9 of the Italian law decree of 12 September 1983, No. 463, which was later confirmed by Parliament and enacted as article 9 of law No. 638 of 11 November 1983. [ ] They contend that this provision infringes article 26 of the International Covenant on Civil and Political Rights in that it violates the right to work of disabled and handicapped persons. No submissions have been made regarding individual cases. The authors apparently seek a pronouncement of the Human Rights Committee that article 9 of law No. 638 was enacted in violation of Italy's commitments under the Covenant.

3. Article 9 contains a modification of the legal regime providing for the compulsory employment of disabled and handicapped persons laid down in law No. 482 of 2 April 1968. According to articles 11 and 12 of that law, private as well as public undertakings whose force exceeds 35 persons are obliged, in principle, to employ 15 percent disabled or handicapped persons, a percentage which may rise to 40 percent for "auxiliary personnel" in the case of public undertakings. At the same time, article 9 of the 1968 law divided the total number of disabled and handicapped persons to be employed compulsorily into different categories, reserving, in particular, 25 percent for military war victims and 10 percent for civilian war victims, while 15 percent were allotted for victims of labor accidents and 15 percent for ordinary disabled or handicapped persons ("*invalidi civili*"). To the extent that any particular category could not be filled with persons within that

---

[2] Art. 44, ACHR.

category, the entitlement was transferred to persons in the other categories. Considering that few war victims remain, the redistribution scheme significantly benefitted disabled and handicapped persons in other categories. By virtue of paragraph 4 of the impugned article 9, this redistribution scheme was abolished. As a consequence, the authors allege that the amendment has considerably reduced the number of work posts available to ordinary disabled or handicapped persons ("*invalidi civili*"). Furthermore, they criticize paragraph 3 of the same article which permits employers to take into account, for the purpose of demonstrating their compliance with the compulsory element of 15 percent of the work force, also those workers whom they have hired outside the special procedure for the employment of disabled and handicapped persons, provided that their disability or handicap exceeds 60 percent.

4. Before proceeding to the merits of a case, the Human Rights Commission must ascertain whether the conditions of admissibility as laid down in the Optional Protocol to the International Covenant on Civil and Political Rights are met.

5. According to article 1 of the Optional Protocol, only individuals have the right to submit a communication. To the extent, therefore, that the communication originates from the Coordinamento, it has to be declared inadmissible because of lack of personal standing.

6.1. As far as the communication has been submitted on their own behalf by the representatives of the different associations forming the Coordinamento it fails to satisfy other requirements laid down in article 1 and 2 of the Optional Protocol.

6.2. The author of a communication must himself claim, in a substantiated manner, to be the victim of a violation by the State party concerned. It is not the task of the Human Rights Committee, acting under the Optional Protocol, to review *in abstracto* national legislation as to its compliance with obligations imposed by the Covenant. It is true that, in some circumstances, a domestic law may be its mere existence directly violate the rights of individuals under the Covenant. In the present case, however, the authors of the communication have not demonstrated that they are themselves actually and personally affected by article 9 of law No. 638 of 11 November 1983. Consequently, the Committee is unable, in accordance with the terms of the Optional Protocol, to consider their complaints.

7. The Human Rights Committee therefore decides: The communication is inadmissible.

∼

QUESTIONS & COMMENTS

(1) Compare the European Court's ruling in *Norris v. Ireland*, 142 Eur. Ct. H.R. (ser. A) (1988), to *A group of associations . . . v. Italy*. In *Norris v. Ireland*, the European Court held that "Article 25 of the Convention entitles individuals to contend that a law violates their rights by itself, in the absence of an individual measure of implementation, if they run the risk of being directly affected by it." *Id.* at §31. Absent an express governmental statement that the government will not enforce the law, the mere existence of a law allegedly in violation of the ECHR is sufficient to allow an individual standing if the law covers them.

In *Norris*, the applicant, an adult homosexual, challenged the Irish antibuggery law. He had not been prosecuted or personally threatened with prosecution, nor had anyone been prosecuted under the law for consensual adult homosexual behavior for many years. In finding that Norris had standing, the European Court noted that

> One of the effects of criminal sanctions against homosexual acts is to reinforce the misapprehension and general prejudice of the public and increase the anxiety and guilt feelings of homosexuals leading, on occasions, to depression and the serious consequences which can follow from that unfortunate disease.

Id. at §33 (*citing* McWilliam, J. in Irish High Court decision of 10 October 1980).

How important should the distinction between criminal and civil sanctions have upon the issue of standing?

(2) The ECHR allows corporations – "juridical beings" as the Inter-American Commission put it – standing or victim status. However, in *Agrotexim and Others v. Greece*, 330 Eur. Ct. H.R. (ser. A) (1995), the European Court rejected the applicant shareholders status as victims and dismissed the case for lack of jurisdiction. In this case, the applicants were shareholders in a bankrupt company that was in the process of liquidation. Two special liquidators were appointed according to Greek law to pay off the creditors. The applicant shareholders argued that the company's property interests – and indirectly their property interests, too – were not being sufficiently protected by the special liquidators. Therefore, the "corporate veil" should be pierced. The European Commission opined that whether a shareholder was the majority shareholder was not the only consideration for piercing the veil. If the special liquidators were effectively under control of the Greek government, it could not be expected that the company would lodge a complaint against the Greek government.

The European Court held that piercing the corporate veil – disregarding the company's legal personality – could be justified only in *exceptional circumstances*. One possible circumstance could be the impossibility of the company through its articles of incorporation or its special liquidators to apply to the ECHR institutions. Furthermore, it must be *clearly established* that such circumstances exist. The European Court found no such circumstances and dismissed for lack of jurisdiction.

(3) Compare U.S. federal law allowing corporations to be recognized as a "legal personality." *Dartmouth College v. Woodward*, 17 U.S. (4 Wheat.) 518 (1819) (*dicta*).

4.3. Exhaustion of Domestic Remedies

As the International Court of Justice has noted,

> [t]he rule that local remedies must be exhausted before international proceedings may be instituted is a well-established rule of customary international law.... Before resort may be had to an international court ... it has been considered necessary that the State where the violation occurred should have an opportunity to redress it by its own means, within the framework of its own domestic legal system.[1]

---

[1] *Interhandel Case* (*Switz. v. U.S.*), [1959] I.C.J. 6, 27 (Mar. 21).

Historically, the exhaustion rule is rooted in the law governing diplomatic protection. It has been incorporated into international human rights law. Under international law, domestic remedies must be effective.[2] The international human rights case law addressing the rule is substantial, and this case law has defined the rule further.

Under international human rights law, local remedies must have been available, effective, and sufficient.[3] The existence of such remedies must have been sufficiently certain, not only in theory but also in practice.[4] Accordingly, a remedy that has no prospect of success does not constitute an effective remedy.[5] According to the UN Human Rights Committee, there need only be a "*reasonable* prospect" that domestic remedies would be ineffective to show exhaustion.[6] For example, in jurisdictions recognizing the principle of *stare decisis* (*e.g.*, Canada, the United States, and the United Kingdom), a controlling case precedent need not be pursued as a remedy.[7] Furthermore, in being effective, the remedy must be capable of producing the result for which it was designed. For example, a habeas corpus petition is not effective if it is not impartially applied or if the party invoking it is thereby placed in danger.[8] When remedies are denied for trivial reasons or without examination on the merits, or if there is proof of the existence of a practice or policy ordered or tolerated by the government, the effect of which is to impede persons from invoking internal remedies that would normally be available to others, resort to such remedies becomes a senseless formality.[9]

Interestingly, under one international arbitration decision, the complainant's failure to call a witness considered essential to his claim before domestic proceedings was found to be a failure to exhaust domestic remedies.[10] However, in a number of UN Human Rights Committee cases from Jamaica addressing the complainant's lawyers' failure to call certain essential witnesses, the Committee has *not* held that there has been no exhaustion of local remedies.[11]

The Inter-American Commission has ruled that the domestic recourse available to a petitioner must be of a judicial rather than a political nature.[12] Furthermore, the Commission has held that where the domestic entity investigating the subject matter of

---

[2] *Claim of Finnish Shipowners* (*Finland v. Great Britain*), 3 R.I.A.A. 1479 (May 9, 1934), Dr. Algot Bagge, Sole Arbitrator, 1934.

[3] *De la Grange v. Italy*, 293-B Eur.Ct.H.R. (ser. A) (1994).

[4] *Van Droogenbroeck v. Belgium*, 50 Eur.Ct.H.R. (ser. A) (1982).

[5] *Kunzi-Brenzikofer and Others v. Denmark*, App. No. 12097/86, 53 Eur. Cm. H.R. Dec. & Rep. 210, 217.

[6] *Altesor v. Uruguay*, UN Hum.Rts.Ctte., Communication No. 10/1977, views adopted 29 March 1982, at §4(b).

[7] *Lovelace v. Canada*, UN Hum. Rts. Ctte, Communication No. 24/1977, admissibility decision adopted 14 August 1979, in 1 Selected Decision under the Optional Protocol (Second to sixteenth sessions) 10, U.N. Doc. CCPR/C/OP/1 (1985) (if highest court has already "substantially decided" the question at issue, author need not pursue national judicial remedy).

[8] *Godínez Cruz v. Honduras*, Inter-Amer. Ct. H.R., Final Judgment of 20 January 1989, Series C No. 5, at §69; see *Robert E. Brown Case* (*U.S. v. Great Britain*), 6 R.I.A.A. 120 (1923) U.N. Rep. Int'l Arbitration Awards (1923) (no need to exhaust where domestic court lacks independence).

[9] *Godínez Cruz v. Honduras, supra*, at §71.

[10] *Ambatielos Claim* (*Greece v. United Kingdom*), 12 R.I.A.A. 83 (6 Mar. 1956).

[11] See, *e.g.*, *Reynolds v. Jamaica*, UN Hum. Rts. Ctte., Communication No. 229/1987, views adopted 8 April 1991; *Collins v. Jamaica*, UN Hum. Rts. Ctte., Communication No. 240/1987, views adopted 1 November 1991; *Sawyers and McLean v. Jamaica*, UN Hum. Rts. Ctte., Communication Nos. 226/1987 and 256/1987, views adopted 11 April 1991.

[12] Case 1697 (Brazil), Report on the Work Accomplished During Its Twenty-eighth Session (Special) May 1–5, 1972, OAS Doc., OEA/ser. L/V/II. 28, doc. 24 rev. 2 (1972), at ¶ 30.

the petition was the body most likely responsible for the alleged violations, an exception to the exhaustion rule would apply.[13] A good example of such a case in where the military are responsible for investigating a disappearance allegedly committed by their members.

Furthermore, in cases where the state party has been found to tolerate and/or instigate a widespread practice of disappearances, the merits of a petitioner's legal claims must be examined in conjunction with exhaustion issues because the government's failure to enforce rights to due process and domestic remedies occasions such a pattern of disappearances.[14] Consider the following case.

Velásquez Rodríguez v. Honduras
Inter-American Court of Human Rights
Preliminary Objections, Judgment of June 26, 1989
ANNUAL REPORT OF THE
INTER-AMERICAN COURT OF HUMAN RIGHTS 1987
OAS/Ser.L/V/III.17, doc. 13.

. . . .

15. According to the petition filed with the Commission on October 7, 1981, and the supplementary information received subsequently, Angel Manfredo Velásquez Rodríguez, a student at the National Autonomous University of Honduras, "was violently detained without a warrant for his arrest by members of the Dirección Nacional de Investigación (DNI) and G-2 of the Armed Forces of Honduras" on the afternoon of September 12, 1981, in Tegucigalpa. According to the petitioners, several eyewitnesses reported that he and others were detained and taken to the cells of Public Security Forces Station No. 2 located in the Barrio El Manchen of Tegucigalpa, where he was "accused of alleged political crimes and subjected to harsh interrogation and cruel torture." The petition added that on September 17, 1981, Velásquez Rodríguez was moved to the First Infantry Battalion, where the interrogation continued, but that the police and security forces, nevertheless, denied that he had been detained.

. . . .

83. The Commission maintains that the issue of exhaustion of domestic remedies must be decided jointly with the merits of this case, rather than in the preliminary phase. Its position is based on two considerations. First, the Commission alleges that this matter is inseparably tied to the merits, since the lack of due process and of effective domestic remedies in the Honduran judiciary during the period when the events occurred is proof of a government practice supportive of the forced disappearance of persons, the case before the Court being but one concrete example of that practice. The Commission also argues that the prior exhaustion of domestic remedies is a requirement for the admissibility of petitions presented to the Commission, but not a prerequisite for filing applications with the Court and that, therefore, the Government's objection should not be ruled upon as a preliminary objection.

84. The Court must first reiterate that, although the exhaustion of domestic remedies is a requirement for admissibility before the Commission, the determination of whether such remedies have been pursued and exhausted or whether one is dealing with one of

---

[13] *Darmburg v. Suriname*, Case 10.117, Res. No. 19/89, Inter-Amer. Cm. H.R. 138, 141, OEA/ser.L/V/II.76, doc.10 (1988–89).

[14] *Velásquez Rodríguez v. Honduras*, Inter-Amer.Ct.H.R., Preliminary Objections, Judgment of 26 June 1987, ANNUAL REPORT OF THE INTER-AMERICAN COURT OF HUMAN RIGHTS 1987, OAS/Ser.L/V/III.17, doc. 13.

the exceptions to such requirement is a matter involving the interpretation or application of the Convention. As such, it falls within the contentious jurisdiction of the Court pursuant to the provisions of Article 62(1) of the Convention [...]. The proper moment for the Court to rule on an objection concerning the failure to exhaust domestic remedies will depend on the special circumstances of each case. There is no reason why the Court should not rule upon a preliminary objection regarding exhaustion of domestic remedies, particularly when the Court rejects the objection, or, on the contrary, why it should not join it with the merits. Thus, in deciding whether to join the Government's objection to the merits in the instant case, the Court must examine the issue in its specific context.

85. Article 46(1)(a) of the Convention shows that the admissibility of petitions under Article 44 is subject to the requirement "that the remedies under domestic law have been pursued and exhausted in accordance with generally recognized principles of international law."

86. Article 46(2) sets out three specific grounds for the inapplicability of the requirement established in Article 46(1)(a), as follows:

The provisions of paragraphs l.a and l.b of this article shall not be applicable when;

> a. the domestic legislation of the state concerned does not afford due process of law for the protection of the right or rights that have allegedly been violated;
> b. the party alleging violation of his rights has been denied access to the remedies under domestic law or has been prevented from exhausting them; or
> c. there has been unwarranted delay in rendering a final judgment under the aforementioned remedies.

87. The Court need not decide here whether the grounds listed in Article 46(2) are exhaustive or merely illustrative. It is clear, however, that the reference to "generally recognized principles of international law" suggests, among other things, that these principles are relevant not only in determining what grounds justify non-exhaustion but also as guidelines for the Court when it is called upon to interpret and apply the rule of Article 46(1)(a) in dealing with issues relating to the proof of the exhaustion of domestic remedies, who has the burden of proof, or, even, what is meant by "domestic remedies." Except for the reference to these principles, the Convention does not establish rules for the resolution of these and analogous questions.

88. Generally recognized principles of international law indicate, first, that this is a rule that may be waived, either expressly or by implication, by the State having the right to invoke it, as this Court has already recognized (*see Viviana Gallardo et al.*, Judgment of November 13, 1981, No. G 101/81. Series A, §26). Second, the objection asserting the non-exhaustion of domestic remedies, to be timely, must be made at an early stage of the proceedings by the State entitled to make it, lest a waiver of the requirement be presumed. Third, the State claiming non-exhaustion has an obligation to prove that domestic remedies remain to be exhausted and that they are effective.

89. The record shows: (a) that the Government failed to make a timely objection when the petition was before the Commission and (b) that when the Government eventually raised the objection, it did so in a contradictory way. For example, in its note of November 18, 1983, the Government stated that domestic remedies had not been exhausted because a writ of *exhibición personal* was still pending, whereas at the hearing the Government argued that such a writ does not exhaust domestic remedies. On other occasions, the Government referred generally to domestic remedies, without specifying what remedies were

available under its domestic law to deal with complaints of the type under consideration. There is also considerable evidence that the Government replied to the Commission's requests for information, including that concerning domestic remedies, only after lengthy delays, and that the information was not always responsive.

90. Under normal circumstances, the conduct of the Government would justify the conclusion that the time had long passed for it to seek the dismissal of this case on the grounds of non-exhaustion of domestic remedies. The Court, however, must not rule without taking into account certain procedural actions by both parties. For example, the Government did not object to the admissibility of the petition on the grounds of non-exhaustion of domestic remedies when it was formally notified of the petition, nor did it respond to the Commission's request for information. On the other hand, when the Commission first became aware of the objection (subsequent to its adoption of Resolution 30/83), not only did it fail to inform the Government that such an objection was untimely but, by note of May 30, 1984, it asked the Government whether "the domestic legal remedies have been exhausted. . . ." Under those circumstances and with no more evidence than that contained in the record, the Court deems that it would be improper to reject the Government's objection *in limine* without giving both parties the opportunity to substantiate their contentions.

91. The rule of prior exhaustion of domestic remedies under the international law of human rights has certain implications that are present in the Convention. Under the Convention, States Parties have an obligation to provide effective judicial remedies to victims of human rights violations (Art. 25), remedies that must be substantiated in accordance with the rules of due process of law (Art. 8(1)), all in keeping with the general obligation of such States to guarantee the free and full exercise of the rights recognized by the Convention to all persons subject to their jurisdiction (Art. 1). Thus, when certain exceptions to the rule of non-exhaustion of domestic remedies are invoked, such as the ineffectiveness of such remedies or the lack of due process of law, not only is it contended that the victim is under no obligation to pursue such remedies, but, indirectly, the State in question is also charged with a new violation of the obligations assumed under the Convention. Thus, the question of domestic remedies is closely tied to the merits of the case.

92. At the hearing, the Government stressed that the requirement of the prior exhaustion of domestic remedies is justified because the international system for the protection of human rights guaranteed in the Convention is ancillary to its domestic law.

93. The observation of the Government is correct. However, it must also be borne in mind that the international protection of human rights is founded on the need to protect the victim from the arbitrary exercise of governmental authority. The lack of effective domestic remedies renders the victim defenseless and explains the need for international protection. Thus, whenever a petitioner alleges that such remedies do not exist or are illusory, the granting of such protection may be not only justified, but urgent. In those cases, not only is Article 37(3) of the Regulations of the Commission on the burden of proof applicable, but the timing of the decision on domestic remedies must also fit the purposes of the international protection system. The rule of prior exhaustion must never lead to a halt or delay that would render international action in support of the defenseless victim ineffective. This is why Article 46(2) of the Convention sets out exceptions to the requirement of recourse to domestic remedies prior to seeking international protection, precisely in situations in which such remedies are, for a variety of reasons,

ineffective. Of course, when the State interposes this objection in timely fashion it should be heard and resolved; however, the relationship between the decision regarding applicability of the rule and the need for timely international action in the absence of effective domestic remedies may frequently recommend the hearing of questions relating to that rule together with the merits, in order to prevent unnecessary delays due to preliminary objections.

94. The foregoing considerations are relevant to the analysis of the application now before the Court, which the Commission presented as a case of the forced disappearance of a person on instructions of public authorities. Wherever this practice has existed, it has been made possible precisely by the lack of domestic remedies or their lack of effectiveness in protecting the essential rights of those persecuted by the authorities. In such cases, given the interplay between the problem of domestic remedies and the very violation of human rights, the question of their prior exhaustion must be taken up together with the merits of the case.

95. The Commission has asserted, moreover, that the pursuit of domestic remedies was unsuccessful and that, during the period in which the events occurred, the three exceptions to the rule of prior exhaustion set forth in the Convention were applicable. The Government contends, on the other hand, that the domestic judicial system offers better alternatives. That difference inevitably leads to the issue of the effectiveness of the domestic remedies and judicial system taken as a whole, as mechanisms to guarantee the respect of human rights. If the Court, then, were to sustain the Government's objection and declare that effective judicial remedies are available, it would be prejudging the merits without having heard the evidence and arguments of the Commission or those of the Government. If, on the other hand, the Court were to declare that all effective domestic remedies had been exhausted or did not exist, it would be prejudging the merits in a manner detrimental to the State.

96. The issues relating to the exhaustion and effectiveness of the domestic remedies applicable to the instant case must, therefore, be resolved together with the merits. . . .

NOW, THEREFORE, THE COURT:

unanimously,

1. Rejects the preliminary objections interposed by the Government of Honduras, except for the issues relating to the exhaustion of the domestic legal remedies, which are herewith ordered joined to the merits of the case.

unanimously,

2. Decides to proceed with the consideration of the instant case.

. . . .

∾

QUESTIONS & COMMENTS

(1) Would refugees residing outside their country and filing claims against their home governments also be covered by the Inter-American Court's decision in *Velásquez Rodríguez v. Honduras*? If refugees have a well-founded fear of persecution compelling them to leave their country, does their fleeing effectively deny them a domestic remedy

that in turn requires that the merits of their claims be examined in conjunction with exhaustion issues?

Exceptions to the Exhaustion of Domestic Remedies in Cases of Indigency
or Inability to Obtain Legal Representation
Because of a Generalized Fear Within the Legal Community
(Arts. 46(1), 46(2)(a) and 46(2)(b) of the American Convention on Human Rights)
Inter-American Court of Human Rights
Advisory Opinion OC-11/90 of August 10, 1990
Inter-Amer. Ct. H.R. (Ser. A) No. 11 (1990)

. . . .

THE COURT [. . .] renders the following Advisory Opinion:

. . . .

2. The request for an advisory opinion poses the following questions:

1. Does the requirement of the exhaustion of internal legal remedies apply to an indigent, who because of economic circumstances is unable to avail himself of the legal remedies within a country?

2. In the event that this requirement is waived for indigents, what criteria should the Commission consider in making its determination of admissibility in such cases?

1. Does the requirement of the exhaustion of internal legal remedies apply to an individual complainant, who because he is unable to retain representation due to a general fear in the legal community cannot avail himself of the legal remedies provided by law in a country?

2. In the event that this requirement is waived for such persons, what criteria should the Commission consider in making its determination of admissibility in these cases?

3. In setting out the considerations that prompted the advisory opinion request, the Commission stated the following:

1. Indigency

The Commission has received certain petitions in which the victim alleges that he has not been able to comply with the requirement of the exhaustion of remedies set forth in the domestic legislation because he cannot afford legal assistance or, in some cases, the obligatory filing fees.

The Commission is aware that some States provide free legal assistance to persons who qualify because of their economic status. However, this practice does not obtain in all of the countries and even in those countries where it exists, it often covers only highly urbanized areas.

When the legal remedies of a State are not in fact available to an alleged victim of a violation of human rights and should the Commission be obligated to dismiss his complaint for failure to meet the requirement of Article 46(1)(a), does this not bring into play the possibility of a discrimination based on "social condition" (Article 1(1) of the Convention)?

2. Lack of Counsel

Complainants have alleged to the Commission that they have been unable to retain counsel to represent them, thereby limiting their ability to effectively pursue the internal legal remedies putatively available at law. This situation has occurred where an atmosphere of fear prevails and lawyers do not accept cases which they believe could place their own lives and those of their families in jeopardy.

When, as a practical matter, such a situation occurs and an alleged victim of a human rights violation brings the matter to the attention of the Inter-American Commission on Human Rights, should the Commission admit such a complaint or dismiss it as inadmissible?

. . . .

5. In a note of February 9, 1989, the Secretariat, acting pursuant to Article 52 of the Rules of Procedure of the Court, requested written observations and other relevant documents on the issues involved in the instant advisory opinion request both from the member states of the Organization of American States (hereinafter "the OAS") and, through the Secretary General of that Organization, from all the organs listed in Chapter VIII of the OAS Charter.

. . . .

14. The questions submitted by the Commission call for an interpretation by the Court of Article 46(1)(a) and 46(2) of the Convention, which reads as follows:

Article 46

1. Admission by the Commission of a petition or communication lodged in accordance with Articles 44 or 45 shall be subject to the following requirements:

a. that the remedies under domestic law have been pursued and exhausted in accordance with generally recognized principles of international law;

2. The provisions of paragraphs 1.a and 1.b of this article shall not be applicable when:

a. the domestic legislation of the state concerned does not afford due process of law for the protection of the right or rights that have allegedly been violated;

b. the party alleging violation of his rights has been denied access to the remedies under domestic law or has been prevented from exhausting them; or

c. there has been unwarranted delay in rendering a final judgment under the afore-mentioned remedies.

15. Article 46(2)(c) does not have any relevance to the questions before the Court. The remaining provisions – sub-paragraphs (a) and (b) – do and require closer analysis.

16. Article 46(1)(a) provides that, for a petition to be ruled admissible by the Commission, it is necessary that the remedies under domestic law have been pursued and exhausted, while sub-paragraph 2 considers the circumstances in which this requirement does not apply.

17. Article 46(2)(a) applies to situations in which the domestic law of a State Party does not provide appropriate remedies to protect rights that have been violated. Article 46(2)(b) is applicable to situations in which the domestic law does provide for remedies, but such remedies are either denied the affected individual or he is otherwise prevented from exhausting them. These provisions thus apply to situations where domestic remedies cannot be exhausted because they are not available either as a matter of law or as a matter of fact.

18. Article 46(2) makes no specific reference to indigents, the subject of the first question, nor to those situations in which a person has been unable to obtain legal representation because of a generalized fear in the legal community to take such cases, which the second question addresses.

19. The answers to the questions presented by the Commission thus depend on a determination of whether a person's failure to exhaust domestic remedies in the circumstances posited falls under one or the other exception spelled out in Article 46(2). That is, whether or under what circumstances a person's indigency or inability to obtain legal representation because of a generalized fear among the legal community will exempt him from the requirement to exhaust domestic remedies.

20. In addressing the issue of indigency, the Court must emphasize that merely because a person is indigent does not, standing alone, mean that he does not have to exhaust domestic remedies, for the provision contained in Article 46(1) is of a general nature. The language of Article 46(2) suggests that whether or not an indigent has to exhaust domestic remedies will depend on whether the law or the circumstances permit him to do so.

21. In analyzing these issues, the Court must bear in mind the provisions contained in Articles 1(1), 24 and the relevant parts of Article 8 of the Convention, which are closely related to the instant matter and read as follows:

Article 1. Obligation to Respect Rights

> 1. The States Parties to this Convention undertake to respect the rights and freedoms recognized herein and to ensure to all persons subject to their jurisdiction the free and full exercise of those rights and freedoms, without any discrimination for reasons of race, color, sex, language, religion, political or other opinion, national or social origin, economic status, birth, or any other social condition.

Article 24. Right to Equal Protection

> All persons are equal before the law. Consequently, they are entitled, without discrimination, to equal protection of the law.

Article 8. Right to a Fair Trial

> 1. Every person has the right to a hearing, with due guarantees and within a reasonable time, by a competent, independent, and impartial tribunal, previously established by law, in the substantiation of any accusation of a criminal nature made against him or for the determination of his rights and obligations of a civil, labor, fiscal, or any other nature.

> 2. Every person accused of a criminal offense has the right to be presumed innocent so long as his guilt has not been proven according to law. During the proceedings, every person is entitled, with full equality, to the following minimum guarantees:
>   . . . .

>> d. the right of the accused to defend himself personally or to be assisted by legal counsel of his own choosing, and to communicate freely and privately with his counsel;
>> e. the inalienable right to be assisted by counsel provided by the state, paid or not as the domestic law provides, if the accused does not defend himself personally or engage his own counsel within the time period established by law; . . . .

22. The final section of Article 1(1) prohibits a state from discriminating on a variety of grounds, among them economic status the meaning of the term discrimination employed by Article 24 must, then, be interpreted by reference to the list enumerated in Article 1(1). If a person who is seeking the protection of the law in order to assert rights which the Convention guarantees finds that his economic status (in this case, his indigency) prevents him from so doing because he cannot afford either the necessary legal counsel or the costs of the proceedings, that person is being discriminated against by reason of his economic status and, hence, is not receiving equal protection before the law.

23. [P]rotection of the law consists, fundamentally, of the remedies the law provides for the protection of the rights guaranteed by the Convention. The obligation to respect and guarantee such rights, which Article 1(1) imposes on the States Parties, implies, as the Court has already stated, the duty of the States Parties to organize the governmental apparatus and, in general, all the structures through which public power is exercised, so that they are capable of juridically ensuring the free and full enjoyment of human rights (*Velásquez Rodríguez Case*, Judgment of July 29, 1988. Series C No. 4, §166; *Godínez Cruz Case*, Judgment of January 20, 1989. Series C No. 5, §175).

24. Insofar as the right to legal counsel is concerned, this duty to organize the governmental apparatus and to create the structures necessary to guarantee human rights is related to the provisions of Article 8 of the Convention. That article distinguishes between accusation[s] of a criminal nature and procedures of a civil, labor, fiscal, or any other nature. Although it provides that [e]very person has the right to a hearing, with due guarantees . . . by a . . . tribunal in both types of proceedings, it spells out in addition certain minimum guarantees for those accused of a criminal offense. Thus, the concept of a fair hearing in criminal proceedings also embraces, at the very least, those minimum guarantees. By labeling these guarantees as minimum guarantees, the Convention assumes that other, additional guarantees may be necessary in specific circumstances to ensure a fair hearing.

25. Sub-paragraphs (d) and (e) of Article 8(2) indicate that the accused has a right to defend himself personally or to be assisted by legal counsel of his own choosing and that, if he should choose not to do so, he has the inalienable right to be assisted by counsel provided by the state, paid or not as the domestic law provides . . . Thus, a defendant may defend himself personally, but it is important to bear in mind that this would only be possible where permitted under domestic law. If a person refuses or is unable to defend himself personally, he has the right to be assisted by counsel of his own choosing. In cases where the accused neither defends himself nor engages his own counsel within the time period established by law, he has the right to be assisted by counsel provided by the state, paid or not as the domestic law provides. To that extent the Convention guarantees the right to counsel in criminal proceedings. But since it does not stipulate that legal counsel be provided free of charge when required, an indigent would suffer discrimination for reason of his economic status if, when in need of legal counsel, the state were not to provide it to him free of charge.

26. Article 8 must, then, be read to require legal counsel only when that is necessary for a fair hearing. Any state that does not provide indigents with such counsel free of charge cannot, therefore, later assert that appropriate remedies existed but were not exhausted.

27. Even in those cases in which the accused is forced to defend himself because he cannot afford legal counsel, a violation of Article 8 of the Convention could be said to

exist if it can be proved that the lack of legal counsel affected the right to a fair hearing to which he is entitled under that Article.

28. For cases which concern the determination of a person's rights and obligations of a civil, labor, fiscal, or any other nature, Article 8 does not specify any minimum guarantees similar to those provided in Article 8(2) for criminal proceedings. It does, however, provide for due guarantees; consequently, the individual here also has the right to the fair hearing provided for in criminal cases. It is important to note here that the circumstances of a particular case or proceeding – its significance, its legal character, and its context in a particular legal system – are among the factors that bear on the determination of whether legal representation is or is not necessary for a fair hearing.

29. Lack of legal counsel is not, of course, the only factor that could prevent an indigent from exhausting domestic remedies. It could even happen that the state might provide legal counsel free of charge but neglect to cover the costs that might be required to ensure the fair hearing that Article 8 prescribes. In such cases, the exceptions to Article 46(1) would apply. Here again, the circumstances of each case and each particular legal system must be kept in mind.

30. In its advisory opinion request, the Commission states that it has received certain petitions in which the victim alleges that he has not been able to comply with the requirement of the exhaustion of remedies set forth in the domestic legislation because he cannot afford legal assistance or, in some cases, the obligatory filing fees. Upon applying the foregoing analysis to the examples set forth by the Commission, it must be concluded that if legal services are required either as a matter of law or fact in order for a right guaranteed by the Convention to be recognized and a person is unable to obtain such services because of his indigency, then that person would be exempted from the requirement to exhaust domestic remedies. The same would be true of cases requiring the payment of a filing fee. That is to say, if it is impossible for an indigent to deposit such a fee, he cannot be required to exhaust domestic remedies unless the state provides some alternative mechanism.

31. Thus, the first question presented to the Court by the Commission is not whether the Convention guarantees the right to legal counsel as such or as a result of the prohibition of discrimination for reason of economic status (Art. 1(1)). Rather, the question is whether an indigent may appeal directly to the Commission to protect a right guaranteed in the Convention without first exhausting the applicable domestic remedies. The answer to this question given what has been said above, is that if it can be shown that an indigent needs legal counsel to effectively protect a right which the Convention guarantees and his indigency prevents him from obtaining such counsel, he does not have to exhaust the relevant domestic remedies. That is the meaning of the language of Article 46(2) read in conjunction with Articles 1(1), 24 and 8.

32. The Court will now turn to the second question. It concerns the exhaustion of domestic remedies in situations where an individual is unable to obtain the necessary legal representation due to a general fear in the legal community of a given country. The Commission explains that, according to what some complainants have alleged, [t]his situation has occurred where an atmosphere of fear prevails and lawyers do not accept cases which they believe could place their own lives and those of their families in jeopardy.

33. In general, the same basic principles govern this question as those which the Court has deemed applicable to the first question. That is to say, if a person, for a reason such as the one stated above, is prevented from availing himself of the domestic legal remedies necessary to assert a right which the Convention guarantees, he cannot be required to

exhaust those remedies. The state's obligation to guarantee such remedies is, of course, unaffected by this conclusion.

34. Article 1 of the Convention provides not only that the States Parties have an obligation to respect the rights and freedoms recognized [t]herein, it also requires them to ensure to all persons subject to their jurisdiction the free and full exercise of those rights and freedoms. The Court has already had occasion to emphasize that this provision imposes an affirmative duty on the States. It is also important to note that the obligation to ensure requires the state to take all necessary measures to remove any impediments which might exist that would prevent individuals from enjoying the rights the Convention guarantees. Any state which tolerates circumstances or conditions that prevent individuals from having recourse to the legal remedies designed to protect their rights is consequently in violation of Article 1(1) of the Convention. As the Court has stated,

> . . . when it is shown that remedies are denied for trivial reasons or without an examination of the merits, or if there is proof of the existence of a practice or policy ordered or tolerated by the government, the effect of which is to impede certain persons from invoking internal remedies that would normally be available to others . . . resort to those remedies becomes a senseless formality. The exceptions of Article 46(2) would be fully applicable in those situations and would discharge the obligation to exhaust internal remedies since they cannot fulfill their objective in that case. (*Velásquez Rodríguez Case,* [ ] §68; *Godínez Cruz Case,* [ ] §71, and *Fairén Garbi and Solís Corrales Case,* Judgment of March 15, 1989. Series C No. 6, §93).

35. It follows therefrom that where an individual requires legal representation and a generalized fear in the legal community prevents him from obtaining such representation, the exception set out in Article 46(2)(b) is fully applicable and the individual is exempted from the requirement to exhaust domestic remedies.

36. The Court is of the opinion that, in the cases posited by the Commission, it is the considerations outlined that render the remedies adequate and effective in accordance with generally recognized principles of international law to which Article 46(1) refers; namely, remedies suitable to address an infringement of a legal right and capable of producing the result for which [they were] designed (*Velásquez Rodríguez Case,* [ ] §§.64 and 66; *Godínez Cruz Case,* [ ], §§.67 and 69, and *Fairén Garbi and Solís Corrales Case,* [ ] §§.88 and 91).

37. The second part of both questions submitted relates to the standards the Commission should apply in determining the admissibility of the claims analyzed herein.

38. In addressing this issue it is clear that the test to be applied must be whether legal representation was necessary in order to exhaust the appropriate remedies and whether such representation was, in fact, available.

39. It is for the Commission to make this determination. It must be emphasized, nevertheless, that all determinations made by the Commission before the case was referred to the Court are fully reviewable by the latter (*Velásquez Rodríguez Case,* Preliminary Objections, Judgment of June 26, 1987. Series C No. 1, §29; *Fairén Garbi and Solís Corrales Case,* Preliminary Objections, Judgment of June 26, 1987. Series C No. 2, §34, and *Godínez Cruz Case,* Preliminary Objections, Judgment of June 26, 1987. Series C No. 3, §32).

40. The exhaustion of domestic remedies is a requirement for admissibility and the Commission must bear this in mind at the appropriate time and provide both the state

and the complainant with the opportunity to present their respective positions on this issue.

41. Under Article 46(1)(a) of the Convention and in accordance with general principles of international law, it is for the state asserting non-exhaustion of domestic remedies to prove that such remedies in fact exist and that they have not been exhausted (*Velásquez Rodríguez Case*, Preliminary Objections,[ ] §88; *Fairén Garbi and Solís Corrales Case*, Preliminary Objections, [ ] §87, and *Godínez Cruz Case*, Preliminary Objections, [ ] §90). Once a State Party has shown the existence of domestic remedies for the enforcement of a particular right guaranteed by the Convention, the burden of proof shifts to the complainant, who must then demonstrate that the exceptions provided for in Article 46(2) are applicable, whether as a result of indigency or because of a generalized fear to take the case among the legal community or any other applicable circumstance. Of course, it must also be shown that the rights in question are guaranteed in the Convention and that legal representation is necessary to assert or enjoy those rights.

42. For these reasons,

THE COURT, IS OF THE OPINION

unanimously

1. That if his indigency or a general fear in the legal community to represent him prevents a complainant before the Commission from invoking the domestic remedies necessary to protect a right guaranteed by the Convention, he is not required to exhaust such remedies.

unanimously

2. That if a State Party has proved that domestic remedies are available, the complainant must then demonstrate that the exceptions contemplated in Article 46(2) apply and that he was prevented from obtaining the legal counsel necessary for the protection of rights guaranteed by the Convention.

∾

QUESTIONS & COMMENTS

(1) The UN Human Rights Committee has held in a number of cases challenging their convictions that the authors did not have to pursue a domestic remedy before the Jamaican Constitutional Court because of the unavailability of legal aid under Jamaican law to press those claims. *See, e.g., Douglas, Gentles & Kerr v. Jamaica*, UN Hum. Rts. Ctte., Communication No. 353/1989, views adopted 19 October 1993, U.N. Doc. CCPR/C/49/D/352/1989 (1993); *Little v. Jamaica*, UN Hum. Rts. Ctte., Communication No. 283/1988, views adopted 1 November 1991.

4.4. Remedies and State Compliance

For a student coming from older legal traditions that employ legal fictions and a rhetoric of rights without real substance, international human rights treaties and their interpretation by international tribunals are refreshingly rational and honest. Unlike, *e.g.*, U.S. law that may *recognize* rights without providing any real *remedy*, international human rights treaties expressly recognize a right to an effective domestic remedy for violations of the rights recognized in the particular treaty or, in some cases, fundamental domestic rights. Depending on the treaty or declaration, these remedies can be judicial, legislative, and/or administrative. They also can entail educational, cultural, and/or informational measures. Most importantly, there is no sovereign immunity attaching to governmental entities or agents. And depending on the particular treaty, this remedy can be in the form of declaratory and injunctive relief, and money damages.

Restitution

The primary remedial means of reparation under international law is a form of injunctive relief: restitution. International tribunals have applied the principle of *restitutio in integrum* directly, ordering states to remedy the consequences of their unlawful acts by taking the necessary steps to reestablish the *status quo ante*. In a case involving a claim by Nicaragua against San Salvador, the Central American Court of Justice found Nicaragua to be under obligation to reestablish and maintain the legal status that existed prior to the Bryan-Chamorro Treaty.[1] Similarly, in the *Case Concerning the Temple of Preah-Vihear*, the International Court of Justice ordered restitution to Cambodia of all the objects that Thai authorities had removed from the temple.[2]

In the case concerning the *United States Diplomatic and Consular Staff in Tehran (U.S. v. Iran)*, the International Court of Justice applied the principle of *restitutio in integrum* as the basis of reparation for a sovereign state's unlawful failure to act. Finding the Iranian government's inaction during the Iran hostage situation to constitute a violation of international law, the ICJ ordered Iran to redress its unlawful omission by specific performance of its legal obligations. The ICJ's order was very specific. The Court specifically directed Iran: (i) to terminate immediately the unlawful detention of the U.S. diplomatic and consular staff, (ii) to ensure that the U.S. staff acquire the necessary means of leaving Iran, and (iii) to restore immediately the premises, property, archives, and documents of the U.S. embassy to the hands of the proper authorities.[3]

Likewise, international arbitration case law provides ample support for *restitutio in integrum* as a fundamental principle of reparation under international law. Most notably, in the dispute between Texaco and Libya concerning compensation for nationalized property, an international arbitral tribunal held that the injured parties were entitled to *restitutio in integrum* and that the sovereign state was obliged to perform specifically its contractual obligations with private foreign investors.[4]

Furthermore, scholars in international law widely recognize *restitutio in integrum* as the normal and proper remedy for violations of international law. According to Lauterpacht, "the rule [is] that in international law, as in private law, *restitutio in integrum* is regarded as the object of redress."[5] Moreover, Oppenheim and Lauterpacht state,

> [t]he principal legal consequences of an international delinquency are reparation of the moral and material wrong done . . . [O]ut of an international delinquency arises a right for the wronged State to request from the delinquent State the performance of such acts as are

---

[1] 11 Am. J. Int'l L. 3 (1917).

[2] *Temple of Preah Vihear (Cambodia v. Thailand)* 1962 I.C.J. 6, 36–37 (June 15).

[3] 1980 I.C.J. 3, 44–45 (May 24).

[4] 17 I.L.M. 1, 36 (1978).

[5] H. Lauterpacht, Private Law Sources and Analogies of International Law 149 (1927).

necessary for reparation of the wrong done. What kind of acts these are depends upon the merits of the case.[6]

Regarding the appropriateness of *restitutio in integrum* as reparation for wrongful state inaction, Mr. Justice E. Jimenez de Arechaga (a former ICJ president) has noted that, among all possible remedies, the equitable remedy of *restitutio in integrum* is fundamental because it is "designed to re-establish the situation which would have existed if the wrongful . . . omission had not taken place, by performance of the obligation which the state failed to discharge."[7] Thus, where a state has failed to fulfill its legal duties, *restitutio in integrum* is justified by the fact that, at least in principle, this remedy satisfies the original obligation as perfectly as possible.

All international human rights tribunals have ordered or recommended restitution, but these tribunals have diverged as to specificity of this injunctive relief. The European Court's "injunctive" remedies are more like declaratory relief. Upon finding an ECHR violation, the European Court usually gives the state party leeway in determining exactly how to "fix" a continuing violation. "The control of the proper execution of the European Court's judgments is . . . mainly performed by the Committee of Ministers,"[8] and under the ECHR, there are no time limits for execution of the judgment.

There are four sorts of injunctive relief possibilities for a state party to comply with the European Court's decision: (i) a change of law by the parliament or government, (ii) a reopening of the case, (iii) acceptance by courts or administrative authorities of the precedent value of the Court's judgment, and/or (iv) pardon, amnesty or abolition.[9] For example, in *Hentrich v. France*,[10] the European Court earlier had found a violation to the applicant's right to property under Protocol No. 1(1) and "that the best form of redress would in principle be for the State to return the land."[11] However, the French government stated that it could not do so under present French law. "Having become part of the private property of the State, the 'pre-empted' land was subject to the provisions of the Code of State Property and it was impracticable to transfer it, let alone without requiring any payment."[12] Accordingly, the Court ordered payment of FRF 1,000,000 to the applicant.[13]

Although the European Court has interpreted the ECHR to allow the states parties the power to choose the specific appropriate measures for complying with their obligations under the Convention,[14] the Inter-American Court has ordered specific and diverse forms of restitution. Consider the following forms of injunctive relief that the Inter-American Court ordered in a massacre case.

---

[6] L. Oppenheim, 1 INTERNATIONAL LAW §156 (H. Lauterpacht ed., 8th ed. 1955).

[7] Eduardo Jiménez de Aréchaga, *International Responsibility*, in MANUAL OF PUBLIC INTERNATIONAL LAW 565 (M. Sorenson, ed., 1968).

[8] Fredrik G. E. Sundberg, *The European Experience of Human Rights Proceedings: The Precedent Value of the European Court's Decisions*, 20 AKRON L. REV. 629, 640 (1987).

[9] *Id.* at 634.

[10] 322 Eur. Ct. H.R. (ser. A) (1995).

[11] *Id.* at §10 (*citing* 296-A Eur. Ct. H.R. (ser. A) (1994) at §21).

[12] *Id.*

[13] *See Papamichalopoulos and Others v. Greece*, 330-B Eur. Ct. H.R. (ser. A) (1995) (money damages awarded instead of return of land).

[14] *See, e.g., McGoff v. Sweden*, 83 Eur. Ct. H.R. (ser. A) (1984) at 28.

96. The compensation fixed for the victims' heirs includes an amount that will enable the minor children to continue their education until they reach a certain age. Nevertheless, these goals will not be met merely by granting compensatory damages; it is also essential that the children be offered a school where they can receive adequate education and basic medical attention. At the present time, this is not available in several of the Saramaka villages.

Most of the children of the victims live in Gujaba, where the school and the medical dispensary have both been shut down. The Court believes that, as part of the compensation due, Suriname is under the obligation to reopen the school at Gujaba and staff it with teaching and administrative personnel to enable it to function on a permanent basis as of 1994. In addition, the necessary steps shall be taken for the medical dispensary already in place there to be made operational and reopen that same year.

Aloeboetoe et al. v. Suriname, Judgment of September 10, 1993, Inter-Am. Ct. H.R. (Ser. C) No. 15 (1994), at §96.

In terms of specificity of injunctive relief, the UN Human Rights Committee has staked out a position between the European Court and the Inter-American Court. Sometimes the Committee has recommended the release or commutation of prison sentences. Other times, the Committee merely declares violations and leaves it to the state party to determine which specific measures are necessary to bring the state party into compliance with its obligations under the ICCPR.

Satisfaction

The second form of reparation is satisfaction. Satisfaction is appropriate for nonmaterial damage. Satisfaction can include both declaratory and injunctive measures. For example, satisfaction can include official regrets, apologies, and/or punishment. Indeed, in international human rights law, satisfaction has included the prevention, investigation, and punishment of serious human rights violations, such as disappearances, summary executions, and sexual assault.

Regarding punishment as satisfaction, the major human rights treaties and declarations do not expressly require states to punish violations of human rights – with the exception of the UN Convention Against Torture. However, the Inter-American Court, European Court, and UN Human Rights Committee have required punishment. Indeed, the UN Human Rights Committee has commented that a state's duty to investigate torture and prosecute its perpetrators is greater than its duty to provide a civil remedy.[15] However, the Committee has rejected a complainant's claim under Article 14(1) (right to fair trial) that individuals have a right to see a particular person criminally prosecuted.[16] However, in one case the Committee held that purely administrative or disciplinary punishment was insufficient for serious human rights violations – especially

---

[15] UN Hum. Rts. Ctte., General Comment 20 (Article 7) (Forty-fourth session, 1992), COMPILATION OF GENERAL COMMENTS AND GENERAL RECOMMENDATIONS, ADOPTED BY HUMAN RIGHTS TREATY BODIES, U.N. Doc. HRI\GEN\1\Rev.1 at 30 (1994).

[16] Diane F. Orentlicher, *Settling Accounts: The Duty to Prosecute Human Rights Violations of a Prior Regime*, 100 YALE L. J. 2537 (1991).

for disappearances.[17] Evidentiary constraints also can limit the state's duty to prosecute – if these constraints were not a consequence of governmental malfeasance. Accordingly, a civil remedy may be more appropriate because the burden of proof is not as great.

However, international criminal tribunals have express authority through UN Security Council Resolutions (as in the cases of, *e.g.*, the ICTR and ICTY) or treaties (as in the case of, *e.g.*, the ICC) to impose punishment.

Indemnity

Finally, there is indemnity as a form of reparation. This is a money award for material and/or moral damages. Under the ECHR, the European Court only awards damages if "necessary." However the Inter-American Court has greater latitude: under the ACHR, it can grant a damage award if "appropriate."

Money damages are especially appropriate when the other forms of injunctive relief, restitution and satisfaction, are not feasible. The European Court and Inter-American Court have awarded money damages for both material and nonmaterial losses. However, no international court has awarded punitive damages.[18] As one commentator has explained this in regards to the Inter-American Court,

> [t]his can be attributed to the Court's attitude that the rights exist to protect individuals, and not necessarily to punish wrongdoers as is done in a criminal system. In addition, most countries around the world base their legal system on civil law which does not provide for punitive damages.[19]

This ruling by the Inter-American Court is somewhat inconsistent with is substantial case law recognizing a state party's international obligation to punish perpetrators of serious human rights violations. Although the Inter-American Court itself is not in the business of criminal conviction and imprisonment, it is not clear why punitive damages – a civil remedy – should not be made available to human rights victims.

∼

QUESTIONS & COMMENTS

(1) In *Gangaram Panday v. Suriname*, Judgment of January 21, 1994, Inter-Am. Ct. H.R. (Ser. C) No. 16 (1994), the applicant was detained by Surinamese authorities. Later he was found dead in his cell. Surinamese authorities claimed that the applicant had hung himself, but an examination disclosed that his testicles had been crushed suggesting improper treatment. There were other suspicious injuries to his body, and the Surinamese authorities were reluctant in providing information to the applicant's brother.

---

[17] *Bautista de Arellana v. Colombia*, views adopted 27 October 1995, U.N. Doc. CCPR/C/55/D/1993. See Part Three (VII) ("State Action and Affirmative Duties").

[18] Note, however, that under Rule 91(E) of the Rules of Procedure and Evidence for the International Criminal Tribunals for the Former Yugoslavia and Rwanda, witnesses committing perjury before the tribunals can be fined up to $10,000 and/or imprisoned up to twelve months.

[19] Barbara Fontana, *Damage Awards for Human Rights Violations in the European and Inter-American Courts of Human Rights*, 31 Santa Clara L. Rev. 1127, 1167 (1991).

Consequently, the applicant's brother claimed that Suriname had violated his brother's rights *inter alia*, to life, human treatment, and personal liberty. Although Mr. Gangaram Panday died under suspicious circumstances while in custody of the Surinamese authorities, the Inter-American Court did not award damages for unlawful death. It chose only to award nominal damages for the violation of Mr. Gangaram Panday's deprivation of liberty.

(2) Note that in *Artico v. Italy*, 37 Eur. Ct. H.R. (ser. A) (1980), the European Court awarded monetary compensation on an equitable basis for nonpecuniary damages in a case where the applicant was "left with a distressing sensation of isolation, confusion and neglect" after being denied effective legal assistance in a fraud case. *Id.* at §47. Interestingly, the Court referred to these moral damages as "satisfaction." The Court awarded Mr. Artico 3 million lira.

(3) The European Court has not awarded money damages for loss of profits; however, interest is available from the date of the violation. *Pine Valley Developments et al. v. Ireland*, 246-B Eur. Ct. H.R. (ser. A) (1993).

(4) At least as of 1987 there has never been any refusal to pay promptly the money damages awarded by the European Court.[20] According to one commentator, some contracting parties are slow in paying damage and costs awards – although the examples are very few given the thousands of cases in which the European Court has made awards to applicants. As Christian Tomuschat observes:

> As far as obligations to make specific payments are concerned, in the telephone tapping case of *Kruslin* France took more than one year and four months before it made the required payment to the applicant in respect of costs and expenses ... and in the *Ezelin* case the period amounted to almost one year. ... But the unfortunate top position is held by Italy. It appears that the *Colozza* case, in which Italy was ordered to pay to the victim's widow six million Lira by way of just satisfaction, [still had not been concluded seven years later].[21]

---

[20] Fredrik G. E. Sundberg, *The European Experience of Human Rights Proceedings: The Precedent Value of the European Court's Decisions*, 20 Akron L. Rev. 629, 642 (1987).

[21] Christian Tomuschat, *Quo Vadis, Argentoratum? The Success Story of the European Convention on Human Rights – and a Few Dark Stains*, 13 Hum. Rts. L. J. 401 (1992).

5. Substantive International Human Rights and Humanitarian Law Protections

The following sections address the substantive rights and freedoms guaranteed by major international human rights and humanitarian instruments. These sections employ extended extracts from the major global and regional instruments, international cases, and advisory opinions. We also have included U.S. and other domestic cases and statutes to provide a comparative analysis as well as to provide other legal sources for establishing customary international law as reflected in domestic practice. We have included extracts from law review articles and monographs as well as our own *Questions & Comments* in order to illuminate certain overarching themes and to examine the coherence and consistency of the different legal traditions. We have integrated materials addressing international human rights law and international humanitarian law in order to highlight areas in which they overlap and differ.

5.1. Fundamental International Human Rights Protections

In this section, we examine those fundamental human rights protections that are associated with *jus cogens* and norms *erga omnes*.

5.1.1. Rights to Life and Humane Treatment

Universal Declaration of Human Rights

Article 3.

Everyone has the right to life, liberty and security of person.

Article 5.

No one shall be subjected to torture or to cruel, inhuman or degrading treatment or punishment.

International Covenant on Civil and Political Rights

Article 6

1. Every human being has the inherent right to life. This right shall be protected by law. No one shall be arbitrarily deprived of his life.

2. In countries which have not abolished the death penalty, sentence of death may be imposed only for the most serious crimes in accordance with the law in force at the time of

the commission of the crime and not contrary to the provisions of the present Covenant and to the Convention on the Prevention and Punishment of the Crime of Genocide. This penalty can only be carried out pursuant to a final judgement rendered by a competent court.

3. When deprivation of life constitutes the crime of genocide, it is understood that nothing in this article shall authorize any State Party to the present Covenant to derogate in any way from any obligation assumed under the provisions of the Convention on the Prevention and Punishment of the Crime of Genocide.

4. Anyone sentenced to death shall have the right to seek pardon or commutation of the sentence. Amnesty, pardon or commutation of the sentence of death may be granted in all cases.

5. Sentence of death shall not be imposed for crimes committed by persons below eighteen years of age and shall not be carried out on pregnant women.

6. Nothing in this article shall be invoked to delay or to prevent the abolition of capital punishment by any State Party to the present Covenant.

Article 7

No one shall be subjected to torture or to cruel, inhuman or degrading treatment or punishment. In particular, no one shall be subjected without his free consent to medical or scientific experimentation.

European Convention on Human Rights

ARTICLE 2

1. Everyone's right to life shall be protected by law. No one shall be deprived of his life intentionally save in the execution of a sentence of a court following his conviction of a crime for which this penalty is provided by law.

2. Deprivation of life shall not be regarded as inflicted in contravention of this article when it results from the use of force which is no more than absolutely necessary:

(a) in defence of any person from unlawful violence;
(b) in order to effect a lawful arrest or to prevent escape of a person unlawfully detained;
(c) in action lawfully taken for the purpose of quelling a riot or insurrection.

Article 3

No one shall be subjected to torture or to inhuman or degrading treatment or punishment.

Charter of Fundamental Rights of the European Union

Article 2

Right to life

1. Everyone has the right to life.

2. No one shall be condemned to the death penalty, or executed.

Article 4

Prohibition of torture and inhuman or degrading treatment or punishment

No one shall be subjected to torture or to inhuman or degrading treatment or punishment.

Article 19

Protection in the event of removal, expulsion or extradition

1. Collective expulsions are prohibited.

2. No one may be removed, expelled or extradited to a State where there is a serious risk that he or she would be subjected to the death penalty, torture or other inhuman or degrading treatment or punishment.

American Convention on Human Rights

Article 4. RIGHT TO LIFE.

1. Every person has the right to have his life respected. This right shall be protected by law and, in general, from the moment of conception. No one shall be arbitrarily deprived of his life.

2. In countries that have not abolished the death penalty, it may be imposed only for the most serious crimes and pursuant to a final judgment rendered by a competent court and in accordance with a law establishing such punishment, enacted prior to the commission of the crime. The application of such punishment shall not be extended to crimes to which it does not presently apply.

3. The death penalty shall not be reestablished in states that have abolished it.

4. In no case shall capital punishment be inflicted for political offenses or related common crimes.

5. Capital punishment shall not be imposed upon persons who, at the time the crime was committed, were under 18 years of age or over 70 years of age; nor shall it be applied to pregnant women.

6. Every person condemned to death shall have the right to apply for amnesty, pardon, or commutation of sentence, which may be granted in all cases. Capital punishment shall not be imposed while such a petition is pending decision by the competent authority.

Article 5. RIGHT TO HUMANE TREATMENT.

1. Every person has the right have his physical, mental, and moral integrity respected.

2. No one shall be subjected to torture or to cruel, inhuman, or degrading punishment or treatment. All persons deprived of their liberty shall be treated with respect for the inherent dignity of the human person.

. . . .

Convention Against Torture and Other Cruel, Inhuman or Degrading Treatment or Punishment
Part I

Article 1

1. For the purposes of this Convention, torture means any act by which severe pain or suffering, whether physical or mental, is intentionally inflicted on a person for such purposes as obtaining from him or a third person information or a confession, punishing him for an act he or a third person has committed or is suspected of having committed, or intimidating or coercing him or a third person, or for any reason based on discrimination of any kind, when such pain or suffering is inflicted by or at the instigation of or with the consent or acquiescence of a public official or other person acting in an official capacity.

It does not include pain or suffering arising only from, inherent in or incidental to lawful sanctions.

2. This article is without prejudice to any international instrument or national legislation which does or may contain provisions of wider application.

Article 2

1. Each State Party shall take effective legislative, administrative, judicial or other measures to prevent acts of torture in any territory under its jurisdiction.

2. No exceptional circumstances whatsoever, whether a state of war or a threat or war, internal political instability or any other public emergency, may be invoked as a justification of torture.

3. An order from a superior officer or a public authority may not be invoked as a justification of torture.

Article 3

1. No State Party shall expel, return ("*refouler*") or extradite a person to another State where there are substantial grounds for believing that he would be in danger of being subjected to torture.

2. For the purpose of determining whether there are such grounds, the competent authorities shall take into account all relevant considerations including, where applicable, the existence in the State concerned of a consistent pattern of gross, flagrant or mass violations of human rights.

Article 4

1. Each State Party shall ensure that all acts of torture are offences under its criminal law. The same shall apply to an attempt to commit torture and to an act by any person which constitutes complicity or participation in torture.

2. Each State Party shall make these offences punishable by appropriate penalties which take into account their grave nature.

Article 5

1. Each State Party shall take such measures as may be necessary to establish its jurisdiction over the offences referred to in article 4 in the following cases:

    (a) When the offences are committed in any territory under its jurisdiction or on board a ship or aircraft registered in that State;
    (b) When the alleged offender is a national of that State;
    (c) When the victim os a national of that State if that State considers it appropriate.

2. Each State Party shall likewise take such measures aa may be necessary to establish its jurisdiction over such offences in cases where the alleged offender is present in any territory under its jurisdiction and it does not extradite him pursuant to article 8 to any of the States mentioned in Paragraph 1 of this article.

3. This Convention does not exclude any criminal jurisdiction exercised in accordance with internal law.

Article 6

1. Upon being satisfied, after an examination of information available to it, that the circumstances so warrant, any State Party in whose territory a person alleged to have

committed any offence referred to in article 4 is present, shall take him into custody or take other legal measures to ensure his presence. The custody and other legal measures shall be as provided in the law of that State but may be continued only for such time as is necessary to enable any criminal or extradition proceedings to be instituted.

2. Such State shall immediately make a preliminary inquiry into the facts.

3. Any person in custody pursuant to paragraph 1 of this article shall be assisted in communicating immediately with the nearest appropriate representative of the State of which he is a national, or, if he is a stateless person, to the representative of the State where he usually resides.

4. When a State, pursuant to this article, has taken a person into custody, it shall immediately notify the States referred to in article 5, paragraph 1, of the fact that such person is in custody and of the circumstances which warrant his detention. The State which makes the preliminary inquiry contemplated in paragraph 2 of this article shall promptly report its findings to the said State and shall indicate whether it intends to exercise jurisdiction.

Article 7

1. The State Party in territory under whose jurisdiction a person alleged to have committed any offence referred to in article 4 is found, shall in the cases contemplated in article 5, if it does not extradite him, submit the case to its competent authorities for the purpose of prosecution.

2. These authorities shall take their decision in the same manner as in the case of any ordinary offence of a serious nature under the law of that State. In the cases referred to in article 5, paragraph 2, the standards of evidence required for prosecution and conviction shall in no way be less stringent than those which apply in the cases referred to in article 5, paragraph 1.

3. Any person regarding whom proceedings are brought in connection with any of the offences referred to in article 4 shall be guaranteed fair treatment at all stages of the proceedings.

Article 8

1. The offences referred to in article 4 shall be deemed to be included as extraditable offences in any extradition treaty existing between States Parties. States Parties undertake to include such offences as extraditable offences in every extradition treaty to be concluded between them.

2. If a State Party which makes extradition conditional on the existence of a treaty receives a request for extradition from another State Party with which it has no extradition treaty, it may consider this Convention as the legal basis for extradition in respect of such offenses. Extradition shall be subject to the other conditions provided by the law of the requested State.

3. States Parties which do not make extradition conditional on the existence of a treaty shall recognize such offences as extraditable offences between themselves subject to the conditions provided by the law of the requested state.

4. Such offences shall be treated, for the purpose of extradition between States Parties, as if they had been committed not only in the place in which they occurred but also in the territories of the States required to establish their jurisdiction in accordance with article 5, paragraph 1.

Article 9

1. States Parties shall afford one another the greatest measure of assistance in connection with civil proceedings brought in respect of any of the offences referred to in article 4, including the supply of all evidence at their disposal necessary for the proceedings.

2. States Parties shall carry out their obligations under paragraph 1 of this article in conformity with any treaties on mutual judicial assistance that may exist between them.

Article 10

1. Each State Party shall ensure that education and information regarding the prohibition against torture are fully included in the training of law enforcement personnel, civil or military, medical personnel, public officials and other persons who may be involved in the custody, interrogation or treatment of any individual subjected to any form of arrest, detention or imprisonment.

2. Each State Party shall include this prohibition in the rules or instructions issued in regard to the duties and functions of any such persons.

Article 11

Each State Party shall keep under systematic review interrogation rules, instructions, methods and practices as well as arrangements for the custody and treatment of persons subjected to any form of arrest, detention or imprisonment in any territory under its jurisdiction, with a view to preventing any cases of torture.

Article 12

Each State Party shall ensure that its competent authorities proceed to a prompt and impartial investigation, wherever there is reasonable ground to believe that an act of torture has been committee in any territory under its jurisdiction.

Article 13

Each State Party shall ensure that any individual who alleges he has been subjected to torture in any territory under its jurisdiction has the right to complain to and to have his case promptly and impartially examined its competent authorities. Steps shall be taken to ensure that the complainant and witnesses are protected against all ill-treatment or intimidation as a consequence of his complaint or any evidence given.

Article 14

1. Each State Party shall ensure in its legal system that the victim of an act of torture obtains redress and has an enforceable right to fair and adequate compensation including the means for as full rehabilitation as possible. In the event of the death of the victim as a result of an act of torture, his dependents shall be entitled to compensation.

2. Nothing in this article shall affect any right of the victim or other person to compensation which may exist under national law.

Article 15

Each State Party shall ensure that any statement which is established to have been made as a result of torture shall not be invoked as evidence in any proceedings, except against a person accused of torture as evidence that the statement was made.

Article 16

1. Each State Party shall undertake to prevent in any territory under its jurisdiction other acts of cruel, inhuman or degrading treatment or punishment which do not amount to torture as defined in article 1, when such acts are committed by or at the instigation of or with the consent or acquiescence of a public official or other person acting in an official capacity. In particular, the obligations contained in articles 10, 11, 12 and 13 shall apply with the substitution for references to torture or references to other forms of cruel, inhuman or degrading treatment or punishment.

2. The provisions of this Convention are without prejudice to the provisions of any other international instrument or national law which prohibit cruel, inhuman or degrading treatment or punishment or which relate to extradition or expulsion.

Inter-American Convention to Prevent and Punish Torture

Article 2

For the purposes of this Convention, torture shall be understood to be any act intentionally performed whereby physical or mental pain or suffering is inflicted on a person for purposes of criminal investigation, as a means of intimidation, as personal punishment, as a preventive measure, as a penalty, or for any other purpose. Torture shall also be understood to be the use of methods upon a person intended to obliterate the personality of the victim or to diminish his physical or mental capacities, even if they do not cause physical pain or mental anguish.

The concept of torture shall not include physical or mental pain or suffering that is inherent in or solely the consequence of lawful measures, provided that they do not include the performance of the acts or use of the methods referred to in this article.

Article 3

The following shall be held guilty of the crime of torture:

(a) A public servant or employee who acting in that capacity orders, instigates or induces the use of torture, or who directly commits it or who, being able to prevent it, fails to do so.

(b) A person who at the instigation of a public servant or employee mentioned in subparagraph (a) orders, instigates or induces the use of torture, directly commits it or is an accomplice thereto.

African [Banjul] Charter on Human and Peoples' Rights

Article 4

Human beings are inviolable. Every human being shall be entitled to respect for his life and the integrity of his person. No one may be arbitrarily deprived of this right.

Article 5

Every individual shall have the right to the respect of the dignity inherent in a human being and to the recognition of his legal status. All forms of exploitation and degradation of man particularly slavery, slave trade, torture, cruel, inhuman or degrading punishment and treatment shall be prohibited.

Inter-American Convention on the Prevention, Punishment and Eradication of Violence Against Women

Article I

For the purposes of this Convention, violence against women shall be understood as any act or conduct, based on gender, which causes death or physical, sexual or psychological harm or suffering to women, whether in the public or the private sphere.

Article 2

Violence against women shall be understood to include physical, sexual and psychological violence:

    a. that occurs within the family or domestic unit or within any other interpersonal relationship, whether or not the perpetrator shares or has shared the same residence with the woman, including, among others, rape, battery and sexual abuse;

    b. that occurs in the community and is perpetrated by any person, including, among others, rape, sexual abuse, torture, trafficking in persons, forced prostitution, kidnapping and sexual harassment in the workplace, as well as in educational institutions, health facilities or any other place; and

    c. that is perpetrated or condoned by the state or its agents regardless of where it occurs.

CHAPTER II

RIGHTS PROTECTED

Article 3

Every woman has the right to be free from violence in both the public and private spheres.

U.S. Constitution

Amendment V

No person shall be held to answer for a capital, or otherwise infamous crime, unless on a presentment or indictment of a Grand Jury, except in cases arising in the land or naval forces, or in the Militia, when in actual service in time of War or public danger; . . . nor be deprived of life, liberty, or property, without due process of law. . . .

Amendment VIII

Excessive bail shall not be required, nor excessive fines imposed, nor cruel and unusual punishments inflicted.

Amendment XIV

Section 1. . . . No State shall make or enforce any law which shall abridge the privileges or immunities of citizens of the United States; nor shall any State deprive any person of life, liberty, or property, without due process of law. . . .

～

Torture; Cruel, Inhuman, Degrading Treatment or Punishment; and Sexual Violence

Ireland v. United Kingdom
European Court of Human Rights
25 Eur. Ct. H.R. (1978)
2 E.H.R.R. 25 (1979–80)

. . . .

FACTS:

I. THE EMERGENCY SITUATION AND ITS BACKGROUND:

11. The tragic and lasting crisis in Northern Ireland lies at the root of the present case. In order to combat what the respondent Government describe as 'the longest and most violent terrorist campaign witnessed in either part of the island of Ireland', the authorities in Northern Ireland exercised from August 1971 until December 1975 a series of extrajudicial powers of arrest, detention and internment. The proceedings in this case concern the scope and the operation in practice of those measures as well as the alleged ill-treatment of persons thereby deprived of their liberty.

. . . .

96. .... [Fourteen suspects in Northern Ireland] were submitted to a form of 'interrogation in depth' which involved the combined application of five particular techniques. These methods, sometimes termed 'disorientation' or 'sensory deprivation' techniques . . . consisted of the following:

(a) wall-standing: forcing the detainees to remain for periods of some hours in a 'stress position', described by those who underwent it as being 'spreadeagled against the wall, with their fingers put high above the head against the wall, the legs spread apart and the feet back, causing them to stand on their toes with the weight of the body mainly on the fingers';
(b) hooding: putting a black or navy coloured bag over the detainees' heads and, at least initially, keeping it there all the time except during interrogation;
(c) subjection to noise: pending their interrogations, holding the detainees in a room where there was a continuous loud and hissing noise;
(d) deprivation of sleep: pending their interrogations, depriving the detainees of sleep;
(e) deprivation of food and drink: subjecting the detainees to a reduced diet during their stay at the centre and pending interrogations.

. . . .

97. From the start, it has been conceded by the respondent Government that the use of the five techniques was authorised at 'high level'. Although never committed to writing or authorised in any official document, the techniques had been orally taught to members of the RUC by the English Intelligence Centre as at seminar held in April 1971.

98. The two operations of interrogation in depth by means of the five techniques led to the obtaining of a considerable quantity of intelligence information, including the identification of 700 members of both IRA factions and the discovery of individual responsibility for about 85 previously unexplained criminal incidents.

. . . .

102. At the hearing before the Court on 8 February 1977, the United Kingdom Attorney-General made the following declaration:

> The Government of the United Kingdom have considered the question of the use of the 'five techniques' with very great care and with particular regard to Article 3 of the Convention. They now give this unqualified undertaking, that the 'five techniques' will not in any circumstances be reintroduced as an aid to interrogation.

103. The Irish Government referred to the Commission eight cases of persons submitted to the five techniques during interrogation at the unidentified centre or centres between 11 and 17 August 1971. A further case, that of T22, considered in the Commission's report in the context of Palace Barracks, concerned the use of the five techniques in October 1971. The Commission examined as illustrative the cases of T6 and T13, which were among the 11 cases investigated by the Compton Committee.

104. . . . . The Commission found no physical injury to have resulted from the application of the five techniques as such, but loss of weight by the two case-witnesses and acute psychiatric symptoms developed by them during interrogation were recorded in the medical and other evidence. The Commission was unable to establish the exact degree of any psychiatric after-effects produced on T6 and T13, but on the general level it was satisfied that some psychiatric after-effects in certain of the 14 persons subjected to the techniques could not be excluded.

. . . .

C. QUESTIONS CONCERNING THE MERITS

162. As was emphasised by the Commission, ill-treatment must attain a minimum level of severity if it is to fall within the scope of Article 3. The assessment of this minimum is, in the nature of things, relative; it depends on all the circumstances of the case, such as the duration of the treatment, its physical or mental effects and, in some cases, the sex, age and state of health of the victim, etc.

163. The Convention prohibits in absolute terms torture and inhuman or degrading treatment or punishment, irrespective of the victim's conduct. Unlike most of the substantive clauses of the Convention and of Protocols 1 and 4, Article 3 makes no provision for exceptions and, under Article 15(2), there can be no derogation therefrom even in the event of a public emergency threatening the life of the nation.

. . . .

(a) The 'five techniques'

165. the facts concerning the five techniques are summarised at paragraphs 96–104 and 106–107 above. In the Commission's estimation, those facts constituted a practice not only of inhuman and degrading treatment but also of torture. The applicant Government ask for confirmation of this opinion which is not contested before the Court by the respondent Government.

166. The police used the five techniques on 14 persons in 1971, [ ]. Although never authorised in writing in any official document, the five techniques were taught orally by the English Intelligence Centre to members of the RUC at a seminar held in April 1971. There was accordingly a practice.

167. The five techniques were applied in combination, with premeditation and for hours at a stretch; they caused, if not actual bodily injury, at least intense physical and

mental suffering to the persons subjected thereto and also led to acute psychiatric disturbances during interrogation. They accordingly fell into the category of inhuman treatment within the meaning of Article 3. The techniques were also degrading since they were such as to arouse in their victims feelings of fear, anguish and inferiority capable of humiliating and debasing them and possibly breaking their physical or moral resistance.

On these two points, the Court is of the same view as the Commission.

In order to determine whether the five techniques should also be qualified as torture, the Court must have regard to the distinction, embodied in Article 3, between this notion and that of inhuman or degrading treatment.

In the Court's view, this distinction derives principally from a difference in the intensity of the suffering inflicted.

The Court considers in fact that, whilst there exists on the one hand violence which is to be condemned both on moral grounds and also in most cases under the domestic law of the Contracting States but which does not fall within Article 3 of the Convention, it appears on the other hand that it was the intention that the Convention, with its distinction between 'torture' and 'inhuman or degrading treatment', should by the first of these terms attach a special stigma to deliberate inhuman treatment causing very serious and cruel suffering.

Moreover, this seems to be the thinking lying behind Article 1 *in fine* of Resolution 3452 (XXX) adopted by the General Assembly of the United Nations on 9 December, 1975, which declares: 'Torture constitutes an aggravated and deliberate form of cruel, inhuman or degrading treatment or punishment'.

Although the five techniques, as applied in combination, undoubtedly amounted to inhuman and degrading treatment, although their object was the extraction of confessions, the naming of others and/or information and although they were used systematically, they did not occasion suffering of the particular intensity and cruelty implied by the word torture as so understood.

168. The Court concludes that recourse to the five techniques amounted to a practice of inhuman and degrading treatment, which practice was in breach of Article 3.

    . . . .

[In addition to the "five techniques," the European Court ruled on a number of other practices raised in the Irish Government's petition. The Court thus found that large numbers of people detained and interrogated at a location called Police Barracks were subject to various forms of violence, including severe beatings. The Court determined that although the large number of incidents illustrated a practice[1], and constituted inhuman treatment, it did not rise to the level of torture:]

174. . . . The evidence before the Court reveals that, at the time in question, quite a large number of those held in custody at Palace Barracks were subjected to violence by members of the RUC. This violence, which was repeated violence occurring in the same place and taking similar forms, did not amount merely to isolated incidents; it definitely constituted a practice. It also led to intense suffering and to physical injury which on occasion was substantial; it thus fell into the category of inhuman treatment.

---

[1] Article 3, ECHR, does not require a showing of a general practice in order to find a violation. The Court in this case limited its inquiry to violations that constituted a general practice rather than individual cases, since that was the claim brought by the Irish Government before the Commission. *See* §157.

According to the applicant Government, the violence in question should also be classified, in some cases, as torture.

On the basis of the data before it, the Court does not share this view. Admittedly, the acts complained of often occurred during interrogation and, to this extent, were aimed at extracting confessions, the naming of others and/or information, but the severity of the suffering that they were capable of causing did not attain the particular level inherent in the notion of torture as understood by the Court (see §167 above).

. . . .

[The Court also found that forced exercises "which caused considerable strain and hardship," and consisted of "sitting on the floor with the legs outstretched and the hands raised high above, or clasped behind, the head, [or] . . . kneeling on the floor with the forehead touching the ground and the hands clasped behind the back" did not constitute a violation of Article 3. *Id.* at §125. The Court noted that while the practices in question "involved some degree of compulsion and must have caused hardship, they were the result of lack of judgment rather than an intention to hurt or degrade." *Id.* at §181. Regarding the requested remedies, the Court noted:]

186. In a letter dated 5 January 1977, the applicant Government requested the Court to order that the respondent Government

> – refrain from reintroducing the five techniques, as a method of interrogation or otherwise;
> – proceed as appropriate, under the criminal law of the United Kingdom and the relevant disciplinary code, against those members of the security forces who have committed acts in breach of Article 3 referred to in the Commission's findings and conclusions, and against those who condoned or tolerated them.

At the hearings, the applicant Government withdrew the first request following the solemn undertaking given on behalf of the United Kingdom Government on 8 February 1977 (see §153 above); on the other hand, the second request was maintained.

187. The Court does not have to consider in these proceedings whether its functions extend, in certain circumstances, to addressing consequential orders to Contracting States. In the present case, the Court finds that the sanctions available to it do not include the power to direct one of those States to institute criminal law or disciplinary proceedings in accordance with its domestic law.

. . . .

[Judge Zekia dissented from the Court's rejection of the Commission's finding of torture. He argued for the introduction of a subjective test to a determination of whether a particular practice amounts to torture, and thus greater deference to the Commission as fact-finder:]

With respect, I subscribe to the main part of the judgment of the Court. I maintain, however, a different view as to the notion and concept of the word "torture" occurring in Article 3 of the Convention. Moreover, I entertain a lot of doubt whether the Court is justified in setting aside a unanimous conclusion of the Commission in respect of torture which has not been contested by the representatives of the two High Contracting States who took part in the proceedings before the Court.

. . . .

A. Torture

Admittedly the word "torture" included in Article 3 of the Convention is not capable of an exact and comprehensive definition. It is undoubtedly an aggravated form of inhuman treatment causing intense physical and/or mental suffering. Although the degree of intensity and the length of such suffering constitute the basis elements of torture, a lot of other relevant factors had to be taken into account. Such as: the nature of ill-treatment inflicted, the means and methods employed, the repetition and duration of such treatment, the age, sex and health condition of the person exposed to it, the likelihood that such treatment might injure the physical, mental, and psychological condition of the persons exposed and whether the injuries inflicted caused serious consequences for short or long duration are all relevant matters to be considered together and arrive at a conclusion whether torture has been committed.

It seems to me permissible, in ascertaining whether torture or inhuman treatment has been committed or not, to apply not only the objective test but also the subjective test.

As an example I can refer to the case of an elderly sick man who is exposed to a harsh treatment – after being given several blows and beaten to the floor, he is dragged and kicked on the floor for several hours. I would say without hesitation that the poor man has been tortured. If such treatment is applied on a wrestler or even a young athlete, I would hesitate a lot to describe it as an inhuman treatment and I might regard it as a mere rough handling. Another example: if a mother, for interrogation, is separated from her suckling baby by keeping them apart in adjoining rooms and the baby, on account of hunger, starts yelling for hours within the hearing of the mother and she is not allowed to attend her baby, again I should say both the mother and the baby have been subjected to inhuman treatment, the mother being agonized and the baby being deprived of the urgent attention of the mother. Neither the mother nor the child has been assaulted.

. . . .

I do not share the view that extreme intensity of physical or mental suffering is a requisite for a case of ill-treatment to amount to "torture" within the purport and object of Article 3 of the Convention. The nature of torture admits gradation in its intensity, in its severity and in the methods adopted. It is, therefore, primarily the duty and responsibility of the authority conducting the enquiries from close quarters, after taking into account all the surrounding circumstances, evidence and material available, to say whether in a particular case inhuman ill-treatment reached the degree of torture. In other words, this is a finding of fact for the competent authority dealing with the case in the first instance and which, for reasons we given hereunder, we should not interfere with.

. . . .

[In addition to Judge Zekia, Judge O'Donoghue (who was a member of the subcommission that investigated *The Greek Case*) dissented, also arguing that the Court should have given more deference to the unanimous finding of the Commission. Judge Fitzmaurice wrote a lengthy dissent explaining why he voted against the holding that the five techniques constitute inhuman or degrading treatment. While not condoning the use of the "five techniques," Judge Fitzmaurice concluded that, even when used in concert, they did not rise to the level of "inhuman" or "degrading" treatment. Finally, Judges Evrigenis and Matscher wrote separate opinions to explain their dissent from the holding that the five techniques did not constitute torture. Judge Matscher offered the following alternative definition of torture:]

According to the majority of the Court in the present case, the distinguishing criterion between inhuman treatment and torture lies primarily in the intensity of suffering imposed. I regret that I cannot accept that interpretation.

My position is close to that of the unanimous opinion of the Commission in the present case [ ], which rests on the interpretation of the essential elements of Article 3 of the Convention as developed in previous cases, particularly in *The Greek Case* [ ]. In my view, the distinguishing test of the concept of torture is the systematic, calculated (and so deliberate) and prolonged infliction of treatment causing physical or psychological suffering of a certain intensity, the aims including the extraction of admissions, the obtaining of information or simply the breaking of a person's will in order to force him to do something which he would not otherwise do, or even to cause suffering to a person for other reasons (sadism, aggravation of a penalty, etc).

There is no doubt that the word torture as it is used in Article 3 can only be used when treatment inflicted on a person is such as to cause in him physical or psychological suffering of a certain grievousness. But I consider the intensity factor to be supplementary to the systematic: the more the method is studied and refined, the less sharp will be the pain (physical pain, in the first place) which it needs to cause in order to attain its purpose. One is aware of those modern methods of torture which, superficially, are quite different from the brutal and primitive methods which were used in the past. In that sense, torture is in no wise inhuman treatment raised to a greater degree. On the contrary, one can think of brutality causing much more painful bodily suffering but which does not thereby necessarily fall within the concept of torture.

Besides, this concept of torture, which I adopt, does not differ in its essentials from those which have been developed recently by various international organs, particularly in the United Nations. (See, for example, Art 1 of Resolution 3452 (xxx), adopted by the General Assembly, 9 December 1975.) It seeks solely to emphasise certain of the elements also adopted by the latter and which appear to me to be more significant.

As regards the facts unanimously found by the Commission and by the Court [ ], the five techniques, as they were used in unidentified interrogation centres, represented a very studied and refined system having the aim of obtaining information or admissions. Used cumulatively, with premeditation and for many hours at a time, they caused to those subjected to them, if not real injury, at least severe psychological and mental suffering; in addition, they caused in them acute psychological disturbances during the interrogation. They thus constitute a typical example of torture within the meaning of Article 3 of the Convention.

∽

QUESTIONS & COMMENTS

(1) Did the Court adopt the purposive definition of torture as set forth by the Commission in *The Greek Case*?

(2) What role does an alleged violator's intent play in determining whether an act constitutes cruel, inhuman, or degrading treatment (CIDT) or torture?

(3) The difference between torture and CIDT is important not only as a measure of determining damages but also for building political pressure. Allegations of torture are

more effective than those of CIDT in linking economic assistance with human rights violations.

(4) Shortly after its decision in *Ireland v. United Kingdom*, the European Court of Human Rights found that the "birching" of a 15-year-old schoolboy by the police at a police station amounted to "degrading," but not "inhuman," "punishment," and thus violated Article 3 of the European Convention. *Tyrer v. United Kingdom*, 26 Eur. Ct. H.R. (ser. A) (1978).

(5) In *Yagiz v. Turkey*, 22 E.H.R.R. 573 (1996), the European Commission of Human Rights unanimously found that a woman who was sexually assaulted and beaten on the soles of her feet while naked and blindfolded, was a victim of torture. The Commission concluded that the violations constituted torture in part because of the petitioner's "cruel and extreme suffering," including psychological trauma and mental disorder. The European Court of Human Rights subsequently dismissed the case, since the violations took place prior to Turkey's agreement to be subject to the Court's jurisdiction.

(6) These decisions involved direct state responsibility for torture or cruel, inhuman, or degrading treatment performed by its officials. Under a number of human rights treaties, a State is obligated not only to ensure that an individual is not subject to torture or CIDT but also to refrain from returning an individual to a country where he may be subjected to such treatment.[2] In *Mutombo v. Switzerland, Mutombo v. Switzerland*, Communication No. 13/1993, U.N. Doc. A/49/44 at 45 (1994), the Committee Against Torture[3] found that Switzerland had an obligation not to return to Zaire an asylum seeker who "had substantial grounds for believing that he would be in danger of being subjected to torture." At the time of this decision, Zaire was not a party to the Convention Against Torture, and thus, as the Committee notes in its decision, the petitioner could only take advantage of the convention protections outside of Zaire.

(7) In 2004, photographs of Iraqi detainees surfaced showing that U.S. military personnel had used a variety of inhumane and degrading methods of "softening up" the detainees for interrogation. Such methods included prolonged standing, hooding, the placement of naked detainees in sexually degrading positions, putting women's underwear on their heads, the use of guard dogs, attaching electrical wires to their bodies, and smearing feces on their bodies. Other reported methods included "waterboarding" during which the detainee is placed prone on a board and submersed in water in order to instill the fear of imminent death by drowning. Which of these methods constitute torture? inhumane treatment? degrading treatment?

(8) U.S. law prohibits torture under 18 U.S.C. §114. Torture is defined under 18 U.S.C. §2340 as follows:

> (1) "torture" means an act committed by a person acting under the color of law specifically intended to inflict severe physical or mental pain or suffering (other than pain or suffering

---

[2] *See, e.g.*, Art. 3, Convention Against Torture; Art. 33(1), Convention Relating to the Status of Refugees.

[3] The UN Committee Against Torture is the body established to implement the provisions of the Convention Against Torture and Other Cruel, Inhuman or Degrading Treatment or Punishment. A state must make a declaration pursuant to Article 22 of the Convention before the Committee has the authority to entertain publicly an individual petition against that State. Unlike other similar treaty-monitoring bodies, however, the Committee Against Torture has the power under Article 20 to initiate a confidential inquiry concerning an allegation of torture.

incidental to lawful sanctions) upon another person within his custody or physical control; (2) "severe mental pain or suffering" means the prolonged mental harm caused by or resulting from – (A) the intentional infliction or threatened infliction of severe physical pain or suffering; (B) the administration or application, or threatened administration or application, of mind-altering substances or other procedures calculated to disrupt profoundly the senses or the personality; (C) the threat of imminent death; or (D) the threat that another person will imminently be subjected to death, severe physical pain or suffering, or the administration or application of mind-altering substances or other procedures calculated to disrupt profoundly the senses or personality; ....

Note that Section 2340 does not address cruel, inhuman, or degrading treatment. The Senate earlier had conditioned its consent to the Convention Against Torture by insisting on a reservation "that the United States considers itself bound by the obligation under Article 16 to prevent 'cruel, inhuman or degrading treatment or punishment,' only insofar as the term 'cruel, inhuman or degrading treatment or punishment' means the cruel, unusual and inhumane treatment or punishment prohibited by the Fifth, Eighth, and/or Fourteenth Amendments to the Constitution of the United States." U.S. reservations, declarations, and understandings, Convention Against Torture and Other Cruel, Inhuman or Degrading Treatment or Punishment, Cong. Rec. S17486–01 (daily ed., Oct. 27, 1990).

Did the United States fail to comply with the Convention Against Torture and other international law prohibiting cruel, inhuman, or degrading treatment by failing to also provide criminal penalties for such treatment?

Hernández Rivas v. El Salvador
Inter-American Commission on Human Rights
Case 10.911, Report No. 7/94, Inter-Am.C.H.R.
OEA/Ser.L/V/II.85 Doc. 9 rev. at 188 (1994)

BACKGROUND

1. On June 25, 1991, the Inter-American Commission on Human Rights received a petition based on the following:

At approximately 4:00 p.m. on March 30, 1990, Flor de María Hernández Rivas, age 14, was taken by force by National Guardsmen who accused her of having participated in the November 1989 FMLN offensive.

That day the young girl was near the San Miguelito Market in San Salvador when National Guardsmen patrolling the area apprehended her and forced her into a vehicle, threatening to kill her. Even though the young girl protested that she was innocent and even though they had no warrant to arrest and hold her in custody, the agents took her to the National Guard's Central headquarters where they blindfolded her, put a hood over her head, mauled her breasts and hit her on the head to force her to cooperate with them. When she asked for water, they told her she would get no water until she told them the "truth." When she refused to acknowledge the charges made against her, electric shocks were applied to her breasts.

The next day, March 31, she was transferred to a small, cold cell, where she spent the entire day listening to the screams of others being tortured. She was given no food. The only time she was taken from the room was when she was fingerprinted.

On April 1, she was removed from that cell and taken elsewhere, where she was again physically and verbally abused. At one time, she was taken to yet another room, where three men raped her. The questioning lasted until April 2, at which point the guards returned her to her cell and gave her drugs to "ease the pain." She did not take the drugs, however, because she was afraid. That afternoon, they removed the blindfold, returned her clothes and released her, but not without threatening her. The guards told her they would kill her if they picked her up again.

On the day she was taken, her mother, María Amparo Hernández Atlas, went to the National Guard to inquire about her daughter. Although the authorities' first reaction was to deny that the young girl had been taken into custody, they later told her that her daughter was "being investigated."

2. On July 2, 1991, the Inter-American Commission began processing the case and requested the Government of El Salvador to supply information on the material facts in the petition and any other information to apprise the Commission of the case history and to enable it to determine whether the remedies under domestic had been exhausted. The Government was given 90 days in which to reply.

. . . .

5. On August 20, 1992, the Government of El Salvador sent a note of reply to the Commission, with regard to the following:

Apprehended on March 30 by the National Guard in this city [San Salvador] on suspicion of being a terrorist; released on April 2, 1990, and turned over to the Human Rights Commission.

Since none of the Hernández Rivas child's rights were violated and because she continues to enjoy full exercise of her rights, the Government of El Salvador respectfully requests that this case be closed.

. . . .

ANALYSIS

. . . .

2. *Of the Commission's competence in this case*:

a. The Commission is competent in the instant case because it concerns violations of rights recognized in the American Convention on Human Rights, chiefly Article 5 guaranteeing the right to humane treatment; Article 7 on the right to personal liberty, Article 8 on the right to a fair trial, Article 19 on the rights of the child, and Article 25 on judicial protection, as provided in Article 44 of that Convention, of which El Salvador is a State party.

. . . .

3. *On the content of the petition*:

a. Despite the fact that more than three years have passed since the events transpired and despite the seriousness of the charges, the Government of El Salvador has not provided a satisfactory response to the specific facts brought by the petitioner concerning the reasons for and lawfulness of the arrest of the minor Hernández Rivas, the charges of mistreatment during her confinement, or the investigations conducted into those complaints.

. . . .

c. In the instant case, the victim is a minor and must be given all the necessary guarantees of due process and the special treatment that is her right as a minor. The United National Convention on the Rights of the Child, which El Salvador signed on January 26, 1990 and ratified on 20 July of that year, making it a State Party, prescribes the following in this regard:

Article 37: States Parties shall ensure that: (a) No child shall be subjected to torture or other cruel, inhuman or degrading treatment of punishment (...)

Article 40:

1. States Parties recognize the right of every child alleged as, accused of, or recognized as having infringed the penal law to be treated in a manner consistent with the promotion of the child's sense of dignity and worth, which reinforces the child's respect for the human rights and fundamental freedoms of others and which takes into account the child's age and the desirability of promoting the child's re-integration and the child's assuming a constructive role in society.

2. To this end, and having regard to the relevant provisions of international instruments, States Parties shall, in particular ensure that:

a) No child shall be alleged as, be accused as, or recognized as having infringed the penal law by reasons of acts or omissions which were not prohibited by national or international law at the time they were committed;

b) Every child alleged as or accused of having infringed the penal law has at least the following guarantees:

i) to be presumed innocent until proven guilty according to law;

ii) to be informed promptly and directly of the charges against him or her, and if appropriate through his or her parents or legal guardian, and to have legal or other appropriate assistance in the preparation and presentation of his or her defense;

iii) to have the matter determined without delay by the competent, independent and impartial authority or judicial body in a fair hearing according to law, in the presence of legal or other appropriate assistance and, unless it is considered not to be in the best interest of the child, in particular, taking into account his or her age or situation, his or her parents or legal guardians;

iv) not to be compelled to give testimony or to confess guilt; to examine or have examined adverse witnesses and to obtain the participation and examination of witnesses on his or her behalf under conditions of equality;

v) if considered to have infringed the penal law, to have this decision and any measures imposed in consequence thereof reviewed by a higher competent, independent and impartial authority or judicial body according to law;

vi) to have the free assistance of an interpreter if the child cannot understand or speak the language used;

vii) to have his or her privacy fully respected at all stages of the proceedings.

d. A brief review of the petition and of the communications received from the Government of El Salvador makes it apparent that the above rules were not respected in the instant case. To make matters worse, Salvadoran authorities informed neither the International Committee of the Red Cross nor any other humanitarian agency to be present to examine the child's condition at the time of her arrest, while she was in custody and at the time of her release, for effective and reliable confirmation of the physical and psychological state of Flor de María de Hernández Rivas.

. . . .

CONCLUSIONS:

1. The Inter-American Commission on Human Rights finds that the Government of El Salvador is responsible for the facts denounced in the communication of June 25, 1991, to the effect that on March 30, 1990, at approximately 4:00 p.m., Flor de María Hernández Rivas, age 14, was violently seized by National Guardsmen, who accused her of having participated in the November 1989 FMLN offense. Denied the most elementary judicial guarantees and with no regard for her status as a minor, she was subjected to physical and psychological mistreatment while in custody at National Guard Headquarters. Before being released on April 2, she was threatened by her captors.

2. The Commission further finds that the Government of El Salvador has violated the American Convention on Human Rights, chiefly Article 5, which guarantees the right to humane treatment; Article 7, on the right to personal liberty; Article 8, on the right to a fair trial; Article 19 on the rights of children, and Article 25 on judicial protection, in relation to Article 1.1 of that Convention, of which El Salvador is a State Party.

3. The Commission makes the following recommendation to the Government of El Salvador:

> a. That it conduct an exhaustive, rapid and impartial investigation into the facts denounced to identify those who arbitrarily arrested and tortured the child Flor María Hernández Rivas and those National Guardsmen who threatened her, and that they be brought to trial so that they may receive the punishment that such serious conduct demands.

> b. That the consequences of the situation caused by the violation of the aforementioned rights be redressed and that the aggrieved party be paid a fair compensation.

> c. That the necessary measures be taken to avoid a recurrence of similar events hereinafter, particularly the following measures:

> – That the law clearly and unequivocally proscribe torture and other cruel, inhuman and degrading punishment or treatment, and establish punishment for the guilty parties and compensation for victims, making allowance for aggravating circumstances if the victim is a minor.

> – That respect for the provisions of Article 19 on the rights of children to the American Convention on Human Rights and Article 40 of the Convention on the Rights of the Child be demanded; those provisions are intended to provide real and effective protection for the rights of minors, particularly minors involved in criminal proceedings.

4. It invites the Government of El Salvador to accept the jurisdiction of the Inter-American Court of Human Rights in this specific case which is the subject of this report.

5. To publish this report pursuant to Article 48 of the Commission's Regulations and Article 53.1 of the Convention, because the Government of El Salvador did not adopt measures to correct the situation denounced within the time period.

∾

QUESTIONS & COMMENTS

(1)   While women have been subject to sexual violence by state officials, both in war and peace, much sexual violence occurs in what is called the "private" sphere – that is, it is violence perpetrated by one private individual against another.[4] International human rights law applies primarily to acts of state officials. This does not mean that nonstate actors cannot violate international human rights law. For example, the laws prohibiting genocide, war crimes, and crimes against humanity specifically apply to state and nonstate actors. Furthermore, states are obligated to ensure that the protections provided under international human rights law are provided to persons within their jurisdiction. A state's failure to protect an individual from human rights violations by nonstate actors may thus violate international human rights law. The Inter-American Court of Human Rights has stated that "[a]n illegal act which violates human rights and which is initially not directly imputable to a state (for example, because it is the act of a private person or because the person responsible has not been identified) can lead to international responsibility of the State, not because of the act itself, but because of the lack of due diligence to prevent the violation or to respond to it as required by the Convention" (*Velásquez Rodríguez v. Honduras* at §172, reproduced in Section 2.3.1).[5]

A major problem facing advocates for women's rights is the failure of states to investigate or even acknowledge acts of violence against women. Thus many states do not legally recognize that a husband can rape his wife. However, the European Court of Human Rights has held that spousal immunity for rape is incompatible with the ECHR, and the OAS has adopted a convention that recognizes the unlawfulness of spousal rape.[6] Some states require that a victim produce eyewitnesses to prove a rape, effectively making almost all rapes unprovable. Many states do not adequately investigate and prosecute acts of violence against women.

General Comment 20 (Article 7)
UN Human Rights Committee
(Forty-fourth session, 1992)
Compilation of General Comments and General Recommendations
Adopted by Human Rights Treaty Bodies
U.N. Doc. HRI\GEN\1\Rev. 1 at 30 (1994)

. . . .

1. This general comment replaces general comment 7 (the sixteenth session, 1982) reflecting and further developing it.

---

[4] On the public/private distinction and violence against women, see Karen Engle, *After the Collapse of the Public/Private Distinction: Strategizing Women's Rights*, in Reconceiving Reality: Women and International Law 143 (Dorinda Dallmeyer ed., 1993).

[5] On state responsibility for private acts of violence against women in the Inter-American system, *see* Ewing, *Establishing State Responsibility for Private Acts of Violence Against Women under the American Convention on Human Rights*, 26 Colum. Hum. Rts. L. Rev. 751 (1995).

[6] *See S.W./C.R. v. United Kingdom*, 355-B-C Eur. Ct. H.R (ser. A) (1996); Inter-American Convention on the Prevention, Punishment and Eradication of Violence Against Women ("Convention of Belem Do Para"), 9 June 1994, art. 2 (a), 33 I.L.M. 1534 (1994).

2. The aim of the provisions of article 7 of the International Covenant on Civil and Political Rights is to protect both the dignity and the physical and mental integrity of the individual. It is the duty of the State party to afford everyone protection through legislative and other measures as may be necessary against the acts prohibited by article 7, whether inflicted by people acting in their official capacity, outside their official capacity or in a private capacity. The prohibition in article 7 is complemented by the positive requirements of article 10, paragraph 1, of the Covenant, which stipulates that "All persons deprived of their liberty shall be treated with humanity and with respect for the inherent dignity of the human person".

3. The text of article 7 allows of no limitation. The Committee also reaffirms that, even in situations of public emergency such as those referred to in article 4 of the Covenant, no derogation from the provision of article 7 is allowed and its provisions must remain in force. The Committee likewise observes that no justification or extenuating circumstances may be invoked to excuse a violation of article 7 for any reasons, including those based on an order from a superior officer or public authority.

4. The Covenant does not contain any definition of the concepts covered by article 7, nor does the Committee consider it necessary to draw up a list of prohibited acts or to establish sharp distinctions between the different kinds of punishment or treatment; the distinctions depend on the nature, purpose and severity of the treatment applied.

5. The prohibition in article 7 relates not only to acts that cause physical pain but also to acts that cause mental suffering to the victim. In the Committee's view, moreover, the prohibition must extend to corporal punishment, including excessive chastisement ordered as punishment for a crime or as an educative or disciplinary measure. It is appropriate to emphasize in this regard that article 7 protects, in particular, children, pupils and patients in teaching and medical institutions.

6. The Committee notes that prolonged solitary confinement of the detained or imprisoned person may amount to acts prohibited by article 7. As the Committee has stated in its general comment No. 6 (16), article 6 of the Covenant refers generally to abolition of the death penalty in terms that strongly suggest that abolition is desirable. Moreover, when the death penalty is applied by a State party for the most serious crimes, it must not only be strictly limited in accordance with article 6 but it must be carried out in such a way as to cause the least possible physical and mental suffering.

7. Article 7 expressly prohibits medical or scientific experimentation without the free consent of the person concerned. The Committee notes that the reports of States parties generally contain little information on this point. More attention should be given to the need and means to ensure observance of this provision. The Committee also observes that special protection in regard to such experiments is necessary in the case of persons not capable of giving valid consent, and in particular those under any form of detention or imprisonment. Such persons should not be subjected to any medical or scientific experimentation that may be detrimental to their health.

. . . .

9. In the view of the Committee, States parties must not expose individuals to the danger of torture or cruel, inhuman or degrading treatment or punishment upon return to another country by way of their extradition, expulsion or *refoulement*. States parties should indicate in their reports what measures they have adopted to that end.

10. The Committee should be informed how States parties disseminate, to the population at large, relevant information concerning the ban on torture and the treatment

prohibited by article 7. Enforcement personnel, medical personnel, police officers and any other persons involved in the custody or treatment of any individual subjected to any form of arrest, detention or imprisonment must receive appropriate instruction and training. States parties should inform the Committee of the instruction and training given and the way in which the prohibition of article 7 forms an integral part of the operational rules and ethical standards to be followed by such persons.

11. In addition to describing steps to provide the general protection against acts prohibited under article 7 to which anyone is entitled, the State party should provide detailed information on safeguards for the special protection of particularly vulnerable persons. It should be noted that keeping under systematic review interrogation rules, instructions, methods and practices as well as arrangements for the custody and treatment of persons subjected to any form of arrest, detention or imprisonment is an effective means of preventing cases of torture and ill-treatment. To guarantee the effective protection of detained persons, provisions should be made for detainees to be held in places officially recognized as places of detention and for their names and places of detention, as well as for the names of persons responsible for their detention, to be kept in registers readily available and accessible to those concerned, including relatives and friends. To the same effect, the time and place of all interrogations should be recorded, together with the names of all those present and this information should also be available for purposes of judicial or administrative proceedings. Provisions should also be made against incommunicado detention. In that connection, States parties should ensure that any places of detention be free from any equipment liable to be used for inflicting torture or ill-treatment. The protection of the detainee also requires that prompt and regular access be given to doctors and lawyers and, under appropriate supervision when the investigation so requires, to family members.

12. It is important for the discouragement of violations under article 7 that the law must prohibit the use of admissibility in judicial proceedings of statements or confessions obtained through torture or other prohibited treatment.

13. States parties should indicate when presenting their reports the provisions of their criminal law which penalize torture and cruel, inhuman and degrading treatment or punishment, specifying the penalties applicable to such acts, whether committed by public officials or other persons acting on behalf of the State, or by private persons. Those who violate article 7, whether by encouraging, ordering, tolerating or perpetrating prohibited acts, must be held responsible. Consequently, those who have refused to obey orders must not be punished or subjected to any adverse treatment.

14. Article 7 should be read in conjunction with article 2, paragraph 3, of the Covenant. In their reports, States parties should indicate how their legal system effectively guarantees the immediate termination of all the acts prohibited by article 7 as well as appropriate redress. The right to lodge complaints against maltreatment prohibited by article 7 must be recognized in the domestic law. Complaints must be investigated promptly and impartially by competent authorities so as to make the remedy effective. The reports of States parties should provide specific information on the remedies available to victims of maltreatment and the procedure that complainants must follow, and statistics on the number of complaints and how they have been dealt with.

15. The Committee has noted that some States have granted amnesty in respect of acts of torture. Amnesties are generally incompatible with the duty of States to investigate such acts; to guarantee freedom from such acts within their jurisdiction; and to ensure

that they do not occur in the future. States may not deprive individuals of the right to an effective remedy, including compensation and such full rehabilitation as may be possible.

～

The "Baby Boy" Case
Inter-American Commission on Human Rights
Case 2141, Resolution No. 23/81
1980–81 Inter-Amer. Cm. H.R. 25,
OEA/Ser. 6/v/II.54, doc. 9 rev. 1 (1981)

. . . .

18. The first violation denounced in the petition concerns Article I of the American Declaration of Rights and Duties of Man: "Every human being has the right to life. . . . " The petitioners admitted that the Declaration does not [answer] "when life begins," "when a pregnancy product becomes a human being," or other such questions. However, they try to answer these fundamental questions with two different arguments:

a) The *travaux préparatoires*, the discussion of the draft Declaration during the IX International Conference of American States at Bogotá in 1948 and the final vote, demonstrate that the intention of the Conference was to protect the right to life "from the moment of conception."

b) The American Convention on Human Rights, promulgated to advance the Declaration's high purposes and to be read as a corollary document, gives a definition of the right to life in Article 4.1: "This right shall be protected by law from the moment of conception."

19. A brief legislative history of the Declaration does not support the petitioner's argument, as may be concluded from the following information and documents:

a) Pursuant to Resolution XL of the Inter-American Conference on Problems of War and Peace (Mexico, 1945), the Inter-American Juridical Committee of Rio de Janeiro formulated a preliminary draft of an International Declaration of the Rights and Duties of Man to be considered by the Ninth International Conference of American States (Bogotá, 1948). . . .

b) Article I – Right to Life – of the draft submitted by the Juridical Committee reads: "Every person has the right to life. This right extends to the right to life from the moment of conception; to the right to life of incurables, imbeciles and the insane. Capital punishment may only be applied in cases in which it has been prescribed by pre-existing law for crimes of exceptional gravity."

c) A Working Group was organized to consider the observations and amendments introduced by the Delegates and to prepare an acceptable document. As a result of its work, the Group submitted to the Sixth Committee a new draft entitled *American Declaration of the Fundamental Rights and Duties of Man*, Article I of which reads: "Every human being has the right to life, liberty, security and integrity of her person."

d) This completely new Article I and some substantial changes introduced by the Working Group in other articles have been explained in its Report of the Working Group to the Committee, as a compromise to resolve the problems raised by the Delegations of Argentina, Brazil, Cuba, United States of America, Mexico, Peru, Uruguay, and Venezuela, mainly as a consequence of the conflict existing between the laws of those States and the draft of the Juridical Committee.

e) In connection with the right to life, the definition given in the Juridical Committee's draft was incompatible with the laws governing the death penalty and abortion in the majority of the American States. In effect, the acceptance of this absolute concept – the right to life from the moment of conception – would imply the obligation to derogate the articles of the Penal Codes in force in 1948 in many countries because such articles excluded the penal sanction for the crime of abortion if performed in one or more of the following cases: A – when necessary to save the life of the mother; B – to interrupt the pregnancy of the victim of a rape; C – to protect the honor of an honest woman; D – to prevent the transmission to the fetus of a hereditary or contagious disease; E – for economic reasons (*angustia económica*).

f) In 1948 the American States that permitted abortion in one of such cases and, consequently, would be affected by the adoption of article I of the Juridical Committee, were: Argentina...; Brazil...; Costa Rica...; Cuba...; Ecuador...; Mexico (Distrito y Territorios Federales)...; Nicaragua...; Paraguay...; Peru...; Uruguay...; Venezuela...; United States of America...; Puerto Rico....

h) Consequently, the defendant is correct in challenging the petitioners' assumption that Article I of the Declaration has incorporated the notion that the right to life exists from the moment of conception. Indeed the conference faced this question but chose not to adopt language which would clearly have stated that principle.

20. The second argument of the petitioners, related to the possible use of the Convention as an element for the interpretation of the Declaration, requires also a study of the motives that prevailed at the San José Diplomatic Conference with the adoption of the definition of the right to life....

25. To accommodate the views that insisted on the concept "from the moment of conception," with the objection raised, since the Bogotá conference, based on the legislation of American States that permitted abortion, *inter alia*, to save the mother's life, and in case of rape, the IACHR, redrafting Article 2 [of the Convention] (Right to life), decided by majority vote, to introduce the words "in general." This compromise was the origin of the new text of Article 2: "1. Every person has the right to have his life respected. This right shall be protected by law, *in general*, from the moment of conception."

26. The rapporteur of the *Opinion* proposed, at this second opportunity for discussion of the definition of the right [to] life, to delete the entire final phrase " ... in general, from the moment of conception." He repeated the reasoning of his dissenting opinion in the Commission; based on the abortion laws in force in the majority of the American States, with an addition: "to avoid any possibility of conflict with article 6, paragraph 1, of the United Nations Covenant on Civil and Political Rights, which states this right in a general way only."...

27. However, the majority of the Commission believed that, for reasons of principle, it was fundamental to state the provision on the protection of the right to life in the form recommended to the Council of the OAS in its *Opinion* (Part One). It was accordingly decided to keep the text of paragraph 1 without change....

30. In the light of this [drafting] history, it is clear that the petitioners' interpretation of the definition given by the American Convention on the right to life in incorrect. The addition of the phrase "in general, from the moment of conception" does not mean that the drafters of the Convention intended to modify the concept of the right to life that prevailed in Bogotá, when they approved the American Declaration. The legal implications of the clause "in general, from the moment of conception" are substantially different from the shorter clause "from the moment of conception" as appears repeatedly in the petitioners' briefs.

31. However, accepting *gratia argumentandi* [for the sake of argument], that the American Convention had established the absolute concept of the right to life from the moment of conception – it would be impossible to impose upon the United States Government or that of any other Member State of the OAS, by means of 'interpretation," an international obligation based upon a treaty that such State has not duly accepted or ratified.

∾

QUESTIONS & COMMENTS

(1) Given that the Inter-American Court of Human Rights has not addressed the question of whether abortion is a violation of the right to life, should pro-choice advocates be concerned about the United States ratifying the ACHR? For example, could an OAS member ratify the ACHR with an understanding or reservation that the ACHR's right to life does not prohibit abortion in light of the UN Human Rights Committee's opinion that reservations that violate a *jus cogens* norm bear a heavy onus of justification and that reservations that violate customary international law are incompatible with the object and purpose of the ICCPR and, hence, are invalid? Could the OAS member seek an advisory opinion as to these issues before ratifying the ACHR?

Vo v. France
European Court of Human Rights
Application No. 53920/00
(8 July 2004)

[Because a French Hospital confused the applicant, Miss Vo, with another patient who was to have a coil removed from her uterus, the hospital mistakenly pierced the applicant's amniotic sac resulting in a substantial loss of amniotic fluid. Consequently, her doctor performed an abortion on the applicant for health reasons. The applicant and her partner filed a criminal complaint alleging unintentional homicide of her child. However, the French Criminal Court subsequently dismissed the criminal charge because the French Criminal Code excluded acts causing fatal injury to a fetus.]

. . . .

1. Existing case-law

75. Unlike Article 4 of the American Convention on Human Rights, which provides that the right to life must be protected "in general, from the moment of conception", Article 2 of the Convention is silent as to the temporal limitations of the right to life and, in particular, does not define "everyone" (*"toute personne"*) whose "life" is protected

by the Convention. The Court has yet to determine the issue of the "beginning" of "everyone's right to life" within the meaning of this provision and whether the unborn child has such a right.

To date it has been raised solely in connection with laws on abortion. Abortion does not constitute one of the exceptions expressly listed in paragraph 2 of Article 2 but the Commission has expressed the opinion that it is compatible with the first sentence of Article 2 §1 in the interests of protecting the mother's life and health because "if one assumes that this provision applies at the initial stage of the pregnancy, the abortion is covered by an implied limitation, protecting the life and health of the woman at that stage, of the 'right to life' of the foetus" (see *X v. the United Kingdom*, Commission decision cited above, at p. 253).

76. Having initially refused to examine *in abstracto* the compatibility of abortion laws with Article 2 of the Convention (see *X v. Norway*, no. 867/60, Commission decision of 29 May 1961, Collection of Decisions 6, p. 34, and *X v. Austria*, no. 7045/75, Commission decision of 10 December 1976, DR 7, p. 87), the Commission acknowledged in the case of *Brüggemann and Scheuten v. the Federal Republic of Germany* that women complaining under Article 8 of the Convention about the Constitutional Court's decision restricting the availability of abortions had standing as victims. It stated on that occasion: " . . . pregnancy cannot be said to pertain uniquely to the sphere of private life. Whenever a woman is pregnant her private life becomes closely connected with the developing foetus" (ibid., at p. 116, §59). However, the Commission did not find it "necessary to decide, in this context, whether the unborn child is to be considered as 'life' in the sense of Article 2 of the Convention, or whether it could be regarded as an entity which under Article 8 §2 could justify an interference 'for the protection of others'" (ibid., at p. 116, §60). It expressed the opinion that there had been no violation of Article 8 of the Convention because "not every regulation of the termination of unwanted pregnancies constitutes an interference with the right to respect for the private life of the mother" (ibid., at pp. 116–17, §61), while emphasising: "There is no evidence that it was the intention of the Parties to the Convention to bind themselves in favour of any particular solution" (ibid., at pp. 117–18, §64).

77. In the *X v. the United Kingdom* decision cited above the Commission considered an application by a man complaining that his wife had been allowed to have an abortion on health grounds. While it accepted that the potential father could be regarded as the "victim" of a violation of the right to life, it considered that the term "everyone" in several Articles of the Convention could not apply prenatally, but observed that "such application in a rare case – e.g. under Article 6, paragraph 1 – cannot be excluded" (see *X v. the United Kingdom*, cited above, at p. 259, §7; for such an application in connection with access to a court, see *Reeve v. the United Kingdom*, no. 24844/94, Commission decision of 30 November 1994, DR 79-A, p. 146). The Commission added that the general usage of the term "everyone" ("*toute personne*") and the context in which it was used in Article 2 of the Convention did not include the unborn. As to the term "life" and, in particular, the beginning of life, the Commission noted a "divergence of thinking on the question of where life begins" and added: "While some believe that it starts already with conception, others tend to focus upon the moment of nidation, upon the point that the foetus becomes 'viable', or upon live birth" (see *X v. the United Kingdom*, cited above, at p. 250, §12).

The Commission went on to examine whether Article 2 was "to be interpreted: as not covering the foetus at all; as recognising a 'right to life' of the foetus with certain implied limitations; or as recognising an absolute 'right to life' of the foetus". Although it did not express an opinion on the first two options, it categorically ruled out the third interpretation, having regard to the need to protect the mother's life, which was indissociable from that of the unborn child: "The 'life' of the foetus is intimately connected with, and it cannot be regarded in isolation of, the life of the pregnant woman. If Article 2 were held to cover the foetus and its protection under this Article were, in the absence of any express limitation, seen as absolute, an abortion would have to be considered as prohibited even where the continuance of the pregnancy would involve a serious risk to the life of the pregnant woman. This would mean that the 'unborn life' of the foetus would be regarded as being of a higher value than the life of the pregnant woman" (ibid., at p. 252, §19). The Commission adopted that solution, noting that by 1950 practically all the Contracting Parties had "permitted abortion when necessary to save the life of the mother" and that in the meantime the national law on termination of pregnancy had "shown a tendency towards further liberalisation" (ibid., at p. 252, §20).

78. In the case of *H. v. Norway*, concerning an abortion carried out on non-medical grounds against the father's wishes, the Commission added that Article 2 required the State not only to refrain from taking a person's life intentionally but also to take appropriate steps to safeguard life (see *H. v. Norway*, cited above, at p. 167). It considered that it did not have to decide "whether the foetus may enjoy a certain protection under Article 2, first sentence", but did not exclude the possibility that "in certain circumstances this may be the case notwithstanding that there is in the Contracting States a considerable divergence of views on whether or to what extent Article 2 protects the unborn life" (ibid.). It further noted that in such a delicate area the Contracting States had to have a certain discretion, and concluded that the mother's decision, taken in accordance with Norwegian legislation, had not exceeded that discretion (ibid., p. 168).

79. The Court has only rarely had occasion to consider the application of Article 2 to the foetus. In the case of *Open Door and Dublin Well Woman* the Irish Government relied on the protection of the life of the unborn child to justify their legislation prohibiting the provision of information concerning abortion facilities abroad. The only issue that was resolved was whether the restrictions on the freedom to receive and impart the information in question had been necessary in a democratic society, within the meaning of paragraph 2 of Article 10 of the Convention, to pursue the "legitimate aim of the protection of morals of which the protection in Ireland of the right to life of the unborn is one aspect" (see *Open Door and Dublin Well Woman*, cited above, pp. 27–28, §63), since the Court did not consider it relevant to determine "whether a right to abortion is guaranteed under the Convention or whether the foetus is encompassed by the right to life as contained in Article 2" (ibid., p. 28, §66). Recently, in circumstances similar to those in the above-mentioned case of *H. v. Norway*, where a woman had decided to terminate her pregnancy against the father's wishes, the Court held that it was not required to determine "whether the foetus may qualify for protection under the first sentence of Article 2 as interpreted [in the case-law relating to the positive obligation to protect life]", and continued: "Even supposing that, in certain circumstances, the foetus might be considered to have rights protected by Article 2 of the Convention, . . . in the instant case . . . [the] pregnancy was terminated in conformity with section 5 of Law

no. 194 of 1978" – a law which struck a fair balance between the woman's interests and the need to ensure protection of the foetus (see *Boso v. Italy* (dec.), no. 50490/99, ECHR 2002-VII).

80. It follows from this recapitulation of the case-law that in the circumstances examined to date by the Convention institutions – that is, in the various laws on abortion – the unborn child is not regarded as a "person" directly protected by Article 2 of the Convention and that if the unborn do have a "right" to "life", it is implicitly limited by the mother's rights and interests. The Convention institutions have not, however, ruled out the possibility that in certain circumstances safeguards may be extended to the unborn child. That is what appears to have been contemplated by the Commission in considering that "Article 8 §1 cannot be interpreted as meaning that pregnancy and its termination are, as a principle, solely a matter of the private life of the mother" (see *Brüggeman and Scheuten*, cited above, at pp. 116–17, §61) and by the Court in the above-mentioned *Boso* decision. It is also clear from an examination of these cases that the issue has always been determined by weighing up various, and sometimes conflicting, rights or freedoms claimed by a woman, a mother or a father in relation to one another or *vis-à-vis* an unborn child.

2. Approach in the instant case

81. The special nature of the instant case raises a new issue. The Court is faced with a woman who intended to carry her pregnancy to term and whose unborn child was expected to be viable, at the very least in good health. Her pregnancy had to be terminated as a result of an error by a doctor and she therefore had to have a therapeutic abortion on account of negligence by a third party. The issue is consequently whether, apart from cases where the mother has requested an abortion, harming a foetus should be treated as a criminal offence in the light of Article 2 of the Convention, with a view to protecting the foetus under that Article. This requires a preliminary examination of whether it is advisable for the Court to intervene in the debate as to who is a person and when life begins, in so far as Article 2 provides that the law must protect "everyone's right to life".

82. As is apparent from the above recapitulation of the case-law, the interpretation of Article 2 in this connection has been informed by a clear desire to strike a balance, and the Convention institutions' position in relation to the legal, medical, philosophical, ethical or religious dimensions of defining the human being has taken into account the various approaches to the matter at national level. This has been reflected in the consideration given to the diversity of views on the point at which life begins, of legal cultures and of national standards of protection, and the State has been left with considerable discretion in the matter, as the opinion of the European Group on Ethics at Community level appositely puts it: "the . . . Community authorities have to address these ethical questions taking into account the moral and philosophical differences, reflected by the extreme diversity of legal rules applicable to human embryo research . . . It is not only legally difficult to seek harmonisation of national laws at Community level, but because of lack of consensus, it would be inappropriate to impose one exclusive moral code".

It follows that the issue of when the right to life begins comes within the margin of appreciation which the Court generally considers that States should enjoy in this sphere, notwithstanding an evolutive interpretation of the Convention, a "living instrument which must be interpreted in the light of present-day conditions"[ ]. The reasons for that conclusion are, firstly, that the issue of such protection has not been resolved within the majority of the Contracting States themselves, in France in particular, where it is the subject of debate (see paragraph 83 below) and, secondly, that there is no European consensus on the scientific and legal definition of the beginning of life (see paragraph 84 below).

83. The Court observes that the French Court of Cassation, in three successive judgments delivered in 1999, 2001 and 2002 [ ], considered that the rule that offences and punishment must be defined by law, which required criminal statutes to be construed strictly, excluded acts causing a fatal injury to a foetus from the scope of Article 221–6 of the Criminal Code, under which unintentional homicide of "another" is an offence. However, if, as a result of unintentional negligence, the mother gives birth to a live child who dies shortly after being born, the person responsible may be convicted of the unintentional homicide of the child [ ]. The first-mentioned approach . . . was interpreted as an invitation to the legislature to fill a legal vacuum. That was also the position of the Criminal Court in the instant case: "The court . . . cannot create law on an issue which [the legislature has] not yet succeeded in defining." The French parliament attempted such a definition in proposing to create the offence of involuntary termination of pregnancy [ ], but the Bill containing that proposal was lost, on account of the fears and uncertainties that the creation of the offence might arouse as to the determination of when life began, and the disadvantages of the proposal, which were thought to outweigh its advantages [ ]. The Court further notes that alongside the Court of Cassation's repeated rulings that Article 221–6 of the Criminal Code does not apply to foetuses, the French parliament is currently revising the 1994 bioethics laws, which added provisions to the Criminal Code on the protection of the human embryo [ ] and required re-examination in the light of scientific and technological progress [ ]. It is clear from this overview that in France, the nature and legal status of the embryo and/or the foetus are currently not defined and that the manner in which it is to be protected will be determined by very varied forces within French society.

84. At the European level, the Court observes that there is no consensus on the nature and status of the embryo and/or foetus [ ], although they are beginning to receive some protection in the light of scientific progress and the potential consequences of research into genetic engineering, medically assisted procreation or embryo experimentation. At best, it may be regarded as common ground between States that the embryo/foetus belongs to the human race. The potentiality of that being and its capacity to become a person – enjoying protection under the civil law, moreover, in many States, such as France, in the context of inheritance and gifts, and also in the United Kingdom [ ] – require protection in the name of human dignity, without making it a "person" with the "right to life" for the purposes of Article 2. The Oviedo Convention on Human Rights and Biomedicine, indeed, is careful not to give a definition of the term "everyone" and its explanatory report indicates that, in the absence of a unanimous agreement on the definition, the member States decided to allow domestic law to provide clarifications for the purposes of the application of that Convention [ ]. The same is true of the Additional Protocol on the Prohibition of Cloning Human Beings and the draft Additional Protocol on Biomedical Research, which do not define the concept of "human being" [ ]. . . .

85. Having regard to the foregoing, the Court is convinced that it is neither desirable, nor even possible as matters stand, to answer in the abstract the question whether the

unborn child is a person for the purposes of Article 2 of the Convention ("*personne*" in the French text). As to the instant case, it considers it unnecessary to examine whether the abrupt end to the applicant's pregnancy falls within the scope of Article 2, seeing that, even assuming that that provision was applicable, there was no failure on the part of the respondent State to comply with the requirements relating to the preservation of life in the public-health sphere. With regard to that issue, the Court has considered whether the legal protection afforded the applicant by France in respect of the loss of the unborn child she was carrying satisfied the procedural requirements inherent in Article 2 of the Convention.

86. In that connection, it observes that the unborn child's lack of a clear legal status does not necessarily deprive it of all protection under French law. However, in the circumstances of the present case, the life of the foetus was intimately connected with that of the mother and could be protected through her, especially as there was no conflict between the rights of the mother and the father or of the unborn child and the parents, the loss of the foetus having been caused by the unintentional negligence of a third party.

87. In the aforementioned *Boso v. Italy* decision, the Court said that even supposing that the foetus might be considered to have rights protected by Article 2 of the Convention [ ], Italian law on the voluntary termination of pregnancy struck a fair balance between the woman's interests and the need to ensure protection of the unborn child. In the present case, the dispute concerns the involuntary killing of an unborn child against the mother's wishes, causing her particular suffering. The interests of the mother and the child clearly coincided. The Court must therefore examine, from the standpoint of the effectiveness of existing remedies, the protection which the applicant was afforded in seeking to establish the liability of the doctor concerned for the loss of her child *in utero* and to obtain compensation for the abortion she had to undergo. The applicant argued that only a criminal remedy would have been capable of satisfying the requirements of Article 2 of the Convention. The Court does not share that view, for the following reasons.

88. The Court reiterates that the first sentence of Article 2, which ranks as one of the most fundamental provisions in the Convention and also enshrines one of the basic values of the democratic societies making up the Council of Europe[ ], requires the State not only to refrain from the "intentional" taking of life, but also to take appropriate steps to safeguard the lives of those within its jurisdiction [ ].

89. Those principles apply in the public-health sphere too. The positive obligations require States to make regulations compelling hospitals, whether private or public, to adopt appropriate measures for the protection of patients' lives. They also require an effective independent judicial system to be set up so that the cause of death of patients in the care of the medical profession, whether in the public or the private sector, can be determined and those responsible made accountable (see *Powell v. the United Kingdom* (dec.), no. 45305/99, ECHR 2000-V . . .).

90. Although the right to have third parties prosecuted or sentenced for a criminal offence cannot be asserted independently (see *Perez v. France* [GC], no. 47287/99, §70, ECHR 2004-), the Court has stated on a number of occasions that an effective judicial system, as required by Article 2, may, and under certain circumstances must, include recourse to the criminal law. However, if the infringement of the right to life or to physical integrity is not caused intentionally, the positive obligation imposed by Article 2 to set up an effective judicial system does not necessarily require the provision of a criminal-law remedy in every case. In the specific sphere of medical negligence, "the obligation

may for instance also be satisfied if the legal system affords victims a remedy in the civil courts, either alone or in conjunction with a remedy in the criminal courts, enabling any liability of the doctors concerned to be established and any appropriate civil redress, such as an order for damages and for the publication of the decision, to be obtained. Disciplinary measures may also be envisaged" (see . . . *Lazzarini and Ghiacci v. Italy* (dec.), no. 53749/00, 7 November 2002; and *Mastromatteo v. Italy* [GC], no. 37703/97, §90, ECHR 2002-VIII).

. . . .

FOR THESE REASONS, THE COURT

1. *Joins to the merits* unanimously the Government's preliminary objections of the application's incompatibility *ratione materiae* with the provisions of the Convention and of failure to exhaust domestic remedies, and *dismisses* them;

2. *Declares* unanimously the application *admissible*;

3. *Holds* by fourteen votes to three that there has been no violation of Article 2 of the Convention.

∼

QUESTIONS & COMMENTS

(1) Compare the Inter-American Commission's decision in the *Baby Boy Case* with the European Court's decision in *Vo v. France*? Would the outcome in *Vo* been different if the ECHR defined life from the moment of conception, as the ACHR does? What significance does the fact that Vo wanted to have the child?

(2) How does the European Court's rationale in *Vo* differ from the rationales given by U.S. Supreme Court decisions?

Death Penalty

Second Optional Protocol to the International Covenant on Civil and Political Rights
Aiming at the Abolition of the Death Penalty

Article 1

1. No one within the jurisdiction of a State Party to the present Protocol shall be executed.

2. Each State Party shall take all necessary measures to abolish the death penalty within its jurisdiction.

European Convention on Human Rights, Protocol No. 6

Article 1

The death penalty shall be abolished. No one shall be condemned to such penalty or executed.

Charter of Fundamental Rights of the European Union

Article 2

Right to life

. . . .

2. No one shall be condemned to the death penalty, or executed.

Protocol to the
American Convention on Human Rights
to Abolish the Death Penalty

ARTICLE 1

The States Parties to this Protocol shall not apply the death penalty in their territory to any person subject to their jurisdiction.

Domingues v. United States
Inter-American Commission on Human Rights
Report No. 62/02, Case 12.285
(2002)

. . . .

2. Merits

17. With respect to the merits of the case, the Petitioner indicates that Mr. Domingues is a U.S. citizen who in August 1994 was tried and convicted by a jury in Nevada of one count of burglary, one count of robbery with the use of a deadly weapon, one count of first degree murder and one count of first degree murder with the use of a deadly weapon. Mr. Domingues was sentenced to death for each of the two murder convictions. The Petitioner argues that the imposition of the death penalty upon an offender who was aged sixteen years at the time of his crime is a breach of Articles I, II, VII and XXVI of the American Declaration for which the State must be held responsible.

. . . .

26. As of the date of adoption of the Commission's preliminary report, the Commission had not received any observations or information from the State regarding Mr. Domingues' complaint.

. . . .

C. Merits

1. Standard of Review

38. Before addressing the merits of the present case, the Commission wishes to reaffirm and reiterate its well-established doctrine that a heightened level of scrutiny will be applied in deciding cases involving capital punishment. The right to life is widely-recognized as the supreme right of the human being, and the *conditio sine qua non* to the enjoyment of all other rights. The Commission therefore considers that it has an enhanced obligation to ensure that any deprivation of life that an OAS member state proposes to perpetrate through the death penalty complies strictly with the requirements

of the applicable inter-American human rights instruments, including the American Declaration. This "heightened scrutiny test" is consistent with the restrictive approach taken by other international human rights authorities to the imposition of the death penalty,[1] and has been articulated and applied by the Commission in previous capital cases before it.[2]

39. The Commission further notes that the heightened scrutiny test applicable to death penalty cases is not precluded by the Commission's fourth instance formula. According to this formula, the Commission in principle will not review the judgments issued by domestic courts acting within their competence and with due judicial guarantees.[ ] Where a possible violation of an individual's rights under applicable inter-American human rights instruments is involved, however, the Commission has consistently held that the fourth instance formula has no application.[ ] The Commission will therefore review the allegations made by the Petitioner with a heightened level of scrutiny, to ensure that Mr. Domingues' rights under the American Declaration have been properly respected by the State.

2. The Commission's Decision in Roach and Pinkerton

40. The Commission notes at the outset of its analysis that the Petitioner's arguments draw significantly upon the Commission's 1987 decision in the case of Roach and Pinkerton against the United States.[3] That case concerned two juvenile offenders, James Terry Roach and Jay Pinkerton, who were sentenced to death in the states of, respectively, South Carolina and Texas, for crimes committed when they were seventeen years of age. Both petitioners were subsequently executed by those states. In determining the complaint brought before it on behalf of the Mr. Roach and Mr. Pinkerton, the Commission considered whether the United States had in sentencing the two prisoners to death and subsequently allowing their executions acted contrary to a recognized norm of *jus cogens* or customary international law. While the Commission determined the existence of a *jus cogens* norm prohibiting the execution of children, it found that uncertainty existed as

---

[1] See e.g. I/A Court H.R., Advisory Opinion OC-16/99 (1 October 1999) "The Right to Information on Consular Assistance in the Framework of the Guarantees of the Due Process of Law", para. 136 (finding that "[b]ecause execution of the death penalty is irreversible, the strictest and most rigorous enforcement of judicial guarantees is required of the State so that those guarantees are not violated and a human life not arbitrarily taken as a result"); *Baboheram-Adhin et al. v. Suriname*, Communication Nos. 148–154/1983, adopted 4 April 1985, para. 14.3 (finding that the law must strictly control and limit the circumstances in which a person may be deprived of his life by the authorities of the state.); Report by the U.N. Special Rapporteur on Extra-judicial Executions, Mr. Bacre Waly Ndiaye, submitted pursuant to Commission on Human Rights Resolution 1994/82, Question of the Violation of Human Rights and Fundamental Freedoms in any part of the World, with particular reference to Colonial and Other Dependent Countries and Territories, UN Doc.E/CN.4/1995/61 (14 December 1994) (hereinafter "Ndiaye Report"), para. 378 (emphasizing that in capital cases, it is the application of the standards of fair trials to each and every case that needs to be ensured and, in case of indications to the contrary, verified, in accordance with the obligation under international law to conduct exhaustive and impartial investigations into all allegations of violation of the right to life.).

[2] *See e.g.* IACHR, Andrews v. United States, Report 57/96, Annual Report of the IACHR 1997), paras. 170–171; IACHR, Baptiste v. Grenada, Report No 38/00, Annual Report of the IACHR 1999, paras. 64–66; McKenzie et al. v. Jamaica, Report No 41/00, Annual Report of the IACHR 1999, paras. 169–171.

[3] Roach and Pinkerton v. United States, Case 9647, Res. 3/87, 22 September 1987, Annual Report of the IACHR 1986–87.

to the applicable age of majority under international law. The Commission specifically articulated the issue before it as follows:

> in the member States of the OAS, there is recognized a norm of *jus cogens* which prohibits the State execution of children. This norm is accepted by all the States of the inter-American system including the United States [ ] the Commission finds that this case arises, not because of doubt concerning the existence of an international norm as to the prohibition of the execution of children, but because the US disputes the allegation that there exists consensus as regards the age of majority.

41. The Commission ultimately concluded that there did not exist at that time a norm of *jus cogens* or other customary international law prohibiting the execution of persons under 18 years of age:

> The Commission is convinced by the US Government's argument that there does not now exist a norm of customary international law establishing 18 to be the minimum age for imposition of the death penalty. Nonetheless, in light of the increasing numbers of States which are ratifying the American Convention on Human Rights and the United Nations Covenant on Civil and Political Rights, and modifying their domestic legislation in conformity with these instruments, the norm is emerging. As mentioned, thirteen states and the U.S. capital have abolished the death penalty entirely and nine retentionist states [26] have abolished it for offenders under the age of 18.[27]

42. Accordingly, in determining the present complaint, the Commission must address whether the state of international law concerning the execution of individuals under the age of 18 has evolved since its decision in Roach and Pinkerton.

3. The American Declaration, Customary International Law and Norms of *Jus Cogens*

43. In addressing the claims raised by the Petitioner concerning the present status of rules governing the execution of minors under international law, it is first instructive to provide a brief overview of the categories of rules of international law pertinent to this analysis, namely customary international law and norms of *jus cogens*, as well as the principal means by which the contents of those rules are manifested.

44. In this connection, the Commission recalls that in interpreting and applying the Declaration, its provisions, including Articles I, VII and XXVI, should be considered in the context of the broader international and inter-American human rights systems, in the light of developments in the field of international human rights law since it was first composed.[ ] Due regard should in this respect be given to other relevant rules of international law applicable to member states against which complaints of violations of the Declaration are properly lodged[ ] as well as developments in the *corpus juris gentium* of international human rights law over time and in present-day conditions.[ ]

45. Developments in the corpus of international human rights law relevant to interpreting and applying the American Declaration may in turn be drawn from various sources of international law,[ ] including the provisions of other international and regional human rights instruments[ ] and customary international law,[ ] including those customary norms considered to form a part of *jus cogens*.[ ]

46. With respect to the rules of customary international law in particular, while these rules are of an inherently changeable nature and therefore cannot be the subject of a definitive or exhaustive enumeration, there nevertheless exists a broad consensus in respect of

the component elements required to establish a norm of customary international law. These include:

a) a concordant practice by a number of states with reference to a type of situation falling within the domain of international relations;
b) a continuation or repetition of the practice over a considerable period of time;
c) a conception that the practice is required by or consistent with prevailing international law;
d) general acquiescence in the practice by other states.[ ]

47. These elements in turn suggest that when considering the establishment of such a customary norm, regard must be had to evidence of state practice.[ ] While the value of potential sources of evidence vary depending on the circumstances, state practice is generally interpreted to mean official governmental conduct which would include state legislation, international and national judicial decisions, recitals in treaties and other international instruments, a pattern of treaties in the same form, the practice of international and regional governmental organizations such as the United Nations and the Organization of American States and their organs, domestic policy statements, press releases and official manuals on legal questions.[ ] In summary, state practice generally comprises any acts or statements by a state from which views about customary laws may be inferred.[ ]

48. Once established, a norm of international customary law binds all states with the exception of only those states that have persistently rejected the practice prior to its becoming law. While a certain practice does not require universal acceptance to become a norm of customary international law, a norm which has been accepted by the majority of States has no binding effect upon a State which has persistently rejected the practice upon which the norm is based.[ ]

49. Turning to the rules which govern the establishment of rules of *jus cogens*, this Commission has previously defined the concept of *jus cogens* as having been derived from ancient law concepts of a "superior order of legal norms, which the laws of man or nations may not contravene" and as the "rules which have been accepted, either expressly by treaty or tacitly by custom, as being necessary to protect the public morality recognized by them."[ ] It has been said that the principal distinguishing feature of these norms is their "relative indelibility," in that they constitute rules of customary law which cannot be set aside by treaty or acquiescence but only by the formation of a subsequent customary rule of contrary effect.[ ] More particularly, as customary international law rests on the consent of nations, a state that persistently objects to a norm of customary international law is not bound by that norm. Norms of *jus cogens*, on the other hand, derive their status from fundamental values held by the international community, as violations of such preemptory norms are considered to shock the conscience of humankind and therefore bind the international community as a whole, irrespective of protest, recognition or acquiescence.[ ] Commonly cited examples of rules of customary law that have attained the status of *jus cogens* norms include genocide, slavery, forced disappearances and torture or other cruel, inhuman or degrading treatment or punishment.[ ] It has been suggested that a reliable starting point in identifying those international legal proscriptions that have achieved *jus cogens* status is the list of rights that international human rights treaties render non-derogable.[ ]

50. Therefore, while based on the same evidentiary sources as a norm of customary international law, the standard for determining a principle of *jus cogens* is more rigorous, requiring evidence of recognition of the indelibility of the norm by the international community as a whole. This can occur where there is acceptance and recognition by a large majority of states, even if over dissent by a small number of states.[45]

4. International Legal Status of the Execution of Juveniles

51. Article I of the Declaration provides that "[e]very human being has the right to life, liberty and the security of his person."

52. The Commission notes that while Article I of the American Declaration does not explicitly refer to the issue of capital punishment, the Commission has in past decisions declined to interpret Article I of the Declaration as either prohibiting use of the death penalty *per se*, or conversely as exempting capital punishment from the Declaration's standards and protections altogether. Rather, in part by reference to the drafting history of the American Declaration as well as the terms of Article 4 of the American Convention on Human Rights, the Commission has found that Article I of the Declaration, while not precluding the death penalty altogether, prohibits its application when doing so would result in an arbitrary deprivation of life or would otherwise be rendered cruel, infamous or unusual punishment.[ ]

53. As noted above, the Petitioner argues that in the light of developments since 1986, a norm of customary international law now exists which prevents the execution of offenders aged 16 or 17 years old at the time of their crime. The Petitioner submits that this norm has acquired the status of *jus cogens*.[ ] Consequently, the Petitioner asks that the Commission's decision in the case of Roach and Pinkerton be reviewed and extended, so as to find that Article I of the Declaration prohibits Mr. Domingues' execution as an offender who committed his crime when he was under 18 years of age.

54. In addressing this issue, the Commission must therefore evaluate whether the provisions of the American Declaration, when interpreted in the context of pertinent developments in customary international law and the norms of *jus cogens*, prohibit the execution of individuals who committed their crime when they were under the age of 18. In so doing, it is appropriate for the Commission to take into account evidence of relevant state practice as disclosed by various sources, including recitals in treaties and other international instruments, a pattern of treaties in the same form, the practice of the United Nations and other international governmental organizations, and the domestic legislation and judicial decisions of states.

a. Treaties

55. Since 1987, several notable developments have occurred in relation to treaties that explicitly prohibit the execution of individuals who were under 18 years of age at the time of committing their offense. These developments include the coming into force of new international agreements as well as broadened ratifications of existing treaties.

56. Most significantly, on November 20, 1989 the U.N. General Assembly adopted the United Nations Convention on the Rights of the Child. Article 37(a) of the Convention provides that:

No child shall be subjected to torture or other cruel, inhuman or degrading treatment or punishment. Neither capital punishment nor life imprisonment without possibility of release shall be imposed for offences committed by persons below eighteen years of age.

57. The treaty subsequently entered into force on September 2, 1990, and as of September 2001 the Convention had 191 state parties with no explicit reservations taken to Article 37(a).[48] The United States signed the Convention in February 1995, but has not yet ratified the Convention, joining Somalia as the only two states that are not parties to this treaty. In the Commission's view, the extent of ratification of this instrument alone constitutes compelling evidence of a broad consensus on the part of the international community repudiating the execution of offenders under 18 years of age.

58. The International Covenant on Civil and Political Rights (ICCPR) was adopted by the UN General Assembly in 1966 and entered into force in 1976. There are presently 64 signatories and 147 Parties to the ICCPR.[ ] Since 1986, sixty-four countries have acceded to or ratified the Covenant,[ ] including the United States in 1992.[ ] Article 6(5) of the ICCPR, like Article 37(a) of the Convention on the Rights of the Child, provides that:

Sentence of death shall not be imposed for crimes committed by persons below eighteen years of age and shall not be carried out on pregnant women.

59. Of the states parties to this Convention, only the instruments of ratification of the U.S. and of accession by Thailand are presently accompanied by declarations or reservations in respect of Article 6(5). Thailand provided an interpretive declarations for Article 6(5) that reads as follows:

With respect to article 6, paragraph 5 of the Covenant, the Thai Penal Code enjoins, or in some cases allows much latitude for, the Court to take into account the offender's youth as a mitigating factor in handing down sentences. Whereas Section 74 of the code does not allow any kind of punishment levied upon any person below fourteen years of age, Section 75 of the same Code provides that whenever any person over fourteen years but not yet over seventeen years of age commits any act provided by the law to be an offence, the Court shall take into account the sense of responsibility and all other things concerning him in order to come to decision as to whether it is appropriate to pass judgment inflicting punishment on him or not. If the court does not deem it appropriate to pass judgment inflicting punishment, it shall proceed according to Section 74 (*viz.* to adopt other correction measures short of punishment) or if the court deems it appropriate to pass judgment inflicting punishment, it shall reduce the scale of punishment provided for such offence by one half. Section 76 of the same Code also states that whenever any person over seventeen years but not yet over twenty years of age, commits any act provided by the law to be an offence, the Court may, if it thinks fit, reduce the scale of the punishment provided for such offence by one third or one half. The reduction of the said scale will prevent the Court from passing any sentence of death. As a result, though in theory, sentence of death may be imposed for crimes committed by persons below eighteen years, but not below seventeen years of age, the Court always exercises its discretion under Section 75 to reduce the said scale of punishment, and in practice the death penalty has not been imposed upon any persons below eighteen years of age. Consequently, Thailand considers that in real terms it has already complied with the principles enshrined herein.

60. The effect of Thailand's declaration is therefore to clarify that despite the strict terms of its applicable legislation, in practice it does not execute juvenile offenders and therefore in real terms had already complied with Article 6(5) of the ICCPR.

61. For its part, the United States asserted the following reservation to Article 6(5) upon becoming a party to the ICCPR:

> That the United States reserves the right, subject to its Constitutional constraints, to Impose capital punishment on any person (other than a pregnant woman) duly convicted under existing or future laws permitting the imposition of capital punishment, including such punishment for crimes committed by persons below eighteen years of age.

62. It is noteworthy that this reservation provoked condemnation within the international community and prompted eleven European States Parties to file objections declaring the reservation to be invalid, a majority on the basis that it was inconsistent with the aims and purposes of the ICCPR as provided by Article 19(c) of the Vienna Convention on the Law of Treaties.[ ] Moreover, in 1995 the U.N. Human Rights Committee declared this reservation to be contrary to the object and purpose of the ICCPR and recommended that the United States withdraw it.[ ]

63. Other international and regional human rights treaties that regulate the implementation of the death penalty have likewise witnessed an increase in states parties thereto since 1987. With regard to the inter-American human rights system in particular, Article 4 of the American Convention on Human Rights provides Capital punishment shall not be imposed upon persons who, at the time the crime was committed, were under 18 years of age.

64. There are presently 24 state parties to the American Convention.[ ] Since 1986, the following 5 OAS member states ratified or acceded to the Convention, none of which claimed reservations respecting the prohibition under Article 4(5) of the execution of juveniles: Brazil (1992); Chile (1990); Dominica (1993); Suriname (1987); Trinidad and Tobago (1991, which subsequently denounced the Convention in 1998). The United States signed the American Convention in 1977 but has never ratified the treaty. The Commission considers that this broad hemispheric adherence to the American Convention, including Article 4(5) thereof, constitutes compelling evidence of a regional norm repudiating the application of the death penalty to persons under 18 years of age even amongst those states such as Guatemala, Jamaica and Grenada that, like the United States, have retained the death penalty.

65. These international and regional developments have been accompanied by initiatives in both the inter-American and European systems to prohibit the application of the death penalty altogether. In 1990, for example, the Protocol to the American Convention on Human Rights to Abolish the Death Penalty was approved by the OAS General Assembly at its twentieth regular session in Asuncion, Paraguay. Eight States have since signed and ratified the Protocol. Similarly, Protocol N° 6 to the European Convention on Human Rights concerning the Abolition of the Death Penalty abolishes the death penalty entirely except in times of war. The protocol came into force in March 1985 and presently has been ratified by 39 European States. Three states have signed but not yet ratified the Protocol and Turkey stands alone as the only member state of the Council of Europe which has not signed the protocol.

66. In the Commission's view, these developments in the corpus of international human rights law should also be viewed in light of corresponding provisions in the related field of international humanitarian law.[ ] In this respect, the Fourth Geneva Convention of 1949 and related instruments prohibit the imposition of the death penalty upon juveniles in times of armed conflict or occupation.[ ] Article 68, paragraph 4 of the Fourth Geneva Convention, which governs the application of penal laws to protected persons in situations of occupation, provides in part that [i]n any case, the death penalty may not be pronounced against a protected person who was under eighteen years of age at the time of the offence.

67. As of January 1, 1986, there were 162 state parties to the Fourth Geneva Convention, and as of 2001, the number of state parties had risen to 189.[ ] This includes the United States, which ratified the Convention on August 2, 1955 absent any reservation to paragraph 4 of Article 68. On this point, the Commission can identify no appropriate justification for applying a more restrictive standard for the application of the death penalty to juveniles in times of occupation than in times of peace, relating as this protection does to the most basic and non-derogable protections for human life and dignity of adolescents that are common to both regimes of international law. As the International Committee of the Red Cross observed in its Commentary on Article 68, paragraph 4 of the Fourth Geneva Convention:

> The clause corresponds to similar provisions in the penal codes of many countries, and is based on the idea that a person who has not reached the age of eighteen years is not fully capable of sound judgment, does not always realize the significance of his actions and often acts under the influence of others, if not under constraint.[ ]

68. The foregoing analysis therefore indicates that since 1987, and consistent with events prior to that date, there has been concordant and widespread development and ratification of treaties by which nearly all of the world states have recognized, without reservation, a norm prohibiting the execution of individuals who were under 18 years of age at the time of committing their offense.

b. United Nations Resolutions and Standards

69. The developments in treaty law discussed above have been accompanied by similar initiatives and practices on the part of United Nations bodies. Prior to the Commission's decision in Roach and Pinkerton, the Third Committee of the United Nations General Assembly in 1980 had already recognized Article 6 of the ICCPR as constituting a "minimum standard" for all U.N. members states and not just those that had ratified the ICCPR.[ ] Consistent with this position, on August 24, 1999 the United Nations Subcommittee on the Promotion and Protection of Human Rights passed a resolution condemning the imposition of the death penalty on those who were under 18 at the time of their offence and calling upon countries that continued to execute juveniles to bring an end to the practice.[ ] In addition, the 54th Session of the United Nations Commission on Human Rights passed a resolution calling on States that maintained the death penalty to comply with the International Covenant by not imposing the death penalty for crimes committed by persons below eighteen years of age.[ ]

70. Standards have also been adopted by the United Nations Economic and Social Council that forbid the execution of children who committed their crimes when they were

under eighteen.[ ] Those same standards have been endorsed by the General Assembly and the Seventh United Nations Congress on the Prevention of Crime and Treatment of Offenders.[ ] The United Nations Standard Minimum Rules for the Administration of Juvenile Justice likewise prohibits the execution of juvenile offenders.[ ]

71. It is therefore apparent that the United Nations bodies responsible for human rights and criminal justice have consistently supported the norm expressed in international human rights agreements prohibiting the execution of offenders under the age of 18.

c. Domestic Practice of States

72. The articulation of an international norm proscribing the execution of juvenile offenders through international practice has been accompanied by the expression of a similar standard in the domestic practice of states. In 1986, 46 countries had abolished the death penalty for traditional crimes, with the exception of certain crimes committed under military law or in time of war. Today, according to available statistics the number has more than doubled, with an additional 49 countries having abolished the death penalty during the intervening fifteen years for all but exceptional crimes. Moreover, a further 20 countries have not carried out any executions for ten years or more. It has been stated that the average annual rate at which countries have abolished the death penalty has increased from 1.5 (1965–1988) to 4 per year (1989–1995), or nearly three times as many.[ ] According to statistics compiled by Amnesty International, a leading source of research and information concerning the global application of the death penalty, 109 countries have abolished the death penalty by law or in practice as of the year 2001.[ ]

73. Also according to statistics compiled by Amnesty International, 115 states whose laws maintain the death penalty for some offences either have provisions in their laws which exclude the use of the death penalty against child offenders, or may be presumed to exclude such use by virtue of becoming parties to the International Covenant on Civil and Political Rights, the Convention on the Rights of the Child or the American Convention on Human Rights without entering a reservation to the relevant articles of these treaties.[ ] Since the beginning of 1994 at least 5 countries have changed their laws to eliminate the use of the death penalty against child offenders: Barbados, Pakistan, Yemen, Zimbabwe and China. [ ]

74. A small minority of states persist in executing juvenile offenders. Since 1990, 7 countries are known to have executed prisoners who were under 18 years old at the time of the crime – Congo (Democratic Republic), Iran, Nigeria, Pakistan, Saudi Arabia, U.S. and Yemen.[ ] A study of the worldwide executions of child offenders cite a total of 25 executions within that 10 year period. Fourteen of those executions were carried out by the United States of America, 6 were conducted in Iran and the remaining 5 nations carried out one execution each. Both Pakistan and Yemen are now reported to have abolished the death penalty for 16 and 17 year old offenders.[ ] In the year 2000, only 3 countries carried out any juvenile executions: the U.S., the Democratic Republic of Congo and Iran. In 1999 juvenile executions took place only in Iran and the U.S. In 1998, the U.S. was alone in its execution of 3 juvenile offenders. Yemen's sole execution took place in 1993, and Saudi Arabia's in 1992, with the consequence that since 1998, only three states, the U.S., Congo and Iran, have executed juvenile offenders sentenced to death.[ ]

75. As with adherence to regional treaties in the Western Hemisphere, it is pertinent to note that of the few states that have continued to execute juveniles, none but the United States are counted among the members of the inter-American system. In the Commission's view, this reinforces the existence of a particularly pervasive regional norm repudiating the application of the death penalty to persons under 18 years of age.

76. Domestic practice over the past 15 years therefore evidences a nearly unanimous and unqualified international trend toward prohibiting the execution of offenders under the age of 18 years. This trend crosses political and ideological lines and has nearly isolated the United States as the only country that continues to maintain the legality of the execution of 16 and 17 year old offenders, and then, as the following discussion indicates, only in certain state jurisdictions.

d. Practice of the United States

77. Within the United States, judicial determinations and legislative initiatives over the past 20 years have also demonstrated a trend towards lack of acceptance of the application of the death penalty to those offenders under the age of 18 years. At the time of the decision of the U.S. Supreme Court in the case *Thompson v. Oklahoma* in 1988, 36 states authorized the use of capital punishment and of those, 18 required that the defendant attain at least the age of 16 years at the time of his or her offense, while another 19 provided no minimum age for the imposition of the death penalty.[ ] In the Thompson decision, the U.S. Supreme Court held that the execution of offenders under the age of sixteen years at the time of their crimes was prohibited by the Eighth Amendment to the United States Constitution.[ ] In its analysis of that case, the Supreme Court concluded that it would "offend civilized standards of decency to execute a person who was less than 16 years old at the time of his or her offense," and cited in support of its conclusion the fact that

> [r]elevant state statutes – particularly those of the 18 States that have expressly considered the question of a minimum age for imposition of the death penalty, and have uniformly required that the defendant have attained at least the age of 16 at the time of the capital offense – support the conclusion that it would offend civilized standards of decency to execute a person who was less than 16 years old at the time of his or her offense. That conclusion is also consistent with the views expressed by respected professional organizations, by other nations that share the Anglo-American heritage, and by the leading members of the Western European Community.[ ]

78. Moreover, since this initiative by the U.S. Supreme Court to establish a minimum age of 16 at which an offender may be executed in the United States, additional state jurisdictions have moved toward a higher standard. In 1999, for example, the Florida Supreme Court interpreted the Florida Constitution to prohibit the death penalty for sixteen-year-old offenders, ruling that the execution of a person who was 16 years old at the time of his crime violated the Florida Constitution and its prohibition against cruel and unusual punishment.[ ] On April 30, 1999 a revision of Montana state law raised the minimum age of offenders who are eligible for the death penalty from 16 year to 18 years of age.

79. Currently within the United States, 38 states and the federal military and civilian jurisdictions have statutes authorizing the death penalty for capital crimes. Of those jurisdictions, 16 have expressly chosen the age of 18 at the time of the crime as the minimum age for eligibility the death sentence,[ ] compared to approximately 10 in 1986,[ ] and 23 states allow the execution of those under 18, compared to 27 in 1986.[ ] These statistics complement the international movement toward the establishment of 18 as the minimum age for the imposition of capital punishment. The Commission considers it significant in this respect that the U.S. federal government itself has considered 18 year to be the minimum age for the purposes of federal capital crimes.[ ] As the U.S. government is the authority responsible for upholding that State's obligations under the American Declaration and other international instruments, the Commission considers the federal government's adoption of 18 as the minimum age for the application of the federal death penalty as a significant indication by the United States itself of the appropriate standard on this issue.

e. Related Developments Regarding the Age of Majority

80. The Commission notes that the emergence of 18 as the minimum age for the execution of offenders is consistent with developments in other fields of international law addressing the age of majority for the imposition of serious and potentially fatal obligations and responsibilities. The Commission notes in particular the establishment of 18 as the minimum age for individuals to take direct part in hostilities as members of their state's armed forces. In this respect, the Optional Protocol to the Convention on the Rights of the Child respecting the involvement of children in armed conflicts, which was adopted and opened for signature, ratification and accession on May 25, 2000,[ ] provides in Article I that the age of 18 years represents a threshold below which special protection is required:

Article 1
State parties shall take all feasible measures to ensure that members of their armed forces who have not attained the age of 18 years do not take a direct part in hostilities.

81. The United States signed the Optional Protocol on September 7, 2000, and while it has not yet ratified the Protocol or the underlying Convention, both the President of the United States[ ] and the U.S. Congress expressed support for the rule prescribed in Article I, with Congress encouraging the United States delegation "not to block the drafting of an optional protocol to the Convention on the Rights of the Child that would establish 18 as the minimum age for participation in armed conflict."[ ]

82. Support for this standard has also been expressed by the OAS General Assembly, which by resolution dated June 5, 2000 noted that more than 300,000 children under 18 years of age were at that time participating in armed conflicts worldwide. In light of this statistic, the General Assembly called upon member states to consider signing and ratifying the Optional Protocol to the United Nations Convention on the Rights of the Child regarding the participation of children in armed conflicts.[ ] Similar standards have been recognized internationally and within the United States itself in connection with areas of societal participation, such as the right to vote, in which the attainment of the age of 18 is considered a minimum and necessary prerequisite.[ ]

83. Accordingly, a finding that an international norm has emerged establishing 18 as the minimum age at which an individual is liable to face the ultimate punishment of

death is, in the Commission's view, entirely consistent with corresponding developments relating to obligations of an equivalent or lesser nature, such as participating in armed conflict or electing political leaders. Indeed, it is difficult to rationalize, much less justify, why a lesser standard should apply in the implementation of capital punishment. This is particularly evident given the broadly-recognized international obligation of states to provide enhanced protection to children, which includes ensuring the well-being of juvenile offenders and endeavor their rehabilitation. These obligations are reflected in Article 19 of the American Convention[ ] and Article VII of the American Declaration[ ] and, as interpreted by the Inter-American Court of Human Rights, require that "when the State apparatus has to intervene in offenses committed by minors, it should make substantial efforts to guarantee their rehabilitation in order to 'allow them to play a constructive and productive role in society.'"[ ]

f. Conclusion

84. In the Commission's view, the evidence canvassed above clearly illustrates that by persisting in the practice of executing offenders under age 18, the U.S. stands alone amongst the traditional developed world nations and those of the inter-American system, and has also become increasingly isolated within the entire global community. The overwhelming evidence of global state practice as set out above displays a consistency and generality amongst world states indicating that the world community considers the execution of offenders aged below 18 years at the time of their offence to be inconsistent with prevailing standards of decency. The Commission is therefore of the view that a norm of international customary law has emerged prohibiting the execution of offenders under the age of 18 years at the time of their crime.

85. Moreover, the Commission is satisfied, based upon the information before it, that this rule has been recognized as being of a sufficiently indelible nature to now constitute a norm of *jus cogens*, a development anticipated by the Commission in its Roach and Pinkerton decision. As noted above, nearly every nation state has rejected the imposition of capital punishment to individuals under the age of 18. They have done so through ratification of the ICCPR, U.N. Convention on the Rights of the Child, and the American Convention on Human Rights, treaties in which this proscription is recognized as non-derogable, as well as through corresponding amendments to their domestic laws. The acceptance of this norm crosses political and ideological boundaries and efforts to detract from this standard have been vigorously condemned by members of the international community as impermissible under contemporary human rights standards. Indeed, it may be said that the United States itself, rather than persistently objecting to the standard, has in several significant respects recognized the propriety of this norm by, for example, prescribing the age of 18 as the federal standard for the application of capital punishment and by ratifying the Fourth Geneva Convention without reservation to this standard. On this basis, the Commission considers that the United States is bound by a norm of *jus cogens* not to impose capital punishment on individuals who committed their crimes when they had not yet reached 18 years of age. As a *jus cogens* norm, this proscription binds the community of States, including the United States. The norm cannot be validly derogated from, whether by treaty or by the objection of a state, persistent or otherwise.

86. Interpreting the terms of the American Declaration in light of this norm of *jus cogens*, the Commission therefore concludes in the present case that the United States has failed to respect the life, liberty and security of the person of Michael Domingues

by sentencing him to death for crimes that he committed when he was 16 years of age, contrary to Article I of the American Declaration.

87. As a further consequence of this determination, the Commission finds that the United States will be responsible for a further grave and irreparable violation of Mr. Domingues' right to life under Article I of the American Declaration if he is executed for crimes that he committed when he was 16 years of age.

. . . .

∼

QUESTIONS & COMMENTS

(1) What do you make of the Inter-American Commission's examination of state practice in the United States for determining evidence of a customary international law norm? Does the Commission view states in the United States on the same legal plane as foreign states whose laws can serve as evidence of customary international law?

(2) Recently, the U.S. Supreme Court in *Roper v. Simmons*, No. 03–633, ___ U.S. ___ (2005), held that the execution of persons committing capital crimes under the age of 18 violated the Eighth Amendment's prohibition of cruel and unusual punishment. Although the Court did not find the international law prohibiting such executions "controlling," the Court did rely in part on this international law for "confirming" its decision.

(3) Also recently, the U.S. Supreme Court in *Atkins v. Virginia*, 536 U.S. 304 (2002), held that the execution of mentally retarded persons violated the Eighth Amendment. Again, the Supreme Court partially relied on "world opinion" cited in an amicus curiae brief submitted by the European Union in an earlier case.

Soering v. United Kingdom
European Court of Human Rights
161 Eur. Ct. H.R. (ser. A) (1989)
11 E.H.R.R. 439 (1989)

. . . .

FACTS:

I. Particular circumstances of the case

11. The applicant, Mr Jens Soering, was born on 1 August 1966 and is a German national. He is currently detained in prison in England pending extradition to the United States of America to face charges of murder in the Commonwealth of Virginia.

12. The homicides in question were committed in Bedford County, Virginia, in March 1985. The victims, William Reginald Haysom (aged 72) and Nancy Astor Haysom (aged 53), were the parents of the applicant's girlfriend, Elizabeth Haysom, who is a Canadian national. Death in each case was the result of multiple and massive stab and slash wounds to the neck, throat and body. At the time the applicant and Elizabeth Haysom, aged 18 and 20 respectively, were students at the University of Virginia. They disappeared together from Virginia in October 1985, but were arrested in England in April 1986 in connection with cheque fraud.

. . . .

[Soering applied to the European Commission of Human Rights alleging an Article 3 right to humane treatment violation. The Commission held that there had been no violation.]

DECISION [OF THE EUROPEAN COURT OF HUMAN RIGHTS]:

I. Alleged breach of Article 3

80. The applicant alleged that the decision by the Secretary of State for the Home Department to surrender him to the authorities of the United States of America would, if implemented, give rise to a breach by the United Kingdom of Article 3 of the Convention, which provides:

> No one shall be subjected to torture or to inhuman or degrading treatment or punishment.

. . . .

B. Application of Article 3 in the particular circumstances of the present case

. . . .

2. Whether in the circumstances the risk of exposure to the 'death row phenomenon' would make extradition a breach of Article 3.

(a) General considerations

100. As is established in the court's case law, ill-treatment, including punishment, must attain a minimum level of severity if it is to fall within the scope of Article 3. The assessment of this minimum is, in the nature of things, relative; it depends on all the circumstances of the case, such as the nature and context of the treatment or punishment, the manner and method if its execution, its duration, its physical or mental effects and, in some instances, the sex, age and state of health of the victim. [*See Ireland v. United Kingdom*, 25 Eur. Ct. H.R. (ser. A) at §162 (1978); and *Tyrer v. United Kingdom*, 26 Eur. Ct. H.R. (ser. A0 at §§29 and 80 (1978).]

Treatment has been held by the Court to be both 'inhuman' because it was premeditated, was applied for hours at a stretch and 'caused, if not actual bodily injury, at least intense physical and mental suffering,' and also 'degrading' because it was 'such as to arouse in [its] victims feelings of fear, anguish and inferiority capable of humiliating and debasing them and possibly breaking their physical or moral resistance'. (*See Ireland v. United Kingdom*, §167.) In order for a punishment or treatment associated with it to be 'inhuman' or 'degrading,' the suffering or humiliation involved must in any event go beyond that inevitable element of suffering or humiliation connected with a given form of legitimate punishment. (*See Tyrer v. United Kingdom*, loc cit.) In this connection, account is to be taken not only of the physical pain experienced but also, where there is a considerable delay before execution of the punishment, of the sentenced person's mental anguish of anticipating the violence he is to have inflicted on him.

101. Capital punishment is permitted under certain conditions by Article 2(1) of the convention, which reads:

> 'Everyone's right to life shall be protected by law. No one shall be deprived of his life intentionally save in the execution of a sentence of a court following his conviction of a crime for which this penalty is provided by law.'

In view of this wording, the applicant did not suggest that the death penalty *per se* violated Article 3. He, like the two Government Parties, agreed with the Commission that the extradition of a person to a country where he risks the death penalty does not in itself raise an issue under either Article 2 or Article 3. On the other hand, Amnesty International in their written comments argued that the evolving standards in Western Europe regarding the existence and use of the death penalty required that the death penalty should now be considered as an inhuman and degrading punishment within the meaning of Article 3.

102. Certainly, 'the Convention is a living instrument which . . . must be interpreted in the light of present-day conditions'; and, in assessing whether a given treatment or punishment is to be regarded as inhuman or degrading for the purposes of Article 3, 'the Court cannot but be influenced by the developments and commonly accepted standards in the penal policy of the member States of the Council of Europe in this field.' (*See Tyrer v. United Kingdom*, §31.) *De facto* the death penalty no longer exists in time of peace in the contracting States to the Convention. In the few Contracting States which retain the death penalty in law for some peacetime offences, death sentences, if ever imposed, are nowadays not carried out. This 'virtual consensus in Western European legal systems that the death penalty is, under current circumstances, no longer consistent with regional standards of justice,' to use the words of Amnesty International, is reflected in Protocol No 6 to the Convention, which provides for the abolition of the death penalty in time of peace. Protocol No 6 was opened for signature in April 1983, which in the practice of the Council of Europe indicates the absence of objection on the part of any of the Member States of the Organisation; it came into force in March 1985 and to date has been ratified by 13 Contracting States to the Convention, not however including the United Kingdom.

Whether these marked changes have the effect of bringing the death penalty *per se* within the prohibition of ill-treatment under Article 3 must be determined on the principles governing the interpretation of the Convention.

103. The Convention is to be read as a whole and Article 3 should therefore be construed in harmony with the provisions of Article 2. (*See, mutatis mutandis, Klass v. Germany*, §68.) On this basis Article 3 evidently cannot have been intended by the drafters of the Convention to include a general prohibition of the death penalty since that would nullify the clear wording of Article 2(1).

Subsequent practice in national penal policy, in the form of a generalised abolition of capital punishment, could be taken as establishing the agreement of the Contracting States to abrogate the exception provided for under Article 2(1) and hence to remove a textual limit on the scope for evolutive interpretation of Article 3. However, Protocol No 6, as a subsequent written agreement, shows that the intention of the Contracting Parties as recently as 1983 was to adopt the normal method of amendment of the text in order to introduce a new obligation to abolish capital punishment in time of peace and, what is more, to do so by an optional instrument allowing each State to choose the moment when to undertake such an engagement. In these conditions, notwithstanding the special character of the Convention, Article 3 cannot be interpreted as generally prohibiting the death penalty.

104. That does not mean however that circumstances relating to a death sentence can never give rise to an issue under Article 3. The manner in which it is imposed or executed, the personal circumstances of the condemned person and a disproportionality

to the gravity of the crime committed, as well as the conditions of detention awaiting execution, are examples of factors capable of bringing the treatment or punishment received by the condemned person with the proscription under Article 3. Present-day attitudes in the contracting States to capital punishment are relevant for the assessment whether the acceptable threshold of suffering or degradation has been exceeded.

(b) The particular circumstances

105. The applicant submitted that the circumstances to which he would be exposed as a consequence of the implementation of the Secretary of State's decision to return him to the United States, namely the 'death row phenomenon,' cumulatively constitute such serious treatment that his extradition would be contrary to Article 3. He cited in particular the delays in the appeal and review procedures following a death sentence, during which time he would be subject to increasing tension and psychological trauma; the fact, so he said, that the judge or jury in determining sentence is not obliged to take into account the defendant's age and mental state at the time of the offence; the extreme conditions of his future detention in 'death row' in Mecklenburg Correctional Center, where he expects to be the victim of violence and sexual abuse because of his age, colour and nationality; and the constant spectre of the execution itself, including the ritual of execution. He also relied on the possibility of extradition or deportation, which he would not oppose, to the Federal Republic of Germany as accentuating the disproportionality of the Secretary of State's decision.

The Government of the Federal Republic of Germany took the view that, taking all the circumstances together, the treatment awaiting the applicant in Virginia would go so far beyond treatment inevitably connected with the imposition and execution of a death penalty as to be 'inhuman' within the meaning of Article 3.

On the other hand, the conclusion expressed by the Commission was that the degree of severity contemplated by Article 3 would not be attained.

The United Kingdom Government shared this opinion. In particular, it disputed many of the applicant's factual allegations as to the conditions on death row in Mecklenburg and his expected fate there.

(i) Length of detention prior to execution

106. The period that a condemned prisoner can expect to spend on death row in Virginia before being executed is on average six to eight years. This length of time awaiting death, is, as the commission and the United Kingdom Government noted, in a sense largely of the prisoner's own making in that he takes advantage of all avenues of appeal which are offered to him by Virginia law. The automatic appeal to the Supreme Court of Virginia normally takes no more than six months. The remaining time is accounted for by collateral attacks mounted by the prisoner himself in habeas corpus proceedings before both the State and Federal courts and in applications to the Supreme Court of the United States for *certiorari* review, the prisoner at each stage being able to seek a stay of execution. The remedies available under Virginia law serve the purpose of ensuring that the ultimate sanction of death is not unlawfully or arbitrarily imposed.

Nevertheless, just as some lapse of time between sentence and execution is inevitable if appeal safeguards are to be provided to the condemned person, so it is equally part of human nature that the person will cling to life by exploiting those safeguards to the full. However well-intentioned and even potentially beneficial is the provision of the complex of post-sentence procedures in Virginia, the consequence is that the condemned prisoner has to endure for many years the conditions on death row and the anguish and mounting tension of living in the ever-present shadow of death.

(ii) Conditions on death row

107. As to conditions in Mecklenburg Correctional Center, where the applicant could expect to be held if sentenced to death, the court bases itself on the facts which were uncontested by the United Kingdom Government, without finding it necessary to determine the reliability of the additional evidence adduced by the applicant, notably as to the risk of homosexual abuse and physical attack undergone by prisoners on death row.

The stringency of the custodial regime in Mecklenburg, as well as the services (medical, legal and social) and the controls (legislative, judicial and administrative) provided for inmates, are described in some detail above. In this connection, the United Kingdom Government drew attention to the necessary requirement of extra security for the safe custody of prisoners condemned to death for murder. Whilst it might thus well be justifiable in principle, the severity of a special regime such as that operated on death row in Mecklenburg is compounded by the fact of inmates being subject to it for a protracted period lasting on average six to eight years.

(iii) The applicant's age and mental state

108. At the time of the killings, the applicant was only 18 years old and there is some psychiatric evidence, which was not contested as such, that he 'was suffering from [such] an abnormality of mind ... as substantially impaired his mental responsibility for his acts'.

Unlike Article 2 of the Convention, Article 6 of the 1966 International Covenant on Civil and Political Rights and Article 4 of the 1969 American Convention on Human Rights expressly prohibit the death penalty from being imposed on persons aged less than 18 at the time of commission of the offence. Whether or not such a prohibition be inherent in the brief and general language of Article 2 of the European Convention, its explicit enunciation in other, later international instruments, the former of which has been ratified by a large number of States parties to the European Convention, at the very least indicates that as a general principle the youth of the person concerned is a circumstance which is liable, with others, to put in question the compatibility with Article 3 of measures connected with a death sentence.

It is in line with the Court's case law to treat disturbed mental health as having the same effect for the application of Article 3.

109. Virginia law, as the United Kingdom Government and the Commission emphasised, certainly does not ignore these two factors. Under the Virginia Code account has to be taken of mental disturbance in a defendant, either as an absolute bar to conviction it if is judged to be sufficient to amount to insanity or, like age, as a fact in mitigation at the sentencing stage. Additionally, indigent capital murder defendants are entitled to the appointment of a qualified mental health expert to assist in the preparation of their submissions at the separate sentencing proceedings. These provisions in the Virginia Code undoubtedly serve, as the American courts have stated, to prevent the arbitrary or capricious imposition of the death penalty and narrowly to channel the sentencer's discretion. They do not however remove the relevance of age and mental condition in relation to the acceptability, under Article 3, of the 'death row phenomenon' for a given individual once condemned to death.

Although it is not for this Court to prejudge issues of criminal responsibility and appropriate sentence, the applicant's youth at the time of the offence and his then mental state, on the psychiatric evidence as it stands, are therefore to be taken into consideration as contributory factors tending, in his case, to bring the treatment on death row within the terms of Article 3.

. . .

(c) Conclusion

111. For any prisoner condemned to death, some element of delay, between imposition and execution of the sentence and the experience of severe stress in conditions necessary for strict incarceration are inevitable. The democratic character of the Virginia legal system in general and the positive features of Virginia trial, sentencing and appeal procedures in particular are beyond doubt. The Court agrees with the Commission that the machinery of justice to which the applicant would be subject in the United States is in itself neither arbitrary nor unreasonable, but, rather, respects the rule of law and affords not inconsiderable procedural safeguards to the defendant in a capital trial. Facilities are available on death row for the assistance of inmates, notably through provision of psychological and psychiatric services.

However, in the Court's view, having regard to the very long period of time spent on death row in such extreme conditions, with the ever-present and mounting anguish of awaiting execution of the death penalty, and to the personal circumstances of the applicant, especially his age and mental state at the time of the offence, the applicant's extradition to the United States would expose him to a real risk of treatment going beyond the threshold set by Article 3. A further consideration of relevance is that in the particular instance the legitimate purpose of extradition could be achieved by another means which would not involve suffering of such exceptional intensity or duration.

Accordingly, the Secretary of State's decision to extradite the applicant to the United States would, if implemented, give rise to a breach of Article 3.

. . . .

Concurring Opinion of Judge de Meyer

. . . .

The second sentence of Article 2(1) of the Convention, as it was drafted in 1950, states that 'no one shall be deprived of his life intentionally save in the execution of a sentence of a court following his conviction of a crime for which this penalty is provided by law.'

In the circumstances of the present case, the applicant's extradition to the United States would subject him to the risk of being sentenced to death, and executed, in Virginia for a crime for which that penalty is not provided by the law of the United Kingdom.

When a person's right to life is involved, no requested State can be entitled to allow a requesting State to do what the requested State is not itself allowed to do.

If, as in the present case, the domestic law of a State does not provide the death penalty for the crime concerned, that State is not permitted to put the person concerned in a position where he may be deprived of his life for that crime at the hands of another State.

That consideration may already suffice to preclude the United Kingdom from surrendering the applicant to the United States.

There is also something more fundamental.

The second sentence of Article 2(1) of the Convention was adopted, nearly forty years ago, in particular historical circumstances, shortly after the second World War. In so far as it still may seem to permit, under certain conditions, capital punishment in time of peace, it does not reflect the contemporary situation, and is now overridden by the development of legal conscience and practice. (*See also* Art 6(2) and (6) of the International Covenant on Civil and Political Rights and Article 4(2) and (3) of the American Convention on Human Rights. The very wording of each of these provisions, adopted respectively in 1966 and in 1969, clearly reflects the evolution of legal conscience and practice towards the universal abolition of the death penalty.)

Such punishment is not consistent with the present state of European civilisation.

De facto, it no longer exists in any State Party to the Convention.

Its unlawfulness was recognised by the Committee of Ministers of the Council of Europe when it adopted in December 1982, and opened for signature in April 1983, the Sixth Protocol to the Convention, which to date has been signed by 16, and ratified by 13, Contracting States.

No State party to the Convention can in that context, even if it has not yet ratified the Sixth Protocol, be allowed to extradite any person if that person thereby incurs the risk of being put to death in the requesting State.

Extraditing somebody in such circumstances would be repugnant to European standards of justice, and contrary to the public order of Europe. (*See, mutatis mutandis*, the judgment of 27 February 1987 by the French Conseil d'Etat in the FIDAN case, [1987] Recueil Dalloz Sirey, 305–310.)

The applicant's surrender by the United Kingdom to the United States could only be lawful if the United States were to give absolute assurances that he will not be put to death if convicted of the crime he is charged with. (*See* the French FIDAN judgment referred to above.)

No such assurances were, or can be, obtained.

The Federal Government of the United States is unable to give any undertaking as to what may or may not be decided, or done, by the judicial and other authorities of the Commonwealth of Virginia.

In fact, the Commonwealth's Attorney dealing with the case intends to seek the death penalty and the Commonwealth's Governor has never commuted a death sentence since the imposition of the death penalty was resumed in 1977.

. . . .

∾

QUESTIONS & COMMENTS

(1) The Commonwealth of Virginia subsequently gave assurances that Soering would not be executed if he were returned to Virginia. Consequently, Soering was returned, tried, convicted, and sentenced to two terms of life imprisonment.

(2) In *Soering v. United Kingdom*, the European Court expressly declined to find that the death penalty inherently violated Article 3, on the grounds that Article 2(1), ECHR, allowed the death penalty. Evidence abounds that the death penalty has ceased to be a relevant penal practice in the nations covered by the ECHR, including its Sixth Protocol, which came into force in 1985 and explicitly bound its contracting parties to the complete

abolition of the death penalty in time of peace. Presently, thirty states have ratified the Sixth Protocol. The Court has found the Sixth Protocol reason to refrain from a judicial reinterpretation of Article 2(1). While acknowledging that the Convention was a living document that could develop in line with evolving principles of justice among ECHR states parties, the court took the Sixth Protocol as evidence of a consensus among states parties to resolve the issue through explicit legislative action by member states. The Court's reading of the Sixth Protocol as evidence of the will among the convention members to resolve the matter directly given that it represented the fruit of a long-term and hard-fought effort to begin the institutionalization of abolitionism within the European convention. WILLIAM A. SCHABAS, THE ABOLITION OF THE DEATH PENALTY IN INTERNATIONAL LAW 228–38 (1993); Francisco Forrest Martin, *et al.*, 1 INTERNATIONAL HUMAN RIGHTS LAW & PRACTICE: CASES, TREATIES AND MATERIALS 459–60 (1997). Most significantly, the EU Constitution has incorporated the Charter of Fundamental Rights of the European Union that prohibits the death penalty. The EU Constitution awaits ratification of EU members.

Recently, the Human Rights Chamber for Bosnia and Herzegovina has been examining cases in which military courts have ordered executions. Under Annex 6 of the Dayton Agreement, the Republic of Bosnia and Herzegovina, the Federation of Bosnia and Herzegovina, and the Republika Srpska are bound by the Sixth Protocol. Under Article 2 of the Sixth Protocol, the death penalty can be imposed only "in respect of acts committed in time of war or of imminent threat of war." However, the Dayton Agreement ended the civil war in Bosnia-Herzegovina; therefore, the Chamber found that the military court could not sentence individuals to death.

(3) The UN Human Rights Committee has held that prolonged detention on death row did not *per se* constitute a violation of Article 7, ICCPR, which forbids torture and inhuman treatment. *Pratt and Morgan v. Jamaica*, Communication Nos. 210/1986 and 225/1987, views adopted U.N. Doc. A/44/40, at §13.6. As with the ECHR, attacks on the death penalty itself as inhuman treatment under Article 7 have run into treaty provisions allowing the death penalty. In the case of the ICCPR, Article 6 allows the death penalty. In particular cases, the Committee has found Article 7 violations surrounding the use of the death penalty. However, in cases involving extradition to the United States from a nation obligated under the Covenant, the Committee has declined to find Article 7 violations on death row phenomenon grounds. However, the Committee has held that there are specific limits to using the death penalty.

For example, in *Ng v. Canada*, Communication No. 469/1991, views adopted 5 November 1993, U.N. Doc. CCPR/C/40/D/469/1991 (1994), the author had been charged with twelve murders in California and had been arrested for theft in Canada. When he was extradited, Mr. Ng authored a complaint to the Committee raising the conditions on death row but also adding a detailed attack on the use of gas asphyxiation then practiced in California. The Committee found on the basis of detailed evidence presented about the operation of the gas chamber that its use would violate the Covenant. The Committee concluded that execution by gas asphyxiation, should the death penalty be imposed on the author, would not meet the test of "least possible physical and mental suffering," and constituted cruel and inhuman treatment in violation of article 7. *Id.* at §16.4.

In *Kindler v. Canada*, Communication No. 470/1991, views adopted 30 July 1993, U.N. Doc. CCPR/C/48/D/470/1001 (1993), the Committee upheld an extradition by

Canada of a convicted murderer to the United States. Joseph Kindler was convicted of murder and kidnapping in Pennsylvania. The same jury voted to recommend death, but before his formal sentencing hearing in front of the judge he escaped custody. Some months later he was arrested in Quebec. The United States sought extradition, which was granted by a Canadian court. The Canadian/U.S. extradition treaty allowed a state that does not practice the death penalty for a particular offense to decline extradition unless that penalty is waived. The Canadian government did not exercise this option and instead extradited Mr. Kindler to Pennsylvania. Kindler submitted a communication to the UN Human Rights Committee challenging Canada's actions under the Covenant on a variety of grounds, including the fact that he would face the death row phenomena in Pennsylvania. The Committee reiterated its earlier view that prolonged detention is not a *per se* violation but, citing *Soering*, the Committee held the existence of a violation in a particular case would turn on "relevant personal factors regarding the author, the specific conditions of detention on death row, and whether the proposed method of execution is particularly abhorrent." *Id.* at §15.3. With regard to Mr. Kindler's claim, however, the Committee pointed out that

> important facts leading to the judgement of the European court [in *Soering*] are distinguishable on material points from the facts in the present case. In particular, the facts differ as to the age and mental state of the offender, and the conditions on death row in the respective prison systems. The author's counsel made no specific submissions on prison conditions in Pennsylvania, or about the possibility or the effects of prolonged delay in the execution of a sentence; nor was any submission made about the specific method of execution.

Id. at §15.3; *see also Cox v. Canada*, Communication No. 539/1993, U.N. Doc. CCPR/C/52/D/539/1993, at §17.2 (rejecting death row phenomenon challenge to extradition to Pennsylvania). However, *Kindler v. Canada* subsequently was overruled by the UN Human Rights Committee in *Judge v. Canada* (reproduced below).

(4) *Soering* represents a path toward abolition that leads to heightening the pressure on retentionist states to resolve the contradictory values underlying delay in carrying out the death penalty. The European Court was unwilling to demand that states parties refuse to support the death penalty elsewhere with extradition powers, but it was willing to require members to get involved in policing the integrity of the death penalty in other states. The Inter-American Court of Human Rights has used its advisory jurisdiction to foster a similar transnational influence of abolitionism on retentionist states.

In *Restrictions to the Death Penalty (Arts. 4 Sect. 2 and Article 4 Sect. 4 American Convention on Human Rights)*, Advisory Opinion OC-3/83 of September 8, 1983, the Court opined that Guatemala violated Article 4(2) which provides:

> The application of such punishment [death penalty] shall not be extended to crimes to which it does not presently apply.

Guatemala executed four men under emergency decree laws for crimes that were made capital long after Guatemala signed the convention. Guatemala argued that it had preserved its sovereign right to use capital punishment in social defense. It also argued that its explicit reservation to Article 4(4) ("In no case shall capital punishment be inflicted for political offenses or related common crimes") implied a right to continue expanding the death penalty. The Court opined that the reservation to Article 4(4) could not bear on Guatemala's obligations under Article 4(2). By the time of the hearing, however, a new government in Guatemala had already withdrawn the contested capital crimes. In 1986, Guatemala withdrew its reservation to Article 4(4) altogether.

In *International Responsibility for the Promulgation and Enforcement of Laws in Violation of the Convention (Arts. 1 and 2 of the American Convention on Human Rights)*, Advisory Opinion OC-14/94 of December 9, 1994, Inter-Am. Ct. H.R. (Ser. A.) No. 14 (1994), the Inter-American Commission asked the Inter-American Court to consider the obligations of state parties and their agents in the face of actions by the state that "manifestly violate[ ] the obligations it assumed upon ratifying the Convention." *Id.* at §1. The circumstances giving rise to the Commission's request for an advisory opinion was the Peruvian government's decision to add an additional capital crime for terrorism, a decision taken after the arrest of Abimael Guzman, the leader of a revolutionary group called "the Shining Path." Since Peru's Constitution provided for the death penalty only for treason in time of war, Article 4(2) of the American Convention appeared to bar Peru from subsequently adding the death penalty for terrorism. Without considering the merits of the violation, the Court opined that:

> The enforcement of a law manifestly in violation of the convention by agents or officials of a state results in international responsibility for that state. If the enforcement in question constitutes an international crime, it will also subject the agents or officials who execute it to international responsibility.

Id. at §57.

(5) After *Soering v. United Kingdom*, the Lords of the Judicial Commission of the Privy Council in the United Kingdom addressed the death row phenomenon. In *Earl Pratt and Ivan Morgan v. The Attorney General for Jamaica*, Privy Council Appeal 2, A.C.1, 4 All E.R. 769 (P.C. 1993) (*en banc*), the petitioners had served fourteen years on death row, including three times on which they were moved to a special cell for the condemned. In each case, new legal challenges by their attorneys resulted in stays of execution. Although the Privy Council acknowledged that defendants naturally played a role in extending the delays, it condemned the inherent cruelty of allowing the process to stretch on so long.

The Privy Council concluded that, in all Commonwealth countries, a delay of more than five years would constitute presumptive proof of death row phenomenon. In the wake of vacating scores of death sentences because of the *Pratt & Morgan* holding, several Caribbean countries have reacted by withdrawing from international human rights treaty mechanisms. Jamaica withdrew from the Optional Protocol to the ICCPR, and Trinidad and Tobago has announced its withdrawal from the ACHR. *See* Natalia Schiffrin, *Jamaica Withdraws the Right of Individual Petition under the International Covenant on Civil and Political Rights*, 92 Am. J. Int'l L. 563 (1998).

Although U.S. Supreme Court Justice Antonin Scalia rejected the authority of foreign cases in *Stanford v. Kentucky*, others of his colleagues on the Supreme Court continue to use such cases. Justice John Paul Stevens cited *Pratt and Morgan v. Attorney General* in his dissent to the denial of certiorari in a case involving a prisoner who had spent seventeen years on death row and raised the "death row phenomenon" issue under the Eighth Amendment. *See Lackey v. Texas*, __ U.S. __, 115 S.Ct. 1421 (1995) (Stevens, J. dissenting). Justice Stephen Breyer also joined that dissent. Stevens and Breyer also cited *Pratt and Morgan v. Attorney General* and *Makwanyane & Mchunu* in their dissents in *Gomez v. Fierro*, __ U.S. __, 117 S.Ct. 285 (1996).

Several lower courts also have considered the death row phenomenon but thus far without reversing a death sentence. In *McKenzie v. Day*, 57 F.3d 1461, 1466 (9th Cir. 1995), Judge Alex Kozinski cited *Pratt & Morgan* and *Soering* but rejected the factual analogy, finding that the evidence did not suggest that Montana was at fault for the long delay in executing McKenzie (he had been on death row for twenty years at that point). Further, Judge Kozinski raised the concern that recognizing the death row phenomenon as an Eighth Amendment violation would undermine the administration of capital punishment.

> By and large, the delay in carrying out death sentences has been of benefit to death row inmates, allowing them to extend their lives, obtain commutation or reversal of their sentences, or in rare cases, secure complete exoneration. Sustaining a claim such as McKenzie's would, we fear, wreak havoc with the orderly administration of the death penalty in this country by placing a substantial premium on speed rather than accuracy.

McKenzie v. Day, 57 F.3d 1461, 1467. In a vigorous dissent, Judge William Norris, cited the international cases as powerful support for the substantiality of McKenzie's Eighth Amendment claim and accused the majority of substituting a "policy lecture" for a serious analysis of the penalogical justifications for executing those who have been held on death row for extremely long periods. *Id.* at 1488–89.

(6) Finally, note that the Statutes of the ICT-Y, ICT-R, and ICC do not allow the use of the death penalty. Given the fact that the crimes covered by the these statutes address violations of *jus cogens* (which is not subject to the persistent objector rule governing the rest of customary international law) and that these statutes have and/or shortly will be globally accepted by states, how would you argue that there now is a *jus cogens* prohibition against the death penalty for *all* crimes by virtue of the fact that the crimes covered by the statutes are considerably worse than other common capital crimes?

Judge v. Canada
Communication No. 829/1998
UN Human Rights Committee
UN Doc. CCPR/C/78/D/829/1998   20 October 2003

. . . .

The complaint

3.2 The author claims that "by detaining [him] for ten years despite the fact that he faced certain execution at the end of his sentence, and proposing now to remove him to the United States, Canada has violated [his] right to life, in violation of article 6 of the Covenant."

. . . .

Issues and proceedings before the Committee

. . . .

Question 1. As Canada has abolished the death penalty, did it violate the author's right to life under article 6, his right not to be subjected to torture or to cruel, inhuman or degrading treatment or punishment under article 7, or his right to an effective remedy under article 2, paragraph 3, of the Covenant by deporting him to a State in which he was under sentence of death without ensuring that that sentence would not be carried out?

10.2 In considering Canada's obligations, as a State party which has abolished the death penalty, in removing persons to another country where they are under sentence of death, the Committee recalls its previous jurisprudence in *Kindler v. Canada*, [ ]that it does not consider that the deportation of a person from a country which has abolished the death penalty to a country where he/she is under sentence of death amounts *per se* to a violation of article 6 of the Covenant. The Committee's rationale in this decision was based on an interpretation of the Covenant which read article 6, paragraph 1, together with article 6, paragraph 2, which does not prohibit the imposition of the death penalty for the most serious crimes. It considered that as Canada itself had not imposed the death penalty but had extradited the author to the United States to face capital punishment, a state which had not abolished the death penalty, the extradition itself would not amount to a violation by Canada unless there was a real risk that the author's rights under the Covenant would be violated in the United States. On the issue of assurances, the Committee found that the terms of article 6 did not necessarily require Canada to refuse to extradite or to seek assurances but that such a request should at least be considered by the removing state.

10.3 While recognizing that the Committee should ensure both consistency and coherence of its jurisprudence, it notes that there may be exceptional situations in which a review of the scope of application of the rights protected in the Covenant is required, such as where an alleged violation involves that most fundamental of rights – the right to life – and in particular if there have been notable factual and legal developments and changes in international opinion in respect of the issue raised. The Committee is mindful of the fact that the abovementioned jurisprudence was established some 10 years ago, and that since that time there has been a broadening international consensus in favour of abolition of the death penalty, and in states which have retained the death penalty, a broadening consensus not to carry it out. Significantly, the Committee notes that since *Kindler* the State party itself has recognized the need to amend its own domestic law to secure the protection of those extradited from Canada under sentence of death in the receiving state, in the case of *United States v. Burns*. There, the Supreme Court of Canada held that the government must seek assurances, in all but exceptional cases, that the death penalty will not be applied prior to extraditing an individual to a state where he/she faces capital punishment. It is pertinent to note that under the terms of this judgment, "Other abolitionist countries do not, in general, extradite without assurances."[ ] The Committee considers that the Covenant should be interpreted as a living instrument and the rights protected under it should be applied in context and in the light of present – day conditions.

10.4 In reviewing its application of article 6, the Committee notes that, as required by the Vienna Convention on the Law of Treaties, a treaty should be interpreted in good faith and in accordance with the ordinary meaning to be given to the terms of the treaty in their context and in the light of its object and purpose. Paragraph 1 of article 6, which states that "Every human being has the inherent right to life...", is a general rule: its purpose is to protect life. States parties that have abolished the death penalty have an obligation under this paragraph to so protect in all circumstances. Paragraphs 2 to 6 of article 6 are evidently included to avoid a reading of the first paragraph of article 6, according to which that paragraph could be understood as abolishing the death penalty as such. This construction of the article is reinforced by the opening words of paragraph 2 ("In countries which have not abolished the death penalty...") and by paragraph 6 ("Nothing in this article shall be invoked to delay or to prevent the abolition of capital punishment by any State Party to the present Covenant."). In effect, paragraphs 2 to 6 have the dual function of creating an exception to the right to life in respect of the death penalty and laying down limits on the scope of that exception. Only the death penalty pronounced when certain elements are present can benefit from the exception. Among these limitations are that found in the opening words of paragraph 2, namely, that only States parties that "have not abolished the death penalty" can avail themselves of the exceptions created in paragraphs 2 to 6. For countries that *have* abolished the death penalty, there is an obligation not to expose a person to the real risk of its application. Thus, they may not remove, either by deportation or extradition, individuals from their jurisdiction if it may be reasonably anticipated that they will be sentenced to death, without ensuring that the death sentence would not be carried out.

10.5 The Committee acknowledges that by interpreting paragraphs 1 and 2 of article 6 in this way, abolitionist and retentionist States parties are treated differently. But it considers that this is an inevitable consequence of the wording of the provision itself, which, as becomes clear from the *Travaux Préparatoires*, sought to appease very divergent views on the issue of the death penalty, in an effort at compromise among the drafters of the provision. The Committee notes that it was expressed in the *Travaux* that, on the one hand, one of the main principles of the Covenant should be abolition, but on the other, it was pointed out that capital punishment existed in certain countries and that abolition would create difficulties for such countries. The death penalty was seen by many delegates and bodies participating in the drafting process as an "anomaly" or a "necessary evil." It would appear logical, therefore, to interpret the rule in article 6, paragraph 1, in a wide sense, whereas paragraph 2, which addresses the death penalty, should be interpreted narrowly.

10.6 For these reasons, the Committee considers that Canada, as a State party which has abolished the death penalty, irrespective of whether it has not yet ratified the Second Optional Protocol to the Covenant Aiming at the Abolition of the Death Penalty, violated the author's right to life under article 6, paragraph 1, by deporting him to the United States, where he is under sentence of death, without ensuring that the death penalty would not be carried out. The Committee recognizes that Canada did not itself impose the death penalty on the author. But by deporting him to a country where he was under sentence of death, Canada established the crucial link in the causal chain that would make possible the execution of the author.

10.7 As to the State party's claim that its conduct must be assessed in the light of the law applicable at the time when the alleged treaty violation took place, the Committee considers that the protection of human rights evolves and that the meaning of Covenant rights should in principle be interpreted by reference to the time of examination and not, as the State party has submitted, by reference to the time the alleged violation took place. The Committee also notes that prior to the author's deportation to the United States the Committee's position was evolving in respect of a State party that had abolished capital punishment (and was a State party to the Second Optional Protocol to the International Covenant on Human Rights, aiming at the abolition of the death penalty), from whether capital punishment would subsequent to removal to another State be applied in violation of the Covenant to whether there was a real risk of capital punishment as such (Communication No. 692/1996, *A.R.J. v. Australia*, Views adopted on 28 July 1997 and Communication No. 706/1996, G.T. v. Australia, Views adopted on 4 November 1997). Furthermore, the State party's concern regarding possible retroactivity involved in the present approach has no bearing on the separate issues to be addressed under question 2 below.

. . . .

11. The Human Rights Committee, acting under article 5, paragraph 4, of the Optional Protocol to the International Covenant on Civil and Political Rights, is of the view that the facts as found by the Committee reveal a violation by Canada of articles 6, paragraph 1 alone and, read together with 2, paragraph 3, of the International Covenant on Civil and Political Rights.

12. Pursuant to article 2, paragraph 3 (a) of the Covenant, the Committee concludes that the author is entitled to an appropriate remedy which would include making such representations as are possible to the receiving state to prevent the carrying out of the death penalty on the author.

. . . .

QUESTIONS & COMMENTS

(1) The U.S. Supreme Court has held that international law governs the relations between states of the Union. *Arkansas v. Tennessee*, 310 U.S. 563, 570 (1940); *Wisconsin v. Michigan*, 295 U.S. 455, 461 (1935); *Connecticut v. Massachusetts*, 282 U.S. 660, 670 (1931); *Kansas v. Colorado*, 185 U.S. 125, 143 (1902). In light of *Judge v. Canada*, could a state that has abolished the death penalty constitutionally refuse to allow the extradition of a defendant to a state that is seeking to impose the death penalty on the defendant? The Full Faith and Credit Clause states: "Full Faith and Credit shall be given in each State to the public Acts, Records, and judicial Proceedings of every other State. And the Congress may by general Laws prescribe the Manner in which such Acts, Records and Proceedings shall be proved, and the Effect thereof." U.S. CONST. art. IV (1). Furthermore, Article IV also states that "A Person charged in any State with Treason, Felony, or other Crime, who shall flee from Justice, and be found in another State, shall on Demand of the executive Authority of the State from which he fled, be delivered up, to be removed to the State having Jurisdiction of the Crime." Consider the argument that the Constitution as a treaty must be construed in conformity with customary international law and the status of the ICCPR as part of the supreme law of the land under the Supremacy Clause.

Abductions, Disappearances, and Summary Executions

While international prohibitions against abductions and summary executions are well established, it is only relatively recently that international adjudicatory bodies have explicitly recognized the practice of "disappearances" as a violation of international human rights law. The practice of "disappearances," which rose to international prominence after its systematic use by the military regime in Argentina in the 1970s, is a particularly effective method of state terror. By its very nature it is designed to leave few if any traces linking state officials to the abduction and subsequent torture or killing, thus presenting a difficult problem of proof. There are rarely witnesses to an abduction; when they do exist, witnesses can usually testify only to the fact that an individual was abducted without being able to identify the abductors. The body of the disappeared person is rarely available, having been destroyed by the abductors, thus leaving open to speculation whether the individual is still alive. In response to these problems, international tribunals have developed special rules of evidence and proof for cases involving disappearances.

The international standard holding states responsible for disappearances that take place in their jurisdiction began as a part of international "soft law," and has evolved into an authoritative rule of customary international law through decisions in regional and municipal courts. Concern about the rise of disappearances internationally in the 1970s led to the creation in 1980 of the UN Working Group on Enforced or Involuntary Disappearances, the first UN "theme" procedure established under the UN Human Rights Commission. In its early years, the Working Group played a major role in publicizing the phenomenon of disappearances and developing a precise definition of the violation. Although the UN Working Groups have no formal enforcement powers, they are able to increase political pressure against a state through site visits and other similarly public mechanisms. While such exposure may not successfully halt the violations nor provide an adequate remedy to victims, it usually can lessen ongoing violations and contributes to the development of human rights norms. Once a mechanism under the UN Human Rights Commission had been created for disappearances, the campaign was taken by victims, human rights organizations, and international lawyers to regional and national courts.

In the following two cases, we examine the connection between the right to humane treatment and the right to personal security in the context of abductions and disappearances. In the first case, we will examine an extraterritorial abduction.

Saldías de López v. Uruguay
UN Human Rights Committee
Communication No. 52/1979
Views adopted 29 July 1981
SELECTED DECISIONS UNDER THE OPTIONAL PROTOCOL
U.N. Doc. CCPR/C/OP/1 (1985), at 88

. . . .

1. The author of the communication is Delia Saldías de López, a political refugee of Uruguayan nationality residing in Austria. She submits the communication on behalf of her husband, Sergio Rubén López Burgos, a worker and trade-union leader in Uruguay.

2.1 The author states that mainly because of the alleged victim's active participation in the trade union movement, he was subjected to various forms of harassment by the authorities from the beginning of his trade union involvement. Thus, he was arrested in December 1974 and held without charges for four months. In May 1975, shortly after his release and while still subjected to harassment by the authorities, he moved to Argentina. In September 1975 he obtained recognition as a political refugee by the Office of the United National High Commissioner for Refugees.

2.2 The author claims that on 13 July 1976 her husband was kidnapped in Buenos Aires by members of the "Uruguayan security and intelligence forces" who were aided by Argentine para-military groups, and was secretly detained in Buenos Aires for about two weeks. On 26 July 1976 Mr. López Burgos, together with several other Uruguayan nationals, was illegally and clandestinely transported to Uruguay, where he was detained incommunicado by the special security forces at a secret prison for three months. During his detention of approximately four months both in Argentina and Uruguay, he was continuously subjected to physical and mental torture and other cruel, inhuman or degrading treatment.

2.3 The author asserts that her husband was subjected to torture and ill-treatment as a consequence of which he suffered a broken jawbone and perforation of the eardrums. In substantiation of her allegations, the author furnishes detailed testimony submitted by six ex-detainees who were held, together with Mr. López Burgos, in some of the secret detention places in Argentina and Uruguay, and who were later released....

. . . .

2.8 She alleges that the following articles of the Covenant on Civil and Political Rights have been violated by the Uruguayan authorities in respect of her husband: articles 7, 9 and 12(1) and article 14(3).

. . . .

4. The State party, in its response under rule 91 of the provisional rules of procedure, dated 14 December 1979, states "that the communication concerned is completely devoid of any grounds which would make it admissible by the Committee since, in the course of the proceedings taken against Mr. López Burgos he enjoyed all the guarantees afforded by the Uruguayan legal order." [. . . T]he State party refers in this connection to its previous submissions to the Committee in other cases citing the domestic remedies generally available at present in Uruguay. Furthermore the State party provides some factual evidence in the case as follows: Mr. López Burgos was arrested on 23 October 1976 for his connection with subversive activities and detained under prompt security measures; on 4 November 1976, the second military examining magistrate charged him with presumed commission of the offense of "subversive association" under section 60(V) of the Military Penal Code; on 8 March 1979, the court of first instance sentenced him to seven years' imprisonment for the offenses specified in section 60(V) of the Military Penal Code, section 60(I)(6) in association with 60(XII) of the Military Penal Code and sections 7, 243 and 54 of the Ordinary Penal Code; subsequently, on 4 October 1979, the Supreme Military Court rendered final judgment, reducing his sentence to four years and six months. It is further stated that Mr. López Burgos' defense counsel was Colonel Mario Rodríguez and that Mr. López Burgos is being held at Military Detention Establishment No. 1. The Government of Uruguay also brings to the attention of the Committee a report on a medical examination of Mr. López Burgos, stating in part as follows:

Medical history prior to imprisonment (*Antecedentes personales anteriores a su "reclusión"*): operated on for bilateral inguinal hernia at the age of 12; (2) history of unstable arterial hypertension; (3) fracture of lower left jaw.

Family medical history: (1) father a diabetic.

Medical record in prison (*Antecedentes de "reclusión"*): treated by the dental surgery service of the Armed Forces Central Hospital for the fracture of the jaw with which he entered the Establishment. Discharged from the Armed Forces Central Hospital on 7 May 1977 with the fracture knitted and progressing well; subsequently examined for polyps of larynx on left vocal cord; a biopsy conducted....

. . . .

7.3 Whereas the author claims that her husband was kidnapped by members of the Uruguayan security and intelligence forces on 13 July 1976, the State party asserts that Mr. López Burgos was arrested on 23 October 1976 and claims that the whereabouts of Mr. López Burgos have been known since the date of his detention but no earlier information is available.

. . . .

10.2 The Human Rights Committee has considered the present communication in the light of all information made available to it by the parties, as provided in article 5(1) of the Optional Protocol. The Committee bases its views *inter alia* on the following undisputed facts:

10.2 Sergio Rubén López Burgos was living in Argentina as a political refugee until his disappearance on 13 July 1976; he subsequently reappeared in Montevideo, Uruguay, not later than 23 October 1976, the date of his purported arrest by Uruguayan authorities, and was detained under "prompt security measures." On 4 November 1976 pre-trial proceedings commenced when the second military examining magistrate charged him with the offense of "subversive association," but the actual trial began in April 1978 before a military court of first instance, which sentenced him on 8 March 1979 to seven years' imprisonment; upon appeal the court of second instance reduced the sentence to four years six months. López Burgos was treated for a broken jaw in a military hospital from 5 February to 7 May 1977.

11.1 In formulating its views the Human Rights Committee also takes into account the following considerations:

11.2 As regards the whereabouts of López Burgos between July and October 1976 the Committee requested precise information from the State party on 24 March 1980. In its submission dated 20 October 1980 the State party claimed that it had no information. The Committee notes that the author has made precise allegations with respect to her husband's arrest and detention in Buenos Aires on 13 July 1976 by the Uruguayan security and intelligence forces and that witness testimony submitted by her indicates the involvement of several Uruguayan officers identified by name. The State party has neither refuted these allegations nor adduced any adequate evidence that they had been duly investigated.

11.3 As regards the allegations of ill-treatment and torture, the Committee notes that the author has submitted detailed testimony from six ex-detainees who were held, together with López Burgos, in some of the secret detention places in Argentina and Uruguay. The Committee notes further that the names of five Uruguayan officers allegedly responsible for or personally involved in the ill-treatment are given. The State party should have investigated the allegations in accordance with its laws and its obligations under the Covenant and the Optional Protocol. . . .

. . . .

11.6 The Committee has considered whether acts and treatment, which are *prima facie* not in conformity with the Covenant, could for any reasons be justified under the Covenant in the circumstances of the case. The Government of Uruguay has referred to provisions, in Uruguayan law, of "prompt security measures." However, the Covenant (art. 4) does not allow national measures for derogating from any of its provisions except in strictly defined circumstances, and the Government has not made any submissions of fact or law in relation thereto. Moreover, some of the facts referred to above raise issues under provisions from which the Covenant does not allow any derogation under any circumstances.

. . . .

12.1 The Human Rights Committee further observes that although the arrest and initial detention and mistreatment of López Burgos allegedly took place on foreign territory, the Committee is not barred either by virtue of article 1 of the Optional Protocol ("... individuals subject to its jurisdiction ...") or by virtue of article 2(1) of the Covenant ("... individuals within its territory and subject to its jurisdiction ...") from considering these allegations, together with the claim of subsequent abduction into Uruguayan territory, inasmuch as these acts were perpetrated by Uruguayan agents acting on foreign soil.

12.2 The reference in article 1 of the Optional Protocol to "individuals subject to its jurisdiction" does not affect the above conclusion because the reference in that article is not to the place where the violation occurred, but rather to the relationship between the individual and the State in relation to a violation of any of the rights set forth in the Covenant, wherever they occurred.

12.3 Article 2(1) of the Covenant places an obligation upon a State party to respect and ensure rights "to all individuals within its territory and subject to its jurisdiction," but it does not imply that the State party concerned cannot be held accountable for violations of rights under the Covenant which its agents commit upon the territory of another State, whether with the acquiescence of the Government of that State or in opposition to it. According to article 5(1) of the Covenant:

> Nothing in the present Covenant may be interpreted as implying for any State, group or person any right to engage in any activity or perform any act aimed at the destruction of any of the rights and freedoms recognized herein or at their limitation to a greater extent than is provided for in the present Covenant.

In line with this, it would be unconscionable to so interpret the responsibility under article 2 of the Covenant as to permit a State party to perpetrate violations of the Covenant on the territory of another State, which violations it could not perpetrate on its own territory.

13. The Human Rights Committee, acting under article 5(4) of the Optional Protocol to the International Covenant on Civil and Political Rights is of the view that the communication discloses violations of the Covenant, in particular of:

> Article 7, because of the treatment (including torture) suffered by López Burgos at the hands of Uruguayan military officers in the period from July to October 1976 both in Argentina and Uruguay;

> Article 9(1), because the act of abduction into Uruguayan territory constituted an arbitrary arrest and detention;

> . . . .

14. The Committee, accordingly, is of the view that the State party is under an obligation, pursuant to article 2(3) of the Covenant, to provide effective remedies to López Burgos, including immediate release, permission to leave Uruguay and compensation for the violations which he has suffered, and to take steps to ensure that similar violations do not occur in the future.

〰

QUESTIONS & COMMENTS

(1) Could Delia Saldías de López have filed her petition against Argentina? Assuming that she could, what are the reasons for filing against one state rather than the other?

(2) *See Sosa v. Alvarez-Machain*, reproduced in Section 3.3.2. By demanding that customary international legal norms be universally obligatory, is the Court in *Alvarez-Machain* incorrectly equating customary international legal norms with norms *erga omnes* that do not accommodate the persistent objector rule?

How specific does a norm have to be to acquire customary international legal status under *Alvarez-Machain*? Compare the language of the U.S. Constitution's norms with those of the ICCPR. Generally speaking, are not the ICCPR's norms stated in greater specificity? Can case law be used to provide the needed definition for both constitutional and customary international legal norms?

Did not the right to liberty and personal security crystalize as a customary international legal norm before the United States' 1992 ratification of the ICCPR and its deposit of the non-self-execution declaration?

Do you find the Court's requirement that detention be *prolonged* in order for it to constitute a customary international legal norm reasonable? How much authoritative weight should be given to the RESTATEMENT (THIRD) OF THE FOREIGN RELATIONS LAW OF THE UNITED STATES for its 1985 claim that the detention had to be prolonged in order to be a customary international legal violation? Is the RESTATEMENT's claim outdated?

By demanding specificity in a norm for it to have customary international legal authority, did the Court fail to apply its own standard in *Alvarez-Machain*? The UN Human Rights Committee in *Saldías de López v. Uruguay* already had found that an extraterritorial abduction violated the ICCPR right to liberty and personal security in 1981. Also, the UN Working Group specifically had found Alvarez's detention a violation of customary international law.

Is the court incorrectly imposing a treaty law issue, namely, non-self-execution, upon customary international law? Is the Court saying that the United States' non-self-execution declaration for the ICCPR supercedes a substantive customary international legal norm? Although the Court did not provide either a reasoned basis or authority for this assertion, on what basis could the Court make such a claim?

(3) Summary executions are universally recognized as violations of international human rights law.[4] The right to life has been interpreted not only to prohibit a state from

---

[4] The universal acceptance of this prohibition has been recognized in a long string of U.S. federal court decisions. *See, e.g., Xuncax v. Gramajo*, 886 F.Supp. 162, 185 (D. Mass. 1995); *Forti v. Suarez-Mason*, 694 F.Supp. 707, 711 (N.D. Cal. 1988) ("*Forti II*"); *Trajano v. Marcos*, 978 F.2d 493 (9th Cir. 1992), *cert. denied* 113 S.Ct. 2960 (1993); *Todd v. Panjiatan*, No. 92-12255WD (D. Mass. decided October 25, 1994). The courts looked to, among other things, affidavits submitted by international human rights law scholars to conclude that the prohibition against summary execution had risen to the level of customary international law. *See, e.g., Xuncax v. Gramajo*, 886 F.Supp. at 185 ("An affidavit signed by twenty-seven widely respected scholars of international law attests that every instrument or agreement that has attempted to define the scope of international human rights has 'recognized a right to life coupled with a right to due process to protect that right.'") Congress affirmed the U.S. position that summary execution violates international human rights law when it passed the Torture Victim Protection Act of 1991 (codified at 28 U.S.C. §1350). The TVPA provides that anyone may bring a civil suit in U.S. federal court for torture and summary execution, regardless of where the violations occurred.

arbitrarily depriving an individual of his or her life but also to obligate a state to investigate and to take reasonable steps to bring to justice those responsible for an illegal killing.

(4) The Inter-American Court of Human Rights has played an important role in defining disappearance as a human rights violation and formulating evidentiary rules that address the difficult questions of proof raised by such a claim. The major problem facing a claim of disappearance is the lack of evidence linking the crime to the state; disappearance is a crime that by definition involves the hiding and destruction of evidence. The Inter-American Court first addressed the problem of disappearances in a series of cases brought by the Inter-American Commission against Honduras.[5] They are the *Fairén Garbi and Solís Corrales Case*,[6] the *Godínez Cruz Case*,[7] and the *Velásquez Rodríguez Case*.[8]

Velásquez Rodríguez v. Honduras
Inter-American Court of Human Rights
Judgment of July 29, 1988, Ser. C No. 4
[Reproduced in Section 2.3.1]

∼

QUESTIONS & COMMENTS

(1) Forced disappearances are considered crimes against humanity by both the Inter-American Court in *Velásquez Rodríguez v. Honduras* and the ICC Statute. However, to be considered crimes under the ICC Statute, these disappearances must be committed as part of a widespread or systematic attack directed against a civilian population. Does the Inter-American Court in *Velásquez Rodríguez v. Honduras* require such a condition for a disappearance to create both state liability and individual culpability? Can some international human rights violations – such as a disappearance or sexual assault that are not crimes against humanity because they are not part of a widespread or systemic attack on a civilian population still be considered international crimes because they entail international criminal liability for the state as well as individual culpability for the individual perpetrator?

(2) Note that the Inter-American Convention on the Forced Disappearance of Persons does not include disappearances perpetrated by political organizations as does the ICC Statute.

(3) If you were a prosecutor, how would you prove the commission of a disappearance without a body? How would you defend?

---

[5] Under the rules of the Inter-American Court, individual victims neither have the right to bring an action nor to be formally represented before the Court. Claudio Grossman, who was one of the lawyers representing the victims in the Honduran cases, argues that the Inter-American Court should revise its rules to allow direct representation. Grossman, *Disappearances in Honduras: The Need for Direct Representation in Human Rights Litigation*, 15 HASTINGS INT'L AND COMP. L. REV. 363 (1992).

[6] Ser. C, No. 6 (1989).

[7] Ser. C, No. 5 (1989).

[8] Ser. C, No. 4, 9 Hum Rts. L.J. 212 (1988).

5.1.2. Rights to Personal Security and Liberty

Universal Declaration of Human Rights

Article 9.

No one shall be subjected to arbitrary arrest, detention or exile.

International Covenant on Civil and Political Rights

Article 9

1. Everyone has the right to liberty and security of person. No one shall be subjected to arbitrary arrest or detention. No one shall be deprived of his liberty except on such grounds and in accordance with such procedure as are established by law.

2. Anyone who is arrested shall be informed, at the time of arrest, of the reasons for his arrest and shall be promptly informed of any charges against him.

3. Anyone arrested or detained on a criminal charge shall be brought promptly before a judge or other officer authorized by law to exercise judicial power and shall be entitled to trial within a reasonable time or to release. It shall not be the general rule that persons awaiting trial shall be detained in custody, but release may be subject to guarantees to appear for trial, at any other stage of the judicial proceedings, and, should occasion arise, for execution of the judgement.

4. Anyone who is deprived of his liberty by arrest or detention shall be entitled to take proceedings before a court, in order that that court may decide without delay on the lawfulness of his detention and order his release if the detention is not lawful.

5. Anyone who has been the victim of unlawful arrest or detention shall have an enforceable right to compensation.

European Convention on Human Rights

Article 5

1. Everyone has the right to liberty and security of person. No one shall be deprived of his liberty save in the following cases and in accordance with a procedure prescribed by law:

(a) the lawful detention of a person after conviction by a competent court;

(b) the lawful arrest or detention of a person for non-compliance with the lawful order of a court or in order to secure the fulfilment of any obligation prescribed by law;

(c) the lawful arrest or detention of a person effected for the purpose of bringing him before the competent legal authority of reasonable suspicion of having committed and offence or when it is reasonably considered necessary to prevent his committing an offence or fleeing after having done so;

(d) the detention of a minor by lawful order for the purpose of educational supervision or his lawful detention for the purpose of bringing him before the competent legal authority;

(e) the lawful detention of persons for the prevention of the spreading of infectious diseases, of persons of unsound mind, alcoholics or drug addicts, or vagrants;

(f) the lawful arrest or detention of a person to prevent his effecting an unauthorized entry into the country or of a person against whom action is being taken with a view to deportation or extradition.

2. Everyone who is arrested shall be informed promptly, in a language which he understands, of the reasons for his arrest and the charge against him.

3. Everyone arrested or detained in accordance with the provisions of paragraph 1(c) of this article shall be brought promptly before a judge or other officer authorized by law to exercise judicial power and shall be entitled to trial within a reasonable time or to release pending trial. Release may be conditioned by guarantees to appear for trial.

4. Everyone who is deprived of his liberty by arrest or detention shall be entitled to take proceedings by which the lawfulness of his detention shall be decided speedily by a court and his release ordered if the detention is not lawful.

5. Everyone who has been the victim of arrest or detention in contravention of the provisions of this article shall have an enforceable right to compensation.

Charter of Fundamental Rights of the European Union

Article 6

Right to liberty and security

Everyone has the right to liberty and security of person.

American Declaration on the Rights and Duties of Man

Article I.

Every human being has the right to life, liberty and the security of his person.

American Convention on Human Rights

Article 7. RIGHT TO PERSONAL LIBERTY.

1. Every person has the right to personal liberty and security.

2. No one shall be deprived of his physical liberty except for the reasons and under the conditions established beforehand by the constitution of the State Party concerned or by a law established pursuant thereto.

3. No one shall be subject to arbitrary arrest or imprisonment.

4. Anyone who is detained shall be informed of the reasons for his detention and shall be promptly notified of the charge or charges against him.

5. Any person detained shall be brought promptly before a judge or other officer authorized by law to exercise judicial power and shall be entitled to trial within a reasonable time or to be released without prejudice to the continuation of the proceedings. His release may be subject to guarantees to assure his appearance for trial.

6. Anyone who is deprived of his liberty shall be entitled to recourse to a competent court, in order that the court may decide without delay on the lawfulness of his arrest or detention and order his release if the arrest or detention is unlawful. In States Parties whose laws provide that anyone who believes himself to be threatened with deprivation of his liberty is entitled to recourse to a competent court in order that it may decide on the

lawfulness of such threat, this remedy may not be restricted or abolished. The interested party or another person in his behalf is entitled to seek these remedies.

7. No one shall be detained for debt. This principle shall not limit the orders of a competent judicial authority issued for nonfulfillment of duties of support.

African [Banjul] Charter on Human and Peoples' Rights

Article 6

Every individual shall have the right to liberty and to the security of his person. No one may be deprived of his freedom except for reasons and conditions previously laid down by law. In particular, no one may be arbitrarily arrested or detained.

Convention on Human Rights and Fundamental Freedoms of the Commonwealth of Independent States

Article 5

1. Everyone shall have the right to liberty and security of person. No one shall be deprived of his liberty save in the following cases and in accordance with a procedure established by national legislation;

a. the lawful detention of a person after conviction by a competent court;
b. the lawful arrest or detention of a person;
c. the lawful detention of a minor for the purpose of referring his case for investigation, sentencing, or trial.

2. Everyone who is arrested shall be informed, at the time of his arrest, in a language he understands, of the reasons for his arrest.

3. Everyone who is deprived of his liberty by arrest or detention, in accordance with national legislation, shall be entitled to have the lawfulness of his arrest or detention examined by a court.

4. Everyone who is deprived of his liberty shall be entitled to humane treatment and to respect for his dignity as a human being.

Persons who have been subjected to unlawful arrest or detention shall be entitled, in accordance with national legislation, to compensation for the damage caused.

U.S. Constitution

Article I (9) (2)

The Privilege of the Writ of Habeas Corpus shall not be suspended, unless when in Cases of Rebellion or Invasion the public Safety may require it.

Amendment V

No person shall be . . . deprived of life, liberty, or property, without due process of law. . . .

Amendment XIV

No State shall . . . deprive any person of life, liberty, or property, without due process of law. . . .

Murray v. United Kingdom
European Court of Human Rights
300-A Eur. Ct. H.R. (ser. A) (1994)
19 E.H.R.R. 193 (1995)

. . . .

FACTS:

I. Particular circumstances of the case

A. Introduction

9. The six applicants are members of the same family. The first applicant, Mrs. Margaret Murray, and the second applicant, Mr. Thomas Murray, are husband and wife. The other four applicants are their children, namely their son Mark Murray (born in 1964), their twin daughters Alana and Michaela Murray (born in 1967) and a younger daughter Rossina Murray (born in 1970). At the relevant time in 1982 all six applicants resided together in the same house in Belfast, Northern Ireland.

10. On 22 June 1982 two of the first applicant's brothers were convicted in the United States of America ("USA") of arms offences connected with the purchase of weapons for the Provisional Irish Republican Army ("Provisional IRA"). The Provisional IRA is included among the organisations proscribed under the special legislation enacted in the United Kingdom to deal with terrorism in Northern Ireland.

B. First applicant's arrest

11. On 26 July 1982 at approximately 6.30 am Corporal D, a member of the Women's Royal Army Corps, attended an Army briefing at which she was told that the first applicant was suspected of involvement in the collection of money for the purchase of arms for the IRA in the United States, this being a criminal offence under section 21 of the Northern Ireland (Emergency Provisions) Act 1978 ("the 1978 Act") and section 10 of the Prevention of Terrorism (Temporary Provisions) Act 1976. The corporal was instructed to go to the first applicant's house, arrest her under section 14 of the 1978 Act and bring her back to the Army screening centre at Springfield Road in Belfast.

12. At 7.00 am Corporal D, who was unarmed but accompanied by five armed soldiers, arrived by Army vehicle at the applicants' home. The first applicant herself answered the door and three of the male soldiers, together with Corporal D, entered the house. Corporal D established the identity of the first applicant and asked her to get dressed. Corporal D went upstairs with the first applicant. The other applicants were roused and asked to assemble in the living room. The soldiers did not carry out any search of the contents of the house, but made written notes as to the interior of the house and recorded personal details concerning the applicants. At about 7.30 am in the hallway of the house Corporal D, with one of the soldiers acting as a witness, said to the first applicant, "As a member of Her Majesty's Forces, I arrest you." On being asked twice by the first applicant under what section, Corporal D replied, "Section 14".

C. First applicant's questioning

13. The first applicant was then driven to the Army screening centre at Springfield Road, Belfast. She was escorted into a building and asked to sit for a short time in a small cubicle. At 8.05 am she was taken before Sergeant B who asked her questions with a view to completing part one of a standard form to record, *inter alia*, details of the

arrest and screening procedure and personal details. The first applicant refused to answer any questions save to give her name and she refused to be photographed. The interview ended four minutes later. She was then examined by a medical orderly who endeavoured to establish whether she suffered from certain illnesses, but she again refused to co-operate and did not answer any of his questions.

14. At 8.20 am she was taken to an interview room and questioned by a soldier in civilian clothes in the presence of Corporal D. She was asked, *inter alia*, about her brothers and her contacts with them, but she still refused to answer questions. After the interview, which ended at 9.35 am, she was returned to the reception area and then taken back to the medical orderly who asked her if she had any complaints. She did not reply to this query.

At some stage during her stay in the centre she was photographed without her knowledge or consent. This photograph and the personal details about her, her family and her home were kept on record.

She was released at 9.45 am without being charged.

15. The standard record form, called the "screening pro forma", recorded the first applicant's name, address, nationality, marital and tenancy status, the chronological details about her arrest, the names of the Army personnel involved, the names of the other applicants and their relationship to her, her physique and her attitude to the interview. Under the heading "Additional information . . . concerning the arrestee (as reported by the arresting soldier)", it stated: "Subject is the sister of C . . . M . . . who was arrested in USA. Questioned on the above subject." Nothing however was recorded under the heading "Suspected offence". It noted that the applicant had refused to answer questions and that no information had been gained from the interview.

D. Proceedings before the High Court

16. Some 18 months later, on 9 February 1984, the first applicant brought an action against the Ministry of Defence for false imprisonment and other torts.

17. In those proceedings one of the principal allegations made by the first applicant was that her arrest and detention had been effected unlawfully and for an improper purpose. Her allegations were summarised in the judgment of Murray J given on 25 October 1985:

> The plaintiff's counsel launched a series of attacks on the legality of the plaintiff's arrest and detention which varied in thrust between the very broad and the very narrow. In the former class, for example, was an attack in which they alleged that the use of section 14 of the [1978 Act] in this case was an example of what they called "an institutionalised form of unlawful screening" by the military authorities, with the intention of obtaining what Counsel termed "low level intelligence" from the plaintiff, and without (a) any genuine suspicion on the part of those authorities that she had committed a criminal offence or (b) any genuine intention on their part of questioning her about a criminal offence alleged to have been committed by her.

. . . .

19. The evidence given by the first applicant is recorded in a note drafted by the trial judge, there being no transcript of the first day of the trial as a result of a technical mishap with the recording equipment. The first applicant explained how she had found the conditions of her arrest and detention distressing for her. She had been angry but had not used strong language. She testified that whilst at the Army centre she had refused to be photographed, to be weighed by the medical orderly, to sign any documents and

to answer questions, whether put by Sergeant B, the medical orderly or the interviewer, apart from giving her name. She had made it clear that she would not be answering any questions. She alleged that Sergeant B had told her in so many words that the Army knew that she had not committed any crime but that her file had been lost and the Army wanted to update it. She said that she had been questioned about her brothers in the United States, their whereabouts and her contacts with them, but not about the purchase of arms for the Provisional IRA or about any offence. She accepted that she had been in contact with her brothers and had been to the United States, including a visit that year (1985). She believed that the Army had wanted to obtain information about her brothers. On leaving the centre, she had told the officials that she would be seeing them in court.

20. As appears from the transcript of her evidence, Corporal D gave an account of her briefing on the morning of the arrest. She stated that at the briefing she had been told the first applicant's name and address and the grounds on which she was wanted for questioning, namely her suspected involvement in the collection of money for the purchase of weapons from America. She testified that "my suspicions were aroused by my briefing, and my belief was that Mrs Murray was suspected of collecting money to purchase arms".

Under cross-examination Corporal D maintained that the purpose of an arrest and detention under section 14 of the 1978 Act was not to gather intelligence but to question a suspected person about an offence. She stated that her suspicion of the first applicant had been formed on the basis of everything she had been told at the briefing and which she had read in a document which had been supplied to her then. Corporal D stated that she would not have effected the arrest unless she had been given the grounds on which she was expected to arrest the person. Under repeated questioning, Corporal D maintained that she had been informed at the briefing, and that she had formed the suspicion, that the applicant had been involved in the collection of money for the purchase of arms from America.

. . . .

22. Sergeant B was examined and cross-examined about his completion of part 1 of the standard record form when standing at the reception desk. He said that the first applicant had stated her name but refused to give her address or date of birth or any further information. He expressly denied the applicant's allegation that he had said to her that he knew she was not a criminal and that he just wanted to update her files which had been lost. He gave evidence that information recorded in 1980 on the occasion of a previous arrest of the first applicant had in any event not been lost, since it had been used to complete the details on the first page of the form when she had refused to answer any questions.

Under cross-examination Sergeant B did not accept that the main purpose of questioning a person arrested under section 14 of the 1978 Act was to gather general information about the background, family and associates of the arrested person. He maintained that persons were only arrested and detained if there existed a suspicion against them of involvement in a criminal offence.

. . . .

24. In his judgment of 25 October 1985 Murray J gave detailed consideration to the evidence of Corporal D and Sergeant B on the one hand and the first applicant on the other. Murray J "could not possibly accept the [first applicant's] evidence" that she had been told by Sergeant B that she was not suspected of any offence and that he was just updating his records. He similarly rejected the applicant's claim that Corporal D at no

time genuinely suspected her of having committed an offence. In the light of the evidence of Corporal D herself, who was described as a "transparently honest witness", the judge was quite satisfied that on the basis of her briefing at Musgrave Park she genuinely suspected the [first applicant] of having been involved in the offence of collecting money in Northern Ireland for arms.

25. Murray J also rejected the first applicant's claim that section 14 of the 1978 Act had been used with a view to screening in order to gain low-level intelligence: he accepted the evidence of Corporal D and Sergeant B, which had been tested in cross-examination, that the purpose of the applicant's arrest and detention under the section had been to establish facts concerning the offence of which she was suspected.

Murray J also believed the evidence of Corporal D that there were questions addressed to the matters of which the applicant was suspected. He stated:

As regards the interviewer, the plaintiff accepted that he was interested in the activities of her brothers who shortly before the date of the interview had been convicted on arms charges in the USA connected with the Provisional IRA but the [first applicant], who seems to have been well aware of her rights, obviously had decided not to co-operate with the military staff in the centre. In particular she had decided (it seems) not to answer any of their questions and in this situation, and with the short detention period permitted by the section, there was little that the interviewer or any of the other staff in the centre could do to pursue their suspicions.

. . . .

27. The first applicant's action before the High Court was therefore dismissed.

E. Proceedings before the Court of Appeal

. . . .

29. The Court of Appeal further unanimously rejected the first applicant's complaint that the purpose of her arrest and detention, and the whole purport of her questioning, was a fishing expedition unrelated to the matters of which she was suspected and designed to obtain low-grade intelligence about the applicant and others.

. . . .

F. Proceedings before the House of Lords

. . . .

32. In the House of Lords the applicant did not pursue the allegation that she had not been arrested on the basis of a genuine and honest suspicion that she had committed an offence.

She did however pursue the complaint, previously raised before the Court of Appeal, that since she was only lawfully arrested at 7.30 am she had been unlawfully detained between 7.00 and 7.30 am The House of Lords found that a person is arrested from the moment he is subject to restraint and that the first applicant was therefore under arrest from the moment that Corporal D identified her on entering the house at 7.00 am. It made no difference that the formal words of arrest were communicated to the applicant by 7.30 am. In this respect Lord Griffiths stated [citation omitted]:

If the plaintiff had been told she was under arrest the moment she identified herself, it would not have made the slightest difference to the sequence of events before she left the house. It would have been wholly unreasonable to take her off, half-clad, to the Army centre, and the same half-hour would have elapsed while she gathered herself together and completed her toilet and dressing. It would seem a strange result that in these circumstances, whether or not she has an action for false imprisonment should depend upon whether the words of arrest are spoken on entering or leaving the house, when the practical effect of the difference on the plaintiff is non-existent.

33. The first applicant had also maintained that the failure to inform her that she was arrested until the soldiers were about to leave the house rendered the arrest unlawful. This submission was also rejected by the House of Lords. Lord Griffiths held as follows [citation omitted]:

It is a feature of the very limited power of arrest contained in section 14 that a member of the armed forces does not have to tell the arrested person the offence of which he is suspected, for it is specifically provided by section 14(2) that it is sufficient if he states that he is effecting the arrest as a member of Her Majesty's forces.

Corporal D was carrying out this arrest in accordance with the procedures in which she had been instructed to make a house arrest pursuant to section 14. This procedure appears to me to be designed to make the arrest with the least risk of injury to those involved including both the soldiers and the occupants of the house. When arrests are made on suspicion of involvement with the IRA it would be to close one's eyes to the obvious not to appreciate the risk that the arrest may be forcibly resisted.

The drill the Army follow is to enter the house and search every room for occupants. The occupants are all directed to assemble in one room, and when the person the soldiers have come to arrest has been identified and is ready to leave, the formal words of arrest are spoken just before they leave the house. The Army do not carry out a search for property in the house and, in my view, they would not be justified in doing so. The power of search is given 'for the purpose of arresting a person', not for a search for incriminating evidence. It is however a proper exercise of the power of search for the purpose of effecting the arrest to search every room for other occupants of the house in case there may be those there who are disposed to resist the arrest. The search cannot be limited solely to looking for the person to be arrested and must also embrace a search whose object is to secure that the arrest should be peaceable. I also regard it as an entirely reasonable precaution that all the occupants of the house should be asked to assemble in one room. As Corporal D explained in evidence, this procedure is followed because the soldiers may be distracted by other occupants in the house rushing from one room to another, perhaps in a state of alarm, perhaps for the purpose of raising the alarm and to resist the arrest. In such circumstances a tragic shooting accident might all too easily happen with young, and often relatively inexperienced, armed soldiers operating under conditions of extreme tension. Your Lordships were told that the husband and children either had commenced, or were contemplating commencing, actions for false imprisonment arising out of the fact that they were asked to assemble in the living-room for a short period before the plaintiff was taken from the house. That very short period of restraint when they were asked to assemble in the living room was a proper and necessary part of the procedure for effecting the peaceable arrest of the plaintiff. It was a temporary restraint of very short duration imposed not only for the benefit of those effecting the arrest, but also for the protection of the occupants of the house and would be wholly insufficient to found an action for unlawful imprisonment.

It was in my opinion entirely reasonable to delay speaking the words of arrest until the party was about to leave the house. If words of arrest are spoken as soon as the house is entered before any precautions have been taken to search the house and find the other occupants, it seems to me that there is a real risk that the alarm may be raised and an attempt made to resist arrest, not only by those within the house but also by summoning assistance from those in the immediate neighbourhood. When soldiers are employed on the difficult and potentially dangerous task of carrying out a house arrest of a person suspected of an offence in connection with the IRA, it is I think essential that they should have been trained in the drill they are to follow. It would be impracticable and I think potentially dangerous to leave it to the individual discretion of the particular soldier making the arrest to devise his own procedures for carrying out this unfamiliar military function. It is in everyone's best interest that the arrest is peaceably effected and I am satisfied that the procedures adopted by the Army are sensible, reasonable and designed to bring about the arrest with the minimum of danger and distress to all concerned. I would however add this rider: that if the suspect, for any reason, refuses to accept the fact of restraint in the house he should be informed forthwith that he is under arrest.

34. Before the House of Lords the first applicant also pursued a claim that her period of detention exceeded what was reasonably required to make a decision whether to release her or hand her over to the police. In this regard the applicant complained that the standard record form (the "screening pro forma") constituted an improper basis for questioning a suspect on the ground that it asked questions not directly relevant to the suspected offence; it was also suggested that the evidence did not show that the questioning of the applicant was directed to the matters of which she was suspected. The allegation was unanimously rejected by the House of Lords. Lord Griffiths observed as follows [citation omitted]:

The member of the forces who carried out the interrogation between 8.20 and 9.35 am was not called as a witness on behalf of the Ministry of Defence. There may have been sound reasons for this decision associated with preserving the confidentiality of interrogating techniques and the identity of the interviewer, but be that as it may, the only evidence of what took place at the interview came from Corporal D and the [first applicant] and it is submitted that this evidence is insufficient to establish that the interview was directed towards an attempt to investigate the suspicion upon which the [applicant] was arrested. Corporal D was present at that interview, she was not paying close attention but she gave evidence that she remembered questions about money which were obviously directed towards the offences of which the [applicant] was suspected. The [applicant] also said she was questioned about her brothers.

The judge also had before him a questionnaire that was completed by the interviewer . . . There is nothing in the questionnaire which the Army may not reasonably ask the suspect together with such particular questions as are appropriate to the particular case . . .

The conclusion of the trial judge that the applicant had not been asked unnecessary or unreasonable questions and the conclusion of the Court of Appeal that the interviewer had attempted to pursue with the applicant the suspicion which had been the occasion of the arrest, but had been unable to make any headway, were held by the House of Lords to be justified on the evidence.

II. The relevant domestic law and practice

A. Introduction

35. For more than 20 years the population of Northern Ireland, which totals about 1.5 million people, has been subjected to a campaign of terrorism. During that time thousands of persons in Northern Ireland have been killed, maimed or injured. The campaign of terror has extended to the rest of the United Kingdom and to the mainland of Europe.

The 1978 Act forms part of the special legislation enacted over the years in an attempt to enable the security forces to deal effectively with the threat of terrorist violence.

B. Entry and search; arrest and detention

36. The first applicant was arrested under section 14 of the 1978 Act, which at the relevant time provided as follows:

1. A member of Her Majesty's forces on duty may arrest without warrant, and detain for not more than four hours, a person whom he suspects of committing, having committed or being about to commit any offence.

2. A person effecting an arrest under this section complies with any rule of law requiring him to state the ground of arrest if he states that he is effecting the arrest as a member of Her Majesty's forces.

3. For the purpose of arresting a person under this section a member of Her Majesty's forces may enter and search any premises or other place –

(a) where that person is, or

(b) if that person is suspected of being a terrorist or of having committed an offence involving the use or possession of an explosive, explosive substance or firearm, where that person is suspected of being.

. . . .

38. The scope and exercise of the section 14 powers were considered by the domestic courts in the proceedings in the present case. The applicable law, as stated by the judgments in these proceedings, is that when the legality of an arrest or detention under section 14 is challenged (whether by way of habeas corpus or in proceedings for damages for wrongful arrest or false imprisonment), the burden lies on the military to justify their acts and, in particular, to establish the following elements:

a. compliance with the formal requirements for arrest;

b. the genuineness of the suspicion on which the arrest was based;

c. that the powers of arrest and detention were not used for any improper purpose such as intelligence-gathering;

d. that the power of search was used only to facilitate the arrest and not for the obtaining of incriminating evidence;

e. that those responsible for the arrest and detention did not exceed the time reasonably required to reach a decision whether to release the detainee or hand him over to the police.

. . . .

D. Standard record form

41. As was confirmed in particular by the Court of Appeal and the House of Lords in the present case, the standard record form (known as the "screening pro forma") was an integral part of the examination of the first applicant following her arrest, and the legal authority for recording certain personal details about her in the form derived

from the lawfulness of her arrest, detention and examination under section 14 of the 1978 Act. The implied lawful authority conferred by section 14 of the 1978 Act to record information about the first applicant equally provided the legal basis for the retention of the information.

PROCEEDINGS BEFORE THE [EUROPEAN COMMISSION OF HUMAN RIGHTS]

42. The applicants applied to the Commission on 28 September 1988 (No 14310/88).

The first applicant complained that her arrest and detention for two hours for questioning gave rise to a violation of Article 5(1) and (2), for which she had no enforceable right to compensation as guaranteed by Article 5(5) . . .

. . . .

All six applicants claimed that the entry into and search of their home by the Army were contrary to their right to respect for their private and family life and their home under Article 8 of the Convention; . . . .

. . . .

44. In its report of 17 February 1993 (Made under Art 31) the Commission expressed the opinion:

a. in the case of the first applicant, by 11 votes to three there had been a violation of Article 5(1), Article 5(2) by 10 votes to four and Article 5(5) by 11 votes to three;
b. by 13 votes to one there had been no violation of Article 8. . . .

. . . .

DECISION [OF THE EUROPEAN COURT OF HUMAN RIGHTS]:

I. General approach

47. The applicants' complaints concern the first applicant's arrest and detention by the Army under special criminal legislation enacted to deal with acts of terrorism connected with the affairs of Northern Ireland. As has been noted in several previous judgments by the Court, the campaign of terrorism waged in Northern Ireland over the last quarter of a century has taken a terrible toll, especially in terms of human life and suffering.

The Court sees no reason to depart from the general approach it has adopted in previous cases of a similar nature. Accordingly, for the purposes of interpreting and applying the relevant provisions of the Convention, due account will be taken of the special nature of terrorist crime, the threat it poses to democratic society and the exigencies of dealing with it. [citations omitted]

II. Alleged violation of Article 5(1) of the Convention

48. The first applicant, Mrs. Margaret Murray, alleged that her arrest and detention by the Army were in breach of Article 5(1) of the Convention, which, in so far as relevant, provides:

Everyone has the right to liberty and security of person. No one shall be deprived of his liberty save in the following cases and in accordance with a procedure prescribed by law:

. . . .

(c) the lawful arrest or detention of a person effected for the purpose of bringing him before the competent legal authority on reasonable suspicion of having committed an offence . . . ;

. . . .

A. Lawfulness

49. Before the Convention institutions the first applicant did not dispute that her arrest and detention were "lawful" under Northern Ireland law and, in particular, "in accordance with a procedure prescribed by law", as required by Article 5(1)....

B. "Reasonable suspicion"

50. Mrs. Murray was arrested and detained by virtue of section 14 of the 1978 Act. This provision, as construed by the domestic courts, empowered the Army to arrest and detain persons suspected of the commission of an offence provided, *inter alia*, that the suspicion of the arresting officer was honestly and genuinely held. It is relevant but not decisive that the domestic legislation at the time merely imposed this essentially subjective standard: the Court's task is to determine whether the objective standard of "reasonable suspicion" laid down in Article 5(1) was met in the circumstances of the application of the legislation in the particular case.

51. In its judgment of 30 August 1990 in the case of *Fox, Campbell and Hartley v. United Kingdom*, which was concerned with arrests carried out by the Northern Ireland police under a similarly worded provision of the 1978 Act, the Court stated as follows:

> The 'reasonableness' of the suspicion on which an arrest must be based forms an essential part of the safeguard against arbitrary arrest and detention which is laid down in Article 5 §1(c)... (Having) a 'reasonable suspicion' presupposes the existence of facts or information which would satisfy an objective observer that the person concerned may have committed the offence. What may be regarded as 'reasonable' will however depend upon all the circumstances.
>
> In this respect, terrorist crime falls into a special category. Because of the attendant risk of loss of life and human suffering, the police are obliged to act with utmost urgency in following up all information, including information from secret sources. Further, the police may frequently have to arrest a suspected terrorist on the basis of information which is reliable but which cannot, without putting in jeopardy the source of the information, be revealed to the suspect or produced in court to support a charge.
>
> ... (In) view of the difficulties inherent in the investigation and prosecution of terrorist-type offences in Northern Ireland, the 'reasonableness' of the suspicion justifying such arrests cannot always be judged according to the same standards as are applied in dealing with conventional crime.
>
> Nevertheless, the exigencies of dealing with terrorist crime cannot justify stretching the notion of 'reasonableness' to the point where the essence of the safeguard secured by Article 5 §1(c) is impaired...
>
> ....
>
> Certainly Article 5 §1(c) of the Convention should not be applied in such a manner as to put disproportionate difficulties in the way of the police authorities of the Contracting States in taking effective measures to counter organised terrorism.... It follows that the Contracting States cannot be asked to establish the reasonableness of the suspicion grounding the arrest of a suspected terrorist by disclosing the confidential sources of supporting information or even facts which would be susceptible of indicating such sources or their identity.

Nevertheless the Court must be enabled to ascertain whether the essence of the safeguard afforded by Article 5 §1(c) has been secured. Consequently, the respondent Government have to furnish at least some facts or information capable of satisfying the Court that the arrested person was reasonably suspected of having committed the alleged offence. This is all the more necessary where, as in the present case, the domestic law does not require reasonable suspicion, but sets a lower threshold by merely requiring honest suspicion.

On the facts the Court found in that case that, although the arrest and detention of the three applicants, which lasted respectively 44 hours, 44 hours and 5 minutes and 30 hours and 15 minutes, were based on an honest suspicion, insufficient elements had been furnished by the Government to support the conclusion that there had been a "reasonable suspicion" for the purposes of sub-paragraph (c) of Article 5(1).

52. In the present case the Government maintained that there existed strong and specific grounds, founded on information from a reliable but secret source, for the Army to suspect that Mrs Murray was involved in the collection of funds for terrorist purposes. However, the "primary" information so provided could not be revealed in the interests of protecting lives and personal safety. In the Government's submission, the fact that they had maintained that this was the foundation of the suspicion should be given considerable weight by the Court. They also pointed to a number of other facts capable of supporting, albeit indirectly, the reasonableness of the suspicion, including notably the findings made by the domestic courts in the proceedings brought by Mrs. Murray, the very recent conviction of her brothers in the USA of offences connected with the purchase of weapons for the Provisional IRA, her own visits to the USA and her contacts with her brothers there. They submitted that all these matters taken together provided sufficient facts and information to satisfy an objective observer that there was a reasonable suspicion in the circumstances of the case. Any other conclusion by the Court would, they feared, prohibit arresting authorities from effecting an arrest of a person suspected of being a terrorist based primarily on reliable but secret information and would inhibit the arresting authorities in taking effective measures to counter organised terrorism.

53. The first applicant, on the other hand, considered that the Government had failed to discharge the onus of disclosing sufficient facts to enable the Convention institutions to conclude that the suspicion grounding her arrest was reasonable or anything more than the "honest" suspicion required under Northern Ireland law. As in the case of *Fox, Campbell and Hartley*, the Government's explanation did not meet the minimum standards set by Article 5(1)(c) for judging the reasonableness of her arrest and detention. She did not accept that the reason advanced for non-disclosure was a genuine or valid one. She in her turn pointed to circumstances said to cast doubt on the reasonableness of the suspicion. Thus, had the suspicion really been reasonable, she would not have been arrested under the four-hour power granted by section 14 of the 1978 Act but under more extensive powers; she would have been questioned by the police, not the Army; time would not have been spent in gathering personal details and in photographing her; she would have been questioned for more than one hour and 15 minutes; she would have been questioned about her own alleged involvement and not just about her brothers in the United States; and she would have been cautioned. In reply to the Government the first applicant contended that the issue which the domestic courts inquired into was

not the objective reasonableness of any suspicion but the subjective state of mind of the arresting officer, Corporal D.

54. For the Commission, the Government's explanation in the present case was not materially distinguishable from that provided in the case of *Fox, Campbell and Hartley*. It took the view that no objective evidence to corroborate the unrevealed information had been adduced in support of the suspicion that the first applicant had been involved in collecting money for Provisional IRA arms purchases other than her kinship with her convicted brothers. That, the Commission concluded, was insufficient to satisfy the minimum standard set by Article 5(1)(c).

55. With regard to the level of "suspicion", the Court would note firstly that, as was observed in its judgment in the case of *Brogan and Others v. United Kingdom*, "sub-paragraph (c) of Article 5 §1 does not presuppose that the [investigating authorities] should have obtained sufficient evidence to bring charges, either at the point of arrest or while [the arrested person is] in custody. Such evidence may have been unobtainable or, in view of the nature of the suspected offences, impossible to produce in court without endangering the lives of others". The object of questioning during detention under sub-paragraph (c) of Article 5(1) is to further the criminal investigation by way of confirming or dispelling the concrete suspicion grounding the arrest. Thus, facts which raise a suspicion need not be of the same level as those necessary to justify a conviction or even the bringing of a charge, which comes at the next stage of the process of criminal investigation.

56. The length of the deprivation of liberty at risk may also be material to the level of suspicion required. The period of detention permitted under the provision by virtue of which Mrs Murray was arrested, namely section 14 of the 1978 Act, was limited to a maximum of four hours.

57. With particular regard to the "reasonableness" of the suspicion, the principles stated in the *Fox, Campbell and Hartley* judgment are to be applied in the present case, although as pointed out in that judgment, the existence or not of a reasonable suspicion in a concrete instance depends ultimately on the particular facts.

58. The Court would firstly reiterate its recognition that the use of confidential information is essential in combating terrorist violence and the threat that organised terrorism poses to the lives of citizens and to democratic society as a whole. [citation omitted] This does not mean, however, that the investigating authorities have *carte blanche* under Article 5 to arrest suspects for questioning, free from effective control by the domestic courts or by the Convention supervisory institutions, whenever they choose to assert that terrorism is involved.

59. As to the present case, the terrorist campaign in Northern Ireland, the carnage it has caused over the years and the active engagement of the Provisional IRA in that campaign are established beyond doubt. The Court also accepts that the power of arrest granted to the Army by section 14 of the 1978 Act represented a bona fide attempt by a democratically elected parliament to deal with terrorist crime under the rule of law. That finding is not altered by the fact that the terms of the applicable legislation were amended in 1987 as a result of the Baker Report so as to include a requirement that the arrest should be based on reasonable, rather than merely honest, suspicion.

The Court is accordingly prepared to attach some credence to the respondent Government's declaration concerning the existence of reliable but confidential information grounding the suspicion against Mrs Murray.

60. Nevertheless, in the words of the *Fox, Campbell and Hartley* judgment, the respondent Government must in addition "furnish at least some facts or information capable of satisfying the Court that the arrested person was reasonably suspected of having committed the alleged offence". In this connection, unlike in the case of *Fox, Campbell and Hartley*, the Convention institutions have had the benefit of the review that the national courts conducted of the facts and of Mrs. Murray's allegations in the civil proceedings brought by her.

61. It cannot be excluded that all or some of the evidence adduced before the national courts in relation to the genuineness of the suspicion on the basis of which Mrs. Murray was arrested may also be material to the issue whether the suspicion was "reasonable" for the purposes of Article 5(1)(c) of the Convention. At the very least the honesty and bona fides of a suspicion constitute one indispensable element of its reasonableness.

In the action brought by Mrs. Murray against the Ministry of Defence for false imprisonment and other torts, the High Court judge, after having heard the witnesses and assessed their credibility, found that she had genuinely been suspected of having been involved in the collection of funds for the purchase of arms in the United States for the Provisional IRA. The judge believed the evidence of the arresting officer, Corporal D, who was described as a "transparently honest witness", as to what she had been told at her briefing before the arrest. Likewise as found by the judge, although the interview at the Army centre was later in time than the arrest, the line of questioning pursued by the interviewer also tends to support the conclusion that Mrs. Murray herself was suspected of the commission of a specific criminal offence.

62. Some weeks before her arrest two of Mrs Murray's brothers had been convicted in the United States of offences connected with purchase of arms for the Provisional IRA. As she disclosed in her evidence to the High Court, she had visited the United States and had contacts with her brothers there. The offences of which her brothers were convicted were ones that implied collaboration with "trustworthy" persons residing in Northern Ireland.

63. Having regard to the level of factual justification required at the stage of suspicion and to the special exigencies of investigating terrorist crime, the Court finds, in the light of all the above considerations, that there did exist sufficient facts or information which would provide a plausible and objective basis for a suspicion that Mrs. Murray may have committed the offence of involvement in the collection of funds for the Provisional IRA. On the particular facts of the present case, therefore, the Court is satisfied that, notwithstanding the lower standard of suspicion under domestic law, Mrs. Murray can be said to have been arrested and detained on "reasonable suspicion" of the commission of a criminal offence, within the meaning of sub-paragraph (c) of Article 5(1).

C. Purpose of the arrest

64. In the first applicant's submission, it was clear from the surrounding circumstances that she was not arrested for the purpose of bringing her before a "competent legal authority" but merely for the purpose of interrogating her with a view to gathering general intelligence. She referred to the entries made in her regard on the standard record completed at the Army centre, to the failure of the Army to involve the police in her questioning and to the short (one-hour) period of her questioning.

The Government disputed this contention, pointing to the fact that it was a claim expressly raised by Mrs. Murray in the domestic proceedings and rejected by the trial judge on the basis of evidence which had been tested by cross-examination of witnesses.

The Commission in its report did not find it necessary to examine this complaint in view of its conclusion as to the lack of "reasonable suspicion" for the arrest and detention.

65. Under the applicable law of Northern Ireland the power of arrest and detention granted to the Army under section 14 of the 1978 Act must not be used for any improper purpose such as intelligence-gathering. In the civil action brought by Mrs. Murray against the Ministry of Defence the trial court judge found that on the evidence before him the purpose of her arrest and detention under section 14 of the 1978 Act had been to establish facts concerning the offence of which she was suspected. In reaching this conclusion the trial judge had had the benefit of seeing the various witnesses give their evidence and of evaluating their credibility. He accepted the evidence of Corporal D and Sergeant B as being truthful and rejected the claims of Mrs. Murray, in particular her contention that she had been told by Sergeant B that she was not suspected of any offence and had been arrested merely in order to bring her file up to date. The Court of Appeal, after reviewing the evidence, in turn rejected her argument that the purpose of her arrest and detention had been a "fishing expedition" designed to obtain low-grade intelligence. This argument was not pursued before the House of Lords.

66. The Court's task is to determine whether the conditions laid down by paragraph (c) of Article 5(1), including the pursuit of the prescribed legitimate purpose, have been fulfilled in the circumstances of the particular case. However, in this context it is not normally within the province of the Court to substitute its own finding of fact for that of the domestic courts, which are better placed to assess the evidence adduced before them. [citations omitted] In the present case no cogent elements have been produced by the first applicant in the proceedings before the Convention institutions which could lead the Court to depart from the findings of fact made by the Northern Ireland courts.

67. Mrs. Murray was neither charged nor brought before a court but was released after an interview lasting a little longer than one hour. This does not necessarily mean, however, that the purpose of her arrest and detention was not in accordance with Article 5(1)(c) since "the existence of such a purpose must be considered independently of its achievement". [citation omitted] As the domestic courts pointed out, in view of her persistent refusal to answer any questions at the Army centre it is not surprising that the authorities were not able to make any headway in pursuing the suspicions against her. It can be assumed that, had these suspicions been confirmed, charges would have been laid and she would have been brought before the competent legal authority.

68. The first applicant also alleged absence of the required proper purpose by reason of the fact that in practice persons arrested by the Army under section 14 were never brought before a competent legal authority by the Army but, if the suspicions were confirmed during questioning, were handed over to the police who preferred charges and took the necessary action to bring the person before a court.

The Court sees little merit in this argument. What counts for the purpose of compliance with Convention obligations is the substance rather than the form. Provided that the purpose of the arrest and detention is genuinely to bring the person before the competent legal authority, the mechanics of how this is to be achieved will not be decisive.

69. The arrest and detention of the first applicant must therefore be taken to have been effected for the purpose specified in paragraph 1(c).

D. Conclusion

70. In conclusion, there has been no violation of Article 5(1) in respect of the first applicant.

III. Alleged violation of Article 5(2) of the Convention

71. The first applicant also alleged a violation of Article 5(2) of the Convention, which provides:

> Everyone who is arrested shall be informed promptly, in a language which he understands, of the reasons for his arrest and of any charge against him.

72. The relevant principles governing the interpretation and application of Article 5(2) in cases such as the present one were explained by the Court in its *Fox, Campbell and Hartley* judgment as follows:

> Paragraph 2 of Article 5 contains the elementary safeguard that any person arrested should know why he is being deprived of his liberty. This provision is an integral part of the scheme of protection afforded by Article 5: by virtue of paragraph 2 any person arrested must be told, in simple, non-technical language that he can understand, the essential legal and factual grounds for his arrest, so as to be able, if he sees fit, to apply to a court to challenge its lawfulness in accordance with paragraph 4 . . . Whilst this information must be conveyed 'promptly' (in French: '*dans le plus court dèlai*'), it need not be related in its entirety by the arresting officer at the very moment of the arrest. Whether the content and promptness of the information conveyed were sufficient is to be assessed in each case according to its special features.

In that case the Court found on the facts that the reasons for the applicants' arrest had been brought to their attention during their interrogation within a few hours of their arrest. This being so, the requirements of Article 5(2) were held to have been satisfied in the circumstances.

73. The first applicant maintained that at no time during her arrest or detention had she been given any or sufficient information as to the grounds of her arrest. Although she had realised that the Army was interested in her brothers' activities, she had not, she claimed, understood from the interview at the Army centre that she herself was suspected of involvement in fund-raising for the Provisional IRA. The only direct information she was given was the formal formula of arrest pronounced by Corporal D.

74. The Commission similarly took the view that it was impossible to draw any conclusions from what it described as the vague indications given by Corporal D in evidence before the High Court as to whether the first applicant had been able to understand from the interview why she had been arrested. In the Commission's opinion, it had not been shown that the questions asked of Mrs. Murray during her interview were sufficiently precise to constitute the information as to the reasons for arrest required by Article 5(2).

75. According to the Government, on the other hand, it was apparent from the trial evidence that in the interview it was made clear to Mrs. Murray that she was suspected of the offence of collecting money for the Provisional IRA. The Government did not accept the Commission's conclusion on the facts, which was at variance with the findings of the domestic courts. They considered it established that Mrs. Murray had been given sufficient information as to the grounds of her arrest. In the alternative, even if insufficient information had been given to her to avail herself of her right under Article 5(4) of the

Convention to take legal proceedings to test the lawfulness of her detention, she had suffered no prejudice thereby which would give rise to a breach of Article 5(2) since she had been released rapidly, before any determination of the lawfulness of her detention could have taken place.

76. It is common ground that, apart from repeating the formal words of arrest required by law, the arresting officer, Corporal D, also told Mrs. Murray the section of the 1978 Act under which the arrest was being carried out. This bare indication of the legal basis for the arrest, taken on its own, is insufficient for the purposes of Article 5(2). [citation omitted]

77. During the trial of Mrs. Murray's action against the Ministry of Defence, evidence as to the interview at the Army centre was given by Mrs. Murray and Corporal D, but not by the solider who had conducted the interview. Mrs. Murray testified that she had been questioned about her brothers in the United States and about her contacts with them but not about the purchase of arms for the Provisional IRA or about any offence. Corporal D did not have a precise recollection as to the content of the questions put to Mrs. Murray. This is not perhaps surprising since the trial took place over three years after the events – Mrs. Murray having waited 18 months before bringing her action – and Corporal D, although present, had not taken an active part in the interview. Corporal D did however remember that questions had been asked about money and about America and the trial judge found her to be a "transparently honest witness". Shortly before the arrest two of Mrs. Murray's brothers had, presumably to the knowledge of all concerned in the interview, been convicted in the United States of offences connected with the purchase of weapons for the Provisional IRA.

In the Court's view, it must have been apparent to Mrs. Murray that she was being questioned about her possible involvement in the collection of funds for the purchase of arms for the Provisional IRA by her brothers in the United States. Admittedly, "there was never any probing examination of her collecting money" – to use the words of the trial judge – but, as the national courts noted, this was because of Mrs. Murray's declining to answer any questions at all beyond giving her name. The Court therefore finds that the reasons for her arrest were sufficiently brought to her attention during her interview.

78. Mrs. Murray was arrested at her home at 7.00 am and interviewed at the Army centre between 8.20 am and 9.35 am on the same day. In the context of the present case this interval cannot be regarded as falling outside the constraints of time imposed by the notion of promptness in Article 5(2).

79. In view of the foregoing findings it is not necessary for the Court to examine the Government's alternative submission.

80. In conclusion, there was no breach of Article 5(2) in respect of the first applicant.

. . . .

For these reasons, THE COURT

1. Holds, by 14 votes to four, that there has been no breach of Article 5(1) of the Convention in respect of the first applicant;

2. Holds, by 13 votes to five, that there has been no breach of Article 5(2) of the Convention in respect of the first applicant;

. . . .

∾

QUESTIONS & COMMENTS

(1) The most striking aspect of ECHR law governing arrests is that only "reasonable suspicion" is required – not probable cause, as under U.S. law. *Spinelli v. United States*, 393 U.S. 410 (1969). Under U.S. law, reasonable suspicion is sufficient only for "stop and frisks." *Terry v. Ohio*, 392 U.S. 1 (1968). Neither the Inter-American Court nor Inter-American Commission has addressed the required evidentiary requirement for lawful arrest. However, the UN Human Rights Committee has opined that only reasonable suspicion is required. *See* M. J. Bossuyt, Guide to the "Travaux Prèparatoires" of the International Covenant on Civil and Political Rights 187–219 (1987) (detailing the ICCPR's drafting history and the Committee's Art. 9 comments).

(2) There are several troubling aspects about the European Court's decision in *Murray v. United Kingdom*. Mrs. Murray's arrest was based on her brothers' convictions in the United States and her visit to them. Is it not reasonable and lawful that a sister would visit her brothers if they had been detained? Furthermore, do her brothers' convictions and her visit really form sufficient grounds for reasonable suspicion of her raising funds for the IRA? If these factors constituted sufficient grounds for reasonable suspicion, then anyone who ever visited a prisoner could be stopped, arrested, and detained for questioning.

Although the European Court made reference to secret sources of information on which the U.K. authorities' reasonable suspicion was based, neither the European Court nor the U.K. courts examined the veracity and basis of knowledge of the secret source. How does this comport with the European Court's other case law addressing the right to the examination of witnesses and documents? Under U.S. law, to establish probable cause, a judge must examine the totality of circumstances, including the "veracity" and "basis of knowledge" of confidential sources. *Illinois v. Gates*, 462 U.S. 213 (1983). Even under a "reasonable suspicion" standard, such as provided by *Terry v. Ohio*, "specific and articulatable facts" must be produced. In *Murray v. United Kingdom*, no comparable analyses of the secret source's information was undertaken by either the U.K. courts or European Court.

> [I]n the words of the *Fox, Campbell and Hartley* judgment, the respondent Government must in addition "furnish at least some facts or information capable of satisfying the Court that the arrested person was reasonably suspected of having committed the alleged offence." In this connection, unlike in the case of *Fox, Campbell and Hartley*, the Convention institutions have had the benefit of the review that the national courts conducted of the facts and of Mrs. Murray's allegations in the civil proceedings brought by her.

Murray v. United Kingdom, 300-A Eur. Ct. H.R. at §60 (1994). Did the European Court fail to exercise the appropriate level of "European supervision" given that this case turns on an important factual issue?

Another troubling aspect of the European Court's decision is that while the European Court provided background as to the civil strife in Northern Ireland and accordingly recognized the need to combat IRA terrorism, it did not see fit to discuss the well-established terrorist practices[9] of the United Kingdom's police and military and the

---

[9] In *Ireland v. United Kingdom*, 24 Eur. Ct. H.R. (ser. A) (1978), the European Court found that the U.K. authorities had, as a matter of policy, used interrogation methods that constituted inhuman and degrading treatment in violation of Article 3, ECHR. Also, recall the case of the Guildford Four in which unlawful coercive interrogation methods were used against suspected IRA terrorists.

concomitant need to combat state terrorism. The use of terror – whether by rousing and holding family members in a room where they could be subjected to physical or other threats or by arresting Mrs. Murray – is often effective in extracting information from persons who are not the subject of reasonable suspicion of committing crimes. In rejecting Mrs. Murray's argument that the purpose of her arrest and detention had been a "fishing expedition" designed to obtain low-grade intelligence, the Court seems to have effectively sanctioned the use of coercive measures against innocent persons in criminal investigations.

Does the fact that Mrs. Murray was released after a very brief interrogation in which no information was elicited throw into question the government's claim of "reasonable suspicion" of criminal activity? If she truly was suspected of terrorist-related activity, would not the government have an interest in detaining her until she answered the questions put to her? If the government had held her until she agreed to answer the questions, would this constitute a violation under the European Convention?

(3) For another right to liberty case dealing with Northern Ireland, *see, e.g., Fox, Campbell, and Hartley v. United Kingdom*, 182 Eur. Ct. H.R. (ser. A) (1990).

(4) Compare *Slijivo v. Republika Srpska (Admissibility and Merits)*, Case No. CH/97/34, Hum. Rts. Chamber-BiH (10 September 1998), in which the Human Rights Chamber for Bosnia and Herzegovina held that arresting authorities need not tell the arrestee the reasons for his or her arrest in its entirety at the moment of arrest.

(5) Compare the strength of the Article 5 right to liberty with that of the Article 8 right to respect for private and family life in the context of arrests within the home or other private places. Does Article 8 provide greater protection to individuals?

(6) Compare the ICC Statute's arrest provisions:

Article 58

Issuance by the Pre-Trial Chamber of a warrant of arrest or a summons to appear

1. At any time after the initiation of an investigation, the Pre-Trial Chamber shall, on the application of the Prosecutor, issue a warrant of arrest of a person if, having examined the application and the evidence or other information submitted by the Prosecutor, it is satisfied that:

(a) There are reasonable grounds to believe that the person has committed a crime within the jurisdiction of the Court; and
(b) The arrest of the person appears necessary:

(i) To ensure the person's appearance at trial,
(ii) To ensure that the person does not obstruct or endanger the investigation or the court proceedings, or
(iii) Where applicable, to prevent the person from continuing with the commission of that crime or a related crime which is within the jurisdiction of the Court and which arises out of the same circumstances.

2. The application of the Prosecutor shall contain:

(a) The name of the person and any other relevant identifying information;
(b) A specific reference to the crimes within the jurisdiction of the Court which the person is alleged to have committed;

(c) A concise statement of the facts which are alleged to constitute those crimes;

(d) A summary of the evidence and any other information which establish reasonable grounds to believe that the person committed those crimes; and

(e) The reason why the Prosecutor believes that the arrest of the person is necessary.

3. The warrant of arrest shall contain:

(a) The name of the person and any other relevant identifying information;

(b) A specific reference to the crimes within the jurisdiction of the Court for which the person's arrest is sought; and

(c) A concise statement of the facts which are alleged to constitute those crimes.

4. The warrant of arrest shall remain in effect until otherwise ordered by the Court.

. . . .

Clearly, the ICC Statute's provisions require more than the "reasonable suspicion" interpretation of the European Court of Human Rights. Does it require more than the reasonable suspicion standard in *Terry v. Ohio*? Does it reach the "probable cause" standard in *Spinelli v. United States*?

Suárez Rosero v. Ecuador
Inter-American Court of Human Rights
Judgment of 12 November 1997

. . . .

34. From an examination of the documents, the witnesses' statements, the expert's report, and the remarks of the State and the Commission in the course of the proceedings, the Court deems the following facts to have been proven:

a. Mr. Rafael Iván Suárez-Rosero was arrested at 2:30 a.m. on June 23, 1992, by officers of the National Police of Ecuador, in connection with police Operation "*Ciclón*", the aim of which was to "*disband one of the largest international drug-trafficking organizations*", by a police order issued when residents of the Zámbiza sector of Quito reported that the occupants of a "Trooper" were burning what appeared to be drugs . . . ;

b. Mr. Suárez-Rosero was arrested without a warrant from the competent authority and not *in flagrante delicto* . . . ;

c. on the day of his arrest, Mr. Suárez-Rosero gave an initial statement to police officers in the presence of three prosecutors from the Ministry of Public Affairs. No defense attorney was present during the questioning . . . ;

d. from June 23 to July 23, 1992, Mr. Rafael Iván Suárez-Rosero was held *incommunicado* at the "Quito Number 2" Police Barracks situated at Montúfar and Manabí streets in the city of Quito, in a damp and poorly ventilated cell measuring five meters by three, together with sixteen other persons . . . ;

e. on July 22, 1992, the Commissioner-General of Police of Pichincha ordered the Director of the Men's Social Rehabilitation Center to keep Mr. Suárez-Rosero and other persons in detention until a court had issued an order to the contrary . . . ;

f. on July 23, 1992, Mr. Suárez-Rosero was transferred to the Men's Social Rehabilitation Center of Quito . . . ;

. . . .

i. on August 12, 1992, the Third Criminal Court of Pichincha issued an order of preventive detention against Mr. Suárez-Rosero . . . ;

j. on September 3, 1992, the Third Criminal Court of Pichincha declined to try the case against Mr. Suárez-Rosero and the other persons detained in Operation "*Ciclón,*" inasmuch of one of the accused in that case was promoted to the rank of Infantry Major, and transferred the file to the Superior Court of Justice of Quito . . . ;

k. on two occasions, on September 14, 1992, and January 21, 1993, Mr. Suárez-Rosero requested that the order authorizing his preventive detention be revoked . . . ;

l. on November 27, 1992, the President of the Superior Court of Justice of Quito ordered the initiation of the first phase of the pre-trial proceedings. In that order, Mr. Suárez-Rosero was charged with transporting drugs for the purpose of destroying them and hiding the evidence . . . ;

m. on December 9, 1992, the President of the Superior Court of Justice of Quito ordered investigative proceedings to be instituted in connection with the case; these were held between December 29, 1992, and January 13, 1993 . . . ;

n. on March 29, 1993, Mr. Suárez-Rosero filed a writ of habeas corpus with the President of the Supreme Court of Justice of Ecuador, under the provisions of Article 458 of the Code of Criminal Proceedings of Ecuador . . . ;

o. on August 25, 1993, the President of the Superior Court of Justice of Quito requested the Public Prosecutor of Pichincha to render his opinion on Mr. Suárez-Rosero's request to have his detention order revoked . . . ;

p. on January 11, 1994, the Prosecutor of Pichincha rendered an opinion on the request for abrogation of Mr. Suárez-Rosero's detention order (*supra,* subparagraph o.), stating that

for the time being, the police report which serves as the basis for initiation of the instant criminal case, as well as the preliminary statements, suggests that the accused [. . .]: Iván Suárez-Rosero [. . .] appear[s] to be responsible, so that it would be improper to revoke the order for [his] preventive detention.

. . . .

q. on January 26, 1994, Mr. Suárez-Rosero's request to have the preventive detention order against him revoked was denied (*supra,* subparagraph k.). . . . That same day, the officers who had arrested him were summoned to give statements, but did not appear, nor did they do so when they were again summoned on March 3 and May 9, 1994 . . . ;

r. on June 10, 1994, the President of the Supreme Court of Justice denied the writ of habeas corpus filed by Mr. Suárez-Rosero (*supra,* subparagraph n.), on the ground that

[t]he petition presented [. did] not provide any information showing the category or nature of the proceeding indicating that he was deprived of his liberty, the district in which the President of the Superior Court of Justice that had issued the order was located, the place of detention, the date on which he was deprived of his liberty, the reason, etc., so that it cannot be processed and is therefore denied and ordered to be struck from the list.

. . . .

s. on November 4, 1994, the President of the Superior Court of Justice of Quito declared the preliminary proceedings to be at an end and referred the case to the Public Prosecutor of Pichincha for his final pronouncement. . . . The prosecutor was to make a determination, within six days, but there is no record of the date in which he did so (Art. 235 of the Code of Criminal Proceeding of Ecuador);

t. on July 10, 1995, the President of the Superior Court of Justice of Quito declared open the plenary phase of the case against Mr. Suárez-Rosero, on a charge of being accessory to the crime of drug trafficking. That court also decided that in Mr. Suárez-Rosero's case the requirements of preventive detention had not been met, and ordered his release . . . ;

u. on July 13, 1995, the Public Prosecutor of Pichincha requested the President of the Superior Court of Pichincha to expand his order of July 10, 1995,

so as not to release any person until that order [had been] referred to the Superior Court, in strict compliance with Article 121 of the Law on Narcotic Drugs and Psychotropic Substances

. . . .

v. on July 24, 1995, the President of the Superior Court of Justice of Quito ruled

[the] petition [of the Public Prosecutor of Pichincha of July 13, 1995] to be in order, inasmuch as the norm previously invoked in this type of violation is mandatory, since it deals with the crime of drug trafficking, governed by the Special Law on Narcotic Drugs and Psychotropic Substances [. . . and that] the order of release granted to accessories and to those whose cases were provisionally suspended should also be reviewed.

Consequently, the units were revised by the First Chamber of the Superior Court of Justice of Quito on July 31, 1995 . . . ;

w. on April 16, 1996, the First Chamber of the Superior Court of Justice of Quito ordered Mr. Suárez-Rosero's release. . . . That order was complied with on April 29, 1996 . . . ;

x. the President of the Superior Court of Justice of Quito, in his judgment of September 9, 1996, decided that Mr. Suárez-Rosero is

an accessory [.] to the crime of illegal trafficking in narcotic and drugs and psychotropic substances, defined and punishable under Art. 62 of the Law on Narcotic Drugs and Psychotropic Substances, and that, pursuant to the provisions of Arts. 44 and 88 of the Criminal Code, he was [.] sentenced to two years' imprisonment which he [was to] serve at the Men's Social Rehabilitation Center in [the] city of Quito, and that the time he has remained in preventive [.] detention would be deducted from that sentence.

Mr. Suárez-Rosero was also fined two thousand times the minimum living wage . . . , and

y. at no time was Mr. Suárez-Rosero summoned to appear before a competent judicial authority to be informed of the charges brought against him. . . .

. . . .

VIOLATION OF ARTICLE 7(2) AND 7(3)

38. In its application the Commission asked the Court to declare that Mr. Suárez-Rosero's initial detention was unlawful and arbitrary, in violation of Article 7(2) and 7(3) of the American Convention, since both this instrument and the Ecuadorian laws

require such acts to be performed by order of the competent authority in accordance with the procedures and terms established by law. A further requirement, according to the Commission, is that the detention be necessary and reasonable, which has not been proven in this case. Lastly, the Commission argued that during the initial period of Mr. Suárez-Rosero's arrest, he was held in facilities unsuitable for persons in preventive detention.

39. The State, for its part, contended that Mr. Suárez-Rosero's arrest "*was carried out in connection with a lawful inquiry and as a result of actual events, of which he was one of the protagonists.*"

40. In its brief of closing arguments the Commission stated that, in the course of the proceeding, not only had Ecuador not denied that Mr. Suárez-Rosero had been arrested in violation of Ecuadorian law, but that, on the contrary, the alternate agent of the State had admitted at the public hearing before the Court that Mr. Suárez-Rosero's arrest had been arbitrary.

41. Ecuador maintained in its closing arguments, on the subject of Mr. Suárez-Rosero's arrest, that "[i]*t is surprised* [. . .] *that the defendant has described a frightful scenario of detention and arrest and yet he is the only person to have appealed to the Commission to demonstrate such monstrous facts.*"

42. Article 7(2) and (3) of the American Convention on Human Rights establishes that

> 2. No one shall be deprived of his physical liberty except for reasons and under conditions established beforehand by the constitution of the State Party concerned or by a law established pursuant thereto.

> 3. No one shall be subject to arbitrary arrest or imprisonment.

43. The Court has said that no one may be

> deprived of personal liberty except for reasons, or in cases or circumstances expressly described in the law (material aspect), but, moreover, with strict adherence to the procedures objectively defined by it (formal aspect) (*Gangaram Panday Case*, Judgment of January 21, 1994. Series C No. 16, para. 47).

With regard to the formal requirements, the Court observes that the Political Constitution of Ecuador provides in Article 22(19)(h) that:

> [n]o one shall be deprived of his liberty except by written order of the competent authority, as appropriate, for the period and according to the procedures prescribed by law, save in the case of *in flagrante delicto*, in which case he may not either be held without a trial order for more than twenty-four hours. In either case, he may not be held *incommunicado* for more than twenty-four hours

and that, pursuant to Article 177 of the Code of Criminal Procedure of Ecuador,

> [t]he court may issue a writ of preventive imprisonment when it deems it to be necessary, provided the following procedural data are presented:

> 1. Evidence leading to a presumption of the existence of a crime that warrants the punishment of deprivation of liberty; and,

> 2. Evidence leading to a presumption that the accused is the author of or accomplice in the crime in question.

The evidence on which the order of imprisonment are based shall be stated in the records.

44. It was not demonstrated in the instant Case that Mr. Suárez-Rosero was apprehended *in flagrante delicto*. His arrest should therefore have been effected with a warrant issued by a competent judicial authority. However, the first judicial proceeding relating to his detention only took place on August 12, 1992 (*supra*, para. 34(i)), that is, over a month after his arrest, in violation of procedures previously established by the Political Constitution and the Code of Criminal Procedure of Ecuador.

45. The Court deems it unnecessary to voice an opinion on the evidence or suspicions that may have led to a detention order. The relevant point is that such an order was only produced in this case long after the victim's arrest. This was expressly acknowledged by the State during the public hearing, when it said that "*Mr. Suárez was the victim of arbitrary detention.*"

46. As to the place in which Mr. Suárez-Rosero was held *incommunicado*, the Court deems it to have been proven that he spent from June 23 to July 23, 1992, at a police station unsuitable as accommodation for a prisoner, according to the Commission and the expert (*supra*, para. 34(d)), in addition to all the violations of the right to liberty to the detriment of Mr. Suárez-Rosero.

47. For the above reasons, the Court finds that the Mr. Suárez-Rosero' arrest and his subsequent detention from June 23, 1992, were carried out in violation of the provisions contained in Article 7(2) and (3) of the American Convention.

. . . .

48. The Commission requested the Court to find that the fact that Mr. Suárez-Rosero's *incommunicado* detention for 36 days generated a violation of Article 7(2) of the American Convention, inasmuch as it violated Ecuadorian law, which establishes that such detention may not exceed 24 hours.

49. Ecuador did not challenge that argument in its answer to the application.

50. The Court observes that, pursuant to Article 22(19)(h) of the Political Constitution of Ecuador, the *incommunicado* detention of a person may not exceed 24 hours (*supra*, para. 43). Nevertheless, Mr. Suárez-Rosero was held *incommunicado* from June 23 to July 28, 1992 (*supra*, para. 34(d)), that is, for a total of 35 days in excess of the maximum period established by the Constitution.

51. *Incommunicado* detention is an exceptional measure the purpose of which is to prevent any interference with the investigation of the facts. Such isolation must be limited to the period of time expressly established by law. Even in that case, the State is obliged to ensure that the detainee enjoys the minimum and non-derogable guarantees established in the Convention and, specifically, the right to question the lawfulness of the detention and the guarantee of access to effective defense during his incarceration.

52. The Court, bearing in mind the maximum limit established in the Ecuadorian Constitution, finds that Mr. Rafael Iván Suárez-Rosero's *incommunicado* detention from June 23 to July 28, 1992, violated Article 7(2) of the American Convention.

VIOLATION OF ARTICLE 7(5)

53. The Commission argued in its application that the State had not fulfilled its obligation to bring Mr. Suárez-Rosero before a competent judicial authority, as required by Article 7(5) of the Convention, for, according to the arguments of the petitioner – not

contested by the State before the Commission –, Mr. Suárez-Rosero never appeared in person before such an authority to be informed of the charges against him.

54. In its answer to the application in that regard, Ecuador stated that "*Mr. Suárez-Rosero has been exercising his legal rights to express his views and make his legitimate claims during his legal process.*"

55. Article 7(5) of the American Convention provides that

[a]ny person detained shall be brought promptly before a judge or other officer authorized by law to exercise judicial power and shall be entitled to trial within a reasonable time or to be released without prejudice to the continuation of the proceedings. His release may be subject to guarantees to assure his appearance for trial.

56. The State did not contest the Commission's claim that Mr. Suárez-Rosero never appeared before a judicial authority during the proceeding. The Court therefore deems that claim to have been proved and rules that this omission on the part of the State constitutes a violation of Article 7(5) of the American Convention.

VIOLATION OF ARTICLES 7(6) AND (25)

57. The Commission asked the Court to rule that Mr. Suárez-Rosero's *incommunicado* detention violated Article 7(6) of the American Convention in that it denied him contact with the outside world and did not permit him to exercise his right of habeas corpus.

58. With regard to the aforementioned guarantee, Article 7(6) of the Convention provides that

[a]nyone who is deprived of his liberty shall be entitled to recourse to a competent court, in order that the court may decide without delay on the lawfulness of his arrest or detention and order his release if the arrest or detention is unlawful. In States Parties whose laws provide that anyone who believes himself to be threatened with deprivation of his liberty is entitled to recourse to a competent court in order that it may decide on the lawfulness of such threat, this remedy may not be restricted or abolished. The interested party or another person on his behalf is entitled to seek these remedies.

59. The Court has already ruled that a detained person must be guaranteed the right of habeas corpus at all times, even when he is being held in exceptional circumstances of *incommunicado* detention established by law. That guarantee is doubly entrenched in the law in Ecuador. Article 28 of the Political Constitution provides that

[a]ny person who believes that he is being unlawfully deprived of his liberty may seek the remedy of habeas corpus. He may exercise this right himself or through another person without the need for written mandate ...

The Code of Criminal Procedure of that State establishes in Article 458 that

[a]ny person who is charged with infringing the precepts contained in [that] Code and is kept in detention may apply to be released to a higher Court than the one that has ordered the deprivation of his liberty.

[...]

The application shall be made in writing.

[...]

Immediately upon receipt of the application, the Judge who is to hear it shall order the detained person to be brought before him and shall hear his statements, which shall be included in a record which shall be signed by the Judge, the Secretary and the applicant, or, should the applicant be unable to sign, by a witness on his behalf. Thereupon, the Judge shall seek to obtain all the information he deems necessary for the purpose of arriving to a conclusion and ensuring the lawfulness of his decision and shall, within forty-eight hours, decide what he deems to be lawful.

60. The Court observes, first of all, that the aforesaid articles do not restrict access to the remedy of habeas corpus to the persons who are held *incommunicado*; in addition, the Constitution allows that remedy to be sought by any person "*without the need for written mandate.*" It also points out that no evidence has been submitted to it to show that Mr. Suárez-Rosero attempted to file such an appeal with a competent authority during his *incommunicado* detention, nor did any other person attempt to do so on his behalf. Consequently, the Court deems the Commission's claim in that regard not to have been proven.

. . . .

61. The Commission claimed that Ecuador violated Articles 7(6) and 25 of the American Convention when it denied Mr. Suárez-Rosero the right of habeas corpus. On that point, the Commission claimed that the inordinate time of fourteen and a half months between Mr. Suárez-Rosero's filing the writ of habeas corpus on March 29, 1993, and the ruling on the writ is patently incompatible with the reasonable time provided for in Ecuador's own legislation. It further claimed that the State had therefore failed in its obligation to provide effective judicial recourse. Lastly, the Commission maintained that such recourse was denied for purely procedural reasons, that is, because the petitioner had not indicated the nature of the proceeding or the location of the court that had ordered the detention, nor the place, date or cause of the detention. Such formal requirements are not established in Ecuadorian Law.

62. Ecuador did not contest those arguments in its answer to the application.

63. This Court shares the Commission's view that the right enshrined in Article 7(6) of the American Convention is not exercised with the mere formal existence of the remedies it governs. Those remedies must be effective, since their purpose, in the terms of Article 7(6), is to obtain without delay a decision "*on the lawfulness of* [his] *arrest or detention,*" and, should they be unlawful, to obtain, also without delay, an "*order* [for] *his release*". The Court has also held that

> [i]n order for habeas corpus to achieve its purpose, which is to obtain a judicial determination of the lawfulness of a detention, it is necessary that the detained person be brought before a competent judge or tribunal with jurisdiction over him. Here habeas corpus performs a vital role in ensuring that a person's life and physical integrity are respected, in preventing his disappearance or the keeping of his whereabouts secret and in protecting him against torture or other cruel, inhuman or degrading punishment or treatment *(Habeas Corpus in Emergency Situations (Arts. 27(2), 25(1) and 7(6) American Convention on Human Rights)*, Advisory Opinion OC-8/87 of January 30, 1987. Series A No. 8, para. 35).

64. As indicated above (*supra*, para. 34.(r)), the Court deems it to have been proven that the writ of habeas corpus filed by Mr. Suárez-Rosero on March 29, 1993, was disposed of by the President of the Supreme Court of Justice of Ecuador on June 10, 1994, that

is, more than 14 months after it was filed. This Court also deems it to have been proven that the application was ruled inadmissible, on the ground that Mr. Suárez-Rosero had omitted certain information, whereas, under Ecuadorian Law, such information is not a prerequisite for admissibility.

65. Article 25 of the American Convention provides that everyone has the right to simple and prompt recourse, or any other effective recourse, to a competent court or tribunal. The Court has ruled that this provision

constitutes one of the basic pillars not only of the American Convention, but of the very rule of law in a democratic society in the sense of the Convention.

Article 25 is closely linked to the general obligation contained in Article 1(1) of the American Convention, in assigning protective functions to the domestic law of States Parties. The purpose of habeas corpus is not only to ensure respect for the right to personal liberty and physical integrity, but also to prevent the person's disappearance or the keeping of his whereabouts secret and, ultimately, to ensure his right to life (*Castillo Páez Case*, Judgment of November 3, 1997. Series C No. 34, paras. 82 and 83).

66. On the basis of the foregoing, and especially since Mr. Suárez-Rosero did not have access to simple, prompt and effective recourse, the Court finds that the State violated the provisions of Article 7(6) and 25 of the American Convention.

. . . .

~

QUESTIONS & COMMENTS

(1) Compare the ICT-Y's decision in *The Prosecutor v. Kupreskic and Others*, Case No. IT-95–16, ICTY, Trial Chamber, Decision on Motion for Provisional Release filed by Zoran Kupreskic, Mirjan Kupreskic, Drago Josipovic, and Dragan Papic (Joined by Marinko Katava and Vladimir Santic (15 December 1997). The trial chamber held that "provisional release may only be ordered in extreme and rare circumstances such as where the accused's state of health is incompatible with any form of detention." The chamber held that four conditions must be met for provisional release: (i) there are exceptional circumstances; (ii) the defendant will appear for trial; (iii) if released, the defendant will not pose a danger to any victim, witness, or other person; and (iv) the host country must be heard. The chamber ruled that a defendant's voluntary surrender did not justify his release from preventive detention.

Why is there a higher standard? Is it because of the crimes involved? What if an ICC defendant is charged with a crime against humanity that consists of one of the less than severe forms of persecution?

(2) Compare *Hill v. Spain*, UN Hum. Rts. Ctte., Communication No. 526/1993, U.N. Doc. CCPR/C/59/D/526/1993 (2 April 1997), in which the UN Human Rights Committee held that the mere fact that the defendant is a foreigner does not of itself imply that she or he must be held in detention pending trial on the mere conjecture that they might leave the state's jurisdiction. In *Hill v. Spain*, the Committee found that the authors, who had been charged with arson and were British citizens, should have been released pending trial.

(3) In *Josip, Bozana and Tomislav Matanovic v. Republika Srpska (Merits)*, Case No. CH/96/1, Hum. Rts. Chamber-BiH (1997), the Human Rights Chamber for Bosnia and Herzegovina in a disappearance case found an Article 5 (right to liberty), ECHR violation for the Republika Srpska's failure to produce the applicant after the Dayton Agreement even though he was originally detained before the Agreement.

Judicial Guarantees in States of Emergency
(Arts. 27(2), 25 and 8 of the American Convention on Human Rights)
Inter-American Court of Human Rights
Advisory Opinion OC-9/87 of October 6, 1987
Inter-Am. Ct. H.R. (Ser. A) No. 9 (1987)
(Reproduced in Section 2.1.3.)

≈

QUESTIONS & COMMENTS

(1) The U.S. Constitution guarantees that the "Privilege of the Writ of Habeas Corpus shall not be suspended, unless when in Cases of Rebellion or Invasion the public Safety may require it." Is this consistent with the Inter-American Court of Human Rights' advisory opinion in *Judicial Guarantees in States of Emergency*, Advisory Opinion No. OC-9/87 (reproduced *supra* in Section 2.1.3) in which the Court opined that right to habeas corpus proceedings are nonderogable if they are essential to ensuring the protection of express nonderogable rights, such as the right to life and humane treatment? Under what kind of circumstances could Congress suspend the writ? If the civilian courts are open and operating? What if the detainee is abroad? What if the detainee is an alien?

Consider the following:

FRANCISCO FORREST MARTIN, CHALLENGING HUMAN RIGHTS VIOLATIONS: USING INTERNATIONAL LAW IN U.S. COURTS 169–72 (2001).

> .... In *Johnson v. Eisentrager*,[1] the U.S. Supreme Court held that enemy aliens arrested in China and imprisoned in Germany after World War II could not obtain writs of *habeas corpus* in U.S. federal courts that otherwise would be available under the Fifth Amendment and Article I, §9 of the U.S. Constitution.[2]
>
> The U.S. Supreme Court's interpretation of Article I, §9 and the Fifth Amendment in *Johnson v. Eisentrager* did not address the subsequent U.S. treaty and customary international law

---

[1] 339 U.S. 763 (1950).

[2] The Fifth Amendment states in relevant part:

> No person shall be held to answer for a capital, or otherwise infamous crime, unless on a presentment or indictment of a Grand Jury, except in cases arising in the land or naval forces, or in the Militia, when in actual service in time of War or public danger ... nor shall be compelled in any criminal case to be a witness against himself, nor be deprived of life, liberty, or property, without due process of law. ...

U.S. CONST. amend. V. Article I, §9 states in relevant part:

> The privilege of the Writ of Habeas Corpus shall not be suspended, unless when in Cases of Rebellion or Invasion the public Safety may require it.

U.S. CONST. art. I, §9, cl. 2.

obligations recognizing extraterritorial liability. Article I, §9 and the Fifth Amendment should now be interpreted in light of and in conformity with this international law because of international law's status as federal law. Moreover, the right to liberty is recognized as a *jus cogens* norm – specifically considered non-derogable during states of emergency. The Inter-American Court of Human Rights specifically has opined that the right to the remedy of *habeas corpus* is a non-derogable right during states of emergency.[3] Additionally, the Geneva Convention – Protocol I recognizes the right to release from detention after circumstances requiring detention cease.[4]

. . . .

. . . . The Inter-American Commission on Human Rights in *Coard v. United States*[5] in the context of the Grenada Invasion stated:

> the Commission determined that the analysis of the petitioners' claims under the [American Declaration on the Rights and Duties of Man] within their factual and legal context requires reference to international humanitarian law, which is a source of authoritative guidance and provides the specific normative standards which apply to conflict situations. In the present case, the standards of humanitarian law help to define whether the detention of the petitioners was "arbitrary" or not under the terms of Articles I[[6]] and XXV[[7]] of the American Declaration.[8]
>
> The Geneva Convention (IV) effectively recognizes a right to liberty by allowing detention of protected persons only if it would be "absolutely necessary" for the security of the detaining power.[9] However, the Geneva Convention allows greater deference to the detaining power when the detention is undertaken to protect the safety of protected persons: the detaining power need only demonstrate that it would be "imperative" for the safety of protected persons to detain them.[10] The "absolutely

---

[3] *See Judicial Guarantees in States of Emergency (Arts. 27(2), 25, and 8 of the American Convention on Human Rights)*, Advisory Opinion OC–9/97, Inter-Am. Ct. H.R. (Ser. A) No. 9 (1987).

[4] Article 75(3) states:

> 3. Any person arrested, detained or interned for actions related to the armed conflict shall be informed promptly, in a language he understands, of the reasons why these measures have been taken. Except in cases of arrest or detention for penal offences, such persons shall be released with the minimum delay possible and in any event as soon as the circumstances justifying the arrest, detention or internment have ceased to exist.

Geneva Convention – Protocol I, art. 75(3).

[5] Report No. 109/99, Case 10.951 (29 September 1999), <http://www1.umn.edu/humanrts/cases/commissn. htm#1999> (visited 18 August 2000).

[6] Article I states "[every human being has the right to life, liberty and personal security]." American Declaration, art. I.

[7] Article XXV states in relevant part:

> No person may be deprived of his liberty except in the cases and according to the procedures established by pre-existing law.
>
> . . . .
>
> Every individual who has been deprived of his liberty has the right to have the legality of his detention ascertained without delay by a court, and the right to be tried without undue delay or otherwise, to be released. He also has the right to humane treatment during the time he is in custody.

American Declaration, art. XXV.

[8] *Coard v. United States, supra* at §42.

[9] Article 42 states:

> The internment or placing in assigned residence of protected persons may be ordered only if the security of the Detaining Power makes it absolutely necessary.

Geneva Convention (IV), art. 42.

[10] Geneva Convention (IV), art. 78.

necessary" test would require the detaining authorities to employ less restrictive measures if available.

Reading Article I, §9 and the Fifth Amendment in light of and consistently with the international law recognizing extraterritorial liability, requires that any limitation to the right to writ of *habeas corpus* (and other liberty-related rights) must be only "absolutely necessary" for national security in cases where there is no individualized suspicion, such as enemy aliens who are non-combatants. The phrase, "the public Safety may require it," in Article I, §9 does not say what level of necessity is required. The Geneva Convention (IV) provides the answer.

Because the U.S. is a party to the Geneva Convention (IV), and the Geneva Convention (IV) reflects customary international law (including *jus cogens*), the U.S. is legally bound to observe the "absolutely necessary" rule.

Does the habeas suspension clause in the U.S. Constitution operate as evidence of a persistent objection to a customary international law norm? Could the United States ever have the competence to ratify the ACHR if the habeas suspension provision in the Constitution could serve to invalidate the United States' ability to conclude the treaty under Article 46 of the Vienna Convention on the Law of Treaties ("A State may not invoke the fact that its consent to be bound by a treaty has been expressed in violation of a provision of its internal law regarding competence to conclude treaties as invalidating its consent unless that violation was manifest and concerned a rule of its internal law of fundamental importance.")?

(2) In *Hamdi v. Rumsfeld*, No. 03-6696, _ U.S. _ (2004), U.S. military forces had captured the petitioner, a U.S. citizen, in Afghanistan during an armed conflict and placed him in detention at a U.S. naval brig in South Carolina as a enemy combatant. The petitioner's father subsequently filed a habeas corpus petition on his son's behalf to challenge his detention. The Supreme Court held that the petitioner had a constitutional right to a hearing in which adequate fact-finding is available to him before a neutral decision maker to challenge the underlying factual assertions made by the government. The Court left open the possibility that such due process protections could be afforded the petitioner through a military tribunal. Subsequently, the Bush Administration employed military commissions that had been earlier established by presidential military order to determine whether detainees at Guantánamo were enemy combatants. However, as of early 2005, federal district courts had reached different conclusions about whether these military commissions were providing sufficient due process. Furthermore, after the Supreme Court's decision, the United States decided to release Hamdi.

(3) In *Rasul et al. v. Bush*, No. 03-334, _ U.S. _ (2004), the petitioners, who were foreign nationals, challenged their detention at the U.S. military base in Guantánamo, Cuba, as enemy combatants by habeas corpus. The U.S. Supreme Court held that the statutory right to habeas corpus extended extraterritorially. The Court distinguished its earlier holding in *Eisentrager* by noting that the Court after *Eisentrager* had filled in some statutory gaps in the federal law governing habeas corpus. The issue turned on whether the custodian of the detainees can be reached by service of process.

Furthermore, the right of aliens to invoke district court jurisdiction under the Alien Tort Statute and federal question jurisdiction also extended extraterritorially.

How does the Supreme Court's ruling in *Rasul* comport with the European Court of Human Rights' decision in *Bankovic and Others v. Belgium and Others* discussed in Section 4.1?

(4) What about U.S. immigration control law? Can the right to liberty not apply in extraterritorial contexts? Consider the following:

FRANCISCO FORREST MARTIN, CHALLENGING HUMAN RIGHTS VIOLATIONS: USING INTERNATIONAL LAW IN U.S. COURTS 172–75 (2001).

[Another] context in which the international law governing the extraterritorial right to liberty enhances U.S. law is the context of immigration control. Within this context, there are four more specific scenarios: (i) international waters, (ii) U.S. territorial waters considered "extraterritorial," (iii) points of entry (*e.g.*, international airports in the U.S.), and (iv) cases of indefinitely detained, excludable aliens. In the immigration control context, it is important to note that there usually is no state of emergency that arguably would allow greater limits on the right to liberty.

In international waters, U.S. waters, and other U.S. territory constitutionally considered "extraterritorial"[11] by the U.S. for controlling immigration,[12] the U.S. Supreme Court generally has held that such persons do not have either procedural[13] or substantive[14] due process rights under the U.S. Constitution. However, Congress has enacted legislation providing for some procedural due process guarantees.[15] Also, using the *Charming Betsy* Rule, the U.S. Ninth Circuit Court of Appeals in *Ma v. Reno*[16] recently construed federal legislation in light of the international law (including the ICCPR) prohibition of arbitrary detention to not allow the INS to indefinitely detain removable aliens.

International law does not allow the issue of extraterritoriality to preclude the protection of the right to liberty. This is very important for eliminating the "entry fiction doctrine" in U.S. law that has led to judicial contortions in attempting to rationalize INS and Congressional

---

[11] This is known as the "doctrine of entry fiction." *Ma v. Reno,* 208 F.3d 815 (9th Cir. 2000).

[12] *See, e.g., Sale v. Haitian Centers Council, Inc.* 113 S. Ct. 2549 (1993); *Chen Zhou Chai v. Carrol,* 48 F.3d 1331 (4th Cir. 1995).

[13] *See United States ex rel. Knauff v. Shaughnessy,* 338 U.S. 537 (1950).

[14] *See Shaughnessy v. United States ex rel. Mezei,* 345 U.S. 206 (1953); *see also United States v. Ramsey,* 431 U.S. 606, 615 (1977) (mere permission of Attorney General is sufficient to authorize any type of extraterritorial arrest or seizure); *but cf. Fiallo v. Bell,* 430 U.S. 787 (1977) (requiring federal immigration statute to be supported by "facially legitimate and bona fide reason").

[15] For example, immigration officers can remove inadmissible arriving aliens without a hearing unless the alien intends to apply for asylum:

> If an immigration officer determines that an alien . . . is arriving in the United States . . . is inadmissible . . . the officer shall order the alien removed from the United states without further hearing or review unless the alien indicates either an intention to apply for asylum. . . .

8 U.S.C. §1225(b)(1)(A)(i). If an alien's application for asylum is rejected, the alien has certain procedural due process rights during the removal hearings:

> In proceedings under this section, under regulations of the Attorney General –

> A. the alien shall have the privilege of being represented, at no expense to the Government, by counsel of the alien's choosing who is authorized to practice in such proceedings,
> B. the alien shall have reasonable opportunity to examine the evidence against the alien, to present evidence on the alien's own behalf, and to cross-examine witnesses presented by the Government but these rights shall not entitle the alien to examine such national security information as the Government may proffer in opposition to the alien's admission to the United States or to an application by the alien for discretionary relief under this chapter, and
> C. a complete record shall be kept of all testimony and evidence produced at the proceeding.

8 U.S.C. §1129(b) (4).

[16] *See Ma v. Reno,* 208 F.3d 815 (9th Cir. 2002); *see also Cornejo-Barreto v. Siefert,* 2000 U.S. App. LEXIS 15857 (11 July 2000) (using *Charming Betsy* Rule in extradition case).

actions. The extraterritorial reach of international law simply moots the issue of the entry fiction doctrine.

For example, the European Court of Human Rights in *Amuur v. France* [17] addressed the issue of "extraterritorial" areas in the context of immigration control. In *Amuur v. France*, a Somali family had fled to France. Upon reaching the Paris-Orly Airport, the applicants were denied entry on the basis of falsified passports. The French authorities detained them for twenty days at a location in the airport which the French government considered extraterritorial, *i.e.*, not within French jurisdiction. Not until four days before the French government expelled the family did they receive legal assistance in applying for asylum. Two days after their expulsion, a French court held that the family's detention was unlawful under French law. The European Court of Human Rights held that the transit zone of the airport was not extraterritorial and that the applicants were subject to French law. Because a French court already had found the applicants' detention violative of French law, their detention also violated the right to liberty under Article 5 (1), ECHR, as being not "in accordance with a procedure prescribed by law."

Most importantly, the Court held that the right to liberty requires "that any deprivation of liberty should be in keeping with the purpose of Article 5 . . . namely to protect the individual from arbitrariness."[18] To be "in accordance with a procedure prescribed by law," the Court held that the "quality of the law" must be scrutinized in light of

> the quality of the other legal rules applicable to the persons concerned. Quality in this sense implies that where a national law authorises deprivation of liberty – especially in respect of a foreign asylum-seeker – it must be sufficiently accessible and precise, in order to avoid all risk of arbitrariness. These characteristics are of fundamental importance with regard to asylum-seekers at airports, particularly in view of the need to reconcile the protection of fundamental rights with the requirements of States' immigration policies.[19]

Applying the law to the facts in *Amuur v. France*, the European Court found that the French immigration law and legal directives did not allow French courts

> to review the conditions under which aliens were held or, if necessary, to impose a limit on the administrative authorities as regards the length of time for which they were held. They did not provide for legal, humanitarian and social assistance, nor did they lay down procedures and time-limits for access to such assistance so that asylum-seekers like the applicants could take the necessary steps. The French legal rules in force at the time, as applied in the present case, did not sufficiently guarantee the applicants' right to liberty.[20]

In another case, *Quinn v. France*,[21] the European Court of Human Rights held that deprivation of liberty during extradition hearings is justified only for so long as extradition proceedings are being conducted. If such proceedings are not being conducted with "due diligence," the detention violates the right to liberty.[22] The Court unanimously held that the detention of the applicant for almost two years violated his right to liberty. The Court's holding suggests that if an alien (or national) is being subjected to prolonged detention because no country

---

[17]   22 Eur. H.R. Rep. 533 (1996).

[18]   *Id.* at §50.

[19]   *Id.*

[20]   *Id.* at §53 (citation omitted).

[21]   21 Eur. H.R. Rep. 529 (1996).

[22]   *Id.* at §48.

is willing to accept him/her pursuant to a court order for his/her removal, then there are not any proceedings being conducted – with due diligence or not. Accordingly, the detaining government is violating the removable person's right to liberty.

The European Court of Human Rights' decisions in *Amuur v. France* and *Quinn v. France* reflect conventional customary international law. Although several U.S. Courts of Appeals in the 1980s and 1990s held that the customary international law governing the right to liberty does not trump either federal law or executive orders,[23] the legitimacy of these holdings is highly suspect, as argued above.[24] Anyway, the issue of the relative authority of customary international law under U.S. law probably is moot. The European Court of Human Rights' decisions in *Amuur v. France* and *Quinn v. France* probably also reflect correct interpretations of the right to liberty under the ICCPR (to which the U.S. is a party) because of the materially similar language governing the right to liberty in both the ECHR and ICCPR. Accordingly, the U.S. now would be bound by its treaty law obligations under the ICCPR. And, indeed, the U.S. Ninth Circuit Court of Appeals has held so in *Ma v. Reno* insofar as the U.S.' obligations under the ICCPR.

In the case of indefinitely detained aliens in the U.S. who cannot be deported because there is no country willing to accept them, the conventional customary international law (as reflected in the European Court of Human Rights' decision in *Amuur v. France*) and ICCPR right to liberty would be violated because the U.S. immigration law allowing their indefinite detention fails to meet the quality of law required for restricting the right to liberty "in accordance with a procedure prescribed by law."[25] Under U.S. immigration law, the U.S. courts cannot impose limits on the INS authorities regarding the length of time for which these aliens can be held – unless the INS legislation is interpreted to conform with international law. Also, under *Quinn v. France*, the U.S. government would be violating the right to liberty for those indefinitely detained aliens who are subject to a final deportation order because there are no proceedings pending.

5.1.3. Right to Freedom from Discrimination

Universal Declaration of Human Rights

Article 7.

All are equal before the law and are entitled without any discrimination to equal protection of the law. All are entitled to equal protection against any discrimination in violation of this Declaration and against any incitement to such discrimination.

International Covenant on Civil and Political Rights

Article 26

All persons are equal before the law and are entitled without any discrimination to the equal protection of the law. In this respect, the law shall prohibit any discrimination and guarantee to all persons equal and effective protection against discrimination on any ground such as race, colour, sex, language, religion, political or other opinion, national or social origin, property, birth or other status.

---

[23] *See, e.g., Garcia-Mir v. Meese*, 788 F.2d 1446 (11th Cir.) (executive and legislative acts override customary international law), *cert. denied*, 479 U.S. 889 (1986).

[24] See Section Ed.'s Note Comment.

[25] *Amuur v. France*, 22 Eur. H.R. Rep. 533 at §53 (1996).

Article 27

In those States in which ethnic, religious or linguistic minorities exist persons belonging to such minorities shall not be denied the right, in community with the other members of their group, to enjoy their own culture, to profess and practise their own religion, or to use their own language.

European Convention on Human Rights

Article 14

The enjoyment of the rights and freedoms set forth in this Convention shall be secured without discrimination on any ground such as sex, race, colour, language, religion, political or other opinion, national or social origin, association with a national minority, property, birth or other status.

Charter of Fundamental Rights of the European Union

EQUALITY

Article 20

Equality before the law

Everyone is equal before the law.

Article 21

Non-discrimination

1. Any discrimination based on any ground such as sex, race, colour, ethnic or social origin, genetic features, language, religion or belief, political or any other opinion, membership of a national minority, property, birth, disability, age or sexual orientation shall be prohibited.

2. Within the scope of application of the Treaty establishing the European Community and of the Treaty on European Union, and without prejudice to the special provisions of those Treaties, any discrimination on grounds of nationality shall be prohibited.

Article 22

Cultural, religious and linguistic diversity

The Union shall respect cultural, religious and linguistic diversity.

Article 23

Equality between men and women

Equality between men and women must be ensured in all areas, including employment, work and pay. The principle of equality shall not prevent the maintenance or adoption of measures providing for specific advantages in favour of the under-represented sex.

Article 24

The rights of the child

1. Children shall have the right to such protection and care as is necessary for their well-being. They may express their views freely. Such views shall be taken into consideration on matters which concern them in accordance with their age and maturity.

2. In all actions relating to children, whether taken by public authorities or private institutions, the child's best interests must be a primary consideration. Every child shall have the right to maintain on a regular basis a personal relationship and direct contact with both his or her parents, unless that is contrary to his or her interests.

Article 25

The rights of the elderly

The Union recognises and respects the rights of the elderly to lead a life of dignity and independence and to participate in social and cultural life.

Article 26

Integration of persons with disabilities

The Union recognises and respects the right of persons with disabilities to benefit from measures designed to ensure their independence, social and occupational integration and participation in the life of the community.

American Declaration of the Rights and Duties of Man

Article II. Right to equality before law.

All persons are equal before the law and have the rights and duties established in this Declaration, without distinction as to race, sex, language, creed or any other factor.

American Convention on Human Rights

Article 1. OBLIGATION TO RESPECT RIGHTS.

1. The States Parties to this Convention undertake to respect the rights and freedoms recognized herein and to ensure to all persons subject to their jurisdiction the free and full exercise of those rights and freedoms, without any discrimination for reasons of race. color, sex, language, religion, political or other opinion, national or social origin, economic status, birth, or any other social condition.

Article 24. RIGHT TO EQUAL PROTECTION.

All persons are equal before the law. Consequently, they are entitled, without discrimination, to equal protection of the law.

African [Banjul] Charter on Human and Peoples' Rights

Article 2

Every individual shall be entitled to the enjoyment of the rights and freedoms recognized and guaranteed in the present Charter without distinction of any kind such as race, ethnic group, color, sex, language, religion, political or any other opinion, national and social origin, fortune, birth or other status.

Article 3

1. Every individual shall be equal before the law.
2. Every individual shall be entitled to equal protection of the law.

Article 18 (3)

3. The State shall ensure the elimination of every discrimination against women and also ensure the protection of the rights of the woman and the child as stipulated in international declarations and conventions.

Convention on Human Rights and Fundamental Freedoms of the Commonwealth of Independent States

Article 20

1. All shall be equal before the law and shall be entitled, without any discrimination, to equal protection of the law.

2. The enjoyment of the rights and freedoms set forth in this Convention shall be guaranteed without discrimination on any ground such as sex, race, color, language, religion, political or other opinion, national or social origin, association with a national minority, property or official capacity, place of birth or other status.

U.S. Constitution

Amendment XIV

Section 1. . . . No State shall . . . deny to any person within its jurisdiction the equal protection of the laws.

Other important multilateral human rights treaties addressing discrimination are: the International Convention on the Elimination of All Forms of Racial Discrimination and the Convention on the Elimination of All Forms of Discrimination Against Women.

Intentional Discrimination

Proposed Amendments to the
Naturalization Provisions of the Constitution of Costa Rica
Inter-American Court of Human Rights
Advisory Opinion OC-4/84 of January 19, 1984
Inter-Am. Ct. H.R. (Ser. A) No. 4 (1984)

[The Costa Rican government requested an advisory opinion from the Inter-American Court as to the compatibility of proposed amendments to the Costa Rican Constitution with the American Convention.]

. . . .

II. PROVISIONS TO BE ANALYZED IN THE DETERMINATION OF COMPATIBILITY

a) Domestic legislation:

1) Present text of Articles 14 and 15 of the Constitution of Costa Rica:

Article 14. The following are Costa Ricans by naturalization:

1. Those who have acquired this status by virtue of former laws;

2. Nationals of the other countries of Central America, who are of good conduct, who have resided at least one year in the republic, and who declare before the civil registrar their intention to be Costa Ricans;

3. Native-born Spaniards and Ibero-Americans who obtain the appropriate certificate from the civil registrar, provided they have been domiciled in the country during the two years prior to application;

4. Central Americans, Spaniards and Ibero-Americans who are not native-born, and other foreigners who have been domiciled in Costa Rica for a minimum period of five years immediately preceding their application for naturalization, in accordance with the requirements of the law;

5. A foreign woman who by marriage to a Costa Rican loses her nationality or who indicates her desire to become a Costa Rican;

6. Anyone who receives honorary nationality from the Legislative Assembly.

Article 15. Anyone who applies for naturalization must give evidence in advance of good conduct, must show that he has a known occupation or means of livelihood, and must promise to reside in the republic regularly.

For purposes of naturalization, domicile implies residence and stable and effective connection with the national community, in accordance with regulations established by law. 2) AMENDMENTS PROPOSED by the Special Committee of the Legislative Assembly in its Report of June 22, 1983.

Article 14. The following are Costa Ricans by naturalization:

1) Those who have acquired this status by virtue of previous laws;

2) Native-born nationals of the other countries of Central America, Spaniards and Ibero-Americans with five years official residence in the country and who fulfill the other requirements of the law;

3) Central Americans, Spaniards and Ibero-Americans, who are not native-born, and other foreigners who have held official residence for a minimum period of seven years and who fulfill the other requirements of the law;

4) A foreign woman who, by marriage to a Costa Rican loses her nationality or who after two years of marriage to a Costa Rican and the same period of residence in the country, indicates her desire to take on our nationality; and

5) Anyone who receives honorary nationality from the Legislative Assembly.

Article 15. Anyone who applies for naturalization must give evidence of good conduct, must show that he has a known occupation or means of livelihood, and must know how to speak, write and read the Spanish language. The applicant shall submit to a comprehensive examination on the history of the country and its values and shall, at the same time, promise to reside within the national territory regularly and swear to respect the constitutional order of the Republic.

The requirements and procedures for applications of naturalization shall be established by law.

3) MOTION OF AMENDMENT to Article 14(4) of the Constitution presented by the Deputies of the Special Committee:

A foreigner, who by marriage to a Costa Rican loses his or her nationality and who after two years of marriage to a Costa Rican and the same period of residence in the country, indicates his or her desire to take on the nationality of the spouse.

b) Articles of the Convention

The above-mentioned legal texts should be compared to the following articles of the American Convention on Human Rights in order to determine their compatibility:

Article 17. Rights of the Family

Paragraph 4. The States Parties shall take appropriate steps to ensure the equality of rights and the adequate balancing of responsibilities of the spouses as to marriage, during marriage, and in the event of its dissolution. In case of dissolution, provision shall be made for the necessary protection of any children solely on the basis of their own best interests.

Article 20. Right to Nationality

1. Every person has the right to a nationality.
2. Every person has the right to the nationality of the state in whose territory he was born if he does not have the right to any other nationality.
3. No one shall be arbitrarily deprived of his nationality or of the right to change it.

Article 24. Right to Equal Protection

All persons are equal before the law. Consequently, they are entitled, without discrimination, to equal protection of the law.

III. SPECIFIC QUESTIONS ON WHICH THE OPINION OF THE COURT IS SOUGHT

In accordance with the request originally made by the Special Committee to study amendments to Articles 14 and 15 of the Constitution, the Government of Costa Rica requests that the Court determine:

a) Whether the proposed amendments are compatible with the aforementioned provisions of the American Convention on Human Rights.

Specifically, within the context of the preceding question, the following questions should be answered:

b) Is the right of every person to a nationality, stipulated in Article 20(1) of the Convention, affected in any way by the proposed amendments to Articles 14 and 15 of the Constitution?
c) Is the proposed amendment to Article 14(4), according to the text proposed in the Report of the Special Committee, compatible with Article 17(4) of the Convention with respect to equality between spouses?
d) Is the text of the motion of the Deputies found in their opinion to amend this same paragraph compatible with Article 20(1) of the Convention?

. . . .

52. The provisions of the proposed amendments that have been brought before the Court for interpretation as well as the text of the Constitution that is now in force establish different classifications as far as the conditions for the acquisition of Costa Rican nationality through naturalization are concerned. Thus, under paragraphs 2 and 3 of Article 14 of the proposed amendment, the periods of official residence in the country required as a condition for the acquisition of nationality differ, depending on whether the applicants qualify as native-born nationals of "other countries of Central America, Spaniards and Ibero-Americans" or whether they acquired the nationality of those countries by naturalization. Paragraph 4 of that same Article in turn lays down special conditions applicable to the naturalization of "a foreign woman" who marries a Costa Rican. Article 14 of the Constitution now in force makes similar distinctions which, even though they may not have the same purpose and meaning, suggest the question whether they do not constitute discriminatory classifications incompatible with the relevant texts of the Convention.

53. Article 1(1) of the Convention, a rule general in scope which applies to all the provisions of the treaty, imposes on the States Parties the obligation to respect and guarantee the free and full exercise of the rights and freedoms recognized therein "without any discrimination." In other words, regardless of its origin or the form it may assume, any treatment that can be considered to be discriminatory with regard to the exercise of any of the rights guaranteed under the Convention is *per se* incompatible with that instrument.

54. Article 24 of the Convention, in turn, reads as follows:

Article 24. Right to Equal Protection

> All persons are equal before the law. Consequently, they are entitled, without discrimination, to equal protection of the law.

Although Articles 24 and 1(1) are conceptually not identical – the Court may perhaps have occasion at some future date to articulate the differences – Article 24 restates to a certain degree the principle established in Article 1(1). In recognizing equality before the law, it prohibits all discriminatory treatment originating in a legal prescription. The prohibition against discrimination so broadly proclaimed in Article 1(1) with regard to the rights and guarantees enumerated in the Convention thus extends to the domestic law of the States Parties, permitting the conclusion that in these provisions the States Parties, by acceding to the Convention, have undertaken to maintain their laws free of discriminatory regulations.

55. The notion of equality springs directly from the oneness of the human family and is linked to the essential dignity of the individual. That principle cannot be reconciled with the notion that a given group has the right to privileged treatment because of its perceived superiority. It is equally irreconcilable with that notion to characterize a group as inferior and treat it with hostility or otherwise subject it to discrimination in the enjoyment of rights which are accorded to others not so classified. It is impermissible to subject human beings to differences in treatment that are inconsistent with their unique and congenerous character.

56. Precisely because equality and nondiscrimination are inherent in the idea of the oneness in dignity and worth of all human beings, it follows that not all differences in legal treatment are discriminatory as such, for not all differences in treatment are in themselves offensive to human dignity. The European Court of Human Rights, "following

the principles which may be extracted from the legal practice of a large number of democratic States," has held that a difference in treatment is only discriminatory when it "has no objective and reasonable justification." [*Belgian Linguistics Case*, 6 Eur. Ct. H.R. (ser. A) (1968) at 34.] There may well exist certain factual inequalities that might legitimately give rise to inequalities in legal treatment that do not violate principles of justice. They may in fact be instrumental in achieving justice or in protecting those who find themselves in a weak legal position. For example, it cannot be deemed discrimination on the grounds of age or social status for the law to impose limits on the legal capacity of minors or mentally incompetent persons who lack the capacity to protect their interests.

57. Accordingly, no discrimination exists if the difference in treatment has a legitimate purpose and if it does not lead to situations which are contrary to justice, to reason or to the nature of things. It follows that there would be no discrimination in differences in treatment of individuals by a state when the classifications selected are based on substantial factual differences and there exists a reasonable relationship of proportionality between these differences and the aims of the legal rule under review. These aims may not be unjust or unreasonable, that is, they may not be arbitrary, capricious, despotic or in conflict with the essential oneness and dignity of humankind.

58. Although it cannot be denied that a given factual context may make it more or less difficult to determine whether or not one has encountered the situation described in the foregoing paragraph, it is equally true that, starting with the notion of the essential oneness and dignity of the human family, it is possible to identify circumstances in which considerations of public welfare may justify departures to a greater or lesser degree from the standards articulated above. One is here dealing with values which take on concrete dimensions in the face of those real situations in which they have to be applied and which permit in each case a certain margin of appreciation in giving expression to them.

59. With this approach in mind, the Court repeats its prior observation that as far as the granting of naturalization is concerned, it is for the granting state to determine whether and to what extent applicants for naturalization have complied with the conditions deemed to ensure an effective link between them and the value system and interests of the society to which they wish to belong. To this extent there exists no doubt that it is within the sovereign power of Costa Rica to decide what standards should determine the granting or denial of nationality to aliens who seek it, and to establish certain reasonable differentiations based on factual differences which, viewed objectively, recognize that some applicants have a closer affinity than others to Costa Rica's value system and interests.

60. Given the above considerations, one example of a non-discriminatory differentiation would be the establishment of less stringent residency requirements for Central Americans, Ibero-Americans and Spaniards than for other foreigners seeking to acquire Costa Rican nationality. It would not appear to be inconsistent with the nature and purpose of the grant of nationality to expedite the naturalization procedures for those who, viewed objectively, share much closer historical, cultural and spiritual bonds with the people of Costa Rica. The existence of these bonds permits the assumption that these individuals will be more easily and more rapidly assimilated within the national community and identify more readily with the traditional beliefs, values and institutions of Costa Rica, which the state has the right and duty to preserve.

61. Less obvious is the basis for the distinction, made in paragraphs 2 and 3 of Article 14 of the proposed amendment, between those Central Americans, Ibero-Americans and Spaniards who acquired their nationality by birth and those who obtained it by

naturalization. Since nationality is a bond that exists equally for the one group as for the other, the proposed classification appears to be based on the place of birth and not on the culture of the applicant for naturalization. The provisions in question may, however, have been prompted by certain doubts about the strictness of the conditions that were applied by those states which conferred their nationality on the individuals now seeking to obtain that of Costa Rica, the assumption being that the previously acquired nationality – be it Spanish, Ibero-American or that of some other Central American country – does not constitute an adequate guarantee of affinity with the value system and interests of the Costa Rican society. Although the distinctions being made are debatable on various grounds, the Court will not consider those issues now. Notwithstanding the fact that the classification resorted to is more difficult to understand given the additional requirements that an applicant would have to meet under Article 15 of the proposed amendment, the Court cannot conclude that the proposed amendment is clearly discriminatory in character.

62. In reaching this conclusion, the Court is fully mindful of the margin of appreciation which is reserved to states when it comes to the establishment of requirements for the acquisition of nationality and the determination whether they have been complied with. But the Court's conclusion should not be viewed as approval of the practice which prevails in some areas to limit to an exaggerated and unjustified degree the political rights of naturalized individuals. Most of these situations involve cases not now before the Court that do, however, constitute clear instances of discrimination on the basis of origin or place of birth, unjustly creating two distinct hierarchies of nationals in one single country.

63. Consistent with its clearly restrictive approach, the proposed amendment also provides for new conditions which must be complied with by those applying for naturalization. Draft Article 15 requires, among other things, proof of the ability to "speak, write and read" the Spanish language; it also prescribes a "comprehensive examination on the history of the country and its values." These conditions can be deemed, *prima facie*, to fall within the margin of appreciation reserved to the state as far as concerns the enactment and assessment of the requirements designed to ensure the existence of real and effective links upon which to base the acquisition of the new nationality. So viewed, it cannot be said to be unreasonable and unjustified to require proof of the ability to communicate in the language of the country or, although this is less clear, to require the applicant to "speak, write and read" the language. The same can be said of the requirement of a "comprehensive examination on the history of the country and its values." The Court feels compelled to emphasize, however, that in practice, and given the broad discretion with which tests such as those mandated by the draft amendment tend to be administered, there exists the risk that these requirements will become the vehicle for subjective and arbitrary judgments as well as instruments for the effectuation of discriminatory policies which, although not directly apparent on the face of the law, could well be the consequence of its application.

64. The fourth paragraph of draft Article 14 accords "a foreign woman who [marries] a Costa Rican" special consideration for obtaining Costa Rican nationality. In doing so, it follows the formula adopted in the current Constitution, which gives women but not men who marry Costa Ricans a special status for purposes of naturalization. This approach or system was based on the so-called principle of family unity and is traceable to two assumptions. One has to do with the proposition that all members of a family should have

the same nationality. The other derives from notions about paternal authority and the fact that authority over minor children was as a rule vested in the father and that it was the husband on whom the law conferred a privileged status of power, giving him authority, for example, to fix the marital domicile and to administer the marital property. Viewed in this light, the right accorded to women to acquire the nationality of their husbands was an outgrowth of conjugal inequality.

65. In the early 1930's, there developed a movement opposing these traditional notions. It had its roots in the acquisition of legal capacity by women and the more widespread acceptance of equality among the sexes based on the principle of nondiscrimination. These developments, which can be documented by means of a comparative law analysis, received a decisive impulse on the international plane. In the Americas, the Contracting Parties to the Montevideo Convention on the Nationality of Women of December 26, 1933 declared in Article 1 of that treaty that "There shall be no distinction based on sex as regards nationality, in their legislation or in their practice." [Adopted at the Seventh International Conference of American States, Montevideo, December 3–26, 1933. The Convention is reproduced in International Conferences of American States – Supplement 1933–1940. Washington, Carnegie Endowment for International Peace, 1940, p. 106.] And the Convention on Nationality, signed also in Montevideo on that same date, provided in Article 6 that "Neither matrimony nor its dissolution affects the nationality of the husband or wife or of their children." [*Ibid.*, at 108.] The American Declaration, in turn, declares in Article II that "All persons are equal before the law and have the rights and duties established in this declaration, without distinction as to race, sex, language, creed or any other factor." These same principles have been embodied in Article 1(3) of the United Nations Charter and in Article 3(j) of the OAS Charter.

66. The same idea is reflected in Article 17(4) of the Convention, which reads as follows:

> The States Parties shall take appropriate steps to ensure the equality of rights and the adequate balancing of responsibilities of the spouses as to marriage, during marriage, and in the event of its dissolution. In case of dissolution, provision shall be made for the necessary protection of any children solely on the basis of their own best interests.

Since this provision is consistent with the general rule enunciated in Article 24, which provides for equality before the law, and with the prohibition of discrimination based on sex contained in Article 1(1), Article 17(4) can be said to constitute the concrete application of these general principles to marriage.

67. The Court consequently concludes that the different treatment envisaged for spouses by paragraph 4 of Article 14 of the proposed amendment, which applies to the acquisition of Costa Rican nationality in cases involving special circumstances brought about by marriage, cannot be justified and must be considered to be discriminatory. The Court notes in this connection and without prejudice to its other observations applicable to the amendment proposed by the members of the Special Legislative Committee [*cf. supra*, ¶¶ 45 *et seq.*] that their proposal is based on the principle of equality between the spouses and, therefore, is more consistent with the Convention. The requirements spelled out in that amendment would be applicable not only to "a foreign woman" but to any "foreigner" who marries a Costa Rican national.

68. For the foregoing reasons, responding to the questions submitted by the Government of Costa Rica regarding the compatibility of the proposed amendments to Articles 14 and 15 of its Constitution with Articles 17(4), 20 and 24 of the Convention,

THE COURT IS OF THE OPINION

As regards Article 20 of the Convention,

By five votes to one

1. That the proposed amendment to the Constitution, which is the subject of this request for an advisory opinion, does not affect the right to nationality guaranteed by Article 20 of the Convention.

As regards Articles 24 and 17(4) of the Convention,

By unanimous vote

2. That the provision stipulating preferential treatment in the acquisition of Costa Rican nationality through naturalization, which favors Central Americans, Ibero-Americans and Spaniards over other aliens, does not constitute discrimination contrary to the Convention.

By five votes to one

3. That it does not constitute discrimination contrary to the Convention to grant such preferential treatment only to those who are Central Americans, Ibero-Americans and Spaniards by birth.

By five votes to one

4. That the further requirements added by Article 15 of the proposed amendment for the acquisition of Costa Rican nationality through naturalization do not as such constitute discrimination contrary to the Convention.

By unanimous vote

5. That the provision stipulating preferential treatment in cases of naturalization applicable to marriage contained in Article 14(4) of the proposed amendment, which favors only one of the spouses, does constitute discrimination incompatible with Articles 17(4) and 24 of the Convention.

QUESTIONS & COMMENTS

(1) In his partially dissenting opinion, Judge Buergenthal argues that the proposed amendment, if adopted, would violate Article 24 because it would unlawfully discriminate between Central Americans, Spaniards, and Ibero-Americans who are nationals of those countries by birth and those who have acquired their nationality by naturalization. Although recognizing "the historical, cultural, social, linguistic and political ties that bind Central Americans, Spaniards and Ibero-Americans," Buergenthal argues that the proposed amendment's distinction is a disproportionate means of appreciating these ties. What margin of appreciation should be given to national authorities in establishing distinctions based on national origin for naturalization purposes? Compare the case of Costa Rica to that of the United States. Given the U.S. history of accepting immigrants

from all over the world, would the margin of appreciation be considerably narrower than that given to Costa Rica on issues of naturalization?

(2) Draft Article 15 required, among other things, proof of the ability to "speak, write and read" the Spanish language. The Court opined that

> [t]hese conditions can be deemed, *prima facie*, to fall within the margin of appreciation reserved to the state as far as concerns the enactment and assessment of the requirements designed to ensure the existence of real and effective links upon which to base the acquisition of the new nationality. So viewed, it cannot be said to be unreasonable and unjustified to require proof of the ability to communicate in the language of the country or, although this is less clear, to require the applicant to "speak, write and read" the language.

Consider the "English-only" movement in the United States. Does the requirement of English in the United States ensure "real and effective links" among different ethnic or racial communities?

(3) Consider the following case addressing language discrimination in the context of education. In *Belgian Linguistics Case*, 6 Eur. Ct. H.R. (ser. A) (1968), the European Court of Human Rights examined two claims of language discrimination. In the first claim, the children of French-speaking families residing in a predominantly Dutch-speaking suburb were not allowed to attend French-speaking public schools. The Belgian government justified its denial on the basis of promoting linguistic unity within primarily unilingual areas. The European Court without examining whether this governmental aim was reasonable, found no violation of Article 14 (discrimination) in conjunction with Protocol No. 1(2) (education), which states:

> No person shall be denied the right to education. In the exercise of any functions which it assumes in relation to education and to teaching, the State shall respect the right of parents to ensure such education and teaching with their own religions and philosophical convictions.

However, on the second claim, the European Court did find a violation. In the second claim, the children of French-speaking families lived near a region in which both French and Dutch instruction was available. Although these children were denied admission to the French-speaking schools, children from Dutch-speaking schools also living near this region were allowed admission to the Dutch-speaking schools. The Court found that the Belgian government's purported aim of promoting linguistic unity could not be furthered by this arbitrary discriminatory treatment.

(4) The UN Human Rights Committee has addressed language discrimination in several cases. *See, e.g., Ballantyne, Davidson, McIntyre v. Canada*, Communications Nos. 359/1989 and 385/1989, views adopted 31 March 1993, U.N. Doc. CCPR/C/47/D/359/1989 and 385/1989/Rev. 1 (1993) (Quebec law requiring use of French in business advertising held not violative of freedom against discrimination); *Singer v. Canada*, Communication No. 455/1991, views adopted 26 July 1994, U.N. Doc. CCPR/C/51/D/455/1991 (1994) (outside spheres of public life, freedom of expression guarantees right to use language of choice).

(5) The European Court will scrutinize a discriminatory practice only when (i) another right guaranteed by the ECHR has been violated and (ii) "a clear inequity of treatment is . . . a fundamental aspect of the case." *Airey v. Ireland*, 32 Eur. Ct. H.R.(ser. A) at 16

(1980). Why should a clear inequity of treatment be a fundamental aspect of the case for establishing a discrimination claim?

(6) The ECHR, ACHR, Banjul Charter, and CIS Convention only prohibit discrimination in the exercise of other rights guaranteed by those respective treaties. Should this be the approach for interpreting Article 26 of the ICCPR, or Article II of the American Declaration? Why should a discrimination claim be tied only to those rights already guaranteed by the particular treaty?

(7) Under U.S. constitutional law, the Fifth Amendment requires that the federal government guarantee equal protection of the law under a due process analysis; the Fourteenth Amendment guarantees equal protection by the states. Classifications on the basis of race, national origin, alienage, or ethnicity receive strict scrutiny. Such classifications are inherently suspect. Under the "strict scrutiny" test, the government must proffer a "compelling" state interest and must *narrowly tailor* the means undertaken for achieving its aim. *Cleburne v. Cleburne Living Center, Inc.*, 473 U.S. 432 (1985) and *New Orleans v. Dukes*, 427 U.S. 297 (1976), discuss the general analytic framework in U.S. constitutional law. To be narrowly tailored, measures must not be underexclusive or overinclusive in achieving this end.

In addition to U.S. constitutional law, there is also federal statutory law prohibiting such discrimination. The Civil Rights Act of 1964, 42 U.S.C. §2000a, prohibits discrimination in places of public accommodation. *Heart of Atlanta Motel v. United States*, 379 U.S. 241 (1964). However, in *Daniel v. Paul*, 395 U.S. 298 (1969), the U.S. Supreme Court held that this prohibition did not apply to private clubs, which are not open to the public. However, 42 U.S.C. §1981 prohibits racial discrimination in the making of contracts. *Runyon v. McCrary*, 427 U.S. 160 (1976). And, 42 U.S.C. §1982 prohibits racial discrimination in the sale of property. Title VII of the Civil Rights Act of 1964 also prohibits discrimination on the basis of race, color, religion, sex, or national origin by employers. Refusal to hire on these grounds as well as harassment and hostile working environments are included within the scope of the statute. *McDonald v. Santa Fe Trail Transp. Co.*, 427 U.S. 273 (1976). Furthermore, the Unfair Immigration Related Employment Practices Act, 8 U.S.C. §1324b, protects individuals against both national origin discrimination and citizenship discrimination in hiring, recruitment, referral, or discharge.

Salgueiro da Silva Mouta v. Portugal
Appl. No. 33290/96
European Court of Human Rights
– Eur. Ct. H.R. (ser. A) (1999)

. . . .

ALLEGED VIOLATION OF ARTICLE 8 OF THE CONVENTION TAKEN ALONE AND IN CONJUNCTION WITH ARTICLE 14

21. The applicant complained that the Lisbon Court of Appeal had based its decision to award parental responsibility for their daughter, M., to his ex-wife rather than to himself exclusively on the ground of his sexual orientation. He alleged that this constituted a violation of Article 8 of the Convention taken alone and in conjunction with Article 14.

The Government disputed that allegation.

22. Under Article 8 of the Convention,

> 1. Everyone has the right to respect for his private and family life, his home and his correspondence.
>
> 2. There shall be no interference by a public authority with the exercise of this right except such as is in accordance with the law and is necessary in a democratic society in the interests of national security, public safety or the economic well-being of the country, for the prevention of disorder or crime, for the protection of health or morals, or for the protection of the rights and freedoms of others."

The Court notes at the outset that the judgment of the Court of Appeal in question, in so far as it set aside the judgment of the Lisbon Family Affairs Court of 14 July 1994 which had awarded parental responsibility to the applicant, constitutes an interference with the applicant's right to respect for his family life and thus attracts the application of Article 8. The Convention institutions have held that this provision applies to decisions awarding custody to one or other parent after divorce or separation (see the *Hoffmann v. Austria* judgment of 23 June 1993, Series A no. 255-C, p. 58, §29; see also *Irlen v. Germany*, application no. 12246/86, Commission decision of 13 July 1987, Decisions and Reports 53, p. 225).

That finding is not affected by the Government's submission that since the judgment of the Court of Appeal did not ultimately vary what had been decided by friendly settlement between the parents on 7 February 1991, there was no interference with the rights of Mr Salgueiro da Silva Mouta.

. . . .

A. Alleged violation of Article 8 taken in conjunction with Article 14

23. Given the nature of the case and the allegations of the applicant, the Court considers it appropriate to examine it first under Article 8 taken in conjunction with Article 14, according to which

> The enjoyment of the rights and freedoms set forth in [the] Convention shall be secured without discrimination on any ground such as sex, race, colour, language, religion, political or other opinion, national or social origin, association with a national minority, property, birth or other status.

24. Mr Salgueiro da Silva Mouta stressed at the outset that he had never disputed the fact that his daughter's interests were paramount, one of the main ones consisting in seeing her father and being able to live with him. He argued, nonetheless, that the Court of Appeal's judgment, in awarding parental responsibility to the mother exclusively on the basis of the father's sexual orientation, amounted to an unjustifiable interference with his right to respect for his family life. The applicant submitted that the decision in issue had been prompted by atavistic misconceptions which bore no relation to the realities of life or common sense. In doing so, he argued, the Court of Appeal had discriminated against him in a manner prohibited by Article 14 of the Convention.

The applicant pointed out that judgment had been given in his favour by the court of first instance, that court being the only one to have had direct knowledge of the facts of the case since the Court of Appeal had ruled solely on the basis of the written proceedings.

25. The Government acknowledged that Article 8 could apply to the situation in question, but only as far as the applicant's right to respect for his family life with his child was concerned. They stressed, however, that no act had been done by a public authority which could have interfered with the applicant's right to the free expression and development of his personality or the manner in which he led his life, in particular his sexual life.

With regard to family life, however, the Government pointed out that, as far as parental responsibility was concerned, the Contracting States enjoyed a wide margin of appreciation in respect of the pursuit of the legitimate aims set out in paragraph 2 of Article 8 of the Convention. They added that in this field, in which the child's interests were paramount, the national authorities were naturally better placed than the international court. The Court should not therefore substitute its own interpretation of things for that of the national courts, unless the measures in question were manifestly unreasonable or arbitrary.

In the instant case the Lisbon Court of Appeal had taken account, in accordance with Portuguese law, of the child's interests alone. The intervention of the Court of Appeal had been prescribed by law (Article 1905 §2 of the Civil Code and sections 178 to 180 of the Guardianship Act). Moreover, it had pursued a legitimate aim, namely the protection of the child's interests, and was necessary in a democratic society.

The Government concluded that the Court of Appeal, in reaching its decision, had had regard exclusively to the overriding interests of the child and not to the applicant's sexual orientation. The applicant had not therefore been discriminated against in any way.

26. The Court reiterates that in the enjoyment of the rights and freedoms guaranteed by the Convention, Article 14 affords protection against different treatment, without an objective and reasonable justification, of persons in similar situations (see the Hoffmann judgment cited above, p. 58, §31).

It must be determined whether the applicant can complain of such a difference in treatment and, if so, whether it was justified.

1. Existence of a difference in treatment

27. The Government disputed the allegation that in the instant case the applicant and M.'s mother had been treated differently. They argued that the Lisbon Court of Appeal's decision had been mainly based on the fact that, in the circumstances of the case, the child's interests would be better served by awarding parental responsibility to the mother.

28. The Court does not deny that the Lisbon Court of Appeal had regard above all to the child's interests when it examined a number of points of fact and of law which could have tipped the scales in favour of one parent rather than the other. However, the Court observes that in reversing the decision of the Lisbon Family Affairs Court and, consequently, awarding parental responsibility to the mother rather than the father, the Court of Appeal introduced a new factor, namely that the applicant was a homosexual and was living with another man.

The Court is accordingly forced to conclude that there was a difference of treatment between the applicant and M.'s mother which was based on the applicant's sexual orientation, a concept which is undoubtedly covered by Article 14 of the Convention. The Court reiterates in that connection that the list set out in that provision is illustrative and not exhaustive, as is shown by the words "any ground such as" (in French "*notamment*") (see the *Engel and Others v. the Netherlands* judgment of 8 June 1976, Series A no. 22, pp. 30–31, §72).

2. Justification for the difference in treatment

29. In accordance with the case-law of the Convention institutions, a difference of treatment is discriminatory within the meaning of Article 14 if it has no objective and reasonable justification, that is if it does not pursue a legitimate aim or if there is not a reasonable relationship of proportionality between the means employed and the aim sought to be realised (see the *Karlheinz Schmidt v. Germany* judgment of 18 July 1994, Series A no. 291-B, pp. 32–33, §24).

30. The decision of the Court of Appeal undeniably pursued a legitimate aim, namely the protection of the health and rights of the child; it must now be examined whether the second requirement was also satisfied.

31. In the applicant's submission, the wording of the judgment clearly showed that the decision to award parental responsibility to the mother was based mainly on the father's sexual orientation, which inevitably gave rise to discrimination against him in relation to the other parent.

32. The Government submitted that the decision in question had, on the contrary, merely touched on the applicant's homosexuality. The considerations of the Court of Appeal to which the applicant referred, when viewed in context, were merely sociological, or even statistical, observations. Even if certain passages of the judgment could arguably have been worded differently, clumsy or unfortunate expressions could not in themselves amount to a violation of the Convention.

33. The Court reiterates its earlier finding that the Lisbon Court of Appeal, in examining the appeal lodged by M.'s mother, introduced a new factor when making its decision as to the award of parental responsibility, namely the applicant's homosexuality (see paragraph 28 above). In determining whether the decision which was ultimately made constituted discriminatory treatment lacking any reasonable basis, it needs to be established whether, as the Government submitted, that new factor was merely an *obiter dictum* which had no direct effect on the outcome of the matter in issue or whether, on the contrary, it was decisive.

34. The Court notes that the Lisbon Family Affairs Court gave its decision after a period in which the applicant, his ex-wife, their daughter M., L.G.C. and the child's maternal grandparents had been interviewed by court psychologists. The court had established the facts and had had particular regard to the experts' reports in reaching its decision.

The Court of Appeal, ruling solely on the basis of the written proceedings, weighed the facts differently from the lower court and awarded parental responsibility to the mother. It considered, among other things, that "custody of young children should as a general rule be awarded to the mother unless there are overriding reasons militating against this" (see paragraph 14 above). The Court of Appeal further considered that there were insufficient reasons for taking away from the mother the parental responsibility awarded her by agreement between the parties.

However, after that observation the Court of Appeal added "Even if that were not the case . . . we think that custody of the child should be awarded to the mother" (ibid.). The Court of Appeal then took account of the fact that the applicant was a homosexual and was living with another man in observing that "The child should live in . . . a traditional

Portuguese family" and that "It is not our task here to determine whether homosexuality is or is not an illness or whether it is a sexual orientation towards persons of the same sex. In both cases it is an abnormality and children should not grow up in the shadow of abnormal situations" (ibid.).

35. It is the Court's view that the above passages from the judgment in question, far from being merely clumsy or unfortunate as the Government maintained, or mere *obiter dicta*, suggest, quite to the contrary, that the applicant's homosexuality was a factor which was decisive in the final decision. That conclusion is supported by the fact that the Court of Appeal, when ruling on the applicant's right to contact, warned him not to adopt conduct which might make the child realise that her father was living with another man "in conditions resembling those of man and wife" (ibid.).

36. The Court is therefore forced to find, in the light of the foregoing, that the Court of Appeal made a distinction based on considerations regarding the applicant's sexual orientation, a distinction which is not acceptable under the Convention. [ ]

The Court cannot therefore find that a reasonable relationship of proportionality existed between the means employed and the aim pursued; there has accordingly been a violation of Article 8 taken in conjunction with Article 14.

QUESTIONS & COMMENTS

(1) In *G.L, A.V., and S.L. v. Austria*, Appl. Nos. 39392/98, 39829/98, and 45330/99 (2003), the European Court of Human Rights held that an Austrian statute that criminalized homosexual acts of adult men with consenting adolescents aged between 14 and 18 violated the right against discrimination. The Court rejected the Austrian government's claim that the criminal statute was needed to avoid "a dangerous strain" being "placed by homosexual experiences upon the sexual development of young males."

(2) In *Karner v. Austria*, Appl. No. 40016/98 (2003), the applicant claimed that the Austrian Supreme Court's failure to recognize his right to succeed to a tenancy after the death of his male partner amounted to discrimination on the basis of sexual orientation that interfered with his right to privacy. The applicant had shared an apartment with his gay partner, who subsequently died from AIDS. His partner designated the applicant as his heir. Under the Austrian Rent Act, domestic partners could succeed to a tenancy after the death of one of the partners. Although recognizing that in certain circumstances that the Austrian government may seek to protect the "traditional family," the European Court of Human Rights held that discrimination on the basis of sexual orientation in the applicant's case was disproportionate and, hence, a violation of the right against discrimination because the Austrian government had failed to provide any additional justification besides the aim of protecting the traditional family.

(3) The Hungarian Constitutional Court has examined the constitutionality of legislation prohibiting same-sex marriage and the extension of legal benefits to same-sex partners cohabitating outside of marriage. 14/1995 (III.13.) *AB hatarozat*. In an advisory opinion (known as an "abstract norm control'), the Court examined the Universal Declaration of Human Rights, the ICCPR, the ECHR, and Article 15 of the Hungarian Constitution, which provides for protection of marriage and the family. Although

the Court recognized changing societal attitudes about marriage, the Court concluded that in light of the prevailing culture and relevant legal rules, marriage should still be heterosexual in character.

However, in regard to legal benefits extending to cohabitating same-sex partners, the Court opined that such benefits could not be prohibited. The Court noted that Hungarian law had recognized such benefits to heterosexual partners since the 1960s. Failure to extend such benefits to same-sex partners would violate the personal dignity of those individuals living in both an emotional and financial partnership within the same household.

(4) Under U.S. constitutional law, a "minimum rational basis" test is used in the context of homosexuality: the government's aim must be legitimate, and the means must be rationally related to this aim. *Romer v. Evans*, 517 U.S. 620 (1996) (invalidating under rational basis test state constitutional amendment barring government agencies from adopting rules or policies that provide homosexual, lesbian, and bisexual classes protection against discrimination).

(5) Note that Article 21 of Charter of Fundamental Rights of the European Union prohibits discrimination on the basis of disability. Is this an emerging customary international legal norm? Has the United States accepted the norm by adopting the Americans with Disabilities Act?

Unintentional and Disparate Impact Discrimination

Simunek, Hastings, Tuzilova and Prochazka v. The Czech Republic
UN Human Rights Committee
Communication No. 516/1992
Views adopted 19 July 1995
U.N. Doc. CCPR/C/54/D/516/1992 (1995)

. . . .

The facts as submitted by the authors:

2.1 Alina Simunek, a Polish citizen born in 1960, and Jaroslav Simunek, a Czech citizen, currently reside in Ontario, Canada. They state that they were forced to leave Czechoslovakia in 1987, under pressure of the security forces of the communist regime. Under the legislation then applicable, their property was confiscated. After the fall of the Communist government on 17 November 1989, the Czech authorities published statements which indicated that expatriate Czech citizens would be rehabilitated in as far as any criminal conviction was concerned, and their property restituted.

2.2 In July 1990, Mr. and Mrs. Simunek returned to Czechoslovakia in order to submit a request for the return of their property, which had been confiscated by the District National Committee, a State organ, in Jablonece. It transpired, however, that between September 1989 and February 1990, all their property and personal effects had been evaluated and auctioned off by the District National Committee. Unsaleable items had been destroyed. On 13 February 1990, the authors' real estate was transferred to the Jablonece Sklarny factory, for which Jaroslav Simunek had been working for twenty years.

2.3 Upon lodging a complaint with the District National Committee, an arbitration hearing was convened between the authors, their witnesses and representatives of the factory on 18 July 1990. The latter's representatives denied that the transfer of the authors' property had been illegal. The authors thereupon petitioned the office of the district public prosecutor, requesting an investigation of the matter on the ground that the transfer of their property had been illegal, since it had been transferred in the absence of a court order or court proceedings to which the authors had been parties. On 17 September 1990, the Criminal Investigations Department of the National Police in Jablonece launched an investigation; its report of 29 November 1990 concluded that no violation of (then) applicable regulations could be ascertained, and that the authors' claim should be dismissed, as the Government had not yet amended the former legislation.

2.4 On 2 February 1991, the Czech and Slovak Federal Government adopted Act 87/1991, which entered into force on 1 April 1991. It endorses the rehabilitation of Czech citizens who had left the country under communist pressure and lays down the conditions for restitution or compensation for loss of property. Under Section 3, subsection 1, of the Act, those who had their property turned into State ownership in the cases specified in Section 6 of the Act are entitled to restitution, but only if they are citizens of the Czech and Slovak Federal Republic and are permanent residents in its territory.

2.5 Under Section 5, subsection 1, of the Act, anyone currently in (illegal) possession of the property shall restitute it to the rightful owner, upon a written request from the latter, who must also prove his or her claim to the property and demonstrate how the property was turned over to the State. Under subsection 2, the request for restitution must be submitted to the individual in possession of the property, within six months of the entry into force of the Act. If the person in possession of the property does not comply with the request, the rightful owner may submit his or her claim to the competent tribunal, within one year of the date of entry into force of the Act (subsection 4).

. . . .

The complaint:

3.1 Alina and Jaroslav Simunek contend that the requirements of Act 87/1991 constitute unlawful discrimination, as it only applies to "pure Czechs living in the Czech and Slovak Federal Republic." Those who fled the country or were forced into exile by the ex-communist regime must take a permanent residence in Czechoslovakia to be eligible for restitution or compensation. Alina Simunek, who lived and worked in Czechoslovakia for eight years, would not be eligible at all for restitution, on account of her Polish citizenship. The authors claim that the Act in reality legalizes former Communist practices, as more than 80% of the confiscated property belongs to persons who do not meet these strict requirements.

3.2 Alina Simunek alleges that the conditions for restitution imposed by the Act constitute discrimination on the basis of political opinion and religion, without however substantiating her claim.

. . . .

The State party's explanations:

6.1 In its submission, dated 12 December 1994, the State party argues that the legislation in question is not discriminatory. It draws the Committee's attention to the fact that according to article 11, Section 2, of the Charter of Fundamental Rights and Freedoms, which is part of the Constitution of the Czech Republic, " . . . the law may specify that some things may be owned exclusively by citizens or by legal persons having their seat in the Czech Republic."

6.2 The State party affirms its commitment to the settlement of property claims by restitution of properties to persons injured during the period of 25 February 1948 to 1 January 1990. Although certain criteria had to be stipulated for the restitution of confiscated properties, the purpose of such requirements is not to violate human rights. The Czech Republic cannot and will not dictate to anybody where to live. Restitution of confiscated property is a very complicated and *de facto* unprecedented measure and therefore it cannot be expected to rectify all damages and to satisfy all the people injured by the Communist regime.

7.1 With respect to the communication submitted by Mrs. Alina Simunek the State party argues that the documents submitted by the author do not define the claims clearly enough. It appears from her submission that Mr. Jaroslav Simunek was probably kept in prison by the State Security Police. Nevertheless, it is not clear whether he was kept in custody or actually sentenced to imprisonment. As concerns the confiscation of the property of Mr. and Mrs. Simunek, the communication does not define the measure on the basis of which they were deprived of their ownership rights. In case Mr. Simunek was sentenced for a criminal offence mentioned in Section 2 or Section 4 of Law No. 119/1990 on judicial rehabilitation as amended by subsequent provisions, he could claim rehabilitation under the law or in review proceedings and, within three years of the entry into force of the court decision on his rehabilitation, apply to the Compensations Department of the Ministry of Justice of the Czech Republic for compensation pursuant to Section 23 of the above-mentioned Law. In case Mr. Simunek was unlawfully deprived of his personal liberty and his property was confiscated between 25 February 1948 and 1 January 1990 in connection with a criminal offence mentioned in Section 2 and Section 4 of the Law but the criminal proceedings against him were not initiated, he could apply for compensation on the basis of a court decision issued at the request of the injured party and substantiate his application with the documents which he had at his disposal or which his legal adviser obtained from the archives of the Ministry of the Interior of the Czech Republic.

7.2 As concerns the restitution of the forfeited or confiscated property, the State party concludes from the submission that Alina and Jaroslav Simunek do not comply with the requirements of Section 3 (1) of Law No. 87/1991 on extrajudicial rehabilitations, namely the requirements of citizenship of the Czech and Slovak Federal Republic and permanent residence on its territory. Consequently, they cannot be recognized as persons entitled to restitution. Remedy would be possible only in case at least one of them complied with both requirements and applied for restitution within 6 months from the entry into force of the law on extrajudicial rehabilitations (*i.e.* by the end of September 1991).

. . . .

Authors' comments on the State party's submissions

10.1 By letter of 21 February 1995, Alina and Jaroslav Simunek contend that the State party has not addressed the issues raised by their communication, namely the compatibility of Act No. 87/1991 with the non-discrimination requirement of article 26 of the Covenant. They claim that Czech hard-liners are still in office and that they have no interest in the restitution of confiscated properties, because they themselves benefited from the confiscations. A proper restitution law should be based on democratic principles and not allow restrictions that would exclude former Czech citizens and Czech citizens living abroad.

. . . .

Examination of the merits

. . . .

11.3 As the Committee has already explained in its decision on admissibility [not included], the right to property, as such, is not protected under the Covenant. However, a confiscation of private property or the failure by a State party to pay compensation for such confiscation could still entail a breach of the Covenant if the relevant act or omission was based on discriminatory grounds in violation of article 26 of the Covenant.

11.4 The issue before the Committee is whether the application of Act 87/1991 to the authors entailed a violation of their rights to equality before the law and to the equal protection of the law. The authors claim that this Act, in effect, reaffirms the earlier discriminatory confiscations. The Committee observes that the confiscations themselves are not here at issue, but rather the denial of a remedy to the authors, whereas other claimants have recovered their properties or received compensation therefor.

11.5 In the instant cases, the authors have been affected by the exclusionary effect of the requirement in Act 87/1991 that claimants be Czech citizens and residents of the Czech Republic. The question before the Committee, therefore, is whether these preconditions to restitution or compensation are compatible with the non-discrimination requirement of article 26 of the Covenant. In this context the Committee reiterates its jurisprudence that not all differentiation in treatment can be deemed to be discriminatory under article 26 of the Covenant [*Zwaan de Vries v. The Netherlands*, Communication No. 182/1984, Views adopted on 9 April 1987, para. 13]. A differentiation which is compatible with the provisions of the Covenant and is based on reasonable grounds does not amount to prohibited discrimination within the meaning of article 26.

11.6 In examining whether the conditions for restitution or compensation are compatible with the Covenant, the Committee must consider all relevant factors, including the authors' original entitlement to the property in question and the nature of the confiscations. The State party itself acknowledges that the confiscations were discriminatory, and this is the reason why specific legislation was enacted to provide for a form of restitution. The Committee observes that such legislation must not discriminate among the victims of the prior confiscations, since all victims are entitled to redress without arbitrary distinctions. Bearing in mind that the authors' original entitlement to their respective properties was not predicated either on citizenship or residence, the Committee finds that the conditions of citizenship and residence in Act 87/1991 are unreasonable. In this connection the Committee notes that the State party has not advanced any grounds which would justify these restrictions. Moreover, it has been submitted that the authors and many others in their situation left Czechoslovakia because of their political opinions and that their property was confiscated either because of their political opinions or because of their emigration from the country. These victims of political persecution sought residence and citizenship in other countries. Taking into account that the State party itself is responsible for the departure of the authors, it would be incompatible with the Covenant to require them permanently to return to the country as a prerequisite for the restitution of their property or for the payment of appropriate compensation.

11.7 The State party contends that there is no violation of the Covenant because the Czech and Slovak legislators had no discriminatory intent at the time of the adoption of Act 87/1991. The Committee is of the view, however, that the intent of the legislature is not alone dispositive in determining a breach of article 26 of the Covenant. A politically motivated differentiation is unlikely to be compatible with article 26. But an act which is not politically motivated may still contravene article 26 if its effects are discriminatory.

11.8 In the light of the above considerations, the Committee concludes that Act 87/1991 has had effects upon the authors that violate their rights under article 26 of the Covenant.

12.1 The Human Rights Committee, acting under article 5, paragraph 4, of the Optional Protocol, is of the view that the denial of restitution or compensation to the authors constitutes a violation of article 26 of the International Covenant on Civil and Political Rights.

12.2 In accordance with article 2, paragraph 3 (a), of the Covenant, the State party is under an obligation to provide the authors with an effective remedy, which may be compensation if the properties in question cannot be returned. . . . The Committee further encourages the State party to review its relevant legislation to ensure that neither the law itself nor its application is discriminatory.

~

QUESTIONS & COMMENTS

(1) Note that the UN Human Rights Committee recognized that the Czech Republic had violated Article 26 because the effects of its legislation were discriminatory. The Committee pointed to three factors for why the legislation's discriminatory effects were legally sufficient to establish an Article 26 violation: (i) residence or citizenship were not necessary conditions for the original entitlement to the property, (ii) the Czech Republic offered no justification for this new requirement of residence or citizenship, and (iii) the authors were compelled to abandon their property because of the Czechoslovak government's earlier discrimination against the authors on the basis of political opinion or emigration. Would each of these factors be sufficient standing alone?

(2) U.S. constitutional law distinguishes between intentionally discriminatory actions and those with a disparate impact. Ordinarily, statutes with a disparate impact are required to satisfy only a requirement of rationality, while sometimes statutes that intentionally discriminate must satisfy a more stringent standard. Does the Human Rights Committee take a different approach? What justifications are there for distinguishing between intentional discrimination and disparate impact? Are they relevant to the problem in *Simunek*?

(3) Examine the racial and birth discrimination claims in *Abdulaziz, Cabales and Balkandali v. United Kingdom*, 94 Eur. Ct. H. R. (ser. A) (1985). Would these claims have succeeded under the UN Human Rights Committee's analysis in *Simunek*?

Abdulaziz, Cabales and Balkandali v. United Kingdom
European Court of Human Rights
94 Eur. Ct. H. R. (ser. A) (1985)
7 E.H.R.R. 471 (1985)

. . . .

FACTS:

10. The applicants are lawfully and permanently settled in the United Kingdom. In accordance with the immigration rules in force at the material time, Mr Abdulaziz,

Mr Cabales and Mr Balkandali were refused permission to remain with or join [the applicants] in that country as their husbands. The applicants maintained that, on this account, they had been victims of a practice of discrimination on the grounds of sex, race and also, in the case of Mrs Balkandali, birth. . . .

I. DOMESTIC LAW AND PRACTICE

A. History and background

11. The evolution of immigration controls in the United Kingdom has to be seen in the light of the history of the British Empire and the corresponding developments in nationality laws. Originally all persons born within or having a specified connection with the United Kingdom or the dominions owed allegiance to the Crown and were British subjects. A common British nationality was, however, difficult to reconcile with the independence of the self-governing countries of the Commonwealth into which the Empire was transformed. As the various territories concerned became independent, they introduced their own citizenship laws but, for the purposes of United Kingdom law, persons having a citizenship of an independent Commonwealth country retained a special status, known as 'British subject' or 'Commonwealth citizen' (these terms being synonymous). This status was also held by 'citizens of the United Kingdom and Colonies.' Prior to 1 January 1973, the latter citizenship was, briefly, acquired by birth within the United Kingdom or one of its remaining dependencies, by descent from a father having that citizenship, by naturalisation or by registration. (British Nationality Act 1948)

12. Whereas aliens have been subject to continuing strict immigration controls over a long period of time, the same is not true of Commonwealth citizens. Until 1962, [Commonwealth citizens], irrespective of their local citizenship, all had freedom to enter the United Kingdom for work and permanent residence, without any restriction. A rapid rise in the influx of immigrants, especially in 1960 and 1961, and the consequent danger of the rate of immigration exceeding the country's capacity to absorb them led to a radical change in this situation. The Commonwealth Immigrants Act 1962, and then the Commonwealth Immigrants Act 1968, restricted the right of entry of, and imposed immigration controls on, certain classes of Commonwealth citizens, including citizens of the United Kingdom and Colonies, who did not have close links to Britain.

B. The Immigration Act 1971

13. The existing immigration laws were amended and replaced by the Immigration Act 1971 ('the 1971 Act'), which came into force on 1 January 1973. One of its main purposes was to assimilate immigration controls over incoming Commonwealth citizens having no close links to Britain to the corresponding rules [for] aliens. The Act created two new categories of persons for immigration purposes, namely those having the right of abode in the United Kingdom ('patrials') and those not having the right ('non-patrials').

14. 'Patrials' were to be free from immigration controls. The status of 'patrial' was intended to designate Commonwealth citizens who 'belonged' to the United Kingdom and, in summary, was conferred on:

(a) citizens of the United Kingdom and Colonies who had acquired that citizenship by birth, adoption, naturalisation or registration in British Islands (that is, the United

Kingdom, the Channel Islands and the Isle of Man), or were the children or grandchildren of any such persons;

(b) citizens of the United Kingdom and Colonies who had at any time been settled in the British Islands for at least five years;

(c) other Commonwealth citizens who were the children of a person having citizenship of the United Kingdom and Colonies by virtue of birth in the British Islands;

(d) women, being Commonwealth citizens, who were or had been married to a man falling within any of the preceding categories.

15. Under section 1(2) of the 1971 Act, 'non-patrials' (whether Commonwealth citizens or aliens) 'may live, work and settle in the United Kingdom by permission and subject to such regulation and control of their entry into, stay in the departure from the United Kingdom as is imposed' by the Act.

Subject to certain exceptions not relevant to the present case, a 'non-patrial' shall not enter the United Kingdom unless given leave to do so. (§3(1).) He may be given such leave (or, if he is already in the country, leave to remain) either for a limited or for an indefinite period; in the former case, the leave may be subject to conditions restricting employment or requiring registration with the police or both. (§3(1).) Where limited leave to enter or remain is granted, it may subsequently be varied, either as regards its duration or the conditions attaching thereto but, if the limit on duration is removed, any conditions attached to the leave cease to apply. (§3(3).) The power to give or refuse leave to enter is exercised by immigration officers but the power to give or vary leave to remain can be exercised only by the Home Secretary. (§4(1).)

C. The Immigration Rules

16. Under section 3(2) of the 1971 Act, the Home Secretary is obliged from time to time to lay before Parliament statements of the rules, or of any changes therein, laid down by him as to the practice to be followed in the administration of the Act for regulating entry into the stay in the United Kingdom. These rules contain instructions to immigration officers as to how they shall exercise the statutory discretions given to them by the Act and statements of the manner in which the Home Secretary will exercise his own powers of control after entry. The rules are required to provide for the admission of persons coming for the purpose of taking employment, or for the purposes of study, or as visitors, or as dependants of persons lawfully in or entering the United Kingdom, but uniform provision does not have to be made for these categories and, in particular, account may be taken of citizenship or nationality. (§§1(4) and 3(2)) Thus, different rules can be and are made for nationals of the member States of the European Economic Community under community law, and Irish citizens are in a special position.

17. The rules are subject to a negative resolution procedure whereby, if a resolution disapproving the Home Secretary's statement is passed by either House of Parliament within 40 days of its being laid, he is required as soon as may be to make such changes as appear to him to be required in the circumstances and to lay the rules as amended before Parliament within 40 days of the passing of the resolution. (§3(2).) The statement of rules thus amended is subject to the same procedure as the original statement. Because of the continuous nature of decision-making by immigration officers, the statement originally laid is not abrogated by any negative resolution; it will come into

operation when made or on the date therein provided and will remain in force until replaced.

18. The exact legal status of the rules is of some complexity. This question was considered by the Court of Appeal in *R v. Secretary of State for the Home Department, ex parte Hosenball* ([1977] 3 All E.R. 452) when Lord Denning MR said:

> [The Home Secretary's rules] are not rules of law. They are rules of practice laid down for the guidance of immigration officers and tribunals who are entrusted with the administration of the [1971 Act]. They can be, and often are, prayed in aid by applicants before the courts in immigration cases. To some extent the courts must have regard to them because there are provisions in the Act itself, particularly in section 19, which show that in appeals to an adjudicator, if the immigration rules have not been complied with, then the appeal is to be allowed. In addition the courts always have regard to those rules, not only in matters where there is a right of appeal; but also in cases under prerogative writs where there is a question whether officers have acted fairly. But they are not rules in the nature of delegated legislation so as to amount to strict rules of law.

Geoffrey Lane LJ also doubted whether the rules constituted delegated legislation. He observed: 'These rules are very difficult to categorise or classify. They are in a class of their own. They are certainly a practical guide for . . . immigration officers . . . Indeed they are, as to large parts, . . . little more than explanatory notes of the [1971 Act] itself.' However, he noted that if Parliament disapproved of the rules, they were not thereby abrogated. Furthermore, at least as far as an adjudicator dealing with appeals was concerned, the rules had the force of law, although it seemed that they could be departed from with the consent of the applicant himself.

Cumming-Bruce LJ said:

> [The rules] are a totally different kind of publication from the rules that usually come into being under the authority delegated to Ministers under Acts of Parliament; . . . they are not in my view in any sense of themselves of legislative force. It is true that . . . the rules are given legal effect in the field of the appellate process to the adjudicator or the tribunal . . . But the legal effect that the rules have in that limited field flows not from the fact that they have been published by the Minister and laid before Parliament, but because by section 19(2) of the [1971] Act the rules are given an effect which is in a certain field clearly legally enforceable, and that is a quite different matter.

19. Notwithstanding that an application for entry clearance (see paragraph 22(b) below) or leave to enter or remain may fall to be refused under the relevant immigration rules, the Home Secretary has a discretion, deriving from historic prerogative powers, to authorise in exceptional circumstances the grant of entry clearance or of leave to enter, or to allow a person to remain in the United Kingdom. Where the applicant is a husband seeking to join or remain with his wife settled in the United Kingdom, factors which the Home Secretary will consider include the extent of her ties with that country and of the hardship she might suffer by going to live abroad, and any recommendations by the immigration appellate authorities.

D. Position at the time of the events giving rise to the present case.

1. Introduction

20. The rules in force at the time of the events giving rise to the present case were contained in the 'Statement of Changes in Immigration Rules' (HC 384) laid before Parliament on 20 February 1980 ('the 1980 Rules'); they applied to all decisions taken on or after 1 March 1980, except those relating to applications made on or before 14 November 1979. A draft of the rules had previously been included in a White Paper published in November 1979.

The 1980 Rules, which in paragraph 2 instructed immigration officers to carry out their duties without regard to the race, colour or religion of the intending entrant, detailed firstly the controls to be exercised on the entry into the United Kingdom of 'non-patrials' and then those to be exercised after entry. The former depended on whether the individual concerned was coming for temporary purposes (for example, visitors or students), for employment of business or as a person of independent means, or for settlement. As under the rules previously in force, visitors were normally to be prohibited from taking employment and persons wishing to come for employment were subject to strict regulations as to work permits. The work permit requirements, however, did not apply to nationals of other member States of the European Economic Community nor to persons covered by the 'United Kingdom ancestry rule'; under the latter rule, which had been in force since the 1971 Act came into operation, a Commonwealth citizen having a grandparent born in the British Islands and wishing to take or seek employment in the United Kingdom could obtain indefinite leave to enter even without a work permit. A further exception was to be found in the 'working holiday rule', whereby young Commonwealth citizens could, without a permit, take employment incidental to an extended holiday being spent in the United Kingdom; however, the period of their stay could, under the 1980 Rules, not exceed two years. All these exceptions have been maintained in subsequent immigration rules.

21. A particular feature of the changes introduced by the 1980 Rules was the inclusion of a number of provisions directed towards implementing a policy of protecting the domestic labour market at a time of high unemployment by curtailing 'primary immigration', that is immigration by someone who could be expected to seek full-time work in order to support a family. In taking these measures, the Government were concerned also to advance public tranquility and, by exercising firm and fair immigration control, to assist in securing good community relations.

To these ends, among the changes effected was the introduction of stricter conditions for the grant of leave to a 'non-patrial' husband or fiancé seeking to join or remain with his wife or fiancée settled in the United Kingdom. Previously, any such husband or fiancé would normally have been allowed to settle after a qualifying period, provided that the primary purpose of the marriage was not to obtain settlement in that country. These new measures were not extended to the wives or fiancées of settled men, a fact attributed by the Government to long-standing commitments (based allegedly on humanitarian, social and ethical reasons) to the reunification of the families of male immigrants. Nor did the new measures apply to nationals of other member-States of the European Economic Community.

22. The relevant provisions of the 1980 Rules – and of their successors – are summarised below in terms of the following expressions.

(a) A person is 'settled in the United Kingdom' when he or she is ordinarily resident there without having entered or remained in breach of the immigration laws, and is free from any restriction on the period for which he or she may remain. (¶ 1)

(b) An 'entry clearance' is a document (either a visa, an entry certificate or a Home Office letter of consent, depending on the nationality of the person concerned) which is to be taken by an immigration officer as evidence that the holder, although a 'non-patrial', is eligible under the immigration rules for entry to the United Kingdom. It is obtained at British missions abroad or from the Home Office prior to arrival in the United Kingdom.

(c) A marriage or intended marriage is 'non-qualifying' if there is reason to believe that:

- its primary purpose is to obtain admission to or settlement in the United Kingdom; or
- the parties do not intend to live together permanently as man and wife; or
- the parties have not met (¶¶ 50, 52, 117).

(d) There is 'potential evasion of the rules' if there is reason to believe that a husband has remained in the United Kingdom in breach of the immigration rules before the marriage, that the marriage has taken place after a decision or recommendation that he be deported or that the marriage has terminated. (¶ 117)

(e) The 'financial requirement' is a requirement that varies according to the circumstances of the particular case: basically it means that adequate maintenance and accommodation must be available to the person concerned without the need for recourse to public funds (¶¶ 42, 52 and 55.).

2. 'Non-patrials' seeking to join a spouse or intended spouse settled in the United Kingdom.

23. Where a 'non-patrial' whose spouse or intended spouse was 'settled in the United Kingdom' came to that country for settlement, he or she would be admitted for that purpose provided that he or she held a current 'entry clearance' and unless the circumstances specified in paragraph 13 of the 1980 Rules obtained (for example, false representations, medical grounds, criminal record, exclusion would be conducive to the public good).

(a) Where the intending entrant was a husband or finance, he could, under paragraphs 50 and 52, obtain an 'entry clearance':

(i) unless the marriage or intended marriage was 'non-qualifying';
(ii) if his wife or fiancée was a citizen of the United Kingdom and Colonies who or one of whose parents had been born in the United Kingdom; and
(iii) if, in the cases of fiancés only, the 'financial requirement' was satisfied.

(b) Where the intending entrant was a wife or fiancée, she could, under paragraphs 42, 43 and 55, obtain an 'entry clearance' irrespective of the nationality of her husband or fiancé or of his own or his parents' place of birth. Here, there was no provision as to 'non-qualifying' marriages, but the 'financial requirement' had generally to be satisfied.

(c) Wives admitted under these rules would be given indefinite leave to enter; husbands would be initially admitted for twelve months and fiancés or fiancées for three months, with the possibility, subject to certain safeguards, of applying subsequently to the Home Office for indefinite leave. (¶¶ 44, 51, 53, 55, 114, 116)

3. 'Non-patrials' seeking to remain in the United Kingdom with a spouse settled there.

24. 'Non-patrials' already admitted to the United Kingdom in a temporary capacity who subsequently married a person 'settled in the United Kingdom' could also obtain permission to stay.

(a) Where the 'non-patrial' seeking permission was a man, the basic conditions (¶ 117) were that:

(i) his wife was a citizen of the United Kingdom and Colonies who or one of whose parents had been born in the United Kingdom; and

(ii) the marriage was not 'non-qualifying' and there was not 'potential evasion of the rules'.

(b) Where the 'non-patrial' seeking permission was a woman, she would normally be granted leave to remain on application. (¶ 115)

(c) Leave to remain granted under these rules would be, for wives, indefinite and, for husbands, for an initial period of 12 months with the possibility, subject again to the conditions referred to in sub-paragraph (a)(ii) above, of subsequent removal of the time limit (¶¶ 115 and 117)

4. General considerations regarding leave to remain

25. Decisions on applications for leave to remain were taken in the light of all relevant facts; thus, even where the individual satisfied the formal requirements, permission would normally be refused if the circumstances specified in paragraph 88 of the 1980 Rules obtained (for example, false representations, non-compliance with the time limit or conditions subject to which he or she had been admitted or given leave to remain, undesirable character, danger to national security).

E. Subsequent developments

1. Introduction

26. One result of the 1971 Act was that the right of abode in the United Kingdom became divorced from nationality: thus, a number of citizens of the United Kingdom and Colonies did not have that right (for example, because they had not been born in the British Islands), whereas it was enjoyed by a number of persons who were not such citizens (for example, Commonwealth citizens having an ancestral link with the United Kingdom). With a view to bringing citizenship and immigration laws into line, the position was substantially amended by the British Nationality Act 1981, which came into force on 1 January 1983. So far as is relevant for the present purposes, that Act:

(a) replaced citizenship for the United Kingdom and colonies (see paragraph 11 *in fine* above) with three separate citizenships, 'British', 'British Dependent Territories' and 'British Overseas';

(b) provided, in section 11(1), that on 1 January 1983 'British citizenship' was to be acquired by persons who were then citizens of the United Kingdom and Colonies and had the right of abode in the United Kingdom under the 1971 Act; this category could include a person who was neither born nor had a parent born in the United Kingdom.

(c) laid down detailed provisions on the acquisition of British citizenship by persons born after 1 January 1983;

(d) contained, in section 6 and Schedule 1, detailed provisions on naturalisation as a British citizen on the basis of residence in the United Kingdom, the grant of a certificate of naturalisation being at the discretion of the Home Secretary;

(e) amended the 1971 Act by providing in section 39 that the right of abode in the United Kingdom – use of the expressions 'patrial' and 'non-patrial' was abandoned – and the consequential freedom from immigration controls were in future to be enjoyed only by British citizens and by such Commonwealth citizens as on 31 December 1972 had the right of abode under the 1971 Act.

2. The 1982 immigration rules

. . . .

28. The 1982 Rules made no changes to the regime governing wives and fiancées, described in paragraphs 23–25 above. The regime governing a husband or fiancé was modified in the following main respects.

(a) The requirement that, for him to be eligible for leave to enter or remain, his wife or fiancée had to be a citizen of the United Kingdom and Colonies born or having a parent born in the United Kingdom was, under paragraphs 41, 54 and 126, replaced by a requirement that she be a British citizen. The place of her own or her parents' birth ceased to be material since British citizens could include persons without the territorial birth link (for example, a woman born in a former Colony but having the right of abode in the United Kingdom by virtue of long residence there).

(b) By virtue of paragraphs 41, 54 and 126, the onus of proof was reversed, so that it became for the man seeking leave to enter or remain to show that the marriage was not 'non-qualifying' or, in cases to which paragraph 126 applied, that there was not 'potential evasion of the rules'.

(c) Leave to remain for settlement following marriage, granted to a man admitted in a temporary capacity, would be for an initial period of 12 months, followed by a further period of 12 months and then by the possibility, subject again to the conditions referred to in sub-paragraph (b) above, of subsequent removal of the time limit. (¶ 126)

29. No provision was made in the 1982 Rules for women settled in the United Kingdom who were not British citizens to be joined by their husbands, although leave could be granted by the Home Secretary in the exercise of his extra-statutory discretion. These women could also apply for naturalisation as British citizens on the basis of residence, under section 6 of the British Nationality Act 1981.

3. The 1983 immigration rules

30. On 9 February 1983, a further Statement of Changes in Immigration Rules. (HC 169; 'the 1983 Rules') was laid before Parliament [which] came into force on 16 February 1983.

31. The 1983 rules again did not modify the regime governing wives and fiancées. That governing husbands was amended, so far as is material to the present case, in that, under paragraph 126, the position concerning the length of leave to remain granted to a man the 1980 Rules (that is, initial leave of 12 months, followed by the possibility of indefinite leave). This change was coupled with a transitional provision (¶ 177) concerning men who, whilst the 1982 Rules were in force, had been granted thereunder an extension of stay for a second period of 12 months: they were entitled to apply immediately for indefinite leave without awaiting the expiry of that period.

32. There was no change in the position concerning women settled in the United Kingdom who were not British citizens, described in paragraph 29 above.

F. Sanctions

33. Under section 3(5)(a), 3(6), 5, 6, 7 and 24(1)(b) of the 1971 Act, a person not having the right of abode in the United Kingdom and having only limited leave to enter or remain in that country who overstays the period of leave or fails to observe a condition attached thereto:

(a) commits a criminal offence punishable with a fine of not more than L200 or imprisonment of not more than six months or both, to which penalties the court may, with certain exceptions, add a recommendation for deportation; and

(b) is, with certain exceptions, liable to deportation, although he cannot be compelled to leave unless the Home Secretary decides to make a deportation order against him.

G. Appeals

34. Appellate authorities in immigration matters were established by the Immigration Appeals Act 1969. They consist of:

(a) adjudicators, who sit alone and are appointed by the Home Secretary;

(b) the Immigration Appeal Tribunal which sits in divisions of at least three members; the members are appointed by the Lord Chancellor and a certain number must be lawyers.

There is no further right of appeal as such to the ordinary courts, but decisions of the appellate authorities are susceptible to judicial review by the High Court on the ground of such matters as error of law or unreasonableness. Judicial review of immigration decisions may also cover questions of an abuse or excess of power by the Home Secretary or whether an immigration officer acted impartially and fairly.

35. Under sections 13, 14 and 15 of the 1971 Act, an appeal may, subject to certain exceptions, be made to an adjudicator against, *inter alia*:

(a) refusal of leave to enter the United Kingdom or of an entry clearance;

(b) variation of, or refusal to vary, a limited leave to remain in the United Kingdom;

(c) a decision to make a deportation order.

. . . .

37. Any party to an appeal to an adjudicator may appeal against his decision to the Immigration Appeal Tribunal, which may affirm that decision or make any other decision which the adjudicator could have made; it also had similar duties and powers in the matter of directions and recommendations. As the law stood at the relevant time, leave to appeal had generally to be obtained; it had to be granted, inter alia, if determination of the appeal turned upon an arguable point of law ($20(1) of the 1971 Act and Rule 14 of the Immigration Appeals (Procedure) Rules 1972)

H. Statistics

38. (a) The Government estimated total immigration into the United Kingdom from the New Commonwealth (that is, the Commonwealth except Australia, Canada and New Zealand) at 500,000 in the period from 1955 to mid-1962. It was thought that by the latter date some 600 million people had the right of abode in the United Kingdom. Between mid-1962 and the end of 1981, a further 900,000 people were estimated to have settled in that country from the New Commonwealth and Pakistan, some 420,000

from non-Commonwealth countries other than Pakistan and some 94,000 from the Old Commonwealth (Australia, Canada and New Zealand); relatively few countries were said to have accounted for most of this immigration.

The official estimates for 1981 show that the population of the United Kingdom (53.7 million) included 2.2 million persons of New Commonwealth and Pakistan origin (of whom about 1 million were in the Greater London area) and 1.2 million other persons not born in the United Kingdom (including those born in the Old Commonwealth but not those born in the Republic of Ireland). It is estimated that the population of New Commonwealth and Pakistan origin could rise to 2.5 million by 1986 and 3 million (5 per cent, of the projected total population) by 1991.

(b) According to the Government, some 3,500 persons entered the United Kingdom annually under the 'United Kingdom ancestry rule', but many of them emigrated after a few years.

(c) In 1980–1983, there was an average net annual emigration from the United Kingdom of about 44,000 but the population density in 1981–229 persons per square kilometer or 355 persons per square kilometer for England alone – was higher than that of any other member-State of the European Communities.

(d) Statistics supplied by the Government showed that in Great Britain in 1981 90 per cent of all men of working age and 63 per cent of all women of working age were 'economically active' (that is, either in employment, or self-employed, or unemployed). The corresponding figures for persons coming from the Indian sub-continent were 86 per cent for men and 41 per cent for women and, for persons coming from the West Indies or Guyana, 90 per cent for men and 70 per cent for women. The statistics also disclosed that a considerably higher proportion of 'economically active' women (particularly married women) than men were in part-time employment only – 47 per cent of married women, compared with 2.3 per cent of men.

Recent years have been a high level of unemployment in the United Kingdom. In 1983, 15.3 per cent of 'economically active' men and 8.4 per cent of 'economically active' women were unemployed, as measures by official figures based on persons claiming unemployment benefit. There was a marked increase between 1980 and 1981, when the figures rose from 7.9 to 12.6 per cent and from 4.3 to 6.4 per cent, respectively.

(e) The Government also produced to the court detailed statistics in support of their claim that the overall effect of the 1980 Rules had been to lead to an annual reduction of up to 5,700 (rather than 2,000, as they had estimated before the Commission) in the number of husbands either accepted for settlement or applying successfully to come for settlement from all parts of the world. They recognised, however, that part – though not a major part – of this figure might represent a decrease attributable to economic conditions. In their submission, this reduction was of a considerable scale when viewed in relation to the figures for the total number of persons accepted for settlement into the United Kingdom. The latter figures (about one-half of which were in each year accounted for by wives and children of men already settled in the country) were: over 80,000 in 1975 and 1976; around 70,000 in each year from 1977 to 1980; 59,100 in 1981; 53,900 in 1982; and 53,500 in 1983. The number of men accepted for settlement by reason of marriage was 11,190 in 1975; 11,060 in 1976; 5,610 in 1977; 9,330 in 1978; 9,900 in 1979; 9,160 in 1980; 6,690 in 1981; 6,070 in 1982; and 5,210 in 1983. The number of women so accepted was 19,890 in 1977; 18,950 in 1978; 19,708 in 1979; 15,430 in 1980; 16,760 in 1981; 15,490 in 1982; and 16,900 in 1983.

The claimed reduction of 5,700 per annum was questioned by the applicants on the following grounds: it was based on a comparison with the figures for 1979, a year in which the number of applications from the Indian sub-continent was artificially high; in order to take account of the delays in processing applications and the 12-month waiting period before indefinite leave to remain between the 1981 and the 1983 figures, no account was taken of the natural decline in applications; and no account was taken of persons properly excluded (for example, on the ground that the marriage was not genuine).

II. THE PARTICULAR CIRCUMSTANCES OF THE CASE

A. Mrs Abdulaziz

39. Mrs Nargis Abdulaziz is permanently and lawfully resident in the United Kingdom with the right to remain indefinitely. She was born in Malawi in 1948 and brought up in that country. Her parents were also born there. According to her, she was a citizen of Malawi at birth but, being of Indian origin, was subsequently deprived of that citizenship and is now stateless. She holds a Malawian travel document.

This applicant went to the United Kingdom on 23 December 1977. She was given leave, as a 'non-patrial', to enter as a visitor, leave which was subsequently extended on three occasions. Since special vouchers had been allocated to members of her family enabling them to settle in the United Kingdom, an application was made on her behalf for indefinite leave to remain. On 16 May 1979, as an act of discretion outside the immigration rules, she was given such leave, essentially on the ground that she was an unmarried woman with little prospect of marriage who formed part of a close family, including her father and mother, settled in the United Kingdom.

40. Mr Ibramobai Abdulaziz is a Portuguese national who was born in Daman, a former Portuguese territory in India, in 1951. He emigrated to Portugal in 1978. On 4 October 1979, he was admitted, as a 'non-patrial', to the United Kingdom for six months as a visitor. He met the applicant six days latter and they became engaged to be married on 27 November. They were married on 8 December 1979 and, during the following week, Mrs Abdulaziz applied for leave for her husband to remain permanently in the United Kingdom. Shortly afterwards, the Joint Council for the Welfare of Immigrants also applied for leave for him to remain, for a period of twelve months.

41. After Mr and Mrs Abdulaziz had been interviewed at the Home Office on 6 June 1980, her application was refused, on 1 July, on the ground that she was not a citizen of the United Kingdom and Colonies who, or one of whose parents, had been born in the United Kingdom. (¶ 117 of the 1980 Rules see §24(a)(1) *supra*)

Mr Abdulaziz appealed to an adjudicator against this decision but the appeal was dismissed on 6 October 1981 as he did not qualify for leave to remain under the 1980 Rules. The adjudicator pointed out that, had the application been made before 14 November 1979 or the decision taken before 1 March 1980, Mr Abdulaziz would have been admitted, under the previous rules. Leave to appeal to the Immigration Appeal Tribunal was refused by the Tribunal on 9 December 1981 on the ground that the determination of the appeal did not turn on any arguable point of law and that leave to appeal was not otherwise merited.

42. Subsequently Mr Abdulaziz remained, and still remains, in the United Kingdom, without leave. He is currently employed as a chef in a restaurant; his wife does not work. A son was born to the couple in October 1982. Representations through Members

of Parliament to the Home Office have been rejected, basically on the ground that the couple could live together in Portugal and that the circumstances of the case were not such as to warrant exceptional treatment. In a letter of 24 February 1982 to one Member, the Minister of State at the Home Office indicated that the authorities would shortly be advising Mr Abdulaziz to depart without delay, adding that if he did not, 'consideration will have to be given to enforcing his departure'; however, a letter of 29 November 1982 to another Member stated that '[the Minister did] not propose for the time being to take any action regarding [Mr Abdulaziz's] removal'. In fact, the authorities have not to date instituted any criminal or deportation proceedings against him; their decision, according to the Government, was taken in the light of all the circumstances, including the Commission's decision on the admissibility of Mrs Abdulaziz's application.

The couple's situation has not until now been changed by the 1982 or the 1983 Rules since Mrs Abdulaziz, although settled in the United Kingdom, is not a British citizen. She has, however, applied, on 16 August 1984, for naturalisation as such a citizen, under section 6 of the British Nationality Act 1981.

43. At the Home Office interview, Mr Abdulaziz said that his wife could not be expected to live in Portugal because she had always been close to her family and because her sick father – who in fact died in September 1980 – needed her company. Before the Commission and the Court, she claimed that her health was under strain because of her husband's settlement problems and that humanitarian considerations prevented her going to Portugal, a country where she had no family and whose language she did not speak. The Government maintain that there is no obstacle whatever to her going with her husband to live in Portugal.

B. Mrs Cabales

44. Mrs Arcely Cabales is permanently and lawfully resident in the United Kingdom with the right to remain indefinitely. She was born in the Philippines in 1939 and was brought up there, and is of Asian origin. She had the nationality of that country until 1984. Her parents were born and live in the Philippines.

This applicant went to the United Kingdom in 1967 with a work permit for employment as a nursing assistant and was admitted, as a 'non-patrial' for 12 months. She remained in approved work thereafter and, on 10 June 1971, the conditions attached to her stay were removed and she was allowed to remain in the United Kingdom indefinitely. She is now employed, and has an established career, as a state enrolled nurse.

45. Mr Ludovico Cabales is a citizen of the Philippines, born in that country in 1937. He met the applicant in Manila in 1977 when she was on holiday and again in 1979 when she was there for one or two months. During the latter period, the couple became engaged. On 23 April 1980, they went through a ceremony of marriage in the Philippines. The applicant returned to the United Kingdom shortly afterwards to take up her job again. In May 1980, she informed the Home Office of the marriage and applied for leave for Mr Cabales to enter the United Kingdom, a request which she repeated in August. On 27 November, he, being a 'non-patrial', applied to the British Embassy in Manila for a visa to join his wife for settlement in the United Kingdom.

46. After Mrs Cabales had supplied certain further information requested by it, the Home Office wrote to her on 23 February 1981 to advise her that the visa application had been refused on the ground that she was not a citizen of the United Kingdom and Colonies who, or one of whose parents, had been born in the United Kingdom. (¶ 50 of

the 1980 Rules; see §23(a)(ii) *supra*) Notice of the decision was not handed to Mr Cabales until 12 November 1981 as he had failed to respond to an invitation of March 1981 to attend at the Manila Embassy for that purpose.

On 20 August 1981, the Joint Council for the Welfare of Immigrants wrote to the Home Office Immigration and Nationality Department, seeking a review of this decision. However, on 13 January 1982, the Department, having considered the circumstances, informed the Council of its decision to maintain the refusal. Mr Cabales had on 8 December 1981 lodged an appeal with an adjudicator against the decision but the appeal was dismissed on 25 July 1983 on the ground that the visa officer's decision was in accordance with the law and the immigration rules. The adjudicator, who noted that Mrs Cabales had not taken legal advice but had thought at the time of the marriage ceremony that a forthcoming change in the law would allow Mr Cabales to be admitted, expressed the hope that the authorities would look at the case sympathetically. This was not initially recognised by the authorities as a recommendation, but the Home Secretary subsequently concluded that there were not sufficient grounds for acting outside the immigration rules. There is no record of an application for leave to appeal to the Immigration Appeal Tribunal. Representations to the Home Office were also rejected, basically on the ground that the couple could live together in the Philippines and that there were not sufficient reasons for the Home Secretary to exercise his extra-statutory discretion.

47. Between April 1980 and December 1984, Mr Cabales continued to live in the Philippines and the couple were separated, apart from a short period in 1983 when Mrs Cabales visited that country. However, following an application made by her in November 1982 under section 6 of the British Nationality Act 1981, Mrs Cabales obtained naturalisation as a British citizen with effect from 18 April 1984; she thereby lost her Philippine citizenship. On 10 July 1984, Mr Cabales applied for entry clearance for permanent settlement as the husband of a British citizen, under paragraph 54 of the 1983 Rules. For the reasons and in the circumstances indicated in the following paragraph this application was refused on 1 October 1984 but, on the following day, Mr Cabales applied for and was granted a visa entitling him to enter the United Kingdom for three months for the purposes of marriage. He arrived in that country on 19 December 1984 and the parties were married there on 26 January 1985. On 4 February, he was granted leave to remain as a husband for the next twelve months; on the expiry of that period, he will be eligible to apply for indefinite leave.

   . . . .

49. Before the Commission and the Court, Mrs Cabales submitted that there would have been real obstacles to her returning to live in the Philippines: she was too old, her qualifactions were not recognised there and, by working in the United Kingdom, she was able to support financially her parents and other members of her family. These claims were contested by the Government, in particular on the ground that it was unrealistic to suppose that her nursing skills could not be put to good use in the Philippines.

C. Mrs Balkandali

50. Mrs Sohair Balkandali is permanently and lawfully resident in the United Kingdom with the right to remain indefinitely. She was born in Egypt in 1946 or 1948. Her parents were born and live in that country.

This applicant first went to the United Kingdom in November 1973 and was given leave, as a 'non-patrial', to enter as a visitor for one month. Subsequently, she obtained several further leaves to remain, as a visitor or a student, the last being until August 1976. She has a high level of university education. In 1978, she married a Mr Corbett, a citizen of the United Kingdom and Colonies, and, five days later, was given indefinite leave to remain in the United Kingdom, by virtue of her marriage, under the provisions then in force. On 26 October 1979, again by virtue of her marriage, she obtained registration as a citizen of the United Kingdom and Colonies under the British Nationality Act 1948, as a result of which she became a 'patrial'. At that time, she was already separated from Mr Corbett and the marriage was dissolved in October 1980.

51. Mr Bekir Balkandali is a Turkish national born in Turkey on 9 April 1946. In January 1979, he was granted leave, as a 'non-patrial', to enter the United Kingdom, apparently as a visitor, for one month. Subsequently, he obtained leave to remain as a student until 31 March 1980. His application of 2 April for an extension of this leave was refused on 23 September 1980 because he had not attended his course of studies and the Home Secretary was not satisfied that he was a genuine student who intended to leave the country on their conclusion. Since his application for an extension had been made after his leave had expired, he had no right of appeal under the 1971 Act; he was advised to leave the United Kingdom and warned of the risk of criminal or deportation proceedings if he did not.

52. Since the autumn of 1979, the applicant had been living with Mr Balkandali, In April 1980 they had a son, who has the right of abode in the United Kingdom. On 14 October 1980, an application was made by the Joint Council for the Welfare of Immigrants for leave for Mr Balkandali to remain in the United Kingdom until he married his fiancée, the applicant. They were interviewed together by Home Office officials on 30 March 1981 and produced evidence of their marriage, which had been celebrated in January 1981. The application was therefore treated as one to remain as the husband of a woman settled in the United Kingdom.

Leave was refused on 14 May 1981 on the ground that Mrs Balkandali was not a citizen of the United Kingdom and Colonies who, or one of whose parents, had been born in the United Kingdom (¶ 117 of the 1980 Rules; see §24(a)(i) *supra*) There was no right of appeal against this decision as Mr Balkandali had no current leave to remain at the time when his application was made. Representations through a Member of Parliament to the Home Office were rejected, basically on the ground that the couple could live together in Turkey and that there were not sufficient compelling compassionate circumstances to warrant exceptional treatment outside the immigration rules. In a letter of 18 December 1981 to the Member, the Minister of State at the Home Office wrote that 'Mr Balkandali should now make arrangements to leave the United Kingdom forthwith, otherwise arrangements will be made to enforce his departure'; however, a letter of 3 December 1982 to the Member stated that '[the Minister did] not propose for the time being to take any action against [Mr Balkandali]'. In fact, the authorities did not at any time institute criminal or deportation proceedings against him; their decision, according to the Government, was taken in the light of all the circumstances, including the Commission's decision on the admissibility of Mrs Balkandali's application.

53. On 20 January 1983, as the husband of a British citizen, Mr Balkandali was given 12 months' leave to remain in the United Kingdom in accordance with paragraph 126 of the 1982 Rules; this was possible because, on 1 January 1983, Mrs Balkandali had automatically acquired British citizenship by virtue of the British Nationality Act 1981. Mr Balkandali subsequently applied for indefinite leave to remain and this was granted

on 18 January 1984 under paragraph 177 of the 1983 Rules. In September 1984, he was working in the catering business and planned shortly to open a restaurant; his wife was working two days a week in a creche.

54. Before the Commission and the Court, Mrs Balkandali submitted that there would have been real obstacles to her going with her husband to live in Turkey: she cited her strong ties to the United Kingdom and alleged that as an educated woman and the mother of an illegitimate child she would have been treated as a social outcast in Turkey. The Government maintain that there were no real obstacles.

[The applicants applied to the European Commission of Human Rights, which found that the United Kingdom had unlawfully discriminated on grounds of sex, race, and birth.]

. . . .

DECISION [OF THE EUROPEAN COURT OF HUMAN RIGHTS]:

I. Alleged violation of Article 8

58. The applicants claimed to be victims of a practice in violation of their right to respect for family life, guaranteed by Article 8. . . .

. . . .

In the present case, the applicants have not shown that there were obstacles to establishing family life in their own or their husbands' home countries or that there were special reasons why that could not be expected of them.

. . . .

69. There was accordingly no 'lack of respect' for family life and, hence, no breach of Article 8 taken alone.

II. Alleged violation of Article 14 taken together with Article 8

A. Introduction

70. The applicants claimed that, as a result of unjustified differences of treatment in securing the right to respect for their family life, based on sex, race and also – in the case of Mrs Balkandali – birth, they had been victims of a violation of Article 14 of the Convention, taken together with Article 8.

. . . .

In the event that the Court should find Article 8 to be applicable in the present case, the Government denied that there was any difference of treatment on the ground of race and submitted that since the differences of treatment on the ground of sex and of birth had objective and reasonable justification and were proportionate to the aims pursued, they were compatible with Article 14.

71. According to the Court's established case law, Article 14 complements the other substantive provisions of the Convention and the Protocols. It has no independent existence since it has effect solely in relation to 'the enjoyment of the rights and freedoms' safeguarded by those provisions. Although the application of Article 14 does not necessarily presuppose a breach of those provisions – and to this extent it is autonomous – there can be no room for its application unless the facts at issue fall within the ambit of one or more of the latter. (See *Rasmussen v Denmark* (1985), at §29) The Court has found Article 8 to be applicable. Although the United Kingdom was not obliged to accept Mr Abdulaziz, Mr Cabales and Mr Balkandali for settlement and the Court therefore

did not find a violation of settlement and the Court therefore did not find a violation of Article 8 taken alone, the facts at issue nevertheless fall within the ambit of that Article. In this respect, a parallel may be drawn, *mutatis mutandis*, with the *National Union of Belgian Police Case*. (§45)

Article 14 also is therefore applicable.

72. For the purposes of Article 14, a difference of treatment is discriminatory if it 'has no objective and reasonable justification', that is, if it does not pursue a 'legitimate aim' or if there is not a 'reasonable relationship of proportionality between the means employed and the aim sought to be realised'. (See *Belgian Linguistic Case*, §10; *Marckx v. Belgium*, §33 and *Rasmussen v. Denmark* (1985), §38)

The Contracting States enjoy a certain margin of appreciation in assessing whether and to what extent differences in otherwise similar situations justify a different treatment in law (*See Rasmussen v. Denmark* (1985), §40), but it is for the Court to give the final ruling in this respect.

73. In the particular circumstances of the case, the Court considers that it must examine in turn the three grounds on which it was alleged that a discriminatory difference of treatment was based.

B. Alleged discrimination on the ground of sex

74. As regards the alleged discrimination on the grounds of sex, it was not disputed that under the 1980 Rules it was easier for a man settled in the United Kingdom than for a woman so settled to obtain permission for his or her non-national spouse to enter or remain in the country for settlement. Argument centred on the question whether this difference had an objective and reasonable justification.

75. According to the Government, the difference of treatment complained of had the aim of limiting 'primary immigration,' and was justified by the need to protect the domestic labour market at a time of high unemployment. They placed strong reliance on the margin of appreciation enjoyed by the Contracting States in this area and laid particular stress on what they described as a statistical fact: men were more likely to seek work than women, with the result that male immigrants would have a greater impact than female immigrants on the said market. Furthermore, the reduction, attributed by the government to the 1980 Rules, of approximately 5,700 per annum in the number of husbands accepted for settlement in the United Kingdom was claimed to be significant. This was said to be so especially when the reduction was viewed in relation to its cumulative effect over the years and to the total number of acceptances for settlement.

This view was contested by the applicants. For them, the government's plea ignored the modern role of women and the fact that men may be self-employed and also, as was exemplified by the case of Mr Balkandali, create rather than seek jobs. Furthermore, the Government's figure of 5,700 was said to be insignificant and, for a number of reasons, in any event unreliable.

76. The Government further contended that the measures in question were justified by the need to maintain effective immigration control, which benefitted settled immigrants as well as the indigenous population. Immigration caused strains on society; the Government's aim was to advance public tranquillity, and a firm and fair control secured good relations between the different communities living in the United Kingdom.

To this, the applicants replied that the racial prejudice of the United Kingdom population could not be advanced as a justification for the measures.

77. In its report, the Commission considered that, when seen in the context of the immigration of other groups, annual emigration and unemployment and economic activity rates, the impact on the domestic labour market of an annual reduction of 2,000 (as then estimated by the Government) in the number of husbands accepted for settlement in the United Kingdom was not of a size or importance to justify a difference of treatment on the ground of sex and the detrimental consequences thereof on the family life of the women concerned. Furthermore, the longstanding commitment to the reunification of the families of male immigrants, to which the Government had referred as a reason for accepting wives whilst excluding husbands, no longer corresponded to modern requirements as to the equal treatment of the sexes. Neither was it established that race relations or immigration controls were enhanced by the rules: they might create resentment in part of the immigrant population and it had not been shown that it was more difficult to limit abuses by non-national husbands than by other immigrant groups. The Commission unanimously concluded that there had been discrimination on the ground of sex, contrary to Article 14, in securing the applicants' right to respect for family life, the application of the relevant rules being disproportionate to the purported aims.

At the hearings before the Court, the Commission's Delegate stated that this conclusion was not affected by the Government's revised figure (about 5,700) for the annual reduction in the number of husbands accepted for settlement.

78. The Court accepts that the 1980 Rules had the aim of protecting the domestic labour market. The fact that, as was suggested by the applicants, this aim might have been further advanced by the abolition of the 'United Kingdom ancestry' and the 'working holiday' rules in no way alters this finding. Neither does the Court perceive any conclusive evidence to contradict in the Parliamentary debates, on which the applicants also relied. It is true, as they pointed out, that unemployment in the United Kingdom in 1980 was lower than in subsequent years, but it had nevertheless already attained a significant level and there was a considerable increase as compared with previous years.

Whilst the aforesaid aim was without doubt legitimate, this does not in itself establish the legitimacy of the difference made in the 1980 Rules as to the possibility for male and female immigrants settled in the United Kingdom to obtain permission for, on the one hand, their non-national wives or fiancées and, on the other hand, their non-national husbands or fiancé to enter or remain in the country.

Although the Contracting States enjoy a certain 'margin of appreciation' in assessing whether and to what extent differences in otherwise similar situations justify a different treatment, the scope of this margin will vary according to the circumstances, the subject matter and its background. (See *Rasmussen v. Denmark* (1985), §40)

As to the present matter, it can be said that the advancement of the equality of the sexes is today a major goal in the member-States of the Council of Europe. This means that very weighty reasons would have to be advanced before a difference of treatment on the ground of sex could be regarded as compatible with the Convention.

79. In the Court's opinion, the Government's arguments summarised in paragraph 75 are not convincing.

It may be correct that on average there is a greater percentage of men of working age than of women of working age who are 'economically active' (for Great Britain 90 per cent of the men and 63 per cent of the women) and that comparable figures hold good for immigrants (according to the statistics, 86 per cent for sub-continent and 90 per cent for men and 70 per cent for women for immigrants from the West Indies and Guyana).

Nevertheless, this does not show that similar differences in fact exist – or would but for the effect of the 1980 Rules have existed – [in the economic activity] of immigrant wives and of immigrant husbands. In this connection, other factors must also be taken into account. Being 'economically active' does not always mean that one is seeking to be employed by someone else. Moreover, although a greater number of men and women may be inclined to seek employment, immigrant husbands were already by far outnumbered, before the introduction of the 1980 Rules, by immigrant wives, many of whom were also 'economically active'. Whilst a considerable proportion of those wives, in so far as they were 'economically active', were engaged in part-time work, the impact on the domestic labour market of women immigrants as compared with men ought not to be underestimated.

In any event, the Court is not convinced that the difference that may nevertheless exist between the respective impact of men and of women on the domestic labour market is sufficiently important to justify the difference of treatment, complained of by the applicants, as to the possibility for a person settled in the United Kingdom to be joined by, as the case may be, his wife or her husband.

80. In this context the Government stressed the importance of the effect on the immigration of husbands of the restrictions contained in the 1980 Rules, which had led, according to their estimate, to an annual reduction of 5,700 (rather than 2,000, as mentioned in the Commission's report) in the number of husbands accepted for settlement.

Without expressing a conclusion on the correctness of the figure of 5,700, the Court notes that in point of time the claimed reduction coincided with a significant increase in unemployment in the United Kingdom and that the Government accepted that some part of the reduction was due to economic conditions rather than to the 1980 Rules themselves.

In any event, for the reasons stated in paragraph 79 above, the reduction achieved does not justify the difference in treatment between men and women.

. . . .

82. There remains a more general argument advanced by the Government, namely that the United Kingdom was not in violation of Article 14 by reason of the fact that it acted more generously in some respects – that is, as regards the admission of non-national wives and fiancées of men settled in the country – than the Convention required.

The Court cannot accept this argument. It would point out that Article 14 is concerned with the avoidance of discrimination in the enjoyment of the convention rights in so far as the requirements of the convention as to those rights can be complied with in different ways. The notion of discrimination within the meaning of Article 14 includes in general cases where a person or group is treated, without proper justification, less favourably than another, even though the more favourable treatment is not called for by the Convention.

83. The Court thus concludes that the applicants have been victims of discrimination on the ground of sex, in violation of Article 14 taken together with Article 8.

C. Alleged discrimination on the ground of race

84. As regards the alleged discrimination on the ground of race, the applicants relied on the opinion of a minority of the Commission. They referred, *inter alia*, to the whole history of and background to the United Kingdom immigration legislation and to the Parliamentary debates on the immigration rules.

In contesting this claim, the Government submitted that the 1980 Rules were not racially motivated, their aim being to limit 'primary immigration'.

A majority of the Commission concluded that there had been no violation of Article 14 under this head. Most immigration policies – restricting, as they do, free entry – differentiated on the basis of people's nationality, and indirectly their race, ethnic origin and possibly their colour. Whilst a Contracting State could not implement 'policies of a purely racist nature', to give preferential treatment to its nationals or to persons from countries with which it had the closest links did not constitute 'racial discrimination'. The effect in practice of the United Kingdom rules did not mean that they were abhorrent on the grounds of racial discrimination, there being no evidence of an actual difference of treatment on grounds of race.

A minority of the Commission, on the other hand, noted that the main effect of the rules was to prevent immigration from the New Commonwealth and Pakistan. This was not coincidental: the legislative history showed that the intention was to 'lower the number of coloured immigrants'. By their effect and purpose, the rules were indirectly racist and there had thus been a violation of Article 14 under this head in the cases of Mrs Abdulaziz and Mrs Cabales.

85. The Court agrees in this respect with the majority of the Commission.

The 1980 Rules, which were applicable in general to all 'non-patrials' wanting to enter and settle in the United Kingdom, did not contain regulations differentiating between persons or groups on the ground of their race or ethnic origin. The rules included in paragraph 2 a specific instruction to immigration officers to carry out their duties without regard to the race, colour or religion of the intending entrant, and they were applicable across the board to intending immigrants from all parts of the world, irrespective of their race or origin.

As the Court has already accepted, the main and essential purpose of the 1980 Rules was to curtail 'primary immigration' in order to protect the labour market at a time of high unemployment. This means that their reinforcement of the restrictions on immigration was grounded not on objections regarding the origin of the non-nationals wanting to enter the country but on the need to stem the flow of immigrants at the relevant time.

That the mass immigration against which the rules were directed consisted mainly of would-be immigrants from the New Commonwealth and Pakistan, and that as a result they affected at the material time fewer white people than others, is not a sufficient reason to consider them as racist in character: it is an effect which derives not from the content of the 1980 Rules but from the fact that, among those wishing to immigrate, some ethnic groups outnumbered others.

The Court concludes from the foregoing that the 1980 Rules made no distinction on the ground of race and were therefore not discriminatory on that account. This conclusion is not altered by the following two arguments on which the applicants relied.

(a) The requirement that the wife or fiancée of the intending entrant be born or have a parent born in the United Kingdom and also the 'United Kingdom ancestry rule' were said to favour persons of a particular ethnic origin. However, the Court regards these provisions as being exceptions designed for the benefit of persons having close links with the United Kingdom, which do not affect the general tenor of the rules.

(b) The requirement that the parties to the marriage or intended marriage must have met was said to operate to the disadvantage of individuals from the Indian sub-continent, where the practice of arranged marriages is customary. In the Court's view, however, such a requirement cannot be taken as an indication of racial discrimination: its main purpose was to prevent evasion of the rules by means of bogus marriages or engagements. It is, besides, a requirement that has nothing to do with the present cases.

86. The Court accordingly holds that the applicants have not been victims of discrimination on the ground of race.

D. Alleged discrimination on the ground of birth

87. Mrs Balkandali claimed that she had also been the victim of discrimination on the ground of birth, in that, as between women citizens of the United Kingdom and Colonies settled in the United Kingdom, only those born or having a parent born in that country could, under the 1980 Rules, have their non-national husband accepted for settlement there.

It was not disputed that the 1980 Rules established a difference of treatment on the ground of birth, argument being centred on the question whether it had an objective and reasonable justification.

In addition to relying on the Commission's report, Mrs Balkandali submitted that the elimination of this distinction from subsequent immigration rules demonstrated that it was not previously justified.

The Government maintained that the difference in question was justified by the concern to avoid the hardship which women having close ties to the United Kingdom would encounter if, on marriage, they were obliged to move abroad in order to remain with their husbands.

The Commission considered that, notwithstanding the subsequent elimination of this difference, the general interest and the possibly temporary nature of immigration rules required it to express an opinion. It took the view that a difference of treatment based on the mere accident of birth, without regard to the individual's personal circumstances or merits, constituted discrimination in violation of Article 14.

88. The Court is unable to share the Commission's opinion. The aim cited by the Government is unquestionably legitimate, for the purposes of Article 14. It is true that a person who, like Mrs Balkandali, has been settled in a country for several years may also have formed close ties with it, even if he or she was not born there. Nevertheless, there are in general persuasive social reasons for giving special treatment to those whose link with a country stems from birth within it. The difference of treatment must therefore be regarded as having had an objective and reasonable justification and, in particular, its results have not been shown to transgress the principle of proportionality. This conclusion is not altered by the fact that the immigration rules were subsequently amended on this point.

89. The Court thus holds that Mrs Balkandali was not the victim of discrimination on the ground of birth.

. . . .

QUESTIONS & COMMENTS

(1) Do you find the European Court's reasons for not finding racial discrimination convincing in light of the Rules' legislative history? Consider the *Simunek, Hastings,*

Tuzilova and Prochazka v. The Czech Republic, Communication No. 516/1992, views adopted 19 July 1995, U.N. Doc. CCPR/C/54/D/516/1992 (1995), where the UN Human Rights Committee observes that "[a] politically motivated differentiation is unlikely to be compatible with article 26" [of the ICCPR, which prohibits discrimination]. *Id.* at §11.7.

How would the U.S. Supreme Court view this kind of legislative history in determining whether the legislation was unlawful discrimination?

(2) The UN Human Rights Committee also has addressed gender discrimination in the area of immigration in *Aumeeruddy-Cziffra v. Mauritius*, UN Hum. Rts. Cmtte., Communication No. 35/1978, views adopted 9 April 1981, Selected Decisions Under the Optional Protocol 67, U.N. Doc. CCPR/C/OP/1 (1985). In this case, the Committee found unlawful gender discrimination. Mauritius subsequently invalidated the offending legislation.

(3) A fractured U.S. Supreme Court upheld a federal citizenship statute in *Miller v. Albright*, 118 S.Ct. 1428 (1998). Under the statute, children born abroad to an unmarried U.S. citizen mother and a non–U.S. citizen father became U.S. citizens relatively easily, while children born abroad to an unmarried U.S. citizen father and a non–U.S. citizen mother had to go through a more difficult process, including acknowledgment by the father or other proof of paternity before the child's eighteenth birthday. Two justices found that the distinction satisfied the Constitution's equality requirements because the two situations differed: U.S. citizen mothers would know about and, ordinarily, would develop relationships with the children, whereas U.S. citizen fathers might not know about or develop ties to their children. Two justices concluded that courts lacked the power to "grant" citizenship by overriding a congressional provision, even one that discriminatorily denied citizenship. And two justices found that the only litigant in the case, the child, lacked standing to raise a challenge to discrimination between fathers and mothers; her father would have had standing, but he had been dismissed from the litigation at an early stage and no longer remained in the case. These two justices suggested, however, that the distinction between fathers and mothers could not survive the high standard of scrutiny applicable to gender discrimination. Finally, three justices would have invalidated the statute. (In light of the Court's division, and the fact that five justices either would have held or strongly suggested that the statute is unconstitutional, what should a State Department employee do when a child of a U.S. citizen father seeks a passport on the ground the she is a citizen?) How would the European Court analyze the problem posed by the U.S. statute?

(4) Consider *Schmidt v. Germany*, 291-B Eur. Ct. H.R. (ser. A) (1994). A German law required all male residents – but not female residents – of Tettnang, Germany, to either volunteer to work for the firemen or to pay a fee in contribution to the firemen. The male applicant challenged the fire-service levy as unlawful gender discrimination in violation of Article 14, ECHR. Howerver, Article 4(3)(d), ECHR, allows an exception to the prohibition against compulsory labor for normal civic obligations to ECHR states parties. The compulsory fire service in Schmidt's town fell within this exception. The alternative financial contribution was considered a "compensatory charge" and because of its close links with the obligation to serve, also fell within the scope of Article 4(3)(d).

The European Court stated that very weighty reasons would have to be put forward before the Court could regard a difference of treatment based exclusively on the grounds of sex as compatible with the Convention. Schmidt argued that the state interest in protecting women could not in itself justify a difference of treatment in this context. He pointed out that a more proportionate means for protecting women would be to take the biological differences between the sexes into account by a sensible division of the various tasks performed in the fire brigade. He also pointed out that as of 1992, close to seventy thousand women had served in fire brigades in Germany, and in his own town, the fire brigades had accepted women since 1978. Finally, Schmidt contended that since no man had ever been required to serve on the brigade, the regulation was really a purely fiscal one that women were as capable of complying with as men. This last claim is what ultimately swayed the European Court to decide the regulation was unlawful discrimination. The European Court did not rule on whether there existed any justification for treating men and women differently in regard to compulsory service in the fire brigade. The Court pointed out that this issue was not decisive in the present case in light of the continuing existence of a sufficient number of volunteers. No one had ever been obliged to serve in a fire brigade. Instead, the financial contribution had become effectively the only actual duty required by the Fire Brigades Act. In the imposition of such a financial burden, a difference of treatment on the ground of sex could "hardly be justified." Accordingly, the European Court found there had been a violation of Article 14 taken in conjunction with Article 4(3)(d) of the Convention.

(5) For a case finding a gender discrimination violation in which an insurance court had dismissed a woman's invalid pension on the assumption that women give up work after giving birth, see *Schuler-Zgraggen*, 263 Eur. Ct. H.R. (ser. A) (1993).

(6) Consider Article 119 of the EC Treaty, which states in relevant part:

> Each Member State shall during the first stage ensure and subsequently maintain the application of the principle that men and women should receive equal pay for equal work.

In *Defrenne v. Sabena* (*No. 2*), Case 43/75, 1976 E.C.R. 455, the European Court of Justice held that Article 119 had direct effect in member states to outlaw direct discrimination as to pay. In *Jenkins v. Kingsgate*, Case 96/80, 1981 E.C.R. 911, the Court extended this protection to less-direct discrimination. The Court held that the payment of lower hourly rates to part-time workers – most of whom were women – as compared with full-time workers violated Article 119. Finally, the Court in *Bilka-Kraufhaus GmbH v. Hartz*, Case 170/84, 1986 E.C.R. 1607, held that Article 119 also outlawed discriminatory practice or policy regarding pay that was neutral on its face.

Another EU antidiscrimination measure is Article 1 of the Equal Treatment Directive:

> The purpose of this Directive is to put into effect in the Member States the principle of equal treatment for men and women as regards access to employment, including promotion, and to vocational training and as regards working conditions. . . .

In *Dekker v. Stichting Vormingscentrum voor Jong Volwassenen* (*VJV-Centrum*), Case 177/88, 1991 E.C.R. I-3941, and *Hertz v. Aldi*, Case 179/88, 1990 E.C.R. I-3979, the European Court of Justice held that the refusal to hire or the dismissal of a pregnant woman was sex discrimination in violation of Article 1 of the Equal Treatment Directive.

(7) Under U.S. constitutional law, a "heightened rational basis" test is used in the context of gender discrimination: the classification must serve "important" governmental objectives, and the discriminatory means employed must be "substantially related" to the achievement of these ends. *Mississippi University for Women v. Hogan*, 458 U.S. 718 (1982); *see also United States v. Virginia*, 116 S.Ct. 2264 (1996) (gender discrimination unconstitutional in absence of "exceedingly persuasive justification").

Under U.S. federal statutory law, Title VII of the Civil Rights Act of 1964 prohibits discrimination on the basis of sex by employers. The Pregnancy Discrimination Act of 1978 extended the definition of sex to include pregnancy. *International Union, UAW v. Johnson Controls*, 499 U.S. 187 (1991). Refusal to hire on these grounds as well as harassment and hostile working environments are included within the scope of the statute. *Meritor Savings Bank v. Vinson*, 477 U.S. 57 (1986) (holding that sexual harassment in violation of Title VII exists in a workplace that creates a "hostile environment"). In addition, sex-based wage discrimination claims can also be brought under Title VII. *County of Washington v. Gunther*, 452 U.S. 161 (1981).

The main exception to the prohibition on purposeful discrimination is the bona fide occupational qualification (BFOQ), which provides that employers may refuse to hire on the basis of race, color, religion, sex, or national origin if members of the excluded class cannot perform the essential job duties. *See, e.g., Dothard v. Rawlinson*, 433 U.S. 321 (1977) (upholding Alabama prison practice of not hiring women guards because of unusually dangerous prison conditions). However, the federal courts have drawn this exception quite narrowly, refusing to accept stereotypes and customer preferences as justifications. *See, e.g., Diaz v. Pan Am. World Airways, Inc.*, 442 F.2d 385 (5th Cir. 1971) (rejecting customer preference for female flight attendants as BFOQ); *Weeks v. Southern Bell Tel. & Tel. Co.*, 408 F.2d 228 (5th Cir. 1969) (rejecting concern for welfare of women performing dangerous jobs as BFOQ).

Affirmative Action

Marschall v. Land Nordrhein-Westfalen (Case C-409/95)
European Court of Justice
[1997] All ER (EC) 865

. . . .

1. By order of 21 December 1995, received at the Court of Justice of the European Communities on 29 December 1995, the Verwaltungsgericht (the Administrative Court) Gelsenkirchen referred to the Court of Justice for a preliminary ruling under art 177 of the EC Treaty a question on the interpretation of art 2(1) and (4) of Council Directive (EEC) 76/207 on the implementation of the principle of equal treatment for men and women as regards access to employment, vocational training and promotion, and working conditions.

2. That question has been raised in proceedings between Hellmut Marschall and Land Nordrhein-Westfalen (the Land) concerning his application for a higher grade post at the Gesamtschule (comprehensive school) Schwerte in Germany.

3. The second sentence of para 25(5) of the Beamtengesetz fur das Land Nordrhein-Westfalen (the Law on Civil Servants of the Land), in the version published on 1 May 1981 (GVNW, p 234), as last amended by para 1 of the Seventh Law amending certain

rules relating to the civil service, of 5 February 1995 (GVNW, p 102), provides:

'Where, in the sector of the authority responsible for promotion, there are fewer women than men in the particular higher grade post in the career bracket, women are to be given priority for promotion in the event of equal suitability, competence and professional performance, unless reasons specific to an individual [male] candidate tilt the balance in his favour.'

4. According to the observations of the Land, the rule of priority laid down by that provision introduced an additional promotion criterion, that of being a female, in order to counteract the inequality affecting female candidates as compared with male candidates applying for the same post: where qualifications are equal, employers tend to promote men rather than women because they apply traditional promotion criteria which in practice put women at a disadvantage, such as age, seniority and the fact that a male candidate is a head of household and sole breadwinner for the household.

5. In providing that priority is to be given to the promotion of women 'unless reasons specific to an individual [male] candidate tilt the balance in his favour', the legislature deliberately chose, according to the Land, a legally imprecise expression in order to ensure sufficient flexibility and, in particular, to allow the administration latitude to take into account any reasons which may be specific to individual candidates. Consequently, notwithstanding the rule of priority, the administration can always give preference to a male candidate on the basis of promotion criteria, traditional or otherwise.

6. According to the order for reference, Mr Marschall works as a tenured teacher for the Land, his salary being that attaching to the basic grade in career bracket A12.

7. On 8 February 1994 he applied for promotion to an A13 post (teacher qualified for teaching in a first-grade secondary school and so employed) at the Gesamtschule Schwerte. The Bezirksregierung (the District Authority) Arnsberg informed him, however, that it intended to appoint a female candidate to the position.

8. Mr Marschall lodged an objection which the Bezirksregierung rejected by decision of 29 July 1994 on the ground that, in view of the provision in question, the female candidate must necessarily be promoted to the position since, according to their official performance assessments, both candidates were equally qualified and since at the time when the post was advertised there were fewer women than men in career bracket A13.

9. Mr Marschall then brought legal proceedings before the Verwaltungsgericht Gelsenkirchen for an order requiring the Land to promote him to the post in question.

10. The Verwaltungsgericht, finding that Mr Marschall and the woman candidate selected were equally qualified for the post, decided that the outcome of the proceedings depended on the compatibility of the provision in question with art 2(1) and (4) of the directive.

11. Relying on the judgment of this court in *Kalanke v Freie Hansestadt Bremen Case C-450/93* [1996] All ER (EC) 66, [1995] ECR I-3051, the Verwaltungsgericht considers that the priority which the provision in question accords in principle to women seems to constitute discrimination within the meaning of art 2(1) of the directive and that such discrimination is not eliminated by the possibility of giving preference, exceptionally, to male candidates.

12. That court also doubts whether the provision in question is covered by the exception provided for in art 2(4) of the directive concerning measures to promote equality of opportunity between men and women. The basis for assessing candidates is unduly

narrowed since only the numerical proportion of men to women at the level concerned is taken into account. Furthermore, the provision in question does not improve women's ability to compete on the labour market and to pursue a career on an equal footing with men but prescribes a result, whereas art 2(4) of the directive allows only measures for promoting equality of opportunity.

13. The Verwaltungsgericht therefore decided to stay proceedings and to refer the following question to the Court of Justice for a preliminary ruling:

'Does Article 2(1) and (4) of Council Directive 76/207/EEC of 9 February 1976 on the implementation of the principle of equal treatment for men and women as regards access to employment, vocational training and promotion, and working conditions, preclude a rule of national law which provides that, in sectors of the public service in which fewer women than men are employed in the relevant higher grade post in a career bracket, women must be given priority where male and female candidates for promotion are equally qualified (in terms of suitability, competence and professional performance), unless reasons specific to an individual male candidate tilt the balance in his favour . . . ?'

14. The Land, the Spanish, Austrian, Finnish, Swedish and Norwegian governments and the European Commission consider that a national rule such as the provision in question constitutes a measure for promoting equality of opportunity between men and women which falls within the scope of art 2(4) of the directive.

15. The Land observes in this regard that the priority accorded to female candidates is intended to counteract traditional promotion criteria without, however, replacing them. The Austrian government considers that a national rule such as that in question is designed to correct discriminatory procedures in the selection of staff.

16. The Finnish, Swedish and Norwegian governments add that the national rule in question promotes access by women to posts of responsibility and thus helps to restore balance to labour markets which, in their present state, are still broadly partitioned on the basis of gender in that they concentrate female labour in lower positions in the occupational hierarchy. According to the Finnish government, past experience shows in particular that action limited to providing occupational training and guidance for women or to influencing the sharing of occupational and family responsibilities is not sufficient to put an end to this partitioning of labour markets.

17. Finally, the Land and all those governments take the view that the provision in question does not guarantee absolute and unconditional priority for women and that it is therefore within the limits outlined by the court in *Kalanke*.

18. The French and the UK governments, on the other hand, consider that the provision in question is not covered by the derogation provided for in art 2(4) of the directive.

19. Those two governments submit that in providing for priority to be accorded to female candidates the provision goes further than promoting equality of opportunity and aims to bring about equality of representation between men and women, so that the court's reasoning in *Kalanke* applies.

20. Nor, in their view, does the presence of a saving clause make the provision in question any less discriminatory. That clause applies only exceptionally and therefore has no impact in a 'normal' case where there are no reasons specific to the male candidate which are such as to outweigh the general requirement to appoint the female candidate.

Since, moreover, it is formulated in terms that are both general and imprecise the clause is contrary to the principle of legal certainty.

21. The court observes that the purpose of the directive, as is clear from art 1(1), is to put into effect in the member states the principle of equal treatment for men and women as regards, inter alia, access to employment, including promotion. Article 2(1) states that the principle of equal treatment means that 'there shall be no discrimination whatsoever on grounds of sex either directly or indirectly'.

22. According to art 2(4), the directive is to –

'be without prejudice to measures to promote equal opportunity for men and women, in particular by removing existing inequalities which affect women's opportunities in the areas referred to in Article 1(1).'

23. In its judgment in *Kalanke* [1996] All ER (EC) 66, [1995] ECR I-3051 (para 16), the court held that a national rule which provides that, where equally qualified men and women are candidates for the same promotion in fields where there are fewer women than men at the level of the relevant post, women are automatically to be given priority, involves discrimination on grounds of sex.

24. However, unlike the provisions in question in *Kalanke*, the provision in question in this case contains a clause (*Vffnungsklausel*: 'saving clause') to the effect that women are not to be given priority in promotion if reasons specific to an individual male candidate tilt the balance in his favour.

25. It is therefore necessary to consider whether a national rule containing such a clause is designed to promote equality of opportunity between men and women within the meaning of art 2(4) of the directive.

26. Article 2(4) is specifically and exclusively designed to authorise measures which, although discriminatory in appearance, are in fact intended to eliminate or reduce actual instances of inequality which may exist in the reality of social life (*see EC Commission v France Case* 312/86 [1988] ECR 6315 (para 15) and *Kalanke* [1996] All ER (EC) 66, [1995] ECR I-3051 (para 18)).

27. It thus authorises national measures relating to access to employment, including promotion, which give a specific advantage to women with a view to improving their ability to compete on the labour market and to pursue a career on an equal footing with men (*see Kalanke* [1996] All ER (EC) 66, [1995] ECR I-3051 (para 19)).

28. As the Council stated in the third recital in the preamble to Council Recommendation (EEC) 84/635 on the promotion of positive action for women:

'. . . existing legal provisions on equal treatment, which are designed to afford rights to individuals, are inadequate for the elimination of all existing inequalities unless parallel action is taken by governments, both sides of industry and other bodies concerned, to counteract the prejudicial effects on women in employment which arise from social attitudes, behaviour and structures . . .' (*See Kalanke* [1996] All ER (EC) 66, [1995] ECR I-3051 (para 20).)

29. As the Land and several governments have pointed out, it appears that even where male and female candidates are equally qualified, male candidates tend to be promoted in preference to female candidates particularly because of prejudices and stereotypes concerning the role and capacities of women in working life and the fear, for example,

that women will interrupt their careers more frequently, that owing to household and family duties they will be less flexible in their working hours, or that they will be absent from work more frequently because of pregnancy, childbirth and breastfeeding.

30. For these reasons, the mere fact that a male candidate and a female candidate are equally qualified does not mean that they have the same chances.

31. It follows that a national rule in terms of which, subject to the application of the saving clause, female candidates for promotion who are equally as qualified as the male candidates are to be treated preferentially in sectors where they are under-represented may fall within the scope of art 2(4) if such a rule may counteract the prejudicial effects on female candidates of the attitudes and behaviour described above and thus reduce actual instances of inequality which may exist in the real world.

32. However, since art 2(4) constitutes a derogation from an individual right laid down by the directive, such a national measure specifically favouring female candidates cannot guarantee absolute and unconditional priority for women in the event of a promotion without going beyond the limits of the exception laid down in that provision (*see Kalanke* [1996] All ER (EC) 66, [1995] ECR I-3051 (paras 21–22)).

33. Unlike the rules at issue in *Kalanke*, a national rule which, as in the case in point in the main proceedings, contains a saving clause does not exceed those limits if, in each individual case, it provides for male candidates who are equally as qualified as the female candidates a guarantee that the candidatures will be the subject of an objective assessment which will take account of all criteria specific to the individual candidates and will override the priority accorded to female candidates where one or more of those criteria tilts the balance in favour of the male candidate. In this respect, however, it should be remembered that those criteria must not be such as to discriminate against female candidates.

34. It is for the national court to determine whether those conditions are fulfilled on the basis of an examination of the scope of the provision in question as it has been applied by the Land.

. . . .

On those grounds, the Court of Justice, in answer to the question referred to it by the Verwaltungsgericht Gelsenkirchen by order of 21 December 1995, hereby rules: a national rule which, in a case where there are fewer women than men at the level of the relevant post in a sector of the public service and both female and male candidates for the post are equally qualified in terms of their suitability, competence and professional performance, requires that priority be given to the promotion of female candidates unless reasons specific to an individual male candidate tilt the balance in his favour is not precluded by art 2(1) and (4) of Council Directive (EEC) 76/207 on the implementation of the principle of equal treatment for men and women as regards access to employment, vocational training and promotion, and working conditions, provided that: – in each individual case the rule provides for male candidates who are equally as qualified as the female candidates a guarantee that the candidatures will be the subject of an objective assessment which will take account of all criteria specific to the candidates and will override the priority accorded to female candidates where one or more of those criteria tilts the balance in favour of the male candidate, and such criteria are not such as to discriminate against the female candidates.

∾

QUESTIONS & COMMENTS

(1) In *Wygant v. Jackson Board of Education*, 476 U.S. 267 (1986), the U.S. Supreme Court held that a layoff policy protecting minority schoolteachers violated equal protection as being neither a narrowly tailored policy nor based on convincing evidence of prior discrimination by the governmental unit involved that required a remedy. Would Marschall have won under the *Wygant* test?

How relevant are the submissions of other national governments arguing the need for such an affirmative action program? Is the European Court of Justice as an *international* court more concerned with inter-governmental consensus rather than in-depth factual and statistical analyses of discrimination? Should it be? *See* Laurence R. Helfer, *Consensus, Coherence and the European Convention on Human Rights*, 26 CORNELL INT'L L.J. 133 (1993) (discussing problems posed by consensus approach of European Court of Human Rights); MARTIN ET AL., 1 INTERNATIONAL HUMAN RIGHTS LAW & PRACTICE: CASES, TREATIES AND MATERIALS 56 (1997).

(2) What relevance – if any – is there to the fact that racial discrimination is involved in *Wygant* but not *Marschall* in light of the heightened rational basis test articulated in *Mississippi University for Women v. Hogan*, 458 U.S. 718 (1982)? What relevance is there to the fact that *Wygant* involved layoffs, whereas *Marschall* involved promotion?

(3) In *Grutter v. Bollinger*, 539 U.S. _, (2003), the U.S. Supreme Court examined an equal protection challenge to the University of Michigan Law School's affirmative action program for minority students. In a concurring opinion, Justice Ginsburg noted what international law says about affirmative action programs:

> The Court's observation that race-conscious programs "must have a logical end point,"[ ] accords with the international understanding of the office of affirmative action. The International Convention on the Elimination of All Forms of Racial Discrimination, . . . endorses "special and concrete measures to ensure the adequate development and protection of certain racial groups or individuals belonging to them, for the purpose of guaranteeing them the full and equal enjoyment of human rights and fundamental freedoms." [CERD, art. 2(2)] But such measures, the Convention instructs, "shall in no case entail as a consequence the maintenance of unequal or separate rights for different racial groups after the objectives for which they were taken have been achieved." [*Ibid*; *see also* art. 1(4) (similarly providing for temporally limited affirmative action); Convention on the Elimination of All Forms of Discrimination against Women, art. 4(1) (authorizing "temporary special measures aimed at accelerating *de facto* equality" that "shall be discontinued when the objectives of equality of opportunity and treatment have been achieved")].

How wide a margin of appreciation should be given to states in determining when such temporary measures are no longer required?

(4) Note that many international human rights treaties prohibit discrimination on the basis of wealth, property, economic status, and/or fortune. How would you make out a customary international law claim that discrimination on the basis of wealth is unlawful? How may these different terms undercut such an argument? Would such a customary international law right create affirmative duties for the state? Under what kind of circumstances?

Given the number and similarity of welfare regimes in other countries, how would you argue that these regimes establish affirmative duties for maintaining a certain subsistence level of income for individuals?

5.2. International Humanitarian Law Protections and Human Rights-Related International Crimes

In this section, we examine international humanitarian law protections and human rights–related international crimes. Most of the following crimes occur in the context of armed conflicts (both international and noninternational) and, hence, are humanitarian law violations. However, some of these human rights–related crimes do not legally require a connection to armed conflict to be international crimes and, hence, are not, strictly speaking, humanitarian law violations.

5.2.1. Genocide

Convention on the Prevention and Punishment of the Crime of Genocide

Article II

In the present Convention, genocide means any of the following acts committed with intent to destroy, in whole or in part, a national, ethnical, racial or religious group, as such:

(a) Killing members of the group;
(b) Causing serious bodily or mental harm to members of the group;
(c) Deliberately inflicting on the group conditions of life calculated to bring about its physical destruction in whole or in part;
(d) Imposing measures intended to prevent births within the group;
(e) Forcibly transferring children of the group to another group.

Article III

The following acts shall be punishable:

(a) Genocide;
(b) Conspiracy to commit genocide;
(c) Direct and public incitement to commit genocide;
(d) Attempt to commit genocide;
(e) Complicity in genocide.

Statute of the International Criminal Tribunal for Rwanda

Article 2

Genocide

1. The International Tribunal for Rwanda shall have the power to prosecute persons committing genocide as defined in paragraph 2 of this article or of committing any of the other acts enumerated in paragraph 3 of this article.

2. Genocide means any of the following acts committed with intent to destroy, in whole or in part, a national, ethnical, racial or religious group, as such:

(a) Killing members of the group;
(b) Causing serious bodily or mental harm to members of the group;
(c) Deliberately inflicting on the group conditions of life calculated to bring about its physical destruction in whole or in part;
(d) Imposing measures intended to prevent births within the group;
(e) Forcibly transferring children of the group to another group.

3. The following acts shall be punishable:

    (a) Genocide;
    (b) Conspiracy to commit genocide;
    (c) Direct and public incitement to commit genocide;
    (d) Attempt to commit genocide;
    (e) Complicity in genocide.

Statute of the International Criminal Court

Article 5

Crimes within the jurisdiction of the Court

1. The jurisdiction of the Court shall be limited to the most serious crimes of concern to the international community as a whole. The Court has jurisdiction in accordance with this Statute with respect to the following crimes:

(a) The crime of genocide;

   . . . .

Article 6

Genocide

For the purpose of this Statute, "genocide" means any of the following acts committed with intent to destroy, in whole or in part, a national, ethnical, racial or religious group, as such:

    (a) Killing members of the group;
    (b) Causing serious bodily or mental harm to members of the group;
    (c) Deliberately inflicting on the group conditions of life calculated to bring about its physical destruction in whole or in part;
    (d) Imposing measures intended to prevent births within the group;
    (e) Forcibly transferring children of the group to another group.

The Prosecutor v. Jean-Paul Akayesu
Case No. ICTR-96-4-T
Trial Chambers Judgment
International Criminal Tribunal for Rwanda
2 September 1998

   . . . .

Genocide (Article 2 of the Statute)

6.3.1. Genocide

Article 2 of the Statute stipulates that the Tribunal shall have the power to prosecute persons responsible for genocide, direct and public incitement to commit genocide, attempt to commit genocide and complicity in genocide.

In accordance with the said provisions of the Statute, the Prosecutor has charged Akayesu with the crimes legally defined as genocide (count 1), complicity in genocide (count 2) and incitement to commit genocide (count 4).

Crime of Genocide, punishable under Article 2(3)(a) of the Statute

The definition of genocide, as given in Article 2 of the Tribunal's Statute, is taken verbatim from Articles 2 and 3 of the Convention on the Prevention and Punishment of the Crime of Genocide (the "Genocide Convention"). It states:

"Genocide means any of the following acts committed with intent to destroy, in whole or in part, a national, ethnical, racial or religious group, as such:

(a) Killing members of the group;
(b) Causing serious bodily or mental harm to members of the group;
(c) Deliberately inflicting on the group conditions of life calculated to bring about its physical destruction in whole or in part;
(d) Imposing measures intended to prevent births within the group;
(e) Forcibly transferring children of the group to another group."

The Genocide Convention is undeniably considered part of customary international law, as can be seen in the opinion of the International Court of Justice on the provisions of the Genocide Convention, and as was recalled by the United Nations' Secretary-General in his Report on the establishment of the International Criminal Tribunal for the former Yugoslavia.

The Chamber notes that Rwanda acceded, by legislative decree, to the Convention on Genocide on 12 February 1975. Thus, punishment of the crime of genocide did exist in Rwanda in 1994, at the time of the acts alleged in the Indictment, and the perpetrator was liable to be brought before the competent courts of Rwanda to answer for this crime.

Contrary to popular belief, the crime of genocide does not imply the actual extermination of [a] group in its entirety, but is understood as such once any one of the acts mentioned in Article 2(2)(a) through 2(2)(e) is committed with the specific intent to destroy "in whole or in part" a national, ethnical, racial or religious group.

Genocide is distinct from other crimes inasmuch as it embodies a special intent or *dolus specialis*. Special intent of a crime is the specific intention, required as a constitutive element of the crime, which demands that the perpetrator clearly seeks to produce the act charged. Thus, the special intent in the crime of genocide lies in "the intent to destroy, in whole or in part, a national, ethnical, racial or religious group, as such".

Thus, for a crime of genocide to have been committed, it is necessary that one of the acts listed under Article 2(2) of the Statute be committed, that the particular act be committed against a specifically targeted group, it being a national, ethnical, racial or religious group. Consequently, in order to clarify the constitutive elements of the crime of genocide, the Chamber will first state its findings on the acts provided for under Article 2(2)(a) through Article 2(2)(e) of the Statute, the groups protected by the Genocide Convention, and the special intent or *dolus specialis* necessary for genocide to take place.

Killing members of the group (paragraph (a)):

With regard to Article 2(2)(a) of the Statute, like in the Genocide Convention, the Chamber notes that the said paragraph states "*meurtre*" in the French version while the English version states "killing". The Trial Chamber is of the opinion that the term "killing" used in the English version is too general, since it could very well include both intentional and unintentional homicides, whereas the term "*meurtre*", used in the French version, is more precise. It is accepted that there is murder when death has been caused with the intention to do so, as provided for, incidentally, in the Penal Code of Rwanda which stipulates in its Article 311 that "Homicide committed with intent to cause death shall be treated as murder".

Given the presumption of innocence of the accused, and pursuant to the general principles of criminal law, the Chamber holds that the version more favourable to the accused should be upheld and finds that Article 2(2)(a) of the Statute must be interpreted in accordance with the definition of murder given in the Penal Code of Rwanda, according to which "*meurtre*" (killing) is homicide committed with the intent to cause death. The Chamber notes in this regard that the *travaux préparatoires* of the Genocide Convention, show that the proposal by certain delegations that premeditation be made a necessary condition for there to be genocide, was rejected, because some delegates deemed it unnecessary for premeditation to be made a requirement; in their opinion, by its constitutive physical elements, the very crime of genocide, necessarily entails premeditation.

Causing serious bodily or mental harm to members of the group (paragraph b).

Causing serious bodily or mental harm to members of the group does not necessarily mean that the harm is permanent and irremediable.

In the Adolf Eichmann case, who was convicted of crimes against the Jewish people, genocide under another legal definition, the District Court of Jerusalem stated in its judgment of 12 December 1961, that serious bodily or mental harm of members of the group can be caused

> "by the enslavement, starvation, deportation and persecution [...] and by their detention in ghettos, transit camps and concentration camps in conditions which were designed to cause their degradation, deprivation of their rights as human beings, and to suppress them and cause them inhumane suffering and torture".

For purposes of interpreting Article 2 (2)(b) of the Statute, the Chamber takes serious bodily or mental harm, without limiting itself thereto, to mean acts of torture, be they bodily or mental, inhumane or degrading treatment, persecution.

Deliberately inflicting on the group conditions of life calculated to bring about its physical destruction in whole or in part (paragraph c):

The Chamber holds that the expression deliberately inflicting on the group conditions of life calculated to bring about its physical destruction in whole or in part, should be construed as the methods of destruction by which the perpetrator does not immediately kill the members of the group, but which, ultimately, seek their physical destruction.

For purposes of interpreting Article 2(2)(c) of the Statute, the Chamber is of the opinion that the means of deliberate inflicting on the group conditions of life calculated to bring about its physical destruction, in whole or part, include, *inter alia*, subjecting a group of people to a subsistence diet, systematic expulsion from homes and the reduction of essential medical services below minimum requirement.

Imposing measures intended to prevent births within the group (paragraph d).

For purposes of interpreting Article 2(2)(d) of the Statute, the Chamber holds that the measures intended to prevent births within the group, should be construed as sexual mutilation, the practice of sterilization, forced birth control, separation of the sexes and prohibition of marriages. In patriarchal societies, where membership of a group is determined by the identity of the father, an example of a measure intended to prevent births within a group is the case where, during rape, a woman of the said group is deliberately impregnated by a man of another group, with the intent to have her give birth to a child who will consequently not belong to its mother's group.

Furthermore, the Chamber notes that measures intended to prevent births within the group may be physical, but can also be mental. For instance, rape can be a measure intended to prevent births when the person raped refuses subsequently to procreate, in the same way that members of a group can be led, through threats or trauma, not to procreate.

Forcibly transferring children of the group to another group (paragraph e).

With respect to forcibly transferring children of the group to another group, the Chamber is of the opinion that, as in the case of measures intended to prevent births, the objective is not only to sanction a direct act of forcible physical transfer, but also to sanction acts of threats or trauma which would lead to the forcible transfer of children from one group to another.

Since the special intent to commit genocide lies in the intent to "destroy, in whole or in part, a national, ethnical, racial or religious group, as such", it is necessary to consider a definition of the group as such. Article 2 of the Statute, just like the Genocide Convention, stipulates four types of victim groups, namely national, ethnical, racial or religious groups.

On reading through the *travaux préparatoires* of the Genocide Convention, it appears that the crime of genocide was allegedly perceived as targeting only "stable" groups, constituted in a permanent fashion and membership of which is determined by birth, with the exclusion of the more "mobile" groups which one joins through individual voluntary commitment, such as political and economic groups. Therefore, a common criterion in the four types of groups protected by the Genocide Convention is that membership in such groups would seem to be normally not challengeable by its members, who belong to it automatically, by birth, in a continuous and often irremediable manner.

Based on the *Nottebohm* decision rendered by the International Court of Justice, the Chamber holds that a national group is defined as a collection of people who are perceived to share a legal bond based on common citizenship, coupled with reciprocity of rights and duties.

An ethnic group is generally defined as a group whose members share a common language or culture.

The conventional definition of racial group is based on the hereditary physical traits often identified with a geographical region, irrespective of linguistic, cultural, national or religious factors.

The religious group is one whose members share the same religion, denomination or mode of worship.

Moreover, the Chamber considered whether the groups protected by the Genocide Convention, echoed in Article 2 of the Statute, should be limited to only the four groups expressly mentioned and whether they should not also include any group which is stable and permanent like the said four groups. In other words, the question that arises is whether it would be impossible to punish the physical destruction of a group as such under the Genocide Convention, if the said group, although stable and membership is by birth, does not meet the definition of any one of the four groups expressly protected by the Genocide Convention. In the opinion of the Chamber, it is particularly important to respect the intention of the drafters of the Genocide Convention, which according to the *travaux préparatoires*, was patently to ensure the protection of any stable and permanent group.

As stated above, the crime of genocide is characterized by its *dolus specialis*, or special intent, which lies in the fact that the acts charged, listed in Article 2 (2) of the Statute, must have been "committed with intent to destroy, in whole or in part, a national, ethnical, racial or religious group, as such".

Special intent is a well-known criminal law concept in the Roman-continental legal systems. It is required as a constituent element of certain offences and demands that the perpetrator have the clear intent to cause the offence charged. According to this meaning, special intent is the key element of an intentional offence, which offence is characterized by a psychological relationship between the physical result and the mental state of the perpetrator.

As observed by the representative of Brazil during the *travaux préparatoires* of the Genocide Convention,

"genocide [is] characterised by the factor of particular intent to destroy a group. In the absence of that factor, whatever the degree of atrocity of an act and however similar it might be to the acts described in the convention, that act could still not be called genocide."

With regard to the crime of genocide, the offender is culpable only when he has committed one of the offences charged under Article 2(2) of the Statute with the clear intent to destroy, in whole or in part, a particular group. The offender is culpable because he knew or should have known that the act committed would destroy, in whole or in part, a group.

In concrete terms, for any of the acts charged under Article 2 (2) of the Statute to be a constitutive element of genocide, the act must have been committed against one or several individuals, because such individual or individuals were members of a specific group, and specifically because they belonged to this group. Thus, the victim is chosen not because of his individual identity, but rather on account of his membership of a national, ethnical, racial or religious group. The victim of the act is therefore a member of a group, chosen as such, which, hence, means that the victim of the crime of genocide is the group itself and not only the individual.

The perpetration of the act charged therefore extends beyond its actual commission, for example, the murder of a particular individual, for the realisation of an ulterior motive, which is to destroy, in whole or part, the group of which the individual is just one element.

On the issue of determining the offender's specific intent, the Chamber considers that intent is a mental factor which is difficult, even impossible, to determine. This is the reason why, in the absence of a confession from the accused, his intent can be inferred from a certain number of presumptions of fact. The Chamber considers that it is possible to deduce the genocidal intent inherent in a particular act charged from the general context of the perpetration of other culpable acts systematically directed against that same group, whether these acts were committed by the same offender or by others. Other factors, such as the scale of atrocities committed, their general nature, in a region or a country, or furthermore, the fact of deliberately and systematically targeting victims on account of their membership of a particular group, while excluding the members of other groups, can enable the Chamber to infer the genocidal intent of a particular act.

Trial Chamber I of the International Criminal Tribunal for the former Yugoslavia also stated that the specific intent of the crime of genocide

> "may be inferred from a number of facts such as the general political doctrine which gave rise to the acts possibly covered by the definition in Article 4, or the repetition of destructive and discriminatory acts. The intent may also be inferred from the perpetration of acts which violate, or which the perpetrators themselves consider to violate the very foundation of the group – acts which are not in themselves covered by the list in Article 4(2) but which are committed as part of the same pattern of conduct".

Thus, in the matter brought before the International Criminal Tribunal for the former Yugoslavia, the Trial Chamber, in its findings, found that "this intent derives from the combined effect of speeches or projects laying the groundwork for and justifying the acts, from the massive scale of their destructive effect and from their specific nature, which aims at undermining what is considered to be the foundation of the group".

6.3.2. Complicity in Genocide

The Crime of Complicity in Genocide, punishable under Article 2(3)e) of the Statute

Under Article 2(3)e) of the Statute, the Chamber shall have the power to prosecute persons who have committed complicity in genocide. The Prosecutor has charged Akayesu with such a crime under count 2 of the Indictment.

Principle VII of the "Nuremberg Principles" reads

> "complicity in the commission of a crime against peace, a war crime, or a crime against humanity as set forth in Principle VI is a crime under international law."

Thus, participation by complicity in the most serious violations of international humanitarian law was considered a crime as early as Nuremberg.

The Chamber notes that complicity is viewed as a form of criminal participation by all criminal law systems, notably, under the Anglo-Saxon system (or Common Law) and the Roman-Continental system (or Civil Law). Since the accomplice to an offence may be defined as someone who associates himself in an offence committed by another, complicity necessarily implies the existence of a principal offence.

According to one school of thought, complicity is "borrowed criminality" (*criminalité d'emprunt*). In other words, the accomplice borrows the criminality of the principal perpetrator. By borrowed criminality, it should be understood that the physical act which constitutes the act of complicity does not have its own inherent criminality, but rather it borrows the criminality of the act committed by the principal perpetrator of the criminal enterprise. Thus, the conduct of the accomplice emerges as a crime when the crime has been consummated by the principal perpetrator. The accomplice has not committed an autonomous crime, but has merely facilitated the criminal enterprise committed by another.

Therefore, the issue before the Chamber is whether genocide must actually be committed in order for any person to be found guilty of complicity in genocide. The Chamber notes that, as stated above, complicity can only exist when there is a punishable, principal act, in the commission of which the accomplice has associated himself. Complicity, therefore, implies a predicate offence committed by someone other than the accomplice.

Consequently, the Chamber is of the opinion that in order for an accused to be found guilty of complicity in genocide, it must, first of all, be proven beyond a reasonable doubt that the crime of genocide has, indeed, been committed.

The issue thence is whether a person can be tried for complicity even where the perpetrator of the principal offence himself has not being tried. Under Article 89 of the Rwandan Penal Code, accomplices

"may be prosecuted even where the perpetrator may not face prosecution for personal reasons, such as double jeopardy, death, insanity or non-identification". [unofficial translation]

As far as the Chamber is aware, all criminal systems provide that an accomplice may also be tried, even where the principal perpetrator of the crime has not been identified, or where, for any other reasons, guilt could not be proven.

The Chamber notes that the logical inference from the foregoing is that an individual cannot thus be both the principal perpetrator of a particular act and the accomplice thereto. An act with which an accused is being charged cannot, therefore, be characterized both as an act of genocide and an act of complicity in genocide as pertains to this accused. Consequently, since the two are mutually exclusive, the same individual cannot be convicted of both crimes for the same act.

As regards the physical elements of complicity in genocide (*actus reus*), three forms of accomplice participation are recognized in most criminal Civil Law systems: complicity by instigation, complicity by aiding and abetting, and complicity by procuring means. It should be noted that the Rwandan Penal Code includes two other forms of participation, namely, incitement to commit a crime through speeches, shouting or threats uttered in public places or at public gatherings, or through the sale or dissemination, offer for sale or display of written material or printed matter in public places or at public gatherings, or through the public display of placards or posters, and complicity by harbouring or aiding a criminal. Indeed, according to Article 91 of the Rwandan Penal Code:
"An accomplice shall mean:

1. A person or persons who by means of gifts, promises, threats, abuse of authority or power, culpable machinations or artifice, directly incite(s) to commit such action or order(s) that such action be committed.

2. A person or persons who procure(s) weapons, instruments or any other means which are used in committing such action with the knowledge that they would be so used.

3. A person or persons who knowingly aid(s) or abet(s) the perpetrator or perpetrators of such action in the acts carried out in preparing or planning such action or in effectively committing it.

4. A person or persons who, whether through speeches, shouting or threats uttered in public places or at public gatherings, or through the sale or dissemination, offer for sale or display of written material or printed matter in public places or at pubic gatherings or through the public display of placards or posters, directly incite(s) the perpetrator or perpetrators to commit such an action without prejudice to the penalties applicable to those who incite others to commit offences, even where such incitement fails to produce results.

5. A person or persons who harbour(s) or aid(s) perpetrators under the circumstances provided for under Article 257 of this Code." [unofficial translation]

The Chamber notes, first of all, that the said Article 91 of the Rwandan Penal Code draws a distinction between "instigation" (*instigation*), on the one hand, as provided for by paragraph 1 of said Article, and "incitation" (*incitement*), on the other, which is referred to in paragraph 4 of the same Article. The Chamber notes in this respect that, as pertains to the crime of genocide, the latter form of complicity, *i.e.* by incitement, is the offence which under the Statute is given the specific legal definition of "direct and public incitement to commit genocide," punishable under Article 2(3)c), as distinguished from "complicity in genocide." The findings of the Chamber with respect to the crime of direct and public incitement to commit genocide will be detailed below. That said, instigation, which according to Article 91 of the Rwandan Penal Code, assumes the form of incitement or instruction to commit a crime, only constitutes complicity if it is accompanied by, "gifts, promises, threats, abuse of authority or power, machinations or culpable artifice". In other words, under the Rwandan Penal Code, unless the instigation is accompanied by one of the aforesaid elements, the mere fact of prompting another to commit a crime is not punishable as complicity, even if such a person committed the crime as a result.

The ingredients of complicity under Common Law do not appear to be different from those under Civil Law. To a large extent, the forms of accomplice participation, namely "aid and abet, counsel and procure", mirror those conducts characterized under Civil Law as "*l'aide et l'assistance, la fourniture des moyens*".

Complicity by aiding or abetting implies a positive action which excludes, in principle, complicity by failure to act or omission. Procuring means is a very common form of complicity. It covers those persons who procured weapons, instruments or any other means to be used in the commission of an offence, with the full knowledge that they would be used for such purposes.

For the purposes of interpreting Article 2(3)e) of the Statute, which does not define the concept of complicity, the Chamber is of the opinion that it is necessary to define complicity as per the Rwandan Penal Code, and to consider the first three forms of criminal participation referred to in Article 91 of the Rwandan Penal Code as being the elements of complicity in genocide, thus:

complicity by procuring means, such as weapons, instruments or any other means, used to commit genocide, with the accomplice knowing that such means would be used for such a purpose;

complicity by knowingly aiding or abetting a perpetrator of a genocide in the planning or enabling acts thereof;

complicity by instigation, for which a person is liable who, though not directly participating in the crime of genocide crime, gave instructions to commit genocide, through gifts, promises, threats, abuse of authority or power, machinations or culpable artifice, or who directly incited to commit genocide.

The intent or mental element of complicity implies in general that, at the moment he acted, the accomplice knew of the assistance he was providing in the commission of the principal offence. In other words, the accomplice must have acted knowingly.

Moreover, as in all criminal Civil law systems, under Common law, notably English law, generally, the accomplice need not even wish that the principal offence be committed. In the case of *National Coal Board v. Gamble*, Justice Devlin stated

"an indifference to the result of the crime does not of itself negate abetting. If one man deliberately sells to another a gun to be used for murdering a third, he may be indifferent about whether the third lives or dies and interested only in the cash profit to be made out of the sale, but he can still be an aider and abettor."

In 1975, the English House of Lords also upheld this definition of complicity, when it held that willingness to participate in the principal offence did not have to be established. As a result, anyone who knowing of another's criminal purpose, voluntarily aids him or her in it, can be convicted of complicity even though he regretted the outcome of the offence.

As far as genocide is concerned, the intent of the accomplice is thus to knowingly aid or abet one or more persons to commit the crime of genocide. Therefore, the Chamber is of the opinion that an accomplice to genocide need not necessarily possess the *dolus specialis* of genocide, namely the specific intent to destroy, in whole or in part, a national, ethnic, racial or religious group, as such.

Thus, if for example, an accused knowingly aided or abetted another in the commission of a murder, while being unaware that the principal was committing such a murder, with the intent to destroy, in whole or in part, the group to which the murdered victim belonged, the accused could be prosecuted for complicity in murder, and certainly not for complicity in genocide. However, if the accused knowingly aided and abetted in the commission of such a murder while he knew or had reason to know that the principal was acting with genocidal intent, the accused would be an accomplice to genocide, even though he did not share the murderer's intent to destroy the group.

This finding by the Chamber comports with the decisions rendered by the District Court of Jerusalem on 12 December 1961 and the Supreme Court of Israel on 29 May 1962 in the case of Adolf Eichmann. Since Eichmann raised the argument in his defence that he was a 'small cog' in the Nazi machine, both the District Court and the Supreme Court dealt with accomplice liability and found that,

"[...] even a small cog, even an insignificant operator, is under our criminal law liable to be regarded as an accomplice in the commission of an offence, in which case he will be dealt with as if he were the actual murderer or destroyer."

The District Court accepted that Eichmann did not personally devise the "Final Solution" himself, but nevertheless, as the head of those engaged in carrying out the "Final Solution" – "acting in accordance with the directives of his superiors, but [with] wide discretionary powers in planning operations on his own initiative," he incurred individual criminal liability for crimes against the Jewish people, as much as his superiors. Likewise, with respect to his subordinates who actually carried out the executions, "[. . .] the legal and moral responsibility of he who delivers up the victim to his death is, in our opinion, no smaller, and may be greater, than the responsibility of he who kills the victim with his own hands." The District Court found that participation in the extermination plan with knowledge of the plan rendered the person liable As an accomplice to the extermination of all [. . .] victims from 1941 to 1945, irrespective of the extent of his participation."

The findings of the Israeli courts in this case support the principle that the *mens rea*, or special intent, required for complicity in genocide is knowledge of the genocidal plan, coupled with the *actus reus* of participation in the execution of such plan. Crucially, then, it does not appear that the specific intent to commit the crime of genocide, as reflected in the phrase "with intent to destroy, in whole or in part, a national, ethnical, racial or religious group, as such," is required for complicity or accomplice liability.

In conclusion, the Chamber is of the opinion that an accused is liable as an accomplice to genocide if he knowingly aided or abetted or instigated one or more persons in the commission of genocide, while knowing that such a person or persons were committing genocide, even though the accused himself did not have the specific intent to destroy, in whole or in part, a national, ethnical, racial or religious group, as such.

At this juncture, the Chamber will address another issue, namely that which, with respect to complicity in genocide covered under Article 2(3)(e) of the Statute, may arise from the forms of participation listed in Article 6 of the Statute entitled, "Individual Criminal Responsibility," and more specifically, those covered under paragraph 1 of the same Article. Indeed, under Article 6(1), "A person who planned, instigated, ordered, committed or otherwise aided and abetted in the planning, preparation or execution of a crime referred to in articles 2 to 4 of the present Statute, shall be individually responsible for the crime." Such forms of participation, which are summarized in the expression "[. . .] or otherwise aided or abetted [. . .]," are similar to the material elements of complicity, though they in and of themselves, characterize the crimes referred to in Articles 2 to 4 of the Statute, which include namely genocide.

Consequently, where a person is accused of aiding and abetting, planning, preparing or executing genocide, it must be proven that such a person acted with specific genocidal intent, *i.e.* the intent to destroy, in whole or in part, a national, ethnical, racial or religious group as such, whereas, as stated above, there is no such requirement to establish accomplice liability in genocide.

Another difference between complicity in genocide and the principle of abetting in the planning, preparation or execution a genocide as per Article 6(1), is that, in theory, complicity requires a positive act, *i.e.* an act of commission, whereas aiding and abetting may consist in failing to act or refraining from action. Thus, in the *Jefferson* and *Coney* cases, it was held that "The accused [. . .] only accidentally present [. . .] must know that his presence is actually encouraging the principal(s)." Similarly, the French Court of Cassation found that,

> "A person who, by his mere presence in a group of aggressors provided moral support
> to the assailants, and fully supported the criminal intent of the group, is liable as an
> accomplice" [unofficial translation].

The International Criminal Tribunal for the Former Yugoslavia also concluded in the *Tadic* judgment that:

"if the presence can be shown or inferred, by circumstantial or other evidence, to be knowing and to have a direct and substantial effect on the commission of the illegal act, then it is sufficient on which to base a finding of participation and assign the criminal culpability that accompanies it."

....

[Later in its decision, the Chambers applied the foregoing legal analysis to the facts in the case.]

7.8. Count 1 – Genocide, Count 2 – Complicity in Genocide

Count 1 relates to all the events described in the Indictment. The Prosecutor submits that by his acts alleged in paragraphs 12 to 23 of the Indictment, Akayesu committed the crime of genocide, punishable under Article 2(3)(a) of the Statute.

Count 2 also relates to all the acts alleged in paragraphs 12 to 23 of the Indictment. The Prosecutor alleges that, by the said acts, the accused committed the crime of complicity in genocide, punishable under Article 2(3)(e) of the Statute.

In its findings on the applicable law, the Chamber indicated *supra* that, in its opinion, the crime of genocide and that of complicity in genocide were two distinct crimes, and that the same person could certainly not be both the principal perpetrator of, and accomplice to, the same offence. Given that genocide and complicity in genocide are mutually exclusive by definition, the accused cannot obviously be found guilty of both these crimes for the same act. However, since the Prosecutor has charged the accused with both genocide and complicity in genocide for each of the alleged acts, the Chamber deems it necessary, in the instant case, to rule on counts 1 and 2 simultaneously, so as to determine, as far as each proven fact is concerned, whether it constituted genocide or complicity in genocide.

Hence the question to be addressed is against which group the genocide was allegedly committed. Although the Prosecutor did not specifically state so in the Indictment, it is obvious, in the light of the context in which the alleged acts were committed, the testimonies presented and the Prosecutor's closing statement, that the genocide was committed against the Tutsi group. Article 2(2) of the Statute, like the Genocide Convention, provides that genocide may be committed against a national, ethnical, racial or religious group. In its findings on the law applicable to the crime of genocide *supra*, the Chamber considered whether the protected groups should be limited to only the four groups specifically mentioned or whether any group, similar to the four groups in terms of its stability and permanence, should also be included. The Chamber found that it was necessary, above all, to respect the intent of the drafters of the Genocide Convention which, according to the *travaux préparatoires*, was clearly to protect any stable and permanent group.

In the light of the facts brought to its attention during the trial, the Chamber is of the opinion that, in Rwanda in 1994, the Tutsi constituted a group referred to as "ethnic" in official classifications. Thus, the identity cards at the time included a reference to "*ubwoko*" in Kinyarwanda or "*ethnie*" (ethnic group) in French which, depending on the case, referred to the designation Hutu or Tutsi, for example. The Chamber further noted that all the Rwandan witnesses who appeared before it invariably answered spontaneously and without hesitation the questions of the Prosecutor regarding their ethnic identity. Accordingly, the Chamber finds that, in any case, at the time of the alleged events, the

Tutsi did indeed constitute a stable and permanent group and were identified as such by all.

In the light of the foregoing, with respect to each of the acts alleged in the Indictment, the Chamber is satisfied beyond reasonable doubt, based on the factual findings it has rendered regarding each of the events described in paragraphs 12 to 23 of the Indictment, of the following:

The Chamber finds that, as pertains to the acts alleged in paragraph 12, it has been established that, throughout the period covered in the Indictment, Akayesu, in his capacity as *bourgmestre*, was responsible for maintaining law and public order in the commune of Taba and that he had effective authority over the communal police. Moreover, as "leader" of Taba commune, of which he was one of the most prominent figures, the inhabitants respected him and followed his orders. Akayesu himself admitted before the Chamber that he had the power to assemble the population and that they obeyed his instructions. It has also been proven that a very large number of Tutsi were killed in Taba between 7 April and the end of June 1994, while Akayesu was *bourgmestre* of the Commune. Knowing of such killings, he opposed them and attempted to prevent them only until 18 April 1994, the date after which he not only stopped trying to maintain law and order in his commune, but was also present during the acts of violence and killings, and sometimes even gave orders himself for bodily or mental harm to be caused to certain Tutsi, and endorsed and even ordered the killing of several Tutsi.

In the opinion of the Chamber, the said acts indeed incur the individual criminal responsibility of Akayesu for having ordered, committed, or otherwise aided and abetted in the preparation or execution of the killing of and causing serious bodily or mental harm to members of the Tutsi group. Indeed, the Chamber holds that the fact that Akayesu, as a local authority, failed to oppose such killings and serious bodily or mental harm constituted a form of tacit encouragement, which was compounded by being present to such criminal acts.

With regard to the acts alleged in paragraphs 12 (A) and 12 (B) of the Indictment, the Prosecutor has shown beyond a reasonable doubt that between 7 April and the end of June 1994, numerous Tutsi who sought refuge at the Taba Bureau communal were frequently beaten by members of the Interahamwe[1] on or near the premises of the Bureau communal. Some of them were killed. Numerous Tutsi women were forced to endure acts of sexual violence, mutilations and rape, often repeatedly, often publicly and often by more than one assailant. Tutsi women were systematically raped, as one female victim testified to by saying that "each time that you met assailants, they raped you". Numerous incidents of such rape and sexual violence against Tutsi women occurred inside or near the Bureau communal. It has been proven that some communal policemen armed with guns and the accused himself were present while some of these rapes and sexual violence were being committed. Furthermore, it is proven that on several occasions, by his presence, his attitude and his utterances, Akayesu encouraged such acts, one particular witness testifying that Akayesu, addressed the Interahamwe who were committing the rapes and said that "never ask me again what a Tutsi woman tastes like". In the opinion of the Chamber, this constitutes tacit encouragement to the rapes that were being committed.

---

[1] [The Interahamwe was the militia of the Mouvement révolutionnaire national pour le développement [MRND]. Ed.'s note.]

In the opinion of the Chamber, the above-mentioned acts with which Akayesu is charged indeed render him individually criminally responsible for having abetted in the preparation or execution of the killings of members of the Tutsi group and the infliction of serious bodily and mental harm on members of said group.

The Chamber found *supra*, with regard to the facts alleged in paragraph 13 of the Indictment, that the Prosecutor failed to demonstrate beyond reasonable doubt that they are established.

As regards the facts alleged in paragraphs 14 and 15 of the Indictment, it is established that in the early hours of 19 April 1994, Akayesu joined a gathering in Gishyeshye and took this opportunity to address the public; he led the meeting and conducted the proceedings. He then called on the population to unite in order to eliminate what he referred to as the sole enemy: the accomplices of the Inkotanyi; and the population understood that he was thus urging them to kill the Tutsi. Indeed, Akayesu himself knew of the impact of his statements on the crowd and of the fact that his call to fight against the accomplices of the Inkotanyi would be understood as exhortations to kill the Tutsi in general. Akayesu who had received from the Interahamwe documents containing lists of names did, in the course of the said gathering, summarize the contents of same to the crowd by pointing out in particular that the names were those of RPF [Rwanda Patriotic Front] accomplices. He specifically indicated to the participants that Ephrem Karangwa's name was on of the lists. Akayesu admitted before the Chamber that during the period in question, that to publicly label someone as an accomplice of the RPF would put such a person in danger. The statements thus made by Akayesu at that gathering immediately led to widespread killings of Tutsi in Taba.

Concerning the acts with which Akayesu is charged in paragraphs 14 and 15 of the Indictment, the Chamber recalls that it has found *supra* that they constitute direct and public incitement to commit genocide, a crime punishable under Article 2(3)(c) of the Statute as distinct from the crime of genocide.

With respect to the Prosecutor's allegations in paragraph 16 of the Indictment, the Chamber is satisfied beyond a reasonable doubt that on 19 April 1994, Akayesu on two occasions threatened to kill victim U, a Tutsi woman, while she was being interrogated. He detained her for several hours at the Bureau communal, before allowing her to leave. In the evening of 20 April 1994, during a search conducted in the home of victim V, a Hutu man, Akayesu directly threatened to kill the latter. Victim V was thereafter beaten with a stick and the butt of a rifle by a communal policeman called Mugenzi and one Francois, a member of the Interahamwe militia, in the presence of the accused. One of victim V's ribs was broken as a result of the beating.

In the opinion of the Chamber, the acts attributed to the accused in connection with victims U and V constitute serious bodily and mental harm inflicted on the two victims. However, while Akayesu does incur individual criminal responsibility by virtue of the acts committed against victim U, a Tutsi, for having committed or otherwise aided and abetted in the infliction of serious bodily and mental harm on a member of the Tutsi group, such acts as committed against victim V were perpetrated against a Hutu and cannot, therefore, constitute a crime of genocide against the Tutsi group.

. . . .

As for the allegations made in paragraph 18 of the Indictment, it is established that on or about 19 April 1994, Akayesu and a group of men under his control were looking for Ephrem Karangwa and destroyed his house and that of his mother. They then went to search the house of Ephrem Karangwa's brother-in-law, in Musambira commune and found his three brothers there. When the three brothers, namely Simon Mutijima, Thaddee Uwanyiligira and Jean-Chrysostome, tried to escape, Akayesu ordered that they be captured, and ordered that they be killed, and participated in their killing.

The Chamber holds that these acts indeed render Akayesu individually criminally responsible for having ordered, committed, aided and abetted in the preparation or execution of the killings of members of the Tutsi group and the infliction of serious bodily and mental harm on members of said group.

Regarding the allegations in paragraph 19, the Chamber is satisfied that it has been established that on or about 19 April 1994, Akayesu took from Taba communal prison eight refugees from Runda commune, handed them over to Interahamwe militiamen and ordered that they be killed. They were killed by the Interahamwe using various traditional weapons, including machetes and small axes, in front of the Bureau communal and in the presence of Akayesu who told the killers "do it quickly". The refugees were killed because they were Tutsi.

The Chamber holds that by virtue of such acts, Akayesu incurs individual criminal liability for having ordered, aided and abetted in the perpetration of the killings of members of the Tutsi group and in the infliction of serious bodily and mental harm on members of said group.

The Prosecutor has proved that, as alleged in paragraph 20 of the Indictment, on that same day, Akayesu ordered the local people to kill intellectuals and to look for one Samuel, a professor who was then brought to the Bureau communal and killed with a machete blow to the neck. Teachers in Taba commune were killed later, on Akayesu's instructions. The victims included the following: Tharcisse Twizeyumuremye, Theogene, Phoebe Uwineze and her fiancé whose name is unknown. They were killed on the road in front of the Bureau communal by the local people and the Interahamwe with machetes and agricultural tools. Akayesu personally witnessed the killing of Tharcisse.

In the opinion of the Chamber, Akayesu is indeed individually criminally responsible by virtue of such acts for having ordered, aided and abetted in the preparation or execution of the killings of members of the Tutsi group and in the infliction of serious bodily and mental harm on members of said group.

The Chamber finds that the acts alleged in paragraph 21 have been proven. It has been established that on the evening of 20 April 1994, Akayesu, and two Interahamwe militiamen and a communal policeman, one Mugenzi, who was armed at the time of the events in question, went to the house of Victim Y, a 69 year old Hutu woman, to interrogate her on the whereabouts of Alexia, the wife of Professor Ntereye. During the questioning which took place in the presence of Akayesu, the victim was hit and beaten several times. In particular, she was hit with the barrel of a rifle on the head by the communal policeman. She was forcibly taken away and ordered by Akayesu to lie on the ground. Akayesu himself beat her on her back with a stick. Later on, he had her lie down in front of a vehicle and threatened to drive over her if she failed to give the information he sought.

Although the above acts constitute serious bodily and mental harm inflicted on the victim, the Chamber notes that they were committed against a Hutu woman. Consequently, they cannot constitute acts of genocide against the Tutsi group.

As regards the allegations in paragraphs 22 and 23 of the Indictment, the Chamber is satisfied beyond reasonable doubt that on the evening of 20 April 1994, in the course of an interrogation, Akayesu forced victim W to lay down in front of a vehicle and threatened to drive over her. That same evening, Akayesu, accompanied by Mugenzi, a communal policeman, and one François, an Interahamwe militiaman, interrogated victims Z and Y. The accused put his foot on the face of victim Z, causing the said victim to bleed, while the police officer and the militiaman beat the victim with the butt of their rifles. The militiaman forced victim Z to beat victim Y with a stick. The two victims were tied together, causing victim Z to suffocate. Victim Z was also beaten on the back with the blade of a machete.

The Chamber holds that by virtue of the above-mentioned acts Akayesu is individually criminally responsible for having ordered, committed, aided and abetted in the preparation or infliction of serious bodily or mental harm on members of the Tutsi group.

From the foregoing, the Chamber is satisfied beyond a reasonable doubt, that Akayesu is individually criminally responsible, under Article 6(1) of the Statute, for having ordered, committed or otherwise aided and abetted in the commission of the acts described above in the findings made by the Chamber on paragraphs 12, 12A, 12B, 16, 18, 19, 20, 22 and 23 of the Indictment, acts which constitute the killing of members of the Tutsi group and the infliction of serious bodily and mental harm on members of said group.

Since the Prosecutor charged both genocide and complicity in genocide with respect to each of the above-mentioned acts, and since, as indicated *supra*, the Chamber is of the opinion that these charges are mutually exclusive, it must rule whether each of such acts constitutes genocide or complicity in genocide.

In this connection, the Chamber recalls that, in its findings on the applicable law, it held that an accused is an accomplice to genocide if he or she knowingly and wilfully aided or abetted or instigated another to commit a crime of genocide, while being aware of his genocidal plan, even where the accused had no specific intent to destroy, in whole or in part, a national, ethnical, racial or religious group, as such. It also found that Article 6(1) of the Statute provides for a form of participation through aiding and abetting which, though akin to the factual elements of complicity, nevertheless entails, in and of itself, the individual responsibility of the accused for the crime of genocide, in particular, where the accused had the specific intent to commit genocide, that is, the intent to destroy a particular group; this latter requirement is not needed where an accomplice to genocide is concerned.

Therefore, it is incumbent upon the Chamber to decide, in this instant case, whether or not Akayesu had a specific genocidal intent when he participated in the above-mentioned crimes, that is, the intent to destroy, in whole or in part, a group as such.

As stated in its findings on the law applicable to the crime of genocide, the Chamber holds the view that the intent underlying an act can be inferred from a number of facts. The Chamber is of the opinion that it is possible to infer the genocidal intention that presided over the commission of a particular act, *inter alia*, from all acts or utterances of the accused, or from the general context in which other culpable acts were perpetrated systematically against the same group, regardless of whether such other acts were committed by the same perpetrator or even by other perpetrators.

First of all, regarding Akayesu's acts and utterances during the period relating to the acts alleged in the Indictment, the Chamber is satisfied beyond reasonable doubt, on the basis of all evidence brought to its attention during the trial, that on several occasions the accused made speeches calling, more or less explicitly, for the commission of genocide. The Chamber, in particular, held in its findings on Count 4, that the accused incurred individual criminal responsibility for the crime of direct and public incitement to commit genocide. Yet, according to the Chamber, the crime of direct and public incitement to commit genocide lies in the intent to directly lead or provoke another to commit genocide, which implies that he who incites to commit genocide also has the specific intent to commit genocide: that is, to destroy, in whole or in part, a national, ethnical, racial or religious group, as such.

Furthermore, the Chamber has already established that genocide was committed against the Tutsi group in Rwanda in 1994, throughout the period covering the events alleged in the Indictment. Owing to the very high number of atrocities committed against the Tutsi, their widespread nature not only in the commune of Taba, but also throughout Rwanda, and to the fact that the victims were systematically and deliberately selected because they belonged to the Tutsi group, with persons belonging to other groups being excluded, the Chamber is also able to infer, beyond reasonable doubt, the genocidal intent of the accused in the commission of the above-mentioned crimes.

With regard, particularly, to the acts described in paragraphs 12(A) and 12(B) of the Indictment, that is, rape and sexual violence, the Chamber wishes to underscore the fact that in its opinion, they constitute genocide in the same way as any other act as long as they were committed with the specific intent to destroy, in whole or in part, a particular group, targeted as such. Indeed, rape and sexual violence certainly constitute infliction of serious bodily and mental harm on the victims and are even, according to the Chamber, one of the worst ways of inflict harm on the victim as he or she suffers both bodily and mental harm. In light of all the evidence before it, the Chamber is satisfied that the acts of rape and sexual violence described above, were committed solely against Tutsi women, many of whom were subjected to the worst public humiliation, mutilated, and raped several times, often in public, in the Bureau Communal premises or in other public places, and often by more than one assailant. These rapes resulted in physical and psychological destruction of Tutsi women, their families and their communities. Sexual violence was an integral part of the process of destruction, specifically targeting Tutsi women and specifically contributing to their destruction and to the destruction of the Tutsi group as a whole.

The rape of Tutsi women was systematic and was perpetrated against all Tutsi women and solely against them. A Tutsi woman, married to a Hutu, testified before the Chamber that she was not raped because her ethnic background was unknown. As part of the propaganda campaign geared to mobilizing the Hutu against the Tutsi, the Tutsi women were presented as sexual objects. Indeed, the Chamber was told, for an example, that before being raped and killed, Alexia, who was the wife of the Professor, Ntereye, and her two nieces, were forced by the Interahamwe to undress and ordered to run and do exercises "in order to display the thighs of Tutsi women". The Interahamwe who raped Alexia said, as he threw her on the ground and got on top of her, "let us now see what the vagina of a Tutsi woman tastes like". As stated above, Akayesu himself, speaking to the Interahamwe who were committing the rapes, said to them: "don't ever ask again what a Tutsi woman tastes like". This sexualized representation of ethnic identity graphically illustrates that Tutsi women were subjected to sexual violence because they were Tutsi.

Sexual violence was a step in the process of destruction of the Tutsi group – destruction of the spirit, of the will to live, and of life itself.

On the basis of the substantial testimonies brought before it, the Chamber finds that in most cases, the rapes of Tutsi women in Taba, were accompanied with the intent to kill those women. Many rapes were perpetrated near mass graves where the women were taken to be killed. A victim testified that Tutsi women caught could be taken away by peasants and men with the promise that they would be collected later to be executed. Following an act of gang rape, a witness heard Akayesu say "tomorrow they will be killed" and they were actually killed. In this respect, it appears clearly to the Chamber that the acts of rape and sexual violence, as other acts of serious bodily and mental harm committed against the Tutsi, reflected the determination to make Tutsi women suffer and to mutilate them even before killing them, the intent being to destroy the Tutsi group while inflicting acute suffering on its members in the process.

In light of the foregoing, the Chamber finds firstly that the acts described *supra* are indeed acts as enumerated in Article 2 (2) of the Statute, which constitute the factual elements of the crime of genocide, namely the killings of Tutsi or the serious bodily and mental harm inflicted on the Tutsi. The Chamber is further satisfied beyond reasonable doubt that these various acts were committed by Akayesu with the specific intent to destroy the Tutsi group, as such. Consequently, the Chamber is of the opinion that the acts alleged in paragraphs 12, 12A, 12B, 16, 18, 19, 20, 22 and 23 of the Indictment and proven above, constitute the crime of genocide, but not the crime of complicity; hence, the Chamber finds Akayesu individually criminally responsible for genocide.

. . . .

[Earlier in its decision, the ICT-R addressed the charge of incitement.]

6.3.3. Direct and Public Incitement to Commit Genocide

. . . .

Under count 4, the Prosecutor charges Akayesu with direct and public incitement to commit genocide, a crime punishable under Article 2(3)(c) of the Statute.

Perhaps the most famous conviction for incitement to commit crimes of international dimension was that of Julius Streicher by the Nuremberg Tribunal for the virulently anti-Semitic articles which he had published in his weekly newspaper DER STÜRMER. The Nuremberg Tribunal found that: "Streicher's incitement to murder and extermination, at the time when Jews in the East were being killed under the most horrible conditions, clearly constitutes persecution on political and racial grounds in connection with War Crimes, as defined by the Charter, and constitutes a Crime against Humanity".

At the time the Convention on Genocide was adopted, the delegates agreed to expressly spell out direct and public incitement to commit genocide as a specific crime, in particular, because of its critical role in the planning of a genocide, with the delegate from the USSR stating in this regard that, "It was impossible that hundreds of thousands of people should commit so many crimes unless they had been incited to do so and unless the crimes had been premeditated and carefully organized. He asked how in those circumstances, the inciters and organizers of the crime could be allowed to escape punishment, when they were the ones really responsible for the atrocities committed".

Under Common law systems, incitement tends to be viewed as a particular form of criminal participation, punishable as such. Similarly, under the legislation of some Civil law countries, including Argentina, Bolivia, Chili, Peru, Spain, Uruguay and Venezuela, provocation, which is similar to incitement, is a specific form of participation in an offence; but in most Civil law systems, incitement is most often treated as a form of complicity.

The Rwandan Penal Code is one such legislation. Indeed, as stated above, in the discussion on complicity in genocide, it does provide that direct and public incitement or provocation is a form of complicity. In fact, Article 91 subparagraph 4 provides that an accomplice shall mean "A person or persons who, whether through speeches, shouting or threats uttered in public places or at public gatherings, or through the sale or dissemination, offer for sale or display of written material or printed matter in public places or at public gatherings or through the public display of placards or posters, directly incite(s) the perpetrator or perpetrators to commit such an action without prejudice to the penalties applicable to those who incite others to commit offences, even where such incitement fails to produce results."

Under the Statute, direct and public incitement is expressly defined as a specific crime, punishable as such, by virtue of Article 2(3)(c). With respect to such a crime, the Chamber deems it appropriate to first define the three terms: incitement, direct and public.

Incitement is defined in Common law systems as encouraging or persuading another to commit an offence. One line of authority in Common law would also view threats or other forms of pressure as a form of incitement. As stated above, Civil law systems punish direct and public incitement assuming the form of provocation, which is defined as an act intended to directly provoke another to commit a crime or a misdemeanour through speeches, shouting or threats, or any other means of audiovisual communication. Such a provocation, as defined under Civil law, is made up of the same elements as direct and public incitement to commit genocide covered by Article 2 of the Statute, that is to say it is both direct and public.

The public element of incitement to commit genocide may be better appreciated in light of two factors: the place where the incitement occurred and whether or not assistance was selective or limited. A line of authority commonly followed in Civil law systems would regard words as being public where they were spoken aloud in a place that were public by definition. According to the International Law Commission, public incitement is characterized by a call for criminal action to a number of individuals in a public place or to members of the general public at large by such means as the mass media, for example, radio or television. It should be noted in this respect that at the time Convention on Genocide was adopted, the delegates specifically agreed to rule out the possibility of including private incitement to commit genocide as a crime, thereby underscoring their commitment to set aside for punishment only the truly public forms of incitement.

The "direct" element of incitement implies that the incitement assume a direct form and specifically provoke another to engage in a criminal act, and that more than mere vague or indirect suggestion goes to constitute direct incitement. Under Civil law systems, provocation, the equivalent of incitement, is regarded as being direct where it is aimed at causing a specific offence to be committed. The prosecution must prove a definite causation between the act characterized as incitement, or provocation in this case, and a specific offence. However, the Chamber is of the opinion that the direct element of incitement should be viewed in the light of its cultural and linguistic content. Indeed, a particular speech may be perceived as "direct" in one country, and not so in another, depending on the audience. The Chamber further recalls that incitement may be direct, and nonetheless implicit. Thus, at the time the Convention on Genocide was being drafted, the Polish delegate observed that it was sufficient to play skillfully on mob psychology by casting suspicion on certain groups, by insinuating that they were responsible for economic or other difficulties in order to create an atmosphere favourable to the perpetration of the crime.

The Chamber will therefore consider on a case-by-case basis whether, in light of the culture of Rwanda and the specific circumstances of the instant case, acts of incitement can be viewed as direct or not, by focusing mainly on the issue of whether the persons for whom the message was intended immediately grasped the implication thereof.

In light of the foregoing, it can be noted in the final analysis that whatever the legal system, direct and public incitement must be defined for the purposes of interpreting Article 2(3)(c), as directly provoking the perpetrator(s) to commit genocide, whether through speeches, shouting or threats uttered in public places or at public gatherings, or through the sale or dissemination, offer for sale or display of written material or printed matter in public places or at public gatherings, or through the public display of placards or posters, or through any other means of audiovisual communication.

The *mens rea* required for the crime of direct and public incitement to commit genocide lies in the intent to directly prompt or provoke another to commit genocide. It implies a desire on the part of the perpetrator to create by his actions a particular state of mind necessary to commit such a crime in the minds of the person(s) he is so engaging. That is to say that the person who is inciting to commit genocide must have himself the specific intent to commit genocide, namely, to destroy, in whole or in part, a national, ethnical, racial or religious group, as such.

Therefore, the issue before the Chamber is whether the crime of direct and public incitement to commit genocide can be punished even where such incitement was unsuccessful. It appears from the *travaux préparatoires* of the Convention on Genocide that the drafters of the Convention considered stating explicitly that incitement to commit genocide could be punished, whether or not it was successful. In the end, a majority decided against such an approach. Nevertheless, the Chamber is of the opinion that it cannot thereby be inferred that the intent of the drafters was not to punish unsuccessful acts of incitement. In light of the overall *travaux*, the Chamber holds the view that the drafters of the Convention simply decided not to specifically mention that such a form of incitement could be punished.

There are under Common law so-called inchoate offences, which are punishable by virtue of the criminal act alone, irrespective of the result thereof, which may or may not have been achieved. The Civil law counterparts of inchoate offences are known as [*infractions formelles*] (acts constituting an offence per se irrespective of their results), as opposed to [*infractions matérielles*] (strict liability offences). Indeed, as is the case with inchoate offenses, in [*infractions formelles*], the method alone is punishable. Put another way, such offenses are "deemed to have been consummated regardless of the result achieved [unofficial translation]" contrary to [*infractions matérielles*]. Indeed, Rwandan lawmakers appear to characterize the acts defined under Article 91(4) of the Rwandan

Penal Code as so-called [*infractions formelles*], since provision is made for their punishment even where they proved unsuccessful. It should be noted, however, that such offences are the exception, the rule being that in theory, an offence can only be punished in relation to the result envisaged by the lawmakers. In the opinion of the Chamber, the fact that such acts are in themselves particularly dangerous because of the high risk they carry for society, even if they fail to produce results, warrants that they be punished as an exceptional measure. The Chamber holds that genocide clearly falls within the category of crimes so serious that direct and public incitement to commit such a crime must be punished as such, even where such incitement failed to produce the result expected by the perpetrator.

. . . .

[Later in its decision, the Chambers applied the facts to the foregoing legal analysis.]

7.5 Count 4 – Direct and Public Incitement to Commit Genocide

Count 4 deals with the allegations described in paragraphs 14 and 15 of the Indictment, relating, essentially, to the speeches that Akayesu reportedly made at a meeting held in Gishyeshye on 19 April 1994. The Prosecutor alleges that, through his speeches, Akayesu committed the crime of direct and public incitement to commit genocide, a crime punishable under Article 2(3)(c) of the Statute.

The Trial Chamber made the following factual findings on the events described in paragraphs 14 and 15 of the Indictment. The Chamber is satisfied beyond a reasonable doubt that: (i) Akayesu, in the early hours of 19 April 1994, joined a crowd of over 100 people which had gathered around the body of a young member of the Interahamwe in Gishyeshye. (ii) He seized that opportunity to address the people and, owing, particularly, to his functions as *bourgmestre* and his authority over the population, he led the gathering and the proceedings. (iii) It has been established that Akayesu then clearly urged the population to unite in order to eliminate what he termed the sole enemy: the accomplices of the Inkotanyi. (iv) On the basis of consistent testimonies heard throughout the proceedings and the evidence of Dr. Ruzindana, appearing as expert witness on linguistic matters, the Chamber is satisfied beyond a reasonable doubt that the population understood Akayesu's call as one to kill the Tutsi. Akayesu himself was fully aware of the impact of his speech on the crowd and of the fact that his call to fight against the accomplices of the Inkotanyi would be construed as a call to kill the Tutsi in general. (v) During the said meeting, Akayesu received from the Interahamwe documents which included lists of names, and read from the lists to the crowd by stating, in particular, that the names were those of RPF accomplices. (vi) Akayesu testified that the lists contained, especially, the name of Ephrem Karangwa, whom he named specifically, while being fully aware of the consequences of doing so. Indeed, he admitted before the Chamber that, at the time of the events alleged in the Indictment, to label anyone in public as an accomplice of the RPF would put such a person in danger. (vii) The Chamber is of the opinion that there is a causal relationship between Akayesu's speeches at the gathering of 19 April 1994 and the ensuing widespread massacres of Tutsi in Taba.

From the foregoing, the Chamber is satisfied beyond a reasonable doubt that, by the above-mentioned speeches made in public and in a public place, Akayesu had the intent to directly create a particular state of mind in his audience necessary to lead to the destruction of the Tutsi group, as such. Accordingly, the Chamber finds that the said acts constitute the crime of direct and public incitement to commit genocide, as defined above.

In addition, the Chamber finds that the direct and public incitement to commit genocide as engaged in by Akayesu, was indeed successful and did lead to the destruction of a great number of Tutsi in the commune of Taba.

∾

QUESTIONS & COMMENTS

(1) Could private arms dealers who provide weapons to persons committing genocide be considered guilty of complicity?

(2) Consider the following excerpt from ICT-Y Trial Chamber's decision in *The Prosecutor v. Furundzija*:

> 12. The application of the Appeals Chamber's finding by the Defence is flawed. All grave breaches [of the Geneva Conventions] are violations of the laws and customs of war. Theoretically, they can be charged as both if the criteria are satisfied. However, there is a general principle of international law (the doctrine of speciality/*lex specialis derogat generali*) which provides that in a choice between two provisions where one has a broader scope and completely encompasses the other, the more specific charge should be chosen. Nevertheless, the situation at hand is not one where the Trial Chamber is faced with different charges under separate articles of the Statute. The Prosecution has already made a choice and has withdrawn the specific charge alleging grave breaches of the Geneva Conventions. It is the finding of the Trial Chamber that the Prosecution is justified in relying on the residual clause to ensure that no serious violation of international humanitarian law escapes the jurisdiction of the International Tribunal. This is fully in line with the reasoning of the Appeals Chamber Decision.

The Prosecutor v. Furundzija, Int'l Crim Trib.-Yugo, Decision on the Defendant's Motion to Dismiss Counts 13 and 14 of the Indictment (Lack of Subject Matter Jurisdiction), Order of 29 May 1998, at §12. Recall that genocide is considered a crime against humanity. *Prosecutor v. Tadic*, at §655. Does the international law doctrine of speciality preclude the possibility that someone can be held culpable for both genocide and crimes against humanity?

(3) In *Prosecutor v. Brdjanin*, Case No. IT-99-36 (19 March 2004), the ICTY Appeals Chamber clarified that a person can be found guilty of genocide even though that person does not have a specific intent to destroy an ethnic or religious group in whole or in part. All that is required is that the person enter into a joint criminal enterprise of which genocide is a reasonably foreseeable consequence and it occurs.

Has the ICTY unlawfully expanded the definition of genocide?

(4) The ICTR in *Prosecutor v. Ruggiu*, Case No. ICTR-97-32-I, ICTR-Trial Chamber (1 June 2000), noted that "at the time the Convention on Genocide was adopted, the delegates agreed to expressly spell out direct and public incitement to commit genocide as a specific crime, in particular, because of its critical role in the planning of a genocide." Is it helpful to understand incitement as an act in furtherance of a conspiracy to commit genocide? Is it possible to incite genocide without a receptive audience?

(5) U.S. law prohibits genocide under 18 U.S.C. §1091:

(a) Basic Offense. – Whoever, whether in time of peace or in time of war, in a circumstance described in subsection (d) and with the specific intent to destroy, in whole or in substantial part, a national, ethnic, racial, or religious group as such –

(1) kills members of that group;

(2) causes serious bodily injury to members of that group;

(3) causes the permanent impairment of the mental faculties of members of the group through drugs, torture, or similar techniques;

(4) subjects the group to conditions of life that are intended to cause the physical destruction of the group in whole or in part;
...shall be punished as provided in subsection (b).

(b) Punishment for Basic Offense. – The punishment for an offense under subsection (a) is –

(1) in the case of an offense under subsection (a)(1),...where death results, by death or imprisonment for life and a fine of not more than $1,000,000, or both; and....

(2) a fine of not more than $1,000,000 or imprisonment for not more than twenty years, or both, in any other case.

(c) Incitement Offense. – Whoever in a circumstance described in subsection (d) directly and publicly incites another to violate subsection (a) shall be fined not more than $500,000 or imprisoned not more than five years, or both.

(d) Required Circumstance for Offenses. – The circumstance referred to in subsections (a) and (c) is that –

(1) the offense is committed within the United States; or

(2) the alleged offender is a national of the United States (as defined in section 101 of the Immigration and Nationality Act (8 U.S.C. 1101)).

(e) Nonapplicability of Certain Limitations. – Notwithstanding section 3282 of this title, in the case of an offense under subsection (a)(1), an indictment may be found, or information instituted, at any time without limitation.

(7) Would Ruggiu's conviction for inciting genocide withstand First Amendment scrutiny?

(8) Compare the international human rights law guaranteeing freedom of expression in Section 5.6 to the humanitarian law prohibiting incitement of genocide.

5.2.2. Crimes Against Humanity

Charter of the International Military Tribunal

Article 6

. . . .

The following acts, or any of them, are crimes coming within the jurisdiction of the Tribunal for which there shall be individual responsibility:

. . . .

(c) CRIMES AGAINST HUMANITY: namely, murder, extermination, enslavement, deportation, and other inhumane acts committed against any civilian population, before or during the war; or persecutions on political, racial or religious grounds in execution of or in connection with any crime within the jurisdiction of the Tribunal, whether or not in violation of the domestic law of the country where perpetrated.

Statute of the International Criminal Court

Article 5

Crimes within the jurisdiction of the Court

1. The jurisdiction of the Court shall be limited to the most serious crimes of concern to the international community as a whole. The Court has jurisdiction in accordance with this Statute with respect to the following crimes:

. . .

(b) Crimes against humanity;

. . . .

Article 7

Crimes against humanity

1. For the purpose of this Statute, "crime against humanity" means any of the following acts when committed as part of a widespread or systematic attack directed against any civilian population, with knowledge of the attack:

(a) Murder;

(b) Extermination;

(c) Enslavement;

(d) Deportation or forcible transfer of population;

(e) Imprisonment or other severe deprivation of physical liberty in violation of fundamental rules of international law;

(f) Torture;

(g) Rape, sexual slavery, enforced prostitution, forced pregnancy, enforced sterilization, or any other form of sexual violence of comparable gravity;

(h) Persecution against any identifiable group or collectivity on political, racial, national, ethnic, cultural, religious, gender as defined in paragraph 3, or other grounds that are universally recognized as impermissible under international law, in connection with any act referred to in this paragraph or any crime within the jurisdiction of the Court;

(i) Enforced disappearance of persons;

(j) The crime of apartheid;

(k) Other inhumane acts of a similar character intentionally causing great suffering, or serious injury to body or to mental or physical health.

2. For the purpose of paragraph 1:

(a) "Attack directed against any civilian population" means a course of conduct involving the multiple commission of acts referred to in paragraph 1 against any civilian population, pursuant to or in furtherance of a State or organizational policy to commit such attack;

(b) "Extermination" includes the intentional infliction of conditions of life, *inter alia* the deprivation of access to food and medicine, calculated to bring about the destruction of part of a population;

(c) "Enslavement" means the exercise of any or all of the powers attaching to the right of ownership over a person and includes the exercise of such power in the course of trafficking in persons, in particular women and children;

(d) "Deportation or forcible transfer of population" means forced displacement of the persons concerned by expulsion or other coercive acts from the area in which they are lawfully present, without grounds permitted under international law;

(e) "Torture" means the intentional infliction of severe pain or suffering, whether physical or mental, upon a person in the custody or under the control of the accused; except that torture shall not include pain or suffering arising only from, inherent in or incidental to, lawful sanctions;

(f) "Forced pregnancy" means the unlawful confinement, of a woman forcibly made pregnant, with the intent of affecting the ethnic composition of any population or carrying out other grave violations of international law. This definition shall not in any way be interpreted as affecting national laws relating to pregnancy;

(g) "Persecution" means the intentional and severe deprivation of fundamental rights contrary to international law by reason of the identity of the group or collectivity;

(h) "The crime of apartheid" means inhumane acts of a character similar to those referred to in paragraph 1, committed in the context of an institutionalized regime of systematic oppression and domination by one racial group over any other racial group or groups and committed with the intention of maintaining that regime;

(i) "Enforced disappearance of persons" means the arrest, detention or abduction of persons by, or with the authorization, support or acquiescence of, a State or a political organization, followed by a refusal to acknowledge that deprivation of freedom or to give information on the fate or whereabouts of those persons, with the intention of removing them from the protection of the law for a prolonged period of time.

3. For the purpose of this Statute, it is understood that the term "gender" refers to the two sexes, male and female, within the context of society. The term "gender" does not indicate any meaning different from the above.

Statute of the International Tribunal for the Former Yugoslavia

Article 5

Crimes against humanity

The International Tribunal shall have the power to prosecute persons responsible for the following crimes when committed in armed conflict, whether international or internal in character, and directed against any civilian population:

(a) murder;
(b) extermination;
(c) enslavement;
(d) deportation;

(e) imprisonment;

(f) torture;

(g) rape;

(h) persecutions on political, racial and religious grounds;

(i) other inhumane acts.

The Prosecutor v. Tadić (Final Judgment)
Case No. IT-94-1-T
Trial Chamber
International Criminal Tribunal for the Former Yugoslavia
(7 May 1997)

[Tadic was indicted for committing grave breaches of the Geneva Conventions (*viz.*, wilful killing, torture or inhuman treatment, and wilfully causing great suffering or serious injury to body and health), violations of the laws and customs of war (*viz.*, murder and cruel treatment), and crimes against humanity (*viz.*, murder, persecution, and inhumane acts) at Kozarac and the Omarska concentration camp in the former Yugoslavia in June 1992. He was arrested in Germany in February 1994 and turned over to the ICT-Y. He pleaded not guilty.

The Chamber of the ICT-Y examined the testimony of dozens of witnesses and documentary evidence. The following excerpts from the Chamber's judgment address the international law governing the substantive offenses.]

557. Having considered the evidence offered at trial, it is now appropriate to discuss the law relating to the offences charged.

558. The competence of this International Tribunal and hence of this Trial Chamber is determined by the terms of the Statute. Article 1 of the Statute confers power to prosecute persons responsible for serious violations of international humanitarian law committed in the territory of the former Yugoslavia since 1991. The Statute then, in Articles 2, 3, 4 and 5, specifies the crimes under international law over which the International Tribunal has jurisdiction. In the present case, only Articles 2, 3 and 5 are relevant. . . .

559. Each of the relevant Articles of the Statute, either by its terms or by virtue of the customary rules which it imports, proscribes certain acts when committed "within the context of" an "armed conflict". Article 2 of the Statute directs the Trial Chamber to the grave breaches regime of the Geneva Conventions which applies only to armed conflicts of an international character and to offences committed against persons or property regarded as "protected", in particular civilians in the hands of a party to a conflict of which they are not nationals[ ]. Article 3 of the Statute directs the Trial Chamber to those sources of customary international humanitarian law that comprise the "laws or customs of war". Article 3 is a general provision covering, subject to certain conditions, all violations of international humanitarian law which do not fall under Article 2 or are not covered by Articles 4 or 5. This includes violations of the rules contained in Article 3 common to the Geneva Conventions ("Common Article 3"), applicable to armed conflicts in general, with which the accused has been charged under Article 3 of the Statute[ ]. Article 5 of the Statute directs the Trial Chamber to crimes against humanity proscribed by customary international humanitarian law. By virtue of the Statute, those crimes must also occur in the context of an armed conflict, whether international or non-international

in character. An armed conflict exists for the purposes of the application of Article 5 if it is found to exist for the purposes of either Article 2 or Article 3.[ ]

. . . .

[Article 5 Crimes Against Humanity]

. . . .

623. . . . [S]ince the Nürnberg Charter, the customary status of the prohibition against crimes against humanity and the attribution of individual criminal responsibility for their commission have not been seriously questioned. It would seem that this finding is implicit in *the Appeals Chamber Decision* which found that "[i]t is by now a settled rule of customary international law that crimes against humanity do not require a connection to international armed conflict"[ ].

. . . .

626. Article 5 of the Statute grants the International Tribunal jurisdiction to prosecute crimes against humanity only "when committed in armed conflict" (whether international or internal) and they must be "directed against any civilian population". These conditions contain within them several elements. The Prosecution argues that the elements of crimes against humanity are: (1) that the accused committed one of the acts enumerated in Article 5; (2) the acts were committed during an armed conflict; (3) at the time of the commission of the acts or omissions there was an ongoing widespread or systematic attack directed against a civilian population; and (4) the accused knew or had reason to know that by his acts or omission, he was participating in the attack on the population. The Defence for the most part agrees with these elements, although it argues that: (1) the crimes must be committed *in* an armed conflict; and (2) the attack must be widespread *and* systematic. The Trial Chamber's determination of the conditions of applicability, as elaborated below, is that, first, "when committed in armed conflict" necessitates the existence of an armed conflict and a nexus between the act and that conflict. Secondly, "directed against any civilian population" is interpreted to include a broad definition of the term "civilian". It furthermore requires that the acts be undertaken on a widespread or systematic basis and in furtherance of a policy. The *Report of the Secretary-General* and the interpretation of several Security Council members reveal the additional requirement that all relevant acts must be undertaken on discriminatory grounds. Finally, the perpetrator must have knowledge of the wider context in which his act occurs.

627. Article 5 of the Statute, addressing crimes against humanity, grants the International Tribunal jurisdiction over the enumerated acts "when committed in armed conflict". The requirement of an armed conflict is similar to that of Article 6(c) of the Nürnberg Charter which limited the Nürnberg Tribunal's jurisdiction to crimes against humanity committed "before or during the war", although in the case of the Nürnberg Tribunal jurisdiction was further limited by requiring that crimes against humanity be committed "in execution of or in connection with" war crimes or crimes against peace[ ] . Despite this precedent, the inclusion of the requirement of an armed conflict deviates from the development of the doctrine after the Nürnberg Charter, beginning with Control Council Law No. 10, which no longer links the concept of crimes against humanity with an armed conflict. As the Secretary-General stated: "Crimes against humanity are aimed at any civilian population and are prohibited regardless of whether they are

committed in an armed conflict, international or internal in character."[ ] In the Statute of the International Tribunal for Rwanda the requirement of an armed conflict is omitted, requiring only that the acts be committed as part of an attack against a civilian population[ ]. The Appeals Chamber has stated that, by incorporating the requirement of an armed conflict, "the Security Council may have defined the crime in Article 5 more narrowly than necessary under customary international law"[ ], having stated earlier that "[s]ince customary international law no longer requires any nexus between crimes against humanity and armed conflict... Article 5 was intended to reintroduce this nexus for the purposes of this Tribunal."[ ] Accordingly, its existence must be proved, as well as the link between the act or omission charged and the armed conflict.

628. The Appeals Chamber ... stated that "an armed conflict exists whenever there is a resort to armed force between States or protracted armed violence between governmental authorities and organized armed groups or between such groups within a State."[ ] Consequently, this is the test which the Trial Chamber has applied and it has concluded that the evidence establishes the existence of an armed conflict.

629. The next issue which must be addressed is the required nexus between the act or omission and the armed conflict. The Prosecution argues that to establish the nexus necessary for a violation of Article 5 it is sufficient to demonstrate that the crimes were committed at some point in the course or duration of an armed conflict, even if such crimes were not committed in direct relation to or as part of the conduct of hostilities, occupation, or other integral aspects of the armed conflict. In contrast the Defence argues that the act must be committed "in" armed conflict.

630. The Statute does not elaborate on the required link between the act and the armed conflict. Nor, for that matter, does the *Appeals Chamber Decision*, although it contains several statements that are relevant in this regard. First is the finding, noted above, that the Statute is more restrictive than custom in that "customary international law no longer requires any nexus between crimes against humanity and armed conflict"[ ]. Accordingly, it is necessary to determine the degree of nexus which is imported by the Statute by its inclusion of the requirement of an armed conflict. This, then, is a question of statutory interpretation.

631. The *Appeals Chamber Decision* is relevant to this question of statutory interpretation. In addressing Article 3 the Appeals Chamber noted that where interpretative declarations are made by Security Council members and are not contested by other delegations "they can be regarded as providing an authoritative interpretation" of the relevant provisions of the Statute[ ]. Importantly, several permanent members of the Security Council commented that they interpret "when committed in armed conflict" in Article 5 of the Statute to mean "during a period of armed conflict"[ ]. These statements were not challenged and can thus, in line with the *Appeals Chamber Decision*, be considered authoritative interpretations of this portion of Article 5.[ ]

632. The Appeals Chamber, in dismissing the Defence argument that the concept of armed conflict covers only the precise time and place of actual hostilities, said: "It is sufficient that the alleged crimes were closely related to the hostilities occurring in other parts of the territories controlled by the parties to the conflict"[ ]. Thus it is not necessary that the acts occur in the heat of battle....

633. On the basis of the foregoing the Trial Chamber accepts, with some caveats, the Prosecution proposition that it is sufficient for purposes of crimes against humanity that

the act occurred in the course or duration of an armed conflict. The first such caveat, a seemingly obvious one, is that the act be linked geographically as well as temporally with the armed conflict. In this regard it is important to note that the Appeals Chamber found that:

> the temporal and geographic scope of both internal and international armed conflicts extends beyond the exact time and place of hostilities.
>
> . . . .

International humanitarian law applies from the initiation of such armed conflicts and extends beyond the cessation of hostilities until a general conclusion of peace is reached; or, in the case of internal conflicts, a peaceful settlement is achieved. Until that moment, international humanitarian law continues to apply in the whole territory of the warring States or, in the case of internal conflicts, the whole territory under the control of a party, whether or not actual combat takes place there.

634. Secondly, the act and the conflict must be related or, to reverse this proposition, the act must not be *unrelated* to the armed conflict, must not be done for purely personal motives of the perpetrator. This is further discussed below in regard to the level of intent required.

635. The requirement in Article 5 that the enumerated acts be "directed against any civilian population" contains several elements. The inclusion of the word "any" makes it clear that crimes against humanity can be committed against civilians of the same nationality as the perpetrator or those who are stateless, as well as those of a different nationality. However, the remaining aspects, namely the definition of a "civilian" population and the implications of the term "population", require further examination.

636. That the prohibited act must be committed against a "civilian" population itself raises two aspects: what must the character of the targeted population be and how is it to be determined whether an individual victim qualifies as a civilian such that acts taken against the person constitute crimes against humanity?

637. The Statute does not provide any guidance regarding the definition of "civilian" nor, for that matter, does the *Report of the Secretary-General*. The Prosecution in its pre-trial brief argues that the term "civilian" covers "all non-combatants within the meaning of common Article 3 to the [Geneva] Conventions" because of the finding that the language of Common Article 3 reflects "elementary considerations of humanity" which are "applicable under customary international law to any armed conflict"[ ]. The Defence agrees that "civilians" under Article 5 covers all non-combatants, arguing however that the concept of "non-combatants" is not always clear in application. The Defence notes that particularly in situations such as that in Bosnia and Herzegovina, "where groups are mobilising without necessarily being under the direct control of the central government," there is a "grey area" between combatants and non-combatants. Thus the Defence concludes that the notion of non-combatants may not be sufficiently defined to determine in all cases whether the victims were civilians.

638. Regarding the first aspect, it is clear that the targeted population must be of a predominantly civilian nature. The presence of certain non-civilians in their midst does not change the character of the population.[2]

---

2 *See* Article 50(3) of the Protocol Additional to the Geneva Conventions of 12 August 1949, and relating to the Protection of Victims of International Armed Conflicts ("Protocol I") (ICRC, Geneva, 1977); *see also*

639. The second aspect, determining which individual[s] of the targeted population qualify as civilians for purposes of crimes against humanity, is not, however, quite as clear. Common Article 3, the language of which reflects "elementary considerations of humanity" which are "applicable under customary international law to any armed conflict"[ ], provides that in an armed conflict "not of an international character" Contracting States are obliged "as a minimum" to comply with the following: "Persons taking no active part in the hostilities, including members of armed forces who have laid down their arms and those placed *hors de combat* by sickness, wounds, detention, or any other cause, shall in all circumstances be treated humanely...." Protocol Additional to the Geneva Conventions of 12 August 1949, and Relating to the Protection of Victims in International Armed Conflicts (Protocol I)[ ] defines civilians by the exclusion of prisoners of war and armed forces, considering a person a civilian in case of doubt. However, this definition of civilians contained in Common Article 3 is not immediately applicable to crimes against humanity because it is a part of the laws or customs of war and can only be applied by analogy. The same applies to the definition contained in Protocol I and the *Commentary*, Geneva Convention IV, on the treatment of civilians, both of which advocate a broad interpretation of the term "civilian". They, and particularly Common Article 3, do, however, provide guidance in answering the most difficult question: specifically, whether acts taken against an individual who cannot be considered a traditional "non-combatant" because he is actively involved in the conduct of hostilities by membership in some form of resistance group can nevertheless constitute crimes against humanity if they are committed in furtherance or as part of an attack directed against a civilian population.

640. In this regard the United Nations War Crimes Commission stated in reference to Article 6(c) of the Nürnberg Charter that "[t]he words '*civilian* population' appear to indicate that 'crimes against humanity' are restricted to inhumane acts committed against civilians as opposed to members of the armed forces..."[ ]. In contrast, the Supreme Court of the British zone determined that crimes against humanity were applicable in all cases where the perpetrator and the victim were of the same nationality, regardless of whether the victim was civilian or military[ ]. Similarly, the possibility of considering members of the armed forces as potential victims of crimes against humanity was recognized as early as 1946[ ]. The Commission of Experts Established Pursuant to Security Council Resolution 780 ("Commission of Experts") observed: "It seems obvious that article 5 applies first and foremost to civilians, meaning people who are not combatants. This, however, should not lead to any quick conclusions concerning people who at one particular point in time did bear arms."[ ] The Commission of Experts then provided an example based on the situation in the former Yugoslavia and concluded: "A Head of a family who under such circumstances tries to protect his family gun-in-hand does not thereby lose his status as a civilian. Maybe the same is the case for the sole policeman or local defence guard doing the same, even if they joined hands to try to prevent the cataclysm."[ ]

641. Precisely this issue was considered in the case of *Fédération Nationale des Déportés et Internés Résistants et Patriotes and Others v. Barbie* (*Barbie* case). In this case the

---

Fédération Nationale des Déportés et Internés Résistants et Patriotes and Others v. Barbie (*Barbie* case); Final Report of the Commission of Experts Established Pursuant to Security Council Resolution 780 (1992), ("*Final Report of the Commission of Experts*"), paras. 77–78, U.N. Doc. S/1994/674.

Chambre d'accusation of the Court of Appeal of Lyons ordered that an indictment for crimes against humanity be issued against Klaus Barbie, head of the Gestapo of Lyons during the Second World War, but only for "persecutions against innocent Jews", and held that prosecution was barred by the statute of limitations for crimes committed by Barbie against combatants who were members of the Resistance or whom Barbie thought were members of the Resistance, even if they were Jewish, because these acts could only constitute war crimes and not crimes against humanity[ ]. The order of the examining magistrate along the same lines was confirmed by the *Cour d'Assises* and an appeal was lodged. On appeal the *Cour de Cassation* quashed and annulled the judgment in part, holding that members of the Resistance could be victims of crimes against humanity as long as the necessary intent for crimes against humanity was present[ ]. As the court stated, "[n]either the driving force which motivated the victims, nor their possible membership of the Resistance, excludes the possibility that the accused acted with the element of intent necessary for the commission of crimes against humanity."[ ] Thus, according to the *Cour de Cassation*, not only was the general population considered to be one of a civilian character despite the presence of Resistance members in its midst but members of the Resistance themselves could be considered victims of crimes against humanity if the other requisite elements are met.[ ]

642. While instructive, it should be noted that the court in the *Barbie* case was applying national legislation that declared crimes against humanity not subject to statutory limitation, although the national legislation defined crimes against humanity by reference to the United Nations resolution of 13 February 1946, which referred back to the Nürnberg Charter ...; and the fact that a crime against humanity is an international crime was relied upon to deny the accused's appeal on the bases of disguised extradition[ ] and an elapsed statute of limitations[ ].

643. Despite the limitations inherent in the use of these various sources, from Common Article 3 to the *Barbie* case, a wide definition of civilian population, as supported by these sources, is justified. Thus the presence of those actively involved in the conflict should not prevent the characterization of a population as civilian and those actively involved in a resistance movement can qualify as victims of crimes against humanity. As noted by Trial Chamber I of the International Tribunal in its Review of the Indictment Pursuant to Rule 61 of the Rules of Procedure and Evidence in *The Prosecutor v. Mile Msksic, Miroslav Radic, and Veselin Sljivancanin* ("*Vukovar Hospital Decision*")[3], although crimes against humanity must target a civilian population, individuals who at one time performed acts of resistance may in certain circumstances be victims of crimes against humanity[ ]. In the context of that case patients in a hospital, either civilians or resistance fighters who had laid down their arms, were considered victims of crimes against humanity[ ].

644. The requirement in Article 5 of the Statute that the prohibited acts must be directed against a civilian "population" does not mean that the entire population of a given State or territory must be victimised by these acts in order for the acts to constitute a crime against humanity. Instead the "population" element is intended to imply crimes of a collective nature and thus exclude single or isolated acts which, although possibly

---

[3]   *The Prosecutor v. Mile Msksic, Miroslav Radic, and Veselin Sljivancanin*, Review of the Indictment Pursuant to Rule 61 of the Rules of Procedure and Evidence, Case No. IT-95-13-R61, T.Ch.I, 3 Apr. 1996.

constituting war crimes or crimes against national penal legislation, do not rise to the level of crimes against humanity[ ]. As explained by this Trial Chamber in its *Decision on the Form of the Indictment*, the inclusion in Article 5 of the requirement that the acts "be 'directed against any civilian population' ensures that what is to be alleged will not be one particular act but, instead, a course of conduct."[ ] The purpose of this requirement was clearly articulated by the United Nations War Crimes Commission when it wrote that:

> Isolated offences did not fall within the notion of crimes against humanity. As a rule systematic mass action, particularly if it was authoritative, was necessary to transform a common crime, punishable only under municipal law, into a crime against humanity, which thus became also the concern of international law. Only crimes which either by their magnitude and savagery or by their large number or by the fact that a similar pattern was applied at different times and places, endangered the international community or shocked the conscience of mankind, warranted intervention by States other than that on whose territory the crimes had been committed, or whose subjects had become their victims.[ ]

Thus the emphasis is not on the individual victim but rather on the collective, the individual being victimised not because of his individual attributes but rather because of his membership of a targeted civilian population. This has been interpreted to mean, as elaborated below, that the acts must occur on a widespread or systematic basis, that there must be some form of a governmental, organizational or group policy to commit these acts and that the perpetrator must know of the context within which his actions are taken, as well as the requirement imported by the Secretary-General and members of the Security Council that the actions be taken on discriminatory grounds[ ].

645. The Prosecution argues that the term "population" in Article 5 contemplates that by his actions the accused participated in a widespread or systematic attack against a relatively large victim group, as distinct from isolated or random acts against individuals. The Defence, while generally in agreement, argues that in order to constitute a crime against humanity the violations must be both widespread and systematic.

646. While this issue has been the subject of considerable debate, it is now well established that the requirement that the acts be directed against a civilian "population" can be fulfilled if the acts occur on either a widespread basis or in a systematic manner. Either one of these is sufficient to exclude isolated or random acts. The *Report of the Secretary-General* stipulates that crimes against humanity "refer to inhumane acts of a very serious nature ... committed as part of a widespread or systematic attack against any civilian population"[ ]. The Defence points to the fact that later in that same paragraph the Secretary-General states that in the conflict in the former Yugoslavia rape occurred on a "widespread and systematic" basis as support for its proposition that both widespreadness and systematicity are required. However, in the Trial Chamber's view, this passage is no more than a reflection of the situation as the Secretary-General saw it, as was the well-known finding by the Nürnberg Tribunal that "[t]he persecution of the Jews at the hands of the Nazi Government has been proved in the greatest detail before the Tribunal. It is a record of *consistent and systematic* inhumanity on the greatest scale."[ ]

647. In addition to the *Report of the Secretary-General* numerous other sources support the conclusion that widespreadness and systematicity are alternatives. For example,

Trial Chamber I came to this conclusion in the Vukovar Hospital Decision.[ ] The Report of the Ad Hoc Committee on the Establishment of a Permanent International Criminal Court provides that crimes against humanity "usually involved a widespread or systematic attack against the civilian population rather than isolated offences"[4]. Article 18 of the International Law Commission Draft Code of Crimes Against the Peace and Security of Mankind[ ] ("I.L.C. Draft Code") requires that the act be committed "in a systematic manner or on a large scale" and explicitly states that these are two alternative requirements. Similarly in its 1994 Report the International Law Commission stated that "the definition of crimes against humanity encompasses inhumane acts of a very serious character involving widespread *or* systematic violations aimed at the civilian population", although it also stated that "[t]he hallmarks of such crimes lie in their large-scale *and* systematic nature", and that the "particular forms of unlawful acts (murder, enslavement, deportation, torture, rape, imprisonment etc.) are less crucial to the definition [sic] the factors of scale and deliberate policy."[ ] Despite this seeming inconsistency the prevailing opinion was for alternative requirements, as is evident from the article addressing crimes against humanity in the 1991 Report of the International Law Commission which was entitled "Systematic or mass violations of human rights"[ ].

648. It is therefore the desire to exclude isolated or random acts from the notion of crimes against humanity that led to the inclusion of the requirement that the acts must be directed against a civilian "population", and either a finding of widespreadness, which refers to the number of victims, or systematicity, indicating that a pattern or methodical plan is evident, fulfils this requirement. As explained by the commentary to the I.L.C. Draft Code:

> (3) The opening clause of this definition establishes the two general conditions which must be met for one of the prohibited acts to qualify as a crime against humanity covered by the present Code. The first condition requires that the act was "committed in a systematic manner or on a large scale". This first condition consists of two alternative requirements... Consequently, an act could constitute a crime against humanity if either of these conditions is met.

The commentary to the I.L.C. Draft Code further explains these requirements and their origins. It states:

> The first alternative requires that the inhumane acts *be committed in a systematic manner* meaning pursuant to a preconceived plan or policy. The implementation of this plan or policy could result in the repeated or continuous commission of inhumane acts. The thrust of this requirement is to exclude a random act that was not committed as part of a broader plan or policy. The Nürnberg Charter did not include such a requirement. None the less the Nürnberg Tribunal emphasized that the inhumane acts were committed as part of the *policy of terror* and were "in many cases... organized and systematic" in considering whether such acts constituted crimes against humanity.

> (4) The second alternative requires that the inhumane acts be *committed on a large scale* meaning that the acts are directed against a multiplicity of victims. This requirement excludes an isolated inhumane act committed by a perpetrator acting on his

---

[4] *Report of the Committee on the Establishment of a Permanent International Criminal Court* ("Report of the Ad Hoc Committee"), U.N. Doc. G.A.O.R. A/50/22 (1995) at 17.

own initiative and directed against a single victim. The Nürnberg Charter did not include this second requirement either. Nonetheless the Nürnberg Tribunal further emphasized that the policy of terror was "certainly carried out on a vast scale" in its consideration of inhumane acts as possible crimes against humanity.... The term "large scale" in the present text ... is sufficiently broad to cover various situations involving multiplicity of victims, for example, as a result of the cumulative effect of a series of inhumane acts or the singular effect of an inhumane act of extraordinary magnitude[ ].

649. A related issue is whether a single act by a perpetrator can constitute a crime against humanity. A tangential issue, not at issue before this Trial Chamber, is whether a single act in and of itself can constitute a crime against humanity. This issue has been the subject of intense debate, with the jurisprudence immediately following the Second World War being mixed. The American tribunals generally supported the proposition that a massive nature was required[5], while the tribunals in the British Zone came to the opposite conclusion, finding that the mass element was not essential to the definition, in respect of either the number of acts or the number of victims and that "what counted was not the mass aspect, but the link between the act and the cruel and barbarous political system, specifically, the Nazi regime."[6] Clearly, a single act by a perpetrator taken within the context of a widespread or systematic attack against a civilian population entails individual criminal responsibility and an individual perpetrator need not commit numerous offences to be held liable. Although it is correct that isolated, random acts should not be included in the definition of crimes against humanity, that is the purpose of requiring that the acts be directed against a civilian *population* and thus "[e]ven an isolated act can constitute a crime against humanity if it is the product of a political system based on terror or persecution"[ ]. The decision of Trial Chamber I of the International Tribunal in the *Vukovar Hospital Decision* is a recent recognition of the fact that a single act by a perpetrator can constitute a crime against humanity. In that decision the Trial Chamber stated:

> 30. Crimes against humanity are to be distinguished from war crimes against individuals. In particular, they must be widespread or demonstrate a systematic character. However, as long as there is a link with the widespread or systematic attack against a civilian population, a single act could qualify as a crime against humanity. As such, an individual committing a crime against a single victim or a limited number of victims might be recognized as guilty of a crime against humanity if his acts were part of the specific context identified above[ ].

Additional support is found in national cases adjudicating crimes arising from the Second World War where individual acts by perpetrators were held to constitute crimes against humanity.[7]

---

[5] See the *Trial of Josef Altstötter and Others ("Justice case")*, Vol. VI, Law Reports of Trials of War Criminals (U.N. War Crimes Commission London, 1949) *("Law Reports")* 79–80 *and see* the *Trial of Fredrich Flick and Five Others (* "*Flick* case"*)*, Vol. IX, *Law Reports*, 51, in which isolated cases of atrocities and persecution were held to be excluded from the definition of crimes against humanity.

[6] Report of I.L.C. Special Rapporteur D. Thiam, Ybk I.L.C. 1986, Vol. II, I.L.C. A/CN.4/466 (*"Report of the Special Rapporteur"*), para. 93, referring to the conclusion of Henri Meyrowitz.

[7] *See, e.g.*, cases 2, 4, 13, 14, 15, 18, 23, 25, 31 and 34 of Entscheidungen Des Obersten Gerichtshofes Für Die Britische Zone in Strafsachen, Vol. I.

650. Another related issue is whether the widespread or systematic acts must be taken on, for example, racial, religious, ethnic or political grounds, thus requiring a discriminatory intent for all crimes against humanity and not only persecution. The law in this area is quite mixed. Many commentators and national courts have found that some form of discriminatory intent is inherent in the notion of crimes against humanity, and thus required for the "inhumane acts" group, as well as persecution, because the acts are taken against the individual as a result of his membership in a group that is for some reason targeted by the perpetrator[8].

651. This requirement of discrimination was not contained in the Nürnberg Charter, which clearly recognized two categories of crimes against humanity: those related to inhumane acts such as murder, extermination, enslavement and deportation; and persecution on political, racial or religious grounds. Nor can support for this position be found in Control Council Law No. 10, as well as cases taken on the basis of this law, such as those concerning medical experiments where criminal medical experiments on non-German nationals, both prisoners of war and civilians, including Jews and "asocial" persons were considered war crimes and crimes against humanity, as was the program of euthanasia for "incurables" which was extended to the Jews[9]. Likewise, the Tokyo Charter does not contain this requirement. The analysis of the Nürnberg Charter and Judgment prepared by the United Nations shortly after the trial of the major war criminals stated:

> It might perhaps be argued that the phrase "on political, racial or religious grounds" refers not only to persecutions but also to the first type of crimes against humanity. The British Chief Prosecutor possibly held that opinion as he spoke of "murder, extermination, enslavement, persecution on political racial or religious grounds". This interpretation, however, seems hardly to be warranted by the English wording and still less by the French text.... Moreover, in its statement with regard to von Schirach's guilt the Court designated the crimes against humanity as "murder, extermination, enslavement, deportation, and other inhumane acts" and "persecutions on political, racial or religious grounds."[10]

652. Additionally this requirement is not contained in the Article on crimes against humanity in the I.L.C. Draft Code nor does the Defence challenge its exclusion in the Prosecution's definition of the offence. Significantly, discriminatory intent as an additional requirement for all crimes against humanity was not included in the Statute of this International Tribunal as it was in the Statute for the International Tribunal for Rwanda[ ], the latter of which has, on this very point, recently been criticised. Nevertheless, because the requirement of discriminatory intent on national, political, ethnic, racial or religious grounds for all crimes against humanity was included in the *Report of the Secretary-General*[ ], and since several Security Council members stated that they interpreted

---

[8]   *See, e.g., Barbie case supra, the Final Report of the Commission of Experts*, para. 84, *supra*, J. Graven, *Les crimes contre l'humanité*, Receuil de Cours (1950) and Catherine Grynfogel, *Le concept de crime contre l'humanité: Hier, aujourd'hui et demain*, Revue de Droit Pénal et de Criminologie 13 (1994); *but see* Leila Sadat Wexler, *The Interpretation of the Nuremberg Principles by the French Court of Cassation: From Touvier to Barbie and Back Again*, 32 Colum. J. Trans. L. 289 (1994).

[9]   *See* the Medical Case, Vol. II Trials of War Criminals before the Nürnberg Military Tribunals under Control Council Law No. 10, 181, 196–98 (Washington: US Govt. Printing Office 1950).

[10]   Memorandum of the Secretary-General on the Charter and Judgment of the Nürnberg Tribunal, 67.

Article 5 as referring to acts taken on a discriminatory basis[ ], the Trial Chamber adopts the requirement of discriminatory intent for all crimes against humanity under Article 5. Factually, the inclusion of this additional requirement that the inhumane acts must be taken on discriminatory grounds is satisfied by the evidence discussed above that the attack on the civilian population was conducted against only the non-Serb portion of the population because they were non-Serbs.

653. As mentioned above the reason that crimes against humanity so shock the conscience of mankind and warrant intervention by the international community is because they are not isolated, random acts of individuals but rather result from a deliberate attempt to target a civilian population. Traditionally this requirement was understood to mean that there must be some form of policy to commit these acts. As explained by the Netherlands' *Hoge Raad* in *Public Prosecutor v. Menten*[11]:

> The concept of 'crimes against humanity' also requires – although this is not expressed in so many words in the above definition Article 6(c) of the Nürnberg Charter – that the crimes in question form a part of a system based on terror or constitute a link in a consciously pursued policy directed against particular groups of people [ ].

Importantly, however, such a policy need not be formalized and can be deduced from the way in which the acts occur. Notably, if the acts occur on a widespread or systematic basis that demonstrates a policy to commit those acts, whether formalized or not. Although some doubt the necessity of such a policy the evidence in this case clearly establishes the existence of a policy.

654. An additional issue concerns the nature of the entity behind the policy. The traditional conception was, in fact, not only that a policy must be present but that the policy must be that of a State, as was the case in Nazi Germany. The prevailing opinion was, as explained by one commentator, that crimes against humanity, as crimes of a collective nature, require a State policy "because their commission requires the use of the state's institutions, personnel and resources in order to commit, or refrain from preventing the commission of, the specified crimes described in Article 6(c) [of the Nürnberg Charter]"[ ]. While this may have been the case during the Second World War, and thus the jurisprudence followed by courts adjudicating charges of crimes against humanity based on events alleged to have occurred during this period, this is no longer the case. As the first international tribunal to consider charges of crimes against humanity alleged to have occurred after the Second World War, the International Tribunal is not bound by past doctrine but must apply customary international law as it stood at the time of the offences. In this regard the law in relation to crimes against humanity has developed to take into account forces which, although not those of the legitimate government, have *de facto* control over, or are able to move freely within, defined territory. The Prosecution in its pre-trial brief argues that under international law crimes against humanity can be committed on behalf of entities exercising *de facto* control over a particular territory but without international recognition or formal status of a *de jure* state, or by a terrorist group or organization. The Defence does not

---

[11] 75 I.L.R. 362–63 (1987).

challenge this assertion, which conforms with recent statements regarding crimes against humanity.

655. For example, Trial Chamber I of the International Tribunal stated in relation to crimes against humanity in its Review of the Indictment Pursuant to Rule 61 of the Rules of Procedure and Evidence in *Prosecutor v. Dragan Nikolic*: "Although they need not be related to a policy established at State level, in the conventional sense of the term, they cannot be the work of isolated individuals alone."[12] The I.L.C. Draft Code is more explicit in this regard. It contains the requirement that in order to constitute a crime against humanity the enumerated acts must be "instigated or directed by a Government or by any organization or group". The commentary clarifies that by stating:

> This alternative is intended to exclude the situation in which an individual commits an inhumane act while acting on his own initiative pursuant to his own criminal plan in the absence of any encouragement or direction from either a Government or a group or organization. This type of isolated criminal conduct on the part of a single individual would not constitute a crime against humanity.... The instigation or direction of a Government or *any* organization or group, which may or may not be affiliated with a Government, gives the act its great dimension and makes it a crime against humanity imputable to private persons or agents of a State[ ].

Thus, according to the International Law Commission, the acts do not even have to be directed or instigated by a group in permanent control of territory. It is important to keep in mind that the 1996 version of the I.L.C. Draft Code contains the final text of the article on crimes against humanity adopted by the International Law Commission[ ], which was established pursuant to General Assembly resolution 174 (II) and whose members are elected by the General Assembly. Importantly, the commentary to the draft articles of the Draft Code prepared by the International Law Commission in 1991, which were transmitted to Governments for their comments and observations, acknowledges that non-State actors are also possible perpetrators of crimes against humanity. It states that

> [i]t is important to point out that the draft article does not confine possible perpetrators of the crimes [crimes against humanity] to public officials or representatives alone . . . the article does not rule out the possibility that private individuals with de facto power or organized in criminal gangs or groups might also commit the kind of systematic or mass violations of human rights covered by the article; in that case, their acts would come under the draft Code[ ].

Similarly, the United States Court of Appeals for the Second Circuit recently recognized that "non-state actors" could be liable for committing genocide, the most egregious form of crimes against humanity, as well as war crimes[13]. Therefore, although a policy must exist to commit these acts, it need not be the policy of a State.

656. As discussed above in relation to the nexus, the act must not be unrelated to the armed conflict. This contains two aspects. First, it is the occurrence of the act within the context of a widespread or systematic attack on a civilian population that makes the act a

---

[12] *The Prosecutor v. Dragan Nikolic*, Review of the Indictment Pursuant to Rule 61 of the Rules of Procedure and Evidence, Case No. IT-94-2-R61, para. 26, T.Ch.I, 20 Oct. 1995.

[13] *Kadic v. Karadzic*, 70 F.3d 232 (2nd Cir. 1995), *cert. denied*, 64 U.S.L.W. 3832 (18 Jun. 1996).

crime against humanity as opposed to simply a war crime or crime against national penal legislation, thus adding an additional element, and therefore in addition to the intent to commit the underlying offence the perpetrator must know of the broader context in which his act occurs. Secondly, the act must not be taken for purely personal reasons unrelated to the armed conflict.

657. Regarding the first aspect, the knowledge by the accused of the wider context in which his act occurs, the approach taken by the majority in *R. v. Finta*,[14] in Canada is instructive. In that case the majority decided that "[t]he mental element required to be proven to constitute a crime against humanity is that the accused was aware of or wilfully blind to facts or circumstances which would bring his or her acts within crimes against humanity. However, it would not be necessary to establish that the accused knew that his actions were inhumane."[ ] While knowledge is thus required, it is examined on an objective level and factually can be implied from the circumstances. Several cases arising under German penal law following the Second World War are relevant in this regard. In a case decided by the *Spruchgericht* at Stade, Germany, the accused, who had been stationed near the concentration camp at Buchenwald, was assumed to have known that numerous persons were deprived of their liberty there on political grounds.[15] In addition, it is not necessary that the perpetrator has knowledge of exactly what will happen to the victims and several German cases stressed the fact that denunciations, without more, constitute crimes against humanity.[16] One case in particular is relevant. In that case two accused in 1944 informed the police that the director of the company for which they both worked had criticised Hitler. After the denouncement the director was arrested, temporarily released and then arrested again and brought to a concentration camp. Both of the accused were acquitted due to a lack of "mens rea" as they had not had either a concrete idea of the consequences of their action or an "abominable attitude". However, the *Obersten Gerichthofes* ("OGH") remanded the case to the trial court, finding that a crime against humanity does not require either a concrete idea of the consequences or an "abominable attitude".

658. As for the second aspect, that the act cannot be taken for purely personal reasons unrelated to the armed conflict, while personal motives may be present they should not be the sole motivation for the act. Again one of the German cases arising from the Second World War is relevant. In that case the accused had denounced his wife for her pro-Jewish, anti-Nazi remarks. The OGH found it sufficient that with the purpose of separating from his wife the accused had ensured that the Gestapo knew about her anti-Nazi remarks and that the connection between the action of the accused and the "despotism of the Nazi Regime" was established because the victim was denounced for her anti-Nazi attitude. The OGH found that he had committed a crime against humanity because his behaviour fitted into the plan of persecution against Jews in Germany and that although his intent was only to harm this one individual, it was closely related to the general mass persecution of the Jews.[17]

---

[14] [1994] 1 R.C.S., 701.

[15] Case No 38, Annual Digest and Reports of Public International Law Cases for the Year 1947, 100–101 (Butterworth & Co., London 1951).

[16] *See, e.g.*, Vol. I Entscheidungen des Obersten Gerichtshofes Für Die Britische Zone in Strafsachen, case 2, 6–10; case 4, 19–25; case 23, 91–95; case 25, 105–110; case 31, 122–126; case 34, 141–143.

[17] OGHBZ, Decision of the District Court (Landgericht) Hamburg of 11 Nov. 1948, STS 78/48, Justiz und NS-Verbrechen II, 1945–1966, 491, 499 (unofficial translation).

659. Thus if the perpetrator has knowledge, either actual or constructive, that these acts were occurring on a widespread or systematic basis and does not commit his act for purely personal motives completely unrelated to the attack on the civilian population, that is sufficient to hold him liable for crimes against humanity. Therefore the perpetrator must know that there is an attack on the civilian population, know that his act fits in with the attack and the act must not be taken for purely personal reasons unrelated to the armed conflict.

660. As discussed, this Trial Chamber has found that an armed conflict existed in the territory of Opstina Prijedor at the relevant time and that an aspect of this conflict was a policy to commit inhumane acts against the civilian population of the territory, in particular the non-Serb population, in the attempt to achieve the creation of a Greater Serbia. In furtherance of this policy these inhumane acts were committed against numerous victims and pursuant to a recognisable plan. As such the conditions of applicability for Article 5 are satisfied: the acts were directed against a civilian population on discriminatory grounds, they were committed on both a widespread basis and in a systematic fashion pursuant to a policy and they were committed in the context of, and related to, an armed conflict.

. . . .

[The chamber then applied the foregoing legal analysis to its factual findings. Tadić was found guilty of crimes against humanity.]

~

QUESTIONS & COMMENTS

(1) The ICC Statute defines "crime against humanity" as

> any of the following acts when committed as part of a widespread or systematic attack directed against any civilian population, with knowledge of the attack: . . . (h) Persecution against any identifiable group or collectivity on . . . grounds that are universally recognized as impermissible under international law, in connection with any act referred to in this paragraph or any crime within the jurisdiction of the Court. . . .

Art. 7, ICC Statute. What other bases of persecution may be universally impermissible under international law? What about persecution of gay, lesbian, and/or bisexual persons? Consider that several regional and global tribunals have ruled that antisodomy-related domestic laws are unlawful. *See, e.g., Toonen v. Australia,* UN Hum. Rts. Ctte., Communication No. 488/1992, views adopted 31 March 1994, U.N. Doc. CCPR/C/50/D/488 (1992) (criminalization of homosexual activity violative of international right to privacy); *Dudgeon v. United Kingdom,* 45 Eur. Ct. H.R. (ser. A) (1981) (same); *Modinos v. Cyprus,* 259 Eur. Ct. H.R. (ser. A) (1993) (extending protection to carnal knowledge "against the order of nature"); *Norris v. Ireland,* 142 Eur. Ct. H.R. (ser. A) (1988) (protection extended to anal intercourse between adult men). Do these cases establish a customary international legal right against the criminalization of gay/lesbian/bisexual activity? Does a widespread persecution against these persons constitute a crime against humanity? Does a customary international legal protection have to be a "universally" recognized legal protection whose violation rises to the level of a "crime against humanity"? Does "universal" mean that every state must recognize the protected class? Does the persistent objector rule create an exception to the universality requirement?

Consider U.S. law. Under U.S. law, for a particular norm to have the status of customary international law, the norm must be "universal, definable and obligatory." *Zuncax v. Gramajo*, 886 F. Supp. 162, 184 (D. Mass. 1991) (citing *Forti v. Suarez-Mason*, 672 F. Supp. 1531, 1540 (N.D. Cal. 1987)). However, it is not necessary to define every aspect of what might comprise the norm to be "fully defined and universally agreed upon." *Id.* at 187. Therefore, because the right to privacy is a customary international law norm that includes the right of same-sex adults to participate in private, consensual sexual activity, this right also should be guaranteed by customary international law. Accordingly, does this conclusion establish that the systematic persecution of gays, lesbians, and/or bisexuals is a crime against humanity?

(2) Consider the following:

> ... the requirement of action "against a civilian population" suggests that even the most atrocious acts are not crimes against humanity if they are truly isolated. Similarly, the discriminatory intent requirement for persecutions suggests that some actions undertaken without regard for specific traits of the victims' identity – *e.g.*, an order by an insane leader to persecute a group picked arbitrarily – is not of international concern. (Indeed, an order to destroy a city for purportedly military reasons alone, without regard to the identity of the inhabitants, might conceivably not qualify presently as a crime against humanity.) The emphasis on some form of official action – though not necessarily that of the recognized government – remains more justifiable because of the focus of human rights and humanitarian law on protecting individuals from those with power over them; yet it is equally clear that profit-driven entities may commit horrendous acts as well.

STEVEN R. RATNER & JASON S. ABRAMS, ACCOUNTABILITY FOR HUMAN RIGHTS ATROCITIES IN INTERNATIONAL LAW: BEYOND THE NUREMBERG LEGACY 79 (2d ed. 2001).

(3) In giving a wide definition to "civilian population" in *Tadic* (¶ 643), did the trial chamber violate the principle that criminal statutes are to be construed narrowly?

The Prosecutor v. Jean-Paul Akayesu
Case No. ICTR-96-4-T
Trial Chambers Judgment
International Criminal Tribunal for Rwanda
2 September 1998

Factual Findings[18]

Having carefully reviewed the testimony of the Prosecution witnesses regarding sexual violence, the Chamber finds that there is sufficient credible evidence to establish beyond a reasonable doubt that during the events of 1994, Tutsi girls and women were subjected to sexual violence, beaten and killed on or near the bureau communal premises, as well

---

[18] [The accused, Jean-Paul Akayesu, was the *bourgmestre* or mayor of the commune of Taba and had effective authority over the communal police. Ed.'s note.]

as elsewhere in the commune of Taba. Witness H, Witness JJ, Witness OO, and Witness NN all testified that they themselves were raped, and all, with the exception of Witness OO, testified that they witnessed other girls and women being raped. Witness J, Witness KK and Witness PP also testified that they witnessed other girls and women being raped in the commune of Taba. Hundreds of Tutsi, mostly women and children, sought refuge at the bureau communal during this period and many rapes took place on or near the premises of the bureau communal – Witness JJ was taken by Interahamwe[19] from the refuge site near the bureau communal to a nearby forest area and raped there. She testified that this happened often to other young girls and women at the refuge site. Witness JJ was also raped repeatedly on two separate occasions in the cultural center on the premises of the bureau communal, once in a group of fifteen girls and women and once in a group of ten girls and women. Witness KK saw women and girls being selected and taken by the Interahamwe to the cultural center to be raped. Witness H saw women being raped outside the compound of the bureau communal, and Witness NN saw two Interahamwes take a woman and rape her between the bureau communal and the cultural center. Witness OO was taken from the bureau communal and raped in a nearby field. Witness PP saw three women being raped at Kinihira, the killing site near the bureau communal, and Witness NN found her younger sister, dying, after she had been raped at the bureau communal. Many other instances of rape in Taba outside the bureau communal – in fields, on the road, and in or just outside houses – were described by Witness J, Witness H, Witness OO, Witness KK, Witness NN and Witness PP. Witness KK and Witness PP also described other acts of sexual violence which took place on or near the premises of the bureau communal – the forced undressing and public humiliation of girls and women. The Chamber notes that much of the sexual violence took place in front of large numbers of people, and that all of it was directed against Tutsi women.

With a few exceptions, most of the rapes and all of the other acts of sexual violence described by the Prosecution witnesses were committed by Interahamwe.... [W]ith regard to all evidence of rape and sexual violence which took place on or near the premises of the bureau communal, the perpetrators were all identified as Interahamwe. Interahamwe are also identified as the perpetrators of many rapes which took place outside the bureau communal.... There is no suggestion in any of the evidence that the Accused or any communal policemen perpetrated rape, and both Witness JJ and Witness KK affirmed that they never saw the Accused rape anyone.

In considering the role of the Accused in the sexual violence which took place and the extent of his direct knowledge of incidents of sexual violence, the Chamber has taken into account only evidence which is direct and unequivocal. Witness H testified that the Accused was present during the rape of Tutsi women outside the compound of the bureau communal, but as she could not confirm that he was aware that the rapes were taking place, the Chamber discounts this testimony in its assessment of the evidence. Witness PP recalled the Accused directing the Interahamwe to take Alexia and her two nieces to Kinihira, saying "Don't you know where killings take place, where the others have been

---

[19] [The Interahamwe was the militia of the Mouvement révolutionnaire national pour le développement [MRND]. Ed.'s note.]

killed?" The three women were raped before they were killed, but the statement of the Accused does not refer to sexual violence and there is no evidence that the Accused was present at Kinihira. For this reason, the Chamber also discounts this testimony in its assessment of the evidence.

On the basis of the evidence set forth herein, the Chamber finds beyond a reasonable doubt that the Accused had reason to know and in fact knew that sexual violence was taking place on or near the premises of the bureau communal, and that women were being taken away from the bureau communal and sexually violated. There is no evidence that the Accused took any measures to prevent acts of sexual violence or to punish the perpetrators of sexual violence. In fact there is evidence that the Accused ordered, instigated and otherwise aided and abetted sexual violence. The Accused watched two Interahamwe drag a woman to be raped between the bureau communal and the cultural center. The two commune policemen in front of his office witnessed the rape but did nothing to prevent it. On the two occasions Witness JJ was brought to the cultural center of the bureau communal to be raped, she and the group of girls and women with her were taken past the Accused, on the way. On the first occasion he was looking at them, and on the second occasion he was standing at the entrance to the cultural center. On this second occasion, he said, "Never ask me again what a Tutsi woman tastes like." Witness JJ described the Accused in making these statements as "talking as if someone were encouraging a player." More generally she stated that the Accused was the one "supervising" the acts of rape. When Witness OO and two other girls were apprehended by Interahamwe in flight from the bureau communal, the Interahamwe went to the Accused and told him that they were taking the girls away to sleep with them. The Accused said "take them." The Accused told the Interahamwe to undress Chantal and march her around. He was laughing and happy to be watching and afterwards told the Interahamwe to take her away and said "you should first of all make sure that you sleep with this girl." The Chamber considers this statement as evidence that the Accused ordered and instigated sexual violence, although insufficient evidence was presented to establish beyond a reasonable doubt that Chantal was in fact raped.

In making its factual findings, the Chamber has carefully considered the cross-examination by the Defence of Prosecution witnesses and the evidence presented by the Defence. With regard to cross-examination, the Chamber notes that the Defence did not question the testimony of Witness J or Witness H on rape at all, although the Chamber itself questioned both witnesses on this testimony. Witness JJ, OO, KK, NN and PP were questioned by the Defence with regard to their testimony of sexual violence, but the testimony itself was never challenged. Details such as where the rapes took place, how many rapists there were, how old they were, whether the Accused participated in the rapes, who was raped and which rapists used condoms were all elicited by the Defence, but at no point did the Defence suggest to the witnesses that the rapes had not taken place. The main line of questioning by the Defence with regard to the rapes and other sexual violence, other than to confirm the details of the testimony, related to whether the Accused had the authority to stop them. In cross-examination of the evidence presented by the Prosecution, specific incidents of sexual violence were never challenged by the Defence.

[The Law]

5.4. Crimes against Humanity (Article 3 of the Statute)

Crimes against Humanity – Historical development

Crimes against humanity were recognized in the Charter and Judgment of the Nuremberg Tribunal, as well as in Law No. 10 of the Control Council for Germany. Article 6(c) of the Charter of Nuremberg Tribunal defines crimes against humanity as

> murder, extermination, enslavement, deportation, and other inhumane acts committed against any civilian population, before or during the war, or persecutions on political, racial or religious grounds in execution of or in connexion with any crime within the jurisdiction of the Chamber, whether or not in violation of the domestic law of the country where perpetrated.

Article II of Law No. 10 of the Control Council Law defined crimes against humanity as:

> Atrocities and Offenses, including but not limited to murder, extermination, enslavement, deportation, imprisonment, torture, rape, or other inhumane acts committed against any civilian population or persecution on political, racial or religious grounds, whether or not in violation of the domestic laws of the country where perpetrated.

Crimes against humanity are aimed at any civilian population and are prohibited regardless of whether they are committed in an armed conflict, international or internal in character. In fact, the concept of crimes against humanity had been recognised long before Nuremberg. On 28 May 1915, the Governments of France, Great Britain and Russia made a declaration regarding the massacres of the Armenian population in Turkey, denouncing them as "crimes against humanity and civilisation for which all the members of the Turkish government will be held responsible together with its agents implicated in the massacres". The 1919 Report of the Commission on the Responsibility of the Authors of the War and on Enforcement of Penalties formulated by representatives from several States and presented to the Paris Peace Conference also referred to "offences against . . . the laws of humanity".

These World War I notions derived, in part, from the Martens clause of the Hague Convention (IV) of 1907, which referred to "the usages established among civilised peoples, from the laws of humanity, and the dictates of the public conscience". In 1874, George Curtis called slavery a "crime against humanity". Other such phrases as "crimes against mankind" and "crimes against the human family" appear far earlier in human history (*see* 12 N.Y.L. Sch. J. Hum. Rts 545 (1995)).

The Chamber notes that, following the Nuremberg and Tokyo trials, the concept of crimes against humanity underwent a gradual evolution in the *Eichmann, Barbie, Touvier* and *Papon* cases.

In the *Eichmann* case, the accused, Otto Adolf Eichmann, was charged with offences under Nazi and Nazi Collaborators (punishment) Law, 5710/1950, for his participation in the implementation of the plan know as "the Final Solution of the Jewish problem". Pursuant to Section I (b) of the said law:

> Crime against humanity means any of the following acts: murder, extermination, enslavement, starvation or deportation and other inhumane acts committed against

any civilian population, and persecution on national, racial, religious or political grounds.

The district court in the Eichmann stated that crimes against humanity differs from genocide in that for the commission of genocide special intent is required. This special intent is not required for crimes against humanity. Eichmann was convicted by the District court and sentenced to death. Eichmann appealed against his conviction and his appeal was dismissed by the supreme court.

In the *Barbie* case, the accused, Klaus Barbie, who was the head of the Gestapo in Lyons from November 1942 to August 1944, during the wartime occupation of France, was convicted in 1987 of crimes against humanity for his role in the deportation and extermination of civilians. Barbie appealed in Cassation, but the appeal was dismissed. For the purposes of the present Judgment, what is of interest is the definition of crimes against humanity employed by the Court. The French Court of Cassation, in a Judgment rendered on 20 December 1985, stated:

> Crimes against humanity, within the meaning of Article 6(c) of the Charter of the International Military Tribunal annexed to the London Agreement of 8 August 1945, which were not subject to statutory limitation of the right of prosecution, even if they were crimes which could also be classified as war crimes within the meaning of Article 6(b) of the Charter, *were inhumane acts and persecution committed in a systematic manner in the name of a State practising a policy of ideological supremacy, not only against persons by reason of their membership of a racial or religious community, but also against the opponents of that policy, whatever the form of their opposition.* (Words italicized by the Court)

This was affirmed in a Judgment of the Court of Cassation of 3 June 1988, in which the Court held that:

> The fact that the accused, who had been found guilty of one of the crimes enumerated in Article 6(c) of the Charter of the Nuremberg Tribunal, in perpetrating that crime took part in the execution of a common plan to bring about the deportation or extermination of the civilian population during the war, or persecutions on political, racial or religious grounds, constituted not a distinct offence or an aggravating circumstance but rather *an essential element of the crime against humanity, consisting of the fact that the acts charged were performed in a systematic manner in the name of a State practising by those means a policy of ideological supremacy.* (Emphasis added)

The definition of crimes against humanity developed in Barbie was further developed in the *Touvier* case. In that case, the accused, Paul Touvier, had been a high-ranking officer in the Militia (Milice) of Lyons, which operated in "Vichy" France during the German occupation. He was convicted of crimes against humanity for his role in the shooting of seven Jews at Rillieux on 29 June 1994 as a reprisal for the assassination by members of the Resistance, on the previous day, of the Minister for Propaganda of the "Vichy" Government.

The Court of Appeal applied the definition of crimes against humanity used in Barbie, stating that:

> The specific intent necessary to establish a crime against humanity was the intention to take part in the execution of a common plan by committing, in a systematic

manner, inhuman acts or persecutions in the name of a State practising a policy of ideological supremacy.

Applying this definition, the Court of Appeal held that Touvier could not be guilty of crimes against humanity since he committed the acts in question in the name of the "Vichy" State, which was not a State practising a policy of ideological supremacy, although it collaborated with Nazi Germany, which clearly did practice such a policy.

The Court of Cassation allowed appeal from the decision of the Court of Appeal, on the grounds that the crimes committed by the accused had been committed at the instigation of a Gestapo officer, and to that extent were linked to Nazi Germany, a State practising a policy of ideological supremacy against persons by virtue of their membership of a racial or religious community. Therefore the crimes could be categorised as crimes against humanity. Touvier was eventually convicted of crimes against humanity by the Cour d'Assises des Yvelines on 20 April 1994.

The definition of crimes against humanity used in Barbie was later affirmed by the ICTY in its *Vukovar Rule 61 Decision* of 3 April 1996 (IT-95-13-R61), to support its finding that crimes against humanity applied equally where the victims of the acts were members of a resistance movement as to where the victims were civilians:

> 29. ... Although according to the terms of Article 5 of the Statute of this Tribunal Y combatants in the traditional sense of the term cannot be victims of a crime against humanity, this does not apply to individuals who, at one particular point in time, carried out acts of resistance. As the Commission of Experts, established pursuant to Security Council resolution 780, noted, "it seems obvious that Article 5 applies first and foremost to civilians, meaning people who are not combatants. This, however, should not lead to any quick conclusions concerning people who at one particular point in time did bear arms. ... Information of the overall circumstances is relevant for the interpretation of the provision in a spirit consistent with its purpose." (Doc S/1994/674, para. 78).

This conclusion is supported by case law. In the *Barbie* case, the French Cour de Cassation said that:

> "inhumane acts and persecution which, in the name of a State practising a policy of ideological hegemony, were committed systematically or collectively not only against individuals because of their membership in a racial or religious group but also against the adversaries of that policy whatever the form of the opposition" could be considered a crime against humanity. (Cass. Crim. 20 December 1985).

Article 7 of the Statute of the International Criminal Court defines a crime against humanity as any of the enumerated acts committed as part of a widespread of systematic attack directed against any civilian population, with knowledge of the attack. These enumerated acts are murder; extermination; enslavement; deportation or forcible transfer of population; imprisonment or other severe deprivation of physical liberty in violation of fundamental rules of international law; torture; rape, sexual slavery, enforced prostitution, forced pregnancy, enforced sterilization, or any other form of sexual violence of comparable gravity; persecution against any identifiable group or collectively on political, racial, national, ethnic, cultural, religious, gender or other grounds that are universally recognised as impermissible under international law, in connection with any act referred to in this article or any other crime within the jurisdiction of the Court; enforced disappearance of persons; the crime of apartheid; other inhumane acts of a similar character intentionally causing great suffering, or serious injury to body or mental or physical health.

Crimes against Humanity in Article 3 of the Statute of the Tribunal

The Chamber considers that Article 3 of the Statute confers on the Chamber the jurisdiction to prosecute persons for various inhumane acts which constitute crimes against humanity. This category of crimes may be broadly broken down into four essential elements, namely:

(i) the act must be inhumane in nature and character, causing great suffering, or serious injury to body or to mental or physical health;

(ii) the act must be committed as part of a wide spread or systematic attack;

(iii) the act must be committed against members of the civilian population;

(iv) the act must be committed on one or more discriminatory grounds, namely, national, political, ethnic, racial or religious grounds.

The act must be committed as part of a wide spread or systematic attack.

The Chamber considers that it is a prerequisite that the act must be committed as part of a wide spread or systematic attack and not just a random act of violence. The act can be part of a widespread or systematic attack and need not be a part of both.

The concept of "widespread" may be defined as massive, frequent, large scale action, carried out collectively with considerable seriousness and directed against a multiplicity of victims. The concept of "systematic" may be defined as thoroughly organised and following a regular pattern on the basis of a common policy involving substantial public or private resources. There is no requirement that this policy must be adopted formally as the policy of a state. There must however be some kind of preconceived plan or policy.

The concept of "attack" maybe defined as a unlawful act of the kind enumerated in Article 3(a) to (I) of the Statute, like murder, extermination, enslavement *etc.* An attack may also be non violent in nature, like imposing a system of apartheid, which is declared a crime against humanity in Article 1 of the Apartheid Convention of 1973, or exerting pressure on the population to act in a particular manner, may come under the purview of an attack, if orchestrated on a massive scale or in a systematic manner.

The act must be directed against the civilian population

The Chamber considers that an act must be directed against the civilian population if it is to constitute a crime against humanity. Members of the civilian population are people who are not taking any active part in the hostilities, including members of the armed forces who laid down their arms and those persons placed *hors de combat* by sickness, wounds, detention or any other cause. Where there are certain individuals within the civilian population who do not come within the definition of civilians, this does not deprive the population of its civilian character.

The act must be committed on discriminatory grounds

The Statute stipulates that inhumane acts committed against the civilian population must be committed on "national, political, ethnic, racial or religious grounds." Discrimination on the basis of a person's political ideology satisfies the requirement of "political" grounds as envisaged in Article 3 of the Statute. For definitions on national, ethnic, racial or religious grounds. . . .

Inhumane acts committed against persons not falling within any one of the discriminatory categories could constitute crimes against humanity if the perpetrator's intention was to further his attacks on the group discriminated against on one of the grounds mentioned in Article 3 of the Statute. The perpetrator must have the requisite intent for the commission of crimes against humanity.

The enumerated acts

Article 3 of the Statute sets out various acts that constitute crimes against humanity, namely: murder; extermination; enslavement; deportation; imprisonment; torture; rape; persecution on political, racial and religious grounds; and; other inhumane acts. Although the category of acts that constitute crimes against humanity are set out in Article 3, this category is not exhaustive. Any act which is inhumane in nature and character may constitute a crime against humanity, provided the other elements are met. This is evident in (i) which caters for all other inhumane acts not stipulated in (a) to (h) of Article 3.

The Chamber notes that the accused is indicted for murder, extermination, torture, rape and other acts that constitute inhumane acts. The Chamber in interpreting Article 3 of the Statute, shall focus its discussion on these acts only.

. . . .

Rape

Considering the extent to which rape constitute crimes against humanity, pursuant to Article 3(g) of the Statute, the Chamber must define rape, as there is no commonly accepted definition of this term in international law. While rape has been defined in certain national jurisdictions as non-consensual intercourse, variations on the act of rape may include acts which involve the insertion of objects and/or the use of bodily orifices not considered to be intrinsically sexual.

The Chamber considers that rape is a form of aggression and that the central elements of the crime of rape cannot be captured in a mechanical description of objects and body parts. The Convention against Torture and Other Cruel, Inhuman and Degrading Treatment or Punishment does not catalogue specific acts in its definition of torture, focusing rather on the conceptual frame work of state sanctioned violence. This approach is more useful in international law. Like torture, rape is used for such purposes as intimidation, degradation, humiliation, discrimination, punishment, control or destruction of a person. Like torture, rape is a violation of personal dignity, and rape in fact constitutes torture when inflicted by or at the instigation of or with the consent or acquiescence of a public official or other person acting in an official capacity.

The Chamber defines rape as a physical invasion of a sexual nature, committed on a person under circumstances which are coercive. Sexual violence which includes rape, is considered to be any act of a sexual nature which is committed on a person under circumstances which are coercive. This act must be committed:

(a) as part of a wide spread or systematic attack;
(b) on a civilian population;

(c) on certain catalogued discriminatory grounds, namely: national, ethnic, political, racial, or religious grounds.

. . . .

[Legal Findings]

7.7. Count 13 (rape) and Count 14 (other inhumane acts) – Crimes against Humanity

In the light of its factual findings with regard to the allegations of sexual violence set forth in paragraphs 12A and 12B of the Indictment, the Tribunal considers the criminal responsibility of the Accused on Count 13, crimes against humanity (rape), punishable by Article 3(g) of the Statute of the Tribunal and Count 14, crimes against humanity (other inhumane acts), punishable by Article 3(i) of the Statute.

In considering the extent to which acts of sexual violence constitute crimes against humanity under Article 3(g) of its Statute, the Tribunal must define rape, as there is no commonly accepted definition of the term in international law. The Tribunal notes that many of the witnesses have used the term "rape" in their testimony. At times, the Prosecution and the Defence have also tried to elicit an explicit description of what happened in physical terms, to document what the witnesses mean by the term "rape". The Tribunal notes that while rape has been historically defined in national jurisdictions as non-consensual sexual intercourse, variations on the form of rape may include acts which involve the insertion of objects and/or the use of bodily orifices not considered to be intrinsically sexual. An act such as that described by Witness KK in her testimony – the Interahamwes thrusting a piece of wood into the sexual organs of a woman as she lay dying – constitutes rape in the Tribunal's view.

The Tribunal considers that rape is a form of aggression and that the central elements of the crime of rape cannot be captured in a mechanical description of objects and body parts. The Tribunal also notes the cultural sensitivities involved in public discussion of intimate matters and recalls the painful reluctance and inability of witnesses to disclose graphic anatomical details of sexual violence they endured. The United Nations Convention Against Torture and Other Cruel, Inhuman and Degrading Treatment or Punishment does not catalogue specific acts in its definition of torture, focusing rather on the conceptual framework of state-sanctioned violence. The Tribunal finds this approach more useful in the context of international law. Like torture, rape is used for such purposes as intimidation, degradation, humiliation, discrimination, punishment, control or destruction of a person. Like torture, rape is a violation of personal dignity, and rape in fact constitutes torture when it is inflicted by or at the instigation of or with the consent or acquiescence of a public official or other person acting in an official capacity.

The Tribunal defines rape as a physical invasion of a sexual nature, committed on a person under circumstances which are coercive. The Tribunal considers sexual violence, which includes rape, as any act of a sexual nature which is committed on a person under circumstances which are coercive. Sexual violence is not limited to physical invasion of the human body and may include acts which do not involve penetration or even physical contact. The incident described by Witness KK in which the Accused ordered the Interahamwe to undress a student and force her to do gymnastics naked in the public courtyard of the bureau communal, in front of a crowd, constitutes sexual violence. The Tribunal notes in this context that coercive circumstances need not be evidenced by a show of physical force. Threats, intimidation, extortion and other forms of duress which prey on fear or desperation may constitute coercion, and coercion may be inherent in certain circumstances, such as armed conflict or the military presence of Interahamwe among refugee Tutsi women at the bureau communal. Sexual violence falls within the scope of "other inhumane acts", set forth Article 3(i) of the Tribunal's Statute, "outrages upon personal dignity," set forth in Article 4(e) of the Statute, and "serious bodily or mental harm," set forth in Article 2(2)(b) of the Statute.

The Tribunal notes that as set forth by the Prosecution, Counts 13–15 are drawn on the basis of acts as described in paragraphs 12(A) and 12(B) of the Indictment. The allegations in these paragraphs of the Indictment are limited to events which took place "on or near the bureau communal premises." Many of the beatings, rapes and murders established by the evidence presented took place away from the bureau communal premises, and therefore the Tribunal does not make any legal findings with respect to these incidents pursuant to Counts 13, 14 and 15.

The Tribunal also notes that on the basis of acts described in paragraphs 12(A) and 12(B), the Accused is charged only pursuant to Article 3(g) (rape) and 3(i) (other inhumane acts) of its Statute, but not Article 3(a) (murder) or Article 3(f) (torture). Similarly, on the basis of acts described in paragraphs 12(A) and 12(B), the Accused is charged only pursuant to Article 4(e) (outrages upon personal dignity) of its Statute, and not Article 4(a) (violence to life, health and physical or mental well-being of persons, in particular murder as well as cruel treatment such as torture, mutilation or any form of corporal punishment). As these paragraphs are not referenced elsewhere in the Indictment in connection with these other relevant Articles of the Statute of the Tribunal, the Tribunal concludes that the Accused has not been charged with the beatings and killings which have been established as Crimes Against Humanity or Violations of Article 3 Common to the Geneva Conventions. The Tribunal notes, however, that paragraphs 12(A) and 12(B) are referenced in Counts 1–3, Genocide and it considers the beatings and killings, as well as sexual violence, in connection with those counts.

The Tribunal has found that the Accused had reason to know and in fact knew that acts of sexual violence were occurring on or near the premises of the bureau communal and that he took no measures to prevent these acts or punish the perpetrators of them. The Tribunal notes that it is only in consideration of Counts 13, 14 and 15 that the Accused is charged with individual criminal responsibility under Section 6(3) of its Statute. As set forth in the Indictment, under Article 6(3) "an individual is criminally responsible as a superior for the acts of a subordinate if he or she knew or had reason to know that the subordinate was about to commit such acts or had done so and the superior failed to take the necessary and reasonable measures to prevent such acts or punish the perpetrators thereof." Although the evidence supports a finding that a superior/subordinate relationship existed between the Accused and the Interahamwe who were at the bureau communal, the Tribunal notes that there is no allegation in the Indictment that the Interahamwe, who are referred to as "armed local militia," were subordinates of the Accused. This relationship is a fundamental element of the criminal offence set forth in Article 6(3). The amendment of the Indictment with additional charges pursuant to

Article 6(3) could arguably be interpreted as implying an allegation of the command responsibility required by Article 6(3). In fairness to the Accused, the Tribunal will not make this inference. Therefore, the Tribunal finds that it cannot consider the criminal responsibility of the Accused under Article 6(3).

The Tribunal finds, under Article 6(1) of its Statute, that the Accused, by his own words, specifically ordered, instigated, aided and abetted the following acts of sexual violence:

(i) the multiple acts of rape of ten girls and women, including Witness JJ, by numerous Interahamwe in the cultural center of the bureau communal; (ii) the rape of Witness OO by an Interahamwe named Antoine in a field near the bureau communal; (iii) the forced undressing and public marching of Chantal naked at the bureau communal.

The Tribunal finds, under Article 6(1) of its Statute, that the Accused aided and abetted the following acts of sexual violence, by allowing them to take place on or near the premises of the bureau communal, while he was present on the premises in respect of (i) and in his presence in respect of (ii) and (iii), and by facilitating the commission of these acts through his words of encouragement in other acts of sexual violence, which, by virtue of his authority, sent a clear signal of official tolerance for sexual violence, without which these acts would not have taken place:

(i) the multiple acts of rape of fifteen girls and women, including Witness JJ, by numerous Interahamwe in the cultural center of the bureau communal; (ii) the rape of a woman by Interahamwe in between two buildings of the bureau communal, witnessed by Witness NN; (iii) the forced undressing of the wife of Tharcisse after making her sit in the mud outside the bureau communal, as witnessed by Witness KK;

The Tribunal finds, under Article 6(1) of its Statute, that the Accused, having had reason to know that sexual violence was occurring, aided and abetted the following acts of sexual violence, by allowing them to take place on or near the premises of the bureau communal and by facilitating the commission of such sexual violence through his words of encouragement in other acts of sexual violence which, by virtue of his authority, sent a clear signal of official tolerance for sexual violence, without which these acts would not have taken place:

(i) the rape of Witness JJ by an Interahamwe who took her from outside the bureau communal and raped her in a nearby forest; (ii) the rape of the younger sister of Witness NN by an Interahamwe at the bureau communal; (iii) the multiple rapes of Alexia, wife of Ntereye, and her two nieces Louise and Nishimwe by Interahamwe near the bureau communal; (iv) the forced undressing of Alexia, wife of Ntereye, and her two nieces Louise and Nishimwe, and the forcing of the women to perform exercises naked in public near the bureau communal.

The Tribunal has established that a widespread and systematic attack against the civilian ethnic population of Tutsis took place in Taba, and more generally in Rwanda, between April 7 and the end of June, 1994. The Tribunal finds that the rape and other inhumane acts which took place on or near the bureau communal premises of Taba were committed as part of this attack.

COUNT 13

The Accused is judged criminally responsible under Article 3(g) of the Statute for the following incidents of rape:

(i) the rape of Witness JJ by an Interahamwe who took her from outside the bureau communal and raped her in a nearby forest; (ii) the multiple acts of rape of fifteen girls and women, including Witness JJ, by numerous Interahamwe in the cultural center of the bureau communal; (iii) the multiple acts of rape of ten girls and women, including Witness JJ, by numerous Interahamwe in the cultural center of the bureau communal; (iv) the rape of Witness OO by an Interahamwe named Antoine in a field near the bureau communal; (v) the rape of a woman by Interahamwe in between two buildings of the bureau communal, witnessed by Witness NN; (vi) the rape of the younger sister of Witness NN by an Interahamwe at the bureau communal; (vii) the multiple rapes of Alexia, wife of Ntereye, and her two nieces Louise and Nishimwe by Interahamwe near the bureau communal.

COUNT 14

The Accused is judged criminally responsible under Article 3(i) of the Statute for the following other inhumane acts:

(i) the forced undressing of the wife of Tharcisse outside the bureau communal, after making her sit in the mud, as witnessed by Witness KK; (ii) the forced undressing and public marching of Chantal naked at the bureau communal; (iii) the forced undressing of Alexia, wife of Ntereye, and her two nieces Louise and Nishimwe, and the forcing of the women to perform exercises naked in public near the bureau communal.

. . . .

~

QUESTIONS & COMMENTS

(1) As noted earlier in regard to forced disappearances, some human rights violations that are not crimes against humanity because they are not part of a widespread or systemic attack on a civilian population may still entail international criminal liability for the state as well as individual culpability for the individual perpetrator.

(2) In *The Prosecutor v. Delalic and Delic (The Celebici Case)*, Case No. IT-96-21-T, Int'l Crim. Trib.-Yugo., Judgment (16 November 1998), the trial chamber stated that "there can be no question that acts of rape may constitute torture under customary law." What kinds of rape or other sexual assault would not rise to the level of torture? Consider the European Court of Human Rights' analysis of the difference between torture and inhuman or degrading treatment in *Ireland v. United Kingdom*: "Torture constitutes an aggravated and deliberate form of cruel, inhuman or degrading treatment or punishment." 25 Eur. Ct. H.R. (ser. A) at §167 (1978) (quoting UNGA Res. No. 3452). Is there any form of sexual assault that is *not* an aggravated and deliberate form of degrading treatment?

5.2.3. War Crimes

Hague Convention (IV)
respecting the Laws and Customs of War on Land and its annex:
Regulations concerning the Laws and Customs of War on Land
18 October 1907

SECTION I

ON BELLIGERENTS

CHAPTER

The qualifications of belligerents

Article 1. The laws, rights, and duties of war apply not only to armies, but also to militia and volunteer corps fulfilling the following conditions:

1. To be commanded by a person responsible for his subordinates;
2. To have a fixed distinctive emblem recognizable at a distance;
3. To carry arms openly; and
4. To conduct their operations in accordance with the laws and customs of war.

In countries where militia or volunteer corps constitute the army, or form part of it, they are included under the denomination "army."

Art. 2. The inhabitants of a territory which has not been occupied, who, on the approach of the enemy, spontaneously take up arms to resist the invading troops without having had time to organize themselves in accordance with Article 1, shall be regarded as belligerents if they carry arms openly and if they respect the laws and customs of war.

Art. 3. The armed forces of the belligerent parties may consist of combatants and non-combatants. In the case of capture by the enemy, both have a right to be treated as prisoners of war.

CHAPTER II

Prisoners of war

Art. 4. Prisoners of war are in the power of the hostile Government, but not of the individuals or corps who capture them.

They must be humanely treated.

All their personal belongings, except arms, horses, and military papers, remain their property.

Art. 5. Prisoners of war may be interned in a town, fortress, camp, or other place, and bound not to go beyond certain fixed limits; but they cannot be confined except as in indispensable measure of safety and only while the circumstances which necessitate the measure continue to exist.

CHAPTER I

Means of injuring the enemy, sieges, and bombardments

Art. 22. The right of belligerents to adopt means of injuring the enemy is not unlimited.

Art. 23. In addition to the prohibitions provided by special Conventions, it is especially forbidden

(a) To employ poison or poisoned weapons;

(b) To kill or wound treacherously individuals belonging to the hostile nation or army;

(c) To kill or wound an enemy who, having laid down his arms, or having no longer means of defence, has surrendered at discretion;

(d) To declare that no quarter will be given;

(e) To employ arms, projectiles, or material calculated to cause unnecessary suffering;

(f) To make improper use of a flag of truce, of the national flag or of the military insignia and uniform of the enemy, as well as the distinctive badges of the Geneva Convention;

(g) To destroy or seize the enemy's property, unless such destruction or seizure be imperatively demanded by the necessities of war;

(h) To declare abolished, suspended, or inadmissible in a court of law the rights and actions of the nationals of the hostile party. A belligerent is likewise forbidden to compel the nationals of the hostile party to take part in the operations of war directed against their own country, even if they were in the belligerent's service before the commencement of the war.

Art. 24. Ruses of war and the employment of measures necessary for obtaining information about the enemy and the country are considered permissible.

Art. 25. The attack or bombardment, by whatever means, of towns, villages, dwellings, or buildings which are undefended is prohibited.

Art. 26. The officer in command of an attacking force must, before commencing a bombardment, except in cases of assault, do all in his power to warn the authorities.

Art. 27. In sieges and bombardments all necessary steps must be taken to spare, as far as possible, buildings dedicated to religion, art, science, or charitable purposes, historic monuments, hospitals, and places where the sick and wounded are collected, provided they are not being used at the time for military purposes.

It is the duty of the besieged to indicate the presence of such buildings or places by distinctive and visible signs, which shall be notified to the enemy beforehand.

Art. 28. The pillage of a town or place, even when taken by assault, is prohibited.

Charter of the International Military Tribunal

Article 6

. . . .

The following acts, or any of them, are crimes coming within the jurisdiction of the Tribunal for which there shall be individual responsibility:

. . . .

(b) WAR CRIMES: namely, violations of the laws or customs of war. Such violations shall include, but not be limited to, murder, ill-treatment or deportation to slave labor or for any other purpose of civilian population of or in occupied territory, murder or ill-treatment of prisoners of war or persons on the seas, killing of hostages, plunder of public or private property, wanton destruction of cities, towns or villages, or devastation not justified by military necessity;

. . . .

Geneva Convention (I) for the Amelioration of the Condition of the Wounded and Sick in Armed Forces in the Field, 12 August 1949

Art 1. The High Contracting Parties undertake to respect and to ensure respect for the present Convention in all circumstances.

Art. 2. In addition to the provisions which shall be implemented in peacetime, the present Convention shall apply to all cases of declared war or of any other armed conflict which may arise between two or more of the High Contracting Parties, even if the state of war is not recognized by one of them.

The Convention shall also apply to all cases of partial or total occupation of the territory of a High Contracting Party, even if the said occupation meets with no armed resistance. Although one of the Powers in conflict may not be a party to the present Convention, the Powers who are parties thereto shall remain bound by it in their mutual relations. They shall furthermore be bound by the Convention in relation to the said Power, if the latter accepts and applies the provisions thereof.

Art. 3. In the case of armed conflict not of an international character occurring in the territory of one of the High Contracting Parties, each Party to the conflict shall be bound to apply, as a minimum, the following provisions:

(1) Persons taking no active part in the hostilities, including members of armed forces who have laid down their arms and those placed hors de combat by sickness, wounds, detention, or any other cause, shall in all circumstances be treated humanely, without any adverse distinction founded on race, colour, religion or faith, sex, birth or wealth, or any other similar criteria.

To this end, the following acts are and shall remain prohibited at any time and in any place whatsoever with respect to the above-mentioned persons:

(a) violence to life and person, in particular murder of all kinds, mutilation, cruel treatment and torture;
(b) taking of hostages;
(c) outrages upon personal dignity, in particular humiliating and degrading treatment;
(d) the passing of sentences and the carrying out of executions without previous judgement pronounced by a regularly constituted court, affording all the judicial guarantees which are recognized as indispensable by civilized peoples.

(2) The wounded and sick shall be collected and cared for. An impartial humanitarian body, such as the International Committee of the Red Cross, may offer its services to the Parties to the conflict.

The Parties to the conflict should further endeavour to bring into force, by means of special agreements, all or part of the other provisions of the present Convention.

The application of the preceding provisions shall not affect the legal status of the Parties to the conflict.

Art. 49. The High Contracting Parties undertake to enact any legislation necessary to provide effective penal sanctions for persons committing, or ordering to be committed, any of the grave breaches of the present Convention defined in the following Article.

Each High Contracting Party shall be under the obligation to search for persons alleged to have committed, or to have ordered to be committed, such grave breaches, and shall bring such persons, regardless of their nationality, before its own courts. It may also, if it prefers, and in accordance with the provisions of its own legislation, hand such persons over for trial to another High Contracting Party concerned, provided such High Contracting Party has made out a prima facie case.

Each High Contracting Party shall take measures necessary for the suppression of all acts contrary to the provisions of the present Convention other than the grave breaches defined in the following Article.

In all circumstances, the accused persons shall benefit by safeguards of proper trial and defence, which shall not be less favourable than those provided by Article 105 and those following, of the Geneva Convention relative to the Treatment of Prisoners of War of 12 August 1949.

Art. 50. Grave breaches to which the preceding Article relates shall be those involving any of the following acts, if committed against persons or property protected by the Convention: wilful killing, torture or inhuman treatment, including biological experiments, wilfully causing great suffering or serious injury to body or health, and extensive destruction and appropriation of property, not justified by military necessity and carried out unlawfully and wantonly.

Geneva Convention (II) for the Amelioration of the Condition of Wounded, Sick and Shipwrecked Members of Armed Forces at Sea, 12 August 1949

Art. 51. Grave breaches to which the preceding Article relates shall be those involving any of the following acts, if committed against persons or property protected by the Convention: wilful killing, torture or inhuman treatment, including biological experiments, wilfully causing great suffering or serious injury to body or health, and extensive destruction and appropriation of property, not justified by military necessity and carried out unlawfully and wantonly.

Geneva Convention (III) Relative to the Treatment of Prisoners of War, 12 August 1949

Art 4.

A. Prisoners of war, in the sense of the present Convention, are persons belonging to one of the following categories, who have fallen into the power of the enemy:

(1) Members of the armed forces of a Party to the conflict, as well as members of militias or volunteer corps forming part of such armed forces.

(2) Members of other militias and members of other volunteer corps, including those of organized resistance movements, belonging to a Party to the conflict and operating in or outside their own territory, even if this territory is occupied, provided that such militias or volunteer corps, including such organized resistance movements, fulfil the following conditions:

(a) that of being commanded by a person responsible for his subordinates;
(b) that of having a fixed distinctive sign recognizable at a distance;
(c) that of carrying arms openly;
(d) that of conducting their operations in accordance with the laws and customs of war.

(3) Members of regular armed forces who profess allegiance to a government or an authority not recognized by the Detaining Power.

(4) Persons who accompany the armed forces without actually being members thereof, such as civilian members of military aircraft crews, war correspondents, supply contractors, members of labour units or of services responsible for the welfare of the armed forces, provided that they have received authorization, from the armed forces which they accompany, who shall provide them for that purpose with an identity card similar to the annexed model.

(5) Members of crews, including masters, pilots and apprentices, of the merchant marine and the crews of civil aircraft of the Parties to the conflict, who do not benefit by more favourable treatment under any other provisions of international law.

(6) Inhabitants of a non-occupied territory, who on the approach of the enemy spontaneously take up arms to resist the invading forces, without having had time to form themselves into regular armed units, provided they carry arms openly and respect the laws and customs of war.

B. The following shall likewise be treated as prisoners of war under the present Convention:

(1) Persons belonging, or having belonged, to the armed forces of the occupied country, if the occupying Power considers it necessary by reason of such allegiance to intern them, even though it has originally liberated them while hostilities were going on outside the territory it occupies, in particular where such persons have made an unsuccessful attempt to rejoin the armed forces to which they belong and which are engaged in combat, or where they fail to comply with a summons made to them with a view to internment.

(2) The persons belonging to one of the categories enumerated in the present Article, who have been received by neutral or non-belligerent Powers on their territory and whom these Powers are required to intern under international law, without prejudice to any more favourable treatment which these Powers may choose to give and with the exception of Articles 8, 10, 15, 30, fifth paragraph, 58–67, 92, 126 and, where diplomatic relations exist between the Parties to the conflict and the neutral or non-belligerent Power concerned, those Articles concerning the Protecting Power. Where such diplomatic relations exist, the Parties to a conflict on whom these persons depend shall be allowed to perform towards them the functions of a Protecting Power as provided in the present Convention, without prejudice to the functions which these Parties normally exercise in conformity with diplomatic and consular usage and treaties.

C. This Article shall in no way affect the status of medical personnel and chaplains as provided for in Article 33 of the present Convention.

Art. 5. The present Convention shall apply to the persons referred to in Article 4 from the time they fall into the power of the enemy and until their final release and repatriation.

Should any doubt arise as to whether persons, having committed a belligerent act and having fallen into the hands of the enemy, belong to any of the categories enumerated in Article 4, such persons shall enjoy the protection of the present Convention until such time as their status has been determined by a competent tribunal.

. . . .

Art. 130. Grave breaches to which the preceding Article relates shall be those involving any of the following acts, if committed against persons or property protected by the Convention: wilful killing, torture or inhuman treatment, including biological experiments, wilfully causing great suffering or serious injury to body or health, compelling a prisoner of war to serve in the forces of the hostile Power, or wilfully depriving a prisoner of war of the rights of fair and regular trial prescribed in this Convention.

Geneva Convention (IV)
Relative to the Protection of Civilian Persons in Time of War,
12 August 1949

Article 1. The High Contracting Parties undertake to respect and to ensure respect for the present Convention in all circumstances.

Art. 2. In addition to the provisions which shall be implemented in peace-time, the present Convention shall apply to all cases of declared war or of any other armed conflict which may arise between two or more of the High Contracting Parties, even if the state of war is not recognized by one of them.

The Convention shall also apply to all cases of partial or total occupation of the territory of a High Contracting Party, even if the said occupation meets with no armed resistance.

Although one of the Powers in conflict may not be a party to the present Convention, the Powers who are parties thereto shall remain bound by it in their mutual relations. They shall furthermore be bound by the Convention in relation to the said Power, if the latter accepts and applies the provisions thereof.

Art. 3. In the case of armed conflict not of an international character occurring in the territory of one of the High Contracting Parties, each Party to the conflict shall be bound to apply, as a minimum, the following provisions:

(1) Persons taking no active part in the hostilities, including members of armed forces who have laid down their arms and those placed *hors de combat* by sickness, wounds, detention, or any other cause, shall in all circumstances be treated humanely, without any adverse distinction founded on race, colour, religion or faith, sex, birth or wealth, or any other similar criteria. To this end the following acts are and shall remain

prohibited at any time and in any place whatsoever with respect to the above-mentioned persons:

(a) violence to life and person, in particular murder of all kinds, mutilation, cruel treatment and torture;

(b) taking of hostages;

(c) outrages upon personal dignity, in particular humiliating and degrading treatment;

(d) the passing of sentences and the carrying out of executions without previous judgment pronounced by a regularly constituted court, affording all the judicial guarantees which are recognized as indispensable by civilized peoples.

(2) The wounded and sick shall be collected and cared for.

An impartial humanitarian body, such as the International Committee of the Red Cross, may offer its services to the Parties to the conflict.

The Parties to the conflict should further endeavour to bring into force, by means of special agreements, all or part of the other provisions of the present Convention.

The application of the preceding provisions shall not affect the legal status of the Parties to the conflict.

Art. 4. Persons protected by the Convention are those who, at a given moment and in any manner whatsoever, find themselves, in case of a conflict or occupation, in the hands of a Party to the conflict or Occupying Power of which they are not nationals.

Nationals of a State which is not bound by the Convention are not protected by it. Nationals of a neutral State who find themselves in the territory of a belligerent State, and nationals of a co-belligerent State, shall not be regarded as protected persons while the State of which they are nationals has normal diplomatic representation in the State in whose hands they are.

The provisions of Part II are, however, wider in application, as defined in Article 13.

Persons protected by the Geneva Convention for the Amelioration of the Condition of the Wounded and Sick in Armed Forces in the Field of 12 August 1949, or by the Geneva Convention for the Amelioration of the Condition of Wounded, Sick and Shipwrecked Members of Armed Forces at Sea of 12 August 1949, or by the Geneva Convention relative to the Treatment of Prisoners of War of 12 August 1949, shall not be considered as protected persons within the meaning of the present Convention.

Art. 146. The High Contracting Parties undertake to enact any legislation necessary to provide effective penal sanctions for persons committing, or ordering to be committed, any of the grave breaches of the present Convention defined in the following Article.

Each High Contracting Party shall be under the obligation to search for persons alleged to have committed, or to have ordered to be committed, such grave breaches, and shall bring such persons, regardless of their nationality, before its own courts. It may also, if it prefers, and in accordance with the provisions of its own legislation, hand such persons over for trial to another High Contracting Party concerned, provided such High Contracting Party has made out a prima facie case.

Each High Contracting Party shall take measures necessary for the suppression of all acts contrary to the provisions of the present Convention other than the grave breaches defined in the following Article.

In all circumstances, the accused persons shall benefit by safeguards of proper trial and defence, which shall not be less favourable than those provided by Article 105 and those following of the Geneva Convention relative to the Treatment of Prisoners of War of 12 August 1949.

Art. 147. Grave breaches to which the preceding Article relates shall be those involving any of the following acts, if committed against persons or property protected by the present Convention: wilful killing, torture or inhuman treatment, including biological experiments, wilfully causing great suffering or serious injury to body or health, unlawful deportation or transfer or unlawful confinement of a protected person, compelling a protected person to serve in the forces of a hostile Power, or wilfully depriving a protected person of the rights of fair and regular trial prescribed in the present Convention, taking of hostages and extensive destruction and appropriation of property, not justified by military necessity and carried out unlawfully and wantonly.

Protocol Additional (I) to the Geneva Conventions of 12 August 1949, and Relating to the Protection of Victims of International Armed Conflicts

Article 1 – General principles and scope of application

1. The High Contracting Parties undertake to respect and to ensure respect for this Protocol in all circumstances.

2. In cases not covered by this Protocol or by other international agreements, civilians and combatants remain under the protection and authority of the principles of international law derived from established custom, from the principles of humanity and from dictates of public conscience.

3. This Protocol, which supplements the Geneva Conventions of 12 August 1949 for the protection of war victims, shall apply in the situations referred to in Article 2 common to those Conventions.

4. The situations referred to in the preceding paragraph include armed conflicts which peoples are fighting against colonial domination and alien occupation and against racist regimes in the exercise of their right of self-determination, as enshrined in the Charter of the United Nations and the Declaration on Principles of International Law concerning Friendly Relations and Co-operation among States in accordance with the Charter of the United Nations.

. . . .

SECTION I: METHODS AND MEANS OF WARFARE

Article 35 – Basic rules

1. In any armed conflict, the right of the Parties to the conflict to choose methods or means of warfare is not unlimited.

2. It is prohibited to employ weapons, projectiles and material and methods of warfare of a nature to cause superfluous injury or unnecessary suffering.

3. It is prohibited to employ methods or means of warfare which are intended, or may be expected, to cause widespread, long-term and severe damage to the natural environment.

Article 36 – New weapons

In the study, development, acquisition or adoption of a new weapon, means or method of warfare, a High Contracting Party is under an obligation to determine whether its employment would, in some or all circumstances, be prohibited by this Protocol or by any other rule of international law applicable to the High Contracting Party.

Article 37 – Prohibition of Perfidy

1. It is prohibited to kill, injure or capture an adversary by resort to perfidy. Acts inviting the confidence of an adversary to lead him to believe that he is entitled to, or is obliged to accord, protection under the rules of international law applicable in armed conflict, with intent to betray that confidence, shall constitute perfidy. The following acts are examples of perfidy:

(a) the feigning of an intent to negotiate under a flag of truce or of a surrender;
(b) the feigning of an incapacitation by wounds or sickness;
(c) the feigning of civilian, non-combatant status; and
(d) the feigning of protected status by the use of signs, emblems or uniforms of the United Nations or of neutral or other States not Parties to the conflict.

2. Ruses of war are not prohibited. Such ruses are acts which are intended to mislead an adversary or to induce him to act recklessly but which infringe no rule of international law applicable in armed conflict and which are not perfidious because they do not invite the confidence of an adversary with respect to protection under that law. The following are examples of such ruses: the use of camouflage, decoys, mock operations and misinformation.

Article 38 – Recognized emblems

1. It is prohibited to make improper use of the distinctive emblem of the red cross, red crescent or red lion and sun or of other emblems, signs or signals provided for by the Conventions or by this Protocol. It is also prohibited to misuse deliberately in an armed conflict other internationally recognized protective emblems, signs or signals, including the flag of truce, and the protective emblem of cultural property.

2. It is prohibited to make use of the distinctive emblem of the United Nations, except as authorized by that Organization.

Article 39 – Emblems of nationality

1. It is prohibited to make use in an armed conflict of the flags or military emblems, insignia or uniforms of neutral or other States not Parties to the conflict.

2. It is prohibited to make use of the flags or military emblems, insignia or uniforms of adverse Parties while engaging in attacks or in order to shield, favour, protect or impede military operations.

3. Nothing in this Article or in Article 37, paragraph 1 (d), shall affect the existing generally recognized rules of international law applicable to espionage or to the use of flags in the conduct of armed conflict at sea.

Article 40 – Quarter

It is prohibited to order that there shall be no survivors, to threaten an adversary therewith or to conduct hostilities on this basis.

Article 41 – Safeguard of an enemy *hors de combat*

1. A person who is recognized or who, in the circumstances should be recognized to be *hors de combat* shall not be made the object of attack.

2. A person is *hors de combat* if:

(a) he is in the power of an adverse Party;
(b) he clearly expresses an intention to surrender; or
(c) he has been rendered unconscious or is otherwise incapacitated by wounds or sickness, and therefore is incapable of defending himself; provided that in any of these cases he abstains from any hostile act and does not attempt to escape.

3. When persons entitled to protection as prisoners of war have fallen into the power or an adverse Party under unusual conditions of combat which prevent their evacuation as provided for in Part III, Section I, of the Third Convention, they shall be released and all feasible precautions shall be taken to ensure their safety.

Article 42 – Occupants of aircraft

1. No person parachuting from an aircraft in distress shall be made the object of attack during his descent.

2. Upon reaching the ground in territory controlled by an adverse Party, a person who has parachuted from an aircraft in distress shall be given an opportunity to surrender before being made the object of attack, unless it is apparent that he is engaging in a hostile act.

3. Airborne troops are not protected by this Article.

. . . .

PART IV

CIVILIAN POPULATION

SECTION I: GENERAL PROTECTION AGAINST EFFECTS OF HOSTILITIES

Chapter I

BASIC RULE AND FIELD OF APPLICATION

Article 48 – Basic rule

In order to ensure respect for and protection of the civilian population and civilian objects, the Parties to the conflict shall at all times distinguish between the civilian population and combatants and between civilian objects and military objectives and accordingly shall direct their operations only against military objectives.

Article 49 – Definition of attacks and scope of application

1. "Attacks" means acts of violence against the adversary, whether in offence or in defence.

2. The provisions of this Protocol with respect to attacks apply to all attacks in whatever territory conducted, including the national territory belonging to a Party to the conflict but under the control of an adverse Party.

3. The provisions of this section apply to any land, air or sea warfare which may affect the civilian population, individual civilians or civilian objects on land. They further apply to all attacks from the sea or from the air against objectives on land but do not otherwise affect the rules of international law applicable in armed conflict at sea or in the air.

4. The provisions of this section are additional to the rules concerning humanitarian protection contained in the Fourth Convention, particularly in part II thereof, and in other international agreements binding upon the High Contracting Parties, as well as to other rules of international law relating to the protection of civilians and civilian objects on land, at sea or in the air against the effects of hostilities.

Chapter II

CIVILIANS AND CIVILIAN POPULATION

Article 50 – Definition of civilians and civilian population

1. A civilian is any person who does not belong to one of the categories of persons referred to in Article 4 (A) (1), (2), (3) and (6) of the Third Convention and in Article 43 of this Protocol. In case of doubt whether a person is a civilian, that person shall be considered to be a civilian.

2. The civilian population comprises all persons who are civilians.

3. The presence within the civilian population of individuals who do not come within the definition of civilians does not deprive the population of its civilian character.

Article 51 – Protection of the civilian population

1. The civilian population and individual civilians shall enjoy general protection against dangers arising from military operations. To give effect to this protection, the following rules, which are additional to other applicable rules of international law, shall be observed in all circumstances.

2. The civilian population as such, as well as individual civilians, shall not be the object of attack. Acts or threats of violence the primary purpose of which is to spread terror among the civilian population are prohibited.

3. Civilians shall enjoy the protection afforded by this section, unless and for such time as they take a direct part in hostilities.

4. Indiscriminate attacks are prohibited. Indiscriminate attacks are:

(a) those which are not directed at a specific military objective;
(b) those which employ a method or means of combat which cannot be directed at a specific military objective; or
(c) those which employ a method or means of combat the effects of which cannot be limited as required by this Protocol;
(d) and consequently, in each such case, are of a nature to strike military objectives and civilians or civilian objects without distinction.

5. Among others, the following types of attacks are to be considered as indiscriminate:

(a) an attack by bombardment by any methods or means which treats as a single military objective a number of clearly separated and distinct military objectives located in a city, town, village or other area containing a similar concentration of civilians or civilian objects; and

(b) an attack which may be expected to cause incidental loss of civilian life, injury to civilians, damage to civilian objects, or a combination thereof, which would be excessive in relation to the concrete and direct military advantage anticipated.

6. Attacks against the civilian population or civilians by way of reprisals are prohibited.

7. The presence or movements of the civilian population or individual civilians shall not be used to render certain points or areas immune from military operations, in particular in attempts to shield military objectives from attacks or to shield, favour or impede military operations. The Parties to the conflict shall not direct the movement of the civilian population or individual civilians in order to attempt to shield military objectives from attacks or to shield military operations.

8. Any violation of these prohibitions shall not release the Parties to the conflict from their legal obligations with respect to the civilian population and civilians, including the obligation to take the precautionary measures provided for in Article 57.

. . . .

SECTION II
REPRESSION OF BREACHES
OF THE CONVENTIONS AND OF THIS PROTOCOL

Article 85 – Repression of breaches of this Protocol

1. The provisions of the Conventions relating to the repression of breaches and grave breaches, supplemented by this Section, shall apply to the repression of breaches and grave breaches of this Protocol.

2. Acts described as grave breaches in the Conventions are grave breaches of this Protocol if committed against persons in the power of an adverse Party protected by Articles 44, 45 and 73 of this Protocol, or against the wounded, sick and shipwrecked of the adverse Party who are protected by this Protocol, or against those medical or religious personnel, medical units or medical transports which are under the control of the adverse Party and are protected by this Protocol.

3. In addition to the grave breaches defined in Article 11, the following acts shall be regarded as grave breaches of this Protocol, when committed wilfully, in violation of the relevant provisions of this Protocol, and causing death or serious injury to body or health:

(a) making the civilian population or individual civilians the object of attack;
(b) launching an indiscriminate attack affecting the civilian population or civilian objects in the knowledge that such attack will cause excessive loss of life, injury to civilians or damage to civilian objects, as defined in Article 57, paragraph 2 (a)(iii);
(c) launching an attack against works or installations containing dangerous forces in the knowledge that such attack will cause excessive loss of life, injury to civilians or damage to civilian objects, as defined in Article 57, paragraph 2 (a)(iii);
(d) making non-defended localities and demilitarized zones the object of attack;
(e) making a person the object of attack in the knowledge that he is *hors de combat*;
(f) the perfidious use, in violation of Article 37, of the distinctive emblem of the red cross, red crescent or red lion and sun or of other protective signs recognized by the Conventions or this Protocol.

4. In addition to the grave breaches defined in the preceding paragraphs and in the Conventions, the following shall be regarded as grave breaches of this Protocol, when committed wilfully and in violation of the Conventions or the Protocol:

(a) the transfer by the occupying Power of parts of its own civilian population into the territory it occupies, or the deportation or transfer of all or parts of the population of the occupied territory within or outside this territory, in violation of Article 49 of the Fourth Convention;

(b) unjustifiable delay in the repatriation of prisoners of war or civilians;

(c) practices of apartheid and other inhuman and degrading practices involving outrages upon personal dignity, based on racial discrimination;

(d) making the clearly-recognized historic monuments, works of art or places of worship which constitute the cultural or spiritual heritage of peoples and to which special protection has been given by special arrangement, for example, within the framework of a competent international organization, the object of attack, causing as a result extensive destruction thereof, where there is no evidence of the violation by the adverse Party of Article 53, subparagraph (b), and when such historic monuments, works of art and places of worship are not located in the immediate proximity of military objectives;

(e) depriving a person protected by the Conventions or referred to in paragraph 2 or this Article of the rights of fair and regular trial.

5. Without prejudice to the application of the Conventions and of this Protocol, grave breaches of these instruments shall be regarded as war crimes.

Article 86 – Failure to act

1. The High Contracting Parties and the Parties to the conflict shall repress grave breaches, and take measures necessary to suppress all other breaches, of the Conventions or of this Protocol which result from a failure to act when under a duty to do so.

2. The fact that a breach of the Conventions or of this Protocol was committed by a subordinate does not absolve his superiors from penal disciplinary responsibility, as the case may be, if they knew, or had information which should have enabled them to conclude in the circumstances at the time, that he was committing or was going to commit such a breach and if they did not take all feasible measures within their power to prevent or repress the breach.

Article 87 – Duty of commanders

1. The High Contracting Parties and the Parties to the conflict shall require military commanders, with respect to members of the armed forces under their command and other persons under their control, to prevent and, where necessary, to suppress and to report to competent authorities breaches of the Conventions and of this Protocol.

2. In order to prevent and suppress breaches, High Contracting Parties and Parties to the conflict shall require that, commensurate with their level of responsibility, commanders ensure that members of the armed forces under their command are aware of their obligations under the Conventions and this Protocol.

3. The High Contracting Parties and Parties to the conflict shall require any commander who is aware that subordinates or other persons under his control are going to commit or

have committed a breach of the Conventions or of this Protocol, to initiate such steps as are necessary to prevent such violations of the Conventions or this Protocol, and, where appropriate, to initiate disciplinary or penal action against violators thereof.

Protocol Additional (II) to the Geneva Conventions of 12 August 1949, and Relating to the Protection of Victims of Non-International Armed Conflicts

PART I

SCOPE OF THIS PROTOCOL

Article 1 – Material field of application

1. This Protocol, which develops and supplements Article 3 common to the Geneva Conventions of 12 August 1949 without modifying its existing conditions or application, shall apply to all armed conflicts which are not covered by Article 1 of the Protocol Additional to the Geneva Conventions of 12 August 1949, and relating to the Protection of Victims of International Armed Conflicts (Protocol I) and which take place in the territory of a High Contracting Party between its armed forces and dissident armed forces or other organized armed groups which, under responsible command, exercise such control over a part of its territory as to enable them to carry out sustained and concerted military operations and to implement this Protocol.

2. This Protocol shall not apply to situations of internal disturbances and tensions, such as riots, isolated and sporadic acts of violence and other acts of a similar nature, as not being armed conflicts.

Article 2 – Personal field of application

1. This Protocol shall be applied without any adverse distinction founded on race, colour, sex, language, religion or belief, political or other opinion, national or social origin, wealth, birth or other status, or on any other similar criteria (hereinafter referred to as "adverse distinction") to all persons affected by an armed conflict as defined in Article 1.

2. At the end of the armed conflict, all the persons who have been deprived of their liberty or whose liberty has been restricted for reasons related to such conflict, as well as those deprived of their liberty or whose liberty is restricted after the conflict for the same reasons, shall enjoy the protection of Articles 5 and 6 until the end of such deprivation or restriction of liberty.

Article 3 – Non-intervention

1. Nothing in this Protocol shall be invoked for the purpose of affecting the sovereignty of a State or the responsibility of the government, by all legitimate means, to maintain or re-establish law and order in the State or to defend the national unity and territorial integrity of the State.

2. Nothing in this Protocol shall be invoked as a justification for intervening, directly or indirectly, for any reason whatever, in the armed conflict or in the internal or external affairs of the High Contracting Party in the territory of which that conflict occurs.

PART II

HUMANE TREATMENT

Article 4 – Fundamental guarantees

1. All persons who do not take a direct part or who have ceased to take part in hostilities, whether or not their liberty has been restricted, are entitled to respect for their person, honour and convictions and religious practices. They shall in all circumstances be treated humanely, without any adverse distinction. It is prohibited to order that there shall be no survivors.

2. Without prejudice to the generality of the foregoing, the following acts against the persons referred to in paragraph I are and shall remain prohibited at any time and in any place whatsoever:

(a) violence to the life, health and physical or mental well-being of persons, in particular murder as well as cruel treatment such as torture, mutilation or any form of corporal punishment;
(b) collective punishments;
(c) taking of hostages;
(d) acts of terrorism;
(e) outrages upon personal dignity, in particular humiliating and degrading treatment, rape, enforced prostitution and any form or indecent assault;
(f) slavery and the slave trade in all their forms;
(g) pillage;
(h) threats to commit any or the foregoing acts.

3. Children shall be provided with the care and aid they require, and in particular:

(a) they shall receive an education, including religious and moral education, in keeping with the wishes of their parents, or in the absence of parents, of those responsible for their care;
(b) all appropriate steps shall be taken to facilitate the reunion of families temporarily separated;
(c) children who have not attained the age of fifteen years shall neither be recruited in the armed forces or groups nor allowed to take part in hostilities;
(d) the special protection provided by this Article to children who have not attained the age of fifteen years shall remain applicable to them if they take a direct part in hostilities despite the provisions of subparagraph (c) and are captured;
(e) measures shall be taken, if necessary, and whenever possible with the consent of their parents or persons who by law or custom are primarily responsible for their care, to remove children temporarily from the area in which hostilities are taking place to a safer area within the country and ensure that they are accompanied by persons responsible for their safety and well-being.

Statute of the International Criminal Tribunal for Rwanda

Article 4

Violations of Article 3 common to the Geneva Conventions and of Additional Protocol II

The International Tribunal for Rwanda shall have the power to prosecute persons committing or ordering to be committed serious violations of Article 3 common to the Geneva Conventions of 12 August 1949 for the Protection of War Victims, and of Additional Protocol II thereto of 8 June 1977. These violations shall include, but shall not be limited to:

(a) Violence to life, health and physical or mental well-being of persons, in particular murder as well as cruel treatment such as torture, mutilation or any form of corporal punishment;
(b) Collective punishments;
(c) Taking of hostages;
(d) d) Acts of terrorism;
(e) Outrages upon personal dignity, in particular humiliating and degrading treatment, rape, enforced prostitution and any form of indecent assault;
(f) Pillage;
(g) The passing of sentences and the carrying out of executions without previous judgement pronounced by a regularly constituted court, affording all the judicial guarantees which are recognized as indispensable by civilized peoples;
(h) Threats to commit any of the foregoing acts.

Statute of the International Tribunal for the Former Yugoslavia

Article 2

Grave breaches of the Geneva Conventions of 1949

The International Tribunal shall have the power to prosecute persons committing or ordering to be committed grave breaches of the Geneva Conventions of 12 August 1949, namely the following acts against persons or property protected under the provisions of the relevant Geneva Convention:

(a) wilful killing;
(b) torture or inhuman treatment, including biological experiments;
(c) wilfully causing great suffering or serious injury to body or health;
(d) extensive destruction and appropriation of property, not justified by military necessity and carried out unlawfully and wantonly;
(e) compelling a prisoner of war or a civilian to serve in the forces of a hostile power;
(f) wilfully depriving a prisoner of war or a civilian of the rights of fair and regular trial;
(g) unlawful deportation or transfer or unlawful confinement of a civilian;
(h) taking civilians as hostages.

Article 3

Violations of the laws or customs of war

The International Tribunal shall have the power to prosecute persons violating the laws or customs of war. Such violations shall include, but not be limited to:

(a) employment of poisonous weapons or other weapons calculated to cause unnecessary suffering;

(b) wanton destruction of cities, towns or villages, or devastation not justified by military necessity;

(c) attack, or bombardment, by whatever means, of undefended towns, villages, dwellings, or buildings;

(d) seizure of, destruction or wilful damage done to institutions dedicated to religion, charity and education, the arts and sciences, historic monuments and works of art and science;

(e) plunder of public or private property.

Statute of the International Criminal Court

Article 5

Crimes within the jurisdiction of the Court

1. The jurisdiction of the Court shall be limited to the most serious crimes of concern to the international community as a whole. The Court has jurisdiction in accordance with this Statute with respect to the following crimes:

. . .

(c) War crimes;

. . . .

Article 8

War crimes

1. The Court shall have jurisdiction in respect of war crimes in particular when committed as a part of a plan or policy or as part of a large-scale commission of such crimes.

2. For the purpose of this Statute, "war crimes" means:

(a) Grave breaches of the Geneva Conventions of 12 August 1949, namely, any of the following acts against persons or property protected under the provisions of the relevant Geneva Convention:

(i) Wilful killing;

(ii) Torture or inhuman treatment, including biological experiments;

(iii) Wilfully causing great suffering, or serious injury to body or health;

(iv) Extensive destruction and appropriation of property, not justified by military necessity and carried out unlawfully and wantonly;

(v) Compelling a prisoner of war or other protected person to serve in the forces of a hostile Power;

(vi) Wilfully depriving a prisoner of war or other protected person of the rights of fair and regular trial;

(vii) Unlawful deportation or transfer or unlawful confinement;

(viii) Taking of hostages.

(b) Other serious violations of the laws and customs applicable in international armed conflict, within the established framework of international law, namely, any of the following acts:

(i) Intentionally directing attacks against the civilian population as such or against individual civilians not taking direct part in hostilities;

(ii) Intentionally directing attacks against civilian objects, that is, objects which are not military objectives;

(iii) Intentionally directing attacks against personnel, installations, material, units or vehicles involved in a humanitarian assistance or peacekeeping mission in accordance with the Charter of the United Nations, as long as they are entitled to the protection given to civilians or civilian objects under the international law of armed conflict;

(iv) Intentionally launching an attack in the knowledge that such attack will cause incidental loss of life or injury to civilians or damage to civilian objects or widespread, long-term and severe damage to the natural environment which would be clearly excessive in relation to the concrete and direct overall military advantage anticipated;

(v) Attacking or bombarding, by whatever means, towns, villages, dwellings or buildings which are undefended and which are not military objectives;

(vi) Killing or wounding a combatant who, having laid down his arms or having no longer means of defence, has surrendered at discretion;

(vii) Making improper use of a flag of truce, of the flag or of the military insignia and uniform of the enemy or of the United Nations, as well as of the distinctive emblems of the Geneva Conventions, resulting in death or serious personal injury;

(viii) The transfer, directly or indirectly, by the Occupying Power of parts of its own civilian population into the territory it occupies, or the deportation or transfer of all or parts of the population of the occupied territory within or outside this territory;

(ix) Intentionally directing attacks against buildings dedicated to religion, education, art, science or charitable purposes, historic monuments, hospitals and places where the sick and wounded are collected, provided they are not military objectives;

(x) Subjecting persons who are in the power of an adverse party to physical mutilation or to medical or scientific experiments of any kind which are neither justified by the medical, dental or hospital treatment of the person concerned nor carried out in his or her interest, and which cause death to or seriously endanger the health of such person or persons;

(xi) Killing or wounding treacherously individuals belonging to the hostile nation or army;

(xii) Declaring that no quarter will be given;

(xiii) Destroying or seizing the enemy's property unless such destruction or seizure be imperatively demanded by the necessities of war;

(xiv) Declaring abolished, suspended or inadmissible in a court of law the rights and actions of the nationals of the hostile party;

(xv) Compelling the nationals of the hostile party to take part in the operations of war directed against their own country, even if they were in the belligerent's service before the commencement of the war;

(xvi) Pillaging a town or place, even when taken by assault;

(xvii) Employing poison or poisoned weapons;

(xviii) Employing asphyxiating, poisonous or other gases, and all analogous liquids, materials or devices;

(xix) Employing bullets which expand or flatten easily in the human body, such as bullets with a hard envelope which does not entirely cover the core or is pierced with incisions;

(xx) Employing weapons, projectiles and material and methods of warfare which are of a nature to cause superfluous injury or unnecessary suffering or which are inherently indiscriminate in violation of the international law of armed conflict, provided that such weapons, projectiles and material and methods of warfare are the subject of a comprehensive prohibition and are included in an annex to this Statute, by an amendment in accordance with the relevant provisions set forth in articles 121 and 123;

(xxi) Committing outrages upon personal dignity, in particular humiliating and degrading treatment;

(xxii) Committing rape, sexual slavery, enforced prostitution, forced pregnancy, as defined in article 7, paragraph 2 (f), enforced sterilization, or any other form of sexual violence also constituting a grave breach of the Geneva Conventions;

(xxiii) Utilizing the presence of a civilian or other protected person to render certain points, areas or military forces immune from military operations;

(xxiv) Intentionally directing attacks against buildings, material, medical units and transport, and personnel using the distinctive emblems of the Geneva Conventions in conformity with international law;

(xxv) Intentionally using starvation of civilians as a method of warfare by depriving them of objects indispensable to their survival, including wilfully impeding relief supplies as provided for under the Geneva Conventions;

(xxvi) Conscripting or enlisting children under the age of fifteen years into the national armed forces or using them to participate actively in hostilities.

(c) In the case of an armed conflict not of an international character, serious violations of article 3 common to the four Geneva Conventions of 12 August 1949, namely, any of the following acts committed against persons taking no active part in the hostilities, including members of armed forces who have laid down their arms and those placed *hors de* combat by sickness, wounds, detention or any other cause:

(i) Violence to life and person, in particular murder of all kinds, mutilation, cruel treatment and torture;

(ii) Committing outrages upon personal dignity, in particular humiliating and degrading treatment;

(iii) Taking of hostages;

(iv) The passing of sentences and the carrying out of executions without previous judgement pronounced by a regularly constituted court, affording all judicial guarantees which are generally recognized as indispensable.

(d) Paragraph 2 (c) applies to armed conflicts not of an international character and thus does not apply to situations of internal disturbances and tensions, such as riots, isolated and sporadic acts of violence or other acts of a similar nature.

(e) Other serious violations of the laws and customs applicable in armed conflicts not of an international character, within the established framework of international law, namely, any of the following acts:

(i) Intentionally directing attacks against the civilian population as such or against individual civilians not taking direct part in hostilities;

(ii) Intentionally directing attacks against buildings, material, medical units and transport, and personnel using the distinctive emblems of the Geneva Conventions in conformity with international law;

(iii) Intentionally directing attacks against personnel, installations, material, units or vehicles involved in a humanitarian assistance or peacekeeping mission in accordance with the Charter of the United Nations, as long as they are entitled to the protection given to civilians or civilian objects under the law of armed conflict;

(iv) Intentionally directing attacks against buildings dedicated to religion, education, art, science or charitable purposes, historic monuments, hospitals and places where the sick and wounded are collected, provided they are not military objectives;

(v) Pillaging a town or place, even when taken by assault;

(vi) Committing rape, sexual slavery, enforced prostitution, forced pregnancy, as defined in article 7, paragraph 2 (f), enforced sterilization, and any other form of sexual violence also constituting a serious violation of article 3 common to the four Geneva Conventions;

(vii) Conscripting or enlisting children under the age of fifteen years into armed forces or groups or using them to participate actively in hostilities;

(viii) Ordering the displacement of the civilian population for reasons related to the conflict, unless the security of the civilians involved or imperative military reasons so demand;

(ix) Killing or wounding treacherously a combatant adversary;

(x) Declaring that no quarter will be given;

(xi) Subjecting persons who are in the power of another party to the conflict to physical mutilation or to medical or scientific experiments of any kind which are neither justified by the medical, dental or hospital treatment of the person concerned nor carried out in his or her interest, and which cause death to or seriously endanger the health of such person or persons;

(xii) Destroying or seizing the property of an adversary unless such destruction or seizure be imperatively demanded by the necessities of the conflict;

(f) Paragraph 2 (e) applies to armed conflicts not of an international character and thus does not apply to situations of internal disturbances and tensions, such as riots, isolated and sporadic acts of violence or other acts of a similar nature. It applies to armed conflicts that take place in the territory of a State when there is protracted armed conflict between governmental authorities and organized armed groups or between such groups.

3. Nothing in paragraphs 2 (c) and (d) shall affect the responsibility of a Government to maintain or re-establish law and order in the State or to defend the unity and territorial integrity of the State, by all legitimate means.

International and Noninternational Conflicts

The Prosecutor v. Tadić (Final Judgment)
Case No. IT-94-1-T
Trial Chamber
International Criminal Tribunal for the Former Yugoslavia
(7 May 1997)

[Tadic was indicted for committing grave breaches of the Geneva Conventions (*viz.,* wilful killing, torture or inhuman treatment, and wilfully causing great suffering or serious injury to body and health), violations of the laws and customs of war (*viz.,* murder and cruel treatment), and crimes against humanity (*viz.*, murder, persecution, and inhumane acts) at Kozarac and the Omarska concentration camp in the former Yugoslavia in June 1992. He was arrested in Germany in February 1994 and turned over to the ICT-Y. He pleaded not guilty.

The Chamber of the ICT-Y examined the testimony of dozens of witnesses and documentary evidence. The following excerpts from the Chamber's judgment address the international law governing the war crimes.]

557. Having considered the evidence offered at trial, it is now appropriate to discuss the law relating to the offences charged.

558. The competence of this International Tribunal and hence of this Trial Chamber is determined by the terms of the Statute. Article 1 of the Statute confers power to prosecute persons responsible for serious violations of international humanitarian law committed in the territory of the former Yugoslavia since 1991. The Statute then, in Articles 2, 3, 4 and 5, specifies the crimes under international law over which the International Tribunal has jurisdiction. In the present case, only Articles 2, 3 . . . are relevant. . . .

559. Each of the relevant Articles of the Statute, either by its terms or by virtue of the customary rules which it imports, proscribes certain acts when committed "within the context of" an "armed conflict". Article 2 of the Statute directs the Trial Chamber to the grave breaches regime of the Geneva Conventions which applies only to armed conflicts of an international character and to offences committed against persons or property regarded as "protected", in particular civilians in the hands of a party to a conflict of which they are not nationals[ ]. Article 3 of the Statute directs the Trial Chamber to those sources of customary international humanitarian law that comprise the "laws or customs of war". Article 3 is a general provision covering, subject to certain conditions, all violations of international humanitarian law which do not fall under Article 2 or are not covered by Articles 4 or 5. This includes violations of the rules contained in Article 3 common to the Geneva Conventions ("Common Article 3"), applicable to armed conflicts in general, with which the accused has been charged under Article 3 of the Statute[ ]. . . .

560. Consequently, it is necessary to show, first, that an armed conflict existed at all relevant times in the territory of the Republic of Bosnia and Herzegovina and, secondly, that the acts of the accused were committed within the context of that armed conflict and for the application of Article 2, that the conflict was international in character and that the offences charged were committed against protected persons.

561. According to [*Prosecutor v. Tadic*, Appeals Chamber Decision on the Defence Motion for Interlocutory Appeal on Jurisdiction, Int'l Crim. Trib.-Yugo. (2 Oct. 1995) (hereinafter "the *Appeals Chamber Decision*)], the test for determining the existence of such a conflict is that

an armed conflict exists whenever there is a resort to armed force between States or protracted armed violence between governmental authorities and organized armed groups or between such groups within a State[ ].

562. The test applied by the Appeals Chamber to the existence of an armed conflict for the purposes of the rules contained in Common Article 3 focuses on two aspects of a conflict; the intensity of the conflict and the organization of the parties to the conflict. In an armed conflict of an internal or mixed character, these closely related criteria are used solely for the purpose, as a minimum, of distinguishing an armed conflict from banditry, unorganized and short-lived insurrections, or terrorist activities, which are not subject to

international humanitarian law[ ]. Factors relevant to this determination are addressed in the Commentary to Geneva Convention for the Amelioration of the Condition of the Wounded and Sick in Armed Forces in the Field, Convention I, ("*Commentary*, Geneva Convention I") [ ]....

568. Having regard then to the nature and scope of the conflict in the Republic of Bosnia and Herzegovina and the parties involved in that conflict, and irrespective of the relationship between the Federal Republic of Yugoslavia (Serbia and Montenegro) and the Bosnian Serb forces, the Trial Chamber finds that, at all relevant times, an armed conflict was taking place between the parties to the conflict in the Republic of Bosnia and Herzegovina of sufficient scope and intensity for the purposes of the application of the laws or customs of war embodied in Article 3 common to the four Geneva Conventions of 12 August 1949, applicable as it is to armed conflicts in general, including armed conflicts not of an international character.

. . . .

578. According to the Appeals Chamber, the Statute specifically restricts the prosecution of grave breaches to those committed against "persons or property protected under the provisions of the relevant Geneva Conventions". In this case, each of the victims of the crimes alleged to have been committed by the accused were civilians caught up in the ongoing armed conflict in the Republic of Bosnia and Herzegovina. Some of the victims were in towns and villages captured by the [Bosnian Serb forces], while others fell victim to the acts of the accused while detained at one of the camps established in opstina Prijedor to facilitate the ethnic cleansing of that area. As such, their status under the Geneva Conventions is governed by the terms of Article 4 of Geneva Convention Relative to the Protection of Civilian Persons in Time of War ("Geneva Convention IV"), which defines those civilians who fall under the protection of that Convention ("protected persons") as follows:

> Persons protected by the Convention are those who, at a given moment and in any manner whatsoever, find themselves, in case of a conflict or occupation, in the hands of a Party to the conflict or Occupying Power of which they are not nationals[ ].

The central question is thus whether at all relevant times the victims of the accused were in the hands of "a Party to the conflict or Occupying Power of which they are not nationals". Implicit in this expression is a threefold requirement. The first and second requirements are that the victims be "in the hands of" a "Party to the conflict or Occupying Power". The third is that the civilian victims not be nationals of that Party or Occupying Power. [The Chamber found that Tadic's victims were not "protected persons" because they were nationals (Bosnian Muslims and Croats) of the Occupying Power (Bosnian Serbs) even though the army of the Federal Republic of Yugoslavia (Serbia and Montenegro) earlier had occupied the Republic of Bosnia and Herzegovina and earlier had supported the Bosnian Serb forces.]

608. The consequence of this finding, as far as this trial is concerned, is that, since Article 2 of the Statute is applicable only to acts committed against "protected persons" within the meaning of the Geneva Conventions, and since it cannot be said that any of the victims, all of whom were civilians, were at any relevant time in the hands of a party to the conflict of which they were not nationals, the accused must be found not guilty of the counts which rely upon [Article 2's "grave breaches" provision].

609. Article 3 of the Statute directs the Trial Chamber to the laws or customs of war, being that body of customary international humanitarian law not covered by Articles 2,

4 or 5 of the Statute. As previously noted, that body of law includes the regime of protection established under Common Article 3 applicable to armed conflicts not of an international character, as a reflection of elementary considerations of humanity, and which is applicable to armed conflicts in general[ ]. Two aspects must be considered. First, there are the requirements imposed by Article 3 of the Statute for the inclusion of a law or custom of war within the jurisdiction of this International Tribunal. Secondly, there are the additional requirements for the applicability of the proscriptive rules contained in paragraph 1 of Common Article 3 in addition to the elements of the proscribed acts contained therein.[ ]

610. According to the Appeals Chamber, the conditions that must be satisfied to fulfil the requirements of Article 3 of the Statute are:

(i) the violation must constitute an infringement of a rule of international humanitarian law;

(ii) the rule must be customary in nature or, if it belongs to treaty law, the required conditions must be met;

(iii) the violation must be "serious", that is to say, it must constitute a breach of a rule protecting important values, and the breach must involve grave consequences for the victim . . . ; and

(iv) the violation of the rule must entail, under customary or conventional law, the individual criminal responsibility of the person breaching the rule[ ].

Those requirements apply to any and all laws or customs of war which Article 3 covers.

611. In relation to requirements (i) and (ii), it is sufficient to note that the Appeals Chamber has held, on the basis of [*Military and Paramilitary Activities in and against Nicaragua (Nicaragua v. United States)*, Int'l Ct. J. (1986)], that Common Article 3 satisfies these requirements as part of customary international humanitarian law[ ].

612. While, for some laws or customs of war, requirement (iii) may be of particular relevance, each of the prohibitions in Common Article 3: against murder; the taking of hostages; outrages upon personal dignity, in particular humiliating and degrading treatment; and the passing of sentences and the carrying-out of executions without previous judgment pronounced by a regularly constituted court, affording all the judicial guarantees which are recognized as indispensable by civilised peoples, constitute, as the Court put it, "elementary considerations of humanity", the breach of which may be considered to be a "breach of a rule protecting important values" and which "must involve grave consequences for the victim". Although it may be possible that a violation of some of the prohibitions of Common Article 3 may be so minor as to not involve "grave consequences for the victim", each of the violations with which the accused has been charged clearly does involve such consequences.

613. Finally, in relation to the fourth requirement, namely that the rule of customary international humanitarian law imposes individual criminal responsibility, the Appeals Chamber held in the *Appeals Chamber Decision* that

customary international law imposes criminal liability for serious violations of common Article 3, as supplemented by other general principles and rules on the protection of victims of internal armed conflict, and for breaching certain fundamental principles and rules regarding means and methods of combat in civil strife.

Consequently, this Trial Chamber has the competence to hear and determine the charges against the accused under Article 3 of the Statute relating to violations of the customary international humanitarian law applicable to armed conflicts, as found in Common Article 3.[ ] The rules contained in paragraph 1 of Common Article 3 proscribe a number of acts which: (i) are committed within the context of an armed conflict; (ii) have a close connection to the armed conflict; and (iii) are committed against persons taking no active part in hostilities. The first and second of these requirements have already been dealt with above. Consequently, the Trial Chamber turns to the third requirement.

615. The customary international humanitarian law regime governing conflicts not of an international character extends protection, from acts of murder, torture and other acts proscribed by Common Article 3, to:

> Persons taking no active part in the hostilities, including members of armed forces who have laid down their arms and those placed *hors de combat* by sickness, wounds, detention, or any other cause … without any adverse distinction founded on race, colour, religion or faith, sex, birth or wealth, or any other similar criteria. …

This protection embraces, at the least, all of those protected persons covered by the grave breaches regime applicable to conflicts of an international character: civilians, prisoners of war, wounded and sick members of the armed forces in the field and wounded sick and shipwrecked members of the armed forces at sea. Whereas the concept of "protected person" under the Geneva Conventions is defined positively, the class of persons protected by the operation of Common Article 3 is defined negatively. For that reason, the test the Trial Chamber has applied is to ask whether, at the time of the alleged offence, the alleged victim of the proscribed acts was directly taking part in hostilities, being those hostilities in the context of which the alleged offences are said to have been committed. If the answer to that question is negative, the victim will enjoy the protection of the proscriptions contained in Common Article 3.

616. It is unnecessary to define exactly the line dividing those taking an active part in hostilities and those who are not so involved. It is sufficient to examine the relevant facts of each victim and to ascertain whether, in each individual's circumstances, that person was actively involved in hostilities at the relevant time. Violations of the rules contained in Common Article 3 are alleged to have been committed against persons who, on the evidence presented to this Trial Chamber, were captured or detained by Bosnian Serb forces, whether committed during the course of the armed take-over of the Kozarac area or while those persons were being rounded-up for transport to each of the camps in opstina Prijedor. Whatever their involvement in hostilities prior to that time, each of these classes of persons cannot be said to have been taking an active part in the hostilities. Even if they were members of the armed forces of the Government of the Republic of Bosnia and Herzegovina or otherwise engaging in hostile acts prior to capture, such persons would be considered "members of armed forces" who are "placed *hors de combat* by detention". Consequently, these persons enjoy the protection of those rules of customary international humanitarian law applicable to armed conflicts, as contained in Article 3 of the Statute.

617. For the purposes of the application of the rules of customary international humanitarian law contained in Common Article 3, this Trial Chamber finds, in the present case, that: (i) an armed conflict existed at all relevant times in relation to the alleged offences; (ii) each of the victims of the acts charged was a person protected by those provisions being a person taking no active part in the hostilities; and (iii) the

offences charged were committed within the context of that armed conflict. Accordingly, the requirements of Article 3 of the Statute are met.

. . . .

[The chamber then applied the foregoing legal analysis to its factual findings. Tadiç was found guilty of violating the laws and customs of war.].

∼

QUESTIONS & COMMENTS

(1) Although the language of Common Article 3 of the Geneva Conventions suggests that its protections do not extend to international conflicts, the ICT has held that it does. In *Prosecutor v. Mucic et al.*, ¶¶ 140–150 (20 Feb. 2001), the ICT Appeals Chamber held that

> [i]t is indisputable that [C]ommon Article 3, which sets forth a minimum core of mandatory rules, reflects the fundamental humanitarian principles which underlie international humanitarian law as a whole, and upon which the Geneva Conventions in their entirety are based. . . . It is both legally and morally untenable that the rules contained in [C]ommon Article 3, which constitute mandatory minimum rules applicable to internal conflicts, in which rules are less developed than in respect of international conflicts, would not be applicable to conflicts of an international character. The rules of [C]ommon Article 3 are encompassed and further developed in the body of rules applicable to international conflicts. It is logical that this minimum be applicable to international conflicts as the substance of these core rules is identical. [S]omething which is prohibited in internal conflicts is necessarily outlawed in an international conflict where the scope of the rules is broader."

See also Prosecutor v. Naletilic and Martinovic, ICT-Trial Chamber, ¶ 228 (31 Mar. 2003) (Common Article 3 "applies regardless of the internal or international character of the conflict.").

(2) Article 4 of the Fourth Geneva Conventions governing civilians states:

> Persons protected by the Convention are those who, at a given moment and in any manner whatsoever, find themselves, in case of a conflict or occupation, in the hands of a Party to the conflict or Occupying Power of which they are not nationals.

> Nationals of a State which is not bound by the Convention are not protected by it. Nationals of a neutral State who find themselves in the territory of a belligerent State, and nationals of a co-belligerent State, shall not be regarded as protected persons while the State of which they are nationals has normal diplomatic representation in the State in whose hands they are.

In *Prosecutor v. Aleksovski*, ¶ 151 (24 Mar. 2000), the ICTY-Appeals Chamber held that "in certain circumstances, Article 4 [of Geneva Convention IV] may be given a wider construction so that a person may be accorded protected status, notwithstanding the fact that he is of the same nationality as his captors." Under what circumstances could such wider construction be given? If Common Article 3 also applies to international conflicts, could the other provisions of the Geneva Conventions (*e.g.*, due process protections) that are associated with Common Article 3 protections (*e.g.*, prohibition of passing sentences without judicial guarantees) be used for extending protections to persons not covered by Article 4 (*e.g.*, nationals who are in the hands of their own government, nationals belonging to neutral states)?

(3) U.S. law prohibits war crimes under 18 U.S.C. §2441:

(a) Offense. – Whoever, whether inside or outside the United States, commits a war crime, in any of the circumstances described in subsection (b), shall be fined under this title or imprisoned for life or any term of years, or both, and if death results to the victim, shall also be subject to the penalty of death.

(b) Circumstances. – The circumstances referred to in subsection (a) are that the person committing such war crime or the victim of such war crime is a member of the Armed Forces of the United States or a national of the United States (as defined in section 101 of the Immigration and Nationality Act).

(c) Definition. – As used in this section the term "war crime" means any conduct –

(1) defined as a grave breach in any of the international conventions signed at Geneva 12 August 1949, or any protocol to such convention to which the United States is a party;

(2) prohibited by Article 23, 25, 27, or 28 of the Annex to the Hague Convention IV, Respecting the Laws and Customs of War on Land, signed 18 October 1907;

(3) which constitutes a violation of common Article 3 of the international conventions signed at Geneva, 12 August 1949, or any protocol to such convention to which the United States is a party and which deals with non-international armed conflict; or

(4) of a person who, in relation to an armed conflict and contrary to the provisions of the Protocol on Prohibitions or Restrictions on the Use of Mines, Booby-Traps and Other Devices as amended at Geneva on 3 May 1996 (Protocol II as amended on 3 May 1996), when the United States is a party to such Protocol, willfully kills or causes serious injury to civilians.

(4) President Bush on February 7, 2002 stated the following in a memorandum:

I accept the legal conclusion of the attorney general and the Department of Justice that I have the authority under the Constitution to suspend [the Geneva Conventions] as between the United States and Afghanistan, but I decline to exercise that authority at this time.

He directed the U.S. military to adhere to Geneva Conventions' guidelines "to the extent appropriate and consistent with military necessity." He based this determination on the claim that Afghanistan was a "failed state" and that the Taliban and al Qaeda members were not parties to the Geneva Conventions.

How valid are President Bush's and his Administration's claims? What is a "failed state," and was Afghanistan a failed state? If Afghanistan was a failed state, how is that relevant to whether the Geneva Conventions still applied? Do not treaty obligations continue to bind successor states? *See, e.g.*, SAMUEL PUFENDORF, ON THE LAW OF NATURE AND OF NATIONS, bk. VIII, ch. ix, §8 (1672) (recognizing successor state responsibility for complying with treaties entered into by earlier state). Is it relevant that the Taliban and al Qaeda members were not parties to the Geneva Conventions? Consider that the Interahamwe were not parties to the Geneva Conventions, yet the ICTR still found that its members had violated the Geneva Conventions. Is it relevant that the Taliban and al Qaeda members did not adhere to the Geneva Conventions. Consider that the violation of humanitarian treaties does not constitute sufficient legal grounds for terminating or suspending the treaty. *See* Vienna Convention on the Law of Treaties, art. 60 (5). What do you make of President Bush's direction that the U.S. military adhere to the Geneva Conventions "to the extent appropriate and consistent with military necessity" given that the Geneva Conventions often do not allow the consideration of military necessity to limit their protections?

The Proportionality Rule and Superfluous Injury and Unnecessary Suffering (SIrUS) Rule

International human rights and humanitarian law recognize a state's authority to use force in maintaining domestic public order and, internationally, in the exercise of its right of self-defense.[1] The use of organized military force by states is regulated by the law of armed conflict as set forth in, *inter alia*, the Hague Conventions, the Geneva Conventions of 1949, and the 1977 Protocols to the Geneva Conventions. The law of armed conflict requires that military forces protect civilians and minimize loss of life and property.[2]

Certain violations of the Geneva Conventions give rise to universal criminal jurisdiction. In other words, any state has jurisdiction to prosecute an individual who has violated one of these "grave breaches" of the Geneva Conventions, regardless of the nationality of the individual and regardless of where the violation occurred. Universal jurisdiction has been the basis for many of the prosecutions of Nazi war criminals in the United States, Europe, and Israel.[3] The prosecutions currently taking place in The Hague and Arusha concerning the recent conflicts in the former Yugoslavia and Rwanda also use the Geneva Conventions as one justification for establishing international criminal jurisdiction over those violations.[4]

International human rights law also governs the use of force both during armed conflicts (international and noninternational) and a state's exercise of its police powers during peacetime. International human rights law also provides noncriminal fora for determining whether a specific instance of use of force by a state violates international human rights law.

Francisco Forrest Martin

Using International Human Rights Law for Establishing a Unified Use of Force Rule in the Law of Armed Conflict

64(2) SASK. L. REV. 347 (2002)

. . . .

Until the end of World War II, the normative understanding of armed conflict generally had been bifurcated into issues dealing with (i) whether the war itself was

---

[1] Under Article 51 of the UN Charter, a state may use force in furtherance of its legitimate right to self-defense, as well as pursuant to a Security Council resolution. In addition, there is an emerging norm of international law permitting the use of force internationally when undertaken as part of a humanitarian mission.

[2] *See, e.g.*, Protocol I, Articles 48 (distinction must be made between civilian population and military targets), 51 (civilians shall not be object of attack), 52 (civilian objects shall not be object of attack), and 57 (collateral damage to civilians resulting from attack on military objective must be minimized).

[3] In fact, many of those prosecutions are authorized by national legislation of the state prosecuting, but the international law justification for such assertion of jurisdiction by the state is the universal jurisdiction granted by the Geneva Conventions and related customary international law.

[4] For a further discussion of individual liability under international law, see Section 2.3.

just,[1] and (ii) whether the war was being waged in a morally or legally acceptable manner. The examination of whether a war was just took place apart from the examination of the conduct of warfare, hence the distinction between *jus ad bellum* and *jus in bello*.[2] This bifurcation was reflected in textual codifications of legal norms. For example, on one hand the *Hague*[3] and *Geneva Conventions*[4] only governed the conduct of warfare;[5] and, on the other hand, the *Kellogg-Briand Pact*[6] only addressed the lawfulness of war itself. This normative conception of war has changed as the dichotomy between just war and lawful waging of war has begun to collapse. The beginning of this conceptual change emerged near the end of World War II with the adoption of the *London Agreement and Charter*,[7] which established the Nuremberg War Crimes Tribunal. This Agreement and Charter addressed both crimes against peace and war crimes in the same instrument, thereby encouraging the integration of *jus ad bellum* and *jus in bello*.[8] Most

---

[1] This inquiry also includes whether *any* war was just.

[2] See R. Lagoni, "Comments: Methods or Means of Warfare, Belligerent Reprisals, and the Principle of Proportionality" in I. F. Dekker & H. H. G. Post, eds., *The Gulf War of 1980–1988* (The Hague: T.M.C. Asser Instituut, 1992) 115 at 118–19 (noting historical bifurcation of *jus in bello* and *jus ad bellum*).

[3] See *e.g.*, *Hague Convention (IV) Respecting the Laws and Customs of War on Land, with Annex of Regulations*, 18 October 1907, T.S. No. 539, 1 Bevans 631, 36 Stat. 2277 (entered into force 26 January 1910) [hereinafter *Hague Convention (IV)*]; *Hague Convention (V) respecting the Rights and Duties of Neutral Powers and Persons in Case of War on Land*, 18 October 1907, 205 Consol. T.S. 299 (entered into force 26 January 1910); *Hague Convention (VI) relative to the Status of Enemy Merchant Ships at the Outbreak of Hostilities*, 18 October 1970, 205 Consol. T.S. 305 (entered into force 26 January 1910); *Hague Convention (VII) relative to the Conversion of Merchant-Ships into War-Ships*, 18 October 1907, 205 Consol. T.S. 319 (entered into force 26 January 1910); *Hague Convention (VIII) relative to the Laying of Automatic Submarine Contact Mines*, 18 October 1907, 205 Consol. T.S. 331 (entered into force 26 January 1910).

[4] See *e.g.*, *Geneva Convention for the Amelioration of the Condition of the Wounded and Sick in Armed Forces in the Field*, 12 August 1949, 75 U.N.T.S. 31 (entered into force 21 October 1950); *Geneva Convention for the Amelioration of the Condition of Wounded, Sick and Shipwrecked Members of Armed Forces at Sea*, 12 August 1949, 75 U.N.T.S. 85 (entered into force 21 October 1950); *Geneva Convention relative to the Treatment of Prisoners of War*, 12 August 1949, 75 U.N.T.S. 135, 6 U.S.T. 3316. T.I.A.S. No. 3364 (entered into force 21 October 1950); *Geneva Convention Relative to the Protection of Civilian Persons in Time of War*, 12 August 1949, 75 U.N.T.S. 287, 6 U.S.T. 3516, T.I.A.S. No. 3365 (entered into force 21 October 1950) [hereinafter *Fourth Geneva Convention*]; *Protocol Additional to the Geneva Conventions of 12 August 1949, and Relating to the Protection of Victims of International Armed Conflicts (Protocol I)*, 7 December 1978, 16 I.L.M. 1391, (entered into force 7 December 1978) [hereinafter *Geneva Convention-Protocol I*]; *Protocol Additional to the Geneva Conventions of 12 August 1949, and Relating to the Protection of Victims of Non-International Armed Conflicts (Protocol II)*, 8 June 1977, 16 I.L.M. 1442, (entered into force 7 December 1978) [hereinafter *Geneva Convention-Protocol II*].

[5] Other instruments included the *Declaration Renouncing the Use, in Time of War, of Explosive Projectiles under 400 Grammes Weight*, 11 December 1868, adopted by International Military Commission at St. Petersburg (outlawing projectiles under 400 grammes that are explosive, or charged with fulminating or inflammable substances) in L. Henkin *et al.*, eds., *Basic Documents Supplement to International Law: Cases and Materials*, 3d ed. (St. Paul, Minn.: West Publishing Co., 1993) at 406.

[6] *Treaty Providing for the Renunciation of War as an Instrument of National Policy*, 27 August 1928, L.N.T.S. 57, 46 Stat. 2343, T.S. No. 796, 2 Bevans 732 (entered into force for the U.S. 24 July 1929).

[7] *Agreement for the Prosecution and Punishment of the Major War Criminals of the European Axis, and Charter of the International Military Tribunal*, 8 August 1945, 82 U.N.T.S. 280, 59 Stat. 1544 (entered into force 8 August 1945) [hereinafter *London Charter*].

[8] Although war crimes and crimes against peace remain two different *crimes*, it does not necessarily follow that *jus in bello* and *jus ad bellum* cannot be integrated and unified insofar as the use of force is concerned [ ]. Furthermore, it is important to note that the law of armed conflict (and especially its criminal aspects) has not had the opportunity to develop as much as international human rights law because international human rights law has been interpreted by numerous global and regional tribunals, unlike the law of armed

recently, the *Treaty of Rome* establishing the International Criminal Court has done the same.[9]

One cause of the collapsing of this dichotomy was the emergence of the idea that certain wars or other armed conflicts are "police actions." The Korean Conflict was described as a police action because of North Korea's aggression against South Korea. The war conducted against North Korea (and later China) was justified under the *UN Charter*, which allows use of armed force for self-defense or international security.[10] Recently, humanitarian military intervention in Kosovo by NATO was justified as necessary to protect international security in a region that was being threatened by the commission of genocidal acts and crimes against humanity. Accordingly, the humanitarian military intervention in Kosovo also could be considered a police action because it arguably sought to stop and prevent further international criminal acts. While such police actions could be taken unilaterally by a state (although UN Security Council approval probably would be required), most police actions today are international efforts (called "peace-enforcement" operations) under chapter VII of the *UN Charter*.

The second cause of this change in the normative conception of armed conflict has been growing technological advances in the means of warfare. On the one hand, technological "advances" have resulted in increased casualty rates for both combatants and civilians. For example, the improvement of air defenses during World War II compelled bomber aircrafts to fly at higher altitudes. This resulted in target-area bombardment instead of bombardment aimed at individual and discrete military targets.[11] As a result, unfortunately, more civilians and combatants were killed.[12] This trend of growing casualties continued with the deployment of landmines and nuclear and chemical weapons.

---

conflict. There is a substantially greater number of international human rights cases that have flushed out the international law governing armed conflict than cases decided by international criminal tribunals, and many of these human rights cases addressed the use of force in armed conflict. See F. F. Martin *et al.*, *International Human Rights Law & Practice: Cases, Treaties and Materials* (The Hague: Kluwer Law International, 1997) for a discussion of cases adjudicated by international human rights and war crimes tribunals.

9   See *Rome Statute of the International Criminal Court*, 17 July 1998, art. 5, U.N. Doc. A/CONF.183/9 [hereinafter ICC Statute].

10   Article 2(4) of the *Charter of the United Nations*, 26 June 1945, Can. T.S. 1945 No. 7 (entered into force 24 October 1945) [hereinafter *UN Charter*] states:

All members shall refrain in their international relations from the threat or use of force against the territorial integrity or political independence of any state, or in any other manner inconsistent with the Purposes of the United Nations.

Article 51 states:

Nothing in the present Charter shall impair the inherent right of individual or collective self-defense if an armed attack occurs against a Member of the United Nations, until the Security Council has taken measures necessary to maintain international peace and security. Measures taken by Members in the exercise of this right of self-defense shall be immediately reported to the Security Council and shall not in any way affect the authority and responsibility of the Security Council under the present Charter to take at any time such action as it deems necessary in order to maintain or restore international peace and security.

11   G. H. Aldrich, "The Laws of War on Land" (2000) 94 A.J.I.L. 42 at 49.

12   "In 1950, noncombatants accounted for about one half of world-wide casualties during war; in 1980 the rate rose to about 80 percent": *ibid.*; Col. J. Siniscalchi, "Non-Lethal Technologies: Implications for Military Strategy", Occasional Paper No. 3 at 21 (Maxwell Air Force Base, Ala.: Center for Strategy and Technology, Air War College & Air University, 1998), online: Center for Strategy and Technology <http://www.au.af.mil/au/awc/awcgate/cst/occppr03.htm> (last modified: 23 May 2002).

The international concern with collateral civilian casualties led to the adoption of several treaties and declarations seeking to curb or eliminate casualties produced by this indiscriminate or unnecessarily injurious weaponry.[13]

On the other hand, as evidenced by the Gulf War and Kosovo Conflict, growing technological advances have recently decreased casualty rates among both civilians and combatants.[14] As Capt. Robert G. Hanseman observed in regard to the U.S.' advanced military capabilities:

> The U.S. is enhancing its power to "leapfrog" over traditional combat units, strike at their command and control centers, and then target the enemy combat units at a leisurely pace as they scramble for intelligence. If this is the case, it could well result in decreased casualties, because enemy units would be more likely to surrender after being cut off from their chain of command, and U.S. forces would have time to put on a display of force designed to convince them that surrender is their best option, rather than simply targeting and killing them.[15]

Smart weaponry and non-lethal measures have allowed military forces to protect not only their own military personnel but also the military forces and civilian populations of an enemy state. In order to remedy the growing casualty rates of civilians, governments ironically have also effectively decreased the casualty rates of enemy combatants. Combatants have become, in a sense, "civilians" in that the protections afforded to civilians by international treaty and use of smart and non-lethal weapon technologies have impacted combatants, too.

The fact that armed conflicts have increasingly become non-international is contributing to the collapse of the civilian-combatant distinction. Wars of national liberation and ethnic conflicts have blurred the distinction between regular forces and irregular forces, making the civilian-combatant distinction difficult to recognize.[16] As a result, the meaning of threats to "international peace and security" has arguably expanded to include

---

[13] See *e.g. Geneva Convention-Protocols I and II, supra; Treaty on the Non-Proliferation of Nuclear Weapons*, 1 July 1968, 21 U.S.T. 483, T.I.A.S. No. 6389, 729 U.N.T.S. 161, 7 I.L.M. 811 (1968) (entered into force 5 March 1970); *Convention on the Prohibition of the Development, Production, and Stockpiling of Bacteriological (Biological) and Toxin Weapons and on Their Destruction*, 10 April 1972, 11 I.L.M. 309; *Declaration on the Prohibition of Chemical Weapons*, 11 January 1989, 28 I.L.M. 1020; *Convention on Prohibitions or Restrictions on the Use of Certain Conventional Weapons Which May Be Deemed to be Excessively Injurious or to Have Indiscriminate Effects*, 10 October 1980, 19 I.L.M. 1524 (entered into force 2 December 1983); *Protocol on Prohibitions or Restrictions on the Use of Mines, Booby Traps and Other Devices (Protocol II)*, 10 October 1980, 19 I.L.M. 1529 (entered into force 2 December 1983); *Amended Protocol on Prohibitions or Restrictions on the Use of Mines, Booby-Traps and Other Devices (Amended Protocol II)*, 3 May 1996, 35 I.L.M. 1206–1218 (entered into force 3 December 1998); *Protocol on Prohibitions or Restrictions on the Use of Incendiary Weapons (Protocol III)*, 10 October 1980, 19 I.L.M. 1534 (entered into force 2 December 1983); *Convention on the Prohibition of the Use, Stockpiling, Production and Transfer of Anti-Personnel Mines and on their Destruction*, 18 September 1997, 36 I.L.M. 1507–1519 (entered into force 1 March 1999).

[14] Of course, the superior military capabilities of the Gulf War Coalition forces and NATO, respectively, also contributed to fewer casualties in the Gulf War and Kosovo Conflict by bringing these conflicts to a quick end.

[15] Capt. R. G. Hanseman, "The Realities and Legalities of Information Warfare" (1997) 42 Air Force L.R. 173 at 186.

[16] See W. J. Fenrick, "The Development of the Law of Armed Conflict through the Jurisprudence of the International Criminal Tribunal for the Former Yugoslavia" in M. N. Schmitt & L. C. Green, eds., *The Law of Armed Conflict: Into the Next Millennium* (Newport, RI: Naval War College, 1998) at 77–78 (the nature of future conflicts will create pressures to dissolve distinction between law governing international conflicts and law governing non-international conflicts).

conflicts that appear at first glance to be only internal in order to extend international legal protection to non-combatants.[17] Moreover, with the development of peacekeeping operations over the last fifty years, military peacekeeping forces often take on domestic police roles. Thus, civilians are increasingly becoming targets for use of force.

These developments reflect a new kind of warfare, and this new warfare represents a revolution in military affairs. There has been a fundamental change in four areas: "information operations, weapons systems, and space",[18] and – particularly relevant to this article – "militarization of civilians and civilian activities".[19] This last area of change is visible in many facilities shared by military and civilian operations (*e.g.*, airports, office buildings), and in the center of technological advances in weaponry, communications, and computers, which lie in the commercial, non-defense sectors.

Together, these opposing results from technological advances in weaponry are collapsing the bifurcation of the normative concept of armed conflict because, in conjunction with the implementation of the idea of "international police actions", combatants have effectively become either "criminal suspects" or "international police", depending on one's opinion as to the underlying legality of the conflict.[20] Persons once characterized as "enemies" should now be characterized in international police actions as "criminal suspects" under international law. As criminal suspects, they have political and civil rights as do civilians who are less blameworthy. It does not matter if these criminal suspects are terrorists or enemy forces possessing substantial weaponry. As the character of armed conflict changes into one characterized best as law enforcement actions, so too should the law governing the conduct of armed conflict.

. . . .

∾

QUESTIONS & COMMENTS

(1) In the United States, challenges to the use of force by the police are brought under 42 U.S.C. §1983. There is a substantial body of case law regarding the correct standard to be applied in evaluating these use of force claims. The U.S. Supreme Court has held that such claims are to be evaluated using an objective reasonableness standard under the U.S. Constitution's Fourth Amendment prohibition against unreasonable seizures. In other words, the police only need to show that they used force in "good faith." In *Tennessee v. Garner*, 471 U.S. 1 (1985), the Supreme Court articulated the test as follows:

> if the suspect threatens the officer with a weapon or there is probable cause to believe that he has committed a crime involving the infliction or threatened infliction of serious physical harm, deadly force may be used if necessary to prevent escape, and if, where feasible, some warning has been given.

---

[17] Two examples are the UN's approval of intervention in Somalia and Haiti, with their "international" aspects being cross-border refugee flows.

[18] Lt. Col. M. N. Schmitt, "Bellum Americanum: The U.S. View of Twenty-First Century War and Its Possible Implications for the Law of Armed Conflict" (1998) 19 Mich. J. Int'l L. 1051 at 1059–60.

[19] *Ibid.*

[20] Regardless of subjective viewpoint, the *Convention on the Safety of United Nations and Associated Personnel* makes it a crime to harm UN peacekeepers operating under Article VI of the UN Charter, but it applies the law of armed conflict to Article VII peace-enforcement operations: 9 December 1994, UN GA 84th Plen. Mtg., GA/Res/49/59 at art. 2(2), online: United Nations <http://www.un.org/gopher-data/ga/recs/49/59> (last modified: 29 November 1999).

471 U.S. at 11–12. The Court later affirmed the use of this objective test, noting that the reasonableness of a particular use of force is to be judged from the "perspective of a reasonable officer on the scene." *Graham v. Connor*, 490 U.S. 386, 396 (1989).[21] Subsequently, several U.S. Courts of Appeal have held that the police are not required to exhaust every alternative before using deadly force.[22]

Prosecutor v. Galiç
International Criminal Tribunal for Former Yugoslavia
(Trial Chamber I Section B)
Memorial *Amicus Curiae* submitted by Rights International
3 March 2003

Introduction

Defendant Galic has been charged with "Violations of the Laws or Customs of War (attacks on civilians as set forth in Article 51 of Additional Protocol I . . . to the Geneva Conventions of 1949) punishable under Article 3 of the Statute of the Tribunal." *The Prosecutor v. Galic*, Case No. IT-98-29-T, Indictment, Count 7 (26 March 1999) [hereinafter Indictment]. The instant case addresses, in part, armed attacks on mixed combatant/civilian targets during armed conflict. *Id.* Amicus will restrict his arguments to this issue.

"[A]n international instrument must be interpreted and applied within the overall framework of the [international] juridical system in force at the time of the interpretation." *Legal Consequences for States of the Continued Presence of South Africa in Namibia (South West Africa) notwithstanding Security Council Resolution 276 (1970)*, Advisory Opinion, 1971 I.C.J. Reports 16, 31 (1971); *Interpretation of the American Declaration of the Rights and Duties of Man within the Framework of Article 64 of the American Convention on Human Rights*, Advisory Opinion OC-10/89, Inter-Am. Ct. H.R. Ser. A, No. 10, at ¶ 37 (1989); *Coard v. United States*, Inter-Am. Cm. H.R., No. 109/99 at ¶ 40 (1999) (available at <http://www.cidh.oas.org/annualrep/99eng/Merits/UnitedStates10.951.htm>). Furthermore, as the Martens Clause restatement in the *Protocol Additional to the Geneva Conventions of 12 August 1949, and Relating to the Protection of Victims of International Armed Conflicts (Protocol I)*, 7 December 1978, 16 I.L.M. 1391 (entered into force 7 December 1978) [hereinafter *Protocol I*], states:

> In cases not covered by this Protocol or by other international agreements, civilians and combatants remain under the protection and authority of the principles of international law derived from established custom, from the principles of humanity and from the dictates of public conscience.

---

[21] Although the objective reasonableness test under the Fourth Amendment applies to the use of force by police in effecting an arrest of a suspect, it is not clear whether the same test applies to the use of force applied to a pretrial detainee. For a recent discussion of the different tests applied to use of force claims in the United States, see F. Taylor, *Use of Force Claims and the Fourth Amendment from Screws to Albright*, 4 POLICE MISCONDUCT AND CIVIL RIGHTS LAW REPORT 146 (January–February 1995).

[22] *See, e.g., Forrett v. Richardson*, 112 F.3d 416 (9th Cir. 1997); *Hegarty v. Somerset County*, 53 F.3d 1367 (1st Cir. 1995); *Scott v. Henrich*, 39 F.3d 912 (9th Cir. 1994); *Menuel v. City of Atlanta*, 25 F.3d 990 (11th Cir. 1994).

Protocol I at art. 1 (2).

The rights to life and humane treatment under international human rights law constitute the *lex specialis* governing armed attacks because these rights are non-derogable during armed conflict. *International Covenant on Civil and Political Rights*, 16 December 1966, art. 4, 999 U.N.T.S. 171 (entered into force 23 March 1976) [hereinafter *ICCPR*] (rights to life and humane treatment are non-derogable); UN Human Rights Committee, *General Comment No. 29, States of Emergency (art. 4)*, adopted 24 July 2001, at ¶ 11 (available at <http://www1.umn.edu/humanrts/gencomm/hrc29.html>) (rights to life and humane treatment are non-derogable and peremptory); *European Convention for the Protection of Human Rights and Fundamental Freedoms*, 4 November 1950, art. 15, 213 U.N.T.S. 221 (entered into force 3 February 1953) [hereinafter *ECHR*] (right to humane treatment is non-derogable). Although the right to life under the *ECHR* is derogable in respect to "deaths resulting from lawful acts of war," states may only take those measures that are "strictly required by the exigencies of the situation." *ECHR*, art. 15 (1).

Furthermore, as the Inter-American Commission on Human Rights has noted:

> while international humanitarian law pertains primarily in times of war and the international law of human rights applies most fully in times of peace, the potential application of one does not necessarily exclude or displace the other. There is an integral linkage between the law of human rights and humanitarian law because they share a "common nucleus of non-derogable rights and a common purpose of protecting human life and dignity," and there may be a substantial overlap in the application of these bodies of law. Certain core guarantees apply in all circumstances, including situations of conflict, and this is reflected, *inter alia*, in the designation of certain protections pertaining to the person as peremptory norms (*jus cogens*) and obligations *erga omnes*, in a vast body of treaty law, in principles of customary international law, and in the doctrine and practice of international human rights bodies such as this Commission.

Coard v. United States, supra, at ¶ 39. Therefore, Amicus will address the "relevant rules of international law" governing use of force established by the law of armed conflict and international human rights law guaranteeing the rights to life and humane treatment.

1. The Proportionality Rule under Protocol I.

Intentionally directing attacks against the civilian population as such or against individual civilians not taking direct part in hostilities is prohibited under the law of armed conflict for both international and non-international conflicts.[1] However, the observation of this "Combatant/Civilian Distinction Rule" is often problematic in contemporary conflicts[2] in which irregular military forces are not clearly identified as hostile

---

[1] *Geneva Convention Relative to the Protection of Civilian Persons in Time of War*, 12 August 1949, arts. 3 and 27, 75 U.N.T.S. 287 (entered into force 21 October 1950) (international and non-international conflicts); *Protocol I*, art. 51(2) (international conflicts); *Rome Statute of the International Criminal Court*, 17 July 1998, arts. 8(2)(b)(i), 8(2)(c)(i), and 8(2)(e)(i), U.N. Doc. A/CONF.183/9 (entered into force 1 July 2002) (international and non-international conflicts) [hereinafter *ICC Statute*].

[2] *See* W. J. Fenrick, "The Development of the Law of Armed Conflict through the Jurisprudence of the International Criminal Tribunal for the Former Yugoslavia" in M. N. Schmitt & L. C. Green, eds., *The Law of Armed Conflict: Into the Next Millennium* (Newport, RI: Naval War College, 1998) at 77–78 (the

combatants.[3] Therefore, when the combatant/civilian distinction is blurred by the presence of such irregular forces, it is essential that attacks on mixed combatant/civilian targets are undertaken in a manner calculated to reduce the probability of harm to civilians.

The Proportionality Rule in the *Protocol I* prohibits launching attacks on such mixed targets with the knowledge that these attacks would be expected to cause incidental civilian casualties that would be "excessive in relation to the concrete and direct military advantage anticipated." *Protocol I*, art. 51(5)(b).[4]

2. The Proportionality Rule Does Not Define What is "Excessive."

However, the *Protocol I* does not define what is "excessive." In determining whether an attack is excessive or disproportionate, some jurists use calculi comparing the number of civilian casualties with the number of combatant casualties. However, there are several problems with these approaches. One such comparative calculation approaches the issue from hindsight by measuring actual casualties, but the Rendulic Rule prohibits commanders being judged by knowledge only gained in hindsight. *List and Others [Hostages Trial]*, [1948] 15 Ann. Dig. I.L.C. No. 215, 632, 647.[5]

Another, somewhat visceral approach is to define the Proportionality Rule in an ad hoc manner employing an extreme numerical casualty standard. For example, if the attack on one enemy combatant is expected to cause, say, 100 civilian casualties, this would be excessive. However, this approach is ambiguous. What if the expected civilian casualties amount to only 50 persons?... to only 10 persons? Where do we establish a numerical threshold for excessive civilian casualty rates that is not arbitrary? Furthermore, even two civilian casualties would not be excessive given that only one combatant using a machine gun or a grenade easily can harm an indefinitely great number of hostile combatants, a very common scenario that would make the Proportionality Rule unworkable because no attack against such a combatant would be disproportional. In other words, this comparative casualty approach to defining the Proportionality Rule is indeterminate.

Most importantly, these comparative approaches do not reflect the test set by the Proportionality Rule itself. The anticipated military advantage against which civilian

---

nature of future conflicts will create pressures to dissolve distinction between law governing international conflicts and law governing non-international conflicts).

[3] *See, e.g., Hague Convention (IV) Respecting the Laws and Customs of War on Land, with Annex of Regulations,* 18 October 1907, art. 1, T.S. No. 539, 1 Bevans 631, 36 Stat. 2277 (entered into force 26 January 1910) (requiring belligerents to have "fixed distinctive emblem recognizable at a distance; to carry arms openly"); *Geneva Convention relative to the Treatment of Prisoners of War,* 12 August 1949, art. 4 (A) (2), 75 U.N.T.S. 135 (entered into force 21 October 1950) (same).

[4] The Proportionality Rule in the *ICC Statute* prohibits those attacks that "would be excessive in relation to the concrete and direct *overall* military advantage anticipated," which indicates a more liberal standard for use of force. *ICC Statute,* art. 8(2)(b)(iv) (emphasis provided).

[5] International criminal law only allows intentional or reckless acts and omissions for establishing criminal culpability. In the *Delalic* case, the ICTY held that "the necessary intent ... required to establish the crimes of wilful killing and murder ... is present where there is demonstrated an intention on the part of the accused to kill, or inflict serious injury in reckless disregard of human life." *The Prosecutor v. Delalic et al.,* Judgment, Case No. IT-96-21-T, at ¶ 439 (16 November 1998). In the case of wilful killing committed by omission, intent can be inferred if death is the foreseeable consequence of such an omission. Jean S. Pictet (ed.), Commentary, IV, Geneva Convention relative to the Protection of Civilian Persons in Time of War, art. 147, p. 597 (1958). *Cf. Osman v. United Kingdom,* 29 E.H.R.R. 245 (2000) (foreseeability requirement for right to life violations); *Soering v. United Kingdom,* 11 E.H.R.R. 439 (1989) (foreseeability requirement for right to humane treatment violations).

casualties is weighed is not limited to combatant casualties. The Proportionality Rule uses "military advantage," which is an unfortunately nebulous concept not conducive to measure. How does one measure injury or the loss of life against "concrete and direct military advantage anticipated"? In other words, civilian casualties and "concrete and direct military advantage" are "apples and oranges."

In order to overcome these problems, the Proportionality Rule must be construed in conformity with the international human rights law governing the rights to life and humane treatment because this law is more precise in establishing the proper necessity threshold for use of armed force.

3. The Proportionality Rule Must Be Construed in Conformity with the Rights to Life and Humane Treatment.

The restatement of the Martens Clause in the *Protocol I* incorporates other "international agreements" into the Geneva Conventions, – which includes human rights treaties establishing use of force standards during armed conflicts. *Protocol I*, art. 1(2).[6] Because armed attacks on mixed combatant/civilian targets result in loss of life and suffering, determining the lawfulness of such attacks requires that this law be construed with the international human rights law governing the rights to life and humane treatment.

3.1. The Proportionality Rule as Construed by International Human Rights Law Allows Attacks on Mixed Combatant/Civilian Targets Only When Absolutely Necessary.

International human rights law recognizes a proportionality rule. In a case involving aerial missile attacks on civilian aircraft in international airspace that resulted in loss of life, the Inter-American Commission on Human Rights held that such attacks violated the right to life by being indiscriminate and disproportionate. The Commission noted that:

> the agents of the Cuban State made no effort to use means other than lethal force to guide the aircraft out of the restricted or danger area. The Commission believes that the indiscriminate use of force, and particularly the use of firearms, is an affront to the right to life and personal integrity. In this particular case, the military airplanes acted irregularly: without prior warning, without evidence that their actions were necessary, without keeping things in their correct proportion, and without the existence of due motivation.

Alejandre et al. v. Cuba, Case 11.589, Report No. 86/99, Inter-Am. Cm. H.R., OEA/Ser.L/ V/II.106 Doc. 3 rev. 586 at ¶ 42 (1999).

Furthermore, international human rights law recognizes that a proportionality rule also applies to armed attacks against combatants or those persons suspected of being combatants even if authorities did not believe that civilians would also be subject to the same attacks. In *Camargo v. Colombia*, Comm. No. 45/1979, U.N. Doc. CCPR/C/OP/1 (1985) (views adopted 31 March 1982), the UN Human Rights Committee examined a case in which the Colombian police killed a number of persons (including Mrs. Camargo) whom the police had mistakenly suspected of belonging to a guerilla organization and

---

[6] The *ICC Statute* also requires that its Elements of Crimes, and its Rules of Procedure and Evidence be applied and interpreted "consistent[ly] with internationally recognized human rights." *ICC Statute*, art. 21 (3).

kidnapping a former ambassador. The Human Rights Committee held that the killing of Mrs. Camargo was a disproportionate use of force in violation of her right to life.[7] The Committee noted the following in reaching its conclusion:

> [T]he police action was apparently taken without warning to the victims and without giving them any opportunity to surrender to the police patrol or to offer any explanation of their presence or intentions. There is no evidence that the action of the police was necessary in their own defense or that of others, or that it was necessary to effect the arrest or prevent the escape of the persons concerned. Moreover, the victims were no more than suspects of the kidnapping. . . .

Id. at §13.2. The extension of the Proportionality Rule under the *Protocol I* to attacks solely against combatants ensures that civilians who are mistakenly believed to be combatants are less likely to be the subject of such attacks.

Most importantly, this extension of the Proportionality Rule also ensures that when armed force actually is used against clearly hostile, irregular military forces who are indistinguishable from and situated among civilians, violence to civilian life and person is minimalized. The rights to life and humane treatment under international human rights law establish an absolute or strict necessity test for the use of force during armed conflicts.[8] In *Satik and Others v. Turkey*, Application No. 31866/96 (2000), the European Court of Human Rights held that the right to humane treatment allows "recourse to physical force" only if it is made "strictly necessary" by the victim's own conduct. In *Satik*, a case concerning a detainee, the Court held that "recourse to physical force which had not been made *strictly necessary* by [the victim's] own conduct diminishes human dignity and is in principle an infringement" of the right to humane treatment. *Id.* at §54 [emphasis added]. In cases involving unlawful actions by the victim, the Court recognized that some acts causing suffering may be lawful if strictly necessary to achieve a lawful objective. In *Satik*, the European Court noted the absence of governmental justification for the commission of certain harmful acts and then held that such acts were unlawfully inhumane. The European Court stated: "In particular, it has not been *suggested* by the Government that the intervention of the gendarme officers was considered *necessary* to quell a riot or a planned attack on the internal security of Buca Prison." *Id.* at 57 [emphasis added]. The Court's language indicates that if the Turkish government had provided a justification for the use of force, demonstrating that it was strictly necessary for achieving lawful objectives, then the Court would not have found a violation of the right to humane treatment.

The right to life under international human rights law allows the taking of life only when "absolutely necessary" in the defense of any person from unlawful violence, in order to effect a lawful arrest, or in action lawfully taken for the purpose of quelling an insurrection. *ECHR*, art.2 (2). In *McCann and Others v. United Kingdom*, 21 E.H.R.R. 97 (1995), the European Court of Human Rights considered a case involving the shootings of three suspected Irish Republican Army terrorists by members of the Special Air Service (SAS) and the police in Gibralter. The UK, Spanish, and Gibralter authorities had reason to believe that a terrorist attack was planned in Gibralter, and that the target was probably the Band and Guard of the Royal Anglican Regiment during a ceremony. The authorities

---

[7] The right to life is guaranteed under article 6 (1) of the *ICCPR*: "Every human being has the inherent right to life. This right shall be protected by law. No one shall be arbitrarily deprived of his life."

[8] There appears to be no material difference between "strict" and "absolute" necessity tests. Both require that there be no other alternative available for achieving a lawful objective.

knew that the suspects were active IRA members and were attempting to enter Gibralter. However, the authorities did not prevent the suspects from entering because the authorities had insufficient evidence to successfully prosecute them. Fearing that the suspects would detonate a remote-controlled bomb, the authorities shot and killed them. Although the suspects, indeed, had planned an attack and planted a bomb, the method of detonation was not a remote device that could be set off instantaneously. Moreover, the evidence claiming that it was such a device was dubious, having been provided by a non-expert.

The European Court found a violation of the right to life because the authorities had used lethal force that was not absolutely necessary in defence of persons from unlawful violence. The Court's decision was based on the facts that the authorities (i) had not prevented the IRA suspects from travelling to Gibralter; (ii) had "failed to make sufficient allowances for the possibility that their intelligence assessments might, in some respects at least, be erroneous"; and (iii) had failed to stop their soldiers from automatically using lethal force. *Id.* at §213. The deprivation of life must be subjected to the most careful scrutiny, taking into consideration both the actions of the authorities and the surrounding circumstances, including the planning and control of the operation.

The Court accepted that the soldiers honestly believed that it was necessary to shoot the suspects in order to prevent remote detonation of the device. Their beliefs were based on erroneous information with which they had been supplied. However, the Court found that their commanders had failed to organize the operation as a whole in conformity with the right to life, including the information and instructions given to the soldiers. Consequently, the organization of the operation inevitably required the use of lethal force and failed to adequately respect the suspects' right to life.

. . . .

Although the right to life is subject to derogation under the *ECHR* "in respect of deaths resulting from lawful acts of war,"[9] and therefore, the absolute necessity test arguably[10] may be non-applicable when States exercise their right of derogation, the absolute necessity test still applies to all uses of force because it is foreseeable that any use of force would create a "real risk" of causing physical or mental suffering in violation of the right to humane treatment, which remains non-derogable even during war. *Cf. Chahal v. United Kingdom*, Appl. No. 22414/93 (1996) (forcible deportation foreseeably would place applicant at "real risk" of inhumane treatment in violation of Art. 3). Although use of force may result in loss of life without physical or mental suffering, it is still a violation of the right to humane treatment if it was foreseeable that the victim would face a real risk of being subjected to physical and mental suffering that was not strictly necessary. Therefore, both the rights to life and humane treatment employ an identical absolute or strict necessity test regardless of whether a State has exercised its right of derogation in respect to loss of life resulting from lawful acts of war.[11]

---

[9] *ECHR*, art. 15 (2).

[10] *See* Jordan J. Paust, *The Right to Life in Human Rights and the Law of War*, 65(2) Sask. L. Rev. 411 (2002) [hereinafter Paust, *Right to Life*] (arguing that absolute necessity test does not apply to "lawful acts of war" resulting in loss of life); *but see* Francisco Forrest Martin, *The Unified Use of Force Rule: Amplifications in Light of the Comments of Professors Green and Paust*, 65 Sask. L. Rev. 515 (2002) [hereinafter Martin, *Amplifications*] (arguing that absolute necessity test still applies to "lawful acts of war" resulting in loss of life).

[11] Although the *ECHR*, strictly speaking, did not create treaty law obligations for the warring parties during the Yugoslavian conflict, the right to humane treatment under the *ECHR* reflected global customary

In both *McCann* and *Satik*, the Court only dealt with cases involving violations of the rights to life and humane treatment of persons who were either committing or suspected of planning to commit hostile acts. The Court did not articulate any test concerning the lawful use of force against mixed combatant/civilian targets. For determining whether use of force is lawful against such targets, it is necessary to examine other international human rights law governing levels of force employed.

3.2 The Rights to Life and Humane Treatment Require That When Force is Used, It May Only Cause the Least, Foreseeable Physical and Mental Suffering.

The decision to use force *per se* is different from the decision of which kinds of force lawfully can be used because different kinds of force cause different levels of harm that can implicate the rights to life and humane treatment. The UN Human Rights Committee has articulated a specific rule governing the exact level of force allowed. In *Ng* v. *Canada*, Communication No. 469/1991, 98 I.L.R. 479 (1993), the UN Human Rights Committee held that the lawful execution of a convicted prisoner "must be carried out in such a way as to cause the *least possible physical and mental suffering*" in order to comply with the right to humane punishment under the *ICCPR*.[12] *Id.* at §16.2 [emphasis added]. Although *Ng v. Canada* did not deal with mixed combatant/civilian targets, the Committee's holding suggests that civilians and other innocent persons may receive greater protection than persons who have committed or are planning to commit unlawful acts, and that civilians and other innocent persons may not be subjected to *any* physical or mental suffering. However, because there appears to be no international law explicitly stating this, it is at least safe to say that the subjection of civilians to any use of force because they constitute part of a mixed civilian-combatant target must be carried out in such a way as to cause the least physical and mental suffering. This conclusion is confirmed by *Protocol I* that requires combatants to "take all feasible precautions in the choice of means and methods of attack with a view to avoiding, and in any event minimizing, incidental loss of civilian life, [and] injury to civilians." *Protocol I*, 57 (2) (a) (ii).

Although a State can kill arguably without making the victim endure physical or mental suffering, the European Court of Human Rights has held that a State must make non-lethal weapons available to their military forces for their use against mixed combatant/civilian targets. In *Güleç* v. *Turkey*, 28 E.H.R.R. 121 (1998), the Court examined a case in which the applicant's son was shot by the Turkish security forces on his way home from school during an unauthorised demonstration. The Turkish Government alleged that he was a terrorist belonging to the Kurdish Worker's Party (PKK) and that there were armed terrorists among the demonstrators, requiring police to open fire on the protestors in order to disperse the demonstration. (Subsequently, it was shown that the protestors were not armed.) The applicant claimed that the police could have used less force, but the government stated that no other weapons were available at the scene of the incident. The Court held that the lack of equipment such as tear gas, rubber bullets, water cannons, and

---

international law binding on the parties because of the identical language of the right to humane treatment in the *ICCPR*, which clearly reflects customary international law. Compare *ECHR*, art. 3 ("No one shall be subjected to ... inhuman ... treatment....") with *ICCPR*, art. 7 ("No one shall be subjected to ... inhuman ... treatment...."); *see Rodriguez Fernandez v. Wilkinson*, 505 F. Supp. 787, 797 (D. Kan. 1980) (right to humane treatment under the *ECHR* "indicative of the customs and uses of civilized nations").

[12] Article 7, ICCPR, guarantees the right to humane treatment and states in relevant part: "No one shall be subjected to torture or to cruel, inhuman or degrading treatment or punishment."

truncheons was "incomprehensible," given that the province of Sirnak where the protest took place was "in a region in which a state of emergency had been declared" and where disorder could therefore be expected. *Id.* at §§71–72. In these circumstances, the Court unanimously declared that the force used was not absolutely necessary and, therefore, constituted a violation of the right to life. Therefore, states must make non-lethal weapons available to their military forces for their use against mixed combatant/civilian targets. This conclusion is also consistent with *Protocol I*'s prohibition of employing "weapons, projectiles and material and methods of warfare of a nature to cause superfluous injury or unnecessary suffering." *Protocol I*, art. 35 (2).

There are a diverse range of non-lethal means and methods for achieving lawful military objectives.[13] For instance, the containment of hostile forces by siege and negotiation for surrender of hostile forces can be viable non-violent methods of achieving lawful military objectives. Also, in cases of where hostile forces are (or are reasonably believed to be) situated among civilians, use of force can be suspended until such hostile forces extract themselves from civilians. Indeed, *Protocol I* requires that combatants "refrain from deciding to launch any attack which may be expected to cause incidental loss of civilian life, [and] injury to civilians . . . or a combination thereof, which would be excessive in relation to the concrete and direct military advantage anticipated." *Protocol I*, art. 57 (2) (a) (iii). Another non-lethal alternative is for artillery or mortars to fire smoke shells[14] as warnings to civilians allowing them an opportunity to flee the vicinity of hostile forces. Furthermore, *Protocol I* requires that "effective advance warning shall be given of attacks which may affect the civilian population, unless circumstances do not permit." *Protocol I*, art. 57 (2) (c). However, such "circumstances" still are subject to the absolute necessity and minimal use of force test.

3.3 Injury and Suffering May Be Escalated Incrementally Through Additional Use of Force Only If At Each Increment the Additional Use of Force is Absolutely Necessary.

There are circumstances in which the use of force does not achieve its lawful objective. In such cases, the additional use of force that results in escalation of injury and suffering may be necessary. Such uses of force could include lethal means. However, such additional use of force still must be absolutely or strictly necessary. *McCann and Others v. United Kingdom, supra* (right to life); *Satik and Others v. Turkey, supra* (right to humane treatment). Therefore, when injury and suffering are escalated through additional use(s) of force, such use(s) of additional force still must be absolutely necessary to pass muster under international human rights law. Furthermore, such use of additional force can only be escalated *incrementally* because international human rights law still requires that the use of force cause the "least possible physical and mental suffering." *Ng v. Canada, supra,* at §16.2 (right to humane treatment); cf. *Güleç v. Turkey, supra* (right to life requires availability and use of non-lethal measures).

In cases where the use of force absolutely must be incrementally increased, there is a range of available options that are scaled according to their respective consequential

---

[13] *See* Col. J. Siniscalchi, "Non-Lethal Technologies: Implications for Military Strategy", Occasional Paper No. 3 at 21 (Maxwell Air Force Base, Ala.: Center for Strategy and Technology, Air War College & Air University, 1998), online: Center for Strategy and Technology (available at <http://www.au.af.mil/au/awc/awcgate/cst/occppr03.htm>) (detailing new and old non-lethal technologies).

[14] Military forces customarily use smoke shells as preparation for targeting artillery and mortar fire.

harms. At the outset, it should be noted that the use of artillery and mortar fire is inherently indiscriminate against mixed combatant/civilian targets. Therefore, use of artillery or mortar fire must be avoided. There are other means and methods of armed force that are less indiscriminate. For example, in cases where there the hostile target is in a clear line of sight, the use of snipers against hostile combatants can eliminate collateral civilian casualties.[15] In cases where there is no clear line of sight because of obstructions that require the use of artillery or mortar fire, artillery or mortar shell airbursts should be avoided because such airbursts cause greater indiscriminate harm by distributing shrapnel over a larger field – as opposed to using impact shells that explode upon hitting the ground or a structure. However, before using these any of these lethal measures, all viable non-violent and non-lethal measures must be tried.

Conclusion

In summary, the Proportionality Rule as construed by international human rights law establishes a three-part test.[16] First, armed attacks on mixed combatant/civilian targets are lawful only if there was no alternative to using force for obtaining a lawful objective. Second, if such use of force was absolutely necessary, the means or method of force employed may only cause the least amount of foreseeable, [ ] physical or mental suffering. Armed force may only be used for the neutralization or deterrence of hostile force, which can take place by surrender, arrest, withdrawal, or isolation of enemy combatants – not only by killing or wounding. This rule requires that military authorities refrain from attacking, provide warnings, and make available and use non-lethal weapons systems. Third, if such a means or method of using force did not achieve its lawful objective, then force may be incrementally escalated to achieve these objectives. This includes the use of snipers against hostile combatants. When it is difficult to distinguish civilians from military forces, compliance with these requirements become all the more important in order to ensure that civilians are not unnecessarily harmed and that such harm is not unnecessarily aggravated.[17]

. . . .

∾

QUESTIONS & COMMENTS

(1) Does the Unified Use of Force Rule adequately address suicide bombers? The rule assumes that nonlethal uses of force often can persuade enemy combatants to surrender

---

[15] Sniper weapons include the Yugoslavian-made Zastava M76 and the Soviet-made Dragunov SVD, the latter of which has an effective range of 1000 meters. *See* Ian Hogg, *Jane's Guns Recognition Guide* 326, 355 (2002).

[16] This three-part test is called the "Unified Use of Force Rule." *See* Francisco Forrest Martin, *Using International Human Rights Law for Establishing a Unified Use of Force Rule in the Law of Armed Conflict*, 64(2) Sask. L. Rev. 347 (2002); Paust, *Right to Life, supra*; L. C. Green, *The "Unified Use of Force Rule" and the Law of Armed Conflict: A Reply to Professor Martin*, 65(2) Sask. L. Rev. 427 (2002); Martin, *Amplifications, supra.*

[17] Furthermore, this rule also serves to ensure that when friendly forces are mistaken for hostile forces, the harm resulting from attacks on such forces are minimized. The aerial bombardment of Canadian ground forces by a U.S. aircraft during the recent Afghanistan conflict highlights the importance of only using force when absolutely necessary and only using force that causes the least amount of physical and mental suffering. *See* BBC News, "Canada Angry at 'Friendly Fire' Deaths" (20 April 2002) (available at <http://news.bbc.co.uk/1/hi/world/americas/1940768.stm>).

or to withdraw. However, in the case of enemy bombers who are willing to kill themselves, the desire for self-preservation is absent; therefore, any use of force – lethal or nonlethal – has no persuasive weight with the suicide bomber.

(2) Consider the following excerpt addressing the justiciability of use of force decisions under U.S. law.

Francisco Forrest Martin

CHALLENGING HUMAN RIGHTS VIOLATIONS:
USING INTERNATIONAL LAW IN U.S. COURTS 130–41 (2001)

. . . .

c. U.S. Law: Justiciability of Lethal Use of Force Decisions Under the "Political Question" Doctrine

In the context of U.S. constitutional law, the observance of the *McCann* Rule[1] must be examined in light of whether it is a justiciable issue under the "political question doctrine." The political question doctrine reflects the constitutional concern for maintaining the separation of powers between the three branches of the federal government. In the context of war-making, two general kinds of issues have come before the federal courts: (i) whether a particular use of military force requires a declaration of war by Congress[2] and (ii) whether the conduct of the war is constitutional. In this section, we only will address the conduct of war.[3]

The President's discretionary power under Article II, §2 of *how* to wage a war historically has been interpreted differently by U.S. federal courts.[4] On one hand, some federal courts have held that the political question doctrine prohibits federal courts from scrutinizing how the President executes military operations. The U.S. Supreme Court in examining the shooting of civilians by the Ohio National Guard at Kent State University in *Gilligan v. Morgan* made the following sweeping statement:

> [I]t is difficult to conceive of an area of governmental activity in which the courts have less competence. The complex, subtle, and professional decisions as to the composition, training, equipping, and control of a military force are essentially

---

[1] [For a discussion of the *McCann Case*, see above Memorial Amicus Curiae. Ed.'s Note.]

[2] In the context of war-making, the federal courts have the power to decide whether the nation's military actions constitute "war" for the purposes of the war clause in Article I §8 of the U.S. Constitution. *Dellums v. Bush*, 752 F. Supp. 1141 (D.D.C. 1990); *see also* Thomas Franck, "The President, The Constitution, and Nuclear Weapons," 363, 366 *in* NUCLEAR WEAPONS AND LAW (Arthur Miller & Martin Fernrider eds., 1984) (President's authority to go to war is justiciable issue); Velvel, *The War in Viet Nam: Unconstitutional, Justiciable, and Jurisdictionally Attackable*, 16 KAN. L. REV. 449 (1968).

[3] This book will not address the international law governing the lawful declaration of war because this area of law presently is ambiguous. The Preparatory Committee for the Statute of the International Criminal Court presently is in the process of developing a clearer definition of the war of aggression. Complicating the impact of any eventual international law governing the initiation of war is the U.S.' refusal to sign or ratify the ICC Statute.

[4] *See, e.g., Sanchez-Espinoza v. Reagan*, 770 F.2d 202 (D.C. Cir. 1985); *Nejad v. United States*, 724 F. Supp. 753 (C. D. Cal. 1989); *Saltany v. Reagan*, 702 F. Supp. 319 (D.D.C. 1988); *Greenham Women Against Cruise Missiles v. Reagan*, 591 F. Supp. 1332 (S.D.N.Y. 1984), *aff'd*, 755 F.2d 34 (2d Cir. 1985); *Crockett v. Reagan*, 558 F. Supp. 893 (D.D.C. 1982), *aff'd*, 720 F.2d 1355 (D.C. Cir. 1983), *cert. denied*, 467 U.S. 1251 (1984); *see also* Thomas Franck, *The President, The Constitution, and Nuclear Weapons, in* NUCLEAR WEAPONS AND LAW 363, 366 (Arthur Miller & Martin Fernrider eds., 1984) (international law cannot alter President's power to conduct war).

professional military judgments, subject *always* to civilian control of the Legislative and Executive Branches.[5]

The Supreme Court reversed the appeals court's instructions to the district court to evaluate the "pattern of training, weaponry and orders in the Ohio National Guard" so as to determine whether it made "inevitable the use of fatal force in suppressing civilian disorders."[6] Therefore, injunctive relief was unavailable.

In *United States v. Sisson*, a federal district court in the context of the Vietnam War held that "[b]ecause a domestic tribunal is incapable of eliciting the facts during a war, and because it is probably incapable of exercising a disinterested judgment which would command the confidence of sound judicial opinion," the determination of whether U.S. military operations violated international law was not within the court's jurisdiction under the political question doctrine.[7] In *Nejad v. United States*,[8] a federal district court noted the following:

[T]he same considerations which preclude judicial examination of the decision to act must necessarily bar examination of the manner in which that decision was executed by the President's subordinates. The textual commitment to the President as commander in chief of authority for military decisions entails that his decision may be implemented without judicial scrutiny. Moreover, courts lack standards with which to judge whether reasonable care was taken to achieve tactical objectives in combat while minimizing injury and loss of life.[9]

However, the U.S. Supreme Court itself has warned of the limitations of the political question doctrine in *Baker v. Carr*:

Much confusion results from the capacity of the "political question" label to obscure the need for case-by-case inquiry. . . .

. . . There are sweeping statements to the effect that all questions touching [upon] foreign relations are political questions. Not only does resolution of such issues frequently turn on standards that defy judicial application, or involve the exercise of a discretion demonstrably committed to the executive or legislature; but many such questions uniquely demand single-voiced statements of the Government's views. Yet it is error to suppose that every case or controversy which touches foreign relations lies beyond judicial cognizance.[10]

As the U.S. Court of Appeals for the D.C. Circuit has held, the President's "power to conduct foreign relations free from unwarranted supervision of the Judiciary cannot give the [President] *carte blanche* to trample the most fundamental liberty . . . rights of this country's citizenry."[11]

---

[5] *Gilligan v. Morgan*, 413 U.S. 1, 10 (1973) (emphasis in original).

[6] *Id.* at 4.

[7] 294 F. Supp. 515, 517–18 (D. Mass. 1968).

[8] 724 F. Supp. 753 (C.D. Cal. 1989).

[9] *Id.* at 755 (citing *Rappenecker v. United States*, 509 F. Supp. 1024, 1030 (N.D. Cal. 1980).

[10] 369 U.S. 186, 210–11 (1962).

[11] *Ramirez de Arellano v. Weinberger*, 745 F.2d 1500, 1515 (D.C. Cir. 1984) (*en banc*).

In *Koohi v. United States*,[12] a U.S. Court of Appeals scrutinized the USS Vincennes' shoot down of Iran Air Flight 655 (an Iranian passenger jet) during the hostilities against Iraq. The appeals court held that a law suit is not

> rendered judicially unmanageable because the challenged conduct took place as part of an authorized military operation. The Supreme Court has made clear that the federal courts are capable of reviewing military decisions, particularly when those decisions cause injury to civilians. The controlling case is *The Paquete Habana*.... The Supreme Court found that the question whether the seizure of the vessels was militarily justified could be reviewed by the Court.... The Court then held that the decision to seize the vessels was not justified by military necessity and that the vessels must be returned.... More recently in *Scheuer v. Rhodes*, 416 U.S. 232 (1974), the Court allowed a civil action alleging the unlawful operation of the national guard during the incident at Kent State.... These cases make clear that the claim of military necessity will not, without more, shield governmental operations from judicial review.[13]

Most importantly, the appeals court recognized that suits for money damages are judicially manageable as opposed to those suits seeking injunctive relief in the context of U.S. military operations.[14] However, the court also noted that "no duty of reasonable care is owed to those against whom force is directed as a result of authorized military action."[15]

To overcome the limits imposed by the political question doctrine in the context of the use of lethal force by military authorities, one must address three issues:

(i) Is there a "textually demonstrable commitment"[16] to the executive and/or legislative branches of the decision when to use lethal force in the context of war?

(ii) Are there prudential considerations counselling for judicial abstention?[17]

(iii) Are there "judicially discoverable and manageable standards"[18] for determining whether the use of lethal force was absolutely necessary?

Let us examine these issues below.

i. Limiting the "Textually Demonstrable Commitment" to the Executive and Legislative Branches of Decisions When to Use Lethal Force

---

[12] 976 F.2d 1328 (9th Cir. 1992).

[13] *Id.* at 1331.

[14] *Id.* at 1332. However, because the plaintiffs in *Koohi* based their cause of action on the Federal Tort Claims Act (FTCA), which contains a combat exception to the FTCA's waiver of sovereign immunity, the suit was dismissed. This exception also extended to the other defendants who were military contractors.

[15] *Id.* at 37 (dictum).

[16] *Goldwater v. Carter*, 444 U.S. 996, 997 (1979) (Powell, J. *concurring*); *see Baker v. Carr*, 369 U.S. 186, 217 (1962) ("impossibility of a court's undertaking independent resolution without expressing lack of the respect due coordinate branches of government").

[17] *Goldwater v. Carter*, 444 U.S. at 998; *see Baker v. Carr*, 369 U.S. at 217 ("the potentiality of embarrassment from multifarious pronouncements by various departments on one question" and/or "an unusual need for unquestioning adherence to a political decision already made"); *Weinberger v. Catholic Action of Hawaii / Peace Educ. Project*, 454 U.S. 139, 146–47 (1981) (issues involving disclosure of military secrets are "beyond judicial scrutiny"); *Lowry v. Reagan*, 676 F. Supp. 333, 340 (D.D.C. 1987) (recognizing demand for "single-voiced view" on whether hostilities do or do not exist in Persian Gulf).

[18] *Goldwater v. Carter*, 444 U.S. at 999; *see Baker v. Carr*, 369 U.S. at 217 ("impossibility of deciding without an initial policy determination of a kind clearly for nonjudicial discretion").

There are *prima facie* "textually demonstrable commitment[s]" of war-making authority to the President under Article II, §2 and to Congress under Article I, §8.[19] However,
neither Article I, §8 or II, §2 gives Congress or the President authority to wage war in a
manner that conflicts with constitutional or international law (as federal law). The texts
of Articles I, §8 and II, §2 make no mention of such authority, and the Constitution
expressly does limit the U.S. government in how it wages war. The U.S. Supreme Court
has stated in dictum that "the war power.... tolerates no qualifications or limitations,
unless found in the Constitution or in applicable principles of international law."[20] And,
a U.S. district court stated in dictum that customary international law trumps controlling
executive acts in context of Geneva Convention – Protocol I.[21] Indeed, Alexander Hamilton argued that the Executive had a constitutional duty to execute international law in
order "to avoid giving a cause of war to foreign powers,"[22] and the Congress is assumed
to legislate in conformity with international law.[23] Given that conventional customary
international law should and *jus cogens* does trump federal statutory law and executive
orders, [ ] the President's and Congress' constitutional war-making authority should be
interpreted to conform with the *McCann* Rule because it reflects conventional customary
international law and *jus cogens*.

Moreover, Article I, §8 and Article II, §2 should be interpreted to conform with the
McCann Rule in order to reflect the fundamental importance of the right to life under
both U.S. constitutional law and international law. The Fifth Amendment of the U.S.
Constitution states:

> No person shall ... be deprived of life ... without due process of law.... [24]

In discussing the need for the greater use of non-lethal weapons, Col. Joseph Siniscalchi
has noted the importance of the "high regard for life in modern democracies:"[25]

> Recent conflicts validate the importance of this factor in modern conflict.... Presi-
> dent Clinton approved the Bosnia deployment based on the Chairman [of the Joint
> Chiefs of Staff]'s projection of a minimal number of civilian casualties.[26] Dur-
> ing execution, the target selection and approval process for military operations in
> Bosnia required extensive, direct involvement from the senior military commanders
> in an effort to minimize unintended casualties and damage. The desire to minimize
> [casualties] friendly, civilian, and enemy forces permeates the US decision process.[27]

---

[19] The War Powers Resolution, 50 U.S.C. §§1541–1548, imposes upon the President many requirements (*e.g.*,
reporting to and consulting Congress) affecting his/her ability to wage an undeclared war. Accordingly,
Congress pursuant to its constitutional authority to *declare* war under Article I, §8 can limit the President's
power of *how* to wage war. This Resolution has become increasingly relevant in recent years in the context
of international conflicts requiring prompt and, hopefully, short military action (*e.g.*, Gulf War, Somalian
and Yugoslavian peacekeeping operations) often referred to as "operations-other-than-war" ("OOTW")
in military jargon.

[20] *United States v. Macintosh*, 283 U.S. 605, 622 (1931) (dictum).

[21] *United States v. Buck*, 690 F. Supp. 1291 (S.D.N.Y 1988) (dictum).

[22] Alexander Hamilton, *Pacificus* 1 in 15 Papers of Alexander Hamilton 40 (Harold Syrett ed. 1961).

[23] *See Murray v. The Schooner Charming Betsy*, 6 U.S. (2 Cranch.) 64, 118 (1804).

[24] U.S. Const. amend. V.

[25] Joseph Siniscalchi, *Non-Lethal Technologies: Implications for Military Strategy*, Occasional Paper No. 3,
Center for Strategy and Technology, Air War College, Air University, Maxwell Air Force Base, Alabama
(March 1998), available at <http://www.au.af.mil/au/awc/ awcgate/cst/occppr03.htm>.

[26] *Citing* Capt Edward O'Connell and 1st Lt John Dillaplain, *Nonlethal Concepts: Implications for Air Force
Intelligence*, Airpower Journal, 26–33 (Winter 1994).

[27] *See* Siniscalchi, *supra* note 25.

In conclusion, presidential and congressional discretionary war-making authority is limited by both constitutional and international law.

ii. Eliminating Prudential Considerations Counselling for Judicial Abstention from Scrutinizing Use of Lethal Force Decisions

Jurists historically have given great deference to the President's discretionary decision-making in military contexts on the basis of the political question doctrine which is based on the constitutional separation of powers. Furthermore, jurists are not inclined to second-guess the military about its choice of tactics and strategy in the heated and confused context of the battlefield. Jurists have not closely scrutinized military operations because such operations historically fell outside both their area of professional competence and their ability to elicit all the facts.[28] Another compelling state interest – national security – serves further to insulate military choices and information from judicial scrutiny.

However, federal courts over the last forty years have slowly eroded the amount of deference given to governmental policy and practice that had been justified on both the political question doctrine[29] and national security interests.[30] Furthermore, the increasing capability of news gathering organizations and the resulting availability of information (through, e.g., the internet) about once-secreted, military information has undermined the viability of the national security interests rationale for withholding such information.[31] Consequently, jurists are in a better position to elicit information about military operations. Numerous human rights NGOs having expertise in military operations also have enabled the judiciary to critically examine military operations in an informed manner, thereby making judges more competent to examine the lawfulness of military operations and articulate injunctive relief regarding military training and weapons selection.[32]

In terms of specific considerations counselling for judicial abstention, Judge Bork in the context of the Hague Conventions has argued that the possibility of "hundreds of thousands or millions of lawsuits" by individuals claiming violations of the Hague Conventions committed during a large-scale war "might be far beyond the capacity of any legal system to resolve at all, much less accurately and fairly."[33] In the abstract, this would be a consideration counselling for judicial abstention from scrutinizing lethal force decisions. However, other civil suits involving hundreds of thousands of plaintiffs (e.g., asbestos, product liability cases) have been managed competently by U.S. courts using, inter alia, class action vehicles.

---

[28] See United States v. Sisson, 294 F. Supp. 515, 517–18 (D. Mass. 1968).

[29] See, e.g., Baker v. Carr, 369 U.S. 186 (1962) (limiting political question doctrine); Koohi v. United States, 976 F.2d 1328 (9th Cir. 1992) (rejecting political question basis for non-judiciability of war-making decision).

[30] See, e.g., New York Times Co. v. United States (The Pentagon Papers Case), 403 U.S. 713 (1971) (rejecting national security reasons in support of request for restraining order against publication of U.S. Dept. of Defense secret study).

[31] See, e.g., United States v. Progressive, Inc., 467 F. Supp. 990 (W. D. Wis. 1979), case dismissed, 610 F.2d 819 (7th Cir. 1979) (government's suit to enjoin publication of hydrogen bomb data dismissed after publication of data elsewhere); cf. Harold Hongju Koh, Judicial Constraints: The Courts and War Powers, in THE U.S. CONSTITUTION AND THE POWER TO GO TO WAR: HISTORICAL AND CURRENT PERSPECTIVES 121, 123 (Gary M. Stern & Morton H. Halperin eds., 1994) ("even cases involving massive amounts of classified information can be fairly adjudicated by a competent and conscientious judge, particularly if the parties provide the crucial information to the court in camera").

[32] The Lawyers Committee on Nuclear Policy, Center for Constitutional Rights, Human Rights Watch-Arms Project, among other NGOs have litigated or lobbied, respectively, around military operations.

[33] Tel-Oren v. Libyan Arab Republic, 726 F.2d 774, 810 (D.C. Cir. 1984) (Bork, J., concurring).

Judge Bork also raises the issue that such a number of suits may pose "an obstacle to the negotiation of peace and the resumption of normal relations between nations."[34] However, the availability of private redress through the U.S. courts actually probably would be an incentive to negotiating peace and resuming normal relations because the availability of reparations for unlawful uses of lethal force would ensure nationals belonging to the enemy-state (and others) also receive consideration and justice. Accordingly, "prudential considerations" counselling for judicial abstention in litigation scrutinizing military operations are increasingly becoming fewer or absent under close scrutiny.[35]

Moreover, there are a number of prudential considerations that *urge* close judicial scrutiny of military operations. First, for the U.S. to continue to effectively maintain its credibility in international relations, the U.S. must comply with the international law that governs these relations. The U.S. must conform its practices to international law, *a fortiori*, when the U.S. plays a central and supervisory role in these relations as, *e.g.*, a permanent member of the UN Security Council or command head of international military operations. Otherwise, there can be adverse consequences: diplomatic isolation, loss of prestige, countermeasures, and/or economic sanctions.[36]

Secondly, the U.S. military often acts in conjunction with European nations[37] that are bound by the ECHR and, thereby, are governed by the *McCann* Rule. Assuming that the U.S. was not governed by the *McCann* Rule because it reflected only a regional customary international law or treaty norm, practical operational considerations still would require the U.S. military authorities to conform its practices with the *McCann* Rule. In cases where U.S. forces would be placed under European command in a joint U.S.-European military force (if constitutionally permissible), European commanders would be required to ensure that the *McCann* Rule was observed by U.S. forces. [ ] In cases where U.S. forces were not placed under European command, the inconsistent observance of the *McCann* Rule by a U.S.-European military coalition may lead to logistical, strategic, and tactical difficulties for joint operations, and the U.S. would receive severe criticism from the world press for valuing civilian lives less than its European partners.

Third, many future conflicts will be international police actions[38] requiring "civil-military implementation strategies."[39] Such strategies also would require the use of identical lethal force standards by the civil and military authorities.

---

[34] *Id.*

[35] There is an additional prudential concern that military forces enforcing international law should not be exposed to greater risks of harm than their enemies who fail to observe the *McCann* Rule. However, this concern must be dismissed. Just because your enemy has committed war crimes does not legally justify your own commission of war crimes. The *tu quoque* defense has been rejected in international criminal law. *Matter of Von Leeb and Others (German High Command Trial)*, 15 I.L.R. 376 (1949), 11 Trials of War Criminals (1950).

[36] *See* Michael J. Glennon, *Can the President Do No Wrong?*, 80 Am. J. Int'l L. 923, 927–28 (1986).

[37] *Cf.* Col. Howard Olsen & John Davis, *Training U.S. Army Officers for Peace Operations*, United States Institute of Peace Special Report 1 (29 October 1999) ("Future peace operations will likely be joint, multinational, and coalition-based.").

[38] The *McCann* Rule also could apply to other international law enforcement actions, such as anti-drug trafficking and anti-terrorism operations.

[39] Olsen & Davis, *supra* note, at 37; *see* Daphna Shraga, *UN Peacekeeping Operations: Applicability of International Humanitarian Law and Responsibility for Operations-Related Damage*, 94 Am. J. Int'l L. 406, 412 (2000) (UN operations have become "increasingly civilian and multidimensional, involving civilian police, political, humanitarian, human rights, and electoral components").

Fourth, non-lethal weapons may be more effective than traditional lethal means both in terms of tactical objectives and overall strategic goals.[40]

> Non-lethal weapons enable effective conflict termination. The reversibility of most non-lethal effects limits the duration of the "damage." Assuming that the political objective is to re-establish stability, it becomes necessary to assist the failed state to restore economic and political processes. A non-lethal strategy provides one option.[41]

Minimizing permanent collateral damage in terms of deaths by the use of non-lethal weapons maintains an environment more favorable for diplomatic resolution of the crisis.[42]

Finally, U.S. military enforcement of the *McCann* Rule also would serve to avoid any potential suits against the U.S. in both U.S. and international courts.

iii. Availability of "Judicially Discoverable and Manageable Standards" for Limiting the Use of Lethal Force

As discussed above, jurists have been loath to "second-guess" the military who operate often in the heated context and confusion of the battlefield. The reluctance of jurists to do so is certainly understandable. However, there are "judicially discoverable and manageable standards" for determining whether the conduct of war is justiciable.[43] In this past century alone, there have been numerous courts both domestic and international that have scrutinized whether the use of lethal force was lawful in a particular military context. These courts have included the International Military ("Nuremberg") Tribunal,[44] Control Council Law No. 10 Proceedings,[45] U.S. courts martial,[46] the Supreme Court of Germany,[47] the International Criminal Tribunals for Yugoslavia[48] and, of course, the European Court of Human Rights.[49]

The European Court of Human Rights in *McCann* was able to discover and articulate judicially manageable standards because it focused on command planning of operations, thereby, avoiding the problems posed by second-guessing military personnel operating in the heat of battle. The European Court of Human Rights noted that the U.K. authorities could have prevented the need for the use of lethal force by proper planning and use of intelligence. The fault laid not with the soldiers for using lethal force to prevent IRA members from setting off the bomb. The fault laid with their commanders who failed to consider the use of non-lethal means in their operations planning. Accordingly, the

---

[40] For example, economic sanctions traditionally are only marginally effective due to the difficulty of enforcement and the lack of credible means to escalate the sanctions. "The effectiveness of sanctions can be significantly enhanced by concurrent employment of non-lethal weapons." *See* Siniscalchi, *supra* note 25.

[41] *Id.*

[42] *Id.*

[43] *See* Koh, *supra* note, at 31.

[44] *See, e.g., Judgment for the Trial of German Major War Criminals*, I.M.T. (1946).

[45] *See, e.g., United States v. List,* XI Trials of War Criminals Before the Nuernberg Military Tribunals under Control Council Law No. 10 (1948).

[46] *See, e.g., United States v. Calley,* 48 C.M.R. 19 (U.S. Ct. of Military App. 1973).

[47] *See, e.g., Case of Lieutenants Dithmar and Boldt Hospital Ship "Llandovery Castle"*, (1921) (sinking of unarmed hospital ship by German U-boat), *cited in* 16 Am. J. Int'l L. 708 (1922).

[48] *See, e.g., Prosecutor v. Tadic,* Case No. IT-94-1 (ICT-Y 1995).

[49] *See, e.g., McCann and Others v. United Kingdom*, 324 Eur. Ct. H.R. (ser. A) (1995).

application of the *McCann* Rule is especially appropriate in cases involving deficient military operational planning that takes place outside the battlefield.

The *McCann* Rule extends not only to the planning of particular military operations and tactics but also general military strategic planning. Although the facts in *McCann* may be distinguished from other cases involving large scale uses of force, strategic military operations consist of many different, sometimes independent, relatively small operations against military targets. The evolution of war into international police actions also has changed the nature of war-making into one characterized by smaller, isolated actions. Nevertheless, the importance of the *McCann* Rule is that it addresses the *planning* of military operations that could include not only small, isolated operations but also larger operations involving strategic issues.

The U.S. Department of Defense has noted that non-lethal weapon employment is not limited to the lower spectrum of conflict, *viz.*, peace-keeping, peace-enforcement, and humanitarian missions. Rather, their employment can apply across the range of military operations where they can enhance the "effectiveness and efficiency of military operations.[50] Accordingly, military forces would need to be further trained in tactics and strategy using non-lethal measures, and several senior military authorities already have argued for such training.[51] The military would have to learn how to "dial up and dial down" the use of force – exercising their choices along a use of force continuum. No longer should the decision be an "either-or" – between the use of no force and the use of lethal force.[52] To conform with the conventional customary international law reflected in the *McCann* Rule,[53] the U.S. military would have to adopt policy requiring and receive further training in the use of non-lethal tactics, strategy, and weaponry.

a. Availability of Liability Standards for Planning and Other Operations

The judicial standard for demonstrating liability probably will depend on how much one weighs the importance of the facts in *McCann* for developing a rule. As argued above, it is clear that the *McCann* Rule applies to situations involving operations planning. It is less clear whether it applies to other situations, such as those requiring immediate responses for which there has been no planning (*e.g.*, defensive responses to enemy ambushes).

For command failure to consider and use available non-lethal measures during operations planning and training, respectively, the European Court of Human Rights decision

---

[50] Department of Defense, Policy for Non-Lethal Weapons," Department of Defense Directive, 1, 2 (9 July 1996).

[51] *See* comments by Gen. Anthony Zinni in *Shoot Not to Kill* (MacNeil/Lehrer Productions 1999); Siniscalchi, *supra* note 25; *see also* Council on Foreign Relations, Report of an Independent Task Force, Nonlethal Technologies: Military Options and Implications 15 (1995).

[52] Non-lethal weapons technologies cover a broad, diverse range of capabilities. The technology ranges from certain types of chemical warfare, information warfare, crowd control measures, to the latest exotic weapons. These include strobe lights (which cause disequilibrium); tear gas and pepper spray; low frequency sound emissions and other noises (for inducing nausea); carbon fiber chaff, electromagnetic pulse, and microwaves (for disrupting electrical systems); internet viruses (for disrupting command and control communications); and soft projectiles (*e.g.*, rubber bullets, stringball grenades, tennis ball launchers, water cannons). *See* Siniscalchi, *supra* note 25.

[53] *See also Güleç v. Turkey*, 28 Eur. H.R. Rep. 121 (1999) (rejecting Turkish government's defense that non-lethal methods, such as tear gas, rubber bullets, water cannons, and truncheons, could not be used).

in *Osman v. United Kingdom*[54] provides guidance. In *Osman v. United Kingdom*, the Court established a negligence standard in determining liability for violations of the right to life.[55] As for the failure to use non-lethal measures in situations involving immediate response to lethal threats, the liability standard certainly should be very high because of the insufficient opportunity to consider other non-lethal alternatives. An intentional or reckless standard probably would be appropriate.[56]

b. Availability of Standards for Determining Damages and Injunctive Relief

Under *Scheuer v. Rhodes*[57] and *Koohi v. United States*,[58] damages are available for the unlawful use of lethal force by military authorities. However, the availability of injunctive relief through private suits is problematic for compelling the U.S. military to adopt policy and training in the use of non-lethal measures. The European Court of Human Rights did not order injunctive relief in *McCann* because the Court has interpreted the ECHR generally to not include injunctive relief. However, the European Court of Human Rights' failure to order injunctive relief does not reflect conventional customary international law, as reflected in the case law of the Inter-American Court of Human Rights[59] and the International Court of Justice.[60] Moreover, although the European Court of Human Rights does not *order* injunctive relief, it often *declares what kind of performance* would fulfill a state's legal obligations.[61] Also problematic is the U.S. Supreme Court's sweeping statement in *Gilligan v. Morgan* that injunctive relief in terms of military training is unavailable. However, their 1973 decision probably is outdated in light of the information and expertise available to federal courts, as discussed above.[ ]

---

54 29 Eur. H.R. Rep. 245 (2000).

55 Recall that although a federal court in *Koohi v. United States*, noted in dictum that "[n]o duty of reasonable care is owed to those against whom force is directed as a result of authorized military action," this standard does not reflect conventional customary international law, and thereby is inapplicable. *Koohi v. United States*, 976 F.2d 1328, 1337 (9th Cir. 1992)

56 Present UN policy is somewhat similar. The UN has established claims review boards in connection with its peacekeeping operations to settle private claims involving, *e.g.*, loss of life. The UN has adopted limited liability for loss of life. In cases where there has been wilful misconduct or gross negligence, the UN will provide full compensation to the harmed party, while retaining the right to seek reimbursement from the member of the force or his/her troop-contributing state. However, if the harm results from measures that were not operationally necessary, compensation is limited to economic losses (*i.e.*, medical expenses, loss of earnings, and financial support), measured by local standards and not exceeding US $ 50,000. Compensation for non-economic loss (*e.g.*, pain and suffering) is not available. To state a claim, one must demonstrate that the loss of life was not operationally necessary. "Operational necessity" must meet four cumulative conditions: (i) the force commander must be convinced that an operational necessity exists, (ii) the measure itself is strictly necessary and not just a matter of mere convenience or expedience, (iii) the measure is part of an overarching operational plan and not the result of a rash individual action, and (iv) the damage inflicted will be proportional to what is strictly necessary to achieve the operational goal. *See* Shraga, *supra* note 39, at 410–11.

57 416 U.S. 232 (1974).

58 976 F.2d at 1328.

59 *See, e.g., Velásquez Rodríguez v. Honduras*, Inter-Am. Ct. H.R., OEA/ser. C, No. 4 (Judgment of 29 July 1988) (ordering prevention, prosecution, and punishment of persons violating right to life).

60 *See, e.g., United States Diplomatic and Consular Staff in Tehran (U.S. v. Iran)*, 1980 I.C.J. 3, 44–45 (May 24) (ordering Iran to release U.S. diplomatic and consular staff, provide means of travel for staff, and restore property); *see also* L. Oppenheim, 1 International Law §156 (H. Lauterpacht ed., 8th ed. 1955) (injured state's right to performance of acts necessary for reparation).

61 *See, e.g., X. & Y. v. The Netherlands*, 91 Eur. Ct. H.R. (ser. A) at §27 (1985) (declaring need for state to enact criminal-law provisions to fulfill it's ECHR obligations).

In conclusion, there are judicially manageable standards for establishing liability and damages.[62] However, the availability of injunctive relief in the form of requiring future proper operations planning and use of intelligence may not be forthcoming.

. . . .

~

5.3. Criminal and Civil Procedural Rights

In this subection, we examine various due process protections in criminal and civil contexts. Note that many due process rights guaranteed by international human rights law also apply to international criminal proceedings.

Universal Declaration of Human Rights

Article 10.

Everyone is entitled in full equality to a fair and public hearing by an independent and impartial tribunal, in the determination of his rights and obligations and of any criminal charge against him.

Article 11.

1. Everyone charged with a penal offence has the right to be presumed innocent until proved guilty according to law in a public trial at which he has had all the guarantees necessary for his defence.

2. No one shall be held guilty of any penal offence on account of any act or omission which did not constitute a penal offence, under national or international law, at the time when it was committed. Nor shall a heavier penalty be imposed than the one that was applicable at the time the penal offence was committed.

International Covenant on Civil and Political Rights

Article 14.

1. All persons shall be equal before the courts and tribunals. In the determination of any criminal charge against him, or of his rights and obligations in a suit at law, everyone shall be entitled to a fair and public hearing by a competent, independent and impartial tribunal established by law. The Press and the public may be excluded from all or part of a trial for reasons of morals, public order (*ordre public*) or national security in a democratic society, or when the interest of the private lives of the parties so requires, or to the extent strictly necessary in the opinion of the court in special circumstances where publicity would prejudice the interests of justice; but any judgement rendered in a criminal case or in a suit at law shall be made public except where the interest of juvenile persons

---

[62] *See Koohi v. United States*, 976 F.2d at 1332. Although *Koohi* disallows money damages under the FTCA, such damages should be available to aliens under ATCA (28 U.S.C. §1350), as a remedy for extra-judicial killings. If the operations planning took place in the U.S., the *situs* of the injury occurred on U.S. territory for purposes of establishing jurisdiction and a private cause of action.

otherwise requires or the proceedings concern matrimonial disputes or the guardianship of children.

2. Everyone charged with a criminal offence shall have the right to be presumed innocent until proved guilty according to law.

3. In the determination of any criminal charge against him, everyone shall be entitled to the following minimum guarantees, in full equality:

(a) To be informed promptly and in detail in a language which he understands of the nature and cause of the charge against him;
(b) To have adequate time and facilities for the preparation of his defence and to communicate with counsel of his own choosing;
(c) To be tried without undue delay;
(d) To be tried in his presence, and to defend himself in person or through legal assistance of his own choosing; to be informed, if he does not have legal assistance, of this right; and to have legal assistance assigned to him, in any case where the interests of justice so require, and without payment by him in any such case if he does not have sufficient means to pay for it;
(e) To examine, or have examined the witnesses against him and to obtain the attendance and examination of witnesses on his behalf under the same conditions as witnesses against him;
(f) To have the free assistance of an interpreter if he cannot understand or speak the language used in court;
(g) Not to be compelled to testify against himself or to confess guilt.

4. In the case of juvenile persons, the procedure shall be such as will take account of their age and the desirability of promoting their rehabilitation.

5. Everyone convicted of a crime shall have the right to his conviction and sentence being reviewed by a higher tribunal according to law.

6. When a person has by a final decision been convicted of a criminal offence and when subsequently his conviction has been reversed or he has been pardoned on the ground that a new or newly discovered fact shows conclusively that there has been a miscarriage of justice, the person who has suffered punishment as a result of such conviction shall be compensated according to law, unless it is proved that the non-disclosure of the unknown fact in time is wholly or partly attributable to him.

7. No one shall be liable to be tried or punished again for an offence for which he has already been finally convicted or acquitted in accordance with the law and penal procedure of each country.

Article 15

1. No one shall be held guilty of any criminal offence on account of any act or omission which did not constitute a criminal offence, under national or international law, at the time when it was committed. Nor shall a heavier penalty be imposed than the one that was applicable at the time when the criminal offence was committed. If, subsequent to the commission of the offence, provision is made by law for the imposition of a lighter penalty, the offender shall benefit thereby.

2. Nothing in this article shall prejudice the trial and punishment of any person for any act or omission which, at the time when it was committed was criminal according to the general principles of law recognized by the community of nations.

European Convention on Human Rights

Article 6

1. In the determination of his civil rights and obligations or of any criminal charge against him, everyone is entitled to a fair and public hearing within a reasonable time by an independent and impartial tribunal established by law. Judgement shall be pronounced publicly by the press and public may be excluded from all or part of the trial in the interest of morals, public order or national security in a democratic society, where the interests of juveniles or the protection of the private life of the parties so require, or the extent strictly necessary in the opinion of the court in special circumstances where publicity would prejudice the interests of justice.

2. Everyone charged with a criminal offence shall be presumed innocent until proved guilty according to law.

3. Everyone charged with a criminal offence has the following minimum rights:

(a) to be informed promptly, in a language which he understands and in detail, of the nature and cause of the accusation against him;
(b) to have adequate time and the facilities for the preparation of his defence;
(c) to defend himself in person or through legal assistance of his own choosing or, if he has not sufficient means to pay for legal assistance, to be given it free when the interests of justice so require;
(d) to examine or have examined witnesses against him and to obtain the attendance and examination of witnesses on his behalf under the same conditions as witnesses against him;
(e) to have the free assistance of an interpreter if he cannot understand or speak the language used in court.

Article 7

1. No one shall be held guilty of any criminal offence on account of any act or omission which did not constitute a criminal offence under national or international law at the time when it was committed. Nor shall a heavier penalty be imposed than the one that was applicable at the time the criminal offence was committed.

2. This article shall not prejudice the trial and punishment of any person for any act or omission which, at the time when it was committed, was criminal according the general principles of law recognized by civilized nations.

European Convention on Human Rights, Protocol No. 7

Article 2

1. Everyone convicted of a criminal offence by a tribunal shall have the right to have conviction or sentence reviewed by a higher tribunal. The exercise of this right, including the grounds on which it may be exercised, shall be governed by law.

2. This right may be subject to exceptions in regard to offences of a minor character, as prescribed by law, or in cases in which the person concerned was tried in the first instance by the highest tribunal or was convicted following an appeal against acquittal.

Article 4

1. No one shall be liable to be tried or punished again in criminal proceedings under the jurisdiction of the same State for an offence for which he has already been finally acquitted or convicted in accordance with the law and penal procedure of the State.

2. The provisions of the preceding paragraph shall not prevent the re-opening of the case in accordance with the law and penal procedure of the State concerned, if there is evidence of new or newly discovered facts, or if there has been a fundamental defect in the previous proceedings, which could affect the outcome of the case.

3. No derogation from this Article shall be made under Article 15 of the Convention.

Charter of Fundamental Rights of the European Union

Justice

Article 47

Right to an effective remedy and to a fair trial

Everyone whose rights and freedoms guaranteed by the law of the Union are violated has the right to an effective remedy before a tribunal in compliance with the conditions laid down in this Article. Everyone is entitled to a fair and public hearing within a reasonable time by an independent and impartial tribunal previously established by law. Everyone shall have the possibility of being advised, defended and represented. Legal aid shall be made available to those who lack sufficient resources in so far as such aid is necessary to ensure effective access to justice.

Article 48

Presumption of innocence and right of defence

1. Everyone who has been charged shall be presumed innocent until proved guilty according to law.

2. Respect for the rights of the defence of anyone who has been charged shall be guaranteed.

Article 49

Principles of legality and proportionality of criminal offences and penalties

1. No one shall be held guilty of any criminal offence on account of any act or omission which did not constitute a criminal offence under national law or international law at the time when it was committed. Nor shall a heavier penalty be imposed than that which was applicable at the time the criminal offence was committed. If, subsequent to the commission of a criminal offence, the law provides for a lighter penalty, that penalty shall be applicable.

2. This Article shall not prejudice the trial and punishment of any person for any act or omission which, at the time when it was committed, was criminal according to the general principles recognised by the community of nations.

3. The severity of penalties must not be disproportionate to the criminal offence.

Article 50

Right not to be tried or punished twice in criminal proceedings for the same criminal offence

No one shall be liable to be tried or punished again in criminal proceedings for an offence for which he or she has already been finally acquitted or convicted within the Union in accordance with the law.

American Declaration on the Rights and Duties of Man

Article XXVI. Right to due process of law.

Every accused person is presumed to be innocent until proved guilty.

Every person accused of an offense has the right to be given an impartial and public hearing, and to be tried by courts previously established in accordance with pre-existing laws, and not to receive cruel, infamous or unusual punishment.

American Convention on Human Rights

Article 8. RIGHT TO A FAIR TRIAL.

1. Every person has the right to a hearing, with due guarantees and within a reasonable time, by a competent, independent, and impartial tribunal, previously established by law, in the substantiation of any accusation of a criminal nature made against him or for the determination of his rights and obligations of a civil, labor, fiscal, or any other nature.

2. Every person accused of a criminal offense has the right to be presumed innocent so long as his guilt has not been proven according to law. During the proceedings, every person is entitled, with full equality, to the following minimum guarantees:

   a. The right of the accused to be assisted without charge by a translator or interpreter, if he does not understand or does not speak the language of the tribunal or court;
   b. Prior notification in detail to the accused of the charges against him;
   c. Adequate time and means for the preparation of his defense;
   d. The right of the accused to defend himself personally or to be assisted by legal counsel of his own choosing. and to communicate freely and privately with his counsel;
   e. The inalienable right to be assisted by counsel provided by the State, paid or not as the domestic law provides, if the accused does not defend himself personally or engage his own counsel within the time period established by law;
   f. The right of the defense to examine witnesses present in the court and to obtain the appearance, as witnesses, of experts or other persons who may throw light on the facts;
   g. The right not to be compelled to be a witness against himself or to plead guilty; and
   h. The right to appeal the judgment to a higher court.

3. A confession of guilt by the accused shall be valid only if it is made without coercion of any kind.

4. An accused person acquitted by a nonappealable judgment shall not be subjected to a new trial for the same cause.

5. Criminal proceedings shall be public, except insofar as may be necessary to protect the interests of justice.

Article 9. FREEDOM FROM "EX POST FACTO" LAWS.

No one shall be convicted of any act or omission that did not constitute a criminal offense, under the applicable law, at the time it was committed. A heavier penalty shall not be imposed than the one that was applicable at the time the criminal offense was committed. If subsequent to the commission of the offense the law provides for the imposition of a lighter punishment, the guilty person shall benefit therefrom.

African [Banjul] Charter on Human and Peoples' Rights

Article 7

1. Every individual shall have the right to have his cause heard. This comprises: (a) the right to an appeal to competent national organs against acts of violating his fundamental rights as recognized and guaranteed by conventions, laws, regulations and customs in force; (b) the right to be presumed innocent until proved guilty by a competent court or tribunal; (c) the right to defence, including the right to be defended by counsel of his choice; (d) the right to be tried within a reasonable time by an impartial court or tribunal.

2. No one may be condemned for an act or omission which did not constitute a legally punishable offence at the time it was committed. No penalty may be inflicted for an offence for which no provision was made at the time it was committed. Punishment is personal and can be imposed only on the offender.

Convention on Human Rights and Fundamental Freedoms of the Commonwealth of Independent States

Article 6

1. All persons shall be equal before the judicial system.
In the determination of any charge against him, everyone shall be entitled to a fair and public hearing within a reasonable time by an independent and impartial court. The decisions of the court or the sentence shall be pronounced publicly, but all or part of the trial may take place *in camera* for reasons of public order or state secrecy or where the interests of juveniles or the protection of the private life of the parties so require.

2. Everyone charged with a criminal offence shall be presumed innocent until proved guilty according to law.

3. Everyone charged with a criminal offence shall have the following minimum rights:

a. to be informed promptly and in detail, in a language which he understands, of the nature and cause of the accusation against him;
b. to have adequate time and facilities for the preparation of his defence;
c. to defend him in person or through legal assistance of his own choosing or to have legal assistance assigned to him whenever the interests of justice so require, as well as to be provided with legal assistance free of charge in cases specified in national legislation;
d. to make applications to the court concerning the examination of witnesses, the carrying out of investigations, the obtaining of documents, the commissioning of expert appraisals and other procedural acts;

e. to have the free assistance of an interpreter if he cannot understand or speak the language used in court;

f. not to be forced to testify against himself or to plead guilty.

Article 7

1. No one shall be held liable for an act which did not constitute an offence under national legislation or international law at the time when it was committed. Nor shall a heavier penalty by imposed than the one that was applicable at the time the offence was committed. If, after an offence is committed, a law establishes a lesser punishment for it or eliminates liability for it, the new law shall be applicable.

2. No one shall be convicted or punished a second time for an offence for which he has already been convicted or punished in accordance with national legislation. Every convicted person shall be entitled, in accordance with the law, to have the judgment of the court reviewed by a higher judicial body as well as apply for a pardon or request a lighter sentence.

Charter of the International Military Tribunal

Article 16.

In order to ensure fair trial for the Defendants, the following procedure shall be followed:

(a) The Indictment shall include full particulars specifying in detail the charges against the Defendants. A copy of the Indictment and of all the documents lodged with the Indictment, translated into a language which he understands, shall be furnished to the Defendant at reasonable time before the Trial.

(b) During any preliminary examination or trial of a Defendant he will have the right to give any explanation relevant to the charges made against him.

(c) A preliminary examination of a Defendant and his Trial shall be conducted in, or translated into, a language which the Defendant understands.

(d) A Defendant shall have the right to conduct his own defense before the Tribunal or to have the assistance of Counsel.

(e) A Defendant shall have the right through himself or through his Counsel to present evidence at the Trial in support of his defense, and to cross-examine any witness called by the Prosecution.

Article 26.

The judgment of the Tribunal as to the guilt or the innocence of any Defendant shall give the reasons on which it is based, and shall be final and not subject to review.

Statute of the International Criminal Tribunal for Rwanda

Article 9

Non bis in idem

1. No person shall be tried before a national court for acts constituting serious violations of international humanitarian law under the present Statute, for which he or she has already been tried by the International Tribunal for Rwanda.

2. A person who has been tried by a national court for acts constituting serious violations of international humanitarian law may be subsequently tried by the International Tribunal for Rwanda only if:

(a) The act for which he or she was tried was characterized as an ordinary crime; or

(b) The national court proceedings were not impartial or independent, were designed to shield the accused from international criminal responsibility, or the case was not diligently prosecuted.

3. In considering the penalty to be imposed on a person convicted of a crime under the present Statute, the International Tribunal for Rwanda shall take into account the extent to which any penalty imposed by a national court on the same person for the same act has already been served.

Article 20

Rights of the accused

1. All persons shall be equal before the International Tribunal for Rwanda.

2. In the determination of charges against him or her, the accused shall be entitled to a fair and public hearing, subject to article 21 of the Statute.

3. The accused shall be presumed innocent until proved guilty according to the provisions of the present Statute.

4. In the determination of any charge against the accused pursuant to the present Statute, the accused shall be entitled to the following minimum guarantees, in full equality:

(a) To be informed promptly and in detail in a language which he or she understands of the nature and cause of the charge against him or her;

(b) To have adequate time and facilities for the preparation of his or her defence and to communicate with counsel of his or her own choosing;

(c) To be tried without undue delay;

(d) To be tried in his or her presence, and to defend himself or herself in person or through legal assistance of his or her own choosing; to be informed, if he or she does not have legal assistance, of this right; and to have legal assistance assigned to him or her, in any case where the interests of justice so require, and without payment by him or her in any such case if he or she does not have sufficient means to pay for it;

(e) To examine, or have examined, the witnesses against him or her and to obtain the attendance and examination of witnesses on his or her behalf under the same conditions as witnesses against him or her;

(f) To have the free assistance of an interpreter if he or she cannot understand or speak the language used in the International Tribunal for Rwanda;

(g) Not to be compelled to testify against himself or herself or to confess guilt.

Statute of the International Tribunal [for the Former Yugoslavia]

Article 10

Non-bis-in-idem

1. No person shall be tried before a national court for acts constituting serious violations of international humanitarian law under the present Statute, for which he or she has already been tried by the International Tribunal.

2. A person who has been tried by a national court for acts constituting serious violations of international humanitarian law may be subsequently tried by the International Tribunal only if:

(a) the act for which he or she was tried was characterized as an ordinary crime; or

(b) the national court proceedings were not impartial or independent, were designed to shield the accused from international criminal responsibility, or the case was not diligently prosecuted.

3. In considering the penalty to be imposed on a person convicted of a crime under the present Statute, the International Tribunal shall take into account the extent to which any penalty imposed by a national court on the same person for the same act has already been served.

Article 21

Rights of the accused

1. All persons shall be equal before the International Tribunal.

2. In the determination of charges against him, the accused shall be entitled to a fair and public hearing, subject to article 22 of the Statute.

3. The accused shall be presumed innocent until proved guilty according to the provisions of the present Statute.

4. In the determination of any charge against the accused pursuant to the present Statute, the accused shall be entitled to the following minimum guarantees, in full equality:

(a) to be informed promptly and in detail in a language which he understands of the nature and cause of the charge against him;

(b) to have adequate time and facilities for the preparation of his defence and to communicate with counsel of his own choosing;

(c) to be tried without undue delay;

(d) to be tried in his presence, and to defend himself in person or through legal assistance of his own choosing; to be informed, if he does not have legal assistance, of this right; and to have legal assistance assigned to him, in any case where the interests of justice so require, and without payment by him in any such case if he does not have sufficient means to pay for it;

(e) to examine, or have examined, the witnesses against him and to obtain the attendance and examination of witnesses on his behalf under the same conditions as witnesses against him;

(f) to have the free assistance of an interpreter if he cannot understand or speak the language used in the International Tribunal;

(g) not to be compelled to testify against himself or to confess guilt.

Statute of the International Criminal Court

Article 20

Non bis in idem

1. Except as provided in this Statute, no person shall be tried before the Court with respect to conduct which formed the basis of crimes for which the person has been convicted or acquitted by the Court.

2. No person shall be tried before another court for a crime referred to in article 5 for which that person has already been convicted or acquitted by the Court.

3. No person who has been tried by another court for conduct also proscribed under articles 6, 7 or 8 shall be tried by the Court with respect to the same conduct unless the proceedings in the other court:

(a) Were for the purpose of shielding the person concerned from criminal responsibility for crimes within the jurisdiction of the Court; or

(b) Otherwise were not conducted independently or impartially in accordance with the norms of due process recognized by international law and were conducted in a manner which, in the circumstances, was inconsistent with an intent to bring the person concerned to justice.

Article 22

Nullum crimen sine lege

1. A person shall not be criminally responsible under this Statute unless the conduct in question constitutes, at the time it takes place, a crime within the jurisdiction of the Court.

2. The definition of a crime shall be strictly construed and shall not be extended by analogy. In case of ambiguity, the definition shall be interpreted in favour of the person being investigated, prosecuted or convicted.

3. This article shall not affect the characterization of any conduct as criminal under international law independently of this Statute.

Article 23

Nulla poena sine lege

A person convicted by the Court may be punished only in accordance with this Statute.

Article 24

Non-retroactivity ratione personae

1. No person shall be criminally responsible under this Statute for conduct prior to the entry into force of the Statute.

2. In the event of a change in the law applicable to a given case prior to a final judgement, the law more favourable to the person being investigated, prosecuted or convicted shall apply.

Article 55

Rights of persons during an investigation

1. In respect of an investigation under this Statute, a person:

(a) Shall not be compelled to incriminate himself or herself or to confess guilt;

(b) Shall not be subjected to any form of coercion, duress or threat, to torture or to any other form of cruel, inhuman or degrading treatment or punishment; and

(c) Shall, if questioned in a language other than a language the person fully understands and speaks, have, free of any cost, the assistance of a competent interpreter and such translations as are necessary to meet the requirements of fairness;

(d) Shall not be subjected to arbitrary arrest or detention; and shall not be deprived of his or her liberty except on such grounds and in accordance with such procedures as are established in the Statute.

2. Where there are grounds to believe that a person has committed a crime within the jurisdiction of the Court and that person is about to be questioned either by the Prosecutor, or by national authorities pursuant to a request made under Part 9 of this Statute, that person shall also have the following rights of which he or she shall be informed prior to being questioned:

(a) To be informed, prior to being questioned, that there are grounds to believe that he or she has committed a crime within the jurisdiction of the Court;
(b) To remain silent, without such silence being a consideration in the determination of guilt or innocence;
(c) To have legal assistance of the person's choosing, or, if the person does not have legal assistance, to have legal assistance assigned to him or her, in any case where the interests of justice so require, and without payment by the person in any such case if the person does not have sufficient means to pay for it;
(d) To be questioned in the presence of counsel unless the person has voluntarily waived his or her right to counsel.

Article 61

. . . .

3. Within a reasonable time before the hearing, the person shall:

(a) Be provided with a copy of the document containing the charges on which the Prosecutor intends to bring the person to trial; and
(b) Be informed of the evidence on which the Prosecutor intends to rely at the hearing.

. . . .

Article 67

Rights of the accused

1. In the determination of any charge, the accused shall be entitled to a public hearing, having regard to the provisions of this Statute, to a fair hearing conducted impartially, and to the following minimum guarantees, in full equality:

(a) To be informed promptly and in detail of the nature, cause and content of the charge, in a language which the accused fully understands and speaks;
(b) To have adequate time and facilities for the preparation of the defence and to communicate freely with counsel of the accused's choosing in confidence;
(c) To be tried without undue delay;
(d) Subject to article 63, paragraph 2, to be present at the trial, to conduct the defence in person or through legal assistance of the accused's choosing, to be informed, if the accused does not have legal assistance, of this right and to have legal assistance assigned by the Court in any case where the interests of justice so require, and without payment if the accused lacks sufficient means to pay for it;
(e) To examine, or have examined, the witnesses against him or her and to obtain the attendance and examination of witnesses on his or her behalf under the same

conditions as witnesses against him or her. The accused shall also be entitled to raise defences and to present other evidence admissible under this Statute;

(f) To have, free of any cost, the assistance of a competent interpreter and such translations as are necessary to meet the requirements of fairness, if any of the proceedings of or documents presented to the Court are not in a language which the accused fully understands and speaks;

(g) Not to be compelled to testify or to confess guilt and to remain silent, without such silence being a consideration in the determination of guilt or innocence;

(h) To make an unsworn oral or written statement in his or her defence; and

(i) Not to have imposed on him or her any reversal of the burden of proof or any onus of rebuttal.

2. In addition to any other disclosure provided for in this Statute, the Prosecutor shall, as soon as practicable, disclose to the defence evidence in the Prosecutor's possession or control which he or she believes shows or tends to show the innocence of the accused, or to mitigate the guilt of the accused, or which may affect the credibility of prosecution evidence. In case of doubt as to the application of this paragraph, the Court shall decide.

Presumption of Innocence

Allenet de Ribemont v. France
European Court of Human Rights
308 Eur. Ct. H.R. (ser. A) (1995)
20 E.H.R.R. 557 (1995)

FACTS:

. . . .

8. On 24 December 1976 Mr Jean de Broglie, a Member of Parliament . . . and former minister, was murdered in front of the applicant's home. He had just been visiting his financial adviser, Mr Pierre De Varga, who lived in the same building and with whom Mr Allenet de Ribemont was planning to become the joint owner of a Paris restaurant, "La Rotisserie de la Reine Pedauque". The scheme was financed by means of a loan taken out by the victim. He had passed on the borrowed sum to the applicant, who was responsible for repaying the loan.

9. A judicial investigation was begun into the commission by a person or persons unknown of the offence of intentional homicide. On 27 and 28 December 1976 the crime squad at Paris police headquarters arrested a number of people, including the victim's financial adviser. On 29 December it arrested Mr Allenet de Ribemont.

B. The press conference of 29 December 1976 and the implicating of the applicant

10. On 29 December 1976, at a press conference on the subject of the French police budget for the coming years, the Minister of the Interior, Mr Michel Poniatowski, the Director of the Paris Criminal Investigation Department, Mr Jean Ducret, and the Head of the Crime Squad, Superintendent Pierre Ottavioli, referred to the inquiry that was under way.

11. Two French television channels reported this press conference in their news programmes. The transcript of the relevant extracts reads as follows:

TF1 NEWS

Mr Roger Giquel, newsreader: ... Be that as it may, here is how all the aspects of the de Broglie case were explained to the public at a press conference given by Mr Michel Poniatowski yesterday evening.

Mr Poniatowski: The haul is complete. All the people involved are now under arrest after the arrest of Mr De Varga-Hirsch. It is a very simple story. A bank loan guaranteed by Mr Jean de Broglie was to be repaid by Mr Varga-Hirsch and Mr de Ribemont.

A journalist: Superintendent, who was the key figure in this case? De Varga?

Mr Ottavioli: I think it must have been Mr De Varga.

Mr Ducret: The instigator, Mr De Varga, and his acolyte, Mr de Ribemont, were the instigators of the murder. The organiser was Detective Sergeant Simone and the murderer was Mr Freche.

Mr Giquel: As you can see, those statements include a number of assertions. That is why the police are now being criticised by Ministry of Justice officials. Although Superintendent Ottavioli and Mr Ducret were careful to (end of recording).

ANTENNE 2 NEWS:

Mr Daniel Bilalian, newsreader: ... This evening, therefore, the case has been cleared up. The motives and the murderer's name are known.

Mr Ducret: The organiser was Detective Sergeant Simone and the murderer was Mr Freche.

Mr Ottavioli: That is correct. I can ... [unintelligible] the facts for you by saying that the case arose from a financial agreement between the victim, Mr de Broglie, and Mr Allenet de Ribemont and Mr Varga.

Mr Poniatowski: It is a very simple story. A bank loan guaranteed by Mr Jean de Broglie was to be repaid by Mr Varga-Hirsch and Mr de Ribemont.

A journalist: Superintendent, who was the key figure in this case? De Varga?

Mr Ottavioli: I think it must have been Mr De Varga.

Mr Jean-Francois Luciani, journalist: The loan was guaranteed by a life insurance policy for four hundred million old francs taken out by Jean de Broglie. In the event of his death, the sum insured was to be paid to Pierre De Varga-Hirsch and Allenet de Ribemont. The turning-point came last night when Guy Simone, a police officer, was the first to crack. He admitted that he had organised the murder and had lent a gun to have the MP killed. He also hired the contract killer, Gerard Freche, who was promised three million old francs and who in turn found two people to accompany him. The reasons for their downfall were, first, that Simone's name appeared in Jean de Broglie's diary and, second, that they killed him in front of no 2 rue des

Dardanelles. That was not planned. The intention had apparently been to take him somewhere else, but Jean de Broglie perhaps refused to follow his killer. At all events, that was their first mistake. Varga and Ribemont apparently then refused to pay them. That led to the secret meetings in bars, the shadowing by the police and informers – we know the rest of the story – and their arrest. The second mistake was made by Simone. Before contacting Freche he approached another contract killer, who turned down the job but apparently talked to other people about it. To catch the killers, the police realistically based their investigation on two simple ideas. Firstly, the murder was committed in the rue des Dardanelles as Jean de Broglie was leaving De Varga's home. There was necessarily a link between the killer and De Varga. Secondly, De Varga's past did not count in his favour and the police regarded him as a rather dubious legal adviser. Those two simple ideas and over sixty investigators led to the discovery of the murderer.

Mr Bilalian: The epilogue to the case coincided with a Cabinet meeting at which the question of public safety was discussed ...

12. On 14 January 1977 Mr Allenet de Ribemont was charged with aiding and abetting intentional homicide and taken into custody. He was released on 1 March 1977 and a discharge order was issued on 21 March 1980.

[Allenet de Ribemont unsuccessfully sought compensation for the false statements before the French courts.]

. . . .

PROCEEDINGS BEFORE THE COMMISSION

. . . .

100. The Commission concludes unanimously that in this case there has been a violation of Article 6(2) of the Convention;

. . . .

DECISION [OF THE EUROPEAN COURT OF HUMAN RIGHTS]:

I. Alleged Violation of Article 6(2) of the Convention

31. Mr Allenet de Ribemont complained of the remarks made by the Minister of the Interior and the senior police officers accompanying him at the press conference of 29 December 1976. He relied on Article 6(2) of the Convention ...

. . . .

A. Applicability of Article 6(2)

32. The Government contested, in substance, the applicability of Article 6(2), relying on the *Minelli v. Switzerland* judgment of 25 March 1983. They maintained that the presumption of innocence could be infringed only by a judicial authority, and could be shown to have been infringed only where, at the conclusion of proceedings ending in a conviction, the court's reasoning suggested that it regarded the defendant as guilty in advance.

33. The Commission acknowledged that the principle of presumption of innocence was above all a procedural safeguard in criminal proceedings, but took the view that its scope was more extensive, in that it imposed obligations not only on criminal courts determining criminal charges but also on other authorities.

34. The Court's task is to determine whether the situation found in this case affected the applicant's right under Article 6(2)....

35. The presumption of innocence enshrined in paragraph 2 of Article 6 is one of the elements of the fair criminal trial that is required by paragraph 1.... It will be violated if a judicial decision concerning a person charged with a criminal offence reflects an opinion that he is guilty before he has been proved guilty according to law. It suffices, even in the absence of an formal finding, that there is some reasoning suggesting that the court regards the accused as guilty....

However, the scope of Article 6(2) is not limited to the eventuality mentioned by the Government. The Court held that there had been violations of this provision in the *Minelli*...case[ ] previously cited, although the national courts concerned had closed the proceedings...because the limitation period had expired and had acquitted the applicant in the second. It has similarly held it to be applicable in other cases where the domestic courts did not have to determine the question of guilt. [*See, e.g., Adolph v. Austria.* 4 E.H.R.R. 313.]

Moreover, the Court reiterates that the Convention must be interpreted in such a way as to guarantee rights which are practical and effective as opposed to theoretical and illusory. (See, among other authorities.... That also applies to the right enshrined in Article 6(2).

36. The Court considers that the presumption of innocence may be infringed not only by a judge or court but also by other public authorities.

37. At the time of the press conference of 29 December 1976 Mr Allenet de Ribemont had just been arrested by the police. Although he had not yet been charged with aiding and abetting intentional homicide, his arrest and detention in police custody formed part of the judicial investigation begun a few days earlier by a Paris investigating judge and made him a person "charged with a criminal offence" within the meaning of Article 6(2). The two senior police officers present were conducting the inquiries in the case. Their remarks, made in parallel with the judicial investigation and supported by the Minister of the Interior, were explained by the existence of that investigation and had a direct link with it. Article 6(2) therefore applies in this case.

B. Compliance with Article 6(2)

1. Reference to the case at the press conference

38. Freedom of expression, guaranteed by Article 10 of the Convention, includes the freedom to receive and impart information. Article 6(2) cannot therefore prevent the authorities from informing the public about criminal investigations in progress, but it requires that they do so with all the discretion and circumspection necessary if the presumption of innocence is to be respected.

2. Content of the statements complained of

39. Like the applicant, the Commission considered that the remarks made by the Minister of the Interior and, in his presence and under his authority, by the police superintendent in charge of the inquiry and the Director of the Criminal Investigation Department, were incompatible with the presumption of innocence. It noted that in them Mr Allenet de Ribemont was held up as one of the instigators of Mr de Broglie's murder.

40. The Government maintained that such remarks came under the head of information about criminal proceedings in progress and were not such as to infringe the presumption of innocence, since they did not bind the courts and could be proved false by subsequent investigations. The facts of the case bore this out, as the applicant had not been formally charged until two weeks after the press conference and the investigating judge had eventually decided that there was no case to answer.

41. The Court notes that in the instant case some of the highest-ranking officers in the French police referred to Mr Allenet de Ribemont, without any qualification or reservation, as one of the instigators of a murder and thus an accomplice in that murder. This was clearly a declaration of the applicant's guilt which, firstly, encouraged the public to believe him guilty and, secondly, prejudged the assessment of the facts by the competent judicial authority. There has therefore been a breach of Article 6(2).

. . . .

∼

QUESTIONS & COMMENTS

(1) How does the European Court's decision in *Allenet de Ribemont v. France* compare with the U.S. law? Can the difference be attributed to the different form of criminal justice system in the United States? Can the difference be attributed to the role of the judge in pretrial proceedings? Is this difference sufficiently material?

(2) Consider the Inter-American Court of Human Rights decision in *Suárez Rosero v. Ecuador* (reproduced above in Section 5.1.2) in which it addresses the right to the presumption of innocence in a preventive detention case involving drug smuggling:

> 76. The Court now turns to the argument put forward by the Commission to the effect that the proceeding against Mr. Suárez-Rosero was in breach of the principle of the presumption of innocence, enunciated in Article 8(2) of the American Convention. That Article provides that
>
>> [e]very person accused of a criminal offense has the right to be presumed innocent so long as his guilt has not been proven according to the law [. . .].
>
> 77. This Court is of the view that the principle of the presumption of innocence – inasmuch as it lays down that a person is innocent until proven guilty – is founded upon the existence of judicial guarantees. Article 8(2) of the Convention establishes the obligation of the State not to restrict the liberty of a detained person beyond the limits strictly necessary to ensure that he will not impede the efficient development of an investigation and that he will not evade justice; preventive detention is, therefore, a precautionary rather than a punitive measure. This concept is laid down in a goodly number of instruments of international human rights law, including the International Covenant on Civil and Political Rights, which provides that preventive detention should not be the normal practice in relation to persons who are to stand trial (Art. 9(3)). This would be tantamount to anticipating a sentence, which is at odds with universally recognized general principles of law.
>
> 78. The Court considers that Mr. Suárez-Rosero's prolonged preventive detention violated the principle of presumption of innocence, in that he was detained from June 23, 1992, to April 28, 1996, and that the order for his release issued on July 10, 1995, was only executed a year later. In view of the above, the Court rules that the State violated Article 8(2) of the American Convention.

Assistance of Legal Counsel

Grant v. Jamaica
UN Human Rights Committee
Communication No. 353/1988
Views adopted 31 March 1994
U.N. Doc. CCPR/C/50/D/353/1988 (1994)

The facts as submitted by the author

1. The author of the communication is Lloyd Grant, a Jamaican citizen awaiting execution at St. Catherine District Prison, Jamaica. . . .

2.1 The author and his brother, Vincent Grant, were tried in the Hanover Circuit Court between 4 and 7 November 1986 for the murder, on 2 October 1985, of one T.M. Both were convicted and sentenced to death. On 5 October 1987, the Court of Appeal of Jamaica dismissed the author's appeal, but acquitted his brother. The author's petition for special leave to appeal to the Judicial Committee of the Privy Council was dismissed on 21 November 1988. With this, it is submitted, all available domestic remedies have been exhausted.

2.2 The author was interrogated by the police on 7 October 1985 in connection with the murder of T.M., who had been killed during a robbery at his home in the parish of Hanover, over 150 miles away from the author's home. The author explained that, while he knew the deceased from the time when he lived in Hanover, he had not visited that town since June 1985 and knew nothing about the crime. He was none the less arrested and placed in custody. On 25 October 1985, the author was placed on an identification parade, where he was identified by the deceased's wife, E.M., whom he also knew. He and Vincent Grant, who was then living in Hanover, were subsequently charged with the murder of T.M.

. . . .

2.4 E.M. testified that, in the afternoon of 1 October 1985, Vincent Grant, whom she had known all her life, entered the shop. Although she spoke to him he remained silent, staring at her house which was opposite the shop. He then left. Subsequently D.S. entered the shop and told her that he had seen Vincent Grant holding a sharp machete and leaning against the gate to her house, watching her banana field, and that two masked men, both carrying machetes, had been in the field. D.S. further told her that, despite the mask, he had recognized Lloyd Grant, who, when asked what they were doing on the M.'s premises, ran away. E.M. further testified that, after having locked the doors and windows of their house, she and her husband retired to bed; a kerosene lamp was left burning in the living room. At approximately 1 a.m., she was woken up by a noise and she went to the living room where she saw two men who immediately assaulted her. At their request, she gave them all the money kept in the house. She was then forced to lie face down on the floor, and one of the men, whom she identified as Lloyd Grant, bent over her, asking her whether she knew him. When she replied in the negative, he stood up and attacked her husband, who had entered the room. A scuffle ensued and her husband fell to the floor. Lloyd Grant, she stated, then proceeded to humiliate and assault her, during which time she had ample opportunity to see his face. E.M. finally testified that, before both men left the premises, they exchanged words with a third man, who was apparently waiting for them outside in the yard.

. . . .

2.6 In court D.S. further testified that, on 2 October 1985, between 2 a.m. and 3 a.m., he was returning home when he saw Vincent and Lloyd Grant and an unidentified third man run away from the *locus in quo*.

2.7 Statements allegedly made by both defendants to the police on 7 and 11 October 1985 were admitted in evidence by the judge after a challenge on the voire dire. Vincent Grant allegedly told the police that he had been forced by his brother to accompany him and another man to T.M.'s house, but that, after both men had entered the premises, he had run away. In his statement, the author identified Vincent Grant as the mastermind behind the robbery and gave details of the burglary and of his entry into T.M.'s house in the company of his brother and a third person. The author further allegedly stated that while he was outside, holding E.M., the third person came out of the house and told him that he had "chopped up" T.M.

2.8 The author put forward an alibi defence. He made an unsworn statement from the dock, claiming that he had been at his home in Kingston with his girlfriend when the crime occurred. He further claimed that he had been forced by the police to sign, on 11 October 1985, a drawn up statement. Vincent Grant also made an unsworn statement from the dock, stating only that, on 2 October 1985, he was at home with his girlfriend, that he went to bed at 5 o'clock and that he knew nothing about the murder.

2.9 With respect to the identification of Vincent Grant (who had not been identified by E.M.), the testimony of D.S. revealed that his sight had been impaired by the darkness. Before the Court of Appeal, Vincent Grant's counsel argued, *inter alia*, that the trial judge had failed to give the jury adequate warning about the dangers of identification evidence and, in addition, failed to relate such direction as he gave on identification to the evidence presented by D.S. The Court of Appeal agreed with counsel that the trial judge overlooked the fact that the identification evidence offered in respect of the two defendants was materially different and that each case required appropriate and specific treatment. The Court of Appeal subsequently acquitted Vincent Grant.

2.10 Author's counsel before the Court of Appeal admitted that "there was overwhelming evidence against his client, especially in the light of E.M.'s testimony", and that, "although he was of the opinion that the trial judge's directions on identification in relation to the author could have been more helpful, he did not believe that any reasonable argument could be mounted in law as to what the trial judge actually said". He further admitted that "the trial judge gave proper directions on common design" and that "overall he could find no arguable ground to urge on behalf of his client". The Court of Appeal agreed with counsel, stating that, in the case of the author, it found no defects in the instructions to the jury by the judge, and that the evidence against him was "overwhelming".

2.11 Throughout his trial and appeal, the author was represented by legal aid lawyers. A London law firm represented him pro bono before the Judicial Committee of the Privy Council.

. . . .

The complaint

. . . .

3.2 In respect of the allegation of unfair trial under article 14 of the Covenant, it is submitted that:

(a) The author did not receive legal advice during the preliminary hearing. It was not until one month prior to the trial that he was assigned a legal aid attorney, who did not consult with him, despite an earlier adjournment for that purpose, until the day before the start of the trial and then only for 40 minutes;

(b) The circumstances of the case were not investigated before the trial began. The attorney did not attempt to secure the testimony of the author's girlfriend, P.D., or of her mother. Although instructed by the author to do so, the attorney failed to contact P.D., whose evidence would have provided an alibi for the author;

(c) The attorney did not argue the issue of reliability of the identification by E.M. If E.M. had been asked when she had last seen the author, it would have been revealed that she had not seen him for about 10 years, when he was fourteen or fifteen years old;

(d) The attorney did not go through the prosecution statements with the author;

(e) Counsel for the appeal effectively abandoned the appeal or failed to pursue it properly. This is said to have prejudiced the author's case before the Judicial Committee of the Privy Council, which acknowledged that there might have been points of law for the Court of Appeal to look into;

(f) Counsel for the appeal also declined to call P.D. It is contended that the author's legal representation was inadequate and in violation of article 14, paragraph 3 (d), in respect of the proceedings before both the Circuit Court and the Court of Appeal.

. . . .

The Committee's admissibility decision

. . . .

5.3 With regard to the allegations of unfair trial, the Committee noted that the author's claims related primarily to the inadequacy of the preparation of his defence and of his representation before the Jamaican courts. It considered that these claims might raise issues under article 14, paragraphs 3 (b), (d) and (e) of the Covenant, which should be examined on the merits.

. . . .

The State party's request for review of admissibility and counsel's comments

. . . .

6.3 With regard to the alleged violations of article 14, paragraphs 3 (b), (d) and (e), the State party refers to an individual opinion appended to the Committee's views in [Communication No. 253/1987 (*Paul Kelly v. Jamaica*), views adopted on 8 April 1991] and submits that the State party's obligation to provide an accused with legal representation cannot extend beyond the duty to act in good faith in assigning counsel to the accused, and that errors of judgement made by court-appointed lawyers cannot be attributed to the State party any more than errors by privately retained lawyers can be. It concludes that the Committee would be applying a double standard if it were to hold court-appointed lawyers accountable to a higher degree of responsibility than their counterparts, and thus hold the State party responsible for their errors of judgement.

. . . .

7.3 As to the inadequacy of the preparation of the author's defence and of his representation before the Jamaican courts, it is submitted that the author was not represented during police interrogation and during the preliminary hearing. In September 1986, he saw the attorney assigned to him for the trial for the first time. She reportedly requested the judge to adjourn the trial, as she needed more time to prepare the defence. The hearing was rescheduled for 3 November 1986. Although upon requesting the adjournment, the attorney promised the author that she would discuss the case with him that evening, she never came to see him. On 3 November 1986, she visited him in the court lockup. During the interview, which lasted for only 40 minutes, she took the first statement from the author; the attorney did not investigate the circumstances of the case prior to the trial nor did she consider the author's alibi defence. The author affirms that during the course of the trial he again met with his attorney, but that she did not carry out his instructions.

7.4 With regard to the attorney's failure to pursue the evidence of the author's girlfriend, counsel forwards an affidavit, dated 4 December 1989, from P.D. and a questionnaire, dated 22 March 1990; P.D. contends that the author was with her during the whole night of 1 to 2 October 1985, and that her mother and one P.M. could have corroborated this evidence. It further appears from her affidavit that, on one of the days of the court hearing, she was informed by the police that her presence was needed, but that she failed to go because she had no money to travel and the police allegedly told her that it had no car available to transport her to the Circuit Court. According to London counsel, the main reason why witnesses were not traced and called was that the legal aid rates were so inadequate that the attorney was not able to make the necessary inquiries and initiate the necessary steps to prepare the author's defence properly.

7.5 As to the conduct of the trial defence itself, it is submitted that the attorney failed properly to challenge the testimony of E.M. and D.S., in particular with regard to their identification of the author, and that she did not make any interventions when counsel for the prosecution put leading questions to the prosecution witnesses.

7.6 With regard to the preparation of the author's defence on appeal, reference is made to the transcript of an annex to the "Privy Council questionnaire for inmate appealing" where the author claims that: "On one occasion D.C. (counsel assigned to him for the purpose of the appeal) came inside the prison and saw about 10 inmates (including myself) and I spoke with him for approximately 20 minutes. During those 20 minutes he asked me if I had any knowledge of the crime and if I have any witness. I also asked him to get my girlfriend in court and he don't". It is submitted that, since D.C. had not represented him at the trial, it was essential for the author to have adequate time to consult with D.C. prior to the hearing of the appeal, and that the amount of time granted for that purpose was wholly inadequate. The above is said to indicate that the author's rights under article 14, paragraph 3 (d) were not respected, since counsel was not of his own choosing.

7.7 With regard to the claim that D.C. abandoned or failed properly to pursue the appeal, reference is made to the written judgement of the Court of Appeal and to a letter, dated 8 February 1988, from D.C. to the Jamaica Council for Human Rights. In his letter, D.C. states that: "I daresay however that the judge's instructions on identification was certainly not the best but the usual safeguards were complied with and on any legal merit I cannot recommend the case for further consideration". According to London counsel, there were several grounds in the case which could have been argued on appeal, such as P.D.'s evidence (had she been called), and the reliability of the identification evidence of

E.M. and D.S., especially in light of the fact that the weakness in the latter's identification concerned both defendants. [Footnote omitted]

. . . .

Examination of the merits

. . . .

8.4 Concerning the author's claims relating to the preparation of his defence and his legal representation on trial, the Committee recalls that the right of an accused person to have adequate time and facilities for the preparation of his defence is an important element of the guarantee of a fair trial and an important aspect of the principle of equality of arms. The determination of what constitutes "adequate time" requires an assessment of the circumstances of each case. The Committee notes that the material before it does not disclose whether either the author or his attorney complained to the trial judge that the time or facilities for the preparation of the defence had been inadequate. Nor is there any indication that the author's attorney acted negligently in the conduct of the defence. In this context, the Committee notes that the trial transcript discloses that E.M. and D.S. were thoroughly cross-examined on the issue of identification by the defence. The Committee therefore finds no violations of article 14, paragraphs 3 (b) and (d), in respect of the author's trial.

8.5 The author also contends that he was unable to secure the attendance of witnesses on his behalf, in particular the attendance of his girlfriend, P.D. The Committee notes from the trial transcript that the author's attorney did contact the girlfriend, and, on the second day of the trial, made a request to the judge to have P.D. called to court. The judge then instructed the police to contact this witness, who, as indicated in paragraph 7.4 above, had no means to attend. The Committee is of the opinion that, in the circumstances, and bearing in mind that this is a case involving the death penalty, the judge should have adjourned the trial and issued a subpoena to secure the attendance of P.D. in court. Furthermore, the Committee considers that the police should have made transportation available to her. To the extent that P.D.'s failure to appear in court was attributable to the State party's authorities, the Committee finds that the criminal proceedings against the author were in violation of article 14, paragraphs 1 and 3 (e), of the Covenant.

8.6 The author also claims that the preparation of his defence and his representation before the Court of Appeal were inadequate, and that counsel assigned to him for this purpose was not of his own choosing. The Committee recalls that, while article 14, paragraph 3 (d), does not entitle the accused to choose counsel provided to him free of charge, measures must be taken to ensure that counsel, once assigned, provides effective representation in the interest of justice. This includes consulting with, and informing, the accused if he intends to withdraw an appeal or to argue before the appellate instance that the appeal has no merit. [Communication No. 356/1989 (*Trevor Collins v. Jamaica*), views adopted on 25 March 1993, para. 8.2.] While it is not for the Committee to question counsel's professional judgement that there was no merit in the appeal, it is of the opinion that he should have informed Mr. Grant of his intention not to raise any grounds of appeal, so that Mr. Grant could have considered any other remaining options open to him. In the circumstances, the Committee finds that the author's rights under article 14, paragraphs 3 (b) and (d) were violated in respect of his appeal.

. . . .

10. The Committee is of the view that Mr. Lloyd Grant is entitled to a remedy entailing his release. It requests the State party to provide information, within ninety days, on any relevant measures taken by the State party in compliance with the Committee's views.

∼

QUESTIONS & COMMENTS

(1) The UN Human Rights Committee has dealt with a variety of due process and legal access issues in numerous death penalty cases from Jamaica and Trinidad and Tobago. In Jamaica, this phenomenon began in the 1980s when there was a surge in death penalty convictions resulting from an enormous influx of weapons during earlier elections. "Gun Courts" were established that provided little due process protection. For other cases addressing the right to effective legal counsel, *see, e.g., Collins v. Jamaica*, UN Hum. Rts. Ctte., Communication No. 356/1989, views adopted 25 March 1993, U.N.Doc. A/48/40 (Pt. II) (1993) at 85 (court appointed counsel required to consult with client before declining to argue appeal); *Simmonds v. Jamaica*, UN Hum. Rts. Ctte., Communication No. 338/1988, views adopted 23 October 1992, U.N.Doc. A/48/40 (Pt. II) (1993) at 78 (Article 14 violation where appellate counsel did not consult client about grounds of appeal).

(2) The UN Human Rights Committee repeatedly has found violations of the right to effective assistance of counsel where appellate counsel in a death penalty case has stated to an appeals court that his client's appeal has no merit. *Reid v. Jamaica*, UN Hum. Rts. Ctte., Communication No. 250/1987, views adopted 20 July 1990; *Collins v. Jamaica*, UN Hum. Rts. Ctte., Communication No 356/1989, views adopted 25 March 1993. The UN Human Rights Committee has held that due process issues require heightened scrutiny in death penalty cases. Compare *Maxwell v. United Kingdom*, 300-C Eur. Ct. H.R. (ser. A) (1994), in which a legal aid office refused to file an appeal on behalf of the applicant facing a five-year sentence because it believed that the appeal had no merit. The European Court found an Article 6(3)(c) violation because of (i) the limited capacity of the appellant to represent himself without the assistance of counsel before the court of highest instance of appeal, (ii) the importance of the "issue at stake" (*viz.*, a five-year sentence), and (iii) the wide powers of the court to, *e.g.*, affirm, dismiss, or set aside the verdict. In *Maxwell*, the European Court held that this five-year sentence was "above all" the determinative issue for finding an Article 6 legal access violation. Should the UN Human Rights Committee extend their heightened due process scrutiny in death penalty cases to cases in which the "issue at stake" is much lower – as low as a five-year sentence as in *Maxwell*? What factors should the UN Human Rights Committee take into consideration in lowering this standard?

(3) Consider *Boner v. United Kingdom*, 300-B Eur. Ct. H.R. (ser. A) (1994). Boner was charged with assault and armed robbery in Scotland. He received free legal aid. During the trial, a prosecution witness (prior to giving testimony) entered the courtroom and spoke to one of Boner's co-accused, against whom charges subsequently were dropped. A jury convicted Boner. The judge sentenced him to eight years in prison. Boner's lawyer stated that in his view the only possible ground of appeal related to the admissibility of the evidence of the above witness who had inappropriately entered the courtroom.

Boner applied to extend legal aid to the appellate proceedings. The Scottish Legal Aid Board refused his application because it believed that the appeal lacked merit. Despite the advice of his solicitor and counsel, Boner decided to proceed with the appeal. Although he had no legal knowledge and had no assistance with his submissions, he presented his own case before the High Court of Justiciary in 1991. The Crown was represented by counsel at this hearing. The Appeal Court held that there was no miscarriage of justice and unanimously dismissed Boner's appeal.

The European Court held that for determining an Article 6 (3) violation the special features of the proceedings involved must be examined. Account must be taken of the entirety of the proceedings and of the role of the courts therein. In the instant case, the Scottish system grants all persons a right to appeal. No special leave is required. The procedure is not limited to specific grounds; any alleged miscarriage of justice may be challenged.

An independent body (the Scottish Legal Aid Board) determines whether an appellant can obtain free legal assistance. The Scottish government defended its decision to refuse Boner legal aid by stating that in view of professional ethics, Boner could not have found counsel willing to represent him because he had no proper basis for bringing an appeal. They also pointed out that the issues in this case were not particularly complex. The Court, although agreeing with the latter point, held that a certain degree of legal skill and experience is necessary to attack a trial judge's exercise of discretion. That Boner was able to understand the grounds for his appeal and that counsel was not prepared to represent him does not alter the fact that without the services of a legal practitioner he was unable to address the court competently on this legal issue and thus defend himself effectively. The United Kingdom pointed out that if the Court found a violation, they might have to end their automatic right of appeal. However, the European Court replied that its responsibility was solely to determine whether the system states do choose leads to results that are inconsistent with the requirements of Article 6. In a situation involving a heavy penalty, where an appellant is left to present his own defense unassisted before the highest court of appeal, the system is not in conformity with the requirements of Article 6. In the instant case, given the nature of the proceedings, the wide powers of the High Court, Boner's limited capacity as an unrepresented appellant to present a legal argument and, above all, the importance of the issue at stake in view of the severity of the sentence (eight years imprisonment), the Court considered that the interests of justice required that Boner be granted legal aid for representation at his appeal. The Court concluded that there had been a violation Article 6 (3)(c).

Compare *Boner v. United Kingdom* to *Lane v. Brown*, 372 U.S. 477 (1963), in which the U.S. Supreme Court found a violation to effective assistance of counsel where the petitioner filed a *habeas corpus* petition challenging his murder conviction, and his publicly funded counsel refused to file his petition because his attorney believed that his petition had no merit. In *Evitts v. Lucey*, 469 U.S. 387, 394 (1985), the U.S. Supreme Court held that an appellate counsel "must play the role of an active advocate, rather than a mere friend of the court assisting in a detached evaluation of the appellant's claim" in finding a Sixth Amendment violation of right to assistance of counsel. Francisco Forrest Martin et al., 1 International Human Rights Law & Practice: Cases, Treaties and Materials 523–26 (1997).

(4) The above cases were from the United States, the United Kingdom, and Jamaica – countries using adversarial (*vs.* inquisitorial) legal systems. Do you think that either the UN Human Rights Committee or the European Court of Human Rights would take a different position on the right to appellate counsel in criminal cases in an inquisitorial legal system? Why? Francisco Forrest Martin et al., 1 International Human Rights Law & Practice: Cases, Treaties and Materials 526 (1997).

(5) A common complaint of authors in these death penalty cases from Jamaica was their lawyers' failure to call certain witnesses. The UN Human Rights Committee repeatedly held that this failure was not an Article 14 violation of right to effective counsel. The Committee felt that the decision to not call witnesses was a professional judgment call by defense counsel. *See, e.g., Reynolds v. Jamaica*, UN Hum. Rts. Ctte., Communication No. 229/1987, views adopted 8 April 1991, at §6.4; *Sawyers and McLean v. Jamaica*, UN Hum. Rts. Ctte., Communication Nos. 226/1987 and 256/1987, views adopted 11 April 1991, at §13.7.

This rule comports with the general rule, as articulated by Corpus Juris Secundum: "the right to counsel is generally not violated due to an attorney's exercise of discretion regarding tactics or strategy, provided the attorney made a reasoned choice." 22 C.J.S. *Effectiveness of Counsel* §305 (1973) (citations omitted).

However, there is some language in one decision by the UN Human Rights Committee that suggests that this rule may only apply to privately retained lawyers.

> The Committee is of the opinion that the failure of the author's representative to bring these issues to the attention of the trial judge, which purportedly resulted in the negative outcome of the trial, cannot be attributed to the State party, *since the lawyer was privately retained.* The Committee, therefore, finds no violation of article 14, paragraph 1, of the Covenant in this respect.

Berry v. Jamaica, UN Hum. Rts. Ctte., Communication No. 330/1988, views adopted 7 April 1994, U.N. Doc. CCPR/C/50/D/330/1988 (1994) at §11.3 (emphasis provided). An explanation for the Committee's language here may be that because a defendant does not have a right to choose his legal aid lawyer, the defendant has less control over the management of the case – unlike a privately retained lawyer who can be dismissed by the client if the client is unhappy with his lawyer's conduct of his case. Also, the Committee may not consider state action to be present in the case of a privately retained lawyer providing ineffective assistance of counsel. Francisco Forrest Martin et al., 1 International Human Rights Law & Practice: Cases, Treaties and Materials 526 (1997).

(6) For the leading U.S. Supreme Court case governing effective assistance of counsel, *see Strickland v. Washington*, 466 U.S. 668 (1984), which sets out a two-part test:

> A convicted defendant's claim that counsel's assistance was so defective as to require reversal of a conviction . . . has two components. First, the defendant must show that counsel's performance was deficient. . . . Second, the defendant must show that the deficient performance prejudiced the defense. This requires showing that counsel's errors were so serious as to deprive the defendant of a fair trial, a trial whose result is reliable.

(7) In *Lala v. The Netherlands*, 297-A Eur. Ct. H.R. (ser. A) (1994), the fact that the defendant, in spite of having been properly summoned, does not appear, cannot – even

in the absence of an excuse – justify depriving him of his right under Article 6(3) to be defended by counsel. The European Court did not accept the Netherlands' argument that there was no interference because Lala's counsel failed to ask the court's permission to defend him. A state party has an affirmative duty to provide counsel. Francisco Forrest Martin et al., 1 International Human Rights Law & Practice: Cases, Treaties and Materials 517 (1997).

(8) In *Campbell & Fell v. United Kingdom*, 80 Eur. Ct. H.R. (ser. A) (1984), the European Court found an Article 6(1) violation for the U.K. government's failure to provide legal assistance to prisoners facing prison disciplinary proceedings. Contrast this decision with a U.S. Supreme Court decision that refused to recognize a prisoner's right to counsel in prison disciplinary proceedings – even if there is a likelihood of criminal prosecution for the same acts on which the disciplinary proceeding is based. *Baxter v. Palmigiano*, 425 U.S. 308 (1976). Is there any material difference between disciplinary and criminal proceedings in the context of right to counsel? Francisco Forrest Martin et al., 1 International Human Rights Law & Practice: Cases, Treaties and Materials 518 (1997).

(9) A critical aspect of the right to legal access is protection from reprisals for exercising this right. In *Hammel v. Madagascar*, Communication No. 155/1983, views adopted 3 April 1987, 2 Selected Decisions of the Human Rights Committee under the Optional Protocol 179, U.N. Doc. CCPR/C/OP/2 (1990), the author of the communication, a French national, practiced law in Madagascar for over thirty years. After defending leaders of the opposition party in Madagascar, he was detained twice, held incommunicado, and eventually deported. The Committee found a violation of the right to assistance of counsel.

(10) The European Court repeatedly has recognized a prisoner's right to correspond privately with his or her lawyer under both Articles 6 (legal assistance) and 8 (privacy of mail). *See e.g., Domenichini v. Italy*, – Eur. Ct. H.R. (ser. A) (1997) (slip opinion); *S. v. Switzerland*, 220 Eur. Ct. H.R. (ser. A) (1992); *Schoenberger and Durmaz Case*, 137 Eur. Ct. H.R. (1989); *Boyle and Rice v. United Kingdom*, 131 Eur. Ct. H.R. (ser. A) (1988); *Silver v. United Kingdom*, 61 Eur. Ct. H.R. (ser. A) (1983); *Golder v. United Kingdom*, 18 Eur. Ct. H.R. (ser. A) (1975).

Under U.S. law, prisoners have a constitutional right to confidential communication with lawyers whether by telephone, mail, or personal meetings. Incoming letters may be opened and inspected for physical contraband in the prisoner's presence, but these letters cannot be read by prison authorities. *Wolff v. McDonnell*, 418 U.S. 539, 577 (1974). Outgoing letters to lawyers generally may be mailed unopened. *Davidson v. Scully*, 694 F.2d 50, 53 (2d Cir. 1982); *Guajardo v. Estelle*, 580 F.2d 748, 759 (5th Cir. 1978). Furthermore, outgoing mail to lawyers seeking legal representation also cannot be opened or read – even if there is no existing lawyer-client agreement. *Taylor v. Sterrett*, 532 F.2d 462, 474 (5th Cir. 1976). In order for legal mail to receive the protection of confidentiality, it must be marked as legal mail. For U.S. federal prisons, the prison authorities require that the envelopes contain the following exact words: "Special Mail – Open Only in the Presence of the Inmate." Francisco Forrest Martin et al., 1 International Human Rights Law & Practice: Cases, Treaties and Materials 519 (1997).

The Right to Information on Consular Assistance
in the Framework of the Guarantees of the Due Process of Law
Inter-American Court of Human Rights
Advisory Opinion OC-16/99
Inter-Am. Ct. H.R. (Ser A) No. 16 (1999)

. . . .

VI

THE RIGHTS TO INFORMATION ON CONSULAR ASSISTANCE, NOTIFICATION AND
COMMUNICATION, AND OF CONSULAR ASSISTANCE, AND THEIR RELATIONSHIP TO
THE PROTECTION OF HUMAN RIGHTS IN THE AMERICAN STATES

(First question)

68. In its request for an advisory opinion, Mexico asked the Court to interpret whether

Under Article 64(1) of the American Convention, . . . Article 36 of the Vienna Convention [on Consular Relations] [should] be interpreted as containing provisions
concerning the protection of human rights in the American States.

[. . .]

69. As stated previously . . . , the Court has jurisdiction to interpret, in addition to the
American Convention, "other treaties concerning the protection of human rights in the
American States."

70. In Advisory Opinion OC-10, the Court interpreted the word "treaty," as the term
is employed in Article 64.1 of the Convention, to be "at the very least, an international
instrument of the type that is governed by the two Vienna Conventions": the 1969 Vienna
Convention on the Law of Treaties and the 1986 Vienna Convention on the Law of Treaties
among States and International Organizations or among International Organizations.
[ ]The Court has also held that the treaties of which Article 64.1 speaks are those to which
one or more American States is party, with an American State understood to mean a
Member State of the OAS. [ ]Lastly, the Court once again notes that the language of the
article in question indicates a very 'expansive' tendency, one that should also inform its
interpretation. [ ]

71. The Vienna Convention on Consular Relations is an "international agreement
concluded between States in written form and governed by international law," in the
broad sense of the term as defined in the 1969 Vienna Convention on the Law of Treaties.
All the Member States of the OAS but two – Belize and St. Kitts and Nevis- are Party to
the Vienna Convention on Consular Relations.

72. For purposes of this Advisory Opinion, the Court must determine whether this
Treaty concerns the protection of human rights in the 33 American States that are Party
thereto; in other words, whether it has bearing upon, affects or is of interest to this subject
matter. In analyzing this issue, the Court reiterates that the interpretation of any norm is
to be done in good faith in accordance with the ordinary meaning to be given to the terms
used in the treaty in their context and in the light of its object and purpose (Article 31
of the Vienna Convention on the Law of Treaties[ ]) and that an interpretation may, if
necessary, involve an examination of the treaty taken as a whole.

73. Some briefs of comments submitted to the Court observed that the preamble to the Vienna Convention on Consular Relations notes that in the drafting process, the States Party realized that:

> ... the purpose of [consular] privileges and immunities is not to benefit individuals but to ensure the efficient performance of functions by consular posts on behalf of their respective States ... [ ]

Thus, the Vienna Convention on Consular Relations would not appear to be intended to confer rights to individuals; the rights of consular communication and notification are, "first and foremost", rights of States.

74. Having examined the *travaux preparatoire* for the preamble of the Vienna Convention on Consular Relations, the Court finds that the "individuals" to whom it refers are those who perform consular functions, and that the clarification cited above was intended to make it clear that the privileges and immunities granted to them were for the performance of their functions.

75. The Court observes, on the other hand, that in the Case Concerning United States Diplomatic and Consular Staff in Tehran, the United States linked Article 36 of the Vienna Convention on Consular Relations with the rights of the nationals of the sending State. [ ]The International Court of Justice, for its part, cited the Universal Declaration in the respective judgment. [ ]

76. Mexico, moreover, is not requesting the Court's interpretation as to whether the principal object of the Vienna Convention on Consular Relations is the protection of human rights; rather, it is asking whether one provision of that Convention concerns the protection of human rights. This is an important point, given the advisory jurisprudence of this Court, which has held that a treaty can concern the protection of human rights, regardless of what the principal purpose of that treaty might be. [ ]Therefore, while some of the comments made to the Court concerning the principal object of the Vienna Convention on Consular Relations to the effect that the treaty is one intended to 'strike a balance among States' are accurate, this does require that the Treaty be dismissed outright as one that may indeed concern the protection of an individual's fundamental rights in the American hemisphere.

77. The discussions of the wording of Article 36 of the Vienna Convention on Consular Relations turned on the common practice of States in the matter of diplomatic protection. That article reads as follows:

> 1. With a view to facilitating the exercise of consular functions relating to nationals of the sending State:
>
>> a) consular officers shall be free to communicate with nationals of the sending State and to have access to them. Nationals of the sending State shall have the same freedom with respect to communication and access to consular officers of the sending State;
>
> [...]

78. The sub-paragraph cited above recognizes the right to freedom of communication. The text in question makes it clear that both the consular officer and the national of the sending State have that right, and does not stipulate any qualifications as to the circumstances of the nationals in question. Further, the most recent international

criminal law[1] recognizes the detained foreign national's right to communicate with consular officers of the sending State.

79. Therefore, the consular officer and national of the sending State both have the right to communicate with each other, at any time, in order that the former may proper discharge his functions. Under Article 5 of the Vienna Convention on Consular Relations, consular functions consist, *inter alia*, in the following:

a) protecting in the host State the interests of the sending State and of its nationals, both individuals and bodies corporate, within the limits permitted by international law;

[...]

e) helping and assisting nationals, both individuals and bodies corporate, of the sending State;

[...]

i) subject to the practices and procedures obtaining in the host State, representing or arranging appropriate representation for nationals of the sending State before the tribunals and other authorities of the host State, for the purpose of obtaining, in accordance with the laws and regulations of the host State, provisional measures for the preservation of the rights and interests of these nationals, where, because of absence or any other reason, such nationals are unable at the proper time to assume the defence of their rights and interests;

[...]

80. Taking the above-cited texts as a whole, it is evident that the Vienna Convention on Consular Relations recognizes assistance to a national of the sending State for the defense of his rights before the authorities of the host State to be one of the paramount functions of a consular officer. Hence, the provision recognizing consular communication serves a dual purpose: that of recognizing a State's right to assist its nationals through the consular officer's actions and, correspondingly, that of recognizing the correlative right of the national of the sending State to contact the consular officer to obtain that assistance.

81. Sub-paragraphs (b) and (c) of Article 36(1) of the Vienna Convention on Consular Relations concern consular assistance in one particular situation: deprivation of freedom. The Court is of the view that these sub-paragraphs need to be examined separately. Sub-paragraph (b) provides the following:

if he so requests, the competent authorities of the host State shall, without delay, inform the consular post of the sending State if, within its consular district, a national of that State is arrested or committed to prison or to custody pending trial or is detained in any other manner. Any communication addressed to the consular post by the person arrested, in prison, custody or detention shall also be forwarded by the said authorities without delay. The said authorities shall inform the person concerned without delay of his rights under this sub-paragraph.

---

[1] Rules governing the detention of persons awaiting trial or appeal before the Tribunal or otherwise detained on the authority of the International Tribunal for the Prosecution of Persons Responsible for Serious Violations of International Humanitarian Law Committed in the Territory of the Former Yugoslavia since 1991; as amended on 17 November 1997; IT/38/REV.7; Rule 65.

This text recognizes, *inter alia*, a detained foreign national's right to be advised, without delay, that he has:

> a) the right to request and obtain from the competent authorities of the host State that they inform the appropriate consular post that he has been arrested, committed to prison, placed in preventive custody or otherwise detained, and
>
> b) the right to address a communication to the appropriate consular post, which is to be forwarded "without delay".

82. The bearer of the rights mentioned in the preceding paragraph, which the international community has recognized in the Body of Principles for the Protection of All Persons under Any Form of Detention or Imprisonment, is the individual. In effect, this article is unequivocal in stating that rights to consular information and notification are "accorded" to the interested person. In this respect, Article 36 is a notable exception to what are essentially States' rights and obligations accorded elsewhere in the Vienna Convention on Consular Relations. As interpreted by this Court in the present Advisory Opinion, Article 36 is a notable advance over international law's traditional conceptions of this subject.

83. The rights accorded to the individual under sub-paragraph (b) of Article 36(1), cited earlier, tie in with the next sub-paragraph, which reads:

> (c) consular officers shall have the right to visit a national of the sending State who is in prison, custody or detention, to converse and correspond with him and to arrange for his legal representation. They shall also have the right to visit any national of the sending State who is in prison, custody or detention in their district in pursuance of a judgment. Nevertheless, consular officers shall refrain from taking action on behalf of a national who is in prison, custody or detention if he expressly opposes such action.

It can be inferred from the above text that exercise of this right is limited only by the individual's choice, who may "expressly" oppose any intervention by the consular officer on his behalf. This confirms the fact that the rights accorded under Article 36 of the Vienna Convention on Consular Relations are rights of individuals.

84. The Court therefore concludes that Article 36 of the Vienna Convention on Consular Relations endows a detained foreign national with individual rights that are the counterpart to the host State's correlative duties. This interpretation is supported by the article's legislative history. There, although in principle some States believed that it was inappropriate to include clauses regarding the rights of nationals of the sending State [ ], in the end the view was that there was no reason why that instrument should not confer rights upon individuals.

85. The Court must now consider whether the obligations and rights recognized in Article 36 of the Vienna Convention on Consular Relations concern the protection of human rights. [ ]

86. Should the sending State decide to provide its assistance and in so doing exercise its rights under Article 36 of the Vienna Convention on Consular Relations, it may assist the detainee with various defence measures, such as providing or retaining legal representation, obtaining evidence in the country of origin, verifying the conditions under which the legal assistance is provided and observing the conditions under which the accused is being held while in prison.

87. Therefore, the consular communication to which Article 36 of the Vienna Convention on Consular does indeed concern the protection of the rights of the national of the sending State and may be of benefit to him. This is the proper interpretation of the functions of 'protecting the interests' of that national and the possibility of his receiving "help and assistance," particularly with arranging appropriate "representation . . . before the tribunals". The relationship between the rights accorded under Article 36 and the concepts of "the due process of law" or "judicial guarantees" is examined in another section of this Advisory Opinion (infra 110).

VII

THE ENFORCEABILITY OF THE RIGHTS RECOGNIZED IN ARTICLE 36 OF THE
VIENNA CONVENTION ON CONSULAR RELATIONS

(Second question)

88. In its second question, Mexico asked the Court for its interpretation as to the following:

> From the point of view of international law, is the enforceability of individual rights conferred on foreigners by the above-mentioned Article 36 on behalf of the interested parties in regard to the host State subject to the protests of the State of which they are nationals?

89. In the opinion of this Court, compliance with the State's duty corresponding to the right of consular communication (Article 36(1), sub-paragraph (a)) is not subject to the requirement that the sending State first file a protest. This is obvious from the language of Article 36(1)(a), which states that:

> Nationals of the sending State shall have the [. . .] freedom with respect to communication with and access to consular officers of the sending State[.]

The same is true in the case of the right to information on consular assistance, which is also upheld as a right that attends the host State's duty. No requirement need be met for this obligation to have effect or currency.

90. Exercise of the right to consular notification is contingent only upon the will of the individual concerned. [ ] It is interesting to note that in the original draft presented to the United Nations Conference on Consular Relations, compliance with the duty to notify the consular officer in the cases provided for in sub-paragraph (b) of Article 36(1) did not hinge on the acquiescence of the person being deprived of his freedom. However, some participants in the Conference objected to this formulation for practical reasons that would have made it impossible to discharge that duty [ ] and because the individual in question should decide of his own free will whether he wanted the consular officer to be notified of his arrest and, if so, authorize the latter's intervention on his behalf. The argument for these positions was, in essence, that the individual's freedom of choice had to be respected. [ ]None of the participating States mentioned any requirements or conditions that the sending State would have to fulfill.

91. Under sub-paragraph (c), any action by a consular officer to "arrange for [the individual's] legal representation" and visit him in his place of confinement requires the consent of the national who is in prison, custody or detention. This sub-paragraph, too, makes no mention of the need for the sending State to file protests.

92. Particularly in the case of sub-paragraphs (b) and (c) of Article 36(1), the object of consular notification is served when the host State discharges its duties immediately. Indeed, the purpose of consular notification is to alert the sending State to a situation of which it is, in principle, unaware. Hence, it would be illogical to make exercise of these rights or fulfillment of these obligations subject to protests from a State that is unaware of its national's predicament.

93. One brief submitted to this Court notes that in some cases it is difficult for the host State to obtain information about the detainee's nationality. [ ] Without that information, the host State will not know that the individual in question has the right to information recognized in Article 36 of the Vienna Convention on Consular Relations.

94. The Court considers that identification of the accused, which is essential for penal individualization programs, is a duty incumbent upon the State that has him in custody. For example, the individual in custody has to be identified in order to determine his age and to make certain that he is treated in a manner commensurate with his circumstances. In discharging this duty to identify a detainee, the State employs that mechanisms created under its domestic laws for this purpose, which necessarily include immigration records in the case of aliens.

95. This Court is aware that individuals in custody may make it difficult to ascertain that they are foreign nationals. Some might conceal the fact because of fear of deportation. In such cases, immigration records will not be useful – or sufficient – for a State to ascertain the subject's identity. Problems also arise when a detainee is in fear of the actions of his State of origin and thus endeavors to hinder any inquiry into his nationality. In both these hypothetical situations, the host State can deal with the problems – for which it is not to blame- in order to comply with its obligations under Article 36. The assessment of each case by the competent national or international authorities will determine whether a host State is or is not responsible for failure to comply with those duties.

96. The foregoing does not alter the principle that the arresting State has a duty to know the identity of the person whom it deprives of his freedom. This will enable it to discharge its own obligations and respect the detainee's rights promptly. Mindful that it may be difficult to ascertain a subject's identity immediately, the Court believes it is no less imperative that the State advise the detainee of his rights if he is an alien, just as it advises him of the other rights accorded to every person deprived of his freedom.

97. For these reasons, the Court considers that enforcement of the rights that Article 36 of the Vienna Convention on Consular Relations confers upon the individual is not subject to the protests of the sending State.

VIII

THE EXPRESSION "WITHOUT DELAY" IN ARTICLE 36(1)(b) OF THE VIENNA
CONVENTION ON CONSULAR RELATIONS

(Third question)

98. The third question that Mexico put to the Court in its request was as follows:

Mindful of the object and purpose of Article 36(1)(b) of the Vienna Convention [on Consular Relations], should the expression "without delay" contained in that provision be interpreted as requiring the authorities of the host State to inform any foreigner detained for crimes punishable by the death penalty of the rights conferred on him by Article 36(1)(b) itself, at the time of the arrest, and in any case before the accused makes any statement or confession to the police or judicial authorities?

99. This question is the first to raise one of the central issues of this Advisory Opinion. While the question mainly concerns whether the expression "without delay" is to be interpreted as pertaining to a particular stage of the criminal justice process, the interpretation being requested is in the context of the cases where the arrest is part of the prosecution of a crime punishable with the death penalty.

100. The requesting State explained that while the request concerned cases punishable with the death penalty, this does not preclude enforcement of the rights conferred in Article 36 in any and all circumstances. The Court concurs with this assessment. Article 36(1)(b) of the Vienna Convention on Consular Relations makes no distinction based on the severity of the penalty for the crime for which the arrest was made. It is interesting to note that the article in question does not require that the consular officer be advised of the reasons for the arrest. Having examined the respective *travaux preparatoire*, the Court found that this was the express decision of the States Party, some of which reasoned that to disclose the reason for the arrest to the consular officer would be to violate the detained person's basic right to privacy. Article 36(1)(b) also makes no distinction for the applicable penalty. It is logical, then, to infer that every detained person has this right.

101. Therefore, the Court's answer to this part of the request applies with equal force to all cases in which a national of a sending State is deprived of his freedom, regardless of the reason, and not just for facts that, when the nature of the crime they constitute has been determined by the competent authority, could involve the death penalty.

102. Having dispatched this aspect of the question, the Court will now proceed to determine whether the expression "without delay" used in Article 36(1)(b) of the Vienna Convention on Consular Relations should be interpreted as requiring the authorities of the host State to inform any detained foreign national of the rights accorded to him in that article "at the time of the arrest, and in any case before the accused makes any statement or confession to the police or judicial authorities."

103. The legislative history of that article reveals that inclusion of the obligation to inform a detained foreign national of his rights under that article "without delay", was proposed by the United Kingdom and had the support of the vast majority [ ] of the States participating in the Conference as a means to help ensure that the detained person was made duly aware of his right to request that the consular officer be advised of his arrest for purposes of consular assistance. It is clear that these are the appropriate effects (*effet utile*) of the rights recognized in Article 36.

104. Therefore, and in application of a general principle of interpretation that international jurisprudence has repeatedly affirmed, the Court will interpret Article 36 so that those appropriate effects (*effet utile*) are obtained. [ ]

105. The Court's finding as to the second question of the request (*supra* 97) is very relevant here. There the Court determined that the enforceability of the rights conferred upon the individual in Article 36 of the Vienna Convention on Consular Relations was not subject to protests from the State of the individual's nationality. It is, therefore, incumbent upon the host State to fulfill the obligation to inform the detainee of his rights, in accord with the finding in paragraph 96.

106. Consequently, in order to establish the meaning to be given to the expression "without delay," the purpose of the notification given to the accused has to be considered.

It is self-evident that the purpose of notification is that the accused has an effective defense. Accordingly, notification must be prompt; in other words, its timing in the process must be appropriate to achieving that end. Therefore, because the text of the Vienna Convention on Consular Relations is not precise, the Court's interpretation is that notification must be made at the time the accused is deprived of his freedom, or at least before he makes his first statement before the authorities.

. . . .

X

THE RIGHT TO INFORMATION ON CONSULAR ASSISTANCE AND ITS RELATIONSHIP TO THE MINIMUM GUARANTEES OF THE DUE PROCESS OF LAW

(Sixth, seventh, eighth and eleventh questions)

110. In a number of the questions in its request, Mexico put specific issues to the Court concerning the nature of the nexus between the right to information on consular assistance and the inherent rights of the individual as recognized in the International Covenant on Civil and Political Rights and the American Declaration and, through the latter, in the Charter of the OAS. These questions are as follows:

With respect to the International Covenant on Civil and Political Rights

[. . .]

6. In connection with Article 14 of the Covenant, should it be applied and interpreted in the light of the expression "all possible safeguards to ensure a fair trial" contained in paragraph 5 of the United Nations Safeguards guaranteeing protection of the rights of those facing the death penalty, and that concerning foreign defendants or persons convicted of crimes subject to capital punishment that expression includes immediate notification of the detainee or defendant, on the part of the host State, of rights conferred on him by Article 36(1)(b) of the Vienna Convention?

7. As regards aliens accused of or charged with crimes subject to the death penalty, is the host State's failure to notify the person involved as required by Article 36(1)(b) of the Vienna Convention in keeping with their rights to "adequate time and facilities for the preparation of his defense," pursuant to Article 14(3)(b) of the Covenant?

8. As regards aliens accused of or charged with crimes subject to the death penalty, should the term "minimum guarantees" contained in Article 14.3 of the Covenant, and the term "at least equal" contained in paragraph 5 of the corresponding United Nations Safeguards be interpreted as exempting the host State from immediate compliance with the provisions of Article 36(1)(b) of the Vienna Convention on behalf of the detained person or defendant?

[. . .]

With respect to the Charter of the OAS and the American Declaration of the Rights and Duties of Man:

[. . .]

11. With regard to the arrest and detention of aliens for crimes punishable by death and in the framework of Article 3(1) of the Charter and Article II of the Declaration,

is failure to notify the detainee or defendant immediately of the rights conferred on him in Article 36(1)(b) of the Vienna Convention compatible with the Charter of Human Rights, which contains the term without distinction of nationality, and with the right to equality before the law without distinction as to any factor, as enshrined in the Declaration?

111. In these questions, the requesting State is seeking from the Court its opinion on whether nonobservance of the right to information constitutes a violation of the rights recognized in Article 14 of the International Covenant on Civil and Political Rights, Article 3 of the Charter of the OAS and Article II of the American Declaration, mindful of the nature of those rights.

112. Examination of these questions necessarily begins with consideration of the rules governing interpretation of the articles in question. The International Covenant on Civil and Political Rights and the OAS Charter, which are treaties in the meaning given to the term in the Vienna Convention on the Law of Treaties, must be interpreted in accordance with the latter's Article 31 (*supra* 58).

113. Under that article, the interpretation of a treaty must take into account not only the agreements and instruments related to the treaty (paragraph 2 of Article 31), but also the system of which it is part (paragraph 3 of Article 31). As the International Court of Justice has held:

[...] the Court must take into consideration the changes which have occurred in the supervening half-century, and its interpretation cannot remain unaffected by the subsequent development of law [...] Moreover, an international instrument has to be interpreted and applied within the framework of the entire legal system prevailing at the time of the interpretation. In the domain to which the present proceedings relate, the last fifty years [...] have brought important developments. In this domain, as elsewhere, the *corpus iuris gentium* has been considerably enriched, and this the Court, if it is faithfully to discharge its functions, may not ignore.

114. This guidance is particularly relevant in the case of international human rights law, which has made great headway thanks to an evolutive interpretation of international instruments of protection. That evolutive interpretation is consistent with the general rules of treaty interpretation established in the 1969 Vienna Convention. Both this Court, in the Advisory Opinion on the Interpretation of the American Declaration of the Rights and Duties of Man (1989) [ ], and the European Court of Human Rights, in *Tyrer v. United Kingdom* (1978),[ ] *Marckx v. Belgium* (1979),[ ] Loizidou v. Turkey (1995),[ ] among others, have held that human rights treaties are living instruments whose interpretation must consider the changes over time and present-day conditions.

115. The *corpus juris* of international human rights law comprises a set of international instruments of varied content and juridical effects (treaties, conventions, resolutions and declarations). Its dynamic evolution has had a positive impact on international law in affirming and building up the latter's faculty for regulating relations between States and the human beings within their respective jurisdictions. This Court, therefore, must adopt the proper approach to consider this question in the context of the evolution of the fundamental rights of the human person in contemporary international law.

116. The International Covenant on Civil and Political Rights recognizes the right to the due process of law (Article 14) as a right that "derives[s] from the inherent dignity of the human person." [ ] That article enumerates a number of guarantees that apply

to "everyone charged with a criminal offence," and in that respect is consistent with the principal international human rights instruments.

117. In the opinion of this Court, for "the due process of law" a defendant must be able to exercise his rights and defend his interests effectively and in full procedural equality with other defendants. It is important to recall that the judicial process is a means to ensure, insofar as possible, an equitable resolution of a difference. The body of procedures, of diverse character and generally grouped under the heading of the due process, is all calculated to serve that end. To protect the individual and see justice done, the historical development of the judicial process has introduced new procedural rights. An example of the evolutive nature of judicial process are the rights not to incriminate oneself and to have an attorney present when one speaks. These two rights are already part of the laws and jurisprudence of the more advanced legal systems. And so, the body of judicial guarantees given in Article 14 of the International Covenant on Civil and Political Rights has evolved gradually. It is a body of judicial guarantees to which others of the same character, conferred by various instruments of international law, can and should be added.

118. In this regard the Court has held that the procedural requirements that must be met to have effective and appropriate judicial guarantees [ ] "are designed to protect, to ensure, or to assert the entitlement to a right or the exercise thereof"[ ] and are "the prerequisites necessary to ensure the adequate protection of those persons whose rights or obligations are pending judicial determination."[ ]

119. To accomplish its objectives, the judicial process must recognize and correct any real disadvantages that those brought before the bar might have, thus observing the principle of equality before the law and the courts and [ ] the corollary principle prohibiting discrimination. The presence of real disadvantages necessitates countervailing measures that help to reduce or eliminate the obstacles and deficiencies that impair or diminish an effective defense of one's interests. Absent those countervailing measures, widely recognized in various stages of the proceeding, one could hardly say that those who have the disadvantages enjoy a true opportunity for justice and the benefit of the due process of law equal to those who do not have those disadvantages.

120. This is why an interpreter is provided when someone does not speak the language of the court, and why the foreign national is accorded the right to be promptly advised that he may have consular assistance. These measures enable the accused to fully exercise other rights that everyone enjoys under the law. Those rights and these, which are inextricably inter-linked, form the body of procedural guarantees that ensures the due process of law.

121. In the case to which this Advisory Opinion refers, the real situation of the foreign nationals facing criminal proceedings must be considered. Their most precious juridical rights, perhaps even their lives, hang in the balance. In such circumstances, it is obvious that notification of one's right to contact the consular agent of one's country will considerably enhance one's chances of defending oneself and the proceedings conducted in the respective cases, including the police investigations, are more likely to be carried out in accord with the law and with respect for the dignity of the human person.

122. The Court therefore believes that the individual right under analysis in this Advisory Opinion must be recognized and counted among the minimum guarantees essential to providing foreign nationals the opportunity to adequately prepare their defense and receive a fair trial.

123. The inclusion of this right in the Vienna Convention on Consular Relations – and the discussions that took place as it was being drafted – [ ] are evidence of a shared understanding that the right to information on consular assistance is a means for the defense of the accused that has repercussions – sometimes decisive repercussions – on enforcement of the accused's other procedural rights.

124. In other words, the individual's right to information, conferred in Article 36(1)(b) of the Vienna Convention on Consular Relations, makes it possible for the right to the due process of law upheld in Article 14 of the International Covenant on Civil and Political Rights, to have practical effects in tangible cases; the minimum guarantees established in Article 14 of the International Covenant can be amplified in the light of other international instruments like the Vienna Convention on Consular Relations, which broadens the scope of the protection afforded to those accused.

XI

CONSEQUENCES OF THE VIOLATION OF THE RIGHT TO INFORMATION ON CONSULAR ASSISTANCE

(Fourth, tenth and twelfth questions)

125. In its fourth, tenth and twelfth questions, Mexico requested the Court's interpretation of the juridical consequences of the imposition and execution of the death penalty in cases in which the rights recognized in Article 36(1)(b) of the Vienna Convention on Consular Relations were not respected:

In relation to the Vienna Convention on Consular Relations:

[…]

4. From the point of view of international law and with regard to aliens, what should be the juridical consequences of the imposition and application of the death penalty in the light of failure to give the notification referred to in Article 36(1)(b) of the Vienna Convention?

[…]

With regard to the International Covenant on Civil and Political Rights:

[…]

10. In connection with the Covenant and with regard to persons of foreign nationality, what should be the juridical consequences of the imposition and application of the death penalty in the light of failure to give the notification referred to in Article 36(1)(b) of the Vienna Convention [on Consular Relations]?

[…]

With regard to the OAS Charter and the American Declaration of the Rights and Duties of States:

12. With regard to aliens in the framework of Article 3(1) of the OAS Charter and Articles I, II and XXVI of the Declaration, what should be the juridical consequences of the imposition and execution of the death penalty when there has been a failure to make the notification referred to in Article 36(1)(b) of the Vienna Convention [on Consular Relations]?

126. From the questions posed by the requesting State, it is unclear whether it is asking the Court to interpret the consequences of the host State's failure to inform the detained foreign national of his rights under Article 36(1)(b) of the Vienna Convention on Consular Relations, or whether the question concerns cases in which the detainee has expressed a desire to have the consular officer advised of his arrest and the host State has failed to comply.

127. However, from the general context of Mexico's request, [ ] the Court's reading is that the request concerns the first of the two hypotheticals suggested above, which is to say the obligation to inform the detainee of his rights under Article 36(1)(b) of the Vienna Convention on Consular Relations. The Court will address that question below.

128. It is a general principle of international law, recognized in the Vienna Convention on the Law of Treaties (Article 26), that States Party to a treaty have the obligation to perform the treaty in good faith (*pacta sunt servanda*).

129. Because the right to information is an element of Article 36(1)(b) of the Vienna Convention on Consular Relations, the detained foreign national must have the opportunity to avail himself of this right in his own defense. Non-observance or impairment of the detainee's right to information is prejudicial to the judicial guarantees.

130. In a number of cases involving application of the death penalty, the United Nations Human Rights Committee observed that if the guarantees of the due process established in Article 14 of the International Covenant on Civil and Political Rights were violated, then so, too, were those of Article 6.2 of the Covenant if sentence was carried out.

131. In Communication No. 16/1977, for example, which concerned the case of Mr. Daniel Monguya Mbenge (1983), that Committee determined that under Article 6.2 of the International Covenant on Civil and Political Rights:

> ... sentence of death may be imposed only "in accordance with the law [of the State party] in force at the time of the commission of the crime and not contrary to the provisions of the Covenant". This requires that both the substantive and the procedural law in the application of which the death penalty was imposed was not contrary to the provisions of the Covenant and also that the death penalty was imposed in accordance with that law and therefore in accordance with the provisions of the Covenant. Consequently, the failure of the State party to respect the relevant requirements of article 14 (3) leads to the conclusion that the death sentences pronounced against the author of the communication were imposed contrary to the provisions of the Covenant, and therefore in violation of article 6 (2). [ ]

132. In the case of *Reid vs. Jamaica* (no. 250/1987), the Committee stated that:

> [T]he imposition of a sentence of death upon the conclusion of a trial in which the provisions of the Covenant have not been respected constitutes [...] a violation of article 6 of the Covenant. As the Committee noted in its general comment 6(16), the provision that a sentence of death may be imposed only in accordance with the law and not contrary to the provisions of the Covenant implies that 'the procedural guarantees therein prescribed must be observed, including the right to a fair hearing by an independent tribunal, the presumption of innocence, the minimum guarantees for the defence, and the right to review by a higher tribunal'.[ ]

It came to exactly the same conclusion in *Wright vs. Jamaica*[ ] in 1992.

133. The Court has observed that the requesting State directed its questions at those cases in which the death penalty is applicable. It must therefore be determined whether international human rights law gives the right to consular information in death penalty cases special effects.

134. It might be useful to recall that in a previous examination of Article 4 of the American Convention,[ ] the Court observed that the application and imposition of capital punishment are governed by the principle that "no one shall be arbitrarily deprived of his life." Both Article 6 of the International Covenant on Civil and Political Rights and Article 4 of the Convention require strict observance of legal procedure and limit application of this penalty to "the most serious crimes." In both instruments, therefore, there is a marked tendency toward restricting application of the death penalty and ultimately abolishing it.[ ]

135. This tendency, evident in other inter-American[ ] and universal [ ] instruments, translates into the internationally recognized principle whereby those States that still have the death penalty must, without exception, exercise the most rigorous control for observance of judicial guarantees in these cases. It is obvious that the obligation to observe the right to information becomes all the more imperative here, given the exceptionally grave and irreparable nature of the penalty that one sentenced to death could receive. If the due process of law, with all its rights and guarantees, must be respected regardless of the circumstances, then its observance becomes all the more important when that supreme entitlement that every human rights treaty and declaration recognizes and protects is at stake: human life.

136. Because execution of the death penalty is irreversible, the strictest and most rigorous enforcement of judicial guarantees is required of the State so that those guarantees are not violated and a human life not arbitrarily taken as a result.

137. For the foregoing reasons, the Court concludes that nonobservance of a detained foreign national's right to information, recognized in Article 36(1)(b) of the Vienna Convention on Consular Relations, is prejudicial to the guarantees of the due process of law; in such circumstances, imposition of the death penalty is a violation of the right not to be "arbitrarily" deprived of one's life, in the terms of the relevant provisions of the human rights treaties (e.g., the American Convention on Human Rights, Article 4; the International Covenant on Civil and Political Rights, Article 6) with the juridical consequences inherent in a violation of this nature, i.e., those pertaining to the international responsibility of the State and the duty to make reparations.

. . . .

∽

QUESTIONS & COMMENTS

(1) In *The Avena Case* (Mexico–United States) (2004), the International Court of Justice held that the United States had violated the Vienna Convention on Consular Relations in regard to a number of Mexican nationals being held in U.S. prisons. The Court held that the United States must provide "by means of its own choosing, review and reconsideration of the convictions and sentences of the Mexican nationals." To satisfy the ICJ's judgment, the ICJ held that such review and reconsideration must take into account the

rights set forth in Article 36 as well as the relevant portions of the Court's opinion on this issue. Review and reconsideration must be effective and must provide "a procedure which guarantees that full weight is given to the violation of the rights set forth in the Vienna Convention, whatever may be the actual outcome of such review and reconsideration." Thus, U.S. courts cannot apply a procedural default rule to preclude the defendant from raising a Vienna Convention violation if she or he failed to raise the claim at trial level. Furthermore, it is insufficient that such review and reconsideration take place at a clemency hearing. In addition, the Court stated that review and reconsideration must occur "with a view to ascertaining whether in each case the violation of Article 36 committed by the competent authorities caused actual prejudice to the defendant in the process of administration of criminal justice." Thus, the Court declined Mexico's request to find that a Vienna Convention violation must automatically result in the partial or total annulment of conviction or sentence.

In late 2004, the U.S. Supreme Court agreed to hear *Medellin v. Dretke* in light of the ICJ's decision. The petitioner in this case is one of the Mexican nationals whose rights had been violated by the U.S. in *Avena*.

Judicial and Jury Impartiality

Andrews v. United States
Report No. 57/96, Case 11.139
Inter-American Commission on Human Rights
ANNUAL REPORT OF THE INTER-AMERICAN COMMISSION
ON HUMAN RIGHTS 1997
OEA/Ser/L/V/II.98, Doc. 7 rev. (19 February 1998)

I. ALLEGATIONS IN PETITION DATED JULY 28, 1992

1. On July 27, 1992, the Commission received a fax communication informing it of the pending execution of Mr. William Andrews by the State of Utah on July 29, 1992, for three counts of Murder....

2. On July 28, 1992 the Commission received a petition filed by Steven W. Hawkins of the LDF Capital Punishment Project; Richard J. Wilson, Director, International Human Rights Clinic, Washington College of Law, American University; and Bartram S. Brown of Chicago-Kent College of Law, on behalf of William Andrews which alleged that he was an African-American male born in Jonesboro, Louisiana, was now a prisoner on death row in Draper Correctional Institution, Draper, Utah, and was scheduled to be executed at or about 12:01 a.m on July 30, 1992. The petition alleged that in 1974, Mr. Andrews was convicted of three counts of first degree murder and two counts of aggravated robbery in the State of Utah, and that he was subsequently sentenced to death on all three counts by the same jury which convicted him.

3. The petitioners further alleged that both the victims and the jurors were Caucasian, and the sole black member of the jury pool was stricken peremptorily by the prosecution during jury selection. Mr. Andrews had left the premises prior to the offenses, and that his co-defendant, fatally shot the victims. His co-defendant, also African-American was executed by the State of Utah in 1987.

4. It is further alleged that a napkin (note) was found among the jurors during a recess of the trial, which stated "Hang the Nigger's" and that Mr. Andrews' attorney requested a

mistrial and a right to question jurors concerning the note, but this request was denied by the trial judge. Instead the trial judge admonished the jurors to "ignore communications from foolish people". That the denial of the right to question the jury about the note and the mistrial coupled with the known racist Mormon Church doctrine was ground for a mistrial and at minimum, a further inquiry into the authorship, and source of the note, exposure of the note to members of the jury or their response to it.

. . . .

II. ARTICLES ALLEGEDLY VIOLATED

8. Articles 3 (k) and 44 (a) of the Organization of American States' Charter. Articles I, (right to life, liberty and personal security) II, (right to equality before the law without distinction as to race), and XXVI (right to an impartial hearing, and not to receive cruel, infamous or unusual punishment) of the American Declaration of the Rights and Duties of Man.

III. THE PETITIONERS REQUEST THAT:

The Inter-American Commission on Human Rights

9. Find that in the trial, sentencing and execution of William Andrews, the United States violated Articles I, II, and XXVI of the American Declaration of the Rights and Duties of Man.

. . . .

IV. PROCEEDINGS BEFORE THE COMMISSION

. . . .

B. Legal Submissions of the Petitioners

18. ... The petitioners argued that the courts in the United States did not grant Mr. Andrews an evidentiary hearing to remedy the defect in his trial and sentencing. . . .

. . . .

20. The petitioners argued that the OAS Charter and the American Declaration were violated by the racially discriminatory manner in which the death penalty was imposed in Mr. Andrews' case. The tainted procedure by which Mr. Andrews was found guilty and sentenced to death in this case violated Articles 3 (k) and 44 (a) of the Charter of the OAS. It also violated Mr. Andrews' rights to equality before the law without distinction as to race (Article II) and to an impartial hearing (Article XXVI) under the American Declaration of the Rights and Duties of Man.

21. The petitioners further argued that both the International Court of Justice and the European Commission of Human Rights have found that racial distinctions require that international tribunals examine "more seriously" the purported justifications for differences in treatment based on race. [ ] Systematic racial discrimination has been recognized as a peremptory norm of the customary international law of human rights.[2] Moreover, the importance of freedom from racial discrimination is affirmed under Article 27(1) of the American Convention on Human Rights, which prohibits racial discrimination even in time of war or national emergence.

22. The petitioners argued that the U.S., as a signatory to several instruments regarding protection of human rights in the Conference on Security and Co-Operation in Europe,

---

[2] See §702(f), *Restatement of the Law (Third): The Foreign Relations Law of the United States*, vol. 2 (1987).

agreed that "special measures" must sometimes be taken to assure that the rights of national minorities are protected.

23. The petitioners argued that in the past, this Commission has found that another petitioner did not satisfy a burden to produce sufficient evidence of racial discrimination in a capital trial or death sentence in the United States, the facts presented here and below demonstrate a clear satisfaction of any burden of production which can be said to lie with the petitioner, and should result in a shifting of the burden of proof to the United States to demonstrate the absence of racial prejudice in Mr. Andrews' death sentence.[3]

24. The petitioners also argued that the procedures in the trial and in the review of the death sentence imposed in William Andrew's case, when considered in the context of the racist doctrine of the Mormon Church at the time of Mr. Andrews' trial in Utah, a State which is overwhelming Mormon and white, demonstrate invidious racial discrimination in violation of the OAS Charter and the American Declaration. Mr. Andrews was denied his right to racial equality when his lawyer was denied both a request for a mistral and a right to question jurors concerning a note that was found among them saying, "Hang the Nigger's [sic]." [ ] The very fact that such a note was found with the jury, coupled with the known racist Mormon Church doctrine at the time, was grounds for a mistrial or, at minimum, a further inquiry into the authorship, source of the note, exposure of the note to members of the jury or their response to it. Yet, the trial judge – who himself was a Mormon – refused to grant the request, and cut off any questioning of the jury about the note.

25. The petitioners argued that no reviewing court in the United States ever required the production of evidence or the holding of an evidentiary hearing on the issue of the influence of racial prejudice in the trial of William Andrews. These errors require redress as a violation of the law of international human rights. At Mr. Andrews' trial in 1974, the blatantly racist note was brought to the trial judge's attention by a bailiff. The bailiff told the judge that he had been given the note, which was written on a napkin, by a member of the jury over the lunch period. The bailiff was sworn and questioned, but could provide little information beyond hearsay. The bailiff told the judge that a juror had told him that he "found" the note in the jury lunchroom. The bailiff also stated that in his opinion one of the jurors could have written the note.

26. Moreover, the petitioners argued that despite the bailiff's own opinion, the trial judge blindly accepted the explanation of a juror who was never called to the stand to testify. The judge never attempted to determine if the juror's claim that the note was "found" was truthful or not by placing that person on the stand to testify. The judge never saw the juror's demeanor in order to adequately gauge his credibility. The judge's only response to this outrageous incident was to tell the jury to "ignore communications from foolish people."

27. The petitioners also argued that racism alone explains why William Andrews was executed in the State of Utah on July 30, 1992. The denial of his basic human right to be accorded the same level of dignity as that of a person of any other race is clearly the result of racist Mormon Church doctrine. The State of Utah is overwhelmingly Mormon and white. Although no inquiry into the racial views of the jurors was permitted at the time of the revelation of the note described above, it was unquestionably true that some or all

---

[3] *Celestine* Case, Res. No. 23/89, Case 10.031 (Sept. 28, 1989).

of the members of the jury were Mormons, and that the tenets of their faith guided their determination to sentence Mr. Andrews to death.

28. The petitioners argued that members of the jury were unable to show William Andrews mercy or to render him compassion because their religion taught them that no person of the Negro race was worthy of their sympathy and had been already condemned to Hell by God. Tragically, to have shown Mr. Andrews mercy would have been sacrilegious to those Mormons who comprised the jury. They were duty-bound to sentence him to death by the Apartheid-type teachings of their religious faith. The racist Church doctrine has its origins in Brigham Young, a Prophet of the Mormon Church, who instructed the congregation in 1852 that Black skin was a mark of God's curse upon black people: "I tell you, these people that are commonly called negroes are the children of the old Cain. I know they are, I know that they cannot bear rule in the Priesthood for the curse upon them. . . ."

29. The petitioners argued that, a century later, racist teaching had not changed, but was actually even more virulent. A former First President of the Mormon Church, the Church's spiritual leader, expressly told the congregation in 1949 that Black people were "damned to death by God:" "Why are so many of the inhabitants of the earth cursed with a skin of blackness? It comes in consequence of their fathers rejecting the power of the holy priesthood, and the law of God. They will go down to death." Even with the advent of the Civil Rights Movement in the United States, the Mormon Church still clung in 1969 to its racist ideology, believing that God had demanded that Blacks be treated as inferior beings. The First President told the congregation: "The seeming discrimination by the Church toward the Negro is not something that originated with man; but goes back to the beginning with God." This formal statement was made less than five years before Mr. Andrews was sentenced to death in Utah.

30. The petitioners argued that less than three years before Mr. Andrews was put on trial for his life, a poll conducted in Utah showed that over 70 percent of all Mormons vehemently believed that God had cursed black people to a life in Hell. Instead of appreciating criticism of their pre-Civil War view of Blacks, a third of the Mormons polled believed that there was a "black conspiracy" to destroy the Church.

31. The petitioners argued that in 1974, at the time when William Andrews was tried for a capital offense, Mormon Church doctrine still compelled that the jury show him no mercy because God had shown no mercy on Mr. Andrews' race. It was only in June of 1978, four years after the jury sentenced Mr. Andrews to death, that the First President of the Mormon Church announced that he had experienced a "revelation" and that from that day forward blacks could enter the Kingdom of Heaven. For Mr. Andrews, the "revelation" had come too late. He tried many times unsuccessfully to have Utah and federal courts address the obvious effect of the Church doctrine on his sentence of death, all to no avail.

32. The petitioners argued that the U.S. cannot demonstrate that it did not violate its obligation of racial equality as articulated in the OAS Charter and the American Declaration on the Rights and Duties of Man (hereinafter "American Declaration"), as well as in more recent international human rights instruments to which it has become a party. The U.S. Government has internationally recognized obligations to racial equality before the law, binding on it in the Inter-American system in which it participates, pursuant to Article II of the American Declaration, as well as Articles 3 (k) and 44 (a) of the OAS Charter, which provide, in relevant part: Article 3. "The American States reaffirm

the following principles: . . . (k) The American States proclaim the fundamental rights of the individual without distinction as to race . . . " Article 44. "The Member States . . . agree to dedicate every effort to the application of the following principles and mechanisms: a) All human beings, without distinction as to race, . . . have a right to . . . liberty, dignity, [and] equality of opportunity. . . . "

33. The petitioners argued that the "fundamental rights of the individual" referred to in Article 3(k) unquestionably refer to the specific provisions of the American Declaration and its antecedent, the Universal Declaration of Human Rights. The latter instrument specifically protects the right to life (Article 3), the right to equality before the law (Article 7) and the right to due process of law in the face of criminal charges (Article 10). These rights are more specifically developed in the American Declaration. It is particularly noteworthy that the United States recently ratified the International Covenant on Civil and Political Rights. There were no reservations by the United States to Articles 2 and 26, which cover equal treatment under the law.[4] Those rights are non-derogable, pursuant to the provisions of Article 4 (1) of the Covenant. Given its recent affirmation to the right to racial equality before the law, the United States cannot now argue that it has no burden to show adherence to racial equality in the case before the Commission.

34. The petitioners argued that finally, the U.S. has been an active participant in the Conference on Security and Co-Operation in Europe (CSCE). As a full participant in the deliberations of the Conference, the U.S. became a signatory of the Report of the CSCE Meeting of Experts on National Minorities, held in Geneva, Switzerland in 1991. The report states that the participating States "consider that respect for human rights and fundamental freedoms must be accorded on a non-discriminatory basis throughout society."[5] That report, in turn, refers to the concluding document of the Copenhagen conference, in which the states parties, including the United States, agreed to the following: "Persons belonging to national minorities have the right to exercise fully and effectively their human rights and fundamental freedoms without any discrimination and in full equality before the law. The participating States will adopt, where necessary, special measures for the purpose of ensuring to persons belonging to national minorities full equality with the other citizens in the exercise and enjoyment of human rights and fundamental freedoms."[6]

35. The petitioners argued that taken as a whole, the U.S. has an internationally recognized obligation to guarantee racial equality before the law. Moreover, when, as here, overwhelming evidence of governmental complicity in racial discrimination is shown, the burden shifts to that government to prove the absence of discrimination in guaranteeing racial equality. The United States cannot discharge that burden here. The Commission should therefore find that the United States has violated its obligations to racial equality as

---

[4] The U.S. did adopt an understanding with regard to the application of Articles 2 and 26, stating that discrimination based on race is understood in the United States "to be permitted when such distinctions are, at minimum, rationally related to a legitimate governmental objective." See *United States: Senate Committee on Foreign Relations Report on the International Covenant on Civil and Political Rights*, 31 I.L.M. 645, 659 (1992). This understanding applies only when the treaty is sought to be applied domestically and does not affect the obligations of the United States under the international law of human rights.

[5]   *Conference on Security and Co-Operation in Europe: Report of the CSCE Meeting of Experts on National Minorities*, 30 I.L.M. 1692, 1696 (1991).

[6] *Document of the Copenhagen Meeting of the Conference on the Human Dimension of the CSCE*, 29 I.L.M. 1305, 1318 (1990).

found in the OAS Charter and the American Declaration. William Andrews was denied his right to life and to due process of law by the decision of the U.S. Government to execute him without an impartial hearing on the issue of racial discrimination at his trial. Despite his many claims to fundamental fairness and his ultimate efforts to seek the intervention of this Commission to review his case, William Andrews was executed on July 30, 1992. Mr. Andrews was improperly deprived of his life in violation of Article I of the American declaration. Article I, as it relates to the imposition of the death penalty in criminal proceedings, must be read in conjunction with Article XXVI, paragraph 2, which guarantees due process in such proceedings.

. . . .

37. The petitioners argued that Mr. Andrews' right to an impartial hearing was violated in his trial, and more importantly, in his sentencing. In complete disregard of universal notions of an impartial trial, no state or federal court ever granted Mr. Andrews the right to inquire into the origins of the racist note. The Supreme Court of the United States would not grant review of Mr. Andrews' case. Justices Marshall and Brennan were the lone dissenters, calling the note "a vulgar incident of lynch-mob racism reminiscent of Reconstruction days." *Andrews v. Shulsen*, 485 U.S. 919, 920 (1988) (dissent from denial of certiorari). Justice Marshall described the denial of basic due process by pointing out that Mr. Andrews merely sought an evidentiary hearing to determine the origins of the note, and that "the Constitution [of the United States], not to mention common decency, require[d] no less than this modest procedure." *Id.* Justice Marshall gave examples of obvious questions about the note that have never been answered: "Was it one or more of [Mr. Andrews'] jurors who drew a black man hanging on a gallows and attached the inscription, "Hang the Niggers"? How many other jurors saw the incendiary drawing before it was turned over to the bailiff? Might it have had any effect on the deliberations?" *Id.* These questions remain unanswered to this day.

38. The petitioners argued that because no court granted Mr. Andrews the right to question the jurors about the note, the worst scenario cannot be ruled out: the entire jury was involved in the drawing of the note and joked about it before finally giving it to the bailiff; the judge then joined in their conspiracy by telling them to "ignore communications by foolish people." It cannot be ruled out that a "lynch-mob atmosphere" existed within the jury which sentenced Mr. Andrews to death since he has never been accorded a hearing. The failure of the U.S. Government to afford a hearing on the issue of racial discrimination, and its subsequent execution of William Andrews, constitute a violation of Articles I and XXVI of the American Declaration.

. . . .

C. United States Government's Response to Petition

. . . .

62. . . . [T]he United States argued that it rejected the petitioner's effort to shift the burden of proof by claiming a presumptive violation of human rights. [The petitioner] contends that because the United States has a duty under the Charter and the Declaration to secure rights without discrimination based on race, the United States accordingly has an affirmative duty to demonstrate that it did not violate that duty to Mr. Andrews. Pet. at 14. Not only is this argument legally unavailing, it is unsupported by any factual basis. The petition alleges "overwhelming evidence of governmental complicity" but provides no evidence of such "complicity" whatsoever, apart from the fact that the State of Utah

successfully prosecuted Mr. Andrews for his role in an especially gruesome crime. The burden remains upon the petitioner to demonstrate the violations [the petitioner] alleges; that effort proves no more successful in this petition than it was for over a decade in the U.S. Court System.

63. The United States argued that the first and arguably most compelling element of petitioner's claim that Mr. Andrews' trial, sentencing and execution were fatally tainted by racially-motivated discrimination turns on the discovery by a juror of a note bearing a racist slur (an apparent copy of which is appended to the petition). According to the judicial record, the juror found the note while on a lunch break in a restaurant when s/he overturned the napkin on the back of which the note had been sketched. Although the jury had been sequestered during the break, there was no indication that the note had been written by a juror or circulated or discussed among members of the jury. Moreover, the note was promptly disclosed to the bailiff, who in turn brought it to the attention of the trial judge.

64. The United States argued that immediately thereafter, the Court held a hearing at which the bailiff was sworn and testified as to the circumstances of the discovery; defendants and counsel were present. Upon conclusion of the hearing, the Court denied defendants' motion to sequester the jury completely and thereafter admonished the jury to ignore such communications. Contrary to the implications of the petition, the trial judge did not fail to respond to the "napkin incident;" in point of fact, the court investigated the incident promptly and determined that it had not resulted in any prejudice to the defendants. Mr. Andrews' attorneys made their objections at the time; they were fully considered by the trial judge and were overruled.

. . . .

66. Generalized Racism – The United States argued that the petition alleged that Mr. Andrews was deprived of his right to a fair and impartial jury free from outside influence because the State of Utah was at the time (and remains) overwhelmingly Mormon and white, the jurors were all white, some or all of them "unquestionably" were Mormons, and they were "compelled" by the Mormon Churchs "racist doctrine" to sentence him to death. Petitioner adduces no evidence whatsoever for these conclusory allegations. While s/he argues that Mr. Andrews was denied an impartial hearing on the issue of racial discrimination at his trial (pet. at 17), s/he admits that "the obvious effect of the Church doctrine on [Mr. Andrews'] sentence to death" was present to the Utah and federal courts, "many times unsuccessfully, all to no avail."

67. The United States argued that the petitioners were entirely correct on this last point. It is clear that Mr. Andrews raised the issue of outside influence with the courts on numerous occasions, and that the courts repeatedly examined the claim and determined that his constitutional right to a fair and impartial jury had not been transgressed. [ ] The fact is that Mr. Andrews failed to convince any court that his assertions concerning the lack of a fair trial had any merit.

68. As to the racial composition of the jury, the United States bears noting that Andrews and his co-defendants themselves objected to the only African-American who was a member of the jury panel; perhaps because that panel member was a law enforcement officer and knew several members of the Ogden Police Department, the attorneys for Andrews and Pierre both objected to him and the State stipulated to his removal for cause. In any event, this claim too was considered by the courts and rejected on the merits.[ ] Moreover, the third defendant, Keith Roberts, was also an African-American

and the only defendant represented by and African-American attorney at trial; surely, if racist doctrine had prevented the jury from reaching an impartial decision or had "compelled" its members to impose capital punishment, he would also have received the death penalty. [ ]

. . . .

[The Inter-American Commission found the petition admissible.]

. . . .

b. The United States Government's Argument on Merits

. . . .

117. . . . . It argued that the burden of proof always remains on the accuser who has the burden of proving that discrimination occurred. While the burden of producing evidence may shift to the accused government to prove lack of discriminatory animus, it does not shift until and unless a prima facie case is made that discrimination exists. It argued that the Commission understands this because in the Celestine case, the Commission held that the burden of production was on the petitioner to prove a prima facie case. Only then does the burden shift. In the Case of Willie L. Celestine *supra*, para. 45 at 72, the Commission said: "in its opinion, the petitioner has not provided sufficient evidence that the statistical studies presented make a prima facie case to prove the allegations of racial/ethnic discrimination and partiality in the imposition of the death penalty such as to shift the burden of proof (sic) to the United States Government."

118. The Government argued further that there was no credible evidence that any of the twelve jurors, let alone all of them were racist, or that any one connected to the case was racist. The sole African-American juror was peremptorily challenged by the State only after the defense challenged him for cause which was denied by the trial court judge. The prosecution obliged the defendants by peremptorily challenging him for them. The evidence reflected that the jury was impartial, and that the napkin incident did not reflect that the jury was racist. While the person who left the napkin was no doubt racist, there is no evidence that his or her racist appeal to the jury incited the juror who saw it to be racist, it was promptly handed over to the bailiff and the judge reflected awareness of the impropriety of the message. No one, including counsel for Andrews and counsel for the co-defendants asked the judge to voir dire the jury after the incident occurred, nor was it necessary after the napkin incident.

119. The Government stated that the admonition to the jury was appropriate. The judge told them: "Occasionally some foolish person will try to communicate with you. Please disregard the communications from foolish persons and ignore the same."[ ]. It argued that treatment of the third co-defendant reflected that the jury was not racist. Keith Roberts, the third co-defendant, was also charged with murder. He was not convicted of murder, let alone sentenced to death. Yet he was African American, and his counsel was African American. The attorneys for the other two co-defendants were not African American. Had the jury truly been racist, it would have found Keith Roberts guilty of murder and sentenced him to death, regardless of his scope of involvement.

120. The Government argued further that there was substantial evidence of Andrews' guilt at trial. To find "racial" ethnic discrimination in this case, the Commission would have to find that there was no other possible basis for the jury's decision to convict Andrews. It stated that there was substantial and appropriate appellate review of Andrews'

claims, and that the allegation of racism was being used as an indirect means to attempt to abolish the death penalty.

. . . .

e. Other Submissions

. . . .

138. The Commission received a 31 page Amicus brief from . . . Rights International . . . which [argued] that disclosure of specific evidence of possible juror racial bias or taint requires the trial judge to examine each juror individually in order to ensure tribunal impartiality as well as to fulfill the State-Party's affirmative duty to eliminate racial discrimination. This requires the State under both international and domestic law to avoid not only bias in fact but also the appearance of bias. International law employs an "objective test" and the domestic law of countries using juries in criminal cases also requires states to avoid the appearance of bias in their tribunals.[ ]

. . . .

VI. ANALYSIS [BY THE INTER-AMERICAN COMMISSION]

A. Did Mr. Andrews Have a Fair and Impartial Hearing?

147. Article XXVI of the American Declaration, paragraph 2 provides: "Every person accused of an offense has the right to be given an impartial and public hearing, and to be tried by courts previously established in accordance with pre-existing laws, and not to receive cruel, infamous or unusual punishment.". . . .

148. . . . Upon examining all arguments, documentary and testimonial evidence including exhibits submitted to it, the Commission notes that: Mr. Andrews was tried, convicted, sentenced, and executed by the State of Utah on three counts of first degree murder, and two counts of aggravated robbery, which occurred after he participated in the robbery of a radio store. He was tried in the State of Utah where the teaching of the Mormon church doctrine prevailing at the time of his trial, was that all black people were damned to death by God and were inferior beings. This doctrine was changed after the trial and conviction of the victim, Mr. Andrews.

. . . .

b) Proceedings in the Trial Court/Napkin

i. The Bailiff's Testimony

150. The Commission, upon examining the trial transcript of the proceedings referring to the "notation on the napkin," noted, that a hearing was held in the afternoon session of the trial proceedings, on the renewal of a motion to sequester the jury and a motion for a mistrial by the co-defendants attorney, including William Andrews' attorney in the absence of the jury, after the jurors returned from lunch. The trial transcript of the testimony of the bailiff, Thomas R. Linox, to whom the napkin was given by a member of the juror reveals the following:

> On the day in question, November 4, 1974, he was in the company of the jurors in Lee's restaurant where they went for lunch on that day, shortly after they had been seated a Mr. Weaver, one of the jurors said, "bailiff I have some evidence for you . . . ", and gave him a napkin. The bailiff said that "myself as well as some of the other people thought it was one of Mr. Weaver's jokes, he is quite a hilarious gentleman.

So I went up there very honestly at first thinking I was just humoring a joke and that is when he produced that napkin with the writing that you see on it."[footnote omitted]

He had not seen the napkin prior to the time that he had it handed to him, and stated that the napkin was with Mr. Weaver's regular place setting, the blank portion of the napkin showing to anyone who would have cared to walk along the table. It had the appearance of any other napkin until, according to him, he turned it over to open it up and that is when he saw the writing that the judge had before him. The bailiff read the words on the napkin "hang the niggers," and described the drawing on the napkin as "a character of a gallows and a stick figure hanging therefrom."

151. The bailiff was asked the following questions:

"Was this, [People's] exhibit No. 4, discussed or shown to other prospective jurors?"[ ] He replied: "I do believe the people immediately to the left and the right of Mr. Weaver would have had to have seen it. I couldn't say with any degree of certainty." The bailiff was then asked: "After the napkin was handed to you, what, if any conversations existed between jurors and yourself or Mr. Weaver and other jurors, in your presence?" He responded: "Nothing pertinent to that. They felt it was that important that I should have it to show the court and nothing more was discussed. There was no comments one way or another about it. There was some concern shown on the part of some of the jurors who asked me directly, 'do you think this will affect our present situation as far as where we are eating or what the court may do about this.' I said, I have no idea. That is a matter for the court to decide." [footnote omitted]

152. Upon further examination the bailiff was asked by Mr. Davis:

"Mr. Linox, do you think perhaps one of the jurors themselves could have drawn that? Are you able to make such a conclusion that it was possible or not? That is what I want to know?" He responded, "Mr. Davis, I say it is possible, that small amount, that much time could have lapsed." [ ]

ii. The Trial Court's Action

153. The Court asked the bailiff the following question:

"Did I tell you to say anything to Mr. Weaver?" The bailiff stated that: "You did" and stated that "I admonished Mr. Weaver not to mention the incident any further, to let the issue die." The judge then asked the bailiff, "have you been able to do that?" the bailiff responded, "I have." The judge then asked the bailiff, "did he say anything to you?" the bailiff responded, "he said he would." [ ]

154. There is language in the trial transcript which shows concern expressed by a defense attorney. He requested of the Court that, "the jury be sequestered, that they be put under guard that would guard against influencing this jury which is accumulative now, with the talk in the hallway, now this action."[ ] The trial court denied the motions to sequester the jury and for a new trial and stated that "the only thing that this kind of foolishness can do is cause the trial to start all over again. It is that foolish, but I will deny your motions at this time."[ ]

c) Appellate Review of Mr. Andrews' Case

. . . .

156. The United States Supreme Court denied Mr. Andrew's motion for certiorari. However, two of the Justices, Marshall and Brennan in the Supreme Court dissented. The note was referred to as "a vulgar incident of lynch-mob racism reminiscent of Reconstruction days."[ ] Justice Marshal referred to the denial of due process by stating that Mr. Andrews merely sought an evidentiary hearing to determine the origins of the note, and that "the Constitution [of the United States], not to mention common decency, require[d] no less than this modest procedure."[ ] Justice Marshall stated:

> Was it one or more of [Mr. Andrews'] jurors who drew a black man hanging on a gallows and attached the inscription, "Hang the niggers"? How many other jurors saw the incendiary drawing before it was turned over to the bailiff? Might it have had any effect on the deliberations? [ ]

d) United States Domestic Law

157. The Fifth Amendment of the Constitution of the United States of America 1787 provides: "No person shall be held to answer for a capital, or otherwise infamous crime . . . nor deprived of life, . . . without due process of law. . . . " The Sixth Amendment provides: "In all criminal prosecutions, the accused shall enjoy the right to a speedy and public trial, by an impartial jury. . . . " The Commission notes the principles enunciated by the Courts in the United States. The United States Supreme Court held in the *Rosales-Lopez v. United States*, that a "reasonable possibility" of juror bias is sufficient to find reversible error for a federal court's refusal to ask venire-persons about possible racial bias."[7] Jury misconduct concerning outside influences must be fully investigated to determine if any misconduct actually occurred and whether or not it was prejudicial.[8] Failure to hold a hearing in these cases constitutes an abuse of discretion and is thus reversible error.[ ]

158. The Code of Criminal Procedure for the State of Utah requires the Court to admonish the jury at each adjournment . . . that it is their duty not to converse among themselves nor with any one else on any subject connected with the trial, and not to form or express any opinion thereon until the case is finally submitted to them.[ ] Under the Code jurors can be challenged in the State of Utah on "peremptory" grounds, and for "cause" (for bias-opinion) and can be examined as to such bias-opinion[ ] by the Court. Such challenges are made prior to the commencement of a trial.

e) The International Standard on Impartiality

159. The international standard on the issue of "judge and juror impartiality" employs an objective test based on "reasonableness, and the appearance of impartiality." The United Nations Committee to Eliminate Racial Discrimination has held that a reasonable suspicion of bias is sufficient for juror disqualification, and stated that: "it is incumbent upon national judicial authorities to investigate the issue and to disqualify the juror if

---

7 451 U.S. 182 (1981).
8 [*United States v. Harris*, 908 F.2d 728, 733 (11th Cir. 1990); *United States v. Brantley*, 733 F.2d 1429, 1439 (11th Cir. 1984), *cert. denied*, 470 U.S. 1006 (1984)].

there is a suspicion that the juror might be biased."[9] The Commission notes that in the European System of Human Rights an objective test was enunciated in the cases of *Piersack v. Belgium*,[10] and *Gregory v. United Kingdom*.[11]

160. In the case of *Remli v. France* the European Court of Human Rights referred to the principles laid down in its case-law concerning the independence and impartiality of tribunals, which applied to jurors as they did to professional and lay judges and found that there had been a violation of Article 6(1) of the European Convention For the Protection of Human Rights and Fundamental Freedoms.[12] That Article provides that: "In the determination of his civil rights and obligations or of any criminal charge against him, everyone is entitled to a fair and public hearing . . . by an independent and impartial tribunal established by law. . . . "

161. The European Court considered that Article 6(1) of the Convention imposed an obligation on every national court to check whether, as constituted, it was "an impartial tribunal" within the meaning of that provision where, as in the instant case, that was disputed on a ground that did not immediately appear to be manifestly devoid of merit.

---

[9] *Narrainen v. Norway*, UN Ctte. Elim Racial Discrim., Communication No. 3/1991, views adopted 15 March 1994. In that case a Norwegian citizen of Tamil origin, who was charged with a drug-related offense, complained that he had not obtained a fair and impartial trial. He alleged that racial views had played a large part in the decision against him, pointing to a statement of one of the jurors that people such as him, living on taxpayers' money, should be sent back from where they had come, and alleged that slurs were made about the color of his skin.

[10] 5 HRR 169 (1982). The European Court of Human Rights held that there was a violation of Article 6 of the European Convention which guarantees the right to a fair and impartial trial. The European Commission stated that: "Whilst impartiality normally denotes absence of prejudice or bias, its existence or otherwise can . . . be tested in various ways. A distinction can be drawn in this context between a subjective approach, that is endeavoring to ascertain the personal conviction of a given judge in a given case, and an objective approach, that is determining whether he offered guarantees sufficient to exclude any legitimate doubt in this respect."

[11] 16 H.R.L.J. 238 (1995). In this case an Afro-Caribbean male had been convicted of armed robbery. During jury deliberations, the trial judge received a handwritten note from a juror stating: "Jury showing racial overtones 1 member to be excused." The trial judge redirected the jury and did not hold an evidentiary hearing. The European Commission found the case admissible and found that the defendant essentially makes the case that it was clear from the jury note that there was, at the very least, a strong objective indication of racial bias within the jury. It looked at the international standard and stated:

[i]f the possibility of bias on the part of the juror comes to the attention of the trial judge in the course of a trial, the trial judge should consider whether there is actual bias or not (subjective test). If this has not been established, that trial judge or appeal court must then consider whether there is "a real danger of bias affecting the mind of the relevant juror or jurors" (objective test). Note, the real danger test originated in the English common law in the case of *R. v. Gough*, 4 A.E.R. (Court of Appeal, Criminal Division 1992).

However, the European Commission concluded that the judge's detailed and careful redirection of the jury was sufficient. The *Gregory* case is now before the European Court of Human Rights.

[12] [1996] HRCD Vol. VIII No. 7, European Court of Human Rights: Judgments, at 608–613. Judgment was delivered on April 23, 1996. The case involves the trial of an Algerian national in France for escape, during which a prison guard was struck and killed. The applicant and another person (both of them were of North African origin) were tried and convicted for international homicide and attempted escape in the Rhone Assize Court. The applicant was sentenced to life imprisonment on April 14, 1989. He submitted evidence that during his trial, a person overheard one of the jurors say, "What's more, I'm a racist." That person so certified in writing, and defense counsel asked that the court take formal note of the racist remark, and that the court append the written statement to the record. The trial court refused the first request but granted the second. As to the first request, the Assize judge stated that it was "not able to take formal note of events alleged to have occurred out of its presence."

In Remli's case the Rhone Assize Court had not made any such check, thereby depriving Mr. Remli of the possibility of remedying, if it had proved necessary, a situation contrary to the requirements of the Convention.[13]

162. The Commission has noted the United States Government's argument that the admonishment by the trial court to the jury to disregard communications from foolish people was appropriate. It has also noted its argument that the jury was not racist because Mr. Andrews' co-defendant, Keith Roberts, who was African American, and whose counsel was African American and also charged with murder, was not convicted of murder, nor sentenced to death; and the attorneys for the other two co-defendants were not African American. The Commission finds that these factors are not dispositive of whether the United States violated the Articles of the American Declaration as pertaining to Mr. William Andrews' right to an "impartial hearing." The Commission has also noted that Mr. Andrews' other co-defendant who was African American was convicted and sentenced to death by the State of Utah, and executed in 1987.

163. The United States Government's evidence produced at the hearing on the merits of the case before the Commission through the testimony of its own witness Mr. Yocum, Assistant Attorney General of Utah substantiates the petitioners' case. Mr. Yocum testified that the jury members were not questioned by the trial judge about the note. The trial judge held a hearing, but only the bailiff was questioned. The judge denied the motion for a mistrial and proceeded to trial with the same members of the jury.

164. Conclusion: The Commission finds that the United States has not disputed that a napkin was found by one of the jurors, and given to the bailiff (who took the jurors to lunch in a restaurant) with words written in black stating "hang the nigger's" and a figure drawn in black hanging therefrom. Nor has it disputed that the napkin was brought to the attention of the trial judge who questioned the bailiff as to its origin.

165. The Commission finds that in assessing the totality of the facts in an objective and reasonable manner the evidence indicates that Mr. Andrews did not receive an impartial hearing because there was a reasonable appearance of "racial bias" by some members of the jury, and the omission of the trial court to voir dire the jury tainted his trial and resulted in him being convicted, sentenced to death and executed. The record before the Commission reflects ample evidence of "racial basis."

166. First, Mr. Andrews was a black male, and was tried by an all white jury some of whom were members of the Mormon Church and adhered to its teachings that black people were inferior beings.[14] The transcript reveals that the bailiff testified that when the juror told him he had some evidence for him, both the bailiff and some of the other jurors thought that it was one of the juror's jokes which they were humoring and there was discussion among the jurors concerning the "napkin."[ ]

167. Second, was the conduct and manner, in which the note was handed to the bailiff by the juror. (See trial transcript, the bailiff thought he was humoring a joke.)

---

[13] In Remli's case the Rhone Assize Court dismissed the application without even examining the evidence submitted to it, on the ground that it was "not able to take formal note of events alleged to have occurred out of its presence." Nor had it ordered that evidence should be taken to verify what had been reported and, if had been established, take formal note of it as requested by the defence, although it could have done so. The applicant had been unable either to have the juror in question replaced by one of the additional jurors or to rely on the fact in issue in support of his appeal on points of law. Nor had he been able to challenge the juror, since the jury had been finally empaneled and no appeal lay against the Assize Court's judgment other than on points of law. *Id.* at 612.

[14] In Davis County, Utah, 73.9% of the people who resided there were Mormons.

The note depicts racial words "hang the nigger's," written on the napkin that was given to the Court. (See the opinions of Justices Brennan and Marshall.) The trial transcript states "Hang the Niggers," and the drawing on the napkin was described by the bailiff as "a gallows and a stick figure hanging therefrom."[ ] The transcript refers to express language by the bailiff, that the jurors who were immediate to the left and the right of Mr. Weaver, (the juror who found the napkin) would have had to have seen it. The jurors asked the bailiff, if it would affect their present situation and what the court may do about it.[ ] The bailiff himself stated under oath that it was possible that one of the jurors could have drawn that note because "that small amount, that much time could have elapsed".[ ]

168. Third, the admonishment by the trial court to the jury was inadequate. The trial judge at the very least if he did not want to grant a mistrial, should have conducted an evidentiary hearing of the jury members to ascertain whether some of them had seen the note and they had been influenced by it. The trial judge instead, warned them against foolish people, and questioned the bailiff and left such an important and fundamental issue for the bailiff, whom he instructed to admonish the juror who found the note. The trial judge appeared to be more concerned to continue the trial with the same members of the jury without questioning them, as to whether they had seen the note, and denied both motions to sequester the jury and for a mistrial.

169. Fourth, in addition to the note being found, there is language in the trial transcript which indicates the concern expressed by the defense attorneys, that two things had occurred during the trial, "the talk in the hallway, and the note," which would influence the jury members in their deliberations and in making their decisions, and which language had become accumulative.

170. It should be noted that while it is not the function of the Inter-American Commission on Human Rights to act as a quasi-judicial fourth instance court and to review the holdings of the domestic courts of the OAS member states,[ ] it is mandated by its Statute and its Regulations to examine petitions alleging violations of human rights under the American Declaration against member States who are not parties to the American Convention.[ ]

171. The Commission finds that Mr. Andrews did not receive an impartial trial because there was evidence of "racial bias" present during his trial, and because the trial court failed to conduct an evidentiary hearing of the jury in order to ascertain whether members of the jury found the napkin as the juror claimed or whether the jurors themselves wrote and drew the racial words on the napkin. If the note did not originate from the jurors and was "found" by the juror then the trial court could have inquired of the jurors by conducting an evidentiary hearing as to whether they would be influenced or their judgment impaired by the napkin depicting the racial words and drawing so that they would be unable to try the case impartially. Had the Court conducted the hearing it would have had the possibility of remedying, if it had proved necessary so to do, a situation contrary to the requirements of the American Declaration.

172. Therefore, the Commission finds the United States in violation of Article XXVI, paragraph 2, of the American Declaration, because Mr. Andrews had the right to receive an impartial hearing as provided by the Article, and he did not receive an impartial trial in United States Courts. In capital punishment cases, the States Parties have an obligation to observe rigorously all the guarantees for an impartial trial. . . .

QUESTIONS & COMMENTS

(1) The U.S. federal government and the state of Utah failed to stay Andrews' execution. The U.S. government had taken the position that the American Declaration is not legally binding on the United States. President Clinton issued an executive order that states in part:

> It shall also be the policy and practice of the Government of the United States to promote respect for international human rights, both in our relationships with all other countries and by working with and strengthening the various international mechanisms for the promotion of human rights, including, *inter alia*, those of the United Nations, the International Labor Organization, and the Organization of American States.

Sec. 1(b), Exec. Order No. 13107, Implementation of Human Rights Treaties (10 Dec. 1998), 63 F.R. 68991 (1998). Does the United States' new policy of promoting respect for international human rights by working with and strengthening the Inter-American Commission entail compliance with the Commission's future requests for stays? What about compliance with the Commission's recommendations?

Assuming that a stay is issued – but the United States does not comply with the Commission's recommendations – and you go into federal or state court to order state compliance with the Commission's recommendation as evidence of customary international law, how would you argue such a claim?

(2) Consider *Rizvanovic v. Federation of Bosnia & Herzegovina (Admissibility and Merits)*, Case No. CH/97/59, Hum. Rts. Chamber-BiH (12 June 1998), in which the Human Rights Chamber for Bosnia and Herzegovina in a death penalty case found that because members of a military court were "operating in a situation of conflict where outside pressure on its members was likely" and were subject to dismissal on the proposal of the Ministry of Defence, these factors could give rise to legitimate doubts as to whether the court meets the standard of independence required in a death penalty case. Accordingly, the chamber concluded that the military court lacked a sufficient appearance of independence and the applicant could not be executed on order from this military court.

Is there a higher standard for death penalty cases in the international law governing judicial impartiality and independence? Should there be?

Equality of Arms: Examination of Witnesses and Documents

Harward v. Norway
UN Human Rights Committee
Communication No. 451/1991
Views adopted 15 July 1994
U.N. Doc. CCPR/C/51/D/451/1991 (1994)

. . . .

2.1 The author [a British citizen] states that he was arrested on 27 September 1986 in Tenerife, Spain, and informed that his extradition had been requested on suspicion of drug trafficking. He was kept in detention until his extradition on 21 August 1987 to Norway. He submits that, at that time, he was still waiting for the outcome of the appeal against his extradition, which he had filed with the Spanish Constitutional Court.

2.2 In Norway, the author was charged with having imported a considerable quantity of heroin into the country during 1985 and 1986. A legal-aid lawyer, who spoke only little

English, was appointed. On 31 August 1987, a formal indictment was issued against him and his co-defendants, including his two brothers.

2.3 The trial started on 12 October 1987, in the Eidsivating High Court. On 3 November 1987, the author and his co-defendants were found guilty as charged; the author, who claims to be innocent, was sentenced to 10 years' imprisonment. On 25 March 1988, the Supreme Court rejected the author's appeal.

The complaint:

. . . .

3.3 The author further claims to be a victim of a violation of article 14, paragraph 3(a), of the Covenant, since he was allegedly misinformed about the charges against him in Spain. He further submits that the 1,100 document pages used in the trial against him were in the Norwegian language, which he did not understand; only the indictment and a small proportion of the other papers were translated.

3.4 The author also claims that article 14, paragraph 3(b), was violated in his case. He claims that he was hindered in the preparation of his defence because the indictment was issued only six weeks before the start of the trial and his lawyer's request to have all documents pertaining to the case translated was refused. He further alleges that his defence was obstructed, since the most damaging evidence against him was only introduced during the trial, and not included in the documents which were available beforehand. According to the author, this evidence consisted of uncorroborated and unsigned statements made by his co-defendants during their detention in solitary confinement, in the absence of an interpreter or lawyer.

. . . .

Issues and proceedings before the Committee:

. . . .

9.2 The Committee notes that the facts, to which the parties agree, show that Mr. Harward was assigned a lawyer on 28 August 1987 and that the trial against him started on 12 October 1987, that the indictment, the statements of co-defendants to the Norwegian police and the court records were provided in written translation to the author, and that the author's defence counsel had access to the entire case file. It is also undisputed that an interpreter was available to the defence for all meetings between counsel and Mr. Harward and that simultaneous interpretation was provided during the court hearings.

9.3 The Committee further notes that the State party has argued that not all documents in the case file were of relevance to the defence and that only fifteen documents were presented by the prosecution in Court and therefore available to the jurors, out of which only four police reports were not available in English or in English translation. The Committee has also taken note of counsel's argument that all documents in the case file, although not presented during the trial, were of relevance to the defence, since they had been used by the police and the prosecution in their preparation of the trial.

9.4 Article 14 of the Covenant protects the right to a fair trial. An essential element of this right is that an accused must have adequate time and facilities to prepare his defence, as is reflected in paragraph 3(b) of article 14. Article 14, however, does not contain an explicit right of an accused to have direct access to all documents used in the preparation of the trial against him in a language he can understand. The question before the Committee is whether, in the specific circumstances of the author's case, the failure of the State party to provide written translations of all the documents used in the preparation of the trial has violated Mr. Harward's right to a fair trial, more specifically his right under article 14, paragraph 3(b), to have adequate facilities to prepare his defence.

9.5 In the opinion of the Committee, it is important for the guarantee of fair trial that the defence has the opportunity to familiarize itself with the documentary evidence against an accused. However, this does not entail that an accused who does not understand the language used in court, has the right to be furnished with translations of all relevant documents in a criminal investigation, provided that the relevant documents are made available to his counsel. The Committee notes that Mr. Harward was represented by a Norwegian lawyer of his choice, who had access to the entire file, and that the lawyer had the assistance of an interpreter in his meetings with Mr. Harward. Defence counsel therefore had opportunity to familiarize himself with the file and, if he thought it necessary, to read out Norwegian documents to Mr. Harward during their meetings, so that Mr. Harward could take note of its contents through interpretation. If counsel would have deemed the time available to prepare the defence (just over six weeks) inadequate to familiarize himself with the entire file, he could have requested a postponement of the trial, which he did not do. The Committee concludes that, in the particular circumstances of the case, Mr. Harward's right to a fair trial, more specifically his right to have adequate facilities to prepare his defence, was not violated.

9.6 The Human Rights Committee, acting under article 5, paragraph 4, of the Optional Protocol to the International Covenant on Civil and Political Rights, is of the view that the facts before it do not reveal a violation of any of the articles of the Covenant.

∾

QUESTIONS & COMMENTS

(1) The European Court has held that Article 6(3)(c) requires that state parties pay for translation costs – even though the criminal defendant eventually was convicted. *Luedicke, Belkaçem and Koç v. Federal Republic of Germany*, 29 Eur. Ct. H. R. (ser. A) (1978); *Öztürk v. Federal Republic of Germany*, 73 Eur. Ct. H.R. (ser. A) (1984).

(2) Consider the rules governing the production of evidence for the International Criminal Tribunal for the Former Yugoslavia:

Section 4: Production of Evidence

Rule 66

Disclosure by the Prosecutor

(A) Subject to the provisions of Rules 53 and 69, the Prosecutor prosecutor shall make available to the defence in a language which the accused understands

(i) within thirty days of the initial appearance of the accused, copies of the supporting material which accompanied the indictment when confirmation was sought as well as all prior statements obtained by the Prosecutor from the accused; and

(ii) within the time-limit prescribed by the Trial Chamber or by the pre-trial Judge appointed pursuant to Rule 65 *ter*, copies of the statements of all witnesses whom the Prosecutor intends to call to testify at trial, and copies of all written statements taken in accordance with Rule 92 *bis*; copies of the statements of additional prosecution witnesses shall be made available to the defence when a decision is made to call those witnesses.

(B) The Prosecutor shall, on request, permit the defence to inspect any books, documents, photographs and tangible objects in the Prosecutor's custody or control, which are material to the preparation of the defence, or are intended for use by the Prosecutor as evidence at trial or were obtained from or belonged to the accused.

(C) Where information is in the possession of the Prosecutor, the disclosure of which may prejudice further or ongoing investigations, or for any other reasons may be contrary to the public interest or affect the security interests of any State, the Prosecutor may apply to the Trial Chamber sitting in camera to be relieved from an obligation under the Rules to disclose that information. When making such application the Prosecutor shall provide the Trial Chamber (but only the Trial Chamber) with the information that is sought to be kept confidential.

Rule 67

Additional Disclosure

(A) Within the time-limit prescribed by the Trial Chamber or by the pre-trial Judge appointed pursuant to Rule 65 *ter*:

(i) the defence shall notify the Prosecutor of its intent to offer:

(a) the defence of alibi; in which case the notification shall specify the place or places at which the accused claims to have been present at the time of the alleged crime and the names and addresses of witnesses and any other evidence upon which the accused intends to rely to establish the alibi;

(b) any special defence, including that of diminished or lack of mental responsibility; in which case the notification shall specify the names and addresses of witnesses and any other evidence upon which the accused intends to rely to establish the special defence; and

(ii) the Prosecutor shall notify the defence of the names of the witnesses that the Prosecutor intends to call in rebuttal of any defence plea of which the Prosecutor has received notice in accordance with paragraph (i) above.

(B) Failure of the defence to provide notice under this Rule shall not limit the right of the accused to testify on the above defences.

(C) If either party discovers additional evidence or material which should have been disclosed earlier pursuant to the Rules, that party shall immediately disclose that evidence or material to the other party and the Trial Chamber.

Rule 68

Disclosure of Exculpatory and Other Relevant Material

(A) The Prosecutor shall, as soon as practicable, disclose to the Defence any material which in the actual knowledge of the Prosecutor may suggest the innocence or mitigate the guilt of the accused or affect the credibility of Prosecution evidence.

(B) Without prejudice to paragraph (A), the Prosecutor shall make available to the defence, in electronic form, collections of relevant material held by the Prosecutor, together with appropriate computer software with which the defence can search such collections electronically.

(C) The Prosecutor shall take reasonable steps, if confidential information is provided to the Prosecutor by a person or entity under Rule 70 (B) and contains material referred to in paragraph (A) above, to obtain the consent of the provider to disclosure of that material, or the fact of its existence, to the accused.

(D) The Prosecutor shall apply to the Chamber sitting *in camera* to be relieved from an obligation under the Rules to disclose information in the possession of the Prosecutor, if its disclosure may prejudice further or ongoing investigations, or for any other reason may be contrary to the public interest or affect the security interests of any State, and when making such application, the Prosecutor shall provide the Trial Chamber (but only the Trial Chamber) with the information that is sought to be kept confidential.

(E) Notwithstanding the completion of the trial and any subsequent appeal, the Prosecutor shall disclose to the other party any material referred to in paragraph (A) above.

Rule 68 *bis*

Failure to Comply with Disclosure Obligations

The pre-trial Judge or the Trial Chamber may decide *proprio motu*, or at the request of either party, on sanctions to be imposed on a party which fails to perform its disclosure obligations pursuant to the Rules.

(3) Compare U.S. law on the prosecution's duty to disclose. In *Brady v. Maryland*, 373 U.S. 83 (1963), the U.S. Supreme Court held that "the suppression by the prosecution of evidence favorable to an accused upon request violates due process where the evidence is material either to guilt or punishment." *Id.* at 87. A prosecutor is not required to deliver his entire file to defense counsel. *United States v. Bagley*, 105 S. Ct. 3375 (1985). The level of "materiality" required is a "reasonable probability" that the evidence will contribute to guilt or punishment. *Id.*

Note that the ICT-Y requires a level of materiality that "may suggest the innocence or mitigate the guilt of the accused or affect the credibility of Prosecution evidence." Rule 68, ROP of ICT-Y. Are both the European Court's decision in *Edwards v. United Kingdom* (reproduced below) and the U.S. Supreme Court's caselaw out-of-step with the ICT-Y's rules on the prosecution's duty to disclose evidence to the defense? Are there any good reasons for this difference? Francisco Forrest Martin, et al., 1 International Human Rights Law & Practice: Cases, Treaties and Materials 577 (1997).

(4) Consider Rule 70 of the ICT-Y's Rules of Procedure:

Rule 70

Matters not Subject to Disclosure

(A) Notwithstanding the provisions of Rules 66 and 67, reports, memoranda, or other internal documents prepared by a party, its assistants or representatives in connection with the investigation or preparation of the case, are not subject to disclosure or notification under those Rules.

(B) If the Prosecutor is in possession of information which has been provided to the Prosecutor on a confidential basis and which has been used solely for the purpose of generating new evidence, that initial information and its origin shall not be disclosed by the Prosecutor without the consent of the person or entity providing the initial information and shall in any event not be given in evidence without prior disclosure to the accused.

(C) If, after obtaining the consent of the person or entity providing information under this Rule, the Prosecutor elects to present as evidence any testimony, document or other material so provided, the Trial Chamber, notwithstanding Rule 98, may not order either party to produce additional evidence received from the person or entity providing the initial information, nor may the Trial Chamber for the purpose of obtaining such additional evidence itself summon that person or a representative of that entity as a witness or order their attendance. A Trial Chamber may not use its power to order the attendance of witnesses or to require production of documents in order to compel the production of such additional evidence.

(D) If the Prosecutor calls a witness to introduce in evidence any information provided under this Rule, the Trial Chamber may not compel that witness to answer any question relating to the information or its origin, if the witness declines to answer on grounds of confidentiality.

(E) The right of the accused to challenge the evidence presented by the Prosecution shall remain unaffected subject only to the limitations contained in paragraphs (C) and (D).

(F) The Trial Chamber may order upon an application by the accused or defence counsel that, in the interests of justice, the provisions of this Rule shall apply *mutatis mutandis* to specific information in the possession of the accused.

(G) Nothing in paragraph (C) or (D) above shall affect a Trial Chamber's power under Rule 89 (D) to exclude evidence if its probative value is substantially outweighed by the need to ensure a fair trial.

(5) In *The Prosecutor v. Blaskic*, Case No. IT-95–14, Int'l Crim. Trib.-Yugo., Trial Chamber (19 January 1998), the Trial Chamber rejected the defense claim that the admission of documents written by persons who did not appear as witnesses violated his right to examine witnesses against him. Compare the European Court of Human Rights decision in *Mantovanelli v. France*, – Eur. Ct. H.R. (ser. A) (1997), in which the Court held that the applicants' inability to have their lawyers present at the interviews held by an independent expert appointed by an administrative court and to have an opportunity to inspect numerous documents to which the expert's report referred, violated their right to a fair hearing. The Court noted that the right to a fair hearing guaranteed by Article 6(1), ECHR, included the right to adversarial proceedings. Most importantly, the Court noted that expert's report contained technical knowledge outside the administrative judge's expertise. Can the difference between the European Court's decision and the ICT-Y's be attributed to the character of evidence in both cases?

Edwards v. United Kingdom
European Court of Human Rights
247-B Eur. Ct. H. R. (ser. A) (1992)
E.H.R.R. 417 (1993)

. . . .

FACTS:

. . . .

A. The trial and appeal proceedings

6. On 9 November 1984 the applicant was convicted at Sheffield Crown Court, *inter alia*, of one count of robbery and two counts of burglary. The jury's decision was by a

majority verdict of ten to two. He received a sentence of imprisonment of ten years for the robbery, and two sentences of eight years each for the burglary offences. All three sentences were to be served concurrently.

The evidence against the applicant consisted of detailed oral admissions that he had allegedly made to the police concerning his involvement in the three offences. According to the police he was questioned on three separate occasions and contemporaneous notes were taken of his statements. However, he had declined to sign them.

His defence during the trial was to maintain that these statements had been concocted by the police. He protested his innocence pointing out that he had not denied his numerous misdeeds in the past. The only witnesses called by the defence during the trial were the two police officers who had interviewed him.

. . . .

8. The victim of the robbery (Miss Sizer) which took place on 14 April 1984 was a lady of 82 years of age who was awakened from her sleep to find a man standing over her. Before having her hands tied behind her back and being blindfolded she was able to take a quick glance at him. She remained tied up until she was freed the next morning. In a statement to the police she gave a description of the man which corresponded with the applicant and stated that she thought she would recognise him again. She was not called as a witness during the trial but her written statement was read to the jury.

The two counts of burglary related to separate incidents which occurred on 19 April and 10 June 1984 also involving the home of an elderly woman. On the latter occasion the police arrested the applicant's co-defendant in the vicinity. It was his statement to the police which lead to the applicant's arrest.

9. On 16 May 1985, the applicant petitioned the Secretary of State for the Home Department with complaints against police officers who had investigated his case and given evidence at his trial. An independent police investigation was ordered in the course of which certain facts came to the applicant's attention. On 3 December 1985, the applicant applied for leave to appeal against conviction out of time. The police report (The Carmichael Report), dated 5 December 1985, was delivered to the Police Complaints Authority which directed it to the Director of Public Prosecutions. The report was requested by the applicant's advisers but its disclosure was refused on the grounds of public interest immunity.

In February 1986, the Director of Public Prosecutions decided that there was insufficient evidence to support criminal charges against the police officers, but recommended that disciplinary charges be brought against three police officers. At the disciplinary hearing, on 13 to 15 June 1988, the tribunal decided that there was no case to answer and dismissed the charges.

B. Reference by the Secretary of State to the Court of Appeal

10. On 21 March 1986, the Secretary of State for the Home Department referred the applicant's case to the Court of Appeal (Criminal Division) under section 17(1)(a) of the Criminal Appeal Act 1968 ('the 1968 Act'). The case was heard on 18 July 1986 and judgment delivered on the same date.

11. The applicant submitted to the Court of Appeal that the verdict should be set aside as unsafe and unsatisfactory because of certain shortcomings in the prosecution case, in particular, that certain information had been withheld by the police. At the trial one of

the police witnesses had stated under cross-examination that no fingerprints were found at the scene of the crime. In fact two fingerprints had been found which later turned out to be those of the next door neighbour who was a regular visitor to the house. The applicant had not been informed of this by the prosecution before his trial.

It was argued by the applicant that the police officer had told lies and that his veracity as regards the admission statements was thus called into question.

The Court of Appeal rejected this submission as follows:

We do not accept that interpretation of Detective Sergeant Hoyland's evidence. We think quite plainly what he was indicating there and intended to indicate was that no fingerprints relating to either of the two alleged burglars were discovered at the scene: neither the fingerprint of Rose nor the fingerprint of Edwards, the present appellant.

We do not think, had the matter been carried further, it would have been demonstrated that Hoyland was a person who to that extent could not be believed on his own.

12. A further shortcoming complained of by the applicant related to the fact that the police had shown two volumes of photographs of possible burglars (including a photograph of himself) to the elderly victim of the robbery who said that she had caught a fleeting glimpse of the burglar. Her statement, read to the jury, said that she thought she would be able to recognise her assailant. Yet she did not pick out the applicant from the photographs.

This fact was not, however, mentioned by one of the police witnesses who had made a written statement which was read out to the jury and had not been indicated to the applicant before or during his trial. Counsel for the applicant submitted to the Court of Appeal that this omission cast such doubt on the evidence of the prosecution that it might have led the jury to believe that the confession statements had indeed been 'manufactured' by the police as the applicant alleged.

The Court of Appeal also rejected this argument:

The fact that Miss Sizer had a fleeting glimpse of her assailant, and the fact that such identification as she did make was largely directed to other matters of identification rather than his features, leads us to believe that the jury would not have been influenced to act other than they did if they had the full story of the photographs and of Police Constable Esdon's activities with regard to that.

13. The Court of Appeal examined other impugned shortcomings which it did not consider to cast any doubt on the verdict. It was of the opinion that even if these matters had been investigated, it would have made no difference to the outcome.

14. The Court concluded as follows:

It is clear that there was some slipshod police work in the present case, no doubt because they took the view that here was a man who had admitted these crimes fully, and consequently there was very little need for them to indulge in a further verification of whether what he said was true. Although this is a matter which perhaps casts the police in a somewhat lazy or idle light, we do not think in the circumstances there was anything unsafe or unsatisfactory in the end about these convictions. Consequently, treating this matter as we have to according to section 17 of the Act, we think this appeal fails and must be dismissed.

15. Counsel for the applicant did not request the Court of Appeal to exercise its discretionary power to rehear evidence under section 23 of the 1968 Act with a view, for example, to cross-examining the police officers who gave evidence at the applicant's trial. He considered that there was little prospect of such a request being granted. Nor did he request the Court to order the production of the Carmichael Report.

16. The applicant took advice concerning the possibility of appealing to the House of Lords but was informed, in an opinion of counsel dated 8 September 1986, that there were no grounds on which an appeal could successfully be pursued before the House of Lords.

He petitioned the Secretary of State for Home Affairs on 3 June 1987 without success. He is currently serving a sentence of two years' imprisonment following his conviction on 26 March 1992 at Sheffield Crown Court on three counts of burglary.

II. Relevant domestic law and practice

A. Duty of prosecution to disclose certain information to the defence

17. Under the Attorney-General's Guidelines issued in December 1981, the prosecution is obliged (subject to specified discretionary exceptions) to disclose to the defence 'unused material,' which includes all witness statements not enclosed in the bundle of statements served on the defence at the stage of committal of the case by the magistrates' court to the Crown Court.

The prosecution is also under a duty to inform the defence of any earlier written or oral statement of a prosecution witness which is inconsistent with evidence given by that witness at the trial. (*R v. Clarke* (1930) 22 Cr. App. R. 58.) Consequently where evidence of a prosecution witness is given before the court stating that the witness would recognise the accused again, and the prosecution knows that when shown a photograph of the accused the witness in fact failed to identify him, it is required to inform the prosecution of that fact.

For the purpose, among others, of ensuring compliance with this duty, the Court of Appeal has stated that all the statements which have been taken by the police should be put before counsel for the Crown, and that it should not be left to the police to decide which statements he is to receive. (*R v. Fellowes*, 12 July 1985, unreported)

B. Jury verdicts

18. A jury's verdict may be either unanimous or by a majority. It must be unanimous unless the trial judge, in accordance with section 17 of the Juries Act 1974, has directed, after at least two hours of unsuccessful jury deliberations, that a majority verdict will be accepted. A majority verdict will be effective if, where there are not less than 11 jurors, ten of them agree on the verdict, or, where there are ten jurors, nine of them agree. If the jury do not agree on either a unanimous or majority verdict, they may, at the discretion of the trial judge, be discharged, but such a discharge does not amount to acquittal and the accused may be tried again by a second jury. In the event of a second jury disagreeing, it is common practice for the prosecution formally to offer no evidence.

. . . .

E. New evidence on appeal

21. Section 23 of the 1968 Act provides, *inter alia*, as follows:

(1) For purposes of this part of the Act, the Court of Appeal may, if they think it necessary or expedient in the interests of justice –

(a) order the production of any document, exhibit or other thing connected with the proceedings, the production of which appears to them necessary for the determination of the case;

(b) order any witness who would have been a compellable witness in the proceedings from which the appeal lies to attend for examination and be examined before the Court, whether or not he was called in those proceedings; and

(c) ...

(2) Without prejudice to subsection (1) above, where evidence is tendered to the Court of Appeal thereunder the Court shall, unless they are satisfied that the evidence, if received, would not afford ground for allowing the appeal, exercise their power of receiving it if –

(a) it appears to them that the evidence is likely to be credible and would have been admissible in the proceedings from which the appeal lies on an issue which is the subject of the appeal; and

(b) they are satisfied that it was not adduced in those proceedings but there is a reasonable explanation for the failure to adduce it.

(3) ...

It falls to the Court to determine, if necessary, claims by the Crown that documents should not be disclosed on the grounds of public interest in immunity. (*see, inter alia, R v. Judith Ward* (1993) 96 Cr App R 1.)

22. The approach to be adopted by the Court of Appeal when considering under section 2(1)(a) of the 1968 Act whether a trial verdict was unsafe or unsatisfactory was discussed by the Appellate Committee of the House of Lords in the context of a section 17 reference in *Stafford v. Director of Public Prosecutions* [1974] AC 878). Viscount Dilhorne, with whom the other members of the Appellate Committee agreed, stated:

> I do not suggest that in determining whether a verdict is unsafe or unsatisfactory, it is a wrong approach for the court to pose the question – 'Might this new evidence have led to the jury returning a verdict of not guilty?' If the court thinks that it would or might, the court will no doubt conclude that the verdict was unsafe or unsatisfactory ...
>
> It would, in my opinion, be wrong for the court to say: 'In our view this evidence does not give rise to any reasonable doubt about the guilt of the accused. We do not ourselves consider that an unsafe or unsatisfactory verdict was returned but as the jury who heard the case might conceivably have taken a different view from ours, we quash the conviction' for Parliament has, in terms, said that the court should only quash a conviction if, there being no error of law or material irregularity at the trial, 'they think' the verdict was unsafe or unsatisfactory. They have to decide and Parliament has not required them or given them power to quash a verdict if they think that a jury might conceivably reach a different conclusion from that to which they have come. If the court has no reasonable doubt about the verdict, it follows that the court does not think that the jury could have one; and, conversely, if the court says that a jury might in the light of the new evidence have a reasonable doubt, that means that the court has a reasonable doubt.

23. The Court of Appeal has held that the powers under section 23 of the 1968 Act extend to rehearing evidence which has already been given at the trial, if this is necessary or expedient in the interests of justice. The Court has also held that it has a general power under section 23(1) to admit further evidence, not restricted to the circumstances set out in section 23(2). (*R v. Lattimore and Others* (1976) 62 Cr. App. R. 53.) However, it is unusual for the Court of Appeal to exercise that power since it is reluctant to substitute its own findings of fact for those of the jury which has already seen and heard the relevant witness. In practice, the exercise of the power to receive evidence is thus mainly confined to fresh evidence which has arisen since the trial and which the jury did not have the benefit of hearing. No statistics are available on the frequency with which the power to rehear evidence is exercised.

24. In March 1991 the Secretary of State for the Home Department announced the appointment of a Royal Commission on Criminal Justice which is expected to consider, *inter alia*, the general application the 1968 Act.

PROCEEDINGS BEFORE THE COMMISSION

25. In his application before the Commission (No 13071/87) lodged on 29 September 1986, the applicant complained that he had not received a fair trial, in breach of Article 6(1) of the Convention and, in particular, that he was denied the right to cross-examine police witnesses on the basis of the new evidence which had come to light, contrary to Article 6(3)(d)....

. . . .

[The European Commission of Human Rights found no violation of Article 6, and it referred the case to the Court.]

. . . .

DECISION [OF THE EUROPEAN COURT OF HUMAN RIGHTS]:

I. Alleged violation of Article 6

29. The applicant complained that he did not receive a fair trial, in breach of Article 6(1) and (3)(d), the relevant parts of which read:

1. In the determination . . . of any criminal charge against him, everyone is entitled to a fair . . . hearing . . . by an independent and impartial tribunal . . .

2. . . . .

3. Everyone charged with a criminal offence has the following minimum rights:

. . . .

(d) to examine or have examined witnesses against him and to obtain the attendance and examination of witnesses on his behalf under the same conditions as witnesses against him.

30. He submitted that the trial proceedings were unfair because of the failure of the police to disclose to the defence (1) the fact that one of the victims, who had made a statement that she thought she would be able to recognise her assailant, had failed to identify the applicant from a police photograph albums and (2) the existence of fingerprints which had been found at the scene of the crime. If his counsel had been aware of these facts he would have been able to attack the credibility of police testimony.

Bearing in mind that this was the main evidence against him there existed a possibility that one more juror might have been persuaded that he was innocent which would have led to his acquittal. As a result, the defence was denied an adequate opportunity to examine the police witnesses and was not on an equal footing with the prosecution as required by Article 6(3)(d).

In the applicant's view the proceedings before the Court of Appeal did not remedy the defects at the trial since it neither heard the police witnesses nor called for the production of the report of the independent police investigation (The Carmichael Report) which had not been disclosed to his legal advisers. In consequence, he had two incomplete hearings before two separate courts.

31. The Government maintained that, in determining whether there had been unfairness, the proceedings must be considered as a whole including those before the Court of Appeal. The applicant who had been provided with all the relevant information concerning the undisclosed facts had every opportunity, through his lawyer, to submit to the Court of Appeal that his conviction should be quashed. Moreover, that court had examined his conviction in the light of the new evidence thoroughly and conscientiously but had concluded that it should be upheld. It was not open to the European Court to substitute its judgment on the facts for that of the Court of Appeal. Finally, the Government contended that Article 6(3)(d) was not relevant to the issue of non-disclosure of evidence to the defence which fell more appropriately to be considered under Article 6(1).

32. The Commission was of the view that paragraph (3)(d) was relevant to the applicant's complaint but concluded that, having regard to the proceedings as a whole, there had been no breach of Article 6(1) read in conjunction with this provision.

33. The Court recalls that the guarantees in Article 6(3) are specific aspects of the right to a fair trial set forth in paragraph 1.... In the circumstances of the case it finds it unnecessary to examine the relevance of paragraph (3)(d) to the case since the applicant's allegations, in any event, amount to a complaint that the proceedings have been unfair. It will therefore confine its examination to this point.

34. In so doing, the Court must consider the proceedings as a whole including the decisions of the appellate courts. (*see*, amongst other authorities, *Helmers v. Sweden* (1993), at §31) Moreover, it is not within the province of the European Court to substitute its own assessment of the facts for that of the domestic courts and, as a general rule, it is for these courts to assess the evidence before them. The Court's task is to ascertain whether the proceedings in their entirety, including the way in which evidence was taken, were fair. (*see, inter alia, Vidal v. Belgium*, 235-B Eur. Ct. H.R. (ser. A) (1992) at §33)

35. The applicant's conviction was based mainly on police evidence, which he contested, that he had confessed to the offences. It subsequently came to light that certain facts had not been disclosed by the police to the defence which would have enabled it to attack the credibility and veracity of police testimony.

36. The Court considers that it is a requirement of fairness under Article 6(1), indeed one which is recognised under English law, that the prosecution authorities disclose to the defence all material evidence for or against the accused and that the failure to do so in the present case gave rise to a defect in the trial proceedings.

However, when this was discovered, the Secretary of State, following an independent police investigation, referred the case to the Court of Appeal, which examined the transcript of the trial including the applicant's alleged confession and considered in detail the impact of the new information on the conviction.

37. In the proceedings before the Court of Appeal the applicant was represented by senior and junior counsel who had every opportunity to seek to persuade the Court that the conviction should not stand in view of the evidence of non-disclosure. Admittedly the police officers who had given evidence at the trial were not heard by the Court of Appeal. It was, nonetheless, open to counsel for the applicant to make an application to the Court – which they chose not to do – that the police officers be called as witnesses.

38. In the course of the hearing before the European Court the applicant claimed, for the first time, that without the disclosure of the Carmichael Report to the applicant or to the Court of Appeal the proceedings, considered as a whole, could not be fair. However, it is not disputed that he could have applied to the Court of Appeal for the production of this report but did not do so. It is no answer to the failure to make such an application that the Crown might have resisted by claiming public interest immunity since such a claim would have been for the Court to determine.

39. Having regard to the above, the Court concludes that the defects of the original trial were remedied by the subsequent procedure before the Court of Appeal. (*see,* in this respect, *Adolf v. Austria* (1982), at §§38–41, and *mutatis mutandis, DeCubber v. Belgium* (1984), at §33). Moreover, there is no indication that the proceedings before the Court of Appeal were in any respect unfair. Accordingly there has been no breach of Article 6.

.....

Dissenting Opinion of Judge Pettiti (provisional translation)

I did not join the majority in voting that there had not been a breach, as in my opinion there was an undeniable violation of Article 6 of the European Convention on Human Rights.

First, because the Court of Appeal prejudged what the jury's decision would have been if they had had to decide and, secondly, because the essential question raised by the *Edwards* case was that of the principle of public interest immunity, which in English law allows the prosecution, in the public interest, not to disclose or communicate to the defence all the evidence in his possession and to 'reserve' certain evidence. Such non-disclosure took place in the Crown Court. The Court made no express statement of its views on this point and its silence might be understood as approval of this principle, which is not the case. The Court had regard primarily to the failure by the defence to rely on this ground of appeal.

To be sure, it is understandable that the plea of 'defence secrets' or state secrets' should be invoked at the stage of duly authorised telephone taps. (*See Klass v. Germany* (1978); *Malone v. United Kingdom* (1984); *Huvig v. France* (1990); *Kruslin v. France* (1990).)) But once there are criminal proceedings and an indictment, the whole of the evidence, favourable or unfavourable to the defendant, must be communicated to the defence in order to be the subject of adversarial argument in accordance with Article 6 of the Convention. It is conceivable that a hearing may be held *in camera* so as to protect defence secrets or state secrets. In the *Edwards* case such a secret was not even involved; it was simply a question of documents and items of ordinary criminal evidence to the effect that Miss Sizer had not recognised the applicant and that the police had neglected to investigate the fingerprints.

In his memorial the applicant made the following pertinent observations:

At present the law of England and Wales permits the use in evidence of uncorroborated and disputed confession statements provided that the trial judge gives a
suitably worded warning to the jury in relation to the confession. A conviction can
be founded on such a confession.

The law in relation to this matter is presently under review by a Royal Commission.

Even if the jury did not accept such a submission, the fact of Miss Sizer's failure
to identify the applicant could itself have raised a reasonable doubt as to the identification of the applicant as the offender and accordingly a reasonable doubt as to
his guilt.

The applicant asks the Court to note that the jury convicted him by a majority
of ten to two, which indicates that two of the jurors entertained reasonable doubts
as to the applicant's guilt. Under domestic law, the applicant could not have been
convicted if three or more jurors had entertained such doubt. It would have required
only one more juror to entertain reasonable doubt in order for the applicant to be
acquitted. The evidence which was withheld from the applicant and the jury might
have produced such doubt in the mind of one more juror.

The fact that Miss Sizer had not identified the applicant was material obtained by
the prosecution but not used by it in its presentation of the case. As such, it should
have been disclosed to the applicant under the Attorney-General's Guidelines and
applying the principles of domestic law stated in *R v. Bryant* ((1946) 31 Cr. App. R.
146) and *R v. Clark* ((1930) 22 Cr. App. R. 58).

The fact that Miss Sizer had failed to identify the applicant, which fact was known
to the police before the trial, was unfairly, and in breach of Article 6(1) and (3)(d)
withheld from the applicant.

. . . .

In English criminal proceedings, the prosecution is required to disclose information of
the kind referred to above to the defence. It cannot be denied that such information was
not disclosed to the applicant in this case. The United Kingdom has failed to put forward
any explanation or justification for this failure to adhere to principles of domestic law
which ought, if adhered to, to secure compliance with Article 6.

The concealment of exonerating evidence and in other cases the fabrication of evidence
have plagued police investigations (remember the Birmingham Six and the *Ward* case).

This shows the importance of the assessment of such a situation in criminal proceedings, and the reservations called for by the decision of the Court of Appeal.

As the defence submitted, the essential point was the credibility of the police officers.
Before the Court the applicant argued as follows:

In those circumstances, it was vital for Mr Edwards to know that, when shown a
photograph of the various persons including himself (Mr Edwards), Miss Sizer had
failed to pick out Mr Edwards as the offender . . .

. . . .

If I may leave the trial at this stage and move to the Court of Appeal procedure,
the applicant accepts the well-established principle in the case law of this Court that in
considering the fairness of trial procedure under Article 6, the criminal proceedings taken

as a whole must be examined. It is also, however, clear that Article 6 requires a tribunal to carry out a fair and public hearing. In this case no one tribunal considered the case fully and with reference to all of the available material.

The submission of Mr Edwards is that the end result of the procedure, taking the trial and the appeal as one sequence of procedure, was a fragmentary procedure. Neither the individual elements of that procedure nor the procedure as a whole can be described as full and fair. Mr Edwards had two incomplete hearings before two separate courts. The trial hearing was an incomplete hearing in that evidence available to the prosecution was not made available to Mr Edwards. The Court of Appeal was similarly an incomplete hearing. Mr Edwards disagrees with the submission of the United Kingdom that all relevant material was before the Court of Appeal. Mr Edwards reminds the Court that the police conduct of the case against him was investigated by Detective Superintendent Robert Carmichael of the Humberside police force. That investigation followed upon complaints made by Mr Edwards himself about the conduct of the police.

Superintendent Carmichael concluded his report in December 1985. The Carmichael report was submitted to the Police Complaints Authority which in turn submitted the report to the Director of Public Prosecutions. The submission of the report led to the referral of the case to the Court of Appeal by the Secretary of State for Home Affairs.

The Carmichael report should not have been protected by any immunity, and should have been disclosed.

With respect to the failure by the defence to raise this ground of appeal in the Court of Appeal, this argument does not seem to me to be relevant. Such concealment is comparable to a ground of nullity for reasons of public policy in the continental system. Grounds of nullity can and must be raised by the court itself *ex officio*, even if the defence does not rely on them. For one cannot leave to a possibly inexperienced defence alone the burden of ensuring respect for the fundamental procedural rule which prohibits the concealment of documents or evidence. In the continental system such a fault on the part of the police may lead to criminal proceedings for malfeasance in public office. Cases where evidence has been hidden from the trial court have left bitter memories in the history of justice.

It seems clear to me that the Court of Appeal should have raised this ground of nullity of the proceedings of its own motion and remitted the case to a jury without prejudging what that jury's decision would have been, especially as the original jury had reached its decision by ten votes to two and one vote more would have meant an acquittal.

Under the European Convention an old doctrine such as that of 'public interest' must be revised in accordance with Article 6.

The European Court has on numerous occasions stated that it is essential that proceedings are 'adversarial' and the favourable and unfavourable evidence is subjected to adversarial examination. (*see, inter alia, Kostovski v. The Netherlands* (1989); *Cardot v. France* (1991); *Delta v. France*, 191 Eur. Ct. H.R. (ser. A) (1990)) This means that the prosecution must communicate the evidence to the defence. For this reason I find that there was a violation of Article 6 in the present case.

⁓

QUESTIONS & COMMENTS

(1) The UN Human Rights Committee has held that the state has an affirmative obligation to provide transportation to an alibi witness in a death penalty case. *Grant v. Jamaica*, Communication No. 353/1988, views adopted 31 March 1994, U.N. Doc. CCPR/C/50/D/353/1988 (1994) at §8.4 (reproduced above in Chapter 12(A)). Would such an affirmative right extend to noncapital cases? Should it?

(2) In *The Prosecutor v. Blaskic*, Case No. IT-95–14, Int'l Crim. Trib.-Yugo., Trial Chamber (21 January 1998), the trial chamber rejected the defense's argument that hearsay evidence was not admissible. The chamber noted that Rule 89(A) of the Rules of Procedure and Evidence states that "Chambers shall not be bound by national rules of evidence." Accordingly, the chamber held that

> neither the rules issuing from the common law tradition in respect of the admissibility of hearsay evidence nor the general principle prevailing in the civil law systems, according to which, barring exceptions, all relevant evidence is admissible, including hearsay evidence, because it is the judge who finally takes a decision on the weight to ascribe to it, are directly applicable before this Tribunal. The International Tribunal is, in fact, a *sui generis* institution with its own rules of procedure which do not merely constitute a transposition of national legal systems. The same holds for the conduct of the trial which, contrary to the Defence arguments, is not similar to an adversarial trial, but is moving towards a more hybrid system.

Given the hybrid character of the ICT-Y, in what other areas might the ICT-Y make a ruling that departs from the civil or common law?

Kostovski v. The Netherlands
European Court of Human Rights
166 Eur. Ct. H. R. (ser. A) (1989)
12 E.H.R.R.434 (1990)

. . . .

FACTS:

I. The particular circumstances of the case

9. Mr Slobodan Kostovski is a Yugoslav citizen born in 1953. He has a very long criminal record, including convictions for various crimes in the Netherlands, notably armed robbery at a jeweller's shop in 1979 for which he was sentenced to six years' imprisonment.

In November 1980 the Amsterdam District Court (*arrondissements-rechtbank*) had declared admissible a request by Sweden for his extradition to stand trial for serious offences committed in Stockholm in September 1979, namely two armed robberies and assisting in an escape from a court building, involving in each case attempted manslaughter.

On 8 August 1981 the applicant escaped from Scheveningen prison together with one Stanley Hillis and others; he remained on the run until the following April.

10. On 20 January 1982 three masked men conducted an armed raid on a bank in Baarn and made off with a substantial amount of currency and cheques.

Police suspicions centred on Stanley Hillis and his associates because, being on the run, they probably needed money and because some years previously Stanley Hillis had been directly involved in a robbery carried out at the same bank with exactly the same *modus operandi* as the 1982 raid. These suspicions were strengthened on 25 January, when the Amsterdam police received an anonymous telephone call from a man who said:

A few days ago a hold-up took place at a bank in Baarn. Those responsible for the hold-up are Stanley Hillis, Paul Molhoek and a Yugoslav. Stanley Hillis and the Yugoslav escaped from prison in The Hague in August last year.

11. On 26 January 1982 a man visited the police in The Hague. The reporting officer drew up, on 18 March, the following account of the interview:

On 26 January there appeared before me a man who for fear of reprisals desired to remain anonymous but whose identity is known to me. He stated as follows:

"A few months ago four men escaped from the remand centre (*huis van bewaring*) in The Hague, among them a Yugoslav and an Amsterdammer. They are now living with an acquaintance of theirs in Utrecht. I do not know the address. They are also in touch with Paul Molhoek of The Hague. The Yugoslav and the Amsterdammer sometimes spend the night at Aad Denie's home in Paul Krugerlaan in The Hague. Paul Molhoek sleeps there almost every night. The Yugoslav and the Amsterdammer now drive a blue BMW car; I do not know the registration number. Paul Molhoek drives a new white Mercedes sports car. The Yugoslav, the Amsterdammer and Paul Molhoek carried out a hold-up a few days ago on a bank in Baarn, in the course of which the staff of the bank were locked up. Aad Denie, who otherwise had nothing to do with the affair, takes Paul Molhoek to the two men in Utrecht every day because Paul Molhoek does not have a driving licence. Aad Denie drives a silver-grey BMW car, registration mark 84-PF-88."

I wish to add that, after being shown various photographs included in the police file, he picked out photos of the following persons: Slobodan Kostovski . . . as being the Yugoslav to whom he had referred; Stanley Marshall Hillis . . . as being the Amsterdammer in question.

12. On 27 January the Utrecht police, acting on information received that Stanley Hillis was hiding with a brother of Paul Molhoek at an address in that town, conducted a search there. Whilst they found no one, they did find fingerprints of Stanley Hillis and Paul Molhoek.

13. On 23 February 1982 a person visited the police in The Hague. The two reporting officers drew up, on 22 March, the following account of the interview:

On Tuesday 23 February 1982 there appeared before us a person who for security reasons wishes to remain anonymous but whose identity is known to us. He/she stated that he/she knew that Stanley Hillis, Slobodan Kostovski, Paul Molhoek and Aad Denie, who were known to him/her, were guilty of the armed raid on a branch of the Nederlandse Middenstands Bank at Nieuwstraat 1 in Baarn on or about 19 January 1982. According to the said person, the first three of the aforementioned persons had carried out the raid and Aad Denie had acted as driver or at least he had picked them up in a car after the raid.

The said person also stated that the proceeds of the raid, amounting to about Fl 600,000, had been divided into more or less equal parts by Hillis, Kostovski and Molhoek and that Aad Denie had received a small part thereof. From what he/she said, this would have been about Fl 20,000. The said person also stated that Hillis, Kostovski and Molhoek knew each other from when they were detained in Scheveningen prison.

Hillis and Kostovski escaped from prison on 8 August 1981 and Molhoek was released at a later date. The said person stated that Paul Molhoek lived most of the time with Aad Denie at Paul Krugerlaan 216 in The Hague. Hillis and Kostovski were said to have lived for a while at Oude Gracht 76 in Utrecht, which they had rented in another name. A brother of Paul Molhoek also lived there; he was called Peter. The said person stated in this connection that the Utrecht police had raided the said premises but had not found the abovementioned people. He/she said that Hillis, Kostovski and Molhoek were in a room on a higher floor of the same building in the Oude Gracht at the time of the police raid. The police had not searched that floor. The person in question also stated that Hillis was now believed to be living in Amsterdam.

Paul Molhoek and Hillis were said to meet each other quite regularly there, near Amstel Station, which was their usual meeting place.

According to the person in question, Hillis, Kostovski and Molhoek were in possession of powerful weapons. He/she knew that Hillis and Kostovski each had a Sten gun among other things and that Paul Molhoek had a revolver, possibly a Colt.45.

The person interviewed by us stated that he/she might later be able to provide more details about the abovementioned persons and the offences they had committed.

14. On 1 April 1982 Stanley Hillis and Slobodan Kostovski were arrested together in Amsterdam. They were in a car driven by one V, who had helped them to escape from prison and had had various contacts with them in and after January 1982.

On his arrest Slobodan Kostovski was in possession of a loaded revolver. Subsequently, firearms were also found in the home of Paul Molhoek, who was arrested on 2 April, in the home of V and in another room in the house previously searched in Utrecht.

Like the applicant, Stanley Hillis, Paul Molhoek, Aad Denie and V all have very long criminal records.

15. A preliminary judicial investigation (*gerechtelijk vooronderzoek*) was instituted in respect of Stanley Hillis, Slobodan Kostovski, Paul Molhoek and Aad Denie. On 8 April 1982 Mr Nuboer, the examining magistrate (*rechter-commissaris*), interviewed, in the presence of the police but in the absence of the public prosecutor and of the applicant and his counsel, the witness who had made a statement to the police in The Hague on 23 February. The magistrate, who did not know the person's identity, considered his/her fear of reprisals to be well-founded and therefore respected his/her wish to remain anonymous. His report on the hearing recorded that the witness made the following sworn statement:

On 23 February 1982 I made a statement to the police in The Hague which was included in a report drawn up on 22 March 1982. You read out that statement to me. I declared that it is the truth and that I stand by it, on the understanding that I was not aware that the bank in Baarn was at No 1 Nieuwstraat. My knowledge stems from the fact that both Stanley Hillis and Paul Molhoek, as well as Aad Denie, had all told me about the hold-up. They said that they had taken not only cash, but also American travellers' cheques and Eurocheques. I myself saw a number of the Eurocheques.

16. On 2 June 1982 the examining magistrate wrote to the lawyers acting for those concerned, enclosing copies of the official reports, including the statements of the anonymous person he had seen. He indicated that they could submit written questions on the basis of the statements made, pointing out that they would not be invited to the hearing before him. Amongst those who responded was Mr Kostovski's lawyer, Mrs Spronken, who submitted fourteen questions in a letter of 14 June.

On 22 June, as a result of those questions, the anonymous witness whom Mr Nuboer had heard was interviewed again, this time by Mr Weijsenfeld, an examining magistrate deputising for Mr Nuboer. The police were present but neither the public prosecutor nor the applicant or his counsel was. The magistrate's report of the hearing recorded that the witness – whose anonymity was respected on this occasion also – made the following sworn statement:

> I stand by the statement which I made on 8 April 1982 to the examining magistrate in Utrecht. My answers to the questions posed by Mrs Spronken are as follows.

> I am not the person who telephoned anonymously to the police communications centre in Amsterdam on 25 January 1982, nor the person who made a statement on 26 January 1982 at the police station in The Hague. I did not state to the police that I knew that the bank was at Nieuwestraat 1 in Baarn. I knew that it was in Baarn, but not the street. I learned the latter from the police and it was included as being part of my own statement by mistake. Although Mrs Sponken did not ask this, I would add that I did not inform the municipal police in Utrecht.

> As regards the questions posed by Van Straelen, I would in the first instance refer to the statement I have just made. I am acquainted with Hillis, Kostovski, Molhoek and Denie and have no doubts as to their identity.

In the event, only two of Mrs Spronken's fourteen questions, most of which concerned the circumstances in which the witness had obtained his/her information, were answered. In this connection Mr Weijsenfeld added the following in his report:

> The questions sent in, including those from SM Hillis, which have not been answered were either not asked by me, the examining magistrate, in order to preserve the anonymity of the witness, or not answered by the witness for the same reason.

17. The cases against Stanley Hillis, Slobodan Kostovski and Paul Molhoek came on for trial before the Utrecht District Court on 10 September 1982. Although for procedural reasons each case was dealt with separately and was the subject of a separate judgment, the court held a single sitting, so that the statements made thereat applied to all three suspects.

The witnesses heard in court included the examining magistrates Mr Nuboer and Mr Weijsenfeld and Mr Weijman, one of the police officers who had conducted the interview on 23 February. They had been called at the applicant's request, but the court, pursuant to Article 288 of the Code of Criminal Procedure, did not allow the defence to put to them certain questions designed to clarify the anonymous witnesses' reliability and sources of information, where answers would have revealed the latter's identity.

Mr Nuboer stated that he believed the witness he had heard on 8 April 1982, who had 'made a favourable impression' on him; that he did not know the witness's identity and considered the fear of reprisals advanced in support of his/her wish for anonymity to be a real one; that he believed the witness had made his/her statement to the police voluntarily; and that he had refused an offer by the police for him to interview the man they had seen on 26 January 1982 as he could not guarantee the latter's anonymity.

Mr Weijsenfeld stated that he considered to be 'not unreliable' the witness – whose identity he did not know – whom he had interviewed on 22 June 1982; and that he too regarded the witness's fear of reprisals as well-founded.

Mr Weijman stated that, in his view, the person he had interviewed with a colleague on 23 February 1982 was 'completely reliable' because he/she had also given information on other cases which had proved to be correct. He added that certain parts of that person's statement had been omitted from the official report in order to protect his/her identity.

18. The anonymous witnesses themselves were not heard at the trial. Contrary to a defence submission, the official reports drawn up by the police and the examining magistrates on the hearings of those witnesses were used in evidence. Also the sworn statements made by one of them to the magistrates were read out and designated as statements by a witness made at the trial, in accordance with Article 295 of the Code of Criminal Procedure.

In its judgments of 24 September 1982 the Utrecht District Court recognised, with regard to the use of the statements of the anonymous witnesses, that their sources of information could not be checked, that it could not form an independent view as to their reliability and that the accused were deprived of the possibility of being confronted with them. By way of justification for its decision nevertheless to use this material in evidence the court stated that it had been convinced of Mr Kostovski's guilt, considering that the statements strengthened and partly complemented each other and having regard to the views it had heard as to the reliability of one of the anonymous witnesses. Having also noted that the applicant had previously been found guilty of similar offences, the court convicted him and his co-accused of armed robbery and sentenced each of them to six years' imprisonment.

19. Mr Hillis, Mr Kostovski and Mr Molhoek – who have always denied any involvement in the bank raid – appealed to the Amsterdam Court of Appeal (*Gerechtshof*), which set aside the Utrecht District Court's judgments as it arrived at a different assessment of the evidence. However, after a retrial, at which the three cases were dealt with together, the Court of Appeal, by judgment of 27 May 1983, also convicted the applicant and his co-accused and imposed the same sentences as before.

On 13 May the Court of Appeal had heard a number of the witnesses previously heard at first instance, who stood by their earlier testimony. Like the Utrecht District Court, it had not allowed certain questions by the defence to be answered, where this would have revealed the identity of the anonymous witnesses. The following statement had also been made to the Court of Appeal by Chief Superintendent Alferink of The Hague municipal police:

> Consultations take place before anonymous witnesses are interviewed. It is customary for me to ascertain the identity of the witness to be interviewed in order to assess whether he or she could be in danger. In this case the anonymous witnesses were in real danger. The threat was real. Both witnesses decided to make statements on their own initiative. The public prosecutor was contacted, but I cannot remember who it was. The testimony of anonymous witnesses is offered to the examining magistrate after consultation with the public prosecutor. Both anonymous witnesses made a reliable impression on me.

The Court of Appeal likewise did not hear the anonymous witnesses but, again contrary to a defence submission, considered the official reports of their interviews with the police and the examining magistrates to be admissible evidence. The court found that the witnesses, who had made their statements on their own initiative, had good reason to fear reprisals; noted that they had made a reliable impression on Mr Alferink and a reasonably reliable one on Mr Nuboer; and took into account the connections between, and the mutual consistency of, the statements in question.

20. On 25 September 1984 the Supreme Court (*Hoge Raad*) dismissed an appeal by the applicant on points of law. It found that the Amsterdam Court of Appeal had adduced sufficient reasons for admitting the reports in question. It also stated that Article 6 of the Convention[15] did not prevent a judge, if he deemed it necessary in the interest of the proper administration of justice, from curtailing to some extent the obligation to answer questions and, notably, from allowing a witness not to answer questions about the identity of persons.

. . . .

II. Relevant domestic law and practice

A. The Code of Criminal Procedure

22. The Dutch Code of Criminal Procedure ('CCP') came into force on 1 January 1926. The citations appearing in the present judgment are taken from the CCP as it stood at the time of the applicant's trials.

23. Article 168 CCP provides that each District Court has one or more examining magistrates to whom criminal cases are entrusted. They are nominated, as for a term of two years, by the competent Court of Appeal from amongst the members of the District Court.

It is open to the public prosecutor, under Article 181 CCP, to request what is called – in order to distinguish it from the subsequent investigation at the trial – a 'preliminary investigation,' which it is the task of an examining magistrate to conduct. In that event the latter will hear the suspect, witnesses and experts as soon as possible and as often as is required. Both the public prosecutor and defence counsel are, in principle, entitled to be present at those hearings and, even if they are absent, to give notice of questions they wish to have put.

The preliminary investigation provides a basis for a decision with regard to the further prosecution of a suspect and also serves to clarify matters which cannot properly be investigated at the trial. The magistrate must act impartially, by collecting also evidence which might exculpate the suspect.

If the public prosecutor is of the opinion that the results of the preliminary investigation justify further prosecution, he will notify the suspect and refer the case to the court. The investigation at the trial will then follow.

24. Under Article 338 CCP, a finding that the accused has been proved to have committed the acts with which he is charged may be made by a judge only if he has been so convinced through the investigation at the trial, by 'legal means of evidence.' The latter consist, according to Article 339 CCP, exclusively of (i) what the judge has himself observed; (ii) statements made by the accused; (iii) statements made by a witness; (iv) statements made by an expert; and (v) written documents.

---

[15] [Dutch law incorporates the ECHR. Eds.' note.]

Evidence in the third category is defined in Article 342 CCP, which reads:

1. A statement by a witness is understood to be his statement, made in the investigation at the trial, of facts or circumstances which he himself has seen or experienced.

2. The judge cannot accept as proven that the defendant has committed the act with which he is charged, solely on the statement of one witness.

25. Articles 280 and 281–s295 CCP contain various provisions concerning the examination of witnesses at the trial, of which the following are of importance in the context of the present case.

(a) The president of the court must ask the witness to state, after his first names and surname, his age, occupation and address; the same obligation is also laid, by Article 190 CCP, on an examining magistrate when he is hearing witnesses.

(b) Articles 284, 285 and 286 CCP make it clear that the accused is entitled to put questions to a witness. As a general rule witnesses are examined first by the president of the court; however, a witness who has not been heard during the preliminary investigation and has been called at the request of the defence will be examined first by the accused and only afterwards by the president. In any event, Article 288 CCP empowers the court 'to prevent a question put by the accused, counsel for the defence or the public prosecutor being answered.'

(c) Article 292 CCP enables the president of the court to order an accused to leave the courtroom so that a witness may be examined out of his presence. If such an order – for which reasons do not have to be given – is made, counsel for the defence may question the witness and 'the accused shall be told immediately what has happened during his absence and only then will the investigation be resumed. Thus, on returning to the courtroom the accused may avail himself of his right, under Article 285 CCP, to put questions to the witness.

26. Article 295 CCP provides for an exception to the rule in Article 342 CCP that witnesses should be heard at the trial. It reads:

An earlier statement by a witness who, having been sworn in or admonished to speak the truth in accordance with Article 216(2), has died or, in the opinion of the court, is unable to appear at the trial shall be considered as having been made at the trial, on condition that it is read aloud there.

In connection with witnesses unable to appear at the trial, Article 187 CCP provides:

If the examining magistrate is of the opinion that there are grounds for assuming that the witness or the expert will not be able to appear at the trial, he shall invite the public prosecutor, the defendant and counsel to be present at the hearing before him, unless, in the interest of the investigation, that hearing cannot be delayed.

27. The fifth category of evidence listed in Article 339 CCP is defined in Article 344 CCP which, so far as is relevant, reads:

1. Written documents means:
1...;
2. official reports and other documents, drawn up in legal form by bodies and persons who have the proper authority and containing their statement of facts or circumstances which they themselves have seen or experienced;
....

5. all other documents; but these are valid only in conjunction with the content of other means of evidence.

2. The judge can accept as proven that the defendant has committed the act with which he is charged, on the official report of an investigating officer.

An anonymous statement contained in an official police report falls within the scope of sub-paragraph 22 of paragraph 1 of this Article.

B. Criminal procedure in practice

28. In the Netherlands, the procedure in a criminal case follows in actual practice a course that is markedly different from that suggested by the above provisions. This is to a considerable extent due to a leading judgment delivered by the Supreme Court on 20 December 1926, the year in which the CCP came into force. That judgment contains the following rulings, each of which is of importance in the context of the present case:

(a) for a statement by a witness to be considered as having been made at the trial under Article 295 CCP, it is immaterial whether or not the examining magistrate has complied with Article 187 CCP,

(b) a deposition by a witness concerning what he was told by another person (hearsay evidence) may be used as evidence, albeit with the utmost caution;

(c) it is permissible to use as evidence declarations made by the accused or by a witness to a police officer, as recorded in the latter's official report.

29. These rulings permit the use, as 'legal means of evidence' within the meaning of Articles 338 and 339 CCP, of depositions made by a witness not at the trial but before a police officer or the examining magistrate, provided they are recorded in an official report which is read aloud in court. The rulings have had the effect that in practice the importance of the investigation at the trial – which is never conducted before a jury – has dwindled. In the great majority of cases witnessed are not heard at the trial but either only by the police or also by the examining magistrate.

30. The law does not make the presence of counsel for the defence obligatory during the investigation by the police. The same applies to the preliminary investigation by the examining magistrate. Nowadays, however, most examining magistrates invite the accused and his counsel to attend when they are hearing witnesses.

C. The anonymous witness: case law

31. The CCP contains no express provisions on statements by anonymous witnesses.

However, with the increase in violent, organised crime a need was felt to protect those witnesses who had justification for fearing reprisals, by granting them anonymity. In a series of judgments the Supreme Court has made this possible.

32. A precursor to this development was a judgment of 17 January 1938 in which the Supreme Court held that hearsay evidence could be admitted even if the witness did not name his informant. Decisions to the same effect were handed down in the 1980s.

In a judgment of 5 February 1980, concerning a case where the examining magistrate had granted anonymity to and had heard a witness without the accused or his counsel being present, the Supreme Court held – following its judgment of 20 December 1926 – that non-compliance with Article 187 CCP did not prevent the magistrate's official report being used in evidence, 'albeit with the caution called for when assessing the probative value of such evidence.' The same ruling was made in a judgment of 4 May 1981, concerning a case where the witness had been heard anonymously by both the police and the examining magistrate; on that occasion the Supreme Court also held – in accordance with its abovementioned judgment of 17 January 1938 – that the mere fact that the official reports of the hearings did not name the witness was not an obstacle to their utilisation in evidence, subject to an identical proviso as to caution.

It may be inferred from a judgment of 29 November 1983 that the caution called for does not necessarily imply that anonymous witnesses must also have been heard by the examining magistrate.

The next judgments in the series are those given by the Supreme Court on 25 September 1984 in the cases of Mr Kostovski and his co-accused. They contain the following new elements:

> (a) the mere fact that the examining magistrate did not know the identity of the witness does not prevent the use in evidence of the official report of the hearing he conducted;
>
> (b) if the defence contests at the trial the reliability of depositions by an anonymous witness, as recorded in the official report of the hearing of the witness, but the court nevertheless decides to admit them as evidence, it must give reasons justifying that decision.

These principles were confirmed in a judgment of 21 May 1985, which makes it clear that the Supreme Court's review of the reasons given to justify the admission of anonymous statements as evidence is only a marginal one.

D. Law reform

33. In their submissions preceding certain of the Supreme Court's judgments referred to in §32 above, various Advocates General, whilst recognising that the granting of anonymity to witnesses could not always be avoided and sometimes had to be accepted as the lesser evil, nevertheless voiced concern. The learned writers who annotated the judgments did likewise, stressing the need for the courts to be very cautious indeed. The judgments have, however, also been criticised.

34. In 1983 the Association of Judges expressed disquiet at the increase in cases in which witnesses were threatened and at the growing number of witnesses who refused to testify unless they were granted anonymity. The Association recommended that the legislature should direct its attention to the question of anonymous witnesses.

The Minister of Justice consequently set up in September 1984 an external advisory committee, called 'the Commission on Threatened Witnesses,' to examine the problem. In its report of 11 June 1986, which was later submitted for advice to several bodies concerned with the application of the criminal law, the Commission concluded, with only one member dissenting, as follows:

> In some cases one cannot avoid anonymity of witnesses. Reference is made to the fact (which was also pointed out by the Minister) that at present there are forms of organised criminality of a gravity that the legislature of the day would not have considered possible.

The Commission added that 'in a society governed by the rule of law the interference with, or more accurately the frustration of, the course of justice resulting [from this situation] cannot possibly be accepted.'

The Commission proposed that the law should in principle forbid the use as evidence of statements by anonymous witnesses. It should, however, be possible to make an exception where the witness would run an unacceptable risk if his or her identity were known. In such cases an anonymous statement might be admitted as evidence if the witness had been examined by an examining magistrate, the accused being given a right of appeal against the latter's decision to grant anonymity. The report contains a Bill making the necessary modifications to the CCP (with draft explanatory notes) and comparative data.

According to the Government, initiation of legislation in this area has been deferred pending the Court's decision in the present case.

. . . .

[Kostovski applied to the European Commission of Human Rights, which unanimously found violations to Article 6(1) and 3(d) in that he had not been able to cross-examine the anonymous witnesses or challenge their statements.]

DECISION:

I. Alleged violation of Article 6

37. The essence of Mr Kostovski's claim was that he had not received a fair trial. In this connection he relied mainly on the following provisions of Article 6 of the Convention:

1. In the determination of . . . any criminal charge against him, everyone is entitled to a fair and public hearing . . . by an independent and impartial tribunal . . .

. . .

3. Everyone charged with a criminal offence has the following minimum rights:

. . .

(d) to examine or have examined witnesses against him and to obtain the attendance and examination of witnesses on his behalf under the same conditions as witnesses against him;

. . . '

The Commission arrived at the conclusion, which was contested by the Government, that there had been a breach of paragraph (1), taken together with paragraph (3)(d), of Article 6.

38. The source of the applicant's allegation was the use as evidence, by the Utrecht District Court and the Amsterdam Court of Appeal, of reports of statements by two anonymous persons. The latter had been heard by the police and, in one case, also by the examining magistrate but were not themselves heard at either of the trials.

39. It has to be recalled at the outset that the admissibility of evidence is primarily a matter for regulation by national law. Again, as a general rule it is for the national courts to assess the evidence before them.

In the light of these principles the Court sees its task in the present case as being not to express a view as to whether the statements in question were correctly admitted and assessed but rather to ascertain whether the proceedings considered as a whole, including the way in which evidence was taken, were fair.

This being the basic issue, and also because the guarantees in Article 6(3) are specific aspects of the right to a fair trial set forth in paragraph (1), the Court will consider the applicant's complaints from the angle of paragraphs (3)(d) and (1) taken together.

40. The Court notes that only one of the authors of the statements – namely the person whose statements were read out at the trial – was, under Dutch law, regarded as a 'witness.'

However, in view of the autonomous interpretation to be given to this term, both authors should be so regarded for the purposes of Article 6(3)(d) of the Convention, since the statements of both of them, whether read out at the trial or not, were in fact before the court and were taken into account by it.

41. In principle, all the evidence must be produced in the presence of the accused at a public hearing with a view to adversarial argument. This does not mean, however, that in order to be used as evidence statements of witnesses should always be made at a public hearing in court: to use as evidence such statements obtained at the pre-trial stage is not in itself inconsistent with paragraphs (3)(d) and (1) of Article 6, provided the rights of the defence have been respected.

As a rule, these rights require that an accused should be given an adequate and proper opportunity to challenge and question a witness against him, either at the time the witness was making his statement or at some later stage of the proceedings.

42. Yet such an opportunity was not afforded to the applicant in the present case, although there could be no doubt that he desired to challenge and question the anonymous persons involved. Not only were the latter not heard at the trials but also their declarations were taken, whether by the police or the examining magistrate, in the absence of Mr Kostovski and his counsel. Accordingly, at no stage could they be questioned directly by him or on his behalf.

It is true that the defence was able, before both the Utrecht District Court and the Amsterdam Court of Appeal, to question one of the police officers and both of the examining magistrates who had taken the declarations. It was also able, but as regards only one of the anonymous persons, to submit written questions to him/her indirectly through the examining magistrate. However, the nature and scope of the questions it could put in either of these ways was considerably restricted by reason of the decision that the anonymity of the authors of the statements should be preserved.

The latter feature of the case compounded the difficulties facing the applicant. If the defence is unaware of the identity of the person it seeks to question, it may be deprived of the very particulars enabling it to demonstrate that he or she is prejudiced, hostile or unreliable. Testimony or other declarations inculpating an accused may well be designedly untruthful or simply erroneous and the defence will scarcely be able to bring this to light if it lacks the information permitting it to test the author's reliability or cast doubt on his credibility. The dangers inherent in such a situation are obvious.

43. Furthermore, each of the trial courts was precluded by the absence of the anonymous persons from observing their demeanour under questioning and thus forming its own impression of their reliability. The courts admittedly heard evidence on the latter point and no doubt – as is required by Dutch law – they observed caution in evaluating the statements in question, but this can scarcely be regarded as a proper substitute for direct observation.

It is true that one of the anonymous persons was heard by examining magistrates. However, the Court is bound to observe that – in addition to the fact that neither the applicant nor his counsel was present at the interviews – the examining magistrates themselves were unaware of the person's identity, a situation which cannot have been without implications for the testing of his/her reliability. As for the other anonymous person, he was not heard by an examining magistrate at all, but only by the police.

In these circumstances it cannot be said that the handicaps under which the defence laboured were counterbalanced by the procedures followed by the judicial authorities.

44. The Government stressed the fact that case law and practice in the Netherlands in the matter of anonymous evidence stemmed from an increase in the intimidation of witnesses and were based on a balancing of interests of society, the accused and the witnesses. It pointed out that in the present case it had been established that the authors of the statements in question had good reason to fear reprisals.

As on previous occasions the Court does not underestimate the importance of the struggle against organised crime. Yet the Government's line of argument, whilst not without force, is not decisive.

Although the growth in organised crime doubtless demands the introduction of appropriate measures, the Government's submissions appear to the Court to lay insufficient weight on what the applicant's counsel described as 'the interest of everybody in a civilised society in a controllable and fair judicial procedure.' The right to a fair administration of justice holds so prominent a place in a democratic society that it cannot be sacrificed to expediency. The Convention does not preclude reliance, at the investigation stage of criminal proceedings, on sources such as anonymous informants. However, the subsequent use of anonymous statements as sufficient evidence to found a conviction, as in the present case, is a difficult matter. It involved limitations on the rights of the defence which were irreconcilable with the guarantees contained in Article 6. In fact, the Government accepted that the applicant's conviction was based 'to a decisive extent' on the anonymous statements.

45. The Court therefore concludes that in the circumstances of the case the constraints affecting the rights of the defence were such that Mr Kostovski cannot be said to have received a fair trial. There was accordingly a violation of paragraph (3)(d), taken together with paragraph (1), of Article 6.

. . . .

~

QUESTIONS & COMMENTS

(1) In a later case, *Doorson v. The Netherlands*, – Eur. Ct. H.R. (ser. A) (1996), the European Court found that the use of anonymous witnesses was compatible with Article 6 if the accused's lawyer were present during the questioning of the witnesses and able to cross-examine these witnesses. Although it may have been preferable for the accused to have attended the questioning of the witnesses, the presence and participation of his counsel was sufficient for the purposes of Article 6(3)(d), ECHR. In addition, although the witnesses did not identify the accused in person, they did identify him through a photograph that he himself acknowledged to be of himself. Because of the foregoing, the "counterbalancing" procedure followed by the authorities in obtaining the evidence of the witnesses was considered sufficient to have enabled the defense to challenge or impeach their testimony. Furthermore, the national court did not base its finding of guilt solely or even to a decisive extent on the evidence of these anonymous witnesses.

(2) Compare the ruling governing witness identification issued by the International Criminal Tribunal for the Former Yugoslavia. For the identity of witnesses to be withheld from the accused, the trial chamber identified five criteria:

(i) there must exist a "real fear" for the safety of the witness or her/his family;

(ii) the testimony of the witness must be "important enough to the Prosecutor's case . . . to make it unfair . . . to compel the Prosecutor to proceed without it";

(iii) the Trial Chamber must be satisfied that there is no prima facie evidence that the witness is untrustworthy or partial;

(iv) the ineffectiveness or non-existence of a witness protection program must be taken into account; and

(v) the measures taken "should be strictly necessary" so that the accused suffers "no undue avoidable prejudice."

Furthermore, the trial chamber proposed the following procedural safeguards:

(i) the judges must be able to observe the demeanour of the witness in order to assess the reliability of the testimony;

(ii) the judges must know the identity of the witness in order to test the reliability of the witness;

(iii) the defense must be allowed ample opportunity to question the witness on issues unrelated to his/her identity or current whereabouts; and

(iv) the identity of the witness must be released when there are no longer reasons to fear for the witness' security.

International Criminal Tribunal for the Former Yugoslavia, 17 *Bulletin* 6–7 (22 April 1997); *see also The Prosecutor v. Tadic*, Case No. IT-94–1, Decision on Prosecutor's Motion Requesting Protective Measures for Victims and Witnesses, Int'l Crim. Trib.-Yugo. Chamber (18 August 1995); Christine M. Chinkin, *Due Process and Witness Anonymity*, 91 AM. J. INT'L L. 75 (1997).

Do you think this is fair? Consider the underlying reasons for not allowing anonymous witnesses given by the U.S. Supreme Court. In *Smith v. Illinois*, 390 U.S. 129 (1968), the prosecution's key witness was an informer who testified that he had bought heroin from the defendant. This witness identified himself using an alias, and the defense counsel's questions about his real name and address were rejected by the court. The U.S. Supreme Court held that the trial court's ruling violated the defendant's right to confrontation. The Supreme Court noted that witnesses' names and addresses are essential to the defense in opening "countless avenues of in-court examination and out-of-court investigation." *Id.* at 131. Is this concern sufficiently addressed by the ICT-Y and the European Court of Human Rights in *Doorson*? FRANCISCO FORREST MARTIN ET AL., 1 INTERNATIONAL HUMAN RIGHTS LAW & PRACTICE: CASES, TREATIES AND MATERIALS 590 (1997).

(3) The trial chamber for the ICT-Y has ruled that in cases of victims of sexual assault testifying, the use of screens to prevent the witness from seeing the accused (but not the accused from seeing the witness) is sufficient. Closed-circuit television is not necessary. International Criminal Tribunal for the Former Yugoslavia, 17 *Bulletin* 6 (22 April 1997).

(4) In *Compass v. Jamaica*, Communication No. 375/1989, views adopted 19 October 1993, U.N. Doc. CCPR/C/49/D/375/1989 (1993), the UN Human Rights Committee held that the failure of the trial judge to instruct the jury as to the dangers of dock identifications during the trial did not violate the right to a fair trial under Article 14, ICCPR. Relying on its previous caselaw, the Committee held that the review of jury instructions by the Committee is beyond the scope of Article 14 – "unless it can be ascertained that the instructions to the jury were clearly arbitrary or amounted to a denial of justice." *Id.* at §4.6. Do you think that other international tribunals would rule differently?

Prosecutor v. Kayishema & Ruzindana
Case No. ICTR-95-1-A
International Criminal Tribunal for Rwanda – Appeals Chamber
(1 June 2001)

. . . .

2. Inequality of arms

(a) Kayishema's arguments

63. During proceedings before the Trial Chamber, Counsel for Kayishema filed a Motion calling for full equality of arms between the Prosecution and the Defence [ ] (that is, both parties must be afforded the same means and resources). The Trial Chamber rejected this argument and held that "the rights of the accused and equality between the parties should not be confused with the equality of means and resources" [ ] and that "the rights of the accused should not be interpreted to mean that the Defence is entitled to same means and resources as the Prosecution". [ ] Kayishema submits that this holding constitutes an error in law. [ ]

64. Furthermore, Kayishema submits that due to the lack of permission from Rwanda his Counsel could not visit before trial the sites referred to in the Indictment so as to verify the Prosecutor's assertions *in situ*. The fact that the Prosecutor was able to visit the said sites while the Defence Counsel could not, is, in Kayishema's submission, an error of fact under Article 24 of the Statute [ ].

65. Kayishema also argues that Defence witnesses were very few since the Defence could only locate and contact a few. [ ] Kayishema further contends that the fact that the Judgement failed to address this issue is an error of fact and of law under Article 24 of the Statute.

66. It is Kayishema's submission that the proceedings were also characterized by the inequality of arms between the parties since the Prosecution was afforded one month to prepare its submissions, while the Defence was allowed only eight days.

(b) Discussion

67. The right of an accused to a fair trial implies the principle of equality of arms between the Prosecution and the Defence. [ ] The Appeals Chamber finds that the Trial Chamber rightly held that:

> "The notion of equality of arms is laid down in Article 20 of the Statute. Specifically, Article 20(2) states, '... the accused shall be entitled to a fair and public hearing ...' Article 20(4) also provides, '... the accused shall be entitled to the following minimum guarantees, in full equality ...,' then follows a series of rights that must be respected, including the right to a legal counsel and the right to have adequate time and facilities to prepare his or her defence." [ ]

68. The Trial Chamber dismissed Kayishema's motion suggesting a duty to seek full equality between the Prosecutor and the Defence. [ ]

69. The Appeals Chamber observes in this regard that equality of arms between the Defence and the Prosecution does not necessarily amount to the material equality of possessing the same financial and/or personal resources. [ ] In deciding on the scope of

the principle of equality of arms, ICTY Appeals Chamber in Tadič held that "equality of arms obligates a judicial body to ensure that neither party is put at a disadvantage when presenting its case". [ ]

70. The Appeals Chamber endorses the Trial Chamber's ruling. [ ]This is to ensure that the guarantees set forth in Article 20(2) and (4) of the Statute are respected. [ ]

71. Consequently, the Appeals Chamber holds that the Trial Chamber did not commit an error on a question of law under Article 24 of the Statute.

72. Regarding the fact that Counsel for Kayishema were unable to travel to sites in Rwanda referred to in the Indictment, the Appeals Chamber wishes, firstly, to recall the Trial Chamber's finding:

> "The question of equality of arms was verbally raised on other occasions. The Defence Counsel complained, for example, of the impossibility to verify the technical and material data about Kibuye *préfecture* submitted by the Prosecution. However, the Trial Chamber is aware that investigators, paid [for] by the Tribunal, [was] put at the disposal of the Defence. Furthermore, Article 17 (C) establishes that any expenses incurred in the preparation of the Defence case relating, *inter alia*, to investigative costs are to be met by the Tribunal. *The Trial Chamber is satisfied that all the necessary provisions for the preparation of a comprehensive defence were available*, and were afforded to all Defence Counsel in this case. The utilisation of those resources is not a matter for the Trial Chamber". [ ]

Kayishema alleges that there was an error in law within the meaning of Article 24 of the Statute as "the Prosecutor herself visited the sites and Defence Counsel did not." [ ] In his Brief, Kayishema does not present any argument nor does he adduce evidence in support of this allegation. Similarly, he does not present any arguments to demonstrate that the fact that Defence Counsel were unable to visit Rwanda in person deprived him of a reasonable opportunity to plead his case. The Appeals Chamber agrees with the Trial Chamber's position and finds that the mere fact of not being able to travel to Rwanda is not sufficient to establish inequality of arms between the Prosecution and the Defence. Investigators, paid by the Tribunal, were put at the disposal of the Defence and the Trial Chamber was satisfied that "all the necessary provisions for the preparation of a comprehensive defence were available, and were afforded to all Defence Counsel in this case." [ ]

73. The Appeals Chamber concurs with ICTY Appeals Chamber's position expressed in *Tadič*, that the principle of equality of arms does not apply to "conditions, outside the control of a court", [ ] that prevented a party from securing the attendance of certain witnesses. Consequently, the Appeals Chamber dismisses Kayishema's claim that problems encountered in locating and contacting potential witnesses allegedly constitutes an error in fact and in law under Article 20 of the Statute.

74. The Appeals Chamber notes that the question of equality of arms with respect to the procedure was examined by the Trial Chamber, which found that designated time-limits had been accorded to both parties. [ ]The Appeals Chamber holds that the Defence closing arguments do not constitute a response to the Prosecutor's closing brief and that the Defence had no cause to wait for the Prosecutor's closing remarks to prepare their

closing arguments. The Appeals Chamber endorses the opinion expressed by the Trial Chamber that:

> "(...) were any particular issues of dispute or dissatisfaction to have arisen, the Trial Chamber should have been seized of these concerns in the appropriate manner and at the appropriate time. A cursory reference in the closing brief, and a desultory allusion in Counsel's closing remarks is not an appropriate mode of raising the issue before the Chamber." [ ]

The Appeals Chamber finds that the Trial Chamber did not commit any error in the exercise of its discretion and that there is nothing in Kayishema's Brief to support his allegation.

   . . . .

∼

QUESTIONS & COMMENTS

(1) If the defense counsel did not avail himself of the investigators provided by the ICTR, could have the defendant successfully raised the issue of the adequacy of counsel provided by his defense counsel?

Self-Incrimination

Funke v. France
European Court of Human Rights
256-A Eur. Ct. H. R. (ser. A) (1993)

   . . . .

FACTS:

THE CIRCUMSTANCES OF THE CASE

6. Mr Jean-Gustave Funke, a German national, was born in 1925 and died on 22 July 1987. He worked as a sales representative and lived in France, at Lingolsheim (Bas-Rhin). His widow, Mrs Ruth Funke, nee Monney, is French and lives in Strasbourg.

The house search and the seizures

7. On 14 January 1980 three Strasbourg customs officers, accompanied by a senior police officer (*officier de police judiciaire*), went to the house of the applicant and his wife to obtain 'particulars of their assets abroad'; they were acting on information received from the tax authorities in Metz.

Mr Funke admitted having, or having had, several bank accounts abroad for professional and family reasons and said that he did not have any bank statements at his home.

The customs officers searched the premises from 10.30 am to 3.00 pm, and discovered statements and cheque-books from foreign banks, together with a German car-repair bill and two cameras. They seized all these items and on the same day drew up a report.

8. The customs officers' search and the seizures did not lead to any criminal proceedings for offences against the regulations governing financial dealings with foreign

countries. They did, however, give rise to parallel proceedings for disclosure of documents and for interim orders.

The proceedings for disclosure of documents (14 January 1980-18 December 1990)

The main proceedings

9. During their search on 14 January 1980 the customs officers asked the applicant to produce the statements for the previous three years – that is to say 1977, 1978 and 1979 – of his accounts at the Postsparkasse in Munich, the PKO in Warsaw, the Societe de Banque Suisse in Basle and the Deutsche Bank in Kehl and of his house-purchase savings plan at the Wurttembergische Bausparkasse in Leonberg and, lastly, his share portfolio at the Deutsche Bank in Kehl.

10. Mr Funke undertook to do so but later changed his mind.

(i) In the Strasbourg police court

11. On 3 May 1982 the customs authorities summoned him before the Strasbourg police court seeking to have him sentenced to a fine (*amende*) and a further penalty (*astreinte*) of 50 FF a day until such [ ] time as he produced the bank statements; they also made an application to have him committed to prison.

12. On 27 September 1982 the court imposed a fine of 1,200 FF on the applicant and ordered him to produce to the customs authorities the bank statements of his accounts at the Societe de Banque Suisse in Basle, the PKO in Warsaw and the Deutsche Bank in Kehl and of his savings account at the Wurttembergische Bausparkasse in Leonberg and all documents concerning the financing of the flat he had bought at Schonach (Federal Republic of Germany), on penalty of 20 FF per day's delay.

The reasons given for its judgment were the following:

...

On 12 February 1980 Mr Funke told the Customs Service that he was unable to make available the documents that he had undertaken to produce.

He has provided no reason for this and has submitted no correspondence that would show he took the necessary steps to obtain the required documents or would prove that the foreign banks refused to supply him with any such document.

Mr Funke acknowledged that, together with his brother, he bought a bedsitter at Schonach (Federal Republic of Germany) and produced photocopies of the contract of sale and of the entry in the land register; but he refused to produce documents concerning the financing of the purchase.

Section 65 of the Customs Code provides: 'Customs officers with the rank of at least inspector . . . may require production of papers and documents of any kind relating to operations of interest to their department.'

It appears from the present proceedings taken by the customs authorities that the prosecuting officer has the rank of inspector.

The documents sought, namely the bank statements and the documents relating to the financing of the purchase of the flat, can be brought within the category of documents covered by section 65 of the Customs Code.

The same section 65 provides in paragraph 1(i) that such requests for production may be made 'on the premises of (*chez*) any natural or legal person directly or indirectly concerned in lawful or unlawful operations falling within the jurisdiction of the Customs Service.'

In this context the term '*chez*' must not be restricted to 'at the home of' (*au domicile de*) but must be construed as meaning 'wherever . . . may be' (*auprès de*).

Any other construction would enable the person concerned to evade the Customs Service's investigations by keeping any compromising papers elsewhere than at his home.

The house search and Mr Funke's own statements provided sufficient evidence that there were bank accounts and financing operations concerning the defendant to enable the Customs Service to exercise their right of inspection in relation to the relevant documents notwithstanding that these were not at Mr Funke's home.

As the holder of an account used abroad, Mr Funke, like any account-holder, must receive statements following any transaction on the account. A statement is an extension, a reflection of the situation, of an account at a given time. The holder of the account is the owner of his statements and may at any time ask for them from his bank, which cannot refuse them.

(ii) In the Colmar Court of Appeal

13. Appeals were brought by Mr Funke, the public prosecutor and the customs authorities. On 14 March 1983 the Colmar Court of Appeal upheld the judgment of the court below other than as regards the inspection of documents relating to the flat at Schonach, and increased the pecuniary penalty to 50 FF per day's delay.

It dealt with Mr Funke's argument based on the Convention as follows:

> Section 413 *bis* of the Customs Code, which applies to financial dealings with foreign countries by virtue of section 451 of the same code, makes any refusal to produce documents and any concealment of documents in the cases provided for, *inter alia*, in section 65 of the aforementioned code punishable by imprisonment for a period ranging from ten days to one month and a fine of 400 to 2,000 FF.
>
> Under section 65, customs officers may require production of documents of any kind relating to operations of interest to their department, in general, on the premises of any natural or legal person directly or indirectly concerned in lawful or unlawful operations falling within the jurisdiction of the Customs Service.
>
> In the instant case Funke is liable only to a fiscal penalty: to a fine, therefore.
>
> It does not appear that the power conferred by the aforementioned provisions on a revenue authority conflicts with the protection of human rights and fundamental freedoms which it is the purpose of the instrument of international law relied on to guarantee.
>
> The defendant had a fair hearing.
>
> Obviously, no offences which performance of the duty to produce documents may disclose are yet before the courts; that being so, Funke's objections of principle are premature.
>
> Moreover, while everyone charged with a criminal offence is to be presumed innocent until proved guilty according to law, Article 6(2) of the Convention does not otherwise restrict the type of evidence which the *lex fori* places at the disposal of the prosecuting party in order to satisfy the court.
>
> Lastly, the obligation on a defendant to produce in proceedings evidence likely to be used against him by the opposing side is not a special feature of customs or tax proceedings since it is enacted in Article 11 of the New Code of Civil Procedure likewise.
>
> On the other hand, while Article 8 of the Convention provides that everyone has the right to respect for his private life and his correspondence, there may be

interference by a public authority with the exercise of this right so long as it is in accordance with the law and amounts to a measure which is necessary in a democratic society, *inter alia* in the interests of the economic well-being of the country or for the prevention of disorder or crime.

In most of the countries signatories to the Convention, moreover, the customs and revenue authorities have a right of direct investigation in banks.

(iii) In the Court of Cassation

14. On 21 November 1983 the Court of Cassation (Criminal Division) dismissed an appeal on points of law by Mr Funke. The third and final ground, in which Articles 6 and 8 of the Convention were prayed in aid, was rejected in the following terms:

> The Court of Appeal held that, while everyone charged with a criminal offence was to be presumed innocent until proved guilty according to law, Article 6 of the Convention ... did not otherwise restrict the types of evidence that the '*lex fori*' placed at the disposal of the prosecuting party in order to satisfy the court; and that while it was true that Article 8 of the Convention provided that everyone has the right to respect for his private life and his correspondence, there might ... be interference by a public authority with the exercise of this right so long as the interference was in accordance with the law and amounted to a measure which was necessary in a democratic society, *inter alia*, in the interests of the economic well-being of the country or for the prevention of disorder or crime.
>
> In so stating, and irrespective of any superfluous reasoning, the Court of Appeal justified its decision and the ground therefore cannot be upheld.

. . . .

RELEVANT CUSTOMS LAW

26. The criminal provisions of customs law in France are treated as a special body of criminal law.

. . . .

30. Section 65–1 of the Customs Code gives the customs authorities a special right of inspection:

> Customs officers with the rank of at least inspector (*inspecteur or officier*) and those performing the duties of collector may require production of papers and documents of any kind relating to operations of interest to their department;
>
> . . .
>
> (i) in general, on the premises of any natural or legal person directly or indirectly concerned in lawful or unlawful operations falling within the jurisdiction of the Customs Service.

The Sanction

31. Anyone refusing to produce documents is liable to imprisonment for a period ranging from 10 days to one month and to a fine of 600 to 3,000 FF (section 413 bis-1) of the Customs Code.

Furthermore, a pecuniary penalty of not less than 10 FF per day's delay may be imposed on him (section 431) and he may be committed to prison for non-payment (section 382).

. . . .

[Funke applied to the European Commission of Human Rights which found that his criminal conviction for refusal to produce the documents requested by the customs had violated his right to a fair trial under Article 6(1).]

DECISION [OF THE EUROPEAN COURT OF HUMAN RIGHTS]:

I. ALLEGED VIOLATION OF ARTICLE 6(1) AND (2)

Mr Funke claimed to be the victim of breaches of Articles 6(1) and (2)....

A. Fairness of the proceedings and presumption of innocence

....

2. Merits of the complaint

(a) Article 6(1)

In the applicant's submission, his conviction for refusing to disclose the documents asked for by the customs (*see* §§9 to 14 above) had infringed his right to a fair trial as secured in Article 6(1). He claimed that the authorities had violated the right not to give evidence against oneself, a general principle enshrined both in the legal orders of the Contracting States and in the European Convention and the International Covenant on Civil and Political Rights, as although they had not lodged a complaint alleging an offence against the regulations governing financial dealings with foreign countries, they had brought criminal proceedings calculated to compel Mr Funke to co-operate in a prosecution mounted against him. Such a method of proceeding was, he said, all the more unacceptable as nothing prevented the French authorities from seeking international assistance and themselves obtaining the necessary evidence from the foreign States.

The Government emphasised the declaratory nature of the French customs and exchange-control regime, which saved taxpayers having their affairs systematically investigated but imposed duties in return, such as the duty to keep papers concerning their income and property for a certain length of time and to make them available to the authorities on request. This right of the State to inspect certain documents, which was strictly supervised by the Court of Cassation, did not mean that those concerned were obliged to incriminate themselves, a requirement that was prohibited by the United Nations Covenant (Article 14) and had been condemned by the Court of Justice of the European Communities (*Orkem* judgment)'; it was not contrary to the guidelines laid down in the Convention institutions' case law on what constituted a fair trial.

In the instant case the customs had not required Mr Funke to confess to an offence or to provide evidence of one himself; they had merely asked him to give particulars of evidence found by their officers and which he had admitted, namely the bank statements and cheque-books discovered during the house search. As to the courts, they had assessed, after adversarial proceedings, whether the customs' application was justified in law and in fact.

The Commission reached the same conclusion, mainly on the basis of the special features of investigation procedures in business and financial matters. It considered that neither the obligation to produce bank statements nor the imposition of pecuniary penalties offended the principle of a fair trial; the former was a reflection of the State's confidence in all its citizens in that no use was made of stricter supervisory measures, while responsibility for the detriment caused by the latter lay entirely with the person affected where he refused to co-operate with the authorities.

The Court notes that the customs secured Mr Funke's conviction in order to obtain certain documents which they believed must exist, although they were not certain of the fact. Being unable or unwilling to procure them by some other means, they attempted to compel the applicant himself to provide the evidence of offences he had allegedly committed. The special features of customs law (*see* §§30 to 31 above) cannot justify such an infringement of the right of anyone 'charged with a criminal offence,' within the autonomous meaning of this expression in Article 6, to remain silent and not to contribute to incriminating himself.

There has accordingly been a breach of Article 6(1).

. . . .

～

QUESTIONS & COMMENTS

(1) The European Court has allowed the drawing of adverse inferences from a criminal defendant's silence under strict conditions. In *Murray v. United Kingdom*, Case No. 41/1994/488/570, – Eur. Ct. H.R. (ser. A) (1996), the applicant, an alleged IRA member, was arrested in a house where an informer had been held captive. The informer testified that he had been forced to make a tape-recorded confession and that he later saw the applicant pulling a tape out of cassette recorder at the house after his release by the police.

After his arrest, the applicant declined to answer police questions eight times during his interrogation. Police warned him each time that adverse inferences could be drawn from his silence. This police practice was based on a new and controversial statute that had superceded the commonlaw, which held the opposite. The new statute had been enacted for security reasons, *viz.*, to suppress illegal IRA operations.

For the first forty-eight hours, the police denied the applicant access to his lawyer, and even after the applicant was given access, his solicitor was not allowed to attend the interrogation. During his trial, the applicant continued to remain silent. In finding the applicant guilty for aiding and abetting false imprisonment, the judge relied on the applicant's refusal to answer questions both during this police interrogation and trial.

The European Court held that there was no Article 6 violation for the judge's drawing of adverse inferences. Although noting that silence in itself cannot be regarded as an indication of guilt, there were conditions in which adverse inferences could be drawn lawfully under Article 6. First, the Court noted that the judge was experienced. Second, warnings were given to the applicant. Third, the evidence was sufficiently strong against the applicant to call for an explanation that the applicant could give.

[However, the Court found an Article 6 violation for the police's refusal to allow the applicant access to his lawyer for forty-eight hours.] FRANCISCO FORREST MARTIN ET AL., 1 INTERNATIONAL HUMAN RIGHTS LAW & PRACTICE: CASES, TREATIES AND MATERIALS 598 (1997).

(2) Unlike Article 14(3)(g) of the ICCPR, the European Convention has no express right to silence. Furthermore, the European Commission of Human Rights has found such a right under Article 10's freedom of expression. In *K. v. Austria*, Report of 13 October 193, Ser. B, No. 236-B, the applicant was forced to testify against his will by being fined and detained for five days in a heroin case. Finding a violation of Article 10, the Commission

held that Article 10 "by implication also guarantees a 'negative right' not to be compelled to express oneself, *i.e.* to remain silent." *Id.* at §45.

(3) Compare the ICT-Y's ruling that a defendant need not provide a handwriting sample to the prosecution because it would violate his right against self-incrimination. *The Prosecutor v. Mucic*, Case No. IT-96–21, Int'l Crim. Trib.-Yugo., Trial Chamber, Decision on the Prosecution's Oral Requests for the Admission of Exhibit 155 into Evidence and for an Order to Compel the Accused, Zdravko Mucic, to Provide a Handwriting Sample (19 January 1998).

(4) Under the Fifth Amendment to the U.S. Constitution, individuals have the right to remain silent in criminal proceedings. Furthermore, a prosecutor or judge cannot make an adverse comment on a defendant's exercise of this right. *Griffin v. California*, 380 U.S. 609 (1965). However, the right against self-incrimination does not extend to evidence obtained in violation of this right in foreign prosecutions. *United States v. Balsys*, 118 S.Ct. 2218 (1998). How would you argue a customary international law claim challenging the Court's ruling in *Balsys*?

Length of Proceedings

Firmenich v. Argentina
Inter-American Commission on Human Rights
Resolution 17/89, Report Case 10037 (13 April 1989)
ANNUAL REPORT OF THE
INTER-AMERICAN COMMISSION ON HUMAN RIGHTS
OEA/Ser.L/V/II. 76 (10 Sept. 1989)

BACKGROUND

1. Case 10,037 refers to an alleged violation of the right of personal freedom stipulated in Article 7 of the American Convention on Human Rights (thereinafter the Convention) and, particularly, to the guarantees set out in subsection 5 of the aforesaid provision. According to the complaint, Argentine citizen Mario Eduardo Firmenich, being tried in two proceedings in the regular Argentine courts and currently imprisoned, has been denied the benefit of release requested under Article 379 (title 18)(6), of the Code of Criminal Procedure of the Argentine Republic which, in essence, corresponds to the guarantee established under Article 7(5) of the Convention [guaranteeing the right to a prompt trial].

. . . .

. . . . The guarantee mentioned in the referenced article of the Convention would have been infringed because of "judicial procrastination" during proceedings against Firmenich, since the above-mentioned term has been exceeded.

In summary, the petitioner states that since more than three and a half years have elapsed since the arrest of Mario Eduardo Firmenich, the period mentioned in Article 379(6) of the Code of Criminal Procedure as well as the one mentioned in Article 701 of the same Code has been exceeded by far, said periods consecrating in internal law the "reasonable length of time" mentioned in the Convention within which a person is entitled to be tried or "to be set free, without prejudice to continuing trial." The claimant states, in keeping with the above, that Article 379(6) is the instrument ("inclusion") of

Article 7(7) of the Convention in the Argentine legal system, since if this were not the case, the foregoing would represent a void that prevents the application of the guarantee in Article 7(5) and would also be a violation of the Convention by Argentina in view of provisions in Article 1 and 2 thereof.

The Argentine Government, also in summary, rejects the criterion of the complainant, commenting that "Argentine law must be construed as having adopted the two year term, mentioned in Article 379(6) in connection with Article 380, as one of the foundations of a "reasonable length of time" and that, therefore, two years could be considered a reasonable period, after which the judge can consider a request for release but which is not, at all, imposed on the judge without consideration for the personal characteristics of the accused, nor should said period be computed as if it consisted of calendar days, overlooking the behavior of the parties and its effect on the greater or lesser speed of the proceedings."

. . . .

The Commission believes that Article 379(6) is supplemented and "moderated" by Article 380 of the said Code, so that the definition of a "reasonable length of time" in Argentina's internal law is the result in each case of the harmonious consideration of these two provisions, leaving said consideration to the judge's criterion, since he must decide based on the parameters specifically determined by law for their joint weighing. As the Argentine Government states: " . . . the norm indicates the channels to be followed by the judge's criterion, that is: the objective assessment of the characteristics of the event and the personal characteristics of the accused." The judge fulfills a natural role entrusted to him: administering justice with the means expressly provided thereto by law.

Two important concepts are derived from the above in connection with the problem of a "reasonable length of time": first, that it is not possible to define this period *in abstracto* but, instead, that it shall be defined in each case after the circumstances mentioned in Article 380 have been considered and weighed. The Commission, in connection with these comments, agrees with the opinion that the referenced State party is "not bound (by the Convention) to fix a valid period for all cases, independently from the circumstances." This viewpoint is also shared by the European Court; second, releasing prisoners under conditions such as those in which Mario Eduardo Firmenich finds himself cannot be done based on a simple chronological consideration of years, months, and days. This has also been made explicit by the European Court . . . since the concept of "reasonable period" is left to the consideration of "the seriousness of the violation," when determining whether the detention has ceased to be reasonable.

The pronouncement of the European Court coincides, in this case, with what has been stated by the Court in San Martin, when deciding on the remedies submitted by counsel for Mr. Firmenich and stating:

Said norm only requires that the person charged be tried within a reasonable period and, if not, be released on bail. The "amount" of reasonable length of time does not have to be set as being two years, as is claimed without additional basis, since if that period is appropriate for a simple and easily investigated case it might not be, when related to another, such as this one, whose complexity, scope and difficulties impose a longer period for it to expire. This last reasoning has been reflected by legislation in the very Article 701 of the ritual order, when it includes the caveat that a trial can take longer than two years when, as in this case, the delays cannot be attributed to the Judge's activity.

In view of the above, it must be concluded that the reasonableness of the period is set by the extremes of Article 380 of the Argentine Code of Criminal Procedure, together with the assessment thereof by the trial judge. This conclusion coincides with what has been stated by the European Court, when it states:

> The Court also believes that to decide whether, in a given case, the detention of the accused does not exceed the limits of what is reasonable, it behooves the national judicial authorities to investigate all circumstances which, because of their nature, lead to acknowledge or reject the existence of true public interest which justifies the repeal of the rule of respect for individual liberty (Neumeister case, sentence dated 27 June 1968, TEDH-5.p.83, Legal Consideration #5).

[ ] It does seem necessary, for brevity's sake, to engage in a detailed analysis of the criteria or factors which the European Commission of Human Rights examined in connection with the problem of a "reasonable period" in order to define an old and vague concept of international law. Both the interested petitioner and Government have made their views known at length.

Nevertheless, the Commission wishes to refer to three factors or features: a) the actual duration of imprisonment; b) the nature of the acts which led to proceedings against Firmenich; and c) the difficulties or judicial problems encountered when conducting said trials.

a. The duration of imprisonment

The claimant holds that the term indicated in Article 379(6) as related to Article 701 of the Code of Criminal Procedure must be computed starting on 13 February 1984, when he was arrested in Rio de Janeiro (Brazil).

The Government holds that the accused was turned over to Argentine authorities on 20 October 1984, and that, therefore, the "reasonable period" mentioned in Article 7(5) of the Convention must be computed as of that date, "... without prejudice to the time between both dates which must be credited to the sentence."

The Commission believes that the opinion of the claimant cannot be entertained since between the date of arrest in Rio and the delivery of the prisoner to the Argentine authorities, extradition proceedings were conducted and that they and the pertinent decision are subject (except insofar as the filing of the petition by the requesting State is concerned) to the authorities with jurisdiction in the State to whom the request for extradition is submitted, according to the latter's internal law and terms of the treaty applicable between both States, if any, or in the absence thereof, international practice.

The foregoing is also valid when applied to the petitioner's claim that the procedural responsibility of the accused cannot be taken into consideration during the extradition proceedings since the latter takes place without the participation of the accused. Firmenich's extradition followed provisions set out in the treaty applicable between Argentina and Brazil (1961), whose Article V indicates that the individual whose extradition is requested must be granted "the opportunity to exercise all the remedies and appeal to all instances foreseen by the legislation of the State receiving the request," remedies and instances which were actually employed by Mr. Firmenich to prevent or delay his extradition.

b. The nature of the crimes

The claimant was extradited for trial in connection with two different crimes (*non bis in idem*): one by the Federal courts (in Buenos Aires) for charges of double aggravated homicide in connection with attempted homicide, also with doubly aggravating circumstances and a request for life imprisonment; the other (Federal Court in San Martin), for twofold homicide with aggravating circumstances and kidnapping or ransom and a request for life and additional imprisonment.

In conclusion and in the light of the provisions in Article 380 of the Argentine Code of Criminal Procedure, the Commission is of the opinion that the characteristics of the (punishable) actions as described in the initial briefs of these proceedings and the penalties which could be imposed in the accused make it possible to assume, on a solid basis, that measures must be taken to forestall an avoidance of justice and that, hence, a request for release must be turned down.

c. Difficulties encountered during the trials

In the two trials against the claimant as is evidenced by the record, an intense investigation was conducted with the active participation of the accused, so that:

i. Case tried in San Martin (Province of Buenos Aires) wherein charges were filed in November of 1985, and the defense requested several extensions to answer the charges. Testimony was frequently waived, or offered extemporaneously on other occasions, "new facts" were introduced and international letters rogatory were dispatched to elicit depositions and during which the judge declared the defense negligent in submitting evidence or portions thereof. Summary investigations lasted one year, trial starting in approximately November 1986, as far as the Commission is able to deduce from the evidence submitted to it. Approximately 90 witnesses and an indeterminate number of accused, but not tried, and linked in one way or another to the case testified during the trial. It must be pointed out that, according to the record, some testimony was given after difficult proceedings and international letters rogatory requested by the defense. The trial phase, as such, was completed in 1987 and sentence passed in May of that year. The sentence of the first instance has been appealed by the defense, and the appeal is still pending. The sentence is prior to submission of the case to the IACHR.

ii. The case before the federal courts (Federal Capital) as evidenced by the record, the investigation was interrupted from February 1982 until February 1984. The accused was charged in October 1986. Ninety witnesses testified, three ballistic tests were conducted, two tests were conducted on explosives, two expert witnesses testified in connection with scopametorics, two handwriting experts testified, one expert witness testified on mechanics and another on typewriters during the investigation. Thirty Official Letters were sent, many through Interpol and others through the Ministry of Foreign Affairs, requesting evidence which would serve information purposes. Charges were made on 2 October 1986, but the defense made an appearance only on 16 March 1987, because of a request for release it had submitted and three requests for extension which were granted by the judge. On 15 May 1987, the defense suggested taking depositions from several witnesses outside the country, that a mechanical expert be called and 40 letters be sent, all of which was done in addition to granting a 90 day (extraordinary) term for submission of evidence, which had twice to be extended. On 14 June 1988, sentence was passed in the first instance.

The foregoing makes it possible to draw the conclusion that although four years is not a reasonable period, in this case because of its unique features and the complexity of the reasons affecting its progress such a period is not an unjustified delay in the administration of justice.

. . . .

∼

QUESTIONS & COMMENTS

(1) Although the Inter-American Commission "for brevity's sake" refers to only three considerations in determining whether Firmenich's proceedings were unreasonably long, it earlier made note of nine more specific considerations. The Argentine government suggested the first seven, the Inter-American Commission added the final two:

   (i) actual duration of imprisonment,
   (ii) duration of preventive detention in relation to the nature of the acts which gave rise to the trial,
   (iii) 'the material, moral or other effects of detention when normal consequences are exceeded,"
   (iv) defendant's behavior and failure to cooperate,
   (v) investigatory difficulties resulting from the nature of the alleged crimes,
   (vi) conduct of investigation,
   (vii) conduct of judicial authorities,
   (viii) judicial opinions regarding release of the defendant, and
   (ix) the undisputed facts mentioned by the petitioner in his appeal.

Firmenich v. Argentina at §12.

(2) Article 6(1), ECHR, recognizes the right to a fair and public hearing within a reasonable time by an independent and impartial tribunal. Furthermore, the reasonableness of the length of detention and the reasonableness of the length of time until final judgment are assessed independently. *Maznetter v. Austria*, 10 Eur. Ct. H.R. (ser. A) (1969). In *Vendittelli v. Italy*, the European Court addressed a criminal prosecution lasting over four years. The European Court analyzed the circumstances surrounding the case and determined this period of time was not unreasonable. The European Court undertook the following analysis for determining Article 6(1) violations on the basis of length. Once the court determines how long the proceedings have lasted, the court determines whether the case is sufficiently complex to merit the delays. If the case is not justifiably complex, the court will look to both the applicant's conduct and that of the relevant authorities. It is important to note that an applicant is under no duty to take steps to shorten the proceedings. *Moreira de Acevedo v. Portugal*, 13 E.H.R.R. 721, §72 (1991). Moreover the applicant's full use of available domestic remedies cannot be used against him or her in

establishing unreasonable length of proceedings. *Eckle v. Fed. Rep. of Germany*, 51 Eur. Ct. H.R. (ser. A) (1982). Finally, in cases where the applicant has a significant stake in the case's outcome, the court will hold states parties to a higher standard. FRANCISCO FORREST MARTIN ET AL., 1 INTERNATIONAL HUMAN RIGHTS LAW & PRACTICE: CASES, TREATIES AND MATERIALS 603–604 (1997).

(3) Are the Inter-American Commission and the European Court using substantially the same test?

(4) Consider *Suárez Rosero v. Ecuador*, Inter-Am. Ct. H.R., Judgment of 12 November 1997 (reproduced above in subsection 5.1.2):

> 70. . . . In the instant case, the first act of the proceeding was Mr. Suárez-Rosero's arrest on June 23, 1992, and, therefore, the time must be calculated from that moment.
>
> 71. The Court considers the proceeding to be at an end when a final and firm judgment is delivered and the jurisdiction thereby ceases (cf. *Cour Eur. D.H., arrêt Guincho du 10 juillet 1984, Serie A n° 81*, para. 29) and that, particularly in criminal matters, that time must cover the entire proceeding, including any appeals that may be filed. On the basis of the evidence contained in the Case before it, the Court considers that the proceeding against Mr. Suárez-Rosero ended in the Ecuadorian jurisdiction on September 9, 1996, the date on which he was convicted by the President of the Superior Court of Justice of Quito. Although at the public hearing Mr. Suárez-Rosero referred to an appeal of that conviction, his statement was not substantiated.
>
> 72. This Court shares the view of the European Court of Human Rights, which in a number of decisions analyzed the concept of reasonable time and decided that three points should be taken into account in determining the reasonableness of the time in which a proceeding takes place: a) the complexity of the case, b) the procedural activity of the interested party, and c) the conduct of the judicial authorities (cf. *Genie Lacayo Case*, Judgment of January 29, 1997. Series C No. 30, para. 77; and cf. *Eur. Court H.R., Motta judgment of 19 February 1991, Series A No. 195-A*, para. No. 30; *Eur. Court H.R., Ruiz-Mateos case v. Spain judgment of 23 June 1993, Series A No. 262*, para. 30).
>
> 73. On the basis of the above considerations, after comprehensive analysis of the proceeding against Mr. Suárez-Rosero in the domestic courts, the Court observes that that proceeding lasted more than 50 months. In the Court's view, this period far exceeds the "*reasonable time*" contemplated in the American Convention.
>
> 74. Likewise, the Court considers that the fact that an Ecuadorian tribunal has found Mr. Suárez-Rosero guilty of complicity in a crime does not justify his being deprived of his liberty for more than three years and ten months, when two years is the maximum in Ecuadorian law for that offense.
>
> 75. In view of the foregoing, the Court finds that the State of Ecuador violated, to the detriment of Mr. Rafael Iván Suárez-Rosero, the right to be tried within a reasonable time or be released, as established in Articles 7(5) and 8(1) of the American Convention.

(5) Compare *The Prosecutor v. Aleksovski*, Case No. IT-95–14/1, Int'l Crim. Trib.-Yugo, Trial Chamber (23 January 1998), in which the trial chamber rejected the defense's claim that 577 days of preventive detention was excessive. The trial chamber was not convinced (i) that the 577 days he had spent in preventive detention was excessive in view of the crimes alleged, (ii) that the condition of defendant's physical health justified his release, (iii) that the effects on his family were unusual, or (iv) that his behavior in prison needed to be taken into account.

(6) Compare U.S. law governing length of proceedings. In *Barker v. Wingo*, 407 U.S. 514 (1972), the U.S. Supreme Court adopted a balancing test. The Court identified four

factors in the balancing test: "[l]ength of delay, the reason for the delay, the defendant's assertion of his right, and prejudice to the defendant." *Id.* at 530.

Retrospective Criminal Laws

Welch v. United Kingdom
European Court of Human Rights
307 Eur. Ct. H.R.(ser. A) (1995)
20 E.H.R.R.247 (1995)

. . . .

FACTS:

I. The circumstances of the case

7. On 3 November 1986 Mr Welch was arrested for suspected drug offences. On 4 November he was charged in respect of offences concerning the importation of large quantities of cannabis. Prosecuting Counsel advised, prior to February 1987, that there was insufficient evidence to charge Mr Welch with possession of cocaine with intent to supply.

8. After further investigations, including forensic examinations, further evidence came to light and on 24 February 1987, the applicant was charged with the offence of possession with intent to supply cocaine, alleged to have been committed on 3 November 1986. Subsequently, on 5 May 1987, he was charged with conspiracy to obtain cocaine with intent to supply in respect of activities which occurred between 1 January 1986 and 3 November.

9. On 24 August 1988, Mr Welch was found guilty on five counts and was given an overall sentence of 22 years' imprisonment. In addition, the trial judge imposed a confiscation order pursuant to the Drug Trafficking Offences Act 1986 ("the 1986 Act") in the amount of £66,914. In default of the payment of this sum he would be liable to serve a consecutive two years' prison sentence. The operative provisions of the 1986 Act had come into force on 12 January 1987. The Act applies only to offences, proceedings for which were instituted after this date.

10. On 11 June 1990 the Court of Appeal reduced Mr Welch's overall sentence by two years. In addition it reduced the confiscation order by £7,000 to £59,914.

II. Relevant domestic law

11. The intended purpose of the 1986 Act was to extend existing confiscation powers to enable the court to follow drug trafficking money which had been "laundered" into legitimate property. In the words of the Secretary of State who introduced the Bill in the House of Commons:

> By attacking the profits made from drug trafficking, we intend to make it much less attractive to enter the trade. We intend to help guard against the possibility that the profits from one trafficking operation will be used to finance others, and, not least, to remove the sense of injury which ordinary people are bound to feel at the idea of traffickers, who may have ruined the lives of children, having the benefit of the profits that they have made from doing so.

. . .

We need the legislation because the forfeiture powers in existing law have proved inadequate. The Courts cannot order the forfeiture of the proceeds of an offence once they have been converted into another asset – a house, stocks and shares, or valuables of any sort. The Operation Julie case was the most notorious example of the courts being unable to deprive convicted traffickers, as they wished, of the proceeds of their offences...the Bill is designed to remedy those defects. It will provide powers for courts to confiscate proceeds even after they have been converted into some other type of asset. (Hansard of 21 January 1986, cols 242 and 243).

A. Drug Trafficking Offences Act 1986

12. The relevant parts of the 1986 Act provide as follows:

1. Confiscation orders

(1) ...where a person appears before the Crown Court to be sentenced in respect of one or more drug trafficking offences (and has not previously been sentenced or otherwise dealt with in respect of his conviction for the offence or, as the case may be, any of the offences concerned), the court shall act as follows:

(2) the court shall first determine whether he has benefitted from drug trafficking.

(3) For the purposes of this Act, a person who has at any time (whether before or after the commencement of this section) received any payment or other reward in connection with drug trafficking carried on by him or another has benefitted from drug trafficking.

(4) If the court determines that he has so benefitted, the court shall, before sentencing...determine...the amount to be recovered in his case by virtue of this section.

(5) The court shall then in respect of the offence or offences concerned –

(a) order him to pay that amount...

2. Assessing the proceeds of drug trafficking

(1) For the purposes of this Act –

(a) any payments or other rewards received by a person at any time (whether before or after the commencement of section 1 of this Act) in connection with drug trafficking carried on by him or another are his proceeds of drug trafficking, and

(b) the value of his proceeds of drug trafficking is the aggregate of the values of the payments or other rewards.

(2) The court may, for the purpose of determining whether the defendant has benefitted from drug trafficking and, if he has, of assessing the value of his proceeds of drug trafficking, make the following assumptions, except to the extent that any of the assumptions are shown to be incorrect in the defendant's case.

(3) Those assumptions are –

(a) that any property appearing to the court –

i. to have been held by him at any time since his conviction, or
ii. to have been transferred to him at any time since the beginning of the period of six years ending when the proceedings were instituted against him, was received

by him, at the earliest time at which he appears to the court to have held it, as a payment or reward in connection with drug trafficking carried on by him,

(b) that any expenditure of his since the beginning of that period was met out of payments received by him in connection with drug trafficking carried on by him, and

(c) that, for the purpose of valuing any property received or assumed to have been received by him at any time as such a reward, he received the property free of any other interests in it . . .

. . .

4. Amount to be recovered under confiscation order

1. Subject to subsection (3) below, the amount to be recovered in the defendant's case shall be the amount the Crown Court assesses to be the value of the defendant's proceeds of drug trafficking.

2. If the court is satisfied as to any matter relevant for determining the amount that might be realised at the time the confiscation order is made . . . the court may issue a certificate giving the court's opinion as to the matters concerned and shall do so if satisfied as mentioned in sub-section (3) below.

3. If the court is satisfied that the amount that may be realised at the time of the confiscation order is made is less than the amount the court assesses to be the value of his proceeds of drug trafficking, the amount to be recovered in the defendant's case under the confiscation order shall be the amount appearing to the court to be the amount that might, be so realised.

B. Discretion of the trial judge

13. In determining the amount of the confiscation order, the trial judge may take into consideration the degree of culpability of the offender. For example, in *R. v. Porter* [12 Crim. App. 377 (1990)] the Court of Appeal held that where more than one conspirator was before the Court the total proceeds of a drug trafficking conspiracy could be unequally allocated as their respective share of the proceeds if there was evidence that the defendants had played unequal roles and had profited to a different extent. Similarly, in the present case, the trial judge made a much smaller order in respect of the applicant's co-defendant in recognition of his lesser involvement in the offences.

C. Imprisonment in default of payment

14. After a confiscation order has been made, the Crown Court decides upon the period of imprisonment which the offender has to serve if he fails to pay. The maximum periods of imprisonment are provided for in section 31 of the Powers of Criminal Courts Act 1973. The maximum period for an order between the sums of £50,000 and £100,000 is two years.

D. Statements by domestic courts concerning the nature of forfeiture and confiscation provisions

15. Prior to the passing of the 1986 Act, Lord Salmon expressed the view that forfeitures of money had both a punitive and deterrent purpose. (House of Lords decision in *R. v. Menocal* [2 W.L.R. 876 (1979)].

16. The domestic courts have commented in various cases on the draconian nature of the confiscation provisions in the 1986 Act and have occasionally referred to the orders, expressly or impliedly, as constituting penalties. (*R. v. Dickens* [91 Crim. App 164 (1990)]; *R. v. Porter*, 12 Crim. App. 377 (1990); *In re Lorenzo Baretto*, High Court decision of 30 November 1992 and Court of Appeal decision of 19 October 1993).

In the Court of Appeal decision in the last mentioned case, which concerned the question whether a power to vary confiscation orders introduced by the Criminal Justice (International Co-operation) Act 1990 could be applied retrospectively, the Master of the Rolls (Sir Thomas Bingham) stated as follows:

> While it is true that a confiscation order is made before sentence is passed for the substantive offence, and the term of imprisonment in default is passed to procure compliance and not by way of punishment, these are in a broad sense penal provisions, inflicting the vengeance of society on those who have transgressed in this field.

17. However, the domestic courts have also referred to the confiscation provisions as not being punitive but reparative in purpose. (Re T (Restraint Order; Disclosure of Assets) [1 W.L.R. 949 (1992)]).

. . . .

[Welch filed an application with the European Commission alleging that the confiscation order imposed upon him constituted the imposition of a retrospective criminal penalty in violation of Article 7. The Commission found no Article 7 violation.]

. . . .

DECISION [OF THE EUROPEAN COURT OF HUMAN RIGHTS]:

I. Alleged Violation of Article 7(1) of the Convention

22. The applicant complained that the confiscation order that was made against him amounted to the imposition of a retrospective criminal penalty, contrary to Article 7. . . .

. . . .

He emphasised that his complaint was limited to the retrospective application of the confiscation provisions of the 1986 Act and not the provisions themselves.

23. He submitted that in determining whether a confiscation order was punitive the Court should look beyond its stated purpose and examine its real effects. The severity and extent of such an order identified it as a penalty for the purposes of the Convention.

In the first place, under section 2(3) of the 1986 Act the national court was entitled to assume that any property which the offender currently held or which had been transferred to him in the preceding six years, or any gift which he had made during the same period, were the proceeds of drug trafficking. In addition, by seeking to confiscate the proceeds, as opposed to the profits, of drug dealing, irrespective of whether there had in fact been any personal enrichment, the order went beyond the notions of reparation and prevention into the realm of punishment.

Moreover, the fact that an order could not be made unless there had been a criminal conviction and that the degree of culpability of an accused was taken into consideration by the court in fixing the amount of the order also pointed in the direction of a penalty. Indeed, prior to the passing of the 1986 Act, the courts had regarded forfeiture orders as having the dual purpose of punishment and deterrence. Finally, confiscation orders had been recognised as having a punitive character in various domestic court decisions and in several decisions of the Supreme Court of the United States concerning similar legislation. *See Austin v. United States,* 509 U.S. 602 (1993) and *Alexander v. United States,* 509 U.S. 544 (1993).

24. The Government contended that the true purpose of the order was two-fold: first, to deprive a person of the profits which he had received from drug trafficking and secondly, to remove the value of the proceeds from possible future use in the drugs trade. It thus did not seek to impose a penalty or punishment for a criminal offence but was essentially a confiscatory and preventive measure. This could be seen from the order in the present case, which had been made for the purpose of depriving the defendant of illegal gains. Had no order been made, the money would have remained within the system for use in further drug dealing enterprises.

It was stressed that a criminal conviction for drug trafficking was no more than a "trigger" for the operation of the statutory provisions. Once the triggering event had occurred, there was no further link with any conviction. Thus, the court could consider whether a person had benefitted from drug-trafficking at any time and not merely in respect of the offence with which he had been charged. Moreover, an order could be made in relation to property which did not form part of the subject matter of the charge against the defendant or which had been received by him in a period to which no drug dealing conviction related.

Furthermore, the fact that a period of imprisonment could be imposed in default of payment could be of no assistance in characterising the nature of the confiscation order since there were many non-penal court orders which attracted such a penalty in the event of non-compliance. Similarly, the harsh effect of the order was of no assistance, since the effectiveness of a preventive measure required that a drug trafficker be deprived not only of net profits but of money which would otherwise remain available for use in the drug trade.

25. For the Commission, the order in the present case was not punitive in nature but reparative and preventive and, consequently, did not constitute a penalty within the meaning of Article 7(1) of the Convention.

26. The Court first observes that the retrospective imposition of the confiscation order is not in dispute in the present case. The order was made following a conviction in respect of drugs offences which had been committed before the 1986 Act came into force. The only question to be determined therefore is whether the order constitutes a penalty within the meaning of Article 7(1), second sentence.

27. The concept of a "penalty" in this provision is, like the notions of "civil rights and obligations" and "criminal charge" in Article 6(1), an autonomous Convention concept. (*See inter alia* – as regards "civil rights" – *X. v. France* [234 Eur. Ct. H.R. (ser. A) at 90 (1992)], and – as regards "criminal charge" – *Demicoli v. Malta* [210 Eur. Ct. H.R. (ser. A) at 15–16 (1992)]. To render the protection offered by Article 7 effective, the Court must remain free to go behind appearances and assess for itself whether a particular measure amounts in substance to a "penalty" within the meaning of this provision. (*See, mutatis mutandis, Van Droogenbroeck v. Belgium* [50 Eur. Ct. H.R. (ser. A) at 20–21 (1982)], and *Duinhof v. The Netherlands* [79 Eur. Ct. H.R. (ser. A) at 15–16 (1984)]).

28. The wording of Article 7(1), second sentence, indicates that the starting point in any assessment of the existence of a penalty is whether the measure in question is imposed following conviction for a "criminal offence". Other factors that may be taken

into account as relevant in this connection are the nature and purpose of the measure in question; its characterisation under national law; the procedures involved in the making and implementation of the measure; and its severity.

29. As regards the connection with a criminal offence, it is to be observed that before an order can be made under the 1986 Act the accused must have been convicted of one or more drug trafficking offences. (*See* §1(1) of the 1986 Act at §12 above). This link is in no way diminished by the fact that, due to the operation of the statutory presumptions concerning the extent to which the applicant has benefitted from trafficking, the court order may affect proceeds or property which are not directly related to the facts underlying the criminal conviction. While the reach of the measure may be necessary to the attainment of the aims of the 1986 Act, this does not alter the fact that its imposition is dependent on there having been a criminal conviction.

30. In assessing the nature and purpose of the measure, the Court has had regard to the background of the 1986 Act, which was introduced to overcome the inadequacy of the existing powers of forfeiture and to confer on the courts the power to confiscate proceeds after they had been converted into other forms of assets. The preventive purpose of confiscating property that might be available for use in future drug trafficking operations as well as the purpose of ensuring that crime does not pay are evident from the ministerial statements that were made to Parliament at the time of the introduction of the legislation. However, it cannot be excluded that legislation which confers such broad powers of confiscation on the courts also pursues the aim of punishing the offender. Indeed, the aims of prevention and reparation are consistent with a punitive purpose and may be seen as constituent elements of the very notion of punishment.

31. In this connection, confiscation orders have been characterised in some United Kingdom court decisions as constituting "penalties", and, in others, as pursuing the aim of reparation as opposed to punishment. Although on balance these statements point more in the direction of a confiscation order being a punitive measure, the Court does not consider them to be of much assistance since they were not directed at the point at issue under Article 7 but rather made in the course of examination of associated questions of domestic law and procedure.

32. The Court agrees with the Government and the Commission that the severity of the order is not in itself decisive, since many non-penal measures of a preventive nature may have a substantial impact on the person concerned.

33. However, there are several aspects of the making of an order under the 1986 Act which are in keeping with the idea of a penalty as it is commonly understood even though they may also be considered as essential to the preventive scheme inherent in the 1986 Act. The sweeping statutory assumptions in section 2(3) of the 1986 Act that all property passing through the offender's hands over a six-year period is the fruit of drug trafficking unless he can prove otherwise; the fact that the confiscation order is directed to the proceeds involved in drug dealing and is not limited to actual enrichment or profit (*See* §§1 and 2 of the 1986 Act in §12 above); the discretion of the trial judge, in fixing the amount of the order, to take into consideration the degree of culpability of the accused; and the possibility of imprisonment in default of payment by the offender – are all elements which, when considered together, provide a strong indication of *inter alia* a regime of punishment.

34. Finally, looking behind appearances at the realities of the situation, whatever the characterisation of the measure of confiscation, the fact remains that the applicant faced

more far-reaching detriment as a result of the order than that to which he was exposed at the time of the commission of the offences for which he was convicted. (*See, mutatis mutandis, Campbell and Fell v. United Kingdom*, [80 Eur. Ct. H.R. (ser. A) at 37–38 (1985)]).

35. Taking into consideration the combination of punitive elements outlined above, the confiscation order amounted, in the circumstances of the present case, to a penalty. Accordingly, there has been a breach of Article 7(1).

36. The Court would stress, however, that this conclusion concerns only the retrospective application of the relevant legislation and does not call into question in any respect the powers of confiscation conferred on the courts as a weapon in the fight against the scourge of drug trafficking.

. . . .

~

QUESTIONS & COMMENTS

(1) In *Jamil v. France*, 320 Eur.Ct.H.R. (ser. A) (1995), the applicant was convicted of smuggling and conspiracy to smuggle prohibited goods (cocaine). The French authorities imprisoned him and ordered him to pay a fine. Furthermore, if he did not pay the fine, he was subject to additional time in prison. The specific amount of time to be served in default of payment was established by a law enacted *after* his conviction. The European Court found a violation of Article 7.

(2) The *ex post facto* doctrine arguably can apply to civil proceedings; however, it has been recognized more generally as a criminal law rule. Related to the *ex post facto* prohibition are the legality doctrines of *nullum crimen sine lege* (which expressly addresses *criminal* liability) and *nulla poena sine lege* (which expressly addresses penalties).

Whether a proceeding is criminal or not, the European Court of Human Rights in *E.L., R.L. and J.O.-L v. Switzerland*, – Eur. Ct. H.R. (ser. A) (1997), ruled that three criteria must be considered for determining whether a person was being "charged with a criminal offence" for purposes of Article 6, ECHR: (i) classification of the offense under national law, (ii) the nature of the offense, and (iii) the nature and degree of severity of the penalty that the person risked incurring.

(3) The Nuremberg Tribunal did not feel that it violated *nullum crimen sine lege* doctrine even though the war crimes defendants were prosecuted under treaties that contained no language about individual criminal liability. The ICT-Y also has felt that it has not violated this doctrine even though prosecution of war crimes under common Article 3 of the Geneva Conventions is not mentioned in those treaties. Only until after the perpetration of those crimes was the ICT-Y Statute enacted that expressly allowed the prosecution of such crimes. The ICT-Y explained that the substantive prohibitions in the common Article 3 provisions were undoubtedly part of customary international law. *Prosecutor v. Tadic*, Decision on the Defence Motion on Jurisdiction (10 Aug. 1995) at 830.

Compare this approach to the U.S. Supreme Court's in *Cook v. United States*, 138 U.S. 157 (1891) in which the Court stated that as long as the crime was prohibited and there was no change in punishment, "[a]n *ex post facto* law does not involve, in any of its definitions, a change of the place of trial of an alleged offense after its commission." *Id.* at

183. For a fuller discussion of these issues, *see* Jordan J. Paust, *Nullum Crimen and Related Claims*, 25 Denver J. In'l L. & Pol'y 321 (1997).

Punishment

Charter of the International Military Tribunal

Article 27.

The Tribunal shall have the right to impose upon a Defendant, on conviction, death or such other punishment as shall be determined by it to be just.

Article 28.

In addition to any punishment imposed by it, the Tribunal shall have the right to deprive the convicted person of any stolen property and order its delivery to the Control Council for Germany.

Article 29.

In case of guilt, sentences shall be carried out in accordance with the orders of the Control Council for Germany, which may at any time reduce or otherwise alter the sentences, but may not increase the severity thereof. If the Control Council for Germany, after any Defendant has been convicted and sentenced, discovers fresh evidence which, in its opinion, would found a fresh charge against him, the Council shall report accordingly to the Committee established under Article 14 hereof, for such action as they may consider proper, having regard to the interests of justice.

Statute of the International Criminal Tribunal (for the fmr. Yugoslavia)

Article 24

1. The penalty imposed by the Trial Chamber shall be limited to imprisonment. In determining the terms of imprisonment, the Trial Chambers shall have recourse to the general practice regarding prison sentences in the courts of the former Yugoslavia.

2. In imposing the sentences, the Trial Chambers should take into account such factors as the gravity of the offence and the individual circumstances of the convicted person.

3. In addition to imprisonment, the Trial Chambers may order the return of any property and proceeds acquired by criminal conduct, including by means of duress, to their rightful owners.

Statute of the International Criminal Tribunal for Rwanda

Article 23

1. The penalty imposed by the Trial Chamber shall be limited to imprisonment. In determining the terms of imprisonment, the Trial Chambers shall have recourse to the general practice regarding prison sentences in the courts of Rwanda.

2. In imposing the sentences, the Trial Chambers should take into account such factors as the gravity of the offence and the individual circumstances of the convicted person.

3. In addition to imprisonment, the Trial Chambers may order the return of any property and proceeds acquired by criminal conduct, including by means of duress, to their rightful owners.

Statute of the International Criminal Court

Article 77 Applicable penalties

1. Subject to article 110, the Court may impose one of the following penalties on a person convicted of a crime under article 5 of this Statute:

(a) Imprisonment for a specified number of years, which may not exceed a maximum of 30 years; or
(b) A term of life imprisonment when justified by the extreme gravity of the crime and the individual circumstances of the convicted person.

2. In addition to imprisonment, the Court may order:

(a) A fine under the criteria provided for in the Rules of Procedure and Evidence;
(b) A forfeiture of proceeds, property and assets derived directly or indirectly from that crime, without prejudice to the rights of bona fide third parties.

Article 78 Determination of the sentence

1. In determining the sentence, the Court shall, in accordance with the Rules of Procedure and Evidence, take into account such factors as the gravity of the crime and the individual circumstances of the convicted person.

2. In imposing a sentence of imprisonment, the Court shall deduct the time, if any, previously spent in detention in accordance with an order of the Court. The Court may deduct any time otherwise spent in detention in connection with conduct underlying the crime.

3. When a person has been convicted of more than one crime, the Court shall pronounce a sentence for each crime and a joint sentence specifying the total period of imprisonment. This period shall be no less than the highest individual sentence pronounced and shall not exceed 30 years' imprisonment or a sentence of life imprisonment in conformity with article 77, paragraph 1 (b).

Article 110 Review by the Court concerning reduction of sentence

1. The State of enforcement shall not release the person before expiry of the sentence pronounced by the Court.

2. The Court alone shall have the right to decide any reduction of sentence, and shall rule on the matter after having heard the person.

3. When the person has served two thirds of the sentence, or 25 years in the case of life imprisonment, the Court shall review the sentence to determine whether it should be reduced. Such a review shall not be conducted before that time.

4. In its review under paragraph 3, the Court may reduce the sentence if it finds that one or more of the following factors are present:

(a) The early and continuing willingness of the person to cooperate with the Court in its investigations and prosecutions;
(b) The voluntary assistance of the person in enabling the enforcement of the judgements and orders of the Court in other cases, and in particular providing assistance in locating assets subject to orders of fine, forfeiture or reparation which may be used for the benefit of victims; or

(c) Other factors establishing a clear and significant change of circumstances sufficient to justify the reduction of sentence, as provided in the Rules of Procedure and
Evidence.

5. If the Court determines in its initial review under paragraph 3 that it is not appropriate to reduce the sentence, it shall thereafter review the question of reduction of sentence
at such intervals and applying such criteria as provided for in the Rules of Procedure and
Evidence.

Prosecutor v. Kambanda
Case No. ICTR97-23-A
International Criminal Tribunal for Rwanda – Appeals Chamber
(19 October 2000)

. . . .

114. The main issue raised by the Appellant in the fourth, fifth, seventh and eighth
grounds of appeal is that the Trial Chamber erred in law in failing to properly take certain
mitigating circumstances into account. As a result the sentence imposed by the Trial
Chamber was excessive. The Appellant submits that the Trial Chamber erred in failing to
consider that his plea of guilty as a mitigating factor carries a discount in sentence; failing
to take into account both his personal circumstances and his substantial co-operation
with the Prosecutor (both in the past and in the future) [ ]; and failing to take into
account the general practice regarding prison sentences in the courts of Rwanda in the
determination of sentence. In addition, he submits that the Trial Chamber erred in law
and on the facts in taking into account the non-explanation of the Appellant when asked
if he had anything to say himself in mitigation before sentence.

115. For the Appellant's appeal to succeed on these grounds, he must show that the Trial
Chamber abused its discretion, so invalidating the sentence. The sentence must be shown
to be outside the discretionary framework provided by the Statute and the Rules.

116. The Appeals Chamber notes that a Trial Chamber is required as a matter of law,
under both the Statute and the Rules, to take account of mitigating circumstances and
the general practice regarding prison sentences in Rwanda. Therefore if it fails to do
so, it commits an error of law. Article 23 provides *inter alia*, that "[i]n determining the
terms of imprisonment, the Trial Chambers shall have recourse to the general practice
regarding prison sentences in the courts of Rwanda" [ ] and that in imposing sentence
it "should take into account such factors as the gravity of the offence and the individual
circumstances of the convicted person." [ ] Rule 101(B) provides:

> In determining the sentence, the Trial Chamber shall take into account the factors
> mentioned in Article 23(2) of the Statute, as well as such factors as:
>
> (i) Any aggravating circumstances;
> (ii) Any mitigating circumstances including the substantial cooperation with the
> Prosecutor by the convicted person before or after conviction;
> (iii) The general practice regarding prison sentences in the courts of Rwanda:
> (iv) The extent to which any penalty imposed by a court of any State on the
> convicted person for the same act has already been served, as referred to in
> Article 9 (3) of the Statute.

117. Rule 101(B) is expressed in the imperative in that the Trial Chamber "shall take into account" the factors listed and therefore if it does not, it will commit an error of law. Whether or not this would invalidate the decision is of course another question.

118. In the Judgement the Trial Chamber considered both the Appellant's guilty plea on each count on the indictment, together with the Plea Agreement, [ ] wherein the Appellant made full admissions of all the relevant facts alleged in the indictment and his involvement as Prime Minister. He "acknowledge[d] that . . . he as Prime Minister, instigated, aided and abetted the *Prefets, Bourgmestres*, and members of the population to commit massacres and killings of civilians, in particular Tutsi and moderate Hutu." [ ] The Trial Chamber noted the gravity of the crimes in question and found as an aggravating factor the fact that the Appellant abused his position of authority and trust of the civilian population when he, as Prime Minister, was responsible for maintaining peace and security. [ ] It considered the factors put forward by the Appellant in mitigation: plea of guilty; remorse, which the Appellant claimed was evident from the act of pleading guilty; and cooperation with the Prosecutor. [ ]Nevertheless, it found that the Appellant had "offered no explanation for his voluntary participation in the genocide; nor [had] he expressed contrition, regret or sympathy for the victims in Rwanda, even when given the opportunity to do so by the Chamber, during the [pre-sentencing] hearing of 3 September 1998." [ ]

119. Weighing up the submissions of both parties, in particular regarding the Appellant's past and future cooperation with the Prosecutor, the fact that the guilty plea would encourage others to come forward and recognize their responsibilities and that it was in itself a mitigating circumstance, the Trial Chamber nevertheless determined that, in view of the "intrinsic gravity" of the crimes and the Appellant's position of authority, "the aggravating circumstances surrounding the crimes . . . negate the mitigating circumstances, especially since [the Appellant] occupied a high ministerial post, at the time he committed the said crimes." [ ]The Appellant was therefore sentenced *"à la peine d'emprisonnement à vie,"* (translated in the English text, as "life imprisonment"). [ ]

120. The Judgement illustrates that the Trial Chamber clearly considered the mitigating factors put forward by both the Appellant and the Prosecutor, the principle that a guilty plea as part of this mitigation carries with it a reduction in sentence and the general practice regarding prison sentences in the courts of Rwanda. The Trial Chamber acknowledged that the Prosecutor had asked the Trial Chamber "to regard as a significant mitigating factor, not only the substantial co-operation so far extended, but also the future co-operation . . . " of the Appellant. [ ] It noted the early guilty plea of the Appellant and the fact that both the Appellant and the Prosecutor

> urged the Chamber to interpret [the Appellant's] guilty pleas as a signal of his remorse, repentance and acceptance of responsibility for his actions. The Chamber is mindful that remorse is not the only reasonable inference that can be drawn from a guilty plea; nevertheless it accepts that most national jurisdictions consider admissions of guilt as matters properly to be considered in mitigation of punishment. [ ]

121. In addition, with regard to consideration of the general practice regarding prison sentences in the courts of Rwanda, the Trial Chamber analysed this issue at some length in paragraphs 18–25 and having reviewed the scale of sentences applicable in Rwanda,

properly concluded that "the reference to this practice can be used for guidance, but is not binding." [ ]

122. The Appeals Chamber therefore finds that the Trial Chamber clearly considered each of the above factors put forward by the Appellant in mitigation in reaching its decision and as required in the Statute and Rules and therefore to this extent did not commit an error of law.

123. However, the second question is whether the Trial Chamber properly took these factors into account. This turns on the question of the weight attached by the Trial Chamber to the mitigating factors. As the Prosecutor submits, "the Appellant's Brief does not appear to argue that the Trial Chamber failed to recognize this as a mitigating circumstance, but rather, that the Trial Chamber failed to give this mitigating circumstance sufficient weight." [ ]

124. The weight to be attached to mitigating circumstances is a matter of discretion for the Trial Chamber and unless the Appellant succeeds in showing that the Trial Chamber abused its discretion, resulting in a sentence outside the discretionary framework provided by the Statute and the Rules, these grounds of appeal will fail.

125. The Appeals Chamber notes that the crimes for which the Appellant was convicted were of the most serious nature. A sentence imposed should reflect the inherent gravity of the criminal conduct. The Appeals Chamber of the ICTY has observed that "[c]onsideration of the gravity of the conduct of the accused is normally the starting point for consideration of an appropriate sentence." [ ] In sentencing the Appellant, the Trial Chamber found that

(v) the crimes for which Jean Kambanda is responsible carry an intrinsic gravity, and their widespread, atrocious and systematic character is particularly shocking to the human conscience;

(vi) Jean Kambanda committed the crimes knowingly and with premeditation;

(vii) and, moreover, Jean Kambanda, as Prime Minister of Rwanda was entrusted with the duty and authority to protect the population and he abused this trust. [ ]

126. In this case, the Trial Chamber balanced the mitigating factors against the aggravating factors and concluded that "the aggravating circumstances surrounding the crimes negate the mitigating circumstances." [ ] The Appeals Chamber considers that this sentence falls within the discretionary framework provided by the Statute and the Rules, and so sees no reason to disturb the decision of the Trial Chamber.

~

QUESTIONS & COMMENTS

(1) Principles governing the international law of punishment are codified in international instruments, such as the Statutes of the ICT-Y, ICT-R, and ICC. But, there are other international law principles that can be gleaned by discovering that social, moral, and political interests are served by international criminal law sanctions but not by sanctions from domestic criminal law traditions that do not incorporate international law.

Assuming that the imposition of the death penalty is no longer a viable sentence under international criminal law,[1] let us list existing and potential measures for imposing punishment under both domestic and international criminal law:

  a. Imprisonment for varying lengths of time
  b. Restriction to "half-way house," probation, and/or parole
  c. Monetary penalties (both compensatory and punitive)
  d. Return of property, assets, and proceeds
  e. Ineligibility to participate in activities of government, political party, military, firm, or enterprise
  f. Public censure
  g. Public statement of contrition and full disclosure of crimes and assets
  h. Community service (in and/or outside prison)

What are the interests served by these measures, respectively? They include:

  a. Restriction of liberty to protect the public from further harm
  b. Compensating the victim and the public for the crime
  c. Deterring offenders and others from committing similar crimes in the future[2]
  d. Eliminating head of state and other official immunities for crimes
  e. Preventing peculiarly systemic or widespread criminal acts
  f. Punishing the offenders through the restriction of his/her liberty, comfort, and forced labor
  g. Shaming the offender
  h. Disclosure of other criminals and criminal acts
  i. Public education
  j. Societal reconciliation[3]
  k. Rehabilitation of the offender[4] and reintegration into society
  l. Safeguard offenders against excessive, disproportionate or arbitrary punishment
  m. Define, coordinate, and harmonize powers, duties, and functions of courts and administrative agencies responsible for dealing with offenders[5]
  n. Differentiation among offenders with a view to just individuation in their treatment[6]

Of these interests that are not generally considered shared with domestic criminal justice systems that do not incorporate international law are (i) the elimination of official immunities, (ii) the prevention of systemic or widespread crimes, and (iii) societal reconciliation. Accordingly, these three goals are particularly associated with *international criminal law* and serve to formulate distinctive principles of the international criminal law of punishment.

---

[1] In recent years, the death penalty has become less an option with the adoption of several abolitionist protocols to human rights treaties (see Section 5.1.1) and the disallowance of the death penalty by the Statutes of the ICT-Y, ICT-R, and ICC.

[2] MODEL PENAL CODE §1.02(2) (1985).

[3] One commentator has noted that the ICC "will help end cycles of violence by offering justice as an alternative to revenge, and it will contribute to the process of reconciliation by replacing the stigma of collective guilt with the catharsis of individual responsibility." Norman Dorsen, "The U.S. and the War Crimes Court: A Glass Half Full," 2 *Lawyers Committee for Human Rights Advisor* 1 (Fall 1998).

[4] MODEL PENAL CODE §1.02(2) (1985).

[5] *Id.*

[6] MODEL PENAL CODE §1.02(2) (1985).

Can these interests be used to justify deviation from domestic criminal law sanctions? Recall that in determining the terms of imprisonment, the trial chambers of the ICT-Y and ICT-R have recourse to the general practice regarding prison sentences in the courts of Rwanda and the former Yugoslavia, respectively. However, the ICC does not mention using domestic law to determine terms of imprisonment.

Can these interests be used both to determine the particular sanction employed as well as the severity of sanction? For example, if the offender was a military commander, an appropriate sanction would be ineligibility to continue military service. This sanction serves to prevent the perpetration of future systemic or widespread crimes whose perpetration is facilitated by the military command structure.[7] However, if a offender committed a single crime while acting in a private capacity, probably none of the goals would come into play, and no deviation from domestic criminal justice sanctions should take place.[8]

In summary, aside from the codification of principles governing punishment contained in the Statutes of the ICT-Y, ICT-R, and ICC, there appear to be three additional principles that can be extracted from international criminal law:

> In imposing sanctions, deviation from domestic law practice is allowed only to achieve any of the following goals:
>
> 1. eliminating official immunities
> 2. preventing systemic or widespread crimes
> 3. societal reconciliation

(2) What other methods can be used to glean international law principles of punishment?

(3) Why do you think the ICC Statute only authorizes imprisonment of up to thirty years or life imprisonment?

(4) The ICT-Y in *The Prosecutor v. Drazen Erdemovic,* Int'l Crim. Trib.-Yugo, Trial Chamber, Sentencing Decision (5 March 1998), examined the following mitigating factors in sentencing: (i) personal circumstances (*e.g.,* age, family situation, background, character), (ii) admission of guilt, (iii) remorse, and (iv) duress. Int'l Crim. Trib.-Yugo, 20 *Bulletin* 2 (20 March 1998).

(5) The sentences imposed so far by the ICT-Y have been comparatively lenient. For example, Tadic received only twenty years for committing both crimes against humanity and war crimes. Erdemovic received only five years for committing a war crime. Compare these sentences to U.S. sentences of life-imprisonment for nonviolent drug trafficking.

5.4. Rights to Privacy and Respect for Family Life

Universal Declaration of Human Rights

Article 12.

No one shall be subjected to arbitrary interference with his privacy, family, home or correspondence, nor to attacks upon his honour and reputation. Everyone has the right to the protection of the law against such interference or attacks.

---

[7] The Inter-American Commission has held that the prohibition of the presidential candidacy of a former chief of state who had been put in power by a military coup d'etat is compatible with the ACHR. *Ríos Montt v. Guatemala*, Report 30/93, Case 10,804, ANNUAL REPORT OF THE INTER-AMERICAN COMMISSION ON HUMAN RIGHTS 1993 206 (1994).

[8] Indeed, it is doubtful that an international criminal tribunal would prosecute such a person, unless the domestic courts failed to do so. *See* Art. 17(1)(a)–(b), ICC Statute.

International Covenant on Civil and Political Rights

Article 17

1. No one shall be subjected to arbitrary or unlawful interference with his privacy, family, home or correspondence, nor to unlawful attacks on his honour and reputation.

2. Everyone has the right to the protection of the law against such interference or attacks.

European Convention on Human Rights

Article 8

1. Everyone has the right to the respect for his private and family life, his home and his correspondence.

2. There shall be no interference by a public authority with the exercise of this right except such as is in accordance with the law and is necessary in a democratic society in the interests of national security, public safety or the economic well-being of the country, for the prevention of disorder or crime, for the protection of health or morals, or for the protection of the rights and freedoms of others.

Charter of Fundamental Rights of the European Union

Article 7

Respect for private and family life

Everyone has the right to respect for his or her private and family life, home and communications.

Article 8

Protection of personal data

1. Everyone has the right to the protection of personal data concerning him or her.

2. Such data must be processed fairly for specified purposes and on the basis of the consent of the person concerned or some other legitimate basis laid down by law. Everyone has the right of access to data which has been collected concerning him or her, and the right to have it rectified.

3. Compliance with these rules shall be subject to control by an independent authority.

Article 9

Right to marry and right to found a family

The right to marry and the right to found a family shall be guaranteed in accordance with the national laws governing the exercise of these rights.

American Declaration on the Rights and Duties of Man

Article V. Right to protection of honor, personal reputation, and private and family life.

Every person has the right to the protection of the law against abusive attacks upon his honor, his reputation, and his private and family life.

Article IX. Right to inviolability of the home.

Every person has the right to the inviolability of his home.

Article X. Right to the inviolability and transmission of correspondence

Every person has the right to the inviolability and transmission of his correspondence.

American Convention on Human Rights

Article 11. RIGHT TO PRIVACY.

1. Everyone has the right to have his honor respected and his dignity recognized.

2. No one may be the object of arbitrary or abusive interference with his private life, his family, his home, or his correspondence, or of unlawful attacks on his honor or reputation.

3. Everyone has the right to the protection of the law against such interference or attacks.

Convention on Human Rights and Fundamental Freedoms of the Commonwealth of Independent States

Article 9

1. Everyone shall have the right to respect for his private and family life, his home and his correspondence.

2. There shall be no interference by a public authority with the exercise of this right except as is in accordance with the law and is necessary in a democratic society in the interests of national security, public safety, public order, public health and moral or for the protection of the rights and freedoms of others.

U.S. Constitution

Amendment IV

The right of the people to be secure in their persons, houses, papers, and effects, against unreasonable searches and seizures, shall not be violated, and no Warrants shall issue, but upon probable cause, supported by Oath or affirmation, and particularly describing the place to be searched, and the persons or things to be seized.

Amendment V

No person shall be ... deprived of ... liberty, ... without due process of law; ...

Amendment IX

The enumeration in the Constitution, of certain rights, shall not be construed to deny or disparage others retained by the people.

Amendment XIV

Section 1. All persons born or naturalized in the United States, and subject to the jurisdiction thereof, are citizens of the United States and of the State wherein they reside. No State shall make or enforce any law which shall abridge the privileges or immunities of citizens of the United States; nor shall any State deprive any person of life, liberty, or property, without due process of law; nor deny to any person within its jurisdiction the equal protection of the laws.

Surveillance, Search and Seizure, and the Exclusionary Rule

Peck v. United Kingdom
Application No. 44647/98
European Court of Human Rights
– Eur. Ct. H.R. (ser. A) (2003)

[The applicant, who was suffering from depression, attempted suicide by cutting his wrists while walking down a public street. He was unaware that he was being filmed by a closed-circuit television camera installed by the city government. Subsequently, the film was aired on television without the applicant's image being sufficiently masked to protect his identity. Later, the applicant made several media appearances in order to protest the airing of this film footage. He filed an application with the European Commission of Human Rights complaining that his right to privacy under Article 8, ECHR, had been violated. The application subsequently was referred to the European Court of Human Rights.]

. . . .

52. The applicant complained that the disclosure by Brentwood Borough Council of the relevant CCTV footage, which resulted in the publication and broadcasting of identifiable images of him, constituted a disproportionate interference with his right to respect for his private life guaranteed by Article 8 of the Convention. . . .

A. The existence of an interference with private life

1. The parties' submissions

53. The Government contended that the applicant's right to private life had not been engaged. They mainly argued that the incident in question did not form part of his private life given the substance of what was filmed and the location and circumstances of the filming. The applicant's actions were already in the public domain. Disclosure of those actions simply distributed a public event to a wider public and could not change the public quality of the applicant's original conduct and render it more private. The Government also maintained that the applicant waived his rights by choosing to do what he did, where he did, and submitted that the fact that the applicant did not complain about being filmed, as such, amounted to an acknowledgment that the filming did not engage his right to the protection of his private life. They further considered that the question of whether there was an interference with his private life was not clear cut and submitted that certain factors should be borne in mind in this respect, including the nature of the impugned act and the parties' conduct.

54. The applicant maintained that the disclosure of the footage constituted a serious interference with his private life. The relevant footage related to an attempted suicide, he was unaware that he was being filmed and the footage showed the immediate aftermath of this episode while he still held the knife. The footage was disclosed to the written and audiovisual media with large audiences, without his consent or knowledge and without masking at all or adequately his identity. His image, even in those circumstances, was broadcast to millions and he was recognised by a large number of persons who knew him, including family members, friends and colleagues. While he was not complaining

about being filmed by CCTV (as this saved his life), he took issue with the disclosure by the Council of the CCTV material which resulted in the impugned publications and broadcasts.

55. While the CCTV material disclosed did not show him actually cutting his wrists, the applicant argued that it concerned a period immediately following his suicide attempt and thus related to that personal and private matter. He may have been in the street, but it was late at night, he was not taking part in a public demonstration (the main reason for demonstrating is to be seen) and, given his psychological state, it could not be said that he was there voluntarily at all. He was unaware that he was being filmed and the disclosure took place without his knowledge or consent and the footage was later broadcast, and the stills published, without his permission and in a manner which did not exclude his identification by family, friends, neighbours and colleagues. The [Broadcasting Standards Commission,] the ITC and the High Court found that his privacy had been invaded and, given those findings, the [Press Complaints Commission]'s view to the contrary was not tenable.

56. In addition, the applicant maintained that the jurisprudence of the Convention institutions accepted that the occurrence of an event in a public place was only one element in the overall assessment of whether there was an interference with private life, other relevant factors including the use made of the material obtained and the extent to which it was made available to the public. In contrast to that jurisprudence, not only was disclosure of the CCTV material specifically foreseen by the Council, but that disclosure was made to the media. Moreover, the applicant contended that it could not be said that he "unequivocally" waived his rights under the Convention on 20 August 1995.

2. The Court's assessment

57. Private life is a broad term not susceptible to exhaustive definition. The Court has already held that elements such as gender identification, name, sexual orientation and sexual life are important elements of the personal sphere protected by Article 8. That Article also protects a right to identity and personal development, and the right to establish and develop relationships with other human beings and the outside world and it may include activities of a professional or business nature. There is, therefore, a zone of interaction of a person with others, even in a public context, which may fall within the scope of "private life" (see *P.G. and J.H. v. the United Kingdom*, no. 44787/98, §56, ECHR 2001-IX, with further references).

58. In *P.G. and J.H.* (§57) the Court further noted as follows:

There are a number of elements relevant to a consideration of whether a person's private *life is concerned in measures* effected outside a person's home or private premises. Since there are occasions when people knowingly or intentionally involve themselves in activities which are or may be recorded or reported in a public manner, a person's reasonable expectations as to privacy may be a significant, although not necessarily conclusive, factor. A person who walks down the street will, inevitably, be visible to any member of the public who is also present. Monitoring by technological means of the same public scene (for example, a security guard viewing through closed-circuit television) is of a similar character. Private life considerations may arise, however, once any systematic or permanent record comes into existence of such material from the public domain.

59. The monitoring of the actions of an individual in a public place by the use of photographic equipment which does not record the visual data does not, as such, give rise to an interference with the individual's private life (see, for example, *Herbecq and the association "Ligue des droits de l'homme" v. Belgium*, applications nos. 32200/96 and 32201/96, Commission decision of 14 January 1998, DR 92-B, p. 92). On the other hand, the recording of the data and the systematic or permanent nature of the record may give rise to such considerations. Accordingly, in both *Rotaru* and *Amann* (to which *P.G. and J.H.* referred) the compilation of data by security services on particular individuals, even without the use of covert surveillance methods, constituted an interference with the applicants' private lives (*Rotaru v. Romania* [GC], no. 28341/95, §§43–44, ECHR 2000-V, and *Amann v. Switzerland* [GC], no. 27798/95, §§65–67, ECHR 2000-II). While the permanent recording of the voices of P.G. and J.H. was made while they answered questions in a police cell as police officers listened to them, the recording of their voices for further analysis was regarded as the processing of personal data about them amounting to an interference with their right to respect for their private lives (see *P.G. and J.H.*, cited above, §§59–60).

60. However, the Court notes that the present applicant did not complain that the collection of data through the CCTV-camera monitoring of his movements and the creation of a permanent record of itself amounted to an interference with his private life. Indeed, he admitted that that function of the CCTV system, together with the consequent involvement of the police, may have saved his life. Rather, he argued that it was the disclosure of that record of his movements to the public in a manner in which he could never have foreseen which gave rise to such an interference.

61. In this connection, the Court recalls both *Lupker* and *Friedl* decided by the Commission, which concerned the unforeseen use by the authorities of photographs which had been previously voluntarily submitted to them (*Lupker and Others v. the Netherlands*, no. 18395/91, Commission decision of 7 December 1992, unreported) and the use of photographs taken by the authorities during a public demonstration (*Friedl v. Austria*, judgment of 31 January 1995, Series A no. 305-B, opinion of the Commission, p. 21, §§49–52). In those cases, the Commission attached importance to whether the photographs amounted to an intrusion into the applicant's privacy (as, for instance, by entering and taking photographs in a person's home), whether the photograph related to private or public matters and whether the material thus obtained was envisaged for a limited use or was likely to be made available to the general public. In *Friedl* the Commission noted that there was no such intrusion into the "inner circle" of the applicant's private life, that the photographs taken of a public demonstration related to a public event and that they had been used solely as an aid to policing the demonstration on the relevant day. In this context, the Commission attached weight to the fact that the photographs taken remained anonymous in that no names were noted down, the personal data recorded and photographs taken were not entered into a data-processing system and no action had been taken to identify the persons photographed on that occasion by means of data processing (ibid.). Similarly, in *Lupker*, the Commission specifically noted that the police used the photographs to identify offenders in criminal proceedings only and that there was no suggestion that the photographs had been made available to the general public or would be used for any other purpose.

62. The present applicant was in a public street but he was not there for the purposes of participating in any public event and he was not a public figure. It was late at night, he was

deeply perturbed and in a state of distress. While he was walking in public wielding a knife, he was not later charged with any offence. The actual suicide attempt was neither recorded nor therefore disclosed. However, footage of the immediate aftermath was recorded and disclosed by the Council directly to the public in its *CCTV News* publication. In addition, the footage was disclosed to the media for further broadcasting and publication purposes. Those media included the audiovisual media: Anglia Television broadcast locally to approximately 350,000 people and the BBC broadcast nationally, and it is "commonly acknowledged that the audiovisual media have often a much more immediate and powerful effect than the print media" (*Jersild v. Denmark*, judgment of 23 September 1994, Series A no. 298, pp. 23–24, §31). The *Yellow Advertiser* was distributed in the applicant's locality to approximately 24,000 readers. The applicant's identity was not adequately, or in some cases not at all, masked in the photographs and footage so published and broadcast. He was recognised by certain members of his family and by his friends, neighbours and colleagues.

As a result, the relevant moment was viewed to an extent which far exceeded any exposure to a passer-by or to security observation (as in *Herbecq and the association "Ligue des droits de l'homme"*, cited above) and to a degree surpassing that which the applicant could possibly have foreseen when he walked in Brentwood on 20 August 1995.

63. Accordingly, the Court considers that the disclosure by the Council of the relevant footage constituted a serious interference with the applicant's right to respect for his private life.

B. Whether the interference was in accordance with the law and pursued a legitimate aim

64. The Government submitted that any interference was "in accordance with the law" in that it fell within section 163 of the Criminal Justice and Public Order Act 1994 ("the 1994 Act") and section 111 of the Local Government Act 1972 ("the 1972 Act"), both of which provisions complied with the Convention's "quality of law" requirements. They added that any interference pursued a legitimate aim: as accepted during the judicial review proceedings, the Council's intention in installing and operating the CCTV system and in disclosing footage to the media was the detection and prevention of crime, thereby securing public safety and private property.

65. The applicant considered that the interference in question was not "in accordance with the law" because it was not foreseeable. He argued that the scope and conditions of the exercise of the discretionary power of disclosure in the 1972 and 1994 Acts were not indicated with sufficient clarity and thereby failed to protect him against arbitrary interferences with his rights. He also considered that the disclosure of the CCTV material had no legitimate aim because any connection between the aim of detecting and deterring crime and his conduct was too remote.

66. The Court has noted the terms of section 163 of the 1994 Act and section 111(1) of the 1972 Act and the judgment of, in particular, the High Court. That court noted that the purpose of section 163 of the 1994 Act was to empower a local authority to provide CCTV equipment in order to promote the prevention of crime and the welfare of victims of crime. It further noted that the publicising of information about the successful operation of the CCTV system reinforced the deterrent effect of its operation. The Council had the power to distribute the CCTV footage to the media for transmission by virtue of section 111(1) of the 1972 Act in the discharge of their functions under section 163 of the 1994 Act.

67. Accordingly, the Court considers that the disclosure did have a basis in law and was, with appropriate legal advice, foreseeable (see *The Sunday Times v. the United Kingdom (no. 1)*, judgment of 26 April 1979, Series A no. 30, p. 31, §49).

It also regards the disclosure as having pursued the legitimate aim of public safety, the prevention of disorder and crime and the protection of the rights of others.

C. Whether the interference was justified

1. The parties' submissions

68. The Government considered that any interference was proportionate. They pointed out that the domestic courts had already assessed the reasonableness of the disclosure, and that this Court should not substitute its own assessment for that of the domestic institutions.

69. As to the reasons why any such interference was proportionate, the Government emphasised the obligation to protect the life and property of citizens. Given the margin of appreciation open to States to implement the most suitable measures to combat crime, the Government's view of CCTV as a powerful weapon in that battle should be accepted. Disclosure of CCTV footage complemented this aim: the policy was to give CCTV as prominent a role as possible in order to avoid covert surveillance, to inspire public confidence and support for the system and to deter criminals. This aim of deterrence was expressly accepted by the High Court as one of the bases of the Council's conduct, and crime had decreased since the installation of the CCTV system. An important element of the publicity given to CCTV had been the release of footage to the media and the CCTV footage of the applicant was an entirely suitable illustration of the type of situation constituting good publicity for CCTV. It was not a private tragedy sensationalised by the disclosure of the footage since it did not show the applicant's attempted suicide and it was not apparent from the footage disclosed that he had made such an attempt or tried to injure himself in any way. This was not obvious to the Council operator, who did not know on the relevant evening that the applicant had tried to commit suicide. Rather, the footage evidenced the police defusing a potentially dangerous situation.

70. In addition, they argued that cooperation with the media to publicise the CCTV system would be undermined if it were necessary to obtain the consent of everyone who appeared on the images; the Government referred to scenes on crowded streets and to footage which might include missing persons whose consent could not be obtained.

71. Moreover, the Government submitted that the nature of the impugned act and the parties' conduct were relevant considerations in this context also. As to the impugned act, they pointed out that the disclosed footage was obtained neither covertly, intrusively or selectively and the degree of intrusion was limited. The applicant, the Government suggested, courted attention by going to a busy junction at the centre of Brentwood clearly brandishing a knife, and he compounded the publicity thereafter by his voluntary appearances in the media. Indeed, it was during those appearances that his identity was first made known to the public and that the first public reference was made to his attempted suicide. The Council, the Government contended, acted in good faith in the public interest with no commercial motive. Since it had no facilities to mask faces on CCTV footage, it released the footage to the media on the understanding that the relevant television companies would mask the applicant's image. The fact that those companies did not do so, or did so inadequately, was not the responsibility of the Council.

72. The applicant maintained that the interference was not proportionate given the serious nature of the interference. The Council should have, and could have, taken reasonable steps to identify the applicant and inform themselves of his situation. It should have, since the purpose of disclosing the film was to advertise widely the benefits of CCTV and not to identify a criminal. It could have, because there was only one person visible, whose identification would have been possible through the police, who had been called by the CCTV operator to the scene.

73. Moreover, he considered that the Council's attempt at ensuring the masking of the relevant image was inadequate. If the Council did not have the facilities themselves, they should have ensured that the media properly carried out the masking. Written agreements would be a step in the right direction, but none were completed prior to the disclosures in his case.

74. Furthermore, the applicant submitted that there was no sufficiently important countervailing public interest. He was not a public figure and he had no public role. The disclosure was made not to catch a criminal or find a missing person but to satisfy the general aim of publicising the effectiveness of the CCTV system, with which aim properly masked images or other less intrusive footage would have been consistent.

75. The applicant contested the Government's assertion that the High Court had assessed the proportionality of the interference. He also rejected their contention that he courted attention on 20 August 1995. He further disputed their questioning of his motivation by their reference to his voluntary media appearances in 1996: his image had already been published and broadcast without his consent and he was identified by those who knew him. He then correctly pursued any remedies available, which procedures were public, and he could not be criticised for speaking about his predicament to responsible media. He faced the classic dilemma of one whose privacy has been interfered with: seeking a remedy and defending one's position by speaking out inevitably led to further publicity.

2. The Court's assessment

76. In determining whether the disclosure was "necessary in a democratic society", the Court will consider whether, in the light of the case as a whole, the reasons adduced to justify the disclosure were "relevant and sufficient" and whether the measures were proportionate to the legitimate aims pursued.

77. In cases concerning the disclosure of personal data, the Court has recognised that a margin of appreciation should be left to the competent national authorities in striking a fair balance between the relevant conflicting public and private interests. However, this margin goes hand in hand with European supervision (see *Funke v. France*, judgment of 25 February 1993, Series A no. 256-A, p. 24, §55) and the scope of this margin depends on such factors as the nature and seriousness of the interests at stake and the gravity of the interference (see *Z v. Finland*, judgment of 25 February 1997, *Reports of judgments and Decisions* 1997-I, p. 348, §99).

78. *Z v. Finland* related to the disclosure in court proceedings without the applicant's consent of her health records, including her HIV status. The Court noted that the protection of personal data was of fundamental importance to a person's enjoyment of his or her right to respect for private life and that the domestic law must therefore afford appropriate safeguards to prevent any such disclosure as may be inconsistent with the guarantees in Article 8 of the Convention. In so finding, the Court referred, *mutatis mutandis*, to Articles 3 §2 (c), 5, 6 and 9 of the Convention for the Protection of Individuals with

regard to Automatic Processing of Personal Data (European Treaty Series no. 108, Strasbourg, 1981). It went on to find that the above considerations were "especially valid" as regards the protection of the confidentiality of information about a person's HIV status, noting that the interests in protecting the confidentiality of such information weighed heavily in the balance in determining whether the interference was proportionate to the legitimate aim pursued. Such interference could not be compatible with Article 8 of the Convention unless it was justified by an overriding requirement in the public interest. Any State measures compelling disclosure of such information without the consent of the patient and any safeguards designed to secure an effective protection called for the most careful scrutiny on the part of the Court.

79. As to the present case, the Court would note at the outset that the applicant was not charged with, much less convicted of, an offence. The present case does not therefore concern disclosure of footage of the commission of a crime.

The Court has also noted, on the one hand, the nature and seriousness of the interference with the applicant's private life (see paragraph 63 above). On the other hand, the Court appreciates the strong interest of the State in detecting and preventing crime. It is not disputed that the CCTV system plays an important role in these respects and that that role is rendered more effective and successful through advertising the CCTV system and its benefits.

80. However, the Court notes that the Council had other options available to it to allow it to achieve the same objectives. In the first place, it could have identified the applicant through enquiries with the police and thereby obtained his consent prior to disclosure. Alternatively, the Council could have masked the relevant images itself. A further alternative would have been to take the utmost care in ensuring that the media, to which the disclosure was made, masked those images. The Court notes that the Council did not explore the first and second options and considers that the steps taken by the Council in respect of the third were inadequate.

81. As to the first option, it is true that individuals may not give their consent or that such an exercise may not be feasible where the footage includes images of numerous persons. In such circumstances, it could be argued that a consent-based system of disclosure could in practice undermine any action aimed at promoting the effectiveness of the CCTV system. However, in the present case, such limitations were not particularly relevant. The relevant footage clearly focused on and related to one individual only. It is not disputed that the Council, whose CCTV operator had alerted the police and observed their intervention, could have made enquiries with the police to establish the identity of the applicant and thereby request his consent to disclosure. Indeed, it appears from the Council's own *CCTV News* article of 9 October 1995 that certain enquiries had been made with the police to establish that the relevant individual had been questioned and assisted, but not to establish his identity.

82. Alternatively, the Council could have masked such images itself. While the Government confirmed that the Council did not have a masking facility, the Court notes that the Council's own guidelines indicate that it was intended to have such a facility. Indeed, the Court notes that the Council itself directly disclosed in its own publication, the *CCTV News*, stills taken from the relevant footage and that no attempt was made to mask those images.

83. As to the third option of ensuring appropriate and sufficient masking by the media to whom footage is disclosed, the Court notes that the High Court found that Anglia Television and the producers of the BBC programme had been orally requested

to mask the applicant. The Court considers, contrary to the view of the High Court, that it would have been reasonable for the Council to demand written undertakings of the media to mask images, which requirement would have emphasised the need to maintain confidentiality. Indeed the High Court suggested that lessons could be learnt from this "unfortunate incident" and that, with the benefit of hindsight, the Council might see if it could tighten up its guidelines to avoid similar incidents in the future. The Council itself clearly intended to have a written licence agreement with the producers of "Crime Beat" but this does not appear to have been concluded as no final and signed agreement was disclosed to the applicant or submitted by the Government to this Court. The Essex police guidelines recommend written agreements with clauses on masking. Moreover, there is no evidence that the *Yellow Advertiser* was requested to mask the applicant's image at all.

84. Furthermore, the relevant CCTV material was released with the aim of promoting the effectiveness of the CCTV system in the prevention and detection of crime and it was not therefore unlikely that the footage would be used in such contexts. This proved to be the case, most notably in the BBC's "Crime Beat" programme. In such circumstances, and even though the applicant does not directly complain about damage to his reputation, the Court considers that particular care was required of the Council, which would reasonably have included verifying with the police whether the individual had, in fact, been charged or not. It is difficult to accept the Government's explanation that the Council was unaware of his identity. As noted above, the Council's own *CCTV News* article of 9 October 1995 would seem to imply that the Council had established that the relevant individual had been questioned and given assistance for his problems and could therefore have verified whether the applicant had, in fact, been charged. Indeed, the *Yellow Advertiser* had established by 13 October 1995 that the applicant had not been charged by the police.

85. In sum, the Court does not find that, in the circumstances of this case, there were relevant or sufficient reasons which would justify the direct disclosure by the Council to the public of stills from the footage in its own *CCTV News* article without the Council obtaining the applicant's consent or masking his identity, or which would justify its disclosures to the media without the Council taking steps to ensure so far as possible that such masking would be effected by the media. The crime-prevention objective and context of the disclosures demanded particular scrutiny and care in these respects in the present case.

86. Finally, the Court does not find that the applicant's later voluntary media appearances diminish the serious nature of the interference or reduce the correlative requirement of care concerning disclosures. The applicant was the victim of a serious interference with his right to privacy involving national and local media coverage: it cannot therefore be held against him that he sought thereafter to avail himself of the media to expose and complain about that wrongdoing.

87. Accordingly, the Court considers that the disclosures by the Council of the CCTV material in the *CCTV News* and to the *Yellow Advertiser*, Anglia Television and the BBC were not accompanied by sufficient safeguards to prevent disclosure inconsistent with the guarantees of respect for the applicant' private life contained in Article 8. As such, the disclosure constituted a disproportionate and therefore unjustified interference with his private life and a violation of Article 8 of the Convention.

. . . .

~

QUESTIONS & COMMENTS

(1) How far could the state's liability extend for similar photographs or videos taken by private individuals?

Klass and Others v. Federal Republic of Germany
European Court of Human Rights
28 Eur. Ct. H.R. (ser. A) (1978)
2 E.H.R.R. 214 (1979–80)

. . . .

FACTS:

10. The applicants, who are German nationals, are Gerhard Klass, an *Oberstaatsanwalt*, Peter Lubberger, a lawyer, Jurgen Nussbruch, a judge, Hans-Jurgen Pohl and Dieter Selb, lawyers. All five applicants claim that article 10(2) of the Basic Law (*Grundgesetz*) and a statute enacted in pursuance of that provision, namely the Act of 13 August 1968 on Restrictions on the Secrecy of the Mail, Post and Telecommunications (*Gesetz zur Beschränkung des Brief- Post- und Fernmeldegeheimnisses*, hereinafter referred to as 'the G 10'), are contrary to the Convention. They do not dispute that the State has the right to have recourse to the surveillance measures contemplated by the legislation; they challenge this legislation in that it permits those measures without obliging the authorities in every case to notify the persons concerned after the event, and in that it excludes any remedy before the courts against the ordering and execution of such measures.

11. Before lodging their application with the Commission, the applicants had appealed to the Federal Constitutional Court. By judgment of 15 December 1970, that Court held that article 1(5) (5) of the G 10 was void, being incompatible with the second sentence of article 10(2) of the Basic Law, insofar as it excluded notification of the person concerned about the measures of surveillance even when such notification could be given without jeopardising the purpose of the restriction. The Constitutional Court dismissed the remaining claims. (30 COLLECTED DECISIONS OF THE CONSTITUTIONAL COURT [BVerfGE] 1.)

Since the operative provisions of that judgment have the force of law, the competent authorities are bound to apply the G 10 in the form and subject to the interpretation decided by the Constitutional Court. Furthermore, the Government of the Federal Republic of Germany were prompted by this judgment to propose amendments to the G 10, but the parliamentary proceedings have not yet been completed.

. . . .

DECISION:

. . . .

II. On the alleged violation of Article 8

39. The applicants claim that the contested legislation[,] notably because the person concerned is not informed of the surveillance measures and cannot have recourse to the courts when such measures are terminated, violates Article 8 of the Convention which provides as follows:

1. Everyone has the right to respect for his private and family life, his home and his correspondence.

2. There shall be no interference by a public authority with the exercise of this right except such as is in accordance with the law and is necessary in a democratic society in the interests of national security, public safety or the economic well-being of the country, for the prevention of disorder or crime, for the protection of health or morals or for the protection of the rights and freedoms of others.

40. According to article 10(2) of the Basic Law, restrictions upon the secrecy of the mail, post and telecommunications may be ordered but only pursuant to a statute. Article 1(1) of the G 10 allows certain authorities to open and inspect mail and post, to read telegraphic messages and to monitor and record telephone conversations [citation omitted]. The Court's examination under Article 8 is thus limited to the authorisation of such measures alone and does not extend, for instance, to the secret surveillance effected in pursuance of the Code of Criminal Procedure [citation omitted].

41. The first matter to be decided is whether and, if so, in what respect the contested legislation in permitting the above-mentioned measures of surveillance, constitutes an interference with the exercise of the right guaranteed to the applicants under Article 8(1).

Although telephone conversations are not expressly mentioned in paragraph 1 of Article 18, the Court considers, as did the Commission, that such conversations are covered by the notions of 'private life' and 'correspondence' referred to by this provision.

In its report, the Commission expressed the opinion that the secret surveillance provided for under the German legislation amounted to an interference with the exercise of the right set forth in Article 8(1). Neither before the Commission nor before the Court did the Government contest this issue. Clearly, any of the permitted surveillance measures, once applied to a given individual, would result in an interference by a public authority with the exercise of that individual's right to respect for his private and family life and his correspondence. Furthermore, in the mere existence of the legislation itself, there is involved, for all those to whom the legislation could be applied, a menace of surveillance; this menace necessarily strikes at freedom of communication between users of the postal and telecommunication services and thereby constitutes an 'interference by a public authority' with the exercise of the applicants' right to respect for private and family life and for correspondence.

The Court does not exclude that the contested legislation, and therefore the measures permitted thereunder, could also involve an interference with the exercise of a person's right to respect for his home. However, the Court does not deem it necessary in the present proceedings to decide this point.

42. The cardinal issue arising under Article 8 in the present case is whether the interference so found is justified by the terms of paragraph 2 of the Article. This paragraph, since it provides for an exception to a right guaranteed by the Convention, is to be narrowly interpreted. Powers of secret surveillance of citizens, characterising as they do the police state, are tolerable under the Convention only in so far as strictly necessary for safeguarding the democratic institutions.

43. In order for the 'interference' established above not to infringe Article 8, it must, according to paragraph 2, first of all have been 'in accordance with the law'. This requirement is fulfilled in the present case since the 'interference' results from Acts passed by Parliament, including one Act which was modified by the Federal Constitutional Court,

in the exercise of its jurisdiction, by its judgment of 15 December 1970 (*see* §11 above). In addition, the Court observes that, as both the Government and the Commission pointed out, any individual measure of surveillance has to comply with the strict conditions and procedures laid down in the legislation itself.

44. It remains to be determined whether the other requisites laid down in paragraph 2 of Article 8 were also satisfied. According to the Government and the Commission, the interference permitted by the contested legislation was 'necessary in a democratic society in the interests of national security' and/or 'for the prevention of disorder or crime'. Before the Court, the Government submitted that the interference was additionally justified 'in the interests of... public safety' and 'for the protection of the rights and freedoms of others'.

45. The G 10 defines precisely, and thereby limits, the purposes for which the restrictive measures may be imposed. It provides that, in order to protect against 'imminent dangers' threatening 'the free democratic constitutional order', 'the existence or security of the Federation or of a Land', 'the security of the [allied] armed forces' stationed on the territory of the Republic or the security of 'the troops of one of the Three Powers stationed in the Land of Berlin', the responsible authorities may authorise the restrictions referred to above [citation omitted].

46. The Court, sharing the view of the Government and the Commission, finds that the aim of the G 10 is indeed to safeguard national security and/or to prevent disorder to crime in pursuance of Article 8(2). In these circumstances, the Court does not deem it necessary to decide whether the further purposes cited by the Government are also relevant.

On the other hand, it has to be ascertained whether the means provided under the impugned legislation for the achievement of the above-mentioned aim remain in all respects within the bounds of what is necessary in a democratic society.

47. The applicants do not object to the German legislation in that it provides for wide-ranging powers of surveillance; they accept such powers, and the resultant encroachment upon the right guaranteed by Article 8(1), as being a necessary means of defence for the protection of the democratic State. The applicants consider, however, that paragraph 2 of Article 8 lays down for such powers certain limits which have to be respected in a democratic society in order to ensure that the society does not slide imperceptibly towards totalitarianism. In their view, the contested legislation lacks adequate safeguards against possible abuse.

48. As the Delegates observed, the Court, in its appreciation of the scope of the protection offered by Article 8, cannot but take judicial notice of two important facts. The first consists of the technical advances made in the means of espionage and, correspondingly, of surveillance; the second is the development of terrorism in Europe in recent years. Democratic societies nowadays find themselves threatened by highly sophisticated forms of espionage and by terrorism, with the result that the State must be able, in order effectively to counter such threats, to undertake the secret surveillance of subversive elements operating within its jurisdiction. The Court has therefore to accept that the existence of some legislation granting powers of secret surveillance over the mail, post and telecommunications is, under exceptional conditions, necessary in a democratic society in the interests of national security and/or for the prevention of disorder or crime.

49. As concerns the fixing of the conditions under which the system of surveillance is to be operated, the Court points out that the domestic legislature enjoys a certain discretion. It is certainly not for the Court to substitute for the assessment of the national

authorities any other assessment of what might be the best policy in this field. [citation omitted]

Nevertheless, the Court stresses that this does not mean that the Contracting States enjoy an unlimited discretion to subject persons within their jurisdiction to secret surveillance. The Court, being aware of the danger such a law poses of undermining or even destroying democracy on the ground of defending it, affirms that the Contracting States may not, in the name of the struggle against espionage and terrorism, adopt whatever measures they deem appropriate.

50. The Court must be satisfied that, whatever system of surveillance is adopted, there exist adequate and effective guarantees against abuse. This assessment has only a relative character: it depends on all the circumstances of the case, such as the nature, scope and duration of the possible measures, the grounds required for ordering such measures, the authorities competent to permit, carry out and supervise such measures, and the kind of remedy provided by the national law.

The functioning of the system of secret surveillance established by the contested legislation, as modified by the Federal Constitutional Court's judgment of 15 December 1970, must therefore be examined in the light of the Convention.

51. According to the G 10, a series of limitative conditions have to be satisfied before a surveillance measure can be imposed. Thus, the permissible restrictive measures are confined to cases in which there are factual indications for suspecting a person of planning, committing or having committed certain serious criminal acts; measures may only be ordered if the establishment of the facts by another method is without prospects of success or considerably more difficult; even then, the surveillance may cover only the specific suspect or his presumed 'contact-persons' [citation omitted]. Consequently, so-called exploratory or general surveillance is not permitted by the contested legislation.

Surveillance may be ordered only on written application giving reasons, and such an application may be made only by the head, or his substitute, of certain services; the decision thereon must be taken by a Federal Minister empowered for the purpose by the Chancellor or, where appropriate, by the supreme Land authority [citation omitted]. Accordingly, under the law, there exists an administrative procedure designed to ensure that measure are not ordered haphazardly, irregularly or without due and proper consideration. In addition, although not required by the Act, the competent Minister in practice and except in urgent cases seeks the prior consent of the G 10 Commission [citation omitted].

52. The G 10 also lays down strict conditions with regard to the implementation of the surveillance measures and to the processing of the information thereby obtained. The measures in question remain in force for a maximum of three months and may be renewed only on fresh application; the measures must immediately be discontinued once the required conditions have ceased to exist or the measures themselves are no longer necessary; knowledge and documents thereby obtained may not be used for other ends, and documents must be destroyed as soon as they are no longer needed to achieve the required purpose [citation omitted].

As regards the implementation of the measures, an initial control is carried out by an official qualified or judicial office. This official examines the information obtained from transmitting to the competent services such information as may be used in accordance with the Act and is relevant to the purpose of the measure; he destroys any other intelligence that may have been gathered [citation omitted].

53. Under the G 10, while recourse to the courts in respect of the ordering and implementation of measures of surveillance is excluded, subsequent control or review is provided instead, in accordance with article 10(2) of the Basic Law, by two bodies appointed by the people's elected representatives, namely, the Parliamentary Board and the G 10 Commission.

The competent Minister must, at least once every six months, report on the application of the G 10 to the Parliamentary Board consisting of five members of Parliament; the members of Parliament are appointed by the Bundestag in proportion to the parliamentary groupings, the opposition being represented on the Board. In addition, the Minister is bound every month to provide the G 10 Commission with an account of the measures he has ordered. In practice, he seeks the prior consent of this Commission. The latter decides, *ex officio* or on application by a person believing himself to be under surveillance, on both the legality of and the necessity for the measures in question; if it declares any measures to be illegal or unnecessary, the Minister must terminate them immediately. The Commission members are appointed for the current term of the Bundestag by the Parliamentary Board after consultation with the Government; they are completely dependent in the exercise of their functions and cannot be subject to instructions [citation omitted].

54. The Government maintains that Article 8(2) does not require judicial control of secret surveillance and that the system of review established under the G 10 does effectively protect the rights of the individual. The applicants, on the other hand, qualify this system as a 'form of political control', inadequate in comparison with the principle of judicial control which ought to prevail.

It therefore has to be determined whether the procedures for supervising the ordering and implementation of the restrictive measures are such as to keep the 'interference' resulting from the contested legislation to what is 'necessary in a democratic society'.

55. Review of surveillance may intervene at three stages: when the surveillance is first ordered, while it is being carried out, or after it has been terminated. As regards the first two stages, the very nature and logic of secret surveillance dictate that not only the surveillance itself but also the accompanying review should be effected without the individual's knowledge. Consequently, since the individual will necessarily be prevented from seeking an effective remedy of his own accord or from taking a direct part in any review proceedings, it is essential that the procedures established should themselves provide adequate and equivalent guarantees safeguarding the individual's rights. In addition, the values of a democratic society must be followed as faithfully as possible in the supervisory procedures if the bounds of necessity, within the meaning of Article 8(2), are not to be exceeded. One of the fundamental principles of a democratic society is the rule of law, which is expressly referred to in the Preamble to the Convention. (*See Golder v. United Kingdom*, 18 Eur. Ct. H.R. (ser. A) at 16–17 (1975).). The rule of law implies, *inter alia*, that an interference by the executive authorities with an individual's rights should be subject to an effective control which should normally be assured by the judiciary, at least in the last resort, judicial control offering the best guarantees of independence, impartiality and a proper procedure.

56. Within the system of surveillance established by the G 10, judicial control was excluded, being replaced by an initial control effected by an official qualified for judicial office and by the control provided by the Parliamentary Board and the G 10 Commission.

The Court considers that, in a field where abuse is potentially so easy in individual cases and could have such harmful consequences for democratic society as a whole, it is in principle desirable to entrust supervisory control to a judge.

Nevertheless, having regard to the nature of the supervisory and other safeguards provided for by the G 10, the Court concludes that the exclusion of judicial control does not exceed the limits of what may be deemed necessary in a democratic society. The Parliamentary Board and the G 10 Commission are independent of the authorities carrying out the surveillance, and are vested with sufficient powers and competence to exercise an effective and continuous control. Furthermore, the democratic character is reflected in the balanced membership of the Parliamentary Board. The opposition is represented on this body and is therefore able to participate in the control of the measures ordered by the competent Minister who is responsible to the Bundestag. The two supervisory bodies may, in the circumstances of the case, be regarded as enjoying sufficient independence to give an objective ruling.

The Court notes in addition that an individual believing himself to be under surveillance has the opportunity of complaining to the G 10 Commission and of having recourse to the Constitutional Court [citation omitted]. However, as the Government conceded, these are remedies which can come into play only in exceptional circumstances.

57. As regards review *a posteriori*, it is necessary to determine whether judicial control, in particular with the individual's participation, should continue to be excluded even after surveillance has ceased. Inextricably linked to this issue is the question of subsequent notification, since there is in principle little scope for recourse to the courts by the individual concerned unless he is advised of the measures taken without his knowledge and thus able retrospectively to challenge their legality.

The applicants' main complaint under Article 8 is in fact that the person concerned is not always subsequently informed after the suspension of surveillance and is not therefore in a position to seek an effective remedy before the courts. Their preoccupation is the danger of measures being improperly implemented without the individual knowing or being able to verify the extent to which his rights have been interfered with. In their view, effective control by the courts after the suspension of surveillance measures is necessary in a democratic society to ensure against abuses; otherwise adequate control of secret surveillance is lacking and the right conferred on individuals under Article 8 is simply eliminated.

In the Government's view, the subsequent notification which must be given since the Federal Constitutional Court's judgment [citation omitted] corresponds to the requirements of Article 8(2). In their submission, the whole efficacy of secret surveillance requires that, both before and after the event, information cannot be divulged if thereby the purpose of the investigation is, or would be retrospectively, thwarted. They stressed that recourse to the courts is no longer excluded after notification has been given, various legal remedies then becoming available to allow the individual, *inter alia*, to seek redress for any injury suffered [citation omitted].

58. In the opinion of the court, it has to be ascertained whether it is even feasible in practice to require subsequent notification in all cases.

The activity or danger against which a particular series of surveillance measures is directed may continue for years, even decades, after the suspension of those measures. Subsequent notification to each individual affected by a suspended measure might well jeopardise the long-term purpose that originally prompted the surveillance. Furthermore, as the Federal Constitutional Court rightly observed, such notification might serve to reveal the working methods and fields of operation of the intelligence services and even possibly to identify their agents. In the Court's view, in so far as the 'interference' resulting from the contested legislation is in principle justified under Article 8(2) [citation omitted], the fact of not informing the individual once surveillance has ceased cannot itself be incompatible with this provision, since it is this very fact which ensures the efficacy of the 'interference'. Moreover, it is to be recalled that, in pursuance of the Federal Constitutional Court's judgment of 15 December 1970, the person concerned must be informed after the termination of the surveillance measures as soon as notification can be made without jeopardising the purpose of the restriction [citation omitted].

59. Both in general and in relation to the question of subsequent notification, the applicants have constantly invoked the danger of abuse as a ground for their contention that the legislation they challenge does not fulfil the requirements of Article 8(2) of the Convention. While the possibility of improper action by a dishonest, negligent or over-zealous official can never be completely ruled out whatever the system, the considerations that matter for the purposes of the Court's present review are the likelihood of such action and the safeguards provided to protect against it.

The Court has examined above [citation omitted] the contested legislation in the light, *inter alia*, of these considerations. The Court notes in particular that the G 10 contains various provisions designed to reduce the effect of surveillance measures to an unavoidable minimum and to ensure that the surveillance is carried out in strict accordance with the law. In the absence of any evidence or indication that the actual practice followed is otherwise, the Court must assume that, in the democratic society of the Federal Republic of Germany, the relevant authorities are properly applying the legislation in issue.

The Court agrees with the Commission that some compromise between the require-ments for defending democratic society and individual rights is inherent in the system of the Convention. (*See, mutatis mutandis, Belgian Linquistics Case* [6 Eur. Ct. H.R. (ser. A) at 32 (1968)]) As the Preamble to the Convention states, 'Fundamental Freedoms ... are best maintained on the one hand by an effective political democracy and on the other by a common understanding and observance of the Human Rights upon which [the Contracting States] depend'. In the context of Article 8, this means that a balance must be sought between the exercise by the individual of the right guaranteed to him under paragraph 1 and the necessity under paragraph 2 to impose secret surveillance for the protection of the democratic society as a whole.

60. In the light of these considerations and of the detailed examination of the contested legislation, the Court concludes that the German legislature was justified to consider the interference resulting from that legislation with the exercise of the right guaranteed by Article 8(1) as being necessary in a democratic society in the interests of national security and for the prevention of disorder or crime (Art 8(2)). Accordingly, the Court finds no breach of Article 8 of the Convention.

....

∾

QUESTIONS & COMMENTS

(1) The European Court seems to treat the existence of terrorism as a sufficient reason to bypass judicial forms of review. In a country like the United States, however, far more people are killed in violence associated with the drug trade than from terrorism. Would the Court accept nonreviewable surveillance over drug trafficking as well? Is there something

about terrorism that requires a different approach? How would the Court's decision in *Peck v. United Kingdom* affect this issue?

The European Court stresses the need for adequate guarantees against abuse. Does the administrative procedure provided here seem enough? In the United States, secret surveillance of mail or telephones requires judicial approval beforehand. Is the inclusion of opposition members of parliament on the oversight board a sufficient alternative to judicial review? In what ways might a parliamentary body be better than judicial oversight? In what ways might judicial oversight be better?

(2) In *Huvig v. France*, 176-B Eur. Ct. H.R. (ser. A) (1990), the French authorities investigated Jacques Huvig and his wife for tax evasion. As part of the investigation, a judge issued a warrant to the gendarmerie to monitor and transcribe all of the Huvigs' telephone calls for part of one day and all of another. The telephone taps lasted a total of twenty-eight hours. The Huvigs were eventually tried and convicted of tax evasion although no evidence collected from the telephone taps was used. The Huvigs raised the telephone taps in several motions to dismiss their charges. After their convictions were final, they applied to the European Commission and Court of Human Rights that found an Article 8 violation.

Following their analysis in *Klass*, the Court first considered whether the "interference" with the "right to respect for his private and family life, his home and his correspondence" was "in accordance with the law." Although the application of existing French law to telephone taps was contestable, the Court felt bound to follow the interpretation of French law by the French courts that the judicial warrant was authorized by law. But the Court went on to hold that the exception for interferences "in accordance with the law" is not a mere formal requirement. To approve the surveillance, the Court must determine that the authorizing national law meets the convention's norms for the substantive quality of the law, *i.e.*, its accessibility, protectiveness, and foreseeability.

The Court held that, unlike *Klass*, the law here did not provide for adequate procedural protection. Specifically, the French law set no temporal limits on the investigation, leaving to police's discretion to determine when the public's investigatory needs were met. Under the German "G-10" rules, every surveillance order had to be renewed every three months, requiring reapplication and reconfirmation of the appropriateness of the mission. Even without a requirement of judicial review, Germany's procedures required oversight and responsibility by higher political officials over the information collected and its use by the government. The French surveillance procedures allowed investigators to make their own judgment without the involvement of higher officials on a continuing basis.

(3) Note that the European Court in *Klass* recognized that the German law could have a chilling effect on persons using the mail and telecommunication services.

> [I]n the mere existence of the legislation itself, there is involved, for all those to whom the legislation could be applied, a menace of surveillance; this menace necessarily strikes at freedom of communication between users of the postal and telecommunication services and thereby constitutes an 'interference by a public authority' with the exercise of the applicants' right to respect for private and family life and for correspondence.

Id. at §41. Article 10, ECHR, guarantees the right to freedom of expression. If the applicant in *Klass* had raised a freedom-of-expression claim along with his privacy claim, do you think the European Court would have decided this case differently, given the interests involved?

García Pérez v. Peru
Inter-American Commission on Human Rights
Report No. 1/95, Case 11.006
Inter-Am. Cm. H.R. 71,
OEA/Ser.L/V/II.88, Doc. 9 rev. (1995)

. . . .

[T]he petitioners have stated that on the night of April 5, 1992, Army soldiers under the command of General Hermoza Ríos entered the home of [former Peruvian President] Dr. Alan García and unlawfully seized private family papers, such as identification papers, passports, property deeds, tax declarations and legal documents used in the defense of the former President in the case brought against him for the crime of unlawful enrichment.

Article 11 of the American Convention on Human Rights protects the right to privacy and stipulates that no one may be the object of arbitrary or abusive interference in his private life or family.

By explicitly protecting the home and private correspondence of individuals, this article serves to guarantee that the right to privacy will be respected. This protection is consistent with the American Declaration of the Rights and Duties of Man inasmuch as it upholds the inviolability of domicile and private papers as guarantees arbitrary State interference in the private lives of individuals [Arts. IX and X].

However, the right to privacy is not absolute; quite the contrary, exercise of this right is routinely restricted by the domestic laws of States.

The guarantee of the inviolability of the domicile and of private papers must give way when there is a well-substantiated search warrant issued by a competent judicial authority, spelling out the reasons for the measure being adopted and specifying the place to be searched and the objects that will be seized.

The 1979 Constitution of Peru stipulated the inviolability of domicile and of private papers except when an order has been issued by a competent judicial authority authorizing the search, explaining its reasons and, where appropriate, authorizing the seizure of private papers, while respecting the guarantees stipulated by law.[1]

Based on these concepts, the Commission concludes that the warrantless search of Dr. García's home and the seizure of private family papers – actions committed by Peruvian soldiers – were committed in complete disregard of the procedural requirements stipulated in the Constitution. The violation of those requirements indicates that the Government of Peru failed to guarantee to Dr. Alan García and to his family the full exercise of their right to privacy.

The arguments made by the Government of Peru to the effect that the Army soldiers surrounded the residence of Dr. García Perez in order to protect him are, in themselves, insufficient. Protection of a private residence does not call for action by heavily armed soldiers nor for the use of war tanks equipped with canons, small tanks or armored troop carriers.

2. Criminal prosecution for the crime of illegal possession of weapons

As the petitioners indicated, Dr. Alan García Perez is charged in two criminal cases for the illegal possession of weapons, wherein the only incriminating evidence – firearms,

---

[1] See Article 2, subparagraphs 7 and 8 of the Constitution in force until December 31, 1993.

munitions and explosives – was unlawfully obtained by searching his private residence, in one case, and the headquarters of the Aprista Party of which the former President is Secretary General in the other case.

Article 8.1 of the American Convention provides that every person has the right to a hearing, with due guarantees, in the substantiation of any action of a criminal nature made against him.

Similarly, Article 8.2 provides that during proceedings, every person is entitled, with full equality, to certain minimum guarantees. The enumeration contained in this clause has been interpreted as a list of the minimum guarantees, but not an exhaustive list. Hence, there are other guarantees recognized in the domestic laws of that State that, although not explicitly included in the text of the Convention, are equally protected under the broad wording of paragraph 1 of Article 8 of the Convention. [note omitted]

.... In effect, inviolability of domicile is one of the implicit guarantees of that article. In effect, inviolability of domicile is more than a guarantee of privacy; it is a guarantee of due process inasmuch as it establishes what can be seized, that being incriminating evidence against an individual charged with a crime. When a search of a domicile is conducted without observing the proper constitutional procedures, that guarantee prevents any evidence thus obtained from being used to arrive at a subsequent court decision. Thus, in practice it functions as an exclusionary rule, one that eliminates illegally obtained evidence.

The *raison d'etre* of this guarantee and of the rule excluding evidence obtained by violating that guarantee has been explained by Maier as follows:

> The justification of the methods used to arrive at the truth depends upon the observance of juridical rules governing how they can be validly weighed in the proceedings. Not all methods are allowed and authorities must compile evidence according to the discipline imposed by procedural law. The judicial procedures are not mere formalities; instead, since they work directly to protect human dignity, they act as a material category... [2]

The proceedings instituted against Dr. García Perez for illegal possession of weapons were based exclusively on unlawfully obtained evidence. The searches conducted of his private residence and of the headquarters of the Aprista Party were effected by means of intimidating tactics by Army troopers, in total disregard for the procedures stipulated by Peru's domestic laws.

For this reason, the Commission considers that the "procedural guarantees" protected by the American Convention were not respected in processing the criminal cases against former President Alan García.

....

[The Commission recommended that the Government undertake the necessary measures to re-establish the "*status quo ante.*"]

∾

---

[2] Julio B. J. Maier, *Derecho Procesal Penal Argentino*, Buenos Aires, Editorial Hammurabi, 1989, pp. 470 and 471.

QUESTIONS & COMMENTS

(1) Many supporters of limiting the exclusionary rule in the United States emphasize the importance of truth finding as the central value of the criminal process. Does the Commission reject that view? Does it matter that this case involves highly charged political antagonisms, while the typical exclusionary rule case in the United States involves drugs seized from low-level dealers and users?

(2) In *The Prosecutor v. Muciç*, Case No. IT-96-21, ICT-Y (9 Feb. 1998), the trial chamber allowed the admission of documents seized by the Austrian police. The seizure may have entailed minor breaches of the Austrian law on search and seizure. The trial chamber allowed the admission because not admitting the evidence "would constitute a dangerous obstacle to the administration of justice." If evidence is obtained illegally by the police, how reliable is that evidence? Consider the ICT-Y's own rules of procedure:

> Rule 95. Evidence Obtained by Means Contrary to Internationally Protected Human Rights
>
> No evidence shall be admissible if obtained by methods which cast substantial doubt on its reliability or if its admission is antithetical to, and would seriously damage, the integrity of the proceedings.

Rule 95, ICT-Y Rules of Procedure.

How does the ICT-Y's ruling comport with the Inter-American Commission's in *García Pérez v. Peru*? How does the ICT-Y's ruling compare with the ICC Statute:

> States Parties shall, in accordance with the provisions of this Part and under *procedures of national law*, comply with requests by the Court to provide the following assistance in relation to investigations or prosecutions:
>
> . . .
>
> (h) The execution of searches and seizures; . . . .

Art. 93, ICC Statute (emphasis provided).

(3) Does the exclusionary rule apply to the use of evidence acquired during an international armed conflict? If evidence is found during, *e.g.*, a warrantless search of houses during a general military operation, could such evidence be used in a subsequent criminal trial? What if the defendant was a nonstate actor charged with terrorism? A state actor charged with war crimes?

Crèmieux v. France
European Court of Human Rights
256-B Eur. Ct. H.R. (ser. A) (1993)
16 E.H.R.R. 357 (1993)

. . . .

FACTS:

I. The circumstances of the case

6. Mr Paul Crèmieux, a French citizen born in 1908, is retired and lives at his female companion's home in Marseilles. At the material time he was chairman and managing director of SAPVIN, a wholesale wine firm, whose head office is in Marseilles.

A. The house searches and seizures of documents

7. In October 1976, in the course of an investigation into the SODEVIM company, customs officers seized documents relating to business transactions between SAPVIN and foreign firms.

8. Thereafter, from 27 January 1977 to 26 February 1980, the customs authorities carried out 83 investigative operations in the form of interviews and of raids on SAPVIN's head office, on the applicant's home and at other addresses of his and on the homes of other people, during which further items were seized.

Each of the house searches was made under Articles 64 and 454 of the Customs Code. They were conducted by officials from the National Customs Investigations Department ('the DNED') in the presence of a senior police officer (*officier de police judiciaire*); a report was made on each of them and they all led to Mr Crèmieux's being subsequently interviewed.

9. Several such searches were made on 23 January 1979.

One of them began at 7 am at the applicant's Paris home, in his absence. The customs officers were received by Mr Crèmieux's son; they inspected the office and took away 518 documents, some of which, according to Mr Crèmieux, had no connection with the customs investigation. The son initialed the inventory of documents. The applicant, who had arrived at 9.10 am, signed the report together with his son; he denied having been able, as the Government maintained, to go through the documents.

Another search began at 8 am at the home of Mr Crèmieux's female companion, whom, the applicant claimed, the DNED officials had followed into the bathroom when she said she wanted to put on a dressing-gown. Numerous personal papers were seized.

Searches were also made of the homes of other people, who had business relations with the applicant and his company.

10. On 24 January and 17 May 1979, Mr Crèmieux was questioned by customs officers.

On 16 February 1979 they opened the private strongbox he had at SAPVIN's head office and took 17 documents from it.

[Crèmieux applied to the European Commission of Human Rights claiming an Article 8 violation to this right to respect for private life. The Commission found no violation and referred the case to the European Court of Human Rights.]

. . . .

DECISION [OF THE EUROPEAN COURT OF HUMAN RIGHTS]

. . . .

B. Merits of the complaint

31. The Government conceded that there had been an interference with Mr Crèmieux's right to respect for his private life, and the Commission additionally found that there had been an interference with his right to respect for his home.

Like Mr Crèmieux, the Court considers that all the rights secured in Article 8(1) are in issue, except for the right to respect for family life. It must accordingly be determined whether the interferences in question satisfied the conditions in paragraph 2.

1. 'In accordance with the law'

32. The applicant contended that the interferences had no legal basis. As worded at the time, Article 64 of the Customs Code was, he claimed, contrary to the 1958 Constitution

because it did not make house searches and seizures subject to judicial authorisation. Admittedly, its constitutionality could not be reviewed, since it had come into force before the Constitution had. Nevertheless, in the related field of taxation the Constitutional Council had rejected section 89 of the Budget Act for 1984, concerning the investigation of income tax and turnover tax offences, holding, *inter alia*:

> While the needs of the Revenue's work may dictate that tax officials should be authorised to make investigations in private places, such investigations can only be conducted in accordance with Article 66 of the Constitution, which makes the judiciary responsible for protecting the liberty of the individual in all its aspects, in particular the inviolability of the home. Provision must be made for judicial participation in order that the judiciary's responsibility and supervisory power may be maintained in their entirety. (Decision no 83-164 DC of 29 December 1983, OFFICIAL GAZETTE (*JOURNAL OFFICIEL*), 30 December 1983, p 3874.)

33. The Government, whose arguments the Commission accepted in substance, maintained that in Article 64 of the Customs Code, as supplemented by a fairly substantial body of case law, the power to search houses was defined very closely and represented a transposition to customs legislation and the regulations governing financial dealings with foreign countries of the power of search provided for in ordinary criminal procedure. Provision was first made for it in an Act of 6 August 1791 and subsequently in a legislative decree of 12 July 1934, and it had been widened in 1945 to cover investigations into exchange-control offences and confirmed on several occasions. In the Government's submission, its constitutionality could not be put in doubt, any more than that of Article 454 of the same code, since review of the constitutionality of statutes took place between their enactment by Parliament and promulgation and was within the sole competence of the Constitutional Council, to the exclusion of all other courts.

As to the 'quality' of the national legal rules *vis-a-vis* the Convention, it was ensured by the precision with which the legislation and case law laid down the scope and manner of exercise of the relevant power, and this eliminated any risk of arbitrariness. Thus, even before the reform of 1986–89, the courts had supervised customs investigations *ex post facto* but very efficiently. And in any case, Article 8 of the Convention contained no requirement that house searches and seizures should be judicially authorised in advance.

34. The Court does not consider it necessary to determine the issue in this instance, as at all events the interferences complained of are incompatible with Article 8 in other respects.

2. Legitimate aim

35. The Government and the Commission considered that the interferences in question were in the interests of 'the economic well-being of the country' and 'the prevention of crime.'

Notwithstanding the applicant's arguments to the contrary, the Court is of the view that the interferences were in pursuit of at any rate the first of these legitimate aims.

3. 'Necessary in a democratic society'

36. In Mr Crèmieux's submission, the interferences could not be regarded as 'necessary in a democratic society.' Their scope was unlimited and they had also been carried out in an unacceptable manner. In the first place, their sheer scale was, he said, striking:

83 investigative operations spread over three years, although the case was neither serious nor complex and ended with a composition; furthermore, none of the documents removed had proved that any exchange-control offence had been committed. The interferences further reflected a lack of discrimination on the part of the customs officers, who took possession of purely private papers and correspondence and lawyer's letters and subsequently returned a very large number of the documents seized, which they deemed unnecessary for the investigation. Lastly, the interferences illustrated the authorities' hounding of the applicant, with the customs searches (*visites domiciliaires*) being turned into thoroughgoing general searches (*perquisitions*).

37. The Government, whose contentions the Commission accepted in substance, argued that house searches and seizures were the only means available to the authorities for investigating offences against the legislation governing financial dealings with foreign countries and thus preventing the flight of capital and tax evasion. In such fields there was a *corpus delicti* only very rarely if at all; the 'physical manifestation' of the offence therefore lay mainly in documents which a guilty party could easily conceal or destroy. Such persons, however, had the benefit of substantial safeguards, strengthened by very rigorous judicial supervision: decision-making by the head of the customs district concerned, the rank of the officers authorised to establish offences, the presence of a senior police officer (*officier de police judiciaire*), the timing of searches, the preservation of lawyers' and doctors' professional secrecy, the possibility of invoking the liability of the public authorities, *etc.* In short, even before the reform of 1986–89, the French system had ensured that there was a proper balance between the requirements of law enforcement and the protection of the rights of the individual.

As regards the circumstances of the case, the Government made two observations. First, the composition agreed to by the authorities was tantamount to acknowledgement by Mr Crèmieux of the offence committed; far from demonstrating that the case was of little importance, it was an efficient procedure commonly used by the customs to obviate more cumbersome proceedings with identical consequences. Secondly, the many house searches had been made necessary by the number of different places where Mr Crèmieux might keep documents.

38. The Court has consistently held that the Contracting States have a certain margin of appreciation in assessing the need for an interference, but it goes hand in hand with European supervision. The exceptions provided for in Article 8(2) are to be interpreted narrowly (*See Klass and Others v. Germany*, 28 Eur. Ct. H.R. (ser. A) at 21 (1978)), and the need for them in a given case must be convincingly established.

39. Undoubtedly, in the field under consideration – the prevention of capital outflows and tax evasion – States encounter serious difficulties owing to the scale and complexity of banking systems and financial channels and to the immense scope for international investment, made all the easier by the relative porousness of national borders. The Court therefore recognises that they may consider it necessary to have recourse to measures such as house searches and seizures in order to obtain physical evidence of exchange-control offences and, where appropriate, to prosecute those responsible. Nevertheless, the relevant legislation and practice must afford adequate and effective safeguards against abuse. (*See*, among other authorities and, *mutatis mutandis, Klass and Others v. Germany*, 28 Eur. Ct. H.R. at 23.)

40. This was not so in the instant case. At the material time – and the Court does not have to express an opinion on the legislative reforms of 1986 and 1989, which were

designed to afford better protection for individuals – the customs authorities had very wide powers; in particular, they had exclusive competence to assess the expediency, number, length and scale of inspections. Above all, in the absence of any requirement of a judicial warrant the restrictions and conditions provided for in law, which were emphasised by the Government, appear too lax and full of loopholes for the interferences in the applicant's right to have been strictly proportionate to the legitimate aim pursued.

41.   In sum, there has been a breach of Article 8.

. . . .

∼

QUESTIONS & COMMENTS

(1) The European Court found that the procedures did little to check the discretion of customs officials. In fact, the existing domestic statutory rules forbade searches at night and required the accompaniment of a municipal officer. What is more important, to limit the occasions on which the police may intrude into private spaces or to make sure that such intrusions are done with respect for the dignity of the individual? Both are presumably important values in democratic nations but courts often fail to recognize both. The U.S. Supreme Court, for example, has emphasized the person's interest in secrecy rather than their interest in the dignity and autonomy of their private spaces and activities. Thus the Court has reprimanded police officers for reading a product identification serial number on the back of a stereo, even though the police were lawfully in the apartment investigating a shooting incident but has tended to ignore the quality of police interventions and especially the routine indignities that young urban males, especially persons of color, experience in street encounters with the police. Compare *Arizona v. Hicks*, 480 U.S. 321 (1987) (police look at the back of stereo equipment without probable cause violated Fourth Amendment), with *Terry v. Ohio*, 392 U.S. 1 (1968) (police do not need probable cause for brief investigative seizures and external "pat-down" type search).

(2) How would you distinguish this case from *Klass*? Does the Court simply believe that terrorism is a more serious threat to democracy then currency flight? Is that an appropriate call for the Court to make?

(3) In 1986, the law was changed to add extensive new regulations to search and seizure powers of the customs officials. Did this change make it easier for the Court to condemn what was essentially a superceded procedure?

(4) Compare *X. & Y. v. Argentina*, Inter-Am. Cm. H.R., Case No. 10.056, ANNUAL REPORT OF THE INTER-AMERICAN COMMISSION ON HUMAN RIGHTS 1996 50, OEA/Ser.L/V/II/95 Doc. 7 rev. (14 March 1997). In *X. & Y. v. Argentina*, the petitioners (a mother and daughter) complained that prison officials routinely performed vaginal inspections during their prison visits with their husband/father. The petitioners alleged the practice violated their right to privacy. The Commission found that the law allowing such searches failed to specify the conditions or types of visits to which such searches were applicable, thereby allowing very wide discretion for prison officials. Accordingly, the Commission found it doubtful that the legislation was precise enough for the searches to be "prescribed by law." The Commission held that such inspections must be "absolutely necessary" for achieving the aim of prison security and that no other options exist to achieve that security. If such

searches were necessary, prison authorities must obtain a judicial order and the search must be executed by qualified medical personnel.

Sexual Orientation and Practice

Toonen v. Australia
UN Human Rights Committee
Communication No. 488/1992
Views adopted 31 March 1994
U.N. Doc. CCPR/C/50/D/488 (1992)

. . . .

The facts as submitted by the author:

2.1 The author is an activist for the promotion of the rights of homosexuals in Tasmania, one of Australia's six constitutive states. He challenges two provisions of the Tasmanian Criminal Code, namely Sections 122(a) and (c) and 123, which criminalize various forms of sexual contacts between men, including all forms of sexual contacts between consenting adult homosexual men in private.

2.2 The author observes that the above sections of the Tasmanian Criminal Code empower Tasmanian police officers to investigate intimate aspects of his private life and to detain him, if they have reason to believe that he is involved in sexual activities which contravene the above sections. He adds that the Director of Public Prosecutions announced, in August 1988, that proceedings pursuant to Sections 122(a), (c) and 123 *would* be initiated if there was sufficient evidence of the commission of a crime.

2.3 Although in practice the Tasmanian police have not charged anyone either with "unnatural sexual intercourse" or "intercourse against nature" (Section 122) nor with "indecent practice between male persons" (Section 123) for several years, the author argues that because of his long-term relationship with another man, his active lobbying of Tasmanian politicians and the reports about his activities in the local media, and because of his activities as a gay rights activist and gay HIV/AIDS worker, his private life and his liberty are threatened by the continued existence of Sections 122(a), (c) and 123 of the Criminal Code.

2.4 Mr. Toonen further argues that the criminalization of homosexuality in private has not permitted him to expose openly his sexuality and to publicize his views on reform of the relevant laws on sexual matters, as he felt that this would have been extremely prejudicial to his employment. In this context, he contends that Sections 122(a), (c) and 123 have created the conditions for discrimination in employment, constant stigmatization, vilification, threats of physical violence and the violation of basic democratic rights.

2.5–2.6 [setting out examples of such treatment]

2.7 . . . .

The Complaint:

3.1 The author affirms that Sections 122 and 123 of the Tasmanian Criminal Code violate articles 2, paragraph 1, 17, and 26 of the Covenant because:

(a) they do not distinguish between sexual activity in private and sexual activity in public and bring private activity into the public domain. In their enforcement, these provisions result in a violation of the right to privacy, since they enable the police to enter a household on the mere suspicion that two consenting homosexual men may be committing a criminal offense. Given the stigma attached to homosexuality in Australian society (and especially in Tasmania), the violation of the right to privacy may lead to unlawful attacks on the honor and the reputation of the individuals concerned.

(b) they distinguish between individuals in the exercise of their right to privacy on the basis of sexual activity, sexual orientation and sexual identity. . . .

. . . .

3.2 For the author, the only remedy for the rights infringed by Sections 122(a), (c) and 123 of the Criminal Code through the criminalization of all forms of sexual activity between consenting adult homosexual men to private would be the repeal of these provisions.

. . . .

The State party's information and observations:

. . . .

4.2. The State party notes that the laws challenged by Mr. Toonen are those of the state of Tasmania and only apply within the jurisdiction of that state. Laws similar to those challenged by the author once applied in other Australian jurisdictions but have since been repealed.

. . . .

The State party's observations on the merits and author's comments thereon:

6.1 In its submission under article 4, paragraph 2, of the Optional Protocol, dated 15 September 1993, the State party concedes that the author has been a victim of arbitrary interference with his privacy, and that the legislative provisions challenged by him cannot be justified on public health or moral grounds. It incorporates into its submission the observations of the government of Tasmania, which denies that the author has been the victim of a violation of the Covenant.

6.2 With regard to article 17, the Federal Government notes that the Tasmanian Government submits that article 17 does not create a "right to privacy" but only a right to freedom from arbitrary or unlawful interference with privacy, and that as the challenged laws were enacted by democratic process, they cannot be an unlawful interference with privacy. The Federal Government, after reviewing the *travaux préparatoires* of article 17, subscribes to the following definition of "private:" "matters which are individual, personal, or confidential, or which are kept or removed from public observation." The State party acknowledges that based on this definition, consensual sexual activity in private is encompassed by the concept of "privacy" in article 17.

6.3 As to whether Sections 122 and 123 of the Tasmanian Criminal Code "interfere" with the author's privacy, the State party notes that the Tasmanian authorities advised that there is no policy to treat investigations or the prosecution of offenses under the disputed provisions any differently from the investigation or prosecution of offenses under the Tasmanian Criminal Code in general, and that the most recent prosecution under the challenged provisions dates back to 1984. The State party acknowledges, however, that in the absence of any specific policy on the part of the Tasmanian authorities not to enforce the laws, the risk of the provisions being applied to Mr. Toonen remains, and that this risk is relevant to the assessment of whether the provisions "interfere" with his privacy. On balance, the State party concedes that Mr. Toonen is personally and actually affected by the Tasmanian laws.

6.4 As to whether the interference with the author's privacy was arbitrary or unlawful, the State party refers to the *travaux préparatoires* of article 17 and observes that the drafting history of the provision in the Commission on Human Rights appears to indicate that the term "arbitrary" was meant to cover interference which, under Australian law, would be covered by the concept of "unreasonableness." Furthermore, the Human Rights Committee, in its General Comment on article 17, states that the concept of arbitrariness is intended to guarantee that even interference provided for by law should be in accordance with the provisions, aims and objectives of the [Covenant] and should be ... reasonable in the particular circumstances. On the basis of this and the Committee's jurisprudence on the concept of "reasonableness," the State party interprets "reasonable" interferences with privacy as measures which are based on reasonable and objective criteria and which are proportional to the purpose for which they are adopted.

6.5 The State party does not accept the argument of the Tasmanian authorities that the retention of the challenged provisions is partly motivated by a concern to protect Tasmania from the spread of HIV/AIDS, and that the laws are justified on public health and moral grounds. This assessment, in fact, goes against the Australian Government's National HIV/AIDS Strategy, which emphasizes that laws criminalizing homosexual activity obstruct public health programs promoting safer sex. The State party further disagrees with the Tasmanian authorities' contention that the laws are justified on moral grounds, noting that moral issues were not at issue when article 17 of the Covenant was drafted.

6.6 None the less, the State party cautions that the formulation of article 17 allows for *some* infringement of the right to privacy if there are reasonable grounds, and that domestic social mores may be relevant to the reasonableness of an interference with privacy. The State party observes that while laws penalizing homosexual activity existed in the past in other Australian states, they have since been repealed with the exception of Tasmania. Furthermore, discrimination on the basis of homosexuality or sexuality is unlawful in three of six Australian states and the two self-governing internal Australian territories. The Federal Government has declared sexual preference to be a ground of discrimination that may be invoked under ILO Convention No. 111 (Discrimination in Employment or Occupation Convention), and created a mechanism through which complaints about discrimination in employment on the basis of sexual preference may be considered by the Australian Human Rights and Equal Opportunity Commission.

6.7 On the basis of the above, the State party contends there is now a general Australian acceptance that no individual should be disadvantaged on the basis of his or her sexual orientation. Given the legal and social situation in all of Australia except Tasmania, the State party acknowledges that a complete prohibition on sexual activity between men is unnecessary to sustain the moral fabric of Australian society. On balance, the State party "does not seek to claim that the challenged laws are based on reasonable and objective criteria."

6.8 Finally, the State party examines, in the context of article 17, whether the challenged laws are a proportional response to the aim sought. It does not accept the argument of the Tasmanian authorities that the extent of interference with personal privacy occasioned by Sections 122 and 123 of the Tasmanian Criminal Code is a proportional response to the perceived threat to the moral standards of Tasmanian society. In this context, it notes that the very fact that the laws are not enforced against individuals engaging in private, consensual sexual activity indicates that the laws are not essential to the protection of that society's moral standards. In light of all the above, the State party concludes that the challenged laws are not reasonable in the circumstances, and that their chief interference with privacy is arbitrary. It notes that the repeal of the laws has been proposed at various times in the recent past by Tasmanian governments.

. . . .

7.1 In his comments, the author welcomes the State party's concession that Sections 122 and 123 violate article 17 of the Covenant but expresses concern that the Australian Government's argumentation is entirely based on the fact that he is threatened with prosecution under the aforementioned provisions and does not take into account the general adverse effect of the laws on himself. He further expresses concern, in the context of the "arbitrariness" of the interference with his privacy, that the State party has found it difficult to ascertain with certainty whether the prohibition of private homosexual activity represents the moral position of a significant portion of the Tasmanian populace. He contends that, in fact, there is significant popular and institutional support for the repeal of Tasmania's anti-gay criminal laws, and provides a detailed list of associations and groups from a broad spectrum of Australian and Tasmanian society, as well as a detailed survey of national and international concern about gay and lesbian rights in general and Tasmania's anti-gay statutes in particular.

7.2 In response to the Tasmanian authorities' argument that moral considerations must be taken into account when dealing with the right to privacy, the author notes that Australia is a pluralistic and multi-cultural society whose citizens have different and at times conflicting moral codes. In these circumstances, it must be the proper rule of criminal laws to entrench these different codes as little as possible; insofar as some values must be entrenched in criminal codes, these values would relate to human dignity and diversity.

....

Examination of the merits:

8.1 The Committee is called upon to determine whether Mr. Toonen has been the victim of an unlawful or arbitrary interference with his privacy, contrary to article 17, paragraph 1....

8.2 Inasmuch as article 17 is concerned, it is undisputed that adult consensual sexual activity in private is covered by the concept of "privacy," and that Mr. Toonen is actually and currently affected by the continued existence of the Tasmanian laws. The Committee considers that Sections 122(a), (c) and 123 of the Tasmanian Criminal Code "interfere" with the author's privacy, even if these provisions have not ben enforced for a decade. In this context, it notes that the policy of the Department of Public Prosecutions not to initiate criminal proceedings in respect to private homosexual conduct does not amount to a guarantee that no actions will be brought against homosexuals in the future, particularly in the light of undisputed statements of the Director of Public Prosecutions of Tasmania in 1988 and those of members of the Tasmanian Parliament. The continued existence of the challenged provisions therefore continuously and directly "interferes" with the author's privacy.

8.3 The prohibition against private homosexual behavior is provided for by law, namely, Sections 122 and 123 of the Tasmanian Criminal Code. As to whether it may be deemed arbitrary, the Committee recalls that pursuant to its General Comment 16[32] in article 17, the "introduction of the concept of arbitrariness is intended to guarantee that even interference provided for by the law should be in accordance with the provisions, aims and objectives of the Covenant and should be, in any event, reasonable in the circumstances." [Citation omitted.] The Committee interprets the requirement of reasonableness to imply that any interference with privacy must be proportional to the end sought and be necessary in the circumstances of any given case.

8.4 While the State party acknowledges that the impugned provisions constitute an arbitrary interference with Mr. Toonen's privacy, the Tasmanian authorities submit that the challenged laws are justified on public health and moral grounds, as they are intended in part to prevent the spread of HIV/AIDS in Tasmania, and because, in the absence of specific limitation clauses in article 17, moral issues must be deemed a matter for domestic decision.

8.5 As far as the public health argument of the Tasmanian authorities is concerned, the Committee notes that the criminalization of homosexual practices cannot be considered a reasonable means or proportionate measure to achieve the aim of preventing the spread of HIV/AIDS. The Australian Government observes that statutes criminalizing homosexual activity tend to impede public health programs "by driving underground many of the people at the risk of infection." Criminalization of homosexual activity thus would appear to run counter to the implementation of effective education programs in respect of the HIV/AIDS implementation of effective education programs in respect to the HIV/AIDS prevention. Secondly, the Committee notes that no link has been shown between the continued criminalization of homosexual activity and the effective control of the spread of the HIV/AIDS virus.

8.6 The Committee cannot accept either that for the purposes of article 17 of the Covenant, moral issues are exclusively a matter of domestic concern, as this would open the door to withdrawing from the Committee's scrutiny a potentially large number of statutes interfering with privacy. It further notes that with the exception of Tasmania, all laws criminalizing homosexuality have been repealed throughout Australia and that, even in Tasmania, it is apparent that there is no consensus as to whether Sections 122 and 123 should not also be repealed. Considering further that these provisions are not currently enforced, which implies that they are not deemed essential to the protection of morals in Tasmania, the Committee concludes that the provisions do not meet the "reasonableness" test in the circumstances of the case, and that they arbitrarily interfere with Mr. Toonen's right under article 17, paragraph 1.

. . . .

9. The Human Rights Committee, acting under article 5, paragraph 4, of the Optional Protocol to the International Covenant on Civil and Political Rights, is of the view that the facts before it reveal a violation of articles 17, paragraph 1, *juncto* 2, paragraph 1, of the Covenant.

10. Under article 2(3)(a) of the Covenant, the author, victim of a violation of articles 17, paragraph 1, *juncto* 2, paragraph 1, of the Covenant, is entitled to a remedy. In the opinion of the Committee, an effective remedy would be the repeal of Sections 122(a), (c) and 123 of the Tasmanian Criminal Code.

. . . .

∿

QUESTIONS & COMMENTS

(1) In the field of sexual orientation law, the ECHR provides greater legal protection to persons than most domestic legal traditions. For example, in the area of gay and lesbian rights, the right to privacy under Article 8 of the European Convention has been

interpreted repeatedly by the European Court of Human Rights to extend to an adult's right to participate in private, consensual homosexual activity. *See Modinos v. Cyprus*, 259 Eur. Ct. H.R. (ser. A) (1993) (protection extended to carnal knowledge "against the order of nature"); *Norris v. Ireland*, 142 Eur. Ct. H.R. (ser. A) (1988) (protection extended to anal intercourse between adult men); *Dudgeon v. United Kingdom*, 45 Eur. Ct. H.R. (ser. A) (1981) (protection extended to mutual masturbation, oral-genital contact, and anal intercourse between adult men).

However, the South African Constitution has been interpreted by the Cape High Court to invalidate the common law offense of sodomy as unconstitutional. *National Coalition for Gay and Lesbian Equality and Others v. Minister of Justice and Others*, South African High Ct. (6), BCLR 726 (W) (Witwatersrand Local Div.1998).

Recall *Laurence v. Texas*, reproduced in Section 3.1.1.2. Note that the Supreme Court in *Lawrence* cites *Dudgeon*, it does not cite *Toonen* – even though the United States is a party to the ICCPR? Why do you think that the Court does this? Is it because the Supreme Court wanted to avoid the issue of the United States' deposit of a declaration stating that the ICCPR's rights provisions are non-self-executing? Regardless of the lawfulness of the United States' declaration, are not the ICCPR's rights provisions strong evidence of the United States' customary international legal obligations that constitutionally can be used as persuasive authority for construing constitutional rights' protections?

(2) In *Laskey, Jaggard & Brown v. United Kingdom*, – Eur. Ct. H.R. (ser. A) (1997) (slip opinion), the European Court examined the state's interest in protecting public health in the context of adult males participating in private, consensual, sado-masochistic activities. Although neither the Commission or the Court described in detail the applicants' behavior, the Court reported that the acts consisted of "maltreatment of the genitalia (with, for example, hot wax, sandpaper, fish hooks and needles) and ritualistic beatings either with the assailant's bare hands or a variety of implements, including stinging nettles, spiked belts and a cat-o'-nine tails." *Id.* at §8. No injuries had required medical attention. The applicants had been convicted of assault and wounding.

The European Court found that "from the facts established by the national courts [. . .] the applicants' sado-masochistic activities involved a significant degree of injury or wounding which could not be characterised as trifling or transient." *Id.* at §45. Also, Lord Templeman of the House of Lords had found the activities "unpredictably dangerous." Accordingly, the European Court held that the "significance" of the harm and the "potential for harm inherent in the acts" were legitimate state interests. *Id.* at §46. As to proportionality, the Court found that because the charges of assault were numerous, the acts occurred over more than ten years, a degree of organization was involved, the applicants did not believe their acts to be criminal, only a few acts were prosecuted, and sentences were reduced on appeal, the prosecution of the applicants was proportionate. Therefore, there was no Article 8 violation.

Under the European Court's analysis, what kinds of sexual behavior involving a high risk of HIV transmission could be considered criminal by the State and still compatible with Article 8?

(3) Both the European Court of Human Rights in *Dudgeon v. United Kingdom* and the UN Human Rights Committee in *Toonen* did not find it necessary to reach a decision on the discrimination claims in both cases because of the success of the complainants' privacy claims. [The Committee did note that sex discrimination included sexual orientation

discrimination. *Toonen* at §8.7.] However, in an individual opinion, committee member Wennergren agreed that the Tasmanian code violated the ICCPR but argued that finding a discrimination violation under Article 26, ICCPR, was an essential prerequisite to finding a violation of Article 17, ICCPR. Article 26 was violated for two reasons. First, Tasmanian Criminal Code §122 prohibited "sexual intercourse between men and between women, thereby making a distinction between heterosexuals and homosexuals;" this constituted discrimination on the ground of sexual orientation in violation of Article 26. Second, Tasmanian Criminal Code §123 outlawed indecent sexual contacts between men but not between women, thereby discriminating on the basis of gender in violation of Article 26. He continued:

> Unlike the majority of the articles in the Covenant, article 17 does not establish any true right or freedom. There is no right to freedom or liberty of privacy, comparable to the right of liberty of the person.... [Article 17(1)] merely mandates that no one shall be subject to arbitrary or unlawful interference with his privacy, family etc.
>
> ...
>
> The discriminatory criminal legislation at issue here is not strictly speaking "unlawful" but it is incompatible with the Covenant, as it limits the right to equality before the law. In my view,... the Tasmanian Criminal Code interferes with privacy to an unjustifiable extent and, therefore, also constitutes a violation of article 17, paragraph 1.

(4) Australia's domestic legal system is dualist: Parliament must enact domestic legislation to give effect to its international legal obligations. In response to *Toonen*, the Australian Parliament enacted a statute eliminating the criminalization of consensual homosexual conduct and discrimination on the basis of sexual orientation. The Human Rights (Sexual Conduct) Act of 1994, ch. 4 §1, provides that "sexual conduct involving only consenting adults in private is not to be subject... to any arbitrary interference with privacy within the meaning of Article 17 [of the ICCPR]." However, some questioned the constitutional legitimacy of Parliament's action. Although the Australian Parliament can make laws with respect to "external affairs," Austl. Const. ch. I, pt. V, §51 (xxix), which includes the incorporation of treaties into domestic law, it is not clear whether it can do so solely within the "external affairs" power and not in conjunction with any of the other enumerated federal powers. Arguably, only the individual Australian states have the authority to do so because individual liberties and criminal law are subjects that fall within the states' jurisdiction. How valid is this argument in light of the international community's embracing of human rights over the past fifty years as a subject of international concern (or "external affairs" for individual states)?

However, this issue is moot. The Tasmanian legislature repealed its antigay law in 1997.

(5) Would the facts in the *Toonen* case satisfy the U.S. Supreme Court's requirements for a "case or controversy"?

(a) Note that the nominally adverse party to the complainant is Australia, not Tasmania, and that all Australian states other than Tasmania had repealed their laws prohibiting consensual homosexual conduct. What interest did Australia (not Tasmania) have in defending the Tasmanian statute? Consider also that Australia's concessions on many subordinate issues made it difficult to avoid the ultimate conclusion of invalidity. Do these aspects of the case make it a suitable one for resolution on the merits? Would you recommend any changes in adjudicatory procedure to address them?

(b) Has Toonen suffered an "injury" sufficient to satisfy U.S. requirements for standing?

(6) Sometimes it has been suggested that statutes that are rarely enforced, or selectively enforced, should be held unconstitutional under a doctrine akin to the common law idea of desuetude, according to which a legal norm that has not been enforced for a sufficiently long period loses its binding effect. Would laws against homosexual sodomy satisfy such a standard? William Eskridge argues that there has been more enforcement of statutes in cases of consensual relations among adults than many people assume, at a level above what might trigger invalidation under a sensible desuetude doctrine. WILLIAM ESKRIDGE, GAY LAW (1999).

(7) Balancing versus categorical approaches. Some scholars of comparative constitutional law have suggested that U.S. law typically is more "categorical" than law elsewhere. *See, e.g.,* KENT GREENAWALT, FIGHTING WORDS (1995). Note the doctrinal formulation that leads to such balancing. In U.S. law, finding that a right is infringed is ordinarily the end of the analysis; the right violation cannot ordinarily be justified by considerations of "necessity" as it may be under the European Court's approach.

Transgendered Persons

Goodwin v. United Kingdom
Application 28957/95
European Court of Human Rights
– Eur. Ct. H.R. (ser. A) (2002)

. . . .

THE FACTS

I. THE CIRCUMSTANCES OF THE CASE

12. The applicant is a United Kingdom citizen born in 1937 and is a post-operative male to female transsexual.

13. The applicant had a tendency to dress as a woman from early childhood and underwent aversion therapy in 1963–64. In the mid-1960s, she was diagnosed as a transsexual. Though she married a woman and they had four children, her conviction was that her "brain sex" did not fit her body. From that time until 1984 she dressed as a man for work but as a woman in her free time. In January 1985, the applicant began treatment in earnest, attending appointments once every three months at the Gender Identity Clinic at the Charing Cross Hospital, which included regular consultations with a psychiatrist as well as on occasion a psychologist. She was prescribed hormone therapy, began attending grooming classes and voice training. Since this time, she has lived fully as a woman. In October 1986, she underwent surgery to shorten her vocal chords. In August 1987, she was accepted on the waiting list for gender re-assignment surgery. In 1990, she underwent gender re-assignment surgery at a National Health Service hospital. Her treatment and surgery was provided for and paid for by the National Health Service.

14. The applicant divorced from her former wife on a date unspecified but continued to enjoy the love and support of her children.

15. The applicant claims that between 1990 and 1992 she was sexually harassed by colleagues at work. She attempted to pursue a case of sexual harassment in the Industrial Tribunal but claimed that she was unsuccessful because she was considered in law to be a man. She did not challenge this decision by appealing to the Employment Appeal Tribunal. The applicant was subsequently dismissed from her employment for

reasons connected with her health, but alleges that the real reason was that she was a transsexual.

16. In 1996, the applicant started work with a new employer and was required to provide her National Insurance (NI) number. She was concerned that the new employer would be in a position to trace her details as once in the possession of the number it would have been possible to find out about her previous employers and obtain information from them. Although she requested the allocation of a new NI number from the Department of Social Security (DSS), this was rejected and she eventually gave the new employer her NI number. The applicant claims that the new employer has now traced back her identity as she began experiencing problems at work. Colleagues stopped speaking to her and she was told that everyone was talking about her behind her back.

17. The DSS Contributions Agency informed the applicant that she would be ineligible for a State pension at the age of 60, the age of entitlement for women in the United Kingdom. In April 1997, the DSS informed the applicant that her pension contributions would have to be continued until the date at which she reached the age of 65, being the age of entitlement for men, namely April 2002. On 23 April 1997, she therefore entered into an undertaking with the DSS to pay direct the NI contributions which would otherwise be deducted by her employer as for all male employees. In the light of this undertaking, on 2 May 1997, the DSS Contributions Agency issued the applicant with a Form CF 384 Age Exemption Certificate (see Relevant domestic law and practice below).

18. The applicant's files at the DSS were marked "sensitive" to ensure that only an employee of a particular grade had access to her files. This meant in practice that the applicant had to make special appointments for even the most trivial matters and could not deal directly with the local office or deal with queries over the telephone. Her record continues to state her sex as male and despite the "special procedures" she has received letters from the DSS addressed to the male name which she was given at birth.

19. In a number of instances, the applicant stated that she has had to choose between revealing her birth certificate and foregoing certain advantages which were conditional upon her producing her birth certificate. In particular, she has not followed through a loan conditional upon life insurance, a re-mortgage offer and an entitlement to winter fuel allowance from the DSS. Similarly, the applicant remains obliged to pay the higher motor insurance premiums applicable to men. Nor did she feel able to report a theft of 200 pounds sterling to the police, for fear that the investigation would require her to reveal her identity.

II. RELEVANT DOMESTIC LAW AND PRACTICE

A. Names

20. Under English law, a person is entitled to adopt such first names or surname as he or she wishes. Such names are valid for the purposes of identification and may be used in passports, driving licences, medical and insurance cards, etc. The new names are also entered on the electoral roll.

B. Marriage and definition of gender in domestic law

21. Under English law, marriage is defined as the voluntary union between a man and a woman. In the case of *Corbett v. Corbett* ([1971] Probate Reports 83), Mr Justice Ormrod ruled that sex for that purpose is to be determined by the application of chromosomal,

gonadal and genital tests where these are congruent and without regard to any surgical intervention. This use of biological criteria to determine sex was approved by the Court of Appeal in *R. v. Tan* ([1983] Queen's Bench Reports 1053) and given more general application, the court holding that a person born male had been correctly convicted under a statute penalising men who live on the earnings of prostitution, notwithstanding the fact that the accused had undergone gender reassignment therapy.

22. Under section 11(b) of the Matrimonial Causes Act 1973, any marriage where the parties are not respectively male and female is void. The test applied as to the sex of the partners to a marriage is that laid down in the above-mentioned case of *Corbett v. Corbett*. According to that same decision a marriage between a male-to-female transsexual and a man might also be avoided on the basis that the transsexual was incapable of consummating the marriage in the context of ordinary and complete sexual intercourse (*obiter per* Mr Justice Ormrod).

This decision was reinforced by Section 12(a) of the Matrimonial Causes Act 1973, according to which a marriage that has not been consummated owing to the incapacity of either party to consummate may be voidable. Section 13(1) of the Act provides that the court must not grant a decree of nullity if it is satisfied that the petitioner knew the marriage was voidable, but led the respondent to believe that she would not seek a decree of nullity, and that it would be unjust to grant the decree.

C. Birth certificates

23. Registration of births is governed by the Births and Deaths Registration Act 1953 ("the 1953 Act"). Section 1(1) of that Act requires that the birth of every child be registered by the Registrar of Births and Deaths for the area in which the child is born. An entry is regarded as a record of the facts at the time of birth. A birth certificate accordingly constitutes a document revealing not current identity but historical facts.

24. The sex of the child must be entered on the birth certificate. The criteria for determining the sex of a child at birth are not defined in the Act. The practice of the Registrar is to use exclusively the biological criteria (chromosomal, gonadal and genital) as laid down by Mr Justice Ormrod in the above-mentioned case of *Corbett v. Corbett*.

25. The 1953 Act provides for the correction by the Registrar of clerical errors or factual errors. The official position is that an amendment may only be made if the error occurred when the birth was registered. The fact that it may become evident later in a person's life that his or her "psychological" sex is in conflict with the biological criteria is not considered to imply that the initial entry at birth was a factual error. Only in cases where the apparent and genital sex of a child was wrongly identified, or where the biological criteria were not congruent, can a change in the initial entry be made. It is necessary for that purpose to adduce medical evidence that the initial entry was incorrect. No error is accepted to exist in the birth entry of a person who undergoes medical and surgical treatment to enable that person to assume the role of the opposite sex.

26. The Government point out that the use of a birth certificate for identification purposes is discouraged by the Registrar General, and for a number of years birth certificates have contained a warning that they are not evidence of the identity of the person presenting it. However, it is a matter for individuals whether to follow this recommendation.

D. Social security, employment and pensions

27. A transsexual continues to be recorded for social security, national insurance and employment purposes as being of the sex recorded at birth.

1. National Insurance

28. The DSS registers every British citizen for National Insurance purposes ("NI") on the basis of the information in their birth certificate. Non-British citizens who wish to register for NI in the United Kingdom may use their passport or identification card as evidence of identity if a birth certificate is unavailable.

29. The DSS allocates every person registered for NI with a unique NI number. The NI number has a standard format consisting of two letters followed by three pairs of numbers and a further letter. It contains no indication in itself of the holder's sex or of any other personal information. The NI number is used to identify each person with a NI account (there are at present approximately 60 million individual NI accounts). The DSS are thereby able to record details of all NI contributions paid into the account during the NI account holder's life and to monitor each person's liabilities, contributions and entitlement to benefits accurately. New numbers may in exceptional cases be issued to persons e.g. under the witness protection schemes or to protect the identity of child offenders.

30. Under Regulation 44 of the Social Security (Contributions) Regulations 1979, made under powers conferred by paragraph 8(1)(p) of Schedule 1 to the Social Security Contributions and Benefits Act 1992, specified individuals are placed under an obligation to apply for a NI number unless one has already been allocated to them.

31. Under Regulation 45 of the 1979 Regulations, an employee is under an obligation to supply his NI number to his employer on request.

32. Section 112(1) of the Social Security Administration Act 1992 provides:

(1) If a person for the purpose of obtaining any benefit or other payment under the legislation ... [as defined in section 110 of the Act] ... whether for himself or some other person, or for any other purpose connected with that legislation –

(a) makes a statement or representation which he knows to be false; or
(b) produces or furnishes, or knowingly causes or knowingly allows to be produced or furnished, any document or information which he knows to be false in a material particular, he shall be guilty of an offence.

33. It would therefore be an offence under this section for any person to make a false statement in order to obtain a NI number.

34. Any person may adopt such first name, surname or style of address (e.g. Mr, Mrs, Miss, Ms) that he or she wishes for the purposes of the name used for NI registration. The DSS will record any such amendments on the person's computer records, manual records and NI number card. But, the DSS operates a policy of only issuing one NI number for each person regardless of any changes that occur to that person's sexual identity through procedures such as gender re-assignment surgery. A renewed application for leave to apply for judicial review of the legality of this policy brought by a male-to-female transsexual was dismissed by the Court of Appeal in the case of *R v. Secretary of State for Social Services ex parte Hooker* (1993) (unreported). McCowan LJ giving the judgment of the Court stated [ ]:

... since it will not make the slightest practical difference, far from the Secretary of State's decision being an irrational one, I consider it a perfectly rational decision. I would further reject the suggestion that the applicant had a legitimate expectation that a new number would be given to her for psychological purposes when, in fact, its practical effect would be nil.

35. Information held in the DSS NI records is confidential and will not normally be disclosed to third parties without the consent of the person concerned. Exceptions are possible in cases where the public interest is at stake or the disclosure is necessary to protect public funds. By virtue of Section 123 of the Social Security Administration Act 1992, it is an offence for any person employed in social security administration to disclose without lawful authority information acquired in the course of his or her employment.

36. The DSS operates a policy of normally marking records belonging to persons known to be transsexual as nationally sensitive. Access to these records is controlled by DSS management. Any computer printer output from these records will normally be referred to a special section within the DSS to ensure that identity details conform with those requested by the relevant person.

37. NI contributions are made by way of deduction from an employee's pay by the employer and then by payment to the Inland Revenue (for onward transmission to the DSS). Employers at present will make such deductions for a female employee until she reaches the pensionable age of 60 and for a male employee until he reaches the pensionable age of 65. The DSS operates a policy for male-to-female transsexuals whereby they may enter into an undertaking with the DSS to pay direct to the DSS any NI contributions due after the transsexual has reached the age of 60 which have ceased to be deducted by the employer in the belief that the employee is female. In the case of female-to-male transsexuals, any deductions which are made by an employer after the age of 60 may be reclaimed directly from the DSS by the employee.

38. In some cases employers will require proof that an apparent female employee has reached, or is about to reach, the age of 60 and so entitled not to have the NI deductions made. Such proof may be provided in the form of an Age Exemption Certificate (form CA4180 or CF384). The DSS may issue such a certificate to a male-to-female transsexual where such a person enters into an undertaking to pay any NI contributions direct to the DSS.

2. State pensions

39. A male-to-female transsexual is currently entitled to a State pension at the retirement age of 65 applied to men and not the age of 60 which is applicable to women. A full pension will be payable only if she has made contributions for 44 years as opposed to the 39 years required of women.

40. A person's sex for the purposes of pensionable age is determined according to biological sex at birth. This approach was approved by the Social Security Commissioner (a judicial officer, who specialises in social security law) in a number of cases:

In the case entitled R(P) 2/80, a male-to-female transsexual claimed entitlement to a pensionable age of 60. The Commissioner dismissed the claimant's appeal and stated at paragraph 9 of his decision:

(a) In my view, the word "woman" in section 27 of the Act means a person who is biologically a woman. Sections 28 and 29 contain many references to a woman in terms which indicate that a person is denoted who is capable of forming a valid marriage with a husband. That can only be a person who is biologically a woman.

(b) I doubt whether the distinction between a person who is biologically, and one who is socially, female has ever been present in the minds of the legislators when enacting relevant statutes. However that may be, it is certain that Parliament has never conferred on any person the right or privilege of changing the basis of his national insurance rights from those appropriate to a man to those appropriate to a woman. In my judgment, such a fundamental right or privilege would have to be expressly granted. . . .

(d) I fully appreciate the unfortunate predicament of the claimant, but the merits are not all on her side. She lived as a man from birth until 1975, and, during the part of that period when she was adult, her insurance rights were those appropriate to a man. These rights are in some respects more extensive than those appropriate to a woman. Accordingly, an element of unfairness to the general public might have to be tolerated so as to allow the payment of a pension to her at the pensionable age of a woman.

41. The Government have instituted plans to eradicate the difference between men and women concerning age of entitlement to State pensions. Equalisation of the pension age is to begin in 2010 and it is anticipated that by 2020 the transition will be complete. As regards the issue of free bus passes in London, which also differentiated between men and women concerning age of eligibility (65 and 60 respectively), the Government have also announced plans to introduce a uniform age.

3. Employment

42. Under section 16(1) of the Theft Act 1968, it is a criminal offence liable to a sentence of imprisonment to dishonestly obtain a pecuniary advantage by deception. Pecuniary advantage includes, under section 16(2)(c), being given the opportunity to earn remuneration in employment. Should a post-operative transsexual be asked by a prospective employer to disclose all their previous names, but fail to make full disclosure before entering into a contract of employment, an offence might be committed. Furthermore, should the employer discover the lack of full disclosure, there might also be a risk of dismissal or an action by the employer for damages.

43. In its judgment of 30 April 1996, in the case of *P. v. S. and Cornwall County Council*, the European Court of Justice (ECJ) held that discrimination arising from gender reassignment constituted discrimination on grounds of sex and, accordingly, Article 5 §1 of Council Directive 76/207/EEC of 9 February 1976 on the implementation of the principle of equal treatment for men and women as regards access to employment, vocational training and promotion and working conditions, precluded dismissal of a transsexual for a reason related to a gender reassignment. The ECJ held, rejecting the argument of the United Kingdom Government that the employer would also have dismissed P. if P. had previously been a woman and had undergone an operation to become a man, that

. . . where a person is dismissed on the ground that he or she intends to undergo or has undergone gender reassignment, he or she is treated unfavourably by comparison with persons of the sex to which he or she was deemed to belong before undergoing gender reassignment.

To tolerate such discrimination would be tantamount, as regards such a person, to a failure to respect the dignity and freedom to which he or she is entitled and which the Court has a duty to safeguard.[ ]

44. The ruling of the ECJ was applied by the Employment Appeal Tribunal in a decision handed down on 27 June 1997 (*Chessington World of Adventures Ltd v. Reed* [1997] 1 Industrial Law Reports).

45. The Sexual Discrimination (Gender Re-assignment) Regulations 1999 were issued to comply with the ruling of the European Court of Justice in *P. v. S. and Cornwall County Council* (30 April 1996). This provides generally that transsexual persons should not be treated less favourably in employment because they are transsexual (whether pre- or post-operative).

E. Rape

46. Prior to 1994, for the purposes of the law of rape, a male-to-female transsexual would have been regarded as a male. Pursuant to section 142 of the Criminal Justice and Public Order Act 1994, for rape to be established there has to be "vaginal or anal intercourse with a person". In a judgment of 28 October 1996, the Reading Crown Court found that penile penetration of a male to female transsexual's artificially constructed vagina amounted to rape: *R. v. Matthews* (unreported).

F. Imprisonment

47. Prison rules require that male and female prisoners shall normally be detained separately and also that no prisoner shall be stripped and searched in the sight of a person of the opposite sex (Rules 12(1) and 41(3) of the Prison Rules 1999 respectively).

48. According to the Report of the Working Group on Transsexual People (Home Office April 2000, see further below, paragraphs 49–50), which conducted a review of law and practice, post-operative transsexuals where possible were allocated to an establishment for prisoners of their new gender. Detailed guidelines concerning the searching of transsexual prisoners were under consideration by which post-operative male to female transsexuals would be treated as women for the purposes of searches and searched only by women[ ].

G. Current developments

1. Review of the situation of transsexuals in the United Kingdom

49. On 14 April 1999, the Secretary of State for the Home Department announced the establishment of an Interdepartmental Working Group on Transsexual People with the following terms of reference:

> to consider, with particular reference to birth certificates, the need for appropriate legal measures to address the problems experienced by transsexuals, having due regard to scientific and societal developments, and measures undertaken in other countries to deal with this issue.

50. The Working Group produced a report in April 2000 in which it examined the current position of transsexuals in the United Kingdom, with particular reference to their status under national law and the changes which might be made. It concluded:

> 5.1. Transsexual people deal with their condition in different ways. Some live in the opposite sex without any treatment to acquire its physical attributes. Others take hormones so as to obtain some of the secondary characteristics of their chosen sex. A smaller number will undergo surgical procedures to make their bodies resemble, so far as possible, those of their acquired gender. The extent of treatment may be determined by individual choice, or by other factors such as health or financial

resources. Many people revert to their biological sex after living for some time in the opposite sex, and some alternate between the two sexes throughout their lives. Consideration of the way forward must therefore take into account the needs of people at these different stages of change.

5.2. Measures have already been taken in a number of areas to assist transsexual people. For example, discrimination in employment against people on the basis of their transsexuality has been prohibited by the Sex Discrimination (Gender Reassignment) Regulations 1999 which, with few exceptions, provide that a transsexual person (whether pre- or post-operative) should not be treated less favourably because they are transsexual. The criminal justice system (*i.e.* the police, prisons, courts, etc.) try to accommodate the needs of transsexual people so far as is possible within operational constraints. A transsexual offender will normally be charged in their acquired gender, and a post-operative prisoner will usually be sent to a prison appropriate to their new status. Transsexual victims and witnesses will, in most circumstances, similarly be treated as belonging to their acquired gender.

5.3. In addition, official documents will often be issued in the acquired gender where the issue is identifying the individual rather than legal status. Thus, a transsexual person may obtain a passport, driving licence, medical card etc, in their new gender. We understand that many non-governmental bodies, such as examination authorities, will often re-issue examination certificates etc. (or otherwise provide evidence of qualifications) showing the required gender. We also found that at least one insurance company will issue policies to transsexual people in their acquired gender.

5.4. Notwithstanding such provisions, transsexual people are conscious of certain problems which do not have to be faced by the majority of the population. Submissions to the Group suggested that the principal areas where the transsexual community is seeking change are birth certificates, the right to marry and full recognition of their new gender for all legal purposes.

5.5. We have identified three options for the future;

  – to leave the current situation unchanged;
  – to issue birth certificates showing the new name and, possibly, the new gender;
  – to grant full legal recognition of the new gender subject to certain criteria and procedures.

We suggest that before taking a view on these options the Government may wish to put the issues out to public consultation.

51. The report was presented to Parliament in July 2000. Copies were placed in the libraries of both Houses of Parliament and sent to 280 recipients, including Working Group members, Government officials, Members of Parliament, individuals and organisations. It was publicised by a Home Office press notice and made available to members of the public through application to the Home Office in writing, E-mail, by telephone or the Home Office web site.

2. Recent domestic case-law

52. In the case of *Bellinger v. Bellinger*, EWCA Civ 1140 [2001], 3 FCR 1, the appellant who had been classified at birth as a man had undergone gender re-assignment surgery

and in 1981 had gone through a form of marriage with a man who was aware of her background. She sought a declaration under the Family Law Act 1986 that the marriage was valid. The Court of Appeal held, by a majority, that the appellant's marriage was invalid as the parties were not respectively male and female, which terms were to be determined by biological criteria as set out in the decision of *Corbett v. Corbett* [1971]. Although it was noted that there was an increasing emphasis upon the impact of psychological factors on gender, there was no clear point at which such factors could be said to have effected a change of gender. A person correctly registered as male at birth, who had undergone gender reassignment surgery and was now living as a woman was biologically a male and therefore could not be defined as female for the purposes of marriage. It was for Parliament, not for the courts, to decide at what point it would be appropriate to recognise that a person who had been assigned to one sex at birth had changed gender for the purposes of marriage. Dame Elizabeth Butler-Sloss, President of the Family Division noted the warnings of the European Court of Human Rights about continued lack of response to the situation of transsexuals and observed that largely as a result of these criticisms an interdepartmental working group had been set up, which had in April 2000 issued a careful and comprehensive review of the medical condition, current practice in other countries and the state of English law in relevant aspects of the life of an individual:

[95.] ... We inquired of Mr Moylan on behalf of the Attorney-General, what steps were being taken by any government department, to take forward any of the recommendations of the Report, or to prepare a consultation paper for public discussion.

[96.] To our dismay, we were informed that no steps whatsoever have been, or to the knowledge of Mr Moylan, were intended to be, taken to carry this matter forward. It appears, therefore, that the commissioning and completion of the report is the sum of the activity on the problems identified both by the Home Secretary in his terms of reference, and by the conclusions of the members of the working group. That would seem to us to be a failure to recognise the increasing concerns and changing attitudes across western Europe which have been set out so clearly and strongly in judgments of Members of the European Court at Strasbourg, and which in our view need to be addressed by the UK ...

[109.] We would add however, with the strictures of the European Court of Human Rights well in mind, that there is no doubt that the profoundly unsatisfactory nature of the present position and the plight of transsexuals requires careful consideration. The recommendation of the interdepartmental working group for public consultation merits action by the government departments involved in these issues. The problems will not go away and may well come again before the European Court sooner rather than later.

53. In his dissenting judgment, Lord Justice Thorpe considered that the foundations of the judgment in *Corbett v. Corbett* were no longer secure, taking the view that an approach restricted to biological criteria was no longer permissible in the light of scientific, medical and social change.

[155.] To make the chromosomal factor conclusive, or even dominant, seems to me particularly questionable in the context of marriage. For it is an invisible feature of an individual, incapable of perception or registration other than by scientific test. It makes no contribution to the physiological or psychological self. Indeed in the context of the institution of marriage as it is today it seems to me right as a matter of principle and logic to give predominance to psychological factors just as it seem right to carry out the essential assessment of gender at or shortly before the time of marriage rather than at the time of birth . . .

[160.] The present claim lies most evidently in the territory of the family justice system. That system must always be sufficiently flexible to accommodate social change. It must also be humane and swift to recognise the right to human dignity and to freedom of choice in the individual's private life. One of the objectives of statute law reform in this field must be to ensure that the law reacts to and reflects social change. That must also be an objective of the judges in this field in the construction of existing statutory provisions. I am strongly of the opinion that there are not sufficiently compelling reasons, having regard to the interests of others affected or, more relevantly, the interests of society as a whole, to deny this appellant legal recognition of her marriage. I would have allowed this appeal.

He also noted the lack of progress in domestic reforms:

[151.] . . . although the [interdepartmental] report has been made available by pub-lication, Mr Moylan said that there has since been no public consultation. Further-more when asked whether the Government had any present intention of initiating public consultation or any other process in preparation for a parliamentary Bill, Mr Moylan said that he had no instructions. Nor did he have any instructions as to whether the Government intended to legislate. My experience over the last 10 years suggests how hard it is for any department to gain a slot for family law reform by primary legislation. These circumstances reinforce my view that it is not only open to the court but it is its duty to construe s 11(c) either strictly, alternatively liberally as the evidence and the submissions in this case justify.

3. Proposals to reform the system of registration of births, marriages and deaths

54. In January 2002, the Government presented to Parliament the document "Civil Registration: Vital Change (Birth, Marriage and Death Registration in the 21st Century)" which set out plans for creating a central database of registration records which moves away from a traditional snapshot of life events towards the concept of a living record or single "through life" record:

In time, updating the information in a birth record will mean that changes to a person's names, and potentially, sex will be able to be recorded.

5.5 Making changes

There is strong support for some relaxation to the rules that govern corrections to the records. Currently, once a record has been created, the only corrections that can be made are where it can be shown that an error was made at the time of registration and that this can be established. Correcting even the simplest spelling error requires formal procedures and the examination of appropriate evidence. The final records contains the full original and corrected information which is shown on subsequently issued certificates. The Government recognises that this can act as a disincentive. In future, changes (to reflect developments after the original record was made) will be made and formally recorded. Documents issued from the records will contain only the information as amended, though all the information will be retained. . . .

H. Liberty's third party intervention

55. Liberty updated the written observations submitted in the case of *Sheffield and Horsham* concerning the legal recognition of transsexuals in comparative law (*Sheffield and Horsham v. the United Kingdom* judgment of 30 July 1998, Reports of Judgments and Decisions 1998-V, p. 2021, §35). In its 1998 study, it had found that over the previous decade there had been an unmistakable trend in the member States of the Council of Europe towards giving full legal recognition to gender re-assignment. In particular, it noted that out of thirty seven countries analysed only four (including the United Kingdom) did not permit a change to be made to a person's birth certificate in one form or another to reflect the re-assigned sex of that person. In cases where gender re-assignment was legal and publicly funded, only the United Kingdom and Ireland did not give full legal recognition to the new gender identity.

56. In its follow up study submitted on 17 January 2002, Liberty noted that while there had not been a statistical increase in States giving full legal recognition of gender re-assignment within Europe, information from outside Europe showed developments in this direction. For example, there had been statutory recognition of gender re-assignment in Singapore, and a similar pattern of recognition in Canada, South Africa, Israel, Australia, New Zealand and all except two of the States of the United States of America. It cited in particular the cases of *Attorney-General v. Otahuhu* Family Court [1995] 1 NZLR 60 and *Re Kevin* [2001] FamCA 1074 where in New Zealand and Australia transsexual persons' assigned sex was recognised for the purposes of validating their marriages: In the latter case, Mr Justice Chisholm held:

> I see no basis in legal principle or policy why Australian law should follow the decision in Corbett. To do so would, I think, create indefensible inconsistencies between Australian marriage law and other Australian laws. It would take the law in a direction that is generally contrary to development in other countries. It would perpetuate a view that flies in the face of current medical understanding and practice. Most of all, it would impose indefensible suffering on people who have already had more than their share of difficulty, with no benefit to society . . .

> . . . Because the words 'man' and 'woman' have their ordinary contemporary meaning, there is no formulaic solution to determining the sex of an individual for the purpose of the law of marriage. That is, it cannot be said as a matter of law that the question in a particular case will be determined by applying a single criterion, or limited list of criteria. Thus it is wrong to say that a person's sex depends on any single factor, such as chromosomes or genital sex; or some limited range of factors, such as the state of the person's gonads, chromosomes or genitals (whether at birth or at some other time). Similarly, it would be wrong in law to say that the question can be resolved by reference solely to the person's psychological state, or by identifying the person's 'brain sex'.

> To determine a person's sex for the law of marriage, all relevant matters need to be considered. I do not seek to state a complete list or suggest that any factors necessarily have more importance than others. However the relevant matters include,

in my opinion, the person's biological and physical characteristics at birth (including gonads, genitals and chromosomes); the person's life experiences, including the sex in which he or she was brought up and the person's attitude to it; the person's self-perception as a man or a woman; the extent to which the person has functioned in society as a man or a woman; any hormonal, surgical or other medical sex re-assignment treatments the person has undergone, and the consequences of such treatment; and the person's biological, psychological and physical characteristics at the time of the marriage...

For the purpose of ascertaining the validity of a marriage under Australian law the question whether a person is a man or a woman is to be determined as of the date of marriage..

57. As regarded the eligibility of post-operative transsexuals to marry a person of sex opposite to their acquired gender, Liberty's survey indicated that 54% of Contracting States permitted such marriage (Annex 6 listed Austria, Belgium, Denmark, Estonia, Finland, France, Germany, Greece, Iceland, Italy, Latvia, Luxembourg, the Netherlands, Norway, Slovakia, Spain, Sweden, Switzerland, Turkey and Ukraine), while 14% did not (Ireland and the United Kingdom did not permit marriage, while no legislation existed in Moldova, Poland, Romania and Russia). The legal position in the remaining 32% was unclear.

III. INTERNATIONAL TEXTS

58. Article 9 of the Charter of Fundamental Rights of the European Union, signed on 7 December 2000, provides:

The right to marry and the right to found a family shall be guaranteed in accordance with the national laws governing the exercise of these rights.

THE LAW

I. ALLEGED VIOLATION OF ARTICLE 8 OF THE CONVENTION

59. The applicant claims a violation of Article 8 of the Convention, the relevant part of which provides as follows:

1. Everyone has the right to respect for his private ... life ...

2. There shall be no interference by a public authority with the exercise of this right except such as is in accordance with the law and is necessary in a democratic society in the interests of national security, public safety or the economic well-being of the country, for the prevention of disorder or crime, for the protection of health or morals, or for the protection of the rights and freedoms of others.?

A. Arguments of the parties

1. The applicant

60. The applicant submitted that despite warnings from the Court as to the importance for keeping under review the need for legal reform the Government had still not taken any constructive steps to address the suffering and distress experienced by the applicant and other post-operative transsexuals. The lack of legal recognition of her changed gender had been the cause of numerous discriminatory and humiliating experiences in her

everyday life. In the past, in particular from 1990 to 1992, she was abused at work and did not receive proper protection against discrimination. She claimed that all the special procedures through which she had to go in respect of her NI contributions and State retirement pension constituted in themselves an unjustified difference in treatment, as they would have been unnecessary had she been recognised as a woman for legal purposes. In particular, the very fact that the DSS operated a policy of marking the records of transsexuals as sensitive was a difference in treatment. As a result, for example, the applicant cannot attend the DSS without having to make a special appointment.

61. The applicant further submitted that the danger of her employer learning about her past identity was real. It was possible for the employer to trace back her employment history on the basis of her NI number and this had in fact happened. She claimed that her recent failure to obtain a promotion was the result of the employer realising her status.

62. As regarded pensionable age, the applicant submitted that she had worked for 44 years and that the refusal of her entitlement to a State retirement pension at the age of 60 on the basis of the pure biological test for determining sex was contrary to Article 8 of the Convention. She was similarly unable to apply for a free London bus pass at the age of 60 as other women were but had to wait until the age of 65. She was also required to declare her birth sex or disclose her birth certificate when applying for life insurance, mortgages, private pensions or car insurance, which led her not to pursue these possibilities to her advantage.

63. The applicant argued that rapid changes, in respect of the scientific understanding of, and the social attitude towards, transsexualism were taking place not only across Europe but elsewhere. She referred, *inter alia*, to Article 29 of the Netherlands Civil Code, Article 6 of Law No. 164 of 14 April 1982 of Italy, and Article 29 of the Civil Code of Turkey as amended by Law No. 3444 of 4 May 1988, which allowed the amendment of civil status. Also, under a 1995 New Zealand statute, Part V, Section 28, a court could order the legal recognition of the changed gender of a transsexual after examination of medical and other evidence. The applicant saw no convincing reason why a similar approach should not be adopted in the United Kingdom. The applicant also pointed to increasing social acceptance of transsexuals and interest in issues of concern to them reflected by coverage in the press, radio and television, including sympathetic dramatisation of transsexual characters in mainstream programming.

2. The Government

64. Referring to the Court's case-law, the Government maintained that there was no generally accepted approach among the Contracting States in respect of transsexuality and that, in view of the margin of appreciation left to States under the Convention, the lack of recognition in the United Kingdom of the applicant's new gender identity for legal purposes did not entail a violation of Article 8 of the Convention. They disputed the applicant's assertion that scientific research and "massive societal changes" had led to wide acceptance, or consensus on issues, of transsexualism.

65. The Government accepted that there may be specific instances where the refusal to grant legal recognition of a transsexual's new sexual identity may amount to a breach of Article 8, in particular where the transsexual as a result suffered practical and actual detriment and humiliation on a daily basis (see the *B. v. France* judgment of 25 March 1992, Series A no. 232-C, pp. 52–54, §§59–63). However, they denied that the applicant

faced any comparable practical disadvantages, as she had been able *inter alia* to obtain important identification documents showing her chosen names and sexual identity (*e.g.* new passport and driving licence).

66. As regards the specific difficulties claimed by the applicant, the Government submitted that an employer was unable to establish the sex of the applicant from the NI number itself since it did not contain any encoded reference to her sex. The applicant had been issued with a new NI card with her changed name and style of address. Furthermore, the DSS had a policy of confidentiality of the personal details of a NI number holder and, in particular, a policy and procedure for the special protection of transsexuals. As a result, an employer had no means of lawfully obtaining information from the DSS about the previous sexual identity of an employee. It was also in their view highly unlikely that the applicant's employer would discover her change of gender through her NI number in any other way. The refusal to issue a new NI number was justified, the uniqueness of the NI number being of critical importance in the administration of the national insurance system, and for the prevention of the fraudulent use of old NI numbers.

67. The Government argued that the applicant's fear that her previous sexual identity would be revealed upon reaching the age of 60, when her employer would no longer be required to make NI contribution deductions from her pay, was entirely without foundation, the applicant having already been issued with a suitable Age Exemption Certificate on Form CF384.

68. Concerning the impossibility for the applicant to obtain a State retirement pension at the age of 60, the Government submitted that the distinction between men and women as regarded pension age had been held to be compatible with European Community law (Article 7(1)(a) of Directive 79/7/EEC; European Court of Justice, R. v. Secretary of State for Social Security ex parte Equal Opportunities Commission Case C-9/91 [1992] ECR I-4927). Also, since the preserving of the applicant's legal status as a man was not contrary as such to Article 8 of the Convention, it would constitute favourable treatment unfair to the general public to allow the applicant's pension entitlement at the age of 60.

69. Finally, as regards allegations of assault and abuse at work, the Government submitted that the applicant could have pressed charges under the criminal law against harassment and assault. Harassment in the workplace on the grounds of transsexuality would also give rise to a claim under the Sex Discrimination Act 1975 where the employers knew of the harassment and took no steps to prevent it. Adequate protection was therefore available under domestic law.

70. The Government submitted that a fair balance had therefore been struck between the rights of the individual and the general interest of the community. To the extent that there were situations where a transsexual may face limited disclosure of their change of sex, these situations were unavoidable and necessary e.g. in the context of contracts of insurance where medical history and gender affected the calculation of premiums.

B. The Court's assessment

1. Preliminary considerations

71. This case raises the issue whether or not the respondent State has failed to comply with a positive obligation to ensure the right of the applicant, a post-operative male to female transsexual, to respect for her private life, in particular through the lack of legal recognition given to her gender re-assignment.

72. The Court recalls that the notion of "respect" as understood in Article 8 is not clear cut, especially as far as the positive obligations inherent in that concept are concerned: having regard to the diversity of practices followed and the situations obtaining in the Contracting States, the notion's requirements will vary considerably from case to case and the margin of appreciation to be accorded to the authorities may be wider than that applied in other areas under the Convention. In determining whether or not a positive obligation exists, regard must also be had to the fair balance that has to be struck between the general interest of the community and the interests of the individual, the search for which balance is inherent in the whole of the Convention (*Cossey v. the United Kingdom* judgment of 27 September 1990, Series A no. 184, p. 15, §37).

73. The Court recalls that it has already examined complaints about the position of transsexuals in the United Kingdom (see the *Rees v. the United Kingdom* judgment of 17 October 1986, Series A no. 106, the *Cossey v. the United Kingdom* judgment, cited above; the *X., Y. and Z. v. the United Kingdom* judgment of 22 April 1997, Reports of Judgments and Decisions 1997-II, and the *Sheffield and Horsham v. the United Kingdom* judgment of 30 July 1998, Reports 1998-V, p. 2011). In those cases, it held that the refusal of the United Kingdom Government to alter the register of births or to issue birth certificates whose contents and nature differed from those of the original entries concerning the recorded gender of the individual could not be considered as an interference with the right to respect for private life (the above-mentioned *Rees* judgment, p. 14, §35, and *Cossey* judgment, p. 15, §36). It also held that there was no positive obligation on the Government to alter their existing system for the registration of births by establishing a new system or type of documentation to provide proof of current civil status. Similarly, there was no duty on the Government to permit annotations to the existing register of births, or to keep any such annotation secret from third parties (the above-mentioned *Rees* judgment, p. 17, §42, and *Cossey* judgment, p. 15, §§38–39). It was found in those cases that the authorities had taken steps to minimise intrusive enquiries (for example, by allowing transsexuals to be issued with driving licences, passports and other types of documents in their new name and gender). Nor had it been shown that the failure to accord general legal recognition of the change of gender had given rise in the applicants' own case histories to detriment of sufficient seriousness to override the respondent State's margin of appreciation in this area (the *Sheffield and Horsham* judgment cited above, p. 2028–29, §59).

74. While the Court is not formally bound to follow its previous judgments, it is in the interests of legal certainty, foreseeability and equality before the law that it should not depart, without good reason, from precedents laid down in previous cases (see, for example, *Chapman v. the United Kingdom* [GC], no. 27238/95, ECHR 2001-I, §70). However, since the Convention is first and foremost a system for the protection of human rights, the Court must have regard to the changing conditions within the respondent State and within Contracting States generally and respond, for example, to any evolving convergence as to the standards to be achieved (see, amongst other authorities, the *Cossey* judgment, p. 14, §35, and *Stafford v. the United Kingdom* [GC], no. 46295/99, judgment of 28 May 2002, to be published in ECHR 2002-, §§67–68). It is of crucial importance that the Convention is interpreted and applied in a manner which renders its rights practical and effective, not theoretical and illusory. A failure by the Court to maintain a dynamic and evolutive approach would indeed risk rendering it a bar to reform or improvement (see the above-cited *Stafford v. the United Kingdom* judgment, §68). In the present context the Court has, on several occasions since 1986, signalled its consciousness

of the serious problems facing transsexuals and stressed the importance of keeping the need for appropriate legal measures in this area under review (see the *Rees* judgment, §47; the *Cossey* judgment, §42; the *Sheffield and Horsham* judgment, §60).

75. The Court proposes therefore to look at the situation within and outside the Contracting State to assess "in the light of present-day conditions" what is now the appropriate interpretation and application of the Convention (see the *Tyrer v. the United Kingdom* judgment of 25 April 1978, Series A no. 26, §31, and subsequent case-law).

2. The applicant's situation as a transsexual

76. The Court observes that the applicant, registered at birth as male, has undergone gender re-assignment surgery and lives in society as a female. Nonetheless, the applicant remains, for legal purposes, a male. This has had, and continues to have, effects on the applicant's life where sex is of legal relevance and distinctions are made between men and women, as, *inter alia*, in the area of pensions and retirement age. For example, the applicant must continue to pay national insurance contributions until the age of 65 due to her legal status as male. However as she is employed in her gender identity as a female, she has had to obtain an exemption certificate which allows the payments from her employer to stop while she continues to make such payments herself. Though the Government submitted that this made due allowance for the difficulties of her position, the Court would note that she nonetheless has to make use of a special procedure that might in itself call attention to her status.

77. It must also be recognised that serious interference with private life can arise where the state of domestic law conflicts with an important aspect of personal identity (see, *mutatis mutandis, Dudgeon v. the United Kingdom* judgment of 22 October 1981, Series A no. 45, §41). The stress and alienation arising from a discordance between the position in society assumed by a post-operative transsexual and the status imposed by law which refuses to recognise the change of gender cannot, in the Court's view, be regarded as a minor inconvenience arising from a formality. A conflict between social reality and law arises which places the transsexual in an anomalous position, in which he or she may experience feelings of vulnerability, humiliation and anxiety.

78. In this case, as in many others, the applicant's gender re-assignment was carried out by the national health service, which recognises the condition of gender dysphoria and provides, *inter alia*, re-assignment by surgery, with a view to achieving as one of its principal purposes as close an assimilation as possible to the gender in which the transsexual perceives that he or she properly belongs. The Court is struck by the fact that nonetheless the gender re-assignment which is lawfully provided is not met with full recognition in law, which might be regarded as the final and culminating step in the long and difficult process of transformation which the transsexual has undergone. The coherence of the administrative and legal practices within the domestic system must be regarded as an important factor in the assessment carried out under Article 8 of the Convention. Where a State has authorised the treatment and surgery alleviating the condition of a transsexual, financed or assisted in financing the operations and indeed permits the artificial insemination of a woman living with a female-to-male transsexual (as demonstrated in the case of *X., Y. and Z. v. the United Kingdom*, cited above), it appears illogical to refuse to recognise the legal implications of the result to which the treatment leads.

79. The Court notes that the unsatisfactory nature of the current position and plight of transsexuals in the United Kingdom has been acknowledged in the domestic courts (see

Bellinger v. Bellinger, cited above, paragraph 52) and by the Interdepartmental Working Group which surveyed the situation in the United Kingdom and concluded that, notwithstanding the accommodations reached in practice, transsexual people were conscious of certain problems which did not have to be faced by the majority of the population (paragraph 50 above).

80. Against these considerations, the Court has examined the countervailing arguments of a public interest nature put forward as justifying the continuation of the present situation. It observes that in the previous United Kingdom cases weight was given to medical and scientific considerations, the state of any European and international consensus and the impact of any changes to the current birth register system.

3. Medical and scientific considerations

81. It remains the case that there are no conclusive findings as to the cause of transsexualism and, in particular, whether it is wholly psychological or associated with physical differentiation in the brain. The expert evidence in the domestic case of *Bellinger v. Bellinger* was found to indicate a growing acceptance of findings of sexual differences in the brain that are determined pre-natally, though scientific proof for the theory was far from complete. The Court considers it more significant however that transsexualism has wide international recognition as a medical condition for which treatment is provided in order to afford relief (for example, the Diagnostic and Statistical Manual fourth edition (DSM-IV) replaced the diagnosis of transsexualism with "gender identity disorder"; see also the International Classification of Diseases, tenth edition (ICD-10)). The United Kingdom national health service, in common with the vast majority of Contracting States, acknowledges the existence of the condition and provides or permits treatment, including irreversible surgery. The medical and surgical acts which in this case rendered the gender re-assignment possible were indeed carried out under the supervision of the national health authorities. Nor, given the numerous and painful interventions involved in such surgery and the level of commitment and conviction required to achieve a change in social gender role, can it be suggested that there is anything arbitrary or capricious in the decision taken by a person to undergo gender re-assignment. In those circumstances, the ongoing scientific and medical debate as to the exact causes of the condition is of diminished relevance.

82. While it also remains the case that a transsexual cannot acquire all the biological characteristics of the assigned sex (*Sheffield and Horsham*, cited above, p. 2028, §56), the Court notes that with increasingly sophisticated surgery and types of hormonal treatments, the principal unchanging biological aspect of gender identity is the chromosomal element. It is known however that chromosomal anomalies may arise naturally (for example, in cases of intersex conditions where the biological criteria at birth are not congruent) and in those cases, some persons have to be assigned to one sex or the other as seems most appropriate in the circumstances of the individual case. It is not apparent to the Court that the chromosomal element, amongst all the others, must inevitably take on decisive significance for the purposes of legal attribution of gender identity for transsexuals (see the dissenting opinion of Thorpe LJ in *Bellinger v. Bellinger* cited in paragraph 52 above; and the judgment of Chisholm J in the Australian case, *Re Kevin*, cited in paragraph 55 above).

83. The Court is not persuaded therefore that the state of medical science or scientific knowledge provides any determining argument as regards the legal recognition of transsexuals.

4. The state of any European and international consensus

84. Already at the time of the *Sheffield and Horsham* case, there was an emerging consensus within Contracting States in the Council of Europe on providing legal recognition following gender re-assignment (see §35 of that judgment). The latest survey submitted by Liberty in the present case shows a continuing international trend towards legal recognition (see paragraphs 55–56 above). In Australia and New Zealand, it appears that the courts are moving away from the biological birth view of sex (as set out in the United Kingdom case of *Corbett v. Corbett*) and taking the view that sex, in the context of a transsexual wishing to marry, should depend on a multitude of factors to be assessed at the time of the marriage.

85. The Court observes that in the case of *Rees* in 1986 it had noted that little common ground existed between States, some of which did permit change of gender and some of which did not and that generally speaking the law seemed to be in a state of transition (see §37). In the later case of Sheffield and Horsham, the Court's judgment laid emphasis on the lack of a common European approach as to how to address the repercussions which the legal recognition of a change of sex may entail for other areas of law such as marriage, filiation, privacy or data protection. While this would appear to remain the case, the lack of such a common approach among forty-three Contracting States with widely diverse legal systems and traditions is hardly surprising. In accordance with the principle of subsidiarity, it is indeed primarily for the Contracting States to decide on the measures necessary to secure Convention rights within their jurisdiction and, in resolving within their domestic legal systems the practical problems created by the legal recognition of post-operative gender status, the Contracting States must enjoy a wide margin of appreciation. The Court accordingly attaches less importance to the lack of evidence of a common European approach to the resolution of the legal and practical problems posed, than to the clear and uncontested evidence of a continuing international trend in favour not only of increased social acceptance of transsexuals but of legal recognition of the new sexual identity of post-operative transsexuals.

5. Impact on the birth register system

86. In the Rees case, the Court allowed that great importance could be placed by the Government on the historical nature of the birth record system. The argument that allowing exceptions to this system would undermine its function weighed heavily in the assessment.

87. It may be noted however that exceptions are already made to the historic basis of the birth register system, namely, in the case of legitimisation or adoptions, where there is a possibility of issuing updated certificates to reflect a change in status after birth. To make a further exception in the case of transsexuals (a category estimated as including some 2,000–5,000 persons in the United Kingdom according to the Interdepartmental Working Group Report, p. 26) would not, in the Court's view, pose the threat of overturning the entire system. Though previous reference has been made to detriment suffered by third parties who might be unable to obtain access to the original entries and to complications occurring in the field of family and succession law (see the *Rees* judgment, p. 18, §43), these assertions are framed in general terms and the Court does not find, on the basis of the material before it at this time, that any real prospect of prejudice has been identified as likely to arise if changes were made to the current system.

88. Furthermore, the Court notes that the Government have recently issued proposals for reform which would allow ongoing amendment to civil status data (see paragraph 54). It is not convinced therefore that the need to uphold rigidly the integrity of the historic basis of the birth registration system takes on the same importance in the current climate as it did in 1986.

6. Striking a balance in the present case

89. The Court has noted above (paragraphs 76–79) the difficulties and anomalies of the applicant's situation as a post-operative transsexual. It must be acknowledged that the level of daily interference suffered by the applicant in *B. v. France* (judgment of 25 March 1992, Series A no. 232) has not been attained in this case and that on certain points the risk of difficulties or embarrassment faced by the present applicant may be avoided or minimised by the practices adopted by the authorities.

90. Nonetheless, the very essence of the Convention is respect for human dignity and human freedom. Under Article 8 of the Convention in particular, where the notion of personal autonomy is an important principle underlying the interpretation of its guarantees, protection is given to the personal sphere of each individual, including the right to establish details of their identity as individual human beings (see, *inter alia*, *Pretty v. the United Kingdom*, no. 2346/02, judgment of 29 April 2002, §62, and *Mikulic v. Croatia*, no. 53176/99, judgment of 7 February 2002, §53, both to be published in ECHR 2002-...). In the twenty first century the right of transsexuals to personal development and to physical and moral security in the full sense enjoyed by others in society cannot be regarded as a matter of controversy requiring the lapse of time to cast clearer light on the issues involved. In short, the unsatisfactory situation in which post-operative transsexuals live in an intermediate zone as not quite one gender or the other is no longer sustainable. Domestic recognition of this evaluation may be found in the report of the Interdepartmental Working Group and the Court of Appeal's judgment of *Bellinger v. Bellinger* (see paragraphs 50, 52–53).

91. The Court does not underestimate the difficulties posed or the important repercussions which any major change in the system will inevitably have, not only in the field of birth registration, but also in the areas of access to records, family law, affiliation, inheritance, criminal justice, employment, social security and insurance. However, as is made clear by the report of the Interdepartmental Working Group, these problems are far from insuperable, to the extent that the Working Group felt able to propose as one of the options full legal recognition of the new gender, subject to certain criteria and procedures. As Lord Justice Thorpe observed in the *Bellinger* case, any "spectral difficulties", particularly in the field of family law, are both manageable and acceptable if confined to the case of fully achieved and post-operative transsexuals. Nor is the Court convinced by arguments that allowing the applicant to fall under the rules applicable to women, which would also change the date of eligibility for her state pension, would cause any injustice to others in the national insurance and state pension systems as alleged by the Government. No concrete or substantial hardship or detriment to the public interest has indeed been demonstrated as likely to flow from any change to the status of transsexuals and, as regards other possible consequences, the Court considers that society may reasonably be expected to tolerate a certain inconvenience to enable individuals to live in dignity and worth in accordance with the sexual identity chosen by them at great personal cost.

92. In the previous cases from the United Kingdom, this Court has since 1986 emphasised the importance of keeping the need for appropriate legal measures under review

having regard to scientific and societal developments (see references at paragraph 73). Most recently in the Sheffield and Horsham case in 1998, it observed that the respondent State had not yet taken any steps to do so despite an increase in the social acceptance of the phenomenon of transsexualism and a growing recognition of the problems with which transsexuals are confronted (cited above, paragraph 60). Even though it found no violation in that case, the need to keep this area under review was expressly re-iterated. Since then, a report has been issued in April 2000 by the Interdepartmental Working Group which set out a survey of the current position of transsexuals in inter alia criminal law, family and employment matters and identified various options for reform. Nothing has effectively been done to further these proposals and in July 2001 the Court of Appeal noted that there were no plans to do so (see paragraphs 52–53). It may be observed that the only legislative reform of note, applying certain non-discrimination provisions to transsexuals, flowed from a decision of the European Court of Justice of 30 April 1996 which held that discrimination based on a change of gender was equivalent to discrimination on grounds of sex (see paragraphs 43–45 above).

93. Having regard to the above considerations, the Court finds that the respondent Government can no longer claim that the matter falls within their margin of appreciation, save as regards the appropriate means of achieving recognition of the right protected under the Convention. Since there are no significant factors of public interest to weigh against the interest of this individual applicant in obtaining legal recognition of her gender re-assignment, it reaches the conclusion that the fair balance that is inherent in the Convention now tilts decisively in favour of the applicant. There has, accordingly, been a failure to respect her right to private life in breach of Article 8 of the Convention.

. . . .

≈

QUESTIONS & COMMENTS

(1) How would the European Court deal with a case involving the privacy rights of an "intersexed" person, *i.e.*, a person that does not identify with either the male or female gender?

(2) *Goodwin* was a unanimous grand chamber decision on the merits. Why do you think a grand chamber (instead of a panel) took up the case?

Parental Rights and the Right to Familial Integrity

Fei v. Colombia
UN Human Rights Committee
Communication No. 514/1992
Views adopted 4 April 1995
U.N. Doc. CCPR/C/53/D/514/1992 (1995)

. . .

1. The author of the communication is Sandra Fei, of Italian and Colombian citizenship, born in 1957 in Santa Fe de Bogota and currently residing in Milan, Italy. She claims to be a victim of violations by Colombia of articles 2, paragraphs 2 and 3; 14,

paragraphs 1 and 3 (c); 17; 23, paragraph 4; and 24 of the International Covenant on Civil and Political Rights. She is represented by counsel.

The facts as submitted by the author:

2.1 Mrs. Fei married Jaime Ospina Sardi in 1976; in 1977, rifts between the spouses began to emerge, and in 1981 Mrs. Fei left the home; the two children born from the marriage remained with the husband. The author sought to establish a residence in Bogota but, as she was unable to obtain more than temporary employment, finally moved to Paris as a correspondent for the daily newspaper 24 Horas.

2.2 A Colombian court order dating from 19 May 1982 established a separation and custody arrangement, but divorce proceedings subsequently were also instituted by the author before a Paris tribunal, with the consent of her exhusband.

2.3 Under the Colombian court order of May 1982, the custody of the children was granted provisionally to the father, with the proviso that custody would go to the mother if the father remarried or cohabited with another woman. It further established joint parental custody and provided for generous visiting rights. Mr. Rodolfo Segovia Salas, a senator of the Republic, brother-in-law of Mr. Ospina Sardi and close family friend, was designated as guarantor of the agreement.

2.4 On 26 September 1985, Mrs. Fei's children, during a visit to her mother, were allegedly kidnapped by the father, with the help of three men said to be employees of the Colombian Embassy in Paris, when the author was leaving her Paris apartment. Between September 1985 and September 1988, the author did not have any contact with her children and knew nothing of their whereabouts, as Mr. Segovia Salas allegedly refused to cooperate. The author obtained the good offices of the French authorities and of the wife of President Mitterrand, but these demarches proved unsuccessful. Mrs. Fei then requested the assistance of the Italian Ministry of Foreign Affairs, which in turn asked for information and judicial assistance from the Colombian authorities. The author alleges that the latter either replied in evasive terms or simply denied that the author's rights had been violated. During the summer of 1988, an official of the Italian Foreign Ministry managed to locate the children in Bogota. In September 1988, accompanied by the Italian Ambassador to Colombia, the author was finally able to see her two children for five minutes, on the third floor of the American School in Bogota.

2.5 In the meantime, Mr. Ospina Sardi had himself initiated divorce proceedings in Bogota, in which he requested the suspension of the author's parental authority as well as an order that would prohibit the children from leaving Colombia. On 13 March 1989, the First Circuit Court of Bogota (*Juzgado Primero Civil del Circuito de Bogota*) handed down its judgement; the author contends that in essence, the judgement confirmed the terms of the separation agreement reached several years earlier. Mrs. Fei further argues that the divorce proceedings in Colombia deliberately ignored the proceedings still pending before the Paris tribunal, as well as the children's dual nationality.

2.6 Mrs. Fei contends that, since September 1985, she has received, and continues to receive, threats. As a result, she claims, she cannot travel to Colombia alone or without protection. In March 1989, therefore, the Italian Foreign Ministry organized a trip to Bogota for her; after negotiations, she was able to see her children for exactly two hours, "as an exceptional favour". The meeting took place in a small room in Mr. Segovia Salas' home, in the presence of a psychologist who allegedly had sought to obstruct the meeting until the very last moment. Thereafter, the author was only allowed to communicate with her children by telephone or mail; she contends that her letters were frequently tampered with and that it was almost impossible to reach the girls by telephone.

2.7 In May 1989, Mr. Ospina Sardi broke off the negotiations with the author without providing an explanation; only in November 1989 were the Italian authorities informed, upon request, of the "final divorce judgement" of 13 March 1989. Mr. Ospina Sardi refused to comply with the terms of the judgement. On 21 June 1991, Mr. Ospina Sardi filed a request for the revision of the divorce judgement and of the visiting rights granted to the author, on the ground that circumstances had changed and that visiting rights as generous as those agreed upon in 1985 were no longer justifiable in the circumstances; the author contends that she was only informed of those proceedings in early 1992. Mr. Ospina Sardi also requested that the author be refused permission to see the children in Colombia, and that the children should not be allowed to visit their mother in Italy.

2.8 The Italian Foreign Ministry was in turn informed that the matter had been passed on to the office of the Prosecutor-General of Colombia, whose task under article 277 of the Constitution it is, *inter alia*, to review compliance with judgements handed down by Colombian courts. The Prosecutor-General initially ignored the case and did not investigate it; nor did he initiate criminal proceedings against Mr. Ospina Sardi for contempt of court and non-compliance with an executory judgement. Several months later, he asked for his disqualification in the case, on the grounds that he had "strong bonds of friendship" with Mr. Ospina Sardi; the file was transferred to another magistrate. The Italian authorities have since addressed several complaints to the President of Colombia and to the Colombian Ministries of Foreign Affairs and International Trade, the latter having offered, on an unspecified earlier date, to find a way out of the impasse. No satisfactory reply has been provided by the Colombian authorities.

2.9 The author notes that, during her trips to Colombia in May and June 1992, she could only see her children very briefly and under conditions deemed unacceptable, and never for more than one hour at a time. On the occasion of her last visit to Colombia in March 1993, the conditions under which the visits took place allegedly had become worse, and the authorities attempted to prevent Mrs. Fei from leaving Colombia. Mrs. Fei has now herself instituted criminal proceedings against Mr. Ospina Sardi, for non-compliance with the divorce judgement.

2.10 In 1992 and 1993, the Colombian courts took further action in respect of Mr. Ospina Sardi's request for a revision of parental custody and visiting rights, as well as in respect of complaints filed on behalf of the author in the Supreme Court of Colombia. On 24 November 1992, the Family Law Division (*Sala de Familia*) of the Superior Court of Bogota (*Tribunal Superior del Distrito Judicial*) modified the visiting rights regime in the sense that all contacts between the children and the author outside Colombia were suspended; at the same time, the entire visiting rights regime was pending for review before Family Court No. 19 of Bogota.

2.11 Mrs. Fei's counsel initiated proceedings in the Supreme Court of Colombia, directed against the Family Court No. 19 of Bogota, against the office of the Procurator-General and against the judgement of 24 November 1992, for nonobservance of the author's constitutional rights. On 9 February 1993, the Civil Chamber of the Supreme Court (*Sala de Casación Civil*) set aside operative paragraph 1 of the judgement of 24 November 1992 concerning the suspension of contacts between the author and her children outside Colombia, while confirming the rest of said judgement. At the same time, the Supreme Court transmitted its judgement to Family Judge No. 19, with the request that its observations be taken into account in the proceedings filed by Mr. Ospina Sardi, and to the Constitutional Court.

2.12 On 14 April 1993, Family Court No. 19 of Bogota handed down its judgement concerning the request for modification of visiting rights. This judgement placed certain conditions on the modalities of the author's visits to her children, especially outside Colombia, inasmuch as the Government of Colombia had to take the measures necessary to guarantee the exit and the re-entry of the children.

2.13 On 28 July 1993, finally, the Constitutional Court partially confirmed and partially modified the judgement of the Supreme Court of 9 February 1993. The judgement is critical of the author's attitude *vis-a-vis* her children between 1985 and 1989, as it assumes that the author deliberately neglected contact with them between those dates. It denies the author any possibility of a transfer of custody, and appears to hold that the judgement of Family Court No. 19 is final ("*no vacila . . . en oponer como cosa juzgada la sentencia . . . dictada el 14 de abril de 1993*"). This, according to counsel, means that the author must start all over again if she endeavours to obtain custody of the children. Finally, the judgement admonishes the author to assume her duties with more responsibility in the future ("*Previanese a la demandante . . . sobre la necesidad de asumir con mayor responsabilidad los deberes que le corresponden como madre de la niñas*").

2.14 In December 1993, the author's children, after presumed pressure from their father, filed proceedings pursuant to article 86 of the Colombian Constitution (*acción de tutela*; see para. 4.5 below) against their mother. The case was placed before the Superior Tribunal in Bogota (*Tribunal Superior del Distrito Judicial de Santa Fe de Bógota*). Mrs. Fei claims that she was never officially notified of this action. It appears that the Court gave her until 10 January 1994 to present her defence, reserving judgement for 14 January. For an unexplained reason, the hearing was then advanced to the morning of 16 December 1993, with the judgement delivered on the afternoon of the same day. The judgement orders Mrs. Fei to stop publishing her book about her and her children's story (PERDUTE, PERDIDAS) in Colombia.

2.15 The author submits that her lawyer was prevented from attending the hearing of 16 December 1993 and from presenting his client's defence. Counsel thereupon filed a complaint based on violations of fundamental rights of the defence with the Supreme Court. On 24 February 1994, the Supreme Court (*Sala de Casación Penal*) declared, on procedural grounds, that it was not competent to hear the complaint.

2.16 Mrs. Fei notes that apart from the divorce and custody proceedings, her ex-husband has filed complaints for defamation and for perjury/deliberately false testimony against her. She observes that she won the defamation complaint in all instances; furthermore, she has won, on first instance, the perjury complaint against her. This action is pending on appeal. The author submits that these suits were malicious and designed to provide a pretext enabling the authorities to prevent her from leaving Colombia the next time she visits her children.

The complaint:

. . . .

3.3 According to the author, the facts as stated above amount to a violation of article 17, on account of the arbitrary and unlawful interferences in her private life or the interference in her correspondence with the children.

3.4 The author complains that Colombia has violated her and her children's rights under article 23, paragraph 4, of the Covenant. In particular, no provision for the protection of the children was made, as required under article 23, paragraph 4 *in fine*. In this context, the author concedes that her children have suffered through the high exposure that the case has had in the media, both in Colombia and in Italy. As a result, they have become withdrawn. A report and the testimony of a psychologist used during the proceedings before Family Court No. 19 concluded that the children's relationships deteriorated abruptly because of the "publicity campaign" waged against their father; the author observes that this psychologist was hired by her ex-husband after the children returned to Colombia in 1985, that she received instructions as to which treatment was appropriate for the children and that she literally "brainwashed" them.

3.5 The author alleges a violation of article 24, in relation to the children's presumed right to acquire Italian nationality, and their right to equal access to both parents.

3.6 Finally, counsel argues that the Committee should take into account that Colombia also violated articles 9 and 10 of the Convention on the Rights of the Child, which relate to contact between parents and their children. In this context, he notes that the Convention on the Rights of the Child was incorporated into Colombian law by Law No. 12 of 1991, and submits that the courts, in particular Family Court No. 19, failed to apply articles 9 and 10 of the Convention.

. . . .

6.5 The State party rejects as unfounded the author's claim that Colombian authorities interfered arbitrarily and unlawfully with the author's right to privacy, by making contacts between herself and her children unnecessarily difficult. This claim, according to the State party, has not been sufficiently substantiated. In this context, the State party contends that it always gave the author the guarantees and assurances requested by the intermediary of the Italian Embassy, so as to facilitate her travel to Colombia. This is said to have included protection, if so requested. The State party recalls that no impediments exist, or have ever existed, that would prevent the author from entering Colombian territory to visit her children, or with a view to initiating such judicial proceedings she considers opportune to defend her rights.

6.6 Concerning the allegation under article 23, paragraph 4, the State party submits that the author has failed to substantiate how this provision was violated in her case. It recalls that the parents jointly agreed, in 1982, that custody of and care for the children should remain with Mr. Ospina Sardi; this agreement has been challenged on numerous subsequent occasions before the domestic courts.

6.7 The State party rejects as unfounded the author's claim that it did nothing or not enough to protect the "interests of the children", within the meaning of article 23, paragraph 4. In this context, it refers to articles 30 and 31 of the Minors' Code (*Código del Minor*), which governs the protection of children. Article 31, in particular, stipulates that the State will guarantee the protection of children, on a subsidiary basis, if the parents or legal guardians do not fulfil their role. As no circumstances that would have warranted the application of articles 30 and 31 were ever brought to the attention of the competent Colombian authorities, the State party deduces that the author's daughters never were in a situation in which they would have required the State's intervention.

6.8 Still in the context of article 23, paragraph 4, the State party notes that Colombian legislation stipulates that the rights of children shall prevail over the rights of others.

Article 44 of the Constitution lays down a number of fundamental rights that are enjoyed by children. A special jurisdiction for minors is safeguarding those rights.

6.9 The State party recalls that the author's daughters themselves filed proceedings against their mother under article 86 of the Constitution, with a view to enforcing their rights under articles 15, 16, 21, 42 and 44 of the Constitution, *inter alia*, on the grounds that their mother's highly publicized attempts to re-establish contacts with them, as well as the publication of a book about her tribulations, interfered with their privacy and had caused them serious moral prejudice. By judgement of 16 December 1993, a court in Bogota (*Sala Penal del Tribunal Superior del Distrito Judicial de Santa Fe de Bógota*) ordered the author to refrain from publishing her book (*PERDUTE, PERDIDAS*) in Colombia, as well as from any other activity encroaching upon her daughters' rights. This judgement was confirmed by the Constitutional Court (*Corte Constitucional, Sala Quinta de Revisión*) on 27 June 1994.

7.1 In her comments, the author reiterates that she did not benefit from equality of arms before the Colombian tribunals. Thus, the procedures initiated by her took exceedingly long to examine and to resolve, whereas the procedures initiated by her ex-husband, either directly or indirectly, were processed immediately and sometimes resolved before the date of the audience initially communicated to the author.

7.2 As an example, the author refers to the proceedings filed by her daughters late in 1993. She insists that she was only notified at the end of January 1994, whereas the delay for the submission of her defence had been set for 10 January 1994, and the audience scheduled for 14 January 1994. Moreover, these dates were wrong, as the audience in fact took place in the morning of 16 December 1993, and judgement was given on the afternoon of the same day.

7.3 The author also refers to the new custody and visiting rights regime decided by the courts in 1992 and 1993, and detailed in paragraphs 2.10 to 2.13 above. Some of these decisions went against her husband, but the author submits that the judicial authorities did not react to his refusal to execute/accept said decisions. For this reason, the author requested the Colombian authorities to guarantee the enforcement of the decisions of Colombian courts, and a magistrate was charged with an investigation into the matter. Months passed before this magistrate asked for his own discharge because of his friendship with Mr. Ospina Sardi, and before another judge was entrusted with the inquiry. The author recalls that the issue has been under inquiry since mid-1992, without any sign of a decision having been taken.

7.4 As to the violation of article 17, the author notes that while she was free to travel to Colombia, she had to arrange herself for her personal protection. The Colombian authorities never assisted her in enforcing her visiting rights. Numerous demarches undertaken to this effect by the Italian Embassy in Bogota either were left without answer or received dilatory replies. The author submits that by so doing, or by remaining inactive, the State party is guilty of passive interference with her right to privacy.

7.5 Still in the context of article 17, the author contends that on two occasions, the State party arbitrarily interfered with her right to privacy. The first occurred in 1992, on the occasion of one of her visits to Colombia. The author submits that she was not personally notified of proceedings instituted by her ex-husband, and that it required the personal intervention of the Italian Ambassador before the magistrate in charge of the case finally accepted to take her deposition, a few hours before her departure for Italy. The second occurred in 1993 when the Colombian police allegedly tried to prevent her from leaving Colombian territory; again, it took the intervention of the Italian Ambassador before the plane carrying the author was allowed to take off.

7.6 Finally, the author contends that the violation of article 23, paragraph 4, in her case is flagrant. She describes the precarious conditions under which the visits of their daughters took place, out of their home, in the presence of a psychologist hired by Mr. Ospina Sardi, and for extremely short periods of time. The testimonies of Ms. Susanna Agnelli, who accompanied the author during these visits, are said to demonstrate clearly the violation of this provision.

7.7 The author further submits that article 23, paragraph 4, was violated because her daughters were forced to testify against her on several occasions in judicial proceedings initiated by Mr. Ospina Sardi, testimonies that allegedly constituted a serious threat to their mental equilibrium. Furthermore, the procedure filed by the children against the author under article 86 of the Constitution is said to have been prompted by pressure from Mr. Ospina Sardi. This, it is submitted, clearly transpires from the text of the initial deposition: according to the author, it could only have been prepared by a lawyer, but not by a child.

. . . .

Examination of the merits:

8.1 The Human Rights Committee has examined the communication in the light of all the information, material and court documents provided by the parties. It bases its findings on the considerations set out below.

. . . .

8.4. . . . As the Committee has noted in its admissibility decision, the very nature of custody proceedings or proceedings concerning access of a divorced parent to his children requires that the issues complained of be adjudicated expeditiously. In the Committee's opinion, given the delays in the determination of the author's actions, this has not been the case.

8.5 The Committee has further noted that the State party's authorities have failed to secure the author's ex-husband's compliance with court orders granting the author access to her children, such as the court order of May 1982 or the judgement of the First Circuit Court of Bógota of 13 March 1989. Complaints from the author about the non-enforcement of such orders apparently continue to be investigated, more than 30 months after they were filed, or remain in abeyance; this is another element indicating that the requirement of equality of arms and of expeditious procedure has not been met.

8.6 Finally, it is noteworthy that in the proceedings under article 86 of the Colombian Constitution instituted on behalf of the author's daughters in December 1993, the hearing took place, and judgement was given, on 16 December 1993, that is, before the expiration of the deadline for the submission of the author's defence statement. The State party has failed to address this point, and the author's version is thus uncontested. In the Committee's opinion, the impossibility for Mrs. Fei to present her arguments before judgement was given was incompatible with the principle of adversary proceedings, and thus contrary to article 14, paragraph 1, of the Covenant.

8.7 The Committee has noted and accepts the State party's argument that in proceedings which are initiated by the children of a divorced parent, the interests and the welfare of the children are given priority. The Committee does not wish to assert that it is in a better position than the domestic courts to assess these interests. The Committee recalls, however, that when such matters are before a local court that is assessing these matters, the court must respect all the guarantees of fair trial.

8.8 The author has claimed arbitrary and unlawful interferences with her right to privacy. The Committee notes that the author's claim about harassment and threats on the occasions of her visits to Colombia have remained generalized, and the transcript of the court proceedings made available to the Committee do not reveal that this matter was addressed before the courts. Nor has the claim that correspondence with her children was frequently tampered with been further documented. As to the difficulties the author experienced in following the court proceedings before different judicial instances, the Committee notes that even serious inconvenience caused by judicial proceedings to which the author of a communication is a party cannot be qualified as "arbitrary" or "unlawful" interference with that individual's privacy. Finally, there is no indication that the author's honour was unlawfully attacked by virtue of the court proceedings themselves. The Committee concludes that these circumstances do not constitute a violation of article 17.

8.9 As to the alleged violation of article 23, paragraph 4, the Committee recalls that this provision grants, barring exceptional circumstances, a right to regular contact between children and both of their parents upon dissolution of a marriage. The unilateral opposition of one parent generally does not constitute such an exceptional circumstance. [Views on case No. 201/1985 (*Hendriks v. The Netherlands*), adopted on 27 July 1988, para. 10.4.]

8.10 In the present case, it was the author's ex-husband who sought to prevent the author from maintaining regular contact with her daughters, in spite of court decisions granting the author such access. On the basis of the material made available to the Committee, the father's refusal apparently was justified as being "in the best interest" of the children. The Committee cannot share this assessment. No special circumstances have been adduced that would have justified the restrictions on the author's contacts with her children. Rather, it appears that the author's ex-husband sought to stifle, by all means at his disposal, the author's access to the girls, or to alienate them from her. The severe restrictions imposed by Mrs. Fei's ex-husband on Mrs. Fei's rare meetings with her daughters support this conclusion. Her attempts to initiate criminal proceedings against her ex-husband for non-compliance with the court order granting her visiting rights were frustrated by delay and inaction on the part of the prosecutor's office. In the circumstances, it was not reasonable to expect her to pursue any remedy that may have been available under the Code of Civil Procedure. In the Committee's opinion, in the absence of special circumstances, none of which are discernible in the present case, it cannot be deemed to be in the "best interest" of children virtually to eliminate one parent's access to them. That Mrs. Fei has, since 1992–1993, reduced her attempts to vindicate her right of access cannot, in the Committee's opinion, be held against her. In all the circumstances of the case, the Committee concludes that there has been a violation of article 23, paragraph 4. Furthermore, the failure of the prosecutor's office to ensure the right to permanent contact between the author and her daughters also has entailed a violation of article 17, paragraph 1, of the Covenant.

9. The Human Rights Committee, acting under article 5, paragraph 4, of the Optional Protocol to the International Covenant on Civil and Political Rights, is of the view that the facts before the Committee reveal violations by Colombia of articles 14, paragraph 1, and 23, paragraph 4, in conjunction with article 17, paragraph 1, of the Covenant.

10. In accordance with article 2, paragraph 3(a), of the Covenant, the State party is under an obligation to provide the author with an effective remedy. In the Committee's opinion, this entails guaranteeing the author's regular access to her daughters, and that

the State party ensure that the terms of the judgements in the author's favour are complied with. The State party is under an obligation to ensure that similar violations do not occur in the future.

. . . .

∽

QUESTIONS & COMMENTS

(1) Fei brought both diplomatic and popular pressure against the Columbian government. Do you think that such actions helped her cause? How does an international human rights lawyer determine whether such extralegal campaigns would be helpful to their client? One cannot wage such campaigns when an application is pending before the European Court of Human Rights or the UN Human Rights Committee because of their regulations; however, there are no such restrictions on petitioners before the Inter-American Commission. Are such extralegal tactics perfect for making the settlement mechanisms employed by the Inter-American Commission work? Consider the fact that many of the Inter-American Commissioners are diplomats and not lawyers.

(2) Parental abduction of children across national borders is a growing phenomenon. Given that the UN Human Rights Committee recognizes that family court decisions should be especially swift in order to avoid further harm to the children, can this principle be helpful to petitioners in arguing constructive exhaustion of domestic remedies? How would you articulate such a principle in child abduction cases?

(3) Consider *Johansen v. Norway*, – Eur. Ct. H.R (ser. A) (1996), 23 E.H.R.R. 33 (1996). Ms. Johansen gave birth to her second child, S., on 7 December 1989. Immediately prior to giving birth, she spent a day at a shelter for abused women. In view of her difficult situation and the problems with the upbringing of her first child, the child welfare authorities were contacted. The chairman of the Client and Patient Committee decided to take this child into provisional care because of the physical and mental state of Johansen. He considered her incapable of taking care of her daughter and thought the daughter would be at risk if this decision was not implemented immediately. On 19 December 1989, Johansen's daughter was placed in a short-term foster home. Johansen was allowed to visit her twice a week at the Aline Child Care Center. On 29 December 1989, the Client and Patient Committee discussed the issue of public care for Johansen's daughter. They obtained a psychologist's expert opinion on Johansen's ability to take care of her daughter. The opinion concluded that Johansen was incapable of taking care of S. at present. The opinion also stressed the importance of the baby's bonding with stable and secure persons on whom she could depend in her adolescence. Johansen requested the appointment of a second expert. After the child welfare authorities refused her request, she hired a psychologist. This expert found there were insufficient reasons for depriving Johansen of the care of her children. On 3 May 1990, after a hearing, the committee decided to take S. into the state's care, to deprive Johansen of her parental responsibilities, to place S. in a foster home with a view to adoption, to refuse Johansen access to her child, and to keep the address of the foster home secret.

Johansen appealed and requested the decision to deny her access be suspended until her appeal was determined. On 30 May, S. was placed with foster parents. On 31 July, the county governor decided not to give the appeal suspensive effect because it would not be in S.'s best interests. He later upheld the committee's decision. Johansen then instituted proceedings against the Ministry of Child and Family Affairs in the Oslo City Court. At trial, the decision to take S. into state care and to deprive Johansen of parental responsibilities was upheld. On 28 May 1991, Johansen lodged an appeal with the Supreme Court. The Court refused leave to appeal. Johansen applied to the European Commission alleging an Article 8 violation of her right to respect for family life, and the Commission eventually referred the case to the European Court.

The European Court found that the placing of Johansen's daughter in state care and the termination of her parental rights had a basis in Norwegian law; therefore, the Norwegian government's actions were "in accordance with law." Furthermore, the aim of these laws was clearly to protect the health, rights, and freedoms of children; accordingly, this aim was legitimate within the meaning of Article 8(2).

In determining whether the actions of the state were "necessary in a democratic society," the European Court considered whether in the light of the case as a whole, the reasons used to justify these actions were relevant and sufficient for the purposes of Article 8(2). While local authorities enjoy a wide margin of appreciation in assessing the necessity of taking a child into state care, a stricter scrutiny is called for if any further limitations (i.e., deprivation of parental rights and access) are sought. Stricter scrutiny is also appropriate when reviewing the legal safeguards designed to secure an effective protection of the right of parents and children to respect for their family life. These further actions entail the danger that the family relations are effectively curtailed. After applying strict scrutiny to all the actions in this case, the Court determined that the decision to deprive Johansen of her parental rights was not "necessary."

The European Court considered that taking a child into care normally should be regarded as a temporary measure to be discontinued as soon as circumstances permit. The Court also believed that any measure implementing temporary care should be consistent with the ultimate aim of reuniting the natural parents and the child. Here, Johansen had been deprived of her parental rights and access through the permanent placement of her child in foster care. These measures were particularly far-reaching in that they totally deprived Johansen of her family life with S. and were inconsistent with the aim of reuniting them. Such measures should only be applied in exceptional circumstances and could only be justified if they were motivated by an overriding requirement pertaining to the child's best interests. During the period between the birth of S. and the committee's decision on 3 May 1990, Johansen had access to her child twice a week and nobody complained of this as unhealthy or unfeasible. Additionally, during the period between the birth of S. and the committee's decision on 3 May, Johansen's lifestyle had already improved. Indeed, less than a year after the committee decision, the City Court found that Johansen's material conditions had improved to the point where she would have been able to provide her daughter with a satisfactory upbringing. The City Court, however, decided not to alter the current custody arrangement because of the lack of contact between Johansen and S. at the time of the proceedings. This state of affairs, the European Court pointed out, was a direct result of the committee's 3 May decision and could not be held against Johansen. The committee had based its decision on the experiences Johansen had had with her first born. These difficulties, however, were not of such a nature and degree as to dispense the authorities altogether from their normal obligation to take measures with a view of reuniting S. with her mother if the mother were to become able to provide her daughter with a satisfying upbringing. Ignoring this aim was not justified in the child's best interest.

Therefore, the European Court concluded that the Norwegian authorities overstepped their margin of appreciation, thereby violating the Johansen's rights under Article 8 of the Convention.

(4) Consider *Keegan v. Ireland*, 290 Eur. Ct. H.R. (ser. A) (1994). Mr. Keegan and his girlfriend, V., lived together for a year. Keegan and V. decided to have a baby and get married. Shortly after V. became pregnant, however, the relationship soured. Keegan moved out. V. gave birth to a healthy baby girl. V. placed the child up for adoption without Keegan's knowledge or consent. In November 1988, the baby was placed with the prospective adopters. As soon as Keegan became aware of the situation, he instituted proceedings before the Circuit Court to be appointed the child's guardian so he could challenge the adoption. As the child's natural father, he had no standing to challenge the adoption, while as the child's guardian he could. In May 1989, the Circuit Court appointed him guardian of his daughter. V. appealed to the High Court. The High Court upheld the Circuit Court's decision, finding Keegan a fit guardian and finding that there were no circumstances involving the child's welfare which required that the father's rights be denied. V. then applied to the Supreme Court, claiming that the Guardianship of Infants Act was misconstrued by the High Court. The Supreme Court agreed. According to the Supreme Court, since Keegan was not married to the mother, his biological link to the child should only be one of the factors used in evaluating his application along with the prospective adopters. The decision should be made by determining which set of guardians could best provide for the child. The Supreme Court remanded the case. In light of this interpretation, the High Court reevaluated the case, finding that the baby's quality of welfare would be an important extent better if she was not moved away from the adopting family, with whom she had lived since her birth. The family could provide a higher standard of living and would provide more stability and security than a single parent could. The High Court awarded the adopting family custody and condoned the adoption.

Keegan applied to the European Commission, claiming that his Article 8 right to respect for family life had been violated in that his daughter was placed for adoption without his knowledge or consent and that Ireland had not provided him an opportunity to be appointed guardian.

The European Court held that the term "family" in Article 8 is not confined solely to marriage-based relationships. "Family" encompasses other *de facto* family ties where the parties are living together outside of marriage. A child born of such a relationship is *ipso iure* part of that "family" unit from the moment of her birth and by the very fact of it. Here, the relationship between Keegan and V. lasted for two years and they cohabited for one. The couple made a deliberate decision to conceive the child and were planning to be married. At this time, their relationship had the hallmark of "family life" for Article 8. The fact that they subsequently broke up did not alter this conclusion any more than it would for a lawfully married couple in a similar situation. Thus, from the moment of his daughter's birth, a bond amounting to "family" life existed between Keegan and his daughter; therefore, Article 8 was applicable.

Under Article 8(1), the state has both positive and negative obligations. Where the existence of a family tie with a child is established, the state must act in a manner calculated to enable the ties to be developed and legal safeguards must be created that render possible as from the moment of birth the child's integration in her family. The mutual enjoyment by parent and child of each other's company constitutes a fundamental element of family life even when the relationship between the parents has broken down. Therefore, the fact that Irish law permitted the secret placement of the child for adoption without Keegan's knowledge or consent, leading to the child's bonding with the prospective adopters amounted to "interference" with Keegan's Article 8(1) right to respect for family life.

The court found that the decision to place the child up for adoption was in accordance with the Guardianship of Infants Act and that the act's legitimate aim was to protect the rights and freedoms of the child. To be necessary in a democratic society, however, the act must strike a fair balance between the competing interests of the individual and the community as a whole. The act did not succeed in striking this balance. It allowed the child to be placed for adoption without her natural father's knowledge or consent. This child, and others similarly situated, may begin to establish bonds with the alternative caretakers. Once these bonds are established, it may no longer be in the child's best interest to be taken away from these caregivers. This state of affairs jeopardizes the natural parent's rights to his child. It also may prove irreversible by placing the natural parent at a disadvantage in his contest with the prospective adopters for custody of the child. In Keegan's case, this had taken place. A unanimous European Court found that Keegan's Article 8 rights had been violated.

Keegan also complained that his Article 6(1) right of access to a court had been violated because he, as the natural father, didn't have standing before the adoption board. The Irish government claimed that the adoption board is not a court and pointed out that Keegan did have access to court in applying for guardianship and custody. The European Court decided this arrangement was part of the problem. Keegan had no standing in the entire adoption procedure. His only recourse to impede the adoption of his daughter was to bring guardianship and custody proceedings. The actual adoption and placement of his daughter had already occurred by the time Keegan's proceedings had been resolved. The child's welfare had tilted inevitably and irreversibly in favor of the prospective adopters. For Keegan to enjoy his right to access, he must be permitted to stand before the adoption board. The European Court, therefore, concluded that Keegan's Article 6(1) right also had been violated.

(5) Compare *Kroon and Others v. The Netherlands,* 297-C Eur. Ct. H.R. (ser. A) (1994), to *Mathew v. Lucas,* 427 U.S. 495 (1976). These two cases approach the issue of "illegitimacy" from two different rights perspectives: right to family and right to due process.

In *Kroon and Others v. the Netherlands,* Catharina Kroon, a Dutch national, and Ali Zerrouk, a Moroccan national, had a child, Samir, in 1987. However, Ms. Kroon was still legally married to Omar M'Hallem-Driss at the time. The relationship between Kroon and Driss dissolved seven years earlier in 1980, and they subsequently lost contact with each other. When Samir was born, Kroon instituted divorce proceedings in the Amsterdam Regional Court. Samir was entered on the birth register as the son of Mrs. Kroon and Driss, who was still her husband. The divorce became final in 1987.

Kroon then tried to remedy the legal affairs of Samir and get Zerrouk officially named as his father. She requested that the Amsterdam Registrar of Births, Deaths and Marriage allow her to make a statement before him to the effect that Driss was not Samir's father and thus make it possible for Zerrouk to recognize the child. The registrar refused this request. Since Samir was born while Kroon and Driss were married, unless Driss brought proceedings to deny paternity, recognition by another man was impossible under Dutch law. Kroon and Zerrouk then applied to the Amsterdam Regional Court for an order directing the registrar to add Kroon's statement to the register. They relied on Article 8 (right to respect for family life) and Article 14 (prohibition of discrimination) of the European Convention. [Dutch law incorporates the ECHR.] The regional court denied their petition. In the interests of legal certainty about paternity, Dutch law provided only limited exceptions to the rule that the husband of the mother was presumed to be the father of a child born in wedlock. Relying again on Articles 8 and 14, Croon and Zerrouk appealed to the Amsterdam Court of Appeal. Since there was no sound reason for the difference of treatment the law established between a husband and a wife by denying the latter the opportunity to deny paternity, the court found a violation of Article 14. But since the court did not have the power to grant Kroon's petition in view of existing law, the court rejected the appeal. Kroon and Zerrouk then lodged an appeal with the Supreme Court. The Supreme Court rejected the appeal. Even if there had been a violation of Article 14, solving the problem of what should replace the current law went beyond the limits of the judiciary's powers. Only the legislature could decide how best to comply with Article 14 regarding the possibility of denying paternity of a child born in wedlock.

Subsequently, Kroon and Zerrouk had three more children. All were recognized by Zerrouk. The couple never married nor lived together. Zerrouk contributed to the care and upbringing of their children.

In 1991, Kroon and Zerrouk applied to the European Commission, complaining that Article 8 of the ECHR, both taken alone and in conjunction with Article 14, had been violated. The Commission expressed the opinion (by 12 votes to 6) that there had been a violation of Article 8 and (unanimously) that there had been no violation of Article 14.

In examining the application of Article 8, the European Court held that the term "family" in Article 8 encompassed other *de facto* family ties. Although, as a rule living together may be a requirement for such a relationship, exceptionally other factors may also serve to demonstrate that a relationship has sufficient constancy to create *de facto* "family ties." The Court found such factors in the instant case on the basis that the couple had had four children since 1987. A child born of such a relationship was *ipso iure* part of that "family" unit. There thus existed between Samir and Zerrouk a bond amounting to family life, whatever the contribution of the latter to his son's care and upbringing.

Where the existence of a family tie with a child has been established, the state must act in a manner calculated to enable these ties to be developed. Furthermore, the state must undertake affirmative legal measures to ensure that it is possible that the child can integrate into his family from the moment of his birth.

The Netherlands claimed such safeguards were in place. The couple had several options open to them to integrate their family; Zerrouk could have adopted Samir and become his stepparent or Kroon could have given joint custody to Zerrouk. The court found that under Dutch law the ordinary instrument for creating family ties between Zerrouk and Samir was "recognition." However, only Driss could deny his own paternity, thereby allowing Zerrouk's recognition – but Driss could not be found. Not even Kroon, herself, could get Zerrouk recognized. While the Netherlands maintained that there were other ways of achieving an equivalent result, the European Court disagreed. Stepparent adoption would require Zerrouk and Kroon to marry. For whatever reason, they did not wish to do so. A solution that allowed a father to create a legal tie with a child with whom he has a bond amounting to family life only if he marries the child's mother could not be regarded as compatible with the notion of "respect" for family life. Joint custody, the second alternative suggested by the Dutch government, was likewise unacceptable. It would have left the legal ties between Samir and Driss intact and would have continued to preclude the formulation of such ties between Samir and Zerrouk. In the European Court's opinion, "respect for family life" required that biological and social reality prevail over a legal presumption, which, as in the present case, flew in the face of both reality and the wishes of those concerned without actually benefiting anyone. Accordingly, the Court concluded that, even having regard to the margin of appreciation left to the state, the Netherlands had failed to secure to Kroon and Zerrouk the "respect" for their family life to that the Convention entitled them. The Court, therefore, held that Article 8 had been violated. (Having found that violation, the Court did not consider that any separate issue arose under Article 8 in conjunction with Article 14.)

In *Mathews v. Lucas*, 427 U.S. 495 (1976), the U.S. Supreme Court examined the issue of survivor's benefits to "illegitimate" children under a due process analysis. In this case, the appellees had proved that the deceased was their father but had failed to demonstrate their dependency by proof that their father had either lived with them or was contributing to their support. Such a demonstration was a requisite condition under the Social Security scheme for receiving survivor's benefits.

The appellees argued that as "illegitimate" children, they constituted a suspect class, requiring a strict scrutiny of the challenged law. However, the Court rejected their claim because the discrimination against "illegitimate" children "never approached the severity or pervasiveness of the historical legal and political discrimination against ... [for example] Negroes." Congress's purpose in adopting the dependency tests was to serve administrative convenience.

Would the applicants in *Kroon* have succeeded under the due process analysis of *Mathew*? Both Lucas and Kroon were facing evidentiary obstacles: Kroon could not find the biological father; Lucas could not prove dependency. Is the pivotal issue in both cases the amount of harm sustained by the "illegitimate" person?

Abortion

Brüggemann and Scheuten v. Federal Republic of Germany
European Commission of Human Rights
Application No. 6959/75
Decision of 12 July 1977
5 Eur. Comm'n H.R. Dec. & Rep. 130 (1976)
3 E.H.R.R. 244 (1981)

[In this case, the Applicants challenged (i) a decision of the Federal Constitutional Court striking down German legislation that would have removed *criminal* liability for any abortion performed during the first twelve weeks of pregnancy, and (ii) subsequent German legislation that generally criminalized *all* abortions except those undertaken in specific situations of distress during the first twelve weeks of pregnancy. The Federal Constitutional Court had held that such a provision violated the right to life and the right to human dignity embodied in the German Basic Law.]

   . . . .

50. The applicants mainly allege a violation of Article 8 of the Convention by the Federal Republic of Germany in that they are not free to have an abortion carried out in

case of an unwanted pregnancy. They state that, as a result, they either have to renounce sexual intercourse or to apply methods of contraception or to carry out a pregnancy against their will.

. . . .

54. According to Article 8 of the Convention, 'Everyone has the right to respect for his private . . . life . . . '. In its decision on admissibility, the Commission has already found that legislation regulating the interruption of pregnancy touches upon the sphere of private life. The first question which must be answered is whether the legal rules governing abortion in the Federal Republic of Germany since the judgment of the Constitutional Court of 25 February 1975 constitute an interference with the right to respect for private life of the applicants.

55. The right to respect for private life is of such a scope as to secure to the individual a sphere within which he can freely pursue the development and fulfillment of his personality. To this effect, he must also have the possibility of establishing relationships of various kinds, including sexual, with other persons. In principle, therefore, whenever the State sets up rules for the behaviour of the individual within this sphere, it interferes with the respect for private life and such interference must be justified in the light of Article 8(2).

56. However, there are limits to the personal sphere. While a large proportion of the law existing in a given State has some immediate or remote effect on the individual's possibility of developing his personality by doing what he wants to do, not all of these can be considered to constitute an interference with private life in the sense of Article 8 of the Convention. In fact, as the earlier jurisprudence of the Commission has already shown, the claim to respect for private life is automatically reduced to the extent that the individual himself brings his private life into contact with public life or into close connection with other protected interests.

57. Thus, the Commission has held that the concept of private life in Article 8 was broader than the definition given by numerous Anglo-Saxon and French authors, namely, the 'right to live as far as one wishes, protected from publicity', in that it also comprises, '*to a certain degree*, the right to establish and to develop relationships with other human beings, especially in the emotional field for the development and fulfillment of one's own personality'. But it denied 'that the protection afforded by Article 8 of the Convention extends to relationships of the individual with his entire immediate surroundings'. It thus found that the right to keep a dog did not pertain to the sphere of private life of the owner because 'the keeping of dogs is by the very nature of that animal necessarily associated with certain interferences with the life of others and even with public life'. (App No 6825/75, *X v. Iceland* (1976) 5 D & R 86, 87 (emphasis added).

. . . .

60. The Commission does not find it necessary to decide, in this context, whether the unborn child is to be considered as 'life' in the sense of Article 2 of the Convention, or whether it could be regarded as an entity which under Article 8 (2) could justify an interference 'for the protection of others'. There can be no doubt that certain interests relating to pregnancy are legally protected, *e.g.* as shown by a survey of the legal order in 13 High Contracting Parties. (*See* the Commission's Report, App VII.). This survey reveals that, without exception, certain rights are attributed to the conceived but unborn child, in particular the right to inherit. The Commission also notes that Article 6(5) of the

United Nations Covenant on Civil and Political Rights prohibits the execution of death sentences on pregnant women.

61. The Commission therefore finds that not every regulation of the termination of unwanted pregnancies constitutes an interference with the right to respect for the private life of the mother. Article 8(1) cannot be interpreted as meaning that pregnancy and its termination are, as a principle, solely a matter of the private life of the mother. In this respect the Commission notes that there is not one member State of the Convention which does not, in one way or another, set up legal rules in this matter. The applicants complain about the fact that the Constitutional Court declared null and void the Fifth Criminal Law Reform Act, but even this Act was not based on the assumption that abortion is entirely a matter of the private life of the pregnant woman. It only provided that an abortion performed by a physician with the pregnant woman's consent should not be punishable if no more than 12 weeks had elapsed after conception.

62. The legal solutions following the Fifth Criminal Law Reform Act cannot be said to disregard the private-life aspect connected with the problem of abortion. The judgment of the Federal Constitutional Court of 25 February 1975 not only recognised the medical, eugenic and ethical indications but also stated that, where the pregnancy was terminated by a doctor with the pregnant woman's consent within the first 12 weeks after conception 'in order to avert from the pregnant woman the risk of serious distress that cannot be averted in any other way she might reasonably be expected to bear, the Court may abstain from imposing punishment'. [citation omitted]

According to Article 218a of the Criminal code in the version of the Fifteenth Criminal Law Reform Act of 18 May 1976 [citation omitted], an abortion performed by a physician is not punishable if the termination of pregnancy is advisable for any reason in order to avert from the pregnant woman the danger of a distress which is so serious that the pregnant woman cannot be required to continue the pregnancy and which cannot be averted in any other way the pregnant woman might reasonably be expected to bear. In particular, the abortion is admitted if continuation of the pregnancy would create a danger to the life or health of the woman, if it has to be feared that the child might suffer from an incurable injury to its health or if the pregnancy is the result of a crime. The woman is required also to seek advice on medically significant aspects of abortion as well as on the public and private assistance available for pregnant women, mothers and children.

In the absence of any of the above indications, the pregnant woman herself is nevertheless exempt from any punishment if the abortion was performed by a doctor within the first 22 weeks of pregnancy and if she made use of the medical and social counseling.

63. In view of this situation, the Commission does not find that the legal rules complained about by the applicants interfere with their right to respect for their private life.

64. Furthermore, the Commission has had regard to the fact that, when the European Convention of Human Rights entered into force, the law on abortion in all member States was at least as restrictive as the one now complained of by the applicants. In many European countries the problem of abortion is or has been the subject of heated debates on legal reform since. There is no evidence that it was the intention of the Parties to the Convention to bind themselves in favour of any particular solution under discussion – *e.g.* a solution of the kind set out in the Fifth Criminal Law Reform Act (*Fristenlösung* – time

limitation) which was not yet under public discussion at the time the Convention was drafted and adopted.

65. The Commission finally notes that, since 21 June 1974, the relevant legal situation has gradually become more favourable to the applicants.

Conclusion

66. The Commission unanimously concludes that the present case does not disclose a breach of Article 8 of the Convention. (The Committee of Ministers, agreeing with the Commission's opinion, decided that there had been no violation of the Convention: Res DH (78) 1 (17 March 1978)).

~

QUESTIONS & COMMENTS

(1) Since *Brüggemann and Scheuten v. Federal Republic of Germany*, the German Constitutional Court has indicated both that fetal life is entitled to some protection under the German right to life and human dignity and that a pregnant woman has competing rights that in some circumstances may outweigh the rights enjoyed by fetal life. The German Court thus has held that the state is not obligated to *criminalize* all acts of abortion in order to implement the German prohibition against abortion and that a regime of counseling that respected the ultimate decision of the mother in certain circumstances is adequate to protect the rights of the fetus. Decision of the Federal Constitutional Court of 28 May 1993, *BverfGE* A III JZ. How does this comport with the European Court's decision in *Vo v. France* in Section 5.1?

(2) As of 1998, fifty-four countries permit abortion at the woman's request or with the approval of medical practitioners on broad social and economic grounds. The other ninety-seven countries still outlaw abortion in most circumstances. Laura Katzive & Katherine Hall Martinez, "*Roe v. Wade* in the Global Context: International Recognition of Abortion Rights," 8 *A.S.I.L. Human Rts. Interest Group Newsletter* 3, 5 (Winter 1998).

In light of this disparity, what problems would face both the antiabortion and pro-choice advocates in making out a customary international law argument in support of their positions?

(3) The Inter-American Commission rejected a challenge to the legalization of abortion in the United States in the *Baby Boy Case*, Case No. 2141, Inter-Am. Cm. H.R. 25, OEA.Ser.L/V/II.54, doc. 9 rev. 1 (1981), *reprinted in* INTER-AM. CM.H.R., TEN YEARS OF ACTIVITIES, 1971–1981, at 186 (1982). Antiabortion advocates filed a petition charging the United States with violating Article I of the American Declaration of the Rights and Duties of Man guaranteeing the right to life; they claimed to act on behalf of a fetus aborted in Massachusetts after the U.S. Supreme Court's decision in *Roe v. Wade*, 410 U.S. 11 (1973). The Commission rejected this claim. The *travaux préparatoires* of the American Declaration showed that Article I had originally provided: "Every person has the right to life. This right extends to the right to life from the moment of conception; to the right to life of incurables, imbeciles and the insane."

In modifying the language to its final form, the drafters noted that the original version would have conflicted with then-existing laws in many OAS member states, which permitted abortion in certain circumstances. The Commission took the deletion of the reference to "the moment of conception" to mean that the state parties could not have meant for the Declaration to cover abortion. Although the Commission noted that because the United States is not a party to the American Convention, it did address Article 4 of that treaty because the petitioners had raised the issue. The Commission noted that the original draft of what eventually became Article 4 had protected the right to life "from the moment of conception." After some states objected that the provision would conflict with their laws governing abortion, the article was redrafted to protect the right to life "in general, from the moment of conception." The Commission took this drafting history to signify that Article 4 has the same meaning as Article I of the Declaration.

In dissent, Dr. Marco Gerardo Monroy Cabra responded that the Commission had misconstrued the significance of the deletion of the reference to conception in the draft of Article I: "[O]ne cannot thereby conclude that life should not be protected from conception, inasmuch as the statement 'to the right to life of incurables, imbeciles, and the insane' was also eliminated, and no one could reasonably say that the life of incurables, imbeciles, or the insane should not be protected." He suggested that "[s]ince Article I does not define when life begins, one can resort to medical science which has concluded that life has its beginning in the union of two series of chromosomes. Most scientists agree that the fetus is a human being and is genetically complete."

In a separate dissent, Dr. Luis Demetrio Tinoco Castro concurred with Dr. Monroy Cabra that the fetus is, in fact, a person, and is therefore entitled to protection. But he also questioned another aspect of the Commission's holding. It is wrong, he argued,

> that the existence, in the legislation of many American countries – in 1948 – of legal standards that recognized the legality, in certain conditions, of induced abortion, should constitute an insurmountable obstacle for recognition to be given, in the Declaration, to the right of the human being to existence, to life, in the prenatal period.... [T]he international community, or the American community, may, and on certain occasions should revise the rules of international law in force at the moment, including the recent ones for the international protection of human rights, for the purpose of establishing new precepts that will correspond to the advances of science, to the teaching of experience, to the changing realities of social and international life, to the needs determined by the inevitable changes that the new epochs create in the course of the years, and the aspirations that arise as generation follows generation. The international community, the American community, could not refuse to accept innovations that have a logical and just basis, because doing so would imply stopping the progress of the law and repudiating the principle contained in the Declaration that the system of protection of the rights of many should be strengthened more and more in the international field as social and legal circumstances become more propitious.

Who, in your view, has the better argument as to (a) the proper interpretation of the American Declaration; (b) the proper approach to interpreting international human rights instruments?

(4) The U.S. Supreme Court in *Roe v. Wade* found it unnecessary to decide whether a fetus was a person within the meaning of the Fourteenth Amendment, in invalidating restrictive abortion laws. Consider the difference between that assertion and the assertion in *Brüggeman and Scheuten* that the European Commission need not decide whether the fetus is a person in order to reject the challenge to Germany's restrictive abortion law.

Why might tribunals be reluctant to address the question of the fetus's status? See *Vo v. France* (in Section 5.1).

Paton v. United Kingdom
European Commission of Human Rights
Application No 8416/78
Decision of 13 May 1980
3 E.H.R.R. 408 (1981)

. . . .

FACTS:

1. The applicant is a citizen of the United Kingdom. . . .

2. From his statement and the documents submitted by the applicant it appears that he was married to Joan Mary Paton on 10 October 1974. On 12 May 1978 he was told by his wife that she was eight weeks pregnant and intended to have an abortion. On 17 May 1978 the applicant applied to the High Court of Justice for an injunction to prevent the abortion from being carried out. . . .

3. Section 1(1) of the 1967 Act permits the termination of a pregnancy by a registered medical practitioner if two registered medical practitioners find

(a) that the continuance of the pregnancy would involve risk to the life of the pregnant woman, or of injury to the physical or mental health of the pregnant woman or any existing children of her family, greater than if the pregnancy were terminated; or

(b) that there is a substantial risk that if the child were born it would suffer from such physical or mental abnormalities as to be seriously handicapped.

The certificate in the present case was issued under paragraph (a) (injury to the physical or mental health of the pregnant woman). (In an affidavit submitted to the High Court the applicant's wife stated *inter alia*: 'My marriage was increasingly unhappy . . . and . . . has broken down irretrievably. I left the plaintiff on legal advice as I feared for my safety and we live apart . . . and in future I will live as a single woman . . . Because of the plaintiff's behaviour life with him became increasingly impossible and my health suffered and I am receiving treatment from my doctor . . . I could not cope and I verily believe that for months I have been close to a nervous breakdown.')

. . . .

7. The President dismissed the application. He stated that an injunction could be granted only to restrain the infringement of a legal right; that in English law the foetus has no legal rights until it is born and has a separate existence from its mother, and that the father of a foetus, whether or not he is married to the mother, has no legal right to prevent the mother from having an abortion or to be consulted or informed about a proposed abortion, if the provisions of the 1967 Act have been complied with. (*See Paton v. British Pregnancy Advisory Service* [1979] Q.B. 276.)

. . . .

Complaints

The applicant contends that the law of England and Wales violates:

(1) Article[ ] 2 . . . of the Convention in that it allows abortion at all . . . ;

(2) Article[ ] ... 8 ... of the Convention in that, if the provisions of the 1967 Act are complied with, it denies the father of a foetus, whether or not he is married to the mother:

(a) a right to object to a proposed abortion of the foetus; and/or

(b) a right to apply to the Courts for an order to prevent or postpone the proposed abortion; and/or

(c) a right to be consulted about the proposed abortion; and/or

(d) a right to be informed about the proposed abortion; and/or

(e) a right to demand, in a case where registered medical practitioners have given certificates under section 1 of the 1967 Act, that the mother be examined by a different registered medical practitioner or practitioners appointed by the father or by and upon his application to a designated court, tribunal or other body; and/or

(f) a right to demand that the registered medical practitioners, who examine the mother to decide whether or not to give certificates under section 1 of the 1967 Act, should be independent of the institution or organisation at or by which the abortion will be carried out should such certificates be given.

. . . .

THE LAW

. . . .

4. The Commission, therefore, has to examine whether this application discloses any appearance of a violation of the provisions of the Convention invoked by the applicant, in particular Articles 2 and 8. It here recalls that the abortion law of High Contracting Parties to the Convention has so far been the subject of several applications. . . . The applicants either alleged that the legislation concerned violated the (unborn child's) right to life (Article 2) or they claimed that it constituted an unjustified interference with the (parents') right to respect for private life (Article 8). Two applications invoking Article 2 were declared inadmissible by the Commission on the ground that the applicants – in the absence of any measure of abortion directly affecting them by reason of a close link with the foetus – could not claim to be 'victims' of the abortion laws complained of. (*X v. Norway,* 4 Y.B. Eur. Conv. H.R. 270 (1961); and *X v. Austria,* 7 Eur. Cm. H.R. 87 (App No 2045/75) (1977).) One application (*Brüggemann and Scheuten v. Germany,* 10 Eur. Cm. H.R. 100 (App No 6959/75) (1978)), invoking Article 8, was declared admissible by the Commission, in so far as it had been brought by two women. The Commission, and subsequently the Committee of Ministers, concluded that there was no breach of Article 8 (*ibid.* at 122). That conclusion was based on an interpretation of Article 8 which, *inter alia,* took into account the High Contracting Parties' law on abortion as applied at the time when the Convention entered into force. (*Ibid.* at 117, §64 of the Commission's Report).

5. The question whether the unborn child is covered by Article 2 was expressly left open in Application No 6959/75 ((1978) 10 Eur. Cm. H.R. 100, 116, §60) and has not yet been considered by the Commission in any other case. It has, however, been the subject of proceedings before the Constitutional Court of Austria, a High Contracting State in which the Convention has the rank of constitutional law. In those proceedings the Austrian Constitutional Court, noting the different view expressed on this question in legal writings, found that Article 2(1), first sentence, interpreted in the context

of Article 2, §§(1) and (2), does not cover the unborn life. (Decision of 11 October 1974, Erk Slg (Collection of Decisions) No 7400, [1975] *Europäische Grundrechtezeit-schrift* 74.)

6. Article 2(1), first sentence, provides: 'Everyone's right to life shall be protected by law' (in the French text: *'Le droit de toute personne à la vie est protégé par la loi'*). The Commission, in its interpretation of this clause and, in particular, of the terms 'everyone' and 'life', has examined the ordinary meaning of the provision in the context both of Article 2 and of the Convention as a whole, taking into account the object and purpose of the Convention.

7. The Commission first notes that the term 'everyone' (*'toute personne'*) is not defined in the Convention. It appears in Article 1 and in Section I, apart from Article 2(1), in Articles 5, 6, 8 to 11 and 13. In nearly all these instances the use of the word is such that it can apply only postnatally. None indicates clearly that it has any possible prenatal application, although such application in a rare case – *e.g.* under Article 6(1) – cannot be entirely excluded.

8. As regards, more particularly, Article 2, it contains the following limitations of 'everyone's' right to life enounced in the first sentence of paragraph (1):

– a clause permitting the death penalty in paragraph (1), second sentence: 'No one shall be deprived of his life intentionally save in the execution of a sentence of a court following his conviction of a crime for which this penalty is provided by law'; and
– the provision, in paragraph (2), that deprivation of life shall not be regarded as inflicted in contravention of Article 2 when it results from 'the use of force which is no more than absolutely necessary' in the following three cases: 'In defence of any person from unlawful violence'; 'in order to effect a lawful arrest or to prevent the escape of a person lawfully detained'; 'in action lawfully taken for the purpose of quelling a riot or insurrection'.

All the above limitations, by their nature, concern persons already born and cannot be applied to the foetus.

9. Thus both the general usage of the term 'everyone' (*'toute personne'*) of the Convention (§7 above) and the context in which this term is employed in Article 2 (§8 above) tend to support the view that it does not include the unborn.

10. The Commission has next examined, in the light of the above considerations, whether the term 'life' in Article 2(1), first sentence, is to be interpreted as covering only the life of persons already born or also the 'unborn life' of the foetus. The Commission notes that the term 'life', too, is not defined in the Convention.

11. It further observes that another, more recent international instrument for the protection of human rights, the American Convention on Human Rights of 1969, contains in Article 4(1), first and second sentences, the following provisions expressly extending the right to life to the unborn:

Every person has the right to have his life respected. This right shall be protected by law and, in general, from the moment of conception.

12. The Commission is aware of the wide divergence of thinking on the question of where life begins. While some believe that it starts already with conception others tend

to focus upon the moment of nidation, upon the point that the foetus becomes 'viable', or upon live birth.

   . . . .

16. The Commission considers with the Austrian Constitutional Court that, in interpreting the scope of the term 'life' in Article 2(1), first sentence, of the Convention, particular regard must be had to the context of the Article as a whole. It also observes that the term 'life' may be subject to different interpretations in different legal instruments, depending on the context in which it is used in the instrument concerned.

17. The Commission has already noted, when discussing the meaning of the term 'everyone' in Article 2 (§8 above), that the limitations, in paragraphs (1) and (2) of the Article, of 'everyone's' right to 'life', by their nature, concern persons already born and cannot be applied to the foetus. The Commission must therefore examine whether Article 2, in the absence of any express limitation concerning the foetus, is to be interpreted:

- as not covering the foetus at all;
- as recognising a 'right to life' of the foetus with certain implied limitations; or
- as recognising an absolute 'right to life' of the foetus.

18. The Commission has first considered whether Article 2 is to be construed as recognising an absolute 'right to life' of the foetus and has excluded such an interpretation on the following grounds.

19. The 'life' of the foetus is intimately connected with, and cannot be regarded in isolation from, the life of the pregnant woman. If Article 2 were held to cover the foetus and its protection under this Article were, in the absence of any express limitation, seen as absolute, an abortion would have to be considered as prohibited even where the continuance of the pregnancy would involve a serious risk to the life of the pregnant woman. This would mean that the 'unborn life' of the foetus would be regarded as being of a higher value than the life of the pregnant woman. The 'right to life' of a person already born would thus be considered as subject not only to the express limitations mentioned in paragraph 8 above but also to a further, implied limitation.

20. The Commission finds that such an interpretation would be contrary to the object and purpose of the Convention. It notes that, already at the time of the signature of the Convention (4 November 1950), all High Contracting Parties, with one possible exception, permitted abortion when necessary to save the life of the mother and that, in the meanwhile, the national law on termination of pregnancy has shown a tendency towards further liberalisation.

21. Having thus excluded, as being incompatible with the object and purpose of the Convention, one of the three different constructions of Article 2 mentioned in paragraph 17 above, the Commission has next considered which of the two remaining interpretations is to be regarded as the correct one – *i.e.* whether Article 2 does not cover the foetus at all or whether it recognises a 'right to life' of the foetus with certain implied limitations.

22. The Commission here notes that the abortion complained of was carried out at the initial stage of the pregnancy – the applicant's wife was ten weeks pregnant – under section 1(1)(a) of the Abortion Act 1967 in order to avert the risk of injury to the physical or mental health of the pregnant woman. It follows that, as regards the second of the two remaining interpretations, the Commission is in the present case not concerned with

the broad question whether Article 2 recognises a 'right to life' of the foetus during the whole period of the pregnancy but only with the narrower issue whether such a right is to be assumed for the initial stage of the pregnancy. Moreover, as regards implied limitations of a 'right to life' of the foetus at the initial stage, only the limitation protecting the life and health of the pregnant woman, the so-called 'medical indication', is relevant for the determination of the present case and the question of other possible limitations (ethic indication, eugenic indication, social indication, time limitation) does not arise.

23. The Commission considers that it is not in these circumstances called upon to decide whether Article 2 does not cover the foetus at all or whether it recognises a 'right to life' of the foetus with implied limitations. It finds that the authorisation, by the United Kingdom authorities, of the abortion complained of is compatible with Article 2(1), first sentence because, if one assumes that this provision applies at the initial stage of the pregnancy, the abortion is covered by an implied limitation, protecting the life and health of the woman at that stage, of the 'right to life' of the foetus.

24. The Commission concludes that the applicant's complaint under Article 2 is inadmissible as being manifestly ill-founded within the meaning of Article 27(2).

25. In its examination of the applicant's complaints, concerning the Abortion Act 1967 and its application in this case, the Commission has next had regard to Article 8 of the Convention which, in paragraph (1), guarantees to everyone the right to respect for his family life. The Commission here notes, apart from his principal complaint concerning the permission of the abortion, the applicant's ancillary submission that the 1967 Act denies the father of the foetus a right to be consulted, and to make applications, about the proposed abortion.

The Commission also observes that the applicant, who under Article 2 claims to be the victim of a violation of the right to life of the foetus of which he was the potential father, under Article 8 invokes a right of his own.

26. As regards the principal complaint concerning the permission of the abortion, the Commission recalls that the pregnancy of the applicant's wife was terminated in accordance with her wish and in order to avert the risk of injury to her physical or mental health. The Commission therefore finds that this decision, in so far as it interfered in itself with the applicant's right to respect for his family life, was justified under paragraph (2) of Article 8 as being necessary for the protection of the rights of another person. It follows that this complaint is also manifestly ill-founded within the meaning of Article 27(2).

27. The Commission has next considered the applicant's ancillary complaint that the Abortion Act 1967 denies the father of the foetus a right to be consulted, and to make applications, about the proposed abortion. It observes that any interpretation of the husband's and potential father's right, under Article 8 of the Convention, to respect for his private and family life, as regards an abortion which his wife intends to have performed on her, must first of all take into account the right of the pregnant woman, being the person primarily concerned in the pregnancy and its continuation or termination, to respect for her private life. The pregnant woman's right to respect for her private life, as affected by the developing foetus, has been examined by the Commission in its Report in the *Brüggemann and Scheuten* case (*supra*, §§59 *et seq*). In the present case the Commission, having regard to the right of the pregnant woman, does not find that the husband's and potential father's right to respect for his private and family life can be interpreted so widely as to embrace such procedural rights as claimed by the applicant, *i.e.* a right to be

consulted, or a right to make applications, about an abortion which his wife intends to have performed on her. . . .

~

QUESTIONS & COMMENTS

(1) The woman in *Paton* was in her tenth week of pregnancy. What regulations does U.S. constitutional law permit at that point in the pregnancy? *Planned Parenthood of Southeastern Pennsylvania v. Casey*, 505 U.S. 833 (1992), while altering the *Roe v. Wade* framework of analysis, invalidated a statute barring the performance of an abortion at the request of a married woman who had not notified her spouse of her intention to obtain an abortion. The plurality opinion recited a number of factual findings made by the lower court regarding the potential threat to women's safety were they to be required to notify their spouses. The plurality held that the notification requirement placed an "undue burden" on "those whose conduct it affects"; that is, women who would not otherwise notify their spouses. The risks to *that* class of women were substantial even though that class comprised only 1% of all women seeking abortions.

(2) In *Caban v. Mohammed*, 441 U.S. 380 (1979), the U.S. Supreme Court held that a New York statute that allowed the biological mother – but not the father – of an "illegitimate" child the right to veto the child's adoption violated equal protection. However, in cases – unlike *Caban v. Mohammed* – where the father has never participated in the rearing of the child, the Court stated such a distinction could pass constitutional muster. In *Paton v. United Kingdom*, the pregnant wife of the applicant-husband had separated from him. Given that the European Court in other cases consistently has placed a strong emphasis on the issue of whether there is a *de facto* family in place for establishing an Article 8 interference, can you conceive of any case where a biological father separated from his pregnant partner could lawfully prevent an abortion? Can you think of any case where the father could veto the adoption of an "illegitimate" child whom he has not raised? Would the father have a compelling Article 8 right to now adopt the child? What constitutes a *de facto* family?

(3) Should international tribunals consider the right to abortion in terms of the right to freedom from gender discrimination, as Ruth Bader Ginsburg, now a U.S. Supreme Court justice, has argued with regard to *Roe v. Wade*? *See* Ruth Bader Ginsburg, *Some Thoughts on Autonomy and Equality in Relation to* Roe v. Wade, 63 N.C. L. Rev. 375 (1985). Considered only under the antidiscrimination guarantee of Article 14, ECHR, would *Brüggemann* have come out differently? What advantages are there for arguing a gender discrimination claim to protecting abortion rights?

(4) Has *Paton* effectively been overruled by *Vo v. France* (see Section 5.1.1)?

5.5. Freedom of Conscience

Universal Declaration of Human Rights

Article 18.

Everyone has the right to freedom of thought, conscience and religion; this right includes freedom to change his religion or belief, and freedom, either alone or in community with others and in public or private, to manifest his religion or belief in teaching, practice, worship and observance.

International Covenant on Civil and Political Rights

Article 18

1. Everyone shall have the right to freedom of thought, conscience and religion. This right shall include freedom to have or to adopt a religion or belief of his choice, and freedom, either individually or in community with others and in public or private, to manifest his religion or belief in worship, observance, practice and teaching.

2. No one shall be subject to coercion which would impair his freedom to have or to adopt a religion or belief of his choice.

3. Freedom to manifest one's religion or beliefs may be subject only to such limitations as are prescribed by law and are necessary to protect public safety, order, health, or morals or the fundamental rights and freedoms of others.

4. The States Parties to the present Covenant undertake to have respect for the liberty of parents and, when applicable, legal guardians to ensure the religious and moral education of their children in conformity with their own convictions.

European Convention on Human Rights

Article 9

1. Everyone has the right to freedom of thought, conscience and religion; this right includes freedom to change his religion or belief, and freedom, either alone or in community with others and in public or private, to manifest his religion or belief, in worship, teaching, practice and observance.

2. Freedom to manifest one's religion or beliefs shall be subject only to such limitations as are prescribed by law and are necessary in a democratic society in the interests of public safety, for the protection of public order, health or morals, or the protection of the rights and freedoms of others.

Charter of Fundamental Rights of the European Union

Article 10

Freedom of thought, conscience and religion

1. Everyone has the right to freedom of thought, conscience and religion. This right includes freedom to change religion or belief and freedom, either alone or in community with others and in public or in private, to manifest religion or belief, in worship, teaching, practice and observance.

2. The right to conscientious objection is recognised, in accordance with the national laws governing the exercise of this right.

American Declaration of the Rights and Duties of Man

Article III. Right to religious freedom and worship.

Every person has the right freely to profess a religious faith, and to manifest and practice it both in public and in private.

American Convention on Human Rights

Article 12. FREEDOM OF CONSCIENCE AND RELIGION.

1. Everyone has the right to freedom of conscience and of religion. This right includes freedom to maintain or to change one's religion or beliefs, and freedom to profess or disseminate one's religion or beliefs, either individually or together with others, in public or in private.

2. No one shall be subject to restrictions that might impair his freedom to maintain or to change his religion or beliefs.

3. Freedom to manifest one's religion and beliefs may be subject only to the limitations prescribed by law that are necessary to protect public safety, order, health, or morals, or the rights or freedoms of others.

4. Parents or guardians, as the case may be, have the right to provide for the religious and moral education of their children or wards that is in accord with their own convictions.

African [Banjul] Charter on Human and Peoples' Rights

Article 8

Freedom of conscience, the profession and free practice of religion shall be guaranteed. No one may, subject to law and order, be submitted to measures restricting the exercise of these freedoms.

Convention on Human Rights and Fundamental Freedoms of the Commonwealth of Independent States

Article 10

1. Everyone shall have the right to freedom of thought, conscience and faith. This right shall include freedom to choose one's religion or belief and freedom, either alone or in community religious and ritual ceremonies and act in accordance with them.

2. Freedom to manifest one's religion or beliefs shall be subject only to such limitations as are prescribed by law and are necessary in a democratic society in the interests of national security, public safety, public order, public health and moral or for the protection of the rights and freedoms of others.

U.S. Constitution

Amendment I

Congress shall make no law respecting an establishment of religion, or prohibiting the free exercise thereof;. . . .

Kokkinakis v. Greece
European Court of Human Rights
260-A Eur. Ct. H.R. (ser. A) (1993)
17 E.H.R.R. 397 (1994)

. . . .

I. THE CIRCUMSTANCES OF THE CASE

6. Mr Minos Kokkinakis, a retired businessman of Greek nationality, was born into an Orthodox family at Sitia (Crete) in 1919. After becoming a Jehovah's Witness in 1936, he

was arrested more than sixty times for proselytism. He was also interned and imprisoned on several occasions.

. . . .

The periods of imprisonment, to which he was sentenced by the courts, were for acts of proselytism (three sentences of two and a half months in 1939 – he was the first Jehovah's Witness to be convicted under the Laws of the Metaxas Government . . . – four and a half months in 1949 and two months in 1962), conscientious objection (eighteen and a half months in 1941) and holding a religious meeting in a private house (six months in 1952).

Between 1960 and 1970 the applicant was arrested four times and prosecuted but not convicted.

7. On 2 March 1986 he and his wife called at the home of Mrs. Kyriakaki in Sitia and engaged in a discussion with her. Mrs. Kyriakaki's husband, who was the cantor at a local Orthodox church, informed the police, who arrested Mr. and Mrs. Kokkinakis and took them to the local police station, where they spent the night of 2–3 March 1986.

A. Proceedings in the Lasithi Criminal Court

8. The applicant and his wife were prosecuted under section 4 of Law no. 1363/1938 making proselytism an offence and were committed for trial at the Lasithi Criminal Court (*trimeles plimmeliodikio*), which heard the case on 20 March 1986.

9. After dismissing an objection that section 4 of that Law was unconstitutional, the Criminal Court heard evidence from Mr. and Mrs. Kyriakaki, a defence witness and the two defendants and gave judgment on the same day:

> "[The defendants], who belong to the Jehovah's Witnesses sect, attempted to proselytise and, directly or indirectly, to intrude on the religious beliefs of Orthodox Christians, with the intention of undermining those beliefs, by taking advantage of their inexperience, their low intellect and their naïvety. In particular, they went to the home of [Mrs. Kyriakaki] . . . and told her that they brought good news; by insisting in a pressing manner, they gained admittance to the house and began to read from a book on the Scriptures which they interpreted with reference to a king of heaven, to events which had not yet occurred but would occur, *etc.*, encouraging her by means of their judicious, skilful explanations . . . to change her Orthodox Christian beliefs."

The court found Mr. and Mrs. Kokkinakis guilty of proselytism and sentenced each of them to four months' imprisonment, convertible (under Article 82 of the Criminal Code) into a pecuniary penalty of 400 drachmas per day's imprisonment, and a fine of 10,000 drachmas. Under Article 76 of the Criminal Code, it also ordered the confiscation and destruction of four booklets which they had been hoping to sell to Mrs. Kyriakaki.

B. The proceedings in the Crete Court of Appeal

10. Mr. and Mrs. Kokkinakis appealed against this judgment to the Crete Court of Appeal (*Efetio*). The Court of Appeal quashed Mrs. Kokkinakis's conviction and upheld her husband's but reduced his prison sentence to three months and converted it into a pecuniary penalty of 400 drachmas per day. The following reasons were given for its judgment, which was delivered on 17 March 1987:

> " . . . [I]t was proved that, with the aim of disseminating the articles of faith of the Jehovah's Witnesses sect . . . to which the defendant adheres, he attempted, directly and indirectly, to intrude on the religious beliefs of a person of a different religious

persuasion from his own, [namely] the Orthodox Christian faith, with the intention of changing those beliefs, by taking advantage of her inexperience, her low intellect and her naïvety. More specifically, at the time and place indicated in the operative provision, he visited Mrs. Georgia Kyriakaki and after telling her he brought good news, pressed her to let him into the house, where he began by telling her about the politician Olof Palme and by expounding pacifist views. He then took out a little book containing professions of faith by adherents of the aforementioned sect and began to read out passages from Holy Scripture, which he skilfully analysed in a manner that the Christian woman, for want of adequate grounding in doctrine, could not challenge, and at the same time offered her various similar books and importunately tried, directly and indirectly, to undermine her religious beliefs. He must consequently be declared guilty of the above mentioned offence, in accordance with the operative provision hereinafter, while the other defendant, his wife Elissavet, must be acquitted, seeing that there is no evidence that she participated in the offence committed by her husband, whom she merely accompanied. . . .”

One of the appeal judges dissented, and his opinion, which was appended to the judgment, read as follows:

. . . [T]he first defendant should also have been acquitted, as none of the evidence shows that Georgia Kyriakaki . . . was particularly inexperienced in Orthodox Christian doctrine, being married to a cantor, or of particularly low intellect or particularly naïve, such that the defendant was able to take advantage and . . . [thus] induce her to become a member of the Jehovah’s Witnesses sect.

According to the record of the hearing of 17 March 1987, Mrs. Kyriakaki had given the following evidence:

“They immediately talked to me about Olof Palme, whether he was a pacifist or not, and other subjects that I can’t remember. They talked to me about things I did not understand very well. It was not a discussion but a constant monologue by them. . . . If they had told me they were Jehovah’s Witnesses, I would not have let them in. I don’t recall whether they spoke to me about the Kingdom of Heaven. They stayed in the house about ten minutes or a quarter of an hour. What they told me was religious in nature, but I don’t know why they told it to me. I could not know at the outset what the purpose of their visit was. They may have said something to me at the time with a view to undermining my religious beliefs. . . . [However,] the discussion did not influence my beliefs. . . .”

C. The proceedings in the Court of Cassation

11. Mr. Kokkinakis appealed on points of law. He maintained, *inter alia*, that the provisions of Law no. 1363/1938 contravened Article 13 of the Constitution.

12. The Court of Cassation (*Arios Pagos*) dismissed the appeal on 22 April 1988. It rejected the plea of unconstitutionality for the following reasons:

“Section 4 of Law no. 1363/1938, substituted by section 2 of Law no. 1672/1939 providing for the implementation of Articles 1 and 2 of the Constitution and enacted under the 1911 Constitution then in force, Article 1 of which prohibited proselytism and any other interference with the dominant religion in Greece, namely the Christian Eastern Orthodox Church, not only does not contravene Article 13 of the 1975

Constitution but is fully compatible with the Constitution, which recognises the inviolability of freedom of conscience in religious matters and provides for freedom to practise any known religion, subject to a formal provision in the same Constitution prohibiting proselytism in that proselytism is forbidden in general whatever the religion against which it is directed, including therefore the dominant religion in Greece, in accordance with Article 3 of the 1975 Constitution, namely the Christian Eastern Orthodox Church."

. . . .

In the opinion of a dissenting member, the Court of Cassation should have quashed the judgment of the court below for having wrongly applied section 4 of Law no. 1363/1938 in that it had made no mention of the promises whereby the defendant had allegedly attempted to intrude on Mrs. Kyriakaki's religious beliefs and had given no particulars of Mrs. Kyriakaki's inexperience and low intellect.

II. RELEVANT DOMESTIC LAW AND PRACTICE

A. Statutory provisions

1. The Constitution

13. The relevant Articles of the 1975 Constitution read as follows:

Article 3

"1. The dominant religion in Greece is that of the Christian Eastern Orthodox Church. The Greek Orthodox Church, which recognises as its head Our Lord Jesus Christ, is indissolubly united, doctrinally, with the Great Church of Constantinople and with any other Christian Church in communion with it (*omodoxi*), immutably observing, like the other Churches, the holy apostolic and synodical canons and the holy traditions. It is autocephalous and is administered by the Holy Synod, composed of all the bishops in office, and by the standing Holy Synod, which is an emanation of it constituted as laid down in the Charter of the Church and in accordance with the provisions of the Patriarchal Tome of 29 June 1850 and the Synodical Act of 4 September 1928.

2. The ecclesiastical regime in certain regions of the State shall not be deemed contrary to the provisions of the foregoing paragraph.["]

. . . .

Article 13

"1. Freedom of conscience in religious matters is inviolable. The enjoyment of personal and political rights shall not depend on an individual's religious beliefs.

2. There shall be freedom to practise any known religion; individuals shall be free to perform their rites of worship without hindrance and under the protection of the law. The performance of rites of worship must not prejudice public order or public morals. Proselytism is prohibited.

3. The ministers of all known religions shall be subject to the same supervision by the State and to the same obligations to it as those of the dominant religion.

4. No one may be exempted from discharging his obligations to the State or refuse to comply with the law by reason of his religious convictions.

5. No oath may be required other than under a law which also determines the form of it."

14. The Christian Eastern Orthodox Church, which during nearly four centuries of foreign occupation symbolised the maintenance of Greek culture and the Greek language, took an active part in the Greek people's struggle for emancipation, to such an extent that Hellenism is to some extent identified with the Orthodox faith.

A royal decree of 23 July 1833 entitled "Proclamation of the Independence of the Greek Church" described the Orthodox Church as "autocephalous". Greece's successive Constitutions have referred to the Church as being "dominant". The overwhelming majority of the population are members of it, and, according to Greek conceptions, it represents *de jure* and *de facto* the religion of the State itself, a good number of whose administrative and educational functions (marriage and family law, compulsory religious instruction, oaths sworn by members of the Government, *etc.*) it moreover carries out. Its role in public life is reflected by, among other things, the presence of the Minister of Education and Religious Affairs at the sessions of the Church hierarchy at which the Archbishop of Athens is elected and by the participation of the Church authorities in all official State events; the President of the Republic takes his oath of office according to Orthodox ritual (Art. 33 §2 of the Constitution); and the official calendar follows that of the Christian Eastern Orthodox Church.

15. Under the region of Otto I (1832–62), the Orthodox Church, which had long complained of a Bible society's propaganda directed at young Orthodox schoolchildren on behalf of the Evangelical Church, managed to get a clause added to the first Constitution (1844) forbidding "proselytism and any other action against the dominant religion". The Constitutions of 1864, 1911 and 1952 reproduced the same clause. The 1975 Constitution prohibits proselytism in general (Art. 13 §2 *in fine*): the ban covers all "known religions", meaning those whose doctrines are not apocryphal and in which no secret initiation is required of neophytes.

2. Laws Nos. 1363/1938 and 1672/1939

16. During the dictatorship of Metaxas (1936–1940), proselytism was made a criminal offence for the first time by section 4 of Law (*anagastikos nomos*) no. 1363/1938. The following year that section was amended by section 2 of Law no. 1672/1939, in which the meaning of the term "proselytism" was clarified:

"1. Anyone engaging in proselytism shall be liable to imprisonment and a fine of between 1,000 and 50,000 drachmas; he shall, moreover, be subject to police supervision for a period of between six months and one year to be fixed by the court when convicting the offender.

. . . .

2. By 'proselytism' is meant, in particular, any direct or indirect attempt to intrude on the religious beliefs of a person of a different religious persuasion (*eterodoxos*), with the aim of undermining those beliefs, either by any kind of inducement or promise of an inducement or moral support or material assistance, or by fraudulent means or by taking advantage of his inexperience, trust, need, low intellect or naïvety.

3. The commission of such an offence in a school or other educational establishment or a philanthropic institution shall constitute a particularly aggravating circumstance."

B. Case-law

17. In a judgment numbered 2276/1953 a full court of the Supreme Administrative Court (*Symvoulio tis Epikratias*) gave the following definition of proselytism:

"Article 1 of the Constitution, which establishes the freedom to practise any known religion and to perform rites of worship without hindrance and prohibits proselytism and all other activities directed against the dominant religion, that of the Christian Eastern Orthodox Church, means that purely spiritual teaching does not amount to proselytism, even if it demonstrates the errors of other religions and entices possible disciples away from them, who abandon their original religions of their own free will; this is because spiritual teaching is in the nature of a rite of worship performed freely and without hindrance. Outside such spiritual teaching, which may be freely given, any determined, importunate attempt to entice disciples away from the dominant religion by means that are unlawful or morally reprehensible constitutes proselytism as prohibited by the aforementioned provision of the Constitution."

18. The Greek courts have held that persons were guilty of proselytism who had: likened the saints to "figures adorning the wall", St. Gerasimos to "a body stuffed with cotton" and the Church to "a theatre, a market, a cinema"; preached, while displaying a painting showing a crowd of wretched people in rags, that "such are all those who do not embrace my faith" (Court of Cassation, judgment no. 271/1932, *Themis* XVII, p. 19); promised Orthodox refugees housing on specially favourable terms if they adhered to the Uniate faith (Court of Appeal of the Aegean, judgment no. 2950/1930, *Themis* B, p. 103); offered a scholarship for study abroad (Court of Cassation, judgment no 2276/1953); sent Orthodox priests booklets with the recommendation that they should study them and apply their content (Court of Cassation, judgment no. 59/1956, *Nomiko Vima*, 1956, no. 4, p. 736); distributed "so-called religious" books and booklets free to "illiterate peasants" or to "young schoolchildren" (Court of Cassation, judgment no. 201/1961, Criminal Annals XI, p. 472); or promised a young seamstress an improvement in her position if she left the Orthodox Church, whose priests were alleged to be "exploiters of society". (Court of Cassation, judgment no. 498/1961, Criminal Annals XII, p. 212.)

The Court of Cassation has ruled that the definition of proselytism in section 4 of Law no. 1363/1938 does not contravene the principle that only the law can define a crime and prescribe a penalty. The Piraeus Criminal Court followed it in an order (*voulevma*) numbered 36/1962 (Greek Lawyers' Journal, 1962, p. 421), adding that the expression "in particular" in section 4 of Law no. 1363/1938 referred to the means used by the person committing the offence and not to the description of the *actus reus*.

19. Until 1975 the Court of Cassation held that the list in section 4 was not exhaustive. In a judgment numbered 997/1975 (Criminal Annals XXVI, p. 380) it added the following clarification:

"... [I]t follows from the provisions of section 4 ... that proselytism consists in a direct or indirect attempt to impinge on religious beliefs by any of the means separately listed in the Law."

20. More recently courts have convicted Jehovah's Witnesses for professing the sect's doctrine "importunately" and accusing the Orthodox Church of being a "source of suffering for the world" (Salonika Court of Appeal, judgment no. 2567/1988); for entering other people's homes in the guise of Christians wishing to spread the New Testament

(Florina Court of First Instance, judgment no. 128/1989); and for attempting to give books and booklets to an Orthodox priest at the wheel of his car after stopping him (Lasithi Court of First Instance, judgment no. 357/1990).

In a judgment numbered 1304/1982 (Criminal Annals XXXII, p. 502), on the other hand, the Court of Cassation quashed a judgment of the Athens Court of Appeal (no. 5434/1981) as having no basis in law because, when convicting a Jehovah's Witness, the Court of Appeal had merely reiterated the words of the indictment and had thus not explained how "the importunate teaching of the doctrines of the Jehovah's Witnesses sect" or "distribution of the sect's booklets at a minimal price" had amounted to an attempt to intrude on the complainants' religious beliefs, or shown how the defendant had taken advantage of their "inexperience" and "low intellect". The Court of Cassation remitted the case to a differently constituted bench of the Court of Appeal, which acquitted the defendant.

Similarly, it has been held in several court decisions that the offence of proselytism was not made out where there had merely been a discussion about the beliefs of the Jehovah's Witnesses, where booklets had been distributed from door to door (Patras Court of Appeal, judgment no. 137/1988) or in the street (Larissa Court of Appeal, judgment no. 749/1986) or where the tenets of the sect had been explained without any deception to an Orthodox Christian (Trikkala Criminal Court, judgment no. 186/1986). Lastly, it has been held that being an "illiterate peasant" is not sufficient to establish the "naïvety", referred to in section 4, of the person whom the alleged proselytiser is addressing (Court of Cassation, judgment No. 1155/1978).

21. After the revision of the Constitution in 1975, the Jehovah's Witnesses brought legal proceedings to challenge the constitutionality of section 4 of Law No. 1363/1938. They complained that the description of the offence was vague, but above all they objected to the actual title of the Act, which indicated that the Law was designed to preserve Articles 1 and 2 of the Constitution in force at the time (the 1911 Constitution), which prohibited proselytism directed against the dominant religion. In the current Constitution this prohibition is extended to all religions and furthermore is no longer included in the chapter concerning religion but in the one dealing with civil and social rights, and more particularly in Article 13, which guarantees freedom of conscience in religious matters.

The courts have always dismissed such objections of unconstitutionality, although they have been widely supported in legal literature.

III. THE JEHOVAH'S WITNESSES IN GREECE

22. The Jehovah's Witnesses movement appeared in Greece at the beginning of the twentieth century. Estimates of its membership today vary between 25,000 and 70,000. Members belong to one of 338 congregations, the first of which was formed in Athens in 1922.

. . . .

24. According to statistics provided by the applicant, 4,400 Jehovah's Witnesses were arrested between 1975 (when democracy was restored) and 1992, and 1,233 of these were committed for trial and 208 convicted. Earlier, several Jehovah's Witnesses had been convicted under Law no. 117/1936 for the prevention of communism and its effects and Law no. 1075/1938 on preserving the social order.

The Government has not challenged the applicant's figures. It has, however, pointed out that there have been signs of a decline in the frequency of convictions of Jehovah's

Witnesses, only seven out of a total of 260 people arrested having been convicted in 1991 and 1992.

[Kokkinakis applied to the European Commission, which found a violation of Article 9]

....

[DECISION OF THE EUROPEAN COURT OF HUMAN RIGHTS:]

27. Mr Kokkinakis complained of his conviction for proselytism; he considered it contrary to [Article 9]....

I. ALLEGED VIOLATION OF ARTICLE 9

28. The applicant's complaints mainly concerned a restriction on the exercise of his freedom of religion. The Court will accordingly begin by looking at the issues relating to Article 9 ...

29. The applicant did not only challenge what he claimed to be the wrongful application to him of section 4 of Law no. 1363/1938. His submission concentrated on the broader problem of whether that enactment was compatible with the right enshrined in Article 9 of the Convention, which, he argued, having been part of Greek law since 1953, took precedence under the Constitution over any contrary statute. He pointed to the logical and legal difficulty of drawing any even remotely clear dividing-line between proselytism and freedom to change one's religion or belief and, either alone or in community with others, in public and in private, to manifest it, which encompassed all forms of teaching, publication and preaching between people.

....

30. In the Government's submission, there was freedom to practise all religions in Greece; religious adherents enjoyed the right both to express their beliefs freely and to try to influence the beliefs of others, Christian witness being a duty of all churches and all Christians. There was, however, a radical difference between bearing witness and "proselytism that is not respectable", the kind that consists in using deceitful, unworthy and immoral means, such as exploiting the destitution, low intellect and inexperience of one's fellow beings. Section 4 prohibited this kind of proselytism – the "misplaced" proselytism to which the European Court referred in its *Kjeldsen, Busk Madsen and Pedersen v. Denmark*, judgment of 7 December 1976 (Ser. A, no. 23, p. 28, §54) – and not straightforward religious teaching. Furthermore, it was precisely this definition of proselytism that had been adopted by the Greek courts.

A. General principles

31. As enshrined in Article 9, freedom of thought, conscience and religion is one of the foundations of a "democratic society" within the meaning of the Convention. It is, in its religious dimension, one of the most vital elements that go to make up the identity of believers and of their conception of life, but it is also a precious asset for atheists, agnostics, sceptics and the unconcerned. The pluralism indissociable from a democratic society, which has been dearly won over the centuries, depends on it.

While religious freedom is primarily a matter of individual conscience, it also implies, *inter alia*, freedom to "manifest [one's] religion". Bearing witness in words and deeds is bound up with the existence of religious convictions.

According to Article 9, freedom to manifest one's religion is not only exercisable in community with others, "in public" and within the circle of those whose faith one shares, but can also be asserted "alone" and "in private"; furthermore, it includes in principle the right to try to convince one's neighbour, for example through "teaching", failing which, moreover, "freedom to change [one's] religion or belief", enshrined in Article 9, would be likely to remain a dead letter.

32. The requirements of Article 9 are reflected in the Greek Constitution in so far as Article 13 of the latter declares that freedom of conscience in religious matters is inviolable and that there shall be freedom to practise any "known religion". Jehovah's Witnesses accordingly enjoy both the status of a 'known religion' and the advantages flowing from that as regards observance.

33. The fundamental nature of the rights guaranteed in Article 9 §1 is also reflected in the wording of the paragraph providing for limitations on them. Unlike the second paragraphs of Articles 8 [right to privacy], 10 [freedom of expression] and 11 [freedom of association], which cover all the rights mentioned in the first paragraphs of those Articles, that of Article 9 refers only to "freedom to manifest one's religion or belief". In so doing, it recognises that in democratic societies, in which several religions coexist within one and the same population, it may be necessary to place restrictions on this freedom in order to reconcile the interests of the various groups and ensure that everyone's beliefs are respected.

34. According to the Government, such restrictions were to be found in the Greek legal system. Article 13 of the 1975 Constitution forbade proselytism in respect of all religions without distinction; and section 4 of Law no. 1363/1938, which attached a criminal penalty to this prohibition, had been upheld by several successive democratic governments notwithstanding its historical and political origins. The sole aim of section 4 was to protect the beliefs of others from activities which undermined their dignity and personality.

35. The Court will confine its attention as far as possible to the issue raised by the specific case before it. It must nevertheless look at the foregoing provisions, since the action complained of by the applicant arose from the application of them. [citation omitted]

B. Application of the principles

36. The sentence passed by the Lasithi Criminal Court and subsequently reduced by the Crete Court of Appeal amounts to an interference with the exercise of Mr. Kokkinakis's right to "freedom to manifest [his] religion or belief". Such an interference is contrary to Article 9 unless it was "prescribed by law", directed at one or more of the legitimate aims in paragraph 2 and "necessary in a democratic society" for achieving them.

1. "Prescribed by law"

37. The applicant said that his submissions relating to Article 7 also applied to the phrase "prescribed by law". The Court will therefore examine them from this point of view.

38. Mr. Kokkinakis impugned the very wording of section 4 of Law no. 1363/1938. He criticised the absence of any description of the "objective substance" of the offence of proselytism. He thought this deliberate, as it would tend to make it possible for any kind of religious conversation or communication to be caught by the provision. He referred to the risk of "extendibility" by the police and often by the courts too of the vague terms of the section, such as "in particular" and "indirect attempt" to intrude on the religious beliefs of others. Punishing a non-Orthodox Christian even when he was offering "moral

support or material assistance" was tantamount to punishing an act that any religion would prescribe and that the Criminal Code required in certain emergencies. Law no. 1672/1939 had, without more, stripped the initial wording of section 4 of its "repetitive verbiage"; it had retained all the "extendible, catch-all" expressions, merely using a more concise but equally "pendantic" style designed to ensure that non-Orthodox Christians were permanently gagged. Consequently, no citizen could regulate his conduct on the basis of this enactment.

Furthermore, section 4 of Law no. 1363/1938 was incompatible with Article 13 of the Constitution.

39. The Government, on the other hand, maintained that section 4 defined proselytism precisely and specifically; it listed all the ingredients of the offence. The use of the adverbial phrase "in particular" was of no importance, as it related only to the means by which the offence could be committed; indicative lists of this kind were, moreover, commonly included in criminal statutes.

Lastly, the objective substance of the offence was not lacking but consisted in the attempt to change the essentials of the religious beliefs of others.

40. The Court has already noted that the wording of many statutes is not absolutely precise. The need to avoid excessive rigidity and to keep pace with changing circumstances means that many laws are inevitably couched in terms which, to a greater or lesser extent, are vague. Criminal-law provisions on proselytism fall within this category. The interpretation and application of such enactments depend on practice.

In this instance there existed a body of settled national case law. This case law, which had been published and was accessible, supplemented the letter of section 4 and was such as to enable Mr. Kokkinakis to regulate his conduct in the matter.

As to the constitutionality of section 4 of Law no. 1363/1938, the Court reiterates that it is, in the first instance, for the national authorities, and in particular the courts, to interpret and apply domestic law. And the Greek courts that have had to deal with the issue have ruled that there is no incompatibility.

41. The measure complained of was therefore "prescribed by law" within the meaning of Article 9(2) of the Convention.

2. Legitimate aim

42. The Government contended that a democratic State had to ensure the peaceful enjoyment of the personal freedoms of all those living on its territory. If, in particular, it was not vigilant to protect a person's religious beliefs and dignity from attempts to influence them by immoral and deceitful means, Article 9 §2 would in practice be rendered wholly nugatory.

43. In the applicant's submission, religion was part of the "constantly renewable flow of human thought" and it was impossible to conceive of its being excluded from public debate. A fair balance of personal rights made it necessary to accept that others' thought should be subject to a minimum of influence, otherwise the result would be a "strange society of silent animals that [would] think but . . . not express themselves, that [would] talk but . . . not communicate, and that [would] exist but . . . not coexist."

44. Having regard to the circumstances of the case and the actual terms of the relevant courts' decisions, the Court considers that the impugned measure was in pursuit of a legitimate aim under Article 9 §2, namely the protection of the rights and freedoms of others, relied on by the Government.

3. *"Necessary in a democratic society"*

45. Mr. Kokkinakis did not consider it necessary in a democratic society to prohibit a fellow citizen's right to speak when he came to discuss religion with his neighbour. He was curious to know how a disclosure delivered with conviction and based on holy books common to all Christians could infringe the rights of others. Mrs. Kyriakaki was an experienced adult woman with intellectual abilities; it was not possible, without flouting fundamental human rights, to make it a criminal offence for a Jehovah's Witness to have a conversation with a cantor's wife. Moreover, the Crete Court of Appeal, although the facts before it were precise and absolutely clear, had not managed to determine the direct or indirect nature of the applicant's attempt to intrude on the complainant's religious beliefs; its reasoning showed that it had convicted the applicant "not for something he had done but for what he was".

The Commission accepted this argument in substance.

46. The Government maintained, on the contrary, that the Greek courts had based themselves on plain facts which amounted to the offence of proselytism: Mr. Kokkinakis's insistence on entering Mrs. Kyriakaki's home on a false pretext; the way in which he had approached her in order to gain her trust; and his "skilful" analysis of the Holy Scriptures calculated to "delude" the complainant, who did not possess any "adequate grounding in doctrine". They pointed out that if the State remained indifferent to attacks on freedom of religious belief, major unrest would be caused that would probably disturb the social peace.

47. The Court has consistently held that a certain margin of appreciation is to be left to the Contracting States in assessing the existence and extent of the necessity of an interference, but this margin is subject to European supervision, embracing both the legislation and the decisions applying it, even those given by an independent court. The Court's task is to determine whether the measures taken at national level were justified in principle and proportionate.

In order to rule on this latter point, the Court must weigh the requirements of the protection of the rights and liberties of others against the conduct of which the applicant stood accused. In exercising its supervisory jurisdiction, the Court must look at the impugned judicial decisions against the background of the case as a whole.

48. First of all, a distinction has to be made between bearing Christian witness and improper proselytism. The former corresponds to true evangelism, which a report drawn up in 1956 under the auspices of the World Council of Churches describes as an essential mission and a responsibility of every Christian and every Church. The latter represents a corruption or deformation of it. It may, according to the same report, take the form of activities offering material or social advantages with a view to gaining new members for a Church or exerting improper pressure on people in distress or in need; it may even entail the use of violence or brainwashing; more generally, it is not compatible with respect for the freedom of thought, conscience and religion of others.

Scrutiny of section 4 of Law no.1363/1938 shows that the relevant criteria adopted by the Greek legislature are reconcilable with the foregoing if and in so far as they are designed only to punish improper proselytism, which the Court does not have to define in the abstract in the present case.

49. The Court notes, however, that in their reasoning the Greek courts established the applicant's liability by merely reproducing the wording of section 4 and did not

sufficiently specify in what way the accused had attempted to convince his neighbour by improper means. None of the facts they set out warrants that finding.

That being so, it has not been shown that the applicant's conviction was justified in the circumstances of the case by a pressing social need. The contested measure therefore does not appear to have been proportionate to the legitimate aim pursued or, consequently, "necessary in a democratic society . . . for the protection of the rights and freedoms of others".

50. In conclusion, there has been a breach of Article 9 of the Convention.

. . . .

∽

QUESTIONS & COMMENTS

(1) In his partly concurring opinion, Judge Pettiti recognized that the danger of assigning to the state the responsibility of determining the weakness or vulnerability of a person could become dangerous if used by an authoritarian state. Does this danger of paternalism also extend to nonauthoritarian states? What specific conditions should be considered as necessary for establishing such weakness or vulnerability? What kinds of extralegal sources can assist in establishing the vulnerability of individuals or groups?

(2) Does the European Court run the risk of having to make theological pronouncements by examining the veracity of a proselyte's statements to a nonbeliever in determining whether the proselyte has made false statements? What kind of limits would be appropriate in safeguarding against fraud?

(3) Greece defended its ban on proselytization as a measure to protect potentially vulnerable victims against a form of misrepresentation.

> (a) In U.S. constitutional law, would it be more appropriate to analyze a similar ban under the Free Speech Clause or the Free Exercise Clause of the First Amendment to the U.S. Constitution? What differences are there between those clauses in the context of a ban on proselytization?
>
> (b) Could Greece have defended the ban as an effort to protect the established church in Greece from being undermined? In the United States, the Establishment Clause forbidding a state-sponsored religion would deprive governments of that justification. Assuming that some degree of an established state religion is compatible with religious liberty, is a ban on proselytization to protect the established religion appropriate? Consider how the European Court would analyze the "established religion" defense of Greece's ban.

(4) The European Court of Human Rights also has examined the vulnerability of military personnel to proselytization by officers in *Larissis and Others v. Greece*, Case No. 140/1996/759/958–960, – Eur. Ct. H.R. (ser. A) (1998). The Court recognized the special concern of protecting subordinate members of the armed forces from harassment or abuse of power. The applicants, who were officers, attempted to proselytize three airmen who appeared to have felt pressured because of the applicants' superior positions. Considering that the penalties against the applicants were not severe and were mainly preventative, the Court decided that the application of the proselytism law in the matter of the airmen was not disproportionate to the law's aims and therefore did not violate Article 9. However, the applicants also approached civilians, and the Court found that

civilians were not subject to pressures like that of subordinate airmen and did not require special protection from proselytizing. Thus, the measures taken against the applicants for their actions toward civilians were unjustified and violated Article 9.

(5) Religious sects often are the targets of government repression. Jehovah's Witnesses have been targeted especially in the United States, Greece, and Argentina. For example, in Case No. 2137 (Argentina), Inter-Am. Cm. H.R. 1978, OEA/Ser. L/V/II.47, doc. 13 rev. 1, 29 June 1979, the Inter-American Commission found the Argentine government's outlawing of Jehovah's Witnesses violative of freedom of religion. In several central European countries, evangelical protestant groups have been persecuted in recent years through the use of licensing laws.

(6) Consider how the U.S. Supreme Court addressed a religious sect's unusual practice of sacrificing animals. In *Church of Lukumi Babalu Aye, Inc. v. City of Hialeah*, 508 U.S. 520 (1993), the petitioner church and its members belonged to the Santeria religion that practiced animal sacrifice. A city council enacted several ordinances outlawing ritual killing of animals. The U.S. Supreme Court invalidated the ordinances as violative of the Free Exercise Clause. The Court pointed out that, although some people may believe animal sacrifice to be an abhorrent practice, "religious beliefs need not be acceptable, logical, consistent, or comprehensible to others in order to merit First Amendment protection." (citing *Thomas v. Review Bd. of Indiana Employment Security Div.*, 450 U.S. 707, 714 (1981)). As the law restricted religious practice and was neither neutral nor of general application, it was subjected to strict scrutiny. The law must thus advance "interests of the highest order" and be "narrowly tailored in pursuit of those interests." *Id.* at 546. The city did not sufficiently demonstrate a compelling governmental interest and the ordinances were underinclusive or overbroad. As Santeria animal sacrifice occurred during a ritual and its primary purpose was to make an offering, rather than food consumption, Santeria sacrifice was prohibited by the ordinances, although almost all other killings, which are no more humane or necessary, went unpunished. The Court also pointed out that narrower legislation would accomplish the city's interest of prevention of cruelty to animals. If the city was concerned that the method used during the Santeria sacrifice was not humane, the subject of the legislation should have been the method of slaughter, rather than a religious classification.

(7) In *Kokkinakis v. Greece,* the European Court noted the following:

> As enshrined in Article 9, freedom of thought, conscience and religion is one of the foundations of a "democratic society" within the meaning of the Convention. It is, in its religious dimension, one of the most vital elements that go to make up the identity of believers and of their conception of life, but it is also a precious asset for atheists, agnostics, sceptics and the unconcerned. The pluralism indissociable from a democratic society, which has been dearly won over the centuries, depends on it.

Kokkinakis, 260-A Eur. Ct. H.R. at 31. Compare the U.S. Supreme Court case, *Welsh v. United States*, 398 U.S. 333 (1970). Welsh was convicted for refusing to submit to his induction into the Armed Forces. He refused because there was no religious basis for his conscientious objector claim under section 6(j) of the Universal Military and Service Act. That provision exempted those "who, by reason of religious training and belief, [are] conscientiously opposed to participation in war in any form." Religious training and belief were defined, in part, as belief in relation to a Supreme Being. In his exemption application, Welsh had stated he could not definitely affirm or deny his belief in a Supreme Being, and he crossed out the words "my religious training and" on his application. He affirmed that he held profound conscientious scruples against participating in a war. The U.S. Supreme Court reversed the conviction, on the basis of *United States v. Seeger*, 380 U.S. 163 (1965). In *Seeger*, the Court held that the issue was "whether the beliefs professed by a registrant are sincerely held and whether they are, *in his own scheme of things*, religious." *Welsh*, 398 U.S. at 339 (citing *Seeger*, 380 U.S. at 185). In other words, the central issue in deciding whether the registrant's beliefs were religious was whether the beliefs "play the role of a religion and function as a religion in the registrant's life." *Welsh*, 398 U.S. at 339. The Court noted that section 6(j)'s exclusion of "essentially political, sociological, or philosophical views or a merely personal moral code" from the definition of "religious training and belief" did not exclude those "religious" conscientious objectors whose consciousness objection to wars is based on consideration of public policy and the United States' domestic and foreign affairs. *Id.* at 342–43. Because Welsh's beliefs functioned as a religion in his life, he was just as entitled to a "religious" conscientious objector exemption as someone whose conscientious opposition to war stems from traditional, conventional religious convictions.

(8) How one defines "religion" in law may say more about extrareligious or political policy issues than about religious practice and/or belief. In *M.A.B. et al. v. Canada*, Communication No. 570/1993, views adopted 8 April 1994, the UN Human Rights Committee held inadmissible the authors' freedom of religion challenge to Canadian law outlawing the use of marijuana. The authors were members of the Assembly of the Church of the Universe who cultivated, distributed, and worshiped marijuana as a sacrament. The UN Human Rights Committee found that "a belief consisting primarily or exclusively in the worship and distribution of a narcotic drug cannot conceivably be brought within the scope of article 18 of the Covenant (freedom of religion and conscience)." *Id.* at §4.2.

Note the ways in which this problem could be analyzed: (a) The claimants do not sincerely hold a religious belief that they must use marijuana. (b) The claimed belief is not a component of any religion and therefore protections of religious liberty are not triggered. (c) The claimed belief is religious, but the government's justifications for outlawing use of marijuana are sufficient despite the impact that ban has on the claimant's religious practices. What are the advantages and disadvantages of each of these approaches?

U.S. constitutional decisions typically assume that a belief is sincerely held and then analyze only whether the state's justifications are sufficient. *Employment Division, Department of Human Resources v. Smith*, 494 U.S. 872 (1990), upheld a state's ban on the use of peyote, even in the religious services of the Native American Church. Five justices held that the Free Exercise Clause did not invalidate neutral laws generally applicable to all, even if such laws had an adverse effect on some religious practices (unless, as in the Hialeah case in *Comment 6, supra*, the adoption of the law was motivated by a desire to suppress religious practices). Justice O'Connor disagreed with that analysis but found that the ban was justified by the state's interest in suppressing drug use. The four dissenters argued that the characteristics of peyote made it unlikely that anyone other than a religious believer would ingest the drug. They agreed, however, that a state could ban use of marijuana even if that ban adversely affected some religious practices.

(9) Protecting civil liberties – including freedom of conscience – serves to check the tyranny of popular majorities. Consider the following excerpt from a memorial *amicus curiae* submitted in a blasphemy case before the European Court of Human Rights.

> As suggested during the drafting of Article 9 [freedom of religion], in countries where there historically have been state-religious institutions, domestic law affecting these institutions should receive European supervision. This was (and continues to be) an important issue because several state-parties to the ECHR had laws protecting religious institutions[ ] as well as establishing state-religions, including Denmark, Ireland, and the United Kingdom. During the drafting of Article 9(2), the Committee of Experts considered perpetuating certain restrictions rooted in history or custom. J.E.S. FAWCETT, THE APPLICATION OF THE EUROPEAN CONVENTION OF HUMAN RIGHTS 198 (1969). Accordingly, it was proposed that Article 9(2) should contain the proviso that "nothing in this Convention may be considered as derogating from already existing national rules as regards religious institutions..."
> *Id.* (citing 2 *TRAVAUX PRÉPARATOIRES* TO THE EUROPEAN CONVENTION ON HUMAN RIGHTS 452, 457).
>
> However, this proviso eventually was abandoned. FAWCETT, *supra,* at 199. This suggests that the drafters intended that national authorities should be given less deference in cases where the national authorities historically have been sponsors of religious institutions.

Rights International, Written Comments in *Wingrove v. United Kingdom,* – Eur. Ct. H.R. (ser. B) (1996).

If a determinative factor in establishing the appropriate margin of appreciation is whether the government historically has been a sponsor of religious institutions, what kinds of sponsorship are relevant for allowing only a narrow margin of appreciation?

5.6. Freedom of Expression

Universal Declaration of Human Rights

Article 19.

Everyone has the right to freedom of opinion and expression; this right includes freedom to hold opinions without interference and to seek, receive and impart information and ideas through any media and regardless of frontiers.

International Covenant on Civil and Political Rights

Article 19

1. Everyone shall have the right to hold opinions without interference.

2. Everyone shall have the right to freedom of expression; this right shall include freedom to seek, receive and impart information and ideas of all kinds, regardless of frontiers, either orally, in writing or in print, in the form of art, or through any other media of his choice.

3. The exercise of the rights provided for in paragraph 2 of this article carries with it special duties and responsibilities. It may therefore be subject to certain restrictions, but these shall only be such as are provided by law and are necessary:

(a) For respect of the rights or reputations of others;

(b) For the protection of national security or of public order (*ordre public*), or of public health or morals.

Article 20

1. Any propaganda for war shall be prohibited by law.

2. Any advocacy of national, racial or religious hatred that constitutes incitement to discrimination, hostility or violence shall be prohibited by law.

European Convention on Human Rights

Article 10

1. Everyone has the right to freedom of expression. This right shall include freedom to hold opinions and to receive and impart information an ideas without interference by public authority and regardless of frontiers. This article shall not prevent States from requiring the licensing of broadcasting, television or cinema enterprises.

2. The exercise of these freedoms, since it carries with it duties and responsibilities, may be subject to such formalities, conditions, restrictions or penalties as are prescribed by law and are necessary in a democratic society, in the interests of national security, territorial integrity or public safety, for the prevention of disorder or crime, for the protection of health or morals, for the protection of the reputation or the rights of others, for preventing the disclosure of information received in confidence, or for maintaining the authority and impartiality of the judiciary.

Charter of Fundamental Human Rights of the European Union

Article 11

Freedom of expression and information

1. Everyone has the right to freedom of expression. This right shall include freedom to hold opinions and to receive and impart information and ideas without interference by public authority and regardless of frontiers.

2. The freedom and pluralism of the media shall be respected.

American Declaration of the Rights and Duties of Man

Article IV. Right to freedom of investigation, opinion, expression and dissemination.

Every person has the right to freedom of investigation, of opinion, and of the expression and dissemination of ideas, by any medium whatsoever.

American Convention on Human Rights

Article 13. FREEDOM OF THOUGHT AND EXPRESSION

1. Everyone has the right to freedom of thought and expression. This right includes freedom to seek, receive, and impart information and ideas of all kinds, regardless of frontiers, either orally, in writing, in print, in the form of art, or through any other medium of one's choice.

2. The exercise of the right provided for in the foregoing paragraph shall not be subject to prior censorship but shall be subject to subsequent imposition of liability, which shall be expressly established by law to the extent necessary to ensure:

   a. Respect for the rights or reputations of others; or
   b. The protection of national security, public order, or public health or morals.

3. The right of expression may not be restricted by indirect methods or means, such as the abuse of government or private controls over newsprint, radio broadcasting frequencies, or equipment used in the dissemination of information, or by any other means tending to impede the communication and circulation of ideas and opinions.

4. Notwithstanding the provisions of paragraph 2 above, public entertainments may be subject by law to prior censorship for the sole purpose of regulating access to them for the moral protection of childhood and adolescence.

5. Any propaganda for war and any advocacy of national, racial, or religious hatred that constitute incitements to lawless violence or to any other similar illegal action against any person or group of persons on any grounds including those of race, color, religion, language, or national origin shall be considered as offenses punishable by law.

Article 14. RIGHT OF REPLY.

1. Anyone injured by inaccurate or offensive statements or ideas disseminated to the public in general by a legally regulated medium of communication has the right to reply or to make a correction using the same communications outlet, under such conditions as the law may establish.

2. The correction or reply shall not in any case remit other legal liabilities that may have been incurred.

3. For the effective protection of honor and reputation, every publisher, and every newspaper, motion picture, radio, and television company, shall have a person responsible who is not protected by immunities or special privileges.

African [Banjul] Charter on Human and Peoples' Rights

Article 9

1. Every individual shall have the right to receive information.

2. Every individual shall have the right to express and disseminate his opinions within the law.

Convention on Human Rights and Fundamental Freedoms of the Commonwealth of Independent States

Article 11

1. Everyone shall have the right to freedom of expression. This right shall include the right to hold opinions and to receive and impart information and ideas by any legal means without interference by a public authority and regardless of frontiers.

2. The exercise of these freedoms, since it carries with it duties and responsibilities, may be subject to such formalities, conditions and restrictions as are prescribed by law

and are necessary in a democratic society, in the interests of national security, public safety or public order for the protection of the rights and freedoms of others.

U.S. Constitution

Amendment I

Congress shall make no law ... abridging the freedom of speech, or of the press; ....

Defamation

Lingens v. Austria
European Court of Human Rights
103 Eur. Ct. H.R. (ser. A) (1986)
8 E.H.R.R. 407 (1986)

. . . .

FACTS:

8. Mr. Lingens, an Austrian journalist born in 1931, resides in Vienna and is editor of the magazine PROFIL.

I. The applicant's articles and their background

9. On 9 October 1975, four days after the Austrian general elections, in the course of a television interview, Mr. Simon Wiesenthal, President of the Jewish Documentation Centre, accused Mr. Freidrich Peter, the President of the Austrian Liberal Party (*Freiheitliche Partei Österreichs*) of having served in the first SS infantry brigade during the Second World War. This unit had on several occasions massacred civilians behind the German lines in Russia. Mr. Peter did not deny that he was a member of the unit, but stated that he was never involved in the atrocities is committed. Mr. Wiesenthal then said that he had not alleged anything of the sort.

10. The following day, Mr. Bruno Kreisky, the retiring Chancellor and President of the Austrian Socialist Party (*Sozialistische Partei Österreichs*), was questioned on television about these accusations.

Immediately before the television interview, he had met Mr. Peter at the Federal Chancellery. Their meeting was one of the normal consultations between heads of parties with a view to forming a new government; it had aroused great public interest because before the elections of 5 October the possibility of a Kreisky-Peter coalition government had been canvassed.

At the interview, Mr. Kreisky excluded the possibility of such a coalition because his party had won an absolute majority. However, he vigorously supported Mr. Peter and referred to Mr. Wiesenthal's organisation and activities as a 'political mafia' and 'mafia methods'. Similar remarks were reported the next day in a Vienna daily newspaper to which he had given an interview.

11. At this juncture, the applicant published two articles in the Vienna magazine Profil.

12. The first was published on 14 October 1975 under the heading 'The Peter Case' ('*Der Fall Peter*'). It related the above events and in particular the activities of the first SS infantry brigade; it also drew attention to Mr. Peter's role in criminal proceedings instituted in Graz (and later abandoned) against persons who had fought in that brigade.

It drew the conclusion that although Mr. Peter was admittedly entitled to the benefit of the presumption of innocence, his past nevertheless rendered him unacceptable as a politician in Austria. The applicant went on to criticise the attitude of Mr. Kreisky whom he accused of protecting Mr. Peter and other former members of the SS for political reasons. With regard to Mr. Kreisky's criticisms of Mr. Wiesenthal, he wrote 'had they been made by someone else this would probably have been described as the basest opportunism' (*'Bei einem anderen würde man es wahrscheinlich übelsten Opportunismus nennen'*), but added that in the circumstances the position was more complex because Mr Kreisky believed what he was saying.

13. The second article, published on 21 October 1975, was entitled 'Reconciliation with the Nazis, but how?' (*'Versöhnung mit den Nazis – aber wie?'*). It covered several pages and was divided into an introduction and six sections: "Still" or "Already", 'We are all innocent', 'Was it necessary to shoot defenceless people?', 'Why is it still a question for discussion?', 'Helbich and Peter' and 'Politically ignorant'.

14. In the introduction Mr Lingens recalled the facts and stressed the influence of Mr Kreisky's remarks on public opinion. He criticised him not only for supporting Mr Peter, but also for his accommodating attitude towards former Nazis who had recently taken part in Austrian politics.

15. Under the heading '"Still" or "Already"' the applicant conceded that one could not object to such attitudes on grounds of 'Realpolitik'. According to him 'the time has passed when for electoral reasons one had to take account not only of Nazis but also of their victims . . . the former have outlived the latter . . .'. Nevertheless Austria, which had produced Hitler and Eichmann and so many other war criminals, had not succeeded in coming to terms with its past; it had simply ignored it. This policy risked delivering the country into the hands of a future fascist movement.

With regard to the then Chancellor, he added: 'In truth Mr. Kreisky's behaviour cannot be criticised on rational grounds but only on irrational grounds: it is immoral, undignified' (*'In Wahrheit kann man das, was Kreisky tut, auf rationale Weise nicht widerlegen. Nur irrational: es ist unmoralisch. Würdelos'*). It was, moreover, unnecessary because Austrians could reconcile themselves with the past without seeking the favours of the former Nazis, minimising the problem of concentration camps or maligning Mr. Wiesenthal by exploiting anti-Semitism.

What was surprising was not that one 'still' spoke about these things thirty years later but, on the contrary, that so many people were 'already' able to close their eyes to the existence of this mountain of corpses.

Finally, Mr. Lingens criticised the lack of tact with which Mr. Kreisky treated the victims of the Nazis.

16. The second section commented on the attitude of Austrian society in general with regard to Nazi crimes and former Nazis. In the author's opinion, by sheltering behind the philosophic alternative between collective guilt and collective innocence the Austrians had avoided facing up to a real, discernible and assessable guilt.

After a long disquisition on various types of responsibility, he stressed that at the time it had in fact been possible to choose between good and evil and gave examples of persons who had refused to collaborate. He concluded that 'if Bruno Kreisky had used his personal reputation, in the way he used it to protect Mr Peter, to reveal this other and better Austria, he would have given this country – thirty years afterwards – what it most needed to come to terms with its past: a greater confidence in itself'.

17. The third and fourth sections (which together amounted to a third of the article) also dealt with the need to overcome the consciousness of collective guilt and envisage the determination of real guilt.

Under the title 'Was it necessary to shoot defenceless people?', Mr. Lingens drew a distinction between the special units and the regular forces in the armies of the Third Reich; he pointed out that no one was forcibly enlisted in the former: one had to volunteer.

In the following section he stressed the difference between individuals guilty of criminal offences and persons who, morally speaking, had to be regarded as accomplices; he maintained that if Austria had tried its Nazis earlier, more quickly and more thoroughly, it would have been able to view its past more calmly without complexes and with more confidence. He then set out the reasons why that had not been possible and defended Mr. Wiesenthal from the charge of belonging to a 'mafia'. Finally, he considered the possibility of showing clemency after so many years and concluded: 'It behooves every society to show mercy but not to maintain an unhealthy relationship with the law by acquitting obvious murderers and concealing, dissembling or denying manifest guilt.'

18. The fifth section of Mr. Lingens' article compared the Peter case with another affair of a more economic nature relating to Mr. Helbich, one of the leaders of the Austrian People's Party (*Österreichische Volkspartei*), and compared Mr. Kreisky's different reaction in each case. The author argued that the circumstances of the first case made Mr. Peter unfit to be a member of parliament, a politician and a member of the government, and added: 'This is a minimum requirement of political ethics' ('*ein Mindesterfordernis des politischen Anstandes*'). The 'monstrosity' ('*Ungeheuerlichkeit*') was not, in his opinion, the fact that Mr. Wiesenthal had raised the matter, but that Mr. Kreisky wished to hush it up.

19. The article ended with a section criticising the political parties in general owing to the presence of former Nazis among their leaders. The applicant considered that Mr. Peter ought to resign, not to admit his guilt but to prove that he possessed a quality unknown to Mr. Kreisky, namely tact.

II. Private prosecutions brought by Mr. Kreisky

20. On 29 October and 12 November 1975, the then Chancellor brought two private prosecutions against Mr. Lingens. He considered that certain passages in the articles summarised above were defamatory and relied on Article 111 of the Austrian Criminal Code, which reads:

> 1. Anyone who in such a way that it may be perceived by a third person accuses another of possessing a contemptible character or attitude or of behaviour contrary to honour or morality and of such a nature as to make him contemptible or otherwise lower him in public esteem shall be liable to imprisonment not exceeding six months or a fine.
>
> 2. Anyone who commits this offence in a printed document, by broadcasting or otherwise in such a way as to make the defamation accessible to a broad section of the public shall be liable to imprisonment not exceeding one year or a fine.
>
> 3. The person making the statement shall not be punished if it is proved to be true. As regards the offence defined in paragraph 1, he shall also not be liable if circumstances are established which gave him sufficient reason to assume that the statement was true.

Under Article 112, 'evidence of the truth and of good faith shall not be admissible unless the person making the statement pleads the correctness of the statement or his good faith....'

A. First set of proceedings

1. Decision of the Vienna Regional Court

21. On 26 March 1979, the Vienna Regional Court found Mr Lingens. guilty of defamation (Criminal Code, Art 111(2)) for having used the expressions 'the basest opportunism', 'immoral' and 'undignified'. However, it held that certain other expressions were not defamatory in their context ('minimum requirement of political ethics', 'monstrosity'). It fined him 20,000 Schillings, considering as mitigating circumstances the fact that the accused intended to voice political criticism of politicians on political questions and that the latter were expected to show greater tolerance of defamation than other individuals. In view of the defendant's good faith it awarded Mr. Kreisky no damages but, on his application, ordered the confiscation of the articles complained of and the publication of the judgment.

22. In its decision, which contained a lengthy statement of reasons, the Regional Court first examined the objectively defamatory character of each of the passages complained of. It held that the expressions 'basest opportunism', 'immoral' and 'undignified' were defamatory and were directly or indirectly aimed at Mr. Kreisky personally, whereas the words 'minimum requirement of political ethics' and 'monstrosity' did not go beyond the accepted limits of political criticism.

According to Mr. Lingens, the first three expressions were value judgements and therefore as such not contrary to Article 111 of the Criminal Code. However, the Regional Court considered that the unfavourable conclusions drawn with regard to the then Chancellor's behaviour fell within the scope of that provision. Nor could the defendant rely on his right to freedom of expression, since the relevant provisions of the Constitution and Article 10 of the [European Convention of Human Rights] authorised limitations of this right: a balance had to be struck between this right and the right to respect for private life and reputation. In the instant case the applicant had gone beyond the permissible limits.

23. As regards Mr Kreisky's use of a private prosecution, the Regional Court pointed out that he had been criticised not in his capacity as Federal Chancellor but as a leading member of his party and a politician. Article 117(2) of the Criminal Code therefore did not apply in the instant case: it made defamation of an office holder punishable, but solely by means of a public prosecution commenced with the consent of the person concerned, who could not bring a private prosecution unless the prosecuting authorities refused to act.

24. The Regional Court then considered the question of proving truth (*preuve de la vérité*). It held that as the applicant had not provided evidence to justify the expression 'basest opportunism', that was sufficient to lead to his conviction.

With regard to the words 'immoral' and 'undignified', the accused had used them in relation to Mr. Kreisky's attitude consisting in minimising Nazi atrocities, referring to Mr. Wiesenthal's activities as being of a mafia-type and insinuating that the latter had collaborated with the Gestapo. On this last point the Regional Court admitted evidence produced by Mr. Lingens in the form of a court decision finding a journalist guilty of defamation for having made a similar allegation.

In so far as Mr. Kreisky had spoken of 'mafia methods' and 'mafia', the Regional Court pointed out that these expressions normally referred to an organised form of criminal behaviour but were sometimes used in a different sense. Even if one did not accept the argument put forward by the private prosecutor, his conception of the 'mafia' was a possible one and deserved to be examined. It was not for the prosecutor to prove the truth of his allegations but for Mr. Lingens to prove the truth of his. Mr. Wiesenthal himself had conceded that in order to attain his various aims he relied on an organisation with numerous ramifications. Moreover, the then Chancellor's statements must be seen in the context of a political struggle between political opponents, each of them using such weapons as were at his disposal. Seem from this angle they did not reflect an absence of morality or dignity but constituted a possible defence and were in no way unusual in the bitter tussles of politics.

In truth, Mr. Kreisky's attitude towards Nazi victims and Nazi collaborators was far from clear and unambiguous; it appeared in a form which allowed different conclusions. It was therefore logically impossible for the defendant to establish that the only possible interpretation of this attitude was the one he put on it.

2. Appeal to the Vienna Court of Appeal

25. Mr. Kreisky and Mr. Lingens both appealed against the judgment to the Vienna Court of Appeal. On 30 November 1979, the Court of Appeal set the judgment aside without examining the merits, on the ground that the Regional Court had failed to go sufficiently into the question whether the then Chancellor was entitled to bring a private prosecution in spite of the provisions of Article 117 of the Criminal Code.

B. Second set of proceedings

1. Decision of the Vienna Regional Court

26. The Vienna Regional Court, to which the Court of Appeal had returned the case, gave judgment on 1 April 1981.

After examining the circumstances surrounding the statements by the then Chancellor, it came to the conclusion that he had been criticised not in his official capacity but as head of a party and as a private individual who felt himself under an obligation to protect a third person. It followed therefore that he was entitled to bring a private prosecution.

As regards the legal definition of the acts imputed to Mr. Lingens, the Regional Court confirmed its judgment of 26 March 1979.

With regard to the defence of justification, it again noted that the accused had not produced any evidence to prove the truth of the expression 'the basest opportunism'. As regards the expressions 'immoral' and 'undignified', the evidence he had produced related solely to the allegations of collaboration with the Nazis made against Mr Wiesenthal. These, however, were not relevant because Mr Kreisky had made them after the publication of the articles in question. In so far as these expressions were directed at other behaviour and attitudes of the Chancellor, the Regional Court maintained its previous findings unchanged. It considered that Mr Lingens' criticisms went far beyond the question of Mr. Kreisky's attacks on Mr Wiesenthal. The fact that the former had been able to prosecute the applicant but could not himself be prosecuted for defamation by Mr. Wiesenthal was due to the existing legislation on parliamentary immunity. The obligation to prove the truth of his statements was also based on the law and it was not for the courts but for the legislature to make this proof less difficult. Nor was the Regional Court responsible for the lack of tolerance and the litigious tendencies of certain politicians.

It therefore passed the same sentence as in the original judgment.

2. Appeal to the Vienna Court of Appeal

27. Both sides again appealed to the Vienna Court of Appeal, which gave judgment on 29 October 1981; it reduced the fine imposed on the applicant to 15,000 Schillings but confirmed the Regional Court's judgment in all other respects.

28. Mr Kreisky disputed the statement that different criteria applied to private life and to political life. He argued that politicians and private individuals should receive the same treatment as regards the protection of their reputation.

The Court of Appeal, however, pointed out that Article 111 of the Criminal Code applied solely to the esteem enjoyed by a person in his social setting. In the case of politicians, this was public opinion. Yet experience showed that frequent use of insults in political discussion (often under cover of parliamentary immunity) had given the impression that statements in this field could not be judged by the same criteria as those relating to private life. Politicians should therefore show greater tolerance. As a general rule, criticisms uttered in political controversy did not affect a person's reputation unless they touched on his private life. That did not apply in the instant case to the expressions 'minimum requirement of political ethics' and 'monstrosity'. Mr. Kreisky's appeal was therefore dismissed.

29. The Court of Appeal then turned to Mr. Lingens' grounds of appeal and first of all examined the evidence taken at first instance, in order to decide in what capacity Mr. Kreisky had been subjected to his criticism. It too found that he was criticised in his capacity both as a party leader and as a private individual.

The expression 'the basest opportunism' meant that the person referred to was acting for a specific purpose with complete disregard of moral considerations and this in itself constituted an attack on Mr. Kreisky's reputation. The use of the words 'had they been made by someone else' could not be understood as a withdrawal of the criticism. As the defendant had not been succeeded in proving the truth of it, the court of first instance had been right to find him guilty of an offence.

According to the applicant, the expressions 'immoral' and 'undignified' were his personal judgement of conduct which was not disputed, a judgement made in exercise of his freedom of expression, guaranteed by Article 10 of the Convention. The Court of Appeal did not accept this argument; it pointed out that Austrian law did not confer upon the individual an unlimited right to formulate value judgements and that Article 10 authorised limitations laid down by law for the protection, inter alia, of the reputation of others. Furthermore, the task of the press was to impart information, the interpretation of which had to be left primarily to the reader. If a journalist himself expressed an opinion, it should remain within the limits set by the criminal law to ensure the protection of reputations. This, however, was not the position in the instant case. The burden was on Mr. Lingens to establish the truth of his statements; he could not separate his unfavourable value judgement from the facts on which it was based. Since Mr. Kreisky was personally convinced that Mr. Wiesenthal used 'mafia methods', he could not be accused of having acted immorally or in an undignified manner.

30. The appeal judgment was published in Profil on 22 February 1982, as required by the accessory penalty imposed on Mr. Lingens and his publisher.

[Lingens applied to the European Commission which unanimously found a violation of Article 10]

DECISION [OF THE EUROPEAN COURT OF HUMAN RIGHTS]:

I. Alleged violation of Article 10

34. . . . .

Mr. Lingens claimed that the impugned court decisions infringed his freedom of expression to a degree incompatible with the fundamental principles of a democratic society.

This was also the conclusion reached by the Commission. In the Government's submission, on the other hand, the disputed penalty was necessary in order to protect Mr. Kreisky's reputation.

35. It was not disputed that there was 'interference by public authority' with the exercise of the applicant's freedom of expression. This resulted from the applicant's conviction for defamation by the Vienna Regional Court on 1 April 1981, which conviction was upheld by the Vienna Court of Appeal on 29 October 1981.

Such interference contravenes the Convention if it does not satisfy the requirements of paragraph 2 of Article 10. It therefore falls to be determined whether the interference was 'prescribed by law', had an aim or aims that is or are legitimate under Article 10(2) and was 'necessary in a democratic society' for the aforesaid aim or aims. [citation omitted]

36. As regards the first two points, the Court agrees with the Commission and the Government that the conviction in question was indisputably based on Article 111 of the Austrian Criminal Code; it was moreover designed to protect 'the reputation or rights of others' and there is no reason to suppose that it had any other purpose. (Art. 18 of the Convention). The conviction was accordingly 'prescribed by law' and had a legitimate aim under Article 10(2) of the Convention.

37. In their respective submissions the Commission, the Government and the applicant concentrated on the question whether the interference was 'necessary in a democratic society' for achieving the abovementioned aim.

The applicant invoked his role as a political journalist in a pluralist society; as such he considered that he had a duty to express his views on Mr. Kreisky's condemnations of Mr. Wiesenthal. He also considered – as did the Commission – that a politician who was himself accustomed to attacking his opponents had to expect fiercer criticism than other people.

The Government submitted that freedom of expression could not prevent national courts from exercising their discretion and taking decisions necessary in their judgment to ensure that political debate did not degenerate into personal insult. It was claimed that some of the expressions used by Mr. Lingens overstepped the limits. Furthermore, the applicant had been able to make his views known to the public without any prior censorship; the penalty subsequently imposed on him was therefore not disproportionate to the legitimate aim pursued. Moreover, the Government asserted that in the instant case there was a conflict between two rights secured in the Convention – freedom of expression (Article 10) and the right to respect for private life (Article 8). The fairly broad interpretation the Commission had adopted of the first of these rights did not, it was said, make sufficient allowance for the need to safeguard the second right.

38. On this latter point the Court notes that the words held against Mr. Lingens related to certain public condemnations of Mr. Wiesenthal by Mr. Kreisky and to the latter's attitude as a politician towards National Socialism and former Nazis. There is accordingly no need in this instance to read Article 10 in the light of Article 8.

39. The adjective 'necessary', within the meaning of Article 10(2), implies the existence of a 'pressing social need'. [citation omitted] The Contracting States have a certain margin of appreciation in assessing whether such a need exists, but it goes hand in hand with a European supervision, embracing both the legislation and the decisions applying it, even those given by an independent court. [citation omitted] The Court is therefore empowered to give the final ruling on whether a 'restriction' or 'penalty' is reconcilable with freedom of expression as protected by Article 10.

40. In exercising its supervisory jurisdiction, the Court cannot confine itself to considering the impugned court decisions in isolation; it must look at them in the light of the case as a whole, including the articles held against the applicant and the context in which they were written. [citation omitted] The Court must determine whether the interference at issue was 'proportionate to the legitimate aim pursued' and whether the reasons adduced by the Austrian courts to justify it are 'relevant and sufficient'. [citation omitted]

41. In this connection, the Court has to recall that freedom of expression, as secured in paragraph 1 of Article 10, constitutes one of the essential foundations of a democratic society and one of the basic conditions for its progress and for each individual's self-fulfilment. Subject to paragraph 2, it is applicable not only to 'information' or 'ideas' that are favourably received or regarded as inoffensive or as a matter of indifference, but also to those that offend, shock or disturb. Such are the demands of that pluralism, tolerance and broadmindedness without which there is no 'democratic society'. [citation omitted]

These principles are of particular importance as far as the press is concerned. Whilst the press must not overstep the bounds set, *inter alia*, for the 'protection of the reputation of others', it is nevertheless incumbent on it to impart information and ideas on political issues just as on those in other areas of public interest. Not only does the press have the task of imparting such information and ideas: the public also has a right to receive them. [citation omitted] In this connection, the Court cannot accept the opinion, expressed in the judgment of the Vienna Court of Appeal, to the effect that the task of the press was to impart information, the interpretation of which had to be left primarily to the reader.

42. Freedom of the press furthermore affords the public one of the best means of discovering and forming an opinion of the ideas and attitudes of political leaders. More generally, freedom of political debate is at the very core of the concept of a democratic society which prevails throughout the Convention.

The limits of acceptable criticism are accordingly wider as regards a politician as such than as regards a private individual. Unlike the latter, the former inevitably and knowingly lays himself open to close scrutiny of his every word and deed by both journalists and the public at large, and he must consequently display a greater degree of tolerance. No doubt Article 10(2) enables the reputation of others – that is to say, of all individuals – to be protected, and this protection extends to politicians too, even when they are not acting in their private capacity; but in such cases the requirements of such protection have to be weighed in relation to the interests of open discussion of political issues.

43. The applicant was convicted because he had used certain expressions ('basest opportunism', 'immoral' and 'undignified') apropos of Mr Kreisky, who was Federal Chancellor at the time, in two articles published in the Viennese magazine Profil on 14 and 21 October 1975. The articles dealt with political issues of public interest in Austria

which had given rise to many heated discussions concerning the attitude of Austrians in general – and the Chancellor in particular – to National Socialism and to the participation of former Nazis in the governance of the country. The content and tone of the articles were on the whole fairly balanced but the use of the aforementioned expressions in particular appeared likely to harm Mr. Kreisky's reputation.

However, since the case concerned Mr. Kreisky in his capacity as a politician, regard must be had to the background against which these articles were written. They had appeared shortly after the general election of October 1975. many Austrians had thought beforehand that Mr. Kreisky's party would lose its absolute majority and, in order to be able to govern, would have to form a coalition with Mr. Peter's party. When, after the elections, Mr. Wiesenthal made a number of revelations about Mr. Peter's Nazi past, the Chancellor defended Mr. Peter and attacked his detractor, whose activities he described as 'mafia methods'; hence Mr. Lingens' sharp reaction.

The impugned expressions are therefore to be seen against the background of a post-election political controversy; as the Vienna Regional Court noted in its judgment of 26 March 1979, in this struggle each used the weapons at his disposal; and these were in no way unusual in the hard-fought tussles of politics.

In assessing, from the point of view of the Convention, the penalty imposed on the applicant and the reasons for which the domestic courts imposed it, these circumstances must not be overlooked.

44. On final appeal the Vienna Court of Appeal sentenced Mr Lingens to a fine; it also ordered confiscation of the relevant issues of PROFIL and publication of the judgment.

As the Government pointed out, the disputed articles had at the time already been widely disseminated, so that although the penalty imposed on the author did not strictly speaking prevent him from expressing himself, it nonetheless amounted to a kind of censure, which would be likely to discourage him from making criticisms of that kind again in future; the Delegate of the Commission rightly pointed this out. In the context of political debate such a sentence would be likely to deter journalists from contributing to public discussion of issues affecting the life of the community. By the same token, a sanction such as this is liable to hamper the press in performing its task as purveyor of information and public watchdog. [citation omitted]

45. The Austrian courts applied themselves first to determining whether the passages held against Mr Lingens were objectively defamatory; they ruled that some of the expressions used were indeed defamatory – 'the basest opportunism', 'immoral' and 'undignified'.

The defendant had submitted that the observations in question were value judgements made by him in the exercise of his freedom of expression. The Court, like the Commission, shares this view. The applicant's criticisms were in fact directed against the attitude adopted by Mr. Kreisky, who was Federal Chancellor at the time. What was at issue was not his right to disseminate information but his freedom of opinion and his right to impart ideas; the restrictions authorised in paragraph 2 of Article 10 nevertheless remained applicable.

46. The relevant courts then sought to determine whether the defendant had established the truth of his statements; this was in pursuance of Article 111(3) of the Criminal Code. They held in substance that there were different ways of assessing Mr. Kreisky's behaviour and that it could not logically be proved that one interpretation was right to the exclusion of all others; they consequently found the applicant guilty of defamation.

In the Court's view, a careful distinction needs to be made between facts and value judgements. The existence of facts can be demonstrated, whereas the truth of value judgements is not susceptible of proof. The Court notes in this connection that the facts on which Mr. Lingens founded his value judgements were undisputed, as was also his good faith.

Under paragraph 3 of Article 111 of the Criminal Code, read in conjunction with paragraph 2, journalists in a case such as this cannot escape conviction for the matters specified in paragraph 2 unless they can prove the truth of their statements.

As regards value judgements this requirement is impossible of fulfilment and it infringes freedom of opinion itself, which is a fundamental part of the right secured by Article 10 of the Convention.

The Vienna Regional Court held that the burden of proof was a consequence of the law and that it was not for the courts but for the legislature to make it less onerous. (Judgment of 1 April 1981; see §26 *supra*). In this context the court points out that it does not have to specify which national authority is responsible for any breach of the Convention; the sole issue is the State's international responsibility. [citation omitted]

47. From the various foregoing considerations it appears that the interference with Mr Lingens' exercise of the freedom of expression was not 'necessary in a democratic society ... for the protection of the reputation ... of others'; it was disproportionate to the legitimate aim pursued. There was accordingly a breach of Article 10 of the Convention.

. . . .

~

QUESTIONS & COMMENTS

(1) The European Court has addressed many defamation cases. In *Castells v. Spain*, 236 Eur. Ct. H.R. (ser. A) (1992), the allegedly defamatory statements were directed at the government *per se*. In this case, the applicant was a senator and a lawyer in Spain. He was affiliated with a political party supporting Basque independence. A weekly magazine published an article he had written that accused the right-wing Spanish government of complicity in the murders of hundreds of Basque separatists over the preceding two years. During his trial, Castells offered to introduce evidence supporting the veracity of the article, but the Supreme Court ruled the evidence inadmissible because truth was no defense to a charge of insulting the government. Castells was ultimately convicted of proffering insults of a less serious kind and sentenced to one year in jail. Before the European Court of Human Rights, Castells argued that the prosecution and conviction had violated his freedom of expression.

The European Court held that the denial to Castells of his ability to adduce evidence of the truth of the challenged statements was an unnecessary interference with his right to freedom of expression. This freedom was an essential foundation of democratic societies, especially so for an elected representative of the people such as Castells. Freedom of the press was also essential to free political debate, which is necessary for the proper operation of democratic government. It was therefore incompatible with Article 10 to deny an individual the opportunity to establish the truth and good faith of accusations against the government.

(2) The Inter-American Commission on Human Rights has addressed laws prohibiting insults against public officials. These laws are called *leyes de desacato* ("contempt laws"). Desacato laws are very common in Latin America. *See Report on the Incompatibility of "Desacato" Laws with the American Convention on Human Rights,* Inter-Am. Cm. H.R., ANNUAL REPORT OF THE INTER-AMERICAN COMMISSION ON HUMAN RIGHTS 1994, OEA/Ser.L/V/11.99, doc. 9 rev. (17 Feb. 1995). Desacato laws are a class of legislation that criminalizes expression that offends, insults, or threatens a public functionary in the performance of his or her official duties. The Inter-American Commission has opined that desacato laws are incompatible with the right to freedom of expression under Article 13, ACHR, because they suppress the freedom of expression necessary for the proper functioning of a democratic society. In the interest of the democratic public order inherent in the American Convention, freedom of expression must be "scrupulously respected." *Id.* at 203 (citing *Compulsory Membership in an Association Prescribed by Law for the Practice of Journalism (Arts. 13 and 29 American Convention of Human Rights),* Inter-Am. Ct. H.R., Advisory Opinion OC-5/85 of 13 November 1985, Ser. A, No. 5, ¶69, at 122).

According to the Commission, only those measures that are "necessary" to achieve legitimate governmental interests are lawful under Article 13. "The term 'necessary' as used in Article 13(2) must be something more than 'useful,' 'reasonable,' or 'desirable'." *Id.,* at 209. Citing the Inter-American Court, the Commission opined that the restrictions on freedom of expression must be not only proportionate but closely tailored to the achievement of the proffered governmental objective. *Compulsory Membership in an Association Prescribed by Law for the Practice of Journalism (Arts. 13 and 29 American Convention of Human Rights),* Inter-Am. Ct. H.R., Advisory Opinion OC-5/85 of 13 November 1985, Ser. A, No.5, ¶46, at 109.

The Commission noted that to ensure the smooth functioning of a democratic public order, democratic governments must allow individuals to criticize public officials. The right to freedom of expression and thought is "inextricably connected to the very existence of a democratic society." *Report on the Incompatibility of "Desacato" Laws with the American Convention, supra,* at 205. "Indeed, '[f]ull and free discussion keep a society from becoming stagnant and unprepared for the stresses and strains that work to tear all civilizations apart'." *Id.* (quoting *Dennis v. United States,* 341 U.S. 494, 584 (1951) (Douglas, J., dissenting)). As the Commission observed:

> The use of desacato laws to protect the honor of public functionaries acting in their official capacities unjustifiably grants a right to protection to public officials that is not available to other members of society. This distinction inverts the fundamental principle in a democratic system that holds the Government subject to controls, such as pubic scrutiny, in order to preclude or control abuse of its coercive powers. If we consider that public functionaries acting in their official capacity are the Government for all intents and purposes, then it must be the individual and the public's right to criticize and scrutinize the officials' actions and attitudes in so far as they relate to the public office.

Id. at 207. Indeed, public officials must be more – not less – open to public criticism and scrutiny. *Id.* at 210.

Article 13's protection of freedom of expression is particularly important in the case of value judgments and opinions. As the Inter-American Commission noted, value judgments and opinions are not susceptible of proof. "Even those laws which allow truth as a defense inevitably inhibit the free flow of ideas and opinions by shifting the burden of proof onto the speaker." Therefore, political criticism expressed by means of value judgments and opinions receive especial protection under Article 13. *Id.* at 208–209.

The Inter-American Commission addressed an Argentine *desacato* law in *Verbitsky v. Argentina*, Case 11.012, Report No. 22/94, Inter-Am. Cm. H.R., OEA/Ser.L/V/II.88 rev.1 doc. 9 at 40 (1995). Mr. Verbitsky, a journalist, had been convicted for allegedly defaming the minister of the Supreme Court by calling him "*asqueroso*" (which can mean either disgusting or disgusted) in an article.

The parties reached a friendly settlement. In compliance with this settlement, the Argentine prosecutor proposed to the Argentine Appeals Court that Mr. Verbitsky's appeal be granted and that Mr. Verbitsky be exonerated. The appeals court accepted the appeal lodged by Mr. Verbitsky, the conviction of Mr. Verbitsky was reversed, and all its effects canceled. Most importantly, the law of desacato was repealed.

(3) The central U.S. Supreme Court defamation case is *New York Times Co. v. Sullivan*, 376 U.S. 254 (1964), in which an Alabama police commissioner claimed to have been libeled by a New York Times advertisement. The Supreme Court held that the petitioners were not liable for defamation because they had not acted recklessly – or as the Court put it – with "actual malice." *Id.* at 280. The plaintiffs needed to prove that the defendants' statement had been made with "knowledge that it was false or with reckless disregard of whether it was false or not." *Id.* The Court observed that "a rule compelling the critic of official conduct to guarantee the truth of all his factual assertions . . . leads to a comparable 'self-censorship' . . . [T]he rule thus dampens the vigor and limits the variety of public debate. . . . [which is] inconsistent with the First . . . Amendment[ ]." *Id.* at 279.

Other domestic common law traditions have adopted the *Sullivan* test. Consider the U.K. case, *Derbyshire County Council v. Times Newspapers Ltd and Others*, House of Lords, AC 534 (1993). Three articles regarding stock deals and the superannuation fund of the Derbyshire County Council appeared in the SUNDAY TIMES. The articles referred to David Bookbinder, a powerful member of the council, and Owen Oyston, a so-called media tycoon, and questioned the propriety of the investment of council's superannuation fund moneys in three deals with Oyston or companies controlled by him. Following publication of the articles, the council, Bookbinder, and Oyston brought actions in damages for libel against THE SUNDAY TIMES, its editor, and the two authors of the articles. [THE SUNDAY TIMES settled with Oyston. Bookbinder's action was subsequently lost on the merits.] In respect of the action brought by the council, the defendants applied to dismiss the council's claim on the grounds that the council lacked the legal capability to bring a libel action for criticism of the Council's governmental and administrative undertakings.

The court of appeal reversed the trial court's decision for the plaintiffs, ruling that although the common law was ambiguous as to whether local authorities may sue for libel, Article 10 of the European Convention did not allow liability. A public authority's libel action would stifle legitimate public criticism of its activities and would therefore interfere with the right of freedom of expression.

In a unanimous decision, the House of Lords affirmed the decision of the court of appeal. However, the Law Lords found it unnecessary to rely on Article 10 because they found no essential difference between English libel law and Article 10. Instead, the Lords based their decision on English common law, *New York Times v. Sullivan*, and the Illinois Supreme Court's *City of Chicago v. Tribune Co.*, 307 Ill. 595 (1923). The House of Lords held that a local authority does not have the right to maintain a civil action for defamation under any circumstances. The House of Lords overruled a previous precedent, *Bognor Regis Urban District Council v. Campion*, which failed to make the following vital distinction: a County Council is a corporation and a legal subject in English law, but it is also a public authority, a governmental body, democratically elected. The House recognized that in a democratic society individuals must be free to express criticism about a democratically elected governmental body or, indeed, any governmental body openly. The House also used *Attorney-General v. Guardian Newspapers Ltd (No. 2)*, [1990] 1 A.C. 109, 283–84, holding that there are rights available to private citizens that are not available to governmental institutions unless it can be shown that the exercise of these rights would be in the public interest. However, the House found that there was no public interest favoring the right of governmental organs in this case and that there was no pressing social need to extend a corporation's right to sue in libel to a municipal corporation seeking to protect its reputation.

In the Australian case, *Theophanous v. Herald & Weekly Times Ltd.*, High Court of Australia, [1993], 1994 AUSTL. L. J. 713 (1994), the plaintiff was a member of the Australian House of Representatives and chairperson of the Joint Parliamentary Standing Committee on Migration Regulations. The HERALD SUN newspaper published a letter entitled "Give Theophanous the Shove," from Bruce Ruxton. This letter essentially questioned the fitness of Theophanous to remain as chairperson of that parliamentary committee and suggested that his immigration policy preference had a pro-Greek bias, that he wished to undermine the status of English as Australia's main language, and that he was, all in all, an idiot.

Theophanous brought an action for defamation against both the Herald and Weekly Times Ltd (the publisher of the HERALD SUN) and Ruxton. The first defendant pleaded a defense based on an asserted freedom of communication guaranteed by the Constitution to publish discussions of government and political matters. The High Court of Australia addressed the question whether the Australian Constitution was written on the assumption that freedom of expression was protected by the common law. By a 4 to 3 majority the High Court held that there was such a constitutional guarantee. The court rejected the plaintiff's argument that the framers of the Constitution believed that fundamental freedoms "were best left to the protection of the common law in association with the doctrine of parliamentary supremacy." It held that the implied freedom of communication recognized in earlier cases was capable of overriding limits imposed by statute law and that it shapes and controls the common law. The court found that the purpose of freedom of communication is to ensure the efficacy of representative democracy. Mason CJ, Toohey, and Gaudron JJ believed that the constitutional implication did not extend to freedom of speech generally but was limited to "political discussion" or "political discourse" only, including discussion of the conduct, policies or fitness for office of government, political parties, public bodies, public officers and those seeking public office, and discussion of the political views and public conduct of persons who are engaged in activities that have become the subject of political debate. They indicated that commercial speech and defamatory comments made about the private life of a member of parliament or other matters unrelated to his or her conduct as a politician or suitability for office are not protected by the implied implication. They held that the impugned statements in this case were clearly within the concept of "political discussion." Deane J also considered that the extent of "political discussion" depends on the degree to which it supports the constitutional principle of representative government. The court held that the current defamation law was inconsistent with the requirements of the implied freedom because the common law of defamation is balanced too far against the freedom of communication and the existing law seriously inhibited freedom of communication on political matters. However, the court did not believe that "the efficacious working of representative democracy and government demands or needs protection in the form of an absolute immunity"; instead, the court held that "the freedom requires no more than that the person who publishes defamatory material in the course of political discussion does not know that it is false, does not publish recklessly, and does not publish unreasonably."

The High Court concluded the following: (i) there is implied in the Constitution a freedom to publish material discussing government and political matters of and concerning members of the Australian Parliament in relation to the performance by such members of their duties as members of the parliament or parliamentary committees, or in relation to the suitability of persons for office as members of the parliament; and (ii) the publication will not be actionable under the law relating to defamation if the defendant can establish that: (a) it was unaware of the falsity of the material published; (b) it did not publish the material recklessly (*i.e.*, it did not care whether the material was true or false); and (c) the publication was reasonable in the circumstances.

In *Rajagopal v. State of Tamil Nadu*, Supreme Ct. of India, 1994 S.C.C. 632 (1994), the Supreme Court of India, following *New York Times v. Sullivan*, ruled that public officials cannot obtain an injunction to restrain publication of a libel nor can they recover damages for libel with respect to the way in which they discharge their official duties, unless they can prove that the publication made by the defendant was false and made with reckless disregard for the truth. In such a case, it is not necessary for the defendant to prove that what she or he has published is true; instead, it is enough for the defendant to prove that she or he acted after a reasonable verification of the facts. In *dicta,* the court further suggested that in an appropriate case it would likely follow the U.S. Supreme Court's extension of the holding of *Sullivan* to public figures. In doing so, the court held that there is an implied constitutional right to privacy.

(4) *Hustler Magazine v. Falwell,* 485 U.S. 46 (1988), holds that the *New York Times* standard applies when a public figure seeks damages for intentional infliction of emotional distress. The case arose when Falwell, a prominent minister who was active in political affairs, sought damages for a "parody" advertisement in *Hustler* purporting to describe Falwell's first sexual experience. *Falwell* raises the question of whether the law of free expression might contribute to a coarsening of public discourse. Do the international human rights cases take that interest into account in assessing whether the restrictions on speech are necessary in a democratic society? Robert C. Post, *The Constitutional Concept of Public Discourse: Outrageous Opinion, Democratic Deliberation and Hustler Magazine v. Falwell*, 103 Harv. L. Rev. 603 (1990), argues that decisions in this area both express a decisions maker's conception of what democracy is and help define the kind of democracy there is. Can you devise rules of public discourse that could inhibit the coarsening of public discourse without depriving the public of valuable political commentary, or is the former an inevitable cost of the latter?

(5) The international right to freedom of expression protects statements that are not capable of verification. In other words, the right protects statements of opinion. In *Schwabe v. Austria,* 242-B Eur. Ct. H.R. (ser. A) (1992), the European Court of Human Rights addressed the issue of misleading statements. Schwabe, an Austrian citizen, was

a town councilor of St. Andrä and chairman of the local Young Austrian People's Party. When the mayor of a nearby village who belonged to Schwabe's party was involved in a hit-and-run car accident while under the influence of alcohol, the local chairman of the opposing Austrian Socialist Party was quoted in the newspaper calling for the mayor's resignation. In response, Schwabe issued a statement pointing out that a deputy in the Austrian Socialist Party had been involved in a similar accident while under the influence of alcohol twenty years earlier. Schwabe was then prosecuted and convicted for defamation and for having reproached a person with an offense for which he had already served his sentence. With respect to the defamation charge, the Austrian court had considered it decisive that the deputy had not, like the mayor, been convicted of drunken driving even though his blood alcohol was just beyond the legal limit at the time of the accident. Schwabe lost on appeal.

Before the European Court of Human Rights, Schwabe alleged that his convictions had violated his right to freedom of expression. The Court, considering the broader context in which Schwabe made his statement, found that the press release sought only to comment on political morality and to suggest that the two accidents had enough in common to warrant the resignation of both officials. It did not try to compare the two traffic accidents from a legal point of view. The impugned comparison thus amounted to a value judgment for which no proof was possible. And because "under the influence of alcohol" was not meant to be a legal judgment, the facts on which the value judgment was based were substantially correct. Accordingly, Schwabe's convictions violated Article 10.

For a discussion of the U.S. constitutional standards applicable to allegedly libelous statements on matters of fact versus opinion, see *Milkovich v. Lorain Journal Co.*, 497 U.S. 1 (1990), holding that liability can be imposed only with respect to statements that are "provable as false." It is therefore unnecessary in U.S. law to ask whether the statement at issue is factual or opinion.

(6) In several cases, the European Court of Human Rights has held defamation suits filed by judges to be compatible with Article 10. *See, e.g., Prager and Oberschlick v. Austria*, 313 Eur. Ct. H.R. (1995); *Barfod v. Denmark*, 149 Eur. Ct. H.R. (ser. A) (1989). How does U.S. law limit speech critical of judges outside the court?

(7) In *Thorgeirson v. Iceland*, 236 & 239 Eur. Ct. H.R. (ser. A) (1994), the applicant commented on alleged police brutality in a newspaper article. The applicant based his criticism on an undisputed fact and only referred to stories and rumors. The European Court held that his article was "fair comment" protected by Article 10. Is the reporting of rumors as rumors protected by the First Amendment under U.S. Constitutional law?

(8) The disproportionate size of a libel award can also violate freedom of expression because of the chilling effect it can have on other protected speech. In *Tolstoy Miloslavsky v. United Kingdom*, 323 Eur. Ct. H.R. (ser. A) (1995), the applicant had been found liable for defamation in the English courts. An English jury subsequently awarded £1.5 million – three times the amount of the highest libel award previously made in England. The European Court found an Article 10 violation because of (i) the insufficient judicial control in setting aside disproportionate awards and (ii) the disproportionate size of the award.

What other ways can freedom of expression be "chilled" to such an extent that it violates either international law or the First Amendment?

Offensive Expression

J.R.T. and the W.G. Party v. Canada
UN Human Rights Committee
Communication No. 104/1981
Views adopted 6 April 1983
2 SELECTED DECISIONS OF THE HUMAN RIGHTS COMMITTEE
UNDER THE OPTIONAL PROTOCOL 25
U.N. Doc. CCPR/C/OP/2 (1990)

. . . .

1. The Communication [. . .] is submitted by Mr. T., a 69-year old Canadian citizen, residing in Canada, and by the W. G. Party, an unincorporated political party under the leadership of Mr. T. since 1976. It is claimed that Mr. T. and the W. G. Party are victims of infringements by the Canadian authorities of the right to hold and maintain their opinions without interference, in violation of article 19(1) of the International Covenant on Civil and Political Rights, and the right to freedom of expression and of the right to seek, receive and impart information and ideas of all kinds though the media of their choice, in violation of Article 19(2) of the Covenant.

2.1. The W. G. Party was founded as a political party in Toronto, Canada, in February 1972. The Party and Mr. T. attempted over several years to attract membership and promote the Party's policies through the use of tape-recorded messages, which were recorded by Mr. T. and linked up to the Bell Telephone System in Toronto, Ontario, Canada. Any member of the public could listen to the messages by dialling the relevant telephone number. The messages were changed from time to time but the contents were basically the same, namely to warn the callers "of the dangers of international finance and international Jewry leading the world into wars, unemployment and inflation and the collapse of world values and principles".

2.2. The Canadian Human Rights Act was promulgated on 1 March 1978. Section 13(1) of the Act reads as follows:

> It is a discriminatory practice for a person or a group of persons acting in concert to communicate telephonically or to cause to be so communicated, repeatedly, in whole or in part by means of the facilities of a telecommunication undertaking within the legislative authority of Parliament, any matter that is likely to expose a person or persons to hatred or contempt by reason of the fact that the person or those persons are identifiable on the basis of a prohibited ground or discrimination.

2.3. By application of this provision in conjunction with section 3 of the Act, which enumerates "race, national or ethnic origin, color, religion, age, sex, marital status, conviction for which a pardon has been granted and physical handicap" as "prohibited ground of discrimination," the telephone service of the W. G. Party and Mr. T. was curtailed. It is alleged that section 13(1) of the Human Rights Act is clearly in violation of the Canadian Bill of Rights. Section 1(d) of the Bill of Rights guarantees freedom of speech, and section 2 states that it shall not be abrogated, abridged or infringed unless expressly authorized by Act of Parliament. It is claimed that the Canadian Human Rights Act contains no provision authorizing such restriction.

2.4. Section 32 of the Human Rights Act enables any individual having reasonable grounds for believing that a person is engaging in a "discriminatory practice" to file a complaint before the Canadian Human Rights Commission. Under this provision, a number of Jewish groups and individual Jews filed letters complaining about Mr. T's messages. In consequence, the Canadian Human Rights Commission initiated complaint proceedings against Mr. T. and the W. G. Party on 16 January 1979 for messages recorded on 6 July, 27 September, 17 November, 14 and 19 December 1978 and 9 January 1979, and decided to appoint a Human Rights Tribunal to inquire into the complaints and to determine whether the matters communicated telephonically by the W. G. Party and Mr. T. would be likely to expose persons identifiable by race and religion to hatred and contempt. The hearings of the Tribunal were carried out on 12, 13, 14 and 15 June 1979 and a decision was made on 20 July 1979. The Tribunal found that "although some of the messages are somewhat innocuous, the matter for the most part that they have communicated is likely to expose a person or persons to hatred or contempt by reason of the fact that the person is identifiable by race or religion and in particular, the messages identify specific individuals by name". It held, therefore, that the complaints were substantiated and ordered the W. G. Party and Mr. T. to cease using the telephone to communicate the subject matter which had formed the contents of the tape-recorded messages referred to in the complaints.

2.5. The Canadian Human Rights Commission sent the decision of the Tribunal to the Federal Court for the purpose of enforcement on 22 August 1979, pursuant to section 43 of the Canadian Human Rights Act, and it was filed pursuant to Federal Court Rule 201(1a)(a); the decision thereupon became enforceable in the same manner as an order of that Court....

2.6. On 31 August 1979, [...] the Canadian Human Rights Commission recorded a new message from the telephone service of the W. G. Party, complaining that "we are now denied the right to expose the race and religion of certain people, regardless of their guilt in the destruction of Canada" and adding "those who do not believe there is a preponderance of certain racial and religious minorities involved in the corruption of our Christian way of life will never understand the simple basis of our way of life – the common denominator." In this connection, the Canadian Human Rights Commission instructed its Legal Counsel to write to Mr. T. He warned Mr. T. on 2 October 1979, that if these particular passages were not deleted from the recordings by 10 October 1979, he would make an application to the Federal Court to enforce the Tribunal order. Mr. T. responded by letter dated 10 October 1979 that, although he did not agree that the passages were in contravention of the order of the Tribunal, he would change the messages.

2.7. Subsequent to Mr. T.'s letter of reply, Mr. T. and the W. G. Party continued to use messages that were deemed to be in contravention of the Tribunal order, and therefore an *ex parte* application was made to the Federal Court, Trial Division, by the Canadian Human Rights Commission to the effect that acts had been committed by Mr. T. contrary to the order of a Human Rights Tribunal. A transcript of the allegedly offensive messages dated 7 and 31 August 1979, 12 October 1979, and 27 November 1979 was placed before the Federal Court. Mr. T. and the W. G. Party were ordered to appear before the Federal Court on 19 February 1980 to hear proof that they had disobeyed the order and to submit a defence.

2.8. The contempt of court proceedings took place before the Federal Court. After hearing the Legal Counsel for the Canadian Human Rights Commission and Mr. T., it concluded that the Commission had established beyond any doubt that Mr. T. and the W.

G. Party had disobeyed the order made by the Human Rights Tribunal and had made use of the telephone services to convey the type of messages which they were prohibited from disseminating, namely, that "some corrupt Jewish international conspiracy is depriving the callers of their birthright and that the white race should stand up and fight back". The Court decided on 21 February 1980 that Mr. T. was guilty of contempt of court and sentenced him to one year imprisonment and the W. G. Party to pay a fine of $5,000. The sentences were to be suspended as long as Mr. T. and the W. G. Party did not use telephone communications for the dissemination of hate messages.

. . . .

6.1. In its submission dated 10 May 1982, the State party objected to the admissibility of the communication on various grounds.

6.2. As regards the allegation that prosecution under section 13 of the Canadian Human Rights Act resulted in a breach of article 19 and, by inference, articles 2 and 26 of the Covenant, the State party submits that no breach of the Covenant occurred. It states that the impugned provision of the Canadian Human Rights Act does not contravene these provisions of the Covenant, but in fact gives effect to article 20(2) of the Covenant. Thus, not only is the author's "right" to communicate racist ideas not protected by the Covenant, it is in fact incompatible with its provisions, and therefore this part of the communication is in this respect inadmissible under articles 1, 2 and 3 of the Optional Protocol.

. . . .

8. On the basis of the information before it the Human Rights Committee... concludes:

. . . .

(b). . . . [T]he opinions which Mr. T. seeks to disseminate through the telephone system clearly constitute the advocacy of racial or religious hatred which Canada has an obligation under article 20 (2) of the Covenant to prohibit. In the Committee's opinion, therefore, the communication is . . . incompatible with the provisions of the Covenant, within the meaning of article 3 of the Optional Protocol;

. . . .

≈

QUESTIONS & COMMENTS

(1) The European Commission and Court of Human Rights also have addressed racist expression. For example, in *Glimmerveen and Hagenbeek v. the Netherlands*, 18 Eur. Cm. H.R. 187 (1980), the applicants were leading members of the "*Nederlandse Volks Unie*" (NVU), a political party whose basic principle is that the state should be ethnically homogenous. If the NVU attained power, they intended to expel the nonwhite Dutch persons from the Netherlands. In 1977, Gimmerveen was convicted for having possessed with a view to distribute leaflets that a Dutch court found to be inciting racial discrimination. Gimmerveen appealed against his conviction. The Court of Appeal of the Hague upheld the decision. Gimmerveen then lodged a plea of nullity with the Supreme Court in the Hague. He claimed that the Dutch penal code had been wrongly applied and

that his Article 10 rights (under the European Convention[1]) had been disregarded. His political party, he stated, envisaged the realization of its aims only by "lawful means." In 1978, Gimmerveen and Hagenbeek submitted their names on a slate as candidates for the Hague's municipal council. Their submission did not name the NVU party. The central voting board decided their submission was invalid. The NVU had been declared a "prohibited association" earlier by the Amsterdam Regional Court. Because of this, the central voting board considered the proposed slate of candidates unacceptable. Gimmerveen appealed to the provisional board of Southern Holland. The board dismissed the appeal pointing out that the courts had determined that NVU's aims were contrary to public order. Since the party's name could not be submitted for public office, a slate that functioned as a cloak for the prohibited association also could not be submitted for public office.

Gimmerveen and Hagenbeek applied to the European Commission claiming their Article 10 rights had been violated. They argued that the Dutch authorities, by convicting them of possessing leaflets and by preventing them from participating in the elections, disregarded their basic and fundamental rights. In its decision, the European Commission pointed out that Article 10 is designed to protect offensive as well as inoffensive information or ideas. Without pluralism, tolerance and broad-mindedness, there could be no "democratic society." Article 17 of the Convention, however, attempts to prevent totalitarian groups from exploiting these principles for their own interests. It states:

> Nothing in this Convention may be interpreted as implying for any state, group or person any right to engage in any activity or perform any act aimed at the destruction of any of the rights and freedoms set forth herein. . . .

The Commission also discussed Article 14's prohibition against discrimination on racial or color bases. The Commission interpreted the applicant's claims in light of these provisions by first stating that if the Netherlands' authorities had allowed the NVU to proclaim their ideas freely and without penalty, these ideas would encourage the discrimination prohibited by Article 14 of the Convention. The Commission also determined that the expression of NVU's political ideas clearly constituted an activity within the meaning of Article 17, which states:

> Nothing in this Convention may be interpreted as implying for any State, group or person any right to engage in any activity or perform any act aimed at the destruction of any of the rights and freedoms set forth herein or at their limitation to a greater extent than is provided for in the Convention.

The NVU sought to destroy the rights and freedoms of all nonwhite Dutch persons. The NVU were essentially seeking to use Article 10 to provide a basis for a right to engage in these activities that are contrary to the text and spirit of the Convention. If this right were granted, it would contribute to the destruction of others' rights and freedoms. Consequently, the Commission found that the applicants could not, by reason of the provisions of Article 17, rely on Article 10 of the Convention.

(2) International freedom of expression law protects the messenger but often not the message. In *Jersild v. Denmark*, 298 Eur. Ct. H.R. (ser. A) (1994), the European Court of Human Rights upheld the reporting of an interview with racist "skinheads" by a reporter.

---

[1] The Netherlands has incorporated the European Convention into its domestic law.

The European Court in *Weber v. Switzerland,* 177 Eur. Ct. H.R. (ser. A) (1990), earlier used a similar principle. In *Weber,* the Court held that a journalist's report of a criminal complaint of judicial abuse of power was protected under Article 10.

(3) Under *Glimmerveen and Hagenbeek v. the Netherlands, Jersild v. Denmark,* and/or *J.R.T. and the W. G. Party v. Canada,* is there any way that one can express racist ideas without coming into conflict with the international law governing freedom of expression and racial discrimination?

(4) What would the result be in *R.A.V. v. City of St. Paul,* 505 U.S. 377 (1992) (invalidating city ordinance prohibiting "hate speech"), under the standard articulated in *J.R.T. and the W. G. Party v. Canada*? What implications should be drawn if applying this standard would lead to upholding the St. Paul ordinance: (a) international human rights standards are insufficiently sensitive to free expression interests or (b) U.S. constitutional law is insufficiently sensitive to issues of racial discrimination?

(5) In *Faurisson v. France,* Communication No. 550/1993 (views adopted 8 Nov. 1996), [1996] IIHRL 86 (8 Nov. 1996), the UN Human Rights Committee held that the author's right to freedom of expression was not violated when France prosecuted him for his public statements denying the existence of gas chambers during the Holocaust. The UNHRC found that Faurisson was not convicted for holding and expressing an opinion in general but for having violated the rights and reputations of others. The UNHRC further found that because his statements were of a nature to raise or strengthen anti-Semitic feelings, the restriction placed on his freedom of expression by the conviction served to protect the Jewish community's ability to live free from fear of an atmosphere of anti-Semitism.

Müller and Others v. Switzerland
European Court of Human Rights
133 Eur. Ct. H.R. (ser. A) (1988)
13 E.H.R.R. 212 (1991)

. . . .

FACTS:

I. The circumstances of the case

8. The first applicant, Josef Felix Müller, a painter born in 1955, lives in St Gall. The other nine applicants are [omitted]

. . . .

10. In 1981, the nine last-mentioned applicants mounted an exhibition of contemporary art in Fribourg at the former Grand Seminary, a building due to be demolished. The exhibition, entitled 'Fri-Art 81,' was held as part of the celebrations of the 500th anniversary of the Canton of Fribourg's entry into the Swiss Confederation. The organisers invited several artists to take part, each of whom was allowed to invite another artist of his own choosing. The artists were meant to make free use of the space allocated to them. Their works, which they created on the spot from early August 1981 onwards, were to have been removed when the exhibition ended on 18 October 1981.

11. In the space of three nights Josef Felix Müller, who had been invited by one of the other artists, produced three large paintings (measuring 3.11 m × 2.24 m, 2.97 m × 1.98 m and 3.74 m × 2.20 m) entitled '*Drei Nächte, drei Bilder*' ('Three Nights, Three Pictures').

They were on show when the exhibition began on 21 August 1981. The exhibition had been advertised in the press and on posters and was open to all, without any charge being made for admission. The catalogue, specially printed for the preview, contained a photographic reproduction of the paintings.

12. On 4 September 1981, the day of the official opening, the principal public prosecutor of the Canton of Fribourg reported to the investigating judge that the paintings in question appeared to come within the provisions of Article 204 of the Criminal Code, which prohibited obscene publications and required that they be destroyed. The prosecutor thought that one of the three pictures also infringed freedom of religious belief and worship within the meaning of Article 261 of the Criminal Code.

According to the Government, the prosecutor had acted on an information laid by a man whose daughter, a minor, had reacted violently to the paintings on show; some days earlier another visitor to the exhibition had apparently thrown down one of the paintings, trampled on it and crumpled it.

13. Accompanied by his clerk and some police officers, the investigating judge went to the exhibition on 4 September and had the pictures in question removed and seized; ten days later, he issued an attachment order. On 30 September 1981, the Indictment Chamber dismissed an appeal against that decision.

After questioning the ten applicants on 10, 15 and 17 September and 6 November 1981, the investigating judge committed them for trial to the Sarine District Criminal Court.

14. On 24 February 1982, the court sentenced each of them to a fine of 300 [Swiss francs] for publishing obscene material (Art 204(1) of the Criminal Code.) – the convictions to be deleted from the criminal records after one year – but acquitted them on the charge of infringing freedom of religious belief and worship. (Art 261.) It also ordered that the confiscated paintings should be deposited in the Art and History Museum of the Canton of Fribourg for safekeeping. At the hearing on 24 February, it had heard evidence from Mr. Jean-Christophe Ammann, the curator of the Kunsthalle in Basel, as to Josef Felix Müller's artistic qualities.

In its judgment, the court pointed out first of all that 'the law [did] not define obscenity for the purposes of Article 204 CC [Criminal Code] and the concept [had] to be clarified by means of interpretation, having regard to the intent and purpose of the enactment as well as to its place in the legislation and in the overall legal system.' After referring to the Federal Court's case law on the subject, it said among other things:

> In the instant case, although Mr. Müller's three works are not sexually arousing to a person of ordinary sensitivity, they are undoubtedly repugnant at the very least. The overall impression is of persons giving free rein to licentiousness and even perversion. The subjects – sodomy, fellatio, bestiality, the erect penis – are obvious morally offensive to the vast majority of the population. Although allowance has to be made for changes in the moral climate, even for the worse, what we have here would revolutionise it. Comment on the confiscated works is superfluous; their vulgarity is plain to see and needs no elaborating upon.
>
> . . . .
>
> Nor can a person of ordinary sensitivity be expected to go behind what is actually depicted and make a second assessment of the picture independently of what he can actually see. To do that he would have to be accompanied to exhibitions by a

procession of sexologists, psychologists, art theorists or ethnologists in order to have explained to him that what he saw was in reality what he wrongly thought he saw.

Lastly, the comparisons with the works of Michelangelo and J Bosch are specious. Apart from the fact that they contain no depictions of the kind in Müller's paintings, no valid comparison can be made with history-of-art or cultural collections in which sexuality has a place . . . , but without lapsing into crudity. Even with an artistic aim, crude sexuality is not worthy of protection . . . Nor are comparisons with civilisations foreign to western civilisation valid.

On the question whether to order the destruction of the pictures under paragraph 3 of Article 204, the court said:

Not without misgivings, the court will not order the destruction of the three works.

The artistic merit of the three works exhibited in Fribourg is admittedly less obvious than is supposed by the witness Ammann, who nevertheless said that the paintings Müller exhibited in Basel were more "demanding." The court would not disagree. Müller is undoubtedly an artist of some accomplishment, particularly in the matter of composition and in the use of colour, even though the works seized in Fribourg appear rather skimped.

Nonetheless, the court, deferring to the art critic's opinion while not sharing it, and concurring with the relevant findings of the Federal Court in the *Rey* judgment, (ATF 89 IV 136 *et seq.*) takes the view that in order to withhold the three paintings from the general public – to "destroy" them – it is sufficient to place them in a museum, whose curator will be required to make them available only to a few serious specialists capable of taking an exclusively artistic or cultural interest in them as opposed to a prurient interest. The Art and History Museum of the Canton of Fribourg meets the requirements for preventing any further breach of Article 204 of the Criminal Code. The three confiscated paintings will be deposited there.

15. All the applicants appealed on points of law on 24 February 1982; in particular, they challenged the trial court's interpretation as regards the obscenity of the relevant paintings. For example, it was argued by Josef Felix Müller (in pleadings of 16 March 1982) that something which was obscene sought directly to arouse sexual passion, and that this had to be its purpose, with the essential aim of pandering to man's lowest instincts or else for pecuniary gain. This, it was alleged, was never the case 'where artistic or scientific endeavour [was] the primary consideration.'

16. The Fribourg Cantonal Court, sitting as a court of cassation, dismissed the appeals on 26 April 1982.

Referring to the Federal Court's case law, it acknowledged that 'in the recent past, and still today, the public's general views on morality and social mores, which vary at different times and in different places, have changed in a way which enables things to be seen more objectively and naturally.' The trial court had to take account of this change, but that did not mean that it had to show complete permissiveness, which would leave no scope for the application of Article 204 of the Criminal Code.

As for works of art, they did not in themselves have any privileged status. At most they might escape destruction despite their obscenity. Their creators nonetheless fell within the thrust of Article 204, 'since that statutory provision as a whole [was] designed to protect public morals, even in the sphere of the fine arts.' That being so, the court could dispense with deciding the question whether the pictures complained of were the outcome of 'artistic ideas, though even then, intention [was] one thing and realisation of it another.'

Like the trial court, the appellate court found that Josef Felix Müller's paintings aroused 'repugnance and disgust':

> These are not works which, in treating a particular subject or scene, allude to sexual activity more or less discreetly. They place it in the foreground, depicting it not in the embrace of man and woman but in vulgar images of sodomy, fellatio between males, bestiality, erect penises and masturbation. Sexual activity is the main, not to say sole, ingredient of all three paintings, and neither the appellants' explanations nor the witness Mr. Ammann's learned-seeming but wholly unpersuasive remarks can alter that fact. To go into detail, however distasteful it may be, one of the paintings contains no fewer than eight erect members. All the persons depicted are entirely naked and one of them is engaging simultaneously in various sexual practices with two other males and an animal. He is kneeling down and not only sodomising the animal but holding its erect penis in another animal's mouth. At the same time he is having the lower part of his back – his buttocks, even – fondled by another male, whose erect penis a third male is holding towards the first male's mouth. The animal being sodomised has its tongue extended towards the buttocks of a fourth male, whose penis is likewise erect. Even the animals' tongues (especially in the smallest painting) are more suggestive, in shape and aspect, of erect male organs than of tongues. Sexual activity is crudely and vulgarly portrayed for its own sake and not as a consequence of any idea informing the work. Lastly, it should be pointed out that the paintings are large . . . , with the result that their crudeness and vulgarity are all the more offensive.
>
> The court is likewise unconvinced by the appellants' contention that the paintings are symbolic. What counts is their face value, their effect on the observer, not some abstraction utterly unconnected with the visible image or which glosses over it. Furthermore, the important thing is not the artist's meaning or purported meaning but the objective effect of the image on the observer. . . .
>
> Not much of the argument in the appeal was directed to the issues of intention or of awareness of obscenity, nor indeed could it have been. In particular, an author is aware of a publication's obscenity when he knows it deals with sexual matters and that any written or pictorial allusion to such matters is likely, in the light of generally accepted views, grossly to offend the average reader's or observer's natural sense of decency and propriety. That was plainly so here, as the evidence at the trial confirmed. . . . Indeed, several of the defendants admitted that the paintings had shocked them. It should be noted that even someone insensible to obscenity is capable of realising that it may disturb others. As the trial court pointed out, the defendants at the very least acted recklessly.
>
> Lastly, it is immaterial that similar works have allegedly been exhibited elsewhere; the three paintings in issue do not on that account cease to be obscene, as the trial court rightly held them to be. . . .

17. On 18 June 1982, the applicants lodged an application for a declaration of nullity (*Nichtigkeitsbeschwerde*) with the Federal Court. They sought to have the judgment of

26 April set aside and the case remitted with a view to their acquittal and the return of the confiscated paintings or, in the alternative, merely the return of the paintings.

In their submission, the Fribourg Cantonal Court had wrongly interpreted Article 204 of the Criminal Code; in particular, it had taken no account of the scope of the freedom of artistic expression, guaranteed *inter alia* in Article 10 of the Convention. Mr. Ammann, one of the most distinguished experts on modern art, had confirmed that these were works of note. Similar pictures by Josef Felix Müller, moreover, had been exhibited in Basel in February 1982 and it had not occurred to anyone to regard them as being obscene.

As to the 'publication' of the obscene items, which was prohibited under Article 204 of the Criminal Code, this was a relative concept. It should be possible to show in an exhibition which, if they were displayed in the market-place, would fall foul of Article 204; people interested in the arts ought to have an opportunity to acquaint themselves with all the trends in contemporary art. Visitors to an exhibition of contemporary art like 'Fri-Art 81' should expect to be faced with modern works that might be incomprehensible. If they did not like the paintings in issue, they were free to look away from them and pass them by; there was no need for the protection of the criminal law. It was not for the court to undertake indirect censorship of the arts. On a strict construction of Article 204 – that is, one which, having regard to the fundamental right to freedom of artistic expression, left it to art-lovers to decide for themselves what they wanted to see –, the applicants should be acquitted.

Confiscation of the paintings in question, they submitted, could only be ordered if they represented a danger to public order such that returning them could not be justified – and that was a matter the court of cassation had not considered. Since the pictures had been openly on display for ten days without giving rise to any protests, it was difficult to see how such a danger was made out. Josef Felix Müller would certainly not show his paintings in Fribourg in the near future. On the other hand, they could be shown without any difficulty elsewhere, as was proved by his exhibition in Basel in February 1982. It was consequently out of all proportion to deprive him of them.

18. The Criminal Cassation Division of the Federal Court dismissed the appeal on 26 January 1983 for the following reasons:

> The decided cases show that for the purposes of Article 204 of the Criminal Code, any item is obscene which offends, in a manner that is difficult to accept, the sense of sexual propriety; the effect of the obscenity may be to arouse a normal person sexually or to disgust or repel him. . . . The test of obscenity to be applied by the court is whether the overall impression of the item or work causes moral offence to a person of ordinary sensitivity. . . .
>
> The paintings in issue show an orgy of unnatural sexual practices (sodomy, bestiality, petting), which is crudely depicted in large format; they are liable grossly to offend the sense of sexual propriety of persons of ordinary sensitivity. The artistic licence relied on by the appellant cannot in any way alter that conclusion in the instant case.
>
> The content and scope of constitutional freedoms are determined on the basis of the federal law currently in force. This applies *inter alia* to freedom of the press, freedom of opinion and artistic freedom; under Article 113 [of the Federal Constitution], the Federal Court is bound by federal enactments. . . . In the field of artistic creation [it] has held that works of art *per se* do not enjoy any special status. . . . A work of art is not obscene, however, if the artist contrives to present subjects of a sexual

nature in an artistic form such that their offensiveness is toned down and ceases to predominate.... In reaching its decision, the criminal court does not have to view the work through an art critic's spectacles (which would often ill become it) but must decide whether the work is liable to offend the unsuspecting visitor.

Expert opinion as to the artistic merit of the work in issue is therefore irrelevant at this stage, though it might be relevant to the decision as to what action to take in order to prevent fresh offences (destruction or seizure of the item). (Art 204(3) CC.)

The Cantonal Court duly scrutinised the paintings for a predominantly aesthetic element. Having regard in particular to the number of sexual features in each of the three (one of them, for instance, contains eight erect members), it decided that the emphasis was on sexuality in its offensive forms and that this was the predominant, not to say sole, ingredient of the items in dispute. The Cassation Division of the Federal Court agrees. The overall impression created by Müller's paintings is such as to be morally offensive to a person of normal sensitivity. The Cantonal Court's finding that they were obscene was accordingly not in breach of federal law.

The appellants maintained that the publication element of the offences was lacking. They were wrong.

The obscene paintings were on display in an exhibition open to the public which had been advertised on posters and in the press. There was no condition of admission to "Fri-Art 81," such as an age limit. The paintings in dispute were thus made accessible to an indeterminate number of people, which is the criterion of publicity for the purposes of Article 204 CC. . . .

Finally, the Criminal Cassation Division of the Federal Court declared the alternative application for return of the paintings to be inadmissible as it had not first been made before the cantonal courts.

19. On 20 January 1988, the Sarine District Criminal Court granted an application made by Josef Felix Müller on 29 June 1987 and ordered the return of the paintings.

On the basis that it had been requested in effect to reconsider the confiscation order it had made in 1982, the court held that it had to decide whether the order could stand 'almost eight years later.' Hence the reasons for its decision were as follows:

In Swiss law, confiscation is a preventive measure *in rem*. This is already clear from the legislative text, which classifies Article 58 under the heading "other measures" – the heading in the margin for Articles 57–62 CC – and not under the subsidiary penalties prescribed in Articles 51–56 CC. . . .

The confiscation of items or assets may admittedly constitute a serious interference with property rights. It must be proportionate and a more lenient order may thus be justified where it achieves the desired aim. Confiscation however remains the rule. It should be departed from only where a more lenient order achieves the desired aim.... In this case, when the confiscation order was made in 1982, the statutory provision (Art 204(3) CC.) would normally have required the destruction of the paintings. Giving a reasoned decision, the court preferred a more lenient measure which achieved the aim of security, whilst complying with the principle of proportionality.... The measure itself should remain in force only as long as the statutory requirements are satisfied. . . .

It is true that the Code makes no provision for an order under Article 58 to be subsequently discharged or varied. The legislature probably did not address itself to this question at the time, whereas provision was made whereby other measures, which were admittedly much more serious because they restricted personal liberty, could be re-examined by a court of its own motion. (Arts 42–44 CC.) It does not follow that discharge or variation is completely illegal. The Federal Court has, moreover, held that a measure should not remain in force where the circumstances justifying it cease to obtain. . . .

Accordingly, the view must be taken that an order confiscating a work of art may subsequently be discharged or varied, either because the confiscated item is no longer dangerous and a measure is no longer required, or because the necessary degree of security may be achieved by another more lenient measure. (Judgment of the Basel-Urban Court of Appeal of 19 August 1980, in the *Fahrner* case.)

Judgments concerning freedom of expression and its scope often refer to Article 10(1) and (2) [of the Convention].

In this area, the decisions of the Convention authorities have a direct influence on the Swiss legal system, by way of strengthening individual liberties and judicial safeguards. . . .

In this case, where the applicant has availed himself of the possibility of applying for the return of his paintings, the court must consider whether the grounds on which it made the confiscation order in the first place, which restricted JF Müller's freedom of expression, are still valid.

While the restriction was necessary in a democratic society in 1982 and was justified by the need to safeguard and protect morality and the rights of others, the court considers, admittedly with some hesitation, that the order may now be discharged. It should be noted that the confiscation measure was not absolute but merely of indeterminate duration, which left room to apply for a reconsideration.

It appears to the court that the preventive measure has now fulfilled its function, namely to ensure that such paintings are not exhibited in public again without any precautions. Those convicted have themselves admitted that the paintings could shock people. Once the order has achieved its aim, there is no reason why it should continue in force.

Accordingly, the artist is entitled to have his works returned to him.

It is not necessary to attach any obligations to this decision. If JF Müller decided to exhibit the three paintings again elsewhere, he knows that he would be running the risk of further action by the courts under Article 204 of the Criminal Code.

Finally, it appears that by exhibiting three provocative paintings in a former seminary in 1982, JF Müller deliberately intended to draw attention to himself and the organisers. Since then he has become known for more "demanding" works, to use the terms of the art critic who gave evidence in 1982. Having achieved a certain repute, he may find it unnecessary to shock by resorting to vulgarity. In any event, there is no reason to believe that he will use the three paintings in future to offend other people's moral sensibilities. . . .

Josef Felix Müller recovered his paintings in March 1988.

II. Relevant domestic law

20. Article 204 of the Swiss Criminal code provides:

1. Anyone who makes or has in his possession any writings, pictures, films or other items which are obscene with a view to trading in them, distributing them or

displaying them in public, or who, for the above purposes, imports, transports or exports such items or puts them into circulation in any way, or who openly or secretly deals in them or publicly distributes or displays them or by way of trade supplies them for hire, or who announces or makes known in any way, with a view to facilitating such prohibited circulation or trade, that anyone is engaged in any of the aforesaid punishable activities, or who announces or makes known how or through whom such items may be directly or indirectly procured, shall be imprisoned or fined.

2. Anyone supplying or displaying such items to a person under the age of 18 shall be imprisoned or fined.

3. The court shall order the destruction of the items.

The Federal Court has consistently held that any works or items which offend, in a manner that is difficult to accept, the sense of sexual propriety, are obscene; the effect may be to arouse a normal person sexually or to disgust or repel him [citations omitted]; making such items available to an indeterminate number of people amounts to 'publication' of them.

21. The Federal Court held in 1963 that, for the purposes of paragraph 3 of Article 204, if an obscene object was of undoubted cultural interest, it was sufficient to withhold it from the general public in order to 'destroy' it.

In its judgment of 10 May 1963 in the case of *Rey v. Attorney General of Valais*, (ATF vol. 89 (1963), part IV, pp 133–140.) it held *inter alia* 'that, in making destruction mandatory, the legislature had in contemplation only the commonest case, publication of entirely pornographic items.' As 'destruction is a measure as opposed to a punishment,' 'it must not go beyond what is necessary to achieve the desired aim,' that is to say 'the protection of public morality.' The court went on to state:

In other words, "destruction," as prescribed by Article 204(3) of the Criminal Code, must protect public morality but go no further than that requirement warrants.

In the commonest case, that of pornographic publications devoid of artistic, literary or scientific merit, the destruction will be physical and irreversible, not just because of the lack of any cultural value, but also because, in general, this is the only adequate way of ultimately protecting the public from the danger of confiscated items....

It is quite a different matter when one is dealing, as in the present case, with an irreplaceable or virtually irreplaceable work of art. There is then a clash of two opposing interests, both of them important in terms of the civilisation to which Switzerland belongs: the moral and the cultural interest. In such a case, the legislature and the courts must find a way of reconciling the two. This court has thus held, in applying Article 204, that it must always be borne in mind that artistic creativity is itself subject to certain constraints of public morality, but that there must nonetheless be artistic freedom....

It is, accordingly, a matter for the courts to consider in each case in view of all the circumstances, whether physical destruction is essential or whether a more lenient measure suffices. The mandatory requirement of Article 204(3) will, therefore, be complied with where the courts order that an obscene item devoid of any cultural value is to be physically destroyed, and, in respect of an item of undoubted cultural interest, where effective steps are taken to withhold it from the general public and to make it available only to a limited number of serious specialists....

If such precautions are taken, Article 204 of the Criminal Code will not be applicable to items which are inherently obscene but of genuine cultural interest. A distinction must also be drawn between such items and pure pornography. The cultural interest of an item admittedly does not prevent it from being obscene. But it does require the courts to determine with particular care what steps must be taken to prevent general access to the item, while making it available to a well-defined number of serious connoisseurs; this will comply with the requirements of Article 204(3) of the Criminal Code, which, as has been shown, makes destruction mandatory but only as a measure whose effects must be in proportion to the intended aim....

This particular case concerned seven ivory reliefs and thirty prints of antique Japanese art; the court held that the requirement to 'destroy' them was met by placing them in a museum.

22. Previous the Sarine District Criminal Court's decision of 20 January 1988, the Basel-Urban Court of Appeal had already discharged a confiscation order made pursuant to the Criminal Code. In a judgment of 29 August 1980, to which the District Court referred, the Court of Appeal granted an application to restore to the heirs of the painter Kurt Fahrner a painting confiscated in 1960, after he had been convicted of an infringement of freedom of religious belief and worship. (Art 261 of the Criminal Code.)

The Court of Appeal held *inter alia* that as confiscation 'always interferes with the property rights of the person concerned, a degree of restraint is called for and, in accordance with the principle of proportionality, such a measure must go no further than is essential to maintain security.' The Court added (translation from the German):

This principle applies, in particular, where (on account of its distinctiveness) the item subject to confiscation is hard or impossible to replace. Therefore the principle applies more strictly to a work of art (*e.g.*, a painting) than to a weapon used to commit an offence.... Finally, having regard to its preventive character, the measure should remain in force only for as long as the legal requirements are satisfied....

Accordingly, the view had to be taken that 'an order confiscating a work of art may subsequently be discharged or varied, either because the confiscated item is no longer dangerous and the measure no longer required, or because the necessary degree of security may be achieved by another more lenient measure.'

In that particular case, the reasoning of the Court of Appeal was as follows:

To apply present-day criteria, both parties agree with the court that the public's ideas of obscenity, immorality, indecency, blasphemy, etc have changed considerably in the last twenty years and have become distinctly more liberal. Although the confiscated painting is undoubtedly liable to offend a great many people's religious sensibilities even today, there is no reason to fear that, by exhibiting it in a private or suitable public place, one would be endangering religious harmony, public safety, morals or public order within the meaning of Article 58 of the Criminal Code ...

Whether there is a danger thus depends primarily on where the item to be confiscated is liable to end up.... In this case, the exhibition of the painting in a museum would at present clearly be unobjectionable in the context of Article 58 of the Criminal Code. However, even if the picture were to be returned unconditionally, the likelihood of misuse must be regarded as minimal because Fahrner, who deliberately set out, by means of a provocative exhibition, to draw attention to himself as a painter and to his ideas and works, has since died. There is no reason to believe that the applicants have any intention of using the picture to offend other people's religious sensibilities. At any rate, the picture would not lend itself to such a purpose (Art 261 of the Criminal Code.) sufficiently to permit the 1960 confiscation order to stand.... Any danger of that kind arising from the picture is no longer serious enough to justify action under Article 58 of the Criminal Code. Nor is there any reason to hand this picture over to a scientific collection, ie a museum, in order to protect the public and morality. The confiscation order should be discharged and the picture unconditionally returned to the applicants, whose main application is thus granted.

[The applicant applied to the European Commission of Human Rights which found a breach of Article 10 in respect of the confiscation of the paintings but not in respect of the conviction.]

    . . . .

DECISION [OF THE EUROPEAN COURT OF HUMAN RIGHTS]:

26. The applicants complained that their conviction and the confiscation of the paintings in issue violated Article 10 of the Convention....

The Government rejected this contention. The Commission too rejected it with regard to the first of the measures complained of but accepted it with regard to the second.

27. The applicants indisputably exercised their right to freedom of expression – the first applicant by painting and then exhibiting the works in question, and the nine others by giving him the opportunity to show them in public at the 'Fri-Art 81' exhibition they had mounted.

Admittedly, Article 10 does not specify that freedom of artistic expression, in issue here, comes within its ambit; but neither, on the other hand, does it distinguish between the various forms of expression. As those appearing before the court all acknowledged, it includes freedom of artistic expression – notably within freedom to receive and impart information and ideas – which affords the opportunity to take part in the public exchange of cultural, political and social information and ideas of all kinds. Confirmation, if any were needed, that this interpretation is correct, is provided by the second sentence of paragraph (1) of Article 10, which refers to 'broadcasting, television or cinema enterprises,' media whose activities extend to the field of art. Confirmation that the concept of freedom of expression is such as to include artistic expression is also to be found in Article 19(2) of the International Covenant on Civil and Political Rights, which specifically includes within the right of freedom of expression information and ideas 'in the form of art.'

28. The applicants clearly suffered 'interference by public authority' with the exercise of their freedom of expression – firstly, by reason of their conviction by the Sarine District Criminal Court on 24 February 1982, which was confirmed by the Fribourg Cantonal Court on 26 April 1982 and then by the Federal Court on 26 January 1983, and secondly on account of the confiscation of the paintings, which was ordered at the same time but subsequently lifted.

Such measures, which constitute 'penalties' or 'restrictions,' are not contrary to the Convention solely by virtue of the fact that they interfere with freedom of expression, as the exercise of this right may be curtailed under the conditions provided for in paragraph (2). Consequently, the two measures complained of did not infringe Article 10 if they were 'prescribed by law,' had one or more of the legitimate aims under paragraph (2) of that Article and were 'necessary in a democratic society' for achieving the aim or aims concerned.

Like the Commission, the Court will look in turn at the applicants' conviction and at the confiscation of the pictures from this point of view.

I. The applicants' conviction

1. 'Prescribed by law'

29. In the applicants' view, the terms of Article 204(1) of the Swiss Criminal Code, in particular the word 'obscene,' were too vague to enable the individual to regulate his conduct and consequently neither the artist nor the organisers of the exhibition could foresee that they would be committing an offence. This view was not shared by the Government and the Commission.

According to the Court's case law, 'foreseeability' is one of the requirements inherent in the phrase 'prescribed by law' in Article 10(2) of the Convention. A norm cannot be regarded as a 'law' unless it is formulated with sufficient precision to enable the citizen – if need be, with appropriate advice – to foresee, to a degree that is reasonable in the circumstances, the consequences which a given action may entail. [citation omitted] The Court has, however, already emphasised the impossibility of attaining absolute precision in the framing of laws, particularly in fields in which the situation changes according to the prevailing views of society. (*Barthold v. Germany* (1985) [citation omitted]) The need to avoid excessive rigidity and to keep pace with changing circumstances means that many laws are inevitably couched in terms which, to a greater or lesser extent, are vague. (*Olsen v. Sweden*) Criminal law provisions on obscenity fall within this category.

In the present instance, it is also relevant to note that there were a number of consistent decisions by the Federal Court on the 'publication' of 'obscene' items. These decisions, which were accessible because they had been published and which were followed by the lower courts, supplemented the letter of Article 204(1) of the Criminal Code. The applicants' conviction was therefore 'prescribed by law' within the meaning of Article 10(2) of the Convention.

2. The legitimacy of the aim pursued

30. The Government contended that the aim of the interference complained of was to protect morals and the rights of others. On the latter point, it relied above all on the reaction of a man and his daughter who visited the 'Fri-Art 81' exhibition.

The Court accepts that Article 204 of the Swiss Criminal Code is designed to protect public morals, and there is no reason to suppose that in applying it in the instant case the Swiss courts had any other objectives that would have been incompatible with the Convention. Moreover, as the Commission pointed out, there is a natural link between protection of morals and protection of the rights of others.

The applicants' conviction consequently had a legitimate aim under Article 10(2).

3. 'Necessary in a democratic society'

31. The submissions of those appearing before the Court focused on the question whether the disputed interference was 'necessary in a democratic society' for achieving the aforementioned aim.

In the applicants' view, freedom of artistic expression was of such fundamental importance that banning a work or convicting the artist of an offence struck at the very essence of the right guaranteed in Article 10 and had damaging consequences for a democratic society. No doubt the impugned paintings reflected a conception of sexuality that was at odds with the currently prevailing social morality, but, the applicants argued, their symbolical meaning had to be considered, since these were works of art. Freedom of artistic expression would become devoid of substance if paintings like those of Josef Felix Müller could not be shown to people interested in the arts as part of an exhibition of experimental contemporary art.

In the Government's submission, on the other hand, the interference was necessary, having regard in particular to the subject-matter of the paintings and to the particular circumstances in which they were exhibited.

For similar reasons and irrespective of any assessment of artistic or symbolical merit, the Commission considered that the Swiss courts could reasonably hold that the paintings were obscene and were entitled to find the applicants guilty of an offence under Article 204 of the Criminal Code.

32. The Court has consistently held that in Article 10(2) the adjective 'necessary' implies the existence of a 'pressing social need.' [citation omitted] The Contracting States have a certain margin of appreciation in assessing whether such a need exists, but this goes hand in hand with a European supervision, embracing both the legislation and the decisions applying it, even those given by an independent court. The Court is therefore empowered to give the final ruling on whether a 'restriction' or 'penalty' is reconcilable with freedom of expression as protected by Article 10.

In exercising its supervisory jurisdiction, the Court cannot confine itself to considering the impugned court decisions in isolation; it must look at them in the light of the case as a whole, including the paintings in question and the context in which they were exhibited. The Court must determine whether the interference at issue was 'proportionate to the legitimate aim pursued' and whether the reasons adduced by the Swiss courts to justify it are 'relevant and sufficient.'

33. In this connection, the Court must reiterate that freedom of expression, as secured in paragraph (1) of Article 10, constitutes one of the essential foundations of a democratic society, indeed one of the basic conditions for its progress and for the self-fulfilment of the individual. Subject to paragraph (2), it is applicable not only to 'information' or 'ideas' that are favourably received or regarded as inoffensive or as a matter of indifference, but also to those that offend, shock or disturb the State or any section of the population. Such are the demands of that pluralism, tolerance and broadmindedness without which there is no 'democratic society.' [citation omitted] Those who create, perform, distribute or exhibit works of art contribute to the exchange of ideas and opinions which is essential for a democratic society. Hence the obligation on the State not to encroach unduly on their freedom of expression.

34. Artists and those who promote their work are certainly not immune from the possibility of limitations as provided for in paragraph (2) of Article 10. Whoever exercises his freedom of expression undertakes, in accordance with the express terms of that paragraph, 'duties and responsibilities'; their scope will depend on his situation and the means he uses. [citation omitted] In considering whether the penalty was 'necessary in a democratic society,' the Court cannot overlook this aspect of the matter.

35. The applicants' conviction on the basis of Article 204 of the Swiss Criminal Code was intended to protect morals. Today, as at the time of the [*Handyside v. United Kingdom*] judgment, it is not possible to find in the legal and social orders of the Contracting States a uniform European conception of morals. The view taken of the requirements of morals

varies from time to time and from place to place, especially in our era, characterised as it is by a far-reaching evolution of opinions on the subject. By reason of their direct and continuous contact with the vital forces of their countries, State authorities are in principle in a better position than the international judge to give an opinion on the exact content of these requirements as well as on the 'necessity' of a 'restriction' or 'penalty' intended to meet them.

36. In the instant case, it must be emphasised that – as the Swiss courts found both at the cantonal level at first instance and on appeal and at the federal level – the paintings in question depict in a crude manner sexual relations, particularly between men and animals. They were painted on the spot – in accordance with the aims of the exhibition, which was meant to be spontaneous – and the general public had free access to them, as the organisers had not imposed any admission charge or any age limit. Indeed, the paintings were displayed in an exhibition which was unrestrictedly open to – and sought to attract – the public at large.

The Court recognises, as did the Swiss courts, that conceptions of sexual morality have changed in recent years. Nevertheless, having inspected the original paintings, the Court does not find unreasonable the view taken by the Swiss courts that those paintings, with their emphasis on sexuality in some of its crudest forms, were 'liable grossly to offend the sense of sexual propriety of persons of ordinary sensitivity.' In the circumstances, having regard to the margin of appreciation left to them under Article 10(2), the Swiss courts were entitled to consider it 'necessary' for the protection of morals to impose a fine on the applicants for publishing obscene material.

The applicants claimed that the exhibition of the pictures had not given rise to any public outcry and indeed that the press on the whole was on their side. It may also be true that Josef Felix Müller has been able to exhibit works in a similar vein in other parts of Switzerland and abroad, both before and after the 'Fri-Art 81' exhibition. It does not, in all the circumstances of the case, respond to a genuine social need, as was affirmed in substance by all three of the Swiss courts which dealt with the case.

37. In conclusion, the disputed measure did not infringe Article 10 of the Convention.

II. The confiscation of the paintings

38. In the applicants' submission, the confiscation of the paintings was not 'prescribed by law' for it was contrary to the clear and unambiguous terms of Article 204(3) of the Swiss Criminal Code, which lays down that items held to be obscene must be destroyed.

The Government and the Commission rightly referred to the development of Swiss case law with regard to this provision, beginning with the Federal Court's judgment of 10 May 1963 in the *Rey* case; since then, where an obscene item is of cultural interest and difficult or impossible to replace, such as a painting, it has been sufficient, in order to satisfy the requirements of Article 204(3) of the Criminal Code, to take whatever measures the court considers essential to withhold it from the general public. In 1982, confiscation was the measure envisaged under the relevant case law and was as a rule employed for this purpose. Accessible to the public and followed by the lower courts, this case law has alleviated the harshness of Article 204(3). The impugned measure was consequently 'prescribed by law' within the meaning of Article 10(2) of the Convention.

2. The legitimacy of the aim pursued

39. The confiscation of the paintings – the persons appearing before the Court were in agreement on this point – was designed to protect public morals by preventing any

repetition of the offence with which the applicants were charged. It accordingly had a legitimate aim under Article 10(2).

3. 'Necessary in a democratic society'

40. Here again, those appearing before the Court concentrated their submissions on the 'necessity' of the interference.

The applicants considered the confiscation to be disproportionate in relation to the aim pursued. In their view, the relevant courts could have chosen a less Draconian measure or, in the interests of protecting human rights, could have decided to take no action at all. They claimed that by confiscating the paintings the Fribourg authorities in reality imposed their view of morals on the country as a whole and that this was unacceptable, contradictory and contrary to the Convention, having regard to the well-known diversity of opinions on the subject.

The Government rejected these contentions. In deciding to take the drastic measure of destroying the paintings, the Swiss courts took the minimum action necessary. The discharge of the confiscation order on 20 January 1988, which the first applicant could have applied for earlier, clearly showed that the confiscation had not offended the proportionality principle; indeed, it represented an application of it.

The Commission considered the confiscation of the paintings to be disproportionate to the legitimate aim pursued. In its view, the judicial authorities had no power to weigh the conflicting interests involved and order measures less severe than confiscation for an indefinite period.

41. It is clear that notwithstanding the apparently rigid terms of paragraph (3) of Article 204 of the Criminal Code, the case law of the Federal Court allowed a court which had found certain items to be obscene to order their confiscation as an alternative to destruction. In the present case, it is the former measure which has to be considered under Article 10(2) of the Convention.

42. A principle of law which is common to the Contracting States allows confiscation of 'items whose use has been lawfully adjudged illicit and dangerous to the general interest.' [*See Handyside v. United Kingdom* at §63] In the instant case, the purpose was to protect the public from any repetition of the offence.

43. The applicants' conviction responded to a genuine social need under Article 10(2) of the Convention. The same reasons which justified that measure also apply in the view of the Court to the confiscation order made at the same time.

Undoubtedly, as the applicants and the Commission rightly emphasised, a special problem arises where, as in the instant case, the item confiscated is an original painting: on account of the measure taken, the artist can no longer make use of his work in whatever way he might wish. Thus Josef Felix Müller lost, in particular, the opportunity of showing his paintings in places where the demands made by the protection of morals are considered to be less strict than in Fribourg.

It must be pointed out, however, that under case law going back to the *Fahrner* case in 1980 and which was subsequently applied in the instant case, it is open to the owner of a confiscated work to apply to the relevant cantonal court to have the confiscation order discharged or varied if the item in question no longer presents any danger or if some other, more lenient, measure would suffice to protect the interests of public morals. In its decision of 20 January 1988, the Sarine District Criminal Court stated that the original confiscation 'was not absolute but merely of indeterminate duration, which left room to apply for a reconsideration. It granted Mr. Müller's application because 'the preventive measure [had] fulfilled its function, namely to ensure that such paintings [were] not exhibited in public again without any precautions.'

Admittedly, the first applicant was deprived of his works for nearly eight years, but there was nothing to prevent him from applying earlier to have them returned; the relevant case law of the Basel Court of Appeal was public and accessible, and, what is more, the Agent of the Government himself drew attention to it during the Commission's hearing on 6 December 1985; there is no evidence before the Court to show that such an application would have failed.

That being so, and having regard to their margin of appreciation, the Swiss courts were entitled to hold that confiscation of the paintings in issue was 'necessary' for the protection of morals.

44. In conclusion, the disputed measure did not infringe Article 10 of the Convention.

∾

QUESTIONS & COMMENTS

(1) How would a U.S. court analyze an attempt to suppress the exhibition of the paintings at issue in *Müller*? Consider whether the European Court's discussion of the diversity of moral views among the contracting states parallels the U.S. Supreme Court's discussion of federalism in *Miller v. California*, 413 U.S. 15 (1973). Note that the paintings in *Müller* were exhibited in a manner that allowed them to be seen by viewers who did not anticipate what their content would be. Does the European Court's opinion indicate how it would have analyzed the case had potential viewers been warned about the paintings' content? Note that under U.S. obscenity law it is irrelevant that obscene materials are available only to consenting adults. *Paris Adult Theatre I v. Slaton*, 413 U.S. 49 (1973).

Consider whether the confiscation procedure in *Müller* provides some additional protection for expression in light of changing social values. Why did the Swiss courts allow the paintings to be returned to the artist? Does the report indicate whether the European Court would have required return had the artist claimed that social values had changed between the time the pictures were produced and the time return was sought?

(2) Since *Müller v. Switzerland*, the European Court has addressed artistic expression in other cases. In the first case, *Otto-Preminger-Institut v. Austria*, 295-A Eur. Ct. H.R. (ser. A) (1994), the applicant association ("OPI") announced the showing of the film *Das Liebeskonzil* (*The Council in Heaven*) to its members by mail and in its theater's display windows. The announcement described the film as a satirical tragedy set in heaven and in the context of a blasphemy trial in 1895. The announcement also described the film as follows: "Trivial imagery and absurdities of the Christian creed are targeted in a caricatural mode and the relationship between religious beliefs and worldly mechanisms of oppression is investigated." *Id.* at §10. The announcement also stated that persons under seventeen years of age were prohibited from seeing the film.

The film portrayed the God of the Jewish, Christian, and Islamic religions as a "senile old man prostrating himself before the devil with whom he exchanges a deep kiss and calling the devil his friend." *Id.*, at §22. God is also portrayed as swearing by the devil. *Id.*

> Other scenes show the Virgin Mary permitting an obscene story to be read to her and the manifestation of a degree of erotic tension between the Virgin Mary and the devil. The adult Jesus Christ is portrayed as a low grade mental defective and in one scene is shown lasciviously attempting to fondle and kiss his mother's breasts, which she is shown permitting. God, the Virgin Mary, and Christ are shown in the film applauding the devil.

Id. After being prompted by the Roman Catholic diocese in Innsbruck, the Austrian government instituted criminal proceedings against OPI's manager. However, this prosecution was discontinued, and only the forfeiture and seizure aspects of the case were pursued.

Subsequently, the European Commission of Human Rights found that the Austrian government's seizure and forfeiture of the film violated Article 10. However, the European Court later held that the Austrian Government did not violate Article 10.

In its decision, the European Court held:

> the manner in which religious beliefs and doctrines are opposed or denied is a matter which may engage the responsibility of the State, notably its responsibility *to ensure the peaceful enjoyment of the right guaranteed under Article 9* to the holders of those beliefs and doctrines. Indeed, in extreme cases the effect of particular methods of opposing or denying religious beliefs can be such as to inhibit those who hold such beliefs from exercising their freedom to hold and express them.

Id. at §47 (emphasis provided). The Court recognized that national authorities must be given a wide margin of appreciation where the "religious feelings of others" are involved. *Id.* at §50.

Most importantly, the Court noted that it could not disregard "the fact that the Roman Catholic religion is the religion of the overwhelming majority of Tyroleans" and that the Austrian authorities had acted to ensure religious peace in the region. *Id.* at §56. Because the proposed screening of the film was sufficiently public to cause offense to the religious beliefs of some persons, the European Court held that it should defer to the national authorities in assessing the need for seizing the film to ensure peace in "a situation obtaining locally at a given time." *Id.* Accordingly, the Court held the seizure and forfeiture of the film did not violate Article 10.

Does the European Court's decision effectively legitimize the *violent* expression of religious belief by Roman Catholic Tyroleans? Should it not be an affirmative duty of the state to provide police protection to persons whose expression is offensive? Compare *Plattform 'Ärzte für das Leben' v. Austria*, 139 Eur. Ct. H.R. (ser. A) (1988) that discusses the state's affirmative duty to protect protestors from counterdemonstrators. Is *Otto-Preminger-Institut v. Austria* in conflict with *Plattform 'Ärzte für das Leben' v. Austria*? Does the criticism of religious beliefs receive less protection than political expression in the European Court's jurisprudence? If so, what underlying and unarticulated reasons could support the Court's decisions?

(3) The European Court in *Otto-Preminger-Institut v. Austria* points out the relevance of the right to religious belief under Article 9, ECHR. What if an individual ascribed to a religion whose central organizing tenet was the caustic condemnation of another religion? Think of the early Lutheran Church's condemnation of Roman Catholicism.

Would Article 9 and 10, respectively, protect this individual's right of expression and right to manifestation of religious belief? What if a religious individual has a religious viewpoint that other believers find offensive? Consider the following case.

In *Wingrove v. United Kingdom*, – Eur. Ct. H.R. (ser. A) (1996) (slip opinion), the applicant was a video film maker who sought a government-issued distribution certificate for his video film entitled *Visions of Ecstasy*. The U.K. government denied the applicant the certificate because the authorities believed that the film was blasphemous. The film depicted the sexual-religious visions of St. Teresa of Avila that included a depiction of St. Teresa being kissed and caressed by another female character representing her psyche, of St. Teresa kissing and licking the wounds of a crucified Christ, of St. Teresa apparently having sexual intercourse with the crucified Christ, and of a Christ character responding in an apparent receptive manner. There was no attempt to identify the character of St. Teresa or her psyche, nor to explain the historical background. The U.K. authorities claimed that the subject matter was not at issue; it was not blasphemous to speak or to publish opinions hostile to Christianity. It was the *manner* of expressing those opinions.

The European Court found no Article 10 violation. The Court based its decision on a number of factors. First, there was "no uniform European conception of morals," especially in relationship to the religious convictions of others. *Id.* at §58. Therefore, the state should have a wide margin of appreciation for limiting freedom of expression in this field. Second, there was "no attempt … made in the film to explore the meaning of the imagery beyond engaging the viewer in a 'voyeuristic erotic experience'." *Id.* at §61. Finally, the Court rejected the argument of the applicant that the video film's audience would be very small and that the film's description of the film would be on the video film's container, thereby ensuring informed consent by adults. The Court noted that because of the nature of video, the video film could be copied, lent, rented, sold, and viewed in different homes, thereby easily escaping any form of control by U.K. authorities.

As students of the histories of art and religion are aware, the visions of St. Teresa of Avila have been interpreted for centuries as involving sexual relations between herself and Christ, and these visions have provided a rich source of artistic expression for many artists, including Bernini. Does the European Court place itself in the position of art critic and theologian by regulating the manner of artistic expression addressing religious themes?

(4) Compare U.S. law on the subject of film and blasphemy. In *Burstyn v. Wilson*, 343 U.S. 495 (1952), the U.S. Supreme Court struck down a New York state law that required film makers to submit their films to a licensing agency for determining whether the film was sacrilegious. The New York state court had interpreted the statute as requiring that "no religion … shall be treated with contempt, mockery, scorn, or ridicule." *Id.* at 504.

The film at issue in *Burstyn v. Wilson*, The Miracle, told the story of a crazed, shepherd girl who was raped by a god and had a divine birth. The Supreme Court held that a state could not ban a film based on the censor's view that it was sacrilegious.

> [T]he state has no legitimate interest in protecting any or all religions from views distasteful to them. … It is not the business of government to suppress real or imagined attacks upon a particular religious doctrine whether they appear in publications, speeches or motion pictures.

Id. at 505. "The most careful and *tolerant* censor would find it virtually impossible to avoid favoring one religion over another, and he would be subject to an inevitable tendency to ban the expression of unpopular sentiments sacred to a religious majority." *Id.*

In *Nyak v. MCA*, 911 F.2d 1082 (5th Cir. 1990), *cert. denied*, 498 U.S. 1087 (1991), a U.S. Court of Appeals examined a suit challenging the distribution and presentation of THE LAST TEMPTATION OF CHRIST because the film was an allegedly defamatory interpretation of Jesus Christ's life that violated the plaintiff's right to freedom of religion. The film, which was directed by Martin Scorsese, related that Jesus Christ, as a carpenter's son, constructed crosses for the crucifixion of fellow Jews. It also related a story that Jesus imagined having a sexual relationship with Mary Magdalene resulting in the birth of children. The court of appeals affirmed the dismissal of the case holding that the case was nonjusticiable. In a terse decision, the court of appeals noted:

> The Supreme Court has stated:
> "The law knows no heresy, and is committed to the support of no dogma, the establishment of no sect." *Watson v. Jones*, 13 Wall. 679.... Freedom of thought, which includes freedom of religious belief, is basic in a society of free men. It embraces the right to maintain theories of life and death and of the hereafter which are rank heresy to followers of the orthodox faiths. *United States v. Ballard*, 322 U.S. 78, 86 (1944). The plaintiff asked the court to decide the "correct" interpretation of the life of Christ. This is not a justiciable question before the court.

Nyak v. MCA, 911 F.2d at 1082.

(5) One of the earliest European Court cases addressing freedom of expression vis-à-vis offensive expression is *Handyside v. United Kingdom*, 24 Eur. Ct. H.R. (ser. A) (1976). In this case, the U.K. government convicted the applicant for possessing copies of an allegedly obscene book entitled THE LITTLE RED SCHOOLBOOK. The book addressed issues such as masturbation, orgasm, intercourse and petting, contraceptives, wet dreams, menstruation, child molestation, pornography, impotence, homosexuality, abortion, venereal diseases, and other sexually related matters. The book was intended as reference book for schoolchildren aged 12 and older. The applicant was prosecuted under the Obscene Publications Act of 1964 that defined "obscene" as having the effect of tending to "deprave and corrupt" persons. *Id.* at §25.

Handyside applied to the European Commission, which found no Article 10 violation and referred the case to the European Court. Before the European Court, the U.K. government justified its prosecution of the applicant on the basis of protecting morals. Both the U.K. government and the European Commission urged the European Court to adopt a "good faith" test for determining whether a state party had acted within its margin of appreciation in limiting the exercise of Article 10.

Although the European Court rejected this "good faith" test, the Court did find that the U.K. government's prosecution was within its margin of appreciation in protecting the morals of children because the book could be interpreted as encouraging children to indulge in "precocious activities" or to commit criminal acts. *Id.* at §52. Such acts included marijuana smoking and unlawful sexual intercourse by minors. *Id.* at §32. Accordingly, the Court found no Article 10 violation.

How would the U.S. Supreme Court rule in a case similar to *Handyside v. United Kingdom*? Compare *Hazelwood School District v. Kuhlmeier*, 484 U.S. 260 (1988).

Open Door Counselling and Dublin Well Woman v. Ireland
European Court of Human Rights
246 Eur. Ct. H.R. (ser. A) (1992)
15 E.H.R.R. 244 (1992)

. . . .

FACTS

I. Introduction

A. The applicants

9. The applicants in this case are (a) Open Door Counselling Ltd. (hereinafter referred to as "Open Door"), a company incorporated under Irish law, which was engaged, *inter alia*, in counselling pregnant women in Dublin and in other parts of Ireland; (b) Dublin Well Woman Center Ltd. (hereinafter referred to as "Dublin Well Woman"), a company also incorporated under Irish law which provided similar services at two clinics in Dublin; (c) Bonnie Maher and Ann Downes, who worked as trained counsellors for Dublin Well Woman; and (d) Mrs. X., born in 1950, and Mrs. Maeve Geraghty, born in 1970, who join in the Dublin Well Woman application as women of child-bearing age. The applicants complained of an injunction imposed by the Irish courts on Open Door and Dublin Well Woman to restrain them from providing certain information to pregnant women concerning abortion facilities outside the jurisdiction of Ireland by way of nondirective counselling.[ ]

[. . .] The services offered by Dublin Well Woman relate to every aspect of women's health, ranging from smear tests to breast examinations, infertility, artificial insemination and the counselling of pregnant women.

10. In 1983, at the time of the referendum leading to the Eighth Amendment of the Constitution,[ ] Dublin Well Woman issued a pamphlet stating, *inter alia*, that legal advice on the implication of the wording of the provision had been obtained and that 'with this wording anybody could seek a court injunction to prevent us offering' the non-directive counselling service. The pamphlet also warned that 'it would also be possible for an individual to seek a court injunction to prevent a woman travelling abroad if they believe she intends to have an abortion.'

B. The Injunction proceedings

1. Before the High Court

11. The applicant companies were the defendants in proceedings before the High Court which were commenced on 28 June 1985 as a private action brought by the Society for the Protection of Unborn Children (Ireland) Ltd. (hereinafter referred to as S.P.U.C.), which was converted into a relator action brought at the suit of the Attorney-General by order of the High Court of 24 September 1986.[ ]

12. S.P.U.C. sought a declaration that the activities of the applicant companies in counselling pregnant women within the jurisdiction of the court to travel abroad to obtain an abortion were unlawful, having regard to Article 40(3)(3) of the Constitution, which protects the right to life of the unborn[ ] and an order restraining the defendants from such counselling or assistance.

13. No evidence was adduced at the hearing of the action which proceeded on the basis of certain agreed facts. The facts as agreed at that time by Dublin Well Woman may

be summarized as follows:

(a) It counsels in a non-directive manner pregnant women resident in Ireland;
(b) Abortion or termination of pregnancy may be one of the options discussed within the said counselling;
(c) If a pregnant woman wants to consider the abortion option further, arrangements will be made by the applicant to refer her to a medical clinic in Great Britain;
(d) In certain circumstances, the applicant may arrange for the travel of such pregnant women;
(e) The applicant will inspect the medical clinic in Great Britain to ensure that it operates at the highest standards;
(f) At those medical clinics abortions have been performed on pregnant women who have been previously counselled by the applicant;
(g) Pregnant women resident in Ireland have been referred to medical clinics in Great Britain where abortions have been performed for many years including 1984.

The facts agreed by Open Door were the same as above with the exception of point (d).

14. The meaning of the concept of non-directive counselling was described in the following terms by Finlay C.J. in the judgment of the Supreme Court in the case:[ ]

> It was submitted on behalf of each of the Defendants that the meaning of non-directive counselling in these agreed sets of facts was that it was counselling which neither included advice nor was judgmental but that it was a service essentially directed to eliciting from the client her own appreciation of her problem and her own considered choice for its solution. This interpretation of the phrase "non-directive counselling" in the context of the activities of the defendants was not disputed on behalf of the respondent. It follows from this, of course, that non-directive counselling to pregnant women would never involve the actual advising of an abortion as the preferred option but neither, of course, could it permit the giving of advice for any reason to the pregnant women receiving such counselling against choosing to have an abortion.

15. On 19 December 1986, Hamilton J., President of the High Court, found that the activities of Open Door and Dublin Well Women in counselling pregnant women within the jurisdiction of the Court to travel abroad to obtain an abortion or to obtain further advice on abortion within a foreign jurisdiction were unlawful having regard to the provisions of Article 40(3)(3) of the Constitution of Ireland.

He confirmed that Irish criminal law made it an offence to procure or attempt to procure an abortion, to administer an abortion or to assist in an abortion by supplying any noxious thing or instrument.[ ] Furthermore, Irish constitutional law also protected the right to life of the unborn from the moment of conception onwards.

An injunction was accordingly granted '... that the Defendants [Open Door and Dublin Well Woman] and each of them, their servants or agents, be perpetually restrained from counselling or assisting pregnant women within the jurisdiction of this Court to obtain further advice on abortion or to obtain an abortion.' The High Court made no order relating to the costs of the proceedings, leaving each side to bear its own legal costs.

2. Before the Supreme Court

16. Open Door and Dublin Well Woman appealed against this decision to the Supreme Court which, in a unanimous judgment delivered on 16 March 1988 by Finlay C.J., rejected the appeal.

The Supreme Court noted that the appellants did not consider it essential to the service which they provided for pregnant women in Ireland that they should take any part in arranging the travel of women who wished to go abroad for the purpose of having an abortion or that they arranged bookings in clinics for such women. However, they did consider it essential to inform women who wished to have an abortion outside the jurisdiction of the court of the name, address, telephone number and method of communication with a specified clinic which they had examined and were satisfied was one which maintained a high standard.

17. On the question of whether the above activity should be restrained as being contrary to the Constitution, Finlay C.J. stated:

> ... the essential issues in this case do not in any way depend upon the plaintiff establishing that the defendants were advising or encouraging the procuring of abortions. The essential issue in this case, having regard to the nature of the guarantees contained in Article 40(3)(3) of the Constitution, is the issue as to whether the Defendants' admitted activities were assisting pregnant women within the jurisdiction to travel outside that jurisdiction in order to have an abortion. To put the matter in another way, the issue and the question of fact to be determined is: were they thus assisting in the destruction of the life of the unborn?
>
> I am satisfied beyond doubt that having regard to the admitted facts the defendants were assisting in the ultimate destruction of the life of the unborn by abortion in that they were helping the pregnant woman who had decided upon that option to get in touch with a clinic in Great Britain which would provide the service of abortion. It seems to me an inescapable conclusion that if a woman was anxious to obtain an abortion and if she was able by availing of the counselling services of one or other of the defendants to obtain the precise location, address and telephone number of, and method of communication with, a clinic in Great Britain which provided that service, put in plain language, that was knowingly helping her to attain her objective. I am, therefore, satisfied that the finding made by the learned trial Judge that the defendants were assisting pregnant women to travel abroad to obtain further advice on abortion and to secure an abortion is well supported on the evidence ...

The Court further noted that the phrase in Article 40(3)(3), 'with due regard to the equal right to life of the mother,' did not arise for interpretation in the case since the applicants were not claiming that the service they were providing for pregnant women was 'in any way confined to or especially directed towards the due regard to the equal right to life of the mother ... '

18. Open Door and Dublin Well Women had submitted that if they did not provide this counselling service it was likely that pregnant women would succeed nevertheless in obtaining an abortion in circumstances less advantageous to their health. The Court rejected this argument in the following terms:

> Even if it could be established, however, it would not be a valid reason why the Court should not restrain the activities in which the defendants were engaged.

The function of the courts, which is not dependent on the existence of legislation, when their jurisdiction to defend and vindicate a constitutionally guaranteed right has been invoked, must be confined to the issues and to the parties before them.

If the Oireachtas enacts legislation to defend and vindicate a constitutionally guaranteed right it may well do so in wider terms than are necessary for the resolution of any individual case. The courts cannot take that wide approach. They are confined to dealing with the parties and issues before them. I am satisfied, therefore, that it is no answer to the making of an order restraining these defendants' activities that there may be other persons or the activities of other groups or bodies which will provide the same result as that assisted by these defendants' activities.

19. As to whether there was a constitutional right to information about the availability of abortion outside the State, the Court stated as follows:

The performing of an abortion on a pregnant woman terminates the unborn life which she is carrying. Within the terms of Article 40(3)(3) it is a direct destruction of the constitutionally guaranteed right to life of that unborn child.

It must follow from this that there could not be an implied and unenumerated constitutional right to information about the availability of a service of abortion outside the State which, if availed of, would have the direct consequence of destroying the expressly guaranteed constitutional right to life of the unborn. As part of the submission on this issue it was further suggested that the right to receive and give information which, it was alleged, existed and was material to this case was, though not expressly granted, impliedly referred to or involved in the right of citizens to express freely their convictions and opinions provided by Article 40(6)(1)(i) of the Constitution, since, it was claimed, the right to express freely convictions and opinions may, under some circumstances, involve as an ancillary right the right to obtain information. I am satisfied that no right could constitutionally arise to obtain information the purpose of the obtaining of which was to defeat the constitutional right to life of the unborn child.

20. The Court upheld the decision of the High Court to grant an injunction but varied the terms of the order as follows:

... that the defendants and each of them, their servants or agents be perpetually restrained from assisting pregnant women within the jurisdiction to travel abroad to obtain abortions by referral to a clinic, by the making for them of travel arrangements, or by informing them of the identity and location of and the method of communication with a specified clinic or clinics or otherwise.

The costs of the Supreme Court appeal were awarded against the applicant companies on 3 May 1988.

21. Following the judgment of the Supreme Court, Open Door, having no assets, ceased its activities.

. . . .

25. The interpretation to be given Article 40(3)(3) also arose before the Supreme Court in the case of *The Attorney General v. X. and Others* which concerned an application to the courts by the Attorney General for an injunction to prevent a 14-year-old-girl who was pregnant from leaving the jurisdiction to have an abortion abroad. The girl alleged that she had been raped and had expressed the desire to commit suicide. The Supreme Court, in its judgment of 5 March 1992, found that termination of pregnancy was permissible

under Article 40(3)(3), where it was established as a matter of probability that there was a real and substantial risk to the life of the mother if such termination was not effected. Finding that this test was satisfied on the facts of the case the Supreme Court discharged the injunction which had been granted by the High Court at first instance.

. . . .

During the oral hearing before the European Court of Human Rights, the Government made the following statement in the light of the Supreme Court's judgment in this case:

> . . . persons who are deemed to be entitled under Irish law to avail themselves of termination of pregnancy in these circumstances must be regarded as being entitled to have appropriate access to information in relation to the facilities for such operations, whether in Ireland or abroad.

D. Evidence presented by the applicants

26. The applicants presented evidence to the Court that there had been no significant drop in the number of Irish women having abortions in Great Britain since the granting of the injunction, that number being well over 3,500 women per year. They also submitted an opinion from an expert in public health (Dr. J. R. Ashton) which concludes that there are five possible adverse implications for the health of Irish women arising from the injunction in the present case:

1. An increase in the birth of unwanted and rejected children;
2. An increase in illegal and unsafe abortions;
3. A lack of adequate preparation of Irish women obtaining abortions;
4. Increases in delay in obtaining abortions with ensuing increased complication rates;
5. Poor aftercare with a failure to deal adequately with medical complications and a failure to provide adequate contraceptive advice.

In their written comments to the Court, S.P.U.C. claimed that the number of abortions obtained by Irish women in England which had been rising rapidly prior to the enactment of Article 40(3)(3), had increased at a much reduced pace. They further submitted that the number of births to married women has increased at a 'very substantial rate.'

27. The applicants claimed that the impugned information was available in British newspapers and magazines which were imported into Ireland as well as in the yellow pages of the London telephone directory which could be purchased from the Irish telephone service. It was also available in publications such as the *British Medical Journal* which was not obtainable in Ireland.

While not challenging the accuracy of the above information the Government observed that no newspaper or magazine had been produced in evidence to the Court.

II. Relevant domestic law and practice concerning protection of the unborn

A. Constitutional protection

28. Article 40(3)(3) of the Irish Constitution (the Eighth Amendment), which came into force in 1983 following a referendum reads:

> The State acknowledges the right to life of the unborn and, with due regard to the equal right to life of the mother, guarantees in its laws to respect, and, as far as practicable, by its laws to defend and vindicate that right.

This provision has been interpreted by the Supreme Court in the present case in *The Society for the Protection of Unborn Children (Ireland) Ltd. v. Grogan and Others* [1989] I.R. 753 and in *The Attorney General v. X. and Others.* [ ]

B. Statutory protection

29. The statutory prohibition of abortion is contained in sections 58 and 59 of the Offences Against the Person Act 1961. Section 58 provides that:

Every woman, being with child, who, with intent to procure her own miscarriage, shall unlawfully administer to herself any poison or other noxious thing or shall unlawfully use any instrument or other means whatsoever with the like intent, and whosoever, with intent to procure the miscarriage of any woman, whether she be or not be with child, shall unlawfully administer to her or cause to be taken by her any poison or other noxious thing, or shall unlawfully use any instrument or other means whatsoever with the like intent, shall be guilty of a felony, and being convicted thereof shall be liable, [to imprisonment for life] . . .

Section 59 states that:

Whoever shall unlawfully supply or procure any poison or other noxious thing, or any instrument or thing whatsoever, knowing that the same is intended to be unlawfully used or employed with intent to procure the miscarriage of any woman, whether she be or be not with child, shall be guilty of a misdemeanor, and being convicted thereof . . .

30. Section 16 of the Censorship of Publications Act 1929 as amended by section 12 of the Health (Family Planning) Act 1979 provides that:

It shall not be lawful for any person, otherwise than under and in accordance with a permit in writing granted to him under this section

(a) to print or publish or cause or procure to be printed or published; or
(b) to sell or expose, offer or keep for sale; or
(c) to distribute, offer to keep for distribution, any book or periodical publication (whether appearing on the register of prohibited publications or not) which advocates or which might reasonably be supposed to advocate the procurement of abortion or miscarriage or any method, treatment or appliance to be used for the purpose of such procurement.

31. Section 58 of the Civil Liability Act 1961 provides that 'the law relating to wrongs shall apply to an unborn child for his protection in like manner as if the child were born, provided the child is subsequently born alive.'

32. Section 10 of the Health (Family Planning) Act 1979 re-affirms the statutory prohibition of abortion and states as follows:

Nothing in this Act shall be construed as authorizing –
(a) the procuring of abortion
(b) the doing of any other thing the doing of which is prohibited by section 58 or 50 of the Offenses Against the Person Act 1961 (which sections prohibit the administering of drugs or the use of any instrument to procure abortion) or
(c) the sale, importation into the State, manufacture, advertising or display of abortifacients.

C. Case law

33. Apart from the present case and subsequent developments,[ ] reference has been made to the right to life of the unborn in various decisions of the Supreme Court.[ ]

34. In the case of *G. v. An. Bord Uchtala*,[ ] Walsh J. stated as follows:

> [A child] has the right to life itself and the right to be guarded against all threats directed to its existence, whether before or after birth . . . The right to life necessarily implies the right to be born, the right to preserve and defend and to have preserved and defended that life . . .

35. The Supreme Court has also stated that the courts are the custodians of the fundamental rights set out in the Constitution and that their powers in this regard are as ample as the defence of the Constitution requires.[ ] Moreover, an infringement of a constitutional right by an individual may be actionable in damages as a constitutional tort. [ ]

In his judgment in *The People v. Shaw*, [I.R. 1 (1982)] Kenny L.J. observed:

> When the People enacted the Constitution of 1937, they provided (Article 40(3)) that the State guaranteed in its laws to respect, and, as far as practicable, by its laws to defend and vindicate the personal rights of the citizen and that the State should, in particular, by its laws protect as best it might from unjust attack and in the case of injustice done, vindicate the life, person, good name and property rights of every citizen. I draw attention to the use of the words "the State." The obligation to implement this guarantee is imposed not on the Oireachtas only, but on each branch of the State which exercises the powers of legislating, executing and giving judgment on those laws: Article 6, the word "laws" in Article 40(3) is not confined to laws which have been enacted by the Oireachtas, but comprehends the laws made by judges and by ministers of State when they make statutory instruments or regulations.

[The applicants applied to the European Commission of Human Rights which found that the injunctions violated freedom of expression.]

. . . .

DECISION [OF THE EUROPEAN COURT OF HUMAN RIGHTS]:

. . . .

III. Alleged violation of Article 10

53. The applicants alleged that the Supreme Court injunction, restraining them from assisting pregnant women to travel abroad to obtain abortions, infringed the rights of the corporate applicants and the two counsellors to impart information, as well as the rights of Mrs. X and Mrs. Geraghty to receive information. They confined their complaint to that part of the injunction which concerned the provision of information to pregnant women as opposed to the making of travel arrangements or referral to clinics.[ ] They invoked Article 10. . . .

54. In their submissions to the Court the Government contested these claims and also contended that Article 10 should be interpreted against the background of Article 2, 17 and 60 of the Convention the relevant parts of which state:

Article 2

1. Everyone's right to life shall be protected by law. No one shall be deprived of his life intentionally save in the execution of a sentence of a court following his conviction of a crime for which this penalty is provided by law . . .

Article 17

Nothing in [the] Convention may be interpreted as implying for any State, group or person any right to engage in any activity or perform any act aimed at the destruction of any of the rights and freedoms set forth herein or at their limitation to a greater extent that is provided for in the Convention.

Article 60

Nothing in [the] Convention shall be construed as limiting or derogating from any of the human rights and fundamental freedoms which may be ensured under the laws of any High Contracting Party or under any other agreement to which it is a Party.

. . . .

C. Did the restriction have aims that were legitimate under Article 10(2)?

61. The Government submitted that the relevant provisions of Irish law are intended for the protection of the rights of others – in this instance the unborn – for the protection of morals and, where appropriate, for the prevention of crime.

62. The applicants disagreed, contending, *inter alia*, that, in view of the use of the term 'everyone' in Article 10(1) and throughout the Convention, it would be illogical to interpret the 'rights of others' in Article 10(2) as encompassing the unborn.

63. The Court cannot accept that the restrictions at issue pursued the aim of the prevention of crime since, as noted above,[ ] neither the provisions of the information in question nor the obtaining of an abortion outside the jurisdiction involved any criminal offence. However, it is evident that the protection afforded under Irish law to the right to life of the unborn is based on profound moral values concerning the nature of life which were reflected in the stance of the majority of the Irish people against abortion as expressed in the 1983 referendum.[ ] The restriction thus pursued the legitimate aim of the protection of morals of which the protection in Ireland of the right to life of the unborn is one aspect. It is not necessary in the light of this conclusion to decide whether the term 'others' under Article 10(2) extends to the unborn.

D. Was the restriction necessary in a democratic society?

64. The Government submitted that the Court's approach to the assessment of the 'necessity' of the restraint should be guided by the fact that the protection of the rights of the unborn in Ireland could be derived from Articles 2, 17 and 60 of the Convention. They further contended that the 'proportionality' test was inadequate where the rights of the unborn were at issue. The Court will examine these issues in turn.

1. Article 2

65. The Government maintained that the injunction was necessary in a democratic society for the protection of the right to life of the unborn and that Article 10 should be interpreted, *inter alia*, against the background of Article 2 of the Convention which,

it argued, also protected unborn life. The view that abortion was morally wrong was the deeply held view of the majority of the people in Ireland and it was not the proper function of the Court to seek to impose a different viewpoint.

66. The Court observes at the outset that in the present case it is not called upon to examine whether a right to abortion is guaranteed under the Convention or whether the foetus is encompassed by the right to life as contained in Article 2. The applicants have not claimed that the Convention contains a right to abortion, as such, their complaint being limited to that part of the injunction which restricts their freedom to impart and receive information concerning abortion abroad.[ ]

Thus, the only issue to be addressed is whether the restrictions on the freedom to impart and receive information contained in the relevant part of the injunction are necessary in a democratic society for the legitimate aim of the protection of morals as explained above.[ ] It follows from this approach that the Government's argument based on Article 2 of the Convention does not fall to be examined in the present case. On the other hand, the arguments based on Article 17 and 60 fall to be considered below.[ ]

2. Proportionality

67. The Government stressed the limited nature of the Supreme Court's injunction which only restrained the provision of certain information. There was no limitation on discussion in Ireland about abortion generally or the right of women to travel abroad to obtain one. They further contended that the Convention test as regards the proportionality of the restriction was inadequate where a question concerning the extinction of life was at stake. The right to life could not, like other rights, be measured according to a graduated scale. It was either respected or it was not. Accordingly, the traditional approach of weighing competing rights and interests in the balance was inappropriate where the destruction of unborn life was concerned. Since life was a primary value which was antecedent to and a prerequisite for the enjoyment of every other rights, its protection might involve the infringement of other rights such as freedom of expression in a manner which might not be acceptable in the defence of rights of a lesser nature.

The Government also emphasized that, in granting the injunction, the Supreme Court was merely sustaining the logic of Article 40(3)(3) of the Constitution. The determination by the Irish courts that the provision of information by the relevant applicants assisted in the destruction of unborn life was not open to review by the Convention institutions.

68. The Court cannot agree that the State's discretion in the field of the protection of morals is unfettered and unreviewable.[ ]

It acknowledges that the national authorities enjoy a wide margin of appreciation in matters of morals, particularly in an area such as the present which touches on matters of belief concerning the nature of human life. As the Court has observed before, it is not possible to find in the legal and social orders of the Contracting States a uniform European conception of morals, and the State authorities are, in principle, in a better position than the international judge to give an opinion on the exact content of the requirements of morals as well as on the 'necessity' of a 'restriction' or 'penalty' intended to meet them. [ ]

However this power of appreciation is not unlimited. It is for the Court, in this field also, to supervise whether a restriction is compatible with the Convention.

69. As regards the application of the 'proportionality' test, the logical consequence of the Government's argument is that measures taken by the national authorities to protect the right to life of the unborn or to uphold the constitutional guarantee on the subject

would be automatically justified under the Convention where infringement of a right of a lesser stature was alleged. It is, in principle, open to the national authorities to take such action as they consider necessary to respect the rule of law or to give effect to constitutional rights. However, they must do so in a manner which is compatible with their obligations under the Convention and subject to review by the Convention institutions. To accept the Government's pleading on this point would amount to an abdication of the Court's responsibility under Article 19 'to ensure the observance of the engagements undertaken by the High Contracting Parties . . . '

70. Accordingly, the Court must examine the question of 'necessity' in the light of the principles developed in its case law.[ ] It must determine whether there existed a pressing social need for the measures in question and, in particular, whether the restriction complained of was 'proportionate to the legitimate aim pursued.'

71. In this context, it is appropriate to recall that freedom of expression is also applicable to 'information' or 'ideas' that offend, shock or disturb the State or any sector of the population. Such are the demands of that pluralism, tolerance and broadmindedness without which there is no 'democratic society.'[ ]

72. While the relevant restriction, as observed by the Government, is limited to the provision of information, it is recalled that it is not a criminal offence under Irish law for a pregnant woman to travel abroad in order to have an abortion. Furthermore, the injunction limited that freedom to receive and impart information with respect to services which are lawful in other Convention countries and may be crucial to a woman's health and well-being. Limitations on information concerning activities which, notwithstanding their moral implications, have been and continue to be tolerated by national authorities, call for careful scrutiny by the Convention institutions as to their conformity with the tenets of a democratic society.

73. The Court is first struck by the absolute nature of the Supreme Court injunction which imposed a 'perpetual' restraint on the provision of information to pregnant women concerning abortion facilities abroad, regardless of age or state of health or their reasons for seeking counselling on the termination of pregnancy. The sweeping nature of this restriction has since been highlighted by the case of *The Attorney General v. X. and Others* and by the injunction no longer applied to women who, in the circumstances as defined in the Supreme Court's judgment in that case, were now free to have an abortion in Ireland or abroad.[ ]

74. On that ground alone the restriction appears over-broad and disproportionate. Moreover, this assessment is confirmed by other factors.

75. In the first place, it is to be noted that the corporate applicants were engaged in the counselling of pregnant women in the course of which counsellors neither advocated nor encouraged abortion, but confined themselves to an explanation of the available options.[ ] The decision was to whether or not to act on the information so provided was that of the woman concerned. There can be little doubt that following such counselling there were women who decided against a termination of pregnancy. Accordingly, the link between the provision of information and the destruction of unborn life is not as definite as contended. Such counselling had in fact been tolerated by the State authorities even after the passing of the Eighth Amendment in 1983, until the Supreme Court's judgment in the present case. Furthermore, the information that was provided by the relevant applicants concerning abortion facilities abroad was not made available to the public at large.

76. It has not been seriously contested by the Government that information concerning abortion facilities abroad can be obtained from other sources in Ireland, such as magazines and telephone directories[ ] or by persons with contacts in Great Britain. Accordingly, information that the injunction sought to restrict was already available elsewhere although in a manner which was not supervised by qualified personnel and thus less protective of women's health. Furthermore, the injunction appears to have been largely ineffective in protecting the right to life of the unborn since it did not prevent large numbers of Irish women from continuing to obtain abortions in Great Britain.[ ]

77. In addition, the available evidence, which has not been disputed by the Government, suggests that the injunction has created a risk to the health of those women who are now seeking abortions at a later stage in their pregnancy, due to lack of proper counselling, and who are not availing [themselves] of customary medical supervision after the abortion has taken place. [ ] Moreover, the injunction may have had more adverse effects on women who were not sufficiently resourceful or had not the necessary level of education to have access to alternative sources of information.[ ] These are certainly legitimate factors to take into consideration in assessing the proportionality of the restriction.

3. Articles 17 and 60

78. The Government, invoking Articles 17 and 60 of the Convention, has submitted that Article 10 should be interpreted in such a manner as to limit, destroy or derogate from the right to life of the unborn which enjoys special protection under Irish law.

79. Without calling into question under the Convention the regime of protection of unborn life that exists under Irish law, the Court recalls that the injunction did not prevent Irish women from having abortions abroad and that the information it sought to restrain was available from other sources.[ ] Accordingly, it is not the interpretation of Article 10 but the position in Ireland as regards the implementation of the law that makes possible the continuance of the current level of abortions obtained by Irish women abroad.

4. Conclusion

80. In the light of the above, the Court concludes that the restraint imposed on the applicants from receiving or imparting information was disproportionate to the aims pursued. Accordingly there has been a breach of Article 10.

. . . .

～

QUESTIONS & COMMENTS

(1) Consider the Partly Dissenting Opinion of Judge Matscher:

> 3. ...
>   (a) the case under review highlights the tension which exists between two of the conditions provided for in the second paragraphs of Articles 8 to 11 of the Convention which, if satisfied, may render permissible interferences with the rights guaranteed under those Articles, the conditions in issue here being that of a "legitimate aim" and that of "necessity in a democratic society."
>   According to my understanding of the position, the criterion of "necessity" relates exclusively to the measures which the State adopts in order to attain the (legitimate) "aim" pursued;

it therefore concerns the appropriateness and proportionality of such measures, but it in no way empowers the European organs to "weigh up" or to call in question the legitimacy of the aim as such, in other words to inquire into whether it is "necessary" to seek to attain such an aim.

That is why I cannot accept the definition of the term "necessary" as "corresponding to a pressing social need," which in fact expresses the intention of the European Court to assess for itself whether it is "necessary" for a national legislature or a national court to seek to attain an aim which the Convention recognizes as legitimate. . . .

Why does the European Court further scrutinize those state interests allowing the limitation of rights in Articles 8 through 11 by requiring that these interests reflect a "pressing social need"? If a "pressing social need" is comparable to the "compelling state interest" in the strict scrutiny test in U.S. constitutional jurisprudence governing fundamental rights (such as rights to freedom of political expression and freedom from racial discrimination), is not this heightened scrutiny reflective of the special status of the rights in Articles 8 through 11?

(2) Consider the dissenting opinion of Judge Blayney.

> . . . The injunction could not in my opinion be said to be disproportionate. It was the only measure possible to uphold Article 40(3)(3). There was no other course that the Court could have taken. It was inconceivable that it should refuse to grant an injunction since this would have amounted to an abdication of its duty to protect the rights of the unborn and would have fatally undermined the moral values enshrined in Article 40(3)(3). . . .

Is Judge Blayney missing the issue here? As the European Court noted, it was the antiabortion law itself that was too broad. If the law itself was too broad, its enforcement mechanism would also be too broad or disproportionate. Suppose that Ireland modified its abortion law (as it had) and accordingly modified the scope of the injunction at issue in *Open Door Counselling*. Would such a modified injunction survive proportionality scrutiny in light of the Court's analysis in §§76 and 77? Could *any* injunction be proportional in light of §§76 and 77?

The problem of effectively implementing a strongly held local value, which is at odds with values in nearby nations or communities, is common to federal and federal-like systems. For example, *Bigelow v. Virginia*, 421 U.S. 809 (1976), involved Virginia's ban on publication of information about abortion, as applied to an advertisement in a Virginia newspaper regarding the availability of abortions in New York, at a time when abortions were unlawful in Virginia and lawful in New York. The U.S. Supreme Court held the ban unconstitutional. (Note, however, that by the time the Supreme Court decided *Bigelow*, it had invalidated the underlying ban on abortion.) Under modern conditions of communications, including travel, a community may find it nearly impossible to insulate itself from exposure to competing values. Should this be a matter of enough concern to induce courts to modify their approach to problems like those in *Open Door Counselling*?

(3) The UN Human Rights Committee also has addressed the prohibition of information that was considered to encourage immoral behavior. In *Hertzberg et al. v. Finland*, Communication No. 61/1979, views adopted 2 April 1982, in UN Human Rights Committee, 1 SELECTED DECISIONS UNDER THE OPTIONAL PROTOCOL (SECOND TO SIXTEENTH SESSIONS) 124, U.N. Doc. CCPR/C/OP/1 (1985), the UN Human Rights Committee found no Article 19 freedom of expression violation in a case where state-controlled television

prevented a broadcast discussion encouraging homosexual behavior on the basis of protecting the morals of children. However, it is unclear from the Committee's decision how
the broadcast "encouraged" homosexual behavior. It is doubtful whether the UN Human
Rights Committee would consider its 15-year-old decision in *Hertzberg et al. v. Finland*
still authoritative after its decision in *Toonen v. Australia,* Communication No. 488/1992,
views adopted 31 March 1994, U.N. Doc. CCPR/C/50/D/488/1992 (1994) (slip opinion),
which found a Tasmanian statute outlawing homosexuality in violation of the right to
privacy under the ICCPR. *See* Laurence R. Helfer & Alice M. Miller, *Sexual Orientation
and Human Rights: Toward a United States and Transnational Jurisprudence,* 9 HARV.
HUM. RTS. J. 61, 74 (1996) ("the more searching analysis in *Toonen* accurately reflects
the current perspective of the Committee and suggests that *Hertzberg* might have been
decided differently today").

Compare the U.S. Supreme Court case of *FCC v. Pacifica Foundation,* 438 U.S. 726
(1978), in which the respondent's radio station broadcast a monologue, entitled "Filthy
Words." The twelve-minute monologue was a satirical treatment of the seven words
(*viz.,* shit, piss, fuck, motherfucker, cocksucker, cunt, and tits) that could not be said on
public airwaves. Immediately prior to the broadcast, the radio station advised listeners
that the monologue included sensitive language that some might find offensive. The
Federal Communications Commission (FCC) found the broadcast in violation of a federal
statute that forbids the use of any "obscene, indecent or profane language" in radio
broadcasts, and that the radio station was susceptible to future sanctions. 18 U.S.C.
§1464.

The U.S. Supreme Court held that the FCC had not violated Pacifica Foundation's
First Amendment right to freedom of expression. The Court observed that of all forms of
communication, "it is broadcasting that has received the most limited First Amendment
[protection]." *FCC v. Pacifica Foundation,* 438 U.S. at 748.

> Patently offensive, indecent material presented over the airwaves confronts the citizen, not
> only in public, but also in the privacy of the home, where the individual's right to be left
> alone plainly outweighs the First Amendment right of an intruder.... Because the broadcast
> audience is constantly tuning in and out, prior warnings cannot completely protect the
> listener or viewer from unexpected program content.

Id. at 748–49. The Court also noted that broadcasting is uniquely accessible to children,
even those too young to read. Therefore, the FCC was justified in threatening sanctions
against radio station for broadcasting offensive language.

In light of the enormous amount of pornographic material on the Internet, the substantial use of computers and the Internet by children, and the ineffectiveness of laws
prohibiting obscene Internet materials because of the material's origin outside the country, will the UN Human Rights Committee's decision in *Hertzberg et al. v. Finland* become
further irrelevant? Will the U.S. Supreme Court's decision in *FCC v. Pacifica Foundation*
also become irrelevant? Compare the European Court of Human Rights observation in
the following case, THE OBSERVER *and* THE GUARDIAN *v. United Kingdom* ("*The Spycatcher Case*"), 216 Eur. Ct. H.R. (ser. A) (1991), that the publication of national security
sensitive materials in other countries undercuts the U.K. government's claim that it has
a lawful need to issue an injunction prohibiting the publication of such materials in the
United Kingdom.

National Security

THE OBSERVER and THE GUARDIAN v. United Kingdom
("The Spycatcher Case")
European Court of Human Rights
216 Eur. Ct. H.R. (ser. A) (1991)
14 E.H.R.R. 153 (1992)

FACTS

. . . .

9. The applicants in this case (who are hereinafter together referred to as 'OG') are (a) The Observer Ltd, the proprietors and publishers of the United Kingdom national Sunday newspaper OBSERVER, Mr. Donald Trelford, its editor, and Mr. David Leigh and Mr. Paul Lashmar, two of its reporters; and (b) Guardian Newspapers Ltd, the proprietors and publishers of the United Kingdom national daily newspaper THE GUARDIAN, Mr. Peter Preston, its editor, and Mr. Richard Norton-Taylor, one of its reporters. They complain of interlocutory injunctions imposed by the English courts on the publication of details of the book SPYCATCHER and information obtained from its author, Mr. Peter Wright.

. . . .

The principles on which such injunctions will be granted – to which reference was made in the proceedings in the present case – were set out in *American Cyanamid Co. v. Ethicon Ltd.* ([1975] A.C. 396) and may be summarised as follows.

(a) It is not for the court at the interlocutory stage to seek to determine disputed issues of fact or to decide difficult questions of law which call for detailed argument and mature consideration.

(b) Unless the material before the court at that stage fails to disclose that the plaintiff has any real prospect of succeeding in his claim for a permanent injunction, the court should consider, in the light of the particular circumstances of the case, whether the balance of convenience lies in favour of granting or refusing the interlocutory relief that is sought.

(c) If damages would be an adequate remedy for the plaintiff if he were to succeed at the trial, no interlocutory injunction should normally be granted. If, on the other hand, damages would not provide an adequate remedy for the plaintiff but would adequately compensate the defendant under the plaintiff's undertaking if the defendant were to succeed at the trial, there would be no reason to refuse an interlocutory injunction on this ground.

(d) It is where there is doubt as to the adequacy of the respective remedies in damages available to either party or both that the question of balance of convenience arises.

(e) Where other factors appear evenly balanced, it is a counsel of prudence to take such measures as are calculated to preserve the status quo.

. . . .

11. Mr. Peter Wright was employed by the British Government as a senior member of the British Security Service (MI5) from 1955 to 1976, when he resigned. Subsequently, without any authority from his former employers, he wrote his memoirs, entitled SPYCATCHER, and made arrangements for their publication in Australia, where he was

then living. The book dealt with the operational organisation, methods and personnel of MI5 and also included an account of alleged illegal activities by the Security Service. He asserted therein, *inter alia*, that MI5 conducted unlawful activities calculated to undermine the 1974–1979 Labour Government, burgled and 'bugged' the embassies of allied and hostile countries and planned and participated in other unlawful and covert activities at home and abroad, and that Sir Roger Hollis, who led MI5 during the latter part of Mr Wright's employment, was a Soviet agent.

Mr. Wright had previously sought, unsuccessfully, to persuade the British Government to institute an independent inquiry into these allegations. In 1987 such an inquiry was also sought by, amongst others, a number of prominent members of the 1974–1979 Labour Government, but in vain.

12. Part of the material in SPYCATCHER had already been published in a number of books about the Security Service written by Mr. Chapman Pincher. Moreover, in July 1984 Mr. Wright had given a lengthy interview to Granada Television (an independent television company operating in the UK) about the work of the service and the programme was shown again in December 1986. Other books and another television programme on the workings and secrets of the service were produced at about the same time, but little Government action was taken against the authors or the media.

D. Institution of proceedings in Australia

13. In September 1985 the Attorney General of England and Wales ('The Attorney General') instituted, on behalf of the United Kingdom Government, proceedings in the Equity Division of the Supreme Court of New South Wales, Australia, to restrain publication of SPYCATCHER and of any information therein derived from Mr. Wright's work for the Security Service. The claim was based not on official secrecy but on the ground that the disclosure of such information by Mr Wright would constitute a breach of, notably, his duty of confidentiality under the terms of his employment. On 17 September he and his publishers, Heinemann Publishers Australia Pty Ltd, gave undertakings, by which they abided, not to publish pending the hearing of the Government's claim for an injunction.

Throughout the Australian proceedings the Government objected to the book as such; it declined to indicate which passages they objected to as being detrimental to national security.

II. The interlocutory proceedings in England and events occurring whilst they were in progress

A. The Observer and Guardian articles and the ensuing injunctions

14. Whilst the Australian proceedings were still pending, there appeared, on Sunday 22 and Monday 23 June 1986 respectively, short articles on inside pages of the OBSERVER and THE GUARDIAN reporting on the forthcoming hearing in Australia and giving details of some of the contents of the manuscript of SPYCATCHER. These two newspapers had for some time been conducting a campaign for an independent investigation into the workings of the Security Service. The details given included the following allegations of improper, criminal and unconstitutional conduct on the part of MI5 officers:

(a) MI5 'bugged' all diplomatic conferences at Lancaster House in London throughout the 1950s and 1960s, as well as the Zimbabwe independence negotiations in 1979;

(b) MI5 'bugged' diplomats from France, Germany, Greece and Indonesia, as well as Mr. Krushchev's hotel suite during his visit to Britain in the 1950s, and was guilty of routine burglary and 'bugging' (including the entering of Soviet consulates abroad);

(c) MI5 plotted unsuccessfully to assassinate President Nasser of Egypt at the time of the Suez crisis;

(d) MI5 plotted against Harold Wilson during his premiership from 1974 to 1976;

(e) MI5 (contrary to its guidelines) diverted its resources to investigate left-wing political groups in Britain.

The OBSERVER and GUARDIAN articles, which were written by Mr. Leigh and Mr. Lashmar and by Mr. Norton-Taylor respectively, were based on investigations by these journalists from confidential sources and not on generally available international press releases or similar material. However, much of the actual information in the articles had already been published elsewhere. The English courts subsequently inferred that, on the balance of probabilities, the journalists' sources must have come from the offices of the publishers of SPYCATCHER or the solicitors acting for them and the author. [citation omitted]

15. The Attorney General instituted proceedings for breach of confidence in the Chancery Division of the High Court of Justice of England and Wales against OG, seeking permanent injunctions restraining them from making any publication of SPYCATCHER material. He based his claim on the principle that the information in the memoirs was confidential and that a third party coming into possession of information knowing that it originated from a breach of confidence owed the same duty to the original confider as that owed by the original confidant. It was accepted that an award of damages would have been an insufficient and inappropriate remedy for the Attorney General and that only an injunction would serve his purpose.

16. The evidential basis for the Attorney General's claim was two affidavits sworn by Sir Robert Armstrong, Secretary to the British Cabinet, in the Australian proceedings on 9 and 27 September 1985. He had stated therein, *inter alia*, that the publication of any narrative based on information available to Mr. Wright as a member of the Security Service would cause unquantifiable damage, both to the service itself and to its officers and other persons identified, by reason of the disclosures involved. It would also undermine the confidence that friendly countries and other organisations and persons had in the Security Service and create a risk of other employees or former employees of that service seeking to publish similar information.

17. On 27 June 1986 *ex parte* interim injunctions were granted to the Attorney General restraining any further publication of the kind in question pending the substantive trial of the actions. On an application by OG and after an inter partes hearing on 11 July, Millett J (sitting in the Chancery Division) decided that these injunctions should remain in force, but with various modifications. The defendants were given liberty to apply to vary or discharge the orders on giving 24 hours' notice.

18. The reasons for Millett J's decision may briefly be summarised as follows.

(a) Disclosure by Mr. Wright of information acquired as a member of the Security Service would constitute a breach of his duty of confidentiality.

(b) OG wished to be free to publish further information deriving directly or indirectly from Mr. Wright and disclosing alleged unlawful activity on the part of the Security Service, whether or not it had been previously published.

(c) Neither the right to freedom of speech nor the right to prevent the disclosure of information received in confidence was absolute.

(d) In resolving, as in the present case, a conflict between the public interest in preventing and the public interest in allowing such disclosure, the court had to take into account all relevant considerations, including the facts that this was an interlocutory application and not the trial of the action, that the injunctions sought at this stage were only temporary and that the refusal of injunctive relief might cause irreparable harm and effectively deprive the Attorney General of his rights. In such circumstances, the conflict should be resolved in favour of restraint unless the court was satisfied that there was a serious defence of public interest that might succeed at the trial: an example would be when the proposed publication related to unlawful acts, the disclosure of which was required in the public interest. This could be regarded either as an exception to the *American Cyanamid* principles or their application in special circumstances where the public interest was invoked on both sides.

(e) The Attorney General's principal objection was not to the dissemination of allegations about the Security Service but to the fact that those allegations were made by one of its former employees, it being that particular fact which OG wished to publish. There was credible evidence (in the shape of Sir Robert Armstrong's affidavits) that the appearance of confidentiality was essential to the operation of the Security Service and that the efficient discharge of its duties would be impaired, with consequent danger to national security, if senior officers were known to be free to disclose what they had learned whilst employed by it. Although this evidence remained to be tested at the substantive trial, the refusal of an interlocutory injunction would permit indirect publication and permanently deprive the Attorney General of his rights at the trial. Bearing in mind, *inter alia*, that the alleged unlawful activities had occurred some time in the past, there was, moreover, no compelling interest requiring publication immediately rather than after the trial.

In the subsequent stages of the interlocutory proceedings, both the Court of Appeal and all the members of the Appellate Committee of the House of Lords considered that this initial grant of interim injunctions by Millett J was justified.

19. On 25 July 1986 the Court of Appeal dismissed an appeal by OG and upheld the injunctions, with minor modifications. It referred to the *American Cyanamid* principles and considered that Millett J had not misdirected himself or exercised his discretion on an erroneous basis. It refused leave to appeal to the House of Lords. It also certified the case as fit for a speedy trial.

As amended by the Court of Appeal, the injunctions ('The Millett injunctions') restrained OG, until the trial of the action or further order, from:

1. disclosing or publishing or causing or permitting to be disclosed or published to any person any information obtained by Peter Maurice Wright in his capacity as a member of the British Security Service and which they know, or have reasonable grounds to believe, to have come or been obtained, whether directly or indirectly, from the said Peter Maurice Wright;

2. attributing in any disclosure or publication made by them to any person any information concerning the British Security Service to the said Peter Maurice Wright whether by name or otherwise.

The orders contained the following provisos:

1. this Order shall not prohibit direct quotation of attributions to Peter Maurice Wright already made by Mr. Chapman Pincher in published works, or in a television programme or programmes broadcast by Granada Television;

2. no breach of this Order shall be constituted by the disclosure or publication of any material disclosed in open court in the Supreme Court of New South Wales unless prohibited by the Judge there sitting or which, after the trial there in action no 4382 of 1985, is not prohibited from publication;

3. no breach of this Order shall be constituted by a fair and accurate report of proceedings in (a) either House of Parliament in the United Kingdom whose publication is permitted by that House; or (b) a court of the United Kingdom sitting in public.

20. On 6 November 1986 the Appellate Committee of the House of Lords granted leave to appeal against the Court of Appeal's decision. The appeal was subsequently withdrawn in the light of the House of Lords decision of 30 July 1987.

. . . .

C. Further press reports concerning SPYCATCHER; the Independent case

22. On 27 April 1987 a major summary of certain of the allegations in SPYCATCHER, allegedly based on a copy of the manuscript, appeared in the United Kingdom national daily newspaper THE INDEPENDENT. Later the same day reports of that summary were published in the LONDON EVENING STANDARD and the LONDON DAILY NEWS.

On the next day the Attorney General applied to the Queen's Bench Division of the High Court for leave to move against the publishers and editors of these three newspapers for contempt of court, that is conduct intended to interfere with or prejudice the administration of justice. Leave was granted on 29 April. In this application (hereinafter 'the Independent case') the Attorney General was not acting – as he was in the breach of confidence proceedings against OG – as the representative of the Government, but independently and in his capacity as 'the guardian of the public interest in the due administration of justice.'

Reports similar to those of 27 April appeared on 29 April in Australia, in the MELBOURNE AGE and the CANBERRA TIMES, and on 3 May in the United States of America, in the WASHINGTON POST.

23. On 29 April 1987 OG applied for the discharge of the Millett injunctions on the ground that there had been a significant change of circumstances since they were granted. They referred to what had transpired in the Australian proceedings and to the United Kingdom newspaper reports of 27 April.

The Vice-Chancellor, Sir Nicolas Browne-Wilkinson, began to hear these applications on 7 May but adjourned them pending the determination of a preliminary issue of law, raised in the Independent case, on which he thought their outcome to be largely dependent, namely 'whether a publication made in the knowledge of an outstanding injunction against another party, and which if made by that other party would be in breach thereof, constitutes a criminal contempt of court upon the footing that it assaults or interferes with the process of justice in relation to the said injunction.' On 11 May, in response to the Vice-Chancellor's invitation, the Attorney General pursued the proceedings in the Independent case in the Chancery Division of the High Court and the Vice Chancellor ordered the trial of the preliminary issue.

24. On 14 May 1987 Viking Penguin Inc, which had purchased from Mr. Wright's Australian publishers the United States publication rights to SPYCATCHER, announced its intention of publishing the book in the latter country.

25. On 2 June 1987 the Vice-Chancellor decided the preliminary issue of law in the Independent case. He held that the reports that had appeared on 27 April 1987 could not, as a matter of law, amount to contempt of court because they were not in breach of the express terms of the Millett injunctions and the three newspapers concerned had not been a party to those injunctions or to a breach thereof by the persons they enjoined. The Attorney General appealed.

26. On 15 June 1987 OG, relying on the intended publication in the United States, applied to have the hearing of their application for discharge of the Millett injunctions restored. The matter was, however, adjourned pending the outcome of the Attorney General's appeal in the Independent case, the hearing of which began on 22 June.

D. Serialisation of SPYCATCHER begins in the SUNDAY TIMES

27. On 12 July 1987 the United Kingdom national Sunday newspaper the SUNDAY TIMES, which had purchased the British newspaper serialisation rights from Mr. Wright's Australian publishers and obtained a copy of the manuscript from Viking Penguin Inc. in the United States, printed – in its later editions in order to avoid the risk of proceedings for an injunction – the first instalment of extracts from SPYCATCHER. It explained that this was timed to coincide with publication of the book in the United States, which was due to take place on 14 July.

On 13 July the Attorney General commenced proceedings for contempt of court against Times Newspapers Ltd, the publisher of the SUNDAY TIMES, and Mr. Andrew Neil, its editor, (hereinafter together referred to as 'ST') on the ground that the publication frustrated the purpose of the Millett injunctions.

E. Publication of SPYCATCHER in the USA

28. On 14 July 1987 Viking Penguin Inc. published SPYCATCHER in the USA; some copies had, in fact, been put on sale on the previous day. It was an immediate best seller. The British Government, which had been advised that proceedings to restrain publication in the United States would not succeed, took no legal action to that end either in that country or in Canada, where the book also became a best seller.

29. A substantial number of copies of the book were then brought into the UK, notably by British citizens who had bought it whilst visiting the United States or who had purchased it by telephone or post from American bookshops. The telephone number and address of such bookshops willing to deliver the book to the UK were widely advertised in that country. No steps to prevent such imports were taken by the British Government, which formed the view that although a ban was within its powers, it was likely to be ineffective. It did, however, take steps to prevent the book being available at UK booksellers or public libraries.

F. Conclusion of the Independent case

30. On 15 July 1987 the Court of Appeal announced that it would reverse the judgment of the Vice-Chancellor in the Independent case. Its reasons, which were handed down on

17 July, were basically as follows: the purpose of the Millett injunctions was to preserve the confidentiality of the SPYCATCHER material until the substantive trial of the actions against OG; the conduct of THE INDEPENDENT, the LONDON EVENING STANDARD and the LONDON DAILY NEWS could, as a matter of law, constitute a criminal contempt of court because publication of that material would destroy that confidentiality and, hence, the subject-matter of those actions and therefore interfere with the administration of justice. The Court of Appeal remitted the case to the High Court for it to determine whether the three newspapers had acted with the specific intent of so interfering. (§§2(3) and 6(c) of the Contempt of Court Act 1981.)

31. The Court of Appeal refused the defendants leave to appeal to the House of Lords and they did not seek leave to appeal from the House itself. Neither did they apply to the High Court for modification of the Millett injunctions. The result of the Court of Appeal's decision was that those injunctions were effectively binding on all the British media, including the SUNDAY TIMES.

G. Conclusion of the interlocutory proceedings in the OBSERVER, GUARDIAN and SUNDAY TIMES cases; maintenance of the Millett injunctions.

32. ST made it clear that, unless restrained by law, they would publish the second installment of the serialisation of SPYCATCHER on 19 July 1987. On 16 July the Attorney General applied for an injunction to restrain them from publishing further extracts, maintaining that this would constitute a contempt of court by reason of the combined effect of the Millett injunctions and the decision in the Independent case.

On the same day the Vice-Chancellor granted a temporary injunction restraining publication by ST until 21 July 1987. It was agreed that on 20 July he would consider the application by OG for discharge of the Millett injunctions and that, since they effectively bound ST as well, the latter would have a right to be heard in support of that application. It was further agreed that he would also hear the Attorney General's claim for an injunction against ST and that that claim would fail if the Millett injunctions were discharged.

33. Having heard argument from 20 to 22 July 1987, the Vice-Chancellor gave judgment on the last-mentioned date, discharging the Millett injunctions and dismissing the claim for an injunction against ST.

The Vice-Chancellor's reasons may briefly be summarised as follows.

(a) There had, notably in view of the publication in the United States, been a radical change of circumstances, and it had to be considered if it would be appropriate to grant the injunctions in the new circumstances.

(b) Having regard to the case law and notwithstanding the changed circumstances, it had to be assumed that the Attorney General still had an arguable case for obtaining an injunction against OG at the substantive trial; accordingly, the ordinary American Cyanamid principles fell to be applied.

(c) Since damages would be an ineffective remedy for the Attorney General and would be no compensation to the newspapers, it had to be determined where the balance of convenience lay; the preservation of confidentiality should be favoured unless another public interest outweighed it.

(d) Factors in favour of continuing the injunctions were: the proceedings were only interlocutory; there was nothing new or urgent about Mr. Wright's allegations; the injunctions would bind all the media, so that there would be no question of discrimination; undertakings not to publish were still in force in Australia; to discharge the injunctions would mean that the courts were powerless to preserve confidentiality; to continue the injunctions would discourage others from following Mr Wright's example.

(e) Factors in favour of discharging the injunctions were: publication in the United States had destroyed a large part of the purpose of the Attorney General's actions; publications in the press, especially those concerning allegations of unlawful conduct in the public service, should not be restrained unless this was unavoidable; the courts would be brought into disrepute if they made orders manifestly incapable of achieving their purpose.

(f) The matter was quite nicely weighted and in no sense obvious but, with hesitation, the balance fell in favour of discharging the injunctions.

The Attorney General immediately appealed against the Vice-Chancellor's decision; pending the appeal the injunctions against OG, but not the injunction against ST, were continued in force.

34. In a judgment of 24 July 1987 the Court of Appeal held that:

(a) the Vice-Chancellor had erred in law in various respects, so that the Court of Appeal could exercise its own discretion;

(b) in the light of the American publication of SPYCATCHER, it was inappropriate to continue the Millett injunctions in their original form;

(c) it was, however, appropriate to vary these injunctions to restrain publication in the course of business of all or part of the book or other statements by or attributed to Mr Wright on security matters, but to permit 'a summary in very general terms' of his allegations.

The members of the Court of Appeal considered that continuation of the injunctions would: serve to restore confidence in the Security Service by showing that memoirs could not be published without authority (Sir John Donaldson, MR); serve to protect the Attorney General's rights until the trial (Ralph Gibson LJ); or fulfil the courts' duty of deterring the dissemination of material written in breach of confidence. (Russell LJ)

The Court of Appeal gave leave to all parties to appeal to the House of Lords.

35. After hearing argument from 27 to 29 July 1987 (when neither side supported the CA's compromise solution), the Appellate Committee of the House of Lords gave judgment on 30 July, holding, by a majority of three (Lord Brandon of Oakbrook, Lord Templeman and Lord Ackner) to two (Lord Bridge of Harwich – the immediate past Chairman of the Security Commission – and Lord Oliver of Aylmerton), that the Millett injunctions should continue. In fact, they subsequently remained in force until the commencement of the substantive trial in the breach of confidence actions on 23 November 1987.

The majority also decided that the scope of the injunctions should be widened by the deletion of part of the proviso that had previously allowed certain reporting of the Australian proceedings, since the injunctions would be circumvented if English newspapers were to reproduce passages from SPYCATCHER read out in open court. In the events that happened, this deletion had, according to the Government, no practical incidence on the reporting of the Australian proceedings.

36. The members of the Appellate Committee gave their written reasons on 13 August 1987; they may briefly be summarised as follows.

(a) Lord Brandon of Oakbrook

(i) The object of the Attorney General's actions against OG was the protection of an important public interest, namely the maintenance as far as possible of the secrecy of the Security Service; as was recognised in Article 10(2) of the Convention, the right to freedom of expression was subject to certain exceptions, including the protection of national security.

(ii) The injunctions in issue were only temporary, being designed to hold the ring until the trial, and their continuation did not prejudge the decision to be made at the trial on the claim for final injunction.

(iii) The view taken in the courts below, before the American publication, that the Attorney General had a strong arguable case for obtaining final injunctions at the trial was not really open to challenge.

(iv) Publication in the United States had weakened that case, but it remained arguable; it was not clear whether, as a matter of law, that publication had caused the newspapers' duty of non-disclosure to lapse. Although the major part of the potential damage adverted to by Sir Robert Armstrong had already been done, the courts might still be able to take useful steps to reduce the risk of similar damage by other Security Service employees in the future. This risk was so serious that the courts should do all they could to minimise it.

(v) The only way to determine the Attorney General's case justly and to strike the proper balance between the public interests involved was to hold a substantive trial at which evidence would be adduced and subjected to cross-examination.

(vi) Immediate discharge of the injunctions would completely destroy the Attorney General's arguable case at the interlocutory stage, without his having had the opportunity of having it tried on appropriate evidence.

(vii) Continuing the injunctions until the trial would, if the Attorney General's claims then failed, merely delay but not prevent the newspapers' right to publish information which, moreover, related to events that had taken place many years in the past.

(viii) In the overall interests of justice, a course which could only result in temporary and in no way irrevocable damage to the cause of the newspapers was to be preferred to one which might result in permanent and irrevocable damage to the cause of the Attorney General.

(b) Lord Templeman (who agreed with the observations of Lords Brandon and Ackner)

(i) The appeal involved a conflict between the right of the public to be protected by the Security Service and its right to be supplied with full information by the press. It therefore involved consideration of the Convention, the question being whether the interference constituted by the injunctions was, on 30 July 1987, necessary in a democratic society for one or more of the purposes listed in Article 10(2).

(ii) In terms of the Convention, the restraints were necessary in the interests of national security, for protecting the reputation or rights of others, for preventing the disclosure of information received in confidence and for maintaining the authority of the judiciary. The restraints would prevent harm to the Security Service, notably in the form of the mass circulation, both now and in the future, of accusations to which its members could not respond. To discharge the injunctions would surrender to the press the power to evade a court order designed to protect the confidentiality of information obtained by a member of the Service.

(c) Lord Ackner (who agreed with the observations of Lord Templeman)

(i) It was accepted by all members of the Appellate Committee that: the Attorney General had an arguable case for a permanent injunction; damages were a worthless remedy for the Crown which, if the Millett injunctions were not continued, would lose forever the prospect of obtaining permanent injunctions at the trial; continuation of the Millett injunctions was not a 'final locking-out' of the press which, if successful at the trial, would then be able to publish material that had no present urgency; there was a real public interest, that required protection, concerned with the efficient functioning of the Security Service and it extended, as was not challenged by the newspapers, to discouraging the use of the United Kingdom market for the dissemination of unauthorised memoirs of Security Service officers.

(ii) It would thus be a denial of justice to refuse to allow the injunctions to continue until the trial, for that would sweep aside the public interest factor without any trial and would prematurely and permanently deny the Attorney General any protection from the courts.

(d) Lord Bridge of Harwich

(i) The case in favour of maintaining the Millett injunctions – which had been properly granted in the first place – would not be stronger at the trial than it was now; it would be absurd to continue them temporarily if no case for permanent injunctions could be made out.

(ii) Since the SPYCATCHER allegations were now freely available to the public, it was manifestly too late for the injunctions to serve the interest of national security in protecting sensitive information.

(iii) It could be assumed that the Attorney General could still assert a bare duty binding on the newspapers, but the question was whether the Millett injunctions could still protect an interest of national security of sufficient weight to justify the resultant encroachment on freedom of speech. The argument that their continuation would have a deterrent effect was of minimal weight.

(iv) The attempt to insulate the British public from information freely available else-where was a significant step down the road to censorship characteristic of a totalitarian regime and, if pursued, would lead to the Government's condemnation and humiliation by the European Court of Human Rights.

(e) Lord Oliver of Aylmerton

(i) Millett J's initial order was entirely correct.

(ii) The injunctions had originally been imposed to preserve the confidentiality of what were at the time unpublished allegations, but that confidentiality had now been irrevocably destroyed by the publication of SPYCATCHER. It was questionable whether it was right to use the injunctive remedy against the newspapers (who had not been concerned with the publication) for the remaining purpose which the injunctions might serve, namely punishing Mr. Wright and providing an example to others.

(iii) The newspapers had presented their arguments on the footing that the Attorney General still had an arguable case for the grant of permanent injunctions and there was force in the view that the difficult and novel point of law involved should not be determined without further argument at the trial. However, in the light of the public availability of the SPYCATCHER material, it was difficult to see how it could be successfully argued that the newspapers should be permanently restrained from publishing it and the case of the Attorney General was unlikely to improve in the meantime. No arguable case for permanent injunctions at the trial therefore remained and the Millett injunctions should accordingly be discharged.

H. Conclusion of the Australian proceedings; further publication of SPYCATCHER

37. On 24 September 1987 the New South Wales Court of Appeal delivered judgment dismissing the Attorney General's appeal; the majority held that his claim was not justiciable in an Australian court since it involved either an attempt to enforce indirectly the public laws of a foreign State or a determination of the question whether publication would be detrimental to the public interest in the United Kingdom.

The Attorney General appealed to the High Court of Australia. In view of the publication of SPYCATCHER in the United States and elsewhere, that court declined to grant temporary injunctions restraining its publication in Australia pending the hearing; it was published in that country on 13 October. The appeal was dismissed on 2 June 1988, on the ground that, under international law, a claim – such as the Attorney General's – to enforce British governmental interests in its security service was unenforceable in the Australian courts.

Further proceedings brought by the Attorney General against newspapers for injunctions were successful in Hong Kong but not in New Zealand.

38. In the meantime publication and dissemination of SPYCATCHER and its contents continued worldwide, not only in the United States (around 715,000 copies were printed and nearly all were sold by October 1987) and in Canada (around 100,000 copies were printed), but also in Australia (145,000 copies printed, of which half were sold within a month) and Ireland (30,000 copies printed and distributed). Nearly 100,000 copies were sent to various European countries other than the UK and copies were distributed from Australia in Asian countries. Radio broadcasts in English about the book were made in Denmark and Sweden and it was translated into 12 other languages, including ten European.

III. The substantive proceedings in England

A. Breach of confidence

39. On 27 October 1987 the Attorney General instituted proceedings against ST for breach of confidence; in addition to injunctive relief, he sought a declaration and an account of profits. The substantive trial of that action and of his actions against OG – in which, by an amendment of 30 October, he now claimed a declaration as well as an injunction – took place before Scott J in the High Court in November-December 1987. He heard evidence on behalf of all parties, the witnesses including Sir Robert Armstrong. He also continued the interlocutory injunctions, pending delivery of his judgment.

40. Scott J gave judgment on 21 December 1987; it contained the following observations and conclusions.

(a) The ground for the Attorney General's claim for permanent injunctions was no longer the preservation of the secrecy of certain information but the promotion of the efficiency and reputation of the Security Service.

(b) Where a duty of confidence is sought to be enforced against a newspaper coming into possession of information known to be confidential, the scope of its duty will depend on the relative weights of the interests claimed to be protected by that duty and the interests served by disclosure.

(c) Account should be taken of Article 10 of the Convention and the judgments of the European court establishing that a limitation of free expression in the interests of national security should not be regarded as necessary unless there was a 'pressing social need' for the limitation and it was 'proportionate to the legitimate aims pursued.'

(d) Mr. Wright owed a duty to the Crown not to disclose any information obtained by him in the course of his employment in MI5. He broke that duty by writing SPYCATCHER and submitting it for publication, and the subsequent publication and dissemination of the book amounted to a further breach, so that the Attorney General would be entitled to an injunction against Mr. Wright or any agent of his, restraining publication of SPYCATCHER in the United Kingdom.

(e) OG were not in breach of their duty of confidentiality, created by being recipients of Mr. Wright's unauthorised disclosures, in publishing their respective articles of 22 and 23 June 1986; the articles were a fair report in general terms of the forthcoming trial in Australia and, furthermore, disclosure of two of Mr. Wright's allegations was justified on an additional ground relating to the disclosure of 'iniquity.'

(f) ST, on the other hand, had been in breach of the duty of confidentiality in publishing the first instalment of extracts from the book on 12 July 1987, since those extracts contained certain material which did not raise questions of public interest outweighing those of national security.

(g) ST were liable to account for the profits accruing to them as a result of the publication of that instalment.

(h) The Attorney General's claims for permanent injunctions failed because the publication and worldwide dissemination of SPYCATCHER since July 1987 had had the result that there was no longer any duty of confidence lying on newspapers or other third parties in relation to the information in the book; as regards this issue, a weighing of the national security factors relied on against the public interest in freedom of the press showed the latter to be overwhelming.

(i) The Attorney General was not entitled to a general injunction restraining future publication of information derived from Mr. Wright or other members of the Security Service.

After hearing argument, Scott J imposed fresh temporary injunctions pending an appeal to the Court of Appeal; those injunctions contained a proviso allowing reporting of the Australian proceedings.

41. On appeal by the Attorney General and a cross-appeal by ST, the Court of Appeal (Composed of Sir John Donaldson, MR, Dillon LJ and Bingham LJ) affirmed, on 10 February 1988, the decision of Scott J.

However, Sir John Donaldson disagreed with his view that the articles in the OBSERVER and THE GUARDIAN had not constituted a breach of their duty of confidence and that the claim for an injunction against these two newspapers in June 1986 was not 'proportionate to the legitimate aim pursued,' Bingham LJ, on the other hand, disagreed with Scott J's view that ST had been in breach of duty by publishing the first instalment of extracts from SPYCATCHER, that they should account for profits and that the Attorney General had been entitled, in the circumstances as they stood in July 1987, to injunctions preventing further serialisation.

After hearing argument, the Court of Appeal likewise granted fresh temporary injunctions, pending an appeal to the House of Lords; OG and ST were given liberty to apply for variation or discharge if any undue delay arose.

42. On 13 October 1988 the Appellate Committee of the House of Lords (Lord Keith of Kinkel, Lord Brightman, Lord Griffiths, Lord Goff of Chievely and Lord Jauncey of Tullichettle) also affirmed Scott J's judgment. Dismissing an appeal by the Attorney General and a cross-appeal by ST, it held:

(i) That a duty of confidence could arise in contract or in equity and a confidant who acquired information in circumstances importing such a duty should be precluded from disclosing it to others; that a third party in possession of information known to be confidential was bound by a duty of confidence unless the duty was extinguished by the information becoming available to the general public or the duty was outweighed by a countervailing public interest requiring disclosure of the information; that in seeking to restrain the disclosure of government secrets the Crown must demonstrate that disclosure was likely to damage or had damaged the public interest before relief could be granted; that since the worldwide publication of SPYCATCHER had destroyed any secrecy as to its contents, and copies of it were readily available to any individual who wished to obtain them, continuation of the injunctions was not necessary; and that, accordingly, the injunctions should be discharged.

(ii) (Lord Griffiths dissenting) that the articles of 22 and 23 June [1986] had not contained information damaging to the public interest; that the OBSERVER and THE GUARDIAN were not in breach of their duty of confidentiality when they published [those] articles; and that, accordingly, the Crown would not have been entitled to a permanent injunction against both newspapers.

(iii) That the SUNDAY TIMES was in breach of its duty of confidence in publishing its first serialised extract from SPYCATCHER on 12 July 1987; that it was not protected by the defence either of prior publication or disclosure of iniquity; that imminent publication of the book in the United States did not amount to a justification; and that, accordingly, the Sunday Times was liable to account for the profits resulting from that breach.

(iv) That since the information in SPYCATCHER was now in the public domain and no longer confidential no further damage could be done to the public interest that had not already been done; that no injunction should be granted against the OBSERVER and THE GUARDIAN restraining them from reporting on the contents of the book; and that (Lord Griffiths dissenting) no injunction should be granted against the Sunday Times to restrain serialising of further extracts from the book.

(v) That members and former members of the Security Service owed a lifelong duty of confidence to the Crown, and that since the vast majority of them would not disclose confidential information to the newspapers it would not be appropriate to grant a general injunction to restrain the newspapers from future publication of any information on the allegations in SPYCATCHER derived from any member or former member of the Security Service.

B. Contempt of court

43. The substantive trial of the Attorney General's actions for contempt of court against THE INDEPENDENT, the LONDON EVENING STANDARD, the LONDON DAILY NEWS, ST and

certain other newspapers took place before Morritt J in the High Court in April 1989. On 8 May he held, *inter alia*, that THE INDEPENDENT and ST had been in contempt of court and imposed a fine of £50,000 in each case.

44. On 27 February 1990 the Court of Appeal dismissed appeals by the latter two newspapers against the finding that they had been in contempt but concluded that no fines should be imposed. A further appeal by ST against the contempt finding was dismissed by the Appellate Committee of the House of Lords on 11 April 1991.

[The applicants applied to the European Commission which found that in respect to temporary injunctions, Article 10 had been violated.]

. . . .

DECISION [OF THE EUROPEAN COURT OF HUMAN RIGHTS]:

I. Alleged violation of Article 10 of the Convention

48. OG alleged that, by reason of the interlocutory injunctions to which they had been subject from 11 July 1986 to 13 October 1988, they had been victims of a violation of Article 10...

This allegation was contested by the Government. It was accepted by the Commission, by a majority as regards the period from 11 July 1986 to 30 July 1987 and unanimously as regards the period from 30 July 1987 to 13 October 1988.

. . . .

B. Did the interference have aims that are legitimate under Article 10(2)?

55. The Government submitted that the interlocutory injunctions were designed to protect the Attorney General's rights at the substantive trial and therefore had the aim, that was legitimate in terms of paragraph (2) of Article 10, of 'maintaining the authority of the judiciary.' Before the Court, it also asserted that the injunctions indirectly served the aim of protecting national security, since the underlying purpose of the Attorney General's actions was to prevent the effective operation of the Security Service from being undermined.

Although OG expressed certain reservations on the second of these points, they did not seek to deny that the interference had a legitimate aim.

56. The Court is satisfied that the injunctions had the direct or primary aim of 'maintaining the authority of the judiciary,' which phrase includes the protection of the rights of litigants. [citation omitted] Perusal of the relevant domestic judgments makes it perfectly clear that the purpose of the order made against OG was – to adopt the description given by Lord Oliver of Aylmerton [*Attorney General v. Times Newspapers Ltd.*, [1991] 2 WLR 1019G] – 'to enable issues between the plaintiff and the defendants to be tried without the plaintiff's rights in the meantime being prejudiced by the doing of the very act which it was the purpose of the action to prevent.'

It is also incontrovertible that a further purpose of the restrictions complained of was the protection of national security. They were imposed, as has just been seen, with a view to ensuring a fair trial of the Attorney General's claim for permanent injunctions against OG and the evidential basis for that claim was the two affidavits sworn by Sir Robert Armstrong, in which he deposed to the potential damage which publication of the SPYCATCHER material would cause to the Security Service. Not only was that evidence relied on by Millett J when granting the injunctions initially, but considerations of national security featured prominently in all the judgments delivered by the English courts in this case. The Court would only comment – and it will revert to this point in paragraph 69 below – that the precise nature of the national security considerations involved varied over the course of time.

57. The interference complained of thus had aims that were legitimate under paragraph (2) of Article 10.

C. Was the interference 'necessary in a democratic society'?

58. Argument before the Court was concentrated on the question whether the interference complained of could be regarded as 'necessary in a democratic society.' After summarising the relevant general principles that emerge from its case law, the Court will, like the Commission, examine this issue with regard to two distinct periods, the first running from 11 July 1986 (imposition of the Millett injunctions) to 30 July 1987 (continuation of those measures by the House of Lords), and the second from 30 July 1987 to 13 October 1988 (final decision on the merits of the Attorney General's actions for breach of confidence).

1. General principles

59. The Court's judgments relating to Article 10 – starting with [*Handyside v. United Kingdom*] concluding, most recently, with [*Oberschlick v. Austria*] and including, amongst others, [*Sunday Times v. United Kingdom*] and [*Lingens v. Austria*] – [an]nounce the following major principles.

(a) Freedom of expression constitutes one of the essential foundations of a democratic society; subject to paragraph (2) of Article 10, it is applicable not only to 'information' or 'ideas' that are favourably received or regarded as inoffensive or as a matter of indifference, but also to those that offend, shock or disturb. Freedom of expression, as enshrined in Article 10, is subject to a number of exceptions which, however, must be narrowly interpreted and the necessity for any restrictions must be convincingly established.

(b) These principles are of particular importance as far as the press is concerned. Whilst it must not overstep the bounds set, *inter alia*, in the "interests of national security" or for "maintaining the authority of the judiciary," it is nevertheless incumbent on it to impart information and ideas on matters of public interest. Not only does the press have the task of imparting such information and ideas: the public also has a right to receive them. Were it otherwise, the press would be unable to play its vital role of "public watchdog."

(c) The adjective "necessary", within the meaning of Article 10(2), implies the existence of a "pressing social need". The Contracting States have a certain margin of appreciation in assessing whether such a need exists, but it goes hand in hand with a European supervision, embracing both the law and the decisions applying it, even those given by independent courts. The Court is therefore empowered to give the final ruling on whether a "restriction" is reconcilable with freedom of expression as protected by Article 10.

(d) The Court's task, in exercising is supervisory jurisdiction, is not to take place of the competent national authorities but rather to review under Article 10 the decisions they delivered pursuant to their power of appreciation. This does not mean that the supervision is limited to ascertaining whether the respondent State exercised its discretion reasonably, carefully and in good faith; what the Court has to do is to look at the interference complained of in light of the case as a whole and determine whether it was "proportionate to the legitimate aim pursued" and whether the reasons adduced by the national authorities to justify it are "relevant and sufficient."

60. For the avoidance of doubt, and having in mind the written comments that were submitted in this case by Article 19 [*amicus curiae*], the Court would only add to the foregoing that Article 10 of the Convention does not in terms prohibit the imposition of prior restraints on publication, as such. This is evidenced not only by the words 'conditions,' 'restrictions,' 'preventing' and 'prevention' which appear in that provision, but also by the [*Sunday Times* judgment of 26 April 1979 and its *Markt Intern Verlag GmbH and Klaus Beeman* judgment of 20 November 1988]. On the other hand, the dangers inherent in prior restraints are such that they call for the most careful scrutiny on the part of the Court. This is especially so as far as the press is concerned, for news is a perishable commodity and to delay its publication, even for a short period, may well deprive it of all its value and interest.

2. The period from 11 July 1986 to 30 July 1987

61. In assessing the necessity for the interference with OG's freedom of expression during the period from 11 July 1986 to 30 July 1987, it is essential to have a clear picture of the factual situation that obtained when Millett J first imposed the injunctions in question.

At that time OG had only published two short articles which, in their submission, constituted fair reports concerning the issues in the forthcoming hearing in Australia; contained information that was of legitimate public concern, that is to say allegations of impropriety on the part of officers of the British Security Service; and repeated material which, with little or no action on the part of the Government to prevent this, had for the most part already been made public.

Whilst substantially correct, these submissions do not tell the whole story. They omit, in the first place, OG's acknowledgment, before Millett J, that they wished to be free to publish further information deriving directly or indirectly from Mr. Wright and disclosing alleged unlawful activity on the part of the Security Service, whether or not it had been previously published. What they also omit is the fact that in July 1986 SPYCATCHER existed only in manuscript form. It was not then known precisely what the book would contain and, even if the previously-published material furnished some clues in this respect, it might have been expected that the author would seek to say something new. And it was not unreasonable to suppose that where a former senior employee of a security service – an 'insider,' such as Mr. Wright – proposed to publish, without authorisation, his memoirs, there was at least a risk that they would comprise material the disclosure of which might be detrimental to that service; it has to be borne in mind that in such a context damaging information may be gleaned from an accumulation of what appear at first sight to be unimportant details. What is more, it was improbable in any event that all the contents of the book would raise questions of public concern outweighing the interests of national security.

62. Millett J's decision to grant injunctions – which, in the subsequent stages of the interlocutory proceedings, was accepted as correct not only by the Court of Appeal but also by all the members of the Appellate Committee of the House of Lords – was based on the following line of reasoning. The Attorney General was seeking a permanent ban on the publication of material the disclosure of which would, according to the credible evidence

presented on his behalf, be detrimental to the Security Service; to refuse interlocutory injunctions would mean that OG would be free to publish that material immediately and before the substantive trial; this would effectively deprive the Attorney General, if successful on the merits, of his right to be granted a permanent injunction, thereby irrevocably destroying the substance of his actions and, with it, the claim to protect national security.

In the Court's view, these reasons were 'relevant' in terms of the aims both of protecting national security and of maintaining the authority of the judiciary. The question remains whether they were 'sufficient.'

63. In this connection, OG objected that the interlocutory injunctions had been granted on the basis of the *American Cyanamid* principles which, in their opinion, were incompatible with the criteria of Article 10. They maintained that, in a case of this kind, those principles were unduly advantageous to the plaintiff since he had to establish only that he had an arguable case and that the balance of convenience lay in favour of injunctive relief; in their submission, a stricter test of necessity had to be applied when it was a question of restricting publication by the press on a matter of considerable public interest.

The *American Cyanamid* case admittedly related to the alleged infringement of a patent and not to freedom of the press. However, it is not the Court's function to review those principles *in abstracto*, but rather to determine whether the interference resulting from their application was necessary having regard to the facts and circumstances prevailing in the specific case before it. [*See Sunday Times v. United Kingdom*, at §65.]

In any event, perusal of the relevant judgments reveals that the English courts did far more than simply apply the *American Cyanamid* principles inflexibly or automatically; they recognised that the present case involved a conflict between the public interest in preventing and the public interest in allowing a disclosure of the material in question, which conflict they resolved by a careful weighing of the relevant considerations on either side.

In forming its own opinion, the Court has borne in mind its observations concerning the nature and contents of SPYCATCHER and the interests of national security involved; it has also had regard to the potential prejudice to the Attorney General's breach of confidence actions, this being a point that has to be seen in the context of the central position occupied by Article 6 of the Convention and its guarantee of the right to a fair trial. [*See Sunday Times v. United Kingdom* at §55.] Particularly in the light of these factors, the Court takes the view that, having regard to their margin of appreciation, the English courts were entitled to consider the grant of injunctive relief to be necessary and that their reasons for so concluding were 'sufficient' for the purposes of paragraph (2) of Article 10.

64. It has nevertheless to be examined whether the actual restraints imposed were 'proportionate' to the legitimate aims pursued.

In this connection, it is to be noted that the injunctions did not erect a blanket prohibition. Whilst they forbade the publication of information derived from or attributed to Mr. Wright in his capacity as a member of the Security Service, they did not prevent OG from pursuing their campaign for an independent inquiry into the operation of that service. Moreover, they contained provisos excluding certain material from their scope, notably that which had been previously published in the works of Mr. Chapman Pincher and in the Granada Television programmes. Again, it was open to OG at any time to seek – as they in fact did – variation or discharge of the orders.

It is true that although the injunctions were intended to be no more than temporary measures, they in fact remained in force – as far as the period now under consideration is concerned – for slightly more than a year. And this is a long time where the perishable commodity of news is concerned. As against this, it may be pointed out that the Court of Appeal certified the case as fit for a speedy trial – which OG apparently did not seek – and that the news in question, relating as it did to events that had occurred several years previously, could not really be classified as urgent. Furthermore, the Attorney General's actions raised difficult issues of both fact and law: time was accordingly required for the preparation of the trial, especially since, as Lord Brandon of Oakbrook pointed out, they were issues on which evidence had to be adduced and subjected to cross-examination.

65. Having regard to the foregoing, the Court concludes that, as regards the period from 11 July 1986 to 30 July 1987, the national authorities were entitled to think that the interference complained of was 'necessary in a democratic society.'

3. The period from 30 July to 13 October 1988

66. On 14 July 1987 SPYCATCHER was published in the USA. This changed the situation that had obtained since 11 July 1986. In the first place, the contents of the book ceased to be a matter of speculation and their confidentiality was destroyed. Furthermore, Mr. Wright's memoirs were obtainable from abroad by residents of the United Kingdom, the Government having made no attempt to impose a ban on importation.

67. In the submission of the Government, the continuation of the interlocutory injunctions during the period from 30 July 1987 to 13 October 1988 nevertheless remained 'necessary,' in terms of Article 10, for maintaining the authority of the judiciary and thereby protecting the interests of national security. It relied on the conclusion of the House of Lords in July 1987 that, notwithstanding the United States publication: (a) the Attorney General still had an arguable case for permanent injunctions against OG, which case could be fairly determined only if restraints on publication were imposed pending the substantive trial; and (b) there was still a national security interest in preventing the general dissemination of the contents of the book through the press and a public interest in discouraging the unauthorised publication of memoirs containing confidential material.

68. The fact that the further publication of SPYCATCHER material could have been prejudiced to the trial of the Attorney General's claims for permanent injunctions was certainly in terms of the aim of maintaining the authority of the judiciary, a 'relevant' reason for continuing the restraints in question. The Court finds, however, that in the circumstances it does not constitute a 'sufficient' reason for the purposes of Article 10.

It is true that the House of Lords had regard to the requirements of the Convention, even though it is not incorporated into domestic law. It is also true that there is some difference between the casual importation of copies of SPYCATCHER into the United Kingdom and mass publication of its contents in the press. On the other hand, even if the Attorney General had succeeded in obtaining permanent injunctions at the substantive trial, they would have borne on material the confidentiality of which had been destroyed in any event – and irrespective of whether any further disclosures were made by OG – as a result of the publication in the United States. Seen in terms of the protection of the Attorney General's rights as a litigant, the interest in maintaining the confidentiality of that material had, for the purposes of the Convention, ceased to exist by 30 July 1987. [citation omitted]

69. As regards the interests of national security relied on, the Court observes that in this respect the Attorney General's case underwent, to adopt the words of Scott J, 'a curious metamorphosis' [citation omitted]. As emerges from Sir Robert Armstrong's evidence, injunctions were sought at the outset, *inter alia*, to preserve the secret character of information that ought to be kept secret. By 30 July 1987, however, the information had lost that character and, as was observed by Lord Brandon of Oakbrook, the major part of the potential damage adverted to by Sir Robert Armstrong had already been done. By then, the purpose of the injunctions had thus become confined to the promotion of the efficiency and reputation of the Security Service, notably by: preserving confidence in that Service on the part of third parties; making it clear that the unauthorised publication of memoirs by its former members would not be countenanced; and deterring others who might be tempted to follow in Mr. Wright's footsteps.

The Court does not regard these objectives as sufficient to justify the continuation of the interference complained of. It is, in the first place, open to question whether the actions against OG could have served to advance the attainment of these objectives any further than had already been achieved by the steps taken against Mr. Wright himself. Again, bearing in mind the availability or an action for an account of profits, the Court shares the doubts of Lord Oliver of Aylmerton whether it was legitimate, for the purpose of punishing Mr. Wright and providing an example to others, to use the injunctive remedy against persons, such as OG, who had not been concerned with the publication of Spycatcher. Above all, continuation of the restrictions after July 1987 prevented newspapers from exercising their right and duty to purvey information, already available, on a matter of legitimate public concern.

70. Having regard to the foregoing, the Court concludes that the interference complained of was no longer 'necessary in a democratic society' after 30 July 1987.

. . . .

For these reasons, THE COURT

1. Holds, by 14 votes to 10, that there was no violation of Article 10 of the Convention during the period from 11 July 1986 to 30 July 1987;

2. Holds, unanimously, that there was a violation of Article 10 during the period from 30 July 1987 to 13 October 1988

. . . .

Partly Dissenting Opinion of Judge Pettiti, joined by Judge Pinheiro Farinha

. . . .

One gets the impression that the extreme severity of Millett J's injunction and of the course adopted by the Attorney General was less a question of the duty of confidentiality than the fear of disclosure of certain irregularities carried out by the security service in the pursuit of political rather than intelligence aims.

. . . .

The contradiction in the way the two periods were viewed is in my opinion the following: on the one hand, a decision imposing a restriction based on mere suppositions or assumptions by the Attorney General and the competent court is regarded as justified; on the other, the publication of the book in the United States, then its partial circulation, are said to have rendered the continuation of the injunction unjustified.

But freedom of expression in one country cannot be made subject to whether or not the material in question has been published in another country. In the era of satellite television it is impossible territorially to partition thought and its expression or to restrict the right to information of the inhabitants of a country whose newspapers are subject to a prohibition.

. . . .

Partly Dissenting Opinion of Judge de Meyer (concerning prior restraint), joined by Judges Pettiti, Russo, Foighel and Bigi.

I cannot endorse the Court's reasoning concerning prior restraint upon publications. Nor can I agree with its finding that, in the present case, the applicants' right to freedom of expression was not violated before the end of July 1987.

In my view, it was violated not only after that date and until the case was concluded in October 1988, but from the very beginning of the proceedings in June 1986, when the Attorney General set about seeking injunctions against them.

My reasons for so finding are simple.

I firmly believe that 'the press must be left free to publish news, whatever the source, without censorship, injunctions, or prior restraint' (Black J, joined by Douglas J, in the case, very similar to the present one, of the Pentagon Papers, *New York Times v. United States* and *United States v. Washington Post*, 403 U.S. 713, 717 (1971); although they were there used in the context of the Constitution of the USA, these words perfectly express the general principle to be applied in this field: in a free and democratic society there can be no room, in times of peace, for restrictions of that kind, and particularly not if these are resorted to, as they were in the present case, for 'governmental suppression of embarrassing information' (Douglas J, joined by Black J, in the same case, at pp 723–724) or ideas.

Of course, those who publish any material which a pressing social need required should remain unpublished may subsequently be held liable in court, as may those acting in breach of a duty of confidentiality. They may be prosecuted if and in so far as this is prescribed by penal law, and they may in any case be sued for compensation if injury has been caused. They may also be subject to other sanctions provided for by law, including, as the case may be, confiscation and destruction of the material in question and forfeiture of the profit obtained.

Under no circumstances, however, can prior restraint, even in the form of judicial injunctions, either temporary or permanent, be accepted, except in what the Convention describes as a 'time of war or other public emergency threatening the life of the nation' and, even then, only 'to the extent strictly required by the exigencies of the situation,' (Art 15 of the Convention).

QUESTIONS & COMMENTS

(1) For an unsuccessful Article 10 challenge to an applicant's conviction for having disclosed minor military secrets to a private arms manufacturer, *see Hadjianastassiou v. Greece*, 252 Eur. Ct. H.R. (ser. A) (1992).

(2) Consider *Vereniging Weekblad* BLUF! *v. The Netherlands*, 306-A Eur. Ct. H.R. (ser. A) (1995) (slip opinion). In 1987, the applicant association planned to publish a confidential security service document in its weekly periodical, BLUF! The document, a 1981

report intended for security service staff and officials, contained various items of general information regarding the service's activities – items that amounted to state secrets only when taken in sum. Before the applicant association published the report, police searched the association's premises and seized the entire print run of the relevant issue. Three people were arrested for divulging secret information but were released the following day. Because the police did not confiscate the offset plates on the printing presses, the applicant-association managed to reprint the confiscated issue during the night of the seizure and to sell approximately two thousand five hundred copies in the streets on the queen's birthday, a national holiday. The authorities decided not to interfere with the sales in order to avoid creating a public disorder. Then, in 1988, the regional court ordered that the controversial issue of BLUF! be withdrawn from circulation. The applicant association brought unsuccessful legal action in the national courts challenging both the initial seizure and the subsequent withdrawal from circulation. Subsequently, the case came before the European Court.

With respect to whether the seizure and withdrawal were necessary in a democratic society, the European Court found an Article 10 violation. Noting that the various items of information in the confidential report were six years old, were general in nature, and were no longer state secrets when taken individually, the Court doubted whether this information was sufficiently sensitive to justify preventing its distribution. Moreover, the Court concluded that, as a result of the sale of two thousand five hundred copies of the applicant's periodical, the confidential information was widely known by the time the periodical was withdrawn from circulation. As a result, protection of this information as a state secret was no longer necessary to achieve the legitimate aim pursued, and Article 10 was violated.

(3) Compare *New York Times Co. v. United States* ("The Pentagon Papers Case"), 403 U.S. 713 (1971). In 1971, the *New York Times* and the *Washington Post* published portions of a secret study prepared by the U.S. Defense Department, entitled "History of U.S. Decision-Making Process on Viet Nam Policy." Better known as "The Pentagon Papers," the study included detailed accounts of military operations and diplomatic negotiations. The U.S. government sued the *New York Times* and the *Washington Post* seeking restraining orders against publication of more excerpts from the study. The U.S. government argued that publication of the study constituted a threat against national security.

The U.S. Supreme Court held that the newspapers could proceed with publishing the study. Relying on principles first stated in *Near v. Minnesota*, 283 U.S. 696 (1931), the Court held that there is a "heavy presumption" against the constitutionality of prior restraints. The governmental interest in national security could only justify prior restraint if the country was actively engaged in a war and if there were proof that publication would cause a great deal of harm.

Compare also *Snepp v. United States*, 444 U.S. 507 (1980), in which the U.S. Supreme Court upheld the imposition of a "constructive trust" in favor of the government on all profits Snepp, a former Central Intelligence Agency (CIA) employee, earned from the publication of a book about the CIA. The Court relied on Snepp's contract with the CIA, which required him to submit all proposed publications to the CIA before they were published. The "constructive trust," according to the Court, would operate as a deterrent to violation of Snepp's contractual obligation, whereas other remedies, such as damages or even punitive damages, might not. The contractual obligation might also have been enforced by an injunction requiring submission of proposed publications.

(4) With the growing tendency toward effective elimination of national borders by the Internet and other telecommunications media that are difficult if not impossible for national authorities to control, will the state's assertion of an interest in preventing the publication of sensitive national security materials become increasingly attenuated? It is a common occurrence that once one newspaper publishes such a document, as in the *Spycatcher Case*, other newspapers follow suit. *See United States v. Progressive, Inc.*, 467 F.Supp. 990 (W. D.Wis. 1979), case dismissed, Nos. 79-1428, 79-1664 (7th Cir., Oct. 1, 1979) (U.S. government's suit to enjoin publication of hydrogen bomb data dismissed after publication of data elsewhere).

(5) Note that the European Convention does not proscribe prior restraint, in contrast to Article 13(2) of the American Convention on Human Rights. *See Martorell v. Chile*, Case 11.230, Report No. 11/96, Inter-Am. Cm. H.R., OEA/Ser.L/V/II.95 Doc. 7 rev. at 234 (1997) (finding prior restraint of book not narrowly tailored to protecting rights to privacy, honor, and dignity, as well as judicial remedies and therefore violative of Art. 13).

(6) In an early case, the European Court held that a court injunction restraining publication of a newspaper article violated Article 10. In *The Sunday Times v. United Kingdom*, 30 Eur. Ct. H.R. (ser. A) (1979), the applicant newspaper intended to publish an article claiming that a pharmaceutical company had been negligent. The company had manufactured thalidomide, which was responsible for severe birth defects, and was party to pending litigation. The injunction was issued on the grounds that the article would prejudge an issue presently pending before the court. However, the European Court held that the inflexibility of the U.K. law prohibiting "trial by newspaper" violated Article 10.

How do U.S. courts attempt to guard against prejudicial effects of newspaper reports in pending cases? Compare *Allenet de Ribemont v. France*, 308 Eur. Ct. H.R. (ser. A) (1995), in which the European Court of Human Rights held that public statements made by the French Minister of the Interior concluding that the applicant was an instigator to a murder was violative of the applicant's right to presumption of innocence.

(7) *Compare Engle and Others v. The Netherlands*, 22 Eur. Ct. H.R. (ser. A) (1976) and *Vereinigung Demokratischer Soldaten Österreichs and Gubi v. Germany*, 302 Eur. Ct. H.R. (ser. A) (1994) with *Greer v. Spock*, 424 U.S. 828 (1976). In *Engle and Others v. The Netherlands*, the European Court found no Article 10 violation where the publication and distribution of a journal by soldiers were undertaken to undermine military discipline during a period in which the atmosphere in the barracks was strained. The Court held that the concept of public order (*ordre public*) of Article 10(2) applied not only to society-at-large but also specific social groups, where disorder within a specific group, such as the military, could have repercussions on society as a whole. However, in *Vereinigung Demokratischer Soldaten Österreichs and Gubi v. Germany*, the European Court did find an Article 10 violation where the German Minister of Defence disallowed the distribution of a journal that reported complaints about the military and proposals for reform, and encouraged readers to institute legal actions.

In the U.S. Supreme Court case of *Greer v. Spock*, civilians were allowed to visit the unrestricted areas of Fort Dix, a U.S. military base. However, all demonstrations and speeches of a partisan political nature were forbidden as was distributing or posting literature without prior written approval. On the basis of these military regulations, the military authorities denied the respondents (who were candidates for political office) access to Fort Dix to distribute campaign literature and to campaign among the service personnel. Four other respondents were barred from entering Fort Dix after having distributed literature several times without prior approval. The U.S. Supreme Court held the regulations did not violate the First Amendment's right to freedom of expression. The mere fact that citizens were allowed to visit governmental property did not automatically make that place a "public forum" for purposes of the First Amendment. The business of a military installation, such as Fort Dix, was to train soldiers rather than provide a public forum. Federal military reservations historically have not served as a forum for "free public assembly and communication of thoughts by private citizens[,]" as have municipal streets and parks. 424 U.S. at 838. Concerning the regulation forbidding political demonstrations and speeches, Fort Dix was merely pursuing its policy to keep its official military activities free of entanglement with any and all partisan political campaigns and thus it has engaged in no discrimination based on the candidates' political views. This policy was held to be constitutional and in keeping with the tradition of a politically neutral military establishment. The Court then noted that, as to the regulation concerning the distribution of literature, only publications that the military commander finds clearly threatening military "loyalty, discipline or morale" may be prohibited. *Id.* at 840. Thus, a military commander may not ban the distribution of a publication merely "because he does not like its contents" or because it is "critical – even unfairly critical – of government policies or officials." *Id.* The Court then noted that there was no issue concerning the unconstitutional application of this regulation, as no respondent had submitted any literature for review.

Justice William Brennan dissented arguing in part that the "First Amendment does not evaporate with the mere intonation of interests," such as military necessity or national defense, and that the training of soldiers does not demand the exclusion of those who wish to express publicly their opinions from streets and parking lots open to the public. *Id.* at 852 (Brennan, J., dissenting).

Would the outcome have been different in *Greer v. Spock* if the respondents had been soldiers under the U.S. Supreme Court's jurisprudence? The European Court of Human Rights' jurisprudence?

Media Access and Licensing, and Commercial Expression

Barthold v. Federal Republic of Germany
European Court of Human Rights
90 Eur. Ct. H.R. (ser. A) (1985)
7 E.H.R.R. 383 (1985)

. . . .

FACTS:

10. Dr Barthold . . . is a veterinary surgeon practising in Hamburg-Fuhlsbuttel. In 1978 and until March 1980, his practice operated as a 'veterinary clinic', of which there were eight in Hamburg at the time. He closed down this clinic on 5 March 1980 but subsequently re-opened it on 1 January 1983.

11. By virtue of the Hamburg Veterinary Surgeons' Council Act of 26 June 1964 (*Tierärztekammergesetz* – 'the 1964 Act'), the applicant is a member of the Hamburg Veterinary Surgeons' Council, whose task, among other things, is to ensure that its members comply with their professional obligations. (§§1 and 3(2) of the 1964 Act.) These

obligations are laid down principally in the Rules of Professional Conduct of Hamburg Veterinary Surgeons (*Berufsordnung der Hamburger Tierärzteschaft* – 'the Rules of Professional Conduct'), which were promulgated on 16 January 1970 by the Council in pursuance of section 8(1) no 1 of the 1964 Act and approved on 10 February 1970 by the Government (*Senat*) of the Land of Hamburg. (§8(3).)

12. As the director and proprietor of a clinic, Dr Barthold provided around-the-clock emergency service. (Rule 19, Rules of Professional Conduct and Reg 2 of Regulations of 27 August 1975 on the Establishment of Veterinary Clinics – *see* §29 *infra*.) This was not necessarily the case as far as other veterinary surgeons were concerned.

From 1974 onwards, the applicant – who was one of the authors of the abovementioned Regulations and who had insisted on the provision of a round-the-clock service by clinics – advocated within the Council that a regular night service involving the participation, by rota, of all veterinary surgeons should be organised. However, the majority of his colleagues voted on two occasions, on 19 December 1974 and 7 December 1979, against such a proposal.

I. THE CIRCUMSTANCES OF THE CASE

A. The article published on 24 August 1978 in the 'Hamburger Abendblatt'

13. On 24 August 1978, there appeared in the daily newspaper HAMBURGER ABEND-BLATT an article signed by Mrs B, a journalist, and entitled '*Tierärzte ab 20 Uhr schwer erreichbar – Warum "Shalen" die Nacht doch noch überlebte*' ('Veterinary surgeons hard to reach after 8 pm – why 'Shalen' managed to survive the night after all').

The article, 146 lines and 4 columns long, comprised an introductory paragraph and in brackets, in bolder type, the three following sub-heads: '*Auf eine spätere Zeit vertröstet*' ('Put off until later'), '*Unfreundliche Absage*' ('Unfriendly refusal') and '*Zur Not hilft die Polizei*' ('Police to the rescue').

The introductory paragraph, in bold type, read as follows:

> When the owner of a domestic pet needs help at night for his beloved animal, he may often become desperate: not one veterinary surgeon can be contacted. This state of affairs ought now to improve. There are plans to bring in a new Act on veterinary surgeons, along the lines of the Hamburg legislation governing doctors. According to Dr Jurgen Arndt, veterinary surgeon and Chairman of the Hamburg Land Association which is part of the Federal Association of Veterinary Surgeons (*Bundesverband praktischer Tierärzte e V.*), 'it will also regulate the emergency night service'. At present, it is true, a few clinics voluntarily provide an emergency service from time to time, and [other] veterinary surgeons also help, but this is not on a regular basis and does not give pet-owners security. They only do it voluntarily.

The journalist writing the article began by recounting the efforts made by the owners of the cat 'Shalen' to find a veterinary surgeon prepared to help them one evening between 7.30 and 10.00 pm. After telephoning in vain to two veterinary practices and to the emergency service, apparently they at last struck lucky: 'Dr Barthold, director of the Fuhlsbuttel veterinary clinic, intervened'. The journalist then quoted the applicant as saying: 'It was high time; . . . [the cat] would not have survived the night'.

According to the author, Mrs B, the particular case disclosed a problem namely the inadequacy of the emergency service, at least on weekdays between 8 pm and 8 am. The following thirty-eight lines read:

'I think that in a big city such as Hamburg there ought to be a regular service for attending to animals', Dr Sigurd Barthold emphasised.

'Hamburg's animal lovers' – added the journalist, summarising her interview with Dr Barthold – 'would then no longer have to get sore fingers trying to ring up veterinary surgeons, looking for one who is prepared to help. In that case it would not only be the clinics which would voluntarily be on emergency duty round the clock; each of the 53 practising veterinary surgeons would be on night duty once a month if arrangements were made for two of them to be on duty each night.

The fact that there is a demand for an emergency service at night time is illustrated by Dr Barthold by reference to the number of calls received by his practice between 8 pm and 8 am: 'Our telephone rings between two and 12 times each night. Of course these are not all emergency cases. Sometimes advice over the telephone is all that is needed.'

The author concluded the article by presenting under the third sub-head comments of Dr Jurgen Arndt, 'Vice-Chairman of the Hamburg Veterinary Surgeons' Council and himself director of a clinic in Hamburg'. Believing that an emergency service organised on a rotational basis 'would not release clinics from dispensing their voluntary service but would lessen the strain on them', Dr Arndt said that he was actively trying to promote such a service. He added that the appropriate Hamburg authorities envisaged drafting the Act on veterinary surgeons during the fourth quarter of the year. Until it came into force, owners of animals would have to call one veterinary surgeon after another – or else the police, who would normally be prepared to help them.

The article was illustrated by two photographs. The larger, centrally placed, showed a cat and had the caption: '*Um das Leben der kleinen "Shalen" wurde gekämpft – erfolgreich*' ('They fought for the life of little "Shalen" – and won'). The second one was an identity photograph which appeared alongside the title and introductory paragraph of the article; it was a photograph of the applicant, though its caption erroneously gave the name of Dr Arndt.

Below the photograph of the cat and outside the space occupied by the article, there was a short text under the heading '*Hamburg – Stadt der Tiere*' ('Hamburg – city of animals'), giving the number of domestic pets, veterinary surgeons and veterinary clinics in Hamburg and the telephone number of the emergency service available at weekends and on public holidays.

14. On 25 August 1978, the HAMBURGER ABENDBLATT once again published the applicant's photograph under the heading '*Unter dem Foto ein falscher Name*' ('Wrong name under photo'), together with the following explanation: 'An error crept into our report yesterday on the emergency veterinary service. Unfortunately, the wrong name appeared under the photograph. The person in question is in fact Dr Sigurd Barthold, director of the Fulhsbuttel veterinary clinic.'

B. The unfair competition proceedings

15. A number of Dr Barthold's fellow practitioners, who regarded the article in question as publicity conflicting with the Rules of Professional Conduct, referred the matter to the association '*PRO HONORE – Verein für Treu und Glauben im Geschäftsleben e V*' ('Pro Honore Association for fairness and trustworthiness in business' – 'Pro Honore'). This association was founded in 1925 by the businessmen of Hamburg and exists in order to 'ensure honesty and good faith in all spheres of business life' and 'in particular

to combat unfair competition, fraud in connection with moneylending and corruption'. (Art 2 of the Chamber of 26 September 1979).

Between 1978 and 30 September 1980, Pro Honore was operating simultaneously as a branch organisation of the *Zentrale zur Bekämpfung unlauteren Wettbewerbs e V Frankfurt-am-Main* (the Frankfurt-am-Main Central Agency for Combating unfair Competition – 'the Central Agency'). The latter has been active for decades in curbing unfair competition, and counts among its members all the chambers of industry, trade and crafts and some 400 other associations, including the Federal Association of Veterinary Surgeons. The Hamburg Veterinary Surgeons' Council and the *Deutsche Tierärzteschaft e V*, which is the umbrella organisation of the councils and private associations of veterinary surgeons, are not members of the Agency.

Under section 13 of the Unfair Competition Act of 7 June 1909 (*Gesetz gegen den unlauteren Wettbewerb* – 'the 1909 Act'), *Pro Honore* and the Central Agency are empowered to bring against anyone engaged in business proceedings to restrain that person from breaking certain rules set forth in the Act.

16. On 4 September 1978, Pro Honore wrote to the applicant to say that it had been informed by certain veterinary surgeons that he had 'instigated or tolerated, in the *Hamburger Abendblatt* of 24 August 1978, publicity on [his] own behalf'. The letter went on to quote extracts from the article in question. The applicant was said to have thereby infringed section 1 of the 1909 Act in conjunction with Rule 7 of the Rules of Professional Conduct.

Section 1 of the 1909 Act stipulates that: 'a prohibitory injunction (*Unterlassung*) and damages may be sought against anyone who in the course of business commits, for the purpose of unfair competition, acts contrary to proper standards (*gute Sitten*)'.

Rule 7 of the Rules of Professional Conduct deals with advertising and publicity (*Werbung und Anpreisung*) and reads as follows:

> It is contrary to the ethics of the profession (*standeswidrig*):
> (a) to advertise publicly one's veterinary practice,
> (b) to instigate or tolerate publicity or public acknowledgements on television, radio or in the press or other publications,
> (c) to disclose case histories or methods of operation or of treatment elsewhere than in specialised journals (*Fachzeitschriften*),
> (d) to co-operate with non-veterinarians for the purpose of publicising one's own practice.

Pro Honore asserted its right to bring proceedings against the applicant for unfair competition (§13(1) of the 1909 Act) and called on him, for the purposes of a friendly settlement of the matter, to sign an enclosed declaration. Under the terms of this declaration, he would undertake not to make publicity on his own behalf by instigating or tolerating press articles such as that which had appeared in the Hamburger Abendblatt, to pay the Central Agency 1000 DM for each infringement and to pay Pro Honore 120 DM by way of costs incurred in asserting its rights (*Rechtsverfolgung*).

17. A lawyer replied two days later on behalf of the applicant. The request made to Dr Barthold was, he wrote, very close to blackmail. It was presumptuous (*Zumutung*) to speak of unlawful publicity. The reproaches directed against his client, who had not instigated the article complained of, had done considerable damage to his person and professional reputation.

The applicant's lawyer asked Pro Honore to confirm in writing that it would be dropping its claim against his client, withdrawing its accusations and expressing regret. He also asked for reimbursement of his costs and announced that he would sue Pro Honore if it failed to meet his demands within three days.

1. The interim injunction (*einstweilige Verfügung*)

18. The Central Agency then applied to the Hamburg Regional Court (*Landgericht*) for an interim injunction. (Arts 936 and 944 of the Code of Civil Procedure.)

An interim injunction was issued on 15 September 1978 by the presiding judge of the 15th Civil Chamber. This decision forbade the applicant

to report in the press (except in professional journals), giving his full name, a photograph of himself and an indication of his occupation as director of the Fuhlsbuttel veterinary clinic, that at least on working days between 8 pm and 8 am, animal lovers in Hamburg would get sore fingers from trying to telephone veterinary surgeons ready to help them, in conjunction with (*in Verbindung mit*)

(a) the statement that only veterinary clinics were on voluntary emergency duty round the clock, and/or

(b) the statement that in his practice the telephone rang between two and twelve times between 8 pm and 8 am, though not all these calls were emergency cases and advice over the telephone would sometimes be sufficient, and/or

(c) the description of a case in which the owner of an animal had tried in vain one ordinary weekday between 7.30 pm and 10 pm to find a veterinary surgeon to treat his cat, until finally he was lucky enough to contact Dr Barthold, who acted when it was more than 'high time', and/or to contribute to such reports by giving journalists information.

For each and every breach of the injunction, he was liable to a maximum fine (*Ordnungsgeld*) of 500,000 DM or non-criminal imprisonment (*Ordnungshaft*) of up to six months, the precise penalty to be fixed by the court.

19. The applicant lodged an objection (*Widerspruch*) against this injunction. (Arts 936 and 924 of the Code of Civil Procedure.) The competent Chamber of the Regional Court upheld the injunction, however, on 15 November 1978. He thereupon entered an appeal which was dismissed on 22 March 1979 by the 3rd Chamber (*Senat*) of the Hanseatic Court of Appeal (*Hanseatisches Oberlandesgericht*). Finally, on 2 July 1979, the Federal Constitutional Court (*Bundesverfassungsgericht*), sitting as a bench of three judges, decided not to entertain the constitutional application he had brought against the latter judgment and the interim injunction of 15 September 1978, on the ground that the application did not offer sufficient prospects of success.

2. The proceedings in the main action

20. Before completion of the proceedings relating to the interim injunction, Dr Barthold had asked the Regional Court to set a time limit within which the Central Agency should commence the action as to the main issue (Arts 936 and 926 of the Code of Civil Procedure); whereupon the Agency instituted the necessary proceedings on 22 December 1978. It statement of claim was couched in the same terms as the prohibitory injunction issued by the Regional Court on 15 September 1978.

21. On 20 July 1979, the 16th Commercial Chamber of the Regional Court found in favour of the defendant.

The Regional Court rejected certain objections raised by him as to the Agency's right of action. Nor did it accept his argument that the plaintiff, in complaining of an infringement of section 1 of the 1909 Act, could not rely upon Rule 7, paragraph (a), of the Rules of Professional Conduct.

On the other hand, the Regional Court was satisfied that the evidence adduced did not support the charge of infringing the rules governing competition (*Wettbewerbsverstoss*). It had not been established that the applicant had influenced to an appreciable extent or tolerated the publication complained of. In fact, there were important indications pointing in the opposite direction. The author of the article had declared that Dr Barthold's name had been mentioned without his knowledge. It could be inferred from her testimony that the applicant had not asked for his identity to be divulged and must have expected not to find mention of it in the newspaper. He might thus have believed – as indeed he asserted – that the *Hamburger Abendblatt* would do no more than discuss the deplorable situation brought about by the absence of a night service. In addition, it was quite possible that the article in question, instigated by the journalist, was not based solely on the interview with Dr Barthold and that the newspaper or the journalist had included the name of Dr Barthold and of his clinic so as to emphasise the difference between the latter – praiseworthy – clinic and other less helpful veterinary surgeons. The question whether the applicant had taken care, or at least endeavoured, to prevent his name and clinic being given prominence over his fellow practitioners had been impossible to elucidate – and this should not operate to Dr Barthold's detriment – as the journalist had refused to give any further evidence, on the justified ground that she was not obliged to disclose her sources.

22. On 24 January 1980, the Hanseatic Court of Appeal, after declaring admissible the appeal brought by the Central Agency, upheld the Agency's grounds of appeal, which reiterated the terms of the injunction granted on 15 September 1978.

The Court of Appeal held in the first place that the applicant had infringed Rule 7, paragraph (a), of the Rules of Professional Conduct, a legally valid (*formell rechtmassig*) provision that was in conformity with the Basic Law as well as other superior rules of law. That Rule did not unreasonably limit Dr Barthold's right to freedom of expression as guaranteed by Article 5 of the Basic Law, for there was nothing to prevent him from freely stating his opinion and in particular from criticising deplorable situations, even if this had the inevitable effect of producing publicity favourable to himself. The Agency was not seeking to restrain Dr Barthold from making public pronouncements about veterinary assistance. Its application was concerned solely with a given form of conduct comprising – cumulatively – several aspects: the giving of Dr Barthold's full name, the reproduction of his photograph, the mention of his being director of the Fuhlsbüttel veterinary clinic and the statement that, at least between 8 pm and 8 am on working days, animal lovers in Hamburg would get sore fingers trying to telephone a veterinary surgeon willing to help them, plus one of the three assertions set out in the Agency's grounds of appeal (and, previously, in the interim injunction of 15 September 1978.)

Objectively, the article complained of entailed publicity for Dr Barthold: compared to other veterinary surgeons, it presented him as an exemplary practitioner, thereby being particularly likely to incite the owners of sick animals to turn to his clinic. Such publicity exceeded the bounds of objective comment on matters of justified concern for the applicant. If in the future he were to supply the press with information necessary for the writing of an article, he should, in order to avoid any infringement of Rule 7, paragraph (a), of the Rules of Professional Conduct, ensure before hand that the text to be published did not involve any unlawful publicity or advertising, by reserving a right of correction or by agreeing on the form of the article with the journalist.

In the view of the Hanseatic Court of Appeal, the respondent had at the same time contravened section 1 of the 1909 Act. His intention of enhancing his own competitiveness to the detriment of his competitors was to be presumed in the case of this type of publication, and that presumption was not rebutted in the circumstances. It mattered little (*unerheblich*) that he may additionally or even primarily have been pursuing other objectives, as there was an act done for the purposes of commercial competition as long as the intent to stimulate such competition had not been entirely overridden by other motives ('*nicht völlig hinter sonstigen Beweggründen Verschwindet*').

As for the risk of repetition, also presumed in this matter, there were no grounds for concluding that this was non-existent. Contrary to what the Regional Court had found, the applicant had knowingly and substantially contributed to the publication which highlighted his person and his clinic. It was true that the press had itself taken up the case of 'Shalen' and had invited Dr Barthold to comment only after being informed of the incident by the animal's owner. However, the applicant had, by his interview, greatly influenced the content of the article and, what was more, had authorised a photograph to be taken of himself. He had thereby provided the opportunity for producing the article in question, with its character of publicity.

He could not have been unaware of this risk and the Rules of Professional Conduct required him to ensure that the text to be published did not involve illegal publicity favourable to himself, by reserving a right of correction or by agreeing on the form of publication with the journalist. He could also have made an arrangement with Mrs B to remain anonymous, although he was in no way obliged to express his views without disclosing his identity.

In fact, the respondent had acknowledged in his written pleadings of 13 December 1978 and 12 December 1979 that he had authorised the inclusion of his name and photograph. Although he retracted those statements on 29 March and 6 April 1979, he had not shown that he had insisted on publication without inclusion of such details. The testimony of the journalist was not conclusive on this point. It was not necessary to take evidence from Dr Arndt, because Dr Barthold had unquestionably allowed photographs to be taken. That being so, he ought not to have contented himself with obtaining a verbal promise – as he claimed to have done – that he would not himself appear in one of the photographs. Whilst he claimed to have told the journalist that the Rules of Professional Conduct prohibited advertising and publicity, he was wrong to have passed on to her the responsibility of writing an article which complied with those Rules.

The danger of repetition persisted notwithstanding the time that had elapsed. The 'Shalen' affair was no longer topical, but the press was likely to come back to the issues it had raised, by making reference to this incident along with others, after another interview with Dr Barthold.

The Court of Appeal decided finally not to give leave to appeal on points of law against its judgment: the latter did not depart from the established case law of the Federal Court of Justice (*Bundesgerichtshof*), and the case did not raise questions of principle.

23. Dr Barthold challenged the judgment of 24 January 1980 before the Federal Constitutional Court. He repeated various arguments on which he had based his constitutional application in the interim proceedings, namely non-observance of equality before the law, of freedom of expression and of freedom to practise a profession, as safeguarded by Article 3, 5 and 12 of the Basic Law, and incompatibility of the obligation to belong to the Veterinary Surgeons' Council with freedom of association, as guaranteed by Article 9 of the Basic Law. In addition, he alleged violation of his right to be heard, in particular by a legally competent court (*gesetzlicher Richter*). On this latter point, he claimed that it was not within the province of the civil courts to apply the Rules of Professional Conduct.

The Constitutional Court, sitting as a bench of three judges, dismissed the constitutional application on 6 October 1980, on the ground that it lacked sufficient prospects of success.

II. THE RELEVANT LEGISLATION

A. The law governing the veterinary profession

24. In the Federal Republic of Germany, veterinary medicine is governed partly by federal law and partly by the law of the Lander. The principal rules relevant to the present case are to be found in the Federal Veterinary Practitioners Act (*Bundes-Tierärzteordnung*) (Version of 22 August 1977 – 'the Federal Act'), the Hamburg Act of 26 June 1964 on the Veterinary Surgeons' Council (The 1964 Act – *see* §11 *supra*), the Hamburg Act on Disciplinary Tribunals for the Medical Professions (*Gesetz über die Berufsgerichtsbarkeit der Heilberufe*) (Version of 20 June 1972 – 'the 1972 Act'), the Rules of Professional Conduct of 16 January 1970 and the Regulations on the establishment of veterinary clinics.

25. The profession of veterinary surgeon is not an industrial, commercial or craft occupation (*Gewerbe*) but, by its nature, a liberal profession. (§1(2) of the Federal Act). According to subsection 1 of section 1 of the Federal Act,

> It shall be the task of the veterinary surgeon to prevent, alleviate and cure suffering and disease in animals, to contribute to the maintenance and development of productive livestock, to protect man from the dangers and harm arising from animal disease and from foodstuffs and products of animal origin, and to endeavour to improve the quality of foodstuffs of animal origin.

In order to be able to practise on a permanent basis, an authorisation (*Approbation*) issued by the appropriate Land authorities is required; such authorisation is granted if the person concerned satisfies the conditions laid down by law. (§§2 to 4 of the Federal Act.)

26. The veterinary surgeons practising in Hamburg constitute the association. (§§1 and 2 of the 1964 Act.) Its functions include defending the professional interests of the veterinary surgeons, ensuring that the latter meet their professional obligations and assisting the public health services (*öffentlicher Gesundheitsdienst*) in the performance of their duties. (§3 of the 1964 Act.)

The Council's organs are the governing board (*Vorstand*) and the general assembly; the latter adopts the Charter and the Rules of Professional Conduct, which are submitted to the Government of the Land for approval. (§§5 and 8 of the 1964 Act.)

The Council is under the supervision of the State, which supervision extends to observance of the laws and the Charter. (§18 of the 1964 Act.)

27. The Rules of Professional Conduct of the Hamburg Council require each veterinary surgeon to practice in such a way that the profession inspires respect and confidence; the making of pejorative statements about the person, knowledge or skills of another veterinary surgeon is not allowed. (Rules 1(1) and (2).)

The Rules contain a number of provisions forbidding veterinary surgeons from advertising their own practices. Under Rule 5, veterinary surgeons may only intervene if asked to do so; offering or providing their services without being requested is at variance with the rules of the profession. Rule 7 deals more specifically with publicity and lays down the conditions to be observed. In addition there are Rules 8 and 9, which concern advertisements in the press and name-plates respectively.

28. Each veterinary surgeon is required to intervene in the event of an emergency (Rule 1(3)); he must (*soll*) participate in providing a service at weekends and on holidays and hold himself in readiness to replace any other colleague. (Rule 14.)

The question of a night service for veterinary surgeons, a matter not dealt with in the law or the Rules of Professional Conduct, has been the subject of debate within the profession. The Council opted on 11 December 1978 for a voluntary solution whereby veterinary surgeons indicate on a list the times when they may be contacted and the Council communicates to the public, by means of an automatic reply service, the names of those veterinary surgeons who are available even outside normal consultation hours.

According to the Government, it was apparently quite a long time before a relatively sizeable number of veterinary surgeons agreed to participate in this scheme. In 1979, the Council was said to have felt the need to launch an appeal for volunteers for the weekend and emergency service.

Yet again, in 1981, the director of a veterinary clinic publicly criticised the working of the emergency service in Hamburg and stated that he had been unsuccessfully campaigning for two years for a duty rota for all veterinary surgeons. (*See Die Zeit* of 11 December 1981.)

However, according to the applicant, there has existed since 1982 a system along the lines he had proposed. The Government did not contest this assertion.

29. An establishment for the treatment of sick animals may be called a 'veterinary clinic' if it has the requisite premises and equipment and if the Council has given its approval. (Rule 19). The detailed rules are set out in Regulations promulgated by the Council, the most recent version of which dates from December 1982. The 1982 Regulations lay down that henceforth clinics must provide a round-the-clock service for emergencies unless the Council has made other arrangements guaranteeing adequate assistance.

B. The law on unfair competition

30. The 1909 Act applies to any person seeking to derive income from a regular economic activity; it thus covers industrial, commercial and craft activities, services and the liberal professions. It is designed to protect competitors and consumers, and applies independently of the texts, if any, governing the conduct of members of the liberal profession in matters of publicity and advertising.

31. The courts with jurisdiction to deal with infringements of the 1909 Act – principally the civil courts (§13 of the Act) – are not bound by any findings made by such professional tribunals as may have considered the same facts in the light of the professional rules governing publicity. However, it has been consistently held by Federal Court of Justice

that breach of these professional rules will, in the normal course of things, also entail infringement of section 1 of the 1909 Act. The court having to decide the case on the basis of the 1909 Act must nonetheless inquire in each case whether the requirements of section 1 are satisfied.

32. By virtue of section 13, an action for contravention of, for example, section 1 may be brought by any competitor, by trade and professional associations (*gewerbliche und Berufsverbände*) and, since 1965, by consumer associations.

[Barthold applied to the European Commission challenging the injunctions. The Commission found an Article 10 violation.]

. . . .

DECISION [OF THE EUROPEAN COURT OF HUMAN RIGHTS]:

I. ALLEGED VIOLATION OF ARTICLE 10

. . . .

37. The applicant complained of the prohibitory injunction issued against him by the German courts following publication of an article in the *Hamburger Abendblatt* on 24 August 1978. In his submission, these injunctions, namely the interim injunction whose terms were then reiterated in the injunction of the Hanseatic Court of Appeal in the main proceedings, prevented him from making known his views on the need for an emergency veterinary service and thereby violated his freedom of expression.

Dr Barthold further contended before the Commission that the rule of professional conduct obliging veterinary surgeons to abstain from advertising was in itself contrary to Article 10. The injunctions complained of were, however, grounded not on Rule 7, paragraph (a), of the Rules of Professional Conduct but on section 1 of the 1909 Act taken in conjunction with Rule 7, paragraph (a). Moreover, the applicant did not repeat this contention before the Court. Like the Commission, the Court will therefore limit its examination to the application of the two relevant provisions in the particular circumstances of the case before it.

38. The Government's main submission was as follows. The subject matter of the injunctions complained of was not Dr Barthold's critical comments regarding the organisation of a night service for veterinary surgeons in Hamburg, but was exclusively the praise of his own practice and clinic and the disparaging remarks about his professional colleagues. These statements, which in part gave incorrect information, went beyond the objective expression of opinion and amounted to commercial advertising. Article 10, however, did not cover commercial advertising, this being a matter relating to the right freely to exercise a trade or profession, a right not protected by the Convention.

In the alternative, the Government argued that the contested measure was justified under paragraph 2 of Article 10.

39. The Commission found a violation. In its opinion, the circumstances of the case did not involve commercial advertising in the sense in which that term is generally understood and, in any event, commercial advertising did not fall outside the scope and intendment of Article 10. (App No 7805/77, *X and Church of Scientology v. Sweden*, 16 D & R 68 at 72.)

A. Applicability of Article 10

40. According to the Delegate, the Government are estopped from reopening the issue of the applicability of Article 10 since before the Commission they had conceded that the case could be examined under this Article.

The Government considered themselves entitled to raise the point as they had always maintained that certain features of the interview in issue did not relate to the exchange of ideas, which lies at the heart of freedom of expression, but fell within the field of economic activity.

41. The Court is unable to agree with the Delegate. For the purposes of the procedure before the Court, the applicability of one of the substantive clauses of the Convention constitutes, by its very nature, an issue going to the merits of the case, to be examined independently of the previous attitude of the respondent State. (*See Belgian Linguistic Case; Airey v. Ireland*, §18.)

42. Article 10(1) specifies that freedom of expression 'shall include freedom to hold opinions and to . . . impart information and ideas'. The restrictions imposed in the present case relate to the inclusion, in any statement of Dr Barthold's view as to the need for a night veterinary service in Hamburg, of certain factual data and assertions regarding, in particular, his person and the running of his clinic. All these various components overlap to make up a whole, the gist of which is the expression of 'opinions' and the imparting of 'information' on a topic of general interest. It is not possible to dissociate from this whole those elements which go more to manner of presentation than to substance and which, so the German courts held, have a publicity-like effect. This is especially so since the publication prompting the restriction was an article written by a journalist and not a commercial advertisement.

The Court accordingly finds that Article 10 is applicable, without needing to inquire in the present case whether or not advertising as such comes within the scope of the guarantee under this provision.

B. Compliance with Article 10

43. There has clearly been an 'interference by public authority' with the exercise of the applicant's freedom of expression, namely the interference resulting from the judgment delivered at final instance in the main proceedings by the Hanseatic Court of Appeal on 24 January 1980 at the close of the action brought by the Central Agency. This interference will not be compatible with Article 10 unless it satisfies the conditions laid down in paragraph 2, a clause calling for a narrow interpretation. (*See Sunday Times v. United Kingdom*, §65.) Thus, the interference must be 'prescribed by law', have an aim or aims that is or are legitimate under Article 10(2) and be 'necessary in a democratic society' for the aforesaid aim or aims. (*Id.* at §45.)

1. Is the interference 'prescribed by law'?

44. In the submission of Dr Barthold, the injunctions in question were neither grounded on a 'law' nor 'prescribed'. Both the Government and the Commission disagreed with this contention.

45. According to the Court's case law on this point, the interference must have some basis in domestic law, which itself must be adequately accessible and be formulated with sufficient precision to enable the individual to regulate his conduct, if need be with appropriate advice. (*See Sunday Times v. United Kingdom*, §§47 and 49; *Silver v. United Kingdom* (1983), §§85–88; *Malone v. United Kingdom* (1985), §§66–68.)

46. The legal basis of the interference under consideration was provided by section 1 of the 1909 Act, section 8(1) of the 1964 Act and Rule 7, paragraph (a), of the Rules of Professional Conduct, as applied by the Hanseatic Court of Appeal. Unlike the first two of these provisions, the third emanated from the Veterinary Surgeons' Council and not directly from Parliament. It is nonetheless to be regarded as a 'law' within the meaning

of Article 10(2) of the Convention. The competence of the Veterinary Surgeons' Council in the sphere of professional conduct derives from the independent rule-making power that the veterinary profession – in company with other liberal professions – traditionally enjoys, by parliamentary delegation, in the Federal Republic of Germany. (*See* judgment of Federal Constitutional Court 9 May 1972, Entscheidungen des Bundesverfassungsgerichts, vol 33, pp 125–171.) Furthermore, it is a competence exercised by the Council under the control of the State, which in particular satisfies itself as to observance of national legislation, and the Council is obliged to submit its rules of professional conduct to the *Land* Government for approval. (§§8(3) and 18 of the 1964 Act. *See* §§11 and 26 *supra*.)

47. The 'accessibility' of the relevant texts has not been the subject of any dispute. On the other hand, the applicant argued that the injunctions complained of were not 'foreseeable', either subjectively or objectively. In his submission, the relevant legislation did not fix the limits of freedom of expression with sufficient clarity to indicate in advance to each member of the veterinary profession the dividing line between what was permitted and what was not; in particular, section 1 of the 1909 Act was couched in extremely vague terms.

Section 1 of the 1909 Act does indeed employ somewhat imprecise wording, notably the expression 'proper standards'. It therefore confers a broad discretion on the courts. The Court has, however, already had the occasion to recognise the impossibility of attaining absolute precision in the framing of laws. (*Sunday Times v. United Kingdom* at §49 and *Silver v. United Kingdom* (1983) at §88.) Such considerations are especially cogent in the sphere of conduct governed by the 1909 Act, namely competition, this being a subject where the relevant factors are in constant evolution in line with developments in the market and in means of communication. Finally, the Hanseatic Court of Appeal based its judgment of 24 January 1980 on a combined application of section 1 of the 1909 Act and paragraph (a) of Rule 7 of the Rules of Professional Conduct, which is a clearer and more detailed provision.

48. Before the Commission, Dr Barthold also pleaded non-compliance with the domestic law. His arguments ran as follows. The civil courts had no jurisdiction to apply the Rules of Professional Conduct; failure to observe the requirements of those Rules could not automatically entail violation of the 1909 Act, a text which, moreover, was inapplicable to the liberal professions; the ordinary courts had interpreted Rule 7, paragraph (a), differently from the professional tribunals; finally, the Central Agency lacked *locus standi* to sue him.

Whilst it is true that no interference can be considered as 'prescribed by law', for the purposes of Article 10(2) of the Convention, unless the decision occasioning it complied with the relevant domestic legislation, the logic of the system of safeguard established by the Convention sets limits upon the scope of the power of review exercisable by the Court in this respect. It is in the first place for the national authorities, notably the courts, to interpret and apply the domestic law: the national authorities are, in the nature of things, particularly qualified to settle the issues arising in this connection. (*See Winterwerp v. Netherlands*, §46; *X v. United Kingdom*, §43.) The evidence adduced in the present case does not disclose any clear non-observance either of the 1909 Act or of the Rules of Professional Conduct. The applicant's arguments – to which, moreover, he did not revert before the Court – do no more than evince his disagreement with the Hamburg courts.

49. To sum up, the injunctions complained of are 'prescribed by law'.

2. Does the interference have an aim that is legitimate under Article 10(2)?

50. The Government argued that the interference in issue served to protect human 'health' as well as the 'rights' of the applicant's fellow veterinary surgeons and of clients of veterinary surgeons, that is to say, 'others'; and that the interference was also aimed at the protection of 'morals'.

Dr Barthold considered, on the contrary, that the interference was likely to perpetuate a situation which constituted a potential risk to public health. The Commission, for its part, found there to be a legitimate object in the protection of the rights of clients of veterinary surgeons.

51. The Court notes that, according to the reasons given in the judgment of 24 January 1980, the final injunction in the present case was issued in order to prevent the applicant from acquiring a commercial advantage over professional conduct themselves in compliance with the rule of professional conduct that requires veterinary surgeons to refrain from advertising. The Hanseatic Court of Appeal grounded its decision on the protection of the 'rights of others' and there is no cause for believing that it was pursuing other objectives alien to the Convention. The judgment of 24 January 1980 thus had an aim that was in itself legitimate – that is to say, subject to the 'necessity' of the measure in issue – for the purposes of Article 10(2) of the Convention. There is no need to inquire whether that judgment is capable of being justified under Article 10(2) on other grounds as well.

3. Is the interference 'necessary in a democratic society'?

52. The Government considered the restriction imposed to be one that was 'necessary in a democratic society'. Their arguments may be summarised as follows. The statements that the applicant was restrained by the judgment of 24 January 1980 from repeating denigrated his fellow veterinary surgeons and were in part erroneous; by reason of the form they took and the type of publication in which they appeared, these statements went beyond objective criticism and amounted to advertising uncompatible with the Rules of Professional Conduct. Although Dr Barthold was not himself the author of the article in the *Hamburger Abendblatt*, the Hanseatic Court of Appeal was not mistaken to hold him responsible.

In addition, the prohibition complained of was consistent with the principle of proportionality. Being circumscribed within narrow limits, it did not bar Dr Barthold from expressing an opinion on the issue of a night veterinary service in Hamburg. The Commissioner had exaggerated the interest of the people of Hamburg for a statutory scheme for such a service. Nor did the penalties that the applicant risked incurring if he were to repeat the prohibited statements fall foul of the principle of proportionality, since they amounted to no more than an 'abstract threat' that the domestic courts would have to implement in the event of wrongful conduct in the light of the particular circumstances obtaining at that time.

Finally, in the submission of the Government, in the field of the "policing" of unfair competition the Contracting States enjoyed a wide margin of appreciation and the legal traditions of the Contracting States had to be respected by the Convention institutions. In this connection, provisions comparable to those of the relevant German legislation were to be found in other member States of the Council of Europe, in international instruments and in the law of the European Communities.

53. The applicant contested the 'necessity' of the interference, adducing the following arguments. His declarations did not have any advertisement-like effect. The prohibition

on his publicly disseminating his opinion together with an indication of his name and professional activities struck at the very essence of his freedom of expression, as did the precautions that the Hanseatic Court of Appeal directed him to observe in his contacts with the press. Moreover, in a democratic society, it was not necessary to prohibit veterinary surgeons from advertising, at least not in as comprehensive a manner as in his case.

In addition, the injunction imposed on him was capable of harming the legitimate interests of animal owners, especially as the Veterinary Surgeons' Council had not made available to animal owners the information they would need regarding the night service. The effect of the judgment of 24 January 1980 was to prevent journalists from checking or exploring with a qualified person information they had received and from revealing the source of any such information, thereby adversely affecting the credibility of any statements published. The judgment was thus liable, directly or indirectly, to render the task of the press more difficult and to reduce the range of information supplied to readers, a result contrary to one of the objectives of a 'democratic society'. Although the applicant remained free to express his views in professional journals, that would not be sufficient to enable the 200,000 households of animal owners in Hamburg to be informed.

54. In the opinion of the Commission, the article in the *Hamburger Abendblatt* dealt with a topic of general interest. There was no indication that Dr Barthold had intended to exploit the article for advertising purposes. The disclosure of his identity and of various facts relating to his practice constituted an essential element of the exercise of his freedom of expression. The Commission further considered that the precautions which the domestic courts required him to take could not be regarded as necessary in a democratic society. In sum, the principle of proportionality had not been respected in the circumstances.

55. It has been pointed out in the Court's case law that, whilst the adjective 'necessary', within the meaning of Article 10(2) of the Convention, is not synonymous with 'indispensable', neither does it have the flexibility of such expressions as 'admissible', 'ordinary', 'useful', 'reasonable' or 'desirable'; rather, it implies a 'pressing social need'. The Contracting States enjoy a power of appreciation in this respect, but that power of appreciation goes hand in hand with a European supervision which is more or less extensive depending upon the circumstances; it is for the Court to make the final determination as to whether the interference in issue corresponds to such a need, whether it is 'proportionate to the legitimate aim pursued' and whether the reasons given by the national authorities to justify it are 'relevant and sufficient'. (*Sunday Times v United Kingdom*, at §62.)

56. In order to assess the necessity for restraining Dr Barthold from repeating those of his declarations which were adjudged to be incompatible with the 1909 Act and with the Rules of Professional Conduct, the prohibited declarations must be placed in their proper context and examined in the light of the particular circumstances of the case.

The gist of the article in the Hamburger Abendblatt concerned the absence in Hamburg of a night service operated by the entirety of veterinary surgeons. The article explained the general problem to readers by illustrating it with the case of the cat 'Shalen' and then by quoting interviews given by the applicant and by Dr Arndt, who at that time was Vice-Chairman of the local Veterinary Surgeons' Council. In addition, the newspaper indicated to readers the telephone number of the emergency service where they could obtain the name and address of practitioners available at the weekend. The article was thus pursuing a specific object, that is to say, informing the public about the situation obtaining in Hamburg, at a time when, according to the two practitioners interviewed, the enactment of new legislation on veterinary surgeons was under consideration.

57. It has not been disputed that the problem discussed in the article was a genuine one. As recently as 1981, a professional colleague of Dr Barthold criticised in *Die Zeit* the lack of a compulsory night duty for veterinary surgeons in Hamburg. In any event, the applicant felt strongly that such a service should be organised; he had always campaigned to this effect within the Veterinary Surgeons' Council.

The Government maintained that on one point at least Dr Barthold was making a false assertion. According to the Government, clinics provided a round-the-clock emergency service because they were obliged to do so and not of their own volition; as proof of this, the Government pointed to Regulation 2 of the Regulations on the Establishment of Veterinary Clinics. The Court restricts itself to noting that the correctness or incorrectness of the applicant's declarations – which, in fact, would seem to have been corroborated on this point by Dr Arndt, himself the director of a clinic – had no influence on the judgment of 24 January 1980, which did not go into the matter.

58. The Court must come to its decision on the basis of all these various factors.

As the Court has already had the occasion to point out, freedom of expression holds a prominent place in a democratic society. Freedom of expression constitutes one of the essential foundations of a democratic society and one of the basic conditions for its progress and for the development of every man and woman. (*See, in particular, Handyside v. United Kingdom*, §49.) The necessity for restricting that freedom for one of the purposes listed in Article 10(2) must be convincingly established.

When considered from this viewpoint, the interference complained of went further than the requirements of the legitimate aim pursued.

It is true, as was stated in the judgment of the Hanseatic Court of Appeal, that the applicant retained the right to express his opinion on the problem of a night service for veterinary surgeons in Hamburg and even, in so doing, to divulge his name, have a photograph of himself published and disclose that he was the director of the Fuhlsbuttel veterinary clinic. He was, however, directed not to supplement his opinion, when accompanied by such indications, with certain factual examples drawn from his own experience and illustrating the difficulties encountered by animal owners in obtaining the assistance of a veterinary surgeon during the night.

It may well be that these illustrations had the effect of giving publicity to Dr Barthold's own clinic, thereby providing a source of complaint for his fellow veterinary surgeons, but in the particular circumstances this effect proved to be altogether secondary having regard to the principal content of the article and to the nature of the issue being put to the public at large. The injunction issued on 24 January 1980 does not achieve a fair balance between the two interests at stake. According to the Hanseatic Court of Appeal there remains an intent to act for the purposes of commercial competition, within the meaning of section 1 of the 1909 Act, as long as that intent has not been entirely overridden by other motives ('*nicht völlig hinter sonstigen Beweggründen verschwindet*'). A criterion as strict as this in approaching the matter of advertising and publicity in the liberal professions is not consonant with freedom of expression. Its application risks discouraging members of the liberal professions from contributing to public debate on topics affecting the life of the community if ever there is the slightest likelihood of their utterances being treated as entailing, to some degree, an advertising effect. By the same token, application of a criterion such as this is liable to hamper the press in the performance of its task of purveyor of information and public watchdog.

59. In conclusion, the injunctions complained of are not proportionate to the legitimate aim pursued and, accordingly, are not 'necessary in a democratic society' for the 'protection of the rights of others', with the result that they give rise to a violation of Article 10 of the Convention.

. . . .

~

QUESTIONS & COMMENTS

(1) In *Casado Coca v. Spain*, 285-A Eur. Ct. H.R. (ser. A) (1994), the European Court held that a lawyer advertising ban did not violate Article 10. Although the Court recognized that there was developing a tendency of member states of the Council of Europe to allow advertising of lawyer services, at the time the application was filed (1983), the Spanish government was entitled to a wide margin of appreciation. The president of the European Court subsequently has questioned whether such a wide margin of appreciation would be appropriate now. R. Ryssdal, *The Case-Law of the European Court of Human Rights on the Freedom of Expression Guaranteed under the European Convention on Human Rights*, Tenth Conference of the European Constitutional Courts (Budapest, 6–10 May 1996) at 12.

Compare *Bates v. Bar of Arizona*, 433 U.S. 350 (1977), in which the U.S. Supreme Court held that an Arizona Supreme Court rule against a lawyer "publicizing himself" through advertising violated the First Amendment.

The U.S. Supreme Court has imposed stringent limitations on government's power to limit advertising of prices. *See, e.g., 44 Liquormart v. Rhode Island*, 517 U.S. 484 (1996). Note that the European Court reserves judgment on whether advertising "as such" is a protected form of expression. Should the rules applicable to price advertising differ from those applicable to other forms of advertising, such as "image" advertising? The European court uses an analytic approach that requires it to balance a wide range of considerations. Is the U.S. approach to regulating commercial speech different? If so, which better promotes the various social goals at issue?

(2) In *Jacubowski v. Germany*, 291-A Eur. Ct. H.R. (ser. A) (1994), the applicant earlier had been dismissed as editor of a news agency, and the news agency issued a press release openly questioning the applicant's professional abilities. Planning to establish his own agency, the applicant sent newspaper articles critical of his former employer to a number of newspaper publishers and journalists who had received the press release. The newspaper articles gave critical accounts of the applicant's dismissal, the circumstances surrounding the dismissal, and the news agency's activities in general. To these articles, the applicant appended a circular letter mentioning his eagerness to discuss future developments in the news market. A few months later, the applicant set up a public relations agency. Finding that the newspaper articles and the circular letter were intended, above all, to promote the applicant's private business interests at the expense of his former employer and competitor, the national court issued an injunction ordering the applicant to desist from such mailings pursuant to an unfair competition law. The applicant complained that the court order violated Article 10.

Contrary to the European Commission's unanimous opinion, the European Court of Human Rights held, by 6 votes to 3, that Article 10 had not been breached. Emphasizing that the national courts had shown moderation in going no further than prohibiting the applicant from distributing his circular letter, thus allowing the applicant to defend his reputation through other means, the Court, unlike the Commission, concluded that the impugned interference was proportionate. Jacubowski had denigrated a competitor in order to poach clients. Therefore, there had been no violation of Article 10.

Why should unfair competition or a contractual obligation trump a democratic society's interest in the dissemination of information? Would it have made a difference to the European Court in *Jacubowski v. Germany* if the applicant had been joined by a newspaper? What relevance does a party's intent have to limitations on freedom of expression?

(3) Consider cases in which a journalist goes undercover to expose criminal or unethical corporate behavior and in doing so commits fraud by lying on his or her employment application. Does the social harm exposed by the journalist outweigh society's interest in eliminating fraud? Should this be a consideration in determining whether the right to freedom of dissemination of ideas has been violated? Or, should it only be a consideration in the determination of civil – as opposed to – criminal penalties against the journalist?

(4) Consider *Goodwin v. United Kingdom*, – Eur. Ct. H.R. (ser. A) (1996) (slip opinion). Goodwin, a British journalist, was fined by the British courts for not revealing a source. Goodwin was phoned by an informant who gave him information about the financial problems of Tetra Ltd. The information, it turned out, had been derived from a draft of Tetra's confidential corporate plan. There were only eight copies of the plan, one of which had been stolen. Tetra sought an *ex parte* interim injunction to restrain Goodwin and his employer from publishing any information derived from the highly confidential plan. The High Court of Justice granted the injunction. The company informed all the national newspapers and relevant journals of the injunction. The High Court ordered Goodwin to disclose his notes from the conversation with the informant and to identify his source. Goodwin and his employer did not comply with this order.

Goodwin lodged an appeal from the order. He argued that disclosure of his notes was not "necessary in the interests of justice" (responding to the statutory language authorizing U.K. courts to make such an order); the public interest in publication outweighed the interest in preserving confidentiality; and, since he had not facilitated any breach of confidence, the disclosure order against him was invalid. The Court of Appeal proceeded to balance Tetra's interests in identifying the threat to its company and forestalling further damage to their company and reputation with the general public interest in maintaining the confidentiality of journalistic sources. The court found the balance came down in favor of disclosure. Goodwin then appealed to the House of Lords. The House of Lords upheld the decision of the High Court and the Court of Appeal. They found that the importance for Tetra's obtaining disclosure lay in the threat of severe damage to their business and consequentially to the livelihood of their employees. These events would inevitably arise from disclosure of the information contained in their corporate plan. This threat could only be defused if they could identify the source either as the thief or as a means to lead to the identification of the thief. The importance of protecting the source, however, was diminished by the source's complicity, at the very least, in a gross breach of confidentiality, which was not counterbalanced by any legitimate interest that publication of the information was calculated to serve.

The European Commission found that the disclosure order violated Article 10.

Although the European Court agreed that the U.K. court's disclosure order was prescribed by law and pursued the legitimate aim of protecting Tetra's rights, the court found the disclosure order was not necessary in a democratic society. The purpose of the disclosure order was to a large extent the same that had already been achieved by the injunction, to prevent the dissemination of confidential information. A vital component of the threat of damage to the company had thus already largely been neutralized by the injunction. As far as the disclosure order merely served to reinforce the injunction, this additional restriction of freedom of expression was not supported by sufficient reasons for the purposes of paragraph 2 of Article 10. Protection of journalistic sources is one of the basic conditions for freedom of the press. Without such protection, sources may be deterred from assisting the press. As a result, the vital public watchdog role of the press may be undermined and the ability of the press to provide accurate and reliable information may be adversely affected. An order to disclose a source has such a potentially chilling effect on freedom of speech that it cannot be compatible with Article 10 of the Convention unless it is justified by an overriding requirement in the public interest. Here, the Court found that Tetra's interests in eliminating, by proceeding against the source, the residual threat of damage through dissemination of the confidential information, in obtaining compensation, and in unmasking a disloyal employee or collaborator, even if considered cumulatively, were insufficient to outweigh the vital public interest in the protection of the journalist's source. Accordingly, the Court concluded that both the order requiring Goodwin to reveal his source and the fine imposed on him for having refused to do so gave rise to a violation of his Article 10 right to freedom of expression.

Compare *Branzburg v. Hayes*, 408 U.S. 665 (1972), upholding an order that a newspaper reporter disclose to a state grand jury the identities of his sources. Suppose that *Goodwin* had arisen in a similar context, rather than in the commercial context. Would the different context of the inquiry affect the European Court's analysis? A majority of the states in the United States have enacted "shield" legislation that protects journalists against compulsory disclosure of their sources.

(5) Access to media can be limited in a number of ways. A common practice in Latin America is to require journalists to be licensed. The Inter-American Court of Human Rights has opined that such compulsory licensing is incompatible with freedom of expression guaranteed by Article 13, ACHR. *Compulsory Membership in an Association Prescribed by Law for the Practice of Journalism (Arts. 13 and 29 of the American Convention on Human Rights)*, Advisory Opinion OC-5/85 of November 13, 1985, Inter-Am. Ct. H.R. (Ser. A) No. 5 (1985).

Besides the licensing of journalists, access to media outlets can be limited by not enforcing the right of reply or correction. Consider the Inter-American Court of Human Rights' advisory opinion addressing this issue. In *Enforceability of the Right to Reply or Correction (Arts. 14(1), 1(1) and 2 of the American Convention on Human Rights)*, Advisory Opinion OC-7/86 of August 29, 1986, Inter-Am. Ct. H.R., Ser. A, No. 7 (1986), the government of Costa Rica had submitted to the Court a request for an advisory opinion regarding the interpretation and scope of Article 14(1) of the American Convention on Human Rights (the right of reply or correction) in relation to Articles 1(1) (guaranteeing the free and full exercise of rights under the Convention to all persons) and 2 (requiring member states to adopt such measures as are necessary to give effect to those rights) of that instrument. Examining the "ordinary meaning" of Article 14(1), the Court concluded that the Convention guarantees an internationally enforceable right of reply or correction. It ruled further that member States are required by Articles 1(1) and 2 not merely to create a right of reply but also to guarantee it. They are required to establish by law the conditions for exercising the right of reply or correction ("under such conditions as the law may establish"), although the contents of the laws may vary from state to state within reasonable limits and within the framework laid down by the Court.

The fact that a state has enacted laws to protect the right of reply or correction does not, however, preclude the court from hearing a claim against that state for violating the right of reply or correction in a particular instance. What matters, the court said, is not the passage of a law but the exercise of the right:

> If Article 14(1) is read together with Articles 1 and 2 of the Convention, any State Party that does not already ensure the free and full exercise of the right of reply or correction is under an obligation to bring about that result, be it by legislation or whatever measures may be necessary under its domestic legal system.

Id. at 57. Thus the concept of "law" in Article 14(1) includes all measures designed to regulate the right of reply or correction. The Court noted, however that any measure restricting the right of reply or correction (or any other right guaranteed by the Convention) would have to be adopted in the form of a law.

Compare U.S. law. Under U.S. law, the right of reply extends only to broadcast media. In *Red Lion Broadcasting Co. v. FCC,* 395 U.S. 367 (1969), the FCC issued regulations to specify the rules governing political editorials in TV and radio broadcasts and to make the personal attack issues of its fairness doctrine (obligating broadcasters to ensure that both sides are presented) more exact and readily enforceable. When a personal attack is made in the "presentation of views on a controversial issue of public importance[,]" the regulations imposed a duty on the licensees/broadcasters to notify the person or group attacked and to allow them to respond over the broadcasters' facilities. When a licensee, in an editorial, endorses or opposes a candidate, he must notify either the candidate he opposed or the ones he did not endorse and allow them to respond on his facilities. The Supreme Court upheld the regulations. Holding that the FCC had not exceeded their congressionally delegated authority, the Court pointed out that "[t]he right of free speech . . . does not embrace a right to snuff out the free speech of others." *Id.* at 387. The Supreme Court also ruled that the First Amendment, while applicable to broadcasting, protects the rights of the viewers and listeners over the rights of the broadcasters. The public has a right to receive adequate access to political, social, and moral issues. "It is the purpose of the First Amendment to preserve an uninhibited marketplace of ideas in which truth will ultimately prevail" (*id.* at 390), and it would be unconstitutional for broadcasters to engage in private censorship and have an unconditional monopoly of a scarce resource denied to others. *Id.* at 391–392.

Note that the Inter-American Court says that "the contents of the laws [guaranteeing a right of reply] may vary from State to State." Is the limitation of the right to reply in U.S. law to broadcast media a permissible "variation"? What standards should there be for determining the reasonableness of variations?

(6) The European Court of Human Rights has addressed different media of expression. *See, e.g., Informationsverein Lentia v. Austria,* 276 Eur. Ct. H.R. (ser. A) (1993) (holding

state monopoly prohibition of applicants' internal cable television network and radio stations violative of freedom of expression); *Autronic AG v. Switzerland*, 178 Eur. Ct. H.R. (ser. A) (1990) (Swiss prohibition of receipt of aerial uncoded television programs from Soviet telecommunications satellite without Soviet government's permission violative of freedom of expression in light of treaty); *Groppera Radio A.G. and Others v. Switzerland*, 173 Eur. Ct. H.R. (ser. A) (1990) (prohibition of retransmission of Italian radio programs by Swiss radio not violative of freedom of expression).

5.7. Freedom of Association and Assembly

Universal Declaration of Human Rights

Article 20.

(1) Everyone has the right to freedom of peaceful assembly and association.

(2) No one may be compelled to belong to an association.

International Covenant on Civil and Political Rights

Article 21

The right of peaceful assembly shall be recognized. No restrictions may be placed on the exercise of this right other than those imposed in conformity with the law and which are necessary in a democratic society in the interests of national security or public safety, public order (*ordre public*), the protection of public health or morals or the protection of the rights and freedoms of others.

Article 22

1. Everyone shall have the right to freedom of association with others, including the right to form and join trade unions for the protection of his interests.

2. No restrictions may be placed on the exercise of this right other than those which are prescribed by law and which are necessary in a democratic society in the interests of national security or public safety, public order (*ordre public*), the protection of public health or morals or the protection of the rights and freedoms of others. This article shall not prevent the imposition of lawful restrictions on members of the armed forces and of the police in their exercise of this right.

3. Nothing in this article shall authorize States Parties to the International Labour Organisation Convention of 1948 concerning Freedom of Association and Protection of the Right to Organize to take legislative measures which would prejudice, or to apply the law in such a manner as to prejudice, the guarantees provided for in that Convention.

European Convention on Human Rights

Article 11

1. Everyone has the right to freedom of peaceful assembly and to freedom of association with others, including the right to form and to join trade unions for the protection of his interests.

2. No restrictions shall be placed on the exercise of these rights other than such as are prescribed by law and are necessary in a democratic society in the interests of national

security or public safety, for the prevention of disorder or crime, for the protection of health or morals or for the protection of the rights and freedoms of others. This article shall not prevent the imposition of lawful restrictions on the exercise of these rights by members of the armed forces, of the police or of the administration of the State.

Charter of Fundamental Human Rights of the European Union

Article 12

Freedom of assembly and of association

1. Everyone has the right to freedom of peaceful assembly and to freedom of association at all levels, in particular in political, trade union and civic matters, which implies the right of everyone to form and to join trade unions for the protection of his or her interests.

2. Political parties at Union level contribute to expressing the political will of the citizens of the Union.

American Declaration of the Rights and Duties of Man

Article XXI. Right of assembly.

Every person has the right to assemble peaceably with others in a formal public meeting or an informal gathering, in connection with matters of common interest of any nature.

Article XXII. Right of association

Every person has the right to associate with others to promote, exercise and protect his legitimate interests of a political, economic, religious, social, cultural, professional, labor union or other nature.

American Convention on Human Rights

Article 15. RIGHT OF ASSEMBLY.

The right of peaceful assembly, without arms, is recognized. No restrictions may be placed on the exercise of this right other than those imposed in conformity with the law and necessary in a democratic society in the interest of national security, public safety or public order, or to protect public health or morals or the rights or freedoms of others.

Article 16. FREEDOM OF ASSOCIATION.

1. Everyone has the right to associate freely for ideological, religious, political, economic, labor, social, cultural, sports, or other purposes.

2. The exercise of this right shall be subject only to such restrictions established by law as may be necessary in a democratic society, in the interest of national security, public safety or public order, or to protect public health or morals or the rights and freedoms of others.

3. The provisions of this article do not bar the imposition of legal restrictions, including even deprivation of the exercise of the right of association, on members of the armed forces and the police.

African [Banjul] Charter on Human and Peoples' Rights

Article 10

1. Every individual shall have the right to free association provided that he abides by the law.

2. Subject to the obligation of solidarity provided for in 29 no one may be compelled to join an association.

Article 11

Every individual shall have the right to assemble freely with others. The exercise of this right shall be subject only to necessary restrictions provided for by law in particular those enacted in the interest of national security, the safety, health, ethics and rights and freedoms of others.

Convention on Human Rights and Fundamental Freedoms of the Commonwealth of Independent States

Article 12

1. Everyone shall have the right to freedom of peaceful assembly and to freedom of association with others, including the right to form and join trade unions for the protection of his interests.

2. No restrictions shall be placed on the exercise of these rights other than such as are prescribed by law and are necessary in a democratic society in the interests of national security, public safety, public order, public health and moral or for the protection of the rights and freedoms of others. This Article shall not preclude the imposition of lawful restrictions on the exercise of these rights by members of the armed forces or by members of the law enforcement or administrative organs of the State.

U.S. Constitution

Amendment I

Congress shall make no law ... abridging ... the right of the people peaceably to assemble. ...

Plattform 'Ärzte für das Leben' v. Austria
European Court of Human Rights
139 Eur. Ct. H.R. (ser. A) (1988)
13 E.H.R.R. 204 (1986)

FACTS:

8. *Plattform 'Ärzte für das Leben'* is an association of doctors who are campaigning against abortion and are seeking to bring about reform of the Austrian legislation on the subject. In 1980 and 1982 it held two demonstrations which were disrupted by counter-demonstrators despite the presence of a large contingent of police.

I. The demonstration at Stadl-Paura

...9. The applicant association decided to hold a religious service at Stadl-Paura Church (Upper Austria) on 28 December 1980, after which there would be a march to the surgery of a doctor who carried out abortions.... [I]t gave notice [under the Assembly Act], on 30 November, to the police authority for the district of Wels-Land. The police made no objection and gave the participants permission to use the public highway. The police did, however, have to ban two other planned demonstrations, which were subsequently announced by supporters of abortion, as these demonstrations were to be held at the same time and in the same place as the *Plattform* demonstration.

10. As the organisers feared that incidents might nonetheless occur, they sought – shortly before the beginning of the march – to change their plans, in consultation with the local authorities. They gave up the idea of demonstrating outside the doctor's surgery and decided instead to march to an altar erected on a hillside quite a distance away from the church and hold a religious ceremony there.

11. The police representatives pointed out to them that the main body of the police officers had already been deployed along the route originally planned and that because of the lie of the land the new route was not suited to crowd control. They did not refuse to provide protection but stated that – irrespective of the route chosen or to be chosen – it would be impossible to prevent counter-demonstrators from throwing eggs and disrupting both the march and the religious service....

12. During the mass, a large number of counter-demonstrators – who, it seems, had not given the notice required under the Assembly Act – assembled outside the church and were not dispersed by the police. They disrupted the march to the hillside by mingling with the marchers and shouting down their recitation of the rosary. The same thing happened at the service celebrated in the open air: some five hundred people attempted to interrupt it using loudspeakers and threw eggs and clumps of grass at the congregation.

13. At the end of the ceremony, when tempers had risen to the point where physical violence nearly broke out, special riot-control units – which had until then been standing by without intervening – formed a cordon between the opposing groups, and this enabled the procession to return to the church.

14. In a letter to the Upper Austrian Safety Authority, the chairman of the association described the counter-demonstrators' behaviour as 'relatively peaceful': on other occasions, the opponents of *Plattform* had attacked the association's members and had assaulted policemen....

[The Association filed a disciplinary complaint against the police for failure to provide adequate protection against the counter-demonstrators. The Safety Authority rejected the complaint, and the Constitutional Court held that it had no jurisdiction to hear an appeal of the refusal. Criminal complaint investigations against some of the counter-demonstrators were later dropped, except that one person was fined for throwing eggs.] ...

II. The Salzburg demonstration

19. The competent police authority gave permission for a second demonstration against abortion to be held in the cathedral square in Salzburg on 1 May 1982. An anniversary meeting was due to be held in the square by the Socialist Party on the same day, but it had to be cancelled because notice of it had been given after the applicant association had given notice of its own meeting.

The demonstration began at 2.15 pm and ended with an hour of prayers inside the cathedral.

At about 1.30 pm some three hundred and fifty people angrily shouting their opposition had passed through the three archways which provide access to the square and gathered outside the cathedral. A hundred policemen formed a cordon around the *Plattform* demonstrators to protect them from direct attack. Other trouble was caused by sympathisers of an extreme right-wing party, the NDP, who voiced their support for *Plattform*. The police asked the association's chairman to order these people to disperse, but without success.

In order to prevent the religious ceremony being disrupted, the police cleared the square.

20. No proceedings were taken after these incidents . . . .

DECISION:

. . . .

28. Before the Commission, *Plattform* complained that the Austrian authorities had disregarded the true meaning of freedom of assembly by having failed to take practical steps to ensure that its demonstrations passed off without any trouble.

29. In the Government's submission, Article 11 did not create any positive obligation to protect demonstrations. Freedom of peaceful assembly – enshrined in Article 12 of the Austrian Constitution of 1867 – was mainly designed to protect the individual from direct interference by the State. Unlike some other provisions in the Convention and the Austrian Constitution, Article 11 did not apply to relations between individuals. . . .

32. A demonstration may annoy or give offence to persons opposed to the ideas or claims that it is seeking to promote. The participants must, however, be able to hold the demonstration without having to fear that they will be subjected to physical violence by their opponents; such a fear would be liable to deter associations or other groups supporting common ideas or interests from openly expressing their opinions on highly controversial issues affecting the community. In a democracy the right to counter-demonstrate cannot extend to inhibiting the exercise of the right to demonstrate.

Genuine, effective freedom of peaceful assembly cannot, therefore, be reduced to a mere duty on the part of the State not to interfere: a purely negative conception would not be compatible with the object and purpose of Article 11. Like Article 8 [right to privacy and respect for family life], Article 11 sometimes requires positive measures to be taken, even in the sphere of relations between individuals, if need be. . . .

34. While it is the duty of Contracting States to take reasonable and appropriate measures to enable lawful demonstrations to proceed peacefully, they cannot guarantee this absolutely and they have a wide discretion in the choice of the means to be used. . . . In this area the obligation they enter into under Article 11 of the Convention is an obligation as to measures to be taken and not as to results to be achieved. . . .

37. As regards the incidents at Stadl-Paura on 28 December 1980, it must first be noted that the two demonstrations planned by supporters of abortion, which were due to be held at the same time and place as *Plattform*'s demonstration (of which notice had been given on 30 November) had been prohibited. Furthermore, a large number of uniformed and plain-clothes policemen had been deployed along the route originally planned, and the police representatives did not refuse the applicant association their protection even after it decided to change the route despite their objections. Lastly, no damage was done nor were there any serious clashes; the counter-demonstrators chanted slogans, waved banners and threw eggs or clumps of grass, which did not prevent the procession and the open-air religious service from proceeding to their conclusion; special riot-control units

placed themselves between the opposing groups when tempers had risen to the point where violence threatened to break out.

38. For the 1982 demonstration in Salzburg (see §19 above) the organisers had chosen the date of 1 May, the day of the traditional Socialist march which had to be cancelled – as regards the cathedral square – because the applicant association had given notice of its demonstration earlier. Furthermore, a hundred policemen were sent to the scene to separate the participants from their opponents and avert the danger of direct attacks; they cleared the square so as to prevent any disturbance of the religious service.

39. It thus clearly appears that the Austrian authorities did not fail to take reasonable and appropriate measures....

∾

QUESTIONS & COMMENTS

(1) Note the affirmative duty of the state to provide protection to protesters. What measures did the Austrian government undertake that satisfied its Article 11 obligations? Under what circumstances do you think a government should restrict assembly by one group in order to protect another group's right to assembly? Does the Court provide any guidance in that respect?

(2) How would you describe the standard of affirmative obligation the European Court employing in *Plattform*? Is it a "due diligence" test?

(3) Were the measures taken by the government consistent with the rights of the pro-choice demonstrators and the members of the Socialist party?

(4) In U.S. constitutional law, similar issues have arisen when police authorities conclude that they lack sufficient force to control the counterdemonstrators and arrest those against whom the counterdemonstrators are acting. *See, e.g., Terminiello v. Chicago*, 337 U.S. 1 (1949). Most scholars think it inappropriate to create a "heckler's veto," whereby those who disagree with a speaker can be so forceful that the *speaker* becomes subject to criminal punishment.

Note that the principal case frames the issue differently. In *Plattform*, it is the public authorities who were alleged to have failed to take enough steps to ensure that their demonstration could proceed without interruption. Would the U.S. courts sustain such a claim? *See DeShaney v. Winnebago County Dept. of Social Services*, 489 U.S. 189 (1989), which suggests that the U.S. Constitution creates no affirmative obligations on government officials. Under the principles stated in *Platfform*, could a state, consistent with Article 11, ban a proposed demonstration on the ground that it would be too hard to control counterdemonstrators? On the ground that the demonstrators were provoking the likely counterdemonstrators?

(5) Both the European Court of Human Rights and the Inter-American Court of Human Rights have held that governments have an affirmative duty to prosecute and punish gross human rights violations. *See, e.g., Velásquez Rodríquez v. Honduras*, Inter-Am. Ct. H.R., Judgment of 29 July 1988, Ser. C, No. 4; *X. and Y. v. The Netherlands*, 91 Eur. Ct. H.R. (ser. A) (1985). How would you argue that these cases reflect a customary international law obligation for the U.S.?

(6) The U.S. Supreme Court has recognized the government's affirmative duties to provide legal aid for indigent criminal defendants, *Gideon v. Wainwright*, 372 U.S. 335 (1963), and the duty to provide medical care to the government's charges (*e.g.*, prisoners), *Estelle v. Gamble*, 429 U.S. 97 (1976). What kind of principles can be distilled from these and other cases for determining whether the state has an affirmative duty?

(7) Unlike international freedom of assembly cases, most international freedom of association cases to date have addressed negative rights: the right *not* to belong to an association, union, bar, or other group. For example, in *Young, James and Webster v. United Kingdom*, 44 Eur. Ct. H.R. (ser. A) (1981), the European Court addressed the applicants' right not to join a railway workers union. Under an agreement with British rail and three unions, a "closed-shop" was established. The applicants successfully argued that membership in the union would entail their support of political activities of which they did not approve. Although the Court did not hold that compulsion to join an association or closed-shops would always be incompatible with Article 11, the Court found that in this case the applicants faced a "threat of dismissal involving loss of livelihood." *Id.* at §55. Accordingly, they held that this was "a most serious form of compulsion" requiring a finding of Article 11 incompatibility. *Id.*

However, the Inter-American Commission on Human Rights has limited the right to association. In *Bomchil and Meliton Ferrari v. Argentina*, Cases 9777 and 9718, 1988 Annual Report of the Inter-American Commission on Human Rights, OEA/Ser.L/ V/II/74, doc.10 rev. 1, the petitioners challenged an Argentine statute that required registration of attorneys in the Colegio Publico de Abogados (Public Association of Lawyers). The petitioners, two lawyers, argued that the statute's requirement violated their right of association in that it would force them to belong to a group in which they did not wish to belong because there were other bar associations. The Inter-American Commission found no violation because of the "imminently public function" of a bar association in maintaining control of professional practice and disciplining lawyers. Furthermore, the government had a legitimate power in licensing lawyers. Other associations that the Inter-American Commission held to not have this "imminently public function," such as trade unions and journalist associations, were distinguished from bar associations on these grounds. *See Compulsory Membership in an Association Prescribed by Law for the Practice of Journalism (Arts. 13 and 29 of the American Convention on Human Rights)*, Advisory Opinion OC-5/85 of November 13, 1985, Inter-Am. Ct. H.R. (Ser. A) No. 5 (1985).

(8) Closed shops and compelled membership in professional organizations are generally matters of statutory law in the United States. The Supreme Court has, however, limited the uses that these associations can make of required dues and fees. *See Abood v. Detroit Board of Education*, 431 U.S. 209 (1977), barring a union recognized as a collective bargaining agent for an "agency" shop to which all employees were required to pay dues, from using compulsory dues for political and ideological activities. The compulsory dues could be used only to support collective bargaining activities. *See also Keller v. State Bar of California*, 496 U.S. 1 (1990), barring the state bar association from using compulsory dues to finance political and ideological activities that are not "necessarily or reasonably incurred for the purpose of regulating the legal profession or improving the quality of legal services." These unions and professional associations are required to set up procedures by which members who disagree with political or ideological activities can refuse to pay the share of dues attributable to those activities.

5.8. Right to Marriage

Universal Declaration of Human Rights

Article 16.

(1) Men and women of full age, without any limitation due to race, nationality or religion, have the right to marry and to found a family. They are entitled to equal rights as to marriage, during marriage and at its dissolution.

(2) Marriage shall be entered into only with the free and full consent of the intending spouses.

(3) The family is the natural and fundamental group unit of society and is entitled to protection by society and the State.

International Covenant on Civil and Political Rights

Article 23

1. The family is the natural and fundamental group unit of society and is entitled to protection by society and the State.

2. The right of men and women of marriageable age to marry and to found a family shall be recognized.

3. No marriage shall be entered into without the free and full consent of the intending spouses.

4. States Parties to the present Covenant shall take appropriate steps to ensure equality of rights and responsibilities of spouses as to marriage, during marriage and at its dissolution. In the case of dissolution, provision shall be made for the necessary protection of any children.

European Convention on Human Rights

ARTICLE 12

Men and women of marriageable age have the right to marry and to found a family, according to the national laws governing the exercise of this right.

American Convention on Human Rights

Article 17. RIGHTS OF THE FAMILY.

. . . .

2. The right of men and women of marriageable age to marry and to raise a family shall be recognized, if they meet the conditions required by domestic laws, insofar as such conditions do not affect the principle of nondiscrimination established in this Convention.

3. No marriage shall be entered into without the free and full consent of the intending spouses.

4. The States Parties shall take appropriate steps to ensure the equality of rights and the adequate balancing of responsibilities of the spouses as to marriage, during marriage, and in the event of its dissolution. In case of dissolution, provision shall be

made for the necessary protection of any children solely on the basis of their own best interests.

Goodwin v. United Kingdom
Application 28957/95
European Court of Human Rights
– Eur. Ct. H.R. (ser. A) (2002)

[For background, see case excerpts reproduced in Subsection 5.4.]

. . . .

II. ALLEGED VIOLATION OF ARTICLE 12 OF THE CONVENTION

94. The applicant also claimed a violation of Article 12 of the Convention, which provides as follows:

> Men and women of marriageable age have the right to marry and to found a family, according to the national laws governing the exercise of this right.

A. Arguments of the parties

1. The applicant

95. The applicant complained that although she currently enjoyed a full physical relationship with a man, she and her partner could not marry because the law treated her as a man. She argued that the *Corbett v. Corbett* definition of a person's sex for the purpose of marriage had been shown no longer to be sufficient in the recent case of *Bellinger v. Bellinger* and that even if a reliance on biological criteria remained acceptable, it was a breach of Article 12 to use only some of those criteria for determining a person's sex and excluding those who failed to fulfil those elements.

2. The Government

96. The Government referred to the Court's previous case-law (the above-cited *Rees, Cossey* and *Sheffield and Horsham* judgments) and maintained that neither Article 12 nor Article 8 of the Convention required a State to permit a transsexual to marry a person of his or her original sex. They also pointed out that the domestic law approach had been recently reviewed and upheld by the Court of Appeal in *Bellinger v. Bellinger*, the matter now pending before the House of Lords. In their view, if any change in this important or sensitive area were to be made, it should come from the United Kingdom's own courts acting within the margin of appreciation which this Court has always afforded. They also referred to the fact that any change brought the possibility of unwanted consequences, submitting that legal recognition would potentially invalidate existing marriages and leave transsexuals and their partners in same-sex marriages. They emphasised the importance of proper and careful review of any changes in this area and the need for transitional provisions.

B. The Court's assessment

97. The Court recalls that in the cases of *Rees, Cossey* and *Sheffield and Horsham* the inability of the transsexuals in those cases to marry a person of the sex opposite to their re-assigned gender was not found in breach of Article 12 of the Convention. These findings were based variously on the reasoning that the right to marry referred to traditional marriage between persons of opposite biological sex (the *Rees* judgment, p. 19, §49), the view that continued adoption of biological criteria in domestic law for determining a person's sex for the purpose of marriage was encompassed within the power of Contracting States to regulate by national law the exercise of the right to marry and the conclusion that national laws in that respect could not be regarded as restricting or reducing the right of a transsexual to marry in such a way or to such an extent that the very essence of the right was impaired (the *Cossey* judgment, p. 18, §§44–46, the *Sheffield and Horsham* judgment, p. 2030, §§66–67). Reference was also made to the wording of Article 12 as protecting marriage as the basis of the family (*Rees*, loc. cit.).

98. Reviewing the situation in 2002, the Court observes that Article 12 secures the fundamental right of a man and woman to marry and to found a family. The second aspect is not however a condition of the first and the inability of any couple to conceive or parent a child cannot be regarded as per se removing their right to enjoy the first limb of this provision.

99. The exercise of the right to marry gives rise to social, personal and legal consequences. It is subject to the national laws of the Contracting States but the limitations thereby introduced must not restrict or reduce the right in such a way or to such an extent that the very essence of the right is impaired (see the *Rees* judgment, p. 19, §50; the *F. v. Switzerland* judgment of 18 December 1987, Series A no. 128, §32).

100. It is true that the first sentence refers in express terms to the right of a man and woman to marry. The Court is not persuaded that at the date of this case it can still be assumed that these terms must refer to a determination of gender by purely biological criteria (as held by Ormrod J. in the case of *Corbett v. Corbett*, paragraph 21 above). There have been major social changes in the institution of marriage since the adoption of the Convention as well as dramatic changes brought about by developments in medicine and science in the field of transsexuality. The Court has found above, under Article 8 of the Convention, that a test of congruent biological factors can no longer be decisive in denying legal recognition to the change of gender of a post-operative transsexual. There are other important factors: the acceptance of the condition of gender identity disorder by the medical professions and health authorities within Contracting States, the provision of treatment including surgery to assimilate the individual as closely as possible to the gender in which they perceive that they properly belong and the assumption by the transsexual of the social role of the assigned gender. The Court would also note that Article 9 of the recently adopted Charter of Fundamental Rights of the European Union departs, no doubt deliberately, from the wording of Article 12 of the Convention in removing the reference to men and women [ ].

101. The right under Article 8 to respect for private life does not however subsume all the issues under Article 12, where conditions imposed by national laws are accorded a specific mention. The Court has therefore considered whether the allocation of sex in national law to that registered at birth is a limitation impairing the very essence of the right to marry in this case. In that regard, it finds that it is artificial to assert that

post-operative transsexuals have not been deprived of the right to marry as, according to law, they remain able to marry a person of their former opposite sex. The applicant in this case lives as a woman, is in a relationship with a man and would only wish to marry a man. She has no possibility of doing so. In the Court's view, she may therefore claim that the very essence of her right to marry has been infringed.

102. The Court has not identified any other reason which would prevent it from reaching this conclusion. The Government have argued that in this sensitive area eligibility for marriage under national law should be left to the domestic courts within the State's margin of appreciation, adverting to the potential impact on already existing marriages in which a transsexual is a partner. It appears however from the opinions of the majority of the Court of Appeal judgment in *Bellinger v. Bellinger* that the domestic courts tend to the view that the matter is best handled by the legislature, while the Government have no present intention to introduce legislation[ ].

103. It may be noted from the materials submitted by Liberty that though there is widespread acceptance of the marriage of transsexuals, fewer countries permit the marriage of transsexuals in their assigned gender than recognise the change of gender itself. The Court is not persuaded however that this supports an argument for leaving the matter entirely to the Contracting States as being within their margin of appreciation. This would be tantamount to finding that the range of options open to a Contracting State included an effective bar on any exercise of the right to marry. The margin of appreciation cannot extend so far. While it is for the Contracting State to determine *inter alia* the conditions under which a person claiming legal recognition as a transsexual establishes that gender re-assignment has been properly effected or under which past marriages cease to be valid and the formalities applicable to future marriages (including, for example, the information to be furnished to intended spouses), the Court finds no justification for barring the transsexual from enjoying the right to marry under any circumstances.

104. The Court concludes that there has been a breach of Article 12 of the Convention in the present case.

. . . .

QUESTIONS & COMMENTS

(1) What effect might the European Court's ruling in *Goodwin* have on gay marriages? Consider Article 9 of the Charter of Fundamental Human Rights of the European Community: "The right to marry and the right to found a family shall be guaranteed in accordance with the national laws governing the exercise of these rights." Article 9 makes no mention of gender.

(2) Article 12, ECHR, contains a clawback provision ("according to the national laws"). Article 9 of the European Charter also contains a clawback provision ("in accordance with the national laws"). Historically, these clawback provisions have been used to undermine any progressive interpretation of the right to marry. Is this any longer the case after *Goodwin*?

(3) Why is it appropriate for the European Court to construe Article 12 of the ECHR in light of Article 9 of the European Charter?

Johnston v. Ireland
European Court of Human Rights
112 Eur. Ct. H.R. (ser. A) (1986)
9 E.H.R.R. 203 (1987)

. . . .

FACTS:

I. The particular circumstances of the case.

10. The first applicant is Roy HW Johnston . . . [and] resides . . . with the second applicant, Janice Williams-Johnston. . . . The third applicant is their daughter, Nessa Doreen Williams-Johnston, who was born in 1978.

11. The first applicant married a Miss M in 1952 in a Church of Ireland ceremony. Three children were born of this marriage, in 1956, 1959 and 1965.

In 1965, it became clear to both parties that the marriage had irretrievably broken down and they decided to live separately at different levels in the family house. Several years later both of them with the other's knowledge and consent, formed relationships and began to live with third parties. By mutual agreement, the two couples resided in self-contained flats in the house until 1976, when Roy Johnston's wife moved elsewhere.

In 1978, the second applicant, with whom Roy Johnston had been living since 1971, gave birth to Nessa. He consented to his name being included in the Register of Births as the father.

12. Under the Constitution of Ireland, the first applicant is unable to obtain, in Ireland, a dissolution of his marriage to enable him to marry the second applicant. He has taken the following steps to regularise his relationship with her and with his wife and to make proper provision for his dependents.

(a) With his wife's consent, he has consulted solicitors in Dublin and in London as to the possibility of obtaining a dissolution of the marriage outside Ireland. His London solicitors advised that, in the absence of residence within the jurisdiction of the English courts, he would not be able to do so in England, and the matter has therefore not been pursued.

(b) On 19 September 1982, he concluded a formal separation agreement with his wife, recording [a maintenance] agreement implemented some years earlier.

(c) He has made a will leaving his house to the second applicant for life with remainder over to his four children as tenants in common, one half of the residue of his estate to the second applicant, and the other half to his four children in equal shares.

(d) He has supported the third applicant throughout her life and has acted in all respects as a caring father.

(e) He contributed towards the maintenance of his wife until the conclusion of the aforementioned separation agreement and has supported the three children of his marriage during their dependency.

(f) The second applicant has been nominated as beneficiary under the pension scheme attached to his employment.

(g) He has taken out health insurance in the names of the second and third applicants, as members of his family.

13. The second applicant, who is largely dependent on the first applicant for her support and maintenance, is concerned at the lack of security provided by her present legal status, in particular the absence of any legal right to be maintained by him and of any potential rights of succession in the event of intestacy. As is permitted by law, she has adopted the first applicant's surname, which she uses amongst friends and neighbours, but for business purposes continues to use the name Willams. According to her, she has felt inhibited about telling employers of her domestic circumstances and although she would like to become an Irish citizen by naturalisation, she has been reluctant to make an application, not wishing to put those circumstances in issue.

14. The third applicant has, under Irish law, the legal situation of an illegitimate child and her parents are concerned at the lack of any means by which she can, even with their consent, be recognised as their child with full rights of support and succession in relation to them. They are also concerned about the possibility of a stigma attaching to her by virtue of her legal situation, especially when she is attending school.

. . . .

II. Relevant domestic law

A. Constitutional provisions relating to the family

16. The Constitution of Ireland, which came into force in 1937, includes the following provisions:

40.3.1 The State guarantees in its laws to respect, and, as far as practicable, by its laws to defend and vindicate the personal rights of the citizen.

40.3.2 The State shall, in particular, by its laws protect as best it may from unjust attack and, in the case of injustice done, vindicate the life, person, good name, and property rights of every citizen.

41.1.1 The State recognises the Family as the natural primary and fundamental unit group of Society, and as a moral institution possessing inalienable and impre-scriptible rights, antecedent and superior to all positive law.

41.1.2 The State, therefore, guarantees to protect the Family in its constitution and authority, as the necessary basis of social order and as indispensable to the welfare of the Nation and the State.

. . . .

41.3.1 The State pledges itself to guard with special care the institution of Marriage, on which the family is founded, and to protect it against attack.

41.3.2 No law shall be enacted providing for the grant of a dissolution of marriage.

. . . .

42.1 The State acknowledges that the primary and natural educator of the child is the Family and guarantees to respect the inalienable right and duty of parents to provide, according to their means, for the religious and moral, intellectual, physical and social education of their children.

. . . .

42.5 In exceptional cases, where the parents for physical or moral reasons fail in their duty towards their children, the State as guardian of the common good, by appropriate means shall endeavour to supply the place of the parents, but always with due regard for the natural and imprescriptible rights of the child.

17. As a result of Article 41.3.2 of the Constitution, divorce in the sense of dissolution of a marriage (divorce *a vinculo matrimonii*) is not available in Ireland. However, spouses may be relieved of the duty of cohabiting either by a legally binding deed of separation concluded between them or by a court decree of judicial separation (also known as a divorce *a mensa et thoro*); such a decree, which is obtainable only on proof of commission of adultery, cruelty or unnatural offences, does not dissolve the marriage. In the remainder of the present judgement, the word divorce denotes a divorce *a vinculo matrimonii*.

It is also possible on various grounds a degree of nullity, that is a declaration by the High Court that a marriage was invalid and therefore null and void *ab initio*. A marriage may also be annulled by an ecclesiastical tribunal, but this does not affect the civil status of the parties.

18. The Irish courts have consistently held that the Family that is afforded protection by Article 41 of the Constitution is the family based on marriage. Thus, in *The State (Nicolaou) v. An Bord Uchtala* ((1966) I.R. 567), The Supreme Court said:

It is quite clear from the provisions of Article 41, and in particular section 3 thereof, that the family referred to in this Article is the family which is founded on the institution of marriage and, in the context of the Article, marriage means valid marriage under the law for the time being in force in the State.

While it is quite true that unmarried persons cohabiting together and the children of their union may often be referred to as a family and have many, if not all, of the outward appearances of a family, and may indeed for the purposes of a particular law be regarded as such, nevertheless as far as Article 41 is concerned the guarantees therein contained are confined to families based upon marriage.

The Supreme Court has, however, held that an illegitimate child had unenumerated natural rights (as distinct from rights conferred by law) which will be protected under Article 40.3 of the Constitution, such as the right to be fed and to live, to be reared and educated, to have the opportunity of working and of realising his or her full personality and dignity as a human being, as well as the same natural rights under the Constitution as a legitimate child to 'religious and moral, intellectual, physical and social education'. (*G v. An Bord Uchtala* (1980) I.R. 32).

B. Recognition of foreign divorces

19. Article 41.3.3 of the Constitution provides:

No person whose marriage has been dissolved under the civil law of any other State but is a subsisting valid marriage under the law for the time being in force within the jurisdiction of the Government and Parliament established by this Constitution shall be capable of contracting a valid marriage within that jurisdiction during the lifetime of the other party to the marriage dissolved.

20. A series of judicial decisions has established that the foregoing provision does not prevent the recognition by Irish courts, under the general Irish rules of private

international law, of certain decrees of divorce obtained, even by Irish nationals, in another State. Such recognition used to be granted only if the parties to the marriage were domiciled within the jurisdiction of the foreign court at the time of the relevant proceedings (*Re Caffin Deceased; Bank Of Ireland v. Caffin* [1971] I.R. 123; *Gaffney v. Gaffney* [1975] I.R. 133; however, since 2 October 1986 a divorce will be recognised if granted in the country where either spouse is domiciled (Domicile and Recognition of Foreign Divorces Act 1986). To be regarded as domiciled in a foreign State, a person must not only be resident there but also have the intention of remaining there permanently and have lost the *animus revertendi*. Moreover, the foreign divorce will not be recognised if domicile has been fraudulently invoked before the foreign court for the purpose of obtaining the decree.

21. If notice is served for a civil marriage before a Registrar of Births, Marriages and Deaths in Ireland and he is aware that either of the parties has been divorced abroad, he must, under the regulations in force, refer the matter to the Registrar-General. The latter will seek legal advice as to whether on the facts of the case the divorce would be recognised as effective to dissolve the marriage under Irish law and as to whether the intended marriage can consequently be permitted.

C. Legal status of persons in the situation of the first and second applicants

1. Marriage

22. Persons who, like the first and second applicants, are living together in a stable relationship after the breakdown of the marriage of one of them are unable, during the lifetime of the other party to that marriage, to marry each other in Ireland and are not recognised there as a family for the purposes of Article 41 of the Constitution.

2. Maintenance and succession.

23. Such persons, unlike a married couple, have no legal duty to support or maintain one another and no mutual statutory rights of succession. However, there is no impediment under Irish law preventing them from living together and supporting each other and, in particular, from making wills or dispositions *inter vivos* in each other's favour. They can also enter into mutual maintenance agreements, although the Government and the applicants expressed different views as to whether these might be unenforceable as contrary to public policy.

In general, the married member of the couple remains, at least in theory, under a continuing legal obligation to maintain his or her spouse. In addition, testamentary dispositions by that member may be subject to the rights of his or her spouse or legitimate children under the Succession Act 1965.

3. Miscellaneous

24. As compared with married couples, persons in the situation of the first and second applicants:

(a) have no access, in the event of difficulties arising between them, to the system of barring orders instituted to provide remedies in respect of violence within the family (Family Law (Maintenance of Spouses and Children) Act 1976, as amended by the Family Law (Protection of Spouses and Children) Act 1981); they can, however, obtain analogous relief by seeking a court injunction or declaration;

(b) do not enjoy any of the rights conferred by the Family Home Protection Act 1976 in relation to the family home and its contents, notably the prohibition on sale by one spouse without the other's consent and the exemption from stamp duty and Land Registry fees in the event of transfer of title between them;

(c) as regards transfers of property between them are less favourably treated for the purposes of capital acquisition tax;

(d) enjoy different rights under the social welfare code, notably the benefits available to deserted wives;

(e) are unable jointly to adopt a child.

D. Legal situation of illegitimate children

1. Affiliation

25. In Irish law, the principle *mater semper certa est* applies: the maternal affiliation of an illegitimate child, such as the third applicant, is established by the fact of birth, without any requirement of voluntary or judicial recognition.

The Illegitimate Children (Affiliation Orders) Act 1930, as amended by the Family Law (Maintenance of Spouses and Children) Act 1976 and the Courts Act 1983, provides procedures whereby the District Court of the Circuit Court may make an 'affiliation order' against the putative father of a child directing him to make periodic payments in respect of the latter's maintenance and also whereby the court may approve a lump-sum maintenance agreement between a person who admits he is the father of an illegitimate child and the latter's mother. Neither of these procedures establishes the child's paternal affiliation for all purposes, any finding of parentage being effective solely for the purposes of the proceedings in question and binding only on the parties.

26. Under the Registration of Births and Deaths (Ireland) Act 1863, as amended by the Births and Deaths Registration (Ireland) Act 1880, the Registrar may enter in the register the name of a person as the father of an illegitimate child if he is so requested jointly by that person and the mother. The act of registration does not, however, establish paternal affiliation.

2. Guardianship

27. The mother of an illegitimate child is his sole guardian as from the moment of his birth (section 6(4) of the Guardianship of Infants Act 1964) and has the same rights of guardianship as are jointly enjoyed by the parents of a legitimate child. The natural father can apply to the court under section 11(4) of the same Act regarding the child's custody and the right of access thereto by either parent; however, he cannot seek the court's directions on other matters affecting the child's welfare nor is there any means whereby he can be established as guardian of the child jointly with the mother, even if she consents.

3. Legitimation

28. An illegitimate child may be legitimated by the subsequent marriage of his parents, provided that, unlike the first and second applicants, they could have been lawfully married to one another at the time of the child's birth or at some time during the preceding 10 months (section 1(1) and (2) of the Legitimacy Act 1931).

4. Adoption

29. Under the Adoption Act 1952, as amended, an adoption order can only be made in favour of a married couple living together, a widow, a widower, or the mother or natural father or a relative of the child.

5. Maintenance

30. The effect of the Illegitimate Children (Affiliation Orders) Act 1930, as amended by the Family Law (Maintenance of Spouses and Children) Act 1976, is to impose on each of the parents of an illegitimate child an equal obligation to maintain him. This obligation cannot be enforced against the father until an 'affiliation order' has been made against him.

6. Succession.

31. The devolution of estates on intestacy is governed by the Succession Act 1965 which provides, basically, that the estate is to be distributed in specified proportions between any spouse or 'issue' who may survive the deceased. In *O'B v. S* ((1984) I.R. 316), the Supreme Court held that the word 'issue' did not include children who were not the issue of a lawful marriage and that accordingly an illegitimate child had, under the Act, no right to inheritance on the intestacy of his natural father. Whilst also holding that the resultant discrimination in favour of legitimate children was justifiable by reason of sections 1 and 3 of Article 41 of the Constitution, the Supreme Court stated that the decision to change the existing rules of intestate succession and the extent to which they were to be changed were primarily matters for the legislature. The relevant rules in the Act formed part of a statute designed to strengthen the protection of the family in accordance with Article 41, an Article which created not merely a State interest but a State obligation to safeguard the family; accordingly, the said discrimination was not necessarily unjust, unreasonable or arbitrary and the rules were not invalid having regard to the provisions of the Constitution.

An illegitimate child may, on the other hand, in certain circumstances have a right to inheritance on the intestacy of his mother. A special rule (section 9(1) of the Legitimacy Act 1931) lays down that where the mother of an illegitimate child dies intestate leaving no legitimate issue, the child is entitled to take any interest in his mother's estate to which he would have been entitled if he had been born legitimate.

32. As regards testate succession, section 117 of the Succession Act 1965 empowers a court to make provision for a child for whom it considers that the testator has failed in his moral duty to make proper provision. An illegitimate child has no claim against his father's estate under this section, but may be able to claim against his mother's estate provided that she leaves no legitimate issue.

33. An illegitimate child inheriting property from his parents is potentially liable to pay capital acquisition tax on a basis less favourable than a child born in wedlock.

E. Law reform proposals.

1. Divorce.

34. In 1983, a Joint Committee of the *Dáil* (Chamber of Deputies) and the *Seanad* (Senate) was established, *inter alia*, to examine the problems which follow the breakdown of marriage. In its report of 1985, it referred to figures suggesting that approximately

6 percent of marriages in Ireland had broken down to date, but noted the absence of accurate statistics. The Committee considered that the parties to stable relationships formed after marriage breakdown and the children of such relationships currently lacked adequate legal status and protection; however, it expressed no view on whether divorce legislation was at present necessary or desirable.

In a national referendum held on 26 June 1986, a majority voted against an amendment of the Constitution, which would have permitted legislation providing for divorce.

2. Illegitimacy

35. In September 1982, the Irish Law Reform Commission published a Report on Illegitimacy. Its basic recommendation was that legislation should remove the concept of illegitimacy from the law and equalise the rights of children born outside marriage with those of children born within marriage.

After considering the report, the Government announced in October 1983 that they had decided that the law should be reformed, and that reform should be concentrated on the elimination of discrimination against persons born outside marriage and on the rights and obligations of their fathers. However, the Government decided not to accept a proposal by the Law Reform Commission that the father be given automatic rights of guardianship in relation to a child so born.

36. In May 1985, the Minister of Justice laid before both Houses of Parliament a Memorandum entitled 'The Status of Children', indicating the scope and nature of the main changes proposed by the Government. On 9 May 1986, the Status of Children Bill 1986, a draft of which had been annexed to the aforesaid Memorandum, was introduced into the Seanad. If enacted in its present form, the Bill – which has the state purpose of removing as far as possible provisions in existing law which discriminate against children born outside marriage – would have, *inter alia*, the following effects.

(a) Where the name of a person was entered on the register of births as the father of a child born outside marriage, he would be presumed to be the father unless the contrary was shown.

(b) The father of a child born outside marriage would be able to seek a court order making him guardian of the child jointly with the mother. In that event, they would jointly have all the parental rights and responsibilities that are enjoyed and borne by married parents.

(c) The proviso qualifying the possibility of legitimation by subsequent marriage would be removed by the repeal of section 1(2) of the Legitimacy Act 1931.

(d) The legal provisions governing the obligation of both of the parents of a child born outside marriage to maintain him would be similar to those governing the corresponding obligation of married parents.

(e) For succession purposes, no distinction would be made between persons based on whether or not their parents were married to each other. Thus, a child born outside marriage would be entitled to share on the intestacy of either parent and would have the same rights in relation to the estate of a parent who died leaving a will as would a child of a family based on marriage.

The Explanatory Memorandum to the Bill states that any fiscal changes necessitated by the proposed new measures would be a matter for separate legislation promoted by the Minister for Finance.

3. Adoption

37. Work is also in progress on legislation reforming the law of adoption, following the publication in July 1984 of the Report of the Review Committee on Adoption Services. That Committee recommended that, as at present, unmarried couples should not be eligible to adopt jointly even their own natural children.

[The European Commission found no violations of Article 8 or Article 12, which guarantees "the right to marry and found a family".]

. . . .

DECISION [OF THE COURT]:

. . . .

II. SITUATION OF THE FIRST AND SECOND APPLICANTS

A. Inability to divorce and re-marry

1. Articles 12 and 8

49. The first and second applicants alleged that because of the impossibility under Irish law of obtaining a dissolution of Roy Johnston's marriage and of his resultant inability to marry Janice Williams-Johnston, they were victims of breaches of Articles 12 and 8 of the Convention. . . .

50. The applicants stated that, as regards this part of the case, the central issue was not whether the Convention guaranteed the right to divorce but rather whether the fact that they were unable to marry each other was compatible with the right to marry or remarry and with the right to respect for the family life, enshrined in Articles 12 and 8.

The Court does not consider that the issues arising can be separated into watertight compartments in this way. In any society espousing the principle of monogamy, it is inconceivable that Roy Johnston should be able to marry as long as his marriage to Mrs Johnston has not been dissolved. The second applicant, for her part, is not complaining of a general inability to marry but rather of her inability to marry the first applicant, a situation that stems precisely from the fact that he cannot obtain a divorce. Consequently, their case cannot be examined in isolation from the problem of the non-availability of divorce.

(a) Article 12

51. In order to determine whether the applicants can derive a right to divorce from Article 12, the Court will seek to ascertain the ordinary meaning to be given to the terms of this provision in their context and in the light of its object and purpose. (*See Golder v. United Kingdom*, §29 and Art 31(1) of the Vienna Convention on the Law of Treaties, 1969).

52. The Court agrees with the Commission that the ordinary meaning of the words 'right to marry' is clear, in the sense that they cover the formation of marital relationships but not their dissolution. Furthermore, these words are found in a context that includes an express reference to 'national laws'; even if, as the applicants would have it, the prohibition on divorce is to be seen as a restriction on capacity to marry, the Court does not consider that, in a society adhering to the principle of monogamy, such a restriction can be regarded as injuring the substance of the right guaranteed by Article 12.

Moreover, the foregoing interpretation of Article 12 is consistent with its object and purpose as revealed by the *travaux préparatoires*. The text of Article 12 was based on that of Article 16 of the Universal Declaration of Human Rights, paragraph 1 of which reads:

Men and women of full age, without any limitation due to race, nationality or religion, have the right to marry and to found a family. They are also entitled to equal rights as to marriage, during marriage and at its dissolution.

In explaining to the Consultative Assembly why the draft of the future Article 12 did not include the words found in the last sentence of the above-cited paragraph, Mr Teitgen, Rapporteur of the Committee on Legal and Administrative Questions, said:

In mentioning the particular Article (of the Universal Declaration), we have used only that part of the paragraph of the Article which affirms the right to marry and to found a family, but not the subsequent provisions of the Article concerning equal rights after marriage, since we only guarantee the right to marry. (*Travaux Préparatoires*, vol 1, p 268).

In the Court's view, the *travaux préparatoires* disclose no intention to include in Article 12 any guarantee of a right to have the ties of marriage dissolved by divorce.

53. The applicants set considerable store on the social developments that have occurred since the Convention was drafted, notably an alleged substantial increase in marriage breakdown.

It is true that the Convention and its Protocols must be interpreted in the light of present-day conditions. (*See Marckx*, §58). However, the Court cannot, by means of an evolutive interpretation, derive from these instruments a right that was not included therein at the outset. This is particularly so here, where the omission was deliberate.

It should also be mentioned that the right to divorce is not included in Protocol No 7 to the Convention which was opened to signature on 22 November 1984. The opportunity was not taken to deal with this question in Article 5 of the Protocol, which guarantees certain additional rights to spouses, notably in the event of dissolution of marriage. Indeed, paragraph 39 of the explanatory report to the Protocol states that the words 'in the event of its dissolution' found in Article 5 'do not imply any obligation on a State to provide for dissolution of marriage or to provide any special forms of dissolution.'

54. The Court thus concludes that the applicants cannot derive a right to divorce from Article 12. . . .

(b) Article 8

55. The principles which emerge from the Court's case law on Article 8 include the following.

(a) By guaranteeing the right to respect for family life, Article 8 presupposes the existence of a family.

(b) Article 8 applies to the 'family life' of the 'illegitimate' family as well as to that of the 'legitimate' family.

(c) Although the essential object of Article 8 is to protect the individual against arbitrary interference by the public authorities, there may in addition be positive obligations inherent in an effective 'respect' for family life. However, especially as far as those positive obligations are concerned, the notion of 'respect' is not clear-cut: having regard to the diversity of the practices followed and the situations obtaining in the Contracting States, the notion's requirements will vary considerably from case to case. Accordingly, this is an area in which the Contracting Parties enjoy a wide margin of appreciation in determining the steps to be taken to ensure compliance with the Convention with due regard to the needs and resources of the community and of individuals. (*Abdulaziz, Cabales and Balkandali v. United Kingdom* (1985), §67).

56. In the present case, it is clear that the applicants, the first and second of whom have lived together for some fifteen years, constitute a 'family' for the purposes of Article 8. They are thus entitled to its protection, notwithstanding the fact that their relationship exists outside marriage.

The question that arises, as regards this part of the case, is whether an effective 'respect' for the applicants' family life imposes on Ireland a positive obligation to introduce measures that would permit divorce.

57. It is true that, on this question, Article 8, with its reference to the somewhat vague notion of 'respect' for family life, might appear to lend itself more readily to an evolutive interpretation than does Article 12. Nevertheless, the Convention must be read as a whole and the Court does not consider that a right to divorce, which it has found to be excluded from Article 12, can, with consistency, be derived from Article 8, a provision of more general purpose and scope. The Court is not oblivious to the plight of the first and second applicants. However, it is of the opinion that, although the protection of private or family life may sometimes necessitate means whereby spouses can be relieved from the duty to live together [citation omitted], the engagements undertaken by Ireland under Article 8 cannot be regarded as extending to an obligation on its part to introduce measures permitting the divorce and the re-marriage which the applicants seek.

58. On the point, there is therefore no failure to respect the family life of the first and second applicants.

. . . .

For these reasons, THE COURT

. . . .

2. Holds by 16 votes to one that the absence of provision for divorce under Irish law and the resultant inability of the first and second applicants to marry each other does not give rise to a violation of Article 8 or 12 of the Convention;

. . . .

≈

QUESTIONS & COMMENTS

(1) Consider the Separate Opinion, Partly Dissenting and Party Concurring, of Judge de Meyer (translation):

5. . . .

The prohibition, under the Constitution of the respondent State, of any legislation permitting the dissolution of marriage is, as seems already to have been recognised in 1967 by a Committee of that State's Parliament, 'coercive in relation to all persons, Catholics and non-Catholics, whose religious rules do not absolutely prohibit divorce in all circumstances' and 'at variance with the accepted principles of religious liberty as declared at the Vatican Council and elsewhere'. Above all, it is, as that Committee stated, 'unnecessarily harsh and rigid.' [citations omitted].

In what the Convention, in several provisions and notably those concerning respect for private and family life and freedom of conscience and religion, calls 'a democratic society', the prohibition cannot be justified.

On more than one occasion, the Court has pointed out that there can be no such society without pluralism, tolerance and broadmindedness (*Handyside v. United Kingdom*, §49; *Lingens v. Austria* (1986), §41): these are hallmarks of a democratic society. (*Young, James and Webster v. United Kingdom*, §63).

In a society grounded on principles of this kind, it seems to me excessive to impose, in an inflexible and absolute manner, a rule that marriage is indissoluble, without even allowing consideration to be given to the possibility of exceptions in cases of the present kind.

For so draconian a system to be legitimate, it does not suffice that it corresponds to the desire or will of a substantial majority of the population: the Court has also stated that 'although individual interests must on occasion be subordinated to those of a group, democracy does not simply mean that the views of a majority must always prevail: a balance must be achieved which ensures the fair and proper treatment of minorities and avoids any abuse of a dominant position.' (*Young, James and Webster v. United Kingdom*, §63).

In my opinion, this statement must also be applicable in the area of marriage and divorce.

(2) One year later, the European Court did find an Article 12 violation where the applicant was prohibited from remarrying. In *F. v. Switzerland*, 128 Eur. Ct. H.R. (ser. A) (1987), the applicant, had been married four times since 1963. In 1983, after his third divorce, the Lausanne District Civil Court imposed a three-year prohibition on remarriage pursuant to Swiss Civil Code Article 150. The court found that the applicant's attitude and adulterous behavior was the reason for the breakdown of the marriage, which had lasted approximately two weeks.

The European Court held that while the right to marry is subject to the national laws of the contracting states, "the limitations thereby introduced must not restrict or reduce the right in such a way or to such an extent that the very essence of the right is impaired." *Id.* at §32. The Court noted that other states abolished waiting periods in light of "present day conditions." *Id.* at §33. However, given varying cultural and historical traditions about family, a state cannot be penalized for isolated views. The Court recognized that the stability of marriage, as supported by Swiss Civil Code Article 150 is a legitimate aim. Yet, the Court found that the means used were not proportionate for achieving that aim. The Court rejected the argument that the prohibition of remarriage is designed to preserve the future spouse of the divorced person. The Court also found that the prohibition wrongfully affects the applicant's future spouse who had no impediment to marriage. Therefore the prohibition of remarriage was disproportionate to the legitimate aim pursued and violated Article 12.

Compare *Zablocki v. Redhail*, 434 U.S. 374 (1978), holding unconstitutional a Wisconsin statute barring any person under a court order to pay financial support to his or her children from remarrying without a prior judicial determination that the support obligation has been met and that the children "are not likely . . . to become public charges." The Court found that the right to marry was constitutionally protected. Is there a U.S. constitutional right to *divorce*? What doctrine would support the claim that there is such a right? *Boddie v. Connecticut*, 401 U.S. 371 (1971), found that the due process clause was violated by a state statute requiring all persons, including indigents, to pay a $60 filing fee as a prerequisite to obtaining a divorce. "The State's refusal to admit these appellants to its courts, the sole means in Connecticut for obtaining a divorce, must be regarded as the equivalent of denying them an opportunity to be heard upon their claimed right to a dissolution of their marriages. . . . " Why does *Boddie* not establish a constitutional right to divorce?

5.9. Right to Vote

Universal Declaration of Human Rights

Article 21.

(1) Everyone has the right to take part in the government of his country, directly or through freely chosen representatives.

(2) Everyone has the right of equal access to public service in his country.

(3) The will of the people shall be the basis of the authority of government; this will shall be expressed in periodic and genuine elections which shall be by universal and equal suffrage and shall be held by secret vote or by equivalent free voting procedures.

International Covenant on Civil and Political Rights

Article 25

Every citizen shall have the right and the opportunity, without any of the distinctions mentioned in article 2 and without unreasonable restrictions:

(a) To take part in the conduct of public affairs, directly or through freely chosen representatives;

(b) To vote and to be elected at genuine periodic elections which shall be by universal and equal suffrage and shall be held by secret ballot, guaranteeing the free expression of the will of the electors;

(c) To have access, on general terms of equality, to public service in his country.

American Declaration of the Rights and Duties of Man

Article XX. Right to vote and to participate in government.

Every person having legal capacity is entitled to participate in the government of his country, directly or through his representatives, and to take part in popular elections, which shall be by secret ballot, and shall be honest, periodic and free.

Article XXXII. Duty to vote.

It is the duty of every person to vote in the popular elections of the country of which he is a national, when he is legally capable of doing so.

American Convention on Human Rights

Article 23. RIGHT TO PARTICIPATE IN GOVERNMENT.

1. Every citizen shall enjoy the following rights and opportunities:

a. To take part in the conduct of public affairs, directly or through freely chosen representatives;

b. To vote and to be elected in genuine periodic elections, which shall be by universal and equal suffrage and by secret ballot that guarantees the free expression of the will of the voters; and

c. To have access, under general conditions of equality, to the public service of his country.

2. The law may regulate the exercise of the rights and opportunities referred to in the preceding paragraph only on the basis of age, nationality, residence, language, education, civil and mental capacity, or sentencing by a competent court in criminal proceedings.

European Convention on Human Rights – Protocol I

ARTICLE 3

The High Contracting Parties undertake to hold free elections at reasonable intervals by secret ballot, under conditions which will ensure the free expression of the opinion of the people in the choice of the legislature.

Charter of Fundamental Rights of the European Union

Article 39

Right to vote and to stand as a candidate at elections to the European Parliament

1. Every citizen of the Union has the right to vote and to stand as a candidate at elections to the European Parliament in the Member State in which he or she resides, under the same conditions as nationals of that State.

2. Members of the European Parliament shall be elected by direct universal suffrage in a free and secret ballot.

Article 40

Right to vote and to stand as a candidate at municipal elections

Every citizen of the Union has the right to vote and to stand as a candidate at municipal elections in the Member State in which he or she resides under the same conditions as nationals of that State.

African Charter of Human and Peoples' Rights

Article 13

1. Every citizen shall have the right to participate freely in the government of his country, either directly or through freely chosen representatives in accordance with the provisions of the law.

2. Every citizen shall have the right of equal access to the public service of his country.

3. Every individual shall have the right of access to public property and services in strict equality of all persons before the law.

U.S. Constitution

Amendment XIV

Section 1. All persons born or naturalized in the United States, and subject to the jurisdiction thereof, are citizens of the United States and of the State wherein they reside. No State shall make or enforce any law which shall abridge the privileges or immunities of citizens of the United States; nor shall any State deprive any person of life, liberty, or property, without due process of law; nor deny to any person within its jurisdiction the equal protection of the laws.

Section 2. Representatives shall be apportioned among the several States according to their respective numbers, counting the whole number of persons in each State, excluding Indians not taxed. But when the right to vote at any election for the choice of electors for President and Vice President of the United States, Representatives in Congress, the Executive and Judicial officers of a State, or the members of the Legislature thereof, is denied to any of the male inhabitants of such State, being twenty-one years of age, and citizens of the United States, or in any way abridged, except for participation in rebellion, or other crime, the basis of representation therein shall be reduced in the proportion which the number of such male citizens shall bear to the whole number of male citizens twenty-one years of age in such State.

. . . .

Amendment XV

Section 1. The right of citizens of the United States to vote shall not be denied or abridged by the United States or by any State on account of race, color, or previous condition of servitude.

. . . .

Amendment XIX

The right of citizens of the United States to vote shall not be denied or abridged by the United States or by any State on account of sex.

. . . .

Amendment XXIII

Section 1. The District constituting the seat of government of the United States shall appoint in such manner as the Congress may direct:

A number of electors of President and Vice President equal to the whole number of Senators and Representatives in Congress to which the District would be entitled if it were a state, but in no event more than the least populous state; they shall be in addition to those appointed by the states, but they shall be considered, for the purposes of the election of President and Vice President, to be electors appointed by a state; and they shall meet in the District and perform such duties as provided by the twelfth article of amendment.

. . . .

Amendment XXIV

Section 1. The right of citizens of the United States to vote in any primary or other election for President or Vice President, for electors for President or Vice President, or for Senator or Representative in Congress, shall not be denied or abridged by the United States or any state by reason of failure to pay any poll tax or other tax.

. . . .

Amendment XXXI

Section 1. The right of citizens of the United States, who are 18 years of age or older, to vote, shall not be denied or abridged by the United States or any state on account of age.

. . . .

Statehood Solidarity Committee v. United States
Case 11.204, Report No. 98/03
Inter-American Commission on Human Rights
Inter-Am. C.H.R., OEA/Ser./L/V/II.114 Doc. 5 rev. 1 at xx (2003)

. . . .

C. Merits

1. The Petitioners and Representation in the U.S. Congress

. . . .

75. At issue in the present case is the role of the residents of the District of Columbia in the legislative branch of the federal government. As illuminated by the observations of the parties and domestic judicial decisions relating to this issue, it appears undisputed that individuals who live in the District of Columbia and would otherwise be eligible to vote in U.S. federal elections may cast a vote for the U.S. President [ ] but may not vote for or elect full members of the House of Representatives or the Senate. This circumstance stems from the terms of the U.S. Constitution as well as the federal legislation through which the District of Columbia was subsequently created.

76. In particular, the preclusion of the right on the part of residents of the District of Columbia to elect members of the House of Representatives is derived from Article 1, section 2, clause 1 of the U.S. Constitution, which provides:

> The House of Representatives shall be composed of Members chosen every second Year by the People of the several States, and the Electors in each State shall have the Qualifications requisite for Electors of the most numerous Branch of the State Legislature.

77. Judicial authorities in the United States have interpreted this provision, in light of its text, history and judicial precedent, as only permitting states to elect members of the House of Representatives, and have held that the District of Columbia cannot be considered a "state" within the meaning of the provision.[1]

78. Similarly with respect to the U.S. Senate, as originally provided under Article I, section 3 of the U.S. Constitution the Senate was to be "composed of two Senators from each State," chosen not "by the People of the several States," as in the case of the House, but rather "by the Legislature thereof."[2] In 1913 the Seventeenth Amendment granted to the people of "each State," rather than their legislatures, the right to choose Senators [ ] and after that change the provisions concerning qualifications and vacancies for the Senate have essentially paralleled those for the House. [ ] As with the House of Representatives, the U.S. courts have concluded that the framers of the Constitution did not contemplate allocating two Senators to the District of Columbia, as the Senate was expressly viewed as representing the states themselves. Further, the guarantee of two senators for each State was an important element of the "Great Compromise" between the smaller and larger states that ensured ratification of the Constitution, such that

---

[1] [Adams v. Clinton (D.D.C.).]

[2] U.S. Const. Article I, §3, cl. 1.

the smaller states were guaranteed equal representation notwithstanding their smaller population.[3]

79. The findings of the U.S. judiciary as to the absence of Congressional voting rights for D.C. residents have also been based upon the terms of the so-called "District clause" in the Constitution, as well as by the Organic Act of 1801 by which the District of Columbia was created. According to Article I, section 8, clause 17 of the U.S. Constitution, Congress is expressly granted the power to "exercise exclusive Legislation in all Cases whatsoever" over the district that would become the seat of government. [ ]When the District of Columbia was ultimately created from land ceded by Maryland and Virginia through the passage of the Organic Act of 1801, [ ] it appears to have been generally accepted that once Congress assumed jurisdiction over the District, individuals residing in the District would lose their right to vote for Congress. [ ] Likewise, since February 1801 District residents have been unable to vote in either Maryland or Virginia.[ ]

80. As to the purpose underlying the treatment of the District of Columbia, it appears to be generally accepted that the historic rationale for the District Clause was to ensure that Congress would not have to depend upon another sovereign for its protection.[ ] In particular, authorities claim that the District Clause was adopted in response to an incident in Philadelphia in 1783 in which a crowd of disbanded Revolutionary War soldiers, angry at not having been paid, gathered to protest in front of the building in which the Continental Congress was meeting under the Articles of Confederation. As described by the U.S. District Court:

> Despite requests from the Congress, the Pennsylvania state government declined to call out its militia to respond to the threat, and the Congress had to adjourn abruptly to New Jersey. The episode, viewed as an affront to the weak national government, led to the widespread belief that exclusive federal control over the national capital was necessary. "Without it," Madison wrote, "not only the public authority might be insulted and its proceedings be interrupted, with impunity; but a dependence of the members of the general Government, on the State comprehending the seat of the Government for protection in the exercise of their duty, might bring on the national councils an imputation of awe or influence, equally dishonorable to the Government, and dissatisfactory to the other members of the confederacy."[ ]

81. The record before the Commission indicates that since the inception of the District, numerous initiatives have been attempted to provide residents of the District with representation at the local and federal levels. These have included: a constitutional amendment allowing for participation by residents of the District in Presidential elections in 1960; passage of the District of Columbia Delegate Act [ ] in 1970 which provided the District with one non-voting delegate in the House of Representatives who enjoys floor privileges, office space, committee assignments and committee voting rights but was not empowered to vote on legislation brought before the House of Representatives; passage of the District of Columbia Self-Government and Governmental Reorganization Act, or Home Rule Act, [ ] in 1973 which led to the election of a city council and mayor; the election by the District since 1990 of "shadow" representatives, namely two non-voting senators and one non-voting representative whose role is to advocate the cause of statehood; [ ] and the

---

[3] Adams v. Clinton, at 25–27, citing The Federalist Nos. 10, 39, 58, 62 (James Madison) (Jacob E. Cooke ed., 1961); Reynolds v. Simms, 377 U.S. 533 (1964).

granting in 1993 to the District delegate and all territorial non-voting delegates the right to vote in Congress' Committee of the Whole.[ ] With respect to this latter development, it is the Commission's understanding based upon the parties' information that the vote of the District's delegate in the Committee of the Whole is subject to a "saving clause" that prevents the District and territorial delegates from casting a deciding vote on the passage of any Congressional legislation in the Committee of the Whole. [ ]

82. Based upon the record before it, therefore, the Commission finds that the Petitioners, as residents of the District of Columbia, are not permitted to vote for or elect members of the U.S. Senate. While the Petitioners are permitted to elect a member of the House of Representatives, that member cannot cast a deciding vote in respect of any of the matters coming before the House. This is in contrast to the residents of States in the United States, who have the right under the U.S. Constitution to elect members of both the Senate and the House of Representatives. The Commission also finds that the basis for this distinction lay with the desire of the original framers of the Constitution to protect the center of federal authority from undue influence of the various States, and at the same time avoid the possibility that the residents of the District might enjoy a disproportionate influence on governmental affairs by virtue of their contiguity to, and residence among, members of the federal government.

2. Articles II and XX of the American Declaration – Interpretation and Application of the Right to Equal and Effective Participation in Government

83. As particularized above, the Petitioners have alleged that the United States is responsible for violations of Articles II and XX of the American Declaration in respect of the members of the Statehood Solidarity Committee and other residents of the District of Columbia. This allegation is based on the contention that the Petitioners, unlike residents elsewhere in the United States, have no meaningful representation in the federal House of Representatives and no representation whatsoever in the Senate, and are therefore denied effective participation in the national legislature. They also contend that these limitations are manifestly arbitrary and that the State has failed to provide any adequate justification for them.

84. Articles II and XX of the American Declaration provide:

Article II. All persons are equal before the law and have the rights and duties established in this Declaration, without distinction as to race, sex, language, creed or any other factor.

Article XX. Every person having legal capacity is entitled to participate in the government of his country, directly or through his representatives, and to take part in popular elections, which shall be by secret ballot, and shall be honest, periodic and free.

85. The Commission has long recognized the significance of representative democracy and associated political rights to the effective realization and protection of human rights more broadly in the hemisphere. According to the Commission

[t]he participation of citizens in government, which is protected by Article XX of the Declaration forms the basis and support of democracy, which cannot exist without it; for title to government rests with the people, the only body empowered to decide its own immediate and future destiny and to designate its legitimate representatives.

Neither form of political life, nor institutional change, nor development planning or the control of those who exercise public power can be made without representative government.

[...]

The right to political participation leaves room for a wide variety of forms of government; there are many constitutional alternatives as regards the degree of centralization of the powers of the state or the election and attributes of the organs responsible for the exercise of those powers. However, a democratic framework is an essential element for establishment of a political society where human values can be fully realized.[4]

86. The central role of representative democracy in the inter-American system is evidenced in the provisions of the system's founding instruments, including Article 3(d) of the Charter of the OAS [ ] which confirms that "solidarity of the American states and the high aims which are sought through it require the political organization of those States on the basis of the effective exercise of representative democracy." Resolutions adopted by the Organization's political organs have likewise reflected the indispensability of democratic governance to the stability, peace and development of the region. In OAS General Assembly Resolution 837, for example, OAS member states reaffirmed the "inalienable right of all of the peoples of the Americas freely to determine their political, economic and social system without outside interference, through a genuine democratic process and within a framework of social justice in which all sectors of the population will enjoy the guarantees necessary to participate freely and effectively through the exercise of universal suffrage." [ ] Citing these and other similar instruments, the Commission recently reaffirmed that "there is a conception in the inter-American system of the fundamental importance of representative democracy as a legitimate mechanism for achieving the realization of and respect for human rights; and as a human right itself, whose observance and defense was entrusted to the Commission."[5] According to the Commission, this conception implies protecting those civil and political rights in the framework of representative democracy, as well as the existence of institutional control over the acts of the branches of government, and the rule of law.[ ]

87. The Commission is therefore of the view that those provisions of the system's human rights instruments that guarantee political rights, including Article XX of the American Declaration, must be interpreted and applied so as to give meaningful effect to exercise of representative democracy in this Hemisphere. The Commission also considers that insights regarding the specific content of Article XX of the Declaration can properly be drawn from Article 23 of the American Convention and the Commission's previous interpretation of that provision,[6] which parallels in several fundamental respects

---

[4] IACHR, Doctrine of the Inter-American Commission of Human Rights (1971–1981), in Ten Years of Activities 1971–1981, Washington, D.C., 1982, p. 334.

[5] Aylwin Azocar et al. v. Chile (Merits), Case 11.863, Report N° 137/99, Annual Report of the IACHR 1999, at 536 [hereinafter *Aylwin Case*].

[6] The Commission has previously held that in interpreting and applying the Declaration, it is necessary to consider its provisions in light of developments in the field of international human rights law since the Declaration was first composed. These developments may in turn be drawn from the provisions of other prevailing international and regional human rights instruments, including in particular the American Convention on Human Rights which, in many instances, may be considered to represent an authoritative

Article XX of the Declaration. Article 23 provides as follows:

1. Every citizen shall enjoy the following rights and opportunities:

   a. to take part in the conduct of public affairs, directly or through freely chosen representatives;
   b. to vote and to be elected in genuine periodic elections, which shall be by universal and equal suffrage and by secret ballot that guarantees the free expression of the will of the voters; and
   c. to have access, under general conditions of equality, to the public service of his country.

2. The law may regulate the exercise of the rights and opportunities referred to in the preceding paragraph only on the basis of age, nationality, residence, language, education, civil and mental capacity, or sentencing by a competent court in criminal proceedings.

88. In interpreting Article 23 of the American Convention, the Commission has recognized that a degree of autonomy must be afforded to states in organizing their political institutions so as to give effect to these rights, as the right to political participation leaves room for a wide variety of forms of government. [ ] As the Commission has appreciated, its role or objective is not to create a uniform model of representative democracy for all states, but rather is to determine whether a state's laws infringe fundamental human rights. [ ] The Commission has similarly recognized that not all differences in treatment are prohibited under international human rights law, and this applies equally to the right to participate in government. [ ]

89. This does not mean, however, that the conduct of states in giving effect to the right to representative government, whether by way of their constitutions or otherwise,[7] is immune from review by the Commission. Rather, certain minimum standards or conditions exist respecting the manner in which this right is given effect which must be shown to have been satisfied. These standards or conditions relate primarily to the nature of permissible limitations that may be imposed on the exercise of such rights. The Commission has noted in this regard that Article 23(2) of the American Convention provides an exhaustive list of grounds upon which states may properly base limitations of the exercise of the rights and opportunities referred to in Article 23(1) of the Convention, namely on the basis of age, nationality, residence, language, education, civil and mental capacity, or sentencing by a competent court in criminal proceedings.[ ]

---

expression of the fundamental principles set forth in the American Declaration. *See, e.g.,* IACHR, Juan Raul Garza v. United States, Case 12.243, Annual Report of the IACHR 2000, paras. 88, 89; citing I/A Court H.R., Interpretation of the American Declaration of the Rights and Duties of Man Within the Framework of Article 64 of the American Convention on Human Rights, Advisory Opinion OC-10/89 of July 14, 1989, Inter-Am. Ct. H. R. (Ser. A) N° 10 (1989), para. 37. *See also* IACHR, Report on the Situation of Human Rights of Asylum Seekers within the Canadian Refugee Determination System, OEA/Ser.L/V/II.106, doc. 40 rev. (February 28, 2000), para. 38 (confirming that while the Commission clearly does not apply the American Convention in relation to member states that have yet to ratify that treaty, its provisions may well be relevant in informing an interpretation of the principles of the Declaration).

[7] It is well-established that all obligations imposed on a State by international law must be fulfilled in good faith and that domestic law may not be invoked to justify nonfulfillment, even in cases involving constitutional provisions. *See* I/A Court H/R., Advisory Opinion OC-14/94 of December 9, 1994, Ser. A N° 14 (1994), para. 35.

90. More generally, the Commission has held that its role in evaluating the right to participate in government is to ensure that any differential treatment in providing for this right lacks any objective and reasonable justification.[8] In this connection, in securing the equal protection of human rights, states may draw distinctions among different situations and establish categories for certain groups of individuals, so long as it pursues a legitimate end, and so long as the classification is reasonably and fairly related to the end pursued by the legal order.[9] And as with other fundamental rights, restrictions or limitations upon the right to participate in government must be justified by the need of them in the framework of a democratic society, as demarcated by the means, their motives, reasonability and proportionality.[10] At the same time, in making these determinations, the Commission must take due account of the State's degree of autonomy in organizing its political institutions and should only interfere where the State has curtailed the very essence and effectiveness of a petitioner's right to participate in his or her government.[11]

91. This approach to the interpretation and application of the right under Article 23 of the American Convention and Article XX of the American Declaration to participate in government is consistent with jurisprudence from other international human rights systems concerning similar treaty protections. The European Court of Human Rights, for example, had occasion to interpreting Article 3 of Protocol I to the European Convention[12] in the context of a complaint challenging Belgian legislation that transitionally demarcated the territory of Dutch-speaking and French-speaking regions of Belgium and placed linguistic restrictions upon representation and membership for minority language groups in the Community and Regional Councils and Executives of those regions.[13] In disposing of the complaint, the European Court indicated that the rights encompassed in Article 3 of Protocol I are not absolute, but rather that there is room for "implied limitations."[ ] Moreover, the Court proclaimed that states have a "wide margin of appreciation" in implementing the rights under Article 3 of Protocol I, but that

[i]t is for the Court to determine in the last resort whether the requirements of Protocol N° 1 (P1) have been complied with; it has to satisfy itself that the conditions do not curtail the rights in question to such an extent as to impair their very essence and deprive them of their effectiveness; that they are imposed in pursuit of a legitimate aim; and that the means employed are not disproportionate. In particular, such conditions must not thwart "the free expression of the opinion of the people in the choice of the legislature."[14]

92. According to the European Court, any electoral system must also be assessed in the light of the political evolution of the country concerned, for, in its view, "features

---

[8] [*Aylwin Case*, paras. 99, 101.]

[9] I/A Court H.R., Advisory Opinion OC-4/84 of January 19, 1984, para. 57.

[10] [*Aylwin Case*, para. 102.]

[11] *Id.*, para. 103, citing Eur. Court H.R., Case of Mathieu-Mohin and Clerfayt, N° 9/1985/95/143 (28 January 1987).

[12] European Convention for the Protection of Human Rights and Fundamental Freedoms, Protocol 1, Article 3 (providing: "The High Contracting Parties undertake to hold free elections at reasonable intervals by secret ballot, under conditions which will ensure the free expression of the opinion of the people in the choice of the legislature.").

[13] *Case of Mathieu-Mohin and Clerfayt.*

[14] *Id.*

that would be unacceptable in the context of one system may accordingly be justified in the context of another, at least so long as the chosen system provides for conditions which will ensure the "free expression of the opinion of the people on the choice of the legislature."[ ] In ultimately dismissing the applicants' complaint, the Court emphasized that

> [i]n any consideration of the electoral system in issue, its general context must not be forgotten. The system does not appear unreasonable if regard is had to the intentions it reflects and to the respondent State's margin of appreciation within the Belgian parliamentary system – a margin that is all the greater as the system is incomplete and provisional.[15]

93. Similar principles governing the right to political participation have been elucidated in the UN human rights system. Article 25(b) of the International Covenant on Civil and Political Rights provides that "[e]very citizen shall have the right and the opportunity, without any of the distinctions mentioned in article 2 and without unreasonable restrictions: [. . .] (b) to vote and to be elected at genuine periodic elections which shall be by universal and equal suffrage and shall be held by secret ballot, guaranteeing the free expression of the will of the electors." Like the European Court and this Commission, the UN Human Rights Committee has recognized that the rights protected under Article 25 of the ICCPR are not absolute, but that any conditions that apply to the right to political participation protected by Article 25 should be based on "objective and reasonable criteria."[16] The Committee has also found that in light of the fundamental principle of proportionality, greater restrictions on political rights require a specific justification.[17]

94. The Commission also observes that in affording individuals the rights prescribed under Article XX of the Declaration, they must do so on the basis of equality and without discrimination as mandated by Article II of the Declaration. As with permissible restrictions under Article XX itself, Article II of the Declaration allows for differential treatment but only when that treatment is based upon factual differences and there exists a reasonable relationship of proportionality between these differences and the aims of the legal rule under review, due account being taken of the State's prerogative in choosing its political institutions.[18]

---

[15] *Id.*

[16] UNHRC, General Comment 25(57), General Comments under Article 40, paragraph 4 of the International Covenant on Civil and Political Rights, adopted by the Committee at its 1510th mtg., U.N. Doc. CCPR/C/Rev.1/Add.7 (1996), para. 4. According to the *travaux préparatoires* to the ICCPR, permissible restrictions under Article 25 would include, for example, prescription of a minimum age for voting. Marc J. Bossuyt, Guide to the "*Travaux Préparatoires*" of the International Covenant on Civil and Political Rights 473 (1987), citing Third Committee, 16th Session (1961), A/5000, §93, referring to A/C.3/SR/1096, §36 (GH), §37 (CL), §46 (GH); A/C.3/SR.1097, §5 (IQ), §9 (TR), §21 (U).

[17] *See The Pietraroia Case*, Communication N° 44/1979, para. 16. *See similarly* Manfred Nowak, U.N. Covenant on Civil and Political Rights – CCPR Commentary 444–5 (1993). Nowak notes that universal suffrage in various countries is not an absolute precept but rather only a relative principle molded by the respective understanding of democratic participation. At the same time, he emphasizes that the principle of universal suffrage obligates States Parties not only to extend the circle of persons eligible to vote and to be elected to as many citizens as possible, but also to take positive steps to ensure that these persons are truly able to exercise their right to vote.

[18] *See, e.g.*, Ferrer-Mazorra *et al.* v. United States, Case 9903, Annual Report of the IACHR 2000, para. 238; I/A Court H.R., Advisory Opinion OC-4/84 of January 19, 1984, paras. 56, 57.

95. In evaluating the circumstances of the present case in light of the above principles, the Commission must first address whether the rights of the Petitioners under Article XX of the American Declaration to participate in their government have, on the evidence, been limited or restricted by the State. In this respect, the State does not contest that the U.S. Constitution, by its terms and as interpreted by the courts in the United States, does not permit the Petitioners and other residents of the District of Columbia to elect representatives to their national legislature.

96. Nevertheless, the United States appears to suggest that District residents are afforded an adequate right to participate in the government of the United States and to take part in popular elections in compliance with Article XX of the Declaration, by reason of other political activities that are open to them. According to the State, these include their ability to vote in Presidential elections, to elect a mayor and city council, and the presence of one non-voting delegate in the House of Representatives and three "shadow" representatives in Congress. The State also points to the fact that the District's status is freely and openly debated in the government through, for example the presentation of statehood bills in Congress. The State therefore contends that by any measure, District residents have been able to take part in "healthy and robust debate" concerning all issues of national concern, including the status of the District itself.

97. Upon consideration of the parties' observations on the record of the case, the Commission must conclude that the Petitioners' rights to participate in the federal legislature of the United States have been limited or restricted both in law and in fact. As noted, it is agreed that as a matter of domestic constitutional law the Petitioners are not afforded the right to elect members of either chamber of Congress. While the State has contended that the District of Columbia elects a delegate to the House of Representatives who has the right to vote upon legislation in the Committee of the Whole,[19] the record indicates that the delegate is prohibited from casting a deciding vote in respect of any legislation that comes before Congress. On this basis, the State's own courts have proclaimed that the vote extended to the District of Columbia delegate in the Committee of the Whole has no chance of affecting the ultimate result of matters coming before the Committee and is therefore "meaningless."[20] Accordingly, the Commission cannot accept this arrangement as providing the Petitioners with effective participation in their legislature. For similar reasons, the ability of the Petitioners to elect representatives to other levels and

---

[19] The U.S. District Court for the District of Columbia has described the Committee of the Whole as follows:

> The Committee of the Whole is comprised of all the Members of the House of Representatives and convenes on the floor of the House with Members serving as the Chair on a rotating basis. It is in this procedural forum that the House considers, debates and votes on amendments to most of the legislation reported out of the standing or select committees. Only after consideration of amendments in the Committee of the Whole is legislation reported to the floor of the House for final, usually perfunctory, consideration.

Robert H. Michel *et al.* v. Donald K. Anderson *et al.*, U.S. District Court for the District of Columbia, Civil Action N° 93–0039, March 8, 1993 (Greene J.), at 5; *aff'd* U.S. Court of Appeals for the District of Columbia, Case N° 93–5109 (January 25, 1994).

[20] *Id.* (concluding that "[i]n a democratic system, the right to vote is genuine and effective only when, under the governing rules, there is a chance, large or small, that, sooner or later, the vote will affect the ultimate result. The votes of the Delegates in the Committee of the Whole cannot achieve that; by virtue of Rule XXIII they are meaningless. It follows that the House action had no effect on legislative power and that it did not violate Article I or any other provision of the Constitution.").

branches of government and to participate in public debates on the status of the District of Columbia cannot be considered equivalent to the nature of participation contemplated by Article XX of the Declaration, which, in the Commission's view, entitles the Petitioners to a meaningful opportunity, directly or through freely elected representatives, to influence the decisions of government that affect them, including those of the federal legislature.

98. Therefore, to the extent that each of the Petitioners, unlike similarly-situation citizens elsewhere in the United States, does not have the right to vote for a representative in their national legislature who has an effective opportunity to influence legislation considered by Congress, the Commission considers that they have been denied an equal right under law in accordance with Article II of the Declaration to participate in the government of their country by reason of their place of residence, and accordingly that their right under Articles XX of the Declaration to participate in their federal government has been limited or restricted. . . .

99. The Commission must next consider whether this restriction or limitation on the rights under Article XX and II of the Declaration to vote and to participate in government with equality under law is nevertheless justified when analyzed in the general political context of the State concerned and thereby permissible under these articles of the Declaration. As noted above, this entails evaluating whether the restrictions imposed by the State may be considered to curtail the very essence and effectiveness of the Petitioners' right to participate in their government and whether the State has offered a reasonable, objective and proportionate justification for the restrictions.

100. In this respect, the State has provided a number of explanations or justifications for the Petitioners' treatment which, in its view, should preclude the Commission from finding any violations of Articles II and XX of the American Declaration. In particular, as noted above, the State argues that the issue raised by the Petitioners relates at base to the federal structure of the United States and the decision by its founders to constitute a union of relatively autonomous states. According to the State, it is the absence of the District's status as a state, and not any conscious decision by the U.S. government, discriminatory or otherwise, to disenfranchise the Petitioners or other residents of the District of Columbia, that has resulted in their status *vis a vis* the U.S. Congress. The decision of the framers of the U.S. Constitution in turn was, according to the State and the Petitioners alike, based upon the desire to protect the center of federal authority from undue influence of the various States, and at the same time avoid the possibility that the residents of the District might enjoy a disproportionate influence on governmental affairs by virtue of their "contiguity to, and residence among, members of the General government."[ ] As such, the State suggests that these decisions not only justify the limitation on the Petitioners' right to elect members of Congress, but concern the very organization of the United States and therefore should be left to the realm of political debate and decision-making.

101. In entering into this stage of its analysis, the Commission acknowledges the degree of deference that must properly be afforded to states in organizing their political institutions so as to give effect to the right to vote and to participate in government. The Commission should only interfere in cases where the State has curtailed the very essence and effectiveness of an individual's right to participate in his or her government. After considering the information on the record, however, the Commission finds that the restrictions on the Petitioners' rights under Article XX to participate in their national legislature have been curtailed in such a manner as to deprive the Petitioners of the very

essence and effectiveness of that right, without adequate justification being shown by the State for this curtailment.

102. The Commission notes in this regard that the political structure of the United States has been developed so as to provide for both state and federal levels of government, each with exclusive areas of jurisdiction under the Constitution. Consistent with this, the U.S. Congress, as the legislative branch of the federal government, has been afforded extensive powers to consider and enact legislation in areas such as taxation, national defense, foreign affairs, immigration and criminal law. It is also clear that these powers and legislative measures are binding upon or otherwise affect residents of the District of Columbia as they do other citizens of the United States. Indeed, as a consequence of Article I, section 8 of the U.S. Constitution and the Organic Act of 1801, Congress has the exceptional authority to exercise all aspects of legislative control over the District, subject to what aspects of that authority Congress may delegate to District authorities through appropriate federal legislation.

103. Despite the existence of this significant and direct legislative authority that Congress exercises over the Petitioners and other residents of the District of Columbia, however, the Petitioners have no effective right to vote upon those legislative measures, directly or through freely chosen representatives, and it is not apparent from the record that Congress is responsible to the Petitioners for those measures by some other means. In this manner, Congress exercises expansive authority over the Petitioners, and yet it is in no way effectively accountable to the Petitioners or other citizens residing in the District of Columbia. This, in the Commission's view, has deprived the Petitioners of the very essence of representative government, namely that title to government rests with the people governed.

104. Both the Petitioners and the State have suggested that the foundation of the denial to the Petitioners of the right to vote for and elect members of Congress lay upon concerns existing at the time the U.S. Constitution was negotiated over 200 years ago that the seat of the federal government may be disproportionately threatened, or the position of a state correspondingly enriched, by placing Congress within a State.

105. The Commission has recognized and given due consideration to the fact that these concerns may have justified depriving residents of the District of elected representation in Congress at the time that the U.S. Constitution was enacted and indeed may have been indispensable to the Constitution's negotiation. However, as with all protections under the American Declaration, the Commission must interpret and apply Articles II and XX in the context of current circumstances and standards.[21] Not only has the State failed to offer any present-day justification for the Petitioners' denial of effective representation in Congress, but modern developments within the United States and the Western Hemisphere more broadly indicate that the restrictions imposed by the State on the Petitioners' right to participate in government are no longer reasonably justified.

106. Significantly, the State's judicial branch has specifically concluded that the historical rationale for the District Clause in the U.S. Constitution would not today require the exclusion of District residents from the Congressional franchise and has accepted

---

[21] *See* Legal Consequences for States of the Continued Presence of South Africa in Namibia (South West Africa) notwithstanding Security Council Resolution 276 (1970), Advisory Opinion, I.C.J. Reports 1971, p. 16 (stating that an "international instrument must be interpreted and applied within the overall framework of the juridical system in force at the time of the interpretation."). *See also* I/A Court H.R., Advisory Opinion OC-10/89,[ ] para. 37.

that denial of the franchise is not necessary for the effective functioning of the seat of government.[22] It is also notable in this regard that domestic courts in the United States have found that the exclusion of District residents from the Congressional franchise does not violate the right to equal protection under the U.S. Constitution, not because the restriction on their right to elect Congressional representatives have been found to be justified, but because the limitation is one drawn by the Constitution itself and accordingly cannot be overcome by the one person, one vote principle.[23] The American Declaration prescribes no similar limits or qualifications upon the guarantee of the rights under Articles II and XX and, as indicated above, establishes standards that apply to all legislative or other enactment by a state, including its constitutional provisions.

107. Numerous political initiatives have been undertaken in the United States in recent years to extend some measure of national representation for D.C. residents, which similarly recognize the present-day inadequacy of the Petitioners' status in the federal system of government. These have included, for example, granting District residents in 1960 the right to vote in Presidential elections through the 23rd amendment to the U.S. Constitution, the passage of the District of Columbia Delegate Act in 1970 which provided the District of Columbia with a non-voting delegate in the House of Representatives, and the extension to the D.C. delegate in 1993 of a limited right to vote in Congress' Committee of the Whole.

108. The Commission also considers it significant that according to the information available, no other federal state in the Western Hemisphere denies the residents of its federal capital the right to vote for representatives in their national legislature. In Canada, for example, the City of Ottawa constitutes a part of the Province of Ontario and accordingly its residents are entitled to elect Members of Parliament in the federal House of Commons on the same basis as residents in other provincial electoral divisions.[ ] The City of Buenos Aires, while constituting a separate enclave similar to the District of Columbia, is entitled to elect deputies and senators to Argentina's national legislature.[ ] Similarly, the residents of Brasilia, Brazil,[ ] Caracas, Venezuela,[ ] and Mexico City, Mexico,[ ] all of which constitute federal enclaves or districts, have voting representation in their national legislatures.

109. Based upon the foregoing analysis, the Commission concludes that the State has failed to justify the denial to the Petitioners of effective representation in their federal government, and consequently that the Petitioners have been denied an effective right to participate in their government, directly or through freely chosen representatives and in general conditions of equality, contrary to Articles XX and II of the American Declaration.

110. It also follows from the Commission's analysis that securing the Petitioners' rights under Articles II and XX of the Declaration does not necessarily require that they

---

[22] Adams v. Clinton, *supra*, at 27, 56 (stating that "[i]t is also true, as our dissenting colleague argues, that the historical rationale for the District Clause – ensuring that Congress would not have to depend upon another sovereign for its protection – would not by itself require the exclusion of District residents from the congressional franchise", and indicating that the majority of the Court "do not disagree that defendants have failed to offer a compelling justification for denying District residents the right to vote in Congress. As the dissent argues, denial of the franchise is not necessary for the effective functioning of the seat of government.").

[23] *Id.*, pp. 56–59 (noting that the Equal Protection Clause (Article 1, §2) of the U.S. Constitution does not protect the right of all citizens to vote but only the right of all "qualified" citizens to vote and that the right to equal protection cannot overcome the line explicitly drawn by that article. Accordingly, the Court concluded that the doctrine of one person, one vote under U.S. constitutional jurisprudence could not serve as a vehicle for challenging the structure the Constitution itself imposes upon the Congress.).

be afforded the same means or degree of participation as residents of states in the United States. What the Declaration and its underlying principles mandate is that the State extend to the Petitioners the opportunity to exercise a meaningful influence on those matters considered by their governing legislature, and that any limitations and restrictions on those rights are justified by the State as reasonable, objective and proportionate, taking due account of the context of its political system. As Article XX of the Declaration suggests, this is generally achieved through the election of representatives to the legislature who may cast a vote on matters before the legislature that has a meaningful possibility of affecting the outcome of those deliberations. Nevertheless, the mechanisms through which the State may afford these opportunities are clearly a matter for the discretion of the State concerned.

. . . .

~

QUESTIONS & COMMENTS

(1) The Commission wrote that "it is well-established that all obligations imposed on a State by international law must be fulfilled in good faith and that domestic law may not be invoked to justify nonfulfillment, even in cases involving constitutional provisions." How can this statement be squared with Article 46 of the Vienna Convention on the Law of Treaties that recognizes that a state may consider itself not bound by a treaty if the treaty violates "a rule of its internal law of fundamental importance"?

(2) Is the Constitution's denial of voting rights to Washington, D.C., residents in congressional elections evidence of a persistent objection to the customary international legal obligations effectively represented by the American Declaration? If so, how does this affect the United States' treaty obligations under the OAS Charter and, thereby, the United States' derivative obligations under the American Declaration? What effects would the status of the Constitution as a multilateral treaty have on the United States' other international legal obligations?

(3) Canada interprets Article 25 of the ICCPR to grant prisoners the right to vote. *See C.F. v. Canada*, UN Hum.Rts.Ctte., Communication No. 113/1981, admissibility decision adopted 12 April 1985, at §3.1 and follow up.

Under U.S. federal law, states may disenfranchise prisoners. *Richardson v. Ramirez*, 418 U.S. 24 (1974). Given that a disproportionate number of prisoners and ex-convicts in the United States are African American, moreover, the policy has racial implications. *See, e.g.*, Andrew L. Shapiro, *Giving Cons and Ex-cons the Vote*, THE NATION, December 20, 1993, at 767.

Does U.S. law permitting disenfranchisement conflict with the ICCPR? Upon its ratification of the ICCPR, the United States issued an Understanding addressing states' rights. Understanding No. 5 states the following:

> (5) That the United States understands that this Covenant shall be implemented by the Federal Government to the extent that it exercises legislative and judicial jurisdiction over the matters covered therein, and otherwise by the state and local governments; to the extent that state and local governments exercise jurisdiction over such matters, the Federal Government shall take measures appropriate to the Federal system to the end that the competent authorities

of the state or local governments *may* take appropriate measures for the fulfillment of the Covenant.

U.S. Reservations, Declarations, and Understandings to the International Covenant on Civil and Political Rights, 138 Cong. Rec. S4784 (daily ed., April 2, 1992) (emphasis provided). Does this Understanding conflict with the "object and purpose" of the ICCPR?

(4) In *Bravo Mena v. Mexico*, Report No. 14/93, Case 10,956, Inter-Am. Cm. H.R. 259, OEA/ser.L/V/II.85, rev. -, doc. 9 (1993), a petitioner challenged election irregularities and the lack of domestic tribunal impartiality in correcting these irregularities. The Inter-American Commission held that "if Article 23 (right to participate in government) [is] to be fully respected elections [must] be authentic, universal, periodic, and by secret ballot or some other means that enabled voters to express their will freely." *Id.* at 267. The Commission rejected the Mexican government's claim that Article 23 "does not prescribe a prototype or model for either the election process, how the election is to be set up or who the election authorities are to be." *Id.* at 266. The Inter-American Commission held that "any mention of the right to vote and to be elected would be mere rhetoric if unaccompanied by a *precisely described set of characteristics* that elections are required to meet." *Id.* at 272 (*citing* Cases 9768, 9780, and 9828 (Mexico), Inter-Am. Cm. H.R. 118, OEA/Ser.L/II.77, rev. 1, doc. 7 (1989–90) (emphasis provided). Subsequently, the Mexican government brought its election practices and election monitoring bodies into compliance.

Should a state party receive less deference from an international tribunal after it has repeatedly failed to comply with its international obligations?

(5) Consider the following passage from *Mathieu-Mohin and Clerfayt v. Belgium*, 113 Eur. Ct. H.R. (ser. A) (1987):

> For the purposes of Article 3 of Protocol No. 1, any electoral system must be assessed in the light of the political evolution of the country concerned; features that would be unacceptable in the context of one system may accordingly be justified in the context of another, at least so long as the chosen system provides for conditions which will ensure the 'free expression of the opinion of the people in the choice of the legislature'.

Id. at §54. How does the European Court's concern with a country's "political evolution" relate to those problems created by amnesties established after a civil war. Let us use a hypothetical case. As part of a peace settlement to a civil war, the negotiating parties agree that special majorities are necessary for legislation. This agreement quickly results in the political marginalization of certain racial minorities. If a country is politically unstable and is at the beginning of its democratic evolution, how far can the right to participate in government be limited without engendering popular animus and re-creating the very same conditions that gave rise to civil war?

5.10. Economic, Social, and Cultural Rights

Universal Declaration of Human Rights

Article 22.

Everyone, as a member of society, has the right to social security and is entitled to realization, through national effort and international co-operation and in accordance with the organization and resources of each State, of the economic, social and cultural rights indispensable for his dignity and the free development of his personality.

Article 23.

(1) Everyone has the right to work, to free choice of employment, to just and favourable conditions of work and to protection against unemployment.

(2) Everyone, without any discrimination, has the right to equal pay for equal work.

(3) Everyone who works has the right to just and favourable remuneration ensuring for himself and his family an existence worthy of human dignity, and supplemented, if necessary, by other means of social protection.

(4) Everyone has the right to form and to join trade unions for the protection of his interests.

Article 24.

Everyone has the right to rest and leisure, including reasonable limitation of working hours and periodic holidays with pay.

Article 25.

(1) Everyone has the right to a standard of living adequate for the health and well-being of himself and of his family, including food, clothing, housing and medical care and necessary social services, and the right to security in the event of unemployment, sickness, disability, widowhood, old age or other lack of livelihood in circumstances beyond his control.

(2) Motherhood and childhood are entitled to special care and assistance. All children, whether born in or out of wedlock, shall enjoy the same social protection.

Article 26.

(1) Everyone has the right to education. Education shall be free, at least in the elementary and fundamental stages. Elementary education shall be compulsory. Technical and professional education shall be made generally available, and higher education shall be equally accessible to all on the basis of merit.

(2) Education shall be directed to the full development of the human personality and to the strengthening of respect for human rights and fundamental freedoms. It shall promote understanding, tolerance and friendship among all nations, racial or religious groups, and shall further the activities of the United Nations for the maintenance of peace.

(3) Parents have a prior right to choose the kind of education that shall be given to their children.

Article 27.

(1) Everyone has the right freely to participate in the cultural life of the community, to enjoy the arts and to share in scientific advancement and its benefits.

(2) Everyone has the right to the protection of the moral and material interests resulting from any scientific, literary or artistic production of which he is the author.

Article 28.

Everyone is entitled to a social and international order in which the rights and freedoms set forth in this Declaration can be fully realized.

International Covenant on Economic, Social and Cultural Rights

PART I

Article 1.

1. All peoples have the right of self-determination. By virtue of that right they freely determine their political status and freely pursue their economic, social and cultural development.

2. All peoples may, for their own ends, freely dispose of their natural wealth and resources without prejudice to any obligations arising out of international economic co-operation, based upon the principle of mutual benefit, and international law. In no case may a people be deprived of its own means of subsistence.

3. The States Parties to the present Covenant, including those having responsibility for the administration of Non-Self-Governing and Trust Territories, shall promote the realization of the right of self-determination, and shall respect that right, in conformity with the provisions of the Charter of the United Nations.

PART II

Article 2.

1. Each State Party to the present Covenant undertakes to take steps, individually and through international assistance and co-operation, especially economic and technical, to the maximum of its available resources, with a view to achieving progressively the full realization of the rights recognized in the present Covenant by all appropriate means, including particularly the adoption of legislative measures.

2. The States Parties to the present Covenant undertake to guarantee that the rights enunciated in the present Covenant will be exercised without discrimination of any kind as to race, colour, sex, language, religion, political or other opinion, national or social origin, property, birth or other status.

3. Developing countries, with due regard to human rights and their national economy, may determine to what extent they would guarantee the economic rights recognized in the present Covenant to non-nationals.

Article 3. The States Parties to the present Covenant undertake to ensure the equal right of men and women to the enjoyment of all economic, social and cultural rights set forth in the present Covenant.

Article 4. The States Parties to the present Covenant recognize that, in the enjoyment of those rights provided by the State in conformity with the present Covenant, the State may subject such rights only to such limitations as are determined by law only in so far as this may be compatible with the nature of these rights and solely for the purpose of promoting the general welfare in a democratic society.

Article 5.

1. Nothing in the present Covenant may be interpreted as implying for any State, group or person any right to engage in any activity or to perform any act aimed at the destruction of any of the rights or freedoms recognized herein, or at their limitation to a greater extent than is provided for in the present Covenant.

2. No restriction upon or derogation from any of the fundamental human rights recognized or existing in any country in virtue of law, conventions, regulations or custom shall be admitted on the pretext that the present Covenant does not recognize such rights or that it recognizes them to a lesser extent.

PART III

Article 6.

1. The States Parties to the present Covenant recognize the right to work, which includes the right of everyone to the opportunity to gain his living by work which he freely chooses or accepts, and will take appropriate steps to safeguard this right.

2. The steps to be taken by a State Party to the present Covenant to achieve the full realization of this right shall include technical and vocational guidance and training programmes, policies and techniques to achieve steady economic, social and cultural development and full and productive employment under conditions safeguarding fundamental political and economic freedoms to the individual.

Article 7. The States Parties to the present Covenant recognize the right of everyone to the enjoyment of just and favourable conditions of work, which ensure, in particular:

(a) remuneration which provides all workers, as a minimum, with:

(i) fair wages and equal remuneration for work of equal value without distinction of any kind, in particular women being guaranteed conditions of work not inferior to those enjoyed by men, with equal pay for equal work;
(ii) a decent living for themselves and their families in accordance with the provisions of the present Covenant;

(b) safe and healthy working conditions;
(c) equal opportunity for everyone to be promoted in his employment to an appropriate higher level, subject to no considerations other than those of seniority and competence;
(d) rest, leisure and reasonable limitation of working hours and periodic holidays with pay, as well as remuneration for public holidays.

Article 8.

The States Parties to the present Covenant undertake to ensure:

(a) the right of everyone to form trade unions and join the trade union of his choice, subject only to the rules of the organization concerned, for the promotion and protection of his economic and social interests. No restrictions may be placed on the exercise of this right other than those prescribed by law and which are necessary in a democratic society in the interests of national security or public order or for the protection of the rights and freedoms of others;
(b) the right of trade unions to establish national federations or confederations and the right of the latter to form or join international trade-union organizations;
(c) the right of trade unions to function freely subject to no limitations other than those prescribed by law and which are necessary in a democratic society in the interests of national security or public order or for the protection of the rights and freedoms of others;

(d) the right to strike, provided that it is exercised in conformity with the laws of the particular country.

2 This article shall not prevent the imposition of lawful restrictions on the exercise of these rights by members of the armed forces or 'of the police,' or of the administration of the State.

3 Nothing in this article shall authorize States Parties to the International Labour Organisation Convention of 1948 concerning Freedom of Association and Protection of the Right to Organize' to take legislative measures which would prejudice, or apply the law in such a manner as would prejudice, the guarantees provided for in that Convention.

Article 9. The States Parties to the present Covenant recognize the right of everyone to social security, including social insurance.

Article 10.

The States Parties to the present Covenant recognize that:

1. The widest possible protection and assistance should be accorded to the family, which is the natural and fundamental group unit of society, particularly for its establishment and while it is responsible for the care and education of dependent children. Marriage must be entered into with the free consent of the intending spouses.

2. Special protection should be accorded to mothers during a reasonable period before and after childbirth. During such period working mothers should be accorded paid leave or leave with adequate social security benefits.

3. Special measures of protection and assistance should be taken on behalf of all children and young persons without any discrimination for reasons of parentage or other conditions. Children and young persons should be protected from economic and social exploitation. Their employment in work harmful to their morals or health or dangerous to life or likely to hamper their normal development should be punishable by law. States should also set age limits below which the paid employment of child labour should be prohibited and punishable by law.

Article 11.

1. The States Parties to the present Covenant recognize the right of everyone to an adequate standard of living for himself and his family, including adequate food, clothing and housing, and to the continuous improvement of living conditions. The States Parties will take appropriate steps to ensure the realization of this right, recognizing to this effect the essential importance of international co-operation based on free consent.

2. The States Parties to the present Covenant, recognizing the fundamental right of everyone to be free from hunger, shall take, individually and through international co-operation, the measures, including specific programmes, which are needed:

(a) to improve methods of production, conservation and distribution of food by making full use of technical and scientific knowledge, by disseminating knowledge of the principles of nutrition and by developing or reforming agrarian systems in such a way as to achieve the most efficient development and utilization of natural resources;

(b) taking into account the problems of both food-importing and food-exporting countries, to ensure an equitable distribution of world food supplies in relation to need.

Article 12.

1. The States Parties to the present Covenant recognize the right of everyone to the enjoyment of the highest attainable standard of physical and mental health.

2. The steps to be taken by the States Parties to the present Covenant to achieve the full realization of this right shall include those necessary for:

(a) the provision for the reduction of the stillbirth-rate and of infant mortality and for the healthy development of the child;
(b) the improvement of all aspects of environmental and industrial hygiene;
(c) the prevention, treatment and control of epidemic, endemic, occupational and other diseases;
(d) the creation of conditions which would assure to all medical service and medical attention in the event of sickness.

Article 13.

1. The States Parties to the present Covenant recognize the right of everyone to education. They agree that education shall be directed to the full development of the human personality and the sense of its dignity, and shall strengthen the respect for human rights and fundamental freedoms. They further agree that education shall enable all persons to participate effectively in a free society, promote understanding, tolerance and friendship among all nations and all racial, ethnic or religious groups, and further the activities of the United Nations for the maintenance of peace.

2. The States Parties to the present Covenant recognize that, with a view to achieving the full realization of this right:

(a) primary education shall be compulsory and available free to all;
(b) secondary education in its different forms, including technical and vocational secondary education, shall be made generally available and accessible to all by every appropriate means, and in particular by the progressive introduction of free education;
(c) higher education shall be made equally accessible to all, on the basis of capacity by every appropriate means, and in particular by the progressive introduction of free education;
(d) fundamental education shall be encouraged or intensified as far as possible for those persons who have not received or completed the whole period of their primary education;
(e) the development of a system of schools at all levels shall be actively pursued, an adequate fellowship system shall be established, and the material conditions of teaching staff shall be continuously improved.

3. The States Parties to the present Covenant undertake to have respect for the liberty of parents and, when applicable, legal guardians, to choose for their children schools, other than those established by the public authorities, which conform to such minimum educational standards as may be laid down or approved by the State and to ensure the religious and moral education of their children in conformity with their own convictions.

4. No part of this article shall be construed so as to interfere with the liberty of individuals and bodies to establish and direct educational institutions, subject always to the

observance of the principles set forth in paragraph 1 of this article and to the requirement that the education given in such institutions shall conform to such minimum standards as may be laid down by the State.

Article 14.

Each State Party to the present Covenant which, at the time of becoming a Party, has not been able to secure in its metropolitan territory or other territories under its jurisdiction compulsory primary education, free of charge, undertakes, within two years, to work out and adopt a detailed plan of action for the progressive implementation, within a reasonable number of years, to be fixed in the plan, of the principle of compulsory education free of charge for all.

Article 15.

1. The States Parties to the present Covenant recognize the right of everyone:
   (a) to take part in cultural life;
   (b) to enjoy the benefits of scientific progress and its applications;
   (c) to benefit from the protection of the moral and material interests resulting from any scientific, literary or artistic production of which he is the author.

2. The steps to be taken by the States Parties to the present Covenant to achieve the full realization of this right shall include those necessary for the conservation, the development and the diffusion of science and culture.

3. The States Parties to the present Covenant undertake to respect the freedom indispensable for scientific research and creative activity.

4. The States Parties to the present Covenant recognize the benefits to be derived from the encouragement and development of international contacts and cooperation in the scientific and cultural fields.

Article 25.

Nothing in the present Covenant shall be interpreted as impairing the inherent right of all peoples to enjoy and utilize fully and freely their natural wealth and resources.

International Covenant on Civil and Political Rights

Article 1

1. All peoples have the right of self-determination. By virtue of that right they freely determine their political status and freely pursue their economic, social and cultural development.

2. All peoples may, for their own ends, freely dispose of their natural wealth and resources without prejudice to any obligations arising out of international economic co-operation, based upon the principle of mutual benefit, and international law. In no case may a people be deprived of it its own means of subsistence.

. . . .

European Convention on Human Rights – Protocol No. 1

ARTICLE 1

Every natural or legal person is entitled to the peaceful enjoyment of his possessions. No one shall be deprived of his possessions except in the public interest and subject to the conditions provided for by law and by the general principles of international law.

The preceding provisions shall not, however, in any way impair the right of a State to enforce such laws as it deems necessary to control the use of property in accordance with the general interest or to secure the payment of taxes or other contributions or penalties.

ARTICLE 2

No person shall be denied the right to education. In the exercise of any functions which it assumes in relation to education and to teaching, the State shall respect the right of parents to ensure such education and teaching in conformity with their own religions and philosophical convictions.

Article 14. Right to education

1. Everyone has the right to education and to have access to vocational and continuing training.

2. This right includes the possibility to receive free compulsory education.

3. The freedom to found educational establishments with due respect for democratic principles and the right of parents to ensure the education and teaching of their children in conformity with their religious, philosophical and pedagogical convictions shall be respected, in accordance with the national laws governing the exercise of such freedom and right.

Article 15. Freedom to choose an occupation and right to engage in work

1. Everyone has the right to engage in work and to pursue a freely chosen or accepted occupation.

2. Every citizen of the Union has the freedom to seek employment, to work, to exercise the right of establishment and to provide services in any Member State.

3. Nationals of third countries who are authorised to work in the territories of the Member States are entitled to working conditions equivalent to those of citizens of the Union.

Article 16. Freedom to conduct a business

The freedom to conduct a business in accordance with Community law and national laws and practices is recognised.

Article 17. Right to property

1. Everyone has the right to own, use, dispose of and bequeath his or her lawfully acquired possessions. No one may be deprived of his or her possessions, except in the public interest and in the cases and under the conditions provided for by law, subject to fair compensation being paid in good time for their loss. The use of property may be regulated by law in so far as is necessary for the general interest.

2. Intellectual property shall be protected.

Article 22. Cultural, religious and linguistic diversity

The Union shall respect cultural, religious and linguistic diversity.

Article 25. The rights of the elderly

The Union recognises and respects the rights of the elderly to lead a life of dignity and independence and to participate in social and cultural life.

Article 26. Integration of persons with disabilities

The Union recognises and respects the right of persons with disabilities to benefit from measures designed to ensure their independence, social and occupational integration and participation in the life of the community.

CHAPTER IV. SOLIDARITY

Article 27. Workers' right to information and consultation within the undertaking

Workers or their representatives must, at the appropriate levels, be guaranteed information and consultation in good time in the cases and under the conditions provided for by Community law and national laws and practices.

Article 28. Right of collective bargaining and action

Workers and employers, or their respective organisations, have, in accordance with Community law and national laws and practices, the right to negotiate and conclude collective agreements at the appropriate levels and, in cases of conflicts of interest, to take collective action to defend their interests, including strike action.

Article 29. Right of access to placement services

Everyone has the right of access to a free placement service.

Article 30. Protection in the event of unjustified dismissal

Every worker has the right to protection against unjustified dismissal, in accordance with Community law and national laws and practices.

Article 31. Fair and just working conditions

1. Every worker has the right to working conditions which respect his or her health, safety and dignity.

2. Every worker has the right to limitation of maximum working hours, to daily and weekly rest periods and to an annual period of paid leave.

Article 32. Prohibition of child labour and protection of young people at work

The employment of children is prohibited. The minimum age of admission to employment may not be lower than the minimum school-leaving age, without prejudice to such rules as may be more favourable to young people and except for limited derogations. Young people admitted to work must have working conditions appropriate to their age and be protected against economic exploitation and any work likely to harm their safety, health or physical, mental, moral or social development or to interfere with their education.

Article 33. Family and professional life

1. The family shall enjoy legal, economic and social protection.

2. To reconcile family and professional life, everyone shall have the right to protection from dismissal for a reason connected with maternity and the right to paid maternity leave and to parental leave following the birth or adoption of a child.

Article 34. Social security and social assistance

1. The Union recognises and respects the entitlement to social security benefits and social services providing protection in cases such as maternity, illness, industrial accidents,

dependency or old age, and in the case of loss of employment, in accordance with the rules laid down by Community law and national laws and practices.

2. Everyone residing and moving legally within the European Union is entitled to social security benefits and social advantages in accordance with Community law and national laws and practices.

3. In order to combat social exclusion and poverty, the Union recognises and respects the right to social and housing assistance so as to ensure a decent existence for all those who lack sufficient resources, in accordance with the rules laid down by Community law and national laws and practices.

Article 35. Health care

Everyone has the right of access to preventive health care and the right to benefit from medical treatment under the conditions established by national laws and practices. A high level of human health protection shall be ensured in the definition and implementation of all Union policies and activities.

Article 36. Access to services of general economic interest

The Union recognises and respects access to services of general economic interest as provided for in national laws and practices, in accordance with the Treaty establishing the European Community, in order to promote the social and territorial cohesion of the Union.

Article 37. Environmental protection

A high level of environmental protection and the improvement of the quality of the environment must be integrated into the policies of the Union and ensured in accordance with the principle of sustainable development.

Article 38. Consumer protection

Union policies shall ensure a high level of consumer protection.

American Convention on Human Rights

Article 26. PROGRESSIVE DEVELOPMENT.

The States Parties undertake to adopt measures, both internally and through international cooperation, especially those of an economic and technical nature, with a view to achieving progressively, by legislation or other appropriate means, the full realization of the rights implicit in the economic. social, educational, scientific, and cultural standards set forth in the Charter of the Organization of American States as amended by the Protocol of Buenos Aires.

African Charter on Human and Peoples' Rights

Article 15

Every individual shall have the right to work under equitable and satisfactory conditions, and shall receive equal pay for equal work.

Article 16

1. Every individual shall have the right to enjoy the best attainable state of physical and mental health.

2. States parties to the present Charter shall take the necessary measures to protect the health of their people and to ensure that they receive medical attention when they are sick.

Article 21

1. All peoples shall freely dispose of their wealth and natural resources. This right shall be exercised in the exclusive interest of the people. In no case shall a people be deprived of it.

2. In case of spoliation the dispossessed people shall have the right to the lawful recovery of its property as well as to an adequate compensation.

3. The free disposal of wealth and natural resources shall be exercised without prejudice to the obligation of promoting international economic cooperation based on mutual respect, equitable exchange and the principles of international law.

4. States parties to the present Charter shall individually and collectively exercise the right to free disposal of their wealth and natural resources with a view to strengthening African unity and solidarity.

5. States parties to the present Charter shall undertake to eliminate all forms of foreign economic exploitation particularly that practiced by international monopolies so as to enable their peoples to fully benefit from the advantages derived from their national resources.

Article 22

1. All peoples shall have the right to their economic, social and cultural development with due regard to their freedom and identity and in the equal enjoyment of the common heritage of mankind.

Article 25

States parties to the present Charter shall have the duty to promote and ensure through teaching, education and publication, the respect of the rights and freedoms contained in the present Charter and to see to it that these freedoms and rights as well as corresponding obligations and duties are understood.

The Nature of States Parties Obligations (art. 2, para. 1 of the Covenant)
General Comment No. 3
UN Committee on Economic, Social & Cultural Rights
U.N. Doc. E/1991/23, pp. 83–87 (Fifth Sess. 1990)

1. Article 2 is of particular importance to a full understanding of the Covenant and must be seen as having a dynamic relationship with all of the other provisions of the Covenant. It describes the nature of the general legal obligations undertaken by States parties to the Covenant.... While great emphasis has sometimes been placed on the difference between the formulations used in this provision and that contained in the equivalent article 2 of the International Covenant on Civil and Political Rights, it is not always recognized that there are also significant similarities. In particular, while the Covenant provides for progressive realization and acknowledges the constraints due to the limits of available resources, it also imposes various obligations which are of immediate effect. Of these, two are of particular importance in understanding the precise nature of

States parties obligations. One of these, which is dealt with in a separate general comment, and which is to be considered by the Committee at its sixth session, is the "undertaking to guarantee" that relevant rights "will be exercised without discrimination. . . ".

2. The other is the undertaking in article 2 (1) "to take steps", which in itself, is not qualified or limited by other considerations. The full meaning of the phrase can also be gauged by noting some of the different language versions. In English the undertaking is "to take steps", in French it is "to act" ("*s'engage à agir*") and in Spanish it is "to adopt measures" ("*a adoptar medidas*"). Thus while the full realization of the relevant rights may be achieved progressively, steps towards that goal must be taken within a reasonably short time after the Covenant's entry into force for the States concerned. Such steps should be deliberate, concrete and targeted as clearly as possible towards meeting the obligations recognized in the Covenant.

3. The means which should be used in order to satisfy the obligation to take steps are stated in article 2 (1) to be "all appropriate means, including particularly the adoption of legislative measures". The Committee recognizes that in many instances legislation is highly desirable and in some cases may even be indispensable. For example, it may be difficult to combat discrimination effectively in the absence of a sound legislative foundation for the necessary measures. In fields such as health, the protection of children and mothers, and education, as well as in respect of the matters dealt with in articles 6 to 9, legislation may also be an indispensable element for many purposes.

4. The Committee notes that States parties have generally been conscientious in detailing at least some of the legislative measures that they have taken in this regard. It wishes to emphasize, however, that the adoption of legislative measures, as specifically foreseen by the Covenant, is by no means exhaustive of the obligations of States parties. Rather, the phrase "by all appropriate means" must be given its full and natural meaning. While each State party must decide for itself which means are the most appropriate under the circumstances with respect to each of the rights, the "appropriateness" of the means chosen will not always be self-evident. . . . However, the ultimate determination as to whether all appropriate measures have been taken remains one for the Committee to make.

5. Among the measures which might be considered appropriate, in addition to legislation, is the provision of judicial remedies with respect to rights which may, in accordance with the national legal system, be considered justiciable. The Committee notes, for example, that the enjoyment of the rights recognized, without discrimination, will often be appropriately promoted, in part, through the provision of judicial or other effective remedies. Indeed, those States parties which are also parties to the International Covenant on Civil and Political Rights are already obligated (by virtue of arts. 2 (paras. 1 and 3), 3 and 26) of that Covenant to ensure that any person whose rights or freedoms (including the right to equality and non-discrimination) recognized in that Covenant are violated, "shall have an effective remedy" (art. 2 (3) (a)). In addition, there are a number of other provisions in the International Covenant on Economic, Social and Cultural Rights, including articles 3, 7 (a) (i), 8, 10 (3), 13 (2) (a), (3) and (4) and 15 (3) which would seem to be capable of immediate application by judicial and other organs in many national legal systems. Any suggestion that the provisions indicated are inherently non-self-executing would seem to be difficult to sustain.

6. Where specific policies aimed directly at the realization of the rights recognized in the Covenant have been adopted in legislative form, the Committee would wish to be informed, *inter alia*, as to whether such laws create any right of action on behalf of

individuals or groups who feel that their rights are not being fully realized. In cases where constitutional recognition has been accorded to specific economic, social and cultural rights, or where the provisions of the Covenant have been incorporated directly into national law, the Committee would wish to receive information as to the extent to which these rights are considered to be justiciable (i.e. able to be invoked before the courts). The Committee would also wish to receive specific information as to any instances in which existing constitutional provisions relating to economic, social and cultural rights have been weakened or significantly changed.

7. Other measures which may also be considered "appropriate" for the purposes of article 2 (1) include, but are not limited to, administrative, financial, educational and social measures.

8. The Committee notes that the undertaking "to take steps...by all appropriate means including particularly the adoption of legislative measures" neither requires nor precludes any particular form of government or economic system being used as the vehicle for the steps in question, provided only that it is democratic and that all human rights are thereby respected. Thus, in terms of political and economic systems the Covenant is neutral and its principles cannot accurately be described as being predicated exclusively upon the need for, or the desirability of a socialist or a capitalist system, or a mixed, centrally planned, or *laisser-faire* economy, or upon any other particular approach. In this regard, the Committee reaffirms that the rights recognized in the Covenant are susceptible of realization within the context of a wide variety of economic and political systems, provided only that the interdependence and indivisibility of the two sets of human rights, as affirmed *inter alia* in the preamble to the Covenant, is recognized and reflected in the system in question. The Committee also notes the relevance in this regard of other human rights and in particular the right to development.

9. The principal obligation of result reflected in article 2 (1) is to take steps "with a view to achieving progressively the full realization of the rights recognized" in the Covenant. The term "progressive realization" is often used to describe the intent of this phrase. The concept of progressive realization constitutes a recognition of the fact that full realization of all economic, social and cultural rights will generally not be able to be achieved in a short period of time. In this sense the obligation differs significantly from that contained in article 2 of the International Covenant on Civil and Political Rights which embodies an immediate obligation to respect and ensure all of the relevant rights. Nevertheless, the fact that realization over time, or in other words progressively, is foreseen under the Covenant should not be misinterpreted as depriving the obligation of all meaningful content. It is on the one hand a necessary flexibility device, reflecting the realities of the real world and the difficulties involved for any country in ensuring full realization of economic, social and cultural rights. On the other hand, the phrase must be read in the light of the overall objective, indeed the *raison d'être*, of the Covenant which is to establish clear obligations for States parties in respect of the full realization of the rights in question. It thus imposes an obligation to move as expeditiously and effectively as possible towards that goal. Moreover, any deliberately retrogressive measures in that regard would require the most careful consideration and would need to be fully justified by reference to the totality of the rights provided for in the Covenant and in the context of the full use of the maximum available resources.

10. On the basis of the extensive experience gained by the Committee, as well as by the body that preceded it, over a period of more than a decade of examining States

parties' reports the Committee is of the view that a minimum core obligation to ensure the satisfaction of, at the very least, minimum essential levels of each of the rights is incumbent upon every State party. Thus, for example, a State party in which any significant number of individuals is deprived of essential foodstuffs, of essential primary health care, of basic shelter and housing, or of the most basic forms of education is, *prima facie*, failing to discharge its obligations under the Covenant. If the Covenant were to be read in such a way as not to establish such a minimum core obligation, it would be largely deprived of its *raison d'être*. By the same token, it must be noted that any assessment as to whether a State has discharged its minimum core obligation must also take account of resource constraints applying within the country concerned. Article 2 (1) obligates each State party to take the necessary steps "to the maximum of its available resources". In order for a State party to be able to attribute its failure to meet at least its minimum core obligations to a lack of available resources it must demonstrate that every effort has been made to use all resources that are at its disposition in an effort to satisfy, as a matter of priority, those minimum obligations.

11. The Committee wishes to emphasize, however, that even where the available resources are demonstrably inadequate, the obligation remains for a State party to strive to ensure the widest possible enjoyment of the relevant rights under the prevailing circumstances. Moreover, the obligations to monitor the extent of the realization, or more especially of the non-realization, of economic, social and cultural rights, and to devise strategies and programmes for their promotion, are not in any way eliminated as a result of resource constraints. . . .

12. Similarly, the Committee underlines the fact that even in times of severe resources constraints whether caused by a process of adjustment, of economic recession, or by other factors the vulnerable members of society can and indeed must be protected by the adoption of relatively low-cost targeted programmes. . . .

. . . .

14. The Committee wishes to emphasize that in accordance with Articles 55 and 56 of the Charter of the United Nations, with well-established principles of international law, and with the provisions of the Covenant itself, international cooperation for development and thus for the realization of economic, social and cultural rights is an obligation of all States. It is particularly incumbent upon those States which are in a position to assist others in this regard. The Committee notes in particular the importance of the Declaration on the Right to Development adopted by the General Assembly in its resolution 41/128 of 4 December 1986 and the need for States parties to take full account of all of the principles recognized therein. It emphasizes that, in the absence of an active programme of international assistance and cooperation on the part of all those States that are in a position to undertake one, the full realization of economic, social and cultural rights will remain an unfulfilled aspiration in many countries. . . .

∾

QUESTIONS & COMMENTS

(1) Consider economic rights (*e.g.*, right to food) that have derivative *jus cogens* status. As discussed in Professor Martin's article in Section 2.1.3, such rights are justiciable because

the compliance with these norms require state affirmative duties. What effect does the doctrine of self-execution have on such rights?

Five Pensioners Case
Inter-American Court of Human Rights
Judgment of February 28, 2003
Inter-Am. Ct. H.R, (Ser. C) No. 98 (2003).

[In this case, the petitioners who had been civil service employees began receiving pension amounts that were lower that guaranteed by an earlier Peruvian law. They challenged the pension reductions and obtained a favorable decision from the Peruvian Constitutional Court. However, the Peruvian government failed to implement the Court's decision for eight years. Subsequently, the Inter-American Court of Human Rights held that they the reduction in their pensions violated their rights to property and a judicial remedy.]

IX. ARTICLE 26 (PROGRESSIVE DEVELOPMENT OF ECONOMIC, SOCIAL AND CULTURAL RIGHTS)

The Commission's arguments

142. With regard to Article 26 of the Convention, the Commission alleges that:

a) The State violated this article when it drafted Decree Law No. 25792, which "constituted an unjustified setback with regard to the level of development of the right to social security that the victims had achieved in accordance with Decree Law No. 20530 and its related norms," so that it imposed a cap that was substantially lower cap than the amount of the equalized pension the alleged victims were receiving. As of the entry into force of Decree Law No. 25792, the five pensioners began to receive approximately one-fifth of the retirement pension they had been receiving;

b) The obligation established in Article 26 of the Convention implies that the States may not adopt regressive measures in relation to the level of development achieved; although, in exceptional circumstances and by analogous application of Article 5 of the Protocol of San Salvador, laws that impose restrictions and limitations on economic, social and cultural rights may be justified, provided that they have been "promulgated in order to preserve the general welfare in a democratic society and only to the extent that they are not incompatible with the purpose and reason underlying those rights"; and

c) The State did not allege or prove that the setback entailed by Decree Law No. 25792 was effected "in order to preserve the general welfare in a democratic society," "nor did it allege or prove any other circumstance in this respect."

Arguments of the representatives of the alleged victims and their next of kin

143. With regard to Article 26 of the Convention, the representatives of the alleged victims and their next of kin indicated that:

a) According to the provisions of this article, the State has the obligation to progressively achieve the full realization of the right to social security. This obligation implies the "correlative prohibition of regression with regard to recognition of the right to social security, except in circumstances that are absolutely necessary, reasonable and justified for the common good." The adoption of regressive policies, aimed at reducing the degree of enjoyment of economic, social and cultural rights, violates the principle of progressive development;

b) The scope of this article should be determined bearing in mind the evolving interpretation of international instruments and in accordance with the *pro homine* principle established in Article 29(b) of the Convention;

c) The essential content of the right to social security is to ensure to all persons a protection against the consequences of ageing or of any other contingency beyond their control that implies a deprivation of the essential means of support to lead a dignified and decorous life. Peru violated the right to social security when it deprived the five pensioners of the means of support that, in the form of an equalized pension, corresponded to them in the context of the pension regime to which they were assigned and that – until March 1992 in one case, and until September that year with regard to the other four – had permitted them to provide the most immediate vital necessities for themselves and their families;

d) The reduction in the amounts of the pensions of the alleged victims "is a regressive measure that was not justified by the State in the context of the full exercise of economic, social and cultural rights." This measure has violated the principle of progressive development established in Article 26 of the Convention, which "cannot be undermined, under the pretext of a lack of economic resources, and much less in the case of vulnerable groups of the population, such as retirees and pensioners";

e) Overall, it is evident that the measures adopted by the State have implied a grave violation of the human right to social security, because "these measures – even though they may not have had that explicit intention – had the concrete effect of creating a situation that deprived them of their means of support, which – as pensioners and elderly adults – was essential to enable them to lead a dignified and decorous life"; and

f) They request the Court to determine the contents of the article on progressive development of economic, social and cultural rights and also to establish parameters and criteria that instruct the States on how to comply with their juridical obligations, as well as criteria to determine how regressive measures violate their obligations under the Convention. Moreover, it would be "very useful" if the Court would establish guidelines that allow the State to adopt an integrated social security policy.

The arguments of the State

144. With regard to Article 26 of the Convention, the State alleges that:

a) It has not violated the progressive development of the retirement pension of the alleged victims, because the pension they are receiving, as a result of the judicial proceedings they filed, "is considerably higher than the one to which they would be legally entitled, if their pensions had been regulated by the regime that corresponded to them;" in other words, in function of the salary of the employees of the public sector labor regime and not to those of the private sector regime; and

b) This article contains a generic declaration that cannot be interpreted so extensively as to claim that it sustains that, under the Peruvian social security and pension regime, payment of pensions is absolute and cannot be limited by law.

Considerations of the Court

145. Article 26 of the Convention states that:

The States Parties undertake to adopt measures, both internally and through international cooperation, especially those of an economic and technical nature, with a view to achieving progressively, by legislation or other appropriate means, the full realization of the rights implicit in the economic, social, educational, scientific, and cultural standards set forth in the Charter of the Organization of American States as amended by the Protocol of Buenos Aires.

146. The Inter-American Commission and the representatives of the alleged victims and their next of kin alleged that Article 26 of the American Convention had been violated because, by reducing the amount of the pensions of the alleged victims, the State failed to comply with its obligation to progressively develop their economic, social and cultural rights and, in particular, did not ensure the progressive development of their right to a pension.

147. Economic, social and cultural rights have both an individual and a collective dimension. This Court considers that their progressive development, about which the United Nations Committee on Economic, Social and Cultural Rights has already ruled, should be measured in function of the growing coverage of economic, social and cultural rights in general, and of the right to social security and to a pension in particular, of the entire population, bearing in mind the imperatives of social equity, and not in function of the circumstances of a very limited group of pensioners, who do not necessarily represent the prevailing situation.

148. It is evident that this is what is occurring in the instant case; therefore, the Court considers that it is in order to reject the request to rule on the progressive development of economic, social and cultural rights in Peru, in the context of this case.

. . . .

XI. NON-COMPLIANCE WITH ARTICLES 1(1) AND 2 (OBLIGATION TO RESPECT RIGHTS AND DOMESTIC LEGAL EFFECTS)

The arguments of the Commission

158. Regarding Articles 1(1) and 2 of the Convention, the Commission alleges that:

a) The violations of Articles 21, 25 and 26 of the Convention committed by Peru to the detriment of the five pensioners, imply that the State did not comply with the general obligation to respect the rights and freedoms and to ensure their free and full exercise; and

b) When it promulgated and applied article 5 of Decree Law No. 25792, the State violated the rights embodied in Articles 21 and 26 of the Convention. The State did not take adequate measures in domestic law to make effective the rights embodied in the Convention, thus violating the general obligation stipulated in Article 2 thereof.

The arguments of the representatives of the alleged victims and their next of kin

159. Regarding Articles 1(1) and 2 of the Convention, the representatives of the alleged victims and their next of kin allege that:

a) As a consequence of the violation of the rights embodied in Articles 8(1), 21, 25 and 26 of the Convention, the State also violated the obligation to respect the rights and freedoms recognized in the Convention and the obligation to ensure their free and full exercise to all persons subject to its jurisdiction; and

b) With the adoption of article 5 of Decree Law No. 25792 and while it was in force, Peru disregarded the obligation to adapt its domestic legislation to the Convention, pursuant to the provisions of Article 2 thereof.

The arguments of the State

160. The State did not refer expressly to the alleged non-compliance with Articles 1(1) and 2 of the American Convention.

The considerations of the Court

161. Article 1(1) of the Convention establishes that:

The States Parties to this Convention undertake to respect the rights and freedoms recognized herein and to ensure to all persons subject to their jurisdiction the free and full exercise of those rights and freedoms, without any discrimination for reasons of race, color, sex, language, religion, political or other opinion, national or social origin, economic status, birth, or any other social condition.

162. While, Article 2 of the Conventions stipulates that:

Where the exercise of any of the rights or freedoms referred to in Article 1 is not already ensured by legislative or other provisions, the States Parties undertake to adopt, in accordance with their constitutional processes and the provisions of this Convention, such legislative or other measures as may be necessary to give effect to those rights or freedoms.

163. The Court has established that:

Article 1(1) is essential in determining whether a violation of the human rights recognized by the Convention can be imputed to a State Party. In effect, that article charges the States Parties with the fundamental duty to respect and guarantee the rights recognized in the Convention. Any impairment of those rights that can be attributed, under the rules of international law, to the act or omission of any public authority constitutes an act imputable to the State and which entails its responsibility as established in the Convention.

According to Article 1(1), any exercise of public power that violates the rights recognized by the Convention is illegal. Whenever a State organ or official, or a public entity violates one of those rights, this constitutes a failure in the duty to respect the rights and freedoms set forth in the Convention.

This conclusion is independent of whether the organ or official has contravened provisions of internal law or overstepped the limits of his authority. Under international law, a State is responsible for the acts of its agents undertaken in their official capacity and for their omissions, even when those agents act outside the sphere of their authority or violate internal law.

164. With regard to Article 2 of the Convention, the Court has said that:

In international law, customary law establishes that a State which has ratified a human rights treaty must introduce the necessary modifications to its domestic law to ensure the proper compliance with the obligations it has assumed. This law is universally accepted, and is supported by jurisprudence. The American Convention establishes the general obligation of each State Party to adapt its domestic law to the provisions of this Convention, in order to guarantee the rights it embodies. This general obligation of the State Party implies that the measures of domestic law must be effective (the principle of effet utile). This means that the State must adopt all measures so that the provisions of the Convention are effectively fulfilled in its domestic legal system, as Article 2 of the Convention requires. Such measures are only effective when the State adjusts its actions to the Convention's rules on protection.

165. The Court has also stated that:

[t]he general duty of Article 2 of the American Convention implies the adoption of measures in two ways. On the one hand, derogation of rules and practices of any kind that imply the violation of guarantees in the Convention. On the other hand, the issuance of rules and the development of practices leading to an effective enforcement of the said guarantees.

166. As already indicated in this judgment, the Court observes that, the State violated the human rights embodied in Articles 21 and 25 of the Convention, to the detriment of Carlos Torres Benvenuto, Javier Mujica Ruiz-Huidobro, Guillermo Álvarez Hernández, Maximiliano Gamarra Ferreyra and Reymert Bartra Vásquez; it therefore failed to comply with the general obligation established in Article 1(1) to respect the rights and freedoms embodied in the Convention and to ensure their free and full exercise.

167. The Court observes that, by abstaining for an extended period of time from adopting the series of measures necessary to fully comply with the judgments of its judicial organs and, consequently, making effective the rights embodied in the American Convention (Articles 21 and 25), the State failed to comply with the obligation stipulated in Article 2 thereof.

168. In view of the foregoing, the Court concludes that the State failed to comply with the general obligations of Articles 1(1) and 2 of the American Convention.

. . . .

∼

QUESTIONS & COMMENTS

(1) The Inter-American Court stated the following:

This Court considers that their progressive development. . . should be measured in function of the growing coverage of economic, social and cultural rights in general, and of the right to social security and to a pension in particular, of the entire population, bearing in mind the imperatives of social equity, and not in function of the circumstances of a very limited group of pensioners, who do not necessarily represent the prevailing situation.

How would a group of petitioners obtain sufficient standing to make a colorable claim that their right to progressive development has been violated? How representative must the group be?

5.10.1. Employment

Juridical Condition and Rights of the Undocumented Migrants
Inter-American Court of Human Rights
Advisory Opinion OC-18/03, September 17, 2003,
Inter-Am. Ct. H.R. (Ser. A) No. 18 (2003)

. . . .

VII. APPLICATION OF THE PRINCIPLE OF EQUALITY AND NON-DISCRIMINATION
TO MIGRANTS

111. Now that the *jus cogens* character of the principle of equality and non-discrimination and the effects that derive from the obligation of States to respect and guarantee this principle have been established, the Court will refer to migration in general and to the application of this principle to undocumented migrants.

112. Migrants are generally in a vulnerable situation as subjects of human rights; they are in an individual situation of absence or difference of power with regard to non-migrants (nationals or residents). This situation of vulnerability has an ideological dimension and occurs in a historical context that is distinct for each State and is maintained by *de jure* (inequalities between nationals and aliens in the laws) and *de facto* (structural inequalities) situations. This leads to the establishment of differences in their access to the public resources administered by the State.

113. Cultural prejudices about migrants also exist that lead to reproduction of the situation of vulnerability; these include ethnic prejudices, xenophobia and racism, which make it difficult for migrants to integrate into society and lead to their human rights being violated with impunity.

114. In this respect, the resolution on "Protection of migrants" of the General Assembly of the United Nations is pertinent, when it indicates that it is necessary to recall "the situation of vulnerability in which migrants frequently find themselves, owing, *inter alia*, to their absence from their State of origin and to the difficulties they encounter because of differences of language, custom and culture, as well as the economic and social difficulties and obstacles for the return to their States of origin of migrants who are non-documented or in an irregular situation." The General Assembly also expressed its concern "at the manifestations of violence, racism, xenophobia and other forms of discrimination and inhuman and degrading treatment against migrants, especially women and children, in different parts of the world." Based on these considerations, the General Assembly reiterated:

> the need for all States to protect fully the universally recognized human rights of migrants, especially women and children, regardless of their legal status, and to provide humane treatment, particularly with regard to assistance and protection [. . .].

115. The Court is aware that, as the General Assembly of the United Nations also observed, "among other factors, the process of globalization and liberalization, including the widening economic and social gap between and among many countries and the marginalization of some countries in the global economy, has contributed to large flows of peoples between and among countries and to the intensification of the complex phenomenon of international migration."

116. With regard to the foregoing, the Programme of Action of the International Conference on Population and Development held in Cairo in 1994 indicated that:

International economic imbalances, poverty and environmental degradation, combined with the absence of peace and security, human rights violations and the varying degrees of development of judicial and democratic institutions are all factors affecting international migration. Although most international migration flows occur between neighbouring countries, interregional migration, particularly that directed to developed countries, has been growing.

117. In accordance with the foregoing, the international community has recognized the need to adopt special measures to ensure the protection of the human rights of migrants.

118. We should mention that the regular situation of a person in a State is not a prerequisite for that State to respect and ensure the principle of equality and non-discrimination, because, as mentioned above, this principle is of a fundamental nature and all States must guarantee it to their citizens and to all aliens who are in their territory. This does not mean that they cannot take any action against migrants who do not comply with national laws. However, it is important that, when taking the corresponding measures, States should respect human rights and ensure their exercise and enjoyment to all persons who are in their territory, without any discrimination owing to their regular or irregular residence, or their nationality, race, gender or any other reason.

119. Consequently, States may not discriminate or tolerate discriminatory situations that prejudice migrants. However, the State may grant a distinct treatment to documented migrants with respect to undocumented migrants, or between migrants and nationals, provided that this differential treatment is reasonable, objective, proportionate and does not harm human rights. For example, distinctions may be made between migrants and nationals regarding ownership of some political rights. States may also establish mechanisms to control the entry into and departure from their territory of undocumented migrants, which must always be applied with strict regard for the guarantees of due process and respect for human dignity. In this respect, the African Commission on Human and Peoples' Rights has indicated that it:

does not wish to call into question nor is it calling into question the right of any State to take legal action against illegal immigrants and deport them to their countries of origin, if the competent courts so decide. It is however of the view that it is unacceptable to deport individuals without giving them the possibility to plead their case before the competent national courts as this is contrary to the spirit and letter of the Charter [the African Charter of Human and Peoples' Rights] and international law.

120. When dealing with the principle of equality and non-discrimination, the continuing development of international law should be borne in mind. In this respect, the Inter-American Court has indicated, in its Advisory Opinion OC-16/99 on The Right to Information on Consular Assistance within the Framework of the Guarantees of Due Process of Law, that:

The *corpus juris* of international human rights law comprises a set of international instruments of varied content and juridical effects (treaties, conventions, resolutions and declarations). Its dynamic evolution has had a positive impact on international law in affirming and building up the latter's faculty for regulating relations between States and the human beings within their respective jurisdictions. This Court, therefore, must adopt the proper approach to consider this question in the context of the evolution of the fundamental rights of the human person in contemporary international law.

121. Due process of law is a right that must be ensured to all persons, irrespective of their migratory status. In this respect, in the above-mentioned Advisory Opinion on The Right to Information on Consular Assistance within the Framework of the Guarantees of Due Process of Law, this Court indicated that:

> [...] for "the due process of law" a defendant must be able to exercise his rights and defend his interests effectively and in full procedural equality with other defendants. It is important to recall that the judicial process is a means to ensure, insofar as possible, an equitable resolution of a difference. The body of procedures, of diverse character and generally grouped under the heading of the due process, is all calculated to serve that end. To protect the individual and see justice done, the historical development of the judicial process has introduced new procedural rights. An example of the evolutive nature of judicial process are the rights not to incriminate oneself and to have an attorney present when one speaks. These two rights are already part of the laws and jurisprudence of the more advanced legal systems. And so, the body of judicial guarantees given in Article 14 of the International Covenant on Civil and Political Rights has evolved gradually. It is a body of judicial guarantees to which others of the same character, conferred by various instruments of international law, can and should be added.

and that:

> To accomplish its objectives, the judicial process must recognize and correct any real disadvantages that those brought before the bar might have, thus observing the principle of equality before the law and the courts and the corollary principle prohibiting discrimination. The presence of real disadvantages necessitates countervailing measures that help to reduce or eliminate the obstacles and deficiencies that impair or diminish an effective defense of one's interests. Absent those countervailing measures, widely recognized in various stages of the proceeding, one could hardly say that those who have the disadvantages enjoy a true opportunity for justice and the benefit of the due process of law equal to those who do not have those disadvantages.

122. The Court considers that the right to due process of law should be recognized within the framework of the minimum guarantees that should be provided to all migrants, irrespective of their migratory status. The broad scope of the preservation of due process applies not only *ratione materiae* but also *ratione personae*, without any discrimination.

123. As this Court has already indicated, due legal process refers to the:

> all the requirement that must be observed in the procedural stages in order for an individual to be able to defend his rights adequately vis-à-vis any [...] act of the State that could affect them. That it to say, due process of law must be respected in any act or omission on the part of the State bodies in a proceeding, whether of an administrative, punitive or jurisdictional nature.

124. Likewise, the Court has observed that the list of minimum guarantees of due legal process applies when determining rights and obligations of "civil, labor, fiscal or any other nature." This shows that due process affects all these areas and not only criminal matters.

125. In addition, it is important to establish, as the Court has already done, that "[i]t is a human right to obtain all the guarantees which make it possible to arrive at fair decisions, and the administration is not exempt from its duty to comply with this obligation. The minimum guarantees must be observed in administrative processes whose decision may affect the rights of persons."

126. The right to judicial protection and judicial guarantees is violated for several reasons: owing to the risk a person runs, when he resorts to the administrative or judicial instances, of being deported, expelled or deprived of his freedom, and by the negative to provide him with a free public legal aid service, which prevents him from asserting the rights in question. In this respect, the State must guarantee that access to justice is genuine and not merely formal. The rights derived from the employment relation subsist, despite the measures adopted.

127. Now that the Court has established what is applicable for all migrants, it will examine the rights of migrant workers, in particular those who are undocumented.

VIII. RIGHTS OF UNDOCUMENTED MIGRANT WORKERS

128.... [A] migrant worker is any person[ ] who is to be engaged, is engaged or has been engaged in a remunerated activity in a State of which he or she is not a national. This definition is embodied in the International Convention on the Protection of the Rights of all Migrant Workers and Members of their Families (Article 2(1)).

129. Migrant workers who are documented or in a regular situation are those who have been "authorized to enter, stay and engage in a remunerated activity in the State of employment pursuant to the law of the State and to international agreements to which that State is a party." Workers who are undocumented or in an irregular situation do not comply with the conditions that documented workers do; in other words, they are not authorized to enter, stay and engage in a remunerated activity in a State of which they are not nationals.

130. In continuation, the Court will rule on undocumented migrant workers and their rights.

131. The vulnerability of migrant workers as compared to national workers must be underscored. In this respect, the preamble to the International Convention on the Protection of the Rights of all Migrant Workers and Members of their Families refers to "the situation of vulnerability in which migrant workers and members of their families frequently find themselves owing, among other things, to their absence from their State of origin and to the difficulties they may encounter arising from their presence in the State of employment."

132. Nowadays, the rights of migrant workers "have not been sufficiently recognized everywhere" and, furthermore, undocumented workers "are frequently employed under less favorable conditions of work than other workers and [...] certain employers find this an inducement to seek such labor in order to reap the benefits of unfair competition."

133. Labor rights necessarily arise from the circumstance of being a worker, understood in the broadest sense. A person who is to be engaged, is engaged or has been engaged in a remunerated activity, immediately becomes a worker and, consequently, acquires the

rights inherent in that condition. The right to work, whether regulated at the national or international level, is a protective system for workers; that is, it regulates the rights and obligations of the employee and the employer, regardless of any other consideration of an economic and social nature. A person who enters a State and assumes an employment relationship, acquires his labor human rights in the State of employment, irrespective of his migratory status, because respect and guarantee of the enjoyment and exercise of those rights must be made without any discrimination.

134. In this way, the migratory status of a person can never be a justification for depriving him of the enjoyment and exercise of his human rights, including those related to employment. On assuming an employment relationship, the migrant acquires rights as a worker, which must be recognized and guaranteed, irrespective of his regular or irregular status in the State of employment. These rights are a consequence of the employment relationship.

135. It is important to clarify that the State and the individuals in a State are not obliged to offer employment to undocumented migrants. The States and individuals, such as employers, can abstain from establishing an employment relationship with migrants in an irregular situation.

136. However, if undocumented migrants are engaged, they immediately become possessors of the labor rights corresponding to workers and may not be discriminated against because of their irregular situation. This is very important, because one of the principal problems that occurs in the context of immigration is that migrant workers who lack permission to work are engaged in unfavorable conditions compared to other workers.

137. It is not enough merely to refer to the obligations to respect and ensure the labor human rights of all migrant workers, but it should be noted that these obligations have different scopes and effects for States and third parties.

138. Employment relationships are established under both public law and private law and, in both spheres, the State plays an important part.

139. In the context of an employment relationship in which the State is the employer, the latter must evidently guarantee and respect the labor human rights of all its public officials, whether nationals or migrants, documented or undocumented, because non-observance of this obligation gives rise to State responsibility at the national and the international level.

140. In an employment relationship regulated by private law, the obligation to respect human rights between individuals should be taken into consideration. That is, the positive obligation of the State to ensure the effectiveness of the protected human rights gives rise to effects in relation to third parties (*erga omnes*). This obligation has been developed in legal writings, and particularly by the *Drittwirkung* theory, according to which fundamental rights must be respected by both the public authorities and by individuals with regard to other individuals.

141. As of the first contentious cases on which it ruled, the Inter-American Court has outlined the application of the effects of the American Convention in relation to third parties (*erga omnes*), having indicated that:

> Thus, in principle, any violation of rights recognized by the Convention carried out by an act of public authority or by persons who use their position of authority is imputable to the State. However, this does not define all the circumstances in which

a State is obligated to prevent, investigate and punish human rights violations, or all the cases in which the State might be found responsible for an infringement of those rights. An illegal act which violates human rights and which is initially not directly imputable to a State (for example, because it is the act of a private person or because the person responsible has not been identified) can lead to international responsibility of the State, not because of the act itself, but because of the lack of due diligence to prevent the violation or to respond to it as required by the Convention.

142. Likewise, by means of provisional measures, this Court has ordered the protection of members of communities and persons that provide services to them, from threats of death and harm to personal safety allegedly caused by the State and third parties. Likewise, on another occasion, it ordered the protection of persons detained in prison, owing to deaths and threats in that prison, many of which were allegedly perpetrated by the prisoners themselves.

143. The European Court of Human Rights recognized the applicability of the European Convention for the Protection of Human Rights and Fundamental Freedoms to relationships between individuals, when it declared that the State had violated this Convention because it had restricted freedom of association, by establishing that membership in determined trade unions was a necessary condition for the petitioners in the case to be able to continue their employment in a company, since the restriction imposed was not "necessary in a democratic society." In another case, the European Court considered that, although the object of Article 8 of this Convention (the right to respect of private and family life) was essentially that of protecting the individual against arbitrary interference by the public authorities, the State must abstain from such interference; in addition to this obligation to abstain, there are positive obligations inherent in effective respect for private or family life that may involve the adoption of measures designed to secure respect for private life even in the sphere of the relations of individuals among themselves. In this case, the European Court found that the State had violated the right to private and family life of a young mentally disabled woman who had been sexually assaulted, because she could not file criminal proceedings against her aggressor due to a vacuum in the criminal legislation.

144. The United Nations Committee on Human Rights has considered that the right to freedom and personal safety, embodied in article 9 of the International Covenant on Civil and Political Rights, imposes on the State the obligation to take adequate steps to ensure the protection of an individual threatened with death. In other words, an interpretation of this article that authorized States parties to ignore threats against the life of persons subject to their jurisdiction, even though they have not been detained or arrested by State agents, would deprive the guarantees established in the Covenant of any effectiveness. The Committee also considered that the State has the obligation to protect the rights of members of minorities against attacks by individuals. Likewise, in its General Comments Nos. 18 and 20 on non-discrimination and article 7 of the said Covenant, the Committee has indicated that States parties must punish public officials, other persons acting in the name of the State, and individuals, who carry out torture and cruel, inhuman or degrading treatment or punishment, and should also "take affirmative action in order to diminish or eliminate conditions which cause or help to perpetuate discrimination prohibited by the Covenant."

145. In addition, in a decision on the obligation to investigate acts of racial discrimination and violence against persons of another color or ethnic origin committed by individuals, the Committee for the Elimination of Racial Discrimination indicated that "when threats of racial violence are made, and especially when they are made in public and by a group, it is incumbent upon the State to investigate with due diligence and expedition."

146. In this way, the obligation to respect and ensure human rights, which normally has effects on the relations between the State and the individuals subject to its jurisdiction, also has effects on relations between individuals. As regards this Advisory Opinion, the said effects of the obligation to respect human rights in relations between individuals is defined in the context of the private employment relationship, under which the employer must respect the human rights of his workers.

147. The obligation to respect and guarantee the human rights of third parties is also based on the fact that it is the State that determines the laws that regulate the relations between individuals and, thus, private law; hence, it must also ensure that human rights are respected in these private relationships between third parties; to the contrary, the State may be responsible for the violation of those rights.

148. The State is obliged to respect and ensure the labor human rights of all workers, irrespective of their status as nationals or aliens, and not to tolerate situations of discrimination that prejudice the latter in the employment relationships established between individuals (employer-worker). The State should not allow private employers to violate the rights of workers, or the contractual relationship to violate minimum international standards.

149. This State obligation arises from legislation that protects workers – legislation based on the unequal relationship between both parties – which therefore protects the workers as the more vulnerable party. In this way, States must ensure strict compliance with the labor legislation that provides the best protection for workers, irrespective of their nationality, social, ethnic or racial origin, and their migratory status; therefore they have the obligation to take any necessary administrative, legislative or judicial measures to correct *de jure* discriminatory situations and to eradicate discriminatory practices against migrant workers by a specific employer or group of employers at the local, regional, national or international level.

150. On many occasions migrant workers must resort to State mechanisms for the protection of their rights. Thus, for example, workers in private companies have recourse to the Judiciary to claim the payment of wages, compensation, etc. Also, these workers often use State health services or contribute to the State pension system. In all these cases, the State is involved in the relationship between individuals as a guarantor of fundamental rights, because it is required to provide a specific service.

151. In labor relations, employers must protect and respect the rights of workers, whether these relations occur in the public or private sector. The obligation to respect the human rights of migrant workers has a direct effect on any type of employment relationship, when the State is the employer, when the employer is a third party, and when the employer is a natural or legal person.

152. The State is thus responsible for itself, when it acts as an employer, and for the acts of third parties who act with its tolerance, acquiescence or negligence, or with the support of some State policy or directive that encourages the creation or maintenance of situations of discrimination.

153. In summary, employment relationships between migrant workers and third party employers may give rise to the international responsibility of the State in different ways. First, States are obliged to ensure that, within their territory, all the labor rights stipulated in its laws – rights deriving from international instruments or domestic legislation – are recognized and applied. Likewise, States are internationally responsible when they tolerate actions and practices of third parties that prejudice migrant workers, either because they do not recognize the same rights to them as to national workers or because they recognize the same rights to them but with some type of discrimination.

154. Furthermore, there are cases in which it is the State that violates the human rights of the workers directly. For example, when it denies the right to a pension to a migrant worker who has made the necessary contributions and fulfilled all the conditions that were legally required of workers, or when a worker resorts to the corresponding judicial body to claim his rights and this body does not provide him with due judicial protection or guarantees.

155. The Court observes that labor rights are the rights recognized to workers by national and international legislation. In other words, the State of employment must respect and guarantee to every worker the rights embodied in the Constitution, labor legislation, collective agreements, agreements established by law (*convenios-ley*), decrees and even specific and local practices, at the national level; and, at the international level, in any international treaty to which the State is a party.

156. This Court notes that, since there are many legal instruments that regulate labor rights at the domestic and the international level, these regulations must be interpreted according to the principle of the application of the norm that best protects the individual, in this case, the worker. This is of great importance, because there is not always agreement either between the different norms or between the norms and their application, and this could prejudice the worker. Thus, if a domestic practice or norm is more favorable to the worker than an international norm, domestic law should be applied. To the contrary, if an international instrument benefits the worker, granting him rights that are not guaranteed or recognized by the State, such rights should be respected and guaranteed to him.

157. In the case of migrant workers, there are certain rights that assume a fundamental importance and yet are frequently violated, such as: the prohibition of obligatory or forced labor; the prohibition and abolition of child labor; special care for women workers, and the rights corresponding to: freedom of association and to organize and join a trade union, collective negotiation, fair wages for work performed, social security, judicial and administrative guarantees, a working day of reasonable length with adequate working conditions (safety and health), rest and compensation. The safeguard of these rights for migrants has great importance based on the principle of the inalienable nature of such rights, which all workers possess, irrespective of their migratory status, and also the fundamental principle of human dignity embodied in Article 1 of the Universal Declaration, according to which "[a]ll human beings are born free and equal in dignity and rights. They are endowed with reason and conscience and should act towards one another in a spirit of brotherhood."

158. This Court considers that the exercise of these fundamental labor rights guarantees the enjoyment of a dignified life to the worker and to the members of his family. Workers have the right to engage in a work activity under decent, fair conditions and to receive a remuneration that allows them and the members of their family to enjoy a decent standard of living in return for their labor. Likewise, work should be a means of

realization and an opportunity for the worker to develop his aptitudes, capacities and potential, and to realize his ambitions, in order to develop fully as a human being.

159. On many occasions, undocumented migrant workers are not recognized the said labor rights. For example, many employers engage them to provide a specific service for less than the regular remuneration, dismiss them because they join unions, and threaten to deport them. Likewise, at times, undocumented migrant workers cannot even resort to the courts of justice to claim their rights owing to their irregular situation. This should not occur; because, even though an undocumented migrant worker could face deportation, he should always have the right to be represented before a competent body so that he is recognized all the labor rights he has acquired as a worker.

160. The Court considers that undocumented migrant workers, who are in a situation of vulnerability and discrimination with regard to national workers, possess the same labor rights as those that correspond to other workers of the State of employment, and the latter must take all necessary measures to ensure that such rights are recognized and guaranteed in practice. Workers, as possessors of labor rights, must have the appropriate means of exercising them.

IX. STATE OBLIGATIONS WHEN DETERMINING MIGRATORY POLICIES IN LIGHT OF THE INTERNATIONAL INSTRUMENTS FOR THE PROTECTION OF HUMAN RIGHTS

161. The Court will now refer to State obligations when determining migratory policies solely in light of international instruments for the protection of human rights.

162. In this section of the Advisory Opinion, the Court will consider whether the fact that the American States subordinate and condition the observance of human rights to their migratory policies is compatible with international human rights law; it will do so in light of the international obligations arising from the International Covenant on Civil and Political Rights and other obligations of an *erga omnes* nature.

163. The migratory policy of a State includes any institutional act, measure or omission (laws, decrees, resolutions, directives, administrative acts, etc.) that refers to the entry, departure or residence of national or foreign persons in its territory.

164. In this respect, the Durban Declaration and Programme of Action adopted by the World Conference against Racism, Racial Discrimination, Xenophobia and Related Intolerance urged all States to "[t]o review and, where necessary, revise their immigration laws, policies and procedures with a view to eliminating any element of racial discrimination and make them consistent with State obligations by virtue of international human rights instruments." Likewise, in paragraph 9 of the Commission on Human Rights resolution 2001/5 on racism, racial discrimination, xenophobia and related intolerance, "States were asked to review and, where necessary, revise any immigration policies which are inconsistent with international human rights instruments, with a view to eliminating all discriminatory policies and practices against migrants."

165. This Court considers it essential to mention the provisions of Article 27 of the Vienna Convention on the Law of Treaties, which, when referring to domestic law and the observance of treaties, provides that: "[a] party may not invoke the provisions of its internal law as justification for its failure to perform a treaty."

166. In other words, when ratifying or acceding to an international treaty, States manifest their commitment in good faith to guarantee and respect the rights recognized therein. In addition, the States must adapt their domestic law to the applicable international law.

167. In this regard, the Inter-American Court has indicated that the general obligation set forth in Article 2 of the American Convention implies the adoption of measures to eliminate norms and practices of any nature that entail the violation of the guarantees set forth in the Convention, and the issuance of norms and the development of practices leading to the effective observance of the said guarantees. In this respect, the Court has indicated that:

Under the law of nations, a customary rule prescribes that a State that has concluded an international agreement must introduce in its domestic laws whatever changes are needed to ensure execution of the obligations it has undertaken. This principle has been accepted universally, and is supported by case law. The American Convention establishes the general obligation of each State Party to adapt its domestic laws to the provisions of the said Convention, so as to guarantee the rights embodied therein. This general obligation of the State Party implies that measures of domestic law must be effective (the "*effet utile*" principle). This means that the State must adopt all necessary measures to ensure that the provisions of the Convention are complied with effectively in its domestic laws, as required by Article 2 of the Convention. Such measures are only effective when the State adapts its actions to the protective norms of the Convention.

168. The goals of migratory policies should take into account respect for human rights. Likewise, migratory policies should be implemented respecting and guaranteeing human rights. As indicated above . . . , the distinctions that the States establish must be objective, proportionate and reasonable.

169. Considering that this Opinion applies to questions related to the legal aspects of migration, the Court deems it appropriate to indicate that, in the exercise of their power to establish migratory policies, it is licit for States to establish measures relating to the entry, residence or departure of migrants who will be engaged as workers in a specific productive sector of the State, provided this is in accordance with measures to protect the human rights of all persons and, in particular, the human rights of the workers. In order to comply with this requirement, States may take different measures, such as granting or denying general work permits or permits for certain specific work, but they must establish mechanisms to ensure that this is done without any discrimination, taking into account only the characteristics of the productive activity and the individual capability of the workers. In this way, the migrant worker is guaranteed a decent life, he is protected from the situation of vulnerability and uncertainty in which he usually finds himself, and the local or national productive process is organized efficiently and adequately.

170. Therefore, it is not admissible for a State of employment to protect its national production, in one or several sectors by encouraging or tolerating the employment of undocumented migrant workers in order to exploit them, taking advantage of their condition of vulnerability in relation to the employer in the State or considering them an offer of cheaper labor, either by paying them lower wages, denying or limiting their enjoyment or exercise of one or more of their labor rights, or denying them the possibility of filing a complaint about the violation of their rights before the competent authority.

171. The Inter-American Court has established the obligation of States to comply with every international instrument applicable to them. However, when referring to this State obligation, it is important to note that this Court considers that not only

should all domestic legislation be adapted to the respective treaty, but also State practice regarding its application should be adapted to international law. In other words, it is not enough that domestic laws are adapted to international law, but the organs or officials of all State powers, whether the Executive, the Legislature or the Judiciary, must exercise their functions and issue or implement acts, resolutions and judgments in a way that is genuinely in accordance with the applicable international law.

172. The Court considers that the State may not subordinate or condition the observance of the principle of equality before the law and non-discrimination to achieving the goals of its public policies, whatever these may be, including those of a migratory nature. This general principle must be respected and guaranteed always. Any act or omission to the contrary is inconsistent with the international human rights instruments.

X OPINIÓN

173. For the foregoing reasons,

THE COURT, DECIDES

unanimously, that it is competent to issue this Advisory Opinion.

AND IS OF THE OPINION

unanimously,

1. That States have the general obligation to respect and ensure the fundamental rights. To this end, they must take affirmative action, avoid taking measures that limit or infringe a fundamental right, and eliminate measures and practices that restrict or violate a fundamental right.

2. That non-compliance by the State with the general obligation to respect and ensure human rights, owing to any discriminatory treatment, gives rise to international responsibility.

3. That the principle of equality and non-discrimination is fundamental for the safeguard of human rights in both international law and domestic law.

4. That the fundamental principle of equality and non-discrimination forms part of general international law, because it is applicable to all States, regardless of whether or not they are a party to a specific international treaty. At the current stage of the development of international law, the fundamental principle of equality and non-discrimination has entered the domain of *jus cogens*.

5. That the fundamental principle of equality and non-discrimination, which is of a peremptory nature, entails obligations *erga omnes* of protection that bind all States and generate effects with regard to third parties, including individuals.

6. That the general obligation to respect and guarantee human rights binds States, regardless of any circumstance or consideration, including the migratory status of a person.

7. That the right to due process of law must be recognized as one of the minimum guarantees that should be offered to any migrant, irrespective of his migratory status. The broad scope of the preservation of due process encompasses all matters and all persons, without any discrimination.

8. That the migratory status of a person cannot constitute a justification to deprive him of the enjoyment and exercise of human rights, including those of a labor-related nature. When assuming an employment relationship, the migrant acquires rights that must be recognized and ensured because he is an employee, irrespective of his regular

or irregular status in the State where he is employed These rights are a result of the employment relationship.

9. That the State has the obligation to respect and guarantee the labor human rights of all workers, irrespective of their status as nationals or aliens, and not to tolerate situations of discrimination that are harmful to the latter in the employment relationships established between private individuals (employer-worker). The State must not allow private employers to violate the rights of workers, or the contractual relationship to violate minimum international standards.

10. That workers, being possessors of labor rights, must have all the appropriate means to exercise them. Undocumented migrant workers possess the same labor rights as other workers in the State where they are employed, and the latter must take the necessary measures to ensure that this is recognized and complied with in practice.

11. That States may not subordinate or condition observance of the principle of equality before the law and non-discrimination to achieving their public policy goals, whatever these may be, including those of a migratory character.

. . . . .

~

QUESTIONS & COMMENTS

(1) Note that the Inter-American Court opines that even if an employed worker is undocumented, s/he still has labor rights that must be protected by the private employer and State, including its courts.

(2) The Inter-American Court opines that a state may treat its nationals and documented aliens differently in employment as well as documented aliens and undocumented aliens. However, such differences in treatment must be reasonable, objective, and proportionate. How much deference should be given to states in determining what is proportionate?

5.10.2. Property

Universal Declaration of Human Rights

Article 17.

(1) Everyone has the right to own property alone as well as in association with others.

(2) No one shall be arbitrarily deprived of his property.

European Convention on Human Rights, Protocol No. 1

Article 1

Every natural or legal person is entitled to the peaceful enjoyment of his possessions. No one shall be deprived of his possessions except in the public interest and subject to the conditions provided for by law and by the general principles of international law.

The preceding provisions shall not, however, in any way impair the right of a State to enforce such laws as it deems necessary to control the use of property in accordance with the general interest or to secure the payment of taxes or other contributions or penalties.

American Declaration of the Rights and Duties of Man

Article XXIII. Right to property.

Every person has a right to own such private property as meets the essential needs of decent living and helps to maintain the dignity of the individual and of the home.

American Convention on Human Rights

Article 21. RIGHT TO PROPERTY.

1. Everyone has the right to the use and enjoyment of his property. The law may subordinate such use and enjoyment to the interest of society.

2. No one shall be deprived of his property except upon payment of just compensation, for reasons of public utility or social interest, and in the cases and according to the forms established by law.

3. Usury and any other form of exploitation of man by man shall be prohibited by law.

African [Banjul] Charter on Human and Peoples' Rights

Article 14

The right to property shall be guaranteed. It may only be encroached upon in the interest of public need or in the general interest of the community and in accordance with the provisions of appropriate laws.

Article 21

1. All peoples shall freely dispose of their wealth and natural resources. This right shall be exercised in the exclusive interest of the people. In no case shall a people be deprived of it.

2. In case of spoliation the dispossessed people shall have the right to the lawful recovery of its property as well as to an adequate compensation.

3. The free disposal of wealth and natural resources shall be exercised without prejudice to the obligation of promoting international economic cooperation based on mutual respect, equitable exchange and the principles of international law.

4. States parties to the present Charter shall individually and collectively exercise the right to free disposal of their wealth and natural resources with a view to strengthening African unity and solidarity.

5. States parties to the present Charter shall undertake to eliminate all forms of foreign economic exploitation particularly that practiced by international monopolies so as to enable their peoples to fully benefit from the advantages derived from their national resources.

Convention on Human Rights and Fundamental Freedoms
of the Commonwealth of Independent States

Article 26

   1. Every national and legal person shall have the right to own property. No one shall be deprived of his property, except in the public interest, under a judicial procedure and

in accordance with the conditions laid down in national legislation and the generally recognised principles of international law.

2. However, the foregoing provisions shall in now way affect the right of the Contracting Parties to adopt such laws as they deem necessary to control the use of items withdrawn from general circulation in the national or public interest.

The Mayagna (Sumo) Awas Tingni Community v. Nicaragua
Inter-American Court of Human Rights
Judgment of August 31, 2001
Inter-Am. Ct. H.R. (Ser. C) No. 79 (2001)

[The petitioner is an indigenous community whose members belong to the Mayagna ethnic group. The community claimed historical possession of land that they have inhabited for over 300 years. Although Nicaraguan law recognized and protected indigenous communal property, the government had failed to demarcate and provide real property title deeds to the petitioner's land. When private firms began logging operations on their lands, the petitioners brought a claim against the Nicaraguan government for these failures.]

. . . .

143. Article 21 of the American Convention recognizes the right to private property. In this regard, it establishes: a) that "[e]veryone has the right to the use and enjoyment of his property"; b) that such use and enjoyment can be subordinate, according to a legal mandate, to "social interest"; c) that a person may be deprived of his or her property for reasons of "public utility or social interest, and in the cases and according to the forms established by law"; and d) that when so deprived, a just compensation must be paid.

144. "Property" can be defined as those material things which can be possessed, as well as any right which may be part of a person's patrimony; that concept includes all movables and immovables, corporeal and incorporeal elements and any other intangible object capable of having value.

145. During the study and consideration of the preparatory work for the American Convention on Human Rights, the phrase "[e]veryone has the right to the use and enjoyment of private property, but the law may subordinate its use and enjoyment to public interest" was replaced by "[e]veryone has the right to the use and enjoyment of his property. The law may subordinate such use and enjoyment to the social interest." In other words, it was decided to refer to the "use and enjoyment of his property" instead of "private property".

146. The terms of an international human rights treaty have an autonomous meaning, for which reason they cannot be made equivalent to the meaning given to them in domestic law. Furthermore, such human rights treaties are live instruments whose interpretation must adapt to the evolution of the times and, specifically, to current living conditions.

147. Article 29(b) of the Convention, in turn, establishes that no provision may be interpreted as "restricting the enjoyment or exercise of any right or freedom recognized by virtue of the laws of any State Party or by virtue of another convention to which one of the said states is a party".

148. Through an evolutionary interpretation of international instruments for the protection of human rights, taking into account applicable norms of interpretation and

pursuant to article 29(b) of the Convention – which precludes a restrictive interpretation of rights – , it is the opinion of this Court that article 21 of the Convention protects the right to property in a sense which includes, among others, the rights of members of the indigenous communities within the framework of communal property, which is also recognized by the Constitution of Nicaragua.

149. Given the characteristics of the instant case, some specifications are required on the concept of property in indigenous communities. Among indigenous peoples there is a communitarian tradition regarding a communal form of collective property of the land, in the sense that ownership of the land is not centered on an individual but rather on the group and its community. Indigenous groups, by the fact of their very existence, have the right to live freely in their own territory; the close ties of indigenous people with the land must be recognized and understood as the fundamental basis of their cultures, their spiritual life, their integrity, and their economic survival. For indigenous communities, relations to the land are not merely a matter of possession and production but a material and spiritual element which they must fully enjoy, even to preserve their cultural legacy and transmit it to future generations.

150.   In this regard, Law No. 28, published on October 30, 1987 in La Gaceta No. 238, the Official Gazette of the Republic of Nicaragua, which regulates the Autonomy Statute of the Regions of the Atlantic Coast of Nicaragua, states in article 36 that:

Communal property are the lands, waters, and forests that have traditionally belonged to the Communities of the Atlantic Coast, and they are subject to the following provisions:

1. Communal lands are inalienable; they cannot be donated, sold, encumbered nor mortgaged, and they are inextinguishable.

2. The inhabitants of the Communities have the right to cultivate plots on communal property and to the usufruct of goods obtained from the work carried out.

151. Indigenous peoples' customary law must be especially taken into account for the purpose of this analysis. As a result of customary practices, possession of the land should suffice for indigenous communities lacking real title to property of the land to obtain official recognition of that property, and for consequent registration.

152. As has been pointed out, Nicaragua recognizes communal property of indigenous peoples, but has not regulated the specific procedure to materialize that recognition, and therefore no such title deeds have been granted since 1990. Furthermore, in the instant case the State has not objected to the claim of the Awas Tingni Community to be declared owner, even though the extent of the area claimed is disputed.

153. It is the opinion of the Court that, pursuant to article 5 of the Constitution of Nicaragua, the members of the Awas Tingni Community have a communal property right to the lands they currently inhabit, without detriment to the rights of other indigenous communities. Nevertheless, the Court notes that the limits of the territory on which that property right exists have not been effectively delimited and demarcated by the State. This situation has created a climate of constant uncertainty among the members of the Awas Tingni Community, insofar as they do not know for certain how far their communal property extends geographically and, therefore, they do not know until where they can freely use and enjoy their respective property. Based on this understanding, the

Court considers that the members of the Awas Tingni Community have the right that the State

    a) carry out the delimitation, demarcation, and titling of the territory belonging to the Community; and

    b) abstain from carrying out, until that delimitation, demarcation, and titling have been done, actions that might lead the agents of the State itself, or third parties acting with its acquiescence or its tolerance, to affect the existence, value, use or enjoyment of the property located in the geographical area where the members of the Community live and carry out their activities.

Based on the above, and taking into account the criterion of the Court with respect to applying article 29(b) of the Convention (supra para. 148), the Court believes that, in light of article 21 of the Convention, the State has violated the right of the members of the Mayagna Awas Tingni Community to the use and enjoyment of their property, and that it has granted concessions to third parties to utilize the property and resources located in an area which could correspond, fully or in part, to the lands which must be delimited, demarcated, and titled.

154. Together with the above, we must recall what has already been established by this court, based on article 1(1) of the American Convention, regarding the obligation of the State to respect the rights and freedoms recognized by the Convention and to organize public power so as to ensure the full enjoyment of human rights by the persons under its jurisdiction. According to the rules of law pertaining to the international responsibility of the State and applicable under International Human Rights Law, actions or omissions by any public authority, whatever its hierarchic position, are chargeable to the State which is responsible under the terms set forth in the American Convention.

155. For all the above, the Court concludes that the State violated article 21 of the American Convention, to the detriment of the members of the Mayagna (Sumo) Awas Tingni Community, in connection with articles 1(1) and 2 of the Convention.

    . . . .

   ~

QUESTIONS & COMMENTS

(1) The Awas Tingni Case was extremely important for the recognition of indigenous peoples' land rights. In the United States, Native Americans continue to complain about both loss of title to their lands, as previously guaranteed by treaty, as well as the loss of the enjoyment of those lands (through, *e.g.*, government mining concessions to private firms) to which they continue to hold title. The last-in-time rule's application to U.S.-Indian treaties has posed a serious obstacle to remedying these human rights violations.

(2) Note that the right to use and enjoyment of property extends not only to individuals but also communities and peoples. If an individual right to the use and enjoyment of property should conflict with a community's/people's right, whose right should prevail? Consider the following hypothetical: a family belongs to an indigenous group that collectively has had historical possession of lands for hunting, fishing, and so on. However, the individual family inhabits a house on the collectively owned lands. The indigenous

group decides to move the family's house to another location to which the family does not wish to move. Would the family have any property rights to its home and the land on which it sits?

James v. United Kingdom
European Court of Human Rights
98 Eur. Ct. H.R. (ser. A) (1986)
8 E.H.R.R. 123 (1986)

A. Introduction

10. The applicants are or were trustees acting under the will of the Second Duke of Westminster. . . .

In the area of Belgravia in Central London, upon a site which was once farmland on the outskirts of the City of London, the Westminster family and its trustees have developed a large estate comprising about 2,000 houses which has become one of the most desirable residential areas in the capital. The applicants, as trustees, have been deprived of their ownership of a number of properties in this estate through the exercise by the occupants of rights of acquisition conferred by the Leasehold Reform Act 1967, as amended.

11. This legislation confers on tenants residing in houses held on 'long leases' (over, or renewed for periods totalling over, 21 years) at 'low rents' the right to purchase compulsorily the 'freehold' of the property (the ground landlord's interest) on prescribed terms and subject to certain prescribed conditions. Under the system of long leaseholds, a tenant will typically purchase a long lease of property for a capital sum and pay a small or even nominal rent for it thereafter. The lease is a real-property interest, registerable in the Land Registry. The legislation in issue in the present case is not concerned with the ordinary system of rented tenure under which the tenant pays a 'rack rent' reflecting the full annual value of the property. The landlord/tenant relationship under the ordinary system is regulated, for houses under a certain (rateable) value, by separate legislation in the form of the 'Rent Acts', which provide machinery for fixing 'fair rents' and provide certain security of tenure for tenants.

B. The system of long leasehold tenure and the background to the Leasehold Reform Act 1967.

12. Two principal forms of long lease of residential property exist.

The first is a building lease, typically for 99 years, under which the tenant pays a 'ground rent' – a low rent fixed by reference to the value of the bare site – and undertakes to erect a house on the site and in general also to deliver it up in good repair at the end of the lease.

The second is a premium lease where the tenant pays the landlord a capital sum or 'premium' for a house provided by the landlord, and thereafter a rent. The duration of the lease is variable, as are the relative proportions of premium and rent. According to evidence submitted to the Court, the premium charged will typically take into account the building cost and an appropriate profit element. Factors entering into the calculation will normally include the length of the proposed lease, its terms (for example, whether sub-letting is allowed) and the state of the property at the time when the lease is granted.

The method used to calculate the premiums under the leases concerned in the present case is described below. . . .

The tenant holding a property under a long lease may normally sell the lease to a third party, who then acquires the tenant's rights and obligations under the lease for the remainder of its duration. In practice, leases are commonly bought and sold on the property market without the landlord playing any part in the transaction. A tenant may normally also grant an 'under-lease' of the property. As a matter of law, however, whether there is a right to sell the lease or sublet depends on the terms of the particular lease.

13. The capital value of the landlord's interest in a property let on a long lease arises from two sources: firstly, the rent payable under the lease and, secondly, the prospect of reversion of the property to him at the end of the lease. At the beginning of a very long lease the value of the reversion may be very little and the total market value of the landlord's interest may therefore amount to little more than the capitalised value of the rent. The capital value of the tenant's interest arises from his right to occupy the house under the lease, and the time for which that right will subsist is of critical importance in relation to its value. At the beginning of a very long lease, the value of the tenant's interest may be more or less equivalent to a 'freehold' interest if the rent payable is a nominal one.

The lease, however, is a wasting asset. As a lease progresses, the value of the tenant's interest in the property diminishes, whilst the value of the landlord's interest increases. At the end of the lease, the tenant's interest ceases to exist and the buildings, including improvements and repairs made, revert to the landlord without any compensation to the tenant.

The sum of the values of the landlord's and tenant's respective interests is less than the freehold value of the property with vacant possession, since neither the landlord alone nor the tenant alone can offer a third party the freehold with such possession. If, however, the reversion is sold to the occupying tenant, who can then merge both interests into a simple freehold, its value is greater than the investment value to a third party purchasing the reversion subject to the existing lease. In free market transactions, it is usual for the vendor and the purchaser to share this additional value, known as the 'merger value', in agreed proportions.

14. The long-leasehold system of tenure has been widely used in England and Wales, and in particular was associated with much urban development in the nineteenth century following the industrial revolution.

15. From about 1880 onwards, demands began to be made for 'leasehold enfranchisement', that is the right for tenants to purchase compulsorily the freehold of their holdings.

Demand for reform of the law revived soon after the Second World War in 1948 a Committee (the Leasehold Committee) was appointed by the Lord Chancellor to consider various aspects of the leasehold question. . . .

The Conservative Government elected in 1951 . . . enacted . . . the Landlord and Tenant Act 1954 ('the 1954 Act'). In broad terms, the effect of this act was – and still is – that on the expiry of a long residential lease the tenant should have the right to continue occupying the house as a sitting tenant under the Rents Acts, paying a 'fair rent' as defined in those Acts and enjoying the security of tenure afforded by the ordinary rent legislation. This privilege is transferable on death to other members of the tenant's family residing in the property.

17. Public discussion of the matter continued. In 1961, claims were made in Parliament that leaseholders were being subjected to hardship as a result of the onerous terms which

landlords were asking for the sale of reversions or for the extension or renewal of existing leases. . . .

18. For some years compulsory enfranchisement had been part of Labour Party Policy. After the election of a Labour Government in 1964, a further White Paper was published in 1966 setting out the Government's proposals for reform including a scheme of compulsory enfranchisement. The grounds on which the Government considered reform to be necessary were set out as follows:

The purpose

1. This White Paper is concerned with residential long leases particularly those granted originally in the latter half of the last century. In the case of long leases, experience has shown that the system has worked very unfairly against the occupying leaseholder. The freeholder has provided the land; but in the great majority of cases it is the leaseholder or his predecessor in title who at their own expense have built the house on the land. Whether this is so or not in all cases, it is almost universally true that over the years it is the lessee and his predecessors who have borne the cost of improvements and maintenance, and these will probably have cost far more than the original building itself. At their expense the leaseholders have preserved it as a habitable dwelling and have used it as such, and not unnaturally, an occupying leaseholder who at the end of the term has lived in it for such a period of years regards it as his family home. It is in such cases quite indefensible, if justice is to be done as between freeholder and occupying leaseholder, that at the end of the term, the law should allow the ownership of the house to revert to the freeholder without his paying anything for it so that he gets not only the land but also the house, the improvements and everything the leaseholder and his predecessors have added to it.

2. The Government has decided that a solution must be found to right this injustice. In the Government's view the basic principle of a reform which will do justice between the parties should be that the freeholder owns the land and the occupying leaseholder is morally entitled to the ownership of the building which has been put on and maintained on that land.

3. Two circumstances make reform a matter of urgency. First, most people buy their house on mortgage and for them the leasehold system works particularly harshly. A purchaser on mortgage may pay virtually the freehold price for a lease with a good many years to run but as he reaches the end of his mortgage term he will feel a sharpening sense of injustice. He will realise that after he has discharged the mortgage he will have an interest far less valuable than it was when he bought it, and difficult to sell because a subsequent purchaser may not be able to get a mortgage. This is the reality now confronting many owner-occupiers who purchased their houses on setting up home immediately after the war. Second, a great many leasehold estates were built in the second half of the nineteenth century when landowners used their monopoly power to prevent development taking place on other than leasehold terms. This occurred particularly in South Wales and in some English areas. These leases are beginning to fall in and the leaseholders are now experiencing the full harshness of the leasehold system.

The Plan

4. The Government will, therefore, introduce a Bill to give leaseholders with an original long lease greater security and to enable them to acquire the freehold on fair

terms. The Bill will be based on the principle that the land belongs in equity to the landowner and the house belongs in equity to the occupying leaseholder. It follows that the leaseholder will have the right to retain his house after the lease expires and the right to enfranchise his lease.

. . . The Government's proposals as to the terms of enfranchisement were explained as follows in paragraphs 11 and 12 of the White Paper:

> 11. Subject to provision for special cases, a qualified leaseholder will have the right at any time during the original term of the lease to acquire the freehold by buying out the landlord compulsorily. It is important to ensure that the price paid for enfranchisement is a fair price. But present market prices reflect the position under the present law which is inequitable to the leaseholder, and the price for enfranchisement must accordingly be based not on present market values but on the value of the land itself, including any development value attaching to it. The price of enfranchisement must be calculated in accordance with the principle that in equity the bricks and mortar belong to the qualified leaseholder and the land to the landlord.
>
> 12. It follows, and the Bill will so provide, that where there is no development value (and often there will not be) the fair price for enfranchisement will be the value of the freehold interest of the site, subject to the lease and its extension of 50 years. This will completely disregard the value of the building on reversion.

19. Thereafter, following their re-election in 1966, the (Labour) Government introduced a Bill into Parliament to give effect to their proposals. . . .

In the parliamentary debates on the Bill, Members of all political parties expressed the view that the 1954 Act, which provides security of tenure, had not succeeded in relieving the hardship or injustice caused to tenants at the expiry of long leases. Two of the reasons given were the continuing liability of the tenant to pay freshly assessed rents and the potential burden of heavy claims for dilapidations which some landlords used as a means of persuading tenants to give up their statutory right of possession. . . .

After extensive debate in both Houses of Parliament, the Bill introduced by the Government was duly enacted as the Leasehold Reform Act 1967. There were about one and a quarter million dwellinghouses occupied by long leaseholders in England and Wales in 1967. It was estimated at the time by the Government that all but 1 or 2 per cent fell within the scope of the enfranchisement scheme introduced by the Act. Subsequently, as a result of an amendment introduced in 1974, a band of more valuable houses within this remaining 1 or 2 per cent was also made susceptible of enfranchisement.

C. The leasehold reform legislation

20. The legislation governing leasehold enfranchisement now consists of the Leasehold Reform Act 1967 ('the 1967 Act'), as amended by the Housing Act 1969 ('the 1969 Act'), the Housing Act 1974 ('the 1974 Act'), the Leasehold Reform Act 1979, the Housing Act 1980 ('the 1980 Act') and the Housing and Building Control Act 1984. This legislation provides occupying tenants of 'houses' let on long leases in England and Wales with the right to acquire the freehold of the house or an extended lease, on certain terms and conditions. The term 'house' as defined, includes semi-detached and terraced houses but not flats and maisonettes (§2 of the 1967 Act).

21. The following, in broad terms, are the principle conditions which must be satisfied before the tenant of a house becomes entitled to the right of acquisition conferred by the Act:

(a) the tenancy must be a 'long' tenancy that is either for a term certain of 21 years or more or for a lesser term once it has been renewed for periods totalling over 21 years.

(b) With certain exceptions not relevant for present purposes, the 'rateable value' of the house (that is, the notional annual rental value fixed for local taxation purposes) must not exceed £750, or £1,500 if the house is in Greater London. The original rateable-value limits fixed in the 1967 Act (£200 and, for Greater London, £400) were revised (in effect being raised to £500 and £1,000, respectively) by the 1974 Act to take account of the country-wide rating revaluation carried out in 1973. The 1974 Act further extended the scope of the enfranchisement scheme under the 1967 Act by bringing in houses of a still higher rateable value (between £500 and £750 and, for Greater London, between £1,000 and £1,500), in respect of which, however, a different purchase price was payable. Certain even more valuable properties, being outside the global rateable-value limits, remain outside the ambit of legislation altogether.

(c) The annual rent must be a 'low' rent, that is less than two-thirds of the rateable value.

(d) The tenant must occupy the house as his only or main residence and must have done so for at least three years prior to the time when he gives notice of his desire to exercise his rights under the Act.

22. Where the above conditions are satisfied the tenant has two rights:

(a) he can obtain a fifty-year extension of the lease at a rent representing the letting value of the ground (without buildings), the rent being subject to revision after 25 years.

(b) he can purchase the freehold on the terms outlined below. The tenant can set in motion the procedure for exercising his right to purchase the freehold at any time up to the original term date of the lease, but not thereafter.

23. No price or premium is payable for an extended lease other than the rent.

On the purchase of a freehold, a price is payable to the landlord as determined in accordance with one or other of two bases of valuation. These are referred to as the '1967 basis of valuation' which was introduced by the 1967 Act (as amended by the 1969 Act), and the '1974 basis of valuation', which was introduced by the 1974 Act. The 1967 basis applied to less valuable properties, and the 1974 basis to the small percentage of more valuable properties brought within the scope of the legislation for the first time by the 1974 Act. The essential features of the two bases of valuation may be summarised as follows:

(a) The 1967 basis of valuation applies to properties with a rateable value of up to £500, or £1,000 if the house is in Greater London. The price payable is the amount which the house, if sold on the open market by a willing seller, might be expected to realise on the assumptions, *inter alia*, that (i) the tenant has exercised his statutory right to obtain an extension of the lease of fifty years, and (ii) the purchaser is someone other than the tenant. The effect of the assumption as to the extension of the lease is that the tenant pays approximately the site value, and pays nothing for the buildings on the site.

The assumption that the purchaser is someone other than the tenant, introduced by the 1969 Act, also excludes any element of 'merger value' from the price. This basis of valuation reflects the policy outlined in the 1966 White Paper.

(b) The 1974 basis of valuation applies to properties with rateable values of over £500 and up to £750, or over £1,000 and up to £1,500 if the house is in Greater London. The price payable is the amount which the house, if sold on the open market by a willing seller, might be expected to realise on the assumption, *inter alia*, that at the end of the tenancy the tenant had the right to remain in possession of the house under the 1954 Act, that is as a statutory tenant paying a 'fair rent' reflecting his occupation of the house. In principle, this basis of valuation is more favourable to the landlord and is intended to provide a price approximately equivalent to the market value of the site and house, assuming it to be tenanted under the 1954 Act; it also allows the landlord a share of the 'merger value'. . . .

24. The tenant may, at any time before the price of the property has been fixed, institute a procedure to have the rateable value of the house adjusted for the purposes of the legislation so as to leave out of account the value of structural improvements carried out by himself or his predecessors. The County Court is competent to determine disputes as to whether improvements are within the scope of the scheme and, since the 1980 Act came into force, there has been a right of appeal to the High Court for such decisions.

25. The legislation lays down procedures for carrying the relevant transactions into effect and for determining disputes. Where the tenant wishes to acquire the freehold, he must first give the landlord written notice of his desire to do so. Disputes over the tenant's entitlement to acquire the freehold under the Act and related matters are within the jurisdiction of the County Court. In such proceedings, the County Court has powers to penalise in costs a tenant who is guilty of unreasonable delay or default in the performance of the obligations arising from the notice of enfranchisement. In default of agreement, the price payable is now subject to determination by a local Leasehold Valuation Tribunal, with a right of appeal to the London-based Lands Tribunal which forms part of the High Court. Before the 1980 Act came into force, disputes as to price were within the jurisdiction of the Lands Tribunal. It is open to a landlord who believes that the enfranchising tenant is deliberately or unnecessarily delaying the process of enfranchisement to refer the matter to the Leasehold Valuation Tribunal (or, formerly, to the Lands Tribunal). Regulations prescribe a timetable for completion of the purchase after the price has been determined.

26. For the purpose of assessing the price payable, the house is valued as at the date of the tenant's notice to the landlord of his desire to acquire the freehold (§§9(1) and 37(1)(d) of the 1967 Act), and not as at the date when the valuation is being carried out.

D. Transactions affecting the applicants

27. In transactions completed between April 1979 and November 1983, the tenants of some 80 leasehold properties forming part of the residential estate of Belgravia (London) which the Westminster family and its trustees have developed exercised their powers under the contested legislation to acquire compulsorily the applicants' interest as freehold owners of the properties. These transactions related to 77 properties held on 'premium' leases and 3 properties held on 'building leases'. . .

As time passes, according to the applicants, the 1974 Act will affect an increasingly higher ratio of properties on their estate. Since November 1983, another 43 enfranchisements have taken place, bringing up to a total of about 215 the number of properties enfranchised on the estate under the leasehold reform legislation to date. The applicants estimate that there are likely to be between 500 to 800 further enfranchisements on their estate in the future. . . .

29. The applicants drew attention to the following features of the individual transactions in question:

(i) in no case except 3 was the property built either by the tenant who enfranchised or by the tenant's predecessors;

(ii) in only 6 cases was the property occupied by members of the tenant's family continuously since the date of creation of the lease;

(iii) the period of occupation of the tenant prior to the date of his or her notice to acquire had varied from three to 35 years; in 34 out of the 80 instances, it had been under 8 years;

(iv) in all the cases, the tenant was entitled to security of tenure, subject to the conditions laid down by the Rent Acts, upon expiry of the lease.

(v) the period between the tenant's notice (the relevant date for assessment of the price) and completion of the sale varied between one and 13 years, and in 34 of the 80 transactions was more than five years;

(vi) the unencumbered freehold value of the properties (as assessed by the applicants) varied from £44,000 to £225,000, whereas the price paid for enfranchisement by the tenant varied from £2,500 to £111,000.

(vii) the value of the unexpired portion of the lease to the tenants was said to be up to £153,750 – without taking into account the right of enfranchise;

(viii) in 15 cases, the tenant sold the lease, after making the claim but before enfranchising, with the benefit of the right to enfranchise;

(ix) in at least 25 out of the 80 cases, the tenant who enfranchised did not remain in occupation of the property, but sold the freehold within one year of acquiring it, and in 9 of these cases did not occupy after enfranchisement at all;

(x) the profits said to have been made by the tenants on such onward sale varied between £32,000 to £182,000, with a it least 7 cases where the tenant made over £100,000; in particular in one case, the tenant who had come into occupation three months before publication of the 1966 White Paper (see paragraph 18 above) – and who had paid a low price (£9,000) for the lease, without prospect of enfranchisement at that time – was able to buy the freehold at 28 percent of its proper value (as assessed by the applicants), and sold it less than a year later for a profit of 636 percent – a profit of £116,000.

The losses claimed by the applicants to have been sustained through having to sell on the statutory terms as opposed to open-market conditions range from £1,350 to £148,080 on each transaction, and total £1,479,407 for properties in respect of which the 1967 basis of valuation obtained and £1,050,496 for properties in respect of which the 1974 basis of valuation obtained. . . .

I. Article 1 of Protocol No. 1

34. The applicants claimed that the compulsory transfer of their property under the Leasehold Reform Act 1967, as amended, gave rise to a violation of Article 1 of Protocol No. 1 to the Convention. . . .

A. General considerations

35. The applicants maintained that since the grievance concerned in substance the effect of the legislation on the ownership of specific properties formerly belonging to them, each individual act of enfranchisement before the Court should be examined on its merits for compliance with Article 1. . . .

36. The Court has frequently stated the principle that, without losing sight of the general context of the case, it must, in proceedings originating in an individual application, confine its attention, as far as possible, to the concrete case. . . .

In the present case, however, the essence of the applicants' complaint is directed against the terms and conditions of the contested legislation. It does not relate to the manner of execution of the law by a State authority, be it administrative or judicial. Indeed, one of the applicants' criticisms was that the legislation does not allow scope for discretionary and variable implementation according to the particular circumstances of each individual property. The Court must therefore . . . direct its attention primarily to the contested legislation itself, in order to determine whether that legislation is compatible with Article 1 of Protocol No. 1.

This does not mean that the Court will examine the legislation *in abstracto*. The individual enfranchisements complained of are illustrative of the impact in practice of the reform it introduced and, as such, material to the issue of its compatibility with the Convention. In this respect, the consequences of application of the legislation such as occurred in the 80 specific transactions before the Court are to be taken into account.

The Court will accordingly consider the applicants' claims on the basis of the above approach.

37. Article 1 in substance guarantees the right of property. . . . In its judgment of 23 September 1982, in the case of *Sporrong and Lonnroth*, the Court analysed Article 1 as comprising 'three distinct rules': the first rule, set out in the first sentence of the first paragraph, is of a general nature and enunciates the principle of the peaceful enjoyment of property; the second rule, contained in the second sentence of the first paragraph, covers deprivation of possessions and subjects it to certain conditions; the third rule, stated in the second paragraph, recognises that the Contracting States are entitled, amongst other things, to control the use of property in accordance with the general interest (§61). The Court further observed that, before inquiring whether the first general rule has been complied with, it must determine whether the last two are applicable. The three rules are not, however, 'distinct' in the sense of being unconnected. The second and third rules are concerned with particular instances of interference with the right to peaceful enjoyment of property and should therefore be construed in the light of the general principle enunciated in the first rule.

B. Second sentence of the first paragraph ('the deprivation rule')

1. Applicability

38. The Court considers that the applicants were 'deprived of [their] possessions', within the meaning of the second sentence of Article 1, by virtue of the contested legislation. This point was not disputed before the Court.

2. 'In the public interest': private individuals as beneficiaries

39. The applicants' first contention was that the 'public interest' test in the deprivation rule is satisfied only if the property is taken for a public purpose of benefit to the community generally and that, as a corollary, the transfer of property from one person to another for the latter's private benefit alone can never be 'in the public interest'. In their submission, the contested legislation does not satisfy this condition.

The Commission and the Government, on the other hand, were agreed in thinking that a compulsory transfer of property from one individual to another may in principle be considered to be 'in the public interest' if the taking is effected in pursuance of legitimate social policies.

40. The Court agrees with the applicants that a deprivation of property effected for no reason other than to confer a private benefit on a private party cannot be 'in the public interest'. Nonetheless, the compulsory transfer of property from one individual to another may, depending upon the circumstances, constitute a legitimate means for promoting the public interest. In this connection, even where the texts in force employ expressions like 'for the public use', no common principle can be identified in the constitutions, legislation and case law of the Contracting States that would warrant understanding the notion of public interest as outlawing compulsory transfer between private parties. The same may be said of certain other democratic countries; thus, the applicants and the Government cited in argument a judgment of the Supreme Court of the United States of America, which concerned State legislation in Hawaii compulsorily transferring title in real property from lessors to lessees in order to reduce the concentration of land ownership.[1]

41. Neither can it be read into the English expression 'in the public interest' that the transferred property should be put into use for the general public or that the community generally, or even a substantial proportion of it, should directly benefit from the taking. The taking of property in pursuance of a policy calculated to enhance social justice within the community can properly be described as being 'in the public interest'. In particular, the fairness of a system of law governing the contractual or property rights of private parties is a matter of public concern and therefore legislative measures intended to bring about such fairness are capable of being 'in the public interest', even if they involve the compulsory transfer of property from one individual to another.

42. The expression *'pour cause d'utilité publique'* used in the French text of Article 1 may indeed be read as having the narrow sense argued by the applicants, as is shown by the domestic law of some, but not all, of the Contracting States where the expression or its equivalent is found in the context of expropriation of property. That, however, is not decisive, as many Convention concepts have been recognised in the Court's case law as having an 'autonomous' meaning. Moreover, the words *'utilité publique'* are also capable of bearing a wider meaning, covering expropriation measures taken in implementation of policies calculated to enhance social justice.

The Court, like the Commission, considers that such an interpretation best reconciles the language of the English and French texts, having regard to the object and purpose of Article 1, which is primarily to guard against the arbitrary confiscation of property.

---

[1] *Hawaii Housing Authority v. Midkiff*, 104 S. Ct. 2321 (1984).

43. The applicants submitted that the use in the same context of different phrases – 'public interest' in the first paragraph of Article 1 and 'general interest' in the second paragraph – should, according to a generally recognised principle of treaty interpretation, be assumed to indicate an intention to refer to different concepts. They construed Article 1 as granting the State more latitude to control the use of someone's property than to take it away from him.

In the Court's opinion, even if there could be differences between the concepts of 'public interest' and 'general interest' in Article 1, on the point under consideration no fundamental distinction of the kind contended for by the applicants can be drawn between them.

44. The applicants accepted that measures designed to ensure equitable distribution of economic advantages, for example by way of taxation, are licensed by Article 1, but, so they argued, solely by the second paragraph and not by the first paragraph. The Court, however, sees no cogent reason why a State should be prohibited under Article 1 from implementing such a policy by resort of deprivation of property.

45. For these reasons, the Court [concludes that]... a taking of property effected in pursuance of legitimate social, economic or other policies may be 'in the public interest', even if the community at large has no direct use or enjoyment of the property taken. The leasehold reform legislation is not therefore *ipso facto* an infringement of Article 1 on this ground. Accordingly, it is necessary to inquire whether in other respects the legislation satisfied the 'public interest' test and the remaining requirements laid down in the second sentence of Article 1.

3. Whether the leasehold reform legislation complied with the 'public interest' test and the remaining requirements of the deprivation rule

(a) Margin of appreciation

46. Because of their direct knowledge of their society and its needs, the national authorities are in principle better placed than the international judge to appreciate what is 'in the public interest'. Under the system of protection established by the Convention, it is thus for the national authorities to make the initial assessment both of the existence of a problem of public concern warranting measures of deprivation of property and of the remedial action to be taken.... Here, as in other fields to which the safeguards of the Convention extend, the national authorities accordingly enjoy a certain margin of appreciation.

Furthermore, the notion of 'public interest' is necessarily extensive. In particular, ... the decision to enact laws expropriating property will commonly involve consideration of political, economic and social issues on which opinions within a democratic society may reasonably differ widely. The Court, finding it natural that the margin of appreciation available to the legislature in implementing social and economic policies should be a wide one, will respect the legislature's judgment as to what is 'in the public interest' unless that judgment be manifestly without reasonable foundation. In other words, although the Court cannot substitute its own assessment for that of the national authorities, it is bound to review the contested measures under Article 1 of Protocol No. 1 and, in so doing, to make an inquiry into the facts with reference to which the national authorities acted.

*(b) Whether the aim of the contested legislation was a legitimate one, in principle
and on the facts*

47. The aim of the 1967 Act, as spelt out in the 1966 White Paper, was to right the
injustice which was felt to be caused to occupying tenants by the operation of the long
leasehold system of tenure. The Act was designed to reform the existing law, said to be
'inequitable to the leaseholder', and to give effect to what was described as the occupying
tenant's moral entitlement to ownership of the house.

Eliminating what are judged to be social injustices is an example of the functions
of a democratic legislature. More especially, modern societies consider housing of the
population to be a prime social need, the regulation of which cannot entirely be left to
the play of market forces. The margin of appreciation is wide enough to cover legislation
aimed at securing greater social justice in the sphere of people's homes, even where
such legislation interferes with existing contractual relations between private parties and
confers no direct benefit on the State or the Community at large. In principle, therefore,
the aim pursued by the leasehold reform legislation is a legitimate one.

48. The applicants suggested that the 1967 Act was not enacted for purposes of public
benefit but was in reality motivated by purely political considerations as a vote-seeking
measure by the Labour Government then in office.

The Court notes, however, that leasehold reform in England and Wales had been a
matter of public concern for almost a century and that, when the 1967 Act was passed,
enfranchisement was accepted as a principle by all the major political parties, although
they expressed different views as to how it should be implemented. It was not disputed by
the applicants that the main criticisms now made by them of the substantive provisions
of the legislation were voiced at the time and fully debated in Parliament before being
rejected. The Court does not find that such political considerations as may have influenced
the legislative process, socio-economic legislation being bound to reflect political attitudes
to a greater or lesser degree, precluded the objective pursued by the 1967 Act from being
a legitimate one 'in the public interest'. Similar reasoning applies to the applicants' claim
that the amendment introduced by the Conservative Government in 1974, whereby a
small percentage of more valuable dwellinghouses was for the first time brought within
the scope of the legislation, 'was born of political expediency alone'.

49. The applicants further disputed the existence of any problems justifying legislation. According to the applicants, the long leasehold system of tenure, certainly as far
as premium leases were concerned, did not in fact suffer from any unfairness and it
could not be said that the tenant had any 'moral entitlement' to ownership of the house
merely by reason of occupying a house built, repaired or improved by previous tenants
in accordance with the contractual terms of a lease.

As stated above, the Court has jurisdiction to inquire into the factual basis of the
justification pleaded by the respondent Government. That review, however, is limited
to determining whether the legislature's assessment of the relevant social and economic
conditions came within the State's margin of appreciation. The Government conceded
that the convictions on which the 1967 Act was based were by no means universally
shared; and this is borne out by the 1962 White Paper. As the Commission observed
in its report, the justice or injustice of the leasehold system and the respective 'moral
entitlements' of tenants and landlords are matters of judgment on which there is clearly
room for legitimate conflict of opinions. The applicants' view cannot be qualified as

groundless. Nonetheless, there is sufficient evidence to justify the contrary views. In a building lease the original tenant will have built the house, in a premium lease he will have paid an initial capital sum which typically took account of the building cost, and in both kinds of lease the tenant will have been responsible for all running repairs. This means that the long-leasehold tenant and his predecessors will over the years have invested a considerable amount of money in the house which is their home, whereas the landlord will normally have made no contribution towards its maintenance subsequent to the granting of the original lease.

The Court therefore agrees with the [European] Commission's conclusion: the United Kingdom Parliament's belief in the existence of a social injustice was not such as could be characterised as manifestly unreasonable.

(c) Means chosen to achieve the aim

50. This, however does not settle the issue. Not only must a measure depriving a person of his property pursue, on the facts as well as in principle, a legitimate aim 'in the public interest', but there must also be a reasonable relationship of proportionality between the means employed and the aim sought to be realised.... This latter requirement was expressed in other terms in the *Sporrong and Lonnroth* judgment by the notion of the 'fair balance' that must be struck between the demands of the general interest of the community and the requirements of the protection of the individual's fundamental rights. The requisite balance will not be found if the person concerned has had to bear 'an individual and excessive burden'. Although the Court was speaking in that judgment in the context of the general rule of peaceful enjoyment of property enunciated in the first sentence of the first paragraph, it pointed out that 'the search for this balance is ... reflected in the structure of Article 1' as a whole.

It was the applicants' contention that the leasehold reform legislation does not satisfy these conditions. In their submission, even assuming there to be a social injustice, the means chosen to cure it were so inappropriate or disproportionate as to take the legislature's decision outside the margin of appreciation.

The Court considers that a measure must be both appropriate for achieving its aim and not disproportionate thereto. Whether this was so on the facts will be examined below when dealing with the applicants' various arguments.

(i) The principle of enfranchisement

51. According to the applicants, the security of tenure that tenants already had under the law in force provided an adequate response and the draconian nature of the means devised to give effect to the alleged moral entitlement, namely deprivation of property, went too far. This was said to be confirmed by the absence of any true equivalent to the 1967 Act in the municipal legislation of the other Contracting States and, indeed, generally in democratic societies. It is, so the applicants argue, only if there were no other less drastic remedy for the perceived injustice that the extreme remedy of expropriation could satisfy the requirements of Article 1.

This amounts to reading a test of strict necessity into the Article, an interpretation which the Court does not find warranted. The availability of alternative solutions does not in itself render the leasehold reform legislation unjustified; it constitutes one factor, along with others, relevant for determining whether the means chosen could be regarded as reasonable and suited to achieving the legitimate aim being pursued, having regard to the need to strike a 'fair balance'. Provided the legislature remained within these bounds, it is not for the Court to say whether the legislation represented the best solution for dealing with the problem or whether the legislative discretion should have been exercised in another way.

The occupying leaseholder was considered by Parliament to have a 'moral entitlement' to ownership of the house, of which inadequate account was taken under the existing law. (See extracts from the 1966 White Paper quoted at §18 *supra*). The concern of the legislature was not simply to regulate more fairly the relationship of landlord and tenant but to right a perceived injustice that went to the very issue of ownership. Allowing a mechanism for the compulsory transfer of the freehold interest in the house and the land to the tenant, with financial compensation to the landlord, cannot in itself be qualified in the circumstances as an inappropriate or disproportionate method for readjusting the law so as to meet that concern.

(ii) Rateable-value limits

52. As to the conditions laid down for enfranchisement, the applicants contended that the restriction of the scope of the legislation to houses below a certain rateable value introduces an arbitrary element and is inconsistent with the philosophy on which the legislation was based, since the same moral entitlement would arise for the tenant whatever the value of the property.

The Court notes that, on the Government's undisputed estimate, all but 1 or 2 percent of dwellinghouses held on long leases in England and Wales were within the 1967 Act. The explanations given on behalf of the Government during the debates on the Bill for inserting the rateable-value limits cannot be dismissed as irrational. In particular, although the argument of 'moral entitlement' was logically capable of being applied across the board, Parliament cannot be said to have acted unreasonably in restricting, as a matter of judgment, the right of enfranchisement under the 1967 Act to less valuable houses so as to redress what were perceived to be the cases of greatest hardship. Neither can the Court find that the amendment in the 1974 Act, whereby a more valuable class of property was rendered liable to enfranchisement fell outside the State's margin of appreciation.

[The Court noted that applicants objected to the compensation terms.]

. . .

(iv) Absence of independent consideration of the reasonableness of each proposed enfranchisement

68. The applicants contended that the operation of the leasehold reform legislation is indiscriminate since it does not provide any machinery whereby the landlord can seek an independent consideration, in any particular case, of either the justification for enfranchisement or the principles on which the compensation is to be calculated, once only it is established that the tenancy is within the ambit of legislation. They pointed to evident differences between leasehold tenants of modest housing in South Wales and the better off, middle class tenants on their estate in Belgravia, who on the whole could not be classified as needy or deserving of protection. In their submission, in order to avoid injustice for the landlord as well as the tenant, the legislation should have provided for judicial review going into the details and reasonableness of each proposed enfranchisement.

Such a system may have been possible, and indeed a proposal to this effect was made during the debates on the draft legislation. However, Parliament chose instead to lay down broad and general categories within which the right of enfranchisement was to arise. The reason for this choice, according to the Government, was to avoid the uncertainty, litigation, expense and delay that would inevitably be caused for both tenants and landlords under a scheme of individual examination of each of many thousands of cases. Expropriation legislation of wide sweep, in particular if it implements a programme of social and economic reform, is hardly capable of doing entire justice in the diverse circumstances of the very large number of different individuals concerned.

It is in the first place for Parliament to assess the advantages and disadvantages involved in the various legislative alternatives available. In view of the fact that the legislation was estimated to be likely to affect 98 to 99 percent of the one and a quarter million dwellinghouses held on long leases in England and Wales, the system chosen by Parliament cannot in itself be dismissed as irrational or inappropriate.

(v) Individual transactions

69. The applicants finally submitted that even if enfranchisement is capable in principle of being 'in the public interest', the 80 individual transactions complained of were not justified. The applicants drew attention to the factors listed in paragraph 29 above to show that the enfranchising tenants of the 80 houses concerned in Belgravia bore no resemblance to the kind of people, deserving of protection, whom the 1966 White Paper said the legislation was designed to benefit. Irrespective of its possible general compatibility with Article 1, the leasehold reform legislation, as applied in the concrete circumstances of these transactions, was alleged to infringe the principle of proportionality as it resulted in effects going far beyond what was required to achieve its apparent purpose. To illustrate that contention, they referred to one of their former properties where the tenant who purchased the lease near the end of its term for a low price before the introduction of the 1967 Act made a substantial and wholly 'undeserved' gain on reselling the property after enfranchising.

The view taken by Parliament as to the tenant's 'moral entitlement' to ownership of the house, which the Court has found to be within the State's margin of appreciation, is one that applies equally to the applicants' properties in Belgravia. An inevitable consequence of the legislation giving effect to that view is that any tenant who sells the unencumbered freehold of the property (comprising house and land) after enfranchising is bound to make an apparent gain, since the price of enfranchisement, at least on the 1967 basis of valuation, did not include the house and the tenant has benefited from the so-called merger value. In addition, the broad sweep and scale of the redistribution of interests achieved by the reform mean that some anomalies, such as the making of 'windfall profits' by tenants who purchased end-of-term leases at the right time, are unavoidable. Parliament decided that landlords affected by the legislation should be deprived of the enrichment, considered unjust, that would otherwise come to them on reversion of the property, at the risk of a number of 'undeserving' tenants being able to make 'windfall profits'. That was a policy decision by Parliament, which the Court cannot find to be so unreasonable as to be outside the State's margin of appreciation. Neither does the operation of the legislation in practice, notably as illustrated by the 80 transactions concerning the applicants, show the scale of anomalies to be such as to render the legislation unacceptable under Article 1. Furthermore, in all the specific transactions complained of, even those where 'windfall profits' were made by tenants in onward sales, the applicants received the prescribed compensation for what Parliament considered to be their entitlement in equity as landlords. Any hardship as a result of the making of a 'windfall profit' was suffered not by the applicants, whose loss and compensation were unaffected, but rather by the predecessor(s) in title of the enfranchising tenant.

The 80 enfranchisements complained of by the applicants remained within the framework of the legislation, which framework the Court has found to be compatible with the second sentence of Article 1. These enfranchisements did not result in placing an excessive burden on the applicants, over and above the disadvantageous effects generally inherent for landlords in the application of the scheme set up under the leasehold reform legislation. Accordingly, the requisite balance under Article 1 was not destroyed....

C. First sentence of the first paragraph ('the peaceful enjoyment rule')

71. Alternatively and additionally, the applicants asserted a violation of their rights of peaceful enjoyment of property as guaranteed by the first sentence of Article 1.

The rule (in the second sentence) subjecting deprivation of possessions to certain conditions concerns a particular category, indeed the most radical kind, of interference with the right to peaceful enjoyment of property; the second sentence supplements and qualifies the general principle enuniciated in the first sentence. This being so, it is inconceivable that application of that general principle to the present case should lead to any conclusion different from that already arrived at by the Court in application of the second sentence.

[The Court concluded that Article 1 had not been violated.]....

$\sim$

QUESTIONS & COMMENTS

(1) The Court concludes that "[e]xpropriation legislation of wide sweep, in particular if it implements a programme of social and economic reform, is hardly capable of doing entire justice in the diverse circumstances of the very large number of different individuals concerned." *James v. United Kingdom* at §68. Is that an adequate reason for not providing individualized judicial determinations of the reasonableness of the expropriations? Given the fact that the European Court gives a greater margin of appreciation to states in the area of property than in other areas of civil rights, should it?

(2) The European Court has considered other programs of transferring land from one owner to another. In *Holy Monasteries v. Greece*, 301-A Eur. Ct. H.R. (ser. A) (1994), the Court faulted an effort by the Greek government to break up the large property holdings of the monasteries, partly because it provided no compensation and partly because it deprived the monasteries of access to court. It did not, however, find fault with the purpose of the law itself – to transfer property to poor farmers, among others.

In *Erkner and Hofauer v. Austria*, 117 Eur. Ct. H.R. (ser. A) (1987), 9 E.H.RR. 464, 486–489 (1987), the Court found a land consolidation law, involving forced exchanges of land, to violate Article 1 of Protocol No. 1. But the Court questioned the means rather than the end:

75. For the purposes of this provision, the Court must inquire whether a proper balance was struck between the demands of the community's general interest and the requirements of protecting the fundamental rights of the individual.

76. It should first be recalled that more than 16 years have already elapsed since the provisional transfer (10 August 1970–24 March 1987) without the applicants having received, under a final consolidation plan, the compensation in land provided for by law. According to the Government, the length of the proceedings is not a matter for consideration under Article 1 of Protocol No. 1 if the Court has already ruled it to have been in breach of Article 6(1) of the Convention. Such an argument is inconsistent with the Court's case law, from which it is apparent that one and the same fact may fall foul of more than one provision of the Convention and Protocols. Moreover, the complaint made under Article 6(1) can be distinguished from the complaint relating to Article 1 of the Protocol. In the former case, the question was one of determining whether the length of time of the consolidation proceedings had exceeded a 'reasonable time', whereas in the latter case their length – whether excessive or not – is material, together with other elements, in determining whether the disputed transfer was compatible with the guarantee of the right of property.

77. It should also be pointed out that the relevant provincial legislation did not permit any reconsideration of the provisional transfer, notwithstanding the applicants' successful appeals against the consolidation plans. Nor does it provide for the possibility of compensating the applicants financially for the loss they may have sustained on account of the forced exchange of their land for other inferior land pursuant to the provisional transfer.

78. The Court is not unmindful of the legislature's concern, however. In authorising a provisional transfer at an early stage of the consolidation process, its intention is to ensure that the land in question can be continuously and economically farmed in the interests of the landowners generally and of the community. Furthermore, although the applicants lost their land in consequence of the transfer decided on in 1970, they received other land in lieu, even if they are not satisfied with it. The applicable system, however, suffers from a degree of inflexibility: before the entry into force of a consolidation plan, it provides no means of altering the position of landowners or of compensating them for damage they may have sustained in the time up to the final award of the statutory compensation in land.

79. In the circumstances of the present case, therefore, the necessary balance between protection of the right of property and the requirements of the public interest was lacking: the applicants, who remain uncertain as to the final fate of their property, have been made to bear a disproportionate burden. There is no need at this stage to determine whether they have suffered actual prejudice.

80. The Court accordingly finds that there has been a breach of Article 1 of Protocol No. 1.

Id. at 488. *See also Poiss v. Austria*, 10 E.H.R.R. 231 (1988); *Prötsch v. Austria*, No. 67/1995/573/659, Eur. Ct. H.R. (Judgment of November 15, 1996).

(3) How would you argue that governments could have an affirmative customary international law duty to transfer property from one person/corporation to another? Consider the substantial treaty law guaranteeing the right to subsistence. What kind of facts would you need?

Does unfair payment for labor services provide legally sufficient grounds for transferring property to an unfairly compensated laborer? Does the European Court's allowing the U.K. government to have a wide margin of appreciation in transferring property to correct the inequities in *James v. United Kingdom* undercut an individual's claim that the state has a positive duty to transfer property in such a case?

Stran Greek Refineries and Stratis Andreadis v. Greece (Merits)
European Court of Human Rights
301-B Eur. Ct. H.R. (ser. A) (1994)
19 E.H.R.R. 293 (1995)

[In July 1972, Stratis Andreadis entered into a contract with the Greek military junta to build an oil refinery near Athens. The refinery was to be built by Stran Greek Refineries, of which Andreadis would be the sole shareholder. By Decree No. 450, also issued in July 1972, the junta permitted him to import U.S. $58 million to finance the refinery. In addition it agreed in the contract with Andreadis to purchase the land for the refinery no later than the end of 1972. In November 1973, although the land had already been expropriated and construction of the refinery had commenced, the junta decided to halt further work on it.

[After the democratic government was restored to power in 1974, it revoked the Decree and terminated the contract, relying on a special provision of the new Constitution which allowed the government to revoke "preferential" contracts given by the military. Stran sought compensation in the Athens Court of First Instance. The Government defended on the ground that the July 1972 contract provided for arbitration as the exclusive means of resolving disputes. The trial court rejected the defense on the ground that the termination of the contract had voided the arbitration clause, but the government commenced arbitration proceedings nevertheless. In those proceedings, Stran contended that the arbitral tribunal lacked jurisdiction. The arbitral court found that it had jurisdiction. Reaching the merits, the tribunal awarded Stran 116,273,442 drachmas, U.S. $16,054,165, and 614,627 FF, together with interest. It also declared that the government was wrongfully retaining a check for 240 million drachmas that Stran had given the government as security.

[The government then instituted a new action in the Athens Court of First Instance to set aside the arbitral award on the ground that the arbitral tribunal lacked jurisdiction. This time, the Court held that that arbitration clause had not voided the arbitration clause. Stran now withdrew its prior action in the Court. The Athens Court of Appeal upheld the judgment of the Court of First Instance. While the matter was on appeal to the Court of Cassation, the judge-rapporteur for the case sent his own opinion to the parties; the opinion recommended that the Government's appeal be dismissed. Shortly thereafter, before the Court of Cassation issued its judgment, the Greek legislature enacted Act 1701/1987. Section 12 provided:

> 1. The true and lawful meaning of the provisions of section 2(1) of Act 141/1975 concerning the termination of contracts entered into between 21 April 1967 and 24 July 1974 is that, upon the termination of these contracts, all their terms, conditions and clauses, including the arbitration clause, are ipso jure repealed and the arbitration tribunal no longer has jurisdiction.
>
> 2. Arbitration awards covered by paragraph 1 shall no longer be valid or enforceable.
>
> 3. Any principal or ancillary claims against the Greek State, expressed either in foreign or local currency, which arise out of the contracts entered into between 21 April 1967 and 24 July 1974, ratified by statute and terminated by virtue of Statute 141/1975, are now proclaimed time-barred.
>
> 4. Any court proceedings at whatever level pending at the time of the enactment of this statute, in respect of claims within the meaning of the preceding paragraph, are declared void.

[A Chamber of the Court initially held section 12 unconstitutional. Meeting in plenary session, however, the Court upheld the law on the ground that the question whether an arbitration clause survives the termination of a contract is a disputed legal question, and it was proper for the legislature to resolve it. (It did, however, hold that section 4 violated the principle of separation of powers.) The Court declared the arbitration award void. Before the European Court, Stran and Andreadis claimed violations of Article 6 and Article 1 of Protocol No. 1.]

. . . .

III. Alleged Violation of Article 1 of Protocol No. 1

. . .

1. Whether there was a "possession" within the meaning of Article 1

58. The principal thrust of the Government's argument was that no "possession" of the applicants, within the meaning of Article 1 of Protocol No. 1, had been subject to interference through the operation of Act 1701/1987.

In their view, neither judgment no. 13910/79 nor the arbitration award was sufficient to establish the existence of a claim against the State. A judicial decision that had not yet become final, or an arbitration award, could not be equated with the right which might be recognised by such decision or award.

In particular with regard to the arbitration award, an invalid procedure could not produce valid effects. The applicants had known perfectly well that the award would be a precarious legal basis for their financial claims until the question of its validity had been irrevocably settled. Judgment no. 5526/85 of the Athens Court of First Instance and judgment no. 9336/86 of the Athens Court of Appeal, which had initially found in favour of the applicants, were subject to review by the Court of Cassation and, before the latter court's final decision, could not form the basis of reasonable expectations concerning the right of property. Furthermore the applicants had themselves chosen to institute proceedings in the ordinary civil courts and had strenuously opposed the jurisdiction of the arbitration court.

Finally, the Government contended that the Strasbourg institutions should not themselves carry out an assessment of the applicants' complaints without having regard to all the arguments of the parties and their attitude before the arbitration court. The State had not recognised that there was any basis for Stran's alleged claim, the merits of which it had consistently disputed, first in the Athens Court of First Instance and then before the arbitration court. Even the proceedings to have the award set aside had of necessity entailed an indirect but implicit challenge to the merits of the decision.

59. In order to determine whether the applicants had a "possession" for the purposes of Article 1 of Protocol No. 1, the Court must ascertain whether judgment no. 13910/79 of the Athens Court of First Instance and the arbitration award had given rise to a debt in their favour that was sufficiently established to be enforceable.

60. In the nature of things, a preliminary decision prejudges the merits of a dispute by ordering an investigative measure. Although the Athens Court of First Instance would appear to have accepted the principle that the State owed a debt to the applicants – as the Commission likewise noted –, it nevertheless ordered that witnesses be heard before ruling on the existence and extent of the alleged damage. The effect of such a decision was merely to furnish the applicants with the hope that they would secure recognition of the claim put forward. Whether the resulting debt was enforceable would depend on any review by two superior courts.

61. This is not the case with regard to the arbitration award, which clearly recognised the State's liability up to a maximum of specified amounts in three different currencies.

The Court agrees with the Government that it is not its task to approve or disapprove the substance of that award. It is, however, under a duty to take note of the legal position established by that decision in relation to the parties.

According to its wording, the award was final and binding; it did not require any further enforcement measure and no ordinary or special appeal lay against it. Under the Greek legislation arbitration awards have the force of final decisions and are deemed to be enforceable. The grounds for appealing against them are exhaustively listed in Article 897 of the Code of Civil Procedure; no provision is made for an appeal on the merits.

62. At the moment when Act 1701/1987 was passed the arbitration award of 27 February 1984 therefore conferred on the applicants a right in the sums awarded. Admittedly, that right was revocable, since the award could still be annulled, but the ordinary courts had by then already twice held – at first instance and on appeal – that there was no ground for such annulment. Accordingly, in the Court's view, that right constituted a "possession" within the meaning of Article 1 of Protocol No. 1.

2. Whether there was an interference

63. In the applicants' submission, although no property was transferred to the State, the combined effect of paragraphs 2 and 3 of section 12 resulted in a *de facto* deprivation of their possessions because the result was literally to cancel the debt arising out of a final and binding arbitration award.

64. The Commission considered this to be an infringement of the right to the peaceful enjoyment of possessions within the meaning of the first sentence of the first paragraph of Article 1 of Protocol No. 1....

66. The Court finds that there was an interference with the applicants' right of property as guaranteed by Article 1 of Protocol No. 1. Paragraph 2 of section 12 of Act 1701/1987 declared the arbitration award void and unenforceable. Paragraph 3 provided that any claim against the State arising from contracts like those concluded by the applicants was statute-barred. Admittedly the Court of Cassation left open the question of the constitutionality of paragraph 3 and the applicants theoretically have the possibility, as the Government argued, of pursuing their 1978 action or bringing a new one. However, the prospects of success of such a step appear minimal. Indeed the question arises whether a first instance court would go so far as to hold this paragraph to be unconstitutional on the basis of general and abstract provisions of the Constitution, in the light in particular of the plenary Court of Cassation's decision of 16 March 1989 concerning paragraphs 1 and 2 of section 12. Both that decision and the judgment of the Court of Cassation of 11 April 1990 had the effect of closing the proceedings in issue once and for all, which was the real objective of the legislature in enacting section 12. This may be seen from the actual wording of paragraph 4, which was intended to bring to a conclusion the sole dispute of this nature pending before the courts at the time, namely that between the applicants and the State, and from the wording of paragraph 3, which was designed to exclude any future action.

67. It follows that it was impossible for the applicants to secure enforcement of an arbitration award having final effect and under which the State was required to pay them specified sums in respect of expenditure that they had incurred in seeking to fulfil their contractual obligations or even for them to take further action to recover the sums in question through the courts.

In conclusion, there was an interference with the applicants' property right.

3. Whether the interference was justified

68. The interference in question was neither an expropriation nor a measure to control the use of property; it falls to be dealt with under the first sentence of the first paragraph of Article 1.

69. The Court must therefore determine whether a fair balance was struck between the demands of the general interest of the community and the requirements of the protection of the individual's fundamental rights.

70. According to the Government, Acts 141/1975 and 1701/1987 pursued a public interest aim which in the specific context was of much broader significance than the mere elimination of the economic consequences of the dictatorship. These laws were part of a body of measures designed to cleanse public life of the disrepute attaching to the military regime and to proclaim the power and the will of the Greek people to defend the democratic institutions. The applicants' complaints derived from a preferential contract, prejudicial to the national economy, which had helped to sustain the regime and to give the impression at national and international level that it had the support of eminent figures from the Greek business world. The period that had elapsed between the restoration of democracy and the enactment of Act 1701/1987, the State's decision to opt for arbitration – a step of a purely technical nature – and the fact that Stran's claims related solely to the reimbursement of its expenses were immaterial.

71. The applicants did not contest the Government's assertion that the brutal practices of the military regime weighed more heavily on the scales of public interest than claims based on transactions concluded with that regime. However, the public interest that the Court was called upon to assess in the case before it was a different one. It would be unjust if every legal relationship entered into with a dictatorial regime was regarded as invalid when the regime came to an end. Moreover, the contract in question related to the construction of an oil refinery, which was of benefit to the economic infrastructure of the country.

72. The Court does not doubt that it was necessary for the democratic Greek State to terminate a contract which it considered to be prejudicial to its economic interests. Indeed according to the case law of international courts and of arbitration tribunals any State has a sovereign power to amend or even terminate a contract concluded with private individuals, provided it pays compensation. This both reflects recognition that the superior interests of the State take precedence over contractual obligations and takes account of the need to preserve a fair balance in a contractual relationship. However, the unilateral termination of a contract does not take effect in relation to certain essential clauses of the contract, such as the arbitration clause. To alter the machinery set up by enacting an authoritative amendment to such a clause would make it possible for one of the parties to evade jurisdiction in a dispute in respect of which specific provision was made for arbitration.

73. In this connection, the Court notes that the Greek legal system recognises the principle that arbitration clauses are autonomous and that the Athens Court of First Instance, the Athens Court of Appeals and, it would appear, the judge-rapporteur of the Court of Cassation applied this principle in the present case. Moreover the two courts found that the applicants' claims originating before the termination of the contract were not invalidated thereby.

The State was therefore under a duty to pay the applicants the sums awarded against it at the conclusion of the arbitration procedure, a procedure for which it had itself opted and the validity of which had been accepted until the day of the hearing in the Court of Cassation.

74. By choosing to intervene at that stage of the proceedings in the Court of Cassation by a law which invoked the termination of the contract in question in order to declare void the arbitration clause and to annul the arbitration award of 27 February 1984, the legislature upset, to the detriment of the applicants, the balance that must be struck between the protection of the right of property and the requirements of public interest.

75. There has accordingly been a violation of Article 1 of Protocol No. 1.

~

QUESTIONS & COMMENTS

(1) *Stran Greek Refineries* deals with one of the problems that arise when an undemocratic regime is replaced by a democratic one. The successor regime is frequently unwilling to honor the arrangements entered into by its predecessor. Such transitions have occurred twice in U.S. history. During the Revolution, many states seized property owned by Loyalists who had fled. The treaty ending the Revolution sought to stabilize property holdings by barring future confiscations. *Martin v. Hunter's Lessee*, 14 U.S. (1 Wheat.) 304 (1816), a case noted primarily for its discussion of the relation between the Supreme Court and state courts, involved a controversy over the interpretation of this treaty provision. Questions of transition arose again after the Civil War. Section 4 of the Fourteenth Amendment repudiated debts incurred by the rebellious southern states; section 3 disqualified from federal office those who, having previously taken an oath to uphold the Constitution, took part in rebellion against the United States. The Supreme Court held unconstitutional further disqualifications. *See Ex parte Garland*, 71 U.S. (4 Wall.) 333 (1866) (invalidating congressional statute barring lawyers from practice before Supreme Court unless they could swear that they had never fought against the United States, as applied to a lawyer who had received a full presidential pardon). It also held that Congress could not restrict the federal courts' jurisdiction over claims for compensation for property seized from participants in the rebellion who had received full pardons. *United States v. Klein*, 80 U.S. (13 Wall.) 128 (1871).

What policy considerations should affect the way a successor regime deals with obligations made by its predecessor? With participants in the predecessor's activities?

(2) Does the European Court of Human Rights question Greece's power to terminate contracts entered into under the Greek dictatorship?

(3) At what point does an obligation on a debt become sufficiently definite to make it a "possession" for purposes of Protocol No. 1, art. 1? Suppose there had been no arbitration clause, and the case had proceeded through the courts. Would a decision at the trial court level in favor of Stran constituted a "possession"?

(4) Is *Stran* consistent with *Pressos Compania Naviera S. A. and Others v. Belgium*, 332 Eur. Ct. H.R. (ser. A) (1995)? *Stran* determined that the arbitral award was a "possession" because, by its terms, it was final and binding, suggesting that had it been preliminary or subject to further review, it would not have been property. *Pressos* holds that a tort claim became an asset the moment the claim accrued, even if no action had yet been brought. However, note that in both cases, the Court refused to permit a state to work a retroactive

change in the law to its own benefit. How strongly should such concerns influence the definition of property interests?

(5) Where do property rights come from? Are they purely the creature of positive law? If so, then what was wrong with the Greek legislature's enactment of a statute in effect defining a property right – by providing that under Greek law arbitral clauses fell with a terminated contract? If the answer is that Stran had relied on the previous law, how reasonable was the reliance, given that the issue was apparently undecided under Greek law? Suppose a state enacted a statute declaring that it retained the right to redefine property rights from time to time. Should that make a difference? How likely is it that a state concerned with stability of property rights would enact such a statute?

(6) No one would dispute that a legislature could establish a general rule providing that when a contract is terminated, the arbitration clause terminates as well. Does *Stran* imply that Article 6 is violated whenever legislative changes in the law are made applicable to pending proceedings? If so, what implications would this have for common law adjudication, in which courts typically apply new interpretations of rules to the case in which they announce the change? Or is the holding of *Stran* more narrowly confined to cases in which the legislature's action affects a contract to which the state itself is party? *Cf. United States Trust Co. v. New Jersey*, 431 U.S. 1 (1977) (closely scrutinizing state's abrogation of provision of contract to which it was a party).

6. Theory and Critique

In this section, we address the theoretical and critical approaches to international human rights and humanitarian law. By placing these materials at the end of the casebook's treatment of the historical, organizational, procedural, and substantive aspects of human rights and humanitarian law, we believe that students will be in a better position to understand the abstract and critical issues raised by the following works.

Richard Falk
The End of World Order:
Essays on Normative International Relations (1983)

[An] important development in the 350 years that have elapsed since Grotius did his work is the changed character of the sovereign state. The government of such a state can no longer be associated with a series of European Christian princes. In the contemporary world, the state is more typically dominated by a faceless bureaucracy that is governed by leaders who are selected and rejected at short intervals or are kept in power for longer periods by sheer brute force, and whose religious and cultural backgrounds embrace the diversities of the main global traditions. The Grotian solution presupposed the personal character of royal rulership in Europe and is not fully transferable to global bureaucracies and the secularization of power that has evolved into the modern post-seventeenth-century state and that has steadily diffused the responsibility and eroded the spirituality of political leadership. . . .

Given the peculiar burdens posed by nuclear weaponry, ecological decay, population pressures, and expectations of equity, the renewal of the Grotian quest in our time cannot rely credibly on a shared heritage of normative traditions as reinforced by the conscience of contemporary leaders. What makes our situation seem so desperate is the vagueness, and even dubiousness, of the normative heritage (especially for non-Western societies) and uncertain contours of the emergent structure. We seem caught in a historical movement where the burdens on the old order are too great to bear, and yet the new alternative order that hopefully lies beyond the presently perceived horizon of attainability casts no shadow backwards from the future that can be reliably and persuasively discerned. . . .

Perhaps we should regard the faddish prominence temporarily accorded to human rights diplomacy as a pathetic reenactment of the Grotian quest. The normative claim embodied in human rights is, quite simply, that leaders of governments can continue to pursue nationalistic economic, social and political goals, only if in governing peoples within their territory, they will abide by the most minimal decencies required by international

938

law. No further accusation is mounted by most rights advocates against the state system as such. Admittedly, the humanizing potential of adhering to human rights is considerable and should not be belittled even in relation to global concerns about peace, justice, and ecological balance. Whether contemporary global and national structures of power actually will allow this potential to be tapped is doubtful. Repression seems integral to the structure. . . .

Compared to the ferment of the seventeenth century with the new logic of the state system taking over from the feudal logic, our transitional challenge is more dangerous and bewildering. The statist logic has not yet been seriously challenged by an alternative logic.

. . . . Most proposals for global reform have uncritically affirmed the ordering contributions of the state to domestic life and have, in one or another form, sought to make those contributions available to the world as a whole. Indeed, the argument for global reform, at least since World War I, has assumed the strident tones of necessity. Since Hiroshima these claims of necessity have been pitched on an apocalyptic level and have been extended to embrace biosocial survival in light of the apparently deepening ecological crisis – the crowding, poisoning, and straining of planetary facilities. The unexamined premise in world order thinking has been that *only* governmental solutions can organize planetary life, that only existing governmental structures and their leaders can command the authority required for this essential undertaking, and that only argument and persuasion can release the political energy needed to overcome the inertia that sustains the state system in the face of the most unmistakable writing on the wall. A major variant to this line of reformist thinking is that persuasion must be supplemented by tragedy before enough political energy is released to achieve a world order solution.

Generally, such advocacy of bureaucratic centralism is coupled with confidence in the moderating capacities of law and institutionalism. The ideal world order would still consist of a realm of states, but with the venom drawn by substituting "law" for "force." Conflict would remain, but war would disappear. Peaceful methods of resolving conflicts would be accepted since all states would be unanimously committed to upholding the federalist edifice.

C. History of Public International Law and Alternative Perspectives

This kind of mainstream "idealism" often coexists with "realism." Until the existing world system is reconstructed according to the principles of legal architecture, one is thrown back onto the state system with its logic of power and its reliance on force to achieve "security" and to "manage" change. The world order idealist of tomorrow can easily justify being Machiavellian today. Hence, the issue of "transition" emerges as critical, and it is a fascinating indictment of mainstream thinking that no sustained attention has been given to the central challenge of transition – namely, access to and transformation of state power.

The anarchist comes forward with a quite different set of ideas, easily adapted to the world order debate: first of all, a skeptical look at the state and an unwillingness to accept it as "a model" for achieving a just order on any level of social organization; second, a positive belief in the capacities of various other collectivities – communes, cities, provinces, regions, associations – to provide the creative impetus for reorganizing the human enterprise; third, a bias toward decentralization of wisdom, authority, and capability, coupled with an insistence upon the autonomy of smaller units and the absolute status of individual liberty; fourth, a structural critique of the present organi-zation of power, wealth, and prestige coupled with a revolutionary set of demands that existing leaders of society would never voluntarily meet; fifth, a processive view of the future, based on embodying the vision of a new order in immediate personal and political activities; sixth, a substitution of "justice" for "order" as the primary test of the adequacy of a given arrangement of power on world society; seventh, a refusal to blueprint the future in a manner that precludes creativity within the eventual setting that will give rise to the possibility of revolution itself. . . . [T]he anarchist case for radical reform (*i.e.*, for social revolution) was *chimerical within* the confines of the state system. However, the state system is now being superseded. In this context, one set of plausible possibilities is the globalization of social life in a way that allows cooperative organizational forms to flourish. That is, the anarchist vision . . . of a fusion between a universal confederation and organic social forms of a communal character lies at the very center of the *only* hopeful prospect for the future of world order. Needless to say, such a prospect has slim chances for success, but at least the possibility is no longer chimerical, given the change of objective circumstances. The state system is not an immovable form, for many economic, political, technological, and sociological forces are everywhere undermining its bases of potency, if unevenly and at an uncertain rate. Therefore, although the political precondition of scale assumed by anarchism still remains formidable, it may yet prove historically realizable. It may be realizable because the preparatory processes going on throughout the world during this historical period are creating more favorable global conditions for the anar-chist dream than have hitherto existed for centuries. This assessment arises because of several distinct developments. Perhaps the most significant is a growing disenchantment with the values, goals, and methods of industrial society. This sense of disenchantment is coming to be shared by increasing numbers of citizens, particularly in the developed nations of the West, and is finding various forms of expression that reflect revised notions of necessity based on "limits to growth," notions of well-being based on intermediate technology and small-scale institutions, and notions of personal transcendence based on a new spiritual energy that repudiates both conventional religion and secular humanism. In this setting, the quest for an appropriate politics converges rather dramatically with the central tenets of anarchist belief. This modern sensibility understands, at last, that the state is simultaneously *too large* to satisfy human needs and *too small* to cope with the requirements of guidance needed by an increasingly interdependent planet. This realiza-tion is temporarily offset by a rising tide of statism in many other parts of the world where political independence is a forbidden fruit only recently tasted, but where the fruit will be poisoned, as everywhere else, by a world of nuclear weapons, ecological decay, and mass economic privation. The main *problematique* of our age is whether an appropriate politics of global reform, combining a centralized form of functional guidance with decentralized economic, social, and political structures, can be shaped by voluntary action, or whether it must be formed in a crucible of tragedy and catastrophe. . . .

∾

QUESTIONS & COMMENTS

(1)   Professor Falk's essay was written in 1983 – *before* the demise of the Soviet Union and *before* the enormous expansion in the use of telefax, personal computers, and the Internet.

What are the implications of these revolutionary developments for international human rights and humanitarian law advocates in light of Falk's description of the changing global order and his concerns? Can international organizations or the United States completely fill the power vacuum created by the collapse of the Soviet Union? Are they doing so now? Is the use of these telecommunication devices by individuals, NGOs, and large and small businesses now providing a significant means of eroding the state's role in a global community?

In the following passages, Professor Henkin provides a sort of "phenomenology" of international human rights. He describes how international human rights is *now* understood. In reading the following excerpts, keep in mind the changing global order.

Louis Henkin
The Age of Rights (1990)

Introduction: The Human Rights Idea

. . . .

Individual rights as a political idea draws on natural laws and its offspring, natural rights. In its modern manifestation that idea is traced to John Locke, to famous articulations in the American Declaration of Independence and in the French Declaration of the Rights of Man and of the Citizen, and to realizations of the idea in the United States Constitution and its Bill of Rights and in the constitutions and laws of modern states.

The idea of human rights that has received currency and universal (if nominal) acceptance in our day owes much to these antecedents but it is discrete and different from them. The contemporary version does not ground or justify itself in natural law, in social contract, or in any other political theory. In international instruments representatives of states declare and recognize human rights, define their content, and ordain their consequences within political societies and in the system of nation-states. The justification of human rights is rhetorical, not philosophical. Human rights are self-evident, implied in other ideas that are commonly intuited and accepted. Human rights are derived from accepted principles, or are required by accepted ends – societal ends such as peace and justice; individual ends such as human dignity, happiness, and fulfillment.

What the pattern of declared norms amounts to, the idea it reflects, is nowhere articulated. I attempt to do so here, not as a philosophical construct, but as a distillation of what underlies national and international instruments.

Human rights are rights of individuals in society. Every human being has, or is entitled to have, "rights" – legitimate, valid, justified claims – upon his or her society; claims to various "goods" and benefits. . . .

Human rights are universal: they belong to every human being in every human society. They do not differ with geography or history, culture or ideology, political or economic system, or stage of societal development. To call them "human" implies that all human beings have them, equally and in equal measure, by virtue of their humanity, regardless of sex, race, age; regardless of high or low "birth," social class, national origin, ethnic or tribal affiliation; regardless of wealth or poverty, occupation, talent, merit, religion, ideology, or other commitment. Implied in one's humanity, human rights are inalienable and imprescriptible: they cannot be transferred, forfeited, or waived; they cannot be lost by having been usurped, or by one's failure to exercise or assert them.

Human rights are *rights*; they are not merely aspirations, or assertions of the good. To call them rights is not to assert, merely, that the benefits indicated are desirable or necessary; or, merely, that it is "right" that the individual shall enjoy these goods; or even, merely, that it is the duty of society to respect the immunity or provide the benefits. To call them "rights" implies that they are claims "as of right," not by appeal to grace, or charity, or brotherhood or love; they need not be earned or deserved. The idea of rights implies entitlement on the part of the holder in some order under some applicable norm; the idea of human rights implies entitlement in a moral order under a moral law, to be translated into and confirmed as legal entitlement in the legal order of a political society. When a society recognizes that a person has a right, it affirms, legitimates, and justifies that entitlement, and incorporates and establishes it in the society's system of values, giving it important weight in competition with other societal values.

Human rights imply the obligation of society to satisfy those claims. The state must develop institutions and procedures, must plan, must mobilize resources as necessary to meet those claims. Political and civil rights require laws, institutions, procedures, and other safeguards against tyranny, against corrupt, immoral, and inefficient agencies or officials. Economic and social rights in modern society require taxation and spending and a network of agencies for social welfare. The idea of human rights implies also that society must provide some system of remedies to which individuals may resort to obtain the benefits to which they are entitled or be compensated for their loss. Together, the affirmation of entitlement, the recognition by society of an obligation to mobilize itself to discharge it, and the implication of remedy all enhance the likelihood that the rights will be realized, that individuals will actually enjoy the benefits to which they are entitled.

Human rights are claims upon society. These claims may derive from moral principles governing relations between persons, but it is society that bears the obligation to satisfy the claims. Of course, the official representatives of society must themselves respect individual freedoms and immunities; political society must also act to protect the individuals's rights against private invasion. As regards claims to economic and social benefits, society must act as insurer to provide them if individuals cannot provide them for themselves. Thus, government must protect me from assault by my neighbor, or from wolves, and must ensure that I have bread or hospitalization; in human rights terms my rights are against the state, not against the neighbor or the wolves, the baker or the hospital. The state may arrange to satisfy my claims by remedies in tort against my neighbor, or administrative remedies against a corrupt, misguided, or inefficient bureaucrat, or access to public schools or health services. Those legal rights and remedies against individuals or agencies within society give effect to my human rights claims upon society.

. . . .

In sum, the idea of human rights is that the individual counts – independent of and in addition to his or her part in the common good. Autonomy and liberty must be respected, and the individual's basic economic-social needs realized, as a matter of entitlement, not of grace or discretion (even by wise and benevolent authority, or even by "the people").

. . . .

Ch. 1: The Internationalization of Human Rights

. . . .

I stress – and distinguish – those two different manifestations of general, worldwide concern with human rights. "Universalization" has brought acceptance, at least in principle and rhetoric, of the concept of individual human rights by all societies and governments and is reflected in national constitutions and law. "Internationalization" has brought agreement, at least in political-legal principle and in rhetoric, that individual human rights are of "international concern" and a proper subject for diplomacy, international institutions, and international law.

Strictly, "international human rights," that is, human rights as a subject of international law and politics, are to be distinguished from individual rights in national societies under national legal systems, but the two are not unrelated in law or in politics. The international movement accepts human rights as rights that, according to agreed-upon moral principles, the individual should enjoy under the constitutional-legal system of his or her society. But national protections for accepted human rights are often deficient; international human rights were designed to induce states to remedy those deficiencies. That would be done by establishing a common international standard by which to judge national rights systems, and by inducing states to undertake international obligations to abide by those standards and to submit to international "machinery" that would monitor compliance. The law, politics, and institutions of international human rights, then, do not replace national laws and institutions; they provide additional international protections for rights under national law. The international law of human rights is implemented largely by national law and institutions; it is satisfied when national laws and institutions are sufficient.

QUESTIONS & COMMENTS

(1) What about human duties? Many international human rights instruments impose duties on private individuals (*e.g.*, right against discrimination). Does not the assertion of rights entail private duties? If so, in which cases and why?

(2) Professor Henkin states that "[t]he justification of human rights is rhetorical, not philosophical. Human rights are self-evident, implied in other ideas that are commonly intuited and accepted." Compare Henkin's statement with William Gass' essay, *The Case of the Obliging Stranger*, which discusses the sometimes absurd endeavors philosophers and theorists undertake in justifying why something is right or wrong. Gass presents the grotesque – and somewhat humorous – story of a stranger who obliges the essayist his wish to cook the stranger in an oven. Although this is a clear case of evil, explanations for its being evil are often unacceptable to philosophers and theorists:

> For if someone asks me, now [that] I am repentant, why I regard my act of baking the obliging stranger as wrong, what can I do but point again to the circumstances comprising the act? "Well, I put this fellow in an oven, you see. The oven was on, don't you know." And if my questioner persists, saying, "Of course, I know all about *that*; but what I want to know is, why is *that* wrong?" I should recognize there is no use in replying that it is wrong because of the kind of act it is, a wrong one, for my questioner is clearly suffering from a sort of *folie de doute morale*. . . .[1]

A moral philosopher who tries to explain why an act is clearly wrong or right sounds comical, as does anyone who gives elaborate reasons for the obvious. In the end, moral

---

[1] William Gass, *The Case of the Obliging Stranger*, FICTIONS AND THE FIGURES OF LIFE 230 (1970).

explanations *look* like purely factual descriptions, but they do drive toward something else that is not sufficiently expressible. As Ludwig Wittgenstein once observed, when individuals give moral reasons, they "thrust against the limits of language."[2]

With this in mind, Professor Stephen Toulmin has argued for a casuistic approach to moral decision making.[3] Moral justifications should not take the form of syllogistic reasoning with its appeal to universal principles. Such appeals go in the opposite direction that decision making should be taking. Such principles often tell more about the rhetoric of political, economic, religious, or cultural positions. Rather, the best approach in moral decision making is a discerning examination of facts in a case-by-case approach. Such an approach is substantially aided by the use of interdisciplinary insights. Consider the use of case law as a particularly authoritative source of customary international law in light of these ideas.

Yash Ghai

Universalism and Relativism: Human Rights as a Framework for
Negotiating Interethnic Claims
21 CARDOZO L. REV. 1095–1102(2000)

Introduction

The controversy surrounding the universalism or relativism of human rights has intensi-fied in recent years, and has been brought to bear on the credentials of the Universal Dec-laration of Human Rights ("UDHR"). The controversy has relevance not only in the con-text of East-West debates, but also, and more immediately and concretely, in the political and cultural organization of most states which are now multiethnic and multicultural. . . .

There are various reasons for the resurgence of the controversy. An obvious one is the salience that the rights discourse has achieved and the reaction to it. Moreover, until now the non-Western world did not feel able to challenge the West. The rapid economic development of Southeast and East Asian states gave those states the confidence to challenge what they considered the intellectual hegemony of the West. Their assertion of "Asian values" was partly a response to what was perceived to be the imposition on them of Western values in the form of human rights. Therefore, we have to recognize a significant element of "nationalism" rather than some simple notion of culture in the debate on relativism. This factor becomes even more important as more states assume the responsibility to foster their "indigenous" culture. Furthermore, "Asian values" were asserted for domestic reasons as an attempt to legitimize authoritarianism.

Another challenge to universalism has come from schools of Islamic thought, particu-larly in the Middle East, which are also resentful of Western pressures. The globalization of economies has also brought cultures into greater contact, and made most states multi-ethnic, with contradictory consequences. On one hand, there is greater knowledge of other cultures that produces a sympathetic understanding of diversity and emphasis on human solidarity. On the other hand, globalization itself has produced a sense of alienation and powerlessness in the face of new global forces, in which one's identity

---

[2] Ludwig Wittgenstein, "A Lecture on Ethics," delivered sometime between September 1929 and December 1930, first published in 74 PHIL. REV. 12 (1965).

[3] Stephen Toulmin, *Equity and Principles*, 20 Osgoode Hall L. J. 15 (1982).

depends even more fundamentally on one's culture, while that culture may be perceived to be under threat from external forces. Amidst predictions of the clash of cultures, there is the danger that the controversy will become damaging, as it has already proved sterile and unproductive.

The concept of the universality of human rights is based on the notion that: (a) there is a universal human nature; (b) this human nature is knowable; (c) it is knowable by reason; and (d) human nature is essentially different from other reality. This centrality of the human being elevates the autonomy of the individual to the highest value; rights become essentially a means of realizing that autonomy. Each individual is, in a certain sense, absolute. He or she is irreducible to another and separated in his or her autonomy from society. In the formative years for the recognition of human rights in the West, rights were seen as catering to the selfish instincts of man – the bourgeois man of Hobbes and Locke, although Kantian revision introduced the notion of self-esteem which in our own times has been considered the basis for identity.

The relativist challenge to universalism is based on challenging some of these assumptions. Opponents of "universalism" admit that rights are drawn from human nature, but assert that human nature is not an abstraction, because humans are defined by their relation to others and as part of a society of like-minded people. A human person is not separate from, or above, society. Since societies vary from culture to culture, evaluations are relative to the cultural background out of which they arise; a society or culture cannot be criticized on the basis of its external value.

It is often assumed in this debate that "universalists" are westerners and "relativists" are easterners. It is also assumed that the UDHR represents Western concepts of the individual and his or her rights. However, many easterners argue that their cultural and religious texts contain ideas of justice, equality, and fairness, which are the foundations of rights. They compare rights in the UDHR with the values of their own cultures and religion, and thereby support the notion of universalism.

Relativist positions are not based only on culture, although this is the most common source of relativism. Until recently, the view of the People's Republic of China was that rights and rights consciousness were based on the material conditions in society. Rights which are appropriate to, and feasible in, a rich and developed country are not suitable for, or possible in, a poorer country – a kind of materialistic relativism.

The positions of cultural relativists vary widely. The most extreme position is that the validity of human rights depends entirely on the "culture" of the community. It is therefore not possible to criticize the conduct of a state on grounds of some supposed universal norms (although it can, of course, be criticized internally for failing to live up to that culture's standards). Another version of an absolute "relativist" position holds that there are indeed cultural differences which bear on the concept of rights, but that only the Western concept of human rights is acceptable as a basis for universal norms. A similar kind of approach seems to be adopted by some Asian politicians who, resentful of the criticism by the West of their human rights record, now argue that their societies are superior to the West, as they are based on harmony rather than conflict. Duties are a better way to ensure the objectives sought by rights; they are less adversarial and help in the cultivation of virtue. Human rights are not desirable, as they elevate the individual above the community, and can damage the fabric and cohesion of society. The moderate cultural relativist position is that some human rights standards are universal and must be respected by all. There is an overlapping of values which can be used to establish a common core of human rights.

Some commentators argue for cultural pluralism, believing that it is possible to reconcile conscience with love of tradition. They believe that there are some necessary international standards for human rights, but cultures will have various ways of understanding them. If there is to be any legitimacy to these standards among the people of the culture, it will have to come from within that culture by reinterpreting texts. Advocates of intercultural discourse are connected with the preceding view. They argue that all cultures have valuable norms and insights. By acknowledging this, and by seeking intercultural understanding, we can enrich the concept of rights and strive towards a new form of universalism. Just as the mixing of cultures has enriched cultures, so variations in contexts and concepts of rights can be enriching.

Traditional discussions of the controversy on universalism and relativism have been conducted in ideological terms, with relatively little attention paid to the actual practices of states. Some resolution of this controversy is necessary for further progress in developing policies to implement human rights. More recent studies have moved away from the older polarities towards a creative potential on the part of intercultural discourses for enriching the concept and substance of rights. In this article, I criticize many of the assumptions underlying the controversy, and argue for a more pragmatic and historical, and less ideological, approach. There is no simple way to argue about universalism or relativism in light of the expansion of the concepts and contents of rights, which came as a response to the multiplicity of values and traditions in a rapidly changing global culture.

In seeking to go beyond the debates on universalism and relativism, I do not engage them directly. Instead, operating at a more empirical level, I discuss how a multicultural society organizes the protection of human rights by examining debates about the provisions on and (to a lesser extent) the practice of rights in four countries – India, Canada, South Africa, and Fiji. These countries not only represent different cultural and religious traditions, but also share the common experience of struggling to manage conflicts arising from their ethnic and religious diversity. The conclusion that I draw from their experiences is that, in the discourse on rights, concerns with culture are less important than the balance of power and the competition for resources. Rights are rarely absolute; there are various mechanisms for balancing different interests that inhere in or surround the right. Balance must also be struck between different types of rights. Some forms of special treatment are not incompatible with the right to equality. All of these factors allow considerable flexibility in using rights as an organizing matrix. The framework of rights has been used with considerable success in mediating competing ethnic and cultural claims. As the cultural problems of more and more states take on a common form, a new version of universal human rights is emerging.

I. Relativism: A Critical Assessment

The danger in the debate outlined above lies in drawing false polarities. The debate misses many dimensions of rights. It makes a number of assumptions with little, if any, empirical support. There are many contradictions, too. The most strident critics of universalism are themselves ardent proselytizers. Those who decry external criticism are vehement in their own denunciations of foreign cultures or political systems. I shall make several points in a brief and dogmatic manner; they provide the groundwork for my national case studies. The following propositions relate to the nature of rights, to the nature of culture, and to the relationship between the two concepts:

(1) Rights are not necessarily emanations or reflections of culture. In many societies there is much oppression in the name of culture and tradition. "Rights" are valuable because they are ahead of "culture." Rights talk has produced powerful ideas which interrogate culture: equality, feminism, social justice. Most cultures have some notion of rights. In some they are latent – they can germinate when conditions change.

(2) Even more fundamentally, the concept of culture is problematic. Culture is protean: it is usually connected with religion, language, history, folklore, values, dress, cuisine, and, more broadly, the way people live. Which of these is privileged at a particular moment, as the crucial manifestation of "culture," is more a matter of political choice than inherent value to the identity of a community. States have always claimed the right to elaborate the culture of their communities; the current debate is essentially between states advancing different views of culture for reasons only tangentially connected with culture.

(3) No community has a static culture, especially today when each community is confronted with a multiplicity of images, and exposure to others' ways of life. Rights consciousness itself affects culture; knowledge of other cultures or moral ideas may make an individual aware of his or her inferior status in society.

(4) Cultures change and intermix – there are multiple cross-cutting cleavages which blur cultural differences between nations, although there are times when, under manipulation by some, one characteristic seems to dominate all others.

(5) There is no homogeneity of culture in a state. Considerable state effort is expended in creating a common culture, even (or perhaps especially) in states whose leaders pose as champions of relativism. There is, for example, the culture of: the military; bureaucrats; academics; professionals; diplomats; trade unionists; and business people. Each has different interests in "rights." Individual or group perception of rights depends on one's economic or social class in society. It is more important to pay attention to the scope and politics of "rights" than to preconceptions of their cultural lineages.

(6) The material bases of "rights" are stronger than cultural bases. The concept of rights has changed over time. Historically rights have been both revolutionary and conservative. Different political systems use different ideologies of rights. Rights serve different purposes in different societies, making the cultural relativism argument exceedingly complex. It is also possible to periodize phases in the rights movement which owe more to global material factors than to the force of culture.

(7) Rights are primarily a matter that arises between state and citizens. They originate in response to the development of market economies and the centralization of states. They are less cultural than "political," are considered necessary whenever political power separates itself from the community, and therefore are particularly necessary in many Asian and African countries where states, however weak internationally, tend to dominate their civil societies.

(8) It follows that the threat to culture from rights may be exaggerated. Culture, as defined in the debate, is primarily a matter of interpersonal or intrafamily relations, and thus no great concern of rights.

(9) There is little doubt that forcing diverse communities to live together has sharpened the debate about relativism, especially in the post-colonial period. The key moral question of our time is the basis on which diverse peoples can coexist and interact. More specifically, the question is whether in this multicultural world a particular view or belief can be regarded as the overriding international consensus on rights and values. I believe that a regime of rights, because of its inherent diversity, is a suitable foundation for intercultural dialogues and consensus.

(10) There are many kinds of rights now. Much of the debate on relativism takes place in the context of civil and political rights, which are supposed to have their origins in Western philosophy. This view disregards the fact that rights are no longer tied to one dominant tradition. Rights are justified on differing bases – from "natural law," or nature of the human person, to more material explanations. The concept of rights is much more diverse today, in response to different economic or social traditions and to emerging needs. In particular, there is wide acceptance of social, economic, and cultural rights. There is great concern (at least at the level of rhetoric) with the disadvantages or oppression of particular classes of persons: women, children, and indigenous peoples. This has, to some extent, shifted the focus away from individuals and has facilitated the recognition of group rights and remedies. It has also focused attention on the material conditions and civil society as causes of oppression, balancing the obsession with the wickedness of the state.

(11) These enriching developments in the menu of rights have prompted the need for tradeoffs between different categories of rights. The diversity also facilitates the "contextualization" of rights and allows a balance between different values and goals.

(12) The notion of rights as used by anthropologists or philosophers is different from that employed by lawyers. Anthropologists consider rights more absolute, interpersonal, and more comprehensive in their range. Lawyers are less committed to absolutes and often seek to strike balances. They operate under some form of the doctrine of margin of appreciation, permitting qualifications of rights. The grounds for qualifications are drawn from notions of proper conduct embedded in culture. The doctrine leads to the new orthodox view that to accept universality does not mean that each culture has to understand a right in precisely the same way or accept the whole range of rights.

(13) For multicultural states, human rights as a negotiated understanding of the acceptable framework for coexistence and the respect for each culture are more important than for monocultural or mono-ethnic societies, where other forms of solidarity and identity can be invoked to minimize or cope with conflicts. In other words, it is precisely where the concept and conceptions of rights are most difficult that they are most needed. The task is difficult, but possible, even if it may not be always completely successful. And most states today in fact are multicultural, whether as a result of immigration or because their peoples are finding new identities.

. . . .

∼

Abdullah Ahmen An-Na'im
Human Rights in the Muslim World:
Socio-Political Conditions and Scriptural Imperatives
3 HARV. HUM. RTS. J. 13 (1990)[1]

INTRODUCTION

Historical formulations of Islamic religious law, commonly known as Shari'a, include a universal system of law and ethics and purport to regulate every aspect of public and private life. The power of Shari'a to regulate the behavior of Muslims derives from its moral and religious authority as well as the formal enforcement of its legal norms. As such, Shari'a influences individual and collective behavior in Muslim countries through its role in the socialization processes of such nations regardless of its status in their formal legal systems. For example, the status and rights of women in the Muslim world have always been significantly influenced by Shari'a, regardless of the degree of Islamization in public life. Of course, Shari'a is not the sole determinant of human behavior nor the only formative force behind social and political institutions in Muslim countries.

. . . .

I conclude that human rights advocates in the Muslim world must work within the framework of Islam to be effective. They need not be confined, however, to particular historical interpretations of Islam known as Shari'a. Muslims are obliged, as a matter of faith, to conduct their private and public affairs in accordance with the dictates of Islam, but there is room for legitimate disagreement over the precise nature of these dictates in the modern context. Religious texts, like all other texts, are open to a variety of interpretations. Human rights advocates in the Muslim world should struggle to have their interpretations of the relevant texts adopted as the new Islamic scriptural imperatives for the contemporary world.

A. *Cultural Legitimacy for Human Rights*

The basic premise of my approach is that human rights violations reflect the lack or weakness of cultural legitimacy of international standards in a society. Insofar as these standards are perceived to be alien to or at variance with the values and institutions of a people, they are unlikely to elicit commitment or compliance. While cultural legitimacy may not be the sole or even primary determinant of compliance with human rights standards, it is, in my view, an extremely significant one. Thus, the underlying causes of any lack or weakness of legitimacy of human rights standards must be addressed in order to enhance the promotion and protection of human rights in that society.

. . . . This cultural illegitimacy, it is argued, derives from the historical conditions surrounding the creation of the particular human rights instruments. Most African and Asian countries did not participate in the formulation of the Universal Declaration of Human Rights because, as victims of colonization, they were not members of the United Nations. When they did participate in the formulation of subsequent instruments, they did so on the basis of an established framework and philosophical assumptions adopted in their absence. For example, the preexisting framework and assumptions favored individual civil and political rights over collective solidarity rights, such as the right to development, an outcome which remains problematic today. Some authors have gone so far as to argue

---

[1] Most footnotes and citations omitted. Ed.'s Note.

that inherent differences exist between the Western notion of human rights as reflected in the international instruments and non-Western notions of human dignity. In the Muslim world, for instance, there are obvious conflicts between Shari'a and certain human rights, especially of women and non-Muslims.

. . . . In this discussion, I focus on the principles of legal equality and nondiscrimination contained in many human rights instruments. These principles relating to gender and religion are particularly problematic in the Muslim world.

II. ISLAM, SHARI'A AND HUMAN RIGHTS

. . . .

A. *The Development and Current Application of Shari'a*

To the over nine hundred million Muslims of the world, the Qur'an is the literal and final word of God and Muhammad is the final Prophet. During his mission, from 610 A.D. to his death in 632 A.D., the Prophet elaborated on the meaning of the Qur'an and supplemented its rulings through his statements and actions. This body of information came to be known as Sunna. He also established the first Islamic state in Medina around 622 A.D. which emerged later as the ideal model of an Islamic state. . . .

While the Qur'an was collected and recorded soon after the Prophet Muhammad's death, it took almost two centuries to collect, verify and record the Sunna. Because it remained an oral tradition for a long time during a period of exceptional turmoil in Muslim history, some Sunna reports are still controversial in terms of both their authenticity and relationship to the Qur'an.

Because Shari'a is derived from Sunna as well as the Qur'an, its development as a comprehensive legal and ethical system had to await the collection and authentication of Sunna. Shari'a was not developed until the second and third centuries of Islam. . . .

. . . .

Shari'a is not a formally enacted legal code. It consists of a vast body of jurisprudence in which individual jurists express their views on the meaning of the Qur'an and Sunna and the legal implications of those views. Although most Muslims believe Shari'a to be a single logical whole, there is significant diversity of opinion not only among the various schools of thought, but also among the different jurists of a particular school. . . .

Furthermore, Muslim jurists were primarily concerned with the formulation of principles of Shari'a in terms of moral duties sanctioned by religious consequences rather than with legal obligations and rights and specific temporal remedies. They categorized all fields of human activity as permissible or impermissible and recommended or reprehensible. In other words, Shari'a addresses the conscience of the individual Muslim, whether in a private, or public and official, capacity, and not the institutions and corporate entities of society and the state.

. . . .

Whatever may have been the historical status of Shari'a as the legal system of Muslim countries, the scope of its application in the public domain has diminished significantly since the middle of the nineteenth century. Due to both internal factors and external influence, Shari'a principles have been replaced by European law governing commercial, criminal and constitutional matters in almost all Muslim countries. Only family law and inheritance continued to be governed by Shari'a. . . .

Recently, many Muslims have challenged the gradual weakening of Shari'a as the basis for their formal legal systems. Most Muslim countries have experienced mounting demands for the immediate application of Shari'a as the sole, or at least primary, legal system of the land. These movements have either succeeded in gaining complete control, as in Iran, or achieved significant success in having aspects of Shari'a introduced into the legal system, as in Pakistan and the Sudan. Governments of Muslim countries generally find it difficult to resist these demands out of fear of being condemned by their own populations as anti-Islamic. Therefore, it is likely that this so-called Islamic fundamentalism will achieve further successes in other Muslim countries. The possibility of further Islamization may convince more people of the urgency of understanding and discussing the relationship between Shari'a and human rights, because Shari'a would have a direct impact on a wider range of human rights issues if it became the formal legal system of any country. . . .

I believe that a modern version of Islamic law can and should be developed. Such a modern "Shari'a" could be, in my view, entirely consistent with current standards of human rights. These views, however, are appreciated by only a tiny minority of contemporary Muslims. To the overwhelming majority of Muslims today, Shari'a is the sole valid interpretation of Islam, and as such *ought* to prevail over any human law or policy.

B. *Shari'a and Human Rights*

In this part, I illustrate with specific examples how Shari'a conflicts with international human rights standards. . . .

. . . .

The second example is the Shari'a law of apostasy. According to Shari'a, a Muslim who repudiates his faith in Islam, whether directly or indirectly, is guilty of a capital offense punishable by death. This aspect of Shari'a is in complete conflict with the fundamental human right of freedom of religion and conscience. The apostasy of a Muslim may be inferred by the court from the person's views or actions deemed by the court to contravene the basic tenets of Islam and therefore be tantamount to apostasy, regardless of the accused's personal belief that he or she is a Muslim.

The Shari'a law of apostasy can be used to restrict other human rights such as freedom of expression. A person may be liable to the death penalty for expressing views held by the authorities to contravene the official view of the tenets of Islam. Far from being an historical practice or a purely theoretical danger, this interpretation of the law of apostasy was applied in the Sudan as recently as 1985, when a Sudanese Muslim reformer was executed, because the authorities deemed his views to be contrary to Islam.[2]

A third and final example of conflict between Shari'a and human rights relates to the status and rights of non-Muslims. Shari'a classifies the subjects of an Islamic state in terms of their religious beliefs: Muslims, *ahl al-Kitab* or believers in a divinely revealed scripture (mainly Christian and Jews), and unbelievers. In modern terms, Muslims are the only full citizens of an Islamic state, enjoying all the rights and freedoms granted by Shari'a and subject only to the limitations and restrictions imposed on women. *Ahl al-Kitab* are entitled to the status of *dhimma*, a special compact with the Muslim state which

---

[2] . . . The Salman Rushdie affair illustrates the serious negative implications of the law of apostasy to literary and artistic expression. Mr. Rushdie, a British national of Muslim background, published a novel entitled, *The Satanic Verses*, in which irreverent reference is made to the Prophet of Islam, his wives and leading companions. Many Muslim governments banned the book because their populations found the author's style and connotations extremely offensive. The late Imam Khomeini of Iran sentenced Rushdie to death *in absentia* without charge or trial. . . .

guarantees them security of persons and property and a degree of communal autonomy to practice their own religion and conduct their private affairs in accordance with their customs and laws. In exchange for these limited rights, *dhimmis* undertake to pay *jizya* or poll tax and submit to Muslim sovereignty and authority in all public affairs.

According to this scheme, non-Muslim subjects of an Islam state can aspire only to the status of *dhimma*, under which they would suffer serious violations of their human rights. *Dhimmis* are not entitled to equality with Muslims. [Economic and family law illustrations omitted.]

IV. A CASE STUDY: THE ISLAMIC DIMENSION OF THE STATUS OF WOMEN

. . . .

The present focus on Muslim violations of the human rights of women does not mean that these are peculiar to the Muslim world.[3] As a Muslim, however, I am particularly concerned with the situation in the Muslim world and wish to contribute to its improvement.

The following discussion is organized in terms of the status and rights of Muslim women in the private sphere, particularly within the family, and in public fora, in relation to access to work and participation in public affairs. This classification is recommended for the Muslim context because the personal law aspects of Shari'a, family law and inheritance, have been applied much more consistently than the public law doctrines.[4] The status and rights of women in private life have always been significantly influenced by Shari'a regardless of the extent of Islamization of the public debate.

A. Shari'a and the Human Rights of Women

. . . . The most important general principle of Shari'a influencing the status and rights of women is the notion of *qawama*. *Qawama* has its origin in verse 4:34 of the Qur'an: "Men have *qawama* [guardianship and authority] over women because of the advantage they [men] have over them [women] and because they [men] spend their property in supporting them [women]." According to Shari'a interpretations of this verse, men as a group are the guardians of and superior to women as a group, and the men of a particular family are the guardians of and superior to the women of that family.

. . . . For example, Shari'a provides that women are disqualified from holding general public office, which involves the exercise of authority over men, because in keeping with the verse 4:34 of the Qur'an, men are entitled to exercise authority over women and not the reverse.

---

[3] It is difficult to distinguish between Islamic, or rather Shari'a, factors and extra-Shari'a factors affecting the status and rights of women. The fact that women's human rights are violated in all parts of the world suggests that there are universal social, economic, and political factors contributing to the persistence of this state of affairs. Nevertheless, the articulation and operation of these factors varies from one culture of context to the next. In particular, the rationalization of discrimination against and denial of equality for women is based on the values and customs of the particular society. In the Muslim world, these values and customs are supposed to be Islamic or at least consistent with the dictates of Islam. It is therefore useful to discuss the Islamic dimension of the status and rights of women.

[4] The private/public dichotomy, however, is an artificial distinction. The two spheres of life overlap and interact. The socialization and treatment of both men and women at home affect their role in public life and vice versa. While this classification can be used for analysis in the Muslim context, its limitations should be noted. It is advisable to look for both the private and public dimensions of a given Shari'a principle or rule rather than assume that it has only private or public implications.

Another general principle of Shari'a that has broad implications for the status and rights of Muslim women is the motion of *al-hijab*, the veil. This means more than requiring women to cover their bodies and faces in public. According to Shari'a interpretations of verses 24:31, 33:33,[5] 33:53, and 33:59[6] of the Qur'an, women are supposed to stay at home and not leave it except when required to by urgent necessity. When they are permitted to venture beyond the home, they must do so with their bodies and faces covered. *Al-hijab* tends to reinforce women's inability to hold public office and restricts their access to public life. They are not supposed to participate in public life, because they must not mix with men even in public places.

. . . . In family law for example, men have the right to marry up to four wives and the power to exercise complete control over them during marriage, to extent of punishing them for disobedience if the men deem that to be necessary.[7] In contrast, the co-wives are supposed to submit to their husband's will and endure his punishments. While a husband is entitled to divorce any of his wives at will, a wife is not entitled to a divorce, except by judicial order on very specific and limited grounds. Another private law feature of discrimination is found in the law of inheritance, where the general rule is that women are entitled to half the share of men. In addition to their general inferiority under the principle of *qawama* and lack of access to public life as a consequence of the notion of *al-hijab*, women are subjected to further specific limitations in the public domain. For instance, in the administration of justice, Shari'a holds women to be incompetent witnesses in serious criminal cases, regardless of their individual character and knowledge of the facts. In civil cases where a woman's testimony is accepted, it takes two women to make a single witness. *Diya*, monetary compensation to be paid to victims of violent crimes or to their surviving kin, is less for female victims than it is for male victims. . . . . These overlapping and interacting principles and rules play an extremely significant role in the socialization of both women and men. Notions of women's inferiority are deeply embedded in the character and attitudes of both women and men from early childhood.

. . . .

C. Muslim Women in Public Life

A similar and perhaps more drastic conflict exists between reformist and conservative trends in relation to the status and rights of women in the public domain. Unlike personal law matters, where Shari'a was never displaced by secular law, in most Muslim countries, constitutional, criminal and other public law matters have come to be based on secular, mainly Western, legal concepts and institutions. Consequently, the struggle over Islamization of public law has been concerned with the reestablishment of Shari'a where it has been absent for decades, or at least since the creation of the modern Muslim

---

[5] [O Consorts of the Prophet . . .] And stay quietly in your houses, and make not a dazzling display, like that of the former Times of Ignorance; and establish regular prayer, and give regular charity; and obey God and His Apostle. And God only wishes to remove all abomination from you, ye Members of the Family, and to make you pure and spotless.

[6] O Prophet! Tell thy wives and daughters, and the believing women, that they should cast their outer garments over their persons (when abroad): that is most convenient, that they should be known (as such) and not molested. And God is Oft-Forgiving, Most Merciful.

[7] Polygamy is based on verse 4:3 of the Qur'an. The husband's power to chastise his wife to the extent of beating her is based on verse 4:34 of the Qur'an.

nation states in the first half of the twentieth century. In terms of women's rights, the struggle shall determine whether women can keep the degree of equality and rights in public life they have achieved under secular constitutions and laws.

. . . .

. . . . Educated women and other modern segments of society may not be able to articulate their vision of an Islamic state in terms of Shari'a, because aspects of Shari'a are incompatible with certain concepts and institutions which these groups take for granted, including the protection of all human rights. To the extent that efforts for the protection and promotion of human rights in the Muslim world must take into account the Islamic dimension of the political and sociological situation in Muslim countries, a modernist conception of Islam is needed.

V. ISLAMIC REFORM AND HUMAN RIGHTS

. . . .

Islamic reform needs must be based on the Qur'an and Sunna, the primary sources of Islam. Although Muslims believe that the Qur'an is the literal and final word of God, and Sunna are the traditions of his final Prophet, they also appreciate that these sources have to be understood and applied through human interpretation and action. . . .

A. *An Adequate Reform Methodology*

. . . . The basic premise of my position, based on the work of the late Sudanese Muslim reformer *Ustadh* Mahmoud Mohamed Taha, is that the Shari'a reflects a historically-conditioned interpretation of Islamic scriptures in the sense that the founding jurists had to understand those sources in accordance with their own social, economic, and political circumstances. In relation to the status and rights of women, for example, equality between men and women in the eighth and ninth centuries in the Middle East, or anywhere else at the time, would have been inconceivable and impracticable. It was therefore natural and indeed inevitable that Muslim jurists would understand the relevant texts of the Qur'an and Sunna as confirming rather than repudiating the realities of the day.

In interpreting the primary sources of Islam in their historical context, the founding jurists of Shari'a tended not only to understand the Qur'an and Sunna as confirming existing social attitudes and institutions, but also to emphasize certain texts and "enact" them into Shari'a while de-emphasizing other texts or interpreting them in ways consistent with what they believed to be the intent and purpose of the sources. Working with the same primary sources, modern Muslim jurists might shift emphasis from one class of texts to the other, and interpret the previously enacted texts in ways consistent with a new understanding of what is believed to be the intent and purpose of the sources. This new understanding would be informed by contemporary social, economic and political circumstances in the same way that the "old" understanding on which Shari'a jurists acted was informed by the then prevailing circumstances. The new understanding would qualify for Islamic legitimacy, in my view, if it is based on specific texts in opposing the application of other texts, and can be shown to be in accordance with the Qur'an and Sunna as a whole.

For example, the general principle of *qawama*, the guardianship and authority of men over women under Shari'a, is based on verse 4:34 of the Qur'an. . . . This verse presents *qawama* as a consequence of two conditions: men's advantage over and financial support of women. The fact that men are generally physically stronger than most women is not relevant in modern times where the rule of law prevails over physical might. Moreover, modern circumstances are making the economic independence of women from men more readily realized and appreciated. In other words, neither of the conditions – advantages of physical might or earning power – set by verse 4:34 as the justification for the *qawama* of men over women is tenable today.

The fundamental position of the modern human rights movement is that all human beings are equal in worth and dignity, regardless of gender, religion or race. This position can be substantiated by the Qur'an and other Islamic sources, as understood under the radically transformed circumstances of today. For example, in numerous verses the Qur'an speaks of honor and dignity for "humankind" and "children of Adam," without distinction as to race, color, general or religion. By drawing on those sources and being willing to set aside archaic and dated interpretations of other sources, such as the one previously given to verse 4:34 of the Qur'an, we can provide Islamic legitimacy for the full range of human rights for women.

Similarly, numerous verses of the Qur'an provide for freedom of choice and non-compulsion in religious belief and conscience.[8] These verses have been either de-emphasized as having been "overruled" by other verses which were understood to legitimize coercion, or "interpreted" in ways which permitted such coercion. For example, verse 9:29 of the Qur'an was taken as the foundation of the whole system of *dhimma*, and its consequent discrimination against non-Muslims. Relying on those verses which extol freedom of religion rather than those that legitimize religious coercion, one can argue now that the *dhimma* system should no longer be part of Islamic law and that complete equality should be assured regardless of religion or belief. The same argument can be used to abolish all negative legal consequences of apostasy as inconsistent with the Islamic principle of freedom of religion.

. . . .

B. Prospects for Acceptance and Likely Impact of the Proposed Reform

. . . . Governments of Muslim countries, like many other governments, formally subscribe to international human rights instruments because, in my view, they find the human rights idea an important legitimizing force both at home and abroad. . . .

Nevertheless, the proposed reform will probably be resisted because it challenges the vested interests of powerful forces in the Muslim world and may upset male-dominated traditional political and social institutions. These forces probably will try to restrict opportunities for a genuine consideration of this reform methodology.

Consequently, the acceptance and implementation of this reform methodology will involve a political struggle within Muslim nations as part of a larger general struggle for human rights. I would recommend this proposal to participants in that struggle who champion the cause of justice and equality for women and non-Muslims, and freedom of belief and expression in the Muslim world. Given the extreme importance of Islamic legitimacy in Muslim societies, I urge human rights advocates to claim the Islamic platform and not concede it to the traditionalist and fundamentalist forces in their societies. I would also invite outside supporters of Muslim human rights advocates

---

[8]   See, for example, verse 2:256 of the Qur'an which provides: "Let there be no compulsion in religion. Truth stands out clear from error. . . ." In verse 18:29 God instructs the Prophet: "Say, the Trust is from your Lord. Let him who will, believe, and let him who will, reject [it]."

to express their support with due sensitivity and genuine concern for Islamic legitimacy in the Muslim world.

∽

QUESTIONS & COMMENTS

(1) Given the present difficulties of Islamic law *vis-à-vis* international human rights law, what is the likelihood of using Islamic legal sources to buttress an expansive jurisprudence of international human rights law? Instead of using Islamic law as legal authority, can it instead be used for descriptive, anthropological purposes in protecting the rights of Muslims to practice their religion in predominantly non-Islamic countries?

Hilary Charlesworth, Christine Chinkin & Shelley Wright
Feminist Approaches to International Law
85 Am. J. Int'l L. 613 (1991)[1]

Feminist concern with the public/private distinction derives from its centrality to liberal theory. . . .

Although the scientific basis of the public/private distinction has been thoroughly attacked and exposed as a culturally constructed ideology, it continues to have a strong grip on legal thinking. The language of the public/private distinction is built into the language of the law itself: law lays claim to rationality, culture, power, objectivity – all terms associated with the public or male realm. It is defined in opposition to the attributes associated with the domestic, private, female sphere: feeling, emotion, passivity, subjectivity. Moreover, the law has always operated primarily within the public domain; it is considered appropriate to regulate the work place, the economy and the distribution of political power, while direct state intervention in the family and the home has long been regarded as inappropriate. Violence within the home, for example, has generally been given different legal significance from violence outside it; the injuries recognized as legally compensable are those which occur outside the home. Damages in civil actions are typically assessed in terms of ability to participate in the public sphere. Women have difficulty convincing law enforcement officials that violent acts within the home are criminal.

In one sense, the public/private distinction is the fundamental basis of the modern state's function of separating and concentrating juridical forms of power that emanate from the state. The distinction implies that the private world is uncontrolled. In fact, the regulation of taxation, social security, education, health and welfare has immediate effects on the private sphere. The myth that state power is not exercised in the "private" realm allocated to women masks its control. . . .

The grip that the public/private distinction has on international law, and the consequent banishment of women's voices and concerns from the discipline, can be seen in the international prohibition on torture. The right to freedom from torture and other forms of cruel, inhuman or degrading treatment is generally accepted as a paradigmatic civil and political right. It is included in all international catalogs of civil and political rights

---

[1] Reproduced with permission from 85 A.J.I.L. 613 (1991), © The American Society of International Law. Footnotes omitted.

and is the focus of specialized United Nations and regional treaties. The right to be free from torture is also regarded as a norm of customary international law – indeed, like the prohibition on slavery, as a norm of jus cogens.

The basis for the right is traced to "the inherent dignity of the human person." Behavior constituting torture is defined in [Article 1(1) of] the Convention against Torture as

> any act by which severe pain or suffering, whether physical or mental, is intentionally inflicted on a person for such purposes as obtaining from him or a third person information or a confession, punishing him for an act he or a third person has committed or is suspected of having committed, or intimidating or coercing him or a third person, or for any reason based on discrimination of any kind, when such pain or suffering is inflicted by or at the instigation of or with the consent or acquiescence of a public official or other person acting in an official capacity.

This definition has been considered broad because it covers mental suffering and behavior "at the instigation of" a public official. However, despite the use of the term "human person" in the Preamble, the use of the masculine pronoun alone in the definition of the proscribed behavior immediately gives the definition a male, rather than a truly human, context. More importantly, the description of the prohibited conduct relies on a distinction between public and private actions that obscures injuries to their dignity typically sustained by women. The traditional canon of human rights law does not deal in categories that fit the experiences of women. It is cast in terms of discrete violations of rights and offers little redress in cases where there is a pervasive, structural denial of rights.

The international definition of torture requires not only the intention to inflict suffering, but also the secondary intention that the infliction of suffering will fulfill a purpose. Recent evidence suggests that women and children, in particular, are victims of widespread and apparently random terror campaigns by both governmental and guerrilla groups in times of civil unrest or armed conflict. Such suffering is not clearly included in the international definition of torture.

A crucial aspect of torture and cruel, inhuman or degrading conduct, as defined, is that they take place in the public realm: a public official or a person acting officially must be implicated in the pain and suffering. The rationale for this limitation is that "private acts (of brutality) would usually be ordinary criminal offenses which national law enforcement is expected to repress. International concern with torture arises only when the State itself abandons its function of protecting its citizenry by sanctioning criminal action by law enforcement personnel." Many women suffer from torture in this limited sense. The international jurisprudence on the notion of torture arguably extends to sexual violence and psychological coercion if the perpetrator has official standing. However, severe pain and suffering that is inflicted outside the most public context of the state – for example, within the home or by private persons, which is the most pervasive and significant violence sustained by women – does not qualify as torture despite its impact on the inherent dignity of the human person. Indeed, some forms of violence are attributed to cultural tradition. The message of violence against women, argues Charlotte Bunch, is domination:

> [S]tay in your place or be afraid. Contrary to the argument that such violence is only personal or cultural, it is profoundly political. It results from the structural

relationships of power, domination, and privilege between men and women in society. Violence against women is central to maintaining those political relations at home, at work, and in all public spheres.[2]

~

QUESTIONS & COMMENTS

(1) In what sense does Article 1(1) of the Convention against Torture have a "male, rather than a truly human, context," according to Charlesworth, Chinkin & Wright? Would expanding it beyond the context they identify require a revision of the treaty's definition of torture, or could the problem be dealt with adequately by reinterpretation?

(2) Is every act of domestic violence a human rights violation for which the state incurs international responsibility? Does it matter how widespread the problem is and what measures the state has taken (or failed to take) to combat it?

(3) The context in which questions of state responsibility are considered may matter. Consider the question of female genital mutilation carried out by traditional elders in a society in which the government formally disapproves of the practice but does little to end it. What provisions of the ICCPR might the practice violate? As for state responsibility, might one more readily attribute responsibility to the state in an asylum context (*i.e.*, a woman asks not to be returned to a country in which her female children will be forced to undergo female genital mutilation) than in, for example, the context of a lawsuit seeking damages against the state for failing to prevent it? *See In re Fauziya Kasinga*, U.S. Board of Immigration Appeals, 1996 BIA Lexis 15 (June 13, 1996).

Thomas M. Franck
Legitimacy in the International System
82 Am. J. Int'l L. 705 (1988)[1]

The surprising thing about international law is that nations ever obey its strictures or carry out its mandates. This observation is made not to register optimism that the half-empty glass is also half full, but to draw attention to a pregnant phenomenon: that most states observe systemic rules much of the time in their relations with other states. That they should do so is much more interesting than, say, the fact that most citizens usually obey their nation's laws, because the international system is organized in a voluntarist fashion, supported by so little coercive authority. This unenforced rule system can obligate states to profess, if not always to manifest, a significant level of day-to-day compliance even, at times, when that is not in their short-term self-interest. The element of paradox attracts our attention and challenges us to investigate it, perhaps in the hope of discovering a theory that can illuminate more generally the occurrence of voluntary normative compliance and even yield a prescription for enhancing aspects of world order.

---

[2] [Charlotte Bunch, *Women's Rights as Human Rights: Toward a Re-vision of Human Rights*, 12 Hum. Rts. Q. 486, 490–91 (1990). Ed.'s Note.]

[1] Reproduced with permission from 82 A.J.I.L. 705, 707–10, 712–14, 716, 725–26, 735–36, 740–41, 750–51, 759 (1988), © The American Society of International Law. [Most footnotes and citations have been omitted. Ed.'s Note.]

Before going further, however, it is necessary to enter a caveat. This essay attempts a study of why states obey laws in the absence of coercion. That is not the same quest as motivates the more familiar studies that investigate the sources of normative obligation. The latter properly focus on the origins of rules – in treaties, custom, decisions of tribunals, *opinio juris*, state conduct, resolutions of international organizations, and so forth – to determine which sources, qua sources, are to be taken seriously, and how seriously to take them. Our object, on the other hand, is to determine why and under what circumstances a specific rule is obeyed. To be sure, the source of every rule – its *pedigree*, in the terminology of this essay – is *one* determinant of how strong its pull to compliance is likely to be. Pedigree, however, is far from being the only indicator of how seriously the rule will be taken, particularly if the rule conflicts with a state's perceived self-interest. Thus, other indicators are also a focus of this essay insofar as they determine the capacity of rules to affect state conduct.

This essay posits that, in a community organized around rules, compliance is secured – to whatever degree it *is* – at least in part by perception of a rule as legitimate by those to whom it is addressed. Their perception of legitimacy will vary in degree from rule to rule and time to time. It becomes a crucial factor, however, in the capacity of any rule to secure compliance when, as in the international system, there are no other compliance-inducing mechanisms.

Legitimacy is used here to mean that quality of a rule *which derives from a perception on the part of those to whom it is addressed that it has come into being in accordance with right process*. Right process includes the notion of valid sources but also encompasses literary, socio-anthropological and philosophical insights. The elements of right process that will be discussed below are identified as affecting decisively the degree to which any rule is perceived as legitimate.

I. WHY A QUEST FOR LEGITIMACY?

Why study the teleology of law? What are laws *for*? What causes obedience? Such basic questions are the meat and potatoes of jurisprudential inquiry. Any legal system worth taking seriously must address such fundamentals. J. L. Brierly has speculated that jurisprudence, nowadays, regards international law as no more than "an attorney's mantle artfully displayed on the shoulders of arbitrary power" and "a decorous name for a convenience of the chancelleries."[2] That seductive epigram captures the still dominant Austinian positivists' widespread cynicism towards the claim that the rules of the international system can be studied jurisprudentially.[3]

. . . .

That international "law" is not law in the positivist sense may be irrefutable but is also irrelevant. Whatever label is attached to it, the normative structure of the international system is perfectly capable of being studied with a view to generating teleological jurisprudence. Indeed, international law is the best place to study some of the fundamental teleological issues that arise not only in the international, but also in national legal systems. This makes it odd that it is not more frequently used as a field for investigation.

---

[2] J. Brierly, The Outlook for International Law 13 (1944) (quoting Sir Alfred Zimmern).

[3] Austin believed that law was the enforced command of a sovereign to a subject. J. Austin, The Province of Jurisprudence Determined (1832); *see also* Janis, *Jeremy Bentham and the Fashioning of "International Law,"* 78 A.J.I.L. 405, 410 (1984). This Austinian view has been widely shared by critics. *See,* however, H. L. A. Hart, The Concept of Law, ch. 10 (1961); and Williams, *International Law and the Controversy Concerning the Word 'Law,'* 22 Brit. Y.B. Int'l L. 146 (1945).

Up to a point, the Austinians are empirically right. The international system of states is fundamentally different from any national community of persons and of corporate entities. It is not helpful to ignore those differences or to cling to the reifying notion that states are "persons" analogous to the citizens of a nation. Some of the differences are of great potential interest. In a nation, Machiavelli noted, "there cannot be good laws where there are not good arms."[4] In the international community, however, there are ample signs that rules unenforced by good arms are yet capable of obligating states and quite often even achieve habitual compliance. The Austinians, beginning with a defensible empirical observation about the difference between national laws and international rules, deduce from the difference that rules governing conduct which are not "law" in the positivist sense cannot usefully be studied as a system of community-based obligations. It is this deduction – not the empirical observation – which is wrong.

Indeed, it is precisely the curious paradox of obligation in the international rule system that should whet our speculative appetite, provoking the opening, not the closing, of jurisprudential inquiry. *Why should rules, unsupported by an effective structure of coercion comparable to a national police force, nevertheless elicit so much compliance, even against perceived self-interest, on the part of sovereign states?* Perhaps finding an answer to this question can help us to find a key to a better, yet realistic, world order. The answer, if there is one, may also incidentally prove useful in designing more widely obeyed, less coerced, laws for ordering the lives of our cities and states.

A series of events connected with the role of the U.S. Navy in protecting U.S.-flagged vessels in the Persian Gulf serves to illustrate the paradoxical phenomenon of uncoerced compliance in a situation where the rule conflicts with perceived self-interest. Early in 1988, the Department of Defense became aware of a ship approaching the gulf with a load of Chinese-made Silkworm missiles en route to Iran. The Department believed the successful delivery of these potent weapons would increase materially the danger to both protected and protecting U.S. ships in the region. It therefore argued for permission to intercept the delivery. The Department of State countered that such a search and seizure on the high seas, under the universally recognized rules of war and neutrality, would constitute aggressive blockade, an act tantamount to a declaration of war against Iran. In the event, the delivery ship and its cargo of missiles were allowed to pass. Deference to systemic rules had won out over tactical advantage in the internal struggle for control of U.S. policy.

Why should this have been so? In the absence of a world government and a global coercive power to enforce its laws, why did the U.S. Government, with its evident power to do as it wished, choose to "play by the rules" despite the considerable short-term strategic advantage to be gained by seizing the Silkworms before they could be delivered? Why did preeminent American power defer to the rules of the sanctionless system? At least part of the answer to this question, quietly given by the State Department to the Department of Defense, is that the international rules of neutrality have attained a high degree of recognized legitimacy and must not be violated lightly. Specifically, they are well understood, enjoy a long pedigree and are part of a consistent framework of rules – the *jus in bello* – governing and restraining the use of force in conflicts. To violate a set of rules of such widely recognized legitimacy, the State Department argued, would transform the U.S. posture in the gulf from that of a neutral to one of belligerency. That

---

[4] N. Machiavelli, The Prince 71 (L. de Alvarez rev. ed. 1981).

could end Washington's role as an honest broker seeking to promote peace negotiations. It would also undermine the carefully crafted historic "rules of the game" applicable to wars, rules that are widely perceived to be in the interest of all states.

Such explanations for deferring to a rule in preference to taking a short-term advantage are the policymaker's equivalent of the philosopher's quest for a theory of legitimacy. Washington voluntarily chose to obey a rule in the Persian Gulf conflict. Yet it does not always obey all international rules. Some rules are harder to disobey – more persuasive in their pull to compliance – than others. This is known intuitively by the legions of Americans who deliberately underreport the dutiable price of goods purchased abroad, and by the aficionados who smuggle Cuban cigars into the country behind pocket handkerchiefs, but would not otherwise commit criminal fraud. That some rules *in themselves* seem to exert more pull to compliance than others is the starting point in the search for a theory of legitimacy.

The questions raised by such examples of obedience and disobedience, however, are more interesting when examined in the context of the international than of the national community. It is the voluntariness of international compliance that heightens the mystery and lures us with the possibility of discovery....

. . . .

Research into the teleology of national legal systems has led the way to a recognition of the role of legitimacy, as distinct from coercion, as the key to legal order and systematic obedience. While most students of national systems, except perhaps for a few utopians such as Foucault,[5] agree with Machiavelli that governance requires *some* exercise of power by an elite supported by coercive force, few any longer believe the Austinians' claim that this necessary condition is also a sufficient one. Having reached this conclusion, most students of law, power and structure in society have sought to identify other characteristics that conduce to the rule of law. Ronald Dworkin identifies three such characteristics: *fairness, justice* and *integrity* (the last being a principled, more sensitive variant of consistency).[6] Jurgen Habermas emphasizes the role of discursive validation, following the tradition of Aeschylus and Aristotle.[7] Important scholarship on contract theory has demonstrated that coercion need not be an essential element in ensuring the efficacy of a contract, which is more accurately seen as self-enforcing obligation.[8] In fact, much recent work focusing on the phenomenon of obedience and obligation in national

---

[5] Foucault rejects all notions of dominance, whether embodied in theories of sovereignty (divine rule, autocracy, "public rights" and so forth) or embraced in "mechanisms of discipline," including, for example, "power that is tied to scientific knowledge." He visualizes, instead, a new form of "right," which is antidisciplinarian and divorced from concepts of sovereignty. M. Foucault, POWER/KNOWLEDGE: SELECTED INTERVIEWS AND OTHER WRITINGS 106–08 (C. Gordon ed. 1980).

[6] R. Dworkin, LAW'S EMPIRE 176–224 (1986).

[7] According to Habermas:

> Legitimacy means that there are good arguments for a political order's claim to be recognized as right and just; a legitimate order deserves recognition. *Legitimacy means a political order's worthiness to be recognized.* This definition highlights the fact that legitimacy is a contestable validity claim; the stability of the order of domination (also) depends on its (at least) de facto recognition. Thus, historically as well as analytically, the concept is used above all in situations in which the legitimacy of an order is disputed, in which, as we say, legitimation problems arise. One side denies, the other asserts legitimacy. This is a *process....*

J. Habermas, COMMUNICATION AND THE EVOLUTION OF SOCIETY 178–79 (T. McCarthy trans. 1979).

[8] Kronman, *Contract Law and the State of Nature,* 1 J. L., ECON. & ORG. 5 (1985).

societies concerns itself primarily with noncoercive factors conducing to consensual compliance.

While some such studies have emphasized the role of strategic concepts that gain voluntary compliance by mutualizing advantage, others, beginning with the seminal work of Max Weber,[9] have emphasized the role of *legitimacy* and *legitimation*. Weber's analysis stressed process legitimacy. He hypothesized that rules tend to achieve compliance when they, themselves, comply with secondary rules about how and by whom rules are to be made and interpreted. In his view, a sovereign's command is more likely to be obeyed if the subject perceives both the rule and the ruler as legitimate. Somewhat different concepts of legitimacy have been developed by Habermas and by neo-Marxist philosophers. Oscar Schachter, working in the field of international normativity, has elucidated and emphasized the role of "competence and authority" in endowing a rule with capacity to obligate.[10] All have in common, however, their emphasis on noncoercive factors as conducing to rule-compliant behavior.

It thus appears that, despite its residual Austinian propensities, national jurisprudence has quite a bit to say to the international system precisely because there is empirical evidence that, in both systems, noncoercive factors play an important part in conducing to rule/law-compliant behavior. The special value to both national and international jurisprudential inquiry of studying the international system, however, lies in its unalloyed noncoercive state. While the dependence of the international system on voluntary compliance is often (and justly) perceived as a weakness, it happens to afford a singular opportunity. Critics of efforts to study legitimacy as a noncoercive factor conducing to compliance in national legal systems have been able to argue that this factor necessarily eludes researchers because it cannot be isolated from other, authoritarian, elements compelling obedience. That critique loses its force, however, in the international context. Thus, the operation of the noncoercive element, or, specifically, *legitimacy*, becomes easier to isolate and study in the interstate system than in societies of persons, where the coercive sovereign always lurks in the background.

. . . .

Four elements – the indicators of rule legitimacy in the community of states – are identified and studied in this essay. They are *determinacy, symbolic validation, coherence* and *adherence* (to a normative hierarchy). To the extent rules exhibit these properties, they appear to exert a strong pull on states to comply with their commands. To the extent these elements are not present, rules seem to be easier to avoid by a state tempted to pursue its short-term self-interest. This is not to say that the legitimacy of a rule can be deduced solely by counting how often it is obeyed or disobeyed. While its legitimacy may exert a powerful pull on state conduct, yet other pulls may be stronger in a particular circumstance. The

---

[9] Weber postulates the validity of an order in terms of its being regarded by the obeying public "as in some way obligatory or exemplary" for its members because, at least in part, it defines "a model" which is "binding" and to which the actions of others "will in fact conform." At least in part, this legitimacy is perceived as adhering to the authority issuing an order, as opposed to the qualities of legitimacy that inhere in an order itself. This distinction between *an* order (command) and *the* order (authority) is easily overlooked but fundamental. 1 M. Weber, Economy and Society: An Outline of Interpretive Sociology 31 (G. Roth & C. Wittich eds. 1968). For a critique, *see* Hyde, *The Concept of Legitimacy in the Sociology of Law*, 1983 Wis. L. Rev. 379.

[10] [Schachter, *Towards a Theory of International Obligation*, 8 Va. J. Int'l L. 300, 309 (1968).]

chance to take a quick, decisive advantage may overcome the counterpull of even a highly legitimate rule. In such circumstances, legitimacy is indicated not by obedience, but by the discomfort disobedience induces in the violator. (Student demonstrations sometimes are a sensitive indicator of such discomfort.) The variable to watch is not compliance but the strength of the compliance pull, whether or not the rule achieves actual compliance in any one case.

Each rule has an inherent pull power that is independent of the circumstances in which it is exerted, and that varies from rule to rule. This pull power is its index of legitimacy. For example, the rule that makes it improper for one state to infiltrate spies into another state in the guise of diplomats is formally acknowledged by almost every state, yet it enjoys so low a degree of legitimacy as to exert virtually no pull towards compliance. As Schachter observes, "some laws, 'though enacted properly, have so low a degree of probable compliance that they are treated as dead letters' and . . . some treaties, while properly concluded, are considered scraps of paper.'" By way of contrast, we have noted, the rules pertaining to belligerency and neutrality actually exerted a very high level of pull on Washington in connection with the Silkworm missile shipment in the Persian Gulf.

The study of legitimacy thus focuses on the inherent capacity of a rule to exert pressure on states to comply. This focus on the properties of rules, of course, is not a self-sufficient account of the socialization process. How rules are made, interpreted and applied is part of a dynamic, expansive and complex set of social phenomena. That complexity can be approached, however, by beginning with the rules themselves. Those seemingly inert constructs are shaped by other, more dynamic forces and, like tree trunks and seashells, tell their own story about the winds and tides that become an experiential part of their shape and texture.

. . . .

Perhaps the most self-evident of all characteristics making for legitimacy is textual *determinacy*. What is meant by this is the ability of the text to convey a clear message, to appear transparent in the sense that one can see through the language to the meaning. Obviously, rules with a readily ascertainable meaning have a better chance than those that do not to regulate the conduct of those to whom the rule is addressed or exert a compliance pull on their policymaking process. Those addressed will know precisely what is expected of them, which is a necessary first step towards compliance.

. . . .

Indeterminacy . . . has costs. Indeterminate normative standards not only make it harder to know what conformity is expected, but also make it easier to justify non-compliance. Put conversely, the more determinate the standard, the more difficult it is to resist the pull of the rule to compliance and to justify noncompliance. Since few persons or states wish to be perceived as acting in obvious violation of a generally recognized rule of conduct, they may try to resolve the conflicts between the demands of a rule and their desire not to be fettered, by "interpreting" the rule permissively. A determinate rule is less elastic and thus less amenable to such evasive strategy than an indeterminate one.

. . . .

The degree of determinacy of a rule directly affects the degree of its perceived legitimacy. A rule that prohibits the doing of "bad things" lacks legitimacy because it fails to communicate what is expected, except within a very small constituency in which "bad" has achieved a high degree of culturally induced specificity. To be legitimate, a rule must communicate what conduct is permitted and what conduct is out of bounds. These bookends should be close enough together to inhibit incipient violators from offering self-serving exculpatory definitions of the rule. When almost everyone scoffs at such an exculpation, the outer boundary of the rule's determinacy has been established.

There is another sense in which determinacy increases the legitimacy of a rule text. A rule of conduct that is highly transparent – its normative content exhibiting great clarity – actually *encourages* gratification deferral and rule compliance. States, in their relations with one another, frequently find themselves tempted to violate a rule of conduct in order to take advantage of a sudden opportunity. If they do not do so, but choose, instead, to obey the rule and forgo that gratification, it is likely to be because of their longer term interests in seeing a potentially useful rule reinforced. They can visualize future situations in which it will operate to their advantage. But they will only defer the attainable short-term gain if the rule is sufficiently specific to support reasonable expectations that benefit can be derived in a contingent future by strengthening the rule in the present instance.

 . . . .

As determinacy is the linguistic or literary-structural component of legitimacy, so *symbolic validation, ritual* and *pedigree* provide its cultural and anthropological dimension. As with determinacy, so here, the legitimacy of the rule – its ability to exert pull to compliance and to command voluntary obedience – is to be examined in the light of its ability to communicate. In this instance, however, what is to be communicated is not so much content as *authority*: the authority of a rule, the authority of the originator of a validating communication and, at times, the authority bestowed on the recipient of the communication. The communication of authority, moreover, is symbolic rather than literal. We shall refer to these symbolically validating communications as cues.

These three concepts – symbolic validation, ritual and pedigree – are related, but not identical. The *symbolic validation* of a rule, or of a rule-making process or institution, occurs when a signal is used as a cue to elicit compliance with a command. The cue serves as a surrogate for enunciated reasons for such obedience. The singing of the national anthem, for example, is a vocal and (on public occasions) a visual signal symbolically reinforcing the citizen's relationship to the state, a relationship of rights and duties. This compliance reinforcement need not be spelled out in the actual words of the anthem (as it is not in the commonly used stanza of the American one). The act of corporate singing itself is a sufficient cue to validate the fabric of regularized relationships that are implicated in good citizenship. We are not really singing about bombs bursting in the night air, but about free and secret elections, the marketplace of ideas, the rule of valid laws and impartial judges.

Ritual is a specialized form of symbolic validation marked by ceremonies, often – but not necessarily – mystical, that provide unenunciated reasons or cues for eliciting compliance with the commands of persons or institutions. The entry of the mace into the British House of Commons is intended to call to mind the Commons's long and successful struggle to capture control of lawmaking power from the Crown. It functions as a much more direct, literal kind of symbolic validation than the "Star-Spangled Banner." Ritual is often presented as drama, to communicate to a community its unity, its values, its uniqueness in both the exclusive and the inclusive sense.

All ritual is a form of symbolic validation, but the converse is not necessarily true. *Pedigree* is a different subset of cues that seek to enhance the compliance pull of rules or rule-making institutions by emphasizing their historical origins, their cultural or anthropological deep-rootedness. An example is the practice of "recognition." When a government recognizes a new regime, or when the United Nations admits a new state to membership, this partly symbolic act has broad significance. It endows the new entity with a range of entitlements and duties, the concomitants of sovereignty. The capacity of states, and, nowadays, perhaps also of the United Nations, to confer sovereignty and its incidents in this fashion derives not from some treaty or other specific agreement but from the ancient practice of states and groupings of states, which legitimizes the exercise of this power.

. . . .

Symbolic validation, like determinacy, serves to legitimize rules. But like determinacy, symbolic validation is not quite as simple a notion as it may initially appear. For example, as traditional Chinese practice makes clear, ritual invoked to enhance the capacity of a rule to compel compliance will only succeed if the rituals are themselves legitimate and are strictly observed. Similarly, a pedigree only confers actual rights and duties when the standards for pedigreeing are applied *coherently*. When, on the contrary, symbols, ritual and pedigree are dispensed capriciously, the desired effect of legitimization may not accrue.

Both determinacy and symbolic validation are connected to a further variable: coherence. The effect of incoherence on symbolic validation can be illustrated by reference to diplomatic practices pertaining to the ritual validation of governments and states. The most important act of pedigreeing in the international system is the deep-rooted, traditional act that endows a new government, or a new state, with symbolic status. When the endowing is done by individual governments, it is known as *recognition*. The symbolic conferral of status is also performed collectively through a global organization like the United Nations when the members vote to admit a new nation to membership, or when the General Assembly votes to accept the credentials of the delegates representing a new government.

. . . .

To recapitulate: an act of recognition, the symbolic validation of a state or regime, has the capacity to bestow, symbolically, rights and duties on the recognized entity when, *but only if*, it is done in accordance with the applicable principled rules and procedures. Such pedigreed recognition, and its corporate UN equivalent, is everywhere accorded great weight. On the other hand, when the rules and standards for validation are violated, or are themselves unprincipled and capricious, then symbolic validation fails in its objective of bestowing status. Moreover, when validation is seen to be capricious, a failure to validate will do more to undermine the legitimacy of the validating process than of the state or government thus deprived of symbolic validation.

. . . .

There is another aspect of coherence. It encompasses the further notion that a rule, standard or validating ritual gathers force if it is seen to be connected to a network of other rules by an underlying general principle. This latter aspect of coherence merits closer examination.

. . . .

Rules become coherent when they are applied so as to preclude capricious checkerboarding. They preclude caprice when they are applied consistently or, if inconsistently applied, when they make distinctions based on underlying general principles that connect with an ascertainable purpose of the rules and with similar distinctions made throughout the rule system. The resultant skein of underlying principles is an aspect of community, which, in turn, confirms the status of the states that constitute the community. Validated membership in the community accords equal capacity for rights and obligations derived from its legitimate rule system.

By focusing on the connections between specific rules and general underlying principles, we have emphasized the horizontal aspect of our central notion of a community of legitimate rules. However, there are vertical aspects of this community that have even more significant impact on the legitimacy of rules.

. . . .

According to Dworkin, a true community, as distinguished from a mere rabble, or even a system of random primary rules of obligation, is one in which the members

> accept that they are governed by common principles, not just by rules hammered out in political compromise. . . . Members of a society of principle accept that their political rights and duties are not exhausted by the particular decisions their political institutions have reached, but depend, more generally, on the scheme of principles those decisions presuppose and endorse. So each member accepts that others have rights and that he has duties flowing from that scheme. . . .

Nor are these rights and duties "conditional on his wholehearted approval of that scheme; these obligations arise from the historical fact that his community has adopted that scheme, . . . not the assumption that he would have chosen it were the choice entirely his."

Moreover, the community "commands that no one be left out, that we are all in politics together for better or worse." And its legitimizing requirement of rule integrity "assumes that each person is as worthy as any other, that each must be treated with equal concern according to some coherent conception of what that means."

Does that accurately describe the social condition of the nations of the world in their interactive mode? The description does not assume harmony or an absence of strife. According to Dworkin, an "association of principle is not automatically a just community; its conception of equal concern may be defective." What a rule community, a community of principle, does is to validate behavior in accordance with rules and applications of rules that confirm principled coherence and adherence, rather than acknowledging only the power of power. A rule community operates in conformity not only with primary rules but also with secondary ones – rules about rules – which are generated by valid legislative and adjudicative institutions. Finally, a community accepts its ultimate secondary rules of recognition not consensually, but as an inherent concomitant of membership status.

In the world of nations, each of these described conditions of a sophisticated community is observable today, even though imperfectly. This does not mean that its rules will never be disobeyed. It does mean, however, that it is usually possible to distinguish rule compliance from rule violation, and a valid rule or ruling from an invalid one. It also means that it is not necessary to await the millennium of Austinian-type world government to proceed with constructing – perfecting – a system of rules and institutions that will exhibit a powerful pull to compliance and a self-enforcing degree of legitimacy.

$\sim$

David Kennedy
The International Human Rights Movement: Part of the Problem?
15 HARV. HUM. RTS. J. 101 (2002)[1]

There is no question that the international human rights movement has done a great deal of good, freeing individuals from great harm, providing an emancipatory vocabulary and institutional machinery for people across the globe, raising the standards by which governments judge one another, and by which they are judged, both by their own people, and by the elites we refer to collectively as the "international community." A career in the human rights movement has provided thousands of professionals, many of them lawyers, with a sense of dignity and confidence that one sometimes can do well while doing good. The literature praising these, and other, accomplishments is vast. Among well-meaning legal professionals in the United States and Europe – humanist, internationalist, liberal, compassionate in all the best senses of these terms – the human rights movement has become a central object of devotion.

But there are other ways of thinking about human rights. As a well-meaning internationalist and, I hope, compassionate legal professional myself, I thought it might be useful to pull together in a short list some of the questions that have been raised about international human rights by people, including myself, who worry that the human rights movement might, on balance, and acknowledging its enormous achievement, be more part of the problem in today's world than part of the solution. This Essay offers an incomplete and idiosyncratic list of such questions that might be of interest to the human rights practitioner.

I should say at the outset that the arguments I have listed are hypotheses. I have stated them as succinctly as I can, at the risk of their seeming conclusive or overly polemical. In fact, although some of them seem more plausible to me than others, to my knowledge none of them has been proven – they are in the air as assertions, worries, polemical charges. They circulate in the background of conversations about the human rights movement. And even if these potential costs were demonstrated, it would still be necessary to weigh them against the very real accomplishments of the human rights movement.

I. THINKING PRAGMATICALLY ABOUT HUMAN RIGHTS

My purpose in pulling these concerns together is to encourage other well-meaning legal professionals to adopt a more pragmatic attitude toward human rights. My hope is that we will develop a stronger practice of weighing the costs and benefits of their articulation, institutionalization and enforcement. Of course, the best human rights practitioners are already intensely strategic and practical in thinking about their work. But it is often tempting (for those within and without the movement) to set pragmatic concerns aside, to treat human rights as an object of devotion rather than calculation. And even the most intense practical evaluations of human rights initiatives too often stop short of considering the full range of potential down sides or negative knock on consequences in their enthusiasm to move forward with efforts whose up side potential seems so apparent.

A. "Pragmatic" – Always and Forever or Here and Now?

Pragmatic evaluation means specifying the benefits and harms that might attend human rights initiatives in particular cases, under specific conditions, in particular time periods,

---

[1] © (2002) by the President and Fellows of Harvard College.

and so forth. Those cases, conditions, times may be extremely specific (pursuing this petition will make this magistrate less likely to grant this other petition) or very general (articulating social welfare needs as individual "rights" makes people everywhere more passive and isolated) but they need to be articulated, and ultimately demonstrated, in concrete terms. At the same time, concrete does not mean sure or inevitable. The factors that influence policy making are not, by any means, all proven empirically. To count as a cost (or benefit), effects must be articulated in terms plausible enough to persuade people seeking to pursue human rights initiatives to take them into account.

Weighing the costs and benefits of "human rights" is difficult because the costs are often articulated in far more general terms than the benefits. The dangers on my list are often expressed as indictments of the entire human rights "idea" and "movement" in all times and places. The benefits are more often cast in immediate and local terms – these people out of this prison, those people provided with housing, this country's political process opened to elections, monitored in this way, these individuals spared the death penalty. It is certainly plausible that thinking about problems in the language of human rights could entail some costs (or benefits) always and everywhere, which would need to be added to each more particularized calculation. More likely, these general costs will be more or less intense in specific places and times. It may turn out that the entire human rights vocabulary or movement suffers from a blindness or works an effect that we should count as a cost. But it is far more likely that the vocabulary is used in different ways by different people, and that the movement is itself split in ways that make blindnesses more acute in some places and times than others. In weighing all this up, it is terribly hard to isolate the effects of "human rights." People in the movement also speak other languages, perhaps using the movement/vocabulary of human rights to get in the door and then speaking instrumentally or ethically. People in the movement will evaluate risks, costs and benefits in quite different ways. The vocabulary and movement are themselves in flux – many of the open terms are subject to ongoing revision precisely to correct for the sorts of difficulties I have listed here. As a pragmatist, all one can do is take these possibilities into account as best one can, estimating their likelihood and augmenting or discounting risks accordingly. As a movement, one can facilitate open engagement about differing pragmatic assessments.

Imagine, for example, an effort to use the vocabulary and political capital of the international human rights movement to end capital punishment in the Caribbean. It might well turn out that leading corporate lawyers acting pro bono in London define the problem and solution differently than lawyers working with non-governmental groups in London, and differently again from lawyers and organizers in the Caribbean. For some the anti-death penalty campaign might seem a distraction from more pressing issues, might occupy the field, might, if the campaign is successful, even legitimate other governmental (in)action or other social conditions that kill more people in the Caribbean. There might be a struggle within the movement about the usefulness of the vocabulary, or within the vocabulary about the conditions and costs of its deployment in particular places. Some people might use the death penalty, and the human rights vocabulary, to leverage interest in other issues or other vocabularies – others might use it to close off broader inquiries. Wherever you are located, if you are thinking pragmatically about devoting scarce institutional resources to furthering or limiting the effort to bring human rights to bear on the instance of Caribbean death penalty, it will be necessary to come to some conclusion, however tentative and general, about how these conflicts and divergent effects will net out. I hope that this list of critical observations about human rights might provide something of a checklist for discussions of this sort.

In assessing costs and benefits, it is as easy to give human rights too much of the blame for costs as it is too much credit for benefits. It is possible, of course, that the potential costs of human rights – as a vocabulary and as a movement – arise when it is misused, distorted, or co-opted. It is possible that the benefits and burdens of human rights might, in the event, be swamped by the effects of other powers. Human rights may be a drop of liberation in an ocean of oppression, or a fig leaf of legitimation over an evil collapsing of its own weight. In thinking pragmatically about human rights, all we can do is disaggregate and assess these causes and effects as carefully as possible. At the same time, we should be suspicious if costs are always attributed to people and forces outside the movement, just as we should be suspicious of claims that everything bad that happens was somehow always already inherent in the vocabulary used by unwitting human rights advocates. In thinking pragmatically about human rights, we will usually find ourselves somewhere in between, evaluating whether the vocabulary or institutional form of the movement, in particular contexts, makes particular types of "misuse" more or less likely. Again, I hope this list will provide a checklist of possible costs that we might think of (in particular circumstances or under certain conditions) as either potential misuses or as outcomes that may be made more likely by the human rights machinery.

Finally, it only makes sense to think pragmatically about human rights in comparative terms. How do the costs and benefits of pursuing an emancipatory objective in the vocabulary of human rights compare with other available discourses? How do efforts to work more intently within the human rights vocabulary compare with efforts to develop alternative vocabularies? How do human rights initiatives affect these efforts? Human rights might well discourage focus on collective responsibility, might leach the spiritual from emancipatory projects, but how does this stack up against alternative vocabularies and institutions – of family, kinship, nationhood, religious conviction – or with other political or legal emancipatory rhetorics? Whose hand is strengthened or weakened by each? How do we assess the medium or long term effort to develop new vocabularies and institutions for emancipation? Again, my hope is that this list will help spark this sort of comparative analysis.

B. Specifying the Costs and Benefits

To weigh costs and benefits, we will need to be as articulate and concrete about the benefits as about the costs. I have not dwelt on the benefit side here, but it should be clear that people will evaluate the benefits very differently. There will be a struggle, both inside and outside the movement, about what benefits to seek and how to rank gains. Here, I have used the term "emancipation" to capture the broad range of (often conflicting) benefits people of good heart might hope to make of human rights – humanitarian, progressive, internationalist, social welfare enhancing. There might be other benefits – human rights might have aesthetic uses, might stimulate the heart or the imagination, just as they might be psychologically or ethically useful. And, of course, human rights might not be useful only for us, but for all sorts of people pursuing various projects, not all of them good-hearted. I leave the list of benefits to others.

But what about the costs. People who have made the criticisms I have listed here differ about the sorts of costs they feel should be toted up. Some criticisms are ethical, some are political, some are philosophical. For some the problem is aesthetics – the ensemble of characters, identities, vocabularies necessary to achieve what has been achieved by the human rights movement is also an aesthetic blight. Of course, the human rights movement might create bad effects not so much by what it does, as by what it does not do. Costs might include things that happen on the ground to potential victims and violators of human rights, or to other people (innocent bystanders). They might include things that happen to other elites – people doing good things weakened, doing bad things strengthened – or things that happen to participants in the human rights movement itself – professional deformations of various kinds that might be subject to ethical, political or philosophical criticism and then count as a cost of the endeavor.

For some people, it matters (ethically, politically, philosophically, aesthetically) what the human rights movement expresses. If the human rights movement increases the incidence of descriptions of women as mothers-on-pedestals or victimized care givers, in legal decisions or institutional documents, that, for some people, is already a cost – ethically, aesthetically, politically. It is bad if women have been represented in too narrow or stereotypical a fashion, even if the only consequence is to pry loose some resources for redistribution to women. A number of the criticisms I have included here are of this type.

For other people, and I must admit, for me, nothing goes in the "costs" column until the human rights movement has a bad effect. A bad effect means influencing someone to act (or fail to act) or to think in a way that counts as a cost (again, ethically, politically, philosophically, aesthetically) for the person making the argument. Intensifying stereotypical representations of women might be thought to have an effect on at least some women (perhaps only plaintiffs and women using the human rights movement as a vehicle of self-expression and freedom, and others who learn who they are from what the human rights movement says women are), encouraging them to become narrower and more stereotypical or to think of themselves more narrowly than they otherwise might. And, of course, such representations would have an effect if they encouraged people in some positions of authority – judges, men, legislators, other women – to exclude women not meeting this stereotypical profile from benefits they would otherwise receive.

In weighing initiatives pragmatically, it is often more useful to focus on "distributional consequences among individuals or groups" than "costs and benefits." The costs/benefits vocabulary suggests (incorrectly) that one could know at an abstract and general level what to count as a cost or a benefit of the initiative. In fact, of course, the "costs" and the "benefits" will look different and be evaluated differently by different people. For those who feel the death penalty deters, its abolition is a cost, which effects a distribution from victims to criminals. Although I speak here of costs and benefits (or the "problem" and the "solution") as if we shared very vague and general aspirations for a more humanitarian, progressive and egalitarian global society, it would probably be more accurate to think of these "benefits" as distributions of power, status and means toward those who share these objectives and away from those who don't. But let us take this general articulation as a first step. Thereafter we would need to assess, from a more particular point of view, who would win and who would lose from a human rights initiative. In that effort, we would need to recast the criticisms I list here as distributions of power that one might oppose.

C. Some Criticisms Left Off the List

In keeping with this focus on usefulness, I have left off the list criticisms of human rights that are not cast in pragmatic terms. For example, the debate about whether human rights "really exist" or are "just" the product of efforts to articulate and use them. Although I find it hard to take too seriously the idea that rights exist in some way, let us assume that they do, and that the human rights movement is getting better and better at discovering and articulating them. If it turned out that doing so caused more misery than it alleviated, as a good-hearted legal professional, I would advocate our doing all we can to keep the existence of rights a secret. In a similar way, if it turns out that rights are "just" a fantasy, a social construction, and so forth, that tells us nothing about whether they are useful or not. If they are more useful than not, more power to the society that constructed them.

Traditional debates about whether human rights do or do not express a social consensus, in one society or across the globe, are similarly beside the point. Indeed, we could see them as updated ways of asking whether human rights really exist. Let us say they do express a social consensus – how does this affect their usefulness? Perhaps being able to say they express consensus weakens them, thins them out, skews their usefulness in various ways, perhaps it strengthens them. To decide, as my grandmother used to ask "whether that's a good thing or a bad thing" we still need to know whether once strengthened or skewed or weakened or whatever they are useful, and if so for what and for whom. Similarly debate about whether human rights "talk" is or is not coherent. Let's say the human rights vocabulary, institutional apparatus, even the soul of the human rights advocate, is riddled with contradictions that would not stand up to logical scrutiny for a minute. Knowing only this does not move us any closer to an understanding of whether they are part of the problem or the solution. Perhaps ambivalent porosity is their secret strength – to the extent human rights is useful, we should then be grateful for the contradictions. Perhaps incoherence is a fatal weakness, but if human rights creates more problems than it solves, this would be all to the good.

I have also left out criticisms that could be answered by intensifying our commitment to the human rights movement – that often rights are not adequately enforced, that the list of rights on which we focus is underinclusive, that participation in the movement – in rights making and enforcing – could be broader, that rights are poorly or unevenly implemented because of opposition from people outside the movement or the movement's own lack of resources, and so forth. This sort of criticism only makes the list when it becomes structural – when it appears that deficiencies like this will not be solved by more commitment or resources – and when they also can be said to have bad effects. If what is done is good, but much is left undone, we can only feel more committed to what is precious in that which can be accomplished. But if the combination of doing and not doing makes matters worse, we must weigh that loss against the gain. We might decide, for example, that no matter how strong the human rights movement gets, it will always be disproportionate in its attentions to some rights and some regions. Skewed in this way, it might reinforce ideas and practices of elites that treat these regions, or these rights, differently in other ways – adding to the legitimacy of various other discriminations. If both these things seem plausible – the claimed skew is structural and there are plausible bad consequences – it makes the list. If made out, these consequences would, of course, need to be weighed against the good achieved to see whether either the broad human rights movement or any particular initiative undertaken in its name was more part of the problem than the solution.

II. A SHORT LIST OF PRAGMATIC WORRIES AND POLEMICAL CHARGES

This is not a list of things unknown. All of these criticisms have been around for a long time, and the human rights movement has responded to them in a wide variety of ways.

Attention is routinely given to previously under-represented rights, regions, modes of enforcement, styles of work. The human rights movement is, in many ways, now "moving beyond" rights, broadening its engagements and terms of reference. In many ways the movement has developed precisely by absorbing waves of criticism, often from those passionate about its possibilities and importance who cast their doubts in one or another of these terms. It would be interesting to list the reactions and reforms that these and other doubts have generated. Sometimes, of course, reflecting on this sort of criticism can itself become part of the problem. If the costs turn out to be low or speculative, any time spent fleshing them out is time lost to the project of using human rights for emancipation – although having "been through" criticism might also strengthen the movement's ability to be useful. We are all familiar, moreover, with the periodic hand-wringing about possible errors and limits that accompanies the professional practice of human rights. This practice might well do more to stabilize the profession's sense of engagement, entitlement, confidence, than to undermine it, even where it turns out the costs far outweigh the benefits. Nevertheless, I can imagine good hearted legal professionals coming to these criticisms fresh, in a pragmatic spirit. How, and how adequately, has the movement responded to its critics? Have we done all we can to eliminate these down-side costs? Are we right to conclude that overall human rights is more part of the solution than the problem?

A. Human Rights Occupies the Field of Emancipatory Possibility

Hegemony as resource allocation. The claim here is that this institutional and political hegemony makes other valuable, often more valuable, emancipatory strategies less available. This argument is stronger, of course, when one can say something about what those alternatives are – or might be. But there may be something to the claim that human rights has so dominated the imaginative space of emancipation that alternatives can now only be thought, perhaps unhelpfully, as negations of what human rights asserts – passion to its reason, local to its global, etc. As a dominant and fashionable vocabulary for thinking about emancipation, human rights crowds out other ways of understanding harm and recompense. This is easiest to see when human rights attracts institutional energy and resources that would otherwise flow elsewhere. But this is not only a matter of scarce resources.

Hegemony as criticism. Human rights also occupies the field by implicit or explicit delegitimation of other emancipatory strategies. As an increasingly dominant emancipatory vocabulary, human rights is also a mode of criticism, among people of good will and against people of good will, when pursuing projects that, by comparison, can seem "too" ideological and political, insufficiently universal, objective, and so on. Where this is so, pursuing a human rights initiative or promoting the use of human rights vocabulary may have fully untended negative consequences for other existing emancipatory projects. Of course this takes us directly to a comparative analysis – how do we compare the gains and losses of human rights to the (potential) gains and losses of these other vocabularies and projects?

Hegemony as distortion. To the extent emancipatory projects must be expressed in the vocabulary of "rights" to be heard, good policies that are not framed that way go unattended. This also distorts the way projects are imagined and framed for international consideration. For example, it is often asserted that the international human rights movement makes an end run around local institutions and strategies that would often be better – ethically, politically, philosophically, aesthetically. Resources and legitimacy are drawn to the center from the periphery. A "universal" idea of what counts as a problem and a solution snuffs out all sorts of promising local political and social initiatives to contest local conditions in other terms. But there are other lost vocabularies that are equally global – vocabularies of duty, of responsibility, of collective commitment. Encouraging people concerned about environmental harm to rethink their concerns as a human rights violation will have bad consequences if it would have turned out to be more animating, for example, to say there is a duty to work for the environment, rather than a right to a clean environment.

The "right to development" is a classic – and well known – example. Once concerns about global poverty are raised in these terms, energy and resources are drawn to developing a literature and an institutional practice at the international level of a particular sort. Efforts that cannot be articulated in these terms seem less legitimate, less practical, less worth the effort. Increasingly, people of good will concerned about poverty are drawn into debate about a series of ultimately impossible legal quandaries – right of whom, against whom, remediable how, and so on – and into institutional projects of codification and reporting familiar from other human rights efforts, without evaluating how these might compare with other uses for this talent and these resources. Meanwhile, efforts that human rights does not criticize are strengthened. International economic policy affecting global poverty is taken over by neo-liberal players who do not see development as a special problem.

B. Human Rights Views the Problem and the Solution Too Narrowly

Narrow in many ways. People have made many different claims about the narrowness of human rights. Here are some: the human rights movement foregrounds harms done explicitly by governments to individuals or groups – leaving largely unaddressed and more legitimate by contrast harms brought about by governments indirectly or by private parties. Even when addressing private harms, human rights focuses attention on public remedies – explicit rights formalized and implemented by the state. One criticizes the state and seeks public law remedies, but leaves unattended or enhanced the powers and felt entitlements of private actors. Human rights implicitly legitimates ills and delegitimates remedies in the domain of private law and nonstate action.

Insulating the economy. Putting these narrowings together often means defining problems and solutions in ways not likely to change the economy. Human rights foregrounds problems of participation and procedure, at the expense of distribution, implicitly legitimating the existing distributions of wealth, status and power in societies once rights have been legislated, formal participation in government achieved, and institutional remedies for violations provided. However useful saying "that's my right" is in extracting things from the state, it is not good for extracting things from the economy, unless you are a property holder. Indeed, a practice of rights claims against the state may actively weaken the capacity of people to challenge economic arrangements. Whether progressive efforts to challenge economic arrangements are weakened by the overwhelming strength of the "right to property" in the human rights vocabulary, or by the channeling of emancipatory energy and imagination into the modes of institutional and rhetorical interaction that are described as "public," the imbalance between civil/political and social/economic rights is neither an accident of politics nor a matter that could be remedied by more intensive commitment. It is structural, to the philosophy of human rights, to the conditions of political possibility that make human rights an emancipatory strategy in the first place, to the institutional character of the movement, or to the ideology of its participants and supporters.

Foregrounding form. The strong attachment of the human rights movement to the legal formalization of rights and the establishment of legal machinery for their implementation makes the achievement of these forms an end in itself. Elites in a political system – international, national – which has adopted the rules and set up the institutions will often themselves have the impression and insist persuasively to others that they have addressed the problem of violations with an elaborate, internationally respected and "state of the art" response. This is analogous to the way in which holding elections can come to substitute for popular engagement in the political process. These are the traditional problems of form: form can hamper peaceful adjustment and necessary change, can be over or underinclusive. Is the right to vote a floor – or can it become a ceiling? The human rights movement ties its own hands on progressive development.

Backgrounding the background. The effects of a wide array of laws that do not explicitly condone violations but nevertheless affect the incidence of violation in a society are left unattended. As a result, these background laws – which may well be more important in generating the harm than an absence of rights and remedies for victims – are left with clean hands. Moreover, to maintain the claim to universality and neutrality, the human rights movement practices a systematic lack of attention to background sociological and political conditions that will determine the meaning a right has in particular contexts, rendering the evenhanded pursuit of "rights" vulnerable to all sorts of distorted, and distinctly non-neutral outcomes.

Even very broad social movements of emancipation – for women, for minorities of various sorts, for the poor – have their vision blinkered by the promise of recognition in the vocabulary and institutional apparatus of human rights. They will be led away from the economy and toward the state, away from political/social conditions and toward the forms of legal recognition. It has been claimed, for example, that promoting a neutral right to religious expression in Africa without acknowledging the unequal background cultural, economic and political authority of traditional religions and imported evangelical sects will dramatically affect the distribution of religious practice. Even if we limit our thinking to the laws that influence the distribution of wealth, status, and power between men and women, the number of those laws that explicitly address "women's issues," still less "women's rights," would form an extremely small and relatively unimportant percentage. However much the human rights movement reaches out to address other background considerations affecting the incidence of human rights abuse, such "background" norms remain, well, background.

C. Human Rights Generalizes Too Much

Universal goods and evils. The vocabulary and institutional practice of human rights promotion propagates an unduly abstract idea about people, politics and society. A one-size-fits-all emancipatory practice underrecognizes and reduces the instance and possibility for particularity and variation. This claim is not that human rights are too "individualistic." Rather, the claim is that the "person," as well as the "group," imagined and brought to life by human rights agitation is both abstract and general in ways that have bad consequences.

Sometimes this claim is framed as a loss of the pre-existing diversity of experience – as a vocabulary for expressing or representing experience, human rights limits human potential. In this view, limits on pre-existing potentials and experiences are themselves bad consequences. For others who make this argument, the loss of a prior, more authentic, humane, diverse real experience is not the issue. Even if it turns out that behind modes of expression there is no authentic experience, much less an edenic one, this particular vocabulary is less useful in encouraging possibility or hope or emancipation than others that generalize less or differently.

Becoming free only as an instance of the general. To come into understanding of oneself as an instance of a pre-existing general – "I am a 'person with rights'" – exacts a cost, a loss of awareness of the unprecedented and plastic nature of experience, or a loss of a capacity to imagine and desire alternative futures. We could term this "alienation." The human rights movement proposes itself as a vocabulary of the general good – as knowledge about the shape of emancipation and human possibility that can be "applied" and "enforced." As an emancipatory vocabulary, it offers answers rather than questions, answers that are not only outside political, ideological and cultural differences, but also beyond the human experience of specificity and against the human capacity to hope for more, in denial of the tawdry and uncertain quality of our available dreams about and experience with justice and injustice. Rather than enabling a discussion of what it means to be human, of who is human, of how humans might relate to one another, it crushes this discussion under the weight of moral condemnation, legal adjudication, textual certainty and political power. Not just bad for victims. The articulation of concrete good and evil in abstract terms is not only limiting for victims. The human rights vocabulary makes us think of evil as a social machine, a theater of roles, in which people are "victims," "violators," and "bystanders." At its most effective, human rights figures victims as passive and innocent, violators as deviant, and human rights professionals as heroic. Only the bystanders are figured in ambivalent or uncertain terms. To enter the terrain of emancipation through human rights is to enter a world of uncivilised deviants, baby seals and knights errant. There is a narrowing here – other evils and other goods receive less attention. Privileging the baby seals delegitimizes the suffering of people (and animals) who are, if anything, more typical in the complexity of their ethical and political posture, and renders the broader political culture less articulate about, and less able to engage, suffering that is embedded in or understood to express a more ambivalent constellation of characters. But this vocabulary also exacts a cost from those who fit most easily into its terms. No number of carefully elaborated "rights" is sufficient to recover a complex sense for a "violator's" human possibility and ambivalent experience. Differences among "victims," the experience of their particularity and the hope for their creative and surprising self-expression, are erased under the power of an internationally sanctified vocabulary for their self-understanding, self-presentation and representation as "victims" of human rights abuse. Even bad for advocates. To come into experience of oneself as a benevolent and pragmatic actor through the professional vocabulary of legal representation has costs for the human rights advocate, compared with other vocabularies of political engagement or social solidarity. Coming into awareness of oneself as the representative of something else – heroic agent for an authentic suffering elsewhere – mutes one's capacity for solidarity with those cast as victims, violators, bystanders, and stills the habit of understanding oneself to inhabit the world one seeks to affect. This claim is often put in ethical or characterological terms: human rights promotes emancipation by propagating an unbearably normative, earnest, and ultimately arrogant mode of thinking and speaking about what is good for people, abstract people, here and there, now and forever. This is bad for people in the movement – it can demobilize them as political beings in the world while encouraging their sanctimony – as well as those whose sense of the politically possible and desirable is shrunk to fit the uniform size.

D. Human Rights Particularizes Too Much

Emancipating the "right holders." The specific way human rights generalizes is to consolidate people into "identities" on the basis of which rights can be claimed. There are two issues here: a focus on individuals and a focus, whether for individuals or groups, on right-holding identity. The focus on individuals and people who come to think of themselves as individuals blunts articulation of a shared life. The focus on discrete and insular right holding identities blunts awareness of diversity, of the continuity of human experience, of overlapping identities. Together these tendencies inhibit expression of the experience of being part of a community.

Again we find two types of claims. For some, the key point is that human rights reduces and distorts a more promising real experience, of more shifting, less bounded identities, at times fused with a general will or co-participating in identities and social arrangements for which one will turn out to have no corresponding right or privilege. For others, the point is that compared to other vocabularies, human rights renders those who use it inarticulate about and less capable of solidarity and open-ended possibility. Either way, the human rights movement intensifies the sense of entitlement in individuals and groups at great cost to their ability to participate in collective political life and to their understanding of own lives as part of a more diverse community.

Strengthening the state. Although the human rights vocabulary expresses relentless suspicion of the state, by structuring emancipation as a relationship between an individual right holder and the state, human rights places the state at the center of the emancipatory promise. However much one may insist on the priority or pre-existence of rights, in the end rights are enforced, granted, recognized, implemented, their violations remedied, by the state. By consolidating human experience into the exercise of legal entitlements, human rights strengthens the national governmental structure and equates the structure of the state with the structure of freedom. To be free is . . . to have an appropriately organized state. We might say that the right-holder imagines and experiences freedom only as a citizen. This encourages autochthonous political tendencies and alienates the "citizen" from both his or her own experience as a person and from the possibility of alternative communal forms. Encouraging conflict and discouraging politics among right-holders. Encouraging each person and group wishing to be free to tally the rights he/she/it holds in preparation for their assertion against the state reduces inter-group and inter-individual sensitivity. In emancipating itself, the right holder is, in effect, queue jumping. Recognizing, implementing, enforcing rights is distributional work. Encouraging people to imagine themselves as right holders, and rights as absolute, makes the negotiation of distributive arrangements among individuals and groups less likely and less tenable. There is no one to triage among rights and right holders – except the state. The absolutist legal vocabulary of rights makes it hard to assess distribution among favored and less favored right holders and forecloses development of a political process for tradeoffs among them, leaving only the vague suspicion that the more privileged got theirs at the expense of the less privileged.

"Refugees" are people too. For fifty years the human rights movement, and the legal departments (often in opposition to the "humanitarian assistance" departments) of the great international institutions have struggled for legal recognition of the status of "refugee," helping to generate millions of people who think of themselves as "refugees," and whose status has often been so certified by one or another institution in the human rights family. Formalizing a status of disconnection from the state of "origin," the "host" state and the state in whose location one seeks "settlement," has taken an enormous toll on everyone's ability to think about and affect either the causes or consequences of refugee status. It is a status defined by its detachment from both. The thirty year stillborn effort to codify a "right to asylum" as an entailment of refugee status illustrates the difficulty of addressing solutions as matters of legal entitlement. Illustrates it so strikingly that we should question whether the effort to define the identity and rights of "the refugee" is more part of the problem than the solution.

E. Human Rights Expresses the Ideology, Ethics, Aesthetic Sensibility and Political Practice of a Particular Western Eighteenth- through Twentieth-Century Liberalism

Tainted origins. Although there are lots of interesting analogies to human rights ideas in various cultural traditions, the particular form these ideas are given in the human rights movement is the product of a particular moment and place. Post-enlightenment, rationalist, secular, Western, modern, capitalist. From a pragmatist point of view, of course, tainted origins are irrelevant. That human rights claims to be universal but is really the product of a specific cultural and historical origin says nothing – unless that specificity exacts costs or renders human rights less useful than something else. The human rights tradition might itself be undermined by its origin – be treated less well by some people, be less effective in some places – just as its origin might, for other audiences, accredit projects undertaken in its name. This is the sort of thing we might strategize about – perhaps we should downplay the universal claims, or look for parallel developments in other cultural traditions, etc.

The movement's Western liberal origins become part of the problem (rather than a limit on the solution) when particular difficulties general to the liberal tradition are carried over to the human rights movement. When, for example, the global expression of emancipatory objectives in human rights terms narrows humanity's appreciation of these objectives to the forms they have taken in the nineteenth- and twentieth-century Western political tradition. One cost would be the loss of more diverse and local experiences and conceptions of emancipation. Even within the liberal West, other useful emancipatory vocabularies (including the solidarities of socialism, Christianity, the labor movement, and so forth) are diminished by the consolidation of human rights as the international expression of the Western liberal tradition. Other costs would be incurred to the extent the human rights tradition could be seen to carry with it particular down sides of the liberal West.

Down sides of the West. That the emancipations of the modern West have come with costs has long been a theme in critical writing – alienation, loss of faith, environmental degradation, immorality, etc. Seeing human rights as part of the Western liberal package is a way of asserting that at least some of these costs should be attributed to the human rights tradition. This might be asserted in a variety of ways. If you thought secularism was part of what is bad about the modern West, you might assert that human rights shares the secular spirit, that as a sentimental vocabulary of devotion it actively displaces religion, offering itself as a poor substitute. You might claim that the enforcement of human rights, including religious rights, downgrades religion to a matter of private and individual commitment, or otherwise advances the secular project. To the extent human rights can be implicated in the secular project, we might conclude that it leaves the world spiritually less well off. Other criticisms of the modern liberal West have been extended to human rights in a parallel fashion.

In particular, critics have linked the human rights project to liberal Western ideas about the relationships among law, politics, and economics. Western enlightenment ideas that make the human rights movement part of the problem rather than the solution include the following: the economy pre-exists politics, politics pre-exists law, the private pre-exists the public, just as the animal pre-exists the human, faith pre-exists reason, or the feudal pre-exists the modern. In each case, the second term is fragile, artificial, a human creation and achievement, and a domain of choice, while the first term identifies a sturdy and natural base, a domain outside human control.

Human rights encourages people to seek emancipation in the vocabularies of reason rather than faith, in public rather than private life, in law rather than politics, in politics rather than economics. In each case, the human rights vocabulary overemphasizes the difference between what it takes as the (natural) base and as the (artificial) domain of emancipation, and underestimates the plasticity of what it treats as the base. Moreover, human rights is too quick to conclude that emancipation means progress forward from the natural passions of politics into the civilized reason of law. The urgent need to develop a more vigorous human politics is sidelined by the effort to throw thin but plausible nets of legal articulation across the globe. Work to develop law comes to be seen as an emancipatory end in itself, leaving the human rights movement too ready to articulate problems in political terms and solutions in legal terms. Precisely the reverse would be more useful. The posture of human rights as an emancipatory political project that extends and operates within a domain above or outside politics – a political project repackaged as a form of knowledge – delegitimates other political voices and makes less visible the local, cultural, and political dimensions of the human rights movement itself.

As liberal Western intellectuals, we think of the move to rights as an escape from the unfreedom of social conditions into the freedom of citizenship, but we repeatedly forget that there is also a loss. A loss of the experience of belonging, of the habit of willing in conditions of indeterminacy, innovating collectively in the absence of knowledge, unchanneled by an available list of rights. This may represent a loss of either the presence of experience itself, experience not yet channeled and returned to the individual as the universal experience of a right holder, or of the capacity to deploy other vocabularies that are more imaginative, open, and oriented to future possibility.

The West and the rest. The Western/liberal character of human rights exacts particular costs when it intersects with the highly structured and unequal relations between the modern West and everyone else. Whatever the limits of modernization in the West, the form of modernization promoted by the human rights movement in third world societies is too often based only on a fantasy about the modern/liberal/capitalist west. The insistence on more formal and absolute conceptions of property rights in transitional societies than are known in the developed West is a classic example of this problem – using the authority of the human rights movement to narrow the range of socio-economic choices available in developing societies in the name of "rights" that do not exist in this unregulated or compromised form in any developed western democracy.

At the same time, the human rights movement contributes to the framing of polit-ical choices in the third world as oppositions between "local/traditional" and "inter-national/modern" forms of government and modes of life. This effect is strengthened by the presentation of human rights as part of belonging to the modern world, but coming from some place outside political choice, from the universal, the rational, the civilized. By strengthening the articulation of third world politics as a choice between tradition and modernity, the human rights movement impoverishes local political discourse, often strengthening the hand of self-styled "traditionalists" who are offered a common-sense and powerful alternative to modernisation for whatever politics they may espouse.

F. Human Rights Promises More than It Can Deliver

Knowledge. Human rights promises a way of knowing – knowing just and unjust, universal and local, victim and violator, harm and remedy – which it cannot deliver. Justice is something that must be made, experienced, articulated, performed each time anew. Human rights may well offer an index of ways in which past experiences of justice-achieved have retrospectively been described, but the usefulness of this catalog as a stimulus to emancipatory creativity is swamped by the encouragement such lists give to the idea that justice need not be made, that it can be found or simply imported. One result is a loss of the habit of grappling with ambivalence, conflict and the unknown. Taken together, belief in these various false promises demobilizes actors from taking other emancipatory steps and encourages a global misconception of both the nature of evil and the possibilities for good.

Justice. Human rights promises a legal vocabulary for achieving justice outside the clash of political interest. Such a vocabulary is not available: rights conflict with one another, rights are vague, rights have exceptions, many situations fall between rights. The human rights movement promises that "law" – the machinery, the texts, the profession, the institution – can resolve conflicts and ambiguities in society by resolving those within its own materials, and that this can be done on the basis of a process of "interpretation" that is different from, more legitimate than, politics. And different in a particularly stultifying way – as a looser or stricter deduction from a past knowledge rather than as a collective engagement with the future. In particular, the human rights movement fetishizes the judge as someone who functions as an instrument of the law rather than as a political actor, when this is simply not possible – not a plausible description of judicial behavior – given the porous legal vocabulary with which judges must work and the likely political context within which judges are asked to act.

Many general criticisms of law's own tendencies to overpromise are applicable in spades to human rights. The absoluteness of rules makes compromise and peaceful adjustment of outcomes more difficult. The vagueness of standards makes for self-serving interpretation. The gap between law in the books and law in action, between legal institutions and the rest of life, hollows promises of emancipation through law. The human rights movement suggests that "rights" can be responsible for emancipation, rather than people making political decisions. This demobilizes other actors and other vocabularies, and encourages emancipation through reliance on enlightened, professional elites with "knowledge" of rights and wrongs, alienating people from themselves and from the vocabulary of their own governance. These difficulties are more acute in the international arena where law is ubiquitous and unaccompanied by political dialog.

Community. The human rights movement shares responsibility for the widespread belief that the world's political elites form a "community" that is benevolent, disconnected from economic actors and interests, and connected in some diffuse way through the media to the real aspirations of the world's people. The international human rights effort promises the ongoing presence of an entity, a "community," which can support and guarantee emancipation. This fantasy has bad consequences not only when people place too much hope in a foreign emancipatory friend that does not materialize. The transformation of the first world media audience, as that audience is imagined by the media, into "the international community" is itself an astonishing act of disenfranchisement. We might think the loss as one of "real" politics – such as that available in the context of a legislature, or at the national level. But even if we conclude that these are also fantastic – vocabularies of emancipation and oppression and opportunities for their expression – they are more useful vocabularies, more likely to emancipate, more likely to encourage habits of engagement, solidarity, responsibility, more open to surprise and reconfiguration.

Neutral intervention. The human rights vocabulary promises Western constituencies a politics-neutral and universalist mode of emancipatory intervention elsewhere in the world. This leads these constituencies to unwarranted innocence about the range of their other ongoing interventions and unwarranted faith in the neutral or universalist nature of a human rights presence. They intervene more often than they might otherwise. Their interventions are less effective than they would be if pursued in other vocabularies. Effective or not in their own terms, these interventions-without-responsibility-or-engagement have unfortunate consequences that are neither acknowledged nor open to contestation.

Emancipator as emancipation. Human rights offers itself as the measure of emancipation. This is its most striking – and misleading – promise. Human rights narrates itself as a universal/eternal/human truth and as a pragmatic response to injustice – there was the holocaust and then there was the genocide convention, women everywhere were subject to discrimination and then there was CEDAW. This posture makes the human rights movement itself seem redemptive – as if doing something for human rights was, in and of itself, doing something against evil. It is not surprising that human rights professionals consequently confuse work on the movement for emancipatory work in society. But there are bad consequences when people of good will mistake work on the discipline for work on the problem.

Potential emancipators can be derailed – satisfied that building the human rights movement is its own reward. People inside the movement can mistake reform of their world for reform of the world. What seem like improvements in the field's ability to respond to things outside itself may only be improvements in the field's ability to respond to its own internal divisions and contradictions. Yet we routinely underestimate the extent to which the human rights movement develops in response to political conflict and discursive fashion among international elites, thereby overestimating the field's pragmatic potential and obscuring the field's internal dynamics and will to power.

Think of the right to development, born less in response to global poverty than in response to an internal political conflict within the elite about the legitimate balance of concerns on the institutional agenda and to an effort by some more marginal members of that elite to express their political interest in the only available language. The move from a world of "rights" to "remedies" and then to "basic needs" and on to "transnational enforcement" reflected less a changing set of problems in the world than a changing set of attitudes among international legal elites about the value of legal formalism. The result of such initiatives to reframe emancipatory objectives in human rights terms is more often growth for the field – more conferences, documents, legal analysis, opposition and response – than decrease in violence against women, poverty, mass slaughter and so forth. This has bad effects when it discourages political engagement or encourages reliance on human rights for results it cannot achieve.

G. The Legal Regime of "Human Rights," Taken as a Whole, Does More To Produce and Excuse Violations than To Prevent and Remedy Them

Treating symptoms. Human rights remedies, even when successful, treat the symptoms rather than the illness, and this allows the illness not only to fester, but to seem like health itself. This is most likely where signing up for a norm – against discrimination – comes to substitute for ending the practice. But even where victims are recompensed or violations avoided, the distributions of power and wealth that produced the violation may well come to seem more legitimate as they seek other avenues of expression.

Humanitarian norms excuse too much. We are familiar with the idea that rules of warfare may do more to legitimate violence than to restrain it – as a result of vague standards, broad justifications, lax enforcement, or prohibitions that are clear but beside the point. The same can often be said about human rights. The vague and conflicting norms, their uncertain status, the broad justifications and excuses, the lack of enforcement, the attention to problems that are peripheral to a broadly conceived program of social justice – all this may, in some contexts, place the human rights movement in the uncomfortable position of legitimating more injustice than it eliminates. This is particularly likely where human rights discourse has been absorbed into the foreign policy processes of the great powers, indeed, of all powers.

Humanitarian norms justify too much. The human rights movement consistently underestimates the usefulness of the human rights vocabulary and machinery for people whose hearts are hard and whose political projects are repressive. The United States, The United Kingdom, Russia – but also Serbia and the Kosovar Albanians – have taken military action, intervened politically, and justified their governmental policies on the grounds of protecting human rights. Far from being a defense of the individual against the state, human rights has become a standard part of the justification for the external use of force by the state against other states and individuals. The porousness of the human rights vocabulary means that the interventions and exercises of state authority it legitimates are more likely to track political interests than its own emancipatory agenda.

Background norms do the real damage. At the same time, the human rights regime, like the law concerning war, is composed of more than those legal rules and institutions that explicitly concern human rights. The human rights movement acts as if the human rights legal regime were composed only of rights catalogs and institutions for their implementation. In fact, the law concerning torture, say, includes all the legal rules, principles, and institutions that bear on the incidence of torture. The vast majority of these rules – rules of sovereignty, institutional competence, agency, property and contract – facilitate or excuse the use of torture by police and governments.

H. The Human Rights Bureaucracy Is Itself Part of the Problem

Professionalizes the humanitarian impulse. The human rights movement attracts and demobilizes thousands of good-hearted people around the globe every year. It offers many thousands more the confidence that these matters are being professionally dealt with by those whom the movement has enlisted. Something similar has occurred within academic life – a human rights discipline has emerged between fields of public law and international law, promising students and teachers that work in the public interest has an institutional life, a professional routine and status. Professionalization has a number of possible costs. Absolute costs in lost personnel for other humanitarian possibilities. As the human rights profession raises its standards and status to compete with disciplines of private law, it raises the bar for other pro-bono activities that have not been as successful in establishing themselves as disciplines, whose practices, knowledge and projects are less systematic, less analogous to practice in the private interest. Professionalization strengthens lawyers at the expense of priests, engineers, politicians, soothsayers and citizens who might otherwise play a more central role in emancipatory efforts. At the same time, professionalization separates human rights advocates from those they represent and those with whom they share a common emancipatory struggle. The division of labor among emancipatory specialists is not merely about efficient specialization. We need only think of the bureaucratization of human rights in places like East Timor that have come within the orbit of international governance – suddenly an elaborate presence pulling local elites away from their base, or consigning them to the status of local informants, attention turning like sunflowers to Geneva, New York, to the Center, to the Commission. To the work of resolutions and reports.

Downgrades the legal profession. Sometimes the concern here is for the legal profession itself. The human rights movement degrades the legal profession by encouraging a combination of overly formal reliance on textual articulations that are anything but clear or binding and sloppy humanitarian argument. This combination degrades the legal skills of those involved, while encouraging them to believe that their projects are more legitimate precisely because they are presented in (sloppy) legal terms. Others have argued that human rights offers the profession, particularly at its most elite sites, a fig leaf of public interest commitment to legitimate the profession's contributions to global emiseration in its daily practice, in part by making all other legal fields, and particularly commercial legal fields, seem outside politics by contrast. For this, the sloppiness of human rights practice is itself useful – marking a line between the political redemptive profession and the apolitical workaday world of other legal professionals.

Encourages false solidarity. Of course there are many different types of people in the human rights movement and bureaucracy – different generations, different nationalities, different genders. To be a male human rights lawyer in Holland in your thirties is to live a different life altogether from that of a female human rights lawyer in Uruguay in her sixties. The human rights vocabulary encourages a false sense of the unity among these experiences and projects. As a vocabulary for progressive elite solidarity, human rights is particularly ham-handed, making it more difficult to articulate differences in the projects of male and female Palestinian human rights lawyers, Americans and Nigerians, etc.

Promotes bad faith. One thing these professionals do share, however, is a more or less bad faith relationship to their professional work. Every effort to use human rights for new purposes, to "cover" new problems, requires that they make arguments they know to be less persuasive than they claim. Arguments about their representative capacity – speaking for a consensus, a victim, an international community – and about the decisiveness of the vocabularies they invoke. Professional bad faith accumulates the more the movement tries to torque its tools to correct for its shortcomings – to address background conditions that affect the incidence of abuse as if they were themselves violations, for example. We need only think of the earnest advocate re-describing torture or the death penalty or female genital mutilation as a problem of "public health" to feel the movement's characteristic professional deformations at work.

Speaking law to politics is not the same thing as speaking truth to power. The human rights professional's vocabulary encourages an overestimation of the distinction between its own idealism and the hard realpolitik motivations of those it purports to address. Professional human rights performances are, in this sense, exercises in de-solidarization. One intensifies the "legal" marks in one's expression as if one thought this would persuade an actual other person who one imagines, paradoxically, to inhabit an altogether different "political" world. In this, the human rights intervention is always addressed to an imaginary third eye – the bystander who will solidarise with the (unstated) politics of the human rights speaker because it is expressed in an apolitical form. This may often work as a form of political recruitment – but it exacts a terrible cost on the habit of using more engaged and open ended political vocabularies. The result is professional narcissism guising itself as empathy and hoping to recruit others to solidarity with its bad faith.

Perils of "representation." The professionalization of human rights creates a mechanism for people to think they are working "on behalf of" less fortunate others, while externalizing the possible costs of their decisions and actions. The representational dimension of human rights work – speaking "for" others – puts the "victims" both on screen and off. The production of authentic victims, or victim authenticity, is an inherently voyeuristic or pornographic practice that, no matter how carefully or sensitively it is done, transforms the position of the "victim" in his or her society and produces a language of victimization for him or her to speak on the international stage. The injured-one-who-is-not-yet-a-victim, the "subaltern" if you like, can neither speak nor be spoken for, but recedes instead before the interpretive and representational practices of the movement. The remove between human rights professionals and the people they purport to represent can reinforce a global divide of wealth, mobility, information and access to audience. Human rights professionals consequently struggle, ultimately in vain, against a tide of bad faith, orientalism and self-serving sentimentalism.

Irresponsible intervention. The people who work within the human rights field have no incentive to take responsibility for the changes they bring about. Consequences are the result of an interaction between a context and an abstraction – "human rights." At the same time, the simultaneously loose and sanctified nature of the vocabulary and the power of the movement itself opens an enormous terrain for discretionary action – intervening here and not there, this way and not that, this time and not that time. There is no vocabulary for treating this discretion as the responsible act of a person, creating intense psychic costs for human rights professionals themselves, but also legitimating their acts of unaccountable discretion. Belief in the nobility of human rights places blame for whatever goes wrong elsewhere – on local politicians, evil individuals, social pathologies. This imposes ethical, political and aesthetic costs on people in the movement – but also on those elsewhere in the elite who must abide them, and in those who, as the terrain of engagement and the object of representation, become the mirror for this professional self regard.

I. The Human Rights Movement Strengthens Bad International Governance

Weakest link. Even within international law, the modes of possible governance are far broader than the patterns worn by human rights professionals. The human rights movement is the product of a particular moment in international legal history, which foregrounded rules rather than standards and institutional rather than cultural enforcement. If we compare modes of governance in other fields we find a variety of more successful models – a standards/culture based environmental regime, an economic law regime embedded in private law, and so forth. The attachment to rights as a measure of the authenticity, universality, and above all as the knowledge we have of social justice binds our professional feet, and places social justice issues under the governance of the least effective institutional forms available.

Clean hands. More generally, international governance errs when it imagines itself capable of governing, "intervening" if you will, without taking responsibility for the messy business of allocating stakes in society – when it intervenes only economically and not politically, only in public and not in private life, only "consensually" without acknowledging the politics of influence, only to freeze the situation and not to improve it, "neutrally" as between the parties, politically/economically but not culturally, and so forth. The human rights movement offers the well-intentioned intervener the illusion of affecting conditions both at home and abroad without being politically implicated in the distribution of stakes that results, by promising an available set of universal, extra-political legal rules and institutions with which to define, conduct and legitimate the intervention.

Fantasy government. International governance is often asked to do globally what we fantasize or expect national governments to do locally – allocate stakes, constitute a community, articulate differences and similarities, provide for the common good. The human rights movement, by strengthening the habit of understanding international governance in legal rather than political terms, weakens its ability to perform what we understand domestically to be these political functions. The conflation of the law with the good encourages an understanding of international governance – by those within and without its institutions – which is systematically blind to the bad consequences of its own action. The difficulty the human rights movement has in thinking of itself in pragmatic rather than theological terms – in weighing and balancing the usefulness of its interventions in the terms like those included in this list – is characteristic of international governance as a whole. The presence of a human rights movement models this blindness as virtue and encourages it among other governance professionals by presenting itself as insurance of international law's broader humanitarian character. Governing the exception. Human rights shares with the rest of international law a tendency to treat only the tips of icebergs. Deference to the legal forms upon which human rights is built – the forms of sovereignty, territorial jurisdictional divisions, subsidiarity, consensual norms – makes it seem natural to isolate aspects of a problem that "cross borders" or "shock the conscience of mankind" for special handling at the international level – often entrenching the rest of the iceberg more firmly in the national political background. The movement's routine polemical denunciations of sovereignty work more as attestations to its continuity than agents of its erosion, limiting the aspirations of good hearted people with international and global political commitments. The notion that law sits atop culture as well as politics demobilizes people who understand their political projects as "intervention" in a "foreign" "culture." The human rights vocabulary, with its emphasis on the development of law itself, strengthens the tendency of international lawyers more broadly to concern themselves with constitutional questions about the structure of the legal regime itself rather than with questions of distribution in the broader society.

J. Human Rights Promotion Can Be Bad Politics in Particular Contexts

It may be that this is all one can say – promoting human rights can sometimes have bad consequences. All of the first nine types of criticism suggested that human rights suffered from one or another design defect – as if these defects would emerge, these costs would be incurred, regardless of context. Perhaps this is so. But so long as none of these criticisms have been proven in such a general way (and it is hard to see just how they could be), it may be that all we have is a list of possible down sides, open risks, bad results that have sometimes occurred, that might well occur. In some context, for example, it might turn out that pursuing emancipation as entitlement could reduce the capacity and propensity for collective action. Something like this seems to have happened in the United States in the last twenty years – the transformation of political questions into legal questions, and then into questions of legal "rights," has made other forms of collective emancipatory politics less available. But it is hard to see that this is always and everywhere the destiny of human rights initiatives. We are familiar, even in the United States, with moments of collective emancipatory mobilisation achieved, in part, through the vocabulary of rights. If we come to the recent British Human Rights Act, it seems an open question whether it will liberate emancipatory political energies frozen by the current legislative process and party structure, or will harness those political possibilities to the human rights claims of de-politicized individuals and judges. The point of an ongoing pragmatic evaluation of the human rights effort is precisely to develop a habit of making such assessments. But that human rights promotion can and has had bad consequences in some contexts does seem clear.

Strengthens repressive states and anti-progressive international initiatives. In some places, human rights implementation can make a repressive state more efficient. Human rights institutions and rhetoric can also be used in particular contexts to humanize repressive political initiatives and co-opt to their support sectors of civil society that might otherwise be opposed. Human rights can and has also been used to strengthen, defend, legitimate a variety of repressive initiatives, by both individuals and states. To legitimate war, defend the death penalty, the entitlements of majorities, religious repression, access to (or restriction of) abortion, and so forth. The recent embrace of human rights by the international financial institutions may serve both functions – strengthening states that will need to enforce harsh structural adjustment policies while co-opting local and international resistance to harsh economic policies, and lending a shroud of universal/rational inevitability to economic policies that are the product of far narrower political calculations and struggles. As deployed, the human rights movement may do a great deal to take distribution off the national and international development agendas, while excusing and legitimating regressive policies at all levels. These difficulties are particularly hard to overcome because the human rights movement remains tone-deaf to the specific political consequences of its activity in particular locations, on the mistaken assumption that a bit more human rights can never make things worse. This makes the human rights movement particularly subject to capture by other political actors and ideological projects. We need only think of the way the move to "responsibilities" signaled by the Universal Declaration on Human Responsibilities of 1998 was captured by neo-liberal efforts to promote privatization and weaken the emancipatory potentials of government.

Condemnation as legitimation. Finally, in many contexts, transforming a harm into a "human rights violation" may be a way of condoning or denying rather than naming and condemning it. A terrible set of events occurs in Bosnia. We could think of it as a sin and send the religious, as illness and send physicians, as politics and send the politicians, as war and send the military. Or we could think of it as a human rights violation and send the lawyers. Doing so can be a way of doing nothing, avoiding responsibility, simultaneously individualizing the harm and denying its specificity. Thinking of atrocity as a human rights violations captures neither the unthinkable or the banal in evil. Instead we find a strange combination of clinically antiseptic analysis, throwing the illusion of cognitive control over the unthinkable, and hysterical condemnation, asserting the advocate's distance from the quotidian possibility of evil. Renaming Auschwitz "genocide" to recognize its unspeakability, enshrining its status as "shocking the conscience of mankind" can also be a way of unthinking its everyday reality. In this sense, human rights, by criminalizing harm and condensing its origin to particular violators, can serve as denial, apology, legitimation, normalization, and routinization of the very harms it seeks to condemn.

III. CONCLUSION

So that is the list. As I said at the outset, some of these worries seem more plausible to me than others. I would worry about some of these costs more than others. The generation that built the human rights movement focused its attention on the ways in which evil people in evil societies could be identified and restrained. More acute now is how good people, well-intentioned people in good societies, can go wrong, can entrench, support, the very things they have learned to denounce. Answering this question requires a pragmatic reassessment of our most sacred humanitarian commitments, tactics and tools.

Whatever has been the history of human rights, we do not know its future. Perhaps these difficulties will be overcome, avoided. But we will not avoid them by avoiding their articulation, discussion, assessment – by treating the human rights movement as a frail child, in need of protection from critical assessment or pragmatic calculation. At this point these remain suspicions, intuitions, hunches, by people who have seen the human rights movement from one or another point of view. Each person involved in international human rights protection will have his or her own view about which, if any, of these doubts are plausible and worth pursuing. As a profession, it would be good to have a more open conversation about worries of this sort, and to think further about how they should affect our understanding of the human rights project as a whole.

~

QUESTIONS & COMMENTS

(1) Professor Kennedy provides few concrete examples in support of his arguments. Does Kennedy's failure to provide concrete examples reflect his own inability to take sides on a particular case because his critique methodology is indeterminate? Or is the problem with Kennedy's critique of the "international human rights movement" that he does not tell us of whom this movement consists, and, therefore, we cannot know whom or what he is targeting for his criticism?

(2) Can you think of some examples that would support his claims? Can you think of counterexamples?

Index